MOUNTAIN VIEW
PUBLIC LIBRARY
Mountain View, CA
W9-CAY-688

HANDBOOK OF U.S. LABOR STATISTICS

For reference
Not to be taken from the room.

Handbook of U.S. Labor Statistics

Employment, Earnings, Prices, Productivity, and Other Labor Data

23rd Edition
2020

Edited by Mary Meghan Ryan

Bernan Press
Lanham • Boulder • New York • London

Published by Bernan Press
An imprint of The Rowman & Littlefield Publishing Group, Inc.
4501 Forbes Boulevard, Suite 200, Lanham, Maryland 20706
www.rowman.com
800-462-6420

6 Tinworth Street, London SE11 5AL, United Kingdom

Copyright © 2020 by The Rowman & Littlefield Publishing Group, Inc.

All rights reserved. No part of this book may be reproduced
in any form or by any electronic or mechanical means, including
information storage and retrieval systems, without written permission
from the publisher, except by a reviewer who may quote passages in a review.
Bernan Press does not claim copyright in U.S. government information.

ISBN: 978-1-64143-406-5
E-ISBN: 978-1-64143-407-2
ISSN: 1526-2553

CONTENTS

LIST OF TABLES

CHAPTER 1: POPULATION, LABOR FORCE, AND EMPLOYMENT STATUS

Population, Labor Force, and Employment Status

Employment

Unemployment

Work Experience

Employee Tenure

Labor Force and Employment Characteristics of Selected Family Types

Labor Force and Employment Characteristics of Foreign-Born Workers

Labor Force and Employment Characteristics by Education

Persons with a Disability: Labor Force Characteristics

Employment Situation of Veterans

Worker Displacement

CHAPTER 2: EMPLOYMENT, HOURS, AND EARNINGS

Employment and Hours

Earnings

Quarterly Census of Employment and Wages

Business Employment Dynamics

CHAPTER 3: OCCUPATIONAL EMPLOYMENT AND WAGES

CHAPTER 4: LABOR FORCE AND EMPLOYMENT PROJECTIONS BY INDUSTRY AND OCCUPATION

Job Openings, Hires, and Separations

CHAPTER 8: LABOR-MANAGEMENT RELATIONS

CHAPTER 9: PRICES

Producer Price Index

Consumer Price Index

Export and Import Price Indexes

CHAPTER 10: THE WORKING POOR

CHAPTER 11: CONSUMER EXPENDITURES

CHAPTER 12: AMERICAN TIME USE SURVEY

CHAPTER 13: INCOME DATA IN THE UNITED STATES (CENSUS BUREAU)

CHAPTER 14: OCCUPATIONAL SAFETY AND HEALTH

LIST OF FIGURES

PREFACE

Bernan Press is pleased to present a compilation of Bureau of Labor Statistics (BLS) data in this 23rd edition of its award-winning *Handbook of U.S Labor Statistics: Employment, Earnings, Prices, Productivity, and Other Labor Data.* BLS and the U.S. Census Bureau provide a treasure trove of historical information about all aspects of labor and employment in the United States. The current edition maintains the content of previous editions and updates the text with additional data and new features. The data in this *Handbook* are excellent sources of information for analysts in both government and the private sector.

The *Handbook* addresses many of the issues that are being discussed across the United States, such as high unemployment, employment projections for the future, the decline in income, the rapidly increasing costs of health care services, and the dramatic aging of the labor force. In addition, this publication provides an abundance of data on topics such as prices, productivity, consumer expenditures, occupational safety and health, international labor comparisons, and much more. It includes the recently released projections from 2018–2028.

The comprehensive and historical data presented in the *Handbook* allow the user to understand the background of current events and compare today's economy with previous years. Select data in this publication go back to 1913 and several tables have data going back to the 1940s.

FEATURES OF THIS PUBLICATION

- Approximately 220 tables that present authoritative data on labor market statistics, including employment and unemployment, mass layoffs, prices, productivity, and data from the American Time Use Survey (ATUS).

- Each chapter is preceded by a figure that calls attention to noteworthy trends in the data.

- In addition to the figures, the introductory material for to each chapter also contains highlights of other salient data.

- The tables in each section are also preceded by notes and definitions, which contain concise descriptions of the data sources, concepts, definitions, and methodology from which the data are derived.

- The introductory notes also include references to more comprehensive reports. These reports provide additional data and more extensive descriptions of estimation methods, sampling, and reliability measures.

SOURCES OF ADDITIONAL INFORMATION

BLS data are primarily derived from surveys conducted by the federal government or through federal-state cooperative arrangements. The comparability of data over time can be affected by changes in the surveys, which are essential for keeping pace with the current structure of economic institutions and for taking advantage of improved survey techniques. Revisions of current data are also periodically made as a result of the availability of new information. In addition, some tables in this *Handbook* were dropped due to the data being from a one-time survey that is now outdated or due to the survey being entirely restructured. Introductory notes to each chapter summarize specific factors that may affect the data. In the tables, the ellipsis character ("...") indicates that data are not available.

More extensive methodological information, including further discussion of the sampling and estimation procedures used for each BLS program, is contained in the *BLS Handbook of Methods*. This publication is in the process of being updated, and completed chapters are available on the BLS Web site at <https://www.bls.gov>. Other sources of current data and analytical include the *Monthly Labor Review* and a daily Internet publication, *The Editor's Desk* (TED). All of these publications can be found on the BLS Web site as well. Other relevant publications, including those from the Census Bureau, are noted in the notes and definitions in each chapter.

OTHER PUBLICATIONS BY BERNAN PRESS

Handbook of U.S Labor Statistics: Employment, Earnings, Prices, Productivity, and Other Labor Data is just one of a number of publications in Bernan Press's award-winning U.S. DataBook Series. Other titles include *The Almanac of American Education*; *Business Statistics of the United States: Patterns of Economic Change*; *Crime in the United States; Housing Statistics of the United States; States Profiles: The Population and Economy of Each U.S. State;* and *Vital Statistics of the United States: Births, Life Expectancy, Deaths, and Selected Health Data.* In addition, Bernan Press publishes *Employment, Hours, and Earnings: States and Areas* as a special edition of this *Handbook*. Each of these titles provides statistical information from official government sources.

CHAPTER 1: POPULATION, LABOR FORCE, AND EMPLOYMENT STATUS

HIGHLIGHTS

This chapter presents the detailed historical information collected in the Current Population Survey (CPS), a monthly survey of households that gathers data on the employment status of the population. Basic data on labor force, employment, and unemployment are shown for various characteristics of the population, including age, sex, race, Hispanic origin, and marital status.

Figure 1-1. Civilian Labor Force and Participation Rate, 1950–2018

Over 162 million people were in the labor force in 2018 compared with 62 million in 1950. While the labor force has grown considerably, the labor force participation rate has grown much slower increasing from 59.2 percent in 1950 to 62.9 percent in 2018. The labor force participation rate remained steady in 2018. It has declined or remained the same each year from 2007 to 2015 before increasing slightly in 2016 and 2017. (See Table 1-1.)

OTHER HIGHLIGHTS

- In 2018, employment increased 1.6 percent after increasing 1.3 percent in 2017. Employment decreased each year from 2008 to 2010 after increasing each year from 1992 through 2007 except for in 2002. The drop in employment was the steepest between 2008 and 2009 when it fell 3.8 percent. (See Table 1-1.)

- While the proportion of white men in the labor force declined significantly from 1985 to 2018, the proportion of black women in the labor force increased from 5.3 percent to 6.6 percent. In addition, Hispanic representation in the labor force also rose increasing from 6.7 percent in 1985 to 17.5 percent in 2018. (See Table 1-7.)

- While the labor force participation rate increased or remained stable for most age groups in 2018, it declined for the youngest workers. Meanwhile, the labor force participation rate increased again for the older workers—those 65 years and over. Since 1999, the labor force has increased or remained steady for each year except in 2014 for those 65 years and over. (See Table 1-8.)

NOTES AND DEFINITIONS

CURRENT POPULATION SURVEY OF HOUSEHOLDS

Collection and Coverage

The Current Population Survey (CPS) is a monthly survey that analyzes and publishes statistics on the labor force, employment, and unemployment, classified by a variety of demographic, social, and economic characteristics. This survey is conducted by the Census Bureau for the Bureau of Labor Statistics (BLS). The CPS includes the civilian noninstitutional population age 16 years and older in the 50 states and DC. Respondents are interviewed to obtain information about the employment status of each household member age 16 years and over. Persons under 16 years of age are excluded from the official estimates because child labor laws, compulsory school attendance, and general social custom in the United States severely limit the types and amount of work that these children can do.

The inquiry relates to the household member's employment status during the calendar week, Sunday through Saturday that includes the 12th day of the month. This is known as the "reference week." Actual field interviewing is conducted during the following week (the week that contains the 19th day of the month).

Concepts and Definitions

The concepts and definitions underlying the labor force data have been modified—but not substantially altered—since the inception of the survey in 1940 when it began as a Work Projects Administration program. Current definitions of some of the major concepts used in the CPS are described below.

The civilian noninstitutional population includes persons 16 years of age and over who reside in the 50 states and the District of Columbia who are not inmates of institutions (such as penal and mental facilities and homes for the aged) and who are not on active duty in the armed forces.

An *employed person* is any person who, during the reference week: (1) did any work at all (at least one hour) as a paid employees in their own business, profession, or on their own farm, or who worked 15 hours or more as an unpaid worker in an enterprise operated by a member of the family; and (2) any person who was not working but who had a job or business from which he or she was temporarily absent due to vacation, illness, bad weather, childcare problems, maternity or paternity leave, labor-management disputes, job training, or other family or personal reasons, despite whether the employee was being paid for the time off or was seeking other jobs.

Each employed person is counted only once, even if he or she holds more than one job. For purposes of occupation and industry classification, multiple jobholders are counted as being in the job at which they worked the greatest number of hours during the reference week.

Included in the total are employed citizens of foreign countries who were temporarily in the United States but not living on the premises of an embassy. Excluded are persons whose only activity during the reference week consisted of work around their own house (painting, repairing, or own home housework) or volunteer work for religious, charitable, and similar organizations.

Unemployed persons are all persons who had no employment during the reference week, but who were available for work (except for temporary illness) and had made specific efforts to find employment some time during the four-week period ending with the reference week. Persons who were waiting to be recalled to a job from which they had been laid off need not have been looking for work to be classified as unemployed.

Reasons for unemployment are divided into four major groups: (1) job losers, defined as (a) persons on temporary layoff, who have been given a date to return to work or who expect to return to work within six months; (b) permanent job losers, whose employment ended involuntarily and who began looking for work; and (c) persons who completed a temporary job and began looking for work after the job ended; (2) job leavers, defined as persons who quit or otherwise terminated their employment voluntarily and immediately began looking for work; (3) reentrants, defined as persons who previously worked but were out of the labor force prior to beginning their job search; and (4) new entrants, defined as persons who had never worked but were currently searching for work.

Duration of unemployment represents the length of time (through the current reference week) that persons classified as unemployed had been looking for work. For persons on layoff, duration of unemployment represents the number of full weeks they had been on layoff. Mean duration of unemployment is the arithmetic average computed from single weeks of unemployment; median duration of unemployment is the midpoint of a distribution of weeks of unemployment.

A *spell of unemployment* is a continuous period of unemployment of at least one week's duration and is terminated by either employment or withdrawal from the labor force.

Extent of unemployment refers to the number of workers and proportion of the labor force that were unemployed at some time during the year. The number of weeks unemployed is the total number of weeks accumulated during the entire calendar year.

The *unemployment rate* is the number of unemployed persons as a percentage of the civilian labor force.

The *civilian labor force* comprises all civilians classified as employed or unemployed.

The *participation rate* represents the proportion of the civilian noninstitutional population currently in the labor force.

The *employment-population ratio* represents the proportion of the population that is currently employed.

Persons not in the labor force are all persons in the civilian noninstitutional population who are neither employed nor unemployed. Information is collected about their desire for and availability to take a job at the time of the CPS interview, job search activity during the prior year, and reason for not looking for work during the four-week period ending with the reference week. Persons not in the labor force who want and are available for a job and who have looked for work within the past 12 months (or since the end of their last job, if they had held one within the past 12 months), but who are not currently looking, are designated as *marginally attached to the labor force.* The marginally attached are divided into those not currently looking because they believe their search would be futile—so-called *discouraged workers*—and those not currently looking for other reasons, such as family responsibilities, ill health, or lack of transportation.

Discouraged workers are defined as persons not in the labor force who want and are available for a job and who have looked for work sometime in the past 12 months (or since the end of their last job, if they held one within the past 12 months), but who are not currently looking because they believe that there are no jobs available or there are none for which they would qualify. The reasons for not currently looking for work include a person's belief that no work is available in his or her line of work or area; he or she could not find any work; he or she lacks necessary schooling, training, skills, or experience; employers would think he or she is too young or too old; or he or she would encounter hiring discrimination.

Usual full- or part-time status refers to hours usually worked per week. Full-time workers are those who usually work 35 hours or more (at all jobs). This group includes some individuals who worked less than 35 hours during the reference week for economic or noneconomic reasons. Part-time workers are those who usually work less than 35 hours per week (at all jobs), regardless of the number of hours worked during the reference week. These concepts are used to differentiate a person's normal schedule from his or her specific activity during the reference week. Unemployed persons who are looking for full-time work or who are on layoff from full-time jobs are counted as part of the full-time labor force; unemployed persons who are seeking part-time work or who are on layoff from part-time jobs are counted as part of the part-time labor force.

Year-round, full-time workers are workers who primarily worked at full-time jobs for 50 weeks or more during the preceding calendar year. Part-year workers worked either full- or part-time for 1 to 49 weeks.

At work part-time for economic reasons, sometimes called involuntary part-time, refers to individuals who gave an economic reason for working 1 to 34 hours during the reference week. Economic reasons include slack work or unfavorable business conditions, inability to find full-time work, and seasonal declines in demand. Those who usually work part-time must also indicate that they want and are available to work full-time to be classified as working part-time for economic reasons.

At work part-time for noneconomic reasons refers to persons who usually work part-time and were at work 1 to 34 hours during the reference week for a noneconomic reason. Noneconomic reasons include illness or other medical limitations, childcare problems or other family or personal obligations, school or training, retirement or Social Security limits on earnings, and being in a job where full-time work is less than 35 hours. This also includes workers who gave an economic reason for usually working 1 to 34 hours but said they do not want to work full-time or were unavailable for full-time work.

Absences are defined as instances in which persons who usually work 35 or more hours a week worked less than that during the reference period for reasons of illness or family obligations. Excluded are situations in which work was missed for vacation, holidays, or other reasons. The estimates are based on one-fourth of the sample only.

Earnings are a remuneration of a worker or group of workers for services performed during a specific period of time.

Usual weekly earnings for wage and salary workers include any overtime pay, commissions, or tips usually received (at the main job in the case of multiple jobholders). Earnings reported on a basis other than weekly (such as annual, monthly, or hourly) are converted to weekly. The term "usual" is as perceived by the respondent. If the respondent asks for a definition of usual, interviewers are instructed to define the term as more than half the weeks worked during the past 4 or 5 months.

Minimum wage refers to the prevailing federal minimum wage which is $7.25. It increased from $6.55 per hour to $7.25 per hour on July 24, 2009 and has remained at that level since. Data are for wage and salary workers who were paid hourly rates and refer to a person's earnings at the sole or principal job.

A *multiple jobholder* is an employed person who, during the reference week, had two or more jobs as a wage and salary worker, was self-employed and also held a wage and salary job, or worked as an unpaid family worker and also held a wage and salary job.

Self-employed persons with multiple businesses and persons with multiple jobs as unpaid family workers are excluded.

Occupation, industry, and class of worker for members of the employed population are determined by the job held during the reference week. Persons with two or more jobs are classified as being in the job at which they worked the greatest number of hours. The unemployed are classified according to their last job. Beginning with data published in 2003, the systems used to classify occupational and industry data changed. They are currently based on the Standard Occupational Classification (SOC) system and the North American Industry Classification System (NAICS). (See the following section on historical comparability for a discussion of previous classification systems used in the CPS.) The class-of-worker breakdown assigns workers to one of the following categories: private and government wage and salary workers, self-employed workers, and unpaid family workers. Wage and salary workers receive wages, salaries, commissions, tips, or pay in kind from a private employer or from a government unit. Self-employed workers are those who work for profit or fees in their own businesses, professions, trades, or on their own farms. Only the unincorporated self-employed are included in the self-employed category in the class-of-worker typology. Self-employed workers who respond that their businesses are incorporated are included among wage and salary workers, because they are technically paid employees of a corporation. An unpaid family worker is a person working without pay for 15 hours or more per week on a farm or in a business operated by a member of the household to whom he or she is related by birth or marriage.

Educational attainment refers to years of school completed in regular schools, which include graded public, private, and parochial elementary, and high schools, whether day or night school. Colleges, universities, and professional schools are also included.

Tenure refers to length of time a worker has been continuously employed by his or her current employer. These data are collected through a supplement to the CPS. All employed persons were asked how long they had been working continuously for their present employer and, if the length of time was one or two years, a follow-up question was asked about the exact number of months. The follow-up question was included for the first time in the February 1996 supplement to the CPS. CPS supplements that obtained information on tenure in the January of 1983, 1987, and 1991 did not include the follow-up question. Prior to 1983, the question on tenure was asked differently. Data prior to 1983 are thus not strictly comparable to data for subsequent years.

White, Black, and Asian are terms used to describe the race of persons. Persons in these categories are those who selected that race only. Persons in the remaining race categories—American Indian or Alaskan Native, Native Hawaiian or Other Pacific Islander, and persons who selected more than one race category—are included in the estimates of total employment and unemployment but are not shown separately because the number of survey respondents is too small to develop estimates of sufficient quality for monthly publication.

Hispanic origin refers to persons who identified themselves in the enumeration process as being Spanish, Hispanic, or Latino. Persons of Hispanic or Latino origin may be of any race.

Single, never married; married, spouse present; and other marital status are the terms used to define the marital status of individuals at the time of the CPS interview. Married, spouse present, applies to a husband and wife if both were living in the same household, even though one may be temporarily absent on business, vacation, in a hospital, etc. Other marital status applies to persons who are married, spouse absent; widowed; or divorced. Married, spouse absent relates to persons who are separated due to marital problems, as well as husbands and wives living apart because one was employed elsewhere, on duty with the armed forces, or any other reason.

A *household* consists of all persons—related family members and all unrelated persons—who occupy a housing unit and have no other usual address. A house, an apartment, a group of rooms, or a single room is regarded as a housing unit when occupied or intended for occupancy as separate living quarters.

A *householder* is the person (or one of the persons) in whose name the housing unit is owned or rented. The term is not applied to either husbands or wives in married-couple families; it refers only to persons in families maintained by either men or women without a spouse.

A *family* is defined as a group of two or more persons residing together who are related by birth, marriage, or adoption. All such persons are considered as members of one family. Families are classified as either married-couple families or families maintained by women or men without spouses.

Children refer to "own" children of the husband, wife, or person maintaining the family, including sons and daughters, stepchildren, and adopted children. Excluded are other related children, such as grandchildren, nieces, nephews, cousins, and unrelated children.

Persons are referred to as *disabled* if they answer yes to the following questions: 1.) Are you deaf or do you have serious difficulty hearing? 2.) Are you blind or do you serious difficulty seeing even when wearing glasses? 3.) Because of a physical, mental, or emotional condition, do you have serious difficulty concentrating, remembering, or making decisions? 4.) Do you have serious difficulty walking or climbing stairs? 5.) Do you have difficulty dressing or bathing? 6.) Because of a physical, mental, or emotional condition, do you have difficulty doing errands alone such as visiting a doctor's office or shopping? Labor force measures are only tabulated for persons 16 years and over.

Veterans are men and women who previously served on active duty in the U.S. Armed Forces and who were civilians at the time they were surveyed.

Nonveterans are men and women who never served on active duty in the U.S. Armed Forces.

World War II, Korean War, Vietnam-era, and Gulf War-era veterans are men and women who served in the Armed Forces during these periods, regardless of where they served.

Veterans of other service periods are men and women who served in the Armed Forces at any time other than World War II, the Korean War, the Vietnam era, or the Gulf War era.

Veteran status is obtained from responses to the question, "Did you ever serve on active duty in the U.S. Armed Forces?"

Period of service is obtained from answers to the question asked of veterans, "When did you serve on active duty in the U.S. Armed Forces?" The following service periods are identified:

Gulf War era II — September 2001–present

Gulf War era I — August 1990–August 2001

Vietnam era — August 1964–April 1975

Korean War — July 1950–January 1955

World War II — December 1941–December 1946

Other service periods — All other time periods

Veterans who served in Iraq, Afghanistan, or both are individuals who served in Iraq at any time since March 2003, in Afghanistan at any time since October 2001, or in both locations.

Presence of service-connected disability is determined by answers to the question, "Has the Department of Veterans Affairs (VA) or Department of Defense (DoD) determined that you have a service-connected disability, that is, a health condition or impairment caused or made worse by any of your military service?"

Service-connected disability rating is based on answers to the question, "What is your current service connected disability rating?" Answers can range from 0 to 100 percent, in increments of 10 percentage points.

Displaced workers are wage and salary workers 20 years of age and older who lost or left jobs because their plant or company closed or moved, there was insufficient work for them to do, or their position or shift was abolished. Data are often presented for long-tenured displaced workers—those who had worked for their employer for 3 or more years at the time of displacement.

Historical Comparability

While the concepts and methods are very similar to those used for the inaugural survey in 1940, a number of changes have been made over the years to improve the accuracy and usefulness of the data. Only recent major changes are described here.

Major changes to the CPS, such as the complete redesign of the questionnaire and the use of computer-assisted interviewing for the entire survey, were introduced in 1994. In addition, there were revisions to some of the labor force concepts and definitions, including the implementation of changes recommended in 1979 by the National Commission on Employment and Unemployment Statistics (NCEUS, also known as the Levitan Commission). Some of the major changes to the survey at this time were:

1. The introduction of a redesigned and automated questionnaire. The CPS questionnaire was totally redesigned in order to obtain more accurate, comprehensive, and relevant information, and to take advantage of state-of-the-art computer interviewing techniques. Computer-assisted interviewing has important benefits most notably that it facilitates the use of a relatively complex questionnaire that incorporates complicated skip patterns and standardized follow-up questions. Additionally, certain questions are automatically tailored to the individual's situation to make them more understandable.

2. Official labor force measures were defined more precisely. While the labor force status of most people is straightforward, some persons are more difficult to classify correctly, especially if they are engaged in activities that are relatively informal or intermittent. Many of the changes to the questionnaire were made to deal with such cases. This was accomplished by rewording and adding questions to conform more precisely to the official definitions, making the questions easier to understand and answer, minimizing reliance on volunteered responses, revising response categories, and taking advantage of the benefits of an automated interview.

3. The amount of data available was expanded. The questionnaire redesign also made it possible to collect several types of data on topics such as multiple job holding and usual hours regularly for the first time.

4. Several labor definitions were modified. The most important definitional changes concerned discouraged workers. The Levitan Commission had criticized the former definition because it was based on a subjective desire for work and on somewhat arbitrary assumptions about an individual's availability to take a job. As a result of the redesign, two requirements were added: For persons to qualify as discouraged they must have engaged in some job search within the past year (or since they last worked, if they worked within the past year), and they must be currently available to take a job. (Formerly, availability was inferred from responses to

other questions; now, there is a direct question.) Also, beginning in January 1994, questions on this subject are asked of the full CPS sample, permitting estimates of the number of discouraged workers to be published monthly (rather than quarterly).

Beginning in January 2003, several other changes were introduced into the CPS. These changes included the following:

1. Population controls that reflected the results of the 2000 census were introduced into the monthly CPS estimation process. The new controls increased the size of the civilian noninstitutional population by about 3.5 million in May 2002. As a result, they also increased the estimated numbers of people unemployed and employed. Because the increases were roughly proportional, however, the overall unemployment rate did not change significantly. Data from January 2000 through December 2002 were revised to reflect these new controls. Over and above these revisions, the U.S. Census Bureau introduced another large upward adjustment to the controls as part of its annual update of population estimates for 2003. These updated population estimates were not available in time to incorporate them into the revised population controls for January 2000 to December 2002. Thus, the data on employment and unemployment levels for January 2003 (and beyond) are not strictly comparable with those for earlier months. The unemployment rate and other ratios, however, were not substantially affected by the 2003 population control revisions.

2. Questions on race and Hispanic origin were modified to comply with the new standards for maintaining, collecting, and presenting federal data on race and ethnicity for federal statistical agencies. The questions were reworded to indicate that individuals could select more than once race category and to convey more clearly that individuals should report their own perception of what race is. These changes had no impact on the overall civilian noninstitutional population and civilian labor force. However, they did reduce the population and labor force levels of Whites, Blacks, and Asians beginning in January 2003.

3. Improvements were introduced to both the second stage and composite weighting procedures. These changes adapted the weighting procedures to the new race/ethnic classification system and enhanced the stability over time for demographic groups. The second-stage weighting procedure substantially reduced the variability of estimates and corrected, to some extent, for CPS underreporting.

Changes in the Occupational and Industrial Classification System

In January 2003, the CPS adopted the 2002 census industry and occupational classification systems, which were derived, respectively, from the 2002 North American Industry Classification System (NAICS) and the 2000 Standard Occupational Classification (SOC) system. The 1990 Census occupational and industry classifications were replaced. The introduction of the new industry and occupational classification systems in 2003 created a complete break in comparability at all levels of industry and occupation aggregation. The composition of detailed occupations and industries changed substantially in the 2002 systems compared with the 1990 systems, as did the structure for aggregating them into major groups. Therefore, any comparisons of data on the different classifications are not possible without major adjustments.

Historical employment series on the 2002 Census classifications are available at broad levels of occupational and industry aggregation back to 1983. However, historical employment series at the detailed occupational and industry levels on the 2002 classifications are available back to 2000 only.

In 2009, BLS began using the 2007 Census industry classification system, which was derived from the 2007 NAICS series, and still uses it currently. The 2010 Census occupational classification was introduced with data for January 2011 and replaced an earlier version that was based on the 2000 SOC. As a result of the classification change, occupational data beginning with January 2011 are not strictly comparable with earlier years. Although the names of the broad- and intermediate-level occupational groups in the 2010 Census occupational classification remained the same, some detailed occupations were re-classified between the broader groups, affecting comparability over time.

The Current Population Survey currently uses the 2010 Census occupational classification and, beginning with data for January 2014, the 2012 Census industry classification. These classifications were derived from the 2010 Standard Occupational Classification (SOC) and the 2012 North American Industry Classification System (NAICS), respectively, to meet the special classification needs of demographic household surveys.

Sources of Additional Information

A complete description of sampling and estimation procedures and further information on the impact of historical changes in the surveys can be found in the updated version of the *BLS Handbook of Methods*. This can be found on the BLS Web site at <https://www.bls.gov/opub/hom/>.

Table 1-1. Employment Status of the Civilian Noninstitutional Population, 1950–2018

(Thousands of people, percent.)

Year	Civilian noninstitutional population	Civilian labor force								Not in labor force
		Total	Participation rate	Employed				Unemployed		
				Total	Percent of population	Agriculture	Nonagricultural industries	Number	Unemployment rate	
1950	104 995	62 208	59.2	58 918	56.1	7 160	51 758	3 288	5.3	42 787
1951	104 621	62 017	59.2	59 961	57.3	6 726	53 235	2 055	3.3	42 604
1952	105 231	62 138	59.0	60 250	57.3	6 500	53 749	1 883	3.0	43 093
1953	107 056	63 015	58.9	61 179	57.1	6 260	54 919	1 834	2.9	44 041
1954	108 321	63 643	58.8	60 109	55.5	6 205	53 904	3 532	5.5	44 678
1955	109 683	65 023	59.3	62 170	56.7	6 450	55 722	2 852	4.4	44 660
1956	110 954	66 552	60.0	63 799	57.5	6 283	57 514	2 750	4.1	44 402
1957	112 265	66 929	59.6	64 071	57.1	5 947	58 123	2 859	4.3	45 336
1958	113 727	67 639	59.5	63 036	55.4	5 580	57 450	4 602	6.8	46 088
1959	115 329	68 369	59.3	64 630	56.0	5 565	59 065	3 740	5.5	46 960
1960	117 245	69 628	59.4	65 778	56.1	5 458	60 318	3 852	5.5	47 617
1961	118 771	70 459	59.3	65 746	55.4	5 200	60 546	4 714	6.7	48 312
1962	120 153	70 614	58.8	66 702	55.5	4 944	61 759	3 911	5.5	49 539
1963	122 416	71 833	58.7	67 762	55.4	4 687	63 076	4 070	5.7	50 583
1964	124 485	73 091	58.7	69 305	55.7	4 523	64 782	3 786	5.2	51 394
1965	126 513	74 455	58.9	71 088	56.2	4 361	66 726	3 366	4.5	52 058
1966	128 058	75 770	59.2	72 895	56.9	3 979	68 915	2 875	3.8	52 288
1967	129 874	77 347	59.6	74 372	57.3	3 844	70 527	2 975	3.8	52 527
1968	132 028	78 737	59.6	75 920	57.5	3 817	72 103	2 817	3.6	53 291
1969	134 335	80 734	60.1	77 902	58.0	3 606	74 296	2 832	3.5	53 602
1970	137 085	82 771	60.4	78 678	57.4	3 463	75 215	4 093	4.9	54 315
1971	140 216	84 382	60.2	79 367	56.6	3 394	75 972	5 016	5.9	55 834
1972	144 126	87 034	60.4	82 153	57.0	3 484	78 669	4 882	5.6	57 091
1973	147 096	89 429	60.8	85 064	57.8	3 470	81 594	4 365	4.9	57 667
1974	150 120	91 949	61.3	86 794	57.8	3 515	83 279	5 156	5.6	58 171
1975	153 153	93 775	61.2	85 846	56.1	3 408	82 438	7 929	8.5	59 378
1976	156 150	96 158	61.6	88 752	56.8	3 331	85 421	7 406	7.7	59 991
1977	159 033	99 009	62.3	92 017	57.9	3 283	88 734	6 991	7.1	60 025
1978	161 910	102 251	63.2	96 048	59.3	3 387	92 661	6 202	6.1	59 659
1979	164 863	104 962	63.7	98 824	59.9	3 347	95 477	6 137	5.8	59 900
1980	167 745	106 940	63.8	99 303	59.2	3 364	95 938	7 637	7.1	60 806
1981	170 130	108 670	63.9	100 397	59.0	3 368	97 030	8 273	7.6	61 460
1982	172 271	110 204	64.0	99 526	57.8	3 401	96 125	10 678	9.7	62 067
1983	174 215	111 550	64.0	100 834	57.9	3 383	97 450	10 717	9.6	62 665
1984	176 383	113 544	64.4	105 005	59.5	3 321	101 685	8 539	7.5	62 839
1985	178 206	115 461	64.8	107 150	60.1	3 179	103 971	8 312	7.2	62 744
1986	180 587	117 834	65.3	109 597	60.7	3 163	106 434	8 237	7.0	62 752
1987	182 753	119 865	65.6	112 440	61.5	3 208	109 232	7 425	6.2	62 888
1988	184 613	121 669	65.9	114 968	62.3	3 169	111 800	6 701	5.5	62 944
1989	186 393	123 869	66.5	117 342	63.0	3 199	114 142	6 528	5.3	62 523
1990	189 164	125 840	66.5	118 793	62.8	3 223	115 570	7 047	5.6	63 324
1991	190 925	126 346	66.2	117 718	61.7	3 269	114 449	8 628	6.8	64 578
1992	192 805	128 105	66.4	118 492	61.5	3 247	115 245	9 613	7.5	64 700
1993	194 838	129 200	66.3	120 259	61.7	3 115	117 144	8 940	6.9	65 638
1994	196 814	131 056	66.6	123 060	62.5	3 409	119 651	7 996	6.1	65 758
1995	198 584	132 304	66.6	124 900	62.9	3 440	121 460	7 404	5.6	66 280
1996	200 591	133 943	66.8	126 708	63.2	3 443	123 264	7 236	5.4	66 647
1997	203 133	136 297	67.1	129 558	63.8	3 399	126 159	6 739	4.9	66 837
1998	205 220	137 673	67.1	131 463	64.1	3 378	128 085	6 210	4.5	67 547
1999	207 753	139 368	67.1	133 488	64.3	3 281	130 207	5 880	4.2	68 385
2000	212 577	142 583	67.1	136 891	64.4	2 464	134 427	5 692	4.0	69 994
2001	215 092	143 734	66.8	136 933	63.7	2 299	134 635	6 801	4.7	71 359
2002	217 570	144 863	66.6	136 485	62.7	2 311	134 174	8 378	5.8	72 707
2003	221 168	146 510	66.2	137 736	62.3	2 275	135 461	8 774	6.0	74 658
2004	223 357	147 401	66.0	139 252	62.3	2 232	137 020	8 149	5.5	75 956
2005	226 082	149 320	66.0	141 730	62.7	2 197	139 532	7 591	5.1	76 762
2006	228 815	151 428	66.2	144 427	63.1	2 206	142 221	7 001	4.6	77 387
2007	231 867	153 124	66.0	146 047	63.0	2 095	143 952	7 078	4.6	78 743
2008	233 788	154 287	66.0	145 362	62.2	2 168	143 194	8 924	5.8	79 501
2009	235 801	154 142	65.4	139 877	59.3	2 103	137 775	14 265	9.3	81 659
2010	237 830	153 889	64.7	139 064	58.5	2 206	136 858	14 825	9.6	83 941
2011	239 618	153 617	64.1	139 869	58.4	2 254	137 615	13 747	8.9	86 001
2012	243 284	154 975	63.7	142 469	58.6	2 186	140 283	12 506	8.1	88 310
2013	245 679	155 389	63.2	143 929	58.6	2 130	141 799	11 460	7.4	90 290
2014	247 947	155 922	62.9	146 305	59.0	2 237	144 068	9 617	6.2	92 025
2015	250 801	157 130	62.7	148 834	59.3	2 422	146 411	8 296	5.3	93 671
2016	253 538	159 187	62.8	151 436	59.7	2 460	148 976	7 751	4.9	94 351
2017	255 079	160 320	62.9	153 337	60.1	2 454	150 883	6 982	4.4	94 759
2018	257 791	162 075	62.9	155 761	60.4	2 425	153 336	6 314	3.9	95 716

Table 1-2. Employment Status of the Civilian Noninstitutional Population, by Sex, 1980–2018

(Thousands of people, percent.)

Sex and year	Civilian noninstitutional population	Civilian labor force								Not in labor force
		Total	Participation rate	Employed				Unemployed		
				Total	Percent of population	Agriculture	Non-agricultural industries	Number	Unemploy-ment rate	
Men										
1980	79 398	61 453	77.4	57 186	72.0	2 709	54 477	4 267	6.9	17 945
1981	80 511	61 974	77.0	57 397	71.3	2 700	54 697	4 577	7.4	18 537
1982	81 523	62 450	76.6	56 271	69.0	2 736	53 534	6 179	9.9	19 073
1983	82 531	63 047	76.4	56 787	68.8	2 704	54 083	6 260	9.9	19 484
1984	83 605	63 835	76.4	59 091	70.7	2 668	56 423	4 744	7.4	19 771
1985	84 469	64 411	76.3	59 891	70.9	2 535	57 356	4 521	7.0	20 058
1986	85 798	65 422	76.3	60 892	71.0	2 511	58 381	4 530	6.9	20 376
1987	86 899	66 207	76.2	62 107	71.5	2 543	59 564	4 101	6.2	20 692
1988	87 857	66 927	76.2	63 273	72.0	2 493	60 780	3 655	5.5	20 930
1989	88 762	67 840	76.4	64 315	72.5	2 513	61 802	3 525	5.2	20 923
1990	90 377	69 011	76.4	65 104	72.0	2 546	62 559	3 906	5.7	21 367
1991	91 278	69 168	75.8	64 223	70.4	2 589	61 634	4 946	7.2	22 110
1992	92 270	69 964	75.8	64 440	69.8	2 575	61 866	5 523	7.9	22 306
1993	93 332	70 404	75.4	65 349	70.0	2 478	62 871	5 055	7.2	22 927
1994	94 355	70 817	75.1	66 450	70.4	2 554	63 896	4 367	6.2	23 538
1995	95 178	71 360	75.0	67 377	70.8	2 559	64 818	3 983	5.6	23 818
1996	96 206	72 087	74.9	68 207	70.9	2 573	65 634	3 880	5.4	24 119
1997	97 715	73 261	75.0	69 685	71.3	2 552	67 133	3 577	4.9	24 454
1998	98 758	73 959	74.9	70 693	71.6	2 553	68 140	3 266	4.4	24 799
1999	99 722	74 512	74.7	71 446	71.6	2 432	69 014	3 066	4.1	25 210
2000	101 964	76 280	74.8	73 305	71.9	1 861	71 444	2 975	3.9	25 684
2001	103 282	76 886	74.4	73 196	70.9	1 708	71 488	3 690	4.8	26 396
2002	104 585	77 500	74.1	72 903	69.7	1 724	71 179	4 597	5.9	27 085
2003	106 435	78 238	73.5	73 332	68.9	1 695	71 636	4 906	6.3	28 197
2004	107 710	78 980	73.3	74 524	69.2	1 687	72 838	4 456	5.6	28 730
2005	109 151	80 033	73.3	75 973	69.6	1 654	74 319	4 059	5.1	29 119
2006	110 605	81 255	73.5	77 502	70.1	1 663	75 838	3 753	4.6	29 350
2007	112 173	82 136	73.2	78 254	69.8	1 604	76 650	3 882	4.7	30 036
2008	113 113	82 520	73.0	77 486	68.5	1 650	75 836	5 033	6.1	30 593
2009	114 136	82 123	72.0	73 670	64.5	1 607	72 062	8 453	10.3	32 013
2010	115 174	81 985	71.2	73 359	63.7	1 665	71 694	8 626	10.5	33 189
2011	116 317	81 975	70.5	74 290	63.9	1 698	72 592	7 684	9.4	34 343
2012	117 343	82 327	70.2	75 555	64.4	1 626	73 930	6 771	8.2	35 017
2013	118 555	82 667	69.7	76 353	64.4	1 611	74 742	6 314	7.6	35 889
2014	119 748	82 882	69.2	77 692	64.9	1 685	76 007	5 190	6.3	36 865
2015	121 101	83 620	69.1	79 131	65.3	1 826	77 305	4 490	5.4	37 481
2016	122 497	84 755	69.2	80 568	65.8	1 839	78 729	4 187	4.9	37 743
2017	123 275	85 145	69.1	81 402	66.0	1 843	79 559	3 743	4.4	38 130
2018	124 678	86 096	69.1	82 698	66.3	1 797	80 902	3 398	3.9	38 582
Women										
1980	88 348	45 487	51.5	42 117	47.7	656	41 461	3 370	7.4	42 861
1981	89 618	46 696	52.1	43 000	48.0	667	42 333	3 696	7.9	42 922
1982	90 748	47 755	52.6	43 256	47.7	665	42 591	4 499	9.4	42 993
1983	91 684	48 503	52.9	44 047	48.0	680	43 367	4 457	9.2	43 181
1984	92 778	49 709	53.6	45 915	49.5	653	45 262	3 794	7.6	43 068
1985	93 736	51 050	54.5	47 259	50.4	644	46 615	3 791	7.4	42 686
1986	94 789	52 413	55.3	48 706	51.4	652	48 054	3 707	7.1	42 376
1987	95 853	53 658	56.0	50 334	52.5	666	49 668	3 324	6.2	42 195
1988	96 756	54 742	56.6	51 696	53.4	676	51 020	3 046	5.6	42 014
1989	97 630	56 030	57.4	53 027	54.3	687	52 341	3 003	5.4	41 601
1990	98 787	56 829	57.5	53 689	54.3	678	53 011	3 140	5.5	41 957
1991	99 646	57 178	57.4	53 496	53.7	680	52 815	3 683	6.4	42 468
1992	100 535	58 141	57.8	54 052	53.8	672	53 380	4 090	7.0	42 394
1993	101 506	58 795	57.9	54 910	54.1	637	54 273	3 885	6.6	42 711
1994	102 460	60 239	58.8	56 610	55.3	855	55 755	3 629	6.0	42 221
1995	103 406	60 944	58.9	57 523	55.6	881	56 642	3 421	5.6	42 462
1996	104 385	61 857	59.3	58 501	56.0	871	57 630	3 356	5.4	42 528
1997	105 418	63 036	59.8	59 873	56.8	847	59 026	3 162	5.0	42 382
1998	106 462	63 714	59.8	60 771	57.1	825	59 945	2 944	4.6	42 748
1999	108 031	64 855	60.0	62 042	57.4	849	61 193	2 814	4.3	43 175
2000	110 613	66 303	59.9	63 586	57.5	602	62 983	2 717	4.1	44 310
2001	111 811	66 848	59.8	63 737	57.0	591	63 147	3 111	4.7	44 962
2002	112 985	67 363	59.6	63 582	56.3	587	62 995	3 781	5.6	45 621
2003	114 733	68 272	59.5	64 404	56.1	580	63 824	3 868	5.7	46 461
2004	115 647	68 421	59.2	64 728	56.0	546	64 182	3 694	5.4	47 225
2005	116 931	69 288	59.3	65 757	56.2	544	65 213	3 531	5.1	47 643
2006	118 210	70 173	59.4	66 925	56.6	543	66 382	3 247	4.6	48 037
2007	119 694	70 988	59.3	67 792	56.6	490	67 302	3 196	4.5	48 707
2008	120 675	71 767	59.5	67 876	56.2	518	67 358	3 891	5.4	48 908
2009	121 665	72 019	59.2	66 208	54.4	496	65 712	5 811	8.1	49 646
2010	122 656	71 904	58.6	65 705	53.6	541	65 164	6 199	8.6	50 752
2011	123 300	71 642	58.1	65 579	53.2	556	65 023	6 063	8.5	51 658
2012	125 941	72 648	57.7	66 914	53.1	560	66 353	5 734	7.9	53 293
2013	127 124	72 722	57.2	67 577	53.2	519	67 058	5 146	7.1	54 401
2014	128 199	73 039	57.0	68 613	53.5	552	68 061	4 426	6.1	55 159
2015	129 700	73 510	56.7	69 703	53.7	597	69 106	3 807	5.2	56 190
2016	131 040	74 432	56.8	70 868	54.1	621	70 247	3 564	4.8	56 608
2017	131 804	75 175	57.0	71 936	54.6	611	71 324	3 239	4.3	56 629
2018	133 112	75 978	57.1	73 063	54.9	628	72 435	2 916	3.8	57 134

Table 1-3. Employment Status of the Civilian Noninstitutional Population, by Sex, Age, Race, and Hispanic Origin, 1995–2018

(Thousands of people.)

Characteristic	1995	1996	1997	1998	1999	2000	2001	2002	2003	2004	2005	2006
ALL RACES												
Both Sexes												
Civilian noninstitutional population	198 584	200 591	203 133	205 220	207 753	212 577	215 092	217 570	221 168	223 357	226 082	228 815
Civilian labor force	132 304	133 943	136 297	137 673	139 368	142 583	143 734	144 863	146 510	147 401	149 320	151 428
Employed	124 900	126 708	129 558	131 463	133 488	136 891	136 933	136 485	137 736	139 252	141 730	144 427
Agriculture	3 440	3 443	3 399	3 378	3 281	2 464	2 299	2 311	2 275	2 232	2 197	2 206
Nonagricultural industries	121 460	123 264	126 159	128 085	130 207	134 427	134 635	134 174	135 461	137 020	139 532	142 221
Unemployed	7 404	7 236	6 739	6 210	5 880	5 692	6 801	8 378	8 774	8 149	7 591	7 001
Not in labor force	66 280	66 647	66 837	67 547	68 385	69 994	71 359	72 707	74 658	75 956	76 762	77 387
Men, 16 Years and Over												
Civilian noninstitutional population	95 178	96 206	97 715	98 758	99 722	101 964	103 282	104 585	106 435	107 710	109 151	110 605
Civilian labor force	71 360	72 087	73 261	73 959	74 512	76 280	76 886	77 500	78 238	78 980	80 033	81 255
Employed	67 377	68 207	69 685	70 693	71 446	73 305	73 196	72 903	73 332	74 524	75 973	77 502
Agriculture	2 559	2 573	2 552	2 553	2 432	1 861	1 708	1 724	1 695	1 688	1 654	1 663
Nonagricultural industries	64 818	65 634	67 133	68 140	69 014	71 444	71 488	71 179	71 636	72 836	74 319	75 838
Unemployed	3 983	3 880	3 577	3 266	3 066	2 975	3 690	4 597	4 906	4 456	4 059	3 753
Not in labor force	23 818	24 119	24 454	24 799	25 210	25 684	26 396	27 085	28 197	28 730	29 119	29 350
Men, 20 Years and Over												
Civilian noninstitutional population	87 811	88 606	89 879	90 790	91 555	93 875	95 181	96 439	98 272	99 476	100 835	102 145
Civilian labor force	67 324	68 044	69 166	69 715	70 194	72 010	72 816	73 630	74 623	75 364	76 443	77 562
Employed	64 085	64 897	66 284	67 135	67 761	69 634	69 776	69 734	70 415	71 572	73 050	74 431
Agriculture	2 335	2 356	2 356	2 350	2 244	1 756	1 613	1 629	1 614	1 596	1 577	1 579
Nonagricultural industries	61 750	62 541	63 927	64 785	65 517	67 878	68 163	68 104	68 801	69 976	71 473	72 852
Unemployed	3 239	3 146	2 882	2 580	2 433	2 376	3 040	3 896	4 209	3 791	3 392	3 131
Not in labor force	20 487	20 563	20 713	21 075	21 362	21 864	22 365	22 809	23 649	24 113	24 392	24 584
Women, 16 Years and Over												
Civilian noninstitutional population	103 406	104 385	105 418	106 462	108 031	110 613	111 811	112 985	114 733	115 647	116 931	118 210
Civilian labor force	60 944	61 857	63 036	63 714	64 855	66 303	66 848	67 363	68 272	68 421	69 288	70 173
Employed	57 523	58 501	59 873	60 771	62 042	63 586	63 737	63 582	64 404	64 728	65 757	66 925
Agriculture	881	871	847	825	849	602	591	587	580	547	544	543
Nonagricultural industries	56 642	57 630	59 026	59 945	61 193	62 983	63 147	62 995	63 824	64 181	65 213	66 382
Unemployed	3 421	3 356	3 162	2 944	2 814	2 717	3 111	3 781	3 868	3 694	3 531	3 247
Not in labor force	42 462	42 528	42 382	42 748	43 175	44 310	44 962	45 621	46 461	47 225	47 643	48 037
Women, 20 Years and Over												
Civilian noninstitutional population	96 262	97 050	97 889	98 786	100 158	102 790	103 983	105 136	106 800	107 658	108 850	109 992
Civilian labor force	57 215	58 094	59 198	59 702	60 840	62 301	63 016	63 648	64 716	64 923	65 714	66 585
Employed	54 396	55 311	56 613	57 278	58 555	60 067	60 417	60 420	61 402	61 773	62 702	63 834
Agriculture	830	827	798	768	803	567	558	557	550	515	519	520
Nonagricultural industries	53 566	54 484	55 815	56 510	57 752	59 500	59 860	59 863	60 852	61 258	62 182	63 315
Unemployed	2 819	2 783	2 585	2 424	2 285	2 235	2 599	3 228	3 314	3 150	3 013	2 751
Not in labor force	39 047	38 956	38 691	39 084	39 318	40 488	40 967	41 488	42 083	42 735	43 136	43 407
Both Sexes, 16 to 19 Years												
Civilian noninstitutional population	14 511	14 934	15 365	15 644	16 040	15 912	15 929	15 994	16 096	16 222	16 398	16 678
Civilian labor force	7 765	7 806	7 932	8 256	8 333	8 271	7 902	7 585	7 170	7 114	7 164	7 281
Employed	6 419	6 500	6 661	7 051	7 172	7 189	6 740	6 332	5 919	5 907	5 978	6 162
Agriculture	275	261	244	261	234	141	128	124	111	121	100	108
Nonagricultural industries	6 144	6 239	6 417	6 790	6 938	7 049	6 611	6 207	5 808	5 786	5 877	6 054
Unemployed	1 346	1 306	1 271	1 205	1 162	1 081	1 162	1 253	1 251	1 208	1 186	1 119
Not in labor force	6 746	7 128	7 433	7 388	7 706	7 642	8 027	8 409	8 926	9 108	9 234	9 397
WHITE[1]												
Both Sexes												
Civilian noninstitutional population	166 914	168 317	169 993	171 478	173 085	176 220	178 111	179 783	181 292	182 643	184 446	186 264
Civilian labor force	111 950	113 108	114 693	115 415	116 509	118 545	119 399	120 150	120 546	121 086	122 299	123 834
Employed	106 490	107 808	109 856	110 931	112 235	114 424	114 430	114 013	114 235	115 239	116 949	118 833
Agriculture	3 194	3 276	3 208	3 160	3 083	2 320	2 174	2 171	2 148	2 103	2 077	2 063
Nonagricultural industries	103 296	104 532	106 648	107 770	109 152	112 104	112 256	111 841	112 087	113 136	114 872	116 769
Unemployed	5 459	5 300	4 836	4 484	4 273	4 121	4 969	6 137	6 311	5 847	5 350	5 002
Not in labor force	54 965	55 209	55 301	56 064	56 577	57 675	58 713	59 633	60 746	61 558	62 148	62 429
Men, 16 Years and Over												
Civilian noninstitutional population	80 733	81 489	82 577	83 352	83 930	85 370	86 452	87 361	88 249	89 044	90 027	91 021
Civilian labor force	61 146	61 783	62 639	63 034	63 413	64 466	64 966	65 308	65 509	65 994	66 694	67 613
Employed	58 146	58 888	59 998	60 604	61 139	62 289	62 212	61 849	61 866	62 712	63 763	64 883
Agriculture	2 347	2 436	2 389	2 376	2 273	1 743	1 606	1 611	1 597	1 583	1 562	1 554
Nonagricultural industries	55 800	56 452	57 608	58 228	58 866	60 546	60 606	60 238	60 269	61 129	62 201	63 330
Unemployed	2 999	2 896	2 641	2 431	2 274	2 177	2 754	3 459	3 643	3 282	2 931	2 730
Not in labor force	19 587	19 706	19 938	20 317	20 517	20 905	21 486	22 053	22 740	23 050	23 334	23 408

[1]Beginning in 2003, persons who selected this race group only; persons who selected more than one race group are not included. Prior to 2003, persons who reported more than one race group were included in the group they identified as the main race.

Table 1-3. Employment Status of the Civilian Noninstitutional Population, by Sex, Age, Race, and Hispanic Origin, 1995–2018—*Continued*

(Thousands of people.)

Characteristic	2007	2008	2009	2010	2011	2012	2013	2014	2015	2016	2017	2018
ALL RACES												
Both Sexes												
Civilian noninstitutional population	231 867	233 788	235 801	237 830	239 618	243 284	245 679	247 947	250 801	253 538	255 079	257 791
Civilian labor force	153 124	154 287	154 142	153 889	153 617	154 975	155 389	155 922	157 130	159 187	160 320	162 075
Employed	146 047	145 362	139 877	139 064	139 869	142 469	143 929	146 305	148 834	151 436	153 337	155 761
Agriculture	2 095	2 168	2 103	2 206	2 254	2 186	2 130	2 237	2 422	2 460	2 454	2 425
Nonagricultural industries	143 952	143 194	137 775	136 858	137 615	140 283	141 799	144 068	146 411	148 976	150 883	153 336
Unemployed	7 078	8 924	14 265	14 825	13 747	12 506	11 460	9 617	8 296	7 751	6 982	6 314
Not in labor force	78 743	79 501	81 659	83 941	86 001	88 310	90 290	92 025	93 671	94 351	94 759	95 716
Men, 16 Years and Over												
Civilian noninstitutional population	112 173	113 113	114 136	115 174	116 317	117 343	118 555	119 748	121 101	122 497	123 275	124 678
Civilian labor force	82 136	82 520	82 123	81 985	81 975	82 327	82 667	82 882	83 620	84 755	85 145	86 096
Employed	78 254	77 486	73 670	73 359	74 290	75 555	76 353	77 692	79 131	80 568	81 402	82 698
Agriculture	1 604	1 650	1 607	1 665	1 698	1 626	1 611	1 685	1 826	1 839	1 843	1 797
Nonagricultural industries	76 650	75 836	72 062	71 694	72 592	73 930	74 742	76 007	77 305	78 729	79 559	80 902
Unemployed	3 882	5 033	8 453	8 626	7 684	6 771	6 314	5 190	4 490	4 187	3 743	3 398
Not in labor force	30 036	30 593	32 013	33 189	34 343	35 017	35 889	36 865	37 481	37 743	38 130	38 582
Men, 20 Years and Over												
Civilian noninstitutional population	103 555	104 453	105 493	106 596	107 736	108 686	110 017	111 299	112 671	114 023	114 783	116 185
Civilian labor force	78 596	79 047	78 897	78 994	79 080	79 387	79 744	80 056	80 735	81 759	82 206	83 188
Employed	75 337	74 750	71 341	71 230	72 182	73 403	74 176	75 471	76 776	78 084	78 919	80 211
Agriculture	1 514	1 552	1 514	1 589	1 611	1 547	1 532	1 614	1 757	1 767	1 776	1 722
Nonagricultural industries	73 823	73 198	69 828	69 641	70 571	71 856	72 644	73 857	75 019	76 317	77 143	78 489
Unemployed	3 259	4 297	7 555	7 763	6 898	5 984	5 568	4 585	3 959	3 675	3 287	2 976
Not in labor force	24 959	25 406	26 596	27 603	28 656	29 299	30 273	31 243	31 936	32 263	32 577	32 997
Women, 16 Years and Over												
Civilian noninstitutional population	119 694	120 675	121 665	122 656	123 300	125 941	127 124	128 199	129 700	131 040	131 804	133 112
Civilian labor force	70 988	71 767	72 019	71 904	71 642	72 648	72 722	73 039	73 510	74 432	75 175	75 978
Employed	67 792	67 876	66 208	65 705	65 579	66 914	67 577	68 613	69 703	70 868	71 936	73 063
Agriculture	490	518	496	541	556	560	519	552	597	621	611	628
Nonagricultural industries	67 302	67 358	65 712	65 164	65 023	66 353	67 058	68 061	69 106	70 247	71 324	72 435
Unemployed	3 196	3 891	5 811	6 199	6 063	5 734	5 146	4 426	3 807	3 564	3 239	2 916
Not in labor force	48 707	48 908	49 646	50 752	51 658	53 293	54 401	55 159	56 190	56 608	56 629	57 134
Women, 20 Years and Over												
Civilian noninstitutional population	111 330	112 260	113 265	114 333	115 107	117 614	118 875	120 014	121 511	122 801	123 542	124 841
Civilian labor force	67 516	68 382	68 856	68 990	68 810	69 765	69 860	70 212	70 695	71 538	72 213	73 002
Employed	64 799	65 039	63 699	63 456	63 360	64 640	65 295	66 287	67 323	68 387	69 344	70 424
Agriculture	460	491	471	519	534	534	498	536	574	593	586	599
Nonagricultural industries	64 339	64 548	63 228	62 936	62 826	64 106	64 798	65 750	66 749	67 794	68 758	69 824
Unemployed	2 718	3 342	5 157	5 534	5 450	5 125	4 565	3 926	3 371	3 151	2 868	2 578
Not in labor force	43 814	43 878	44 409	45 343	46 297	47 849	49 015	49 802	50 816	51 263	51 330	51 839
Both Sexes, 16 to 19 Years												
Civilian noninstitutional population	16 982	17 075	17 043	16 901	16 774	16 984	16 787	16 633	16 619	16 714	16 754	16 765
Civilian labor force	7 012	6 858	6 390	5 906	5 727	5 823	5 785	5 654	5 700	5 889	5 901	5 885
Employed	5 911	5 573	4 837	4 378	4 327	4 426	4 458	4 548	4 734	4 965	5 074	5 126
Agriculture	121	125	119	98	109	105	100	86	91	100	92	103
Nonagricultural industries	5 790	5 448	4 719	4 281	4 218	4 321	4 358	4 462	4 643	4 865	4 982	5 023
Unemployed	1 101	1 285	1 552	1 528	1 400	1 397	1 327	1 106	966	925	827	759
Not in labor force	9 970	10 218	10 654	10 995	11 048	11 162	11 002	10 979	10 919	10 824	10 853	10 879
WHITE[1]												
Both Sexes												
Civilian noninstitutional population	188 253	189 540	190 902	192 075	193 077	193 204	194 333	195 498	196 868	198 215	198 942	200 221
Civilian labor force	124 935	125 635	125 644	125 084	124 579	123 684	123 412	123 327	123 607	124 658	124 941	125 815
Employed	119 792	119 126	114 996	114 168	114 690	114 769	115 379	116 788	117 944	119 313	120 176	121 461
Agriculture	1 953	2 021	1 968	2 071	2 134	2 033	1 975	2 093	2 262	2 309	2 267	2 251
Nonagricultural industries	117 839	117 104	113 028	112 098	112 556	112 735	113 404	114 695	115 682	117 004	117 909	119 210
Unemployed	5 143	6 509	10 648	10 916	9 889	8 915	8 033	6 540	5 662	5 345	4 765	4 354
Not in labor force	63 319	63 905	65 258	66 991	68 498	69 520	70 920	72 170	73 261	73 557	74 001	74 407
Men, 16 Years and Over												
Civilian noninstitutional population	92 073	92 725	93 433	94 082	94 801	94 266	94 865	95 513	96 147	96 861	97 225	97 933
Civilian labor force	68 158	68 351	68 051	67 728	67 551	66 921	66 842	66 680	67 018	67 564	67 592	68 082
Employed	65 289	64 624	61 630	61 252	71	61 990	62 322	63 108	63 892	64 612	65 000	65 702
Agriculture	1 501	1 539	1 499	1 557	1 602	1 515	1 495	1 571	1 701	1 725	1 694	1 670
Nonagricultural industries	63 788	63 085	60 131	59 695	60 318	60 476	60 827	61 537	62 192	62 887	63 306	64 031
Unemployed	2 869	3 727	6 421	6 476	5 631	4 931	4 520	3 572	3 126	2 952	2 592	2 380
Not in labor force	23 915	24 374	25 382	26 353	27 249	27 345	28 024	28 834	29 129	29 297	29 633	29 850

[1]Beginning in 2003, persons who selected this race group only; persons who selected more than one race group are not included. Prior to 2003, persons who reported more than one race group were included in the group they identified as the main race.

Table 1-3. Employment Status of the Civilian Noninstitutional Population, by Sex, Age, Race, and Hispanic Origin, 1995–2018—*Continued*

(Thousands of people.)

Characteristic	1995	1996	1997	1998	1999	2000	2001	2002	2003	2004	2005	2006
WHITE[1]												
Men, 20 Years and Over												
Civilian noninstitutional population	74 879	75 454	76 320	76 966	77 432	78 966	80 029	80 922	81 860	82 615	83 556	84 466
Civilian labor force	57 719	58 340	59 126	59 421	59 747	60 850	61 519	62 067	62 473	62 944	63 705	64 540
Employed	55 254	55 977	56 986	57 500	57 934	59 119	59 245	59 124	59 348	60 159	61 255	62 259
Agriculture	2 132	2 224	2 201	2 182	2 094	1 640	1 512	1 519	1 517	1 495	1 488	1 473
Nonagricultural industries	53 122	53 753	54 785	55 319	55 839	57 479	57 733	57 605	57 831	58 664	59 767	60 785
Unemployed	2 465	2 363	2 140	1 920	1 813	1 731	2 275	2 943	3 125	2 785	2 450	2 281
Not in labor force	17 161	17 114	17 194	17 545	17 685	18 116	18 510	18 855	19 386	19 671	19 851	19 927
Women, 16 Years and Over												
Civilian noninstitutional population	86 181	86 828	87 417	88 126	89 156	90 850	91 660	92 422	93 043	93 599	94 419	95 242
Civilian labor force	50 804	51 325	52 054	52 380	53 096	54 079	54 433	54 842	55 037	55 092	55 605	56 221
Employed	48 344	48 920	49 859	50 327	51 096	52 136	52 218	52 164	52 369	52 527	53 186	53 950
Agriculture	847	840	819	784	810	578	568	560	551	520	515	510
Nonagricultural industries	47 497	48 080	49 040	49 543	50 286	51 558	51 650	51 604	51 818	52 007	52 672	53 440
Unemployed	2 460	2 404	2 195	2 053	1 999	1 944	2 215	2 678	2 668	2 565	2 419	2 271
Not in labor force	35 377	35 503	35 363	35 746	36 060	36 770	37 227	37 581	38 006	38 508	38 814	39 021
Women, 20 Years and Over												
Civilian noninstitutional population	80 567	81 041	81 492	82 073	82 953	84 718	85 526	86 266	86 905	87 430	88 200	88 942
Civilian labor force	47 686	48 162	48 847	49 029	49 714	50 740	51 218	51 717	52 099	52 212	52 643	53 286
Employed	45 643	46 164	47 063	47 342	48 098	49 145	49 369	49 448	49 823	50 040	50 589	51 359
Agriculture	799	798	771	729	765	546	537	532	522	488	492	488
Nonagricultural industries	44 844	45 366	46 292	46 612	47 333	48 599	48 831	48 916	49 301	49 552	50 097	50 871
Unemployed	2 042	1 998	1 784	1 688	1 616	1 595	1 849	2 269	2 276	2 172	2 054	1 927
Not in labor force	32 881	32 879	32 645	33 044	33 239	33 978	34 308	34 548	34 806	35 218	35 557	35 656
Both Sexes, 16 to 19 Years												
Civilian noninstitutional population	11 468	11 822	12 181	12 439	12 700	12 535	12 556	12 596	12 527	12 599	12 690	12 856
Civilian labor force	6 545	6 607	6 720	6 965	7 048	6 955	6 661	6 366	5 973	5 929	5 950	6 009
Employed	5 593	5 667	5 807	6 089	6 204	6 160	5 817	5 441	5 064	5 039	5 105	5 215
Agriculture	262	254	236	250	224	135	125	121	109	116	97	102
Nonagricultural industries	5 331	5 413	5 571	5 839	5 980	6 025	5 692	5 320	4 955	4 923	5 008	5 113
Unemployed	952	939	912	876	844	795	845	925	909	890	845	794
Not in labor force	4 923	5 215	5 462	5 475	5 652	5 581	5 894	6 230	6 554	6 669	6 739	6 847
BLACK[1]												
Both Sexes												
Civilian noninstitutional population	23 246	23 604	24 003	24 373	24 855	24 902	25 138	25 578	25 686	26 065	26 517	27 007
Civilian labor force	14 817	15 134	15 529	15 982	16 365	16 397	16 421	16 565	16 526	16 638	17 013	17 314
Employed	13 279	13 542	13 969	14 556	15 056	15 156	15 006	14 872	14 739	14 909	15 313	15 765
Agriculture	101	98	117	138	117	77	62	69	63	50	51	60
Nonagricultural industries	13 178	13 444	13 852	14 417	14 939	15 079	14 944	14 804	14 676	14 859	15 261	15 705
Unemployed	1 538	1 592	1 560	1 426	1 309	1 241	1 416	1 693	1 787	1 729	1 700	1 549
Not in labor force	8 429	8 470	8 474	8 391	8 490	8 505	8 717	9 013	9 161	9 428	9 504	9 693
Men, 16 Years and Over												
Civilian noninstitutional population	10 411	10 575	10 763	10 927	11 143	11 129	11 172	11 391	11 454	11 656	11 882	12 130
Civilian labor force	7 183	7 264	7 354	7 542	7 652	7 702	7 647	7 794	7 711	7 773	7 998	8 128
Employed	6 422	6 456	6 607	6 871	7 027	7 082	6 938	6 959	6 820	6 912	7 155	7 354
Agriculture	93	86	103	118	99	67	56	63	52	43	43	51
Nonagricultural industries	6 329	6 371	6 504	6 752	6 952	7 015	6 882	6 896	6 768	6 869	7 111	7 303
Unemployed	762	808	747	671	671	620	709	835	891	860	844	774
Not in labor force	3 228	3 311	3 409	3 386	3 386	3 427	3 525	3 597	3 743	3 884	3 884	4 002
Men, 20 Years and Over												
Civilian noninstitutional population	9 280	9 414	9 575	9 727	9 926	9 952	9 993	10 196	10 278	11 656	10 659	10 864
Civilian labor force	6 730	6 806	6 910	7 053	7 182	7 240	7 200	7 347	7 346	7 773	7 600	7 720
Employed	6 137	6 167	6 325	6 530	6 702	6 741	6 627	6 652	6 586	6 912	6 901	7 079
Agriculture	89	83	101	112	96	67	55	62	51	274	43	49
Nonagricultural industries	6 048	6 084	6 224	6 418	6 606	6 675	55	6 591	6 535	6 638	6 858	7 030
Unemployed	593	639	585	524	480	499	573	695	760	860	699	640
Not in labor force	2 550	2 608	2 665	2 673	2 743	2 711	2 792	2 848	2 932	3 884	3 060	3 144
Women, 16 Years and Over												
Civilian noninstitutional population	12 835	13 029	13 241	13 446	13 711	13 772	13 966	14 187	14 232	14 409	14 635	14 877
Civilian labor force	7 634	7 869	8 175	8 441	8 713	8 695	8 774	8 772	8 815	8 865	9 014	9 186
Employed	6 857	7 086	7 362	7 685	8 029	8 073	8 068	7 914	7 919	7 997	8 158	8 410
Agriculture	8	13	14	20	18	10	6	6	11	7	8	9
Nonagricultural industries	6 849	7 073	7 348	7 665	8 011	8 064	8 062	7 907	7 908	7 990	8 150	8 402
Unemployed	777	784	813	756	684	621	706	858	895	868	856	775
Not in labor force	5 201	5 159	5 066	5 005	4 999	5 078	5 192	5 415	5 418	5 544	5 621	5 691

[1]Beginning in 2003, persons who selected this race group only; persons who selected more than one race group are not included. Prior to 2003, persons who reported more than one race group were included in the group they identified as the main race.

Table 1-3. Employment Status of the Civilian Noninstitutional Population, by Sex, Age, Race, and Hispanic Origin, 1995–2018—*Continued*

(Thousands of people.)

Characteristic	2007	2008	2009	2010	2011	2012	2013	2014	2015	2016	2017	2018
WHITE[1]												
Men, 20 Years and Over												
Civilian noninstitutional population	85 420	86 056	86 789	87 502	88 191	87 780	88 474	89 193	89 865	90 572	90 941	91 662
Civilian labor force	65 214	65 483	65 372	65 265	65 165	64 540	64 505	64 430	64 710	65 169	65 296	65 812
Employed	62 806	62 304	59 626	59 438	60 118	60 193	60 511	61 289	61 959	62 575	63 009	63 719
Agriculture	1 417	1 447	1 410	1 483	1 518	1 438	1 418	1 504	1 638	1 658	1 629	1 600
Nonagricultural industries	61 389	60 857	58 216	57 955	58 600	58 755	59 093	59 785	60 321	60 917	61 380	62 118
Unemployed	2 408	3 179	5 746	5 828	5 046	4 347	3 994	3 141	2 751	2 594	2 288	2 094
Not in labor force	20 206	20 573	21 417	22 236	23 026	23 241	23 969	24 763	25 155	25 403	25 645	25 849
Women, 16 Years and Over												
Civilian noninstitutional population	96 180	96 814	97 469	97 993	98 276	98 938	99 467	99 984	100 720	101 354	101 717	102 289
Civilian labor force	56 777	57 284	57 593	57 356	57 028	56 763	56 571	56 648	56 589	57 095	57 349	57 732
Employed	54 503	54 501	53 366	52 916	52 770	52 779	53 057	53 680	54 052	54 701	55 176	55 759
Agriculture	452	482	469	513	532	519	480	522	562	585	573	581
Nonagricultural industries	54 050	54 019	52 897	52 402	52 238	52 260	52 577	53 158	53 490	54 117	54 603	55 178
Unemployed	2 274	2 782	4 227	4 440	4 257	3 985	3 513	2 968	2 537	2 393	2 173	1 973
Not in labor force	39 403	39 531	39 876	40 638	41 248	42 175	42 897	43 337	44 132	44 260	44 368	44 556
Women, 20 Years and Over												
Civilian noninstitutional population	89 790	90 400	91 078	91 683	92 068	92 766	93 360	93 928	94 680	95 301	95 661	96 242
Civilian labor force	53 925	54 508	54 976	54 957	54 700	54 475	54 299	54 421	54 410	54 871	55 103	55 426
Employed	51 996	52 124	51 231	50 997	50 881	50 911	51 198	51 798	52 161	52 771	53 179	53 682
Agriculture	423	457	444	492	511	493	460	507	540	557	549	553
Nonagricultural industries	51 572	51 667	50 787	50 505	50 371	50 418	50 737	51 291	51 621	52 214	52 630	53 129
Unemployed	1 930	2 384	3 745	3 960	3 818	3 564	3 102	2 623	2 249	2 100	1 923	1 743
Not in labor force	35 864	35 892	36 101	36 725	37 368	38 291	39 060	39 507	40 270	40 430	40 559	40 816
Both Sexes, 16 to 19 Years												
Civilian noninstitutional population	13 043	13 084	13 035	12 891	12 818	12 658	12 499	12 377	12 323	12 342	12 339	12 318
Civilian labor force	5 795	5 644	5 295	4 861	4 714	4 669	4 608	4 476	4 487	4 618	4 542	4 576
Employed	4 990	4 697	4 138	3 733	3 691	3 665	3 671	3 701	3 824	3 967	3 989	4 060
Agriculture	113	118	114	96	105	103	97	82	84	94	89	98
Nonagricultural industries	4 877	4 580	4 025	3 637	3 585	3 563	3 574	3 619	3 740	3 874	3 899	3 962
Unemployed	805	947	1 157	1 128	1 024	1 004	937	775	662	651	554	516
Not in labor force	7 248	7 440	7 740	8 030	8 103	7 988	7 891	7 901	7 836	7 724	7 797	7 741
BLACK[1]												
Both Sexes												
Civilian noninstitutional population	27 485	27 843	28 241	28 708	29 114	29 907	30 376	30 843	31 386	31 889	32 247	32 761
Civilian labor force	17 496	17 740	17 632	17 862	17 881	18 400	18 580	18 873	19 318	19 637	20 088	20 414
Employed	16 051	15 953	15 025	15 010	15 051	15 856	16 151	16 732	17 472	17 982	18 587	19 091
Agriculture	53	55	66	59	52	61	58	62	66	66	75	62
Nonagricultural industries	15 998	15 898	14 959	14 951	14 999	15 795	16 093	16 670	17 406	17 916	18 512	19 030
Unemployed	1 445	1 788	2 606	2 852	2 831	2 544	2 429	2 141	1 846	1 655	1 501	1 322
Not in labor force	9 989	10 103	10 609	10 846	11 233	11 508	11 797	11 970	12 068	12 252	12 159	12 347
Men, 16 Years and Over												
Civilian noninstitutional population	12 361	12 516	12 705	12 939	13 164	13 508	13 747	13 997	14 268	14 525	14 712	14 964
Civilian labor force	8 252	8 347	8 265	8 415	8 454	8 594	8 733	8 909	9 099	9 315	9 508	9 694
Employed	7 500	7 398	6 817	6 865	6 953	7 302	7 497	7 818	8 164	8 471	8 742	9 018
Agriculture	46	49	56	53	47	51	48	54	57	58	67	50
Nonagricultural industries	7 454	7 350	6 761	6 812	6 905	7 252	7 448	7 764	8 107	8 413	8 675	8 968
Unemployed	752	949	1 448	1 550	1 502	1 292	1 236	1 091	935	845	766	676
Not in labor force	4 110	4 169	4 441	4 524	4 710	4 913	5 014	5 089	5 169	5 209	5 204	5 270
Men, 20 Years and Over												
Civilian noninstitutional population	11 057	11 194	11 379	11 626	11 882	12 189	12 471	12 751	13 031	13 278	13 464	13 723
Civilian labor force	7 867	7 962	7 914	8 076	8 125	8 256	8 386	8 586	8 773	8 965	9 163	9 327
Employed	7 245	7 151	6 628	6 680	6 765	7 104	7 304	7 613	7 938	8 228	8 500	8 745
Agriculture	45	47	55	52	46	50	48	54	55	55	66	48
Nonagricultural industries	7 201	7 104	6 573	6 628	6 719	7 053	7 256	7 559	7 883	8 173	8 435	8 696
Unemployed	622	811	1 286	1 396	1 360	1 152	1 082	973	835	737	663	582
Not in labor force	3 189	3 232	3 465	3 550	17	3 932	4 084	4 165	4 258	4 313	4 301	4 396
Women, 16 Years and Over												
Civilian noninstitutional population	15 124	15 328	15 536	15 769	15 950	16 400	16 629	16 846	17 118	17 365	17 535	17 797
Civilian labor force	9 244	9 393	9 367	9 447	9 427	9 805	9 846	9 964	10 218	10 321	10 580	10 720
Employed	8 551	8 554	8 208	8 145	8 098	8 553	8 654	8 915	9 308	9 511	9 845	10 073
Agriculture	7	6	10	6	5	10	9	8	10	8	8	12
Nonagricultural industries	8 544	8 548	8 198	8 139	8 093	8 543	8 645	8 906	9 298	9 503	9 837	10 062
Unemployed	693	839	1 159	1 302	1 329	1 252	1 192	1 050	911	810	735	646
Not in labor force	5 879	5 934	6 169	6 322	6 523	6 595	6 783	6 881	6 899	7 043	6 955	7 077

[1]Beginning in 2003, persons who selected this race group only; persons who selected more than one race group are not included. Prior to 2003, persons who reported more than one race group were included in the group they identified as the main race.

Table 1-3. Employment Status of the Civilian Noninstitutional Population, by Sex, Age, Race, and Hispanic Origin, 1995–2018—*Continued*

(Thousands of people.)

Characteristic	1995	1996	1997	1998	1999	2000	2001	2002	2003	2004	2005	2006
BLACK[1]												
Women, 20 Years and Over												
Civilian noninstitutional population	11 682	11 833	12 016	12 023	12 451	12 561	12 758	12 966	13 026	14 409	13 377	13 578
Civilian labor force	7 175	7 405	7 686	7 912	8 224	8 215	8 323	8 348	8 409	8 865	8 610	8 723
Employed	6 556	6 762	7 013	7 290	7 663	7 703	7 741	7 610	7 636	7 997	7 876	8 068
Agriculture	7	12	13	19	17	9	6	5	10	7	7	7
Nonagricultural industries	6 548	6 749	7 000	7 272	7 646	7 694	7 735	7 604	7 626	7 701	7 868	8 060
Unemployed	620	643	673	622	561	512	582	738	772	868	734	656
Not in labor force	4 507	4 428	4 330	4 291	4 226	4 346	4 434	4 618	4 618	5 544	4 768	4 854
Both Sexes, 16 to 19 Years												
Civilian noninstitutional population	2 284	2 356	2 412	2 443	2 479	2 389	2 388	2 416	2 382	2 423	2 481	2 565
Civilian labor force	911	923	933	1 017	959	941	898	870	771	762	803	871
Employed	586	613	631	736	691	711	637	611	516	520	536	618
Agriculture	5	3	3	8	4	1	1	2	1	0	1	3
Nonagricultural industries	581	611	611	728	687	710	637	609	515	520	535	614
Unemployed	325	310	310	281	268	230	260	260	255	241	267	253
Not in labor force	1 372	1 434	1 434	1 427	1 520	1 448	1 490	1 546	1 611	1 661	1 677	1 694
HISPANIC[2]												
Both Sexes												
Civilian noninstitutional population	18 629	19 213	20 321	21 070	21 650	23 938	24 942	25 963	27 551	28 109	29 133	30 103
Civilian labor force	12 267	12 774	13 796	14 317	14 665	16 689	17 328	17 943	18 813	19 272	19 824	20 694
Employed	11 127	11 642	12 726	13 291	13 720	15 735	16 190	16 590	17 372	17 930	18 632	19 613
Agriculture	604	609	660	742	734	536	423	448	446	441	423	428
Nonagricultural industries	10 524	11 033	12 067	12 549	12 986	15 199	15 767	16 141	16 927	17 489	18 209	19 185
Unemployed	1 140	1 132	1 069	1 026	945	954	1 138	1 353	1 441	1 342	1 191	1 081
Not in labor force	6 362	6 439	6 526	6 753	6 985	7 249	7 614	8 020	8 738	8 837	9 310	9 409
Men, 16 Years and Over												
Civilian noninstitutional population	9 329	9 604	10 368	10 734	10 713	12 174	12 695	13 221	14 098	14 417	14 962	15 473
Civilian labor force	7 376	7 646	8 309	8 571	8 546	9 923	10 279	10 609	11 288	11 587	11 985	12 488
Employed	6 725	7 039	7 728	8 018	8 067	9 428	9 668	9 845	10 479	10 832	11 337	11 887
Agriculture	527	537	571	651	642	449	345	361	350	356	350	347
Nonagricultural industries	6 198	6 502	7 157	7 367	7 425	8 979	9 323	9 484	10 129	10 476	10 987	11 540
Unemployed	651	607	582	552	480	494	611	764	809	755	647	601
Not in labor force	1 952	1 957	2 059	2 164	2 167	2 252	2 416	2 613	2 810	2 831	2 977	2 985
Men, 20 Years and Over												
Civilian noninstitutional population	8 375	8 611	9 250	9 573	9 523	10 841	11 386	11 928	12 797	13 082	13 586	14 046
Civilian labor force	6 898	7 150	7 779	8 005	7 950	9 247	9 595	9 977	10 756	11 020	11 408	11 888
Employed	6 367	6 655	7 307	7 570	7 576	8 859	9 100	9 341	10 063	10 385	10 872	11 391
Agriculture	501	510	544	621	602	423	328	345	336	335	341	337
Nonagricultural industries	5 866	6 145	6 763	6 949	6 974	8 435	8 773	8 996	9 727	10 050	10 532	11 054
Unemployed	530	495	471	436	374	388	495	636	693	635	536	497
Not in labor force	1 477	1 461	1 471	1 568	1 573	1 595	1 791	1 951	2 041	2 061	2 177	2 157
Women, 16 Years and Over												
Civilian noninstitutional population	9 300	9 610	9 953	10 335	10 937	11 764	12 247	12 742	13 452	13 692	14 172	14 630
Civilian labor force	4 891	5 128	5 486	5 746	6 119	6 767	7 049	7 334	7 525	7 685	7 839	8 206
Employed	4 403	4 602	4 999	5 273	5 653	6 307	6 522	6 744	6 894	7 098	7 295	7 725
Agriculture	76	72	89	91	92	87	77	87	96	85	73	80
Nonagricultural industries	4 326	4 531	4 910	5 182	5 561	6 220	6 445	6 657	6 798	7 013	7 222	7 645
Unemployed	488	525	488	473	466	460	527	590	631	587	544	480
Not in labor force	4 409	4 482	4 466	4 589	4 819	4 997	5 198	5 408	5 928	6 007	6 333	6 424
Women, 20 Years and Over												
Civilian noninstitutional population	8 382	8 654	8 950	9 292	9 821	10 574	11 049	11 528	12 211	12 420	12 858	13 262
Civilian labor force	4 779	5 106	5 304	5 666	6 275	6 557	6 863	7 096	7 096	7 257	7 377	7 735
Employed	4 116	4 341	4 705	4 928	5 290	5 903	6 121	6 367	6 541	6 752	6 913	7 321
Agriculture	72	69	83	85	88	81	73	84	91	78	70	77
Nonagricultural industries	4 044	4 272	4 622	4 843	5 202	5 822	6 048	6 283	6 450	6 674	6 843	7 244
Unemployed	404	438	401	376	376	371	436	496	555	504	464	414
Not in labor force	3 863	3 875	3 845	3 988	4 155	4 299	4 492	4 666	5 114	5 163	5 481	5 527
Both Sexes, 16 to 19 Years												
Civilian noninstitutional population	1 872	1 948	2 121	2 204	2 307	2 523	2 508	2 507	2 543	2 608	2 689	2 796
Civilian labor force	850	845	911	1 007	1 049	1 168	1 176	1 103	960	995	1 038	1 071
Employed	645	646	714	793	854	973	969	882	768	792	847	900
Agriculture	31	29	33	36	45	31	22	19	19	25	13	14
Nonagricultural industries	614	617	682	757	809	942	947	863	749	767	834	887
Unemployed	205	199	197	214	196	194	208	221	192	203	191	170
Not in labor force	1 022	1 103	1 210	1 197	1 257	1 355	1 331	1 404	1 583	1 612	1 651	1 725

[1]Beginning in 2003, persons who selected this race group only; persons who selected more than one race group are not included. Prior to 2003, persons who reported more than one race group were included in the group they identified as the main race.
[2]May be of any race.

Table 1-3. Employment Status of the Civilian Noninstitutional Population, by Sex, Age, Race, and Hispanic Origin, 1995–2018—*Continued*

(Thousands of people.)

Characteristic	2007	2008	2009	2010	2011	2012	2013	2014	2015	2016	2017	2018
BLACK[1]												
Women, 20 Years and Over												
Civilian noninstitutional population	13 788	13 974	14 178	14 425	14 638	15 076	15 340	15 584	15 863	16 102	16 272	16 539
Civilian labor force	8 828	8 991	8 988	9 110	9 110	9 433	9 476	9 606	9 843	9 943	10 171	10 324
Employed	8 240	8 260	7 956	7 944	7 906	8 313	8 408	8 663	9 032	9 219	9 514	9 751
Agriculture	7	6	10	6	5	10	9	8	10	8	8	12
Nonagricultural industries	8 233	8 254	7 946	7 938	7 901	8 303	8 399	8 655	9 022	9 211	9 506	9 739
Unemployed	588	732	1 032	1 165	1 204	1 119	1 069	943	811	724	657	573
Not in labor force	4 960	4 982	5 190	5 315	5 529	5 643	5 864	5 978	6 021	6 159	6 101	6 215
Both Sexes, 16 to 19 Years												
Civilian noninstitutional population	2 640	2 676	2 684	2 657	2 594	2 643	2 565	2 508	2 491	2 510	2 511	2 499
Civilian labor force	801	787	729	677	647	711	717	681	701	729	754	763
Employed	566	541	442	386	380	438	439	456	502	535	573	596
Agriculture	1	1	1	1	1	0	1	0	2	3	1	2
Nonagricultural industries	564	540	440	385	379	438	438	456	500	532	571	594
Unemployed	235	246	288	291	267	272	278	225	199	194	181	167
Not in labor force	1 839	1 889	1 954	1 980	1 947	1 932	1 848	1 827	1 790	1 781	1 758	1 736
HISPANIC[2]												
Both Sexes												
Civilian noninstitutional population	31 383	32 141	32 891	33 713	34 438	36 759	37 517	38 400	39 617	40 697	41 371	42 734
Civilian labor force	21 602	22 024	22 352	22 748	22 898	24 391	24 771	25 370	26 126	26 797	27 339	28 336
Employed	20 382	20 346	19 647	19 906	20 269	21 878	22 514	23 492	24 400	25 249	25 938	27 012
Agriculture	426	441	426	480	523	491	495	517	580	604	629	630
Nonagricultural industries	19 956	19 904	19 221	19 426	19 746	21 387	22 019	22 975	23 820	24 645	25 309	26 383
Unemployed	1 220	1 678	2 706	2 843	2 629	2 514	2 257	1 878	1 726	1 548	1 401	1 323
Not in labor force	9 781	10 116	10 539	10 964	11 540	12 368	12 746	13 030	13 491	13 900	14 032	14 398
Men, 16 Years and Over												
Civilian noninstitutional population	16 154	16 524	16 897	17 359	17 753	18 434	18 798	19 244	19 745	20 266	20 578	21 287
Civilian labor force	13 005	13 255	13 310	13 511	13 576	14 026	14 341	14 651	15 054	15 396	15 604	16 113
Employed	12 310	12 248	11 640	11 800	12 049	12 643	13 078	13 655	14 111	14 563	14 874	15 418
Agriculture	352	364	344	377	418	388	392	403	454	464	477	468
Nonagricultural industries	11 958	11 884	11 296	11 423	11 631	12 255	12 686	13 251	13 657	14 099	14 397	14 950
Unemployed	695	1 007	1 670	1 711	1 527	1 383	1 263	996	943	833	730	695
Not in labor force	3 149	3 270	3 588	3 849	4 177	4 408	4 457	4 593	4 691	4 870	4 974	5 174
Men, 20 Years and Over												
Civilian noninstitutional population	14 649	14 971	15 305	15 693	15 941	16 555	16 928	17 371	17 860	18 346	18 627	19 289
Civilian labor force	12 403	12 629	12 730	12 958	13 030	13 407	13 728	14 066	14 444	14 775	14 987	15 464
Employed	11 827	11 769	11 256	11 438	11 685	12 212	12 638	13 202	13 624	14 055	14 355	14 873
Agriculture	337	351	332	367	405	374	378	391	440	454	468	458
Nonagricultural industries	11 490	11 418	10 924	11 071	11 281	11 838	12 259	12 811	13 184	13 602	13 887	14 415
Unemployed	576	860	1 474	1 519	1 345	1 195	1 090	864	820	720	632	591
Not in labor force	2 246	2 342	2 575	2 735	2 911	3 149	3 200	3 305	3 416	3 571	3 640	3 825
Women, 16 Years and Over												
Civilian noninstitutional population	15 229	15 616	15 993	16 353	16 685	18 324	18 719	19 156	19 872	20 430	20 794	21 447
Civilian labor force	8 597	8 769	9 043	9 238	9 322	10 365	10 430	10 720	11 072	11 401	11 735	12 223
Employed	8 072	8 098	8 007	8 106	8 220	9 235	9 437	9 838	10 289	10 686	11 064	11 594
Agriculture	74	77	82	103	105	103	103	114	126	140	153	162
Nonagricultural industries	7 999	8 021	7 925	8 003	8 115	9 131	9 334	9 724	10 163	10 547	10 912	11 433
Unemployed	525	672	1 036	1 132	1 102	1 130	994	882	783	715	671	628
Not in labor force	6 632	6 847	6 951	7 116	7 363	7 959	8 289	8 437	8 800	9 029	9 058	9 224
Women, 20 Years and Over												
Civilian noninstitutional population	13 791	14 127	14 463	14 776	15 090	16 548	16 938	17 367	18 052	18 573	18 900	19 507
Civilian labor force	8 108	8 274	8 560	8 789	8 902	9 853	9 911	10 195	10 539	10 844	11 128	11 592
Employed	7 662	7 707	59	7 788	8 902	8 858	9 056	9 431	9 853	10 217	10 543	11 045
Agriculture	69	75	78	101	104	100	99	111	123	137	148	159
Nonagricultural industries	7 593	7 632	7 570	7 687	7 814	8 758	8 957	9 320	9 730	10 079	10 394	10 886
Unemployed	446	567	911	1 001	984	995	855	764	686	627	585	547
Not in labor force	5 682	5 853	5 903	5 987	6 187	6 695	7 028	7 172	7 513	7 729	7 773	7 915
Both Sexes, 16 to 19 Years												
Civilian noninstitutional population	2 944	3 042	3 123	3 243	3 407	3 656	3 651	3 662	3 705	3 777	3 844	3 938
Civilian labor force	1 091	1 121	1 063	1 002	965	1 131	1 133	1 109	1 144	1 178	1 225	1 280
Employed	894	870	742	680	665	808	821	859	922	977	1 041	1 094
Agriculture	20	15	16	12	14	17	18	15	17	13	13	13
Nonagricultural industries	874	855	726	668	651	791	803	844	906	964	1 027	1 081
Unemployed	197	251	321	322	300	324	312	250	221	201	184	186
Not in labor force	1 853	1 921	2 061	2 242	2 442	2 524	2 518	2 553	2 562	2 599	2 619	2 658

[1]Beginning in 2003, persons who selected this race group only; persons who selected more than one race group are not included. Prior to 2003, persons who reported more than one race group were included in the group they identified as the main race.

[2]May be of any race.

Table 1-4. Employment Status of the Civilian Noninstitutional Population, by Sex and Marital Status, 1995–2018

(Thousands of people.)

Race, marital status, and year	Men				Women			
	Civilian noninstitutional population	Civilian labor force			Civilian noninstitutional population	Civilian labor force		
		Total	Employed	Unemployed		Total	Employed	Unemployed
ALL RACES								
Single								
1995	26 918	19 841	17 833	2 007	23 151	15 467	14 053	1 413
1996	27 387	20 071	18 055	2 016	23 623	15 842	14 403	1 439
1997	28 311	20 689	18 783	1 906	24 285	16 492	15 037	1 455
1998	28 693	21 037	19 240	1 798	24 941	17 087	15 755	1 332
1999	29 104	21 351	19 686	1 665	25 576	17 575	16 267	1 308
2000	29 887	22 002	20 339	1 663	25 920	17 849	16 628	1 221
2001	30 646	22 285	20 298	1 988	26 462	18 021	16 635	1 386
2002	31 072	22 289	19 983	2 306	26 999	18 203	16 583	1 621
2003	31 691	22 297	19 841	2 457	27 802	18 397	16 723	1 674
2004	32 422	22 776	20 395	2 381	28 228	18 616	16 995	1 621
2005	33 125	23 214	21 006	2 209	29 046	19 183	17 588	1 595
2006	33 931	23 974	21 907	2 067	29 624	19 474	17 978	1 496
2007	34 650	24 276	22 143	2 132	30 219	19 745	18 322	1 422
2008	35 274	24 643	21 938	2 705	30 980	20 231	18 513	1 717
2009	36 087	24 640	20 628	4 011	31 500	20 224	17 800	2 424
2010	37 137	24 985	20 850	4 135	32 548	20 592	17 950	2 642
2011	37 782	25 301	21 474	3 827	33 266	20 878	18 266	2 612
2012	38 180	25 494	22 002	3 492	34 267	21 506	18 973	2 533
2013	38 930	26 046	22 648	3 398	35 047	22 070	19 690	2 381
2014	39 676	26 456	23 535	2 921	35 506	22 320	20 222	2 098
2015	40 151	26 803	24 267	2 537	36 145	22 738	20 881	1 857
2016	40 928	27 545	25 217	2 328	36 800	23 321	21 606	1 715
2017	41 059	27 691	25 553	2 138	37 318	23 993	22 442	1 552
2018	41 958	28 394	26 442	1 952	38 079	24 556	23 124	1 432
Married, Spouse Present								
1995	56 100	43 472	42 048	1 424	54 716	33 359	32 063	1 296
1996	56 363	43 739	42 417	1 322	54 970	33 618	32 406	1 211
1997	56 396	43 808	42 642	1 167	54 915	33 802	32 755	1 047
1998	56 670	43 957	42 923	1 034	55 331	33 857	32 872	985
1999	57 089	44 244	43 254	990	56 178	34 372	33 450	921
2000	58 167	44 987	44 078	908	57 557	35 146	34 209	937
2001	58 448	45 233	44 007	1 226	57 610	35 236	34 153	1 083
2002	59 102	45 766	44 116	1 650	58 165	35 477	34 153	1 323
2003	60 063	46 404	44 653	1 751	59 069	36 046	34 695	1 352
2004	60 412	46 550	45 084	1 466	59 278	35 845	34 600	1 244
2005	60 545	46 771	45 483	1 287	59 205	35 941	34 773	1 168
2006	60 751	46 842	45 700	1 142	59 576	36 314	35 272	1 042
2007	61 760	47 520	46 314	1 206	60 474	36 881	35 832	1 049
2008	61 794	47 450	45 860	1 590	60 554	37 194	35 869	1 325
2009	61 773	47 114	43 998	3 115	60 675	37 264	35 207	2 057
2010	61 254	46 430	43 292	3 138	60 257	36 742	34 582	2 160
2011	61 358	45 954	43 283	2 671	60 061	36 141	34 110	2 031
2012	61 757	46 094	43 820	2 274	61 219	36 436	34 521	1 915
2013	61 932	45 971	43 978	1 993	61 386	36 137	34 484	1 653
2014	62 432	45 919	44 377	1 542	61 754	36 082	34 720	1 363
2015	62 975	46 248	44 938	1 310	62 203	36 135	34 997	1 138
2016	63 748	46 586	45 327	1 259	62 852	36 387	35 294	1 093
2017	64 184	46 818	45 705	1 113	63 178	36 776	35 782	994
2018	64 171	46 891	45 932	959	63 353	36 885	35 988	897
Divorced, Widowed, or Separated								
1995	12 160	8 048	7 496	551	25 539	12 118	11 407	712
1996	12 456	8 276	7 735	541	25 791	12 397	11 691	706
1997	13 009	8 764	8 260	504	26 218	12 742	12 082	660
1998	13 394	8 965	8 530	435	26 190	12 771	12 143	628
1999	13 528	8 918	8 507	411	26 276	12 909	12 324	585
2000	13 910	9 291	8 888	403	27 135	13 308	12 748	559
2001	14 188	9 367	8 892	476	27 738	13 592	12 949	642
2002	14 411	9 445	8 804	641	27 821	13 683	12 846	837
2003	14 680	9 537	8 838	699	27 862	13 828	12 986	842
2004	14 875	9 654	9 045	608	28 141	13 961	13 133	828
2005	15 481	10 048	9 484	563	28 680	14 163	13 396	768
2006	15 923	10 440	9 895	545	29 010	14 385	13 675	709
2007	15 763	10 341	9 797	544	29 001	14 362	13 638	724
2008	16 044	10 427	9 688	739	29 141	14 342	13 494	849
2009	16 275	10 370	9 043	1 326	29 490	14 531	13 201	1 330
2010	16 783	10 570	9 217	1 352	29 851	14 570	13 173	1 397
2011	17 177	10 719	9 533	1 186	29 974	14 623	13 203	1 420
2012	17 406	10 738	9 734	1 005	30 454	14 706	13 420	1 286
2013	17 694	10 649	9 726	923	30 691	14 515	13 403	1 112
2014	17 639	10 508	9 780	727	30 938	14 637	13 672	965
2015	17 975	10 569	9 926	643	31 352	14 637	13 825	812
2016	17 821	10 624	10 025	600	31 389	14 725	13 968	757
2017	18 032	10 636	10 144	492	31 308	14 405	13 712	693
2018	18 550	10 811	10 325	487	31 680	14 538	13 951	587

Note: See notes and definitions for information on historical comparability.

Table 1-5. Employment Status of the Civilian Noninstitutional Population, by Region, Division, State, and Selected Territory, 2017–2018

(Thousands of people, percent.)

Region, division, and state	2017						2018					
	Civilian noninstitutional population	Civilian labor force					Civilian noninstitutional population	Civilian labor force				
		Total	Participation rate	Employed	Unemployed	Unemployment rate		Total	Participation rate	Employed	Unemployed	Unemployment rate
UNITED STATES[1]	255 079	160 320	62.9	153 337	6 982	4.4	257 791	162 075	62.9	155 761	6 314	3.9
Northeast	45 074	28 385	63.0	27 110	1 275	4.5	45 168	28 495	63.1	27 362	1 133	4.0
New England	12 045	7 946	66.0	7 638	307	3.9	12 110	8 073	66.7	7 793	280	3.5
Connecticut	2 878	1 897	65.9	1 808	89	4.7	2 883	1 905	66.1	1 827	78	4.1
Maine	1 099	698	63.5	675	24	3.4	1 104	699	63.3	675	24	3.4
Massachusetts	5 586	3 696	66.2	3 557	139	3.8	5 630	3 805	67.6	3 678	127	3.3
New Hampshire	1 105	754	68.2	734	20	2.7	1 114	762	68.4	743	19	2.5
Rhode Island	859	554	64.5	529	24	4.4	861	556	64.6	533	23	4.1
Vermont	516	346	67.1	336	10	3.0	519	346	66.7	337	9	2.7
Middle Atlantic	33 030	20 440	61.9	19 472	968	4.7	33 058	20 422	61.8	19 569	853	4.2
New Jersey	7 058	4 454	63.1	4 248	206	4.6	7 082	4 423	62.5	4 240	183	4.1
New York	15 724	9 561	60.8	9 114	448	4.7	15 705	9 575	61.0	9 181	394	4.1
Pennsylvania	10 248	6 425	62.7	6 111	314	4.9	10 271	6 424	62.5	6 149	276	4.3
Midwest	53 468	34 777	65.0	33 344	1 433	4.1	53 674	34 817	64.9	33 530	1 287	3.7
East North Central	36 961	23 623	63.9	22 570	1 053	4.5	37 072	23 642	63.8	22 687	955	4.0
Illinois	10 049	6 490	64.6	6 171	319	4.9	10 035	6 470	64.5	6 191	278	4.3
Indiana	5 176	3 337	64.5	3 218	119	3.6	5 208	3 382	64.9	3 266	116	3.4
Michigan	7 954	4 886	61.4	4 661	225	4.6	7 986	4 902	61.4	4 699	203	4.1
Ohio	9 193	5 770	62.8	5 483	287	5.0	9 229	5 755	62.4	5 492	263	4.6
Wisconsin	4 589	3 140	68.4	3 037	103	3.3	4 615	3 133	67.9	3 039	94	3.0
West North Central	16 507	11 154	67.6	10 774	380	3.4	16 602	11 176	67.3	10 843	332	3.0
Iowa	2 453	1 678	68.4	1 626	52	3.1	2 465	1 687	68.4	1 644	43	2.5
Kansas	2 217	1 479	66.7	1 425	54	3.7	2 222	1 482	66.7	1 432	50	3.4
Minnesota	4 357	3 057	70.2	2 953	104	3.4	4 395	3 070	69.9	2 981	89	2.9
Missouri	4 776	3 061	64.1	2 946	115	3.8	4 796	3 052	63.6	2 955	98	3.2
Nebraska	1 463	1 012	69.2	982	29	2.9	1 474	1 020	69.2	992	29	2.8
North Dakota	579	410	70.8	399	11	2.7	582	404	69.4	394	11	2.6
South Dakota	662	456	68.9	442	15	3.2	669	459	68.6	446	14	3.0
South	96 100	59 137	61.5	56 571	2 566	4.3	97 203	59 772	61.5	57 497	2 275	3.8
South Atlantic	51 037	31 557	61.8	30 196	1 362	4.3	51 681	31 846	61.6	30 670	1 176	3.7
Delaware	762	477	62.6	455	21	4.5	772	482	62.4	464	18	3.8
District of Columbia	570	401	70.4	377	24	6.1	575	405	70.4	382	22	5.6
Florida	16 940	10 093	59.6	9 669	424	4.2	17 233	10 235	59.4	9 870	365	3.6
Georgia	7 995	5 059	63.3	4 822	237	4.7	8 099	5 108	63.1	4 906	201	3.9
Maryland	4 736	3 193	67.4	3 058	136	4.3	4 755	3 197	67.2	3 072	125	3.9
North Carolina	8 029	4 938	61.5	4 717	221	4.5	8 141	4 982	61.2	4 787	195	3.9
South Carolina	3 946	2 306	58.4	2 207	99	4.3	4 004	2 323	58.0	2 244	80	3.4
Virginia	6 595	4 310	65.4	4 150	159	3.7	6 645	4 331	65.2	4 203	129	3.0
West Virginia	1 464	780	53.3	739	41	5.2	1 456	783	53.8	742	41	5.3
East South Central	14 869	8 703	58.5	8 320	382	4.4	14 958	8 781	58.7	8 431	350	4.0
Alabama	3 833	2 178	56.8	2 082	97	4.4	3 847	2 199	57.2	2 112	86	3.9
Kentucky	3 475	2 054	59.1	1 953	101	4.9	3 490	2 062	59.1	1 972	89	4.3
Mississippi	2 290	1 281	55.9	1 215	65	5.1	2 293	1 276	55.6	1 215	61	4.8
Tennessee	5 270	3 190	60.5	3 070	120	3.8	5 329	3 245	60.9	3 132	113	3.5
West South Central	30 195	18 877	62.5	18 055	822	4.4	30 563	19 145	62.6	18 396	749	3.9
Arkansas	2 324	1 348	58.0	1 298	50	3.7	2 336	1 351	57.8	1 301	50	3.7
Louisiana	3 584	2 104	58.7	1 996	108	5.1	3 582	2 103	58.7	2 001	103	4.9
Oklahoma	3 000	1 836	61.2	1 758	78	4.2	3 011	1 842	61.2	1 779	63	3.4
Texas	21 287	13 589	63.8	13 003	586	4.3	21 635	13 848	64.0	13 314	534	3.9
West	60 358	37 975	62.9	36 269	1 706	4.5	61 046	38 555	63.2	36 954	1 601	4.2
Mountain	18 679	11 916	63.8	11 433	483	4.1	19 028	12 224	64.2	11 736	487	4.0
Arizona	5 492	3 328	60.6	3 165	163	4.9	5 606	3 440	61.4	3 274	166	4.8
Colorado	4 399	2 992	68.0	2 911	81	2.7	4 477	3 096	69.2	2 995	102	3.3
Idaho	1 305	835	64.0	808	27	3.2	1 337	857	64.1	833	24	2.8
Montana	834	525	62.9	504	21	3.9	843	528	62.6	509	20	3.7
Nevada	2 328	1 458	62.6	1 385	74	5.1	2 382	1 500	63.0	1 432	68	4.6
New Mexico	1 625	936	57.6	881	55	5.9	1 633	940	57.6	894	47	4.9
Utah	2 248	1 548	68.9	1 498	50	3.3	2 303	1 572	68.3	1 523	49	3.1
Wyoming	448	293	65.4	281	12	4.2	448	290	64.7	278	12	4.1
Pacific	41 679	26 059	62.5	24 836	1 223	4.7	42 018	26 331	62.7	25 218	1 114	4.2
Alaska	547	361	66.0	336	25	7.0	547	357	65.3	333	24	6.6
California	30 865	19 205	62.2	18 285	920	4.8	31 063	19 398	62.4	18 583	815	4.2
Hawaii	1 093	684	62.6	667	17	2.4	1 092	679	62.2	662	17	2.4
Oregon	3 332	2 091	62.8	2 005	86	4.1	3 376	2 105	62.4	2 017	87	4.2
Washington	5 842	3 719	63.7	3 544	175	4.7	5 941	3 793	63.8	3 622	171	4.5

Note: Data refer to place of residence. Region and division data are derived from summing the component states. Sub-national data reflect revised population controls and model reestimation.

[1]Due to separate processing and weighing procedures, totals for the United States differ from the results obtained by aggregating data for regions, divisions, or states.

Table 1-6. Civilian Noninstitutional Population, by Age, Race, Sex, and Hispanic Origin, 1948–2018

(Thousands of people.)

Race, Hispanic origin, sex, and year	16 years and over	16 to 19 years			20 years and over						
		Total	16 to 17 years	18 to 19 years	Total	20 to 24 years	25 to 34 years	35 to 44 years	45 to 54 years	55 to 64 years	65 years and over
ALL RACES											
Both Sexes											
1948	103 068	8 449	4 265	4 185	94 618	11 530	22 610	20 097	16 771	12 885	10 720
1949	103 994	8 215	4 139	4 079	95 778	11 312	22 822	20 401	17 002	13 201	11 035
1950	104 995	8 143	4 076	4 068	96 851	11 080	23 013	20 681	17 240	13 469	11 363
1951	104 621	7 865	4 096	3 771	96 755	10 167	22 843	20 863	17 464	13 692	11 724
1952	105 231	7 922	4 234	3 689	97 305	9 389	23 044	21 137	17 716	13 889	12 126
1953	107 056	8 014	4 241	3 773	99 041	8 960	23 266	21 922	17 991	13 830	13 075
1954	108 321	8 224	4 336	3 889	100 095	8 885	23 304	22 135	18 305	14 085	13 375
1955	109 683	8 364	4 440	3 925	101 318	9 036	23 249	22 348	18 643	14 309	13 728
1956	110 954	8 434	4 482	3 953	102 518	9 271	23 072	22 567	19 012	14 516	14 075
1957	112 265	8 612	4 587	4 026	103 653	9 486	22 849	22 786	19 424	14 727	14 376
1958	113 727	8 986	4 872	4 114	104 737	9 733	22 563	23 025	19 832	14 923	14 657
1959	115 329	9 618	5 337	4 282	105 711	9 975	22 201	23 207	20 203	15 134	14 985
1960	117 245	10 187	5 573	4 615	107 056	10 273	21 998	23 437	20 601	15 409	15 336
1961	118 771	10 513	5 462	5 052	108 255	10 583	21 829	23 585	20 893	15 675	15 685
1962	120 153	10 652	5 503	5 150	109 500	10 852	21 503	23 797	20 916	15 874	16 554
1963	122 416	11 370	6 301	5 070	111 045	11 464	21 400	23 948	21 144	16 138	16 945
1964	124 485	12 111	6 974	5 139	112 372	12 017	21 367	23 940	21 452	16 442	17 150
1965	126 513	12 930	6 936	5 995	113 582	12 442	21 417	23 832	21 728	16 727	17 432
1966	128 058	13 592	6 914	6 679	114 463	12 638	21 543	23 579	21 977	17 007	17 715
1967	129 874	13 480	7 003	6 480	116 391	13 421	22 057	23 313	22 256	17 310	18 029
1968	132 028	13 698	7 200	6 499	118 328	13 891	22 912	23 036	22 534	17 614	18 338
1969	134 335	14 095	7 422	6 673	120 238	14 488	23 645	22 709	22 806	17 930	18 657
1970	137 085	14 519	7 643	6 876	122 566	15 323	24 435	22 489	23 059	18 250	19 007
1971	140 216	15 022	7 849	7 173	125 193	16 345	25 337	22 274	23 244	18 581	19 406
1972	144 126	15 510	8 076	7 435	128 614	17 143	26 740	22 358	23 338	19 007	20 023
1973	147 096	15 840	8 227	7 613	131 253	17 692	28 172	22 287	23 431	19 281	20 389
1974	150 120	16 180	8 373	7 809	133 938	17 994	29 439	22 461	23 578	19 517	20 945
1975	153 153	16 418	8 419	7 999	136 733	18 595	30 710	22 526	23 535	19 844	21 525
1976	156 150	16 614	8 442	8 171	139 536	19 109	31 953	22 796	23 409	20 185	22 083
1977	159 033	16 688	8 482	8 206	142 345	19 582	33 117	23 296	23 197	20 557	22 597
1978	161 910	16 695	8 484	8 211	145 216	20 007	34 091	24 099	22 977	20 875	23 166
1979	164 863	16 657	8 389	8 268	148 205	20 353	35 261	24 861	22 752	21 210	23 767
1980	167 745	16 543	8 279	8 264	151 202	20 635	36 558	25 578	22 563	21 520	24 350
1981	170 130	16 214	8 068	8 145	153 916	20 820	37 777	26 291	22 422	21 756	24 850
1982	172 271	15 763	7 714	8 049	156 508	20 845	38 492	27 611	22 264	21 909	25 387
1983	174 215	15 274	7 385	7 889	158 941	20 799	39 147	28 932	22 167	22 003	25 892
1984	176 383	14 735	7 196	7 538	161 648	20 688	39 999	30 251	22 226	22 052	26 433
1985	178 206	14 506	7 232	7 274	163 700	20 097	40 670	31 379	22 418	22 140	26 997
1986	180 587	14 496	7 386	7 110	166 091	19 569	41 731	32 550	22 732	22 011	27 497
1987	182 753	14 606	7 501	7 104	168 147	18 970	42 297	33 755	23 183	21 835	28 108
1988	184 613	14 527	7 284	7 243	170 085	18 434	42 611	34 784	24 004	21 641	28 612
1989	186 393	14 223	6 886	7 338	172 169	18 025	42 845	35 977	24 744	21 406	29 173
1990	189 164	14 520	6 893	7 626	174 644	18 902	42 976	37 719	25 081	20 719	29 247
1991	190 925	14 073	6 901	7 173	176 852	18 963	42 688	39 116	25 709	20 675	29 700
1992	192 805	13 840	6 907	6 933	178 965	18 846	42 278	39 852	27 206	20 604	30 179
1993	194 838	13 935	7 010	6 925	180 903	18 642	41 771	40 733	28 549	20 574	30 634
1994	196 814	14 196	7 245	6 951	182 619	18 353	41 306	41 534	29 778	20 635	31 012
1995	198 584	14 511	7 407	7 104	184 073	17 864	40 798	42 254	30 974	20 735	31 448
1996	200 591	14 934	7 678	7 256	185 656	17 409	40 252	43 086	32 167	20 990	31 751
1997	203 133	15 365	7 861	7 504	187 769	17 442	39 559	43 883	33 391	21 505	31 989
1998	205 220	15 644	7 895	7 749	189 576	17 593	38 778	44 299	34 373	22 296	32 237
1999	207 753	16 040	8 060	7 979	191 713	17 968	37 976	44 635	35 587	23 064	32 484
2000	212 577	15 912	7 978	7 934	196 664	18 311	38 703	44 312	37 642	24 230	33 466
2001	215 092	15 929	8 020	7 909	199 164	18 877	38 505	44 195	38 904	25 011	33 672
2002	217 570	15 994	8 099	7 895	201 576	19 348	38 472	43 894	39 711	26 343	33 808
2003	221 168	16 096	8 561	7 535	205 072	19 801	39 021	43 746	40 522	27 728	34 253
2004	223 357	16 222	8 574	7 648	207 134	20 197	38 939	43 226	41 245	28 919	34 609
2005	226 082	16 398	8 778	7 619	209 685	20 276	39 064	43 005	42 107	30 165	35 068
2006	228 815	16 678	9 089	7 589	212 137	20 265	39 230	42 753	42 901	31 375	35 613
2007	231 867	16 982	9 222	7 760	214 885	20 427	39 751	42 401	43 544	32 533	36 228
2008	233 788	17 075	9 133	7 942	216 713	20 409	39 993	41 699	43 960	33 491	37 161
2009	235 801	17 043	8 944	8 100	218 757	20 524	40 280	40 919	44 365	34 671	37 998
2010	237 830	16 901	8 943	7 957	220 929	21 047	40 903	40 090	44 297	35 885	38 706
2011	239 618	16 774	8 727	8 048	222 843	21 423	41 364	39 499	43 842	36 987	39 729
2012	243 284	16 984	8 891	8 093	226 300	21 799	40 975	39 642	43 697	38 318	41 869
2013	245 679	16 787	8 943	7 845	228 892	22 052	41 548	39 613	43 246	39 022	43 412
2014	247 947	16 633	8 898	7 735	231 314	22 079	42 131	39 565	42 815	39 764	44 959
2015	250 801	16 619	8 852	7 767	234 182	21 971	42 771	39 701	42 637	40 594	46 509
2016	253 538	16 714	8 994	7 720	236 824	21 721	43 547	39 817	42 397	41 308	48 035
2017	255 079	16 754	9 073	7 681	238 325	21 396	43 958	39 952	41 787	41 691	49 542
2018	257 791	16 765	8 917	7 848	241 026	21 239	44 581	40 569	41 240	42 114	51 283

Table 1-6. Civilian Noninstitutional Population, by Age, Race, Sex, and Hispanic Origin, 1948–2018 *—Continued*

(Thousands of people.)

Race, Hispanic origin, sex, and year	16 years and over	16 to 19 years			20 years and over						
		Total	16 to 17 years	18 to 19 years	Total	20 to 24 years	25 to 34 years	35 to 44 years	45 to 54 years	55 to 64 years	65 years and over
ALL RACES											
Men											
1948	49 996	4 078	2 128	1 951	45 918	5 527	10 767	9 798	8 290	6 441	5 093
1949	50 321	3 946	2 062	1 884	46 378	5 405	10 871	9 926	8 379	6 568	5 226
1950	50 725	3 962	2 043	1 920	46 763	5 270	10 963	10 034	8 472	6 664	5 357
1951	49 727	3 725	2 039	1 687	46 001	4 451	10 709	10 049	8 551	6 737	5 503
1952	49 700	3 767	2 121	1 647	45 932	3 788	10 855	10 164	8 655	6 798	5 670
1953	50 750	3 823	2 122	1 701	46 927	3 482	11 020	10 632	8 878	6 798	6 119
1954	51 395	3 953	2 174	1 780	47 441	3 509	11 067	10 718	9 018	6 885	6 241
1955	52 109	4 022	2 225	1 798	48 086	3 708	11 068	10 804	9 164	6 960	6 380
1956	52 723	4 020	2 238	1 783	48 704	3 970	10 983	10 889	9 322	7 032	6 505
1957	53 315	4 083	2 284	1 800	49 231	4 166	10 889	10 965	9 499	7 109	6 602
1958	54 033	4 293	2 435	1 858	49 740	4 339	10 787	11 076	9 675	7 179	6 683
1959	54 793	4 652	2 681	1 971	50 140	4 488	10 625	11 149	9 832	7 259	6 785
1960	55 662	4 963	2 805	2 159	50 698	4 679	10 514	11 230	10 000	7 373	6 901
1961	56 286	5 112	2 742	2 371	51 173	4 844	10 440	11 286	10 112	7 483	7 006
1962	56 831	5 150	2 764	2 386	51 681	4 925	10 207	11 389	10 162	7 610	7 386
1963	57 921	5 496	3 162	2 334	52 425	5 240	10 165	11 476	10 274	7 740	7 526
1964	58 847	5 866	3 503	2 364	52 981	5 520	10 144	11 466	10 402	7 873	7 574
1965	59 782	6 318	3 488	2 831	53 463	5 701	10 182	11 427	10 512	7 990	7 649
1966	60 262	6 658	3 478	3 180	53 603	5 663	10 224	11 294	10 598	8 099	7 723
1967	60 905	6 537	3 528	3 010	54 367	5 977	10 495	11 161	10 705	8 218	7 809
1968	61 847	6 683	3 634	3 049	55 165	6 127	10 944	11 040	10 819	8 336	7 897
1969	62 898	6 928	3 741	3 187	55 969	6 379	11 309	10 890	10 935	8 464	7 990
1970	64 304	7 145	3 848	3 299	57 157	6 861	11 750	10 810	11 052	8 590	8 093
1971	65 942	7 430	3 954	3 477	58 511	7 511	12 227	10 721	11 129	8 711	8 208
1972	67 835	7 705	4 081	3 624	60 130	8 061	12 911	10 762	11 167	8 895	8 330
1973	69 292	7 855	4 152	3 703	61 436	8 429	13 641	10 746	11 202	8 990	8 426
1974	70 808	8 012	4 231	3 781	62 796	8 600	14 262	10 834	11 315	9 140	8 641
1975	72 291	8 134	4 252	3 882	64 158	8 950	14 899	10 874	11 298	9 286	8 852
1976	73 759	8 244	4 266	3 978	65 515	9 237	15 528	11 010	11 243	9 444	9 053
1977	75 193	8 288	4 290	4 000	66 904	9 477	16 108	11 260	11 144	9 616	9 297
1978	76 576	8 309	4 295	4 014	68 268	9 693	16 598	11 665	11 045	9 758	9 509
1979	78 020	8 310	4 251	4 060	69 709	9 873	17 193	12 046	10 944	9 907	9 746
1980	79 398	8 260	4 195	4 064	71 138	10 023	17 833	12 400	10 861	10 042	9 979
1981	80 511	8 092	4 087	4 005	72 419	10 116	18 427	12 758	10 797	10 151	10 170
1982	81 523	7 879	3 911	3 968	73 644	10 136	18 787	13 410	10 726	10 215	10 371
1983	82 531	7 659	3 750	3 908	74 872	10 140	19 143	14 067	10 689	10 261	10 573
1984	83 605	7 386	3 655	3 731	76 219	10 108	19 596	14 719	10 724	10 285	10 788
1985	84 469	7 275	3 689	3 586	77 195	9 746	19 864	15 265	10 844	10 392	11 084
1986	85 798	7 275	3 768	3 507	78 523	9 498	20 498	15 858	10 986	10 336	11 347
1987	86 899	7 335	3 824	3 510	79 565	9 195	20 781	16 475	11 215	10 267	11 632
1988	87 857	7 304	3 715	3 588	80 553	8 931	20 937	17 008	11 625	10 193	11 859
1989	88 762	7 143	3 524	3 619	81 619	8 743	21 080	17 590	11 981	10 092	12 134
1990	90 377	7 347	3 534	3 813	83 030	9 320	21 117	18 529	12 238	9 778	12 049
1991	91 278	7 134	3 548	3 586	84 144	9 367	20 977	19 213	12 554	9 780	12 254
1992	92 270	7 023	3 542	3 481	85 247	9 326	20 792	19 585	13 271	9 776	12 496
1993	93 332	7 076	3 595	3 481	86 256	9 216	20 569	20 037	13 944	9 773	12 717
1994	94 355	7 203	3 718	3 486	87 151	9 074	20 361	20 443	14 545	9 810	12 918
1995	95 178	7 367	3 794	3 573	87 811	8 835	20 079	20 800	15 111	9 856	13 130
1996	96 206	7 600	3 955	3 645	88 606	8 611	19 775	21 222	15 674	9 997	13 327
1997	97 715	7 836	4 053	3 783	89 879	8 706	19 478	21 669	16 276	10 282	13 469
1998	98 758	7 968	4 059	3 909	90 790	8 804	19 094	21 857	16 773	10 649	13 613
1999	99 722	8 167	4 143	4 024	91 555	8 899	18 565	21 969	17 335	11 008	13 779
2000	101 964	8 089	4 096	3 993	93 875	9 101	19 106	21 683	18 365	11 583	14 037
2001	103 282	8 101	4 102	3 999	95 181	9 368	19 056	21 643	18 987	11 972	14 155
2002	104 585	8 146	4 140	4 006	96 439	9 627	19 037	21 523	19 379	12 641	14 233
2003	106 435	8 163	4 365	3 797	98 272	9 878	19 347	21 463	19 784	13 305	14 496
2004	107 710	8 234	4 318	3 916	99 476	10 125	19 358	21 255	20 160	13 894	14 684
2005	109 151	8 317	4 481	3 836	100 835	10 181	19 446	21 177	20 585	14 502	14 944
2006	110 605	8 459	4 613	3 846	102 145	10 191	19 568	21 082	20 991	15 095	15 219
2007	112 173	8 618	4 658	3 960	103 555	10 291	19 858	20 910	21 313	15 658	15 525
2008	113 113	8 660	4 625	4 035	104 453	10 249	19 999	20 567	21 512	16 123	16 002
2009	114 136	8 643	4 548	4 095	105 493	10 284	20 167	20 199	21 731	16 698	16 414
2010	115 174	8 578	4 540	4 038	106 596	10 550	20 465	19 807	21 713	17 291	16 769
2011	116 317	8 582	4 486	4 095	107 736	10 844	20 711	19 446	21 451	17 810	17 474
2012	117 343	8 657	4 550	4 107	108 686	10 889	20 205	19 416	21 339	18 416	18 422
2013	118 555	8 539	4 532	4 006	110 017	11 038	20 511	19 404	21 125	18 751	19 189
2014	119 748	8 449	4 513	3 936	111 299	11 067	20 841	19 388	20 920	19 116	19 967
2015	121 101	8 430	4 509	3 920	112 671	11 012	21 142	19 444	20 839	19 518	20 717
2016	122 497	8 475	4 509	3 966	114 023	10 897	21 570	19 514	20 727	19 867	21 448
2017	123 275	8 493	4 587	3 906	114 783	10 726	21 819	19 597	20 435	20 054	22 151
2018	124 678	8 493	4 527	3 967	116 185	10 639	22 205	19 933	20 157	20 263	22 988

Table 1-6. Civilian Noninstitutional Population, by Age, Race, Sex, and Hispanic Origin, 1948–2018 —*Continued*

(Thousands of people.)

Race, Hispanic origin, sex, and year	16 years and over	16 to 19 years			20 years and over						
		Total	16 to 17 years	18 to 19 years	Total	20 to 24 years	25 to 34 years	35 to 44 years	45 to 54 years	55 to 64 years	65 years and over
ALL RACES											
Women											
1948	53 071	4 371	2 137	2 234	48 700	6 003	11 843	10 299	8 481	6 444	5 627
1949	53 670	4 269	2 077	2 195	49 400	5 907	11 951	10 475	8 623	6 633	5 809
1950	54 270	4 181	2 033	2 148	50 088	5 810	12 050	10 647	8 768	6 805	6 006
1951	54 895	4 140	2 057	2 084	50 754	5 716	12 134	10 814	8 913	6 955	6 221
1952	55 529	4 155	2 113	2 042	51 373	5 601	12 189	10 973	9 061	7 091	6 456
1953	56 305	4 191	2 119	2 072	52 114	5 478	12 246	11 290	9 113	7 032	6 956
1954	56 925	4 271	2 162	2 109	52 654	5 376	12 237	11 417	9 287	7 200	7 134
1955	57 574	4 342	2 215	2 127	53 232	5 328	12 181	11 544	9 479	7 349	7 348
1956	58 228	4 414	2 244	2 170	53 814	5 301	12 089	11 678	9 690	7 484	7 570
1957	58 951	4 529	2 303	2 226	54 421	5 320	11 960	11 821	9 925	7 618	7 774
1958	59 690	4 693	2 437	2 256	54 997	5 394	11 776	11 949	10 157	7 744	7 974
1959	60 534	4 966	2 656	2 311	55 570	5 487	11 576	12 058	10 371	7 875	8 200
1960	61 582	5 224	2 768	2 456	56 358	5 594	11 484	12 207	10 601	8 036	8 435
1961	62 484	5 401	2 720	2 681	57 082	5 739	11 389	12 299	10 781	8 192	8 679
1962	63 321	5 502	2 739	2 764	57 819	5 927	11 296	12 408	10 754	8 264	9 168
1963	64 494	5 874	3 139	2 736	58 620	6 224	11 235	12 472	10 870	8 398	9 419
1964	65 637	6 245	3 471	2 775	59 391	6 497	11 223	12 474	11 050	8 569	9 576
1965	66 731	6 612	3 448	3 164	60 119	6 741	11 235	12 405	11 216	8 737	9 783
1966	67 795	6 934	3 436	3 499	60 860	6 975	11 319	12 285	11 379	8 908	9 992
1967	68 968	6 943	3 475	3 470	62 026	7 445	11 562	12 152	11 551	9 092	10 220
1968	70 179	7 015	3 566	3 450	63 164	7 764	11 968	11 996	11 715	9 278	10 441
1969	71 436	7 167	3 681	3 486	64 269	8 109	12 336	11 819	11 871	9 466	10 667
1970	72 782	7 373	3 796	3 578	65 408	8 462	12 684	11 679	12 008	9 659	10 914
1971	74 274	7 591	3 895	3 697	66 682	8 834	13 110	11 553	12 115	9 870	11 198
1972	76 290	7 805	3 994	3 811	68 484	9 082	13 829	11 597	12 171	10 113	11 693
1973	77 804	7 985	4 076	3 909	69 819	9 263	14 531	11 541	12 229	10 290	11 963
1974	79 312	8 168	4 142	4 028	71 144	9 393	15 177	11 627	12 263	10 377	12 304
1975	80 860	8 285	4 168	4 117	72 576	9 645	15 811	11 652	12 237	10 558	12 673
1976	82 390	8 370	4 176	4 194	74 020	9 872	16 425	11 786	12 166	10 742	13 030
1977	83 840	8 400	4 193	4 206	75 441	10 103	17 008	12 036	12 053	10 940	13 300
1978	85 334	8 386	4 189	4 197	76 948	10 315	17 493	12 435	11 932	11 118	13 658
1979	86 843	8 347	4 139	4 208	78 496	10 480	18 070	12 815	11 808	11 303	14 021
1980	88 348	8 283	4 083	4 200	80 065	10 612	18 725	13 177	11 701	11 478	14 372
1981	89 618	8 121	3 981	4 140	81 497	10 705	19 350	13 533	11 625	11 605	14 680
1982	90 748	7 884	3 804	4 081	82 864	10 709	19 705	14 201	11 538	11 694	15 017
1983	91 684	7 616	3 635	3 981	84 069	10 660	20 004	14 865	11 478	11 742	15 319
1984	92 778	7 349	3 542	3 807	85 429	10 580	20 403	15 532	11 501	11 768	15 645
1985	93 736	7 231	3 543	3 688	86 506	10 351	20 805	16 114	11 574	11 748	15 913
1986	94 789	7 221	3 618	3 603	87 567	10 072	21 233	16 692	11 746	11 675	16 150
1987	95 853	7 271	3 677	3 594	88 583	9 776	21 516	17 279	11 968	11 567	16 476
1988	96 756	7 224	3 569	3 655	89 532	9 503	21 674	17 776	12 378	11 448	16 753
1989	97 630	7 080	3 361	3 719	90 550	9 282	21 765	18 387	12 763	11 314	17 039
1990	98 787	7 173	3 359	3 813	91 614	9 582	21 859	19 190	12 843	10 941	17 198
1991	99 646	6 939	3 353	3 586	92 708	9 597	21 711	19 903	13 155	10 895	17 446
1992	100 535	6 818	3 366	3 452	93 718	9 520	21 486	20 267	13 935	10 828	17 682
1993	101 506	6 859	3 415	3 444	94 647	9 426	21 202	20 696	14 605	10 801	17 917
1994	102 460	6 993	3 528	3 465	95 467	9 279	20 945	21 091	15 233	10 825	18 094
1995	103 406	7 144	3 613	3 531	96 262	9 029	20 719	21 454	15 862	10 879	18 318
1996	104 385	7 335	3 723	3 612	97 050	8 798	20 477	21 865	16 493	10 993	18 424
1997	105 418	7 528	3 808	3 721	97 889	8 736	20 081	22 214	17 115	11 224	18 520
1998	106 462	7 676	3 835	3 840	98 786	8 790	19 683	22 442	17 600	11 646	18 625
1999	108 031	7 873	3 917	3 955	100 158	9 069	19 411	22 666	18 251	12 056	18 705
2000	110 613	7 823	3 882	3 941	102 790	9 211	19 597	22 628	19 276	12 647	19 430
2001	111 811	7 828	3 917	3 910	103 983	9 509	19 449	22 552	19 917	13 039	19 517
2002	112 985	7 848	3 959	3 889	105 136	9 721	19 435	22 371	20 332	13 703	19 575
2003	114 733	7 934	4 195	3 738	106 800	9 924	19 674	22 283	20 738	14 423	19 758
2004	115 647	7 989	4 257	3 732	107 658	10 072	19 581	21 970	21 085	15 025	19 925
2005	116 931	8 081	4 297	3 784	108 850	10 095	19 618	21 828	21 521	15 663	20 125
2006	118 210	8 218	4 476	3 742	109 992	10 074	19 662	21 671	21 910	16 280	20 394
2007	119 694	8 364	4 564	3 800	111 330	10 137	19 893	21 491	22 231	16 876	20 703
2008	120 675	8 415	4 508	3 907	112 260	10 160	19 994	21 132	22 448	17 367	21 160
2009	121 665	8 401	4 396	4 004	113 265	10 240	20 113	20 721	22 633	17 973	21 584
2010	122 656	8 323	4 403	3 919	114 333	10 497	20 438	20 283	22 584	18 594	21 937
2011	123 300	8 193	4 241	3 952	115 107	10 579	20 653	20 053	22 391	19 177	22 255
2012	125 941	8 327	4 341	3 986	117 614	10 910	20 770	20 226	22 358	19 902	23 447
2013	127 124	8 249	4 410	3 838	118 875	11 014	21 037	20 209	22 121	20 271	24 222
2014	128 199	8 184	4 385	3 799	120 014	11 012	21 290	20 178	21 894	20 648	24 992
2015	129 700	8 189	4 342	3 847	121 511	10 959	21 629	20 257	21 798	21 076	25 792
2016	131 040	8 239	4 485	3 754	122 801	10 823	21 976	20 303	21 670	21 441	26 587
2017	131 804	8 261	4 486	3 775	123 542	10 669	22 139	20 354	21 352	21 637	27 390
2018	133 112	8 272	4 390	3 882	124 841	10 600	22 376	20 637	21 083	21 851	28 295

Table 1-6. Civilian Noninstitutional Population, by Age, Race, Sex, and Hispanic Origin, 1948–2018 —*Continued*

(Thousands of people.)

Race, Hispanic origin, sex, and year	16 years and over	16 to 19 years			20 years and over						
		Total	16 to 17 years	18 to 19 years	Total	20 to 24 years	25 to 34 years	35 to 44 years	45 to 54 years	55 to 64 years	65 years and over
WHITE											
Both Sexes											
1954	97 705	7 180	3 786	3 394	90 524	7 794	20 818	19 915	16 569	12 993	12 438
1955	98 880	7 292	3 874	3 419	91 586	7 912	20 742	20 110	16 869	13 169	12 785
1956	99 976	7 346	3 908	3 438	92 629	8 106	20 564	20 314	17 198	13 341	13 105
1957	101 119	7 505	4 007	3 498	93 612	8 293	20 342	20 514	17 562	13 518	13 383
1958	102 392	7 843	4 271	3 573	94 547	8 498	20 063	20 734	17 924	13 681	13 645
1959	103 803	8 430	4 707	3 725	95 370	8 697	19 715	20 893	18 257	13 858	13 951
1960	105 282	8 924	4 909	4 016	96 355	8 927	19 470	21 049	18 578	14 070	14 260
1961	106 604	9 211	4 785	4 427	97 390	9 203	19 289	21 169	18 845	14 304	14 581
1962	107 715	9 343	4 818	4 526	98 371	9 484	18 974	21 293	18 872	14 450	15 297
1963	109 705	9 978	5 549	4 430	99 725	10 069	18 867	21 398	19 082	14 681	15 629
1964	111 534	10 616	6 137	4 481	100 916	10 568	18 838	21 375	19 360	14 957	15 816
1965	113 284	11 319	6 049	5 271	101 963	10 935	18 882	21 258	19 604	15 215	16 070
1966	114 566	11 862	5 993	5 870	102 702	11 094	18 989	21 005	19 822	15 469	16 322
1967	116 100	11 682	6 051	5 632	104 417	11 797	19 464	20 745	20 067	15 745	16 602
1968	117 948	11 840	6 225	5 616	106 107	12 184	20 245	20 474	20 310	16 018	16 875
1969	119 913	12 179	6 418	5 761	107 733	12 677	20 892	20 156	20 546	16 305	17 156
1970	122 174	12 521	6 591	5 931	109 652	13 359	21 546	19 929	20 760	16 591	17 469
1971	124 758	12 937	6 750	6 189	111 821	14 208	22 295	19 694	20 907	16 884	17 833
1972	127 906	13 301	6 910	6 392	114 603	14 897	23 555	19 673	20 950	17 250	18 278
1973	130 097	13 533	7 021	6 512	116 563	15 264	24 685	19 532	20 991	17 484	18 607
1974	132 417	13 784	7 114	6 671	118 632	15 502	25 711	19 628	21 061	17 645	19 085
1975	134 790	13 941	7 132	6 808	120 849	15 980	26 746	19 641	20 981	17 918	19 587
1976	137 106	14 055	7 125	6 930	123 050	16 368	27 757	19 827	20 816	18 220	20 064
1977	139 380	14 095	7 150	6 944	125 285	16 728	28 703	20 231	20 575	18 540	20 508
1978	141 612	14 060	7 132	6 928	127 552	17 038	29 453	20 932	20 322	18 799	21 007
1979	143 894	13 994	7 029	6 964	129 900	17 284	30 371	21 579	20 058	19 071	21 538
1980	146 122	13 854	6 912	6 943	132 268	17 484	31 407	22 174	19 837	19 316	22 050
1981	147 908	13 516	6 704	6 813	134 392	17 609	32 367	22 778	19 666	19 485	22 487
1982	149 441	13 076	6 383	6 693	136 366	17 579	32 863	23 910	19 478	19 591	22 945
1983	150 805	12 623	6 089	6 534	138 183	17 492	33 286	25 027	19 349	19 625	23 403
1984	152 347	12 147	5 918	6 228	140 200	17 304	33 889	26 124	19 348	19 629	23 906
1985	153 679	11 900	5 922	5 978	141 780	16 853	34 450	27 100	19 405	19 620	24 352
1986	155 432	11 879	6 036	5 843	143 553	16 353	35 293	28 062	19 587	19 477	24 780
1987	156 958	11 939	6 110	5 829	145 020	15 808	35 667	29 036	19 965	19 242	25 301
1988	158 194	11 838	5 893	5 945	146 357	15 276	35 876	29 818	20 652	18 996	25 739
1989	159 338	11 530	5 506	6 023	147 809	14 879	35 951	30 774	21 287	18 743	26 175
1990	160 625	11 630	5 464	6 166	148 996	15 538	35 661	31 739	21 535	18 204	26 319
1991	161 759	11 200	5 451	5 749	150 558	15 516	35 342	32 854	22 052	18 074	26 721
1992	162 972	11 004	5 478	5 526	151 968	15 354	34 885	33 305	23 364	17 951	27 108
1993	164 289	11 078	5 562	5 516	153 210	15 087	34 365	33 919	24 456	17 892	27 493
1994	165 555	11 264	5 710	5 554	154 291	14 708	33 865	34 582	25 435	17 924	27 776
1995	166 914	11 468	5 822	5 646	155 446	14 313	33 355	35 222	26 418	17 986	28 153
1996	168 317	11 822	6 026	5 796	156 495	13 907	32 852	35 810	27 403	18 136	28 387
1997	169 993	12 181	6 213	5 968	157 812	13 983	32 091	36 325	28 388	18 511	28 514
1998	171 478	12 439	6 264	6 176	159 039	14 138	31 286	36 610	29 132	19 231	28 642
1999	173 085	12 700	6 342	6 358	160 385	14 394	30 516	36 755	30 048	19 855	28 818
2000	176 220	12 535	6 264	6 271	163 685	14 552	30 948	36 261	31 550	20 757	29 617
2001	178 111	12 556	6 291	6 265	165 556	15 001	30 770	36 113	32 475	21 434	29 762
2002	179 783	12 596	6 346	6 250	167 187	15 360	30 676	35 750	33 012	22 540	29 849
2003	181 292	12 527	6 629	5 898	168 765	15 536	30 789	35 352	33 466	23 589	30 033
2004	182 643	12 599	6 561	6 038	170 045	15 817	30 585	34 845	34 005	24 549	30 245
2005	184 446	12 690	6 768	5 921	171 757	15 871	30 592	34 554	34 649	25 534	30 556
2006	186 264	12 856	6 981	5 875	173 408	15 848	30 661	34 217	35 228	26 486	30 968
2007	188 253	13 043	7 026	6 018	175 210	15 945	31 011	33 770	35 665	27 392	31 426
2008	189 540	13 084	6 962	6 122	176 456	15 914	31 234	33 093	35 941	28 109	32 165
2009	190 902	13 035	6 775	6 261	177 867	15 963	31 471	32 378	36 166	29 022	32 867
2010	192 075	12 891	6 799	6 091	179 184	16 280	31 813	31 647	36 064	29 983	33 396
2011	193 077	12 818	6 673	6 145	180 259	16 562	32 136	31 030	35 526	30 799	34 206
2012	193 204	12 658	6 617	6 040	180 547	16 289	31 242	30 597	34 935	31 511	35 973
2013	194 333	12 499	6 690	5 809	181 834	16 357	31 488	30 427	34 413	31 954	37 194
2014	195 498	12 377	6 650	5 727	183 121	16 329	31 782	30 254	33 948	32 450	38 358
2015	196 868	12 323	6 538	5 784	184 545	16 171	32 036	30 186	33 633	33 005	39 513
2016	198 215	12 342	6 639	5 703	185 873	15 947	32 384	30 136	33 266	33 478	40 662
2017	198 942	12 339	6 687	5 652	186 603	15 701	32 541	30 182	32 668	33 709	41 803
2018	200 221	12 318	6 564	5 754	187 904	15 557	32 770	30 538	32 046	33 900	43 094

Table 1-6. Civilian Noninstitutional Population, by Age, Race, Sex, and Hispanic Origin, 1948–2018 —*Continued*

(Thousands of people.)

Race, Hispanic origin, sex, and year	16 years and over	16 to 19 years: Total	16 to 19 years: 16 to 17 years	16 to 19 years: 18 to 19 years	20 years and over: Total	20 years and over: 20 to 24 years	20 years and over: 25 to 34 years	20 years and over: 35 to 44 years	20 years and over: 45 to 54 years	20 years and over: 55 to 64 years	20 years and over: 65 years and over
WHITE											
Men											
1954	46 462	3 455	1 902	1 553	43 007	3 074	9 948	9 688	8 172	6 341	5 787
1955	47 076	3 507	1 945	1 563	43 569	3 241	9 936	9 768	8 303	6 398	5 923
1956	47 602	3 500	1 955	1 546	44 102	3 464	9 851	9 848	8 446	6 455	6 038
1957	48 119	3 556	2 000	1 557	44 563	3 638	9 758	9 917	8 605	6 518	6 127
1958	48 745	3 747	2 140	1 607	44 998	3 783	9 656	10 018	8 765	6 574	6 203
1959	49 408	4 079	2 370	1 710	45 329	3 903	9 499	10 081	8 909	6 639	6 298
1960	50 065	4 349	2 476	1 874	45 716	4 054	9 373	10 131	9 042	6 721	6 395
1961	50 608	4 479	2 407	2 073	46 129	4 204	9 290	10 178	9 148	6 819	6 490
1962	51 054	4 520	2 426	2 094	46 534	4 306	9 080	10 239	9 191	6 917	6 801
1963	52 031	4 827	2 792	2 036	47 204	4 610	9 039	10 309	9 297	7 031	6 919
1964	52 869	5 148	3 090	2 059	47 721	4 862	9 024	10 301	9 417	7 153	6 963
1965	53 681	5 541	3 050	2 492	48 140	5 017	9 056	10 262	9 516	7 261	7 028
1966	54 061	5 820	3 023	2 798	48 241	4 974	9 085	10 136	9 592	7 362	7 092
1967	54 608	5 671	3 058	2 613	48 937	5 257	9 339	10 013	9 688	7 474	7 167
1968	55 434	5 787	3 153	2 635	49 647	5 376	9 752	9 902	9 790	7 585	7 242
1969	56 348	6 005	3 246	2 759	50 343	5 589	10 074	9 760	9 895	7 705	7 320
1970	57 516	6 179	3 329	2 851	51 336	5 988	10 441	9 678	9 999	7 822	7 409
1971	58 900	6 420	3 412	3 008	52 481	6 546	10 841	9 578	10 066	7 933	7 517
1972	60 473	6 627	3 503	3 125	53 845	7 042	11 495	9 568	10 078	8 089	7 573
1973	61 577	6 737	3 555	3 182	54 842	7 312	12 075	9 514	10 099	8 178	7 664
1974	62 791	6 851	3 604	3 247	55 942	7 476	12 599	9 564	10 165	8 288	7 849
1975	63 981	6 929	3 609	3 320	57 052	7 766	13 131	9 578	10 134	8 413	8 031
1976	65 132	6 993	3 609	3 384	58 138	7 987	13 655	9 674	10 063	8 556	8 203
1977	66 301	7 024	3 625	3 399	59 278	8 175	14 139	9 880	9 957	8 708	8 420
1978	67 401	7 022	3 619	3 404	60 378	8 335	14 528	10 236	9 845	8 826	8 608
1979	68 547	7 007	3 568	3 439	61 540	8 470	15 008	10 563	9 730	8 949	8 820
1980	69 634	6 941	3 508	3 433	62 694	8 581	15 529	10 863	9 636	9 059	9 027
1981	70 480	6 764	3 401	3 363	63 715	8 644	16 005	11 171	9 560	9 139	9 195
1982	71 211	6 556	3 249	3 307	64 655	8 621	16 260	11 756	9 463	9 188	9 367
1983	71 922	6 340	3 098	3 242	65 581	8 597	16 499	12 314	9 408	9 208	9 556
1984	72 723	6 113	3 019	3 094	66 610	8 522	16 816	12 853	9 434	9 217	9 768
1985	73 373	5 987	3 026	2 961	67 386	8 246	17 042	13 337	9 488	9 262	10 010
1986	74 390	5 977	3 084	2 894	68 413	8 002	17 564	13 840	9 578	9 201	10 229
1987	75 189	6 015	3 125	2 890	69 175	7 729	17 754	14 338	9 771	9 101	10 481
1988	75 855	5 968	3 015	2 953	69 887	7 473	17 867	14 743	10 114	9 001	10 688
1989	76 468	5 813	2 817	2 996	70 654	7 279	17 908	15 237	10 434	8 900	10 897
1990	77 369	5 913	2 809	3 103	71 457	7 764	17 766	15 770	10 598	8 680	10 879
1991	77 977	5 704	2 805	2 899	72 274	7 748	17 615	16 340	10 856	8 640	11 074
1992	78 651	5 611	2 819	2 792	73 040	7 676	17 403	16 579	11 513	8 602	11 268
1993	79 371	5 650	2 862	2 788	73 721	7 545	17 158	16 900	12 058	8 590	11 470
1994	80 059	5 748	2 938	2 810	74 311	7 357	16 915	17 247	12 545	8 618	11 629
1995	80 733	5 854	2 995	2 859	74 879	7 163	16 653	17 567	13 028	8 653	11 815
1996	81 489	6 035	3 099	2 936	75 454	6 971	16 395	17 868	13 518	8 734	11 968
1997	82 577	6 257	3 209	3 048	76 320	7 087	16 043	18 163	14 030	8 929	12 067
1998	83 352	6 386	3 233	3 153	76 966	7 170	15 644	18 310	14 400	9 286	12 155
1999	83 930	6 498	3 266	3 232	77 432	7 244	15 150	18 340	14 834	9 581	12 283
2000	85 370	6 404	3 224	3 181	78 966	7 329	15 528	18 003	15 578	10 028	12 501
2001	86 452	6 422	3 229	3 194	80 029	7 564	15 486	17 960	16 047	10 369	12 604
2002	87 361	6 439	3 251	3 189	80 922	7 750	15 470	17 792	16 317	10 918	12 676
2003	88 249	6 390	3 378	3 012	81 860	7 856	15 569	17 620	16 555	11 442	12 818
2004	89 044	6 429	3 301	3 129	82 615	8 024	15 486	17 404	16 834	11 922	12 946
2005	90 027	6 471	3 464	3 006	83 556	8 057	15 507	17 286	17 169	12 415	13 123
2006	91 021	6 555	3 551	3 004	84 466	8 052	15 567	17 143	17 467	12 891	13 346
2007	92 073	6 653	3 567	3 086	85 420	8 113	15 762	16 927	17 686	13 341	13 591
2008	92 725	6 669	3 550	3 120	86 056	8 072	15 884	16 599	17 830	13 698	13 972
2009	93 433	6 644	3 469	3 175	86 789	8 076	16 011	16 260	17 956	14 154	14 332
2010	94 082	6 580	3 473	3 107	87 502	8 240	16 174	15 920	17 919	14 634	14 615
2011	94 801	6 610	3 496	3 114	88 191	8 485	16 332	15 540	17 602	15 018	15 213
2012	94 266	6 486	3 387	3 099	87 780	8 211	15 691	15 263	17 287	15 333	15 995
2013	94 865	6 391	3 413	2 978	88 474	8 256	15 824	15 185	17 043	15 547	16 619
2014	95 513	6 321	3 370	2 950	89 193	8 250	15 992	15 110	16 823	15 794	17 224
2015	96 147	6 282	3 328	2 955	89 865	8 164	16 087	15 067	16 677	16 067	17 802
2016	96 861	6 289	3 346	2 943	90 572	8 057	16 280	15 055	16 507	16 300	18 373
2017	97 225	6 284	3 398	2 886	90 941	7 925	16 374	15 088	16 220	16 413	18 922
2018	97 933	6 271	3 374	2 897	91 662	7 848	16 536	15 288	15 920	16 515	19 554

Table 1-6. Civilian Noninstitutional Population, by Age, Race, Sex, and Hispanic Origin, 1948–2018 —*Continued*

(Thousands of people.)

Race, Hispanic origin, sex, and year	16 years and over	16 to 19 years			20 years and over						
		Total	16 to 17 years	18 to 19 years	Total	20 to 24 years	25 to 34 years	35 to 44 years	45 to 54 years	55 to 64 years	65 years and over
WHITE											
Women											
1954	51 242	3 725	1 884	1 841	47 517	4 720	10 870	10 227	8 397	6 652	6 651
1955	51 802	3 785	1 929	1 856	48 017	4 671	10 806	10 342	8 566	6 771	6 862
1956	52 373	3 846	1 953	1 892	48 527	4 642	10 713	10 466	8 752	6 886	7 067
1957	52 998	3 949	2 007	1 941	49 049	4 655	10 584	10 597	8 957	7 000	7 256
1958	53 645	4 096	2 131	1 966	49 549	4 715	10 407	10 716	9 159	7 107	7 442
1959	54 392	4 351	2 337	2 015	50 041	4 794	10 216	10 812	9 348	7 219	7 653
1960	55 214	4 575	2 433	2 142	50 639	4 873	10 097	10 918	9 536	7 349	7 865
1961	55 993	4 732	2 378	2 354	51 261	4 999	9 999	10 991	9 697	7 485	8 091
1962	56 660	4 823	2 392	2 432	51 837	5 178	9 894	11 054	9 681	7 533	8 496
1963	57 672	5 151	2 757	2 394	52 521	5 459	9 828	11 089	9 785	7 650	8 710
1964	58 663	5 468	3 047	2 422	53 195	5 706	9 814	11 074	9 943	7 804	8 853
1965	59 601	5 778	2 999	2 779	53 823	5 918	9 826	10 996	10 088	7 954	9 042
1966	60 503	6 042	2 970	3 072	54 461	6 120	9 904	10 869	10 230	8 107	9 230
1967	61 491	6 011	2 993	3 019	55 480	6 540	10 125	10 732	10 379	8 271	9 435
1968	62 512	6 053	3 072	2 981	56 460	6 809	10 493	10 572	10 520	8 433	9 633
1969	63 563	6 174	3 172	3 002	57 390	7 089	10 818	10 396	10 651	8 600	9 836
1970	64 656	6 342	3 262	3 080	58 315	7 370	11 105	10 251	10 761	8 769	10 060
1971	65 857	6 518	3 338	3 180	59 340	7 662	11 454	10 117	10 841	8 951	10 315
1972	67 431	6 673	3 407	3 267	60 758	7 855	12 060	10 105	10 872	9 161	10 705
1973	68 517	6 796	3 466	3 331	61 721	7 951	12 610	10 018	10 891	9 306	10 943
1974	69 623	6 933	3 510	3 424	62 690	8 026	13 112	10 064	10 896	9 356	11 236
1975	70 810	7 011	3 523	3 488	63 798	8 214	13 615	10 063	10 847	9 505	11 556
1976	71 974	7 062	3 516	3 546	64 912	8 381	14 102	10 153	10 752	9 664	11 860
1977	73 077	7 071	3 525	3 545	66 007	8 553	14 564	10 351	10 618	9 832	12 088
1978	74 213	7 038	3 513	3 524	67 174	8 704	14 926	10 696	10 476	9 974	12 399
1979	75 347	6 987	3 460	3 527	68 360	8 815	15 363	11 017	10 327	10 122	12 717
1980	76 489	6 914	3 403	3 511	69 575	8 904	15 878	11 313	10 201	10 256	13 022
1981	77 428	6 752	3 303	3 449	70 677	8 965	16 362	11 606	10 106	10 346	13 292
1982	78 230	6 519	3 134	3 385	71 711	8 959	16 603	12 154	10 015	10 402	13 579
1983	78 884	6 282	2 991	3 292	72 601	8 895	16 788	12 714	9 941	10 418	13 847
1984	79 624	6 034	2 899	3 135	73 590	8 782	17 073	13 271	9 914	10 412	14 138
1985	80 306	5 912	2 895	3 017	74 394	8 607	17 409	13 762	9 917	10 358	14 342
1986	81 042	5 902	2 953	2 949	75 140	8 351	17 728	14 223	10 009	10 277	14 551
1987	81 769	5 924	2 985	2 939	75 845	8 079	17 913	14 698	10 194	10 141	14 820
1988	82 340	5 869	2 878	2 991	76 470	7 804	18 009	15 074	10 537	9 994	15 052
1989	82 871	5 716	2 690	3 027	77 154	7 600	18 043	15 537	10 853	9 843	15 278
1990	83 256	5 717	2 654	3 063	77 539	7 774	17 895	15 969	10 937	9 524	15 440
1991	83 781	5 497	2 646	2 850	78 285	7 768	17 726	16 514	11 196	9 435	15 647
1992	84 321	5 393	2 659	2 734	78 928	7 678	17 482	16 727	11 851	9 350	15 841
1993	84 918	5 428	2 700	2 728	79 490	7 542	17 206	17 019	12 398	9 302	16 023
1994	85 496	5 516	2 772	2 744	79 980	7 351	16 950	17 335	12 890	9 306	16 148
1995	86 181	5 614	2 827	2 787	80 567	7 150	16 702	17 654	13 390	9 333	16 337
1996	86 828	5 787	2 927	2 860	81 041	6 936	16 457	17 943	13 884	9 402	16 419
1997	87 417	5 924	3 004	2 920	81 492	6 896	16 047	18 162	14 357	9 582	16 447
1998	88 126	6 053	3 031	3 023	82 073	6 969	15 642	18 300	14 732	9 944	16 486
1999	89 156	6 202	3 076	3 127	82 953	7 150	15 366	18 415	15 214	10 274	16 536
2000	90 850	6 131	3 041	3 090	84 718	7 223	15 420	18 258	15 972	10 729	17 116
2001	91 660	6 134	3 062	3 071	85 526	7 438	15 284	18 153	16 428	11 065	17 158
2002	92 422	6 157	3 096	3 061	86 266	7 611	15 207	17 958	16 695	11 622	17 173
2003	93 043	6 137	3 251	2 886	86 905	7 680	15 220	17 731	16 911	12 147	17 216
2004	93 599	6 169	3 260	2 909	87 430	7 794	15 099	17 441	17 170	12 627	17 299
2005	94 419	6 219	3 304	2 915	88 200	7 814	15 086	17 268	17 480	13 119	17 433
2006	95 242	6 301	3 429	2 871	88 942	7 796	15 094	17 074	17 760	13 596	17 623
2007	96 180	6 390	3 458	2 932	89 790	7 832	15 249	16 843	17 979	14 051	17 835
2008	96 814	6 414	3 412	3 003	90 400	7 842	15 349	16 493	18 111	14 411	18 193
2009	97 469	6 391	3 306	3 086	91 078	7 887	15 460	16 118	18 210	14 868	18 535
2010	97 993	6 311	3 327	2 984	91 683	8 040	15 640	15 727	18 146	15 349	18 781
2011	98 276	6 208	3 177	3 031	92 068	8 077	15 803	15 490	17 925	15 781	18 992
2012	98 938	6 172	3 230	2 942	92 766	8 078	15 550	15 334	17 648	16 179	19 978
2013	99 467	6 107	3 277	2 830	93 360	8 101	15 664	15 242	17 370	16 408	20 575
2014	99 984	6 056	3 280	2 777	93 928	8 079	15 790	15 144	17 125	16 656	21 134
2015	100 720	6 040	3 211	2 829	94 680	8 007	15 950	15 119	16 956	16 938	21 711
2016	101 354	6 053	3 293	2 760	95 301	7 890	16 104	15 082	16 758	17 178	22 289
2017	101 717	6 055	3 289	2 767	95 661	7 776	16 168	15 094	16 448	17 296	22 881
2018	102 289	6 047	3 189	2 857	96 242	7 709	16 234	15 250	16 126	17 384	23 540

Table 1-6. Civilian Noninstitutional Population, by Age, Race, Sex, and Hispanic Origin, 1948–2018 *—Continued*

(Thousands of people.)

Race, Hispanic origin, sex, and year	16 years and over	16 to 19 years			20 years and over						
		Total	16 to 17 years	18 to 19 years	Total	20 to 24 years	25 to 34 years	35 to 44 years	45 to 54 years	55 to 64 years	65 years and over
BLACK											
Both Sexes											
1985	19 664	2 160	1 083	1 077	17 504	2 649	4 873	3 290	2 372	2 060	2 259
1986	19 989	2 137	1 090	1 048	17 852	2 625	5 026	3 410	2 413	2 079	2 298
1987	20 352	2 163	1 123	1 040	18 189	2 578	5 139	3 563	2 460	2 097	2 352
1988	20 692	2 179	1 130	1 049	18 513	2 527	5 234	3 716	2 524	2 110	2 402
1989	21 021	2 176	1 116	1 060	18 846	2 479	5 308	3 900	2 587	2 118	2 454
1990	21 477	2 238	1 101	1 138	19 239	2 554	5 407	4 328	2 618	1 970	2 362
1991	21 799	2 187	1 085	1 102	19 612	2 585	5 419	4 538	2 682	1 985	2 403
1992	22 147	2 155	1 086	1 069	19 992	2 615	5 404	4 722	2 809	1 996	2 446
1993	22 521	2 181	1 113	1 069	20 339	2 600	5 409	4 886	2 941	2 016	2 487
1994	22 879	2 211	1 168	1 044	20 668	2 616	5 362	5 038	3 084	2 045	2 524
1995	23 246	2 284	1 198	1 086	20 962	2 554	5 337	5 178	3 244	2 079	2 571
1996	23 604	2 356	1 238	1 118	21 248	2 519	5 311	5 290	3 408	2 110	2 609
1997	24 003	2 412	1 255	1 158	21 591	2 515	5 279	5 410	3 571	2 164	2 653
1998	24 373	2 443	1 241	1 202	21 930	2 546	5 221	5 510	3 735	2 224	2 695
1999	24 855	2 479	1 250	1 229	22 376	2 615	5 197	5 609	3 919	2 295	2 741
2000	24 902	2 389	1 205	1 183	22 513	2 611	5 089	5 488	4 168	2 407	2 750
2001	25 138	2 388	1 212	1 176	22 750	2 686	5 003	5 467	4 343	2 478	2 775
2002	25 578	2 416	1 235	1 181	23 162	2 779	5 015	5 460	4 513	2 571	2 823
2003	25 686	2 382	1 309	1 074	23 304	2 773	4 978	5 387	4 628	2 692	2 846
2004	26 065	2 423	1 350	1 072	23 643	2 821	5 020	5 335	4 739	2 827	2 899
2005	26 517	2 481	1 341	1 140	24 036	2 835	5 075	5 311	4 869	2 980	2 967
2006	27 007	2 565	1 408	1 157	24 442	2 851	5 133	5 302	4 992	3 137	3 027
2007	27 485	2 640	1 497	1 143	24 845	2 891	5 210	5 271	5 110	3 284	3 080
2008	27 843	2 676	1 459	1 217	25 168	2 914	5 262	5 198	5 183	3 429	3 182
2009	28 241	2 684	1 462	1 221	25 557	2 973	5 349	5 109	5 290	3 596	3 239
2010	28 708	2 657	1 438	1 219	26 051	3 097	5 491	5 031	5 322	3 773	3 337
2011	29 114	2 594	1 353	1 240	26 520	3 168	5 606	4 995	5 357	3 955	3 440
2012	29 907	2 643	1 381	1 262	27 265	3 326	5 455	5 107	5 446	4 281	3 650
2013	30 376	2 565	1 344	1 221	27 811	3 425	5 585	5 131	5 429	4 430	3 811
2014	30 843	2 508	1 345	1 163	28 335	3 460	5 742	5 168	5 377	4 573	4 015
2015	31 386	2 491	1 343	1 148	28 895	3 425	5 929	5 232	5 383	4 718	4 207
2016	31 889	2 510	1 377	1 132	29 380	3 338	6 138	5 273	5 380	4 840	4 409
2017	32 247	2 511	1 352	1 159	29 736	3 239	6 308	5 311	5 335	4 934	4 610
2018	32 761	2 499	1 280	1 218	30 262	3 172	6 502	5 408	5 295	5 037	4 848
Men											
1985	8 790	1 059	543	517	7 731	1 202	2 180	1 462	1 060	924	902
1986	8 956	1 049	548	503	7 907	1 195	2 264	1 517	1 072	934	924
1987	9 128	1 065	566	499	8 063	1 173	2 320	1 587	1 092	944	947
1988	9 289	1 074	569	505	8 215	1 151	2 367	1 656	1 121	951	970
1989	9 439	1 075	575	501	8 364	1 128	2 403	1 741	1 145	956	989
1990	9 573	1 094	555	540	8 479	1 144	2 412	1 968	1 183	855	917
1991	9 725	1 072	546	526	8 652	1 168	2 417	2 060	1 211	864	933
1992	9 896	1 056	544	512	8 840	1 194	2 409	2 150	1 268	868	951
1993	10 083	1 075	559	516	9 008	1 181	2 425	2 228	1 330	874	969
1994	10 258	1 087	586	501	9 171	1 207	2 399	2 300	1 392	889	985
1995	10 411	1 131	601	530	9 280	1 161	2 388	2 362	1 462	901	1 006
1996	10 575	1 161	623	538	9 414	1 154	2 373	2 413	1 534	914	1 025
1997	10 763	1 188	634	553	9 575	1 153	2 363	2 471	1 607	936	1 045
1998	10 927	1 201	623	578	9 727	1 166	2 335	2 520	1 682	956	1 068
1999	11 143	1 218	628	589	9 926	1 197	2 321	2 566	1 765	986	1 091
2000	11 129	1 178	605	572	9 952	1 195	2 277	2 471	1 889	1 067	1 053
2001	11 172	1 179	606	573	9 993	1 224	2 212	2 440	1 960	1 096	1 060
2002	11 391	1 195	615	580	10 196	1 281	2 223	2 437	2 042	1 137	1 075
2003	11 454	1 176	661	515	10 278	1 291	2 210	2 401	2 094	1 189	1 093
2004	11 656	1 195	680	516	10 461	1 326	2 242	2 382	2 150	1 250	1 111
2005	11 882	1 223	682	541	10 659	1 341	2 277	2 372	2 202	1 319	1 148
2006	12 130	1 266	713	552	10 864	1 355	2 318	2 369	2 261	1 390	1 170
2007	12 361	1 305	742	563	11 057	1 380	2 366	2 352	2 318	1 454	1 186
2008	12 516	1 322	718	604	11 194	1 384	2 398	2 313	2 335	1 519	1 245
2009	12 705	1 326	736	590	11 379	1 410	2 454	2 271	2 392	1 592	1 260
2010	12 939	1 313	715	598	11 626	1 474	2 540	2 234	2 406	1 673	1 299
2011	13 164	1 282	642	640	11 882	1 510	2 612	2 222	2 435	1 759	1 344
2012	13 508	1 319	707	612	12 189	1 586	2 461	2 286	2 484	1 923	1 449
2013	13 747	1 276	685	591	12 471	1 647	2 536	2 299	2 474	1 992	1 522
2014	13 997	1 246	688	558	12 751	1 675	2 634	2 319	2 448	2 062	1 613
2015	14 268	1 237	697	540	13 031	1 662	2 740	2 353	2 454	2 130	1 692
2016	14 525	1 247	666	580	13 278	1 621	2 861	2 378	2 447	2 189	1 782
2017	14 712	1 249	673	576	13 464	1 571	2 963	2 401	2 430	2 234	1 864
2018	14 964	1 241	633	608	13 723	1 535	3 077	2 454	2 400	2 282	1 974

Table 1-6. Civilian Noninstitutional Population, by Age, Race, Sex, and Hispanic Origin, 1948–2018 —*Continued*

(Thousands of people.)

Race, Hispanic origin, sex, and year	16 years and over	16 to 19 years			20 years and over						
		Total	16 to 17 years	18 to 19 years	Total	20 to 24 years	25 to 34 years	35 to 44 years	45 to 54 years	55 to 64 years	65 years and over
BLACK											
Women											
1985	10 873	1 101	540	560	9 773	1 447	2 693	1 828	1 312	1 136	1 357
1986	11 033	1 088	542	545	9 945	1 430	2 762	1 893	1 341	1 145	1 374
1987	11 224	1 098	557	541	10 126	1 405	2 819	1 976	1 368	1 153	1 405
1988	11 402	1 105	561	544	10 298	1 376	2 867	2 060	1 403	1 159	1 432
1989	11 582	1 100	541	559	10 482	1 351	2 905	2 159	1 441	1 162	1 464
1990	11 904	1 144	546	598	10 760	1 410	2 995	2 360	1 435	1 114	1 446
1991	12 074	1 115	539	576	10 959	1 417	3 003	2 478	1 471	1 121	1 470
1992	12 251	1 099	542	557	11 152	1 421	2 995	2 573	1 542	1 127	1 495
1993	12 438	1 106	554	552	11 332	1 419	2 983	2 659	1 611	1 142	1 518
1994	12 621	1 125	582	543	11 496	1 410	2 963	2 738	1 692	1 156	1 538
1995	12 835	1 153	597	556	11 682	1 392	2 948	2 816	1 782	1 178	1 565
1996	13 029	1 195	615	580	11 833	1 364	2 938	2 877	1 874	1 196	1 584
1997	13 241	1 225	620	604	12 016	1 362	2 916	2 939	1 964	1 228	1 608
1998	13 446	1 243	618	624	12 203	1 380	2 886	2 991	2 053	1 268	1 626
1999	13 711	1 261	621	640	12 451	1 418	2 876	3 043	2 153	1 310	1 650
2000	13 772	1 211	600	611	12 561	1 416	2 812	3 017	2 279	1 340	1 697
2001	13 966	1 209	606	603	12 758	1 462	2 790	3 026	2 383	1 382	1 714
2002	14 187	1 221	620	601	12 966	1 498	2 792	3 023	2 471	1 434	1 747
2003	14 232	1 206	648	558	13 026	1 482	2 768	2 986	2 534	1 504	1 753
2004	14 409	1 227	670	557	13 182	1 495	2 778	2 954	2 590	1 577	1 789
2005	14 635	1 258	659	598	13 377	1 494	2 797	2 939	2 666	1 661	1 819
2006	14 877	1 299	694	605	13 578	1 495	2 815	2 933	2 731	1 747	1 857
2007	15 124	1 336	755	581	13 788	1 511	2 844	2 918	2 792	1 830	1 893
2008	15 328	1 354	741	613	13 974	1 530	2 864	2 885	2 848	1 910	1 937
2009	15 536	1 357	726	631	14 178	1 563	2 895	2 839	2 898	2 004	1 979
2010	15 769	1 344	723	621	14 425	1 623	2 951	2 796	2 916	2 101	2 038
2011	15 950	1 312	712	600	14 638	1 657	2 994	2 773	2 922	2 196	2 096
2012	16 400	1 324	674	650	15 076	1 740	2 994	2 821	2 963	2 358	2 201
2013	16 629	1 289	659	630	15 340	1 778	3 048	2 832	2 955	2 437	2 289
2014	16 846	1 262	656	605	15 584	1 785	3 108	2 849	2 929	2 511	2 402
2015	17 118	1 254	646	609	15 863	1 764	3 190	2 879	2 929	2 588	2 515
2016	17 365	1 263	711	552	16 102	1 717	3 278	2 895	2 933	2 652	2 627
2017	17 535	1 263	679	584	16 272	1 667	3 344	2 909	2 905	2 700	2 747
2018	17 797	1 257	648	610	16 539	1 636	3 425	2 954	2 895	2 755	2 875
HISPANIC											
Both Sexes											
1985	11 915	1 298	638	661	10 617	1 864	3 401	2 117	1 377	1 015	843
1986	12 344	1 302	658	644	11 042	1 899	3 510	2 239	1 496	1 023	875
1987	12 867	1 332	651	681	11 536	1 910	3 714	2 464	1 492	1 061	895
1988	13 325	1 354	662	692	11 970	1 948	3 807	2 565	1 571	1 159	920
1989	13 791	1 399	672	727	12 392	1 950	3 953	2 658	1 649	1 182	1 001
1990	15 904	1 737	821	915	14 167	2 428	4 589	3 001	1 817	1 247	1 084
1991	16 425	1 732	819	913	14 693	2 481	4 674	3 243	1 879	1 283	1 134
1992	16 961	1 737	836	901	15 224	2 444	4 806	3 458	1 980	1 321	1 216
1993	17 532	1 756	855	901	15 776	2 487	4 887	3 632	2 094	1 324	1 353
1994	18 117	1 818	902	916	16 300	2 518	5 000	3 756	2 223	1 401	1 401
1995	18 629	1 872	903	969	16 757	2 528	5 050	3 965	2 294	1 483	1 437
1996	19 213	1 948	962	986	17 265	2 524	5 181	4 227	2 275	1 546	1 512
1997	20 321	2 121	1 088	1 033	18 200	2 623	5 405	4 453	2 581	1 580	1 558
1998	21 070	2 204	1 070	1 135	18 865	2 731	5 447	4 636	2 775	1 615	1 662
1999	21 650	2 307	1 113	1 194	19 344	2 700	5 512	4 833	2 868	1 713	1 718
2000	23 938	2 523	1 214	1 309	21 415	3 255	6 466	5 189	3 061	1 736	1 708
2001	24 942	2 508	1 173	1 334	22 435	3 417	6 726	5 346	3 339	1 816	1 792
2002	25 963	2 507	1 216	1 291	23 456	3 508	7 010	5 606	3 494	1 953	1 885
2003	27 551	2 543	1 346	1 197	25 008	3 533	7 506	6 003	3 845	2 093	2 027
2004	28 109	2 608	1 337	1 270	25 502	3 666	7 470	6 055	3 987	2 208	2 115
2005	29 133	2 689	1 415	1 274	26 444	3 647	7 684	6 293	4 217	2 361	2 242
2006	30 103	2 796	1 518	1 277	27 307	3 603	7 856	6 519	4 466	2 516	2 347
2007	31 383	2 944	1 559	1 385	28 440	3 648	8 129	6 785	4 720	2 685	2 473
2008	32 141	3 042	1 620	1 422	29 098	3 620	8 147	6 946	4 937	2 840	2 609
2009	32 891	3 123	1 602	1 522	29 768	3 623	8 099	7 078	5 192	3 017	2 759
2010	33 713	3 243	1 673	1 570	30 469	3 880	8 084	7 123	5 351	3 167	2 864
2011	34 438	3 407	1 808	1 598	31 031	4 193	8 107	7 103	5 414	3 311	2 903
2012	36 759	3 656	1 906	1 750	33 103	4 502	8 512	7 551	5 831	3 613	3 094
2013	37 517	3 651	1 911	1 740	33 867	4 572	8 564	7 663	6 010	3 791	3 267
2014	38 400	3 662	1 949	1 713	34 738	4 642	8 656	7 792	6 192	3 989	3 467
2015	39 617	3 705	1 970	1 736	35 912	4 697	8 762	8 026	6 474	4 255	3 698
2016	40 697	3 777	2 011	1 766	36 919	4 711	8 914	8 194	6 672	4 483	3 946
2017	41 371	3 844	2 045	1 799	37 528	4 686	8 988	8 263	6 800	4 662	4 129
2018	42 734	3 938	2 086	1 852	38 795	4 744	9 263	8 499	6 983	4 892	4 414

Table 1-6. Civilian Noninstitutional Population, by Age, Race, Sex, and Hispanic Origin, 1948–2018 —*Continued*

(Thousands of people.)

Race, Hispanic origin, sex, and year	16 years and over	16 to 19 years			20 years and over						
		Total	16 to 17 years	18 to 19 years	Total	20 to 24 years	25 to 34 years	35 to 44 years	45 to 54 years	55 to 64 years	65 years and over
HISPANIC											
Men											
1985	5 885	. . .	. . .	. . .	5 232	. . .	. . .	. . .	. . .	. . .	. . .
1986	6 106	. . .	. . .	. . .	5 451	. . .	. . .	. . .	. . .	. . .	. . .
1987	6 371	. . .	. . .	. . .	5 700	. . .	. . .	. . .	. . .	. . .	. . .
1988	6 604	. . .	. . .	. . .	5 921	. . .	. . .	. . .	. . .	. . .	. . .
1989	6 825	. . .	. . .	. . .	6 114	. . .	. . .	. . .	. . .	. . .	. . .
1990	8 041	. . .	. . .	. . .	7 126	. . .	. . .	. . .	. . .	. . .	. . .
1991	8 296	. . .	. . .	. . .	7 392	. . .	. . .	. . .	. . .	. . .	. . .
1992	8 553	. . .	. . .	. . .	7 655	. . .	. . .	. . .	. . .	. . .	. . .
1993	8 824	. . .	. . .	. . .	7 930	. . .	. . .	. . .	. . .	. . .	. . .
1994	9 104	926	472	454	8 178	1 346	2 627	1 871	1 076	644	614
1995	9 329	954	481	473	8 375	1 337	2 657	1 966	1 127	668	619
1996	9 604	992	485	507	8 611	1 321	2 692	2 144	1 111	712	630
1997	10 368	1 119	585	534	9 250	1 439	2 872	2 275	1 266	747	651
1998	10 734	1 161	586	575	9 573	1 462	2 907	2 377	1 342	771	714
1999	10 713	1 190	571	619	9 523	1 398	2 805	2 407	1 397	767	749
2000	12 174	1 333	640	693	10 841	1 784	3 380	2 626	1 527	799	725
2001	12 695	1 310	619	690	11 386	1 846	3 529	2 765	1 650	848	749
2002	13 221	1 293	615	678	11 928	1 890	3 727	2 875	1 716	902	817
2003	14 098	1 301	674	627	12 797	1 905	4 033	3 098	1 910	989	862
2004	14 417	1 336	664	672	13 082	1 981	4 024	3 147	1 990	1 046	894
2005	14 962	1 376	730	646	13 586	1 956	4 155	3 284	2 114	1 123	953
2006	15 473	1 428	763	664	14 046	1 916	4 266	3 414	2 251	1 204	996
2007	16 154	1 505	790	714	14 649	1 928	4 430	3 563	2 384	1 287	1 058
2008	16 524	1 553	838	716	14 971	1 890	4 438	3 655	2 502	1 365	1 121
2009	16 897	1 593	818	774	15 305	1 875	4 405	3 735	2 647	1 459	1 184
2010	17 359	1 666	847	819	15 693	2 016	4 381	3 783	2 741	1 538	1 234
2011	17 753	1 812	951	861	15 941	2 278	4 379	3 702	2 717	1 604	1 260
2012	18 434	1 879	970	909	16 555	2 341	4 424	3 822	2 911	1 729	1 329
2013	18 798	1 870	988	882	16 928	2 364	4 453	3 880	3 012	1 818	1 402
2014	19 244	1 873	1 006	867	17 371	2 389	4 509	3 951	3 104	1 920	1 499
2015	19 745	1 886	1 014	872	17 860	2 396	4 516	4 053	3 241	2 050	1 604
2016	20 266	1 920	1 041	879	18 346	2 396	4 588	4 142	3 347	2 166	1 708
2017	20 578	1 951	1 042	908	18 627	2 374	4 617	4 183	3 404	2 256	1 794
2018	21 287	1 998	1 067	931	19 289	2 402	4 777	4 321	3 498	2 374	1 917
HISPANIC											
Women											
1985	6 029	. . .	. . .	. . .	5 385	. . .	. . .	. . .	. . .	. . .	. . .
1986	6 238	. . .	. . .	. . .	5 591	. . .	. . .	. . .	. . .	. . .	. . .
1987	6 496	. . .	. . .	. . .	5 835	. . .	. . .	. . .	. . .	. . .	. . .
1988	6 721	. . .	. . .	. . .	6 050	. . .	. . .	. . .	. . .	. . .	. . .
1989	6 965	. . .	. . .	. . .	6 278	. . .	. . .	. . .	. . .	. . .	. . .
1990	7 863	. . .	. . .	. . .	7 041	. . .	. . .	. . .	. . .	. . .	. . .
1991	8 130	. . .	. . .	. . .	7 301	. . .	. . .	. . .	. . .	. . .	. . .
1992	8 408	. . .	. . .	. . .	7 569	. . .	. . .	. . .	. . .	. . .	. . .
1993	8 708	. . .	. . .	. . .	7 846	. . .	. . .	. . .	. . .	. . .	. . .
1994	9 014	892	430	462	8 122	1 173	2 373	1 885	1 147	757	787
1995	9 300	918	422	496	8 382	1 191	2 393	1 999	1 167	815	818
1996	9 610	956	477	479	8 654	1 203	2 489	2 082	1 164	834	882
1997	9 953	1 003	503	500	8 950	1 184	2 533	2 178	1 315	833	907
1998	10 335	1 044	483	560	9 292	1 269	2 539	2 259	1 433	844	948
1999	10 937	1 116	542	575	9 821	1 302	2 707	2 425	1 470	947	969
2000	11 764	1 190	574	616	10 574	1 471	3 086	2 564	1 534	937	982
2001	12 247	1 198	554	644	11 049	1 571	3 198	2 581	1 689	968	1 043
2002	12 742	1 214	601	613	11 528	1 617	3 283	2 732	1 777	1 051	1 068
2003	13 452	1 242	672	570	12 211	1 628	3 473	2 905	1 935	1 105	1 166
2004	13 692	1 272	674	598	12 420	1 685	3 447	2 908	1 997	1 162	1 221
2005	14 172	1 313	685	628	12 858	1 692	3 529	3 009	2 103	1 237	1 289
2006	14 630	1 368	755	613	13 262	1 688	3 590	3 105	2 215	1 313	1 351
2007	15 229	1 439	769	670	13 791	1 720	3 698	3 222	2 336	1 398	1 416
2008	15 616	1 489	782	706	14 127	1 730	3 710	3 291	2 435	1 475	1 488
2009	15 993	1 531	783	748	14 463	1 748	3 694	3 343	2 545	1 558	1 576
2010	16 354	1 578	826	752	14 776	1 864	3 703	3 340	2 610	1 628	1 630
2011	16 685	1 595	857	738	15 090	1 915	3 727	3 401	2 696	1 707	1 643
2012	18 324	1 776	936	841	16 548	2 161	4 088	3 729	2 920	1 884	1 765
2013	18 719	1 781	923	858	16 938	2 208	4 110	3 783	2 998	1 973	1 866
2014	19 156	1 790	944	846	17 367	2 253	4 147	3 841	3 088	2 070	1 968
2015	19 872	1 820	956	864	18 052	2 301	4 247	3 973	3 233	2 205	2 094
2016	20 430	1 857	971	887	18 573	2 315	4 326	4 052	3 325	2 317	2 238
2017	20 794	1 893	1 002	891	18 900	2 312	4 371	4 079	3 397	2 406	2 335
2018	21 447	1 940	1 020	921	19 507	2 342	4 486	4 178	3 485	2 518	2 497

. . . = Not available.

Table 1-7. Civilian Labor Force, by Age, Sex, Race, and Hispanic Origin, 1948–2018

(Thousands of people.)

Race, Hispanic origin, sex, and year	16 years and over	16 to 19 years			20 years and over						
		Total	16 to 17 years	18 to 19 years	Total	20 to 24 years	25 to 34 years	35 to 44 years	45 to 54 years	55 to 64 years	65 years and over
ALL RACES											
Both Sexes											
1948	60 621	4 435	1 780	2 654	56 187	7 392	14 258	13 397	10 914	7 329	2 897
1949	61 286	4 288	1 704	2 583	57 000	7 340	14 415	13 711	11 107	7 426	3 010
1950	62 208	4 216	1 659	2 557	57 994	7 307	14 619	13 954	11 444	7 633	3 036
1951	62 017	4 103	1 743	2 360	57 914	6 594	14 668	14 100	11 739	7 796	3 020
1952	62 138	4 064	1 806	2 257	58 075	5 840	14 904	14 383	11 961	7 980	3 005
1953	63 015	4 027	1 727	2 299	58 989	5 481	14 898	15 099	12 249	8 024	3 236
1954	63 643	3 976	1 643	2 300	59 666	5 475	14 983	15 221	12 524	8 269	3 192
1955	65 023	4 092	1 711	2 382	60 931	5 666	15 058	15 400	12 992	8 513	3 305
1956	66 552	4 296	1 878	2 418	62 257	5 940	14 961	15 694	13 407	8 830	3 423
1957	66 929	4 275	1 843	2 433	62 653	6 071	14 826	15 847	13 768	8 853	3 290
1958	67 639	4 260	1 818	2 442	63 377	6 272	14 668	16 028	14 179	9 031	3 199
1959	68 369	4 492	1 971	2 522	63 876	6 413	14 435	16 127	14 518	9 227	3 158
1960	69 628	4 841	2 095	2 747	64 788	6 702	14 382	16 269	14 852	9 385	3 195
1961	70 459	4 936	1 984	2 951	65 524	6 950	14 319	16 402	15 071	9 636	3 146
1962	70 614	4 916	1 919	2 997	65 699	7 082	14 023	16 589	15 096	9 757	3 154
1963	71 833	5 139	2 171	2 966	66 695	7 473	14 050	16 788	15 338	10 006	3 041
1964	73 091	5 388	2 449	2 940	67 702	7 963	14 056	16 771	15 637	10 182	3 090
1965	74 455	5 910	2 486	3 425	68 543	8 259	14 233	16 840	15 756	10 350	3 108
1966	75 770	6 558	2 664	3 893	69 219	8 410	14 458	16 738	15 984	10 575	3 053
1967	77 347	6 521	2 734	3 786	70 825	9 010	15 055	16 703	16 172	10 792	3 097
1968	78 737	6 619	2 817	3 803	72 118	9 305	15 708	16 591	16 397	10 964	3 153
1969	80 734	6 970	3 009	3 959	73 763	9 879	16 336	16 458	16 730	11 135	3 227
1970	82 771	7 249	3 135	4 115	75 521	10 597	17 036	16 437	16 949	11 283	3 222
1971	84 382	7 470	3 192	4 278	76 913	11 331	17 714	16 305	17 024	11 390	3 149
1972	87 034	8 054	3 420	4 636	78 980	12 130	18 960	16 398	16 967	11 412	3 114
1973	89 429	8 507	3 665	4 839	80 924	12 846	20 376	16 492	16 983	11 256	2 974
1974	91 949	8 871	3 810	5 059	83 080	13 314	21 654	16 763	17 131	11 284	2 934
1975	93 775	8 870	3 740	5 131	84 904	13 750	22 864	16 903	17 084	11 346	2 956
1976	96 158	9 056	3 767	5 288	87 103	14 284	24 203	17 317	16 982	11 422	2 895
1977	99 009	9 351	3 919	5 431	89 658	14 825	25 500	17 943	16 878	11 577	2 934
1978	102 251	9 652	4 127	5 526	92 598	15 370	26 703	18 821	16 891	11 744	3 070
1979	104 962	9 638	4 079	5 559	95 325	15 769	27 938	19 685	16 897	11 931	3 104
1980	106 940	9 378	3 883	5 496	97 561	15 922	29 227	20 463	16 910	11 985	3 054
1981	108 670	8 988	3 647	5 340	99 682	16 099	30 392	21 211	16 970	11 969	3 042
1982	110 204	8 526	3 336	5 189	101 679	16 082	31 186	22 431	16 889	12 062	3 030
1983	111 550	8 171	3 073	5 098	103 379	16 052	31 834	23 611	16 851	11 992	3 040
1984	113 544	7 943	3 050	4 894	105 601	16 046	32 723	24 933	17 006	11 961	2 933
1985	115 461	7 901	3 154	4 747	107 560	15 718	33 550	26 073	17 322	11 991	2 907
1986	117 834	7 926	3 287	4 639	109 908	15 441	34 591	27 232	17 739	11 894	3 010
1987	119 865	7 988	3 384	4 604	111 878	14 977	35 233	28 460	18 210	11 877	3 119
1988	121 669	8 031	3 286	4 745	113 638	14 505	35 503	29 435	19 104	11 808	3 284
1989	123 869	7 954	3 125	4 828	115 916	14 180	35 896	30 601	19 916	11 877	3 446
1990	125 840	7 792	2 937	4 856	118 047	14 700	35 929	32 145	20 248	11 575	3 451
1991	126 346	7 265	2 789	4 476	119 082	14 548	35 507	33 312	20 828	11 473	3 413
1992	128 105	7 096	2 769	4 327	121 009	14 521	35 369	33 899	22 160	11 587	3 473
1993	129 200	7 170	2 831	4 338	122 030	14 354	34 780	34 562	23 296	11 599	3 439
1994	131 056	7 481	3 134	4 347	123 576	14 131	34 353	35 226	24 318	11 713	3 834
1995	132 304	7 765	3 225	4 540	124 539	13 688	34 198	35 751	25 223	11 860	3 819
1996	133 943	7 806	3 263	4 543	126 137	13 377	33 833	36 556	26 397	12 146	3 828
1997	136 297	7 932	3 237	4 695	128 365	13 532	33 380	37 326	27 574	12 665	3 887
1998	137 673	8 256	3 335	4 921	129 417	13 638	32 813	37 536	28 368	13 215	3 847
1999	139 368	8 333	3 337	4 996	131 034	13 933	32 143	37 882	29 388	13 682	4 005
2000	142 583	8 271	3 261	5 010	134 312	14 250	32 755	37 567	31 071	14 356	4 312
2001	143 734	7 902	3 088	4 814	135 832	14 557	32 361	37 404	32 025	15 104	4 382
2002	144 863	7 585	2 870	4 715	137 278	14 781	32 196	36 926	32 597	16 309	4 469
2003	146 510	7 170	2 857	4 313	139 340	14 928	32 343	36 695	33 270	17 312	4 792
2004	147 401	7 114	2 747	4 367	140 287	15 154	32 207	36 158	33 758	18 013	4 998
2005	149 320	7 164	2 825	4 339	142 157	15 127	32 341	36 030	34 402	18 979	5 278
2006	151 428	7 281	2 952	4 329	144 147	15 113	32 573	35 848	35 146	19 984	5 484
2007	153 124	7 012	2 771	4 242	146 112	15 205	33 130	35 527	35 697	20 750	5 804
2008	154 287	6 858	2 552	4 306	147 429	15 174	33 332	35 061	36 003	21 615	6 243
2009	154 142	6 390	2 227	4 163	147 752	14 971	33 298	34 239	36 205	22 505	6 534
2010	153 889	5 906	2 000	3 905	147 983	15 028	33 614	33 366	35 960	23 297	6 718
2011	153 617	5 727	1 873	3 853	147 890	15 270	33 724	32 660	35 360	23 765	7 112
2012	154 975	5 823	1 952	3 870	149 152	15 462	33 465	32 734	35 054	24 710	7 727
2013	155 389	5 785	2 023	3 762	149 604	15 595	33 746	32 563	34 467	25 116	8 116
2014	155 922	5 654	1 971	3 683	150 268	15 641	34 199	32 506	34 062	25 502	8 358
2015	157 130	5 700	1 987	3 713	151 430	15 523	34 647	32 603	33 902	25 954	8 801
2016	159 187	5 889	2 127	3 763	153 298	15 313	35 519	32 820	33 909	26 465	9 272
2017	160 320	5 901	2 237	3 664	154 418	15 259	36 086	33 034	33 563	26 899	9 577
2018	162 075	5 885	2 133	3 753	156 190	15 099	36 774	33 619	33 311	27 354	10 032

Table 1-7. Civilian Labor Force, by Age, Sex, Race, and Hispanic Origin, 1948–2018—*Continued*

(Thousands of people.)

Race, Hispanic origin, sex, and year	16 years and over	16 to 19 years			20 years and over						
		Total	16 to 17 years	18 to 19 years	Total	20 to 24 years	25 to 34 years	35 to 44 years	45 to 54 years	55 to 64 years	65 years and over
ALL RACES											
Men											
1948	43 286	2 600	1 109	1 490	40 687	4 673	10 327	9 596	7 943	5 764	2 384
1949	43 498	2 477	1 056	1 420	41 022	4 682	10 418	9 722	8 008	5 748	2 454
1950	43 819	2 504	1 048	1 456	41 316	4 632	10 527	9 793	8 117	5 794	2 453
1951	43 001	2 347	1 081	1 266	40 655	3 935	10 375	9 799	8 205	5 873	2 469
1952	42 869	2 312	1 101	1 210	40 558	3 338	10 585	9 945	8 326	5 949	2 416
1953	43 633	2 320	1 070	1 249	41 315	3 053	10 736	10 437	8 570	5 975	2 543
1954	43 965	2 295	1 023	1 272	41 669	3 051	10 771	10 513	8 702	6 105	2 526
1955	44 475	2 369	1 070	1 299	42 106	3 221	10 806	10 595	8 838	6 122	2 526
1956	45 091	2 433	1 142	1 291	42 658	3 485	10 685	10 663	9 002	6 220	2 602
1957	45 197	2 415	1 127	1 289	42 780	3 629	10 571	10 731	9 153	6 222	2 477
1958	45 521	2 428	1 133	1 295	43 092	3 771	10 475	10 843	9 320	6 304	2 378
1959	45 886	2 596	1 206	1 390	43 289	3 940	10 346	10 899	9 438	6 345	2 322
1960	46 388	2 787	1 290	1 496	43 603	4 123	10 251	10 967	9 574	6 399	2 287
1961	46 653	2 794	1 210	1 583	43 860	4 253	10 176	11 012	9 668	6 530	2 220
1962	46 600	2 770	1 178	1 592	43 831	4 279	9 920	11 115	9 715	6 560	2 241
1963	47 129	2 907	1 321	1 586	44 222	4 514	9 876	11 187	9 836	6 675	2 135
1964	47 679	3 074	1 499	1 575	44 604	4 754	9 876	11 156	9 956	6 741	2 124
1965	48 255	3 397	1 532	1 866	44 857	4 894	9 903	11 120	10 045	6 763	2 132
1966	48 471	3 685	1 609	2 075	44 788	4 820	9 948	10 983	10 100	6 847	2 089
1967	48 987	3 634	1 658	1 976	45 354	5 043	10 207	10 859	10 189	6 937	2 118
1968	49 533	3 681	1 687	1 995	45 852	5 070	10 610	10 725	10 267	7 025	2 154
1969	50 221	3 870	1 770	2 100	46 351	5 282	10 941	10 556	10 344	7 058	2 170
1970	51 228	4 008	1 810	2 199	47 220	5 717	11 327	10 469	10 417	7 126	2 165
1971	52 180	4 172	1 856	2 315	48 009	6 233	11 731	10 347	10 451	7 155	2 090
1972	53 555	4 476	1 955	2 522	49 079	6 766	12 350	10 372	10 412	7 155	2 026
1973	54 624	4 693	2 073	2 618	49 932	7 183	13 056	10 338	10 416	7 028	1 913
1974	55 739	4 861	2 138	2 721	50 879	7 387	13 665	10 401	10 431	7 063	1 932
1975	56 299	4 805	2 065	2 740	51 494	7 565	14 192	10 398	10 401	7 023	1 914
1976	57 174	4 886	2 069	2 817	52 288	7 866	14 784	10 500	10 293	7 020	1 826
1977	58 396	5 048	2 155	2 893	53 348	8 109	15 353	10 771	10 158	7 100	1 857
1978	59 620	5 149	2 227	2 923	54 471	8 327	15 814	11 159	10 083	7 151	1 936
1979	60 726	5 111	2 192	2 919	55 615	8 535	16 387	11 531	10 008	7 212	1 943
1980	61 453	4 999	2 102	2 897	56 455	8 607	16 971	11 836	9 905	7 242	1 893
1981	61 974	4 777	1 957	2 820	57 197	8 648	17 479	12 166	9 868	7 170	1 866
1982	62 450	4 470	1 776	2 694	57 980	8 604	17 793	12 781	9 784	7 174	1 845
1983	63 047	4 303	1 621	2 682	58 744	8 601	18 038	13 398	9 746	7 119	1 842
1984	63 835	4 134	1 591	2 542	59 701	8 594	18 488	14 037	9 776	7 050	1 755
1985	64 411	4 134	1 663	2 471	60 277	8 283	18 808	14 506	9 870	7 060	1 750
1986	65 422	4 102	1 707	2 395	61 320	8 148	19 383	15 029	9 994	6 954	1 811
1987	66 207	4 112	1 745	2 367	62 095	7 837	19 656	15 587	10 176	6 940	1 899
1988	66 927	4 159	1 714	2 445	62 768	7 594	19 742	16 074	10 566	6 831	1 960
1989	67 840	4 136	1 630	2 505	63 704	7 458	19 905	16 622	10 919	6 783	2 017
1990	69 011	4 094	1 537	2 557	64 916	7 866	19 872	17 481	11 103	6 627	1 967
1991	69 168	3 795	1 452	2 343	65 374	7 820	19 641	18 077	11 362	6 550	1 924
1992	69 964	3 751	1 453	2 297	66 213	7 770	19 495	18 347	12 040	6 551	2 010
1993	70 404	3 762	1 497	2 265	66 642	7 671	19 214	18 713	12 562	6 502	1 980
1994	70 817	3 896	1 630	2 266	66 921	7 540	18 854	18 966	12 962	6 423	2 176
1995	71 360	4 036	1 668	2 368	67 324	7 338	18 670	19 189	13 421	6 504	2 201
1996	72 087	4 043	1 665	2 378	68 044	7 104	18 430	19 602	13 967	6 693	2 247
1997	73 261	4 095	1 676	2 419	69 166	7 184	18 110	20 058	14 564	6 952	2 298
1998	73 959	4 244	1 728	2 516	69 715	7 221	17 796	20 242	14 963	7 253	2 240
1999	74 512	4 318	1 732	2 587	70 194	7 291	17 318	20 382	15 394	7 477	2 333
2000	76 280	4 269	1 676	2 594	72 010	7 521	17 844	20 093	16 269	7 795	2 488
2001	76 886	4 070	1 568	2 501	72 816	7 640	17 671	20 018	16 804	8 171	2 511
2002	77 500	3 870	1 431	2 439	73 630	7 769	17 596	19 828	17 143	8 751	2 542
2003	78 238	3 614	1 405	2 209	74 623	7 906	17 767	19 762	17 352	9 144	2 692
2004	78 980	3 616	1 329	2 288	75 364	8 057	17 798	19 539	17 635	9 547	2 787
2005	80 033	3 590	1 368	2 222	76 443	8 054	17 837	19 495	18 053	10 045	2 959
2006	81 255	3 693	1 453	2 240	77 562	8 116	17 944	19 407	18 489	10 509	3 096
2007	82 136	3 541	1 354	2 187	78 596	8 095	18 308	19 299	18 801	10 904	3 188
2008	82 520	3 472	1 238	2 235	79 047	8 065	18 302	18 972	18 928	11 345	3 436
2009	82 123	3 226	1 103	2 123	78 897	7 839	18 211	18 518	19 001	11 730	3 598
2010	81 985	2 991	990	2 002	78 994	7 864	18 352	18 119	18 856	12 103	3 701
2011	81 975	2 895	917	1 978	79 080	8 101	18 469	17 686	18 483	12 350	3 990
2012	82 327	2 940	950	1 990	79 387	8 110	18 083	17 607	18 363	12 879	4 345
2013	82 667	2 923	987	1 936	79 744	8 156	18 287	17 605	18 071	13 117	4 507
2014	82 882	2 827	959	1 868	80 056	8 182	18 478	17 547	17 900	13 361	4 587
2015	83 620	2 885	997	1 888	80 735	8 038	18 776	17 556	17 893	13 627	4 845
2016	84 755	2 995	1 028	1 967	81 759	7 954	19 151	17 686	17 890	13 938	5 141
2017	85 145	2 939	1 057	1 882	82 206	7 948	19 374	17 777	17 662	14 156	5 289
2018	86 096	2 909	1 003	1 906	83 188	7 786	19 789	18 123	17 528	14 436	5 525

Table 1-7. Civilian Labor Force, by Age, Sex, Race, and Hispanic Origin, 1948–2018—*Continued*

(Thousands of people.)

Race, Hispanic origin, sex, and year	16 years and over	16 to 19 years			20 years and over						
		Total	16 to 17 years	18 to 19 years	Total	20 to 24 years	25 to 34 years	35 to 44 years	45 to 54 years	55 to 64 years	65 years and over
ALL RACES											
Women											
1948	17 335	1 835	671	1 164	15 500	2 719	3 931	3 801	2 971	1 565	513
1949	17 788	1 811	648	1 163	15 978	2 658	3 997	3 989	3 099	1 678	556
1950	18 389	1 712	611	1 101	16 678	2 675	4 092	4 161	3 327	1 839	583
1951	19 016	1 756	662	1 094	17 259	2 659	4 293	4 301	3 534	1 923	551
1952	19 269	1 752	705	1 047	17 517	2 502	4 319	4 438	3 635	2 031	589
1953	19 382	1 707	657	1 050	17 674	2 428	4 162	4 662	3 679	2 049	693
1954	19 678	1 681	620	1 028	17 997	2 424	4 212	4 708	3 822	2 164	666
1955	20 548	1 723	641	1 083	18 825	2 445	4 252	4 805	4 154	2 391	779
1956	21 461	1 863	736	1 127	19 599	2 455	4 276	5 031	4 405	2 610	821
1957	21 732	1 860	716	1 144	19 873	2 442	4 255	5 116	4 615	2 631	813
1958	22 118	1 832	685	1 147	20 285	2 501	4 193	5 185	4 859	2 727	821
1959	22 483	1 896	765	1 132	20 587	2 473	4 089	5 228	5 080	2 882	836
1960	23 240	2 054	805	1 251	21 185	2 579	4 131	5 302	5 278	2 986	908
1961	23 806	2 142	774	1 368	21 664	2 697	4 143	5 390	5 403	3 106	926
1962	24 014	2 146	741	1 405	21 868	2 803	4 103	5 474	5 381	3 197	913
1963	24 704	2 232	850	1 380	22 473	2 959	4 174	5 601	5 502	3 331	906
1964	25 412	2 314	950	1 365	23 098	3 209	4 180	5 615	5 681	3 441	966
1965	26 200	2 513	954	1 559	23 686	3 365	4 330	5 720	5 711	3 587	976
1966	27 299	2 873	1 055	1 818	24 431	3 590	4 510	5 755	5 884	3 728	964
1967	28 360	2 887	1 076	1 810	25 475	3 966	4 848	5 844	5 983	3 855	979
1968	29 204	2 938	1 130	1 808	26 266	4 235	5 098	5 866	6 130	3 939	999
1969	30 513	3 100	1 239	1 859	27 413	4 597	5 395	5 902	6 386	4 077	1 057
1970	31 543	3 241	1 325	1 916	28 301	4 880	5 708	5 968	6 532	4 157	1 056
1971	32 202	3 298	1 336	1 963	28 904	5 098	5 983	5 957	6 573	4 234	1 059
1972	33 479	3 578	1 464	2 114	29 901	5 364	6 610	6 027	6 555	4 257	1 089
1973	34 804	3 814	1 592	2 221	30 991	5 663	7 320	6 154	6 567	4 228	1 061
1974	36 211	4 010	1 672	2 338	32 201	5 926	7 989	6 362	6 699	4 221	1 002
1975	37 475	4 065	1 674	2 391	33 410	6 185	8 673	6 505	6 683	4 323	1 042
1976	38 983	4 170	1 698	2 470	34 814	6 418	9 419	6 817	6 689	4 402	1 069
1977	40 613	4 303	1 765	2 538	36 310	6 717	10 149	7 171	6 720	4 477	1 078
1978	42 631	4 503	1 900	2 603	38 128	7 043	10 888	7 662	6 807	4 593	1 134
1979	44 235	4 527	1 887	2 639	39 708	7 234	11 551	8 154	6 889	4 719	1 161
1980	45 487	4 381	1 781	2 599	41 106	7 315	12 257	8 627	7 004	4 742	1 161
1981	46 696	4 211	1 691	2 520	42 485	7 451	12 912	9 045	7 101	4 799	1 176
1982	47 755	4 056	1 561	2 495	43 699	7 477	13 393	9 651	7 105	4 888	1 185
1983	48 503	3 868	1 452	2 416	44 636	7 451	13 796	10 213	7 105	4 873	1 198
1984	49 709	3 810	1 458	2 351	45 900	7 451	14 234	10 896	7 230	4 911	1 177
1985	51 050	3 767	1 491	2 276	47 283	7 434	14 742	11 567	7 452	4 932	1 156
1986	52 413	3 824	1 580	2 244	48 589	7 293	15 208	12 204	7 746	4 940	1 199
1987	53 658	3 875	1 638	2 237	49 783	7 140	15 577	12 873	8 034	4 937	1 221
1988	54 742	3 872	1 572	2 300	50 870	6 910	15 761	13 361	8 537	4 977	1 324
1989	56 030	3 818	1 495	2 323	52 212	6 721	15 990	13 980	8 997	5 095	1 429
1990	56 829	3 698	1 400	2 298	53 131	6 834	16 058	14 663	9 145	4 948	1 483
1991	57 178	3 470	1 337	2 133	53 708	6 728	15 867	15 235	9 465	4 924	1 489
1992	58 141	3 345	1 316	2 030	54 796	6 750	15 875	15 552	10 120	5 035	1 464
1993	58 795	3 408	1 335	2 073	55 388	6 683	15 566	15 849	10 733	5 097	1 459
1994	60 239	3 585	1 504	2 081	56 655	6 592	15 499	16 259	11 357	5 289	1 658
1995	60 944	3 729	1 557	2 172	57 215	6 349	15 528	16 562	11 801	5 356	1 618
1996	61 857	3 763	1 599	2 164	58 094	6 273	15 403	16 954	12 430	5 452	1 581
1997	63 036	3 837	1 561	2 277	59 198	6 348	15 271	17 268	13 010	5 713	1 590
1998	63 714	4 012	1 607	2 405	59 702	6 418	15 017	17 294	13 405	5 962	1 607
1999	64 855	4 015	1 606	2 410	60 840	6 643	14 826	17 501	13 994	6 204	1 673
2000	66 303	4 002	1 585	2 416	62 301	6 730	14 912	17 473	14 802	6 561	1 823
2001	66 848	3 832	1 520	2 313	63 016	6 917	14 690	17 386	15 221	6 932	1 870
2002	67 363	3 715	1 439	2 277	63 648	7 012	14 600	17 098	15 454	7 559	1 926
2003	68 272	3 556	1 452	2 104	64 716	7 021	14 576	16 933	15 919	8 168	2 099
2004	68 421	3 498	1 418	2 080	64 923	7 097	14 409	16 619	16 123	8 466	2 211
2005	69 288	3 574	1 457	2 117	65 714	7 073	14 503	16 535	16 349	8 934	2 319
2006	70 173	3 588	1 499	2 089	66 585	6 997	14 628	16 441	16 656	9 475	2 388
2007	70 988	3 471	1 417	2 055	67 516	7 110	14 822	16 227	16 896	9 846	2 615
2008	71 767	3 385	1 314	2 071	68 382	7 109	15 030	16 089	17 075	10 270	2 808
2009	72 019	3 163	1 124	2 039	68 856	7 132	15 087	15 720	17 204	10 776	2 937
2010	71 904	2 914	1 011	1 904	68 990	7 164	15 263	15 247	17 104	11 194	3 017
2011	71 642	2 832	957	1 875	68 810	7 169	15 255	14 973	16 876	11 414	3 121
2012	72 648	2 883	1 003	1 880	69 765	7 352	15 382	15 127	16 692	11 830	3 383
2013	72 722	2 862	1 036	1 826	69 860	7 440	15 459	14 957	16 396	12 000	3 609
2014	73 039	2 827	1 012	1 815	70 212	7 459	15 721	14 958	16 163	12 141	3 771
2015	73 510	2 815	991	1 824	70 695	7 485	15 871	15 047	16 009	12 326	3 957
2016	74 432	2 894	1 099	1 795	71 538	7 359	16 369	15 134	16 019	12 527	4 130
2017	75 175	2 962	1 180	1 782	72 213	7 311	16 712	15 257	15 901	12 743	4 288
2018	75 978	2 977	1 130	1 847	73 002	7 312	16 985	15 497	15 783	12 918	4 508

Table 1-7. Civilian Labor Force, by Age, Sex, Race, and Hispanic Origin, 1948–2018—*Continued*

(Thousands of people.)

Race, Hispanic origin, sex, and year	16 years and over	16 to 19 years			20 years and over						
		Total	16 to 17 years	18 to 19 years	Total	20 to 24 years	25 to 34 years	35 to 44 years	45 to 54 years	55 to 64 years	65 years and over
WHITE											
Both Sexes											
1954	56 816	3 501	1 448	2 054	53 315	4 752	13 226	13 540	11 258	7 591	2 946
1955	58 085	3 598	1 511	2 087	54 487	4 941	13 267	13 729	11 680	7 810	3 062
1956	59 428	3 771	1 656	2 113	55 657	5 194	13 154	14 000	12 061	8 080	3 166
1957	59 754	3 775	1 637	2 135	55 979	5 283	13 044	14 117	12 382	8 091	3 049
1958	60 293	3 757	1 615	2 144	56 536	5 449	12 884	14 257	12 727	8 254	2 964
1959	60 952	4 000	1 775	2 225	56 952	5 544	12 670	14 355	13 048	8 411	2 925
1960	61 915	4 275	1 071	2 405	57 640	5 787	12 594	14 450	13 322	8 522	2 964
1961	62 656	4 362	1 767	2 594	58 294	6 026	12 503	14 557	13 517	8 773	2 917
1962	62 750	4 354	1 709	2 645	58 396	6 164	12 218	14 695	13 551	8 856	2 912
1963	63 830	4 559	1 950	2 608	59 271	6 537	12 229	14 859	13 789	9 067	2 790
1964	64 921	4 784	2 211	2 572	60 137	6 952	12 235	14 852	14 043	9 239	2 817
1965	66 137	5 267	2 221	3 044	60 870	7 189	12 391	14 900	14 162	9 392	2 839
1966	67 276	5 827	2 367	3 460	61 449	7 324	12 591	14 785	14 370	9 583	2 793
1967	68 699	5 749	2 432	3 318	62 950	7 886	13 123	14 765	14 545	9 817	2 821
1968	69 976	5 839	2 519	3 320	64 137	8 109	13 740	14 683	14 756	9 968	2 884
1969	71 778	6 168	2 698	3 470	65 611	8 614	14 289	14 564	15 057	10 132	2 954
1970	73 556	6 442	2 824	3 617	67 113	9 238	14 896	14 525	15 269	10 255	2 930
1971	74 963	6 681	2 894	3 787	68 282	9 889	15 445	14 374	15 343	10 351	2 880
1972	77 275	7 193	3 096	4 098	70 082	10 605	16 584	14 399	15 283	10 402	2 809
1973	79 151	7 579	3 320	4 260	71 572	11 182	17 764	14 440	15 256	10 240	2 687
1974	81 281	7 899	3 441	4 459	73 381	11 600	18 862	14 644	15 375	10 241	2 656
1975	82 831	7 899	3 375	4 525	74 932	12 019	19 897	14 753	15 308	10 287	2 668
1976	84 767	8 088	3 410	4 679	76 678	12 444	20 990	15 088	15 187	10 371	2 599
1977	87 141	8 352	3 562	4 790	78 789	12 892	22 099	15 604	15 053	10 495	2 647
1978	89 634	8 555	3 715	4 839	81 079	13 309	23 067	16 353	15 004	10 602	2 745
1979	91 923	8 548	3 668	4 881	83 375	13 632	24 101	17 123	14 965	10 767	2 787
1980	93 600	8 312	3 485	4 827	85 286	13 769	25 181	17 811	14 956	10 812	2 759
1981	95 052	7 962	3 274	4 688	87 089	13 926	26 208	18 445	14 993	10 764	2 753
1982	96 143	7 518	3 001	4 518	88 625	13 866	26 814	19 491	14 879	10 832	2 742
1983	97 021	7 186	2 765	4 421	89 835	13 816	27 237	20 488	14 798	10 732	2 766
1984	98 492	6 952	2 720	4 232	91 540	13 733	27 958	21 588	14 899	10 701	2 660
1985	99 926	6 841	2 777	4 065	93 085	13 469	28 640	22 591	15 101	10 679	2 605
1986	101 801	6 862	2 895	3 967	94 939	13 176	29 497	23 571	15 379	10 583	2 732
1987	103 290	6 893	2 963	3 931	96 396	12 764	29 956	24 581	15 792	10 497	2 806
1988	104 756	6 940	2 861	4 079	97 815	12 311	30 167	25 358	16 573	10 462	2 943
1989	106 355	6 809	2 685	4 124	99 546	11 940	30 388	26 312	17 278	10 533	3 094
1990	107 447	6 683	2 543	4 140	100 764	12 397	30 174	27 265	17 515	10 290	3 123
1991	107 743	6 245	2 432	3 813	101 498	12 248	29 794	28 213	18 028	10 129	3 086
1992	108 837	6 022	2 388	3 633	102 815	12 187	29 518	28 580	19 200	10 196	3 135
1993	109 700	6 105	2 458	3 647	103 595	11 987	29 027	29 056	20 181	10 215	3 129
1994	111 082	6 357	2 681	3 677	104 725	11 688	28 580	29 626	21 026	10 319	3 486
1995	111 950	6 545	2 749	3 796	105 404	11 266	28 325	30 112	21 804	10 432	3 466
1996	113 108	6 607	2 780	3 826	106 502	11 003	27 901	30 683	22 781	10 648	3 485
1997	114 693	6 720	2 779	3 941	107 973	11 127	27 362	31 171	23 709	11 086	3 517
1998	115 415	6 965	2 860	4 105	108 450	11 244	26 707	31 221	24 282	11 548	3 448
1999	116 509	7 048	2 849	4 199	109 461	11 436	25 978	31 391	25 102	11 960	3 595
2000	118 545	6 955	2 768	4 186	111 590	11 626	26 336	30 968	26 353	12 463	3 846
2001	119 399	6 661	2 626	4 035	112 737	11 883	26 010	30 778	27 062	13 121	3 883
2002	120 150	6 366	2 445	3 921	113 784	12 073	25 908	30 286	27 405	14 148	3 965
2003	120 546	5 973	2 414	3 560	114 572	12 064	25 752	29 788	27 786	14 944	4 238
2004	121 086	5 929	2 309	3 620	115 156	12 192	25 548	29 305	28 181	15 522	4 408
2005	122 299	5 950	2 390	3 560	116 349	12 109	25 548	29 107	28 685	16 275	4 624
2006	123 834	6 009	2 473	3 536	117 825	12 128	25 681	28 849	29 231	17 132	4 805
2007	124 935	5 795	2 326	3 470	119 139	12 176	26 076	28 394	29 627	17 782	5 085
2008	125 635	5 644	2 126	3 518	119 990	12 142	26 210	27 932	29 780	18 464	5 463
2009	125 644	5 295	1 883	3 413	120 349	11 995	26 277	27 263	29 903	19 199	5 711
2010	125 084	4 861	1 693	3 168	120 223	11 948	26 455	26 510	29 632	19 808	5 869
2011	124 579	4 714	1 581	3 134	119 865	12 120	26 511	25 834	29 036	20 188	6 175
2012	123 684	4 669	1 605	3 065	119 015	11 914	25 806	25 445	28 384	20 752	6 714
2013	123 412	4 608	1 669	2 939	118 804	11 962	25 898	25 167	27 776	20 945	7 056
2014	123 327	4 476	1 591	2 885	118 851	11 927	26 172	25 029	27 336	21 181	7 207
2015	123 607	4 487	1 579	2 908	119 120	11 755	26 305	24 929	27 066	21 534	7 531
2016	124 658	4 618	1 692	2 926	120 040	11 553	26 725	24 996	26 929	21 889	7 948
2017	124 941	4 542	1 766	2 776	120 399	11 481	27 040	25 056	26 474	22 209	8 139
2018	125 815	4 576	1 692	2 884	121 238	11 383	27 332	25 442	26 113	22 464	8 504

Table 1-7. Civilian Labor Force, by Age, Sex, Race, and Hispanic Origin, 1948–2018—*Continued*

(Thousands of people.)

Race, Hispanic origin, sex, and year	16 years and over	16 to 19 years			20 years and over						
		Total	16 to 17 years	18 to 19 years	Total	20 to 24 years	25 to 34 years	35 to 44 years	45 to 54 years	55 to 64 years	65 years and over
WHITE											
Men											
1954	39 759	1 989	896	1 095	37 770	2 654	9 695	9 516	7 913	5 653	2 339
1955	40 197	2 056	935	1 121	38 141	2 803	9 721	9 597	8 025	5 654	2 343
1956	40 734	2 114	1 002	1 110	38 620	3 036	9 595	9 661	8 175	5 736	2 417
1957	40 826	2 108	992	1 114	38 718	3 152	9 483	9 719	8 317	5 735	2 307
1958	41 080	2 116	1 001	1 116	38 964	3 278	9 386	9 822	8 465	5 800	2 213
1959	41 397	2 279	1 077	1 202	39 118	3 409	9 261	9 876	8 581	5 833	2 158
1960	41 743	2 433	1 140	1 293	39 310	3 559	9 153	9 919	8 689	5 861	2 129
1961	41 986	2 439	1 067	1 372	39 547	3 681	9 072	9 961	8 776	5 988	2 068
1962	41 931	2 432	1 041	1 391	39 499	3 726	8 846	10 029	8 820	5 995	2 082
1963	42 404	2 563	1 183	1 380	39 841	3 955	8 805	10 079	8 944	6 090	1 967
1964	42 894	2 716	1 345	1 371	40 178	4 166	8 800	10 055	9 053	6 161	1 942
1965	43 400	2 999	1 359	1 639	40 401	4 279	8 824	10 023	9 130	6 188	1 959
1966	43 572	3 253	1 423	1 830	40 319	4 200	8 859	9 892	9 189	6 250	1 928
1967	44 041	3 191	1 464	1 727	40 851	4 416	9 102	9 785	9 260	6 348	1 944
1968	44 553	3 236	1 504	1 732	41 318	4 432	9 477	9 662	9 340	6 427	1 981
1969	45 185	3 413	1 583	1 830	41 772	4 615	9 773	9 509	9 413	6 467	1 996
1970	46 035	3 551	1 629	1 922	42 483	4 988	10 099	9 414	9 487	6 517	1 978
1971	46 904	3 719	1 681	2 039	43 185	5 448	10 444	9 294	9 528	6 550	1 922
1972	48 118	3 980	1 758	2 223	44 138	5 937	11 039	9 278	9 473	6 562	1 846
1973	48 920	4 174	1 875	2 300	44 747	6 274	11 621	9 212	9 445	6 452	1 740
1974	49 843	4 312	1 922	2 391	45 532	6 470	12 135	9 246	9 455	6 464	1 759
1975	50 324	4 290	1 871	2 418	46 034	6 642	12 579	9 231	9 415	6 425	1 742
1976	51 033	4 357	1 869	2 489	46 675	6 890	13 092	9 289	9 310	6 437	1 657
1977	52 033	4 496	1 949	2 548	47 537	7 097	13 575	9 509	9 175	6 492	1 688
1978	52 955	4 565	2 002	2 563	48 390	7 274	13 939	9 858	9 068	6 508	1 744
1979	53 856	4 537	1 974	2 563	49 320	7 421	14 415	10 183	8 968	6 571	1 761
1980	54 473	4 424	1 881	2 543	50 049	7 479	14 893	10 455	8 877	6 618	1 727
1981	54 895	4 224	1 751	2 473	50 671	7 521	15 340	10 740	8 836	6 530	1 704
1982	55 133	3 933	1 602	2 331	51 200	7 438	15 549	11 289	8 727	6 520	1 677
1983	55 480	3 764	1 452	2 312	51 716	7 406	15 707	11 817	8 649	6 446	1 691
1984	56 062	3 609	1 420	2 189	52 453	7 370	16 037	12 348	8 683	6 410	1 606
1985	56 472	3 576	1 467	2 109	52 895	7 122	16 306	12 767	8 730	6 376	1 595
1986	57 217	3 542	1 502	2 040	53 675	6 986	16 769	13 207	8 791	6 260	1 663
1987	57 779	3 547	1 524	2 023	54 232	6 717	16 963	13 674	8 945	6 200	1 733
1988	58 317	3 583	1 487	2 095	54 734	6 468	17 018	14 068	9 285	6 108	1 787
1989	58 988	3 546	1 401	2 146	55 441	6 316	17 077	14 516	9 615	6 082	1 835
1990	59 638	3 522	1 333	2 189	56 116	6 688	16 920	15 026	9 713	5 957	1 811
1991	59 656	3 269	1 266	2 003	56 387	6 619	16 709	15 523	9 926	5 847	1 763
1992	60 168	3 192	1 260	1 932	56 976	6 542	16 512	15 701	10 570	5 821	1 830
1993	60 484	3 200	1 292	1 908	57 284	6 449	16 244	15 971	11 010	5 784	1 825
1994	60 727	3 315	1 403	1 912	57 411	6 294	15 879	16 188	11 327	5 726	1 998
1995	61 146	3 427	1 429	1 998	57 719	6 096	15 669	16 414	11 730	5 809	2 000
1996	61 783	3 444	1 421	2 023	58 340	5 922	15 475	16 728	12 217	5 943	2 054
1997	62 639	3 513	1 440	2 073	59 126	6 029	15 120	17 019	12 710	6 154	2 094
1998	63 034	3 614	1 487	2 127	59 421	6 063	14 770	17 157	13 003	6 415	2 013
1999	63 413	3 666	1 478	2 188	59 747	6 151	14 292	17 201	13 368	6 618	2 117
2000	64 466	3 615	1 422	2 193	60 850	6 244	14 666	16 880	13 977	6 840	2 243
2001	64 966	3 446	1 334	2 112	61 519	6 363	14 536	16 809	14 400	7 169	2 241
2002	65 308	3 241	1 215	2 026	62 067	6 444	14 499	16 583	14 615	7 665	2 261
2003	65 509	3 036	1 193	1 843	62 473	6 479	14 529	16 398	14 708	7 973	2 386
2004	65 994	3 050	1 127	1 923	62 944	6 586	14 429	16 192	14 934	8 326	2 478
2005	66 694	2 988	1 162	1 826	63 705	6 562	14 426	16 080	15 273	8 734	2 631
2006	67 613	3 074	1 222	1 852	64 540	6 597	14 469	15 962	15 606	9 152	2 753
2007	68 158	2 944	1 147	1 798	65 214	6 567	14 715	15 765	15 846	9 500	2 821
2008	68 351	2 868	1 040	1 829	65 483	6 526	14 715	15 436	15 905	9 855	3 046
2009	68 051	2 679	933	1 746	65 372	6 348	14 669	15 066	15 943	10 160	3 186
2010	67 728	2 463	844	1 619	65 265	6 342	14 734	14 713	15 791	10 422	3 263
2011	67 551	2 386	780	1 606	65 165	6 539	14 785	14 317	15 400	10 629	3 494
2012	66 921	2 382	785	1 596	64 540	6 339	14 256	14 018	15 121	10 970	3 835
2013	66 842	2 337	821	1 516	64 505	6 353	14 325	13 909	14 804	11 125	3 990
2014	66 680	2 250	764	1 486	64 430	6 309	14 401	13 827	14 617	11 266	4 011
2015	67 018	2 308	798	1 511	64 710	6 165	14 533	13 757	14 539	11 489	4 227
2016	67 564	2 395	855	1 539	65 169	6 082	14 675	13 803	14 451	11 694	4 464
2017	67 592	2 296	855	1 441	65 296	6 062	14 765	13 818	14 210	11 863	4 579
2018	68 082	2 270	805	1 465	65 812	5 951	14 958	14 055	14 020	12 031	4 796

Table 1-7. Civilian Labor Force, by Age, Sex, Race, and Hispanic Origin, 1948–2018—*Continued*

(Thousands of people.)

Race, Hispanic origin, sex, and year	16 years and over	16 to 19 years			20 years and over						
		Total	16 to 17 years	18 to 19 years	Total	20 to 24 years	25 to 34 years	35 to 44 years	45 to 54 years	55 to 64 years	65 years and over
WHITE											
Women											
1954	17 057	1 512	552	959	15 545	2 098	3 531	4 024	3 345	1 938	607
1955	17 888	1 542	576	966	16 346	2 138	3 546	4 132	3 655	2 156	719
1956	18 694	1 657	654	1 003	17 037	2 158	3 559	4 339	3 886	2 344	749
1957	18 928	1 667	645	1 021	17 261	2 131	3 561	4 398	4 065	2 356	742
1958	19 213	1 641	614	1 028	17 572	2 171	3 498	4 435	4 262	2 454	751
1959	19 555	1 721	698	1 023	17 834	2 135	3 409	4 479	4 467	2 578	767
1960	20 172	1 842	731	1 112	18 330	2 228	3 441	4 531	4 633	2 661	835
1961	20 670	1 923	700	1 222	18 747	2 345	3 431	4 596	4 741	2 785	849
1962	20 819	1 922	668	1 254	18 897	2 438	3 372	4 666	4 731	2 861	830
1963	21 426	1 996	767	1 228	19 430	2 582	3 424	4 780	4 845	2 977	823
1964	22 027	2 068	866	1 201	19 959	2 786	3 435	4 797	4 990	3 078	875
1965	22 737	2 268	862	1 405	20 469	2 910	3 567	4 877	5 032	3 204	880
1966	23 704	2 574	944	1 630	21 130	3 124	3 732	4 893	5 181	3 333	865
1967	24 658	2 558	968	1 591	22 100	3 471	4 021	4 980	5 285	3 469	877
1968	25 423	2 603	1 015	1 588	22 821	3 677	4 263	5 021	5 416	3 541	903
1969	26 593	2 755	1 115	1 640	23 839	3 999	4 516	5 055	5 644	3 665	958
1970	27 521	2 891	1 195	1 695	24 630	4 250	4 797	5 111	5 781	3 738	952
1971	28 060	2 962	1 213	1 748	25 097	4 441	5 001	5 080	5 816	3 801	958
1972	29 157	3 213	1 338	1 875	25 945	4 668	5 544	5 121	5 810	3 839	963
1973	30 231	3 405	1 445	1 960	26 825	4 908	6 143	5 228	5 811	3 788	947
1974	31 437	3 588	1 520	2 068	27 850	5 131	6 727	5 399	5 920	3 777	897
1975	32 508	3 610	1 504	2 107	28 898	5 378	7 318	5 522	5 892	3 862	926
1976	33 735	3 731	1 541	2 189	30 004	5 554	7 898	5 799	5 877	3 935	940
1977	35 108	3 856	1 614	2 243	31 253	5 795	8 523	6 095	5 877	4 003	959
1978	36 679	3 990	1 713	2 276	32 689	6 035	9 128	6 495	5 936	4 094	1 001
1979	38 067	4 011	1 694	2 318	34 056	6 211	9 687	6 940	5 997	4 196	1 024
1980	39 127	3 888	1 605	2 284	35 239	6 290	10 289	7 356	6 079	4 194	1 032
1981	40 157	3 739	1 523	2 216	36 418	6 406	10 868	7 704	6 157	4 235	1 049
1982	41 010	3 585	1 399	2 186	37 425	6 428	11 264	8 202	6 152	4 313	1 065
1983	41 541	3 422	1 314	2 109	38 119	6 410	11 530	8 670	6 149	4 285	1 074
1984	42 431	3 343	1 300	2 043	39 087	6 363	11 922	9 240	6 217	4 292	1 054
1985	43 455	3 265	1 310	1 955	40 190	6 348	12 334	9 824	6 371	4 303	1 010
1986	44 584	3 320	1 393	1 927	41 264	6 191	12 729	10 364	6 588	4 323	1 069
1987	45 510	3 347	1 439	1 908	42 164	6 047	12 993	10 907	6 847	4 297	1 073
1988	46 439	3 358	1 374	1 984	43 081	5 844	13 149	11 291	7 288	4 354	1 156
1989	47 367	3 262	1 284	1 978	44 105	5 625	13 311	11 796	7 663	4 451	1 259
1990	47 809	3 161	1 210	1 951	44 648	5 709	13 254	12 239	7 802	4 333	1 312
1991	48 087	2 976	1 166	1 810	45 111	5 629	13 085	12 689	8 101	4 282	1 324
1992	48 669	2 830	1 128	1 702	45 839	5 645	13 006	12 879	8 630	4 375	1 305
1993	49 216	2 905	1 167	1 739	46 311	5 539	12 783	13 085	9 171	4 430	1 304
1994	50 356	3 042	1 278	1 764	47 314	5 394	12 702	13 439	9 699	4 593	1 487
1995	50 804	3 118	1 320	1 798	47 686	5 170	12 656	13 697	10 074	4 622	1 466
1996	51 325	3 163	1 360	1 803	48 162	5 081	12 426	13 955	10 563	4 706	1 431
1997	52 054	3 207	1 339	1 867	48 847	5 099	12 242	14 153	10 999	4 932	1 422
1998	52 380	3 351	1 373	1 977	49 029	5 180	11 937	14 064	11 279	5 133	1 435
1999	53 096	3 382	1 371	2 010	49 714	5 285	11 685	14 190	11 734	5 342	1 478
2000	54 079	3 339	1 346	1 993	50 740	5 381	11 669	14 088	12 376	5 623	1 602
2001	54 433	3 215	1 292	1 923	51 218	5 519	11 474	13 969	12 662	5 952	1 642
2002	54 842	3 125	1 229	1 895	51 717	5 628	11 409	13 703	12 790	6 482	1 704
2003	55 037	2 937	1 221	1 716	52 099	5 584	11 223	13 390	13 078	6 970	1 852
2004	55 092	2 879	1 182	1 697	52 212	5 606	11 119	13 114	13 247	7 197	1 930
2005	55 605	2 962	1 228	1 733	52 643	5 546	11 123	13 027	13 413	7 542	1 993
2006	56 221	2 935	1 251	1 684	53 286	5 530	11 212	12 886	13 625	7 980	2 052
2007	56 777	2 851	1 179	1 672	53 925	5 609	11 360	12 629	13 781	8 282	2 264
2008	57 284	2 776	1 086	1 690	54 508	5 616	11 495	12 495	13 875	8 609	2 417
2009	57 593	2 616	950	1 667	54 976	5 647	11 608	12 197	13 960	9 039	2 525
2010	57 356	2 398	849	1 549	54 957	5 607	11 721	11 796	13 841	9 386	2 607
2011	57 028	2 328	800	1 528	54 700	5 581	11 726	11 517	13 636	9 559	2 681
2012	56 763	2 288	819	1 469	54 475	5 575	11 550	11 428	13 263	9 782	2 879
2013	56 571	2 271	848	1 423	54 299	5 609	11 573	11 258	12 973	9 820	3 066
2014	56 648	2 226	827	1 399	54 421	5 618	11 771	11 202	12 719	9 915	3 196
2015	56 589	2 178	782	1 397	54 410	5 589	11 772	11 172	12 527	10 045	3 304
2016	57 095	2 224	837	1 387	54 871	5 471	12 050	11 193	12 478	10 195	3 484
2017	57 349	2 247	911	1 335	55 103	5 419	12 275	11 238	12 264	10 346	3 560
2018	57 732	2 307	887	1 420	55 426	5 432	12 374	11 387	12 093	10 434	3 707

Table 1-7. Civilian Labor Force, by Age, Sex, Race, and Hispanic Origin, 1948–2018—*Continued*

(Thousands of people.)

Race, Hispanic origin, sex, and year	16 years and over	16 to 19 years			20 years and over						
		Total	16 to 17 years	18 to 19 years	Total	20 to 24 years	25 to 34 years	35 to 44 years	45 to 54 years	55 to 64 years	65 years and over
BLACK											
Both Sexes											
1985	12 364	889	311	578	11 476	1 854	3 888	2 681	1 742	1 059	252
1986	12 654	883	322	562	11 770	1 881	4 028	2 793	1 793	1 051	224
1987	12 993	899	336	563	12 094	1 818	4 147	2 942	1 838	1 098	251
1988	13 205	889	344	545	12 316	1 782	4 226	3 069	1 894	1 069	276
1989	13 497	925	353	572	12 573	1 789	4 295	3 227	1 954	1 023	285
1990	13 740	866	306	560	12 874	1 758	4 307	3 566	2 003	977	262
1991	13 797	774	266	508	13 023	1 750	4 254	3 719	2 042	1 001	256
1992	14 162	816	285	532	13 346	1 763	4 309	3 843	2 142	1 029	259
1993	14 225	807	283	524	13 418	1 764	4 232	3 960	2 212	1 013	237
1994	14 502	852	351	501	13 650	1 800	4 199	4 068	2 308	1 007	267
1995	14 817	911	366	545	13 906	1 754	4 267	4 165	2 404	1 046	271
1996	15 134	923	366	556	14 211	1 738	4 305	4 287	2 553	1 073	255
1997	15 529	933	352	580	14 596	1 783	4 329	4 401	2 724	1 093	265
1998	15 982	1 017	370	646	14 966	1 797	4 332	4 531	2 863	1 163	278
1999	16 365	959	352	607	15 406	1 866	4 430	4 653	2 992	1 180	285
2000	16 397	941	356	585	15 456	1 873	4 281	4 515	3 203	1 264	320
2001	16 421	898	332	565	15 524	1 878	4 180	4 483	3 298	1 335	350
2002	16 565	870	297	574	15 695	1 908	4 134	4 458	3 435	1 407	353
2003	16 526	771	289	482	15 755	1 892	4 060	4 465	3 506	1 466	366
2004	16 638	762	272	489	15 876	1 926	4 076	4 380	3 578	1 538	380
2005	17 013	803	279	525	16 209	1 957	4 145	4 370	3 686	1 647	403
2006	17 314	871	318	553	16 443	1 960	4 197	4 348	3 785	1 739	414
2007	17 496	801	300	501	16 695	1 974	4 254	4 357	3 866	1 811	432
2008	17 740	787	270	517	16 953	1 981	4 328	4 316	3 945	1 908	476
2009	17 632	729	231	499	16 902	1 961	4 300	4 175	3 976	1 995	495
2010	17 862	677	203	473	17 186	2 072	4 418	4 095	3 991	2 104	506
2011	17 881	647	188	459	17 234	2 105	4 434	4 029	3 957	2 155	555
2012	18 400	711	213	498	17 689	2 210	4 333	4 120	4 057	2 369	599
2013	18 580	717	218	499	17 863	2 236	4 383	4 144	4 021	2 462	617
2014	18 873	681	227	454	18 192	2 305	4 541	4 159	4 013	2 528	648
2015	19 318	701	233	469	18 616	2 337	4 707	4 226	4 051	2 584	711
2016	19 637	729	240	489	18 908	2 259	4 926	4 283	4 039	2 669	732
2017	20 088	754	250	504	19 334	2 241	5 094	4 368	4 068	2 741	822
2018	20 414	763	232	530	19 651	2 173	5 260	4 441	4 075	2 846	856
Men											
1985	6 220	471	162	310	5 749	950	1 937	1 313	879	544	125
1986	6 373	458	164	294	5 915	957	2 029	1 359	901	552	116
1987	6 486	463	179	284	6 023	914	2 074	1 406	915	586	130
1988	6 596	469	186	283	6 127	913	2 114	1 459	936	565	139
1989	6 701	480	190	291	6 221	904	2 157	1 544	945	530	141
1990	6 802	445	161	284	6 357	879	2 142	1 733	988	496	119
1991	6 851	400	140	260	6 451	896	2 111	1 806	1 010	507	122
1992	6 997	429	149	280	6 568	900	2 121	1 859	1 037	521	130
1993	7 019	425	154	270	6 594	875	2 118	1 918	1 065	506	112
1994	7 089	443	176	266	6 646	891	2 068	1 975	1 102	484	125
1995	7 183	453	184	269	6 730	866	2 089	1 987	1 148	490	150
1996	7 264	458	182	276	6 806	848	2 077	2 036	1 204	509	132
1997	7 354	444	178	266	6 910	832	2 052	2 096	1 287	508	134
1998	7 542	488	181	307	7 053	837	2 034	2 142	1 343	548	150
1999	7 652	470	180	291	7 182	835	2 069	2 206	1 387	547	138
2000	7 702	462	181	281	7 240	875	1 999	2 105	1 497	612	151
2001	7 647	447	166	281	7 200	853	1 915	2 073	1 537	645	177
2002	7 794	446	149	297	7 347	906	1 909	2 064	1 623	664	181
2003	7 711	365	138	228	7 346	918	1 872	2 058	1 627	685	186
2004	7 773	359	128	231	7 414	927	1 931	2 000	1 654	714	188
2005	7 998	399	139	260	7 600	940	1 948	2 028	1 732	756	196
2006	8 128	409	152	256	7 720	971	1 986	1 999	1 792	777	195
2007	8 252	384	137	247	7 867	981	2 037	2 030	1 822	791	206
2008	8 347	385	124	261	7 962	984	2 047	2 008	1 846	852	225
2009	8 265	350	111	239	7 914	954	2 041	1 932	1 852	904	231
2010	8 415	339	96	244	8 076	986	2 118	1 924	1 862	950	236
2011	8 454	329	89	241	8 125	1 012	2 159	1 860	1 854	983	257
2012	8 594	338	99	239	8 256	1 054	2 030	1 908	1 884	1 099	281
2013	8 733	347	105	242	8 386	1 091	2 081	1 934	1 867	1 132	281
2014	8 909	323	115	208	8 586	1 138	2 174	1 931	1 870	1 176	297
2015	9 099	326	112	213	8 773	1 145	2 250	1 956	1 899	1 204	320
2016	9 315	350	92	259	8 965	1 091	2 365	2 003	1 887	1 270	349
2017	9 508	345	103	242	9 163	1 091	2 460	2 041	1 887	1 304	380
2018	9 694	367	98	269	9 327	1 046	2 573	2 087	1 900	1 343	379

Table 1-7. Civilian Labor Force, by Age, Sex, Race, and Hispanic Origin, 1948–2018—*Continued*

(Thousands of people.)

Race, Hispanic origin, sex, and year	16 years and over	16 to 19 years			20 years and over						
		Total	16 to 17 years	18 to 19 years	Total	20 to 24 years	25 to 34 years	35 to 44 years	45 to 54 years	55 to 64 years	65 years and over
BLACK											
Women											
1985	6 144	417	149	268	5 727	904	1 951	1 368	862	515	127
1986	6 281	425	157	268	5 855	924	1 999	1 434	892	499	107
1987	6 507	435	157	278	6 071	904	2 073	1 537	924	512	121
1988	6 609	419	158	262	6 190	869	2 112	1 610	958	504	137
1989	6 796	445	163	281	6 352	885	2 138	1 683	1 009	493	144
1990	6 938	421	145	276	6 517	879	2 165	1 833	1 015	481	143
1991	6 946	374	126	248	6 572	854	2 143	1 913	1 032	494	135
1992	7 166	387	135	252	6 778	863	2 188	1 985	1 105	508	129
1993	7 206	383	129	254	6 824	889	2 116	2 042	1 147	506	125
1994	7 413	409	174	235	7 004	909	2 131	2 093	1 206	523	142
1995	7 634	458	182	276	7 175	887	2 177	2 178	1 256	556	121
1996	7 869	464	184	280	7 405	890	2 228	2 251	1 349	565	122
1997	8 175	489	175	314	7 686	951	2 277	2 305	1 437	585	131
1998	8 441	528	189	339	7 912	960	2 298	2 390	1 520	615	128
1999	8 713	489	172	316	8 224	1 031	2 360	2 447	1 606	633	147
2000	8 695	479	175	305	8 215	998	2 282	2 409	1 706	652	168
2001	8 774	451	166	284	8 323	1 025	2 265	2 410	1 762	690	173
2002	8 772	424	148	276	8 348	1 002	2 225	2 394	1 812	743	171
2003	8 815	406	151	255	8 409	973	2 188	2 407	1 879	781	180
2004	8 865	403	144	259	8 462	999	2 144	2 380	1 924	824	192
2005	9 014	405	140	265	8 610	1 017	2 197	2 342	1 954	891	207
2006	9 186	462	166	297	8 723	989	2 211	2 349	1 993	963	218
2007	9 244	417	163	254	8 828	993	2 218	2 328	2 044	1 019	227
2008	9 393	402	146	256	8 991	997	2 281	2 308	2 099	1 056	251
2009	9 367	379	119	260	8 988	1 008	2 258	2 243	2 124	1 091	264
2010	9 447	337	108	230	9 110	1 086	2 299	2 171	2 129	1 153	270
2011	9 427	318	99	219	9 110	1 093	2 275	2 168	2 104	1 172	298
2012	9 805	373	114	258	9 433	1 157	2 303	2 212	2 173	1 271	317
2013	9 846	370	113	257	9 476	1 145	2 303	2 210	2 153	1 330	336
2014	9 964	358	112	246	9 606	1 167	2 367	2 227	2 142	1 352	351
2015	10 218	376	120	255	9 843	1 192	2 457	2 270	2 152	1 381	391
2016	10 321	379	148	231	9 943	1 168	2 561	2 280	2 152	1 399	383
2017	10 580	409	146	262	10 171	1 151	2 634	2 327	2 181	1 437	441
2018	10 720	395	134	261	10 324	1 128	2 687	2 354	2 175	1 503	478
HISPANIC											
Both Sexes											
1985	7 698	579	199	379	7 119	1 358	2 571	1 595	985	527	82
1986	8 076	571	203	368	7 505	1 414	2 685	1 713	1 097	511	84
1987	8 541	610	206	404	7 931	1 425	2 890	1 904	1 086	545	81
1988	8 982	671	234	437	8 311	1 486	2 957	1 996	1 147	621	103
1989	9 323	680	224	456	8 643	1 483	3 118	2 092	1 205	625	120
1990	10 720	829	276	554	9 891	1 839	3 590	2 386	1 320	647	110
1991	10 920	781	249	532	10 139	1 835	3 596	2 539	1 376	681	111
1992	11 338	796	263	533	10 542	1 815	3 740	2 735	1 442	687	122
1993	11 610	771	246	525	10 839	1 811	3 800	2 865	1 534	684	145
1994	11 975	807	285	522	11 168	1 863	3 865	2 965	1 626	698	151
1995	12 267	850	291	559	11 417	1 818	3 943	3 113	1 671	720	152
1996	12 774	845	284	561	11 929	1 845	4 054	3 361	1 697	806	166
1997	13 796	911	315	596	12 884	2 004	4 298	3 601	1 945	850	186
1998	14 317	1 007	320	688	13 310	2 077	4 372	3 707	2 090	894	169
1999	14 665	1 049	333	717	13 616	2 052	4 330	3 929	2 178	927	199
2000	16 689	1 168	368	800	15 521	2 546	5 197	4 241	2 387	940	209
2001	17 328	1 176	352	824	16 152	2 616	5 380	4 377	2 583	1 000	195
2002	17 943	1 103	335	769	16 840	2 678	5 645	4 545	2 657	1 091	224
2003	18 813	960	322	638	17 853	2 672	5 960	4 867	2 894	1 201	259
2004	19 272	995	297	698	18 277	2 732	5 931	4 931	3 093	1 284	306
2005	19 824	1 038	331	708	18 785	2 651	6 080	5 110	3 256	1 378	311
2006	20 694	1 071	360	710	19 623	2 681	6 295	5 337	3 452	1 490	369
2007	21 602	1 091	347	744	20 511	2 728	6 559	5 552	3 707	1 569	395
2008	22 024	1 121	353	768	20 903	2 668	6 557	5 698	3 862	1 701	417
2009	22 352	1 063	301	762	21 290	2 647	6 435	5 752	4 116	1 866	472
2010	22 748	1 002	264	738	21 747	2 760	6 517	5 783	4 238	1 936	513
2011	22 898	965	251	713	21 933	3 017	6 416	5 702	4 272	2 015	511
2012	24 391	1 131	315	817	23 260	3 205	6 736	6 053	4 569	2 185	512
2013	24 771	1 133	328	805	23 639	3 276	6 705	6 094	4 695	2 311	557
2014	25 370	1 109	314	795	24 261	3 315	6 822	6 224	4 849	2 460	591
2015	26 126	1 144	327	817	24 983	3 365	6 863	6 383	5 070	2 666	637
2016	26 797	1 178	356	823	25 619	3 384	7 029	6 520	5 205	2 765	715
2017	27 339	1 225	384	841	26 115	3 326	7 129	6 649	5 294	2 939	778
2018	28 336	1 280	371	909	27 056	3 399	7 413	6 836	5 475	3 113	819

Table 1-7. Civilian Labor Force, by Age, Sex, Race, and Hispanic Origin, 1948–2018—*Continued*

(Thousands of people.)

Race, Hispanic origin, sex, and year	16 years and over	16 to 19 years			20 years and over						
		Total	16 to 17 years	18 to 19 years	Total	20 to 24 years	25 to 34 years	35 to 44 years	45 to 54 years	55 to 64 years	65 years and over
HISPANIC											
Men											
1985	4 729	334	116	218	4 395	835	1 629	957	591	331	53
1986	4 948	336	114	222	4 612	888	1 669	1 015	661	323	56
1987	5 163	345	112	233	4 818	865	1 801	1 121	652	325	55
1988	5 409	378	123	255	5 031	897	1 834	1 189	686	355	69
1989	5 595	400	129	271	5 195	909	1 899	1 221	719	375	71
1990	6 546	512	165	346	6 034	1 182	2 230	1 403	775	380	65
1991	6 664	466	141	325	6 198	1 202	2 260	1 487	780	401	67
1992	6 900	468	154	314	6 432	1 141	2 366	1 593	844	414	74
1993	7 076	455	145	310	6 621	1 147	2 417	1 675	900	394	88
1994	7 210	463	163	300	6 747	1 184	2 430	1 713	922	410	89
1995	7 376	479	168	311	6 898	1 153	2 469	1 795	965	417	98
1996	7 646	496	156	340	7 150	1 132	2 510	1 966	967	469	105
1997	8 309	531	177	354	7 779	1 267	2 684	2 091	1 112	511	113
1998	8 571	565	188	377	8 005	1 288	2 733	2 173	1 164	541	106
1999	8 546	596	181	415	7 950	1 231	2 633	2 219	1 205	526	136
2000	9 923	676	204	471	9 247	1 590	3 181	2 451	1 337	555	134
2001	10 279	684	200	484	9 595	1 602	3 294	2 562	1 430	582	125
2002	10 609	632	183	449	9 977	1 627	3 484	2 647	1 478	607	134
2003	11 288	532	164	368	10 756	1 642	3 776	2 877	1 630	680	150
2004	11 587	567	156	410	11 020	1 671	3 765	2 934	1 736	728	186
2005	11 985	577	179	398	11 408	1 645	3 879	3 058	1 855	779	192
2006	12 488	600	189	411	11 888	1 646	4 014	3 203	1 960	838	228
2007	13 005	602	189	412	12 403	1 645	4 170	3 346	2 104	904	233
2008	13 255	626	202	424	12 629	1 594	4 172	3 425	2 216	979	243
2009	13 310	580	160	420	12 730	1 542	4 046	3 472	2 350	1 046	273
2010	13 511	553	132	420	12 958	1 612	4 061	3 515	2 407	1 061	302
2011	13 576	545	129	416	13 030	1 811	4 011	3 421	2 372	1 122	293
2012	14 026	620	162	457	13 407	1 837	4 053	3 480	2 542	1 215	280
2013	14 341	613	169	444	13 728	1 857	4 053	3 564	2 644	1 286	324
2014	14 651	584	157	428	14 066	1 862	4 081	3 671	2 724	1 399	329
2015	15 054	610	167	443	14 444	1 851	4 105	3 754	2 862	1 515	356
2016	15 396	621	187	434	14 775	1 848	4 153	3 832	2 966	1 569	407
2017	15 604	617	176	441	14 987	1 829	4 162	3 878	3 015	1 658	446
2018	16 113	649	183	467	15 464	1 841	4 280	4 010	3 085	1 776	472
HISPANIC											
Women											
1985	2 970	245	84	161	2 725	524	943	639	394	196	29
1986	3 128	236	89	147	2 893	526	1 016	698	436	189	28
1987	3 377	265	94	171	3 112	559	1 090	783	434	220	27
1988	3 573	293	111	182	3 281	589	1 123	806	461	267	34
1989	3 728	280	95	185	3 448	574	1 219	871	486	251	49
1990	4 174	318	110	207	3 857	657	1 360	983	545	268	45
1991	4 256	315	107	207	3 941	633	1 336	1 052	596	279	44
1992	4 439	328	110	219	4 110	674	1 374	1 142	599	273	48
1993	4 534	316	101	215	4 218	664	1 383	1 190	633	290	57
1994	4 765	345	122	222	4 421	679	1 435	1 252	704	288	62
1995	4 891	371	123	249	4 520	666	1 473	1 318	706	303	54
1996	5 128	349	128	221	4 779	713	1 544	1 395	729	338	61
1997	5 486	381	138	242	5 106	737	1 614	1 510	833	338	73
1998	5 746	442	132	310	5 304	789	1 639	1 533	927	353	62
1999	6 119	453	151	302	5 666	821	1 698	1 710	973	401	63
2000	6 767	492	164	328	6 275	956	2 016	1 791	1 051	386	75
2001	7 049	492	152	340	6 557	1 014	2 086	1 815	1 153	418	70
2002	7 334	471	152	320	6 863	1 051	2 161	1 897	1 179	484	90
2003	7 525	428	158	271	7 096	1 030	2 183	1 990	1 264	520	109
2004	7 685	429	141	288	7 257	1 060	2 166	1 998	1 357	556	119
2005	7 839	462	152	310	7 377	1 005	2 201	2 052	1 401	599	119
2006	8 206	471	171	300	7 735	1 035	2 280	2 134	1 492	652	141
2007	8 597	489	158	332	8 108	1 083	2 389	2 205	1 604	665	162
2008	8 769	495	151	344	8 274	1 074	2 384	2 274	1 646	722	174
2009	9 043	483	141	342	8 560	1 105	2 388	2 280	1 767	820	200
2010	9 238	449	132	317	8 789	1 147	2 456	2 268	1 831	875	211
2011	9 322	419	122	297	8 902	1 206	2 406	2 282	1 899	893	217
2012	10 365	512	152	360	9 853	1 368	2 683	2 574	2 027	969	232
2013	10 430	520	159	361	9 911	1 419	2 653	2 530	2 051	1 025	233
2014	10 720	525	158	367	10 195	1 453	2 741	2 552	2 125	1 061	262
2015	11 072	533	160	373	10 539	1 514	2 758	2 628	2 207	1 151	280
2016	11 401	557	169	388	10 844	1 536	2 876	2 688	2 239	1 196	308
2017	11 735	608	208	400	11 128	1 497	2 967	2 771	2 280	1 281	332
2018	12 223	631	189	442	11 592	1 558	3 133	2 826	2 390	1 337	347

Table 1-8. Civilian Labor Force Participation Rates, by Age, Sex, Race, and Hispanic Origin, 1948–2018

(Percent.)

Race, Hispanic origin, sex, and year	16 years and over	16 to 19 years	20 years and over						
			Total	20 to 24 years	25 to 34 years	35 to 44 years	45 to 54 years	55 to 64 years	65 years and over
ALL RACES									
Both Sexes									
1948	58.8	52.5	59.4	64.1	63.1	66.7	65.1	56.9	27.0
1949	58.9	52.2	59.5	64.9	63.2	67.2	65.3	56.2	27.3
1950	59.2	51.8	59.9	65.9	63.5	67.5	66.4	56.7	26.7
1951	59.2	52.2	59.8	64.8	64.2	67.6	67.2	56.9	25.8
1952	59.0	51.3	59.7	62.2	64.7	68.0	67.5	57.5	24.8
1953	58.9	50.2	59.6	61.2	64.0	68.9	68.1	58.0	24.8
1954	58.8	48.3	59.6	61.6	64.3	68.8	68.4	58.7	23.9
1955	59.3	48.9	60.1	62.7	64.8	68.9	69.7	59.5	24.1
1956	60.0	50.9	60.7	64.1	64.8	69.5	70.5	60.8	24.3
1957	59.6	49.6	60.4	64.0	64.9	69.5	70.9	60.1	22.9
1958	59.5	47.4	60.5	64.4	65.0	69.6	71.5	60.5	21.8
1959	59.3	46.7	60.4	64.3	65.0	69.5	71.9	61.0	21.1
1960	59.4	47.5	60.5	65.2	65.4	69.4	72.2	60.9	20.8
1961	59.3	46.9	60.5	65.7	65.6	69.5	72.1	61.5	20.1
1962	58.8	46.1	60.0	65.3	65.2	69.7	72.2	61.5	19.1
1963	58.7	45.2	60.1	65.1	65.6	70.1	72.5	62.0	17.9
1964	58.7	44.5	60.2	66.3	65.8	70.0	72.9	61.9	18.0
1965	58.9	45.7	60.3	66.4	66.4	70.7	72.5	61.9	17.8
1966	59.2	48.2	60.5	66.5	67.1	71.0	72.7	62.2	17.2
1967	59.6	48.4	60.9	67.1	68.2	71.6	72.7	62.3	17.2
1968	59.6	48.3	60.9	67.0	68.6	72.0	72.8	62.2	17.2
1969	60.1	49.4	61.3	68.2	69.1	72.5	73.4	62.1	17.3
1970	60.4	49.9	61.6	69.2	69.7	73.1	73.5	61.8	17.0
1971	60.2	49.7	61.4	69.3	69.9	73.2	73.2	61.3	16.2
1972	60.4	51.9	61.4	70.8	70.9	73.3	72.7	60.0	15.6
1973	60.8	53.7	61.7	72.6	72.3	74.0	72.5	58.4	14.6
1974	61.3	54.8	62.0	74.0	73.6	74.6	72.7	57.8	14.0
1975	61.2	54.0	62.1	73.9	74.4	75.0	72.6	57.2	13.7
1976	61.6	54.5	62.4	74.7	75.7	76.0	72.5	56.6	13.1
1977	62.3	56.0	63.0	75.7	77.0	77.0	72.8	56.3	13.0
1978	63.2	57.8	63.8	76.8	78.3	78.1	73.5	56.3	13.3
1979	63.7	57.9	64.3	77.5	79.2	79.2	74.3	56.2	13.1
1980	63.8	56.7	64.5	77.2	79.9	80.0	74.9	55.7	12.5
1981	63.9	55.4	64.8	77.3	80.5	80.7	75.7	55.0	12.2
1982	64.0	54.1	65.0	77.1	81.0	81.2	75.9	55.1	11.9
1983	64.0	53.5	65.0	77.2	81.3	81.6	76.0	54.5	11.7
1984	64.4	53.9	65.3	77.6	81.8	82.4	76.5	54.2	11.1
1985	64.8	54.5	65.7	78.2	82.5	83.1	77.3	54.2	10.8
1986	65.3	54.7	66.2	78.9	82.9	83.7	78.0	54.0	10.9
1987	65.6	54.7	66.5	78.9	83.3	84.3	78.6	54.4	11.1
1988	65.9	55.3	66.8	78.7	83.3	84.6	79.6	54.6	11.5
1989	66.5	55.9	67.3	78.7	83.8	85.1	80.5	55.5	11.8
1990	66.5	53.7	67.6	77.8	83.6	85.2	80.7	55.9	11.8
1991	66.2	51.6	67.3	76.7	83.2	85.2	81.0	55.5	11.5
1992	66.4	51.3	67.6	77.0	83.7	85.1	81.5	56.2	11.5
1993	66.3	51.5	67.5	77.0	83.3	84.9	81.6	56.4	11.2
1994	66.6	52.7	67.7	77.0	83.2	84.8	81.7	56.8	12.4
1995	66.6	53.5	67.7	76.6	83.8	84.6	81.4	57.2	12.1
1996	66.8	52.3	67.9	76.8	84.1	84.8	82.1	57.9	12.1
1997	67.1	51.6	68.4	77.6	84.4	85.1	82.6	58.9	12.2
1998	67.1	52.8	68.3	77.5	84.6	84.7	82.5	59.3	11.9
1999	67.1	52.0	68.3	77.5	84.6	84.9	82.6	59.3	12.3
2000	67.1	52.0	68.3	77.8	84.6	84.8	82.5	59.2	12.9
2001	66.8	49.6	68.2	77.1	84.0	84.6	82.3	60.4	13.0
2002	66.6	47.4	68.1	76.4	83.7	84.1	82.1	61.9	13.2
2003	66.2	44.5	67.9	75.4	82.9	83.9	82.1	62.4	14.0
2004	66.0	43.9	67.7	75.0	82.7	83.6	81.8	62.3	14.4
2005	66.0	43.7	67.8	74.6	82.8	83.8	81.7	62.9	15.1
2006	66.2	43.7	67.9	74.6	83.0	83.8	81.9	63.7	15.4
2007	66.0	41.3	68.0	74.4	83.3	83.8	82.0	63.8	16.0
2008	66.0	40.2	68.0	74.4	83.3	84.1	81.9	64.5	16.8
2009	65.4	37.5	67.5	72.9	82.7	83.7	81.6	64.9	17.2
2010	64.7	34.9	67.0	71.4	82.2	83.2	81.2	64.9	17.4
2011	64.1	34.1	66.4	71.3	81.5	82.7	80.7	64.3	17.9
2012	63.7	34.3	65.9	70.9	81.7	82.6	80.2	64.5	18.5
2013	63.2	34.5	65.4	70.7	81.2	82.2	79.7	64.4	18.7
2014	62.9	34.0	65.0	70.8	81.2	82.2	79.6	64.1	18.6
2015	62.7	34.3	64.7	70.7	81.0	82.1	79.5	63.9	18.9
2016	62.8	35.2	64.7	70.5	81.6	82.4	80.0	64.1	19.3
2017	62.9	35.2	64.8	71.3	82.1	82.7	80.3	64.5	19.3
2018	62.9	35.1	64.8	71.1	82.5	82.9	80.8	65.0	19.6

Table 1-8. Civilian Labor Force Participation Rates, by Age, Sex, Race, and Hispanic Origin, 1948–2018 *—Continued*

(Percent.)

Race, Hispanic origin, sex, and year	16 years and over	16 to 19 years	20 years and over						
			Total	20 to 24 years	25 to 34 years	35 to 44 years	45 to 54 years	55 to 64 years	65 years and over
ALL RACES									
Men									
1948	86.6	63.7	88.6	84.6	95.9	97.9	95.8	89.5	46.8
1949	86.4	62.8	88.5	86.6	95.8	97.9	95.6	87.5	47.0
1950	86.4	63.2	88.4	87.9	96.0	97.6	95.8	86.9	45.8
1951	86.3	63.0	88.2	88.4	96.9	97.5	95.9	87.2	44.9
1952	86.3	61.3	88.3	88.1	97.5	97.8	96.2	87.5	42.6
1953	86.0	60.7	88.0	87.7	97.4	98.2	96.5	87.9	41.6
1954	85.5	58.0	87.8	86.9	97.3	98.1	96.5	88.7	40.5
1955	85.4	58.9	87.6	86.9	97.6	98.1	96.4	87.9	39.6
1956	85.5	60.5	87.6	87.8	97.3	97.9	96.6	88.5	40.0
1957	84.8	59.1	86.9	87.1	97.1	97.9	96.3	87.5	37.5
1958	84.2	56.6	86.6	86.9	97.1	97.9	96.3	87.8	35.6
1959	83.7	55.8	86.3	87.8	97.4	97.8	96.0	87.4	34.2
1960	83.3	56.1	86.0	88.1	97.5	97.7	95.7	86.8	33.1
1961	82.9	54.6	85.7	87.8	97.5	97.6	95.6	87.3	31.7
1962	82.0	53.8	84.8	86.9	97.2	97.6	95.6	86.2	30.3
1963	81.4	52.9	84.4	86.1	97.1	97.5	95.7	86.2	28.4
1964	81.0	52.4	84.2	86.1	97.3	97.3	95.7	85.6	28.0
1965	80.7	53.8	83.9	85.8	97.2	97.3	95.6	84.6	27.9
1966	80.4	55.3	83.6	85.1	97.3	97.2	95.3	84.5	27.1
1967	80.4	55.6	83.4	84.4	97.2	97.3	95.2	84.4	27.1
1968	80.1	55.1	83.1	82.8	96.9	97.1	94.9	84.3	27.3
1969	79.8	55.9	82.8	82.8	96.7	96.9	94.6	83.4	27.2
1970	79.7	56.1	82.6	83.3	96.4	96.9	94.3	83.0	26.8
1971	79.1	56.1	82.1	83.0	95.9	96.5	93.9	82.1	25.5
1972	78.9	58.1	81.6	83.9	95.7	96.4	93.2	80.4	24.3
1973	78.8	59.7	81.3	85.2	95.7	96.2	93.0	78.2	22.7
1974	78.7	60.7	81.0	85.9	95.8	96.0	92.2	77.3	22.4
1975	77.9	59.1	80.3	84.5	95.2	95.6	92.1	75.6	21.6
1976	77.5	59.3	79.8	85.2	95.2	95.4	91.6	74.3	20.2
1977	77.7	60.9	79.7	85.6	95.3	95.7	91.1	73.8	20.0
1978	77.9	62.0	79.8	85.9	95.3	95.7	91.3	73.3	20.4
1979	77.8	61.5	79.8	86.4	95.3	95.7	91.4	72.8	19.9
1980	77.4	60.5	79.4	85.9	95.2	95.5	91.2	72.1	19.0
1981	77.0	59.0	79.0	85.5	94.9	95.4	91.4	70.6	18.4
1982	76.6	56.7	78.7	84.9	94.7	95.3	91.2	70.2	17.8
1983	76.4	56.2	78.5	84.8	94.2	95.2	91.2	69.4	17.4
1984	76.4	56.0	78.3	85.0	94.4	95.4	91.2	68.5	16.3
1985	76.3	56.8	78.1	85.0	94.7	95.0	91.0	67.9	15.8
1986	76.3	56.4	78.1	85.8	94.6	94.8	91.0	67.3	16.0
1987	76.2	56.1	78.0	85.2	94.6	94.6	90.7	67.6	16.3
1988	76.2	56.9	77.9	85.0	94.3	94.5	90.9	67.0	16.5
1989	76.4	57.9	78.1	85.3	94.4	94.5	91.1	67.2	16.6
1990	76.4	55.7	78.2	84.4	94.1	94.3	90.7	67.8	16.3
1991	75.8	53.2	77.7	83.5	93.6	94.1	90.5	67.0	15.7
1992	75.8	53.4	77.7	83.3	93.8	93.7	90.7	67.0	16.1
1993	75.4	53.2	77.3	83.2	93.4	93.4	90.1	66.5	15.6
1994	75.1	54.1	76.8	83.1	92.6	92.8	89.1	65.5	16.8
1995	75.0	54.8	76.7	83.1	93.0	92.3	88.8	66.0	16.8
1996	74.9	53.2	76.8	82.5	93.2	92.4	89.1	67.0	16.9
1997	75.0	52.3	77.0	82.5	93.0	92.6	89.5	67.6	17.1
1998	74.9	53.3	76.8	82.0	93.2	92.6	89.2	68.1	16.5
1999	74.7	52.9	76.7	81.9	93.3	92.8	88.8	67.9	16.9
2000	74.8	52.8	76.7	82.6	93.4	92.7	88.6	67.3	17.7
2001	74.4	50.2	76.5	81.6	92.7	92.5	88.5	68.3	17.7
2002	74.1	47.5	76.3	80.7	92.4	92.1	88.5	69.2	17.9
2003	73.5	44.3	75.9	80.0	91.8	92.1	87.7	68.7	18.6
2004	73.3	43.9	75.8	79.6	91.9	91.9	87.5	68.7	19.0
2005	73.3	43.2	75.8	79.1	91.7	92.1	87.7	69.3	19.8
2006	73.5	43.7	75.9	79.6	91.7	92.1	88.1	69.6	20.3
2007	73.2	41.1	75.9	78.7	92.2	92.3	88.2	69.6	20.5
2008	73.0	40.1	75.7	78.7	91.5	92.2	88.0	70.4	21.5
2009	72.0	37.3	74.8	76.2	90.3	91.7	87.4	70.2	21.9
2010	71.2	34.9	74.1	74.5	89.7	91.5	86.8	70.0	22.1
2011	70.5	33.7	73.4	74.7	89.2	90.9	86.2	69.3	22.8
2012	70.2	34.0	73.0	74.5	89.5	90.7	86.1	69.9	23.6
2013	69.7	34.2	72.5	73.9	89.2	90.7	85.5	70.0	23.5
2014	69.2	33.5	71.9	73.9	88.7	90.5	85.6	69.9	23.0
2015	69.1	34.2	71.7	73.0	90.3	88.8	85.9	69.8	23.4
2016	69.2	35.3	71.7	73.0	88.8	90.6	86.3	70.2	24.0
2017	69.1	34.6	71.6	74.1	88.8	90.7	86.4	70.6	23.9
2018	69.1	34.2	71.6	73.2	89.1	90.9	87.0	71.2	24.0

Table 1-8. Civilian Labor Force Participation Rates, by Age, Sex, Race, and Hispanic Origin, 1948–2018 —*Continued*

(Percent.)

Race, Hispanic origin, sex, and year	16 years and over	16 to 19 years	20 years and over						
			Total	20 to 24 years	25 to 34 years	35 to 44 years	45 to 54 years	55 to 64 years	65 years and over
ALL RACES									
Women									
1948	32.7	42.0	31.8	45.3	33.2	36.9	35.0	24.3	9.1
1949	33.1	42.4	32.3	45.0	33.4	38.1	35.9	25.3	9.6
1950	33.9	41.0	33.3	46.0	34.0	39.1	37.9	27.0	9.7
1951	34.6	42.4	34.0	46.5	35.4	39.8	39.7	27.6	8.9
1952	34.7	42.2	34.1	44.7	35.4	40.4	40.1	28.7	9.1
1953	34.4	40.7	33.9	44.3	34.0	41.3	40.4	29.1	10.0
1954	34.6	39.4	34.2	45.1	34.4	41.2	41.2	30.0	9.3
1955	35.7	39.7	35.4	45.9	34.9	41.6	43.8	32.5	10.6
1956	36.9	42.2	36.4	46.3	35.4	43.1	45.5	34.9	10.8
1957	36.9	41.1	36.5	45.9	35.6	43.3	46.5	34.5	10.5
1958	37.1	39.0	36.9	46.3	35.6	43.4	47.8	35.2	10.3
1959	37.1	38.2	37.1	45.1	35.3	43.4	49.0	36.6	10.2
1960	37.7	39.3	37.6	46.1	36.0	43.4	49.9	37.2	10.8
1961	38.1	39.7	38.0	47.0	36.4	43.8	50.1	37.9	10.7
1962	37.9	39.0	37.8	47.3	36.3	44.1	50.0	38.7	10.0
1963	38.3	38.0	38.3	47.5	37.2	44.9	50.6	39.7	9.6
1964	38.7	37.0	38.9	49.4	37.2	45.0	51.4	40.2	10.1
1965	39.3	38.0	39.4	49.9	38.5	46.1	50.9	41.1	10.0
1966	40.3	41.4	40.1	51.5	39.8	46.8	51.7	41.8	9.6
1967	41.1	41.6	41.1	53.3	41.9	48.1	51.8	42.4	9.6
1968	41.6	41.9	41.6	54.5	42.6	48.9	52.3	42.4	9.6
1969	42.7	43.2	42.7	56.7	43.7	49.9	53.8	43.1	9.9
1970	43.3	44.0	43.3	57.7	45.0	51.1	54.4	43.0	9.7
1971	43.4	43.4	43.3	57.7	45.6	51.6	54.3	42.9	9.5
1972	43.9	45.8	43.7	59.1	47.8	52.0	53.9	42.1	9.3
1973	44.7	47.8	44.4	61.1	50.4	53.3	53.7	41.1	8.9
1974	45.7	49.1	45.3	63.1	52.6	54.7	54.6	40.7	8.1
1975	46.3	49.1	46.0	64.1	54.9	55.8	54.6	40.9	8.2
1976	47.3	49.8	47.0	65.0	57.3	57.8	55.0	41.0	8.2
1977	48.4	51.2	48.1	66.5	59.7	59.6	55.8	40.9	8.1
1978	50.0	53.7	49.6	68.3	62.2	61.6	57.1	41.3	8.3
1979	50.9	54.2	50.6	69.0	63.9	63.6	58.3	41.7	8.3
1980	51.5	52.9	51.3	68.9	65.5	65.5	59.9	41.3	8.1
1981	52.1	51.8	52.1	69.6	66.7	66.8	61.1	41.4	8.0
1982	52.6	51.4	52.7	69.8	68.0	68.0	61.6	41.8	7.9
1983	52.9	50.8	53.1	69.9	69.0	68.7	61.9	41.5	7.8
1984	53.6	51.8	53.7	70.4	69.8	70.1	62.9	41.7	7.5
1985	54.5	52.1	54.7	71.8	70.9	71.8	64.4	42.0	7.3
1986	55.3	53.0	55.5	72.4	71.6	73.1	65.9	42.3	7.4
1987	56.0	53.3	56.2	73.0	72.4	74.5	67.1	42.7	7.4
1988	56.6	53.6	56.8	72.7	72.7	75.2	69.0	43.5	7.9
1989	57.4	53.9	57.7	72.4	73.5	76.0	70.5	45.0	8.4
1990	57.5	51.6	58.0	71.3	73.5	76.4	71.2	45.2	8.6
1991	57.4	50.0	57.9	70.1	73.1	76.5	72.0	45.2	8.5
1992	57.8	49.1	58.5	70.9	73.9	76.7	72.6	46.5	8.3
1993	57.9	49.7	58.5	70.9	73.4	76.6	73.5	47.2	8.1
1994	58.8	51.3	59.3	71.0	74.0	77.1	74.6	48.9	9.2
1995	58.9	52.2	59.4	70.3	74.9	77.2	74.4	49.2	8.8
1996	59.3	51.3	59.9	71.3	75.2	77.5	75.4	49.6	8.6
1997	59.8	51.0	60.5	72.7	76.0	77.7	76.0	50.9	8.6
1998	59.8	52.3	60.4	73.0	76.3	77.1	76.2	51.2	8.6
1999	60.0	51.0	60.7	73.2	76.4	77.2	76.7	51.5	8.9
2000	59.9	51.2	60.6	73.1	76.1	77.2	76.8	51.9	9.4
2001	59.8	49.0	60.6	72.7	75.5	77.1	76.4	53.2	9.6
2002	59.6	47.3	60.5	72.1	75.1	76.4	76.0	55.2	9.8
2003	59.5	44.8	60.6	70.8	74.1	76.0	76.8	56.6	10.6
2004	59.2	43.8	60.3	70.5	73.6	75.6	76.5	56.3	11.1
2005	59.3	44.2	60.4	70.1	73.9	75.8	76.0	57.0	11.5
2006	59.4	43.7	60.5	69.5	74.4	75.9	76.0	58.2	11.7
2007	59.3	41.5	60.6	70.1	74.5	75.5	76.0	58.3	12.6
2008	59.5	40.2	60.9	70.0	75.2	76.1	76.1	59.1	13.3
2009	59.2	37.7	60.8	69.6	75.0	75.9	76.0	60.0	13.6
2010	58.6	35.0	60.3	68.3	74.7	75.2	75.7	60.2	13.8
2011	58.1	34.6	59.8	67.8	73.9	74.7	75.4	59.5	14.0
2012	57.7	34.6	59.3	67.4	74.1	74.8	74.7	59.4	14.4
2013	57.2	34.7	58.8	67.5	73.5	74.0	74.1	59.2	14.9
2014	57.0	34.5	58.5	67.7	73.8	74.1	73.8	58.8	15.1
2015	56.7	34.4	58.2	68.3	73.4	74.3	73.4	58.5	15.3
2016	56.8	35.1	58.3	68.0	74.5	74.5	73.9	58.4	15.5
2017	57.0	35.9	58.5	68.5	75.5	75.0	74.5	58.9	15.7
2018	57.1	36.0	58.5	69.0	75.9	75.1	74.9	59.1	15.9

Table 1-8. Civilian Labor Force Participation Rates, by Age, Sex, Race, and Hispanic Origin, 1948–2018 *—Continued*

(Percent.)

Race, Hispanic origin, sex, and year	16 years and over	16 to 19 years	20 years and over						
			Total	20 to 24 years	25 to 34 years	35 to 44 years	45 to 54 years	55 to 64 years	65 years and over
WHITE									
Both Sexes									
1954	58.2	48.8	58.9	61.0	63.5	68.0	67.9	58.4	23.7
1955	58.7	49.3	59.5	62.4	64.0	68.3	69.2	59.3	23.9
1956	59.4	51.3	60.1	64.1	64.0	68.9	70.1	60.6	24.2
1957	59.1	50.3	59.8	63.7	64.1	68.8	70.5	59.9	22.8
1958	58.9	47.9	59.8	64.1	64.2	68.8	71.0	60.3	21.7
1959	58.7	47.4	59.7	63.7	64.3	68.7	71.5	60.7	21.0
1960	58.8	47.9	59.8	64.8	64.7	68.6	71.7	60.6	20.8
1961	58.8	47.4	59.9	65.5	64.8	68.8	71.7	61.3	20.0
1962	58.3	46.6	59.4	65.0	64.4	69.0	71.8	61.3	19.0
1963	58.2	45.7	59.4	64.9	64.8	69.4	72.3	61.8	17.9
1964	58.2	45.1	59.6	65.8	64.9	69.5	72.5	61.8	17.8
1965	58.4	46.5	59.7	65.7	65.6	70.1	72.2	61.7	17.7
1966	58.7	49.1	59.8	66.0	66.3	70.4	72.5	61.9	17.1
1967	59.2	49.2	60.3	66.8	67.4	71.2	72.5	62.3	17.0
1968	59.3	49.3	60.4	66.6	67.9	71.7	72.7	62.2	17.1
1969	59.9	50.6	60.9	67.9	68.4	72.3	73.3	62.1	17.2
1970	60.2	51.4	61.2	69.2	69.1	72.9	73.5	61.8	16.8
1971	60.1	51.6	61.1	69.6	69.3	73.0	73.4	61.3	16.1
1972	60.4	54.1	61.2	71.2	70.4	73.2	72.9	60.3	15.4
1973	60.8	56.0	61.4	73.3	72.0	73.9	72.7	58.6	14.4
1974	61.4	57.3	61.9	74.8	73.4	74.6	73.0	58.0	13.9
1975	61.5	56.7	62.0	75.2	74.4	75.1	73.0	57.4	13.6
1976	61.8	57.5	62.3	76.0	75.6	76.1	73.0	56.9	13.0
1977	62.5	59.3	62.9	77.1	77.0	77.1	73.2	56.6	12.9
1978	63.3	60.8	63.6	78.1	78.3	78.1	73.8	56.4	13.1
1979	63.9	61.1	64.2	78.9	79.4	79.3	74.6	56.5	12.9
1980	64.1	60.0	64.5	78.7	80.2	80.3	75.4	56.0	12.5
1981	64.3	58.9	64.8	79.1	81.0	81.0	76.2	55.2	12.2
1982	64.3	57.5	65.0	78.9	81.6	81.5	76.4	55.3	12.0
1983	64.3	56.9	65.0	79.0	81.8	81.9	76.5	54.7	11.8
1984	64.6	57.2	65.3	79.4	82.5	82.6	77.0	54.5	11.1
1985	65.0	57.5	65.7	79.9	83.1	83.4	77.8	54.4	10.7
1986	65.5	57.8	66.1	80.6	83.6	84.0	78.5	54.3	11.0
1987	65.8	57.7	66.5	80.7	84.0	84.7	79.1	54.6	11.1
1988	66.2	58.6	66.8	80.6	84.1	85.0	80.3	55.1	11.4
1989	66.7	59.1	67.3	80.2	84.5	85.5	81.2	56.2	11.8
1990	66.9	57.5	67.6	79.8	84.6	85.9	81.3	56.5	11.9
1991	66.6	55.8	67.4	78.9	84.3	85.9	81.8	56.0	11.6
1992	66.8	54.7	67.7	79.4	84.6	85.8	82.2	56.8	11.6
1993	66.8	55.1	67.6	79.5	84.5	85.7	82.5	57.1	11.4
1994	67.1	56.4	67.9	79.5	84.4	85.7	82.7	57.6	12.5
1995	67.1	57.1	67.8	78.7	84.9	85.5	82.5	58.0	12.3
1996	67.2	55.9	68.1	79.1	84.9	85.7	83.1	58.7	12.3
1997	67.5	55.2	68.4	79.6	85.3	85.8	83.5	59.9	12.3
1998	67.3	56.0	68.2	79.5	85.4	85.3	83.4	60.1	12.0
1999	67.3	55.5	68.2	79.5	85.1	85.4	83.5	60.2	12.5
2000	67.3	55.5	68.2	79.9	85.1	85.4	83.5	60.0	13.0
2001	67.0	53.1	68.1	79.2	84.5	85.2	83.3	61.2	13.0
2002	66.8	50.5	68.1	78.6	84.5	84.7	83.0	62.8	13.3
2003	66.5	47.7	67.9	77.7	83.6	84.3	83.0	63.3	14.1
2004	66.3	47.1	67.7	77.1	83.5	84.1	82.9	63.2	14.6
2005	66.3	46.9	67.7	76.3	83.5	84.2	82.8	63.7	15.1
2006	66.5	46.7	67.9	76.5	83.8	84.3	83.0	64.7	15.5
2007	66.4	44.4	68.0	76.4	84.1	84.1	83.1	64.9	16.2
2008	66.3	43.1	68.0	76.3	83.9	84.4	82.9	65.7	17.0
2009	65.8	40.6	67.7	75.1	83.5	84.2	82.7	66.2	17.4
2010	65.1	37.7	67.1	73.4	83.2	83.8	82.2	66.1	17.6
2011	64.5	36.8	66.5	73.2	82.5	83.3	81.7	65.5	18.1
2012	64.0	36.9	65.9	73.1	82.6	83.2	81.2	65.9	18.7
2013	63.5	36.9	65.3	73.1	82.2	82.7	80.7	65.5	19.0
2014	63.1	36.2	64.9	73.0	82.3	82.7	80.5	65.3	18.8
2015	62.8	36.4	64.5	72.7	82.1	82.6	80.5	65.2	19.1
2016	62.9	37.4	64.6	72.4	82.5	82.9	81.0	65.4	19.5
2017	62.8	36.8	64.5	73.1	83.1	83.0	81.0	65.9	19.5
2018	62.8	37.2	64.5	73.2	83.4	83.3	81.5	66.3	19.7

Table 1-8. Civilian Labor Force Participation Rates, by Age, Sex, Race, and Hispanic Origin, 1948–2018
—Continued

(Percent.)

Race, Hispanic origin, sex, and year	16 years and over	16 to 19 years	20 years and over						
			Total	20 to 24 years	25 to 34 years	35 to 44 years	45 to 54 years	55 to 64 years	65 years and over
WHITE									
Men									
1954	85.6	57.6	87.8	86.3	97.5	98.2	96.8	89.1	40.4
1955	85.4	58.6	87.5	86.5	97.8	98.2	96.7	88.4	39.6
1956	85.6	60.4	87.6	87.6	97.4	98.1	96.8	88.9	40.0
1957	84.8	59.2	86.9	86.6	97.2	98.0	96.7	88.0	37.7
1958	84.3	56.5	86.6	86.7	97.2	98.0	96.6	88.2	35.7
1959	83.8	55.9	86.3	87.3	97.5	98.0	96.3	87.9	34.3
1960	83.4	55.9	86.0	87.8	97.7	97.9	96.1	87.2	33.3
1961	83.0	54.5	85.7	87.6	97.7	97.9	95.9	87.8	31.9
1962	82.1	53.8	84.9	86.5	97.4	97.9	96.0	86.7	30.6
1963	81.5	53.1	84.4	85.8	97.4	97.8	96.2	86.6	28.4
1964	81.1	52.7	84.2	85.7	97.5	97.6	96.1	86.1	27.9
1965	80.8	54.1	83.9	85.3	97.4	97.7	95.9	85.2	27.9
1966	80.6	55.9	83.6	84.4	97.5	97.6	95.8	84.9	27.2
1967	80.6	56.3	83.5	84.0	97.5	97.7	95.6	84.9	27.1
1968	80.4	55.9	83.2	82.4	97.2	97.6	95.4	84.7	27.4
1969	80.2	56.8	83.0	82.6	97.0	97.4	95.1	83.9	27.3
1970	80.0	57.5	82.8	83.3	96.7	97.3	94.9	83.3	26.7
1971	79.6	57.9	82.3	83.2	96.3	97.0	94.7	82.6	25.6
1972	79.6	60.1	82.0	84.3	96.0	97.0	94.0	81.1	24.4
1973	79.4	62.0	81.6	85.8	96.2	96.8	93.5	78.9	22.7
1974	79.4	62.9	81.4	86.6	96.3	96.7	93.0	78.0	22.4
1975	78.7	61.9	80.7	85.5	95.8	96.4	92.9	76.4	21.7
1976	78.4	62.3	80.3	86.3	95.9	96.0	92.5	75.2	20.2
1977	78.5	64.0	80.2	86.8	96.0	96.2	92.1	74.6	20.0
1978	78.6	65.0	80.1	87.3	95.9	96.3	92.1	73.7	20.3
1979	78.6	64.8	80.1	87.6	96.0	96.4	92.2	73.4	20.0
1980	78.2	63.7	79.8	87.2	95.9	96.2	92.1	73.1	19.1
1981	77.9	62.4	79.5	87.0	95.8	96.1	92.4	71.5	18.5
1982	77.4	60.0	79.2	86.3	95.6	96.0	92.2	71.0	17.9
1983	77.1	59.4	78.9	86.1	95.2	96.0	91.9	70.0	17.7
1984	77.1	59.0	78.7	86.5	95.4	96.1	92.0	69.5	16.4
1985	77.0	59.7	78.5	86.4	95.7	95.7	92.0	68.8	15.9
1986	76.9	59.3	78.5	87.3	95.5	95.4	91.8	68.0	16.3
1987	76.8	59.0	78.4	86.9	95.5	95.4	91.6	68.1	16.5
1988	76.9	60.0	78.3	86.6	95.2	95.4	91.8	67.9	16.7
1989	77.1	61.0	78.5	86.8	95.4	95.3	92.2	68.3	16.8
1990	77.1	59.6	78.5	86.2	95.2	95.3	91.7	68.6	16.6
1991	76.5	57.3	78.0	85.4	94.9	95.0	91.4	67.7	15.9
1992	76.5	56.9	78.0	85.2	94.9	94.7	91.8	67.7	16.2
1993	76.2	56.6	77.7	85.5	94.7	94.5	91.3	67.3	15.9
1994	75.9	57.7	77.3	85.5	93.9	93.9	90.3	66.4	17.2
1995	75.7	58.5	77.1	85.1	94.1	93.4	90.0	67.1	16.9
1996	75.8	57.1	77.3	85.0	94.4	93.6	90.4	68.0	17.2
1997	75.9	56.1	77.5	85.1	94.2	93.7	90.6	68.9	17.4
1998	75.6	56.6	77.2	84.6	94.4	93.7	90.3	69.1	16.6
1999	75.6	56.4	77.2	84.9	94.3	93.8	90.1	69.1	17.2
2000	75.5	56.5	77.1	85.2	94.5	93.8	89.7	68.2	17.9
2001	75.1	53.7	76.9	84.1	93.9	93.6	89.7	69.1	17.8
2002	74.8	50.3	76.7	83.2	93.7	93.2	89.6	70.2	17.8
2003	74.2	47.5	76.3	82.5	93.3	93.1	88.8	69.7	18.6
2004	74.1	47.4	76.2	82.1	93.2	93.0	88.7	69.8	19.1
2005	74.1	46.2	76.2	81.4	93.0	93.0	89.0	70.4	20.0
2006	74.3	46.9	76.4	81.9	92.9	93.1	89.3	71.0	20.6
2007	74.0	44.3	76.3	80.9	93.4	93.1	89.6	71.2	20.8
2008	73.7	43.0	76.1	80.8	92.6	93.0	89.2	71.9	21.8
2009	72.8	40.3	75.3	78.6	91.6	92.7	88.8	71.8	22.2
2010	72.0	37.4	74.6	77.0	91.1	92.4	88.1	71.2	22.3
2011	71.3	36.1	73.9	77.1	90.5	92.1	87.5	70.8	23.0
2012	71.0	36.7	73.5	77.2	90.9	91.8	87.5	71.6	24.0
2013	70.5	36.6	72.9	76.9	90.5	91.6	86.9	71.6	24.0
2014	69.8	35.6	72.2	76.5	90.0	91.5	86.9	71.3	23.3
2015	69.7	36.7	72.0	75.5	90.3	91.3	87.2	71.5	23.7
2016	69.8	38.1	72.0	75.5	90.1	91.7	87.5	71.7	24.3
2017	69.5	36.5	71.8	76.5	90.2	91.6	87.6	72.3	24.2
2018	69.5	36.2	71.8	75.8	90.5	91.9	88.1	72.8	24.5

Table 1-8. Civilian Labor Force Participation Rates, by Age, Sex, Race, and Hispanic Origin, 1948–2018 —*Continued*

(Percent.)

Race, Hispanic origin, sex, and year	16 years and over	16 to 19 years	20 years and over						
			Total	20 to 24 years	25 to 34 years	35 to 44 years	45 to 54 years	55 to 64 years	65 years and over
WHITE									
Women									
1954	33.3	40.6	32.7	44.4	32.5	39.3	39.8	29.1	9.1
1955	34.5	40.7	34.0	45.8	32.8	40.0	42.7	31.8	10.5
1956	35.7	43.1	35.1	46.5	33.2	41.5	44.4	34.0	10.6
1957	35.7	42.2	35.2	45.8	33.6	41.5	45.4	33.7	10.2
1958	35.8	40.1	35.5	46.0	33.6	41.4	46.5	34.5	10.1
1959	36.0	39.6	35.6	44.5	33.4	41.4	47.8	35.7	10.0
1960	36.5	40.3	36.2	45.7	34.1	41.5	48.6	36.2	10.6
1961	36.9	40.6	36.6	46.9	34.3	41.8	48.9	37.2	10.5
1962	36.7	39.8	36.5	47.1	34.1	42.2	48.9	38.0	9.8
1963	37.2	38.7	37.0	47.3	34.8	43.1	49.5	38.9	9.4
1964	37.5	37.8	37.5	48.8	35.0	43.3	50.2	39.4	9.9
1965	38.1	39.2	38.0	49.2	36.3	44.4	49.9	40.3	9.7
1966	39.2	42.6	38.8	51.0	37.7	45.0	50.6	41.1	9.4
1967	40.1	42.5	39.8	53.1	39.7	46.4	50.9	41.9	9.3
1968	40.7	43.0	40.4	54.0	40.6	47.5	51.5	42.0	9.4
1969	41.8	44.6	41.5	56.4	41.7	48.6	53.0	42.6	9.7
1970	42.6	45.6	42.2	57.7	43.2	49.9	53.7	42.6	9.5
1971	42.6	45.4	42.3	58.0	43.7	50.2	53.6	42.5	9.3
1972	43.2	48.1	42.7	59.4	46.0	50.7	53.4	41.9	9.0
1973	44.1	50.1	43.5	61.7	48.7	52.2	53.4	40.7	8.7
1974	45.2	51.7	44.4	63.9	51.3	53.6	54.3	40.4	8.0
1975	45.9	51.5	45.3	65.5	53.8	54.9	54.3	40.6	8.0
1976	46.9	52.8	46.2	66.3	56.0	57.1	54.7	40.7	7.9
1977	48.0	54.5	47.3	67.8	58.5	58.9	55.3	40.7	7.9
1978	49.4	56.7	48.7	69.3	61.2	60.7	56.7	41.1	8.1
1979	50.5	57.4	49.8	70.5	63.1	63.0	58.1	41.5	8.1
1980	51.2	56.2	50.6	70.6	64.8	65.0	59.6	40.9	7.9
1981	51.9	55.4	51.5	71.5	66.4	66.4	60.9	40.9	7.9
1982	52.4	55.0	52.2	71.8	67.8	67.5	61.4	41.5	7.8
1983	52.7	54.5	52.5	72.1	68.7	68.2	61.9	41.1	7.8
1984	53.3	55.4	53.1	72.5	69.8	69.6	62.7	41.2	7.5
1985	54.1	55.2	54.0	73.8	70.9	71.4	64.2	41.5	7.0
1986	55.0	56.3	54.9	74.1	71.8	72.9	65.8	42.1	7.3
1987	55.7	56.5	55.6	74.8	72.5	74.2	67.2	42.4	7.2
1988	56.4	57.2	56.3	74.9	73.0	74.9	69.2	43.6	7.7
1989	57.2	57.1	57.2	74.0	73.8	75.9	70.6	45.2	8.2
1990	57.4	55.3	57.6	73.4	74.1	76.6	71.3	45.5	8.5
1991	57.4	54.1	57.6	72.5	73.8	76.8	72.4	45.4	8.5
1992	57.7	52.5	58.1	73.5	74.4	77.0	72.8	46.8	8.2
1993	58.0	53.5	58.3	73.4	74.3	76.9	74.0	47.6	8.1
1994	58.9	55.1	59.2	73.4	74.9	77.5	75.2	49.4	9.2
1995	59.0	55.5	59.2	72.3	75.8	77.6	75.2	49.5	9.0
1996	59.1	54.7	59.4	73.3	75.5	77.8	76.1	50.1	8.7
1997	59.5	54.1	59.9	73.9	76.3	77.9	76.6	51.5	8.6
1998	59.4	55.4	59.7	74.3	76.3	76.9	76.6	51.6	8.7
1999	59.6	54.5	59.9	73.9	76.0	77.1	77.1	52.0	8.9
2000	59.5	54.5	59.9	74.5	75.7	77.2	77.5	52.4	9.4
2001	59.4	52.4	59.9	74.2	75.1	77.0	77.1	53.8	9.6
2002	59.3	50.8	60.0	74.0	75.0	76.3	76.6	55.8	9.9
2003	59.2	47.9	59.9	72.7	73.7	75.5	77.3	57.4	10.8
2004	58.9	46.7	59.7	71.9	73.6	75.2	77.1	57.0	11.2
2005	58.9	47.6	59.7	71.0	73.7	75.4	76.7	57.5	11.4
2006	59.0	46.6	59.9	70.9	74.3	75.5	76.7	58.7	11.6
2007	59.0	44.6	60.1	71.6	74.5	75.0	76.6	58.9	12.7
2008	59.2	43.3	60.3	71.6	74.9	75.8	76.6	59.7	13.3
2009	59.1	40.9	60.4	71.6	75.1	75.7	76.7	60.8	13.6
2010	58.5	38.0	59.9	69.7	74.9	75.0	76.3	61.1	13.9
2011	58.0	37.5	59.4	69.1	74.2	74.4	76.1	60.6	14.1
2012	57.4	37.1	58.7	69.0	74.3	74.5	75.2	60.5	14.4
2013	56.9	37.2	58.2	69.2	73.9	73.9	74.7	59.9	14.9
2014	56.7	36.8	57.9	69.5	74.5	74.0	74.3	57.2	14.5
2015	56.2	36.1	57.5	69.8	73.8	73.9	73.9	59.3	15.2
2016	56.3	36.7	57.6	69.3	74.8	74.2	74.5	59.3	15.6
2017	56.4	37.1	57.6	69.7	75.9	74.5	74.6	59.8	15.6
2018	56.4	38.1	57.6	70.5	76.2	74.7	75.0	60.0	15.7

Table 1-8. Civilian Labor Force Participation Rates, by Age, Sex, Race, and Hispanic Origin, 1948–2018 —*Continued*

(Percent.)

Race, Hispanic origin, sex, and year	16 years and over	16 to 19 years	20 years and over						
			Total	20 to 24 years	25 to 34 years	35 to 44 years	45 to 54 years	55 to 64 years	65 years and over
BLACK									
Both Sexes									
1985	62.9	41.2	65.6	70.0	79.8	81.5	73.4	51.4	11.2
1986	63.3	41.3	65.9	71.7	80.1	81.9	74.3	50.6	9.7
1987	63.8	41.6	66.5	70.5	80.7	82.6	74.7	52.4	10.7
1988	63.8	40.8	66.5	70.5	80.8	82.6	75.0	50.6	11.5
1989	64.2	42.5	66.7	72.2	80.9	82.7	75.5	48.3	11.6
1990	64.0	38.7	66.9	68.8	79.7	82.4	76.5	49.6	11.1
1991	63.3	35.4	66.4	67.7	78.5	82.0	76.2	50.4	10.7
1992	63.9	37.9	66.8	67.4	79.7	81.4	76.2	51.6	10.6
1993	63.2	37.0	66.0	67.8	78.3	81.0	75.2	50.2	9.5
1994	63.4	38.5	66.0	68.8	78.3	80.8	74.8	49.3	10.6
1995	63.7	39.9	66.3	68.7	80.0	80.4	74.1	50.3	10.5
1996	64.1	39.2	66.9	69.0	81.1	81.0	74.9	50.9	9.8
1997	64.7	38.7	67.6	70.9	82.0	81.4	76.3	50.5	10.0
1998	65.6	41.6	68.2	70.6	83.0	82.2	76.7	52.3	10.3
1999	65.8	38.7	68.9	71.4	85.2	83.0	76.4	51.4	10.4
2000	65.8	39.4	68.7	71.8	84.1	82.3	76.9	52.5	11.6
2001	65.3	37.6	68.2	69.9	83.6	82.0	75.9	53.9	12.6
2002	64.8	36.0	67.8	68.6	82.4	81.6	76.1	54.7	12.5
2003	64.3	32.4	67.6	68.2	81.6	82.9	75.8	54.4	12.9
2004	63.8	31.4	67.2	68.3	81.2	82.1	75.5	54.4	13.1
2005	64.2	32.4	67.4	69.0	81.7	82.3	75.7	55.3	13.6
2006	64.1	34.0	67.3	68.8	81.8	82.0	75.8	55.4	13.7
2007	63.7	30.3	67.2	68.3	81.7	82.7	75.7	55.1	14.0
2008	63.7	29.4	67.4	68.0	82.2	83.0	76.1	55.6	15.0
2009	62.4	27.2	66.1	66.0	80.4	81.7	75.2	55.5	15.3
2010	62.2	25.5	66.0	66.9	80.5	81.4	75.0	55.7	15.2
2011	61.4	24.9	65.0	66.5	79.1	80.6	73.9	54.5	16.1
2012	61.5	26.9	64.9	66.5	79.4	80.7	74.5	55.3	16.4
2013	61.2	28.0	64.2	65.3	78.5	80.7	74.1	55.6	16.2
2014	61.2	27.2	64.2	66.6	79.1	80.5	74.6	55.3	16.1
2015	61.5	28.1	64.4	68.2	79.4	80.8	75.3	54.8	16.9
2016	61.6	29.0	64.4	67.7	80.3	81.2	75.1	55.1	16.6
2017	62.3	30.0	65.0	69.2	80.8	82.3	76.2	55.6	17.8
2018	62.3	30.5	64.9	68.5	80.9	82.1	77.0	56.5	17.7
Men									
1985	70.8	44.6	74.4	79.0	88.8	89.8	83.0	58.9	13.9
1986	71.2	43.7	74.8	80.1	89.6	89.6	84.1	59.1	12.6
1987	71.1	43.6	74.7	77.8	89.4	88.6	83.7	62.1	13.7
1988	71.0	43.8	74.6	79.3	89.3	88.2	83.5	59.4	14.3
1989	71.0	44.6	74.4	80.2	89.7	88.7	82.5	55.5	14.3
1990	71.0	40.7	75.0	76.8	88.8	88.1	83.5	58.0	13.0
1991	70.4	37.3	74.6	76.7	87.3	87.7	83.4	58.7	13.0
1992	70.7	40.6	74.3	75.4	88.0	86.5	81.8	60.0	13.7
1993	69.6	39.5	73.2	74.1	87.3	86.1	80.0	57.9	11.6
1994	69.1	40.8	72.5	73.9	86.2	85.9	79.1	54.5	12.7
1995	69.0	40.1	72.5	74.6	87.5	84.1	78.5	54.4	14.9
1996	68.7	39.5	72.3	73.4	87.5	84.4	78.5	55.6	12.9
1997	68.3	37.4	72.2	72.1	86.8	84.8	80.1	54.3	12.9
1998	69.0	40.7	72.5	71.8	87.1	85.0	79.9	57.3	14.0
1999	68.7	38.6	72.4	69.8	89.2	86.0	78.5	55.5	12.7
2000	69.2	39.2	72.8	73.3	87.8	85.2	79.2	57.4	14.4
2001	68.4	37.9	72.1	69.7	86.6	84.9	78.4	58.9	16.7
2002	68.4	37.3	72.1	70.7	85.9	84.7	79.5	58.4	16.9
2003	67.3	31.1	71.5	71.1	84.7	85.7	77.7	57.6	17.0
2004	66.7	30.0	70.9	69.9	86.1	84.0	76.9	57.1	17.0
2005	67.3	32.6	71.3	70.1	85.5	85.5	78.6	57.3	17.1
2006	67.0	32.3	71.1	71.6	85.7	84.4	79.2	55.9	16.7
2007	66.8	29.4	71.2	71.1	86.1	86.3	78.6	54.4	17.3
2008	66.7	29.1	71.1	71.1	85.3	86.8	79.1	56.1	18.1
2009	65.0	26.4	69.6	67.6	83.2	85.1	77.4	56.8	18.3
2010	65.0	25.8	69.5	66.9	83.4	86.1	77.4	56.8	18.1
2011	64.2	25.7	68.4	67.0	82.6	83.7	76.1	55.9	19.1
2012	63.6	25.6	67.7	66.4	82.5	83.5	75.9	57.1	19.4
2013	63.5	27.2	67.2	66.2	82.0	84.1	75.5	56.8	18.5
2014	63.6	25.9	67.3	67.9	82.5	83.3	76.4	57.0	18.4
2015	63.8	26.3	67.3	68.9	82.1	83.1	77.4	56.5	18.9
2016	64.1	28.1	67.5	67.3	82.7	84.2	77.1	58.0	19.6
2017	64.6	27.6	68.1	69.4	83.0	85.0	77.6	58.4	20.4
2018	64.8	29.6	68.0	68.1	83.6	85.0	79.2	58.9	19.2

Table 1-8. Civilian Labor Force Participation Rates, by Age, Sex, Race, and Hispanic Origin, 1948–2018 —*Continued*

(Percent.)

Race, Hispanic origin, sex, and year	16 years and over	16 to 19 years	20 years and over						
			Total	20 to 24 years	25 to 34 years	35 to 44 years	45 to 54 years	55 to 64 years	65 years and over
BLACK									
Women									
1985	56.5	37.9	58.6	62.5	72.4	74.8	65.7	45.3	9.4
1986	56.9	39.1	58.9	64.6	72.4	75.8	66.5	43.6	7.8
1987	58.0	39.6	60.0	64.4	73.5	77.8	67.5	44.4	8.6
1988	58.0	37.9	60.1	63.2	73.7	78.1	68.3	43.4	9.6
1989	58.7	40.4	60.6	65.5	73.6	78.0	70.0	42.4	9.8
1990	58.3	36.8	60.6	62.4	72.3	77.7	70.7	43.2	9.9
1991	57.5	33.5	60.0	60.3	71.4	77.2	70.2	44.1	9.2
1992	58.5	35.2	60.8	60.8	73.1	77.1	71.7	45.1	8.6
1993	57.9	34.6	60.2	62.6	70.9	76.8	71.2	44.4	8.3
1994	58.7	36.3	60.9	64.5	71.9	76.4	71.3	45.3	9.2
1995	59.5	39.8	61.4	63.7	73.9	77.3	70.5	47.2	7.7
1996	60.4	38.9	62.6	65.2	75.9	78.2	72.0	47.2	7.7
1997	61.7	39.9	64.0	69.9	78.1	78.4	73.2	47.6	8.2
1998	62.8	42.5	64.8	69.6	79.6	79.9	74.0	48.5	7.9
1999	63.5	38.8	66.1	72.7	82.1	80.4	74.6	48.4	8.9
2000	63.1	39.6	65.4	70.5	81.1	79.9	74.9	48.6	9.9
2001	62.8	37.3	65.2	70.1	81.2	79.6	73.9	49.9	10.1
2002	61.8	34.7	64.4	66.9	79.7	79.2	73.3	51.8	9.8
2003	61.9	33.7	64.6	65.7	79.1	80.6	74.2	51.9	10.3
2004	61.5	32.8	64.2	66.8	77.2	80.6	74.3	52.3	10.7
2005	61.6	32.2	64.4	68.1	78.5	79.7	73.3	53.7	11.4
2006	61.7	35.6	64.2	66.2	78.6	80.1	73.0	55.1	11.8
2007	61.1	31.2	64.0	65.7	78.0	79.8	73.2	55.7	12.0
2008	61.3	29.7	64.3	65.2	79.6	80.0	73.7	55.3	13.0
2009	60.3	27.9	63.4	64.5	78.0	79.0	73.3	54.4	13.3
2010	59.9	25.1	63.2	66.9	77.9	77.7	73.0	54.9	13.3
2011	59.1	24.2	62.2	65.9	76.0	78.2	72.0	53.4	14.2
2012	59.8	28.2	62.6	66.5	76.9	78.4	73.3	53.9	14.4
2013	59.2	28.7	61.8	64.4	75.5	78.0	72.9	54.6	14.7
2014	59.2	28.4	61.6	65.4	76.2	78.2	73.2	53.8	14.6
2015	59.7	29.9	62.0	67.6	77.0	78.9	73.5	53.4	15.6
2016	59.4	30.0	61.8	68.0	78.1	78.7	73.4	52.7	14.6
2017	60.3	32.4	62.5	69.0	78.8	80.0	75.1	53.2	16.1
2018	60.2	31.4	62.4	68.9	78.5	79.7	75.1	54.5	16.6
HISPANIC									
Both Sexes									
1985	64.6	44.6	69.0	. . .	. . .	. . .	. . .	. . .	. . .
1986	65.4	43.9	67.1	. . .	. . .	. . .	. . .	. . .	. . .
1987	66.4	45.8	69.0	. . .	. . .	. . .	. . .	. . .	. . .
1988	67.4	49.6	73.6	. . .	. . .	. . .	. . .	. . .	. . .
1989	67.6	48.6	71.9	. . .	. . .	. . .	. . .	. . .	. . .
1990	67.4	47.8	70.9	. . .	. . .	. . .	. . .	. . .	. . .
1991	66.5	45.1	67.8	. . .	. . .	. . .	. . .	. . .	. . .
1992	66.8	45.8	68.6	. . .	. . .	. . .	. . .	. . .	. . .
1993	66.2	43.9	66.3	. . .	. . .	. . .	. . .	. . .	. . .
1994	66.1	44.4	67.2	74.0	77.3	78.9	73.1	49.8	10.7
1995	65.8	45.4	69.0	71.9	78.1	78.5	72.8	48.6	10.5
1996	66.5	43.4	65.3	73.1	78.2	79.5	74.6	52.2	11.0
1997	67.9	43.0	63.3	76.4	79.5	80.9	75.4	53.8	11.9
1998	67.9	45.7	67.3	76.1	80.3	80.0	75.3	55.4	10.1
1999	67.7	45.5	67.2	76.0	78.6	81.3	75.9	54.1	11.6
2000	69.7	46.3	66.4	78.2	80.4	81.7	78.0	54.2	12.3
2001	69.5	46.9	67.5	76.6	80.0	81.9	77.4	55.1	10.9
2002	69.1	44.0	63.7	76.3	80.5	81.1	76.1	55.8	11.9
2003	68.3	37.7	55.2	75.6	79.4	81.1	75.3	57.4	12.8
2004	68.6	38.2	55.7	74.5	79.4	81.4	77.6	58.1	14.5
2005	68.0	38.6	56.8	72.7	79.1	81.2	77.2	58.4	13.9
2006	68.7	38.3	55.7	74.4	80.1	81.9	77.3	59.2	15.7
2007	68.8	37.1	53.9	74.8	80.7	81.8	78.6	58.5	16.0
2008	68.5	36.9	53.9	73.7	80.5	82.0	78.2	59.9	16.0
2009	68.0	34.0	50.0	73.1	79.5	81.3	79.3	61.9	17.1
2010	67.5	30.9	45.8	71.1	80.6	81.2	79.2	61.1	17.9
2011	66.5	28.3	42.6	72.0	79.1	80.3	78.9	60.8	17.6
2012	66.4	30.9	46.5	71.2	79.1	80.2	78.4	60.5	16.5
2013	66.0	31.0	47.0	71.7	78.3	79.5	78.1	61.0	17.0
2014	66.1	30.3	69.8	71.4	78.8	79.9	78.3	61.7	17.0
2015	65.9	30.9	69.6	71.6	78.3	79.5	78.3	62.7	17.2
2016	65.8	31.2	69.4	71.8	78.9	79.6	78.0	61.7	18.1
2017	66.1	31.9	69.6	71.0	79.3	80.5	77.9	63.0	18.8
2018	66.3	32.5	69.7	71.6	80.0	80.4	78.4	63.6	18.6

. . . = Not available.

Table 1-8. Civilian Labor Force Participation Rates, by Age, Sex, Race, and Hispanic Origin, 1948–2018 *—Continued*

(Percent.)

Race, Hispanic origin, sex, and year	16 years and over	16 to 19 years	20 years and over						
			Total	20 to 24 years	25 to 34 years	35 to 44 years	45 to 54 years	55 to 64 years	65 years and over
HISPANIC									
Men									
1985	80.3	. . .	84.0	. . .	. . .	. . .	. . .	. . .	. . .
1986	81.0	. . .	84.6	. . .	. . .	. . .	. . .	. . .	. . .
1987	81.0	. . .	84.5	. . .	. . .	. . .	. . .	. . .	. . .
1988	81.9	. . .	85.0	. . .	. . .	. . .	. . .	. . .	. . .
1989	82.0	. . .	85.0	. . .	. . .	. . .	. . .	. . .	. . .
1990	81.4	. . .	84.7	. . .	. . .	. . .	. . .	. . .	. . .
1991	80.3	. . .	83.8	. . .	. . .	. . .	. . .	. . .	. . .
1992	80.7	. . .	84.0	. . .	. . .	. . .	. . .	. . .	. . .
1993	80.2	. . .	83.5	. . .	. . .	. . .	. . .	. . .	. . .
1994	79.2	50.0	82.5	88.0	92.5	91.5	85.7	63.6	14.4
1995	79.1	50.2	82.4	86.2	92.9	91.3	85.6	62.4	15.8
1996	79.6	50.0	83.0	85.7	93.2	91.7	87.0	65.9	16.7
1997	80.1	47.4	84.1	88.1	93.5	91.9	87.8	68.4	17.3
1998	79.8	48.7	83.6	88.1	94.0	91.4	86.7	70.2	14.9
1999	79.8	50.1	83.5	88.1	93.9	92.2	86.2	68.6	18.2
2000	81.5	50.7	85.3	89.1	94.1	93.3	87.6	69.4	18.5
2001	81.0	52.2	84.3	86.8	93.4	92.7	86.7	68.6	16.8
2002	80.2	48.8	83.6	86.1	93.5	92.1	86.1	67.3	16.3
2003	80.1	40.9	84.1	86.2	3.6	92.9	85.4	68.8	17.4
2004	80.4	42.4	84.2	84.4	3.6	93.2	87.2	69.6	20.8
2005	80.1	41.9	84.0	84.1	3.3	93.1	87.7	69.3	20.1
2006	80.7	42.0	84.6	85.9	4.1	93.8	87.1	69.6	22.9
2007	80.5	40.0	84.7	85.3	4.1	93.9	88.3	70.3	22.0
2008	80.2	40.3	84.4	84.3	4.0	93.7	88.6	71.7	21.7
2009	78.8	36.4	83.2	82.3	1.9	93.0	88.8	71.7	23.0
2010	77.8	33.2	82.6	80.0	2.7	92.9	87.8	69.0	24.5
2011	76.5	30.1	81.7	79.5	1.6	92.4	87.3	69.9	23.3
2012	76.1	33.0	81.0	78.5	1.6	91.1	87.3	70.3	21.1
2013	76.3	32.8	81.1	78.6	1.0	91.9	87.8	70.7	23.1
2014	76.1	31.2	81.0	77.9	90.5	92.9	87.8	72.9	21.9
2015	76.2	32.4	80.9	77.3	90.9	92.6	88.3	73.9	22.2
2016	76.0	32.3	80.5	77.1	90.5	92.5	88.6	72.4	23.8
2017	75.8	31.6	80.5	77.0	90.1	92.7	88.6	73.5	24.9
2018	75.7	32.5	80.2	76.6	89.6	92.8	88.2	74.8	24.6
HISPANIC									
Women									
1985	49.3	50.6	50.6	. . .	. . .	. . .	. . .	. . .	. . .
1986	50.1	51.7	51.7	. . .	. . .	. . .	. . .	. . .	. . .
1987	52.0	53.3	53.3	. . .	. . .	. . .	. . .	. . .	. . .
1988	53.2	54.2	54.2	. . .	. . .	. . .	. . .	. . .	. . .
1989	53.5	54.9	54.9	. . .	. . .	. . .	. . .	. . .	. . .
1990	53.1	54.8	54.8	. . .	. . .	. . .	. . .	. . .	. . .
1991	52.4	54.0	54.0	. . .	. . .	. . .	. . .	. . .	. . .
1992	52.8	54.3	54.3	. . .	. . .	. . .	. . .	. . .	. . .
1993	52.1	53.8	53.8	. . .	. . .	. . .	. . .	. . .	. . .
1994	52.9	54.4	54.4	57.9	60.5	66.4	61.4	38.1	7.9
1995	52.6	53.9	53.9	55.9	61.6	65.9	60.5	37.2	6.6
1996	53.4	55.2	55.2	59.2	62.0	67.0	62.7	40.5	6.9
1997	55.1	57.0	57.0	62.3	63.7	69.3	63.3	40.6	8.1
1998	55.6	57.1	57.1	62.2	64.5	67.9	64.7	41.9	6.6
1999	55.9	57.7	57.7	63.0	62.7	70.5	66.2	42.4	6.5
2000	57.5	59.3	59.3	65.0	65.3	69.9	68.5	41.2	7.7
2001	57.6	59.3	59.3	64.6	65.2	70.3	68.3	43.2	6.7
2002	57.6	59.5	59.5	65.0	65.8	69.5	66.3	46.1	8.5
2003	55.9	58.1	58.1	63.3	62.9	68.5	65.3	47.1	9.4
2004	56.1	58.4	58.4	62.9	62.9	68.7	67.9	47.8	9.8
2005	55.3	57.4	57.4	59.4	62.4	68.2	66.6	48.4	9.3
2006	56.1	58.3	58.3	61.3	63.5	68.7	67.4	49.7	10.4
2007	56.5	58.8	58.8	62.9	64.6	68.4	68.7	47.6	11.4
2008	56.2	58.6	58.6	62.1	64.3	69.1	67.6	48.9	11.7
2009	56.5	59.2	59.2	63.2	64.7	68.2	69.4	52.6	12.7
2010	56.5	59.5	59.5	61.6	66.3	67.9	70.2	53.7	13.0
2011	55.9	59.0	59.0	63.0	64.5	67.1	70.4	52.3	13.2
2012	56.6	59.5	59.5	63.3	65.6	69.0	69.4	51.4	13.2
2013	55.7	58.5	58.5	64.3	64.5	66.9	68.4	52.0	12.5
2014	56.0	29.3	58.7	64.5	66.1	66.4	68.8	51.3	13.3
2015	55.7	29.3	58.4	65.8	64.9	66.2	68.3	52.2	13.4
2016	55.8	30.0	58.4	66.4	66.5	66.3	67.3	51.6	13.8
2017	56.4	32.1	58.9	64.7	67.9	67.9	67.1	53.2	14.2
2018	57.0	32.5	59.4	66.5	69.8	67.6	68.6	53.1	13.9

. . . = Not available.

Table 1-9. Employed and Unemployed Full- and Part-Time Workers, by Age, Sex, and Race, 2005–2018

(Thousands of people.)

Race, sex, age, and year	Employed[1]								Unemployed	
	Full-time workers				Part-time workers					
	Total	At work		Not at work	Total	At work[2]		Not at work	Looking for full-time work	Looking for part-time work
		35 hours or more	1 to 34 hours for economic or noneco-nomic reasons			For economic reasons	For noneco-nomic reasons			
ALL RACES										
Both Sexes, 16 Years and Over										
2005	117 016	103 044	9 983	3 990	24 714	2 963	20 229	1 522	6 175	1 415
2006	119 688	105 328	10 223	4 137	24 739	2 774	20 356	1 609	5 675	1 326
2007	121 091	106 990	9 976	4 125	24 956	2 851	20 511	1 594	5 789	1 289
2008	120 030	105 575	10 426	4 030	25 332	3 814	20 009	1 509	7 446	1 478
2009	112 634	95 911	12 853	3 870	27 244	6 353	19 327	1 563	12 523	1 741
2010	111 714	97 946	10 217	3 551	27 350	6 965	18 876	1 509	12 970	1 854
2011	112 556	98 976	10 047	3 534	27 313	6 872	18 984	1 525	11 914	1 833
2012	114 809	101 877	9 324	3 607	27 661	6 626	19 509	1 525	10 699	1 807
2013	116 314	104 069	8 756	3 489	27 615	6 479	19 621	1 514	9 726	1 733
2014	118 718	105 416	9 772	3 531	27 587	5 904	20 185	1 498	8 055	1 561
2015	121 492	106 611	11 263	3 618	27 341	5 143	20 750	1 448	6 888	1 409
2016	123 761	110 540	9 507	3 713	27 675	4 684	21 421	1 571	6 345	1 406
2017	125 967	111 686	10 295	3 987	27 370	4 104	21 646	1 620	5 649	1 334
2018	128 572	115 402	9 357	3 814	27 189	3 564	22 072	1 553	5 052	1 262
Both Sexes, 20 Years and Over										
2005	115 206	101 534	9 729	3 942	20 546	2 698	16 489	1 359	5 619	786
2006	117 844	103 779	9 974	4 090	20 421	2 510	16 478	1 433	5 117	765
2007	119 317	105 499	9 738	4 080	20 819	2 587	16 819	1 413	5 234	742
2008	118 404	104 212	10 204	3 989	21 385	3 492	16 543	1 350	6 790	849
2009	111 414	94 928	12 647	3 839	23 626	5 934	16 286	1 406	11 651	1 061
2010	110 622	97 037	10 057	3 528	24 064	6 552	16 138	1 373	12 155	1 142
2011	111 500	98 103	9 888	3 508	24 043	6 457	16 259	1 327	11 180	1 167
2012	113 667	100 919	9 167	3 582	24 376	6 240	16 750	1 385	9 968	1 141
2013	115 106	103 041	8 601	3 464	24 365	6 103	16 877	1 386	9 043	1 090
2014	117 514	104 403	9 604	3 506	24 244	5 551	17 334	1 358	7 503	1 008
2015	120 199	105 523	11 088	3 588	23 901	4 822	17 771	1 308	6 378	953
2016	122 363	109 351	9 332	3 681	24 108	4 399	18 279	1 430	5 881	945
2017	124 525	110 459	10 112	3 953	23 739	3 842	18 439	1 459	5 261	894
2018	127 095	114 129	9 184	3 781	23 540	3 320	18 822	1 398	4 697	858
Men, 16 Years and Over										
2005	67 858	60 825	5 096	1 937	8 115	1 316	6 370	429	3 444	616
2006	69 307	62 087	5 237	1 984	8 194	1 232	6 510	452	3 192	561
2007	70 035	62 965	5 095	1 975	8 220	1 319	6 424	477	3 326	556
2008	68 853	61 436	5 443	1 974	8 634	1 842	6 349	442	4 396	637
2009	63 951	55 317	6 772	1 862	9 719	3 035	6 170	514	7 696	757
2010	63 501	56 425	5 352	1 723	9 858	3 316	6 066	476	7 827	799
2011	64 333	57 413	5 189	1 731	9 957	3 262	6 216	479	6 903	781
2012	65 477	58 956	4 803	1 719	10 078	3 089	6 491	498	5 988	784
2013	66 335	60 112	4 531	1 692	10 017	2 985	6 526	507	5 563	752
2014	67 829	61 128	5 004	1 697	9 863	2 712	6 663	487	4 516	674
2015	69 351	61 892	5 737	1 722	9 780	2 368	6 927	485	3 888	602
2016	70 567	63 943	4 841	1 782	10 002	2 194	7 305	502	3 607	580
2017	71 571	64 472	5 189	1 910	9 831	1 914	7 392	525	3 174	569
2018	72 935	66 314	4 774	1 847	9 764	1 650	7 587	527	2 877	521
Men, 20 Years and Over										
2005	66 803	59 934	4 955	1 914	6 247	1 182	4 705	360	3 118	274
2006	68 193	61 140	5 095	1 958	6 238	1 100	4 762	376	2 861	270
2007	68 968	62 057	4 959	1 952	6 369	1 190	4 782	397	2 990	268
2008	67 895	60 625	5 315	1 955	6 855	1 675	4 802	378	3 994	303
2009	63 242	54 738	6 659	1 845	8 099	2 827	4 828	445	7 151	404
2010	62 854	55 887	5 258	1 710	8 376	3 102	4 857	417	7 336	427
2011	63 690	56 870	5 104	1 715	8 492	3 059	5 010	423	6 461	437
2012	64 810	58 386	4 719	1 705	8 593	2 883	5 271	439	5 547	437
2013	65 631	59 504	4 448	1 679	8 545	2 797	5 301	447	5 144	424
2014	67 093	60 498	4 911	1 684	8 378	2 532	5 422	424	4 192	393
2015	68 588	61 240	5 642	1 706	8 189	2 200	5 570	419	3 594	365
2016	69 747	63 242	4 740	1 765	8 337	2 039	5 857	441	3 329	346
2017	70 729	63 750	5 087	1 892	8 190	1 779	5 962	449	2 941	346
2018	72 061	65 556	4 678	1 828	8 150	1 525	6 162	463	2 658	318

[1]Employed persons are classified as full- or part-time workers based on their usual weekly hours at all jobs, regardless of the number of hours they were at work during the reference week. Persons absent from work are also classified according to their usual status.
[2]Includes some persons at work 35 hours or more classified by their reason for working part time.

Table 1-9. Employed and Unemployed Full- and Part-Time Workers, by Age, Sex, and Race, 2005–2018 —*Continued*

(Thousands of people.)

Race, sex, age, and year	Employed[1]								Unemployed	
	Full-time workers				Part-time workers					
	Total	At work		Not at work	Total	At work[2]		Not at work	Looking for full-time work	Looking for part-time work
		35 hours or more	1 to 34 hours for economic or noneconomic reasons			For economic reasons	For noneconomic reasons			
ALL RACES—*Continued*										
Women, 16 Years and Over										
2005	49 158	42 219	4 887	2 052	16 598	1 647	13 859	1 092	2 732	799
2006	50 380	43 241	4 986	2 153	16 545	1 542	13 846	1 157	2 483	764
2007	51 056	44 025	4 881	2 150	16 736	1 532	14 087	1 117	2 463	732
2008	51 178	44 139	4 983	2 056	16 698	1 972	13 660	1 067	3 050	841
2009	48 683	40 594	6 080	2 009	17 525	3 318	13 157	1 050	4 827	984
2010	48 214	41 521	4 865	1 828	17 491	3 648	12 810	1 033	5 144	1 055
2011	48 224	41 563	4 858	1 802	17 355	3 610	12 767	977	5 011	1 052
2012	49 331	42 921	4 521	1 888	17 583	3 538	13 018	1 026	4 711	1 023
2013	49 979	43 957	4 225	1 797	17 598	3 495	13 095	1 008	4 164	982
2014	50 889	44 287	4 768	1 834	17 724	3 192	13 521	1 011	3 539	887
2015	52 142	44 719	5 527	1 896	17 561	2 775	13 823	963	3 000	807
2016	53 194	46 597	4 666	1 931	17 674	2 490	14 115	1 069	2 739	826
2017	54 396	47 214	5 105	2 077	17 539	2 190	14 254	1 095	2 474	765
2018	55 638	49 088	4 583	1 966	17 425	1 914	14 485	1 026	2 175	741
Women, 20 Years and Over										
2005	48 403	41 600	4 774	2 028	14 299	1 516	11 784	999	2 501	512
2006	49 651	42 639	4 880	2 132	14 183	1 410	11 716	1 057	2 256	495
2007	50 349	43 442	4 779	2 128	14 450	1 397	12 037	1 016	2 244	474
2008	50 509	43 587	4 888	2 034	14 530	1 817	11 740	973	2 796	546
2009	48 171	40 190	5 988	1 994	15 527	3 107	11 459	961	4 500	657
2010	47 767	41 150	4 799	1 818	15 688	3 450	11 282	956	4 819	715
2011	47 810	41 233	4 784	1 792	15 551	3 398	11 249	904	4 719	730
2012	48 857	42 533	4 448	1 877	15 783	3 358	11 480	946	4 420	704
2013	49 475	43 537	4 153	1 785	15 820	3 306	11 575	939	3 900	665
2014	50 421	43 905	4 693	1 823	15 865	3 019	11 912	934	3 311	615
2015	51 611	44 284	5 446	1 881	15 712	2 622	12 201	889	2 784	588
2016	52 616	46 109	4 591	555	15 770	2 360	12 422	989	2 553	599
2017	53 796	46 709	5 025	2 061	15 549	2 062	12 477	1 010	2 320	548
2018	55 033	48 574	4 506	1 953	15 390	1 795	12 660	935	2 039	540
WHITE[3]										
Men, 16 Years and Over										
2005	56 955	50 965	4 334	1 656	6 808	1 014	5 424	370	2 459	471
2006	58 063	51 894	4 484	1 685	6 820	947	5 481	393	2 299	432
2007	58 494	52 460	4 359	1 676	6 795	1 022	5 368	406	2 444	425
2008	57 432	51 104	4 653	1 675	7 192	1 433	5 379	379	3 235	492
2009	53 506	46 153	5 770	1 583	8 124	2 438	5 240	446	5 819	602
2010	53 086	47 055	4 554	1 477	8 166	2 662	5 102	402	5 832	644
2011	53 727	47 865	4 397	1 465	8 193	2 560	5 227	405	5 020	611
2012	53 857	48 409	4 009	1 439	8 133	2 383	5 334	416	4 330	600
2013	54 263	49 091	3 775	1 397	8 059	2 281	5 357	421	3 941	579
2014	55 281	49 766	4 107	1 408	7 827	2 027	5 402	399	3 086	486
2015	56 176	50 088	4 673	1 415	7 716	1 752	5 567	397	2 678	448
2016	56 735	51 333	3 941	1 460	7 877	1 598	5 873	407	2 526	426
2017	57 296	51 552	4 202	1 543	7 704	1 386	5 890	427	2 176	416
2018	58 015	52 678	3 849	1 487	7 687	1 183	6 083	421	1 998	383
Men, 20 Years and Over										
2005	56 050	50 203	4 213	1 634	5 205	905	3 990	310	2 242	209
2006	57 108	51 081	4 365	1 662	5 150	840	3 987	324	2 074	208
2007	57 591	51 691	4 243	1 656	5 216	915	3 967	334	2 204	204
2008	56 623	50 421	4 542	1 660	5 681	1 302	4 055	324	2 944	235
2009	52 899	45 654	5 676	1 569	6 728	2 269	4 075	384	5 421	325
2010	52 530	46 592	4 472	1 466	6 907	2 484	4 071	352	5 481	347
2011	53 186	47 406	4 328	1 451	6 933	2 392	4 184	357	4 702	344
2012	53 302	47 934	3 941	1 427	6 891	2 218	4 306	367	4 014	333
2013	53 660	48 569	3 706	1 386	6 850	2 132	4 349	370	3 657	337
2014	54 671	49 249	4 026	1 395	6 619	1 889	4 382	348	2 855	286
2015	55 533	49 536	4 593	1 403	6 426	1 622	4 460	345	2 480	271
2016	56 071	50 764	3 861	1 447	6 504	1 480	4 668	356	2 344	250
2017	56 620	50 967	4 123	1 530	6 388	1 293	4 730	365	2 028	259
2018	57 312	52 068	3 775	1 470	6 406	1 093	4 944	369	1 858	235

[1]Employed persons are classified as full- or part-time workers based on their usual weekly hours at all jobs, regardless of the number of hours they were at work during the reference week. Persons absent from work are also classified according to their usual status.
[2]Includes some persons at work 35 hours or more classified by their reason for working part time.
[3]Beginning in 2003, persons who selected this race group only; persons who selected more than one race group are not included. Prior to 2003, persons who reported more than one race group were included in the group they identified as their main race.

Table 1-9. Employed and Unemployed Full- and Part-Time Workers, by Age, Sex, and Race, 2005–2018 —*Continued*

(Thousands of people.)

Race, sex, age, and year	Employed[1]								Unemployed	
	Full-time workers				Part-time workers					
		At work				At work[2]				
	Total	35 hours or more	1 to 34 hours for economic or noneconomic reasons	Not at work	Total	For economic reasons	For noneconomic reasons	Not at work	Looking for full-time work	Looking for part-time work
WHITE[3]—*Continued*										
Women, 16 Years and Over										
2005	38 973	33 325	3 976	1 672	14 213	1 207	12 043	963	1 807	612
2006	39 813	33 980	4 082	1 751	14 137	1 157	11 967	1 013	1 670	601
2007	40 238	34 486	4 014	1 738	14 265	1 143	12 148	973	1 694	579
2008	40 292	34 569	4 076	1 647	14 209	1 518	11 761	931	2 119	664
2009	38 456	31 885	4 946	1 626	14 910	2 579	11 418	913	3 442	785
2010	38 158	32 710	3 958	1 490	14 758	2 846	11 029	883	3 612	828
2011	38 152	32 731	3 944	1 477	14 618	2 775	10 994	850	3 450	807
2012	38 362	33 244	3 614	1 504	14 416	2 674	10 875	867	3 191	794
2013	38 629	33 870	3 329	1 430	14 428	2 605	10 986	837	2 756	757
2014	39 241	22 994	3 770	1 477	14 439	2 345	11 242	852	2 304	664
2015	39 823	34 038	4 311	1 474	14 228	2 035	11 395	798	1 945	592
2016	40 477	35 331	3 640	1 506	14 225	1 784	11 560	881	1 781	613
2017	41 145	35 554	3 961	1 630	14 031	1 554	11 571	905	1 593	580
2018	41 825	36 781	3 541	1 504	13 934	1 363	11 740	831	1 414	560
Women, 20 Years and Over										
2005	38 354	32 820	3 882	1 652	12 235	1 108	10 248	879	1 653	401
2006	39 232	33 500	3 998	1 733	12 128	1 050	10 151	927	1 524	402
2007	39 670	34 015	3 932	1 722	12 326	1 037	10 402	887	1 547	383
2008	39 765	34 128	4 005	1 632	12 359	1 392	10 116	851	1 949	435
2009	38 033	31 547	4 872	1 614	13 198	2 411	9 952	835	3 216	529
2010	37 789	32 404	3 904	1 481	13 208	2 684	9 705	818	3 389	571
2011	37 816	32 466	3 882	1 468	13 065	2 597	9 683	785	3 255	563
2012	38 362	32 936	3 556	1 497	12 923	2 533	9 591	799	3 009	555
2013	38 233	33 544	3 269	1 420	12 964	2 462	9 719	783	2 586	516
2014	39 241	33 994	3 770	1 477	14 439	2 345	11 242	852	2 304	664
2015	39 418	33 707	4 249	1 462	12 743	1 915	10 091	736	1 812	437
2016	40 037	34 955	3 587	1 495	12 733	1 689	10 226	819	1 652	448
2017	40 696	35 177	3 899	1 619	12 484	1 460	10 185	838	1 496	427
2018	41 369	36 395	3 480	1 494	12 313	1 271	10 286	756	1 329	415
BLACK[3]										
Men, 16 Years and Over										
2005	6 381	5 745	463	174	773	207	533	33	742	102
2006	6 529	5 907	446	176	825	201	590	34	681	93
2007	6 673	6 068	429	176	826	195	589	42	660	92
2008	6 548	5 935	440	173	850	276	542	32	849	100
2009	5 871	5 166	556	150	946	379	530	36	1 348	100
2010	5 856	5 279	446	130	1 009	419	550	41	1 448	102
2011	5 892	5 293	445	154	1 060	452	566	43	1 393	108
2012	6 185	5 579	453	153	1 117	442	629	46	1 169	123
2013	6 331	5 752	423	156	1 166	471	651	44	1 124	112
2014	6 678	6 032	488	158	1 140	442	651	47	973	118
2015	6 974	6 258	553	164	1 190	400	740	50	839	96
2016	7 279	6 616	490	173	1 192	375	764	53	751	94
2017	7 533	6 791	534	209	1 208	336	818	54	673	93
2018	7 899	7 239	463	197	1 119	299	759	61	591	85

[1]Employed persons are classified as full- or part-time workers based on their usual weekly hours at all jobs, regardless of the number of hours they were at work during the reference week. Persons absent from work are also classified according to their usual status.
[2]Includes some persons at work 35 hours or more classified by their reason for working part time.
[3]Beginning in 2003, persons who selected this race group only; persons who selected more than one race group are not included. Prior to 2003, persons who reported more than one race group were included in the group they identified as their main race.

Table 1-9. Employed and Unemployed Full- and Part-Time Workers, by Age, Sex, and Race, 2005–2018 *—Continued*

(Thousands of people.)

Race, sex, age, and year	Employed[1]								Unemployed	
	Full-time workers				Part-time workers					
	Total	At work		Not at work	Total	At work[2]		Not at work	Looking for full-time work	Looking for part-time work
		35 hours or more	1 to 34 hours for economic or noneconomic reasons			For economic reasons	For noneconomic reasons			
BLACK[3]—*Continued*										
Men, 20 Years and Over										
2005	6 287	5 662	452	174	614	189	397	28	655	44
2006	6 424	5 816	433	175	655	185	441	30	596	44
2007	6 574	5 983	417	174	671	181	452	37	580	43
2008	6 461	5 860	430	171	690	252	409	29	764	46
2009	5 811	5 119	544	148	817	355	428	34	1 238	49
2010	5 803	5 235	439	129	877	392	447	37	1 344	52
2011	5 830	5 242	435	153	935	428	470	38	1 299	61
2012	6 117	5 522	443	152	987	421	526	40	1 081	71
2013	6 279	5 707	416	156	1 025	450	534	41	1 026	56
2014	6 614	5 975	482	158	998	418	539	41	909	64
2015	6 974	6 258	553	164	1 190	400	740	50	839	96
2016	7 192	6 545	476	171	1 036	348	642	47	675	62
2017	7 452	6 724	522	206	1 049	312	688	49	609	53
2018	7 797	7 150	450	197	948	274	619	55	531	51
Women, 16 Years and Over										
2005	6 750	5 871	619	260	1 407	320	1 018	70	723	133
2006	7 001	6 131	605	265	1 410	274	1 054	82	655	120
2007	7 119	6 272	584	263	1 432	273	1 085	75	589	104
2008	7 105	6 238	596	272	1 449	302	1 070	77	717	122
2009	6 666	5 696	718	252	1 542	480	984	78	1 027	132
2010	6 525	5 727	582	215	1 621	528	1 010	82	1 142	160
2011	6 450	5 651	592	207	1 648	573	1 004	72	1 165	164
2012	6 750	5 956	557	236	1 803	559	1 157	88	1 099	153
2013	6 868	6 097	553	218	1 786	572	1 128	86	1 043	150
2014	7 063	6 213	626	224	1 852	538	1 229	85	899	151
2015	7 424	6 457	715	252	1 884	504	1 298	82	777	134
2016	7 591	6 722	622	247	1 920	474	1 342	104	674	136
2017	7 901	6 949	684	267	1 945	435	1 413	97	621	113
2018	8 154	7 261	617	275	1 920	365	1 454	101	534	112
Women, 20 Years and Over										
2005	6 653	5 789	606	258	1 222	298	861	63	660	74
2006	6 893	6 042	588	263	1 175	255	848	72	588	67
2007	7 024	6 194	570	260	1 216	254	897	65	527	61
2008	7 006	6 160	580	267	1 254	283	902	68	654	78
2009	6 600	5 644	705	250	1 356	449	837	71	951	82
2010	6 471	5 681	575	215	1 473	504	894	75	1 063	103
2011	6 402	5 610	586	207	1 504	549	888	67	1 095	108
2012	6 682	5 901	547	235	1 631	531	1 021	79	1 021	98
2013	6 802	6 039	546	216	1 606	541	986	79	969	100
2014	7 063	6 213	626	224	1 852	538	1 229	85	899	151
2015	7 345	6 389	705	250	1 687	482	1 130	74	714	97
2016	7 506	6 651	609	245	1 713	452	1 166	95	630	94
2017	7 803	6 863	675	265	1 711	411	1 210	90	580	77
2018	8 058	7 179	607	272	1 693	350	1 250	93	495	79

[1]Employed persons are classified as full- or part-time workers based on their usual weekly hours at all jobs, regardless of the number of hours they were at work during the reference week. Persons absent from work are also classified according to their usual status.
[2]Includes some persons at work 35 hours or more classified by their reason for working part time.
[3]Beginning in 2003, persons who selected this race group only; persons who selected more than one race group are not included. Prior to 2003, persons who reported more than one race group were included in the group they identified as their main race.

Table 1-10. Persons Not in the Labor Force, by Age, Sex, and Desire and Availability for Work, 2015–2018

(Thousands of people.)

Category	Total		Age						Sex			
			16 to 24 years		25 to 54 years		55 years and over		Men		Women	
	2015	2016	2015	2016	2015	2016	2015	2016	2015	2016	2015	2016
TOTAL, NOT IN THE LABOR FORCE	93 671	94 351	17 367	17 232	23 957	23 513	52 347	53 606	37 481	37 743	56 190	56 608
Do Not Want a Job Now[1]	87 589	88 502	15 525	15 452	21 344	21 032	50 719	52 018	34 681	35 009	52 907	53 492
Want a Job[1]	6 082	5 849	1 842	1 780	2 612	2 481	1 628	1 587	2 799	2 733	3 283	3 116
Did not search for work in the previous year	3 454	3 415	1 030	994	1 357	1 353	1 067	1 069	1 507	1 522	1 947	1 894
Searched for work in the previous year[2]	2 628	2 434	812	787	1 256	1 128	561	519	1 292	1 211	1 336	1 222
Not available to work now	673	630	287	257	307	287	79	86	277	251	395	379
Available to work now	1 956	1 804	525	530	949	841	482	433	1 015	960	941	843
Reason not currently looking:												
Discouragement over job prospects[3]	664	553	159	130	316	267	189	156	404	345	261	208
Reasons other than discouragement	1 291	1 250	366	400	632	573	293	277	611	615	680	635
Family responsibilities	216	199	23	26	138	127	55	46	64	61	153	138
In school or training	212	224	154	171	51	47	7	7	106	120	107	105
Ill health or disability	168	144	16	16	77	67	75	62	84	77	84	67
Other[4]	695	682	174	187	366	333	155	162	358	356	337	326

Category	Total		Age						Sex			
			16 to 24 years		25 to 54 years		55 years and over		Men		Women	
	2017	2018	2017	2018	2017	2018	2017	2018	2017	2018	2017	2018
TOTAL, NOT IN THE LABOR FORCE	94 759	95 716	16 989	17 020	23 014	22 685	54 756	56 010	38 130	38 582	56 629	57 134
Do Not Want a Job Now[1]	89 242	90 467	15 335	15 430	20 732	20 513	53 175	54 524	35 591	36 133	53 650	54 334
Want a Job[1]	5 518	5 249	1 655	1 590	2 282	2 172	1 581	1 487	2 539	2 448	2 979	2 800
Did not search for work in the previous year	3 320	3 161	953	925	1 281	1 195	1 086	1 040	1 450	1 399	1 870	1 762
Searched for work in the previous year[2]	2 198	2 088	702	665	1 001	977	495	447	1 089	1 049	1 109	1 039
Not available to work now	610	571	263	232	258	267	90	72	254	232	357	338
Available to work now	1 587	1 517	439	433	743	709	405	375	835	817	752	700
Reason not currently looking:												
Discouragement over job prospects[3]	476	423	115	93	223	211	138	120	299	266	177	158
Reasons other than discouragement	1 112	1 094	324	340	519	499	268	255	536	551	575	542
Family responsibilities	188	173	23	25	121	114	44	35	53	50	135	123
In school or training	187	184	141	144	41	36	6	4	103	99	84	85
Ill health or disability	139	152	13	16	54	64	71	72	68	85	71	67
Other[4]	598	584	147	156	304	285	147	143	312	317	286	267

[1] Includes some persons who were not asked if they wanted a job.
[2] Persons who had a job during the prior 12 months must have searched since the end of that job.
[3] Includes believes no work available, could not find work, lacks necessary schooling or training, employer thinks too young or old, and other types of discrimination.
[4] Includes those who did not actively look for work in the prior four weeks for reasons such as childcare and transportation problems, as well as a small number for whom reason for nonparticipation was not ascertained.

Figure 1-2. Number of Employed Civilians by Age and Sex, 2018

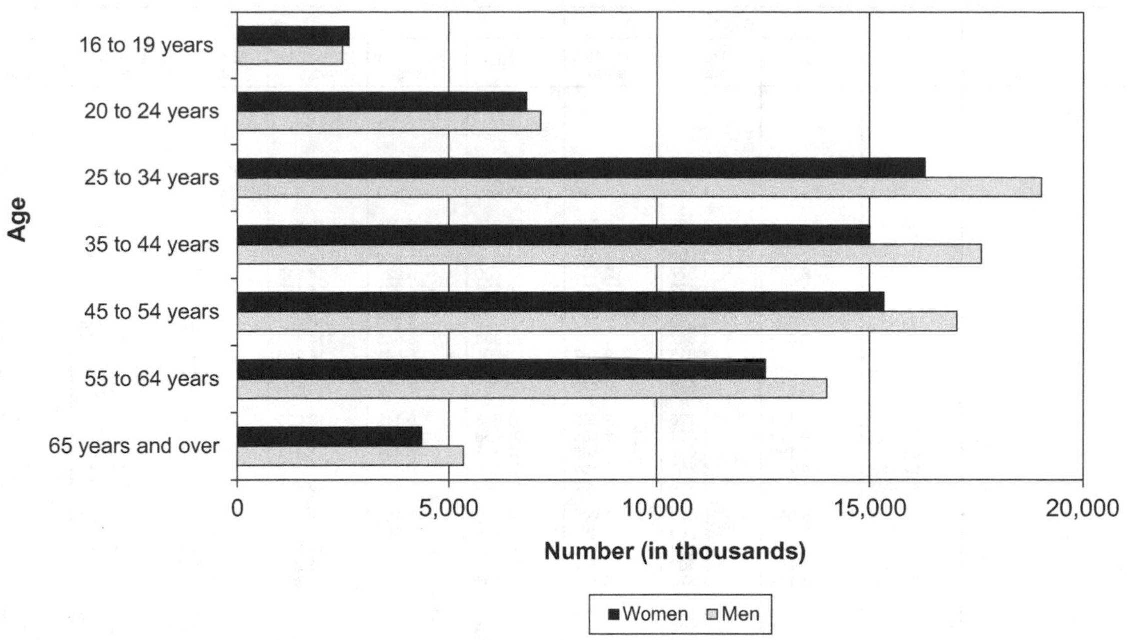

There were nearly 156 million employed civilians in the labor force in 2018—the highest amount ever. This represented an increase of 1.6 percent from 2017. From 2007 to 2011, the number of employed civilians declined 4.2 percent. (See Table 1-11.)

OTHER HIGHLIGHTS

- While men made up 53.1 percent of employed civilians in 2018, they only made up 12.9 percent of employees in healthcare support occupations; 26.8 percent of employees in education, training, and library occupations; and 28.4 percent of employees in office and administrative support occupations. (See Table 1-13.)

- In 2018, employment increased for all groups except for those some college but no degree. It increased 2.5 for those with an associate's degree, 1.0 percent for high school graduates and 3.8 percent for those that are college graduates or higher. (See Table 1-16.)

- The multiple jobholding rate increased to 5.0 percent in May 2019 after declining in 2018. It remained higher for women (5.5 percent) than for men (4.5 percent). (See Table 1-17.)

- In 2018, more than 4.3 million families had an unemployed member—a decline from 4.7 million in 2017, 5.3 million in 2016, and 5.6 million in 2015. (See Table 1-20.)

Table 1-11. Employed Civilians, by Age, Sex, Race, and Hispanic Origin, 1948–2018

(Thousands of people.)

Race, Hispanic origin, sex, and year	16 years and over	16 to 19 years			20 years and over						
		Total	16 to 17 years	18 to 19 years	Total	20 to 24 years	25 to 34 years	35 to 44 years	45 to 54 years	55 to 64 years	65 years and over
ALL RACES											
Both Sexes											
1948	58 343	4 026	1 600	2 426	54 318	6 937	13 801	13 050	10 624	7 103	2 804
1949	57 651	3 712	1 466	2 246	53 940	6 660	13 639	13 108	10 636	7 042	2 864
1950	58 918	3 703	1 433	2 270	55 218	6 746	13 917	13 424	10 966	7 265	2 899
1951	59 961	3 767	1 575	2 192	56 196	6 321	14 233	13 746	11 421	7 558	2 917
1952	60 250	3 719	1 626	2 092	56 536	5 572	14 515	14 058	11 687	7 785	2 919
1953	61 179	3 720	1 577	2 142	57 460	5 225	14 519	14 774	11 969	7 806	3 166
1954	60 109	3 475	1 422	2 053	56 634	4 971	14 190	14 541	11 976	7 895	3 060
1955	62 170	3 642	1 500	2 143	58 528	5 270	14 481	14 879	12 556	8 158	3 185
1956	63 799	3 818	1 647	2 171	59 983	5 545	14 407	15 218	12 978	8 519	3 314
1957	64 071	3 778	1 613	2 167	60 291	5 641	14 253	15 348	13 320	8 553	3 179
1958	63 036	3 582	1 519	2 063	59 454	5 571	13 675	15 157	13 448	8 559	3 045
1959	64 630	3 838	1 670	2 168	60 791	5 870	13 709	15 454	13 915	8 822	3 023
1960	65 778	4 129	1 770	2 360	61 648	6 119	13 630	15 598	14 238	8 989	3 073
1961	65 746	4 108	1 621	2 486	61 638	6 227	13 429	15 552	14 320	9 120	2 987
1962	66 702	4 195	1 607	2 588	62 508	6 446	13 311	15 901	14 491	9 346	3 013
1963	67 762	4 255	1 751	2 504	63 508	6 815	13 318	16 114	14 749	9 596	2 915
1964	69 305	4 516	2 013	2 503	64 789	7 303	13 449	16 166	15 094	9 804	2 973
1965	71 088	5 036	2 075	2 962	66 052	7 702	13 704	16 294	15 320	10 028	3 005
1966	72 895	5 721	2 269	3 452	67 178	7 964	14 017	16 312	15 615	10 310	2 961
1967	74 372	5 682	2 334	3 348	68 690	8 499	14 575	16 281	15 789	10 536	3 011
1968	75 920	5 781	2 403	3 377	70 141	8 762	15 265	16 220	16 083	10 745	3 065
1969	77 902	6 117	2 573	3 543	71 785	9 319	15 883	16 100	16 410	10 919	3 155
1970	78 678	6 144	2 598	3 546	72 534	9 731	16 318	15 922	16 473	10 974	3 118
1971	79 367	6 208	2 596	3 613	73 158	10 201	16 781	15 675	16 451	11 009	3 040
1972	82 153	6 746	2 787	3 959	75 407	10 999	18 082	15 822	16 457	11 044	3 003
1973	85 064	7 271	3 032	4 239	77 793	11 839	19 509	16 041	16 553	10 966	2 886
1974	86 794	7 448	3 111	4 338	79 347	12 101	20 610	16 203	16 633	10 964	2 835
1975	85 846	7 104	2 941	4 162	78 744	11 885	21 087	15 953	16 190	10 827	2 801
1976	88 752	7 336	2 972	4 363	81 416	12 570	22 493	16 468	16 224	10 912	2 747
1977	92 017	7 688	3 138	4 550	84 329	13 196	23 850	17 157	16 212	11 126	2 787
1978	96 048	8 070	3 330	4 739	87 979	13 887	25 281	18 128	16 338	11 400	2 946
1979	98 824	8 083	3 340	4 743	90 741	14 327	26 492	18 981	16 357	11 585	2 999
1980	99 303	7 710	3 106	4 605	91 593	14 087	27 204	19 523	16 234	11 586	2 960
1981	100 397	7 225	2 866	4 359	93 172	14 122	28 180	20 145	16 255	11 525	2 945
1982	99 526	6 549	2 505	4 044	92 978	13 690	28 149	20 879	15 923	11 414	2 923
1983	100 834	6 342	2 320	4 022	94 491	13 722	28 756	21 960	15 812	11 315	2 927
1984	105 005	6 444	2 404	4 040	98 562	14 207	30 348	23 598	16 178	11 395	2 835
1985	107 150	6 434	2 492	3 941	100 716	13 980	31 208	24 732	16 509	11 474	2 813
1986	109 597	6 472	2 622	3 850	103 125	13 790	32 201	25 861	16 949	11 405	2 919
1987	112 440	6 640	2 736	3 905	105 800	13 524	33 105	27 179	17 487	11 465	3 041
1988	114 968	6 805	2 713	4 092	108 164	13 244	33 574	28 269	18 447	11 433	3 197
1989	117 342	6 759	2 588	4 172	110 582	12 962	34 045	29 443	19 279	11 499	3 355
1990	118 793	6 581	2 410	4 171	112 213	13 401	33 935	30 817	19 525	11 189	3 346
1991	117 718	5 906	2 202	3 704	111 812	12 975	33 061	31 593	19 882	11 001	3 300
1992	118 492	5 669	2 128	3 540	112 824	12 872	32 667	31 923	21 022	10 998	3 341
1993	120 259	5 805	2 226	3 579	114 455	12 840	32 385	32 666	22 175	11 058	3 331
1994	123 060	6 161	2 510	3 651	116 899	12 758	32 286	33 599	23 348	11 228	3 681
1995	124 900	6 419	2 573	3 846	118 481	12 443	32 356	34 202	24 378	11 435	3 666
1996	126 708	6 500	2 646	3 853	120 208	12 138	32 077	35 051	25 514	11 739	3 690
1997	129 558	6 661	2 648	4 012	122 897	12 380	31 809	35 908	26 744	12 296	3 761
1998	131 463	7 051	2 762	4 289	124 413	12 557	31 394	36 278	27 587	12 872	3 725
1999	133 488	7 172	2 793	4 379	126 316	12 891	30 865	36 728	28 635	13 315	3 882
2000	136 891	7 189	2 759	4 431	129 701	13 229	31 549	36 433	30 310	14 002	4 179
2001	136 933	6 740	2 558	4 182	130 194	13 348	30 863	36 049	31 036	14 645	4 253
2002	136 485	6 332	2 330	4 002	130 154	13 351	30 306	35 235	31 281	15 674	4 306
2003	137 736	5 919	2 312	3 607	131 817	13 433	30 383	34 881	31 914	16 598	4 608
2004	139 252	5 907	2 193	3 714	133 345	13 723	30 423	34 580	32 469	17 331	4 819
2005	141 730	5 978	2 284	3 694	135 752	13 792	30 680	34 630	33 207	18 349	5 094
2006	144 427	6 162	2 444	3 719	138 265	13 878	31 051	34 569	34 052	19 389	5 325
2007	146 047	5 911	2 286	3 625	140 136	13 964	31 586	34 302	34 563	20 108	5 614
2008	145 362	5 573	1 989	3 584	139 790	13 629	31 383	33 457	34 529	20 812	5 979
2009	139 877	4 837	1 651	3 187	135 040	12 764	30 014	31 517	33 613	21 019	6 114
2010	139 064	4 378	1 418	2 960	134 686	12 699	30 229	30 663	33 191	21 636	6 268
2011	139 869	4 327	1 355	2 972	135 542	13 036	30 537	30 270	32 867	22 186	6 647
2012	142 469	4 426	1 419	3 007	138 043	13 408	30 701	30 576	32 874	23 239	7 245
2013	143 929	4 458	1 487	2 971	139 471	13 599	31 242	30 650	32 523	23 776	7 681
2014	146 305	4 548	1 545	3 003	141 757	13 894	31 975	30 966	32 556	24 395	7 971
2015	148 834	4 734	1 624	3 110	144 099	14 022	32 742	31 252	32 643	24 975	8 465
2016	151 436	4 965	1 747	3 218	146 471	14 027	33 722	31 562	32 720	25 524	8 916
2017	153 337	5 074	1 890	3 184	148 263	14 132	34 439	31 892	32 503	26 064	9 234
2018	155 761	5 126	1 838	3 289	150 635	14 051	35 324	32 616	32 373	26 565	9 705

Table 1-11. Employed Civilians, by Age, Sex, Race, and Hispanic Origin, 1948–2018—*Continued*

(Thousands of people.)

Race, Hispanic origin, sex, and year	16 years and over	16 to 19 years			20 years and over						
		Total	16 to 17 years	18 to 19 years	Total	20 to 24 years	25 to 34 years	35 to 44 years	45 to 54 years	55 to 64 years	65 years and over
ALL RACES											
Men											
1948	41 725	2 344	996	1 348	39 382	4 349	10 038	9 363	7 742	5 587	2 303
1949	40 925	2 124	911	1 213	38 803	4 197	9 879	9 308	7 661	5 438	2 329
1950	41 578	2 186	909	1 277	39 394	4 255	10 060	9 445	7 790	5 508	2 336
1951	41 780	2 156	979	1 177	39 626	3 780	10 134	9 607	8 012	5 711	2 382
1952	41 682	2 107	985	1 121	39 578	3 183	10 352	9 753	8 144	5 804	2 343
1953	42 430	2 136	976	1 159	40 296	2 901	10 500	10 229	8 374	5 808	2 483
1954	41 619	1 985	881	1 104	39 634	2 724	10 254	10 082	8 330	5 830	2 414
1955	42 621	2 095	936	1 159	40 526	2 973	10 453	10 267	8 553	5 857	2 424
1956	43 379	2 164	1 008	1 156	41 216	3 245	10 337	10 385	8 732	6 004	2 512
1957	43 357	2 115	987	1 130	41 239	3 346	10 222	10 427	8 851	6 002	2 394
1958	42 423	2 012	948	1 064	40 411	3 293	9 790	10 291	8 828	5 955	2 254
1959	43 466	2 198	1 015	1 183	41 267	3 597	9 862	10 492	9 048	6 058	2 210
1960	43 904	2 361	1 090	1 271	41 543	3 754	9 759	10 552	9 182	6 105	2 191
1961	43 656	2 315	989	1 325	41 342	3 795	9 591	10 505	9 195	6 155	2 098
1962	44 177	2 362	990	1 372	41 815	3 898	9 475	10 711	9 333	6 260	2 138
1963	44 657	2 406	1 073	1 334	42 251	4 118	9 431	10 801	9 478	6 385	2 038
1964	45 474	2 587	1 242	1 345	42 886	4 370	9 531	10 832	9 637	6 478	2 039
1965	46 340	2 918	1 285	1 634	43 422	4 583	9 611	10 837	9 792	6 542	2 057
1966	46 919	3 253	1 389	1 863	43 668	4 599	9 709	10 764	9 904	6 668	2 024
1967	47 479	3 186	1 417	1 769	44 294	4 809	9 988	10 674	9 990	6 774	2 058
1968	48 114	3 255	1 453	1 802	44 859	4 812	10 405	10 554	10 102	6 893	2 093
1969	48 818	3 430	1 526	1 904	45 388	5 012	10 736	10 401	10 187	6 931	2 122
1970	48 990	3 409	1 504	1 905	45 581	5 237	10 936	10 216	10 170	6 928	2 094
1971	49 390	3 478	1 510	1 968	45 912	5 593	11 218	10 028	10 139	6 916	2 019
1972	50 896	3 765	1 598	2 167	47 130	6 138	11 884	10 088	10 139	6 929	1 953
1973	52 349	4 039	1 721	2 318	48 310	6 655	12 617	10 126	10 197	6 857	1 856
1974	53 024	4 103	1 744	2 359	48 922	6 739	13 119	10 135	10 181	6 880	1 869
1975	51 857	3 839	1 621	2 219	48 018	6 484	13 205	9 891	9 902	6 722	1 811
1976	53 138	3 947	1 626	2 321	49 190	6 915	13 869	10 069	9 881	6 724	1 732
1977	54 728	4 174	1 733	2 441	50 555	7 232	14 483	10 399	9 832	6 848	1 761
1978	56 479	4 336	1 800	2 535	52 143	7 559	15 124	10 845	9 806	6 954	1 855
1979	57 607	4 300	1 799	2 501	53 308	7 791	15 688	11 202	9 735	7 015	1 876
1980	57 186	4 085	1 672	2 412	53 101	7 532	15 832	11 355	9 548	6 999	1 835
1981	57 397	3 815	1 526	2 289	53 582	7 504	16 266	11 613	9 478	6 909	1 812
1982	56 271	3 379	1 307	2 072	52 891	7 197	16 002	11 902	9 234	6 781	1 776
1983	56 787	3 300	1 213	2 087	53 487	7 232	16 216	12 450	9 133	6 686	1 770
1984	59 091	3 322	1 244	2 078	55 769	7 571	17 166	13 309	9 326	6 694	1 703
1985	59 891	3 328	1 300	2 029	56 562	7 339	17 564	13 800	9 411	6 753	1 695
1986	60 892	3 323	1 352	1 971	57 569	7 250	18 092	14 266	9 554	6 654	1 753
1987	62 107	3 381	1 393	1 988	58 726	7 058	18 487	14 898	9 750	6 682	1 850
1988	63 273	3 492	1 403	2 089	59 781	6 918	18 702	15 457	10 201	6 591	1 911
1989	64 315	3 477	1 327	2 150	60 837	6 799	18 952	16 002	10 569	6 548	1 968
1990	65 104	3 427	1 254	2 173	61 678	7 151	18 779	16 771	10 690	6 378	1 909
1991	64 223	3 044	1 135	1 909	61 178	6 909	18 265	17 086	10 813	6 245	1 860
1992	64 440	2 944	1 096	1 848	61 496	6 819	17 966	17 230	11 365	6 173	1 943
1993	65 349	2 994	1 155	1 839	62 355	6 805	17 877	17 665	11 927	6 166	1 916
1994	66 450	3 156	1 288	1 868	63 294	6 771	17 741	18 111	12 439	6 142	2 089
1995	67 377	3 292	1 316	1 977	64 085	6 665	17 709	18 374	12 958	6 272	2 108
1996	68 207	3 310	1 318	1 992	64 897	6 429	17 527	18 816	13 483	6 470	2 172
1997	69 685	3 401	1 355	2 045	66 284	6 548	17 338	19 327	14 107	6 735	2 229
1998	70 693	3 558	1 398	2 161	67 135	6 638	17 097	19 634	14 544	7 052	2 171
1999	71 446	3 685	1 437	2 249	67 761	6 729	16 694	19 811	14 991	7 274	2 263
2000	73 305	3 671	1 394	2 276	69 634	6 974	17 241	19 537	15 871	7 606	2 406
2001	73 196	3 420	1 268	2 151	69 776	6 952	16 915	19 305	16 268	7 900	2 437
2002	72 903	3 169	1 130	2 040	69 734	6 978	16 573	18 932	16 419	8 378	2 455
2003	73 332	2 917	1 115	1 802	70 415	7 065	16 670	18 774	16 588	8 733	2 585
2004	74 524	2 952	1 037	1 915	71 572	7 246	16 818	18 700	16 951	9 174	2 683
2005	75 973	2 923	1 067	1 855	73 050	7 279	16 993	18 780	17 429	9 714	2 857
2006	77 502	3 071	1 182	1 888	74 431	7 412	17 134	18 765	17 920	10 192	3 008
2007	78 254	2 917	1 091	1 827	75 337	7 374	17 452	18 666	18 210	10 556	3 080
2008	77 486	2 736	926	1 810	74 750	7 145	17 183	18 097	18 124	10 919	3 282
2009	73 670	2 328	786	1 543	71 341	6 510	16 223	16 918	17 443	10 890	3 357
2010	73 359	2 129	675	1 454	71 230	6 466	16 358	16 585	17 242	11 140	3 439
2011	74 290	2 108	650	1 459	72 182	6 826	16 674	16 370	17 113	11 469	3 730
2012	75 555	2 152	659	1 493	73 403	6 948	16 607	16 483	17 221	12 068	4 077
2013	76 353	2 177	700	1 477	74 176	7 013	16 907	16 590	17 033	12 276	4 257
2014	77 692	2 222	729	1 493	75 471	7 187	17 293	16 735	17 118	12 762	4 377
2015	79 131	2 354	799	1 555	76 776	7 173	17 746	16 861	17 245	13 092	4 661
2016	80 568	2 484	825	1 659	78 084	7 212	18 185	17 042	17 287	13 410	4 948
2017	81 402	2 483	882	1 601	78 919	7 281	18 490	17 202	17 125	13 710	5 111
2018	82 698	2 487	847	1 640	80 211	7 190	19 027	17 608	17 038	14 001	5 348

Table 1-11. Employed Civilians, by Age, Sex, Race, and Hispanic Origin, 1948–2018—*Continued*

(Thousands of people.)

Race, Hispanic origin, sex, and year	16 years and over	16 to 19 years			20 years and over						
		Total	16 to 17 years	18 to 19 years	Total	20 to 24 years	25 to 34 years	35 to 44 years	45 to 54 years	55 to 64 years	65 years and over
ALL RACES											
Women											
1948	16 617	1 682	604	1 078	14 936	2 588	3 763	3 687	2 882	1 516	501
1949	16 723	1 588	555	1 033	15 137	2 463	3 760	3 800	2 975	1 604	535
1950	17 340	1 517	524	993	15 824	2 491	3 857	3 979	3 176	1 757	563
1951	18 181	1 611	596	1 015	16 570	2 541	4 099	4 139	3 409	1 847	535
1952	18 568	1 612	641	971	16 958	2 389	4 163	4 305	3 543	1 981	576
1953	18 749	1 584	601	983	17 164	2 324	4 019	4 545	3 595	1 998	683
1954	18 490	1 490	541	949	17 000	2 247	3 936	4 459	3 646	2 065	646
1955	19 551	1 547	564	984	18 002	2 297	4 028	4 612	4 003	2 301	761
1956	20 419	1 654	639	1 015	18 767	2 300	4 070	4 833	4 246	2 515	802
1957	20 714	1 663	626	1 037	19 052	2 295	4 031	4 921	4 469	2 551	785
1958	20 613	1 570	571	999	19 043	2 278	3 885	4 866	4 620	2 604	791
1959	21 164	1 640	655	985	19 524	2 273	3 847	4 962	4 867	2 764	813
1960	21 874	1 768	680	1 089	20 105	2 365	3 871	5 046	5 056	2 884	882
1961	22 090	1 793	632	1 161	20 296	2 432	3 838	5 047	5 125	2 965	889
1962	22 525	1 833	617	1 216	20 693	2 548	3 836	5 190	5 158	3 086	875
1963	23 105	1 849	678	1 170	21 257	2 697	3 887	5 313	5 271	3 211	877
1964	23 831	1 929	771	1 158	21 903	2 933	3 918	5 334	5 457	3 326	934
1965	24 748	2 118	790	1 328	22 630	3 119	4 093	5 457	5 528	3 486	948
1966	25 976	2 468	880	1 589	23 510	3 365	4 308	5 548	5 711	3 642	937
1967	26 893	2 496	917	1 579	24 397	3 690	4 587	5 607	5 799	3 762	953
1968	27 807	2 526	950	1 575	25 281	3 950	4 860	5 666	5 981	3 852	972
1969	29 084	2 687	1 047	1 639	26 397	4 307	5 147	5 699	6 223	3 988	1 033
1970	29 688	2 735	1 094	1 641	26 952	4 494	5 382	5 706	6 303	4 046	1 023
1971	29 976	2 730	1 086	1 645	27 246	4 609	5 563	5 647	6 313	4 093	1 021
1972	31 257	2 980	1 188	1 792	28 276	4 861	6 197	5 734	6 318	4 115	1 051
1973	32 715	3 231	1 310	1 920	29 484	5 184	6 893	5 915	6 356	4 109	1 029
1974	33 769	3 345	1 367	1 978	30 424	5 363	7 492	6 068	6 451	4 084	966
1975	33 989	3 263	1 320	1 943	30 726	5 401	7 882	6 061	6 288	4 105	989
1976	35 615	3 389	1 346	2 043	32 226	5 655	8 624	6 400	6 343	4 188	1 017
1977	37 289	3 514	1 403	2 110	33 775	5 965	9 367	6 758	6 380	4 279	1 027
1978	39 569	3 734	1 530	2 204	35 836	6 328	10 157	7 282	6 532	4 446	1 091
1979	41 217	3 783	1 541	2 242	37 434	6 538	10 802	7 779	6 622	4 569	1 124
1980	42 117	3 625	1 433	2 192	38 492	6 555	11 370	8 168	6 686	4 587	1 125
1981	43 000	3 411	1 340	2 070	39 590	6 618	11 914	8 532	6 777	4 616	1 133
1982	43 256	3 170	1 198	1 972	40 086	6 492	12 147	8 977	6 689	4 634	1 147
1983	44 047	3 043	1 107	1 935	41 004	6 490	12 540	9 510	6 678	4 629	1 157
1984	45 915	3 122	1 161	1 962	42 793	6 636	13 182	10 289	6 852	4 700	1 133
1985	47 259	3 105	1 193	1 913	44 154	6 640	13 644	10 933	7 097	4 721	1 118
1986	48 706	3 149	1 270	1 879	45 556	6 540	14 109	11 595	7 395	4 751	1 165
1987	50 334	3 260	1 343	1 917	47 074	6 466	14 617	12 281	7 737	4 783	1 191
1988	51 696	3 313	1 310	2 003	48 383	6 326	14 872	12 811	8 246	4 841	1 286
1989	53 027	3 282	1 261	2 021	49 745	6 163	15 093	13 440	8 711	4 950	1 388
1990	53 689	3 154	1 156	1 998	50 535	6 250	15 155	14 046	8 835	4 811	1 437
1991	53 496	2 862	1 067	1 794	50 634	6 066	14 796	14 507	9 069	4 756	1 440
1992	54 052	2 724	1 032	1 692	51 328	6 053	14 701	14 693	9 657	4 825	1 398
1993	54 910	2 811	1 071	1 740	52 099	6 035	14 508	15 002	10 248	4 892	1 414
1994	56 610	3 005	1 222	1 783	53 606	5 987	14 545	15 488	10 908	5 085	1 592
1995	57 523	3 127	1 258	1 869	54 396	5 779	14 647	15 828	11 421	5 163	1 558
1996	58 501	3 190	1 328	1 862	55 311	5 709	14 549	16 235	12 031	5 269	1 518
1997	59 873	3 260	1 293	1 967	56 613	5 831	14 471	16 581	12 637	5 561	1 532
1998	60 771	3 493	1 364	2 128	57 278	5 919	14 298	16 644	13 043	5 820	1 554
1999	62 042	3 487	1 357	2 130	58 555	6 163	14 171	16 917	13 644	6 041	1 619
2000	63 586	3 519	1 364	2 154	60 067	6 255	14 308	16 897	14 438	6 396	1 773
2001	63 737	3 320	1 289	2 031	60 417	6 396	13 948	16 744	14 768	6 745	1 815
2002	63 582	3 162	1 200	1 962	60 420	6 374	13 733	16 303	14 863	7 296	1 851
2003	64 404	3 002	1 197	1 805	61 402	6 367	13 714	16 106	15 326	7 866	2 023
2004	64 728	2 955	1 156	1 799	61 773	6 477	13 605	15 880	15 518	8 157	2 135
2005	65 757	3 055	1 217	1 838	62 702	6 513	13 687	15 850	15 779	8 635	2 238
2006	66 925	3 091	1 261	1 830	63 834	6 467	13 917	15 804	16 132	9 198	2 316
2007	67 792	2 994	1 195	1 798	64 799	6 590	14 133	15 636	16 353	9 553	2 534
2008	67 876	2 837	1 063	1 774	65 039	6 484	14 200	15 360	16 406	9 893	2 697
2009	66 208	2 509	865	1 644	63 699	6 254	13 791	14 599	16 170	10 128	2 757
2010	65 705	2 249	743	1 506	63 456	6 233	13 870	14 078	15 949	10 496	2 830
2011	65 579	2 219	705	1 514	63 360	6 209	13 863	13 900	15 753	10 717	2 917
2012	66 914	2 274	760	1 514	64 640	6 460	14 094	14 093	15 653	11 171	3 168
2013	67 577	2 281	787	1 494	65 295	6 586	14 336	14 060	15 490	11 400	3 424
2014	68 613	2 326	817	1 510	66 287	6 707	14 682	14 232	15 438	11 634	3 594
2015	69 703	2 380	825	1 555	67 323	6 849	14 996	14 391	15 399	11 884	3 804
2016	70 868	2 481	922	1 559	68 387	6 815	15 537	14 520	15 433	12 114	3 968
2017	71 936	2 591	1 008	1 583	69 344	6 851	15 949	14 690	15 377	12 354	4 124
2018	73 063	2 639	991	1 648	70 424	6 861	16 298	15 008	15 335	12 564	4 358

Table 1-11. Employed Civilians, by Age, Sex, Race, and Hispanic Origin, 1948–2018—*Continued*

(Thousands of people.)

Race, Hispanic origin, sex, and year	16 years and over	16 to 19 years			20 years and over						
		Total	16 to 17 years	18 to 19 years	Total	20 to 24 years	25 to 34 years	35 to 44 years	45 to 54 years	55 to 64 years	65 years and over
WHITE											
Both Sexes											
1954	53 957	3 078	1 257	1 822	50 879	4 358	12 616	13 000	10 811	7 262	2 831
1955	55 833	3 225	1 330	1 896	52 608	4 637	12 855	13 327	11 322	7 510	2 957
1956	57 269	3 389	1 465	1 922	53 880	4 897	12 748	13 637	11 706	7 822	3 068
1957	57 465	3 374	1 442	1 931	54 091	4 952	12 619	13 716	12 009	7 829	2 951
1958	56 613	3 216	1 370	1 847	53 397	4 908	12 128	13 571	12 113	7 849	2 828
1959	58 006	3 475	1 520	1 955	54 531	5 138	12 144	13 830	12 552	8 063	2 805
1960	58 850	3 700	1 598	2 103	55 150	5 331	12 021	13 930	12 820	8 192	2 855
1961	58 913	3 693	1 472	2 220	55 220	5 460	11 835	13 905	12 906	8 335	2 778
1962	59 698	3 774	1 447	2 327	55 924	5 676	11 703	14 173	13 066	8 511	2 795
1963	60 622	3 851	1 600	2 250	56 771	6 036	11 689	14 341	13 304	8 718	2 683
1964	61 922	4 076	1 846	2 230	57 846	6 444	11 794	14 380	13 596	8 910	2 717
1965	63 446	4 562	1 892	2 670	58 884	6 752	11 992	14 473	13 804	9 116	2 748
1966	65 021	5 176	2 052	3 124	59 845	6 986	12 268	14 449	14 072	9 356	2 713
1967	66 361	5 114	2 121	2 993	61 247	7 493	12 763	14 429	14 224	9 596	2 746
1968	67 750	5 195	2 193	3 002	62 555	7 687	13 410	14 386	14 487	9 781	2 804
1969	69 518	5 508	2 347	3 161	64 010	8 182	13 935	14 270	14 788	9 947	2 888
1970	70 217	5 571	2 386	3 185	64 645	8 559	14 326	14 092	14 854	9 979	2 835
1971	70 878	5 670	2 404	3 266	65 208	9 000	14 713	13 858	14 843	10 014	2 780
1972	73 370	6 173	2 581	3 592	67 197	9 718	15 904	13 940	14 845	10 077	2 714
1973	75 708	6 623	2 806	3 816	69 086	10 424	17 099	14 083	14 886	9 983	2 610
1974	77 184	6 796	2 881	3 916	70 388	10 676	18 040	14 196	14 948	9 958	2 568
1975	76 411	6 487	2 721	3 770	69 924	10 546	18 485	13 979	14 555	9 827	2 533
1976	78 853	6 724	2 762	3 962	72 129	11 119	19 662	14 407	14 549	9 923	2 470
1977	81 700	7 068	2 926	4 142	74 632	11 696	20 844	14 984	14 483	10 107	2 518
1978	84 936	7 367	3 085	4 282	77 569	12 251	22 008	15 809	14 550	10 311	2 642
1979	87 259	7 356	3 079	4 278	79 904	12 594	23 033	16 578	14 522	10 477	2 699
1980	87 715	7 021	2 861	4 161	80 694	12 405	23 653	17 071	14 405	10 475	2 684
1981	88 709	6 588	2 645	3 943	82 121	12 477	24 551	17 617	14 414	10 386	2 676
1982	87 903	5 984	2 317	3 667	81 918	12 097	24 531	18 268	14 083	10 283	2 656
1983	88 893	5 799	2 156	3 643	83 094	12 138	24 955	19 194	13 961	10 169	2 678
1984	92 120	5 836	2 209	3 627	86 284	12 451	26 235	20 552	14 239	10 227	2 580
1985	93 736	5 768	2 270	3 498	87 968	12 235	26 945	21 552	14 459	10 247	2 530
1986	95 660	5 792	2 386	3 406	89 869	12 027	27 746	22 515	14 750	10 176	2 654
1987	97 789	5 898	2 468	3 431	91 890	11 748	28 429	23 596	15 216	10 164	2 738
1988	99 812	6 030	2 424	3 606	93 782	11 438	28 796	24 468	16 054	10 153	2 874
1989	101 584	5 946	2 278	3 668	95 638	11 084	29 091	25 442	16 775	10 223	3 024
1990	102 261	5 779	2 141	3 638	96 481	11 498	28 773	26 282	16 933	9 960	3 035
1991	101 182	5 216	1 971	3 246	95 966	11 116	27 989	26 883	17 269	9 719	2 990
1992	101 669	4 985	1 904	3 081	96 684	11 031	27 552	27 097	18 285	9 701	3 019
1993	103 045	5 113	1 990	3 123	97 932	10 931	27 274	27 645	19 273	9 772	3 037
1994	105 190	5 398	2 210	3 188	99 792	10 736	27 101	28 442	20 247	9 912	3 354
1995	106 490	5 593	2 273	3 320	100 897	10 400	27 014	28 951	21 127	10 070	3 335
1996	107 808	5 667	2 325	3 343	102 141	10 149	26 678	29 566	22 071	10 313	3 364
1997	109 856	5 807	2 341	3 466	104 049	10 362	26 294	30 137	23 061	10 785	3 411
1998	110 931	6 089	2 436	3 653	104 842	10 512	25 729	30 320	23 662	11 272	3 347
1999	112 235	6 204	2 435	3 769	106 032	10 716	25 113	30 548	24 507	11 657	3 491
2000	114 424	6 160	2 383	3 777	108 264	10 944	25 500	30 151	25 762	12 169	3 738
2001	114 430	5 817	2 224	3 593	108 613	11 054	24 948	29 793	26 301	12 743	3 774
2002	114 013	5 441	2 037	3 404	108 572	11 096	24 568	29 049	26 401	13 630	3 828
2003	114 235	5 064	1 999	3 065	109 171	11 052	24 399	28 501	26 762	14 375	4 083
2004	115 239	5 039	1 895	3 145	110 199	11 233	24 337	28 176	27 228	14 965	4 260
2005	116 949	5 105	1 999	3 106	111 844	11 231	24 443	28 102	27 801	15 788	4 480
2006	118 833	5 215	2 099	3 117	113 618	11 296	24 652	27 929	28 419	16 652	4 670
2007	119 792	4 990	1 965	3 026	114 802	11 325	25 024	27 492	28 779	17 262	4 921
2008	119 126	4 697	1 703	2 994	114 428	11 055	24 875	26 736	28 686	17 829	5 247
2009	114 996	4 138	1 443	2 696	110 858	10 438	23 957	25 237	27 891	17 978	5 357
2010	114 168	3 733	1 248	2 485	110 435	10 334	24 097	24 540	27 502	18 464	5 496
2011	114 690	3 691	1 189	2 501	111 000	10 574	24 376	24 156	27 176	18 937	5 780
2012	114 769	3 665	1 207	2 458	111 104	10 561	23 925	23 931	26 769	19 608	6 309
2013	115 379	3 671	1 274	2 397	111 708	10 662	24 247	23 833	26 363	19 913	6 690
2014	116 788	3 701	1 289	2 412	113 087	10 842	24 771	23 970	26 251	20 351	6 902
2015	117 944	3 824	1 319	2 505	114 120	10 784	25 111	24 012	26 154	20 783	7 276
2016	119 313	3 967	1 419	2 549	115 346	10 722	25 568	24 159	26 070	21 169	7 658
2017	120 176	3 989	1 520	2 469	116 188	10 738	26 001	24 289	25 716	21 581	7 863
2018	121 461	4 060	1 485	2 575	117 401	10 697	26 400	24 771	25 437	21 855	8 241

Table 1-11. Employed Civilians, by Age, Sex, Race, and Hispanic Origin, 1948–2018—*Continued*

(Thousands of people.)

Race, Hispanic origin, sex, and year	16 years and over	16 to 19 years			20 years and over						
		Total	16 to 17 years	18 to 19 years	Total	20 to 24 years	25 to 34 years	35 to 44 years	45 to 54 years	55 to 64 years	65 years and over
WHITE											
Men											
1954	37 846	1 723	771	953	36 123	2 394	9 287	9 175	7 614	5 412	2 241
1955	38 719	1 824	821	1 004	36 895	2 607	9 461	9 351	7 792	5 431	2 254
1956	39 368	1 893	890	1 002	37 475	2 850	9 330	9 449	7 950	5 559	2 336
1957	39 349	1 865	874	990	37 484	2 930	9 226	9 480	8 067	5 542	2 234
1958	38 591	1 783	852	932	36 808	2 896	8 861	9 386	8 061	5 501	2 103
1959	39 494	1 961	915	1 046	37 533	3 153	8 911	9 560	8 261	5 588	2 060
1960	39 755	2 092	973	1 119	37 663	3 264	8 777	9 589	8 372	5 618	2 043
1961	39 588	2 055	891	1 164	37 533	3 311	8 630	9 566	8 394	5 670	1 961
1962	40 016	2 098	883	1 215	37 918	3 426	8 514	9 718	8 512	5 749	1 998
1963	40 428	2 156	972	1 184	38 272	3 646	8 463	9 782	8 650	5 844	1 887
1964	41 115	2 316	1 128	1 188	38 799	3 856	8 538	9 800	8 787	5 945	1 872
1965	41 844	2 612	1 159	1 453	39 232	4 025	8 598	9 795	8 924	5 998	1 892
1966	42 331	2 913	1 245	1 668	39 418	4 028	8 674	9 719	9 029	6 096	1 871
1967	42 833	2 849	1 278	1 571	39 985	4 231	8 931	9 632	9 093	6 208	1 892
1968	43 411	2 908	1 319	1 589	40 503	4 226	9 315	9 522	9 198	6 316	1 926
1969	44 048	3 070	1 385	1 685	40 978	4 401	9 608	9 379	9 279	6 359	1 953
1970	44 178	3 066	1 374	1 692	41 112	4 601	9 784	9 202	9 271	6 340	1 914
1971	44 595	3 157	1 393	1 764	41 438	4 935	10 026	9 026	9 256	6 339	1 856
1972	45 944	3 416	1 470	1 947	42 528	5 431	10 664	9 047	9 236	6 363	1 786
1973	47 085	3 660	1 590	2 071	43 424	5 863	11 268	9 046	9 257	6 299	1 689
1974	47 674	3 728	1 611	2 117	43 946	5 965	11 701	9 027	9 242	6 304	1 706
1975	46 697	3 505	1 502	2 002	43 192	5 770	11 783	8 818	9 005	6 160	1 656
1976	47 775	3 604	1 501	2 103	44 171	6 140	12 362	8 944	8 968	6 176	1 579
1977	49 150	3 824	1 607	2 217	45 326	6 437	12 893	9 212	8 898	6 279	1 605
1978	50 544	3 950	1 664	2 286	46 594	6 717	13 413	9 608	8 840	6 339	1 677
1979	51 452	3 904	1 654	2 250	47 546	6 868	13 888	9 930	8 748	6 406	1 707
1980	51 127	3 708	1 534	2 174	47 419	6 652	14 009	10 077	8 586	6 412	1 684
1981	51 315	3 469	1 402	2 066	47 846	6 652	14 398	10 307	8 518	6 309	1 662
1982	50 287	3 079	1 214	1 865	47 209	6 372	14 164	10 593	8 267	6 188	1 624
1983	50 621	3 003	1 124	1 879	47 618	6 386	14 297	11 062	8 152	6 084	1 637
1984	52 462	3 001	1 140	1 861	49 461	6 647	15 045	11 776	8 320	6 108	1 564
1985	53 046	2 985	1 185	1 800	50 061	6 428	15 374	12 214	8 374	6 118	1 552
1986	53 785	2 966	1 225	1 741	50 818	6 340	15 790	12 620	8 442	6 012	1 612
1987	54 647	2 999	1 252	1 747	51 649	6 150	16 084	13 138	8 596	5 991	1 690
1988	55 550	3 084	1 248	1 836	52 466	5 987	16 241	13 590	8 992	5 909	1 748
1989	56 352	3 060	1 171	1 889	53 292	5 839	16 383	14 046	9 335	5 891	1 797
1990	56 703	3 018	1 119	1 899	53 685	6 179	16 124	14 496	9 383	5 744	1 760
1991	55 797	2 694	1 017	1 677	53 103	5 942	15 644	14 743	9 488	5 578	1 707
1992	55 959	2 602	990	1 612	53 357	5 855	15 357	14 842	10 027	5 503	1 772
1993	56 656	2 634	1 031	1 603	54 021	5 830	15 230	15 178	10 497	5 514	1 772
1994	57 452	2 776	1 144	1 632	54 676	5 738	15 052	15 562	10 910	5 490	1 925
1995	58 146	2 892	1 169	1 723	55 254	5 613	14 958	15 793	11 359	5 609	1 921
1996	58 888	2 911	1 161	1 750	55 977	5 444	14 820	16 136	11 834	5 755	1 987
1997	59 998	3 011	1 206	1 806	56 986	5 590	14 567	16 470	12 352	5 972	2 037
1998	60 604	3 103	1 233	1 870	57 500	5 659	14 259	16 715	12 661	6 251	1 955
1999	61 139	3 205	1 254	1 951	57 934	5 753	13 851	16 781	13 046	6 447	2 056
2000	62 289	3 169	1 205	1 965	59 119	5 876	14 238	16 477	13 675	6 678	2 175
2001	62 212	2 967	1 102	1 865	59 245	5 870	13 989	16 280	13 987	6 941	2 178
2002	61 849	2 725	987	1 738	59 124	5 882	13 727	15 910	14 060	7 360	2 184
2003	61 866	2 518	972	1 546	59 348	5 890	13 731	15 675	14 117	7 640	2 295
2004	62 712	2 553	903	1 650	60 159	6 026	13 735	15 572	14 418	8 018	2 390
2005	63 763	2 508	942	1 566	61 255	6 041	13 840	15 544	14 810	8 471	2 550
2006	64 883	2 625	1 020	1 605	62 259	6 114	13 903	15 480	15 189	8 893	2 680
2007	65 289	2 483	951	1 531	62 806	6 066	14 112	15 287	15 399	9 215	2 727
2008	64 624	2 320	808	1 512	62 304	5 858	13 931	14 775	15 300	9 518	2 922
2009	61 630	2 004	692	1 312	59 626	5 379	13 230	13 858	14 710	9 465	2 984
2010	61 252	1 815	598	1 217	59 438	5 347	13 282	13 583	14 542	9 637	3 047
2011	61 920	1 802	573	1 229	60 118	5 630	13 548	13 366	14 370	9 932	3 271
2012	61 990	1 797	563	1 234	60 193	5 547	13 212	13 224	14 264	10 334	3 611
2013	62 322	1 811	608	1 203	60 511	5 597	13 381	13 182	14 035	10 541	3 775
2014	63 108	1 819	599	1 219	61 289	5 681	13 627	13 258	14 060	10 817	3 847
2015	63 892	1 934	653	1 280	61 959	5 585	13 866	13 273	14 059	11 088	4 088
2016	64 612	2 037	708	1 328	62 575	5 598	14 022	13 358	14 005	11 284	4 308
2017	65 000	1 991	727	1 264	63 009	5 613	14 190	13 422	13 819	11 531	4 434
2018	65 702	1 983	696	1 287	63 719	5 561	14 450	13 711	13 658	11 692	4 647

Table 1-11. Employed Civilians, by Age, Sex, Race, and Hispanic Origin, 1948–2018—*Continued*

(Thousands of people.)

Race, Hispanic origin, sex, and year	16 years and over	16 to 19 years			20 years and over						
		Total	16 to 17 years	18 to 19 years	Total	20 to 24 years	25 to 34 years	35 to 44 years	45 to 54 years	55 to 64 years	65 years and over
WHITE											
Women											
1954	16 111	1 355	486	869	14 756	1 964	3 329	3 825	3 197	1 850	590
1955	17 114	1 401	509	892	15 713	2 030	3 394	3 976	3 530	2 079	703
1956	17 901	1 496	575	920	16 405	2 047	3 418	4 188	3 756	2 263	732
1957	18 116	1 509	568	941	16 607	2 022	3 393	4 236	3 942	2 287	717
1958	18 022	1 433	518	915	16 589	2 012	3 267	4 185	4 052	2 348	725
1959	18 512	1 514	605	909	16 998	1 985	3 233	4 270	4 291	2 475	745
1960	19 095	1 608	625	984	17 487	2 067	3 244	4 341	4 448	2 574	812
1961	19 325	1 638	581	1 056	17 687	2 149	3 205	4 339	4 512	2 665	817
1962	19 682	1 676	564	1 112	18 006	2 250	3 189	4 455	4 554	2 762	797
1963	20 194	1 695	628	1 066	18 499	2 390	3 226	4 559	4 654	2 874	796
1964	20 807	1 760	718	1 042	19 047	2 588	3 256	4 580	4 809	2 971	845
1965	21 602	1 950	733	1 217	19 652	2 727	3 394	4 678	4 880	3 118	856
1966	22 690	2 263	807	1 456	20 427	2 958	3 594	4 730	5 043	3 260	842
1967	23 528	2 265	843	1 422	21 263	3 262	3 832	4 797	5 131	3 388	854
1968	24 339	2 287	874	1 413	22 052	3 461	4 095	4 864	5 289	3 465	878
1969	25 470	2 438	962	1 476	23 032	3 781	4 327	4 891	5 509	3 588	935
1970	26 039	2 505	1 012	1 493	23 534	3 959	4 542	4 890	5 582	3 640	921
1971	26 283	2 513	1 011	1 502	23 770	4 065	4 687	4 831	5 588	3 675	924
1972	27 426	2 755	1 111	1 645	24 669	4 286	5 240	4 893	5 608	3 714	928
1973	28 623	2 962	1 217	1 746	25 661	4 562	5 831	5 036	5 628	3 684	920
1974	29 511	3 069	1 269	1 799	26 442	4 711	6 340	5 169	5 706	3 654	862
1975	29 714	2 983	1 215	1 767	26 731	4 775	6 701	5 161	5 550	3 667	877
1976	31 078	3 120	1 260	1 860	27 958	4 978	7 300	5 462	5 580	3 746	891
1977	32 550	3 244	1 319	1 923	29 306	5 259	7 950	5 772	5 585	3 829	912
1978	34 392	3 416	1 420	1 996	30 975	5 535	8 595	6 201	5 710	3 972	964
1979	35 807	3 451	1 423	2 027	32 357	5 726	9 145	6 648	5 773	4 071	993
1980	36 587	3 314	1 327	1 986	33 275	5 753	9 644	6 994	5 818	4 064	1 001
1981	37 394	3 119	1 242	1 877	34 275	5 826	10 153	7 311	5 896	4 077	1 013
1982	37 615	2 905	1 103	1 802	34 710	5 724	10 367	7 675	5 816	4 095	1 032
1983	38 272	2 796	1 032	1 764	35 476	5 751	10 659	8 132	5 809	4 084	1 041
1984	39 659	2 835	1 069	1 766	36 823	5 804	11 190	8 776	5 920	4 118	1 015
1985	40 690	2 783	1 085	1 698	37 907	5 807	11 571	9 338	6 084	4 128	978
1986	41 876	2 825	1 160	1 665	39 050	5 687	11 956	9 895	6 307	4 164	1 042
1987	43 142	2 900	1 216	1 684	40 242	5 598	12 345	10 459	6 620	4 172	1 047
1988	44 262	2 946	1 176	1 770	41 316	5 450	12 555	10 878	7 062	4 244	1 126
1989	45 232	2 886	1 107	1 779	42 346	5 245	12 708	11 395	7 440	4 332	1 227
1990	45 558	2 762	1 023	1 739	42 796	5 319	12 649	11 785	7 551	4 217	1 275
1991	45 385	2 523	954	1 569	42 862	5 174	12 344	12 139	7 781	4 141	1 283
1992	45 710	2 383	915	1 468	43 327	5 176	12 195	12 254	8 258	4 198	1 246
1993	46 390	2 479	959	1 520	43 910	5 101	12 044	12 467	8 776	4 258	1 265
1994	47 738	2 622	1 066	1 556	45 116	4 997	12 049	12 880	9 338	4 423	1 429
1995	48 344	2 701	1 104	1 597	45 643	4 787	12 056	13 157	9 768	4 461	1 415
1996	48 920	2 756	1 164	1 592	46 164	4 705	11 858	13 430	10 237	4 558	1 376
1997	49 859	2 796	1 136	1 660	47 063	4 773	11 727	13 667	10 709	4 813	1 374
1998	50 327	2 986	1 203	1 783	47 342	4 853	11 470	13 604	11 001	5 021	1 392
1999	51 096	2 999	1 181	1 817	48 098	4 963	11 262	13 767	11 461	5 211	1 435
2000	52 136	2 991	1 178	1 813	49 145	5 068	11 262	13 674	12 087	5 490	1 564
2001	52 218	2 850	1 122	1 727	49 369	5 184	10 959	13 513	12 314	5 802	1 597
2002	52 164	2 716	1 050	1 665	49 448	5 214	10 842	13 138	12 341	6 269	1 644
2003	52 369	2 546	1 027	1 519	49 823	5 161	10 668	12 826	12 645	6 735	1 788
2004	52 527	2 486	991	1 495	50 040	5 207	10 602	12 604	12 810	6 947	1 870
2005	53 186	2 597	1 057	1 540	50 589	5 190	10 603	12 558	12 991	7 317	1 930
2006	53 950	2 590	1 079	1 512	51 359	5 182	10 750	12 449	13 230	7 758	1 991
2007	54 503	2 507	1 013	1 494	51 996	5 259	10 912	12 205	13 380	8 047	2 193
2008	54 501	2 377	895	1 482	52 124	5 197	10 943	11 961	13 386	8 312	2 325
2009	53 366	2 134	751	1 383	51 231	5 060	10 727	11 379	13 181	8 513	2 373
2010	52 916	1 918	650	1 268	50 997	4 988	10 815	10 958	12 960	8 827	2 450
2011	52 770	1 889	617	1 272	50 881	4 943	10 828	10 789	12 806	9 005	2 509
2012	52 779	1 868	644	1 224	50 911	5 014	10 713	10 708	12 505	9 274	2 698
2013	53 057	1 860	665	1 195	51 198	5 066	10 866	10 651	12 328	9 371	2 915
2014	53 680	1 882	690	1 192	51 798	5 161	11 143	10 712	12 192	9 535	3 055
2015	54 052	1 891	666	1 225	52 161	5 200	11 245	10 739	12 094	9 695	3 188
2016	54 701	1 931	711	1 220	52 771	5 124	11 546	10 800	12 065	9 885	3 350
2017	55 176	1 997	792	1 205	53 179	5 126	11 811	10 867	11 897	10 050	3 428
2018	55 759	2 077	788	1 288	53 682	5 137	11 950	11 060	11 779	10 163	3 594

Table 1-11. Employed Civilians, by Age, Sex, Race, and Hispanic Origin, 1948–2018—*Continued*

(Thousands of people.)

Race, Hispanic origin, sex, and year	16 years and over	16 to 19 years			20 years and over						
		Total	16 to 17 years	18 to 19 years	Total	20 to 24 years	25 to 34 years	35 to 44 years	45 to 54 years	55 to 64 years	65 years and over
BLACK											
Both Sexes											
1985	10 501	532	175	356	9 969	1 399	3 325	2 427	1 598	985	235
1986	10 814	536	183	353	10 278	1 429	3 464	2 524	1 666	982	214
1987	11 309	587	203	385	10 722	1 421	3 614	2 695	1 714	1 036	241
1988	11 658	601	223	378	11 057	1 433	3 725	2 839	1 783	1 018	261
1989	11 953	625	237	388	11 328	1 467	3 801	2 981	1 844	970	265
1990	12 175	598	194	404	11 577	1 409	3 803	3 287	1 897	933	248
1991	12 074	494	161	334	11 580	1 373	3 714	3 401	1 892	957	243
1992	12 151	492	157	335	11 659	1 343	3 699	3 441	1 964	965	246
1993	12 382	494	171	323	11 888	1 377	3 700	3 584	2 059	941	226
1994	12 835	552	224	328	12 284	1 449	3 732	3 722	2 178	953	251
1995	13 279	586	223	363	12 693	1 443	3 844	3 861	2 288	1 004	253
1996	13 542	613	233	380	12 929	1 411	3 851	3 974	2 426	1 025	241
1997	13 969	631	229	401	13 339	1 456	3 903	4 094	2 588	1 048	249
1998	14 556	736	246	490	13 820	1 496	3 967	4 238	2 739	1 118	262
1999	15 056	691	243	448	14 365	1 594	4 091	4 404	2 872	1 134	271
2000	15 156	711	260	451	14 444	1 593	3 993	4 261	3 073	1 226	300
2001	15 006	637	230	408	14 368	1 571	3 840	4 200	3 139	1 283	335
2002	14 872	611	193	417	14 262	1 543	3 726	4 109	3 220	1 332	332
2003	14 739	516	196	320	14 222	1 516	3 618	4 080	3 289	1 373	346
2004	14 909	520	169	351	14 389	1 572	3 635	4 039	3 332	1 452	359
2005	15 313	536	164	372	14 776	1 599	3 722	4 060	3 464	1 555	375
2006	15 765	618	215	402	15 147	1 643	3 809	4 072	3 570	1 659	394
2007	16 051	566	202	364	15 485	1 674	3 888	4 120	3 658	1 732	413
2008	15 953	541	172	369	15 411	1 625	3 870	4 015	3 670	1 791	440
2009	15 025	442	131	310	14 584	1 474	3 582	3 686	3 562	1 827	453
2010	15 010	386	106	280	14 624	1 532	3 641	3 561	3 531	1 899	460
2011	15 051	380	99	281	14 671	1 574	3 632	3 499	3 513	1 943	508
2012	15 856	438	119	319	15 417	1 700	3 693	3 662	3 660	2 161	540
2013	16 151	439	117	322	15 712	1 727	3 780	3 730	3 644	2 263	567
2014	16 732	456	142	315	16 276	1 839	3 936	3 834	3 728	2 342	596
2015	17 472	502	164	338	16 970	1 953	4 190	3 928	3 806	2 433	660
2016	17 982	535	167	368	17 447	1 930	4 492	3 997	3 814	2 526	689
2017	18 587	573	189	384	18 015	1 984	4 667	4 115	3 858	2 606	786
2018	19 091	596	176	420	18 496	1 940	4 910	4 208	3 898	2 728	812
Men											
1985	5 270	278	92	186	4 992	726	1 669	1 187	795	501	114
1986	5 428	278	96	182	5 150	732	1 756	1 211	831	507	112
1987	5 661	304	109	195	5 357	728	1 821	1 283	853	547	124
1988	5 824	316	122	193	5 509	736	1 881	1 348	878	536	131
1989	5 928	327	124	202	5 602	742	1 931	1 415	886	498	131
1990	5 995	303	99	204	5 692	702	1 895	1 586	926	469	114
1991	5 961	255	85	170	5 706	695	1 859	1 634	923	481	114
1992	5 930	249	78	170	5 681	679	1 819	1 650	930	478	124
1993	6 047	254	88	166	5 793	674	1 858	1 717	978	461	106
1994	6 241	276	107	169	5 964	718	1 850	1 795	1 030	455	115
1995	6 422	285	111	174	6 137	714	1 895	1 836	1 085	468	138
1996	6 456	289	109	180	6 167	685	1 867	1 878	1 129	482	126
1997	6 607	282	108	174	6 325	668	1 874	1 955	1 215	487	127
1998	6 871	341	120	221	6 530	686	1 886	2 008	1 284	524	142
1999	7 027	325	120	205	6 702	700	1 926	2 092	1 327	525	131
2000	7 082	341	129	211	6 741	730	1 865	1 984	1 425	596	142
2001	6 938	311	115	196	6 627	703	1 757	1 931	1 452	614	170
2002	6 959	306	95	212	6 652	725	1 729	1 899	1 503	624	172
2003	6 820	234	89	145	6 586	726	1 660	1 868	1 518	638	176
2004	6 912	231	76	155	6 681	739	1 720	1 840	1 534	668	180
2005	7 155	254	76	178	6 901	748	1 759	1 886	1 616	711	182
2006	7 354	275	99	175	7 079	804	1 797	1 882	1 680	734	184
2007	7 500	254	82	172	7 245	816	1 851	1 916	1 717	750	195
2008	7 398	247	70	177	7 151	794	1 805	1 854	1 703	792	204
2009	6 817	189	56	133	6 628	689	1 635	1 662	1 622	813	206
2010	6 865	185	48	137	6 680	692	1 710	1 638	1 594	834	211
2011	6 953	187	49	138	6 765	734	1 733	1 583	1 621	858	236
2012	7 302	198	52	146	7 104	784	1 723	1 667	1 693	988	249
2013	7 497	192	51	141	7 304	818	1 782	1 738	1 675	1 036	256
2014	7 818	205	70	134	7 613	887	1 879	1 772	1 721	1 081	272
2015	8 164	226	75	150	7 938	936	1 995	1 816	1 780	1 115	297
2016	8 471	242	57	185	8 228	906	2 156	1 865	1 779	1 195	327
2017	8 742	241	74	168	8 500	946	2 249	1 920	1 789	1 231	365
2018	9 018	273	69	204	8 745	913	2 408	1 973	1 810	1 281	361

Table 1-11. Employed Civilians, by Age, Sex, Race, and Hispanic Origin, 1948–2018—*Continued*

(Thousands of people.)

Race, Hispanic origin, sex, and year	16 years and over	16 to 19 years			20 years and over						
		Total	16 to 17 years	18 to 19 years	Total	20 to 24 years	25 to 34 years	35 to 44 years	45 to 54 years	55 to 64 years	65 years and over
BLACK											
Women											
1985	5 231	254	83	171	4 977	673	1 656	1 240	804	484	121
1986	5 386	259	87	171	5 128	696	1 708	1 313	835	475	102
1987	5 648	283	93	190	5 365	693	1 793	1 412	860	489	117
1988	5 834	285	101	184	5 548	697	1 844	1 491	905	482	129
1989	6 025	298	113	185	5 727	725	1 870	1 566	959	472	134
1990	6 180	296	96	200	5 884	707	1 907	1 701	971	464	135
1991	6 113	239	76	164	5 874	677	1 855	1 768	969	476	129
1992	6 221	243	79	164	5 978	664	1 880	1 791	1 034	487	123
1993	6 334	239	82	157	6 095	703	1 842	1 867	1 081	480	121
1994	6 595	275	117	158	6 320	731	1 882	1 926	1 147	497	136
1995	6 857	301	112	189	6 556	729	1 949	2 025	1 202	530	114
1996	7 086	324	124	200	6 762	726	1 984	2 096	1 297	543	115
1997	7 362	349	122	227	7 013	789	2 029	2 139	1 373	561	122
1998	7 685	395	126	268	7 290	810	2 081	2 230	1 455	594	120
1999	8 029	366	123	243	7 663	893	2 165	2 312	1 545	609	139
2000	8 073	370	131	240	7 703	862	2 128	2 277	1 647	630	158
2001	8 068	327	115	212	7 741	868	2 084	2 269	1 686	668	165
2002	7 914	304	99	205	7 610	819	1 997	2 209	1 717	708	160
2003	7 919	283	107	175	7 636	790	1 959	2 211	1 770	735	171
2004	7 997	289	93	196	7 707	833	1 914	2 199	1 798	784	179
2005	8 158	282	88	194	7 876	852	1 964	2 175	1 848	844	193
2006	8 410	343	116	227	8 068	839	2 012	2 191	1 890	925	210
2007	8 551	311	120	191	8 240	858	2 037	2 205	1 941	982	218
2008	8 554	294	102	192	8 260	831	2 065	2 161	1 967	1 000	236
2009	8 208	252	75	178	7 956	784	1 947	2 024	1 939	1 014	246
2010	8 145	201	58	143	7 944	841	1 931	1 923	1 936	1 065	248
2011	8 098	193	50	142	7 906	840	1 899	1 916	1 892	1 086	272
2012	8 553	240	67	173	8 313	916	1 970	1 995	1 968	1 173	291
2013	8 654	246	66	180	8 408	909	1 998	1 992	1 970	1 228	311
2014	8 915	252	71	180	8 663	952	2 057	2 061	2 007	1 261	325
2015	9 308	276	89	188	9 032	1 017	2 195	2 112	2 026	1 319	363
2016	9 511	292	110	183	9 219	1 025	2 335	2 132	2 035	1 330	362
2017	9 845	331	115	216	9 514	1 038	2 418	2 194	2 069	1 375	421
2018	10 073	322	107	215	9 751	1 027	2 502	2 235	2 088	1 448	451
HISPANIC											
Both Sexes											
1985	6 888	438	144	294	6 449	1 187	2 316	1 473	913	486	75
1986	7 219	430	146	284	6 789	1 231	2 427	1 570	1 011	474	76
1987	7 790	474	149	325	7 316	1 273	2 668	1 775	1 010	512	76
1988	8 250	523	171	353	7 727	1 341	2 749	1 876	1 078	585	97
1989	8 573	548	165	383	8 025	1 325	2 900	1 968	1 129	589	114
1990	9 845	668	208	460	9 177	1 672	3 327	2 229	1 235	611	103
1991	9 828	602	169	433	9 225	1 622	3 264	2 333	1 266	637	103
1992	10 027	577	169	408	9 450	1 575	3 350	2 468	1 316	628	112
1993	10 361	570	160	410	9 792	1 574	3 446	2 605	1 402	630	135
1994	10 788	609	195	415	10 178	1 643	3 517	2 737	1 495	647	139
1995	11 127	645	194	450	10 483	1 609	3 618	2 889	1 565	666	135
1996	11 642	646	199	447	10 996	1 628	3 758	3 115	1 595	748	152
1997	12 726	714	228	487	12 012	1 798	4 029	3 371	1 846	794	173
1998	13 291	793	230	563	12 498	1 883	4 113	3 504	1 994	846	158
1999	13 720	854	254	600	12 866	1 881	4 097	3 738	2 074	886	190
2000	15 735	973	285	688	14 762	2 356	4 950	4 052	2 308	898	197
2001	16 190	969	268	701	15 221	2 404	5 065	4 149	2 472	944	187
2002	16 590	882	254	628	15 708	2 413	5 272	4 273	2 511	1 029	209
2003	17 372	768	242	525	16 604	2 399	5 541	4 573	2 711	1 132	249
2004	17 930	792	211	581	17 138	2 477	5 560	4 671	2 932	1 210	288
2005	18 632	847	253	595	17 785	2 423	5 756	4 879	3 114	1 317	296
2006	19 613	900	287	614	18 712	2 487	6 001	5 106	3 324	1 441	354
2007	20 382	894	269	625	19 488	2 516	6 237	5 314	3 547	1 499	376
2008	20 346	870	248	622	19 476	2 361	6 119	5 371	3 620	1 619	385
2009	19 647	742	192	550	18 905	2 218	5 704	5 168	3 700	1 680	435
2010	19 906	680	165	515	19 226	2 281	5 781	5 185	3 779	1 737	464
2011	20 269	665	155	510	19 604	2 544	5 747	5 179	3 848	1 820	465
2012	21 878	808	204	604	21 070	2 761	6 119	5 552	4 188	1 983	467
2013	22 514	821	217	604	21 693	2 857	6 157	5 652	4 374	2 140	514
2014	23 492	859	225	634	22 633	2 947	6 354	5 869	4 593	2 313	557
2015	24 400	922	253	669	23 477	3 027	6 432	6 063	4 831	2 523	601
2016	25 249	977	284	693	24 272	3 086	6 652	6 251	4 975	2 627	681
2017	25 938	1 041	311	730	24 898	3 073	6 767	6 395	5 098	2 825	533
2018	27 012	1 094	307	787	25 918	3 160	7 093	6 600	5 305	2 982	778

Table 1-11. Employed Civilians, by Age, Sex, Race, and Hispanic Origin, 1948–2018—*Continued*

(Thousands of people.)

Race, Hispanic origin, sex, and year	16 years and over	16 to 19 years			20 years and over						
		Total	16 to 17 years	18 to 19 years	Total	20 to 24 years	25 to 34 years	35 to 44 years	45 to 54 years	55 to 64 years	65 years and over
HISPANIC											
Men											
1985	4 245	251	82	169	3 994	727	1 473	888	550	308	. . .
1986	4 428	254	82	172	4 174	773	1 510	929	614	297	. . .
1987	4 713	268	81	188	4 444	777	1 664	1 044	606	303	. . .
1988	4 972	292	87	205	4 680	815	1 706	1 120	645	331	. . .
1989	5 172	319	94	225	4 853	821	1 787	1 152	676	350	. . .
1990	6 021	412	126	286	5 609	1 083	2 076	1 312	722	355	. . .
1991	5 979	356	94	263	5 623	1 063	2 050	1 360	719	369	. . .
1992	6 093	336	97	238	5 757	985	2 127	1 437	768	372	. . .
1993	6 328	337	95	242	5 992	1 003	2 200	1 527	822	360	. . .
1994	6 530	341	109	233	6 189	1 056	2 227	1 600	847	379	79
1995	6 725	358	110	248	6 367	1 030	2 284	1 675	908	384	85
1996	7 039	384	107	277	6 655	1 015	2 345	1 842	918	438	96
1997	7 728	420	130	290	7 307	1 142	2 547	1 978	1 059	477	105
1998	8 018	449	133	315	7 570	1 173	2 592	2 077	1 115	512	101
1999	8 067	491	139	352	7 576	1 135	2 524	2 135	1 151	502	130
2000	9 428	570	159	411	8 859	1 486	3 063	2 358	1 295	532	126
2001	9 668	568	149	419	9 100	1 473	3 142	2 446	1 375	545	119
2002	9 845	504	141	363	9 341	1 476	3 271	2 503	1 396	569	125
2003	10 479	415	121	294	10 063	1 485	3 537	2 724	1 533	639	144
2004	10 832	446	108	338	10 385	1 514	3 557	2 801	1 654	687	174
2005	11 337	465	137	328	10 872	1 511	3 711	2 939	1 781	748	183
2006	11 887	496	146	350	11 391	1 535	3 845	3 088	1 894	809	220
2007	12 310	483	145	338	11 827	1 524	3 982	3 220	2 012	869	220
2008	12 248	479	140	340	11 769	1 406	3 897	3 233	2 080	929	224
2009	11 640	383	94	289	11 256	1 287	3 576	3 108	2 104	930	251
2010	11 800	361	78	283	11 438	1 319	3 591	3 169	2 137	949	273
2011	12 049	364	76	287	11 685	1 535	3 615	3 124	2 141	1 006	266
2012	12 643	431	97	334	12 212	1 584	3 714	3 229	2 334	1 097	256
2013	13 078	440	111	329	12 638	1 609	3 748	3 332	2 471	1 181	296
2014	13 655	453	108	344	13 202	1 655	3 830	1 949	2 600	1 317	307
2015	14 111	487	127	359	13 624	1 655	3 873	3 604	2 730	1 432	331
2016	14 563	508	147	361	14 055	1 677	3 952	3 693	2 859	1 490	384
2017	14 874	519	146	373	14 355	1 692	3 972	3 746	2 921	1 601	423
2018	15 418	545	149	396	14 873	1 705	4 125	3 892	3 002	1 704	446
HISPANIC											
Women											
1985	2 642	187	62	125	2 456	460	843	585	362	178	. . .
1986	2 791	176	64	112	2 615	458	917	641	397	177	. . .
1987	3 077	206	69	137	2 872	496	1 004	732	405	209	. . .
1988	3 278	231	84	147	3 047	526	1 042	756	434	254	. . .
1989	3 401	229	71	158	3 172	504	1 114	816	453	239	. . .
1990	3 823	256	82	174	3 567	588	1 251	917	513	256	. . .
1991	3 848	246	76	170	3 603	559	1 214	972	548	268	. . .
1992	3 934	242	72	170	3 693	591	1 223	1 031	548	256	. . .
1993	4 033	233	65	168	3 800	571	1 246	1 077	581	269	. . .
1994	4 258	268	86	182	3 989	587	1 290	1 137	648	268	59
1995	4 403	287	85	202	4 116	579	1 334	1 213	657	282	50
1996	4 602	261	92	169	4 341	612	1 412	1 273	677	310	56
1997	4 999	294	98	196	4 705	656	1 482	1 393	787	318	69
1998	5 273	345	97	247	4 928	710	1 521	1 428	879	334	57
1999	5 653	363	115	248	5 290	746	1 574	1 603	923	384	60
2000	6 307	404	127	277	5 903	870	1 887	1 695	1 013	366	72
2001	6 522	401	119	282	6 121	931	1 923	1 703	1 097	398	67
2002	6 744	378	113	265	6 367	937	2 001	1 770	1 114	460	84
2003	6 894	353	121	231	6 541	914	2 004	1 849	1 178	493	105
2004	7 098	346	103	243	6 752	964	2 003	1 870	1 279	523	114
2005	7 295	382	116	266	6 913	912	2 045	1 940	1 333	569	113
2006	7 725	404	140	264	7 321	951	2 155	2 018	1 430	632	135
2007	8 072	410	124	287	7 662	991	2 255	2 094	1 535	631	155
2008	8 098	391	108	282	7 707	955	2 222	2 138	1 541	690	161
2009	8 007	358	98	261	7 649	931	2 128	2 060	1 596	751	183
2010	8 106	318	87	231	7 788	962	2 189	2 016	1 642	788	191
2011	8 220	301	79	223	7 918	1 010	2 132	2 055	1 707	814	200
2012	9 235	377	107	269	8 858	1 178	2 405	2 323	1 854	887	212
2013	9 437	381	107	274	9 056	1 249	2 409	2 320	1 902	959	217
2014	9 838	407	117	290	9 431	1 291	2 524	2 376	1 993	997	250
2015	10 289	436	126	310	9 853	1 372	2 560	2 460	2 101	1 091	270
2016	10 686	470	138	332	10 217	1 409	2 700	2 557	2 116	1 137	297
2017	11 064	522	165	357	10 543	1 381	2 795	2 649	2 176	1 224	317
2018	11 594	549	158	391	11 045	1 456	2 968	2 708	2 303	1 278	331

. . . = Not available.

Table 1-12. Civilian Employment-Population Ratios, by Sex, Age, Race, and Hispanic Origin, 1948–2018

(Percent.)

Race, Hispanic origin, and year	Both sexes			Men			Women		
	16 years and over	16 to 19 years	20 years and over	16 years and over	16 to 19 years	20 years and over	16 years and over	16 to 19 years	20 years and over
ALL RACES									
1948	56.6	47.7	57.4	83.5	57.5	85.8	31.3	38.5	30.7
1949	55.4	45.2	56.3	81.3	53.8	83.7	31.2	37.2	30.6
1950	56.1	45.5	57.0	82.0	55.2	84.2	32.0	36.3	31.6
1951	57.3	47.9	58.1	84.0	57.9	86.1	33.1	38.9	32.6
1952	57.3	46.9	58.1	83.9	55.9	86.2	33.4	38.8	33.0
1953	57.1	46.4	58.0	83.6	55.9	85.9	33.3	37.8	32.9
1954	55.5	42.3	56.6	81.0	50.2	83.5	32.5	34.9	32.3
1955	56.7	43.5	57.8	81.8	52.1	84.3	34.0	35.6	33.8
1956	57.5	45.3	58.5	82.3	53.8	84.6	35.1	37.5	34.9
1957	57.1	43.9	58.2	81.3	51.8	83.8	35.1	36.7	35.0
1958	55.4	39.9	56.8	78.5	46.9	81.2	34.5	33.5	34.6
1959	56.0	39.9	57.5	79.3	47.2	82.3	35.0	33.0	35.1
1960	56.1	40.5	57.6	78.9	47.6	81.9	35.5	33.8	35.7
1961	55.4	39.1	56.9	77.6	45.3	80.8	35.4	33.2	35.6
1962	55.5	39.4	57.1	77.7	45.9	80.9	35.6	33.3	35.8
1963	55.4	37.4	57.2	77.1	43.8	80.6	35.8	31.5	36.3
1964	55.7	37.3	57.7	77.3	44.1	80.9	36.3	30.9	36.9
1965	56.2	38.9	58.2	77.5	46.2	81.2	37.1	32.0	37.6
1966	56.9	42.1	58.7	77.9	48.9	81.5	38.3	35.6	38.6
1967	57.3	42.2	59.0	78.0	48.7	81.5	39.0	35.9	39.3
1968	57.5	42.2	59.3	77.8	48.7	81.3	39.6	36.0	40.0
1969	58.0	43.4	59.7	77.6	49.5	81.1	40.7	37.5	41.1
1970	57.4	42.3	59.2	76.2	47.7	79.7	40.8	37.1	41.2
1971	56.6	41.3	58.4	74.9	46.8	78.5	40.4	36.0	40.9
1972	57.0	43.5	58.6	75.0	48.9	78.4	41.0	38.2	41.3
1973	57.8	45.9	59.3	75.5	51.4	78.6	42.0	40.5	42.2
1974	57.8	46.0	59.2	74.9	51.2	77.9	42.6	41.0	42.8
1975	56.1	43.3	57.6	71.7	47.2	74.8	42.0	39.4	42.3
1976	56.8	44.2	58.3	72.0	47.9	75.1	43.2	40.5	43.5
1977	57.9	46.1	59.2	72.8	50.4	75.6	44.5	41.8	44.8
1978	59.3	48.3	60.6	73.8	52.2	76.4	46.4	44.5	46.6
1979	59.9	48.5	61.2	73.8	51.7	76.5	47.5	45.3	47.7
1980	59.2	46.6	60.6	72.0	49.5	74.6	47.7	43.8	48.1
1981	59.0	44.6	60.5	71.3	47.1	74.0	48.0	42.0	48.6
1982	57.8	41.5	59.4	69.0	42.9	71.8	47.7	40.2	48.4
1983	57.9	41.5	59.5	68.8	43.1	71.4	48.0	40.0	48.8
1984	59.5	43.7	61.0	70.7	45.0	73.2	49.5	42.5	50.1
1985	60.1	44.4	61.5	70.9	45.7	73.3	50.4	42.9	51.0
1986	60.7	44.6	62.1	71.0	45.7	73.3	51.4	43.6	52.0
1987	61.5	45.5	62.9	71.5	46.1	73.8	52.5	44.8	53.1
1988	62.3	46.8	63.6	72.0	47.8	74.2	53.4	45.9	54.0
1989	63.0	47.5	64.2	72.5	48.7	74.5	54.3	46.4	54.9
1990	62.8	45.3	64.3	72.0	46.6	74.3	54.3	44.0	55.2
1991	61.7	42.0	63.2	70.4	42.7	72.7	53.7	41.2	54.6
1992	61.5	41.0	63.0	69.8	41.9	72.1	53.8	40.0	54.8
1993	61.7	41.7	63.3	70.0	42.3	72.3	54.1	41.0	55.0
1994	62.5	43.4	64.0	70.4	43.8	72.6	55.3	43.0	56.2
1995	62.9	44.2	64.4	70.8	44.7	73.0	55.6	43.8	56.5
1996	63.2	43.5	64.7	70.9	43.6	73.2	56.0	43.5	57.0
1997	63.8	43.4	65.5	71.3	43.4	73.7	56.8	43.3	57.8
1998	64.1	45.1	65.6	71.6	44.7	73.9	57.1	45.5	58.0
1999	64.3	44.7	65.9	71.6	45.1	74.0	57.4	44.3	58.5
2000	64.4	45.2	66.0	71.9	45.4	74.2	57.5	45.0	58.4
2001	63.7	42.3	65.4	70.9	42.2	73.3	57.0	42.4	58.1
2002	62.7	39.6	64.6	69.7	38.9	72.3	56.3	40.3	57.5
2003	62.3	36.8	64.3	68.9	35.7	71.7	56.1	37.8	57.5
2004	62.3	36.4	64.4	69.2	35.9	71.9	56.0	37.0	57.4
2005	62.7	36.5	64.7	69.6	35.1	72.4	56.2	37.8	57.6
2006	63.1	36.9	65.2	70.1	36.3	72.9	56.6	37.6	58.0
2007	63.0	34.8	65.2	69.8	33.8	72.8	56.6	35.8	58.2
2008	62.2	32.6	64.5	68.5	31.6	71.6	56.2	33.7	57.9
2009	59.3	28.4	61.7	64.5	26.9	67.6	54.4	29.9	56.2
2010	58.5	25.9	61.0	63.7	24.8	66.8	53.6	27.0	55.5
2011	58.4	25.8	60.8	63.9	24.6	67.0	53.2	27.1	55.0
2012	58.6	26.1	61.0	64.4	24.9	67.5	53.1	27.3	55.0
2013	58.6	26.6	60.9	64.4	25.5	67.4	53.2	27.7	54.9
2014	59.0	27.3	61.3	64.9	26.3	67.8	53.5	28.4	55.2
2015	59.3	28.5	61.5	65.3	27.9	68.1	53.7	29.1	55.4
2016	59.7	29.7	61.8	65.8	29.3	68.5	54.1	30.1	55.7
2017	60.1	30.3	62.2	66.0	29.2	68.8	54.6	31.4	56.1
2018	60.4	30.6	62.5	66.3	29.3	69.0	54.9	31.9	56.4

Table 1-12. Civilian Employment-Population Ratios, by Sex, Age, Race, and Hispanic Origin, 1948–2018 —*Continued*

(Percent.)

Race, Hispanic origin, and year	Both sexes			Men			Women		
	16 years and over	16 to 19 years	20 years and over	16 years and over	16 to 19 years	20 years and over	16 years and over	16 to 19 years	20 years and over
WHITE									
1954	55.2	42.9	56.2	81.5	49.9	84.0	31.4	36.4	31.1
1955	56.5	44.2	57.4	82.2	52.0	84.7	33.0	37.0	32.7
1956	57.3	46.1	58.2	82.7	54.1	85.0	34.2	38.9	33.8
1957	56.8	45.0	57.8	81.8	52.4	84.1	34.2	38.2	33.9
1958	55.3	41.0	56.5	79.2	47.6	81.8	33.6	35.0	33.5
1959	55.9	41.2	57.2	79.9	48.1	82.8	34.0	34.8	34.0
1960	55.9	41.5	57.2	79.4	48.1	82.4	34.6	35.1	34.5
1961	55.3	40.1	56.7	78.2	45.9	81.4	34.5	34.6	34.5
1962	55.4	40.4	56.9	78.4	46.4	81.5	34.7	34.8	34.7
1963	55.3	38.6	56.9	77.7	44.7	81.1	35.0	32.9	35.2
1964	55.5	38.4	57.3	77.8	45.0	81.3	35.5	32.2	35.8
1965	56.0	40.3	57.8	77.9	47.1	81.5	36.2	33.7	36.5
1966	56.8	43.6	58.3	78.3	50.1	81.7	37.5	37.5	37.5
1967	57.2	43.8	58.7	78.4	50.2	81.7	38.3	37.7	38.3
1968	57.4	43.9	59.0	78.3	50.3	81.6	38.9	37.8	39.1
1969	58.0	45.2	59.4	78.2	51.1	81.4	40.1	39.5	40.1
1970	57.5	44.5	59.0	76.8	49.6	80.1	40.3	39.5	40.4
1971	56.8	43.8	58.3	75.7	49.2	79.0	39.9	38.6	40.1
1972	57.4	46.4	58.6	76.0	51.5	79.0	40.7	41.3	40.6
1973	58.2	48.9	59.3	76.5	54.3	79.2	41.8	43.6	41.6
1974	58.3	49.3	59.3	75.9	54.4	78.6	42.4	44.3	42.2
1975	56.7	46.5	57.9	73.0	50.6	75.7	42.0	42.5	41.9
1976	57.5	47.8	58.6	73.4	51.5	76.0	43.2	44.2	43.1
1977	58.6	50.1	59.6	74.1	54.4	76.5	44.5	45.9	44.4
1978	60.0	52.4	60.8	75.0	56.3	77.2	46.3	48.5	46.1
1979	60.6	52.6	61.5	75.1	55.7	77.3	47.5	49.4	47.3
1980	60.0	50.7	61.0	73.4	53.4	75.6	47.8	47.9	47.8
1981	60.0	48.7	61.1	72.8	51.3	75.1	48.3	46.2	48.5
1982	58.8	45.8	60.1	70.6	47.0	73.0	48.1	44.6	48.4
1983	58.9	45.9	60.1	70.4	47.4	72.6	48.5	44.5	48.9
1984	60.5	48.0	61.5	72.1	49.1	74.3	49.8	47.0	50.0
1985	61.0	48.5	62.0	72.3	49.9	74.3	50.7	47.1	51.0
1986	61.5	48.8	62.6	72.3	49.6	74.3	51.7	47.9	52.0
1987	62.3	49.4	63.4	72.7	49.9	74.7	52.8	49.0	53.1
1988	63.1	50.9	64.1	73.2	51.7	75.1	53.8	50.2	54.0
1989	63.8	51.6	64.7	73.7	52.6	75.4	54.6	50.5	54.9
1990	63.7	49.7	64.8	73.3	51.0	75.1	54.7	48.3	55.2
1991	62.6	46.6	63.7	71.6	47.2	73.5	54.2	45.9	54.8
1992	62.4	45.3	63.6	71.1	46.4	73.1	54.2	44.2	54.9
1993	62.7	46.2	63.9	71.4	46.6	73.3	54.6	45.7	55.2
1994	63.5	47.9	64.7	71.8	48.3	73.6	55.8	47.5	56.4
1995	63.8	48.8	64.9	72.0	49.4	73.8	56.1	48.1	56.7
1996	64.1	47.9	65.3	72.3	48.2	74.2	56.3	47.6	57.0
1997	64.6	47.7	65.9	72.7	48.1	74.7	57.0	47.2	57.8
1998	64.7	49.0	65.9	72.7	48.6	74.7	57.1	49.3	57.7
1999	64.8	48.9	66.1	72.8	49.3	74.8	57.3	48.4	58.0
2000	64.9	49.1	66.1	73.0	49.5	74.9	57.4	48.8	58.0
2001	64.2	46.3	65.6	72.0	46.2	74.0	57.0	46.5	57.7
2002	63.4	43.2	64.9	70.8	42.3	73.1	56.4	44.1	57.3
2003	63.0	40.4	64.7	70.1	39.4	72.5	56.3	41.5	57.3
2004	63.1	40.0	64.8	70.4	39.7	72.8	56.1	40.3	57.2
2005	63.4	40.2	65.1	70.8	38.8	73.3	56.3	41.8	57.4
2006	63.8	40.6	65.5	71.3	40.0	73.7	56.6	41.1	57.7
2007	63.6	38.3	65.5	70.9	37.3	73.5	56.7	39.2	57.9
2008	62.9	35.9	64.8	69.7	34.8	72.4	56.3	37.1	57.7
2009	60.2	31.7	62.3	66.0	30.2	68.7	54.8	33.4	56.2
2010	59.4	29.0	61.6	65.1	27.6	67.9	54.0	30.4	55.6
2011	59.4	28.8	61.6	65.3	27.3	68.2	53.7	30.4	55.3
2012	59.4	29.0	61.5	65.8	27.7	68.6	53.3	30.3	54.9
2013	59.4	29.4	61.4	65.7	28.3	68.4	53.3	30.5	54.8
2014	59.7	29.9	61.8	66.1	28.8	68.7	56.7	36.8	57.9
2015	59.9	31.0	61.8	66.5	30.8	68.9	53.7	31.3	55.1
2016	60.2	32.1	62.1	66.7	32.4	69.1	54.0	31.9	55.4
2017	60.4	32.3	62.3	66.9	31.7	69.3	54.2	33.0	55.6
2018	60.7	33.0	62.5	67.1	31.6	69.5	54.5	34.3	55.8

Table 1-12. Civilian Employment-Population Ratios, by Sex, Age, Race, and Hispanic Origin, 1948–2018 —*Continued*

(Percent.)

Race, Hispanic origin, and year	Both sexes			Men			Women		
	16 years and over	16 to 19 years	20 years and over	16 years and over	16 to 19 years	20 years and over	16 years and over	16 to 19 years	20 years and over
BLACK									
1985	53.4	24.6	57.0	60.0	26.3	64.6	48.1	23.1	50.9
1986	54.1	25.1	57.6	60.6	26.5	65.1	48.8	23.8	51.6
1987	55.6	27.1	58.9	62.0	28.5	66.4	50.3	25.8	53.0
1988	56.3	27.6	59.7	62.7	29.4	67.1	51.2	25.8	53.9
1989	56.9	28.7	60.1	62.8	30.4	67.0	52.0	27.1	54.6
1990	56.7	26.7	60.2	62.6	27.7	67.1	51.9	25.9	54.7
1991	55.4	22.6	59.0	61.3	23.8	66.0	50.6	21.4	53.6
1992	54.9	22.8	58.3	59.9	23.6	64.3	50.8	22.1	53.6
1993	55.0	22.7	58.4	60.0	23.6	64.3	50.9	21.6	53.8
1994	56.1	25.0	59.4	60.8	25.4	65.0	52.3	24.4	55.0
1995	57.1	25.7	60.6	61.7	25.2	66.1	53.4	26.1	56.1
1996	57.4	26.0	60.8	61.0	24.9	65.5	54.4	27.1	57.1
1997	58.2	26.2	61.8	61.4	23.7	66.1	55.6	28.5	58.4
1998	59.7	30.1	63.0	62.9	28.4	67.1	57.2	31.8	59.7
1999	60.6	27.9	64.2	63.1	26.7	67.5	58.6	29.0	61.5
2000	60.9	29.8	64.2	63.6	28.9	67.7	58.6	30.6	61.3
2001	59.7	26.7	63.2	62.1	26.4	66.3	57.8	27.0	60.7
2002	58.1	25.3	61.6	61.1	25.6	65.2	55.8	24.9	58.7
2003	57.4	21.7	61.0	59.5	19.9	64.1	55.6	23.5	58.6
2004	57.2	21.5	60.9	59.3	19.3	63.9	55.5	23.6	58.5
2005	57.7	21.6	61.5	60.2	20.8	64.7	55.7	22.4	58.9
2006	58.4	24.1	62.0	60.6	21.7	65.2	56.5	26.4	59.4
2007	58.4	21.4	62.3	60.7	19.5	65.5	56.5	23.3	59.8
2008	57.3	20.2	61.2	59.1	18.7	63.9	55.8	21.7	59.1
2009	53.2	16.5	57.1	53.7	14.3	58.2	52.8	18.6	56.1
2010	52.3	14.5	56.1	53.1	14.1	57.5	51.7	15.0	55.1
2011	51.7	14.6	55.3	52.8	14.6	56.9	50.8	14.7	54.0
2012	53.0	16.6	56.5	54.1	15.0	58.3	52.2	18.1	55.1
2013	53.2	17.1	56.5	54.5	15.0	58.6	52.0	19.1	54.8
2014	54.3	18.2	57.4	55.9	16.4	59.7	52.9	19.9	55.6
2015	55.7	20.1	58.7	57.2	18.2	60.9	54.4	22.0	56.9
2016	56.4	21.3	59.4	58.3	19.4	62.0	54.8	23.1	57.3
2017	57.6	22.8	60.6	59.4	19.3	63.1	56.1	26.2	58.5
2018	58.3	23.8	61.1	60.3	22.0	63.7	56.6	25.6	59.0
HISPANIC									
1985	57.8	. . .	. . .	72.1	. . .	. . .	43.8	. . .	. . .
1986	58.5	. . .	. . .	72.5	. . .	. . .	44.7	. . .	. . .
1987	60.5	. . .	. . .	74.0	. . .	. . .	47.4	. . .	. . .
1988	61.9	. . .	. . .	75.3	. . .	. . .	48.8	. . .	. . .
1989	62.2	. . .	. . .	75.8	. . .	. . .	48.8	. . .	. . .
1990	61.9	. . .	. . .	74.9	. . .	. . .	48.6	. . .	. . .
1991	59.8	. . .	. . .	72.1	. . .	. . .	47.3	. . .	. . .
1992	59.1	. . .	. . .	71.2	. . .	. . .	46.8	. . .	. . .
1993	59.1	. . .	. . .	71.7	. . .	. . .	46.3	. . .	. . .
1994	59.5	33.5	. . .	71.7	36.8	. . .	47.2	30.1	. . .
1995	59.7	34.4	. . .	72.1	37.5	. . .	47.3	31.3	. . .
1996	60.6	33.1	. . .	73.3	38.8	. . .	47.9	27.3	. . .
1997	62.6	33.7	. . .	74.5	37.6	. . .	50.2	29.3	. . .
1998	63.1	36.0	. . .	74.7	38.6	. . .	51.0	33.0	. . .
1999	63.4	37.0	. . .	75.3	41.2	. . .	51.7	32.5	. . .
2000	65.7	38.6	. . .	77.4	42.8	81.7	53.6	33.9	55.8
2001	64.9	38.6	. . .	76.2	43.3	79.9	53.3	33.5	55.4
2002	63.9	35.2	. . .	74.5	39.0	78.3	52.9	31.1	55.2
2003	63.1	30.2	66.4	74.3	31.9	78.6	51.2	28.4	53.6
2004	63.8	30.4	67.2	75.1	33.4	79.4	51.8	27.2	54.4
2005	64.0	31.5	67.3	75.8	33.8	80.0	51.5	29.1	53.8
2006	65.2	32.2	68.5	76.8	34.8	81.1	52.8	29.5	55.2
2007	64.9	30.4	68.5	76.2	32.1	80.7	53.0	28.5	55.6
2008	63.3	28.6	66.9	74.1	30.9	78.6	51.9	26.2	54.6
2009	59.7	23.7	63.5	68.9	24.1	73.5	50.1	23.4	52.9
2010	59.0	21.0	63.1	68.0	21.7	72.9	49.6	20.2	52.7
2011	58.9	19.5	63.2	67.9	20.1	73.3	49.3	18.9	52.5
2012	59.5	22.1	63.6	68.6	22.9	73.8	50.4	21.2	53.5
2013	60.0	22.5	64.1	69.6	23.5	74.7	50.4	21.4	53.5
2014	61.2	23.5	65.2	71.0	24.2	76.0	51.4	22.7	54.3
2015	61.6	24.9	65.4	71.5	25.8	76.3	51.8	23.9	54.6
2016	62.0	25.9	65.7	71.9	26.4	76.6	52.3	25.3	55.0
2017	62.7	27.1	66.3	72.3	26.6	77.1	53.2	27.6	55.8
2018	63.2	27.8	66.8	72.4	27.3	77.1	54.1	28.3	56.6

. . . = Not available.

Table 1-13. Employed Civilians, by Sex, Race, Hispanic Origin, and Occupation, 2016–2018

(Thousands of people.)

Year and occupation	Total	Men	Women	White	Black	Hispanic[1]
2016						
All Occupations	151 436	80 568	70 868	119 313	17 982	25 249
Management, professional, and related occupations	59 438	28 846	30 593	47 729	5 421	5 551
Management, business, and financial operations occupations	24 941	14 019	10 922	20 664	2 036	2 456
Computer and mathematical occupations	4 601	3 428	1 173	3 122	362	315
Architecture and engineering occupations	3 106	2 665	441	2 499	2 168	273
Life, physical and social science occupations	1 367	765	602	1 032	88	112
Community and social service occupations	2 612	901	1 711	1 944	486	317
Legal occupations	1 808	871	936	1 590	114	151
Education, training, and library occupations	8 948	2 410	6 538	7 405	896	895
Arts, design, entertainment, sports, and media occupations	3 097	1 596	1 502	2 632	204	329
Healthcare practitioner and technical occupations	8 960	2 190	6 769	6 842	1 060	703
Healthcare support occupations	3 554	438	3 116	2 252	971	601
Protective service occupations	3 117	2 423	694	2 296	594	438
Food preparation and serving related occupations	8 542	3 969	4 573	6 470	1 175	2 200
Building and grounds cleaning and maintenance occupations	5 804	3 478	2 326	4 542	847	2 217
Personal care and service occupations	5 795	1 318	4 477	4 084	923	947
Sales and related occupations	15 848	8 088	7 761	12 675	1 742	2 486
Office and administrative support occupations	17 691	4 936	12 755	13 736	2 488	2 758
Farming, fishing, and forestry occupations	1 096	852	244	990	53	493
Construction and extraction occupations	7 929	7 693	236	6 989	535	2 696
Installation, maintenance, and repair occupations	4 879	4 703	177	4 118	429	929
Production occupations	8 459	6 073	2 385	6 577	1 092	8 459
Transportation and material moving occupations	9 284	7 753	1 531	6 855	1 711	9 284
2017						
All Occupations	153 337	81 402	71 936	120 176	18 587	25 938
Management, professional, and related occupations	60 901	29 488	31 413	48 748	5 719	5 826
Management, business, and financial operations occupations	25 379	14 207	11 171	21 065	2 075	2 532
Computer and mathematical occupations	4 804	3 578	1 226	3 258	416	352
Architecture and engineering occupations	3 224	2 702	521	2 556	182	281
Life, physical and social science occupations	1 431	753	678	1 093	81	129
Community and social service occupations	2 635	893	1 742	1 925	524	326
Legal occupations	1 827	862	965	1 582	126	157
Education, training, and library occupations	9 215	2 486	6 729	7 553	987	967
Arts, design, entertainment, sports, and media occupations	3 246	1 723	1 523	2 722	237	332
Healthcare practitioner and technical occupations	9 141	2 285	6 857	6 994	1 091	751
Healthcare support occupations	3 506	451	3 055	2 301	879	661
Protective service occupations	3 113	2 418	694	2 261	638	399
Food preparation and serving related occupations	8 305	3 840	4 465	6 179	1 155	2 117
Building and grounds cleaning and maintenance occupations	5 888	3 491	2 397	4 560	875	2 235
Personal care and service occupations	5 939	1 421	4 518	4 127	955	1 016
Sales and related occupations	15 815	8 045	7 770	12 640	1 756	2 515
Office and administrative support occupations	17 751	4 929	12 823	13 717	2 593	2 824
Farming, fishing, and forestry occupations	1 184	907	278	1 058	58	524
Construction and extraction occupations	8 031	7 788	243	7 050	554	2 890
Installation, maintenance, and repair occupations	4 977	4 778	200	4 232	149	946
Production occupations	8 482	6 031	2 450	6 514	1 132	1 935
Transportation and material moving occupations	9 445	7 815	1 630	6 790	1 844	2 051
2018						
All Occupations	155 761	82 698	73 063	121 461	19 091	27 012
Management, professional, and related occupations	62 436	30 287	32 149	49 555	5 982	6 048
Management, business, and financial operations occupations	25 850	14 464	11 387	21 309	2 127	2 535
Computer and mathematical occupations	5 126	3 814	1 313	3 436	431	382
Architecture and engineering occupations	3 263	2 745	518	2 588	211	290
Life, physical and social science occupations	1 529	815	714	1 194	108	133
Community and social service occupations	2 680	898	1 783	1 925	546	325
Legal occupations	1 891	915	976	1 620	139	187
Education, training, and library occupations	9 313	2 495	6 819	7 588	987	995
Arts, design, entertainment, sports, and media occupations	3 362	1 790	1 572	2 812	247	397
Healthcare practitioner and technical occupations	9 420	2 352	7 068	7 083	1 183	803
Healthcare support occupations	3 629	469	3 161	2 333	952	665
Protective service occupations	3 203	2 483	720	2 353	645	441
Food preparation and serving related occupations	8 220	3 655	4 565	6 014	1 214	2 126
Building and grounds cleaning and maintenance occupations	5 854	3 434	2 421	4 526	869	2 273
Personal care and service occupations	5 947	1 375	4 572	4 118	972	1 059
Sales and related occupations	15 806	7 999	7 807	12 677	1 738	2 582
Office and administrative support occupations	17 655	5 010	12 646	13 614	2 543	2 976
Farming, fishing, and forestry occupations	1 121	848	273	1 007	42	516
Construction and extraction occupations	8 338	8 053	285	7 294	590	3 088
Installation, maintenance, and repair occupations	5 012	4 825	187	4 180	473	1 006
Production occupations	8 621	6 140	2 480	6 604	1 167	2 021
Transportation and material moving occupations	9 918	8 121	1 797	7 186	1 903	2 213

[1]May be of any race.

Table 1-14. Employed Civilians, by Selected Occupation and Industry, 2016–2018

(Thousands of people.)

Year and occupation	Total employed	Agriculture, forestry, fishing, and hunting	Mining	Construction	Manufacturing			Wholesale trade
					Total	Durable goods	Nondurable goods	
2016								
All Occupations	151 436	2 460	792	10 328	15 408	9 704	5 704	3 641
Management, professional, and related occupations	59 438	1 136	291	2 050	4 860	3 325	1 535	741
Management, business, and financial operations occupations	24 941	1 083	157	1 784	2 673	1 731	942	575
Computer and mathematical occupations	4 601	3	24	25	449	352	97	73
Architecture and engineering occupations	3 106	4	70	178	1 162	989	173	26
Life, physical and social science occupations	1 367	33	32	4	256	44	212	9
Community and social service occupations	2 612	4	0	0	3	3	0	2
Legal occupations	1 808	0	3	6	42	25	17	4
Education, training, and library occupations	8 948	4	1	5	33	24	9	6
Arts, design, entertainment, sports, and media occupations	3 097	3	3	40	203	137	66	35
Healthcare practitioner and technical occupations	8 960	1	3	7	39	20	19	11
Healthcare support occupations	3 554	1	0	1	10	8	2	1
Protective service occupations	3 117	14	2	13	29	16	14	3
Food preparation and serving related occupations	8 542	4	2	7	62	7	54	12
Building and grounds cleaning and maintenance occupations	5 804	36	6	47	150	70	81	25
Personal care and service occupations	5 795	53	...	3	11	7	4	5 795
Sales and related occupations	15 848	15	13	103	639	324	315	1 337
Office and administrative support occupations	17 691	88	49	483	1 296	789	507	569
Farming, fishing, and forestry occupations	1 096	945	...	3	59	6	53	33
Construction and extraction occupations	7 929	11	231	6 657	303	240	63	21
Installation, maintenance, and repair occupations	4 879	38	52	559	634	411	223	130
Production occupations	8 459	36	62	151	6 098	3 828	2 270	101
Transportation and material moving occupations	9 284	84	84	252	1 258	674	584	666
2017								
All Occupations	153 337	2 454	748	10 692	15 408	9 698	5 710	3 594
Management, professional, and related occupations	60 901	1 108	257	2 249	4 899	3 316	1 583	686
Management, business, and financial operations occupations	25 379	1 056	146	1 984	2 645	1 692	952	513
Computer and mathematical occupations	4 804	4	19	27	475	369	106	64
Architecture and engineering occupations	3 224	4	60	178	1 182	989	193	31
Life, physical and social science occupations	1 431	31	21	5	260	53	207	9
Community and social service occupations	2 635	1	...	0	3	2	0	2
Legal occupations	1 827	3	6	6	35	22	13	10
Education, training, and library occupations	9 215	1	1	4	31	20	11	11
Arts, design, entertainment, sports, and media occupations	3 246	5	2	41	230	150	80	23
Healthcare practitioner and technical occupations	9 141	3	2	4	39	19	20	23
Healthcare support occupations	3 506	1	0	1	10	7	3	2
Protective service occupations	3 113	14	4	15	36	25	12	3
Food preparation and serving related occupations	8 305	3	2	5	58	8	50	9
Building and grounds cleaning and maintenance occupations	5 888	41	3	40	133	69	64	21
Personal care and service occupations	5 939	32	0	2	15	6	9	2
Sales and related occupations	15 815	18	11	111	608	296	312	1 304
Office and administrative support occupations	17 751	80	52	492	1 292	823	469	542
Farming, fishing, and forestry occupations	1 184	1 001	1	5	61	5	56	52
Construction and extraction occupations	8 031	11	235	6 769	304	234	71	22
Installation, maintenance, and repair occupations	4 977	30	55	612	675	434	241	126
Production occupations	8 482	24	47	161	6 078	3 823	2 255	122
Transportation and material moving occupations	9 445	90	81	232	1 239	654	585	701
2018								
All Occupations	155 761	2 425	784	11 181	15 560	9 831	5 729	3 671
Management, professional, and related occupations	62 436	1 072	253	2 451	4 927	3 311	1 616	695
Management, business, and financial operations occupations	25 850	1 032	144	2 149	2 630	1 661	969	516
Computer and mathematical occupations	5 126	3	13	32	473	375	98	75
Architecture and engineering occupations	3 263	6	55	201	1 229	1 028	200	37
Life, physical and social science occupations	1 529	24	30	10	253	46	207	12
Community and social service occupations	2 680	3	...	0	4	1	3	0
Legal occupations	1 891	1	5	7	26	15	10	8
Education, training, and library occupations	9 313	2	3	5	23	12	11	7
Arts, design, entertainment, sports, and media occupations	3 362	1	1	42	223	137	86	25
Healthcare practitioner and technical occupations	9 420	1	1	6	67	35	32	14
Healthcare support occupations	3 629	0	0	1	11	9	2	5
Protective service occupations	3 203	14	4	18	26	12	14	6
Food preparation and serving related occupations	8 220	9	1	4	70	14	57	13
Building and grounds cleaning and maintenance occupations	5 854	31	8	38	141	64	76	30
Personal care and service occupations	5 947	44	0	6	16	6	10	2
Sales and related occupations	15 806	15	11	124	602	313	289	1 297
Office and administrative support occupations	17 655	83	51	543	1 243	783	460	557
Farming, fishing, and forestry occupations	1 121	966	0	3	56	4	52	33
Construction and extraction occupations	8 338	15	246	6 992	313	246	67	27
Installation, maintenance, and repair occupations	5 012	36	55	585	710	441	269	126
Production occupations	8 621	41	51	185	6 103	3 872	2 231	133
Transportation and material moving occupations	9 918	15	...	18	1 344	757	587	747

... = Not available.

Table 1-14. Employed Civilians, by Selected Occupation and Industry, 2016–2018—*Continued*

(Thousands of people.)

Year and occupation	Retail trade	Transportation and warehousing	Utilities	Information	Finance and insurance	Real estate and rental and leasing	Professional and technical services
2016							
All Occupations	16 577	6 693	1 319	2 855	7 241	3 163	11 228
Management, professional, and related occupations	1 969	760	456	1 685	4 095	1 075	9 160
Management, business, and financial operations occupations	990	610	248	608	3 327	987	3 619
Computer and mathematical occupations	172	67	55	294	509	25	1 860
Architecture and engineering occupations	23	45	99	103	17	10	1 044
Life, physical and social science occupations	3	3	24	5	8	1	343
Community and social service occupations	2	1	0	3	30	5	21
Legal occupations	17	4	7	10	72	34	1 205
Education, training, and library occupations	23	11	5	104	30	3	51
Arts, design, entertainment, sports, and media occupations	208	14	15	553	29	9	734
Healthcare practitioner and technical occupations	530	5	2	4	72	4	283
Healthcare support occupations	37	2	1	2	5	4	48
Protective service occupations	65	20	8	6	43	25	25
Food preparation and serving related occupations	408	11	2	32	10	18	8
Building and grounds cleaning and maintenance occupations	158	55	18	16	26	228	33
Personal care and service occupations	53	...	3	11	7	4	38
Sales and related occupations	8 871	61	33	337	1 151	1 087	325
Office and administrative support occupations	2 660	1 479	195	401	1 849	330	1 251
Farming, fishing, and forestry occupations	10	1	0	...	0	1	5
Construction and extraction occupations	68	69	117	8	3	49	65
Installation, maintenance, and repair occupations	621	301	217	266	19	187	88
Production occupations	441	107	223	33	20	22	129
Transportation and material moving occupations	1 211	3 789	49	42	14	104	51
2017							
All Occupations	16 720	6 810	1 349	2 903	7 288	3 194	11 764
Management, professional, and related occupations	2 020	762	493	1 698	4 182	1 124	9 548
Management, business, and financial operations occupations	984	610	265	564	3 363	1 036	3 774
Computer and mathematical occupations	200	69	57	301	537	23	2 004
Architecture and engineering occupations	26	40	112	95	21	12	1 109
Life, physical and social science occupations	4	1	31	4	14	3	369
Community and social service occupations	1	1	1	2	30	6	20
Legal occupations	13	8	6	13	82	20	1 206
Education, training, and library occupations	29	11	9	124	18	1	39
Arts, design, entertainment, sports, and media occupations	215	18	9	590	36	16	761
Healthcare practitioner and technical occupations	548	3	3	6	80	8	265
Healthcare support occupations	42	2	0	0	7	3	69
Protective service occupations	66	20	14	6	43	19	25
Food preparation and serving related occupations	392	22	1	27	6	20	10
Building and grounds cleaning and maintenance occupations	143	60	16	15	19	227	28
Personal care and service occupations	59	50	0	30	7	37	40
Sales and related occupations	8 824	100	23	330	1 168	1 116	366
Office and administrative support occupations	2 776	1 464	189	428	1 790	323	1 322
Farming, fishing, and forestry occupations	10	2	2	0	...	0	4
Construction and extraction occupations	73	66	110	13	8	42	56
Installation, maintenance, and repair occupations	582	352	191	279	23	163	78
Production occupations	456	114	259	40	25	16	145
Transportation and material moving occupations	1 276	3 797	50	37	10	105	74
2018							
All Occupations	16 599	7 207	1 345	2 919	7 376	3 273	12 105
Management, professional, and related occupations	1 971	809	520	1 770	4 321	1 144	9 913
Management, business, and financial operations occupations	940	629	282	611	3 456	1 042	3 780
Computer and mathematical occupations	209	81	72	319	548	33	2 237
Architecture and engineering occupations	27	42	111	90	21	17	1 070
Life, physical and social science occupations	8	4	29	7	14	...	378
Community and social service occupations	1	2	...	4	26	5	17
Legal occupations	13	12	5	13	104	27	1 252
Education, training, and library occupations	30	18	1	113	27	3	50
Arts, design, entertainment, sports, and media occupations	203	16	16	607	49	12	833
Healthcare practitioner and technical occupations	541	6	4	5	77	5	296
Healthcare support occupations	36	4	...	0	7	4	59
Protective service occupations	55	20	10	6	36	17	24
Food preparation and serving related occupations	366	24	1	28	6	22	4
Building and grounds cleaning and maintenance occupations	162	70	12	10	20	213	31
Personal care and service occupations	57	54	0	29	7	29	43
Sales and related occupations	8 766	99	31	319	1 185	1 196	396
Office and administrative support occupations	2 678	1 547	182	379	1 731	329	1 245
Farming, fishing, and forestry occupations	13	0	1	...	...	...	2
Construction and extraction occupations	74	76	109	14	6	56	76
Installation, maintenance, and repair occupations	577	366	194	291	18	143	89
Production occupations	472	135	242	33	29	14	141
Transportation and material moving occupations	1 372	4 003	41	39	9	106	82

... = Not available.

Table 1-14. Employed Civilians, by Selected Occupation and Industry, 2016–2018—*Continued*

(Thousands of people.)

Year and occupation	Management, administrative, and waste services	Educational services	Health care and social assistance	Arts, entertainment, and recreation	Accommodation and food services	Other services (except public administration)	Public administration
2016							
All Occupations	7 097	13 674	20 589	3 241	10 952	7 320	6 857
Management, professional, and related occupations	1 425	10 732	11 437	1 144	1 700	1 705	3 020
Management, business, and financial operations occupations	1 026	1 503	1 812	292	1 598	744	1 305
Computer and mathematical occupations	125	267	224	32	23	60	312
Architecture and engineering occupations	37	47	36	13	8	10	173
Life, physical and social science occupations	16	210	217	10	1	15	178
Community and social service occupations	13	373	1 127	10	6	662	348
Legal occupations	30	14	17	7	3	12	319
Education, training, and library occupations	24	7 749	665	84	31	53	68
Arts, design, entertainment, sports, and media occupations	62	250	54	685	24	115	60
Healthcare practitioner and technical occupations	90	318	7 285	10	6	32	257
Healthcare support occupations	54	34	3 149	24	5	141	35
Protective service occupations	554	127	78	171	35	20	1 879
Food preparation and serving related occupations	22	430	438	254	6 729	64	29
Building and grounds cleaning and maintenance occupations	2 594	552	453	252	541	478	135
Personal care and service occupations	26	267	2 043	842	102	2 080	161
Sales and related occupations	278	46	75	170	909	358	38
Office and administrative support occupations	1 057	1 039	2 508	215	469	590	1 164
Farming, fishing, and forestry occupations	13	1	0	4	1	2	18
Construction and extraction occupations	101	54	30	20	18	15	88
Installation, maintenance, and repair occupations	210	112	99	59	55	1 103	131
Production occupations	220	30	141	20	114	441	69
Transportation and material moving occupations	540	251	138	66	274	324	89
2017							
All Occupations	7 072	13 763	20 720	3 399	10 891	7 485	7 083
Management, professional, and related occupations	1 422	10 849	11 754	1 252	1 763	1 671	3 163
Management, business, and financial operations occupations	1 067	1 453	1 856	358	1 660	695	1 351
Computer and mathematical occupations	111	276	225	27	14	51	319
Architecture and engineering occupations	38	55	34	11	5	19	193
Life, physical and social science occupations	13	221	223	13	1	20	189
Community and social service occupations	14	366	1 155	9	5	638	381
Legal occupations	32	12	25	8	2	16	321
Education, training, and library occupations	28	7 883	726	108	42	64	84
Arts, design, entertainment, sports, and media occupations	40	272	56	708	22	133	69
Healthcare practitioner and technical occupations	80	311	7 454	10	12	36	255
Healthcare support occupations	52	39	3 060	19	7	151	41
Protective service occupations	532	121	60	160	41	27	1 905
Food preparation and serving related occupations	28	369	387	256	6 634	48	29
Building and grounds cleaning and maintenance occupations	2 780	558	474	255	506	440	127
Personal care and service occupations	32	263	2 023	888	99	2 232	127
Sales and related occupations	278	39	61	159	882	385	31
Office and administrative support occupations	957	1 041	2 497	239	469	603	1 195
Farming, fishing, and forestry occupations	14	1	3	4	1	2	21
Construction and extraction occupations	75	52	30	20	16	24	105
Installation, maintenance, and repair occupations	225	114	87	64	46	1 110	165
Production occupations	166	34	134	19	120	442	80
Transportation and material moving occupations	511	283	149	62	305	349	94
2018							
All Occupations	6 845	13 910	21 133	3 362	10 905	7 742	7 419
Management, professional, and related occupations	1 374	11 047	12 041	1 217	1 862	1 709	3 339
Management, business, and financial operations occupations	997	1 483	1 898	348	1 747	713	1 451
Computer and mathematical occupations	112	238	261	29	23	50	318
Architecture and engineering occupations	46	44	33	13	6	12	204
Life, physical and social science occupations	22	257	231	10	5	17	219
Community and social service occupations	17	382	1 173	7	5	652	383
Legal occupations	19	11	21	5	3	13	349
Education, training, and library occupations	28	8 032	692	89	42	56	92
Arts, design, entertainment, sports, and media occupations	52	280	53	705	20	159	65
Healthcare practitioner and technical occupations	82	319	7 678	11	12	38	257
Healthcare support occupations	53	31	3 207	23	4	137	48
Protective service occupations	597	116	67	171	34	29	1 954
Food preparation and serving related occupations	31	382	384	269	6 522	50	34
Building and grounds cleaning and maintenance occupations	2 664	534	460	234	500	559	138
Personal care and service occupations	24	255	1 985	879	98	2 254	163
Sales and related occupations	252	43	67	149	858	363	35
Office and administrative support occupations	905	1 009	2 516	244	539	638	1 238
Farming, fishing, and forestry occupations	11	2	1	5	1	3	23
Construction and extraction occupations	85	46	31	30	15	16	111
Installation, maintenance, and repair occupations	193	119	97	61	46	1 153	153
Production occupations	162	38	143	17	111	490	79
Transportation and material moving occupations	493	288	134	64	316	343	105

Table 1-15. Employed Civilians in Agriculture and Nonagricultural Industries, by Class of Worker and Sex, 1995–2018

(Thousands of people.)

Sex and year	Total employed	Agriculture				Nonagricultural industries							
		Total	Wage and salary workers	Self-employed workers	Unpaid family workers	Total employed	Wage and salary workers					Self-employed workers	Unpaid family workers
							Total	Govern-ment	Private household	Other industries except private households			
Both Sexes													
1995	124 900	3 440	1 814	1 580	45	121 460	112 448	18 362	963	93 123		8 902	110
1996	126 707	3 443	1 869	1 518	56	123 264	114 171	18 217	928	95 026		8 971	122
1997	129 558	3 399	1 890	1 457	51	126 159	116 983	18 131	915	97 937		9 056	120
1998	131 463	3 378	2 000	1 341	38	128 085	119 019	18 383	962	99 674		8 962	103
1999	133 488	3 281	1 944	1 297	40	130 207	121 323	18 903	933	101 487		8 790	95
2000	136 891	2 464	1 421	1 010	33	134 427	125 114	19 248	718	105 148		9 205	108
2001	136 933	2 299	1 283	988	28	134 635	125 407	19 335	694	105 378		9 121	107
2002	136 485	2 311	1 282	1 003	26	134 174	125 156	19 636	757	104 764		8 923	95
2003	137 736	2 275	1 299	951	25	135 461	126 015	19 634	764	105 616		9 344	101
2004	139 252	2 232	1 242	964	27	137 020	127 463	19 983	779	106 701		9 467	90
2005	141 730	2 197	1 212	955	30	139 532	129 931	20 357	812	108 761		9 509	93
2006	144 427	2 206	1 287	901	18	142 221	132 449	20 337	803	111 309		9 685	87
2007	146 047	2 095	1 220	856	19	143 952	134 283	21 003	813	112 467		9 557	112
2008	145 362	2 168	1 279	860	28	143 194	133 882	21 258	805	111 819		9 219	93
2009	139 877	2 103	1 242	836	25	137 775	128 713	21 178	783	106 752		836	25
2010	139 064	2 206	1 353	821	33	136 858	127 914	21 003	667	106 244		8 860	84
2011	139 869	2 254	1 380	846	28	137 615	128 934	20 536	722	107 676		8 603	78
2012	142 469	2 186	1 377	780	29	140 283	131 452	20 360	738	110 355		8 749	81
2013	143 929	2 130	1 310	789	31	141 799	133 111	20 247	723	112 141		8 619	70
2014	146 305	2 237	1 459	756	22	144 068	135 402	20 135	820	114 446		8 602	64
2015	148 834	2 422	1 547	844	32	146 411	137 678	20 601	798	116 279		8 665	68
2016	151 436	2 460	1 583	853	23	148 976	140 161	20 630	724	118 807		8 751	65
2017	153 337	2 454	1 640	790	24	150 883	142 096	20 835	657	120 603		8 736	52
2018	155 761	2 425	1 632	766	27	153 336	144 326	20 942	777	122 607		8 941	69
Men													
1995	67 377	2 559	1 395	1 138	26	64 818	59 332	8 267	96	50 969		5 461	25
1996	68 207	2 573	1 418	1 124	31	65 634	60 133	8 110	99	51 924		5 465	36
1997	69 685	2 552	1 439	1 084	29	67 133	61 595	8 015	81	53 499		5 506	31
1998	70 693	2 553	1 526	1 005	23	68 140	62 630	8 178	86	54 366		5 480	29
1999	71 446	2 432	1 450	962	20	69 014	63 624	8 278	74	55 272		5 366	25
2000	73 305	1 861	1 116	725	20	71 444	65 838	8 309	71	57 458		5 573	33
2001	73 196	1 708	990	703	15	71 488	65 930	8 342	63	57 524		5 527	31
2002	72 903	1 724	979	731	14	71 179	65 726	8 437	76	57 212		5 425	29
2003	73 332	1 695	991	694	11	71 636	65 871	8 368	59	57 444		5 736	30
2004	74 525	1 687	970	702	15	72 838	66 951	8 616	60	58 275		5 860	27
2005	75 973	1 654	949	688	17	74 319	68 345	8 760	67	59 518		5 944	30
2006	77 502	1 663	989	664	10	75 838	69 811	8 696	60	61 055		6 004	23
2007	78 254	1 604	973	623	8	76 650	70 697	9 022	76	61 599		5 920	32
2008	77 486	1 650	997	637	16	75 836	70 072	9 089	70	60 912		5 736	29
2009	73 670	1 607	977	613	17	72 062	66 517	9 013	74	57 430		5 527	19
2010	73 359	1 665	1 051	598	17	71 694	66 189	9 059	60	57 070		5 472	33
2011	74 290	1 698	1 050	632	16	72 592	67 306	8 922	78	58 307		5 262	24
2012	75 555	1 626	1 048	562	16	73 930	68 629	8 760	82	59 786		5 266	34
2013	76 353	1 611	1 020	571	20	74 742	69 606	8 799	62	60 744		5 111	25
2014	77 692	1 685	1 119	554	12	76 007	70 828	8 633	64	62 131		5 158	22
2015	79 131	1 826	1 194	615	17	77 305	72 016	8 870	58	63 088		5 269	21
2016	80 568	1 839	1 211	614	14	78 729	73 342	8 890	60	64 392		5 366	22
2017	81 402	1 843	1 263	568	13	79 559	74 352	9 043	55	65 255		5 191	15
2018	82 698	1 797	1 236	542	19	80 902	75 456	9 016	53	66 387		5 423	22
Women													
1995	57 523	881	419	442	20	56 642	53 115	10 095	867	42 153		3 440	86
1996	58 501	871	452	394	25	57 630	54 037	10 107	830	43 100		3 506	87
1997	59 873	847	451	373	23	59 026	55 388	10 116	834	44 438		3 550	89
1998	60 770	825	474	336	15	59 945	56 389	10 205	876	45 308		3 482	74
1999	62 042	849	494	335	20	61 193	57 699	10 625	859	46 215		3 424	70
2000	63 586	602	305	285	12	62 983	59 277	10 939	647	47 690		3 631	76
2001	63 737	591	293	284	13	63 147	59 477	10 993	630	47 853		3 594	75
2002	63 582	587	303	272	12	62 995	59 431	11 199	680	47 552		3 499	66
2003	64 404	580	309	257	14	63 824	60 144	11 267	705	48 172		3 609	72
2004	64 728	546	271	262	12	64 182	60 512	11 367	719	48 426		3 607	63
2005	65 757	544	263	267	13	65 213	61 586	11 598	745	49 243		3 565	63
2006	66 925	543	298	237	8	66 382	62 638	11 641	742	50 254		3 681	64
2007	67 792	490	247	233	11	67 302	63 586	11 981	737	50 868		3 637	80
2008	67 876	518	282	224	12	67 358	63 810	12 169	735	50 907		3 483	65
2009	66 208	496	265	223	8	65 712	62 197	12 165	709	49 322		3 468	47
2010	65 705	541	302	223	16	65 164	61 725	11 944	607	49 174		3 388	51
2011	65 579	556	330	214	12	65 023	61 628	11 614	644	49 370		3 341	54
2012	66 914	560	329	218	13	66 353	62 824	11 600	656	50 568		3 483	47
2013	67 577	519	290	218	11	67 058	63 505	11 447	661	51 396		3 508	45
2014	68 613	552	340	202	10	68 061	64 574	11 502	757	52 316		3 444	43
2015	69 703	597	353	229	14	69 106	65 663	11 731	741	53 191		3 396	48
2016	70 868	621	372	239	10	70 247	66 819	11 740	664	54 415		3 385	43
2017	71 936	611	378	222	11	71 324	67 743	11 793	602	55 349		3 544	37
2018	73 063	628	396	224	9	72 435	68 870	11 926	725	56 220		3 518	47

Table 1-16. Number of Employed Persons Age 25 Years and Over, by Educational Attainment, Sex, Race, and Hispanic Origin, 2007–2018

(Thousands of people.)

Race, Hispanic origin, sex, and year	Total	Less than a high school diploma	High school graduate, no college	Some college, no degree	Associate's degree	College graduate or higher	
						Total	Bachelor's degree only
Both Sexes							
2007	126 172	11 521	36 857	22 076	12 535	43 182	28 055
2008	126 161	11 073	36 097	22 092	12 948	43 951	28 460
2009	122 277	10 371	34 487	21 016	12 872	43 531	27 964
2010	121 987	10 115	34 293	20 838	12 910	43 832	27 977
2011	122 507	9 967	33 823	20 712	13 182	44 822	28 333
2012	124 635	9 923	33 718	20 936	13 770	46 288	29 371
2013	125 872	9 798	33 619	20 914	14 011	47 531	30 140
2014	127 863	9 852	33 865	21 159	14 139	48 848	30 789
2015	130 077	10 098	33 402	21 573	14 213	50 792	31 772
2016	132 444	9 884	33 801	21 668	14 718	52 374	32 475
2017	134 132	9 668	34 210	21 440	14 842	53 971	33 620
2018	136 584	9 701	34 550	21 128	15 209	55 995	35 026
Men							
2007	67 963	7 450	20 434	11 382	5 862	22 835	14 680
2008	67 605	7 108	20 093	11 356	6 021	23 027	14 845
2009	64 831	6 569	19 085	10 772	5 864	22 541	14 368
2010	64 765	6 434	19 159	10 737	5 829	22 606	14 359
2011	65 356	6 388	19 059	10 741	6 029	23 138	14 637
2012	66 455	6 309	19 192	10 862	6 364	23 729	15 024
2013	67 163	6 335	19 103	10 946	6 446	24 333	15 487
2014	68 284	6 410	19 403	11 151	6 531	24 791	15 706
2015	69 604	6 573	19 302	11 293	6 660	25 776	16 323
2016	70 872	6 354	19 691	11 311	6 928	26 588	16 670
2017	71 638	6 129	20 013	11 355	6 969	27 172	17 137
2018	73 021	6 201	20 294	11 279	7 182	28 066	17 803
Women							
2007	58 209	4 071	16 423	10 695	6 674	20 346	13 375
2008	58 555	3 965	16 004	10 737	6 926	20 924	13 614
2009	57 445	3 802	15 402	10 244	7 008	20 990	13 597
2010	57 222	3 681	15 134	10 101	7 080	21 226	13 618
2011	57 151	3 579	14 764	9 971	7 153	21 684	13 697
2012	58 180	3 614	14 527	10 074	7 405	22 559	14 347
2013	58 710	3 463	14 516	9 968	7 565	23 198	14 653
2014	59 579	3 442	14 462	10 009	7 609	24 057	15 083
2015	60 474	3 525	14 100	10 280	7 553	25 016	15 449
2016	61 572	3 530	14 110	10 357	7 790	25 786	15 805
2017	62 494	3 540	14 197	10 085	7 873	26 799	16 483
2018	63 563	3 501	14 256	9 850	8 028	27 929	17 223
White[1]							
2007	103 477	9 446	30 140	17 936	10 419	35 535	23 138
2008	103 373	9 036	29 495	17 873	10 742	36 228	23 511
2009	100 419	8 497	28 372	16 983	10 714	35 854	23 109
2010	100 100	8 290	28 128	16 800	10 707	36 176	23 179
2011	100 426	8 248	27 568	16 713	10 922	36 975	23 533
2012	100 543	8 100	27 112	16 594	11 260	37 476	23 942
2013	101 046	7 885	27 049	16 425	11 460	38 228	24 419
2014	102 245	7 895	27 132	16 556	11 556	39 106	24 879
2015	103 336	8 128	26 508	16 820	11 501	40 380	25 395
2016	104 624	7 879	26 623	16 786	11 881	41 454	25 967
2017	105 449	7 690	26 710	16 515	11 872	42 662	26 986
2018	106 704	7 713	26 870	16 281	12 067	43 772	27 708
Black[1]							
2007	13 811	1 293	4 783	2 912	1 389	3 435	2 362
2008	13 786	1 234	4 719	2 972	1 439	3 423	2 354
2009	13 110	1 096	4 375	2 855	1 422	3 363	2 253
2010	13 092	1 103	4 234	2 864	1 482	3 409	2 260
2011	13 097	1 013	4 298	2 792	1 519	3 474	2 257
2012	13 717	1 016	4 397	2 919	1 584	3 801	2 479
2013	13 985	1 064	4 343	3 034	1 583	3 961	2 582
2014	14 437	1 084	4 442	3 119	1 674	4 117	2 623
2015	15 017	1 033	4 549	3 242	1 775	4 418	2 850
2016	15 517	1 069	4 737	4 737	1 817	4 612	2 942
2017	16 031	1 038	4 889	3 335	1 894	4 874	3 050
2018	16 556	1 009	4 986	3 276	1 994	5 291	3 395
Hispanic[2]							
2007	16 973	5 677	5 110	2 382	1 160	2 644	1 898
2008	17 115	5 426	5 232	2 484	1 236	2 736	1 930
2009	18 642	6 064	5 658	2 670	1 357	2 894	2 063
2010	16 946	5 183	5 175	2 474	1 252	2 862	2 025
2011	17 059	5 156	5 216	2 513	1 317	2 857	1 982
2012	18 309	5 269	5 613	2 734	1 482	3 210	2 221
2013	18 836	5 297	5 754	2 781	1 543	3 460	2 428
2014	19 686	5 365	5 954	2 990	1 636	3 741	2 648
2015	20 450	5 592	6 064	3 119	1 739	3 936	2 694
2016	21 186	5 472	6 398	3 227	1 826	4 263	2 884
2017	21 825	5 462	6 642	3 258	1 937	4 525	3 139
2018	22 758	5 488	7 145	3 341	2 012	4 770	3 312

[1]Beginning in 2003, persons who selected this race group only; persons who selected more than one race group are not included. Prior to 2003, persons who reported more than one race group were included in the group they identified as their main race.
[2]May be of any race.

Table 1-16. Number of Employed Persons Age 25 Years and Over, by Educational Attainment, Sex, Race, and Hispanic Origin, 2007–2018—*Continued*

(Thousands of people.)

Race, Hispanic origin, sex, and year	Total	Less than a high school diploma	High school graduate, no college	Some college, no degree	Associate's degree	College graduate or higher	
						Total	Bachelor's degree only
White Men[1]							
2007	56 740	6 364	17 039	9 409	4 964	18 964	12 260
2008	56 446	6 066	16 741	9 397	5 070	19 171	12 482
2009	54 248	5 583	15 966	8 937	4 948	18 813	12 112
2010	54 091	5 461	15 952	8 846	4 922	18 910	12 128
2011	54 488	5 450	15 776	8 878	5 082	19 303	12 344
2012	54 646	5 339	15 711	8 809	5 273	19 513	12 495
2013	54 914	5 286	15 672	9 356	5 611	20 542	13 287
2014	55 608	5 299	15 830	8 942	5 424	20 113	12 957
2015	56 374	5 484	15 617	9 037	5 533	20 702	13 265
2016	56 977	5 258	15 844	8 970	5 705	21 199	13 488
2017	57 396	5 074	16 029	8 954	5 670	21 670	13 966
2018	58 158	5 138	16 122	8 930	5 814	22 153	14 286
White Women[1]							
2007	46 737	3 082	13 102	8 527	5 455	16 571	10 878
2008	46 928	2 970	12 753	8 477	5 672	17 056	11 029
2009	46 172	2 913	12 406	8 046	5 766	17 040	10 997
2010	46 010	2 829	12 176	7 953	5 785	17 266	11 051
2011	45 938	2 798	11 792	7 835	5 840	17 672	11 189
2012	45 897	2 761	11 402	7 784	5 987	17 963	11 447
2013	46 132	2 598	11 377	7 649	6 111	18 396	11 637
2014	46 637	2 596	11 302	7 614	6 132	18 993	11 923
2015	46 962	2 643	10 891	7 782	5 968	19 677	12 131
2016	47 647	2 621	10 779	7 816	6 176	20 255	12 479
2017	48 053	2 616	10 681	7 562	6 203	20 992	13 020
2018	48 546	2 575	10 748	7 351	6 253	21 619	13 422
Black Men[1]							
2007	6 429	653	2 340	1 320	570	1 547	1 076
2008	6 357	616	2 358	1 296	579	1 508	1 036
2009	5 939	551	2 199	1 225	544	1 419	958
2010	5 988	561	2 164	1 270	567	1 426	960
2011	6 031	532	2 225	1 235	591	1 449	968
2012	6 320	530	2 281	1 328	639	1 541	1 024
2013	6 487	569	2 222	1 400	623	1 673	1 134
2014	6 726	592	2 319	1 433	662	1 720	1 136
2015	7 003	545	2 407	1 477	679	1 895	1 283
2016	7 323	562	2 504	1 482	751	2 023	1 342
2017	7 554	535	2 564	1 535	821	2 098	1 361
2018	7 832	505	2 661	1 543	840	2 283	1 549
Black Women[1]							
2007	7 382	641	2 443	1 592	819	1 888	1 286
2008	7 429	617	2 361	1 676	859	1 915	1 318
2009	7 171	544	2 176	1 631	877	1 943	1 295
2010	7 104	542	2 070	1 594	915	1 983	1 300
2011	7 066	481	2 073	1 558	928	2 026	1 289
2012	7 397	487	2 115	1 591	945	2 260	1 455
2013	7 498	495	2 121	1 634	961	2 288	1 448
2014	7 711	492	2 123	1 686	1 012	2 398	1 487
2015	8 014	488	2 142	1 765	1 096	2 523	1 567
2016	8 194	507	2 233	1 799	1 066	2 589	1 600
2017	8 477	503	2 325	1 800	1 073	2 775	1 689
2018	8 724	504	2 325	1 733	1 155	3 007	1 846
Hispanic Men[2]							
2007	10 303	3 947	3 100	1 285	567	1 403	1 000
2008	10 363	3 714	3 231	1 371	607	1 439	1 008
2009	9 969	3 508	3 114	1 321	595	1 431	992
2010	10 120	3 517	3 176	1 341	595	1 491	1 045
2011	10 151	3 487	3 158	1 377	636	1 492	1 044
2012	10 629	3 512	3 391	1 420	693	1 612	1 115
2013	11 029	3 599	3 475	1 486	718	1 751	1 236
2014	11 546	3 651	3 584	1 637	791	1 883	1 362
2015	11 969	3 787	3 664	1 642	875	2 001	1 402
2016	12 378	3 669	3 960	1 697	896	2 156	1 488
2017	12 663	3 662	4 067	1 771	915	2 248	1 598
2018	13 168	3 679	4 369	1 822	951	2 346	1 654
Hispanic Women[2]							
2007	6 670	1 730	2 010	1 097	593	1 241	898
2008	6 752	1 712	2 001	1 113	629	1 297	922
2009	6 718	1 724	1 955	1 093	647	1 298	941
2010	6 826	1 666	1 999	1 133	656	1 371	979
2011	6 908	1 669	2 058	1 136	681	1 365	938
2012	7 680	1 757	2 222	1 315	788	1 598	1 106
2013	7 807	1 698	2 280	1 295	826	1 709	1 192
2014	8 140	1 713	2 370	1 353	845	1 859	1 287
2015	8 481	1 805	2 401	1 477	864	1 935	1 292
2016	8 807	1 803	2 438	1 530	930	2 107	1 396
2017	9 162	1 799	2 575	1 488	1 023	2 277	1 542
2018	9 589	1 809	2 776	1 519	1 061	2 424	1 658

[1]Beginning in 2003, persons who selected this race group only; persons who selected more than one race group are not included. Prior to 2003, persons who reported more than one race group were included in the group they identified as their main race.
[2]May be of any race.

Table 1-17. Multiple Jobholders and Multiple Jobholding Rates, by Selected Characteristics, May of Selected Years, 1970–2019

(Thousands of people, percent, not seasonally adjusted.)

Year	Total employed	Multiple jobholders				Multiple jobholding rate[1]						
		Total	Men	Women: Number	Women: Percent of all multiple jobholders	Total	Men	Women	White	Black[2]	Asian	Hispanic[3]
1970	78 358	4 048	3 412	636	15.7	5.2	7.0	2.2	5.3	4.4	. . .	. . .
1971	78 708	4 035	3 270	765	19.0	5.1	6.7	2.6	5.3	3.8	. . .	. . .
1972	81 224	3 770	3 035	735	19.5	4.6	6.0	2.4	4.8	3.7	. . .	. . .
1973	83 758	4 262	3 393	869	20.4	5.1	6.6	2.7	5.1	4.7	. . .	. . .
1974	85 786	3 889	3 022	867	22.3	4.5	5.8	2.6	4.6	3.8	. . .	. . .
1975	84 146	3 918	2 962	956	24.4	4.7	5.8	2.9	4.8	3.7	. . .	. . .
1976	87 278	3 948	3 037	911	23.1	4.5	5.8	2.6	4.7	2.8	. . .	. . .
1977	90 482	4 558	3 317	1 241	27.2	5.0	6.2	3.4	5.3	2.6	. . .	. . .
1978	93 904	4 493	3 212	1 281	28.5	4.8	5.8	3.3	5.0	3.1	. . .	. . .
1979	96 327	4 724	3 317	1 407	29.8	4.9	5.9	3.5	5.1	3.0	. . .	. . .
1980	96 809	4 759	3 210	1 549	32.5	4.9	5.8	3.8	5.1	3.2	. . .	. . .
1985	106 878	5 730	3 537	2 192	38.3	5.4	5.9	4.7	5.7	3.2	. . .	. . .
1989	117 084	7 225	4 115	3 109	43.0	6.2	6.4	5.9	6.5	4.3	. . .	. . .
1991	116 626	7 183	4 054	3 129	43.6	6.2	6.4	5.9	6.4	4.9	. . .	. . .
1994	122 946	7 316	3 973	3 343	45.7	6.0	6.0	5.9	6.1	4.9	. . .	3.8
1995	124 554	7 952	4 225	3 727	46.9	6.4	6.3	6.5	6.6	5.2	. . .	3.6
1996	126 391	7 846	4 352	3 494	44.5	6.2	6.4	6.0	6.4	5.1	. . .	4.0
1997	129 565	8 197	4 398	3 800	46.4	6.3	6.3	6.4	6.5	5.7	. . .	4.1
1998	131 476	8 126	4 438	3 688	45.4	6.2	6.3	6.1	6.3	5.5	. . .	4.4
1999	133 411	7 895	4 117	3 778	47.9	5.9	5.8	6.1	6.0	5.5	. . .	3.6
2000	136 685	7 751	4 084	3 667	47.3	5.7	5.6	5.8	5.9	4.9	3.4	3.2
2001	137 121	7 540	3 914	3 626	48.1	5.5	5.3	5.7	5.6	5.3	3.7	3.4
2002	136 559	7 247	3 736	3 511	48.4	5.3	5.1	5.5	5.5	4.7	4.0	3.8
2003	137 567	7 338	3 841	3 498	47.7	5.3	5.3	5.4	5.5	4.3	4.2	3.4
2004	138 867	7 258	3 653	3 605	49.7	5.2	4.9	5.6	5.3	5.1	3.7	3.4
2005	141 591	7 348	3 741	3 607	49.1	5.2	4.9	5.5	5.4	4.4	3.5	2.8
2006	144 041	7 641	3 863	3 778	49.4	5.3	5.0	5.7	5.3	5.4	3.7	3.1
2007	145 864	7 693	3 835	3 858	50.1	5.3	4.9	5.7	5.5	4.4	3.7	3.0
2008	145 927	7 653	3 842	3 812	49.8	5.2	4.9	5.6	5.4	4.9	3.8	2.9
2009	140 363	7 265	3 540	3 725	51.3	5.2	4.8	5.6	5.3	4.8	3.9	3.0
2010	139 497	7 261	3 559	3 702	51.0	5.2	4.8	5.6	5.4	4.6	3.1	3.1
2011	140 028	7 084	3 491	3 593	50.7	5.1	4.7	5.5	5.3	4.5	3.1	3.3
2012	142 727	7 174	3 605	3 569	49.7	5.0	4.8	5.3	5.2	4.9	3.3	3.1
2013	144 432	7 123	3 570	3 553	49.9	4.9	4.7	5.2	5.1	4.4	3.7	3.7
2014	146 398	7 305	3 647	3 658	50.1	5.0	4.7	5.3	5.0	4.9	4.0	3.7
2015	149 349	7 081	3 441	3 641	51.4	4.7	4.3	5.2	4.8	5.1	2.9	3.1
2016	151 594	7 472	3 677	3 796	50.8	4.9	4.6	5.4	5.0	5.4	3.0	2.7
2017	153 407	7 584	3 831	3 752	49.5	4.9	4.7	5.2	5.0	5.0	3.8	3.2
2018	156 009	7 411	3 687	3 724	50.2	4.8	4.4	5.1	4.8	4.7	2.9	3.7
2019	157 152	7 857	3 774	4 083	52.0	5.0	4.5	5.5	5.0	5.3	3.4	3.4

Note: Data prior to 1985 reflect 1970 census–based population controls; years 1985–1991 reflect 1980 census–based controls; years 1994–1999 reflect 1990 census–based controls adjusted for the estimated undercount; and data for years 2000–2002 have been revised to incorporate population controls from the 2000 census. Prior to 1994, data on multiple jobholders were collected only through special periodic supplements to the Current Population Survey (CPS) in May of various years; these supplemental surveys were not conducted in 1981–1984, 1986–1988, 1990, or 1992–1993. Beginning in 1994, data reflect the introduction of a major redesign of the CPS, including the collection of monthly data on multiple jobholders.

[1]Multiple jobholders as a percent of all employed persons in specified group.
[2]Data for years prior to 1977 refer to the Black-and-Other population group.
[3]May be of any race.
. . . = Not available.

Table 1-18. Multiple Jobholders, by Sex, Age, Marital Status, Race, Hispanic Origin, and Job Status, 2015–2018

(Thousands of people, percent.)

Characteristic	Both sexes				Men				Women			
	Number		Rate[1]		Number		Rate[1]		Number		Rate[1]	
	2015	2016	2015	2016	2015	2016	2015	2016	2015	2016	2015	2016
Age												
Total, 16 years and over[2]	7 262	7 531	4.9	5.0	3 571	3 645	4.5	4.5	3 692	3 887	5.3	5.5
16 to 19 years	199	205	4.2	4.1	73	81	3.1	3.3	126	124	5.3	5.0
20 to 24 years	799	848	5.7	6.0	329	335	4.6	4.6	470	514	6.9	7.5
25 to 34 years	1 616	1 727	4.9	5.1	810	858	4.6	4.7	806	869	5.4	5.6
35 to 44 years	1 530	1 548	4.9	4.9	796	783	4.7	4.6	734	765	5.1	5.3
45 to 54 years	1 637	1 687	5.0	5.2	803	819	4.7	4.7	834	868	5.4	5.6
55 to 64 years	1 162	1 161	4.7	4.5	587	571	4.5	4.3	575	589	4.8	4.9
65 years and over	319	356	3.8	4.0	174	198	3.7	4.0	145	158	3.8	4.0
Marital Status												
Single	2 318	2 463	5.1	5.3	1 027	1 089	4.2	4.3	1 291	1 374	6.2	6.4
Married, spouse present	3 702	3 761	4.6	4.7	2 121	2 114	4.7	4.7	1 581	1 647	4.5	4.7
Widowed, divorced, or separated	2 318	1 307	5.2	5.4	423	442	4.3	4.4	1 291	865	6.2	6.2
Race and Hispanic Origin												
White	5 881	5 999	5.0	5.0	2 917	2 926	5.0	4.5	2 964	3 072	5.5	5.6
Black	869	958	5.0	5.3	410	449	5.0	5.3	459	510	4.9	5.4
Hispanic[3]	782	820	3.2	3.2	430	433	3.2	3.0	352	387	3.4	3.6
Full- or Part-Time Status												
Primary job full time, secondary job part time	3 909	4 084	. . .	. . .	2 128	2 235	. . .	. . .	1 781	1 849	. . .	. . .
Primary and secondary jobs, both part time	1 951	2 075	. . .	. . .	662	703	. . .	. . .	1 288	1 372	. . .	. . .
Primary and secondary jobs, both full time	242	278	. . .	. . .	156	167	. . .	. . .	86	112	. . .	. . .
Hours vary on primary or secondary job	1 114	1 038	. . .	. . .	600	512	. . .	. . .	514	526	. . .	. . .

Characteristic	Both sexes				Men				Women			
	Number		Rate[1]		Number		Rate[1]		Number		Rate[1]	
	2017	2018	2017	2018	2017	2018	2017	2018	2017	2018	2017	2018
Age												
Total, 16 years and over[2]	7 545	7 769	4.9	5.0	3 748	3 835	4.6	4.6	3 798	3 934	5.3	5.4
16 to 19 years	189	183	3.7	3.6	81	61	3.3	2.4	109	122	4.2	4.6
20 to 24 years	828	780	5.9	5.6	359	328	4.9	4.6	469	452	6.8	6.6
25 to 34 years	1 724	1 867	5.0	5.3	846	915	4.6	4.8	878	952	5.5	5.8
35 to 44 years	1 578	1 646	4.9	5.0	801	834	4.7	4.7	776	811	5.3	5.4
45 to 54 years	1 687	1 684	5.2	5.2	825	847	4.8	5.0	862	837	5.6	5.5
55 to 64 years	1 183	1 220	4.5	4.6	621	629	4.5	4.5	563	591	4.6	4.7
65 years and over	356	390	3.9	4.0	215	221	4.2	4.1	141	169	3.4	3.9
Marital Status												
Single	2 447	2 579	5.1	5.2	1 123	1 160	4.4	4.4	1 324	1 419	5.9	6.1
Married, spouse present	3 769	3 842	4.6	4.7	2 161	2 191	4.7	4.8	1 608	1 651	4.5	4.6
Widowed, divorced, or separated	1 329	1 348	5.6	5.6	463	484	4.4	4.7	866	864	6.3	6.2
Race and Hispanic Origin												
White	5 988	6 166	5.0	5.1	2 995	3 057	5.0	4.7	2 993	3 110	5.4	5.6
Black	979	993	5.3	5.2	469	469	5.3	5.2	510	523	5.2	5.2
Hispanic[3]	880	951	3.4	3.5	464	538	3.3	3.5	388	413	3.5	3.6
Full- or Part-Time Status												
Primary job full time, secondary job part time	4 151	4 290	. . .	. . .	2 268	2 327	. . .	. . .	1 883	1 963	. . .	. . .
Primary and secondary jobs, both part time	1 993	2 031	. . .	. . .	694	717	. . .	. . .	1 298	1 314	. . .	. . .
Primary and secondary jobs, both full time	297	316	. . .	. . .	192	196	. . .	. . .	106	120	. . .	. . .
Hours vary on primary or secondary job	1 052	1 080	. . .	. . .	571	570	. . .	. . .	481	510	. . .	. . .

Note: Estimates for the above race groups (White or Black) do not sum to totals because data are not presented for all races. Beginning in January 2003, data reflect the revised population controls used in the household survey.

[1]Multiple jobholders as a percent of all employed persons in specified group.
[2]Includes a small number of persons who work part time at their primary job and full time at their secondary job(s), not shown separately.
[3]May be of any race.
. . . = Not available.

Table 1-19. Multiple Jobholders, by Sex and Industry of Principal Secondary Job, Annual Averages, 2016–2018

(Thousands of people.)

Year and industry of secondary job	Both sexes	Men	Women
2016			
All Nonagricultural Industries, Wage and Salary Workers	5 466	2 544	2 921
Mining, quarrying, and oil and gas extraction	4	3	1
Construction	118	90	28
Manufacturing	133	90	44
Durable goods	73	56	17
Nondurable goods	60	33	27
Wholesale and retail trade	803	325	479
Wholesale trade	61	39	22
Retail trade	742	285	457
Transportation and utilities	224	170	54
Transportation and warehousing	213	163	50
Utilities	11	7	4
Information	104	49	55
Financial activities	235	138	97
Professional and business services	524	305	219
Education and health services	1 607	570	1 037
Leisure and hospitality	1 080	520	559
Other services	421	154	26
Other services, except private households	356	150	206
Other services, private households	65	4	61
Public administration	212	132	80
2017			
All Nonagricultural Industries, Wage and Salary Workers	5 472	2 575	2 897
Mining, quarrying, and oil and gas extraction	3	2	1
Construction	125	102	23
Manufacturing	128	75	53
Durable goods	62	48	14
Nondurable goods	66	27	39
Wholesale and retail trade	785	313	473
Wholesale trade	46	26	21
Retail trade	739	287	452
Transportation and utilities	217	149	68
Transportation and warehousing	202	140	62
Utilities	15	9	5
Information	110	61	49
Financial activities	235	140	95
Professional and business services	536	317	219
Education and health services	1 526	559	967
Leisure and hospitality	1 141	535	605
Other services	451	189	262
Other services, except private households	386	182	204
Other services, private households	386	182	204
Public administration	217	134	83
2018			
All Nonagricultural Industries, Wage and Salary Workers	5 608	2 631	2 977
Mining, quarrying, and oil and gas extraction	4	2	2
Construction	129	98	30
Manufacturing	125	75	50
Durable goods	54	43	11
Nondurable goods	71	31	39
Wholesale and retail trade	794	329	464
Wholesale trade	34	15	19
Retail trade	759	314	445
Transportation and utilities	244	179	64
Transportation and warehousing	227	169	57
Utilities	17	10	7
Information	115	71	44
Financial activities	263	167	97
Professional and business services	521	293	229
Education and health services	1 666	602	1 064
Leisure and hospitality	1 057	454	603
Other services	466	202	264
Other services, except private households	392	193	199
Other services, private households	74	9	65
Public administration	225	159	66

Table 1-20. Employment and Unemployment in Families, by Race and Hispanic Origin, Annual Averages, 2006–2018

(Thousands of people, percent.)

Characteristic	2006	2007	2008	2009	2010	2011	2012	2013	2014	2015	2016	2017	2018
ALL RACES													
Total Families	77 017	77 894	77 943	78 361	78 246	78 362	80 141	80 445	80 889	81 410	82 092	82 015	82 502
With employed member(s)	63 492	64 330	64 058	63 010	62 560	62 529	64 091	64 318	64 832	65 360	66 023	66 027	66 655
As percent of total families	82.4	82.6	82.2	80.4	80.0	79.8	80.0	80.0	80.1	80.3	80.4	80.5	80.8
Some usually work full time[1]	58 918	59 616	59 116	57 037	56 471	56 498	58 007	58 113	58 762	59 520	60 065	60 395	61 159
With no employed member	13 525	13 564	13 884	15 351	15 686	15 833	16 050	16 127	16 057	16 050	16 069	15 988	15 847
As percent of total families	17.6	17.4	17.8	19.6	20.0	20.2	20.0	20.0	19.9	19.7	19.6	19.5	19.2
With unemployed member(s)	4 913	4 914	6 104	9 381	9 695	9 043	8 444	7 685	6 486	5 615	5 301	4 744	4 300
As percent of total families	6.4	6.3	7.8	12.0	12.4	11.5	10.5	9.6	8.0	6.9	6.5	5.8	5.2
Some member(s) employed	3 419	3 497	4 319	6 438	6 566	6 079	5 702	5 192	4 419	3 831	3 656	3 277	3 012
As percent of families with unemployed member(s)	69.6	71.2	70.8	68.6	67.7	67.2	67.5	67.6	68.1	68.2	69.0	69.1	70.0
Some usually work full time[1]	3 049	3 096	3 830	5 460	5 572	5 211	4 902	4 453	3 819	3 302	3 162	2 870	2 636
As percent of families with unemployed member(s)	62.1	63.0	62.7	58.2	57.5	57.6	58.1	58.0	58.9	58.8	59.7	60.5	61.3
WHITE[2]													
Total Families	62 977	63 667	63 490	63 774	63 551	63 635	64 246	64 294	64 476	64 663	65 083	64 910	65 042
With employed member(s)	52 054	52 669	52 273	51 494	51 048	51 030	51 491	51 471	51 661	51 769	52 209	52 016	52 264
As percent of total families	82.7	82.7	82.3	80.7	80.3	80.2	80.1	80.1	80.1	80.1	80.2	80.1	80.4
Some usually work full time[1]	48 395	48 879	48 271	46 629	46 150	46 203	46 710	46 636	46 937	47 225	47 611	47 621	47 973
With no employed member	10 923	10 997	11 217	12 280	12 502	12 605	12 755	12 822	12 815	12 894	12 873	12 894	12 778
As percent of total families	17.3	17.3	17.7	19.3	19.7	19.8	19.9	19.9	19.9	19.9	19.8	19.9	19.6
With unemployed member(s)	3 556	3 587	4 506	7 089	7 202	6 608	6 133	5 471	4 499	3 908	3 711	3 343	3 042
As percent of total families	5.6	5.6	7.1	11.1	11.3	10.4	9.5	8.5	7.0	6.0	5.7	5.2	4.7
Some member(s) employed	2 582	2 653	3 332	5 072	5 069	4 627	4 321	3 845	3 195	2 784	2 684	2 385	2 184
As percent of families with unemployed member(s)	72.6	73.9	74.0	71.5	70.4	70.0	70.5	70.3	71.0	71.2	72.3	71.3	71.8
Some usually work full time[1]	2 306	2 350	2 955	4 294	4 289	3 964	3 719	3 310	2 767	2 408	2 343	2 098	1 917
As percent of families with unemployed member(s)	64.8	65.5	65.6	60.6	59.6	60.0	60.6	60.5	61.5	61.6	63.1	62.8	63.0
BLACK[2]													
Total Families	9 058	9 184	9 297	9 318	9 404	9 370	9 671	9 737	9 793	9 854	9 976	10 017	10 008
With employed member(s)	7 078	7 249	7 290	7 022	7 030	6 954	7 290	7 373	7 481	7 652	7 764	7 886	7 934
As percent of total families	78.1	78.9	78.4	75.4	74.8	74.2	75.4	75.7	76.4	77.7	77.8	78.7	79.3
Some usually work full time[1]	6 437	6 608	6 622	6 265	6 222	6 105	6 419	6 451	6 596	6 792	6 835	7 053	7 149
With no employed member	1 980	1 935	2 006	2 296	2 374	2 416	2 380	2 363	2 312	2 202	2 212	2 131	2 074
As percent of total families	21.9	21.1	21.6	24.6	25.2	25.8	24.6	24.3	23.6	22.3	22.2	21.3	20.7
With unemployed member(s)	1 036	990	1 188	1 624	1 807	1 767	1 629	1 555	1 376	1 184	1 086	951	837
As percent of total families	11.4	10.8	12.8	17.4	19.2	18.9	16.8	16.0	14.1	12.0	11.0	10.0	8.4
Some member(s) employed	596	591	686	886	1 009	985	885	880	780	666	628	553	504
As percent of families with unemployed member(s)	57.6	59.7	57.8	54.5	55.8	55.7	54.3	56.6	56.7	56.3	57.8	58.1	60.3
Some usually work full time[1]	526	519	605	748	862	835	752	733	666	558	524	469	437
As percent of families with unemployed member(s)	50.8	52.4	50.9	46.0	47.7	47.3	46.1	47.1	48.4	47.2	48.2	49.4	52.3
HISPANIC[3]													
Total Families	9 905	10 332	10 500	10 489	10 561	10 902	11 769	12 023	12 178	12 602	12 900	12 936	13 194
With employed member(s)	8 641	9 048	9 135	8 852	8 897	9 178	9 962	10 231	10 456	10 883	11 182	11 244	11 546
As percent of total families	87.2	87.6	87.0	84.4	84.2	84.2	84.6	85.1	85.9	86.4	86.7	86.9	87.5
Some usually work full time[1]	8 129	8 492	8 466	7 923	7 934	8 201	8 978	9 242	9 429	9 914	10 217	10 383	10 706
With no employed member	1 264	1 285	1 365	1 637	1 664	1 724	1 808	1 792	1 722	1 719	1 718	1 692	1 649
As percent of total families	12.8	12.4	13.0	15.6	15.8	15.8	15.4	14.9	14.1	13.6	13.3	13.1	12.5
With unemployed member(s)	793	876	1 159	1 770	1 841	1 781	1 707	1 547	1 311	1 220	1 117	994	918
As percent of total families	8.0	8.5	11.0	16.9	17.4	16.3	14.5	12.9	10.8	9.7	8.7	7.7	7.0
Some member(s) employed	544	619	846	1 228	1 262	1 226	1 197	1 078	933	864	811	715	657
As percent of families with unemployed member(s)	68.6	70.6	73.0	69.3	68.6	68.8	70.1	69.7	71.1	70.8	72.6	71.9	71.5
Some usually work full time[1]	491	554	743	1 021	1 060	1 030	1 020	919	798	740	702	634	584
As percent of families with unemployed member(s)	61.9	63.2	64.1	57.7	57.6	57.8	59.7	59.4	60.9	60.7	62.9	63.8	63.6

Note: The race or ethnicity of the family is determined by the race of the householder. Estimates for the above race groups (White or Black) do not sum to totals because data are not presented for all races.

[1]Usually work 35 hours or more a week at all jobs.
[2]Beginning in 2003, families where the householder selected this race group only; families where the householder selected more than one race group are excluded. Prior to 2003, families where the householder selected more than one race group were included in the group that the householder identified as the main race.
[3]May be of any race.

Table 1-21. Families, by Presence and Relationship of Employed Members and Family Type, Annual Averages, 2006–2018

(Thousands of people, percent.)

Characteristic	Number of families												
	2006	2007	2008	2009	2010	2011	2012	2013	2014	2015	2016	2017	2018
MARRIED-COUPLE FAMILIES													
Total	57 509	58 145	58 125	58 124	57 524	57 290	58 431	58 529	58 806	59 217	59 747	59 910	60 094
Member(s) employed, total	48 196	48 676	48 541	47 876	47 238	46 910	47 830	47 722	47 852	48 205	48 440	48 525	48 791
Husband only	11 399	11 509	11 351	11 371	11 311	11 426	11 815	11 755	11 713	11 726	11 649	11 425	11 469
Wife only	3 754	3 858	4 036	4 909	4 937	4 764	4 696	4 578	4 422	4 209	4 253	4 265	4 085
Husband and wife	29 799	30 055	29 854	28 211	27 501	27 229	27 708	27 748	28 042	28 434	28 693	28 944	29 317
Other employment combinations	3 244	3 254	3 300	3 384	3 489	3 491	3 612	3 640	3 676	3 837	3 845	3 891	3 921
No member(s) employed	9 313	9 469	9 585	10 248	10 286	10 379	10 601	10 807	10 954	11 012	11 307	11 386	11 302
FAMILIES MAINTAINED BY WOMEN[1]													
Total	14 208	14 423	14 383	14 610	14 913	15 147	15 517	15 507	15 581	15 693	15 669	15 438	15 452
Member(s) employed, total	10 796	11 087	10 929	10 642	10 715	10 867	11 236	11 360	11 585	11 765	12 001	11 861	12 003
Householder only	6 103	6 307	6 250	6 135	6 189	6 248	6 403	6 359	6 368	6 451	6 502	6 333	6 250
Householder and other member(s)	2 955	2 994	2 870	2 642	2 603	2 683	2 896	2 933	3 059	3 181	3 293	3 372	3 484
Other member(s), not householder	1 738	1 785	1 809	1 866	1 923	1 937	1 937	2 069	2 159	2 133	2 205	2 156	2 269
No member(s) employed	3 412	3 336	3 454	3 968	4 198	4 280	4 281	4 147	3 995	3 928	3 668	3 577	3 449
FAMILIES MAINTAINED BY MEN[1]													
Total	5 300	5 327	5 435	5 627	5 809	5 926	6 192	6 410	6 502	6 499	6 676	6 666	6 956
Member(s) employed, total	4 500	4 568	4 589	4 492	4 607	4 752	5 025	5 236	5 394	5 389	5 582	5 641	5 861
Householder only	2 089	2 170	2 178	2 104	2 215	2 399	2 514	2 529	2 568	2 517	2 577	2 564	2 703
Householder and other member(s)	1 715	1 696	1 659	1 557	1 525	1 506	1 622	1 736	1 891	1 932	2 050	2 101	2 173
Other member(s), not householder	696	701	752	831	867	847	889	971	935	940	955	976	985
No member(s) employed	800	759	845	1 135	1 202	1 174	1 168	1 174	1 108	1 110	1 094	1 025	1 096

Characteristic	Percent distribution												
	2006	2007	2008	2009	2010	2011	2012	2013	2014	2015	2016	2017	2018
MARRIED-COUPLE FAMILIES													
Total	100.0	100.0	100.0	100.0	100.0	100.0	100.0	100.0	100.0	100.0	100.0	100.0	100.0
Member(s) employed, total	83.8	83.7	83.5	82.4	82.1	81.9	81.9	81.5	81.4	81.4	81.1	81.0	81.2
Husband only	19.8	19.8	19.5	19.6	19.7	19.9	20.2	20.1	19.9	19.8	19.5	19.1	19.1
Wife only	6.5	6.6	6.9	8.4	8.6	8.3	8.0	7.8	7.5	7.1	7.1	7.1	6.8
Husband and wife	51.8	51.7	51.4	48.5	47.8	47.5	47.4	47.4	47.7	48.0	48.0	48.3	48.8
Other employment combinations	5.6	5.6	5.7	5.8	6.1	6.1	6.2	6.2	6.3	6.5	6.4	6.5	6.5
No member(s) employed	16.2	16.3	16.5	17.6	17.9	18.1	18.1	18.5	18.6	18.6	18.9	19.0	18.8
FAMILIES MAINTAINED BY WOMEN[1]													
Total	100.0	100.0	100.0	100.0	100.0	100.0	100.0	100.0	100.0	100.0	100.0	100.0	100.0
Member(s) employed, total	76.0	76.9	76.0	72.8	71.9	71.7	72.4	73.3	74.4	75.0	76.6	76.8	77.7
Householder only	43.0	43.7	43.5	42.0	41.5	41.2	41.3	41.0	40.9	41.1	41.5	41.0	40.4
Householder and other member(s)	20.8	20.8	20.0	18.1	17.5	17.7	18.7	18.9	19.6	20.3	21.0	21.8	22.5
Other member(s), not householder	12.2	12.4	12.6	12.8	12.9	12.8	12.5	13.3	13.9	13.6	14.1	14.0	14.7
No member(s) employed	24.0	23.1	24.0	27.2	28.1	28.3	27.6	26.7	25.6	25.0	23.4	23.2	22.3
FAMILIES MAINTAINED BY MEN[1]													
Total	100.0	100.0	100.0	100.0	100.0	100.0	100.0	100.0	100.0	100.0	100.0	100.0	100.0
Member(s) employed, total	84.9	85.7	84.4	79.8	79.3	80.2	81.1	81.7	83.0	82.9	83.6	84.6	84.3
Householder only	39.4	40.7	40.1	37.4	38.1	40.5	40.6	39.5	39.5	38.7	38.6	38.5	38.9
Householder and other member(s)	32.4	31.8	30.5	27.7	26.2	25.4	26.2	27.1	29.1	29.7	30.7	31.5	31.2
Other member(s), not householder	13.1	13.2	13.8	14.8	14.9	14.3	14.4	15.1	14.4	14.5	14.3	14.6	14.2
No member(s) employed	15.1	14.3	15.6	20.2	20.7	19.8	18.9	18.3	17.0	17.1	16.4	15.4	15.7

Note: Detail may not sum to total due to rounding.

[1]No spouse present.

Table 1-22. Unemployment in Families, by Presence and Relationship of Employed Members and Family Type, Annual Averages, 2006–2018

(Thousands of people, percent.)

Characteristic	Number												
	2006	2007	2008	2009	2010	2011	2012	2013	2014	2015	2016	2017	2018
MARRIED-COUPLE FAMILIES													
With Unemployed Member(s), Total	2 968	2 978	3 796	6 056	6 147	5 576	5 140	4 586	3 765	3 292	3 122	2 783	2 528
No member employed	526	512	663	1 218	4 884	4 413	4 123	3 639	3 028	2 653	2 511	2 245	2 075
Some member(s) employed	2 442	2 467	3 133	4 838	1 263	1 162	1 017	946	737	639	612	537	452
Husband unemployed	1 061	1 110	1 439	2 808	2 813	2 387	2 066	1 824	1 398	1 194	1 149	1 009	877
Wife employed	679	725	927	1 799	1 783	1 497	1 307	1 134	872	739	702	632	558
Wife unemployed	898	902	1 114	1 630	1 697	1 610	1 567	1 346	1 121	947	913	850	766
Husband employed	772	783	975	1 397	1 455	1 350	1 328	1 129	943	786	775	700	654
Other family member unemployed	1 010	966	1 243	1 618	1 637	1 579	1 507	1 416	1 246	1 151	1 060	923	885
FAMILIES MAINTAINED BY WOMEN[1]													
With Unemployed Member(s), Total	1 429	1 416	1 666	2 309	2 446	2 498	2 372	2 165	1 933	1 666	1 543	1 389	1 233
No member employed	753	701	849	1 244	1 094	1 146	1 081	1 026	936	804	774	691	633
Some member(s) employed	675	714	817	1 065	1 351	1 352	1 290	1 139	997	862	770	697	600
Householder unemployed	688	650	796	1 141	1 227	1 268	1 191	1 053	892	770	710	644	559
Other member(s) employed	132	144	181	225	254	275	250	251	216	181	174	165	154
Other member(s) unemployed	740	766	870	1 168	1 218	1 229	1 180	1 112	1 040	896	833	744	673
FAMILIES MAINTAINED BY MEN[1]													
With Unemployed Member(s), Total	516	520	642	1 016	1 102	970	932	934	789	657	635	573	539
No member employed	215	205	274	482	587	520	497	527	455	375	372	340	303
Some member(s) employed	301	316	368	535	515	450	435	408	333	282	264	233	236
Householder unemployed	284	294	385	626	680	575	535	550	446	378	354	312	306
Other member(s) employed	118	137	164	239	259	231	209	238	200	158	153	132	125
Other member(s) unemployed	232	226	257	391	422	394	397	385	343	280	282	260	233

Characteristic	Percent distribution												
	2006	2007	2008	2009	2010	2011	2012	2013	2014	2015	2016	2017	2018
MARRIED-COUPLE FAMILIES													
With Unemployed Member(s), Total	100.0	100.0	100.0	100.0	100.0	100.0	100.0	100.0	100.0	100.0	100.0	100.0	100.0
No member employed	17.7	17.2	17.5	20.1	79.4	79.2	80.2	79.4	80.4	80.6	80.4	80.7	82.1
Some member(s) employed	82.3	82.8	82.5	79.9	20.6	20.8	19.8	20.6	19.6	19.4	19.6	19.3	17.9
Husband unemployed	35.7	37.3	37.9	46.4	45.8	42.8	40.2	39.8	37.1	36.3	36.8	36.3	34.7
Wife employed	22.9	24.3	24.4	29.7	29.0	26.9	25.4	24.7	23.2	22.5	22.5	22.7	22.1
Wife unemployed	30.3	30.3	29.3	26.9	27.6	28.9	30.5	29.4	29.8	28.8	29.2	30.6	30.3
Husband employed	26.0	26.3	25.7	23.1	23.7	24.2	25.8	24.6	25.1	23.9	24.8	25.1	25.9
Other family member unemployed	34.0	32.4	32.7	26.7	26.6	28.3	29.3	30.9	33.1	35.0	34.0	33.2	35.0
FAMILIES MAINTAINED BY WOMEN[1]													
With Unemployed Member(s), Total	100.0	100.0	100.0	100.0	100.0	100.0	100.0	100.0	100.0	100.0	100.0	100.0	100.0
No member employed	52.7	49.5	50.9	53.9	44.7	45.9	45.6	47.4	48.4	48.2	50.1	49.8	51.4
Some member(s) employed	47.3	50.5	49.1	46.1	55.3	54.1	54.4	52.6	51.6	51.8	49.9	50.2	48.6
Householder unemployed	48.2	45.9	47.8	49.4	50.2	50.8	50.2	48.6	46.2	46.2	46.0	46.4	45.4
Other member(s) employed	9.3	10.2	10.9	9.7	10.4	11.0	10.6	11.6	11.2	10.8	11.3	11.9	12.5
Other member(s) unemployed	51.8	54.1	52.2	50.6	49.8	49.2	49.8	51.4	53.8	53.8	54.0	53.6	54.6
FAMILIES MAINTAINED BY MEN[1]													
With Unemployed Member(s), Total	100.0	100.0	100.0	100.0	100.0	100.0	100.0	100.0	100.0	100.0	100.0	100.0	100.0
No member employed	41.7	39.3	42.7	47.4	53.3	53.6	53.3	56.4	57.7	57.0	58.5	59.4	56.2
Some member(s) employed	58.3	60.7	57.3	52.6	46.7	46.4	46.7	43.6	42.3	43.0	41.5	40.6	43.8
Householder unemployed	55.0	56.6	60.0	61.6	61.7	59.4	57.4	58.8	56.5	57.5	55.6	54.5	56.7
Other member(s) employed	22.8	26.3	25.6	23.5	23.5	23.8	22.5	25.5	25.4	24.1	24.0	23.1	23.2
Other member(s) unemployed	45.0	43.4	40.0	38.4	38.3	40.6	42.6	41.2	43.5	42.5	44.4	45.5	43.3

Note: Detail may not sum to total due to rounding.

[1]No spouse present.

Table 1-23. Employment Status of the Population, by Sex, Marital Status, and Presence and Age of Own Children Under 18 Years, Annual Averages, 2010–2018

(Thousands of people, percent.)

Characteristic	2010			2011			2012			2013			2014		
	Both sexes	Men	Women	Both sexes	Men	Women	Both sexes	Men	Women	Both sexes	Men	Women	Both sexes	Men	Women
With Own Children Under 18 Years, Total															
Civilian noninstitutional population	64 488	28 463	36 025	63 885	28 143	35 743	65 620	28 943	36 676	65 385	28 947	36 438	65 643	29 040	36 602
Civilian labor force	52 159	26 661	25 499	51 521	26 302	25 219	52 754	26 954	25 800	52 335	26 869	25 466	52 580	26 939	25 641
Participation rate	80.9	93.7	70.8	80.6	93.5	70.6	80.4	93.1	70.3	80.0	92.8	69.9	80.1	92.8	70.0
Employed	47 863	24 653	23 210	47 578	24 619	22 959	49 101	25 460	23 641	49 146	25 540	23 606	49 948	25 899	24 049
Employment-population ratio	74.2	86.6	64.4	74.5	87.5	64.2	74.8	88.0	64.5	75.2	88.2	64.8	76.1	89.2	65.7
Full-time workers[1]	7 581	1 477	6 104	7 303	1 374	5 930	41 698	24 055	17 643	41 844	24 207	17 637	42 727	24 615	18 112
Part-time workers[2]	74	87	64	74	88	64	7 403	1 405	5 999	7 302	1 333	5 969	7 221	1 284	5 937
Unemployed	4 296	2 008	2 289	3 943	1 683	2 260	3 653	1 494	2 159	3 189	1 329	1 860	2 632	1 040	1 592
Unemployment rate	8.2	7.5	9.0	7.7	6.4	9.0	6.9	5.5	8.4	6.1	4.9	7.3	5.0	3.9	6.2
Married, Spouse Present															
Civilian noninstitutional population	50 868	25 820	25 049	49 999	25 392	24 607	49 595	25 013	24 582	49 595	25 035	24 560	49 739	25 098	24 641
Civilian labor force	41 600	24 332	17 268	40 783	23 873	16 911	40 277	23 481	16 796	40 096	23 447	16 650	40 220	23 505	16 715
Participation rate	81.8	94.2	68.9	81.6	94.0	68.7	81.2	93.9	68.3	80.8	93.7	67.8	80.9	93.7	67.8
Employed	38 870	22 689	16 181	38 379	22 480	15 900	38 261	22 374	15 886	38 325	22 478	15 847	38 804	22 762	16 042
Employment-population ratio	76.4	87.9	64.6	76.8	88.5	64.6	77.1	89.5	64.6	77.3	89.8	64.5	78.0	90.7	65.1
Full-time workers[1]	5 728	1 245	4 482	5 440	1 158	4 282	32 961	21 277	11 684	33 196	21 436	11 759	33 773	21 751	12 022
Part-time workers[2]	76	88	65	77	88	65	5 299	1 097	4 202	5 130	1 042	4 088	5 032	1 012	4 020
Unemployed	2 730	1 643	1 087	2 404	1 393	1 011	2 017	1 106	910	1 771	969	802	1 415	742	673
Unemployment rate	6.6	6.8	6.3	5.9	5.8	6.0	5.0	4.7	5.4	4.4	4.1	4.8	3.5	3.2	4.0
Other Marital Status[3]															
Civilian noninstitutional population	13 620	2 643	10 977	13 886	2 751	11 135	16 025	3 930	12 095	15 789	3 912	11 878	15 904	3 943	11 961
Civilian labor force	10 559	2 329	8 230	10 737	2 429	8 308	12 477	3 473	9 004	12 238	3 422	8 817	12 360	3 434	8 926
Participation rate	77.5	88.1	75.0	77.3	88.3	74.6	77.9	88.4	74.4	77.5	87.5	74.2	77.7	87.1	74.6
Employed	8 994	1 964	7 029	9 198	2 139	7 059	10 840	3 085	7 755	10 820	3 062	7 759	11 143	3 137	8 007
Employment-population ratio	66.0	74.3	64.0	66.2	77.8	63.4	67.6	78.5	64.1	68.5	78.3	65.3	70.1	79.6	66.9
Full-time workers[1]	1 853	232	1 621	1 864	216	1 647	8 736	2 777	5 959	8 648	2 771	5 878	8 955	2 864	6 090
Part-time workers[2]	66	74	64	66	78	63	2 104	308	1 796	2 172	291	1 881	2 189	272	1 917
Unemployed	1 566	365	1 201	1 539	290	1 249	1 636	388	1 249	1 418	360	1 058	1 217	298	919
Unemployment rate	14.8	15.7	14.6	14.3	11.9	15.0	13.1	11.2	13.9	11.6	10.5	12.0	9.8	8.7	10.3
With Own Children 6 to 17 Years, None Younger															
Civilian noninstitutional population	35 402	15 639	19 763	35 027	15 431	19 596	35 786	15 777	20 009	36 218	16 007	20 212	36 486	16 114	20 372
Civilian labor force	29 625	14 515	15 110	29 193	14 289	14 904	29 573	14 545	15 028	29 815	14 714	15 101	29 989	14 768	15 221
Participation rate	83.7	92.8	76.5	77.6	87.0	70.2	82.6	92.2	75.1	82.3	91.9	74.7	82.2	91.6	74.7
Employed	27 421	13 482	13 939	27 178	13 422	13 756	27 722	13 791	13 931	28 216	14 047	14 169	28 689	14 244	14 445
Employment-population ratio	77.5	86.2	70.5	77.6	87.0	70.2	77.5	87.4	69.6	77.9	87.8	70.1	78.6	88.4	70.9
Full-time workers[1]	4 182	757	3 425	3 992	686	3 306	23 783	13 074	10 709	24 181	13 361	10 819	24 746	13 594	11 153
Part-time workers[2]	78	86	70	78	87	70	3 939	717	3 222	4 035	686	3 349	3 943	650	3 292
Unemployed	2 204	1 032	1 172	2 015	867	1 148	1 851	754	1 097	1 599	667	933	1 300	524	775
Unemployment rate	7.4	7.1	7.8	6.9	6.1	7.7	6.3	5.2	7.3	5.4	4.5	6.2	4.3	3.6	5.1
With Own Children Under 6 Years															
Civilian noninstitutional population	29 086	12 824	16 262	28 858	12 712	16 146	29 834	13 167	16 667	29 166	12 940	16 226	29 157	12 927	16 230
Civilian labor force	22 534	12 146	10 388	22 328	12 013	10 315	23 181	12 409	10 772	22 519	12 155	10 365	22 591	12 171	10 420
Participation rate	77.5	94.7	63.9	77.4	94.5	63.9	77.7	94.2	64.6	77.2	93.9	63.9	77.5	94.2	64.0
Employed	20 442	11 171	9 271	20 400	11 197	9 203	21 379	11 669	9 710	20 930	11 493	9 437	21 259	11 655	9 604
Employment-population ratio	70.3	87.1	57.0	70.7	88.1	57.0	71.7	88.6	58.3	71.8	88.8	58.2	72.9	90.2	59.2
Full-time workers[1]	3 399	720	2 679	3 311	687	2 624	17 915	10 981	6 934	17 663	10 846	6 817	17 981	11 021	6 959
Part-time workers[2]	70	87	57	71	88	57	3 464	688	2 776	3 267	647	2 620	3 278	634	2 644
Unemployed	2 092	975	1 117	1 928	816	1 112	1 802	740	1 062	1 589	662	928	1 332	516	816
Unemployment rate	9.3	8.0	10.8	8.6	6.8	10.8	7.8	6.0	9.9	7.1	5.4	8.9	5.9	4.2	7.8
With No Own Children Under 18 Years															
Civilian noninstitutional population	173 342	86 711	86 631	175 732	88 175	87 558	177 665	88 400	89 264	180 295	89 609	90 686	182 304	90 707	91 596
Civilian labor force	101 729	55 324	46 405	102 096	55 673	46 423	102 221	55 373	46 848	103 055	55 798	47 256	103 342	55 943	47 399
Participation rate	58.7	63.8	53.6	58.1	63.1	53.0	57.5	62.6	52.5	57.2	62.3	52.1	56.7	61.7	51.7
Employed	91 201	48 706	42 495	92 291	49 671	42 620	93 368	50 096	43 272	94 783	50 813	43 971	96 357	51 793	44 564
Employment-population ratio	52.6	56.2	49.1	52.5	56.3	48.7	52.6	56.7	48.5	52.6	56.7	48.5	52.9	57.1	48.7
Full-time workers[1]	19 769	8 381	11 387	20 010	8 584	11 426	73 111	41 423	31 688	74 470	42 128	32 342	75 991	43 214	32 777
Part-time workers[2]	53	56	49	52	56	49	20 257	8 673	11 584	20 313	8 685	11 629	20 366	8 579	11 787
Unemployed	10 528	6 618	3 910	9 805	6 002	3 803	8 853	5 277	3 575	8 271	4 986	3 285	6 985	4 150	2 835
Unemployment rate	10.3	12.0	8.4	9.6	10.8	8.2	8.7	9.5	7.6	8.0	8.9	7.0	6.8	7.4	6.0

Note: Own children include sons, daughters, stepchildren, and adopted children. Not included are nieces, nephews, grandchildren, and other related and unrelated children. Detail may not sum to total due to rounding.

[1]Usually work 35 hours or more a week at all jobs.
[2]Usually work less than 35 hours a week at all jobs.
[3]Includes never-married, divorced, separated, and widowed persons.

Table 1-23. Employment Status of the Population, by Sex, Marital Status, and Presence and Age of Own Children Under 18 Years, Annual Averages, 2010–2018—*Continued*

(Thousands of people, percent.)

Characteristic	2015			2016			2017			2018		
	Both sexes	Men	Women	Both sexes	Men	Women	Both sexes	Men	Women	Both sexes	Men	Women
With Own Children Under 18 Years, Total												
Civilian noninstitutional population	65 564	29 095	36 469	65 055	28 992	36 063	64 188	28 740	35 448	64 235	28 913	35 321
Civilian labor force	52 476	26 978	25 498	52 321	26 902	25 419	51 875	26 662	25 213	52 206	26 967	25 239
Participation rate	80.0	92.7	69.9	80.4	92.8	70.5	80.8	92.8	71.1	81.3	93.3	71.5
Employed	50 238	26 079	24 159	50 240	26 039	24 201	50 036	25 920	24 117	50 590	26 316	24 274
Employment-population ratio	76.6	89.6	66.2	77.2	89.8	67.1	78.0	90.2	68.0	78.8	91.0	68.7
Full-time workers[1]	43 250	24 880	18 370	43 352	24 896	18 456	43 433	24 807	18 626	44 177	25 231	18 946
Part-time workers[2]	6 989	1 199	5 790	6 887	1 143	5 744	6 604	1 113	5 491	6 414	1 085	5 328
Unemployed	2 238	899	1 339	2 082	864	1 218	1 838	742	1 096	1 616	651	965
Unemployment rate	4.3	3.3	5.3	4.0	3.2	4.8	3.5	2.8	4.3	3.1	2.4	3.8
Married, Spouse Present												
Civilian noninstitutional population	49 822	25 122	24 700	49 472	25 007	24 465	48 974	24 779	24 195	49 007	24 809	24 198
Civilian labor force	40 226	23 532	16 694	40 016	23 409	16 607	39 781	23 172	16 609	40 043	23 341	16 703
Participation rate	80.7	93.7	67.6	80.9	93.6	67.9	81.2	93.5	68.6	81.7	94.1	69.0
Employed	39 026	22 889	16 137	38 866	22 791	16 075	38 775	22 633	16 142	39 183	22 895	16 288
Employment-population ratio	78.3	91.1	65.3	78.6	91.1	65.7	79.2	91.3	66.7	80.0	92.3	67.3
Full-time workers[1]	34 148	21 958	12 190	34 112	21 899	12 214	34 081	21 746	12 334	34 625	22 044	12 581
Part-time workers[2]	4 877	931	3 947	4 754	892	3 861	4 695	887	3 808	4 558	851	3 707
Unemployed	1 200	643	557	1 150	618	532	1 006	539	467	860	445	415
Unemployment rate	3.0	2.7	3.3	2.9	2.6	3.2	2.5	2.3	2.8	2.1	1.9	2.5
Other Marital Status[3]												
Civilian noninstitutional population	15 742	3 973	11 769	15 583	3 985	11 598	15 213	3 961	11 253	15 228	4 104	11 123
Civilian labor force	12 250	3 446	8 804	12 305	3 494	8 811	12 093	3 490	8 603	12 163	3 627	8 536
Participation rate	77.8	86.7	74.8	79.0	87.7	76.0	79.5	88.1	76.5	79.9	88.4	76.7
Employed	11 213	3 190	8 022	11 374	3 248	8 125	11 261	3 287	7 975	11 407	3 421	7 987
Employment-population ratio	71.2	80.3	68.2	73.0	81.5	70.1	74.0	83.0	70.9	74.9	83.3	71.8
Full-time workers[1]	9 101	2 922	6 179	9 240	2 997	6 243	9 352	3 061	6 291	9 552	3 187	6 365
Part-time workers[2]	2 111	268	1 843	2 134	251	1 883	1 909	226	1 683	1 856	234	1 622
Unemployed	1 038	256	782	931	246	686	832	203	629	755	206	550
Unemployment rate	8.5	7.4	8.9	7.6	7.0	7.8	6.9	5.8	7.3	6.2	5.7	6.4
With Own Children 6 to 17 Years, None Younger												
Civilian noninstitutional population	36 616	16 171	20 445	36 491	16 152	20 338	36 286	16 153	20 133	35 880	15 995	19 886
Civilian labor force	30 057	14 840	15 218	30 088	14 836	15 252	30 060	14 812	15 248	29 936	14 753	15 183
Participation rate	82.1	91.8	74.4	82.5	91.9	75.0	82.8	91.7	75.7	83.4	92.2	76.4
Employed	28 923	14 392	14 531	28 998	14 393	14 605	29 063	14 428	14 635	29 097	14 429	14 668
Employment-population ratio	79.0	89.0	71.1	79.5	89.1	71.8	80.1	89.3	72.7	81.1	90.2	73.8
Full-time workers[1]	25 073	13 785	11 288	25 166	13 785	11 381	25 391	13 830	11 561	25 604	13 860	11 744
Part-time workers[2]	3 850	607	3 243	3 831	607	3 224	3 672	598	3 074	3 493	569	2 924
Unemployed	1 134	448	687	1 090	444	646	997	384	612	840	324	515
Unemployment rate	3.8	3.0	4.5	3.6	3.0	4.2	3.3	2.6	4.0	2.8	2.2	3.4
With Own Children Under 6 Years												
Civilian noninstitutional population	28 948	12 924	16 024	28 565	12 840	15 724	27 902	12 587	15 315	28 354	12 919	15 436
Civilian labor force	22 419	12 138	10 281	22 233	12 066	10 167	21 815	11 849	9 965	22 270	12 214	10 056
Participation rate	77.4	93.9	64.2	77.8	94.0	64.7	78.2	94.1	65.0	78.5	94.5	65.1
Employed	21 315	11 687	9 628	21 242	11 646	9 596	20 973	11 492	9 481	21 494	11 888	9 606
Employment-population ratio	73.6	90.4	60.1	74.4	90.7	61.0	18041.0	10977.0	7064.0	18573.0	11371.0	7201.0
Full-time workers[1]	18 177	11 095	7 082	18 186	11 110	7 076	75	91	62	76	92	62
Part-time workers[2]	3 139	592	2 547	3 056	536	2 520	2 932	515	2 417	2 921	516	2 405
Unemployed	1 104	451	652	992	420	572	841	358	484	776	327	449
Unemployment rate	4.9	3.7	6.3	4.5	3.5	5.6	3.9	3.0	4.9	3.5	2.7	4.5
With No Own Children Under 18 Years												
Civilian noninstitutional population	185 237	92 006	93 231	188 482	93 505	94 978	190 891	94 535	96 356	193 556	95 765	97 791
Civilian labor force	104 654	56 643	48 011	106 866	57 852	49 014	108 445	58 483	49 962	109 869	59 129	50 740
Participation rate	56.5	61.6	51.5	56.7	61.9	51.6	56.8	61.9	51.9	56.8	61.7	51.9
Employed	98 595	53 052	45 544	101 196	54 529	46 667	103 301	55 482	47 819	105 171	56 382	48 789
Employment-population ratio	53.2	57.7	48.9	53.7	58.3	49.1	54.1	58.7	49.6	54.3	58.9	49.9
Full-time workers[1]	78 243	44 471	33 772	80 408	45 671	34 738	82 535	46 764	35 770	84 396	47 704	36 692
Part-time workers[2]	20 353	8 581	11 772	20 788	8 858	11 930	20 766	8 718	12 048	20 775	8 678	12 096
Unemployed	6 058	3 591	2 468	5 670	3 323	2 346	5 144	3 001	2 143	4 698	2 747	1 951
Unemployment rate	5.8	6.3	5.1	5.3	5.7	4.8	4.7	5.1	4.3	4.3	4.6	3.8

Note: Own children include sons, daughters, stepchildren, and adopted children. Not included are nieces, nephews, grandchildren, and other related and unrelated children. Detail may not sum to total due to rounding.

[1]Usually work 35 hours or more a week at all jobs.
[2]Usually work less than 35 hours a week at all jobs.
[3]Includes never-married, divorced, separated, and widowed persons.

Table 1-24. Employment Status of Mothers with Own Children Under 3 Years of Age, by Age of Youngest Child and Marital Status, Annual Averages, 2009–2018

(Thousands of people, percent.)

Year and characteristic	Civilian noninsti-tutional population	Civilian labor force		Employed				Unemployed	
		Total	Percent of population	Total	Percent of population	Full-time workers[1]	Part-time workers[2]	Number	Percent of labor force
2009									
Total Mothers with Own Children Under 3 Years	9 476	5 787	61.1	5 191	54.8	3 626	1 565	595	10.3
2 years	2 848	1 855	65.1	1 693	59.4	1 195	498	162	8.7
1 year	3 398	2 104	61.9	1 880	55.3	1 314	566	224	10.6
Under 1 year	3 231	1 828	56.6	1 619	50.1	1 117	502	209	11.4
Married, Spouse Present with Own Children Under 3 Years	6 784	4 047	59.7	3 780	55.7	2 657	1 123	267	6.6
2 years	2 053	1 288	62.7	1 208	58.8	858	350	80	6.2
1 year	2 425	1 465	60.4	1 369	56.4	963	406	96	6.6
Under 1 year	2 306	1 293	56.1	1 204	52.2	836	368	90	7.0
Other Marital Status with Own Children Under 3 Years[3]	2 693	1 740	64.6	1 411	52.4	969	442	328	18.9
2 years	795	567	71.3	485	61.0	337	148	82	14.4
1 year	973	639	65.6	511	52.5	351	160	127	20.0
Under 1 year	925	534	57.8	415	44.9	281	134	119	22.3
2010									
Total Mothers with Own Children Under 3 Years	9 503	5 770	60.7	5 114	53.8	3 570	1 543	656	11.4
2 years	2 968	1 908	64.3	1 708	57.5	1 200	509	199	10.5
1 year	3 351	2 062	61.5	1 815	54.2	1 243	572	246	12.0
Under 1 year	3 184	1 800	56.5	1 590	49.9	1 128	462	210	11.7
Married, Spouse Present with Own Children Under 3 Years	6 642	3 941	59.3	3 670	55.3	2 596	1 074	271	6.9
2 years	2 055	1 275	62.1	1 195	58.2	841	354	80	6.3
1 year	2 344	1 403	59.8	1 301	55.5	896	405	101	7.2
Under 1 year	3 184	1 800	56.5	1 590	49.9	1 128	462	210	11.7
Other Marital Status with Own Children Under 3 Years[3]	2 862	1 828	63.9	1 444	50.5	974	470	385	21.0
2 years	914	633	69.2	514	56.2	359	155	119	18.8
1 year	1 007	659	65.5	514	51.0	346	168	145	22.0
Under 1 year	941	537	57.0	416	44.2	269	147	121	22.5
2011									
Total Mothers with Own Children Under 3 Years	9 259	5 613	60.6	4 977	53.8	3 486	1 492	635	11.3
2 years	2 893	1 848	63.9	1 645	56.9	1 169	476	202	11.0
1 year	3 353	2 083	62.1	1 844	55.0	1 296	548	239	11.5
Under 1 year	3 013	1 682	55.8	1 488	49.4	1 021	467	194	11.5
Married, Spouse Present with Own Children Under 3 Years	6 488	3 854	59.4	3 603	55.5	2 594	1 009	251	6.5
2 years	1 999	1 220	61.0	1 138	56.9	822	316	82	6.7
1 year	2 381	1 434	60.2	1 342	56.4	967	375	92	6.4
Under 1 year	2 109	1 200	56.9	1 123	53.3	805	318	77	6.4
Other Marital Status with Own Children Under 3 Years[3]	2 771	1 759	63.5	1 375	49.6	892	483	384	21.8
2 years	894	628	70.3	508	56.8	347	161	120	19.2
1 year	973	649	66.8	502	51.6	329	173	147	22.6
Under 1 year	905	482	53.2	365	40.3	216	149	117	24.2
2012									
Total Mothers with Own Children Under 3 Years	9 540	5 839	61.2	5 245	55.0	3 690	1 555	594	10.2
2 years	2 922	1 890	64.7	1 708	58.5	1 215	493	181	9.6
1 year	3 393	2 119	62.5	1 909	56.3	1 314	595	210	9.9
Under 1 year	3 224	1 830	56.7	1 628	50.5	1 161	467	202	11.0
Married, Spouse Present with Own Children Under 3 Years	6 334	3 808	60.1	3 600	56.8	2 595	1 005	208	5.5
2 years	1 940	1 198	61.8	1 134	58.5	816	318	64	5.4
1 year	2 288	1 409	61.6	1 332	58.2	928	405	77	5.5
Under 1 year	2 106	1 200	57.0	1 134	53.8	852	282	66	5.5
Other Marital Status with Own Children Under 3 Years[3]	3 206	2 031	63.4	1 645	51.3	1 095	550	386	19.0
2 years	982	691	70.4	574	58.5	399	175	117	17.0
1 year	1 105	710	64.2	577	52.2	386	191	133	18.8
Under 1 year	1 119	630	56.3	494	44.2	309	185	136	21.6
2013									
Total Mothers with Own Children Under 3 Years	9 211	5 626	61.1	5 113	55.5	3 615	1 497	514	9.1
2 years	2 877	1 875	65.2	1 723	59.9	1 240	482	152	8.1
1 year	3 266	1 995	61.1	1 798	55.0	1 251	547	197	9.9
Under 1 year	3 069	1 757	57.3	1 593	51.9	1 124	469	164	9.3
Married, Spouse Present with Own Children Under 3 Years	6 224	3 689	59.3	3 503	56.3	2 541	962	186	5.0
2 years	1 913	1 194	62.4	1 141	59.6	835	305	54	4.5
1 year	2 232	1 299	58.2	1 224	54.9	867	357	75	5.8
Under 1 year	2 080	1 196	57.5	1 138	54.7	839	299	58	4.8
Other Marital Status with Own Children Under 3 Years[3]	2 987	1 937	64.9	1 610	53.9	1 075	535	327	16.9
2 years	964	681	70.6	582	60.3	405	177	99	14.5
1 year	1 034	695	67.3	573	55.5	384	189	122	17.5
Under 1 year	989	561	56.7	455	46.0	285	169	107	19.0

Note: Own children include sons, daughters, stepchildren, and adopted children. Not included are nieces, nephews, grandchildren, and other related and unrelated children. Detail may not sum to total due to rounding. Updated population controls are introduced annually with the release of January data.

[1]Usually work 35 hours or more a week at all jobs.
[2]Usually work less than 35 hours a week at all jobs.
[3]Includes never-married, divorced, separated, and widowed persons.

Table 1-24. Employment Status of Mothers with Own Children Under 3 Years of Age, by Age of Youngest Child and Marital Status, Annual Averages, 2009–2018—*Continued*

(Thousands of people, percent.)

Year and characteristic	Civilian noninstitutional population	Civilian labor force						Unemployed	
		Total	Percent of population	Employed				Number	Percent of labor force
				Total	Percent of population	Full-time workers[1]	Part-time workers[2]		
2014									
Total Mothers with Own Children Under 3 Years	9 224	5 624	61.0	5 169	56.0	3 685	1 484	456	8.1
2 years	2 834	1 799	63.5	1 661	58.6	1 185	477	137	7.6
1 year	3 293	2 056	62.4	1 880	57.1	1 325	555	176	8.6
Under 1 year	3 097	1 770	57.1	1 628	52.6	1 175	453	142	8.0
Married, Spouse Present with Own Children Under 3 Years	6 243	3 691	59.1	3 526	56.5	2 602	925	165	4.5
2 years	1 934	1 153	59.6	1 104	57.1	807	296	49	4.3
1 year	2 300	1 376	59.8	1 307	56.8	950	357	68	5.0
Under 1 year	2 009	1 163	57.9	1 116	55.5	844	271	47	4.1
Other Marital Status with Own Children Under 3 Years[3]	2 981	1 933	64.9	1 642	55.1	1 083	559	291	15.0
2 years	900	646	71.8	558	62.0	377	180	88	13.6
1 year	993	681	68.6	573	57.7	375	197	108	15.8
Under 1 year	1 088	607	55.8	512	47.0	330	182	95	15.6
2015									
Total Mothers with Own Children Under 3 Years	9 308	5 714	61.4	5 336	57.3	3 882	1 455	377	6.6
2 years	2 920	1 869	64.0	1 741	59.6	1 280	462	127	6.8
1 year	3 254	2 024	62.2	1 897	58.3	1 370	526	128	6.3
Under 1 year	3 134	1 821	58.1	1 698	54.2	1 232	466	123	6.7
Married, Spouse Present with Own Children Under 3 Years	6 341	3 772	59.5	3 628	57.2	2 698	931	144	3.8
2 years	1 974	1 198	60.7	1 149	58.2	864	285	49	4.1
1 year	2 252	1 356	60.2	1 300	57.7	961	339	55	4.1
Under 1 year	2 114	1 218	57.6	1 179	55.8	873	306	39	3.2
Other Marital Status with Own Children Under 3 Years[3]	2 967	1 942	65.4	1 708	57.6	1 184	524	234	12.0
2 years	946	670	70.9	592	62.6	415	177	78	11.6
1 year	1 001	669	66.8	596	59.5	409	187	72	10.8
Under 1 year	1 020	603	59.1	519	50.9	359	160	84	13.9
2016									
Total Mothers with Own Children Under 3 Years	9 158	5 662	61.8	5 343	58.3	3 870	1 473	319	5.6
2 years	2 850	1 858	65.2	1 764	61.9	1 312	452	94	5.0
1 year	3 322	2 055	61.9	1 933	58.2	1 392	540	123	6.0
Under 1 year	2 985	1 749	58.6	1 645	55.1	1 165	480	103	5.9
Married, Spouse Present with Own Children Under 3 Years	6 335	3 768	59.5	3 648	57.6	2 691	957	120	3.2
2 years	1 964	1 210	61.6	1 171	59.6	876	294	39	3.3
1 year	2 302	1 367	59.4	1 321	57.4	966	356	46	3.4
Under 1 year	2 069	1 191	57.6	1 156	55.9	849	307	35	3.0
Other Marital Status with Own Children Under 3 Years[3]	2 823	1 894	67.1	1 695	60.0	1 179	516	199	10.5
2 years	886	648	73.1	594	67.0	436	158	54	8.4
1 year	1 020	689	67.5	612	60.0	427	185	77	11.2
Under 1 year	917	557	60.8	489	53.4	316	173	68	12.2
2017									
Total Mothers with Own Children Under 3 Years	8 877	5 528	62.3	5 250	59.1	3 837	1 413	277	5.0
2 years	2 804	1 835	65.4	1 742	62.1	1 315	427	93	5.1
1 year	3 208	2 016	62.8	1 923	59.9	1 385	538	93	4.6
Under 1 year	2 865	1 677	58.5	1 585	55.3	1 138	447	92	5.5
Married, Spouse Present with Own Children Under 3 Years	6 193	3 716	60.0	3 618	58.4	2 660	958	98	2.6
2 years	1 951	1 207	61.9	1 167	59.8	871	296	40	3.3
1 year	2 253	1 354	60.1	1 324	58.8	970	353	30	2.2
Under 1 year	1 989	1 155	58.1	1 128	56.7	819	309	27	2.4
Other Marital Status with Own Children Under 3 Years[3]	2 684	1 812	67.5	1 632	60.8	1 177	455	180	9.9
2 years	853	628	73.6	575	67.4	443	131	53	8.5
1 year	956	662	69.3	600	62.7	415	185	62	9.4
Under 1 year	876	522	59.6	457	52.2	319	138	64	12.3
2018									
Total Mothers with Own Children Under 3 Years	8 825	5 462	61.9	5 210	59.0	3 827	1 383	251	4.6
2 years	2 842	1 858	65.4	1 775	62.5	1 323	452	83	4.5
1 year	3 133	1 956	62.4	1 866	59.6	1 347	519	90	4.6
Under 1 year	2 849	1 648	57.8	1 569	55.1	1 157	412	78	4.8
Married, Spouse Present with Own Children Under 3 Years	6 195	3 694	59.6	3 597	58.1	2 656	940	97	2.6
2 years	1 996	1 221	61.2	1 187	59.4	881	306	35	2.9
1 year	2 195	1 328	60.5	1 294	59.0	945	349	33	2.5
Under 1 year	2 004	1 145	57.1	1 116	55.7	831	285	29	2.5
Other Marital Status with Own Children Under 3 Years[3]	2 630	1 768	67.2	1 614	61.4	1 170	443	154	8.7
2 years	846	637	75.2	589	69.5	442	147	48	7.6
1 year	938	628	67.0	572	60.9	402	170	57	9.0
Under 1 year	845	503	59.5	453	53.6	327	127	50	9.8

Note: Own children include sons, daughters, stepchildren, and adopted children. Not included are nieces, nephews, grandchildren, and other related and unrelated children. Detail may not sum to total due to rounding. Updated population controls are introduced annually with the release of January data.

[1]Usually work 35 hours or more a week at all jobs.
[2]Usually work less than 35 hours a week at all jobs.
[3]Includes never-married, divorced, separated, and widowed persons.

UNEMPLOYMENT

Figure 1-3. Unemployment Rate by Race and Sex, 1975–2018

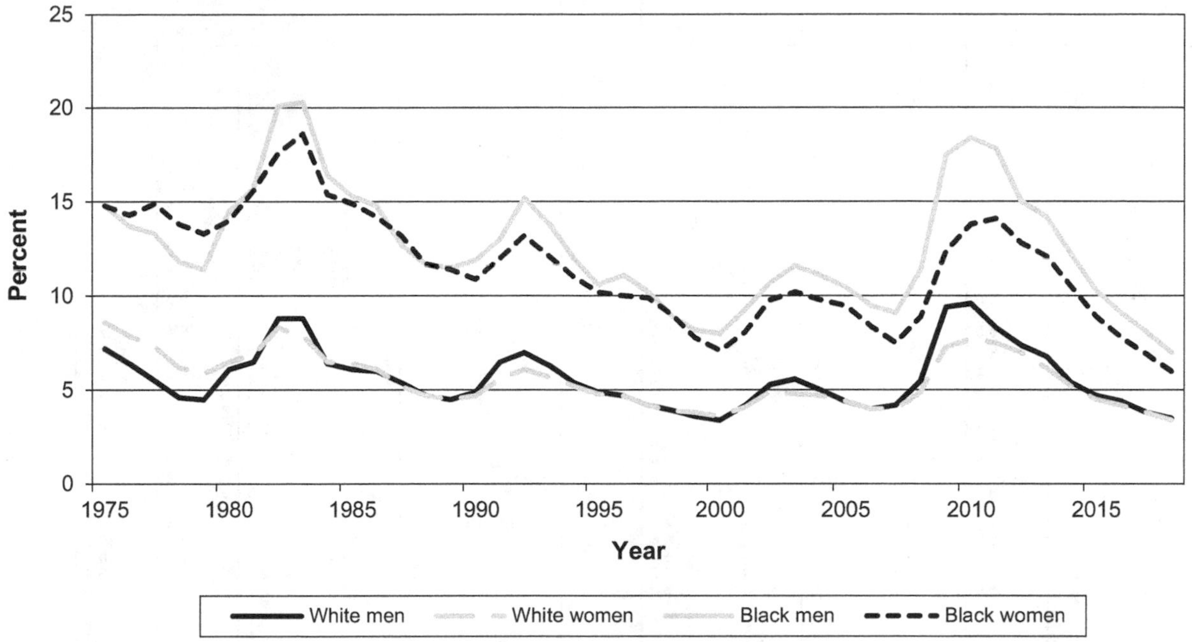

The unemployment rate declined for the eighth consecutive year in 2018 from 4.4 percent in 2017 to 3.9 percent in 2018. Although the unemployment rate was slightly higher for men (3.9 percent) than for women (3.8 percent), the gap is getting far more narrow. In 2010, men had an unemployment rate of 10.5 percent compared with an unemployment rate of 8.6 percent for women. In 2018, Black men had the highest unemployment rate at 7.0 percent followed by Black women with an unemployment rate of 6.0 percent. From 2017 to 2018, the unemployment rate decreased by 1.0 percent for both Blacks and 0.3 percent for Whites. (See Table 1-27.)

OTHER HIGHLIGHTS

- While the unemployment rate decreased or remained steady for every age group again in 2018, the disparity in unemployment rates among age groups continued to be substantial as younger workers typically experience much higher levels of unemployment. In 2018, the unemployment rate for those age 16 to 19 years was 12.9 percent, while it was only 2.9 percent for those age 55 to 64 years. (See Table 1-27.)

- Among the major industries, agriculture and private wage salary workers continued to have the highest unemployment rate at 7.2 percent, followed by and leisure and hospitality workers at 5.7 percent. Financial activities had the lowest unemployment rate at 2.2 percent. (See Table 1-29.)

- The number of persons unemployed 27 weeks and over declined again in 2017 to 1.3 million. Although this was a 78 percent decline from 2010, it was still significantly higher than the number of unemployed people in 2006 shortly before the Great Recession (1.2 million). (See Table 1-31.)

- In 2018, the unemployment rate declined in 45 states and the District of Columbia, remained stable in Maine, Arkansas, and Hawaii, and increased in three states (West Virginia, Colorado, and Oregon). (See Table 1-5.)

Table 1-25. Unemployment Rate, by Selected Characteristics, 1948–2018

(Unemployment as a percent of civilian labor force.)

Year	All civilian workers	Both sexes, 16 to 19 years	Men, 20 years and over	Women, 20 years and over	White[1]	Black[1]	Asian[1]	Hispanic[2]	Marital status and sex: Men: Single, never married	Men: Married, spouse present	Men: Widowed, divorced, or separated	Women: Single, never married	Women: Married, spouse present	Women: Widowed, divorced, or separated
1948	3.8	9.2	3.2	3.6	...	...	...	...	...	...	...	...	...	...
1949	5.9	13.4	5.4	5.3	...	...	...	...	...	...	...	...	...	...
1950	5.3	12.2	4.7	5.1	...	...	...	...	...	...	...	...	...	...
1951	3.3	8.2	2.5	4.0	...	...	...	...	...	...	...	...	...	...
1952	3.0	8.5	2.4	3.2	...	...	...	...	...	...	...	...	...	...
1953	2.9	7.6	2.5	2.9	...	...	...	...	...	...	...	...	...	...
1954	5.5	12.6	4.9	5.5	5.0	...	...	...	...	...	...	...	...	...
1955	4.4	11.0	3.8	4.4	3.9	...	...	...	8.6	2.6	7.1	5.0	3.7	5.0
1956	4.1	11.1	3.4	4.2	3.6	...	...	...	7.7	2.3	6.2	5.3	3.6	5.0
1957	4.3	11.6	3.6	4.1	3.8	...	...	...	9.2	2.8	6.8	5.6	4.3	4.7
1958	6.8	15.9	6.2	6.1	6.1	...	...	...	13.3	5.1	11.2	7.4	6.5	6.7
1959	5.5	14.6	4.7	5.2	4.8	...	...	...	11.6	3.6	8.6	7.1	5.2	6.2
1960	5.5	14.7	4.7	5.1	5.0	...	...	...	11.7	3.7	8.4	7.5	5.2	5.9
1961	6.7	16.8	5.7	6.3	6.0	...	...	...	13.1	4.6	10.3	8.7	6.4	7.4
1962	5.5	14.7	4.6	5.4	4.9	...	...	...	11.2	3.6	9.9	7.9	5.4	6.4
1963	5.7	17.2	4.5	5.4	5.0	...	...	...	12.4	3.4	9.6	8.9	5.4	6.7
1964	5.2	16.2	3.9	5.2	4.6	...	...	...	11.5	2.8	8.9	8.7	5.1	6.4
1965	4.5	14.8	3.2	4.5	4.1	...	...	...	10.1	2.4	7.2	8.2	4.5	5.4
1966	3.8	12.8	2.5	3.8	3.4	...	...	...	8.6	1.9	5.5	7.9	3.7	4.7
1967	3.8	12.9	2.3	4.2	3.4	...	...	...	8.3	1.8	4.9	7.5	4.5	4.6
1968	3.6	12.7	2.2	3.8	3.2	...	...	...	8.0	1.6	4.2	7.6	3.9	4.2
1969	3.5	12.2	2.1	3.7	3.1	...	...	...	8.0	1.5	4.0	7.3	3.9	4.0
1970	4.9	15.3	3.5	4.8	4.5	...	...	...	11.2	2.6	6.4	9.0	4.9	5.2
1971	5.9	16.9	4.4	5.7	5.4	...	...	...	13.2	3.2	7.4	10.5	5.7	6.3
1972	5.6	16.2	4.0	5.4	5.1	10.4	...	...	12.4	2.8	7.0	10.1	5.4	6.1
1973	4.9	14.5	3.3	4.9	4.3	9.4	...	7.5	10.4	2.3	5.4	9.4	4.7	5.8
1974	5.6	16.0	3.8	5.5	5.0	10.5	...	8.1	11.8	2.7	6.2	10.5	5.3	6.3
1975	8.5	19.9	6.8	8.0	7.8	14.8	...	12.2	16.1	5.1	11.0	13.0	7.9	8.9
1976	7.7	19.0	5.9	7.4	7.0	14.0	...	11.5	14.9	4.2	9.8	12.1	7.1	8.7
1977	7.1	17.8	5.2	7.0	6.2	14.0	...	10.1	13.5	3.6	8.2	12.1	6.5	7.9
1978	6.1	16.4	4.3	6.0	5.2	12.8	...	9.1	11.7	2.8	6.6	10.9	5.5	6.9
1979	5.8	16.1	4.2	5.7	5.1	12.3	...	8.3	11.1	2.8	6.5	10.4	5.1	6.7
1980	7.1	17.8	5.9	6.4	6.3	14.3	...	10.1	13.6	4.2	8.6	10.9	5.8	7.2
1981	7.6	19.6	6.3	6.8	6.7	15.6	...	10.4	14.6	4.3	9.1	11.9	6.0	8.1
1982	9.7	23.2	8.8	8.3	8.6	18.9	...	13.8	17.7	6.5	12.4	13.6	7.4	9.5
1983	9.6	22.4	8.9	8.1	8.4	19.5	...	13.7	17.3	6.5	13.0	13.1	7.0	9.9
1984	7.5	18.9	6.6	6.8	6.5	15.9	...	10.7	13.5	4.6	9.4	11.1	5.7	8.4
1985	7.2	18.6	6.2	6.6	6.2	15.1	...	10.5	12.7	4.3	9.2	10.7	5.6	8.3
1986	7.0	18.3	6.1	6.2	6.0	14.5	...	10.6	12.2	4.4	8.8	10.7	5.2	7.7
1987	6.2	16.9	5.4	5.4	5.3	13.0	...	8.8	11.1	3.9	7.6	9.5	4.3	7.0
1988	5.5	15.3	4.8	4.9	4.7	11.7	...	8.2	9.9	3.3	7.0	8.6	3.9	6.3
1989	5.3	15.0	4.5	4.7	4.5	11.4	...	8.0	9.6	3.0	6.3	8.4	3.7	5.9
1990	5.6	15.5	5.0	4.9	4.8	11.4	...	8.2	10.1	3.4	6.9	8.7	3.8	6.0
1991	6.8	18.7	6.4	5.7	6.1	12.5	...	10.0	12.4	4.4	9.0	10.1	4.5	6.9
1992	7.5	20.1	7.1	6.3	6.6	14.2	...	11.6	13.2	5.1	9.8	10.8	5.0	7.6
1993	6.9	19.0	6.4	5.9	6.1	13.0	...	10.8	12.4	4.4	9.0	10.3	4.6	7.3
1994	6.1	17.6	5.4	5.4	5.3	11.5	...	9.9	11.0	3.7	7.4	9.7	4.1	6.6
1995	5.6	17.3	4.8	4.9	4.9	10.4	...	9.3	10.1	3.3	6.9	9.1	3.9	5.9
1996	5.4	16.7	4.6	4.8	4.7	10.5	...	8.9	10.0	3.0	6.5	9.1	3.6	5.7
1997	4.9	16.0	4.2	4.4	4.2	10.0	...	7.7	9.2	2.7	5.8	8.8	3.1	5.2
1998	4.5	14.6	3.7	4.1	3.9	8.9	...	7.2	8.5	2.4	4.8	7.8	2.9	4.9
1999	4.2	13.9	3.5	3.8	3.7	8.0	...	6.4	7.8	2.2	4.6	7.4	2.7	4.5
2000	4.0	13.1	3.3	3.6	3.5	7.6	3.6	5.7	7.6	2.0	4.3	6.8	2.7	4.2
2001	4.7	14.7	4.2	4.1	4.2	8.6	4.5	6.6	8.9	2.7	5.1	7.7	3.1	4.7
2002	5.8	16.5	5.3	5.1	5.1	10.2	5.9	7.5	10.3	3.6	6.8	8.9	3.7	6.1
2003	6.0	17.5	5.6	5.1	5.2	10.8	6.0	7.7	11.0	3.8	7.3	9.1	3.7	6.1
2004	5.5	17.0	5.0	4.9	4.8	10.4	4.4	7.0	10.5	3.1	6.3	8.7	3.5	5.9
2005	5.1	16.6	4.4	4.6	4.4	10.0	4.0	6.0	9.5	2.8	5.6	8.3	3.3	5.4
2006	4.6	15.4	4.0	4.1	4.0	8.9	3.0	5.2	8.6	2.4	5.2	7.7	2.9	4.9
2007	4.6	15.7	4.1	4.0	4.1	8.3	3.2	5.6	8.8	2.5	5.3	7.2	2.8	5.0
2008	5.8	18.7	5.4	4.9	5.2	10.1	4.0	7.6	11.0	3.4	7.1	8.5	3.6	5.9
2009	9.3	24.3	9.6	7.5	8.5	14.8	7.3	12.1	16.3	6.6	12.8	12.0	5.5	9.2
2010	9.6	25.9	9.8	8.0	8.7	16.0	7.5	12.5	16.5	6.8	12.8	12.8	5.9	9.6
2011	8.9	24.4	8.7	7.9	7.9	15.8	7.0	11.5	15.1	5.8	11.1	12.5	5.6	9.7
2012	8.1	24.0	7.5	7.3	7.2	13.8	5.9	10.3	13.7	4.9	9.4	11.8	5.3	8.7
2013	7.4	22.9	7.0	6.5	6.5	13.1	5.2	9.1	13.0	4.3	8.7	10.8	4.6	7.7
2014	6.2	19.6	5.7	5.6	5.3	11.3	5.0	7.4	11.0	3.4	6.9	9.4	3.8	6.6
2015	5.3	16.9	4.9	4.8	4.6	9.6	3.8	6.6	9.5	2.8	6.1	8.2	3.1	5.5
2016	4.9	15.7	4.5	4.4	4.3	8.4	3.6	5.8	8.5	2.7	5.6	7.4	3.0	5.1
2017	4.4	14.0	4.0	4.0	3.8	7.5	3.4	5.1	7.7	2.4	4.6	6.5	2.7	4.8
2018	3.9	12.9	3.6	3.5	3.5	6.5	3.0	4.7	6.9	2.0	4.5	5.8	2.4	4.0

Note: See notes and definitions for information on historical comparability.

[1]Beginning in 2003, persons who selected this race group only; persons who selected more than one race group are not included. Prior to 2003, persons who reported more than one race group were included in the group they identified as their main race.
[2]May be of any race.
. . . = Not available.

Table 1-26. Unemployed Persons, by Age, Sex, Race, and Hispanic Origin, 1948–2018

(Thousands of people.)

Race, Hispanic origin, sex, and year	16 years and over	16 to 19 years			20 years and over						
		Total	16 to 17 years	18 to 19 years	Total	20 to 24 years	25 to 34 years	35 to 44 years	45 to 54 years	55 to 64 years	65 years and over
ALL RACES											
Both Sexes											
1948	2 276	409	180	228	1 869	455	457	347	290	226	93
1949	3 637	576	238	337	3 060	680	776	603	471	384	146
1950	3 288	513	226	287	2 776	561	702	530	478	368	137
1951	2 055	336	168	168	1 718	273	435	354	318	238	103
1952	1 883	345	180	165	1 539	268	389	325	274	195	86
1953	1 834	307	150	157	1 529	256	379	325	280	218	70
1954	3 532	501	221	247	3 032	504	793	680	548	374	132
1955	2 852	450	211	239	2 403	396	577	521	436	355	120
1956	2 750	478	231	247	2 274	395	554	476	429	311	109
1957	2 859	497	230	266	2 362	430	573	499	448	300	111
1958	4 602	678	299	379	3 923	701	993	871	731	472	154
1959	3 740	654	301	354	3 085	543	726	673	603	405	135
1960	3 852	712	325	387	3 140	583	752	671	614	396	122
1961	4 714	828	363	465	3 886	723	890	850	751	516	159
1962	3 911	721	312	409	3 191	636	712	688	605	411	141
1963	4 070	884	420	462	3 187	658	732	674	589	410	126
1964	3 786	872	436	437	2 913	660	607	605	543	378	117
1965	3 366	874	411	463	2 491	557	529	546	436	322	103
1966	2 875	837	395	441	2 041	446	441	426	369	265	92
1967	2 975	839	400	438	2 140	511	480	422	383	256	86
1968	2 817	838	414	426	1 978	543	443	371	314	219	88
1969	2 832	853	436	416	1 978	560	453	358	320	216	72
1970	4 093	1 106	537	569	2 987	866	718	515	476	309	104
1971	5 016	1 262	596	665	3 755	1 130	933	630	573	381	109
1972	4 882	1 308	633	676	3 573	1 132	878	576	510	368	111
1973	4 365	1 235	634	600	3 130	1 008	866	451	430	290	88
1974	5 156	1 422	699	722	3 733	1 212	1 044	559	498	321	99
1975	7 929	1 767	799	968	6 161	1 865	1 776	951	893	520	155
1976	7 406	1 719	796	924	5 687	1 714	1 710	849	758	510	147
1977	6 991	1 663	781	881	5 330	1 629	1 650	785	666	450	147
1978	6 202	1 583	796	787	4 620	1 483	1 422	694	552	345	123
1979	6 137	1 555	739	816	4 583	1 442	1 446	705	540	346	104
1980	7 637	1 669	778	890	5 969	1 835	2 024	940	676	399	94
1981	8 273	1 763	781	981	6 510	1 976	2 211	1 065	715	444	98
1982	10 678	1 977	831	1 145	8 701	2 392	3 037	1 552	966	647	107
1983	10 717	1 829	753	1 076	8 888	2 330	3 078	1 650	1 039	677	114
1984	8 539	1 499	646	854	7 039	1 838	2 374	1 335	828	566	97
1985	8 312	1 468	662	806	6 844	1 738	2 341	1 340	813	518	93
1986	8 237	1 454	665	789	6 783	1 651	2 390	1 371	790	489	91
1987	7 425	1 347	648	700	6 077	1 453	2 129	1 281	723	412	78
1988	6 701	1 226	573	653	5 475	1 261	1 929	1 166	657	375	87
1989	6 528	1 194	537	657	5 333	1 218	1 851	1 159	637	379	91
1990	7 047	1 212	527	685	5 835	1 299	1 995	1 328	723	386	105
1991	8 628	1 359	587	772	7 269	1 573	2 447	1 719	946	473	113
1992	9 613	1 427	641	787	8 186	1 649	2 702	1 976	1 138	589	132
1993	8 940	1 365	606	759	7 575	1 514	2 395	1 896	1 121	541	108
1994	7 996	1 320	624	696	6 676	1 373	2 067	1 627	971	485	153
1995	7 404	1 346	652	695	6 058	1 244	1 841	1 549	844	425	153
1996	7 236	1 306	617	689	5 929	1 239	1 757	1 505	883	406	139
1997	6 739	1 271	589	683	5 467	1 152	1 571	1 418	830	369	127
1998	6 210	1 205	573	632	5 005	1 081	1 419	1 258	782	343	122
1999	5 880	1 162	544	618	4 718	1 042	1 278	1 154	753	367	124
2000	5 692	1 081	502	579	4 611	1 022	1 207	1 133	762	355	132
2001	6 801	1 162	531	632	5 638	1 209	1 498	1 355	989	458	129
2002	8 378	1 253	540	714	7 124	1 430	1 890	1 691	1 315	635	163
2003	8 774	1 251	545	706	7 523	1 495	1 960	1 815	1 356	713	183
2004	8 149	1 208	554	653	6 942	1 431	1 784	1 578	1 288	682	179
2005	7 591	1 186	541	645	6 405	1 335	1 661	1 400	1 195	630	184
2006	7 001	1 119	509	610	5 882	1 234	1 521	1 279	1 094	595	159
2007	7 078	1 101	485	616	5 976	1 241	1 544	1 225	1 135	642	190
2008	8 924	1 285	563	722	7 639	1 545	1 949	1 604	1 473	803	264
2009	14 265	1 552	576	976	12 712	2 207	3 284	2 722	2 592	1 487	421
2010	14 825	1 528	582	945	13 297	2 329	3 386	2 703	2 769	1 660	449
2011	13 747	1 400	519	881	12 348	2 234	3 187	2 389	2 493	1 579	465
2012	12 506	1 397	533	863	11 109	2 054	2 764	2 158	2 181	1 470	482
2013	11 460	1 327	536	791	10 133	1 997	2 504	1 913	1 945	1 340	435
2014	9 617	680	426	1 106	8 511	1 747	2 224	1 539	1 507	1 107	387
2015	8 296	966	363	603	7 330	1 501	1 905	1 351	1 259	978	337
2016	7 751	925	380	545	6 826	1 286	1 797	1 258	1 189	941	355
2017	6 982	827	347	480	6 155	1 127	1 647	1 143	1 060	835	343
2018	6 314	759	295	464	5 555	1 048	1 450	1 003	938	789	327

Table 1-26. Unemployed Persons, by Age, Sex, Race, and Hispanic Origin, 1948–2018—*Continued*

(Thousands of people.)

Race, Hispanic origin, sex, and year	16 years and over	16 to 19 years			20 years and over						
		Total	16 to 17 years	18 to 19 years	Total	20 to 24 years	25 to 34 years	35 to 44 years	45 to 54 years	55 to 64 years	65 years and over
ALL RACES											
Men											
1948	1 559	256	113	142	1 305	324	289	233	201	177	81
1949	2 572	353	145	207	2 219	485	539	414	347	310	125
1950	2 239	318	139	179	1 922	377	467	348	327	286	117
1951	1 221	191	102	89	1 029	155	241	192	193	162	87
1952	1 185	205	116	89	980	155	233	192	182	145	73
1953	1 202	184	94	90	1 019	152	236	208	196	167	60
1954	2 344	310	142	168	2 035	327	517	431	372	275	112
1955	1 854	274	134	140	1 580	248	353	328	285	265	102
1956	1 711	269	134	135	1 442	240	348	278	270	216	90
1957	1 841	300	140	159	1 541	283	349	304	302	220	83
1958	3 098	416	185	231	2 681	478	685	552	492	349	124
1959	2 420	398	191	207	2 022	343	484	407	390	287	112
1960	2 486	426	200	225	2 060	369	492	415	392	294	96
1961	2 997	479	221	258	2 518	458	585	507	473	375	122
1962	2 423	408	188	220	2 016	381	445	404	382	300	103
1963	2 472	501	248	252	1 971	396	445	386	358	290	97
1964	2 205	487	257	230	1 718	384	345	324	319	263	85
1965	1 914	479	247	232	1 435	311	292	283	253	221	75
1966	1 551	432	220	212	1 120	221	239	219	196	179	65
1967	1 508	448	241	207	1 060	235	219	185	199	163	60
1968	1 419	426	234	193	993	258	205	171	165	132	61
1969	1 403	440	244	196	963	270	205	155	157	127	48
1970	2 238	599	306	294	1 638	479	391	253	247	198	71
1971	2 789	693	346	347	2 097	640	513	320	313	239	71
1972	2 659	711	357	355	1 948	628	466	284	272	227	73
1973	2 275	653	352	300	1 624	528	439	211	219	171	57
1974	2 714	757	394	362	1 957	649	546	266	250	183	63
1975	4 442	966	445	521	3 476	1 081	986	507	499	302	103
1976	4 036	939	443	496	3 098	951	914	431	411	296	94
1977	3 667	874	421	453	2 794	877	869	373	326	252	97
1978	3 142	813	426	388	2 328	768	691	314	277	198	81
1979	3 120	811	393	418	2 308	744	699	329	272	196	67
1980	4 267	913	429	485	3 353	1 076	1 137	482	357	243	58
1981	4 577	962	431	531	3 615	1 144	1 213	552	390	261	55
1982	6 179	1 090	469	621	5 089	1 407	1 791	879	550	393	69
1983	6 260	1 003	408	595	5 257	1 369	1 822	947	613	433	73
1984	4 744	812	348	464	3 932	1 023	1 322	728	450	356	53
1985	4 521	806	363	443	3 715	944	1 244	706	459	307	55
1986	4 530	779	355	424	3 751	899	1 291	763	440	301	58
1987	4 101	732	353	379	3 369	779	1 169	689	426	258	49
1988	3 655	667	311	356	2 987	676	1 040	617	366	240	49
1989	3 525	658	303	355	2 867	660	953	619	351	234	49
1990	3 906	667	283	384	3 239	715	1 092	711	413	249	59
1991	4 946	751	317	433	4 195	911	1 375	990	550	305	64
1992	5 523	806	357	449	4 717	951	1 529	1 118	675	378	67
1993	5 055	768	342	426	4 287	865	1 338	1 049	636	336	64
1994	4 367	740	342	398	3 627	768	1 113	855	522	281	88
1995	3 983	744	352	391	3 239	673	961	815	464	233	94
1996	3 880	733	347	387	3 146	675	903	786	484	223	76
1997	3 577	694	321	373	2 882	636	772	732	457	217	69
1998	3 266	686	330	355	2 580	583	699	609	420	201	69
1999	3 066	633	295	338	2 433	562	624	571	403	203	70
2000	2 975	599	281	317	2 376	547	602	557	398	189	83
2001	3 690	650	300	350	3 040	688	756	714	536	272	74
2002	4 597	700	301	399	3 896	792	1 023	897	725	373	87
2003	4 906	697	291	407	4 209	841	1 097	988	764	412	107
2004	4 456	664	292	372	3 791	811	980	839	684	373	104
2005	4 059	667	300	367	3 392	775	844	715	624	331	102
2006	3 753	622	271	352	3 131	705	810	642	569	318	88
2007	3 882	623	263	360	3 259	721	856	634	591	349	108
2008	5 033	736	312	425	4 297	920	1 119	875	804	425	153
2009	8 453	898	317	581	7 555	1 329	1 988	1 600	1 558	840	241
2010	8 626	863	315	548	7 763	1 398	1 993	1 534	1 614	962	262
2011	7 684	786	267	520	6 898	1 275	1 795	1 316	1 370	882	261
2012	6 771	787	291	497	5 984	1 163	1 476	1 124	1 142	811	268
2013	6 314	746	287	459	5 568	1 143	1 381	1 015	1 039	741	250
2014	5 190	605	230	375	4 585	996	1 185	813	782	600	210
2015	4 490	531	197	333	3 959	865	1 030	695	649	536	184
2016	4 187	512	203	309	3 675	742	966	644	602	528	193
2017	3 743	457	175	282	3 287	667	884	575	537	445	179
2018	3 398	422	156	266	2 976	596	763	515	490	435	177

Table 1-26. Unemployed Persons, by Age, Sex, Race, and Hispanic Origin, 1948–2018—*Continued*

(Thousands of people.)

Race, Hispanic origin, sex, and year	16 years and over	16 to 19 years			20 years and over						
		Total	16 to 17 years	18 to 19 years	Total	20 to 24 years	25 to 34 years	35 to 44 years	45 to 54 years	55 to 64 years	65 years and over
ALL RACES											
Women											
1948	717	153	67	86	564	131	168	114	89	49	12
1949	1 065	223	93	130	841	195	237	189	124	74	21
1950	1 049	195	87	108	854	184	235	182	151	82	20
1951	834	145	66	79	689	118	194	162	125	76	16
1952	698	140	64	76	559	113	156	133	92	50	13
1953	632	123	56	67	510	104	143	117	84	51	10
1954	1 188	191	79	79	997	177	276	249	176	99	20
1955	998	176	77	99	823	148	224	193	151	90	18
1956	1 039	209	97	112	832	155	206	198	159	95	19
1957	1 018	197	90	107	821	147	224	195	146	80	28
1958	1 504	262	114	148	1 242	223	308	319	239	123	30
1959	1 320	256	110	147	1 063	200	242	266	213	118	23
1960	1 366	286	125	162	1 080	214	260	256	222	102	26
1961	1 717	349	142	207	1 368	265	305	343	278	141	37
1962	1 488	313	124	189	1 175	255	267	284	223	111	38
1963	1 598	383	172	210	1 216	262	287	288	231	120	29
1964	1 581	385	179	207	1 195	276	262	281	224	115	32
1965	1 452	395	164	231	1 056	246	237	263	183	101	28
1966	1 324	405	175	229	921	225	202	207	173	86	27
1967	1 468	391	159	231	1 078	277	261	237	184	93	26
1968	1 397	412	180	233	985	285	238	200	149	87	27
1969	1 429	413	192	220	1 015	290	248	203	163	89	24
1970	1 855	506	231	275	1 349	387	327	262	229	111	33
1971	2 227	568	250	318	1 658	489	420	310	260	142	38
1972	2 222	598	276	322	1 625	503	413	293	237	141	38
1973	2 089	583	282	301	1 507	480	427	240	212	119	31
1974	2 441	665	305	360	1 777	564	497	294	248	137	36
1975	3 486	802	355	447	2 684	783	791	444	395	219	52
1976	3 369	780	352	429	2 588	763	795	417	346	214	53
1977	3 324	789	361	428	2 535	752	782	412	340	198	50
1978	3 061	769	370	399	2 292	714	731	381	275	148	43
1979	3 018	743	346	396	2 276	697	748	375	268	150	38
1980	3 370	755	349	407	2 615	760	886	459	318	155	36
1981	3 696	800	350	450	2 895	833	998	513	325	184	43
1982	4 499	886	362	524	3 613	985	1 246	673	416	254	38
1983	4 457	825	344	481	3 632	961	1 255	703	427	244	41
1984	3 794	687	298	390	3 107	815	1 052	607	378	211	45
1985	3 791	661	298	363	3 129	794	1 098	634	355	211	39
1986	3 707	675	310	365	3 032	752	1 099	609	350	189	33
1987	3 324	616	295	321	2 709	674	960	592	298	155	30
1988	3 046	558	262	297	2 487	585	889	550	291	136	38
1989	3 003	536	234	302	2 467	558	897	540	286	144	41
1990	3 140	544	243	301	2 596	584	902	617	310	137	46
1991	3 683	608	270	338	3 074	662	1 071	728	396	168	49
1992	4 090	621	283	338	3 469	698	1 173	858	463	210	66
1993	3 885	597	264	333	3 288	648	1 058	847	485	205	45
1994	3 629	580	282	298	3 049	605	954	772	449	204	66
1995	3 421	602	299	303	2 819	571	880	735	381	193	60
1996	3 356	573	270	303	2 783	564	854	720	399	183	63
1997	3 162	577	268	310	2 585	516	800	686	373	152	58
1998	2 944	519	242	277	2 424	498	720	650	362	141	53
1999	2 814	529	249	280	2 285	480	654	584	350	163	54
2000	2 717	483	221	262	2 235	475	604	577	364	165	50
2001	3 111	512	230	282	2 599	521	742	641	453	187	55
2002	3 781	553	238	315	3 228	638	866	795	591	263	76
2003	3 868	554	255	299	3 314	654	863	827	592	302	76
2004	3 694	543	262	281	3 150	619	804	739	605	309	75
2005	3 531	519	240	278	3 013	560	817	685	571	299	82
2006	3 247	496	238	258	2 751	530	711	637	524	277	71
2007	3 196	478	222	256	2 718	520	688	591	544	293	81
2008	3 891	549	251	297	3 342	625	830	730	669	377	111
2009	5 811	654	259	395	5 157	878	1 296	1 121	1 034	647	180
2010	6 199	665	268	397	5 534	931	1 392	1 169	1 156	698	187
2011	6 063	613	252	362	5 450	960	1 392	1 073	1 123	697	204
2012	5 734	609	242	367	5 125	891	1 288	1 034	1 039	659	214
2013	5 146	581	249	332	4 565	854	1 123	898	906	600	185
2014	4 426	501	196	305	3 926	751	1 039	726	725	507	177
2015	3 807	435	166	269	3 371	636	874	656	610	442	153
2016	3 564	413	177	236	3 151	545	832	614	586	413	162
2017	3 239	371	172	199	2 868	460	763	568	523	389	164
2018	2 916	338	139	198	2 578	452	687	488	448	354	150

Table 1-26. Unemployed Persons, by Age, Sex, Race, and Hispanic Origin, 1948–2018—*Continued*

(Thousands of people.)

Race, Hispanic origin, sex, and year	16 years and over	16 to 19 years			20 years and over						
		Total	16 to 17 years	18 to 19 years	Total	20 to 24 years	25 to 34 years	35 to 44 years	45 to 54 years	55 to 64 years	65 years and over
WHITE											
Both Sexes											
1954	2 859	423	191	232	2 436	394	610	540	447	329	115
1955	2 252	373	181	191	1 879	304	412	402	358	300	105
1956	2 159	382	191	191	1 777	297	406	363	355	258	98
1957	2 289	401	195	204	1 888	331	425	401	373	262	98
1958	3 680	541	245	297	3 139	541	756	686	614	405	136
1959	2 946	525	255	270	2 421	406	526	525	496	348	120
1960	3 065	575	273	302	2 490	456	573	520	502	330	109
1961	3 743	669	295	374	3 074	566	668	652	611	438	139
1962	3 052	580	262	318	2 472	488	515	522	485	345	117
1963	3 208	708	350	358	2 500	501	540	518	485	349	107
1964	2 999	708	365	342	2 291	508	441	472	447	323	100
1965	2 691	705	329	374	1 986	437	399	427	358	276	91
1966	2 255	651	315	336	1 604	338	323	336	298	227	80
1967	2 338	635	311	325	1 703	393	360	336	321	221	75
1968	2 226	644	326	318	1 582	422	330	297	269	187	80
1969	2 260	660	351	309	1 601	432	354	294	269	185	66
1970	3 339	871	438	432	2 468	679	570	433	415	275	95
1971	4 085	1 011	491	521	3 074	887	732	517	500	338	100
1972	3 906	1 021	515	506	2 885	887	679	459	439	324	95
1973	3 442	955	513	443	2 486	758	664	358	371	257	77
1974	4 097	1 104	561	544	2 993	925	821	448	427	283	88
1975	6 421	1 413	657	755	5 007	1 474	1 413	774	753	460	136
1976	5 914	1 364	649	715	4 550	1 326	1 329	682	637	448	128
1977	5 441	1 284	636	648	4 157	1 195	1 255	621	569	388	129
1978	4 698	1 189	631	558	3 509	1 059	1 059	543	453	290	104
1979	4 664	1 193	589	603	3 472	1 038	1 068	545	443	290	87
1980	5 884	1 291	625	666	4 593	1 364	1 528	740	550	335	74
1981	6 343	1 374	629	745	4 968	1 449	1 658	827	578	379	77
1982	8 241	1 534	683	851	6 707	1 770	2 283	1 223	796	549	86
1983	8 128	1 387	609	778	6 741	1 678	2 282	1 294	837	563	88
1984	6 372	1 116	510	605	5 256	1 282	1 723	1 036	660	475	81
1985	6 191	1 074	507	567	5 117	1 235	1 695	1 039	642	432	75
1986	6 140	1 070	509	561	5 070	1 149	1 751	1 056	629	407	78
1987	5 501	995	495	500	4 506	1 017	1 527	984	576	333	68
1988	4 944	910	437	473	4 033	874	1 371	890	520	309	69
1989	4 770	863	407	456	3 908	856	1 297	871	503	311	70
1990	5 186	903	401	502	4 283	899	1 401	983	582	330	88
1991	6 560	1 029	461	568	5 532	1 132	1 805	1 330	759	410	96
1992	7 169	1 037	484	553	6 132	1 156	1 967	1 483	915	495	116
1993	6 655	992	468	523	5 663	1 057	1 754	1 411	907	442	92
1994	5 892	960	471	489	4 933	952	1 479	1 184	779	407	132
1995	5 459	952	476	476	4 507	866	1 311	1 161	676	362	131
1996	5 300	939	456	484	4 361	854	1 223	1 117	709	336	122
1997	4 836	912	438	475	3 924	765	1 068	1 035	648	302	106
1998	4 484	876	424	451	3 608	731	978	901	620	276	101
1999	4 273	844	414	430	3 429	720	865	843	595	303	104
2000	4 121	795	386	409	3 326	682	835	817	591	294	107
2001	4 969	845	402	443	4 124	829	1 062	985	761	378	109
2002	6 137	925	407	518	5 212	977	1 340	1 237	1 004	518	137
2003	6 311	909	414	495	5 401	1 012	1 354	1 287	1 025	569	155
2004	5 847	890	414	476	4 957	959	1 211	1 130	953	557	148
2005	5 350	845	391	454	4 505	878	1 106	1 006	884	488	144
2006	5 002	794	375	419	4 208	832	1 029	920	813	480	135
2007	5 143	805	361	444	4 338	851	1 052	902	848	520	164
2008	6 509	947	422	524	5 562	1 087	1 336	1 196	1 094	634	216
2009	10 648	1 157	440	717	9 491	1 556	2 320	2 026	2 012	1 221	355
2010	10 916	1 128	445	683	9 788	1 614	2 358	1 969	2 130	1 344	373
2011	9 889	1 024	391	633	8 865	1 546	2 135	1 678	1 859	1 251	395
2012	8 915	1 004	397	607	7 911	1 353	1 881	1 514	1 614	1 144	405
2013	8 033	937	395	542	7 096	1 299	1 651	1 334	1 414	1 032	366
2014	6 540	775	302	473	5 764	1 084	1 402	1 059	1 085	829	305
2015	5 662	662	260	402	5 000	970	1 194	917	913	751	255
2016	5 345	651	273	378	4 694	831	1 157	837	858	720	290
2017	4 765	554	247	307	4 211	743	1 039	766	759	628	277
2018	4 354	516	207	309	3 837	685	932	671	677	610	262

Table 1-26. Unemployed Persons, by Age, Sex, Race, and Hispanic Origin, 1948–2018—*Continued*

(Thousands of people.)

Race, Hispanic origin, sex, and year	16 years and over	16 to 19 years			20 years and over						
		Total	16 to 17 years	18 to 19 years	Total	20 to 24 years	25 to 34 years	35 to 44 years	45 to 54 years	55 to 64 years	65 years and over
WHITE											
Men											
1954	1 913	266	125	142	1 647	260	408	341	299	241	98
1955	1 478	232	114	117	1 246	196	260	246	233	223	89
1956	1 366	221	112	108	1 145	186	265	212	225	177	81
1957	1 477	243	118	124	1 234	222	257	239	250	193	73
1958	2 489	333	149	184	2 156	382	525	436	404	299	110
1959	1 903	318	162	156	1 585	256	350	316	320	245	98
1960	1 988	341	167	174	1 647	295	376	330	317	243	86
1961	2 398	384	176	208	2 014	370	442	395	382	318	107
1962	1 915	334	158	176	1 581	300	332	311	308	246	84
1963	1 976	407	211	196	1 569	309	342	297	294	246	80
1964	1 779	400	217	183	1 379	310	262	255	266	216	70
1965	1 556	387	200	186	1 169	254	226	228	206	190	67
1966	1 241	340	178	162	901	172	185	173	160	154	57
1967	1 208	342	186	156	866	185	171	153	167	140	52
1968	1 142	328	185	143	814	206	162	140	142	111	55
1969	1 137	343	198	145	794	214	165	130	134	108	43
1970	1 857	485	255	230	1 372	388	316	212	216	177	64
1971	2 309	562	288	275	1 747	513	418	268	272	211	66
1972	2 173	564	288	276	1 610	506	375	231	237	199	60
1973	1 836	513	284	229	1 323	411	353	166	188	153	51
1974	2 169	584	311	274	1 585	505	434	218	213	161	53
1975	3 627	785	369	416	2 841	871	796	412	411	265	86
1976	3 258	754	368	385	2 504	750	730	346	341	259	78
1977	2 883	672	342	330	2 211	660	682	297	276	213	82
1978	2 411	615	338	277	1 797	558	525	250	227	169	68
1979	2 405	633	319	313	1 773	553	526	253	220	165	56
1980	3 345	716	347	369	2 629	827	884	378	291	206	44
1981	3 580	755	349	406	2 825	869	943	433	317	221	42
1982	4 846	854	387	467	3 991	1 066	1 385	696	460	331	53
1983	4 859	761	328	433	4 098	1 019	1 410	755	497	362	54
1984	3 600	608	280	328	2 992	722	991	572	363	302	42
1985	3 426	592	282	310	2 834	694	931	553	356	257	43
1986	3 433	576	276	299	2 857	645	978	586	349	248	51
1987	3 132	548	272	276	2 584	568	879	536	350	209	43
1988	2 766	499	239	260	2 268	480	777	477	293	200	40
1989	2 636	487	230	257	2 149	476	694	470	280	191	38
1990	2 935	504	214	290	2 431	510	796	530	330	214	51
1991	3 859	575	249	327	3 284	677	1 064	780	438	269	55
1992	4 209	590	270	319	3 620	686	1 155	858	543	318	58
1993	3 828	565	261	305	3 263	619	1 015	793	512	270	53
1994	3 275	540	259	280	2 735	555	827	626	417	236	74
1995	2 999	535	260	275	2 465	483	711	621	371	200	79
1996	2 896	532	260	273	2 363	478	655	592	383	188	67
1997	2 641	502	234	268	2 140	439	553	549	358	182	58
1998	2 431	510	254	257	1 920	405	512	441	342	164	58
1999	2 274	461	223	237	1 813	398	441	419	322	172	61
2000	2 177	446	217	229	1 731	368	428	403	302	162	68
2001	2 754	479	232	247	2 275	494	547	529	413	229	64
2002	3 459	516	228	288	2 943	562	772	672	554	305	77
2003	3 643	518	221	298	3 125	589	798	723	591	333	91
2004	3 282	497	224	274	2 785	560	694	620	516	307	88
2005	2 931	480	220	260	2 450	522	586	536	463	263	81
2006	2 730	449	202	247	2 281	483	567	482	417	259	73
2007	2 869	461	195	266	2 408	501	604	478	447	285	93
2008	3 727	548	231	317	3 179	668	784	662	604	337	124
2009	6 421	675	241	434	5 746	969	1 439	1 208	1 233	695	202
2010	6 476	648	246	402	5 828	995	1 452	1 131	1 249	785	216
2011	5 631	585	208	377	5 046	909	1 237	951	1 030	697	223
2012	4 931	584	222	362	4 347	792	1 044	794	856	637	224
2013	4 520	526	213	313	3 994	756	944	727	769	583	215
2014	3 572	431	165	266	3 141	628	774	568	558	449	164
2015	3 126	375	144	231	2 751	581	667	484	480	400	139
2016	2 952	358	147	211	2 594	484	653	444	446	410	156
2017	2 592	304	128	177	2 288	449	575	396	391	331	144
2018	2 380	286	109	178	2 094	390	508	344	363	339	149

Table 1-26. Unemployed Persons, by Age, Sex, Race, and Hispanic Origin, 1948–2018—*Continued*

(Thousands of people.)

Race, Hispanic origin, sex, and year	16 years and over	16 to 19 years			20 years and over						
		Total	16 to 17 years	18 to 19 years	Total	20 to 24 years	25 to 34 years	35 to 44 years	45 to 54 years	55 to 64 years	65 years and over
WHITE											
Women											
1954	946	157	66	90	789	134	202	199	148	88	17
1955	774	141	67	74	633	108	152	156	125	77	16
1956	793	161	79	83	632	111	141	151	130	81	17
1957	812	158	77	80	654	109	168	162	123	69	25
1958	1 191	208	96	113	983	159	231	250	210	106	26
1959	1 043	207	93	114	836	150	176	209	176	103	22
1960	1 077	234	106	128	843	161	197	190	185	87	23
1961	1 345	285	119	166	1 060	196	226	257	229	120	32
1962	1 137	246	104	142	891	188	183	211	177	99	33
1963	1 232	301	139	162	931	192	198	221	191	103	27
1964	1 220	308	148	159	912	198	179	217	181	107	30
1965	1 135	318	129	188	817	183	173	199	152	86	24
1966	1 014	311	137	174	703	166	138	163	138	73	23
1967	1 130	293	125	169	837	209	189	183	154	81	23
1968	1 084	316	141	175	768	216	168	157	127	76	25
1969	1 123	317	153	164	806	218	189	164	135	77	23
1970	1 482	386	183	202	1 096	291	254	221	199	98	31
1971	1 777	449	203	246	1 328	376	314	249	228	126	34
1972	1 733	457	227	230	1 275	381	304	227	202	125	35
1973	1 606	442	228	214	1 164	347	311	192	183	104	26
1974	1 927	519	250	270	1 408	420	387	230	214	122	35
1975	2 794	628	288	340	2 166	602	617	362	342	195	49
1976	2 656	611	280	330	2 045	577	598	336	296	188	49
1977	2 558	612	294	318	1 946	536	573	323	293	175	47
1978	2 287	574	292	281	1 713	500	533	294	226	122	37
1979	2 260	560	270	290	1 699	485	542	293	223	125	32
1980	2 540	576	278	298	1 964	537	645	362	259	129	31
1981	2 762	620	281	339	2 143	580	715	394	261	158	36
1982	3 395	680	296	384	2 715	704	898	527	337	217	33
1983	3 270	626	282	345	2 643	659	872	539	340	201	33
1984	2 772	508	231	277	2 264	559	731	464	297	173	39
1985	2 765	482	225	257	2 283	541	763	486	286	175	32
1986	2 708	495	233	262	2 213	504	773	470	281	159	27
1987	2 369	447	223	224	1 922	449	648	448	227	124	25
1988	2 177	412	198	214	1 766	393	594	413	227	110	30
1989	2 135	376	177	199	1 758	380	603	401	223	120	32
1990	2 251	399	187	212	1 852	389	605	453	251	116	37
1991	2 701	453	212	241	2 248	455	741	550	320	141	41
1992	2 959	447	214	233	2 512	469	811	625	372	177	58
1993	2 827	426	208	219	2 400	438	739	618	395	172	39
1994	2 617	420	211	208	2 197	397	652	558	361	170	58
1995	2 460	418	216	201	2 042	384	600	540	306	162	52
1996	2 404	407	196	211	1 998	376	568	525	326	148	55
1997	2 195	411	204	207	1 784	326	515	486	290	119	49
1998	2 053	365	171	195	1 688	327	467	460	279	112	43
1999	1 999	383	190	193	1 616	322	423	423	273	131	43
2000	1 944	349	168	180	1 595	314	407	414	289	133	39
2001	2 215	366	170	196	1 849	335	515	456	348	150	45
2002	2 678	409	179	230	2 269	415	567	565	449	213	60
2003	2 668	391	194	197	2 276	423	555	564	434	235	64
2004	2 565	393	191	202	2 172	399	516	510	437	250	60
2005	2 419	365	172	193	2 054	356	520	469	421	225	63
2006	2 271	345	173	172	1 927	349	462	437	395	222	62
2007	2 274	344	166	178	1 930	350	448	425	401	235	71
2008	2 782	399	191	207	2 384	419	552	534	489	298	92
2009	4 227	482	199	283	3 745	587	881	818	780	526	153
2010	4 440	480	199	281	3 960	619	906	839	881	559	157
2011	4 257	439	184	255	3 818	637	899	728	829	554	171
2012	3 985	420	176	245	3 564	561	837	720	758	508	181
2013	3 513	411	183	228	3 102	543	707	607	645	449	151
2014	2 968	344	138	207	2 623	457	628	490	527	380	141
2015	2 537	288	116	172	2 249	390	527	433	433	351	116
2016	2 393	293	126	167	2 100	347	504	393	412	310	134
2017	2 173	249	119	130	1 923	293	464	228	367	297	132
2018	1 973	230	99	131	1 743	295	424	327	314	271	113

Table 1-26. Unemployed Persons, by Age, Sex, Race, and Hispanic Origin, 1948–2018—*Continued*

(Thousands of people.)

Race, Hispanic origin, sex, and year	16 years and over	16 to 19 years			20 years and over						
		Total	16 to 17 years	18 to 19 years	Total	20 to 24 years	25 to 34 years	35 to 44 years	45 to 54 years	55 to 64 years	65 years and over
BLACK											
Both Sexes											
1985	1 864	357	135	221	1 507	455	562	254	143	74	18
1986	1 840	347	138	209	1 493	453	564	269	127	69	10
1987	1 684	312	134	178	1 373	397	533	247	124	62	10
1988	1 547	288	121	167	1 259	349	502	230	111	51	15
1989	1 544	300	116	184	1 245	322	494	246	109	53	20
1990	1 565	268	112	156	1 297	349	505	278	106	44	14
1991	1 723	280	105	175	1 443	378	539	318	151	44	13
1992	2 011	324	127	197	1 687	421	610	402	178	64	13
1993	1 844	313	112	201	1 530	387	532	376	153	72	11
1994	1 666	300	127	173	1 366	351	468	346	130	55	16
1995	1 538	325	143	182	1 213	311	423	303	116	42	18
1996	1 592	310	133	177	1 282	327	454	313	127	48	13
1997	1 560	302	123	179	1 258	327	426	307	136	45	16
1998	1 426	281	124	156	1 146	301	366	294	125	45	16
1999	1 309	268	109	159	1 041	273	339	249	121	46	14
2000	1 241	230	96	134	1 011	281	289	254	131	38	20
2001	1 416	260	102	158	1 155	307	340	283	159	52	15
2002	1 693	260	103	156	1 433	365	407	349	215	76	21
2003	1 787	255	93	162	1 532	375	442	385	217	93	20
2004	1 729	241	103	138	1 487	353	441	341	245	86	21
2005	1 700	267	115	152	1 433	358	423	310	222	92	28
2006	1 549	253	102	151	1 296	318	388	276	214	81	19
2007	1 445	235	98	138	1 210	300	367	237	208	79	19
2008	1 788	246	98	148	1 542	355	458	301	275	117	36
2009	2 606	288	99	189	2 319	488	717	489	415	168	42
2010	2 852	291	97	194	2 562	539	776	534	461	204	47
2011	2 831	267	88	179	2 564	531	801	529	444	212	47
2012	2 544	272	94	179	2 272	510	640	457	397	209	59
2013	2 429	278	101	177	2 151	509	603	414	376	199	50
2014	2 141	225	85	139	1 916	466	605	325	284	186	51
2015	1 846	199	69	131	1 646	384	517	298	245	151	51
2016	1 655	194	73	122	1 460	329	435	286	225	143	43
2017	1 501	181	61	120	1 320	258	428	253	210	135	36
2018	1 322	167	56	111	1 155	234	349	234	177	117	44
Men											
1985	951	193	69	124	757	224	268	127	85	43	11
1986	946	180	68	112	765	225	273	148	70	44	5
1987	826	160	70	90	666	186	253	122	61	39	6
1988	771	154	64	90	617	177	233	111	58	30	8
1989	773	153	65	88	619	162	226	129	59	33	10
1990	806	142	62	80	664	177	247	146	62	27	6
1991	890	145	54	91	745	201	252	172	87	25	7
1992	1 067	180	71	109	886	221	301	208	107	42	6
1993	971	170	66	104	801	201	260	201	87	46	7
1994	848	167	69	97	682	173	218	180	72	29	10
1995	762	168	73	95	593	153	195	150	63	21	11
1996	808	169	73	96	639	163	210	158	75	26	7
1997	747	162	70	92	585	165	178	141	72	22	7
1998	671	147	61	86	524	151	148	133	60	24	8
1999	626	145	60	85	480	135	143	114	60	22	7
2000	620	121	52	70	499	145	134	121	72	17	9
2001	709	136	51	85	573	150	159	142	84	31	7
2002	835	140	54	85	695	181	180	165	120	40	9
2003	891	132	49	83	760	192	212	189	109	47	10
2004	860	128	52	75	733	188	211	160	120	46	8
2005	844	145	63	82	699	192	189	143	116	45	14
2006	774	134	53	81	640	167	189	118	112	43	11
2007	752	130	55	75	622	166	186	114	106	41	10
2008	949	138	54	84	811	190	242	154	143	61	21
2009	1 448	161	55	106	1 286	264	406	270	230	91	24
2010	1 550	154	47	107	1 396	294	408	286	268	116	24
2011	1 502	142	39	102	1 360	278	426	277	233	125	21
2012	1 292	140	47	93	1 152	269	308	241	191	110	32
2013	1 236	154	54	101	1 082	273	298	196	193	96	26
2014	1 091	118	44	74	973	251	295	159	149	95	25
2015	935	100	37	63	835	209	254	140	119	89	23
2016	845	108	35	73	737	186	208	138	108	75	22
2017	766	104	29	74	663	144	211	121	90	73	15
2018	676	94	29	65	582	133	165	114	52	62	18

Table 1-26. Unemployed Persons, by Age, Sex, Race, and Hispanic Origin, 1948–2018—*Continued*

(Thousands of people.)

Race, Hispanic origin, sex, and year	16 years and over	16 to 19 years			20 years and over						
		Total	16 to 17 years	18 to 19 years	Total	20 to 24 years	25 to 34 years	35 to 44 years	45 to 54 years	55 to 64 years	65 years and over
BLACK											
Women											
1985	913	164	66	98	750	231	295	913	58	31	7
1986	894	167	70	97	728	228	291	894	57	25	5
1987	858	152	64	88	706	211	280	858	63	23	4
1988	776	134	57	78	642	172	269	776	53	22	7
1989	772	147	51	96	625	160	267	772	50	21	9
1990	758	126	49	76	633	172	258	758	44	17	8
1991	833	135	51	84	698	177	288	833	64	19	6
1992	944	144	56	88	800	200	308	944	71	22	6
1993	872	143	46	97	729	186	272	872	66	26	5
1994	818	133	57	76	685	178	249	818	59	26	6
1995	777	157	. . .	87	620	158	228	777	53	20	7
1996	784	141	60	80	643	164	244	784	52	21	7
1997	813	140	53	87	673	163	248	813	64	24	9
1998	756	134	63	71	622	150	218	756	65	21	8
1999	684	123	49	74	561	138	196	684	61	25	7
2000	621	109	44	65	512	136	154	621	59	22	10
2001	706	124	52	72	582	157	181	706	75	21	8
2002	858	120	49	71	738	183	228	858	95	35	12
2003	895	123	44	79	772	183	230	895	109	46	10
2004	868	114	51	63	755	166	230	868	126	40	13
2005	856	123	52	70	734	166	233	856	106	47	14
2006	775	120	50	70	656	150	199	775	102	38	8
2007	693	106	43	63	588	135	181	693	103	38	9
2008	839	108	44	64	732	166	216	839	132	56	15
2009	1 159	127	44	82	1 032	223	311	1 159	185	77	17
2010	1 302	137	50	87	1 165	245	369	1 302	193	88	22
2011	1 329	125	49	76	1 204	253	376	1 329	211	86	25
2012	1 252	133	47	85	1 119	241	333	1 252	205	98	26
2013	1 192	124	47	77	1 069	235	305	1 192	184	103	24
2014	1 050	106	41	65	943	215	310	166	136	91	26
2015	911	99	32	68	811	174	263	158	126	62	28
2016	810	86	38	48	724	143	226	148	117	68	21
2017	735	77	32	46	657	113	216	133	112	62	21
2018	646	73	27	46	573	101	185	120	87	55	26
HISPANIC											
Both Sexes											
1985	811	141	55	85	670	171	256	123	73	41	7
1986	857	141	57	84	716	183	258	143	85	38	9
1987	751	136	57	79	615	152	222	128	75	33	5
1988	732	148	63	84	585	145	209	120	69	36	6
1989	750	132	59	73	618	158	218	124	76	36	6
1990	876	161	68	94	714	167	263	156	85	36	7
1991	1 092	179	79	99	913	214	332	206	110	44	8
1992	1 311	219	94	124	1 093	240	390	267	126	59	10
1993	1 248	201	86	115	1 047	237	354	261	132	54	10
1994	1 187	198	90	108	989	220	348	227	132	51	12
1995	1 140	205	96	109	934	209	325	224	106	54	16
1996	1 132	199	85	114	933	217	296	246	101	59	14
1997	1 069	197	87	110	872	206	269	229	99	56	13
1998	1 026	214	89	125	812	194	260	203	96	48	11
1999	945	196	79	117	750	171	233	190	104	42	10
2000	954	194	83	112	759	190	247	189	79	42	12
2001	1 138	208	84	123	931	212	315	228	111	56	9
2002	1 353	221	81	140	1 132	265	373	271	146	62	15
2003	1 441	192	79	113	1 249	273	419	294	183	69	10
2004	1 342	203	86	117	1 139	255	371	261	161	74	18
2005	1 191	191	78	113	1 000	227	324	231	142	61	15
2006	1 081	170	74	97	911	194	294	231	128	49	14
2007	1 220	197	78	119	1 023	213	322	238	161	70	19
2008	1 678	251	105	146	1 427	307	437	328	242	81	32
2009	2 706	321	109	212	2 385	429	731	584	416	186	38
2010	2 843	322	99	223	2 520	479	736	598	459	199	49
2011	2 629	300	96	203	2 329	473	669	524	424	195	45
2012	2 514	324	111	213	2 190	444	618	502	381	201	44
2013	2 257	312	111	201	1 945	418	549	442	321	172	43
2014	1 878	250	89	160	1 628	368	469	355	255	147	33
2015	1 726	221	74	147	1 505	338	430	319	239	143	36
2016	1 548	201	71	130	1 347	298	377	269	230	137	34
2017	1 401	184	73	111	1 217	253	362	254	197	113	38
2018	1 323	186	64	122	1 138	239	320	237	170	131	42

. . . = Not available.

Table 1-26. Unemployed Persons, by Age, Sex, Race, and Hispanic Origin, 1948–2018—*Continued*

(Thousands of people.)

Race, Hispanic origin, sex, and year	16 years and over	16 to 19 years			20 years and over						
		Total	16 to 17 years	18 to 19 years	Total	20 to 24 years	25 to 34 years	35 to 44 years	45 to 54 years	55 to 64 years	65 years and over
HISPANIC											
Men											
1985	483	82	34	49	401	108	156	69	40	23	. . .
1986	520	82	33	50	438	115	159	86	46	26	. . .
1987	451	77	32	45	374	88	137	77	46	22	. . .
1988	437	86	36	50	351	83	128	70	42	24	. . .
1989	423	81	36	45	342	88	113	69	43	25	. . .
1990	524	100	40	60	425	99	154	91	53	25	. . .
1991	685	110	47	62	575	139	210	126	62	33	. . .
1992	807	132	56	75	675	156	239	156	75	42	. . .
1993	747	118	50	68	629	144	217	148	79	33	. . .
1994	680	121	54	67	558	128	203	113	75	30	9
1995	651	121	59	63	530	123	185	120	57	33	13
1996	607	112	49	63	495	117	165	124	49	31	9
1997	582	110	47	63	471	125	137	113	54	35	8
1998	552	117	54	62	436	115	142	97	49	29	5
1999	480	106	42	63	374	96	109	83	54	24	7
2000	494	106	46	60	388	105	118	93	42	23	8
2001	611	117	52	65	495	129	152	116	55	36	6
2002	764	127	42	86	636	151	213	144	82	38	8
2003	809	116	42	74	693	157	239	153	98	41	5
2004	755	120	48	72	635	158	207	133	82	41	13
2005	647	112	42	70	536	134	168	119	74	31	9
2006	601	104	43	61	497	110	169	114	66	29	8
2007	695	119	44	74	576	121	189	126	92	35	13
2008	1 007	147	63	84	860	188	275	192	136	50	19
2009	1 670	196	66	131	1 474	255	470	364	246	117	21
2010	1 711	191	54	137	1 519	294	470	346	269	112	28
2011	1 527	182	53	129	1 345	277	395	297	231	116	28
2012	1 383	189	66	123	1 195	254	339	251	208	119	24
2013	1 263	173	58	115	1 090	248	305	232	173	105	28
2014	996	132	48	83	864	207	251	179	124	82	22
2015	943	124	40	84	820	196	232	151	133	83	25
2016	833	113	40	74	720	171	201	139	107	78	23
2017	730	98	30	68	632	137	190	132	93	57	23
2018	695	104	34	70	591	136	155	119	83	73	26
HISPANIC											
Women											
1985	327	58	22	37	269	63	100	54	32	18	. . .
1986	337	59	25	35	278	68	99	57	39	12	. . .
1987	300	59	25	34	241	64	85	51	29	11	. . .
1988	296	62	27	34	234	63	81	50	27	12	. . .
1989	327	51	23	28	276	70	105	55	33	11	. . .
1990	351	62	28	34	289	68	109	65	32	11	. . .
1991	407	69	32	37	339	74	122	80	48	12	. . .
1992	504	87	38	49	418	84	151	111	51	17	. . .
1993	501	83	36	47	418	93	136	113	53	21	. . .
1994	508	77	36	40	431	92	145	115	57	21	2
1995	488	84	38	46	404	86	140	104	50	21	3
1996	525	88	36	52	438	100	131	122	52	27	5
1997	488	87	40	46	401	81	132	117	46	21	4
1998	473	98	35	63	376	80	118	106	48	19	5
1999	466	90	36	54	376	75	124	107	50	17	3
2000	460	88	37	51	371	86	129	96	38	19	4
2001	527	91	33	58	436	83	163	112	56	20	3
2002	590	94	39	54	496	113	160	127	65	24	7
2003	631	76	37	39	555	116	180	141	86	28	5
2004	587	83	38	45	504	97	164	128	78	32	5
2005	544	80	36	43	464	93	156	112	68	30	6
2006	480	67	31	36	414	84	125	116	62	20	6
2007	525	79	34	45	446	92	134	111	69	35	6
2008	672	104	42	62	567	119	162	136	105	32	13
2009	1 036	125	44	81	911	174	260	220	170	70	17
2010	1 132	131	45	86	1 001	186	267	252	190	87	20
2011	1 102	118	44	74	984	196	274	227	192	78	17
2012	1 130	135	45	90	995	190	278	251	173	83	20
2013	994	139	52	86	855	170	244	210	148	67	15
2014	882	118	41	77	764	162	218	176	131	65	11
2015	783	98	34	63	686	142	198	168	107	60	11
2016	715	88	31	56	627	127	176	130	123	59	12
2017	671	86	43	43	585	116	172	122	103	56	15
2018	628	82	31	51	547	103	165	118	87	58	16

. . . = Not available.

Table 1-27. Unemployment Rates of Civilian Workers, by Age, Sex, Race, and Hispanic Origin, 1948–2018

(Percent of labor force.)

Race, Hispanic origin, sex, and year	16 years and over	16 to 19 years			20 years and over						
		Total	16 to 17 years	18 to 19 years	Total	20 to 24 years	25 to 34 years	35 to 44 years	45 to 54 years	55 to 64 years	65 years and over
ALL RACES											
Both Sexes											
1948	3.8	9.2	10.1	8.6	3.3	6.2	3.2	2.6	2.7	3.1	3.2
1949	5.9	13.4	14.0	13.0	5.4	9.3	5.4	4.4	4.2	5.2	4.9
1950	5.3	12.2	13.6	11.2	4.8	7.7	4.8	3.8	4.2	4.8	4.5
1951	3.3	8.2	9.6	7.1	3.0	4.1	3.0	2.5	2.7	3.1	3.4
1952	3.0	8.5	10.0	7.3	2.7	4.6	2.6	2.3	2.3	2.4	2.9
1953	2.9	7.6	8.7	6.8	2.6	4.7	2.5	2.2	2.3	2.7	2.2
1954	5.5	12.6	13.5	10.7	5.1	9.2	5.3	4.5	4.4	4.5	4.1
1955	4.4	11.0	12.3	10.0	3.9	7.0	3.8	3.4	3.4	4.2	3.6
1956	4.1	11.1	12.3	10.2	3.7	6.6	3.7	3.0	3.2	3.5	3.2
1957	4.3	11.6	12.5	10.9	3.8	7.1	3.9	3.1	3.3	3.4	3.4
1958	6.8	15.9	16.4	15.5	6.2	11.2	6.8	5.4	5.2	5.2	4.8
1959	5.5	14.6	15.3	14.0	4.8	8.5	5.0	4.2	4.2	4.4	4.3
1960	5.5	14.7	15.5	14.1	4.8	8.7	5.2	4.1	4.1	4.2	3.8
1961	6.7	16.8	18.3	15.8	5.9	10.4	6.2	5.2	5.0	5.4	5.1
1962	5.5	14.7	16.3	13.6	4.9	9.0	5.1	4.1	4.0	4.2	4.5
1963	5.7	17.2	19.3	15.6	4.8	8.8	5.2	4.0	3.8	4.1	4.1
1964	5.2	16.2	17.8	14.9	4.3	8.3	4.3	3.6	3.5	3.7	3.8
1965	4.5	14.8	16.5	13.5	3.6	6.7	3.7	3.2	2.8	3.1	3.3
1966	3.8	12.8	14.8	11.3	2.9	5.3	3.1	2.5	2.3	2.5	3.0
1967	3.8	12.9	14.6	11.6	3.0	5.7	3.2	2.5	2.4	2.4	2.8
1968	3.6	12.7	14.7	11.2	2.7	5.8	2.8	2.2	1.9	2.0	2.8
1969	3.5	12.2	14.5	10.5	2.7	5.7	2.8	2.2	1.9	1.9	2.2
1970	4.9	15.3	17.1	13.8	4.0	8.2	4.2	3.1	2.8	2.7	3.2
1971	5.9	16.9	18.7	15.5	4.9	10.0	5.3	3.9	3.4	3.3	3.5
1972	5.6	16.2	18.5	14.6	4.5	9.3	4.6	3.5	3.0	3.2	3.6
1973	4.9	14.5	17.3	12.4	3.9	7.8	4.2	2.7	2.5	2.6	3.0
1974	5.6	16.0	18.3	14.3	4.5	9.1	4.8	3.3	2.9	2.8	3.4
1975	8.5	19.9	21.4	18.9	7.3	13.6	7.8	5.6	5.2	4.6	5.2
1976	7.7	19.0	21.1	17.5	6.5	12.0	7.1	4.9	4.5	4.5	5.1
1977	7.1	17.8	19.9	16.2	5.9	11.0	6.5	4.4	3.9	3.9	5.0
1978	6.1	16.4	19.3	14.2	5.0	9.6	5.3	3.7	3.3	2.9	4.0
1979	5.8	16.1	18.1	14.7	4.8	9.1	5.2	3.6	3.2	2.9	3.4
1980	7.1	17.8	20.0	16.2	6.1	11.5	6.9	4.6	4.0	3.3	3.1
1981	7.6	19.6	21.4	18.4	6.5	12.3	7.3	5.0	4.2	3.7	3.2
1982	9.7	23.2	24.9	22.1	8.6	14.9	9.7	6.9	5.7	5.4	3.5
1983	9.6	22.4	24.5	21.1	8.6	14.5	9.7	7.0	6.2	5.6	3.7
1984	7.5	18.9	21.2	17.4	6.7	11.5	7.3	5.4	4.9	4.7	3.3
1985	7.2	18.6	21.0	17.0	6.4	11.1	7.0	5.1	4.7	4.3	3.2
1986	7.0	18.3	20.2	17.0	6.2	10.7	6.9	5.0	4.5	4.1	3.0
1987	6.2	16.9	19.1	15.2	5.4	9.7	6.0	4.5	4.0	3.5	2.5
1988	5.5	15.3	17.4	13.8	4.8	8.7	5.4	4.0	3.4	3.2	2.7
1989	5.3	15.0	17.2	13.6	4.6	8.6	5.2	3.8	3.2	3.2	2.6
1990	5.6	15.5	17.9	14.1	4.9	8.8	5.6	4.1	3.6	3.3	3.0
1991	6.8	18.7	21.0	17.2	6.1	10.8	6.9	5.2	4.5	4.1	3.3
1992	7.5	20.1	23.1	18.2	6.8	11.4	7.6	5.8	5.1	5.1	3.8
1993	6.9	19.0	21.4	17.5	6.2	10.5	6.9	5.5	4.8	4.7	3.2
1994	6.1	17.6	19.9	16.0	5.4	9.7	6.0	4.6	4.0	4.1	4.0
1995	5.6	17.3	20.2	15.3	4.9	9.1	5.4	4.3	3.3	3.6	4.0
1996	5.4	16.7	18.9	15.2	4.7	9.3	5.2	4.1	3.3	3.3	3.6
1997	4.9	16.0	18.2	14.5	4.3	8.5	4.7	3.8	3.0	2.9	3.3
1998	4.5	14.6	17.2	12.8	3.9	7.9	4.3	3.4	2.8	2.6	3.2
1999	4.2	13.9	16.3	12.4	3.6	7.5	4.0	3.0	2.6	2.7	3.1
2000	4.0	13.1	15.4	11.6	3.4	7.2	3.7	3.0	2.5	2.5	3.1
2001	4.7	14.7	17.2	13.1	4.2	8.3	4.6	3.6	3.1	3.0	2.9
2002	5.8	16.5	18.8	15.1	5.2	9.7	5.9	4.6	4.0	3.9	3.6
2003	6.0	17.5	19.1	16.4	5.4	10.0	6.1	4.9	4.1	4.1	3.8
2004	5.5	17.0	20.2	15.0	4.9	9.4	5.5	4.4	3.8	3.8	3.6
2005	5.1	16.6	19.1	14.9	4.5	8.8	5.1	3.9	3.5	3.3	3.5
2006	4.6	15.4	17.2	14.1	4.1	8.2	4.7	3.6	3.1	3.0	2.9
2007	4.6	15.7	17.5	14.5	4.1	8.2	4.7	3.4	3.2	3.1	3.3
2008	5.8	18.7	22.1	16.8	5.2	10.2	5.8	4.6	4.1	3.7	4.2
2009	9.3	24.3	25.9	23.4	8.6	14.7	9.9	7.9	7.2	6.6	6.4
2010	9.6	25.9	29.1	24.2	9.0	15.5	10.1	8.1	7.7	7.1	6.7
2011	8.9	24.4	27.7	22.9	8.3	14.6	9.5	7.3	7.1	6.6	6.5
2012	8.1	24.0	27.3	22.3	7.4	13.3	8.3	6.6	6.2	5.9	6.2
2013	7.4	22.9	26.5	21.0	6.8	12.8	7.4	5.9	5.6	5.3	5.4
2014	6.2	19.6	21.6	18.5	5.7	11.2	6.5	4.7	4.4	4.3	4.1
2015	5.3	16.9	18.3	16.2	4.8	9.7	5.5	4.1	3.7	3.8	3.8
2016	4.9	15.7	17.9	14.5	4.5	8.4	5.1	3.8	3.5	3.6	3.8
2017	4.4	14.0	15.5	13.1	4.0	7.4	4.6	3.5	3.2	3.1	3.6
2018	3.9	12.9	13.8	12.4	3.6	6.9	3.9	3.0	2.8	2.9	3.3

Table 1-27. Unemployment Rates of Civilian Workers, by Age, Sex, Race, and Hispanic Origin, 1948–2018 *—Continued*

(Percent of labor force.)

Race, Hispanic origin, sex, and year	16 years and over	16 to 19 years			20 years and over						
		Total	16 to 17 years	18 to 19 years	Total	20 to 24 years	25 to 34 years	35 to 44 years	45 to 54 years	55 to 64 years	65 years and over
ALL RACES											
Men											
1948	3.6	9.8	10.2	9.5	3.2	6.9	2.8	2.4	2.5	3.1	3.4
1949	5.9	14.3	13.7	14.6	5.4	10.4	5.2	4.3	4.3	5.4	5.1
1950	5.1	12.7	13.3	12.3	4.7	8.1	4.4	3.6	4.0	4.9	4.8
1951	2.8	8.1	9.4	7.0	2.5	3.9	2.3	2.0	2.4	2.8	3.5
1952	2.8	8.9	10.5	7.4	2.4	4.6	2.2	1.9	2.2	2.4	3.0
1953	2.8	7.9	8.8	7.2	2.5	5.0	2.2	2.0	2.3	2.8	2.4
1954	5.3	13.5	13.9	13.2	4.9	10.7	4.8	4.1	4.3	4.5	4.4
1955	4.2	11.6	12.5	10.8	3.8	7.7	3.3	3.1	3.2	4.3	4.0
1956	3.8	11.1	11.7	10.5	3.4	6.9	3.3	2.6	3.0	3.5	3.5
1957	4.1	12.4	12.4	12.3	3.6	7.8	3.3	2.8	3.3	3.5	3.4
1958	6.8	17.1	16.3	17.8	6.2	12.7	6.5	5.1	5.3	5.5	5.2
1959	5.2	15.3	15.8	14.9	4.7	8.7	4.7	3.7	4.1	4.5	4.8
1960	5.4	15.3	15.5	15.0	4.7	8.9	4.8	3.8	4.1	4.6	4.2
1961	6.4	17.1	18.3	16.3	5.7	10.8	5.7	4.6	4.9	5.7	5.5
1962	5.2	14.7	16.0	13.8	4.6	8.9	4.5	3.6	3.9	4.6	4.6
1963	5.2	17.2	18.8	15.9	4.5	8.8	4.5	3.5	3.6	4.3	4.5
1964	4.6	15.8	17.1	14.6	3.9	8.1	3.5	2.9	3.2	3.9	4.0
1965	4.0	14.1	16.1	12.4	3.2	6.4	2.9	2.5	2.5	3.3	3.5
1966	3.2	11.7	13.7	10.2	2.5	4.6	2.4	2.0	1.9	2.6	3.1
1967	3.1	12.3	14.5	10.5	2.3	4.7	2.1	1.7	2.0	2.3	2.8
1968	2.9	11.6	13.9	9.7	2.2	5.1	1.9	1.6	1.6	1.9	2.8
1969	2.8	11.4	13.8	9.3	2.1	5.1	1.9	1.5	1.5	1.8	2.2
1970	4.4	15.0	16.9	13.4	3.5	8.4	3.5	2.4	2.4	2.8	3.3
1971	5.3	16.6	18.7	15.0	4.4	10.3	4.4	3.1	3.0	3.3	3.4
1972	5.0	15.9	18.3	14.1	4.0	9.3	3.8	2.7	2.6	3.2	3.6
1973	4.2	13.9	17.0	11.4	3.3	7.3	3.4	2.0	2.1	2.4	3.0
1974	4.9	15.6	18.4	13.3	3.8	8.8	4.0	2.6	2.4	2.6	3.3
1975	7.9	20.1	21.6	19.0	6.8	14.3	6.9	4.9	4.8	4.3	5.4
1976	7.1	19.2	21.4	17.6	5.9	12.1	6.2	4.1	4.0	4.2	5.1
1977	6.3	17.3	19.5	15.6	5.2	10.8	5.7	3.5	3.2	3.6	5.2
1978	5.3	15.8	19.1	13.3	4.3	9.2	4.4	2.8	2.7	2.8	4.2
1979	5.1	15.9	17.9	14.3	4.2	8.7	4.3	2.9	2.7	2.7	3.4
1980	6.9	18.3	20.4	16.7	5.9	12.5	6.7	4.1	3.6	3.4	3.1
1981	7.4	20.1	22.0	18.8	6.3	13.2	6.9	4.5	4.0	3.6	2.9
1982	9.9	24.4	26.4	23.1	8.8	16.4	10.1	6.9	5.6	5.5	3.7
1983	9.9	23.3	25.2	22.2	8.9	15.9	10.1	7.1	6.3	6.1	3.9
1984	7.4	19.6	21.9	18.3	6.6	11.9	7.2	5.2	4.6	5.0	3.0
1985	7.0	19.5	21.9	17.9	6.2	11.4	6.6	4.9	4.6	4.3	3.1
1986	6.9	19.0	20.8	17.7	6.1	11.0	6.7	5.1	4.4	4.3	3.2
1987	6.2	17.8	20.2	16.0	5.4	9.9	5.9	4.4	4.2	3.7	2.6
1988	5.5	16.0	18.2	14.6	4.8	8.9	5.3	3.8	3.5	3.5	2.5
1989	5.2	15.9	18.6	14.2	4.5	8.8	4.8	3.7	3.2	3.5	2.4
1990	5.7	16.3	18.4	15.0	5.0	9.1	5.5	4.1	3.7	3.8	3.0
1991	7.2	19.8	21.8	18.5	6.4	11.6	7.0	5.5	4.8	4.6	3.3
1992	7.9	21.5	24.6	19.5	7.1	12.2	7.8	6.1	5.6	5.8	3.3
1993	7.2	20.4	22.9	18.8	6.4	11.3	7.0	5.6	5.1	5.2	3.2
1994	6.2	19.0	21.0	17.6	5.4	10.2	5.9	4.5	4.0	4.4	4.0
1995	5.6	18.4	21.1	16.5	4.8	9.2	5.1	4.2	3.5	3.6	4.3
1996	5.4	18.1	20.8	16.3	4.6	9.5	4.9	4.0	3.5	3.3	3.4
1997	4.9	16.9	19.1	15.4	4.2	8.9	4.3	3.6	3.1	3.1	3.0
1998	4.4	16.2	19.1	14.1	3.7	8.1	3.9	3.0	2.8	2.8	3.1
1999	4.1	14.7	17.0	13.1	3.5	7.7	3.6	2.8	2.6	2.7	3.0
2000	3.9	14.0	16.8	12.2	3.3	7.3	3.4	2.8	2.4	2.4	3.3
2001	4.8	16.0	19.1	14.0	4.2	9.0	4.3	3.6	3.2	3.3	3.0
2002	5.9	18.1	21.1	16.4	5.3	10.2	5.8	4.5	4.2	4.3	3.4
2003	6.3	19.3	20.7	18.4	5.6	10.6	6.2	5.0	4.4	4.5	4.0
2004	5.6	18.4	22.0	16.3	5.0	10.1	5.5	4.3	3.9	3.9	3.7
2005	5.1	18.6	22.0	16.5	4.4	9.6	4.7	3.7	3.5	3.3	3.4
2006	4.6	16.9	18.6	15.7	4.0	8.7	4.5	3.3	3.1	3.0	2.8
2007	4.7	17.6	19.4	16.5	4.1	8.9	4.7	3.3	3.1	3.2	3.4
2008	6.1	21.2	25.2	19.0	5.4	11.4	6.1	4.6	4.2	3.8	4.5
2009	10.3	27.8	28.7	27.4	9.6	17.0	10.9	8.6	8.2	7.2	6.7
2010	10.5	28.8	31.8	27.4	9.8	17.8	10.9	8.5	8.6	8.0	7.1
2011	9.4	27.2	29.1	26.3	8.7	15.7	9.7	7.4	7.4	7.1	6.5
2012	8.2	26.8	30.6	25.0	7.5	14.3	8.2	6.4	6.2	6.3	6.2
2013	7.6	25.5	29.1	23.7	7.0	14.0	7.6	5.8	5.7	5.6	5.5
2014	6.3	21.4	24.0	20.1	5.7	12.2	6.4	4.6	4.4	4.5	4.6
2015	5.4	18.4	19.8	17.6	4.9	10.8	5.5	4.0	3.6	3.9	3.8
2016	4.9	17.1	19.7	15.7	4.5	9.3	5.0	3.6	3.4	3.8	3.8
2017	4.4	15.5	16.5	15.0	4.0	8.4	4.6	3.2	3.0	3.1	3.4
2018	3.9	14.5	15.5	13.9	3.6	7.7	3.9	2.8	2.8	3.0	3.2

Table 1-27. Unemployment Rates of Civilian Workers, by Age, Sex, Race, and Hispanic Origin, 1948–2018 —*Continued*

(Percent of labor force.)

Race, Hispanic origin, sex, and year	16 years and over	16 to 19 years			20 years and over						
		Total	16 to 17 years	18 to 19 years	Total	20 to 24 years	25 to 34 years	35 to 44 years	45 to 54 years	55 to 64 years	65 years and over
ALL RACES											
Women											
1948	4.1	8.3	10.0	7.4	3.6	4.8	4.3	3.0	3.0	3.1	2.3
1949	6.0	12.3	14.4	11.2	5.3	7.3	5.9	4.7	4.0	4.4	3.8
1950	5.7	11.4	14.2	9.8	5.1	6.9	5.7	4.4	4.5	4.5	3.4
1951	4.4	8.3	10.0	7.2	4.0	4.4	4.5	3.8	3.5	4.0	2.9
1952	3.6	8.0	9.1	7.3	3.2	4.5	3.6	3.0	2.5	2.5	2.2
1953	3.3	7.2	8.5	6.4	2.9	4.3	3.4	2.5	2.3	2.5	1.4
1954	6.0	11.4	12.7	7.7	5.5	7.3	6.6	5.3	4.6	4.6	3.0
1955	4.9	10.2	12.0	9.1	4.4	6.1	5.3	4.0	3.6	3.8	2.3
1956	4.8	11.2	13.2	9.9	4.2	6.3	4.8	3.9	3.6	3.6	2.3
1957	4.7	10.6	12.6	9.4	4.1	6.0	5.3	3.8	3.2	3.0	3.4
1958	6.8	14.3	16.6	12.9	6.1	8.9	7.3	6.2	4.9	4.5	3.7
1959	5.9	13.5	14.4	13.0	5.2	8.1	5.9	5.1	4.2	4.1	2.8
1960	5.9	13.9	15.5	12.9	5.1	8.3	6.3	4.8	4.2	3.4	2.9
1961	7.2	16.3	18.3	15.1	6.3	9.8	7.4	6.4	5.1	4.5	4.0
1962	6.2	14.6	16.7	13.5	5.4	9.1	6.5	5.2	4.1	3.5	4.2
1963	6.5	17.2	20.2	15.2	5.4	8.9	6.9	5.1	4.2	3.6	3.2
1964	6.2	16.6	18.8	15.2	5.2	8.6	6.3	5.0	3.9	3.3	3.3
1965	5.5	15.7	17.2	14.8	4.5	7.3	5.5	4.6	3.2	2.8	2.9
1966	4.8	14.1	16.6	12.6	3.8	6.3	4.5	3.6	2.9	2.3	2.8
1967	5.2	13.5	14.8	12.8	4.2	7.0	5.4	4.1	3.1	2.4	2.7
1968	4.8	14.0	15.9	12.9	3.8	6.7	4.7	3.4	2.4	2.2	2.7
1969	4.7	13.3	15.5	11.8	3.7	6.3	4.6	3.4	2.6	2.2	2.3
1970	5.9	15.6	17.4	14.4	4.8	7.9	5.7	4.4	3.5	2.7	3.1
1971	6.9	17.2	18.7	16.2	5.7	9.6	7.0	5.2	4.0	3.3	3.6
1972	6.6	16.7	18.8	15.2	5.4	9.4	6.2	4.9	3.6	3.3	3.5
1973	6.0	15.3	17.7	13.5	4.9	8.5	5.8	3.9	3.2	2.8	2.9
1974	6.7	16.6	18.2	15.4	5.5	9.5	6.2	4.6	3.7	3.2	3.6
1975	9.3	19.7	21.2	18.7	8.0	12.7	9.1	6.8	5.9	5.1	5.0
1976	8.6	18.7	20.8	17.4	7.4	11.9	8.4	6.1	5.2	4.9	5.0
1977	8.2	18.3	20.5	16.9	7.0	11.2	7.7	5.7	5.1	4.4	4.7
1978	7.2	17.1	19.5	15.3	6.0	10.1	6.7	5.0	4.0	3.2	3.8
1979	6.8	16.4	18.3	15.0	5.7	9.6	6.5	4.6	3.9	3.2	3.3
1980	7.4	17.2	19.6	15.6	6.4	10.4	7.2	5.3	4.5	3.3	3.1
1981	7.9	19.0	20.7	17.9	6.8	11.2	7.7	5.7	4.6	3.8	3.6
1982	9.4	21.9	23.2	21.0	8.3	13.2	9.3	7.0	5.9	5.2	3.2
1983	9.2	21.3	23.7	19.9	8.1	12.9	9.1	6.9	6.0	5.0	3.4
1984	7.6	18.0	20.4	16.6	6.8	10.9	7.4	5.6	5.2	4.3	3.8
1985	7.4	17.6	20.0	16.0	6.6	10.7	7.4	5.5	4.8	4.3	3.3
1986	7.1	17.6	19.6	16.3	6.2	10.3	7.2	5.0	4.5	3.8	2.8
1987	6.2	15.9	18.0	14.3	5.4	9.4	6.2	4.6	3.7	3.1	2.4
1988	5.6	14.4	16.6	12.9	4.9	8.5	5.6	4.1	3.4	2.7	2.9
1989	5.4	14.0	15.7	13.0	4.7	8.3	5.6	3.9	3.2	2.8	2.9
1990	5.5	14.7	17.4	13.1	4.9	8.5	5.6	4.2	3.4	2.8	3.1
1991	6.4	17.5	20.2	15.9	5.7	9.8	6.8	4.8	4.2	3.4	3.3
1992	7.0	18.6	21.5	16.6	6.3	10.3	7.4	5.5	4.6	4.2	4.5
1993	6.6	17.5	19.8	16.1	5.9	9.7	6.8	5.3	4.5	4.0	3.1
1994	6.0	16.2	18.7	14.3	5.4	9.2	6.2	4.7	4.0	3.9	4.0
1995	5.6	16.1	19.2	14.0	4.9	9.0	5.7	4.4	3.2	3.6	3.7
1996	5.4	15.2	16.9	14.0	4.8	9.0	5.5	4.2	3.2	3.4	4.0
1997	5.0	15.0	17.2	13.6	4.4	8.1	5.2	4.0	2.9	2.7	3.6
1998	4.6	12.9	15.1	11.5	4.1	7.8	4.8	3.8	2.7	2.4	3.3
1999	4.3	13.2	15.5	11.6	3.8	7.2	4.4	3.3	2.5	2.6	3.2
2000	4.1	12.1	13.9	10.8	3.6	7.1	4.1	3.3	2.5	2.5	2.7
2001	4.7	13.4	15.2	12.2	4.1	7.5	5.1	3.7	3.0	2.7	2.9
2002	5.6	14.9	16.6	13.8	5.1	9.1	5.9	4.6	3.8	3.5	3.9
2003	5.7	15.6	17.5	14.2	5.1	9.3	5.9	4.9	3.7	3.7	3.6
2004	5.4	15.5	18.5	13.5	4.9	8.7	5.6	4.4	3.7	3.6	3.4
2005	5.1	14.5	16.5	13.1	4.6	7.9	5.6	4.1	3.5	3.3	3.5
2006	4.6	13.8	15.9	12.4	4.1	7.6	4.9	3.9	3.1	2.9	3.0
2007	4.5	13.8	15.7	12.5	4.0	7.3	4.6	3.6	3.2	3.0	3.1
2008	5.4	16.2	19.1	14.3	4.9	8.8	5.5	4.5	3.9	3.7	3.9
2009	8.1	20.7	23.1	19.4	7.5	12.3	8.6	7.1	6.0	6.0	6.1
2010	8.6	22.8	26.5	20.9	8.0	13.0	9.1	7.7	6.8	6.2	6.2
2011	8.5	21.7	26.3	19.3	7.9	13.4	9.1	7.2	6.7	6.1	6.5
2012	7.9	21.1	24.2	19.5	7.3	12.1	8.4	6.8	6.2	5.6	6.3
2013	7.1	20.3	24.0	18.2	6.5	11.5	7.3	6.0	5.5	5.0	5.1
2014	6.1	17.7	19.3	16.8	5.6	10.1	6.6	4.9	4.5	4.2	4.7
2015	5.2	15.5	16.7	14.8	4.8	8.5	5.5	4.4	3.8	3.6	3.9
2016	4.8	14.3	16.1	13.2	4.4	7.4	5.1	4.1	3.7	3.3	3.9
2017	4.3	12.5	14.6	11.1	4.0	6.3	4.6	3.7	3.3	3.1	3.8
2018	3.8	11.3	12.3	10.7	3.5	6.2	4.0	3.2	2.8	2.7	3.3

Table 1-27. Unemployment Rates of Civilian Workers, by Age, Sex, Race, and Hispanic Origin, 1948–2018 —*Continued*

(Percent of labor force.)

Race, Hispanic origin, sex, and year	16 years and over	16 to 19 years			20 years and over						
		Total	16 to 17 years	18 to 19 years	Total	20 to 24 years	25 to 34 years	35 to 44 years	45 to 54 years	55 to 64 years	65 years and over
WHITE											
Both Sexes											
1954	5.0	12.1	13.2	11.3	4.6	8.3	4.6	4.0	4.0	4.3	3.9
1955	3.9	10.4	12.0	9.2	3.4	6.2	3.1	2.9	3.1	3.8	3.4
1956	3.6	10.1	11.5	9.0	3.2	5.7	3.1	2.6	2.9	3.2	3.1
1957	3.8	10.6	11.9	9.6	3.4	6.3	3.3	2.8	3.0	3.2	3.2
1958	6.1	14.4	15.2	13.9	5.6	9.9	5.9	4.8	4.8	4.9	4.6
1959	4.8	13.1	14.4	12.1	4.3	7.3	4.2	3.7	3.8	4.1	4.1
1960	5.0	13.5	14.6	12.6	4.3	7.9	4.5	3.6	3.8	3.9	3.7
1961	6.0	15.3	16.7	14.4	5.3	9.4	5.3	4.5	4.5	5.0	4.8
1962	4.9	13.3	15.3	12.0	4.2	7.9	4.2	3.6	3.6	3.9	4.0
1963	5.0	15.5	17.9	13.7	4.2	7.7	4.4	3.5	3.5	3.8	3.8
1964	4.6	14.8	16.5	13.3	3.8	7.3	3.6	3.2	3.2	3.5	3.5
1965	4.1	13.4	14.8	12.3	3.3	6.1	3.2	2.9	2.5	2.9	3.2
1966	3.4	11.2	13.3	9.7	2.6	4.6	2.6	2.3	2.1	2.4	2.9
1967	3.4	11.0	12.8	9.8	2.7	5.0	2.7	2.3	2.2	2.3	2.7
1968	3.2	11.0	12.9	9.6	2.5	5.2	2.4	2.0	1.8	1.9	2.8
1969	3.1	10.7	13.0	8.9	2.4	5.0	2.5	2.0	1.8	1.8	2.2
1970	4.5	13.5	15.5	11.9	3.7	7.3	3.8	3.0	2.7	2.7	3.2
1971	5.4	15.1	17.0	13.8	4.5	9.0	4.7	3.6	3.3	3.3	3.5
1972	5.1	14.2	16.6	12.3	4.1	8.4	4.1	3.2	2.9	3.1	3.4
1973	4.3	12.6	15.4	10.4	3.5	6.8	3.7	2.5	2.4	2.5	2.9
1974	5.0	14.0	16.3	12.2	4.1	8.0	4.4	3.1	2.8	2.8	3.3
1975	7.8	17.9	19.5	16.7	6.7	12.3	7.1	5.2	4.9	4.5	5.1
1976	7.0	16.9	19.0	15.3	5.9	10.7	6.3	4.5	4.2	4.3	4.9
1977	6.2	15.4	17.9	13.5	5.3	9.3	5.7	4.0	3.8	3.7	4.9
1978	5.2	13.9	17.0	11.5	4.3	8.0	4.6	3.3	3.0	2.7	3.8
1979	5.1	14.0	16.1	12.4	4.2	7.6	4.4	3.2	3.0	2.7	3.1
1980	6.3	15.5	17.9	13.8	5.4	9.9	6.1	4.2	3.7	3.1	2.7
1981	6.7	17.3	19.2	15.9	5.7	10.4	6.3	4.5	3.9	3.5	2.8
1982	8.6	20.4	22.8	18.8	7.6	12.8	8.5	6.3	5.4	5.1	3.1
1983	8.4	19.3	22.0	17.6	7.5	12.1	8.4	6.3	5.7	5.2	3.2
1984	6.5	16.0	18.8	14.3	5.7	9.3	6.2	4.8	4.4	4.4	3.0
1985	6.2	15.7	18.3	13.9	5.5	9.2	5.9	4.6	4.3	4.0	2.9
1986	6.0	15.6	17.6	14.1	5.3	8.7	5.9	4.5	4.1	3.8	2.9
1987	5.3	14.4	16.7	12.7	4.7	8.0	5.1	4.0	3.7	3.2	2.4
1988	4.7	13.1	15.3	11.6	4.1	7.1	4.5	3.5	3.1	3.0	2.4
1989	4.5	12.7	15.2	11.1	3.9	7.2	4.3	3.3	2.9	3.0	2.3
1990	4.8	13.5	15.8	12.1	4.3	7.3	4.6	3.6	3.3	3.2	2.8
1991	6.1	16.5	19.0	14.9	5.5	9.2	6.1	4.7	4.2	4.0	3.1
1992	6.6	17.2	20.3	15.2	6.0	9.5	6.7	5.2	4.8	4.9	3.7
1993	6.1	16.2	19.0	14.4	5.5	8.8	6.0	4.9	4.5	4.3	3.0
1994	5.3	15.1	17.6	13.3	4.7	8.1	5.2	4.0	3.7	3.9	3.8
1995	4.9	14.5	17.3	12.5	4.3	7.7	4.6	3.9	3.1	3.5	3.8
1996	4.7	14.2	16.4	12.6	4.1	7.8	4.4	3.6	3.1	3.2	3.5
1997	4.2	13.6	15.8	12.0	3.6	6.9	3.9	3.3	2.7	2.7	3.0
1998	3.9	12.6	14.8	11.0	3.3	6.5	3.7	2.9	2.6	2.4	2.9
1999	3.7	12.0	14.5	10.2	3.1	6.3	3.3	2.7	2.4	2.5	2.9
2000	3.5	11.4	13.9	9.8	3.0	5.9	3.2	2.6	2.2	2.4	2.8
2001	4.2	12.7	15.3	11.0	3.7	7.0	4.1	3.2	2.8	2.9	2.8
2002	5.1	14.5	16.7	13.2	4.6	8.1	5.2	4.1	3.7	3.7	3.5
2003	5.2	15.2	17.2	13.9	4.7	8.4	5.3	4.3	3.7	3.8	3.7
2004	4.8	15.0	17.9	13.1	4.3	7.9	4.7	3.9	3.4	3.6	3.3
2005	4.4	14.2	16.4	12.7	3.9	7.2	4.3	3.5	3.1	3.0	3.1
2006	4.0	13.2	15.1	11.9	3.6	6.9	4.0	3.2	2.8	2.8	2.8
2007	4.1	13.9	15.5	12.8	3.6	7.0	4.0	3.2	2.9	2.9	3.2
2008	5.2	16.8	19.9	14.9	4.6	9.0	5.1	4.3	3.7	3.4	4.0
2009	8.5	21.8	23.4	21.0	7.9	13.0	8.8	7.4	6.7	6.4	6.2
2010	8.7	23.2	26.3	21.6	8.1	13.5	8.9	7.4	7.2	6.8	6.4
2011	7.9	21.7	24.7	20.2	7.4	12.8	8.1	6.5	6.4	6.2	6.4
2012	7.2	21.5	24.8	19.8	6.6	11.4	7.3	5.9	5.7	5.5	6.0
2013	6.5	20.3	23.7	18.4	6.0	10.9	6.4	5.3	5.1	4.9	5.2
2014	5.3	17.3	19.0	16.4	4.9	9.1	5.4	4.2	4.0	3.9	4.2
2015	4.6	14.8	16.5	13.8	4.2	8.3	4.5	3.7	3.4	3.5	3.4
2016	4.3	14.1	16.1	12.9	3.9	7.2	4.3	3.3	3.2	3.3	3.7
2017	3.8	12.2	14.0	11.1	3.5	6.5	3.8	3.1	2.9	2.8	3.4
2018	3.5	11.3	12.3	10.7	3.2	6.0	3.4	2.6	2.6	2.7	3.1

Table 1-27. Unemployment Rates of Civilian Workers, by Age, Sex, Race, and Hispanic Origin, 1948–2018 —*Continued*

(Percent of labor force.)

Race, Hispanic origin, sex, and year	16 years and over	16 to 19 years			20 years and over						
		Total	16 to 17 years	18 to 19 years	Total	20 to 24 years	25 to 34 years	35 to 44 years	45 to 54 years	55 to 64 years	65 years and over
WHITE											
Men											
1954	4.8	13.4	14.0	13.0	4.4	9.8	4.2	3.6	3.8	4.3	4.2
1955	3.7	11.3	12.2	10.4	3.3	7.0	2.7	2.6	2.9	3.9	3.8
1956	3.4	10.5	11.2	9.7	3.0	6.1	2.8	2.2	2.8	3.1	3.4
1957	3.6	11.5	11.9	11.1	3.2	7.0	2.7	2.5	3.0	3.4	3.2
1958	6.1	15.7	14.9	16.5	5.5	11.7	5.6	4.4	4.8	5.2	5.0
1959	4.6	14.0	15.0	13.0	4.1	7.5	3.8	3.2	3.7	4.2	4.5
1960	4.8	14.0	14.6	13.5	4.2	8.3	4.1	3.3	3.6	4.1	4.0
1961	5.7	15.7	16.5	15.2	5.1	10.1	4.9	4.0	4.4	5.3	5.2
1962	4.6	13.7	15.2	12.7	4.0	8.1	3.8	3.1	3.5	4.1	4.0
1963	4.7	15.9	17.8	14.2	3.9	7.8	3.9	2.9	3.3	4.0	4.1
1964	4.1	14.7	16.1	13.3	3.4	7.4	3.0	2.5	2.9	3.5	3.6
1965	3.6	12.9	14.7	11.3	2.9	5.9	2.6	2.3	2.3	3.1	3.4
1966	2.8	10.5	12.5	8.9	2.2	4.1	2.1	1.7	1.7	2.5	3.0
1967	2.7	10.7	12.7	9.0	2.1	4.2	1.9	1.6	1.8	2.2	2.7
1968	2.6	10.1	12.3	8.3	2.0	4.6	1.7	1.4	1.5	1.7	2.8
1969	2.5	10.0	12.5	7.9	1.9	4.6	1.7	1.4	1.4	1.7	2.2
1970	4.0	13.7	15.7	12.0	3.2	7.8	3.1	2.3	2.3	2.7	3.2
1971	4.9	15.1	17.1	13.5	4.0	9.4	4.0	2.9	2.9	3.2	3.4
1972	4.5	14.2	16.4	12.4	3.6	8.5	3.4	2.5	2.5	3.0	3.3
1973	3.8	12.3	15.2	10.0	3.0	6.6	3.0	1.8	2.0	2.4	2.9
1974	4.4	13.5	16.2	11.5	3.5	7.8	3.6	2.4	2.2	2.5	3.0
1975	7.2	18.3	19.7	17.2	6.2	13.1	6.3	4.5	4.4	4.1	5.0
1976	6.4	17.3	19.7	15.5	5.4	10.9	5.6	3.7	3.7	4.0	4.7
1977	5.5	15.0	17.6	13.0	4.7	9.3	5.0	3.1	3.0	3.3	4.9
1978	4.6	13.5	16.9	10.8	3.7	7.7	3.8	2.5	2.5	2.6	3.9
1979	4.5	13.9	16.1	12.2	3.6	7.5	3.7	2.5	2.5	2.5	3.2
1980	6.1	16.2	18.5	14.5	5.3	11.1	5.9	3.6	3.3	3.1	2.5
1981	6.5	17.9	19.9	16.4	5.6	11.6	6.1	4.0	3.6	3.4	2.4
1982	8.8	21.7	24.2	20.0	7.8	14.3	8.9	6.2	5.3	5.1	3.2
1983	8.8	20.2	22.6	18.7	7.9	13.8	9.0	6.4	5.7	5.6	3.2
1984	6.4	16.8	19.7	15.0	5.7	9.8	6.2	4.6	4.2	4.7	2.6
1985	6.1	16.5	19.2	14.7	5.4	9.7	5.7	4.3	4.1	4.0	2.7
1986	6.0	16.3	18.4	14.7	5.3	9.2	5.8	4.4	4.0	4.0	3.0
1987	5.4	15.5	17.9	13.7	4.8	8.4	5.2	3.9	3.9	3.4	2.5
1988	4.7	13.9	16.1	12.4	4.1	7.4	4.6	3.4	3.2	3.3	2.2
1989	4.5	13.7	16.4	12.0	3.9	7.5	4.1	3.2	2.9	3.1	2.1
1990	4.9	14.3	16.1	13.2	4.3	7.6	4.7	3.5	3.4	3.6	2.8
1991	6.5	17.6	19.7	16.3	5.8	10.2	6.4	5.0	4.4	4.6	3.1
1992	7.0	18.5	21.5	16.5	6.4	10.5	7.0	5.5	5.1	5.5	3.2
1993	6.3	17.7	20.2	16.0	5.7	9.6	6.2	5.0	4.7	4.7	2.9
1994	5.4	16.3	18.5	14.7	4.8	8.8	5.2	3.9	3.7	4.1	3.7
1995	4.9	15.6	18.2	13.8	4.3	7.9	4.5	3.8	3.2	3.4	4.0
1996	4.7	15.5	18.3	13.5	4.1	8.1	4.2	3.5	3.1	3.2	3.2
1997	4.2	14.3	16.3	12.9	3.6	7.3	3.7	3.2	2.8	3.0	2.7
1998	3.9	14.1	17.1	12.1	3.2	6.7	3.5	2.6	2.6	2.6	2.9
1999	3.6	12.6	15.1	10.8	3.0	6.5	3.1	2.4	2.4	2.6	2.9
2000	3.4	12.3	15.3	10.4	2.8	5.9	2.9	2.4	2.2	2.4	3.0
2001	4.2	13.9	17.4	11.7	3.7	7.8	3.8	3.1	2.9	3.2	2.8
2002	5.3	15.9	18.8	14.2	4.7	8.7	5.3	4.1	3.8	4.0	3.4
2003	5.6	17.1	18.5	16.1	5.0	9.1	5.5	4.4	4.0	4.2	3.8
2004	5.0	16.3	19.8	14.2	4.4	8.5	4.8	3.8	3.5	3.7	3.5
2005	4.4	16.1	18.9	14.3	3.8	7.9	4.1	3.3	3.0	3.0	3.1
2006	4.0	14.6	16.5	13.4	3.5	7.3	3.9	3.0	2.7	2.8	2.7
2007	4.2	15.7	17.0	14.8	3.7	7.6	4.1	3.0	2.8	3.0	3.3
2008	5.5	19.1	22.2	17.3	4.9	10.2	5.3	4.3	3.8	3.4	4.1
2009	9.4	25.2	25.9	24.8	8.8	15.3	9.8	8.0	7.7	6.8	6.3
2010	9.6	26.3	29.2	24.8	8.9	15.7	9.9	7.7	7.9	7.5	6.6
2011	8.3	24.5	26.6	23.5	7.7	13.9	8.4	6.6	6.7	6.6	6.4
2012	7.4	24.5	28.3	22.7	6.7	12.5	7.3	5.7	5.7	5.8	5.8
2013	6.8	22.5	25.9	20.7	6.2	11.9	6.6	5.2	5.2	5.2	5.4
2014	5.4	19.2	21.6	17.9	4.9	9.9	5.4	4.1	3.8	4.0	4.1
2015	4.7	16.2	18.1	15.3	4.3	9.4	4.6	3.5	3.3	3.5	3.3
2016	4.4	14.9	17.2	13.7	4.0	8.0	4.5	3.2	3.1	3.5	3.5
2017	3.8	13.3	14.9	12.3	3.5	7.4	3.9	2.9	2.8	2.8	3.2
2018	3.5	12.6	13.5	12.1	3.2	6.6	3.4	2.4	2.6	2.8	3.1

Table 1-27. Unemployment Rates of Civilian Workers, by Age, Sex, Race, and Hispanic Origin, 1948–2018 —*Continued*

(Percent of labor force.)

Race, Hispanic origin, sex, and year	16 years and over	16 to 19 years			20 years and over						
		Total	16 to 17 years	18 to 19 years	Total	20 to 24 years	25 to 34 years	35 to 44 years	45 to 54 years	55 to 64 years	65 years and over
WHITE											
Women											
1954	5.5	10.4	12.0	9.4	5.1	6.4	5.7	4.9	4.4	4.5	2.8
1955	4.3	9.1	11.6	7.7	3.9	5.1	4.3	3.8	3.4	3.6	2.2
1956	4.2	9.7	12.1	8.3	3.7	5.1	4.0	3.5	3.3	3.5	2.3
1957	4.3	9.5	11.9	7.8	3.8	5.1	4.7	3.7	3.0	2.9	3.4
1958	6.2	12.7	15.6	11.0	5.6	7.3	6.6	5.6	4.9	4.3	3.5
1959	5.3	12.0	13.3	11.1	4.7	7.0	5.2	4.7	3.9	4.0	2.9
1960	5.3	12.7	14.5	11.5	4.6	7.2	5.7	4.2	4.0	3.3	2.8
1961	6.5	14.8	17.0	13.6	5.7	8.4	6.6	5.6	4.8	4.3	3.8
1962	5.5	12.8	15.6	11.3	4.7	7.7	5.4	4.5	3.7	3.5	4.0
1963	5.8	15.1	18.1	13.2	4.8	7.4	5.8	4.6	3.9	3.5	3.3
1964	5.5	14.9	17.1	13.2	4.6	7.1	5.2	4.5	3.6	3.5	3.4
1965	5.0	14.0	15.0	13.4	4.0	6.3	4.9	4.1	3.0	2.7	2.7
1966	4.3	12.1	14.5	10.7	3.3	5.3	3.7	3.3	2.7	2.2	2.7
1967	4.6	11.5	12.9	10.6	3.8	6.0	4.7	3.7	2.9	2.3	2.6
1968	4.3	12.1	13.9	11.0	3.4	5.9	3.9	3.1	2.3	2.1	2.8
1969	4.2	11.5	13.7	10.0	3.4	5.5	4.2	3.2	2.4	2.1	2.4
1970	5.4	13.4	15.3	11.9	4.4	6.9	5.3	4.3	3.4	2.6	3.3
1971	6.3	15.1	16.7	14.1	5.3	8.5	6.3	4.9	3.9	3.3	3.6
1972	5.9	14.2	17.0	12.3	4.9	8.2	5.5	4.4	3.5	3.3	3.7
1973	5.3	13.0	15.8	10.9	4.3	7.1	5.1	3.7	3.2	2.7	2.8
1974	6.1	14.5	16.4	13.0	5.1	8.2	5.8	4.3	3.6	3.2	3.9
1975	8.6	17.4	19.2	16.1	7.5	11.2	8.4	6.5	5.8	5.0	5.3
1976	7.9	16.4	18.2	15.1	6.8	10.4	7.6	5.8	5.0	4.8	5.3
1977	7.3	15.9	18.2	14.2	6.2	9.3	6.7	5.3	5.0	4.4	4.9
1978	6.2	14.4	17.1	12.4	5.2	8.3	5.8	4.5	3.8	3.0	3.7
1979	5.9	14.0	15.9	12.5	5.0	7.8	5.6	4.2	3.7	3.0	3.1
1980	6.5	14.8	17.3	13.1	5.6	8.5	6.3	4.9	4.3	3.1	3.0
1981	6.9	16.6	18.4	15.3	5.9	9.1	6.6	5.1	4.2	3.7	3.4
1982	8.3	19.0	21.2	17.6	7.3	10.9	8.0	6.4	5.5	5.0	3.1
1983	7.9	18.3	21.4	16.4	6.9	10.3	7.6	6.2	5.5	4.7	3.1
1984	6.5	15.2	17.8	13.6	5.8	8.8	6.1	5.0	4.8	4.0	3.7
1985	6.4	14.8	17.2	13.1	5.7	8.5	6.2	4.9	4.5	4.1	3.1
1986	6.1	14.9	16.7	13.6	5.4	8.1	6.1	4.5	4.3	3.7	2.6
1987	5.2	13.4	15.5	11.7	4.6	7.4	5.0	4.1	3.3	2.9	2.4
1988	4.7	12.3	14.4	10.8	4.1	6.7	4.5	3.7	3.1	2.5	2.6
1989	4.5	11.5	13.8	10.1	4.0	6.8	4.5	3.4	2.9	2.7	2.5
1990	4.7	12.6	15.5	10.9	4.1	6.8	4.6	3.7	3.2	2.7	2.8
1991	5.6	15.2	18.2	13.3	5.0	8.1	5.7	4.3	4.0	3.3	3.1
1992	6.1	15.8	18.9	13.7	5.5	8.3	6.2	4.9	4.3	4.0	4.5
1993	5.7	14.7	17.8	12.6	5.2	7.9	5.8	4.7	4.3	3.9	3.0
1994	5.2	13.8	16.6	11.8	4.6	7.4	5.1	4.2	3.7	3.7	3.9
1995	4.8	13.4	16.4	11.2	4.3	7.4	4.7	3.9	3.0	3.5	3.5
1996	4.7	12.9	14.4	11.7	4.1	7.4	4.6	3.8	3.1	3.1	3.8
1997	4.2	12.8	15.2	11.1	3.7	6.4	4.2	3.4	2.6	2.4	3.4
1998	3.9	10.9	12.4	9.8	3.4	6.3	3.9	3.3	2.5	2.2	3.0
1999	3.8	11.3	13.9	9.6	3.3	6.1	3.6	3.0	2.3	2.5	2.9
2000	3.6	10.4	12.5	9.0	3.1	5.8	3.5	2.9	2.3	2.4	2.4
2001	4.1	11.4	13.1	10.2	3.6	6.1	4.5	3.3	2.7	2.5	2.7
2002	4.9	13.1	14.6	12.1	4.4	7.4	5.0	4.1	3.5	3.3	3.5
2003	4.8	13.3	15.9	11.5	4.4	7.6	4.9	4.2	3.3	3.4	3.5
2004	4.7	13.6	16.1	11.9	4.2	7.1	4.6	3.9	3.3	3.5	3.1
2005	4.4	12.3	14.0	11.1	3.9	6.4	4.7	3.6	3.1	3.0	3.2
2006	4.0	11.7	13.8	10.2	3.6	6.3	4.1	3.4	2.9	2.8	3.0
2007	4.0	12.1	14.1	10.6	3.6	6.2	3.9	3.4	2.9	2.8	3.1
2008	4.9	14.4	17.6	12.3	4.4	7.5	4.8	4.3	3.5	3.5	3.8
2009	7.3	18.4	20.9	17.0	6.8	10.4	7.6	6.7	5.6	5.8	6.0
2010	7.7	20.0	23.4	18.1	7.2	11.0	7.7	7.1	6.4	6.0	6.0
2011	7.5	18.9	22.9	16.7	7.0	11.4	7.7	6.3	6.1	5.8	6.4
2012	7.0	18.4	21.4	16.7	6.5	10.1	7.2	6.3	5.7	5.2	6.3
2013	6.2	18.1	21.5	16.0	5.7	9.7	6.1	5.4	5.0	4.6	4.9
2014	5.2	15.5	16.6	14.8	4.8	8.1	5.3	4.4	4.1	3.8	4.4
2015	4.5	13.2	14.8	12.3	4.1	7.0	4.5	3.9	3.5	3.5	3.5
2016	4.2	13.2	15.1	12.0	3.8	6.3	4.2	3.5	3.3	3.0	3.9
2017	3.8	11.1	13.1	9.8	3.5	5.4	3.8	3.3	3.0	2.9	3.7
2018	3.4	10.0	11.1	9.3	3.1	5.4	3.4	2.9	2.6	2.6	3.0

Table 1-27. Unemployment Rates of Civilian Workers, by Age, Sex, Race, and Hispanic Origin, 1948–2018 —*Continued*

(Percent of labor force.)

Race, Hispanic origin, sex, and year	16 years and over	16 to 19 years			20 years and over						
		Total	16 to 17 years	18 to 19 years	Total	20 to 24 years	25 to 34 years	35 to 44 years	45 to 54 years	55 to 64 years	65 years and over
BLACK											
Both Sexes											
1985	15.1	40.2	43.6	38.3	13.1	24.5	14.5	9.5	8.2	7.0	7.0
1986	14.5	39.3	43.0	37.2	12.7	24.1	14.0	9.6	7.1	6.6	4.5
1987	13.0	34.7	39.7	31.6	11.3	21.8	12.8	8.4	6.8	5.6	3.9
1988	11.7	32.4	35.1	30.7	10.2	19.6	11.9	7.5	5.9	4.8	5.5
1989	11.4	32.4	32.9	32.2	9.9	18.0	11.5	7.6	5.6	5.2	6.9
1990	11.4	30.9	36.5	27.8	10.1	19.9	11.7	7.8	5.3	4.6	5.3
1991	12.5	36.1	39.5	34.4	11.1	21.6	12.7	8.5	7.4	4.4	5.2
1992	14.2	39.7	44.7	37.1	12.6	23.8	14.2	10.5	8.3	6.2	4.9
1993	13.0	38.8	39.7	38.4	11.4	21.9	12.6	9.5	6.9	7.1	4.7
1994	11.5	35.2	36.1	34.6	10.0	19.5	11.1	8.5	5.6	5.4	6.2
1995	10.4	35.7	39.1	33.4	8.7	17.7	9.9	7.3	4.8	4.0	6.7
1996	10.5	33.6	36.3	31.7	9.0	18.8	10.5	7.3	5.0	4.4	5.3
1997	10.0	32.4	35.0	30.8	8.6	18.3	9.9	7.0	5.0	4.2	6.1
1998	8.9	27.6	33.6	24.2	7.7	16.8	8.4	6.5	4.4	3.9	5.6
1999	8.0	27.9	31.0	26.2	6.8	14.6	7.6	5.3	4.0	3.9	5.0
2000	7.6	24.5	26.9	22.9	6.5	15.0	6.7	5.6	4.1	3.0	6.1
2001	8.6	29.0	30.8	27.9	7.4	16.3	8.1	6.3	4.8	3.9	4.3
2002	10.2	29.8	34.9	27.2	9.1	19.1	9.9	7.8	6.3	5.4	5.9
2003	10.8	33.0	32.2	33.5	9.7	19.8	10.9	8.6	6.2	6.3	5.4
2004	10.4	31.7	37.8	28.3	9.4	18.4	10.8	7.8	6.9	5.6	5.5
2005	10.0	33.3	41.2	29.0	8.8	18.3	10.2	7.1	6.0	5.6	6.9
2006	8.9	29.1	32.2	27.3	7.9	16.2	9.3	6.3	5.7	4.6	4.7
2007	8.3	29.4	32.6	27.4	7.2	15.2	8.6	5.4	5.4	4.3	4.5
2008	10.1	31.2	36.3	28.5	9.1	17.9	10.6	7.0	7.0	6.1	7.5
2009	14.8	39.5	43.1	37.8	13.7	24.9	16.7	11.7	10.4	8.4	8.5
2010	16.0	43.0	47.8	40.9	14.9	26.0	17.6	13.0	11.5	9.7	9.2
2011	15.8	41.3	47.1	38.9	14.9	25.2	18.1	13.1	11.2	9.8	8.4
2012	13.8	38.3	44.0	35.9	12.8	23.1	14.8	11.1	9.8	8.8	9.8
2013	13.1	38.8	46.2	35.5	12.0	22.8	13.8	10.0	9.4	8.1	8.1
2014	11.3	33.0	37.6	30.7	10.5	20.2	13.3	7.8	7.1	7.3	6.7
2015	9.6	28.4	29.6	27.9	8.8	16.4	11.0	7.1	6.1	5.8	7.2
2016	8.4	26.7	30.4	24.9	7.7	14.5	8.8	6.7	5.6	5.4	5.8
2017	7.5	24.0	24.5	23.8	6.8	11.5	8.4	5.8	5.2	4.9	4.4
2018	6.5	21.9	24.3	20.9	5.9	10.8	6.6	5.3	4.3	4.1	5.2
Men											
1985	15.3	41.0	42.9	40.0	13.2	23.5	13.8	9.6	9.7	7.9	8.9
1986	14.8	39.3	41.4	38.2	12.9	23.5	13.5	10.9	7.8	8.0	4.3
1987	12.7	34.4	39.0	31.6	11.1	20.3	12.2	8.7	6.7	6.6	4.3
1988	11.7	32.7	34.4	31.7	10.1	19.4	11.0	7.6	6.2	5.2	5.6
1989	11.5	31.9	34.4	30.3	10.0	17.9	10.5	8.4	6.2	6.2	7.4
1990	11.9	31.9	38.8	28.0	10.4	20.1	11.5	8.4	6.3	5.4	4.6
1991	13.0	36.3	39.0	34.8	11.5	22.4	11.9	9.5	8.6	5.0	6.1
1992	15.2	42.0	47.5	39.1	13.5	24.6	14.2	11.2	10.3	8.1	4.9
1993	13.8	40.1	42.7	38.6	12.1	23.0	12.3	10.5	8.1	9.0	5.8
1994	12.0	37.6	39.3	36.5	10.3	19.4	10.6	9.1	6.5	6.0	8.2
1995	10.6	37.1	39.7	35.4	8.8	17.6	9.3	7.6	5.5	4.4	7.6
1996	11.1	36.9	39.9	34.9	9.4	19.2	10.1	7.8	6.3	5.2	5.0
1997	10.2	36.5	39.5	34.4	8.5	19.8	8.7	6.7	5.6	4.2	5.5
1998	8.9	30.1	33.9	27.9	7.4	18.0	7.3	6.2	4.4	4.5	5.2
1999	8.2	30.9	33.3	29.4	6.7	16.2	6.9	5.2	4.3	3.9	5.0
2000	8.0	26.2	28.5	24.7	6.9	16.6	6.7	5.8	4.8	2.7	6.3
2001	9.3	30.4	30.5	30.4	8.0	17.6	8.3	6.9	5.5	4.8	4.0
2002	10.7	31.3	36.6	28.7	9.5	20.0	9.4	8.0	7.4	6.1	5.0
2003	11.6	36.0	35.6	36.3	10.3	20.9	11.3	9.2	6.7	6.8	5.6
2004	11.1	35.6	40.8	32.7	9.9	20.3	10.9	8.0	7.2	6.4	4.2
2005	10.5	36.3	45.1	31.5	9.2	20.5	9.7	7.0	6.7	5.9	7.1
2006	9.5	32.7	34.8	31.5	8.3	17.2	9.5	5.9	6.3	5.5	5.8
2007	9.1	33.8	40.1	30.2	7.9	16.9	9.1	5.6	5.8	5.2	5.0
2008	11.4	35.9	43.9	32.0	10.2	19.3	11.8	7.7	7.7	7.1	9.5
2009	17.5	46.0	49.3	44.5	16.3	27.7	19.9	14.0	12.4	10.1	10.6
2010	18.4	45.4	49.4	43.9	17.3	29.8	19.3	14.9	14.4	12.2	10.4
2011	17.8	43.1	44.5	42.5	16.7	27.4	19.7	14.9	12.5	12.7	8.2
2012	15.0	41.3	47.2	38.9	14.0	25.6	15.2	12.6	10.2	10.1	11.5
2013	14.2	44.5	51.2	41.6	12.9	25.1	14.3	10.1	10.3	8.5	9.1
2014	12.2	36.5	38.5	35.5	11.3	22.1	13.6	8.2	7.9	8.0	8.5
2015	10.3	30.8	33.1	29.5	9.5	18.3	11.3	7.2	6.3	7.4	7.2
2016	9.1	30.9	37.8	28.4	8.2	17.0	8.8	6.9	5.7	5.9	6.2
2017	8.1	30.0	28.5	30.7	7.2	13.2	8.6	5.9	5.2	5.6	4.0
2018	7.0	25.7	30.0	24.1	6.2	12.7	6.4	5.5	4.7	4.6	4.7

Table 1-27. Unemployment Rates of Civilian Workers, by Age, Sex, Race, and Hispanic Origin, 1948–2018 —*Continued*

(Percent of labor force.)

Race, Hispanic origin, sex, and year	16 years and over	16 to 19 years			20 years and over						
		Total	16 to 17 years	18 to 19 years	Total	20 to 24 years	25 to 34 years	35 to 44 years	45 to 54 years	55 to 64 years	65 years and over
BLACK											
Women											
1985	14.9	39.2	44.3	36.4	13.1	25.6	15.1	9.3	6.8	7.3	5.2
1986	14.2	39.2	44.6	36.1	12.4	24.7	14.6	8.5	6.4	5.9	4.9
1987	13.2	34.9	40.5	31.7	11.6	23.3	13.5	8.1	6.9	6.0	3.4
1988	11.7	32.0	35.9	29.6	10.4	19.8	12.7	7.4	5.6	5.0	5.4
1989	11.4	33.0	31.1	34.0	9.8	18.1	12.5	7.0	5.0	4.5	6.4
1990	10.9	29.9	34.1	27.6	9.7	19.6	11.9	7.2	4.3	4.3	5.9
1991	12.0	36.0	40.1	33.9	10.6	20.7	13.4	7.6	6.2	4.2	4.4
1992	13.2	37.2	41.7	34.8	11.8	23.1	14.1	9.8	6.4	3.6	5.0
1993	12.1	37.4	36.1	38.1	10.7	20.9	12.9	8.6	5.8	3.8	3.6
1994	11.0	32.6	32.9	32.5	9.8	19.6	11.7	8.0	4.9	4.2	4.4
1995	10.2	34.3	38.5	31.5	8.6	17.8	10.5	7.0	4.2	5.1	5.6
1996	10.0	30.3	32.8	28.6	8.7	18.4	11.0	6.9	3.8	4.9	6.6
1997	9.9	28.7	30.3	27.8	8.8	17.1	10.9	7.2	4.4	3.6	6.1
1998	9.0	25.3	33.2	20.9	7.9	15.7	9.5	6.7	4.3	3.8	5.0
1999	7.8	25.1	28.5	23.3	6.8	13.4	8.3	5.5	3.8	4.1	6.0
2000	7.1	22.8	25.3	21.3	6.2	13.6	6.8	5.5	3.4	3.4	4.6
2001	8.1	27.5	31.2	25.4	7.0	15.3	8.0	5.8	4.3	3.9	6.9
2002	9.8	28.3	33.2	25.6	8.8	18.3	10.2	7.7	5.3	3.3	5.3
2003	10.2	30.3	29.1	31.1	9.2	18.8	10.5	8.1	5.8	3.1	6.8
2004	9.8	28.2	35.2	24.3	8.9	16.6	10.7	7.6	6.5	4.7	6.6
2005	9.5	30.3	37.3	26.6	8.5	16.3	10.6	7.2	5.4	5.9	3.7
2006	8.4	25.9	29.9	23.6	7.5	15.2	9.0	6.7	5.1	4.8	4.0
2007	7.5	25.3	26.4	24.7	6.7	13.6	8.1	5.3	5.0	5.3	5.8
2008	8.9	26.8	29.9	25.0	8.1	16.6	9.5	6.4	6.3	3.9	6.6
2009	12.4	33.4	37.2	31.7	11.5	22.2	13.8	9.7	8.7	3.7	8.2
2010	13.8	40.5	46.4	37.7	12.8	22.6	16.0	11.4	9.1	5.3	8.5
2011	14.1	39.4	49.5	34.8	13.2	23.1	16.5	11.6	10.0	7.1	8.2
2012	12.8	35.6	41.3	33.1	11.9	20.8	14.4	9.8	9.4	7.6	7.2
2013	12.1	33.4	41.6	29.8	11.3	20.6	13.2	9.8	8.5	7.4	7.2
2014	10.5	29.7	36.7	26.6	9.8	18.4	13.1	7.4	7.9	6.7	7.4
2015	8.9	26.4	26.3	26.5	8.2	14.6	10.7	7.0	5.9	4.5	7.2
2016	7.8	22.8	25.7	20.9	7.3	12.3	8.8	6.5	5.4	4.9	5.4
2017	6.9	18.9	21.7	17.4	6.5	9.8	8.2	5.7	5.1	4.3	4.7
2018	6.0	18.4	20.2	17.6	5.6	8.9	6.9	5.1	4.0	3.7	5.5
HISPANIC											
Both Sexes											
1985	10.5	24.3	27.8	22.5	9.4	12.6	9.9	7.7	7.4	7.8	8.1
1986	10.6	24.7	28.1	22.9	9.5	12.9	9.6	8.4	7.8	7.3	10.1
1987	8.8	22.3	27.7	19.5	7.8	10.6	7.7	6.7	6.9	6.0	6.5
1988	8.2	22.0	27.1	19.3	7.0	9.8	7.1	6.0	6.0	5.8	5.6
1989	8.0	19.4	26.4	16.0	7.2	10.7	7.0	5.9	6.3	5.8	5.3
1990	8.2	19.5	24.5	16.9	7.2	9.1	7.3	6.6	6.4	5.6	6.0
1991	10.0	22.9	31.9	18.7	9.0	11.6	9.2	8.1	8.0	6.5	7.0
1992	11.6	27.5	35.7	23.4	10.4	13.2	10.4	9.8	8.8	8.6	8.1
1993	10.8	26.1	35.1	21.8	9.7	13.1	9.3	9.1	8.6	8.0	6.6
1994	9.9	24.5	31.7	20.6	8.9	11.8	9.0	7.7	8.1	7.3	7.9
1995	9.3	24.1	33.1	19.5	8.2	11.5	8.2	7.2	6.4	7.5	10.6
1996	8.9	23.6	30.0	20.3	7.8	11.8	7.3	7.3	6.0	7.3	8.2
1997	7.7	21.6	27.7	18.4	6.8	10.3	6.3	6.4	5.1	6.5	6.8
1998	7.2	21.3	28.0	18.1	6.1	9.4	5.9	5.5	4.6	5.3	6.4
1999	6.4	18.6	23.7	16.3	5.5	8.3	5.4	4.8	4.8	4.5	5.0
2000	5.7	16.6	22.5	13.9	4.9	7.5	4.8	4.5	3.3	4.5	5.7
2001	6.6	17.7	24.0	15.0	5.8	8.1	5.9	5.2	4.3	5.6	4.5
2002	7.5	20.1	24.2	18.2	6.7	9.9	6.6	6.0	5.5	5.7	6.8
2003	7.7	20.0	24.6	17.7	7.0	10.2	7.0	6.0	6.3	5.7	3.9
2004	7.0	20.4	29.0	16.8	6.2	9.3	6.3	5.3	5.2	5.8	6.0
2005	6.0	18.4	23.6	16.0	5.3	8.6	5.3	4.5	4.4	4.4	4.9
2006	5.2	15.9	20.4	13.6	4.6	7.2	4.7	4.3	3.7	3.3	3.9
2007	5.6	18.1	22.5	16.0	5.0	7.8	4.9	4.3	4.3	4.5	4.9
2008	7.6	22.4	29.8	19.0	6.8	11.5	6.7	5.8	6.3	4.8	7.8
2009	12.1	30.2	36.3	27.8	11.2	16.2	11.4	10.2	10.1	10.0	8.0
2010	12.5	32.2	37.6	30.2	11.6	17.4	11.3	10.3	10.8	10.3	9.5
2011	11.5	31.1	38.3	28.5	10.6	15.7	10.4	9.2	9.9	9.7	8.8
2012	10.3	28.6	35.2	26.1	9.4	13.8	9.2	8.3	8.3	9.2	8.7
2013	9.1	27.5	33.7	25.0	8.2	12.8	8.2	7.3	6.8	7.4	7.7
2014	7.4	22.5	28.5	20.2	6.7	11.1	6.9	5.7	5.3	6.0	5.7
2015	6.6	19.3	22.6	18.0	6.0	10.0	6.3	5.0	4.7	5.4	5.8
2016	5.8	17.1	20.0	15.8	5.3	8.8	5.4	4.1	4.4	5.0	4.8
2017	5.1	15.0	19.0	13.2	4.7	7.6	5.1	3.8	3.7	3.9	4.9
2018	4.7	14.5	17.3	13.4	4.2	7.0	4.3	3.5	3.1	4.2	5.1

Table 1-27. Unemployment Rates of Civilian Workers, by Age, Sex, Race, and Hispanic Origin, 1948–2018 —*Continued*

(Percent of labor force.)

Race, Hispanic origin, sex, and year	16 years and over	16 to 19 years			20 years and over						
		Total	16 to 17 years	18 to 19 years	Total	20 to 24 years	25 to 34 years	35 to 44 years	45 to 54 years	55 to 64 years	65 years and over
HISPANIC											
Men											
1985	10.2	24.7	29.1	22.4	9.1	12.9	9.6	7.2	6.8	7.0	. . .
1986	10.5	24.5	28.5	22.4	9.5	13.0	9.5	8.5	7.0	8.0	. . .
1987	8.7	22.2	28.2	19.3	7.8	10.2	7.6	6.9	7.1	6.7	. . .
1988	8.1	22.7	29.5	19.5	7.0	9.2	7.0	5.9	6.1	6.7	. . .
1989	7.6	20.2	27.6	16.8	6.6	9.7	5.9	5.7	6.0	6.6	. . .
1990	8.0	19.5	24.0	17.4	7.0	8.4	6.9	6.5	6.8	6.5	. . .
1991	10.3	23.5	33.6	19.2	9.3	11.6	9.3	8.5	7.9	8.1	. . .
1992	11.7	28.2	36.6	24.0	10.5	13.7	10.1	9.8	8.9	10.2	. . .
1993	10.6	25.9	34.5	21.9	9.5	12.6	9.0	8.8	8.8	8.5	. . .
1994	9.4	26.3	33.3	22.5	8.3	10.8	8.4	6.6	8.1	7.4	10.5
1995	8.8	25.3	34.8	20.2	7.7	10.6	7.5	6.7	5.9	7.9	12.9
1996	7.9	22.5	31.5	18.4	6.9	10.3	6.6	6.3	5.1	6.7	8.3
1997	7.0	20.8	26.5	17.9	6.1	9.8	5.1	5.4	4.8	6.8	7.2
1998	6.4	20.6	29.0	16.4	5.4	8.9	5.2	4.5	4.2	5.3	5.0
1999	5.6	17.8	23.4	15.3	4.7	7.8	4.1	3.8	4.5	4.6	5.0
2000	5.0	15.7	22.3	12.8	4.2	6.6	3.7	3.8	3.1	4.1	6.2
2001	5.9	17.1	25.8	13.4	5.2	8.1	4.6	4.5	3.8	6.3	4.8
2002	7.2	20.2	22.9	19.1	6.4	9.3	6.1	5.4	5.5	6.2	6.3
2003	7.2	21.9	25.9	20.1	6.4	9.6	6.3	5.3	6.0	6.0	3.6
2004	6.5	21.2	30.7	17.6	5.8	9.4	5.5	4.5	4.7	5.7	6.9
2005	5.4	19.3	23.4	17.5	4.7	8.2	4.3	3.9	4.0	4.0	4.8
2006	4.8	17.3	22.6	14.8	4.2	6.7	4.2	3.6	3.4	3.5	3.7
2007	5.3	19.7	23.4	18.0	4.6	7.4	4.5	3.8	4.4	3.9	5.5
2008	7.6	23.4	30.9	19.9	6.8	11.8	6.6	5.6	6.2	5.1	7.8
2009	12.5	33.8	41.1	31.1	11.6	16.6	11.6	10.5	10.5	11.2	7.8
2010	12.7	34.6	41.0	32.6	11.7	18.2	11.6	9.8	11.2	10.6	9.4
2011	11.2	33.3	40.7	31.0	10.3	15.3	9.9	8.7	9.8	10.4	9.5
2012	9.9	30.5	40.6	26.9	8.9	13.8	8.4	7.2	8.2	9.8	8.6
2013	8.8	28.2	34.5	25.8	7.9	13.4	7.5	6.5	6.5	8.2	8.5
2014	6.8	22.5	30.8	19.5	6.1	11.1	6.1	4.9	4.6	5.9	6.6
2015	6.3	20.3	23.8	18.9	5.7	10.6	5.7	4.0	4.6	5.5	5.7
2016	5.4	18.3	21.4	16.9	4.9	9.3	4.8	3.6	3.6	5.0	5.6
2017	4.7	15.9	17.3	15.3	4.2	7.5	4.6	3.4	3.1	3.4	5.1
2018	4.3	16.0	18.5	15.1	3.8	7.4	3.6	3.0	2.7	4.1	5.5
HISPANIC											
Women											
1985	11.0	23.8	26.2	22.6	9.9	12.1	10.6	8.5	8.1	9.2	. . .
1986	10.8	25.1	27.6	23.6	9.6	12.9	9.8	8.2	8.9	6.2	. . .
1987	8.9	22.4	27.1	19.9	7.7	11.4	7.8	6.5	6.7	5.0	. . .
1988	8.3	21.0	24.5	18.9	7.1	10.7	7.2	6.2	5.9	4.6	. . .
1989	8.8	18.2	24.7	14.9	8.0	12.2	8.6	6.3	6.7	4.5	. . .
1990	8.4	19.4	25.4	16.2	7.5	10.4	8.0	6.7	6.0	4.3	. . .
1991	9.6	21.9	29.6	17.9	8.6	11.7	9.1	7.6	8.1	4.1	. . .
1992	11.4	26.4	34.5	22.4	10.2	12.4	11.0	9.7	8.5	6.2	. . .
1993	11.0	26.3	36.0	21.7	9.9	14.0	9.9	9.5	8.3	7.2	. . .
1994	10.7	22.2	29.7	18.1	9.8	13.5	10.1	9.2	8.0	7.1	3.6
1995	10.0	22.6	30.7	18.7	8.9	13.0	9.5	7.9	7.0	6.8	6.4
1996	10.2	25.1	28.2	23.3	9.2	14.1	8.5	8.7	7.2	8.1	8.0
1997	8.9	22.7	29.2	19.1	7.9	11.0	8.2	7.7	5.5	6.1	6.0
1998	8.2	22.1	26.4	20.2	7.1	10.1	7.2	6.9	5.1	5.4	8.8
1999	7.6	19.8	24.0	17.7	6.6	9.1	7.3	6.3	5.1	4.3	4.8
2000	6.8	18.0	22.7	15.6	5.9	9.0	6.4	5.4	3.6	5.0	4.8
2001	7.5	18.5	21.6	17.1	6.6	8.2	7.8	6.2	4.8	4.8	4.0
2002	8.0	19.9	25.8	17.0	7.2	10.8	7.4	6.7	5.5	5.0	7.5
2003	8.4	17.7	23.2	14.4	7.8	11.3	8.2	7.1	6.8	5.3	4.4
2004	7.6	19.3	27.0	15.5	7.0	9.1	7.6	6.4	5.8	5.8	4.6
2005	6.9	17.2	23.8	14.0	6.3	9.2	7.1	5.5	4.8	5.0	5.1
2006	5.9	14.1	18.1	11.9	5.3	8.1	5.5	5.5	4.2	3.1	4.2
2007	6.1	16.1	21.3	13.6	5.5	8.5	5.6	5.1	4.3	5.2	4.0
2008	7.7	21.1	28.1	18.0	6.9	11.1	6.8	6.0	6.4	4.4	7.7
2009	11.5	25.8	30.8	23.8	10.6	15.7	10.9	9.7	9.6	8.5	8.3
2010	12.3	29.1	34.2	27.0	11.4	16.2	10.9	11.1	10.4	9.9	9.6
2011	11.8	28.1	35.7	25.0	11.1	16.3	11.4	9.9	10.1	8.8	8.0
2012	10.9	26.4	29.4	25.1	10.1	13.9	10.4	9.7	8.5	8.5	8.8
2013	9.5	26.7	33.0	23.9	8.6	12.0	9.2	8.3	7.2	6.5	6.7
2014	8.2	22.5	26.1	21.0	7.5	11.1	7.9	6.9	6.2	6.1	4.5
2015	7.1	18.3	21.4	16.9	6.5	9.4	7.2	6.4	4.8	5.2	3.9
2016	6.3	15.8	18.6	14.5	5.8	8.3	6.1	4.8	5.5	4.9	3.7
2017	5.7	14.1	20.5	10.8	5.3	7.7	5.8	4.4	4.5	4.4	4.6
2018	5.1	12.9	16.2	11.6	4.7	6.6	5.3	4.2	3.6	4.4	4.5

. . . = Not available.

Table 1-28. Unemployed Persons and Unemployment Rates, by Selected Occupation, 2005–2018

(Thousands of people, percent of civilian labor force.)

Occupation	2005	2006	2007	2008	2009	2010	2011	2012	2013	2014	2015	2016	2017	2018
Total Unemployed Persons, 16 Years and Over[1]	7 591	7 001	7 078	8 924	14 265	14 825	13 747	12 506	11 460	9 617	8 296	7 751	6 982	6 314
Management, professional, and related	1 172	1 065	1 090	1 463	2 531	2 566	2 458	2 318	2 036	1 777	1 504	1 513	1 383	1 346
Management, business, and financial operations	464	427	429	619	1 105	1 117	1 067	935	831	704	602	629	558	523
Professional and related	708	638	662	844	1 427	1 449	1 392	1 383	1 205	1 073	902	884	825	822
Services	1 587	1 485	1 521	1 769	2 605	2 819	2 727	2 540	2 444	2 048	1 855	1 655	1 530	1 353
Sales and office	1 820	1 667	1 638	2 006	3 143	3 315	3 135	2 775	2 575	2 119	1 792	1 623	1 443	1 337
Sales and related	874	812	835	980	1 501	1 596	1 481	1 318	1 212	1 022	909	799	699	669
Office and administrative support	946	856	804	1 026	1 642	1 719	1 653	1 457	1 363	1 096	883	825	744	668
Natural resources, construction, and maintenance	1 069	1 007	1 052	1 421	2 464	2 504	2 000	1 668	1 423	1 171	1 058	953	903	780
Farming, fishing, and forestry	103	101	89	112	179	193	181	167	124	134	132	127	113	114
Construction and extraction	751	699	781	1 067	1 825	1 809	1 414	1 181	1 016	813	701	618	611	530
Installation, maintenance, and repair	214	207	182	243	459	503	406	320	284	224	225	207	179	136
Production, transportation, and material moving	1 245	1 127	1 128	1 474	2 453	2 365	2 099	1 845	1 690	1 385	1 182	1 160	1 014	881
Production	677	544	564	746	1 322	1 206	1 025	865	792	632	513	516	435	361
Transportation and material moving	568	583	564	727	1 131	1 159	1 073	980	898	754	668	644	579	520
Total Unemployment Rate, 16 Years and Over[1]	5.1	4.6	4.6	5.8	9.3	9.6	8.9	8.1	7.4	6.2	5.3	4.9	4.4	3.9
Management, professional, and related	2.3	2.1	2.1	2.7	4.6	4.7	4.5	4.1	3.6	3.1	2.5	2.5	2.2	2.1
Management, business, and financial operations	2.2	2.0	1.9	2.7	4.9	5.1	4.7	4.0	3.5	2.9	2.4	2.5	2.2	2.0
Professional and related	2.4	2.1	2.1	2.7	4.4	4.5	4.3	4.2	3.6	3.2	2.6	2.5	2.3	2.2
Services	6.4	5.9	5.9	6.7	9.6	10.3	9.9	9.1	8.6	7.3	6.7	5.8	5.4	4.8
Sales and office	4.8	4.4	4.3	5.3	8.5	9.0	8.7	7.7	7.2	6.0	5.1	4.6	4.1	3.8
Sales and related	5.0	4.7	4.8	5.7	8.8	9.4	8.8	7.9	7.3	6.1	5.5	4.8	4.2	4.1
Office and administrative support	4.6	4.2	4.0	5.1	8.3	8.7	8.5	7.6	7.1	5.8	4.7	4.5	4.0	3.6
Natural resources, construction, and maintenance	6.5	6.0	6.3	8.8	15.6	16.1	13.3	11.5	9.8	8.0	7.2	6.4	6.0	5.1
Farming, fishing, and forestry	9.6	9.5	8.5	10.2	16.2	16.3	15.3	14.4	11.4	11.6	10.9	10.4	8.7	9.2
Construction and extraction	7.6	6.8	7.6	11.0	19.7	20.1	16.6	14.4	12.5	9.6	8.4	7.2	7.1	6.0
Installation, maintenance, and repair	3.9	3.7	3.4	4.5	8.5	9.3	7.7	6.2	5.4	4.4	4.3	4.1	3.5	2.6
Production, transportation, and material moving	6.5	5.8	5.8	7.6	13.3	12.8	11.3	9.8	9.1	7.4	6.3	6.1	5.4	4.5
Production	6.7	5.5	5.7	7.7	14.7	13.1	11.2	9.3	8.7	7.0	5.7	5.7	4.9	4.0
Transportation and material moving	6.2	6.2	6.0	7.6	12.0	12.4	11.4	10.3	9.4	7.7	6.8	6.5	5.8	5.0

[1]Includes persons with no work experience and persons whose last job was in the armed forces.

Table 1-29. Unemployed Persons and Unemployment Rates, by Class of Worker and Industry, 2005–2018

(Thousands of people, percent.)

Class of worker and industry	2005	2006	2007	2008	2009	2010	2011	2012	2013	2014	2015	2016	2017	2018
Total Unemployed Persons, 16 Years and Over	7 591	7 001	7 078	8 924	14 265	14 825	13 747	12 506	11 460	9 617	8 296	7 751	6 982	6 314
Nonagricultural private wage and salary workers	5 989	5 523	5 559	7 118	11 654	11 808	10 655	9 531	8 693	7 267	6 299	5 824	5 323	4 798
Mining, quarrying, and oil and gas extraction	20	22	25	25	90	73	52	59	64	52	84	67	31	27
Construction	712	671	757	1 030	1 770	1 801	1 383	1 129	935	762	624	558	559	494
Manufacturing	812	699	706	945	1 890	1 622	1 373	1 122	1 019	754	677	667	563	517
Durable goods	485	410	436	597	1 279	1 074	887	693	612	454	410	412	360	295
Nondurable goods	326	289	270	348	611	548	485	430	407	300	267	255	203	222
Wholesale trade and retail trade	1 137	1 039	975	1 205	1 844	1 963	1 834	1 663	1 463	1 260	1 135	1 009	942	881
Transportation and utilities	232	229	233	312	525	492	484	410	406	357	275	278	271	236
Information	163	126	120	167	294	303	222	218	175	153	108	123	120	99
Financial activities	272	264	289	380	598	626	582	466	424	373	247	266	240	215
Professional and business services	792	746	740	921	1 522	1 561	1 430	1 358	1 284	1 083	894	842	775	671
Education and health services	627	568	575	698	1 100	1 243	1 217	1 232	1 098	935	823	772	714	638
Leisure and hospitality	921	865	896	1 102	1 543	1 592	1 527	1 403	1 379	1 168	1 092	949	856	791
Other services	301	293	241	332	477	533	551	470	445	368	340	293	251	229
Agriculture and related private wage and salary workers	104	95	78	123	200	211	190	188	141	146	155	139	122	124
Government workers	534	473	505	534	799	969	1 013	923	851	678	573	582	527	505
Self-employed and unpaid family workers	298	293	309	383	577	617	605	547	527	440	389	383	319	285
Total Unemployment Rate, 16 Years and Over[1]	5.1	4.6	4.6	5.8	9.3	9.6	8.9	8.1	7.4	6.2	5.3	4.9	4.4	3.9
Nonagricultural private wage and salary workers	5.2	4.7	4.7	5.9	9.8	9.9	9.0	7.9	7.2	5.9	5.1	4.6	4.2	3.7
Mining	3.1	3.2	3.4	3.1	11.6	9.4	6.1	6.0	5.8	4.7	8.6	8.0	4.1	3.4
Construction	7.4	6.7	7.4	10.6	19.0	20.6	16.4	13.9	11.3	8.9	7.3	6.3	6.0	5.1
Manufacturing	4.9	4.2	4.3	5.8	12.1	10.6	9.0	7.3	6.6	4.9	4.3	4.3	3.6	3.3
Durable goods	4.6	3.9	4.2	5.6	12.9	11.2	9.2	7.2	6.3	4.7	4.1	4.2	3.7	3.0
Nondurable goods	5.3	4.8	4.5	6.0	10.6	9.6	8.5	7.5	7.1	5.2	4.6	4.4	3.5	3.8
Wholesale trade and retail trade	5.4	4.9	4.7	5.9	9.0	9.5	8.9	8.1	7.3	6.1	5.5	5.0	4.6	4.3
Transportation and utilities	4.1	4.0	3.9	5.1	8.9	8.4	8.2	6.9	6.6	5.7	4.4	4.2	4.1	3.4
Information	5.0	3.7	3.6	5.0	9.2	9.7	7.3	7.6	6.2	5.2	3.9	4.6	4.5	3.7
Financial activities	2.9	2.7	3.0	3.9	6.4	6.9	6.4	5.1	4.5	4.0	2.6	2.7	2.4	2.2
Professional and business services	6.2	5.6	5.3	6.5	10.8	10.8	9.7	8.9	8.3	6.9	5.6	5.1	4.5	3.9
Education and health services	3.4	3.0	3.0	3.5	5.3	5.8	5.6	5.5	4.9	4.2	3.6	3.3	3.0	2.6
Leisure and hospitality	7.8	7.3	7.4	8.6	11.7	12.2	11.6	10.4	10.0	8.6	7.9	6.8	6.1	5.7
Other services	4.8	4.7	3.9	5.3	7.5	8.5	8.8	7.2	6.9	5.7	5.2	4.4	3.8	3.3
Agriculture and related private wage and salary workers	8.3	7.2	6.3	9.2	14.3	13.9	12.5	12.4	10.1	9.4	9.4	8.3	7.2	7.2
Government workers	2.6	2.3	2.3	2.4	3.6	4.4	4.7	4.3	4.0	3.2	2.7	2.7	2.5	2.3
Self-employed and unpaid family workers	2.7	2.7	2.8	3.6	5.5	5.9	6.0	5.4	5.3	4.4	3.9	3.8	3.2	2.8

Note: See notes and definitions for information on historical comparability.

[1]Includes persons with no work experience and persons whose last job was in the armed forces.

Table 1-30. Unemployed Persons, by Duration of Unemployment, 1948–2018

(Thousands of people, number of weeks.)

Year	Total unemployed	Duration of unemployment											
		Less than 5 weeks		5 to 14 weeks		15 weeks and over						Average duration, in weeks	Median duration, in weeks
								15 to 26 weeks		27 weeks and over			
		Number	Percent	Number	Percent	Number	Percent	Number	Percent	Number	Percent		
1948	2 276	1 300	57.1	669	29.4	309	13.6	193	8.5	116	5.1	8.6	. . .
1949	3 637	1 756	48.3	1 194	32.8	684	18.8	428	11.8	256	7.0	10.0	. . .
1950	3 288	1 450	44.1	1 055	32.1	782	23.8	425	12.9	357	10.9	12.1	. . .
1951	2 055	1 177	57.3	574	27.9	303	14.7	166	8.1	137	6.7	9.7	. . .
1952	1 883	1 135	60.3	516	27.4	232	12.3	148	7.9	84	4.5	8.4	. . .
1953	1 834	1 142	62.3	482	26.3	210	11.5	132	7.2	78	4.3	8.0	. . .
1954	3 532	1 605	45.4	1 116	31.6	812	23.0	495	14.0	317	9.0	11.8	. . .
1955	2 852	1 335	46.8	815	28.6	702	24.6	366	12.8	336	11.8	13.0	. . .
1956	2 750	1 412	51.3	805	29.3	533	19.4	301	10.9	232	8.4	11.3	. . .
1957	2 859	1 408	49.2	891	31.2	560	19.6	321	11.2	239	8.4	10.5	. . .
1958	4 602	1 753	38.1	1 396	30.3	1 452	31.6	785	17.1	667	14.5	13.9	. . .
1959	3 740	1 585	42.4	1 114	29.8	1 040	27.8	469	12.5	571	15.3	14.4	. . .
1960	3 852	1 719	44.6	1 176	30.5	957	24.8	503	13.1	454	11.8	12.8	. . .
1961	4 714	1 806	38.3	1 376	29.2	1 532	32.5	728	15.4	804	17.1	15.6	. . .
1962	3 911	1 663	42.5	1 134	29.0	1 119	28.6	534	13.7	585	15.0	14.7	. . .
1963	4 070	1 751	43.0	1 231	30.2	1 088	26.7	535	13.1	553	13.6	14.0	. . .
1964	3 786	1 697	44.8	1 117	29.5	973	25.7	491	13.0	482	12.7	13.3	. . .
1965	3 366	1 628	48.4	983	29.2	755	22.4	404	12.0	351	10.4	11.8	. . .
1966	2 875	1 573	54.7	779	27.1	526	18.3	287	10.0	239	8.3	10.4	. . .
1967	2 975	1 634	54.9	893	30.0	448	15.1	271	9.1	177	5.9	8.7	2.3
1968	2 817	1 594	56.6	810	28.8	412	14.6	256	9.1	156	5.5	8.4	4.5
1969	2 832	1 629	57.5	827	29.2	375	13.2	242	8.5	133	4.7	7.8	4.4
1970	4 093	2 139	52.3	1 290	31.5	663	16.2	428	10.4	235	5.8	8.6	4.9
1971	5 016	2 245	44.8	1 585	31.6	1 187	23.7	668	13.3	519	10.4	11.3	6.3
1972	4 882	2 242	45.9	1 472	30.2	1 167	23.9	601	12.3	566	11.6	12.0	6.2
1973	4 365	2 224	51.0	1 314	30.1	826	18.9	483	11.1	343	7.9	10.0	5.2
1974	5 156	2 604	50.5	1 597	31.0	955	18.5	574	11.1	381	7.4	9.8	5.2
1975	7 929	2 940	37.1	2 484	31.3	2 505	31.6	1 303	16.4	1 203	15.2	14.2	8.4
1976	7 406	2 844	38.4	2 196	29.6	2 366	32.0	1 018	13.8	1 348	18.2	15.8	8.2
1977	6 991	2 919	41.8	2 132	30.5	1 942	27.8	913	13.1	1 028	14.7	14.3	7.0
1978	6 202	2 865	46.2	1 923	31.0	1 414	22.8	766	12.3	648	10.5	11.9	5.9
1979	6 137	2 950	48.1	1 946	31.7	1 241	20.2	706	11.5	535	8.7	10.8	5.4
1980	7 637	3 295	43.2	2 470	32.3	1 871	24.5	1 052	13.8	820	10.7	11.9	6.5
1981	8 273	3 449	41.7	2 539	30.7	2 285	27.6	1 122	13.6	1 162	14.0	13.7	6.9
1982	10 678	3 883	36.4	3 311	31.0	3 485	32.6	1 708	16.0	1 776	16.6	15.6	8.7
1983	10 717	3 570	33.3	2 937	27.4	4 210	39.3	1 652	15.4	2 559	23.9	20.0	10.1
1984	8 539	3 350	39.2	2 451	28.7	2 737	32.1	1 104	12.9	1 634	19.1	18.2	7.9
1985	8 312	3 498	42.1	2 509	30.2	2 305	27.7	1 025	12.3	1 280	15.4	15.6	6.8
1986	8 237	3 448	41.9	2 557	31.0	2 232	27.1	1 045	12.7	1 187	14.4	15.0	6.9
1987	7 425	3 246	43.7	2 196	29.6	1 983	26.7	943	12.7	1 040	14.0	14.5	6.5
1988	6 701	3 084	46.0	2 007	30.0	1 610	24.0	801	12.0	809	12.1	13.5	5.9
1989	6 528	3 174	48.6	1 978	30.3	1 375	21.1	730	11.2	646	9.9	11.9	4.8
1990	7 047	3 265	46.3	2 257	32.0	1 525	21.6	822	11.7	703	10.0	12.0	5.3
1991	8 628	3 480	40.3	2 791	32.4	2 357	27.3	1 246	14.4	1 111	12.9	13.7	6.8
1992	9 613	3 376	35.1	2 830	29.4	3 408	35.4	1 453	15.1	1 954	20.3	17.7	8.7
1993	8 940	3 262	36.5	2 584	28.9	3 094	34.6	1 297	14.5	1 798	20.1	18.0	8.3
1994	7 996	2 728	34.1	2 408	30.1	2 860	35.8	1 237	15.5	1 623	20.3	18.8	9.2
1995	7 404	2 700	36.5	2 342	31.6	2 363	31.9	1 085	14.6	1 278	17.3	16.6	8.3
1996	7 236	2 633	36.4	2 287	31.6	2 316	32.0	1 053	14.6	1 262	17.4	16.7	8.3
1997	6 739	2 538	37.7	2 138	31.7	2 062	30.6	995	14.8	1 067	15.8	15.8	8.0
1998	6 210	2 622	42.2	1 950	31.4	1 637	26.4	763	12.3	875	14.1	14.5	6.7
1999	5 880	2 568	43.7	1 832	31.2	1 480	25.2	755	12.8	725	12.3	13.4	6.4
2000	5 692	2 558	44.9	1 815	31.9	1 318	23.2	669	11.8	649	11.4	12.6	5.9
2001	6 801	2 853	42.0	2 196	32.3	1 752	25.8	951	14.0	801	11.8	13.1	6.8
2002	8 378	2 893	34.5	2 580	30.8	2 904	34.7	1 369	16.3	1 535	18.3	16.6	9.1
2003	8 774	2 785	31.7	2 612	29.8	3 378	38.5	1 442	16.4	1 936	22.1	19.2	10.1
2004	8 149	2 696	33.1	2 382	29.2	3 072	37.7	1 293	15.9	1 779	21.8	19.6	9.8
2005	7 591	2 667	35.1	2 304	30.4	2 619	34.5	1 130	14.9	1 490	19.6	18.4	8.9
2006	7 001	2 614	37.3	2 121	30.3	2 266	32.4	1 031	14.7	1 235	17.6	16.8	8.3
2007	7 078	2 542	35.9	2 232	31.5	2 303	32.5	1 061	15.0	1 243	17.6	16.8	8.5
2008	8 924	2 932	32.8	2 804	31.4	3 188	35.7	1 427	16.0	1 761	19.7	17.9	9.4
2009	14 265	3 165	22.2	3 828	26.8	7 272	51.0	2 775	19.5	4 496	31.5	24.4	15.1
2010	14 825	2 771	18.7	3 267	22.0	8 786	59.3	2 371	16.0	6 415	43.3	33.0	21.4
2011	13 747	2 677	19.5	2 993	21.8	8 077	58.8	2 061	15.0	6 016	43.8	39.3	21.4
2012	12 506	2 644	21.1	2 866	22.9	6 996	55.9	1 859	14.9	5 136	41.1	39.4	19.3
2013	11 460	2 584	22.5	2 759	24.1	6 117	53.0	1 807	16.0	4 310	37.6	36.5	17.0
2014	9 617	2 471	25.7	2 432	25.3	4 714	49.0	1 497	16.0	3 218	33.5	33.7	14.0
2015	8 296	2 399	28.9	2 302	27.7	3 595	43.0	1 267	15.0	2 328	28.1	29.2	11.6
2016	7 751	2 362	30.5	2 226	28.7	3 163	41.0	1 158	15.0	2 005	25.9	27.5	10.6
2017	6 982	2 270	32.5	2 008	28.8	2 704	39.0	1 017	15.0	1 687	24.2	25.0	10.0
2018	6 314	2 170	34.4	1 876	29.7	2 268	36.0	917	15.0	1 350	21.4	22.7	9.3

. . . = Not available.

Table 1-31. Long-Term Unemployment, by Industry and Selected Occupation, 2005–2018

(Thousands of people.)

Characteristic	2005	2006	2007	2008	2009	2010	2011	2012	2013	2014	2015	2016	2017	2018
UNEMPLOYED 15 WEEKS AND OVER														
Total	2 619	2 266	2 303	3 188	7 272	8 786	8 077	6 996	6 117	4 714	3 595	3 163	2 704	2 268
Wage and Salary Workers, by Industry														
Agriculture and related	29	30	28	42	96	100	99	92	71	71	62	53	37	47
Mining [1]	8	5	6	7	44	46	31	25	27	23	28	28	17	12
Construction	216	177	215	339	907	1 083	822	643	476	340	264	195	206	178
Manufacturing	326	257	259	385	1 059	1 122	922	702	611	410	311	304	229	199
Durable goods	199	140	162	246	702	773	611	443	367	246	189	180	148	112
Nondurable goods	127	116	97	139	357	350	311	259	244	165	122	124	81	87
Wholesale and retail trade	415	337	334	440	962	1 215	1 118	971	834	635	522	432	383	344
Transportation and utilities	91	87	95	142	290	343	343	262	249	212	135	133	117	99
Information	76	55	49	66	170	204	146	142	109	84	53	63	56	46
Financial activities	91	103	100	168	357	446	411	312	261	220	130	139	115	89
Professional and business services	299	266	247	346	810	985	878	793	739	541	429	356	315	249
Education and health services	271	263	253	320	691	898	910	907	772	588	443	388	351	305
Leisure and hospitality	277	259	274	356	755	898	830	740	682	562	441	358	309	248
Other services	117	97	80	132	245	310	336	261	236	179	295	122	109	80
Public administration	62	34	51	55	107	164	185	144	141	101	74	67	68	54
Experienced Workers, by Occupation														
Management, professional, and related	436	373	368	569	1 331	1 600	1 482	1 362	1 116	884	662	634	566	509
Services	511	464	482	595	1 243	1 557	1 500	1 356	1 261	984	788	649	582	447
Sales and office	641	561	560	741	1 675	2 048	1 949	1 622	1 446	1 099	809	679	591	505
Natural resources, construction, and maintenance	341	294	299	463	1 224	1 445	1 150	914	715	534	436	356	325	277
Production, transportation, and material moving	461	380	384	570	1 302	1 498	1 290	1 041	944	683	508	485	373	310
UNEMPLOYED 27 WEEKS AND OVER														
Total	1 490	1 235	1 243	1 761	4 496	6 415	6 016	5 136	4 310	3 218	2 328	2 005	1 687	1 350
Wage and Salary Workers, by Industry														
Agriculture and related	16	13	14	17	51	57	58	55	39	40	33	27	17	23
Mining [1]	4	3	3	4	23	37	22	17	15	13	15	18	11	5
Construction	108	92	107	168	530	773	617	464	324	218	161	117	109	94
Manufacturing	195	140	152	230	657	888	725	533	439	291	202	196	139	121
Durable goods	124	75	93	150	428	619	486	341	273	172	123	114	86	69
Nondurable goods	71	64	58	80	229	269	239	192	166	118	79	82	54	52
Wholesale and retail trade	230	183	171	237	607	904	833	731	604	427	336	278	240	200
Transportation and utilities	50	42	58	77	180	263	265	198	180	141	90	88	78	64
Information	41	30	29	38	115	159	116	107	77	60	40	47	36	32
Financial activities	56	56	50	97	232	332	315	245	185	156	130	86	77	54
Professional and business services	172	144	130	184	510	722	641	580	518	369	429	221	204	153
Education and health services	156	144	132	182	432	644	671	668	561	417	443	234	216	182
Leisure and hospitality	148	135	142	196	445	624	596	519	472	379	441	212	178	145
Other services	74	51	43	73	161	223	249	192	161	126	156	79	77	48
Public administration	38	21	29	29	66	121	140	112	101	74	74	45	43	33
Experienced Workers, by Occupation														
Management, professional, and related	269	206	207	569	840	6 415	1 121	1 022	801	625	442	414	370	312
Services	284	249	251	595	750	1 094	1 086	971	896	673	513	398	360	257
Sales and office	354	299	285	741	1 067	1 513	1 486	1 211	1 042	760	521	429	375	315
Natural resources, construction, and maintenance	186	158	157	463	724	1 042	855	676	487	346	265	218	194	151
Production, transportation, and material moving	261	206	219	570	814	1 142	973	773	656	461	331	306	221	185

[1]Starting in 2009, mining includes quarrying, and oil and gas extraction.

Table 1-32. Unemployed Persons and Unemployment Rates, by Reason for Unemployment, Sex, and Age, 1985–2018

(Thousands of people, percent.)

Sex, age, and year	Number of unemployed					Unemployed as a percent of the total civilian labor force			
	Total	Job losers and persons who completed temporary jobs	Job leavers	Entrants		Job losers and persons who completed temporary jobs	Job leavers	Entrants	
				Reentrants	New entrants			Reentrants	New entrants
Both Sexes, 16 Years and Over									
1985	8 312	4 139	877	2 256	1 039	3.6	0.8	2.0	0.9
1986	8 237	4 033	1 015	2 160	1 029	3.4	0.9	1.8	0.9
1987	7 425	3 566	965	1 974	920	3.0	0.8	1.6	0.8
1988	6 701	3 092	983	1 809	816	2.5	0.8	1.5	0.7
1989	6 528	2 983	1 024	1 843	677	2.4	0.8	1.5	0.5
1990	7 047	3 387	1 041	1 930	688	2.7	0.8	1.5	0.5
1991	8 628	4 694	1 004	2 139	792	3.7	0.8	1.7	0.6
1992	9 613	5 389	1 002	2 285	937	4.2	0.8	1.8	0.7
1993	8 940	4 848	976	2 198	919	3.8	0.8	1.7	0.7
1994	7 996	3 815	791	2 786	604	2.9	0.6	2.1	0.5
1995	7 404	3 476	824	2 525	579	2.6	0.6	1.9	0.4
1996	7 236	3 370	774	2 512	580	2.5	0.6	1.9	0.4
1997	6 739	3 037	795	2 338	569	2.2	0.6	1.7	0.4
1998	6 210	2 822	734	2 132	520	2.1	0.5	1.5	0.4
1999	5 880	2 622	783	2 005	469	1.9	0.6	1.4	0.3
2000	5 692	2 517	780	1 961	434	1.8	0.5	1.4	0.3
2001	6 801	3 476	835	2 031	459	2.4	0.6	1.4	0.3
2002	8 378	4 607	866	2 368	536	3.2	0.6	1.6	0.4
2003	8 774	4 838	818	2 477	641	3.3	0.6	1.7	0.4
2004	8 149	4 197	858	2 408	686	2.8	0.6	1.6	0.5
2005	7 591	3 667	872	2 386	666	2.5	0.6	1.6	0.4
2006	7 001	3 321	827	2 237	616	2.2	0.5	1.5	0.4
2007	7 078	3 515	793	2 142	627	2.3	0.5	1.4	0.4
2008	8 924	4 789	896	2 472	766	3.1	0.6	1.6	0.5
2009	14 265	9 160	882	3 187	1 035	5.9	0.6	2.1	0.7
2010	14 825	9 250	889	3 466	1 220	6.0	0.6	2.3	0.8
2011	13 747	8 106	956	3 401	1 284	5.3	0.6	2.2	0.8
2012	12 506	6 877	967	3 345	1 316	4.4	0.6	2.2	0.8
2013	11 460	6 073	932	3 207	1 247	3.9	0.6	2.1	0.8
2014	9 617	4 878	824	2 829	1 086	3.1	0.5	1.8	0.7
2015	8 296	4 063	819	2 535	879	2.6	0.5	1.6	0.6
2016	7 751	3 740	858	2 330	823	2.3	0.5	1.5	0.5
2017	6 982	3 434	778	2 079	690	2.1	0.5	1.3	0.4
2018	6 314	2 990	794	1 928	602	1.8	0.5	1.2	0.4
Both Sexes, 16 to 19 Years									
1985	1 468	275	113	390	689	3.5	1.4	4.9	8.7
1986	1 454	240	145	374	695	3.0	1.8	4.7	8.8
1987	1 347	210	146	375	617	2.7	1.8	4.7	7.7
1988	1 226	207	159	310	550	2.6	2.0	3.9	6.8
1989	1 194	198	200	345	452	2.5	2.5	4.3	5.7
1990	1 212	233	181	338	460	3.0	2.3	4.3	5.9
1991	1 359	289	180	365	524	4.0	2.5	5.0	7.2
1992	1 427	259	149	377	643	3.6	2.1	5.3	9.1
1993	1 365	233	151	353	628	3.3	2.1	4.9	8.8
1994	1 320	185	84	634	416	2.5	1.1	8.5	5.6
1995	1 346	214	102	615	415	2.8	1.3	7.9	5.3
1996	1 306	182	91	625	409	2.3	1.2	8.0	5.2
1997	1 271	174	104	606	388	2.2	1.3	7.6	4.9
1998	1 205	181	86	577	361	2.2	1.0	7.0	4.4
1999	1 162	173	114	547	328	2.1	1.4	6.6	3.9
2000	1 081	157	109	516	299	1.9	1.3	6.2	3.6
2001	1 162	185	98	568	311	2.3	1.2	7.2	3.9
2002	1 253	197	91	597	368	2.6	1.2	7.9	4.9
2003	1 251	188	85	554	424	2.6	1.2	7.7	5.9
2004	1 208	165	76	510	456	2.3	1.1	7.2	6.4
2005	1 186	155	76	489	466	2.2	1.1	6.8	6.5
2006	1 119	145	78	461	435	2.0	1.1	6.3	6.0
2007	1 101	176	71	435	419	2.5	1.0	6.2	6.0
2008	1 285	203	80	490	511	3.0	1.2	7.1	7.5
2009	1 552	271	56	548	677	4.2	0.9	8.6	10.6
2010	1 528	220	42	487	778	3.7	0.7	8.2	13.2
2011	1 400	181	52	429	739	3.2	0.9	7.5	12.9
2012	1 397	176	43	419	758	3.0	0.7	7.2	13.0
2013	1 327	170	53	386	718	2.9	0.9	6.7	12.4
2014	1 106	140	44	327	595	2.5	0.8	5.8	10.5
2015	966	132	51	301	481	2.6	0.5	1.6	0.6
2016	925	113	53	307	453	1.9	0.9	5.2	7.7
2017	827	116	44	267	399	2.0	0.7	4.5	6.8
2018	759	111	52	256	340	1.9	0.9	4.3	5.8

Note: See notes and definitions for information on historical comparability.

Table 1-32. Unemployed Persons and Unemployment Rates, by Reason for Unemployment, Sex, and Age, 1985–2018—*Continued*

(Thousands of people, percent.)

Sex, age, and year	Number of unemployed					Unemployed as a percent of the total civilian labor force			
	Total	Job losers and persons who completed temporary jobs	Job leavers	Entrants		Job losers and persons who completed temporary jobs	Job leavers	Entrants	
				Reentrants	New entrants			Reentrants	New entrants
Men, 20 Years and Over									
1985	3 715	2 568	352	671	124	4.3	0.6	1.1	0.2
1986	3 751	2 568	444	611	128	4.1	0.7	1.0	0.2
1987	3 369	2 289	413	558	108	3.7	0.7	0.9	0.2
1988	2 987	1 939	416	534	98	3.1	0.7	0.9	0.2
1989	2 867	1 843	394	541	88	2.9	0.6	0.8	0.1
1990	3 239	2 100	431	626	82	3.2	0.7	1.0	0.1
1991	4 195	2 982	411	698	105	4.6	0.6	1.1	0.2
1992	4 717	3 420	421	765	111	5.2	0.6	1.2	0.2
1993	4 287	2 996	429	747	114	4.5	0.6	1.1	0.2
1994	3 627	2 296	367	898	65	3.4	0.5	1.3	0.1
1995	3 239	2 051	356	775	57	3.0	0.5	1.2	0.1
1996	3 146	2 043	322	731	51	3.0	0.5	1.1	0.1
1997	2 882	1 795	358	675	55	2.6	0.5	1.0	0.1
1998	2 580	1 588	318	611	63	2.3	0.5	0.9	0.1
1999	2 433	1 459	336	592	46	2.1	0.5	0.8	0.1
2000	2 376	1 416	328	577	55	2.0	0.5	0.8	0.1
2001	3 040	1 999	372	612	56	2.7	0.5	0.8	0.1
2002	3 896	2 702	386	743	65	3.7	0.5	1.0	0.1
2003	4 209	2 899	376	846	88	3.9	0.5	1.1	0.1
2004	3 791	2 503	398	791	99	3.3	0.5	1.0	0.1
2005	4 059	2 188	445	1 067	359	2.7	0.5	1.0	0.1
2006	3 131	1 927	368	757	78	2.5	0.5	1.0	0.1
2007	3 259	2 064	371	723	101	2.6	0.5	0.9	0.1
2008	4 297	2 918	410	969	856	3.7	0.5	1.1	0.1
2009	7 555	5 796	407	1 190	162	7.3	0.5	1.5	0.2
2010	7 763	5 773	433	1 346	211	7.3	0.5	1.7	0.3
2011	6 898	4 856	464	1 312	267	6.1	0.6	1.7	0.3
2012	5 984	3 996	464	1 250	274	5.0	0.6	1.6	0.3
2013	5 568	3 582	440	1 285	261	4.5	0.6	1.6	0.3
2014	4 585	2 839	392	1 109	245	3.5	0.5	1.4	0.3
2015	3 959	2 361	379	1 014	206	4.9	0.5	1.3	0.3
2016	3 675	2 165	388	936	185	2.6	0.5	1.1	0.2
2017	3 287	1 970	359	815	142	2.4	0.4	1.0	0.2
2018	2 976	1 706	381	759	130	2.1	0.5	0.9	0.2
Women, 20 Years and Over									
1985	3 129	1 296	412	1 195	227	2.7	0.9	2.5	0.5
1986	3 032	1 225	426	1 175	206	2.5	0.9	2.4	0.4
1987	2 709	1 067	406	1 041	194	2.2	0.8	2.1	0.4
1988	2 487	946	408	965	168	1.9	0.8	1.9	0.3
1989	2 467	942	430	958	137	1.8	0.8	1.8	0.3
1990	2 596	1 054	429	966	146	2.0	0.8	1.8	0.3
1991	3 074	1 423	413	1 075	163	2.6	0.8	2.0	0.3
1992	3 469	1 710	433	1 142	183	3.1	0.8	2.1	0.3
1993	3 288	1 619	395	1 098	176	2.9	0.7	2.0	0.3
1994	3 049	1 334	339	1 253	122	2.4	0.6	2.2	0.2
1995	2 819	1 211	366	1 135	107	2.1	0.6	2.0	0.2
1996	2 783	1 145	361	1 156	120	2.0	0.6	2.0	0.2
1997	2 585	1 069	333	1 057	126	1.8	0.6	1.8	0.2
1998	2 424	1 053	330	944	97	1.8	0.6	1.6	0.2
1999	2 285	990	333	866	96	1.6	0.5	1.4	0.2
2000	2 235	943	343	868	80	1.5	0.6	1.4	0.1
2001	2 599	1 291	365	850	92	2.0	0.6	1.3	0.1
2002	3 228	1 708	389	1 028	102	2.7	0.6	1.6	0.2
2003	3 314	1 751	357	1 076	130	2.7	0.6	1.7	0.2
2004	3 150	1 529	384	1 107	131	2.4	0.6	1.7	0.2
2005	3 013	1 417	391	1 103	101	2.2	0.6	1.7	0.2
2006	2 751	1 249	380	1 019	103	1.9	0.6	1.5	0.2
2007	2 718	1 276	351	984	107	1.9	0.5	1.7	0.4
2008	3 342	1 668	406	1 126	143	2.4	0.6	1.6	0.2
2009	5 157	3 093	419	1 449	196	4.5	0.6	2.1	0.3
2010	5 534	3 257	413	1 633	231	4.7	0.6	2.4	0.3
2011	5 450	3 070	441	1 661	279	4.5	0.6	2.4	0.4
2012	5 125	2 705	460	1 676	284	3.9	0.7	2.4	0.4
2013	4 565	2 322	439	1 536	269	3.3	0.6	2.2	0.4
2014	3 926	1 899	388	1 393	245	2.7	0.6	2.0	0.3
2015	3 371	1 570	389	1 220	192	2.2	0.6	1.7	0.3
2016	3 151	1 461	417	1 087	186	2.0	0.6	1.5	0.3
2017	2 868	1 348	375	996	149	1.9	0.5	1.5	0.4
2018	2 578	1 173	361	912	132	1.6	0.5	1.2	0.2

Note: See notes and definitions for information on historical comparability.

Table 1-33. Percent of the Population with Work Experience During the Year, by Age and Sex, 1995–2018

(Percent.)

Sex and year	Total	16 to 17 years	18 to 19 years	20 to 24 years	25 to 34 years	35 to 44 years	45 to 54 years	55 to 59 years	60 to 64 years	65 to 69 years	70 years and over
Both Sexes											
1995	69.6	44.4	71.2	82.0	85.6	85.9	83.4	72.2	53.3	28.0	10.2
1996	69.9	43.3	70.5	83.1	86.1	85.7	84.3	73.3	54.3	27.8	10.4
1997	70.1	43.6	70.5	83.0	87.1	85.9	84.4	73.8	53.8	28.5	10.0
1998	70.1	42.1	69.9	82.9	86.7	86.3	84.2	73.7	54.5	29.2	10.6
1999	70.7	43.7	71.2	82.7	87.3	86.9	85.0	72.3	55.8	30.5	11.6
2000	70.5	42.2	69.6	82.6	87.1	87.0	84.6	72.9	55.1	30.8	11.4
2001	69.4	37.7	66.7	80.8	86.1	85.8	83.7	73.5	56.7	30.6	10.5
2002	68.5	34.5	62.8	78.5	84.4	85.0	83.7	74.7	56.8	33.1	10.4
2003	67.8	32.0	61.7	77.5	83.7	84.0	82.9	73.9	56.5	33.2	11.4
2004	67.7	32.6	59.8	76.9	83.3	84.2	82.6	73.9	57.0	32.7	12.2
2005	67.8	31.1	60.1	77.3	83.7	84.1	82.8	74.4	58.2	32.0	12.1
2006	67.9	30.9	58.3	76.9	84.4	84.3	82.8	74.5	58.2	33.6	12.6
2007	67.8	28.5	57.3	76.6	84.2	84.4	82.4	75.6	59.7	35.2	13.0
2008	67.1	24.6	55.3	76.0	84.1	83.9	81.8	74.6	60.3	34.9	13.5
2009	65.0	21.9	48.7	71.0	81.6	82.0	80.5	73.8	59.3	35.3	12.8
2010	63.8	17.8	43.9	69.1	80.2	81.3	79.2	73.8	58.4	37.1	13.0
2011	63.4	17.0	44.8	69.8	79.7	81.3	79.0	72.0	59.5	36.5	13.3
2012	63.9	19.9	47.1	70.1	80.6	81.3	79.4	74.5	59.2	37.5	14.0
2013	63.6	19.9	46.3	71.0	80.2	81.0	79.9	72.4	59.3	36.8	14.7
2014	63.7	20.4	46.7	70.0	80.5	82.0	79.5	73.0	60.4	37.7	14.7
2015	64.3	22.4	48.6	71.3	81.7	82.3	80.1	74.6	60.5	38.2	14.9
2016	64.4	23.6	49.0	72.7	82.8	82.6	80.3	73.4	60.9	38.0	15.6
2017	64.3	23.5	49.1	73.1	82.5	83.0	80.8	73.4	62.2	38.0	15.5
2018	64.5	22.4	49.4	73.2	83.3	82.9	81.8	74.2	61.9	39.2	15.9
Men											
1995	77.0	43.7	73.6	86.4	92.6	92.2	89.7	81.5	62.1	34.5	14.9
1996	77.2	44.1	71.8	86.7	93.4	92.1	90.4	81.8	62.5	33.6	15.2
1997	77.1	43.4	70.3	86.6	94.1	92.3	90.7	81.4	62.9	33.8	13.9
1998	76.9	40.4	71.6	86.4	93.5	92.7	90.1	81.7	63.5	35.5	14.7
1999	77.3	44.7	72.3	85.5	93.9	93.2	89.9	79.2	65.1	37.4	16.5
2000	77.1	42.1	70.2	85.1	93.4	93.6	89.8	80.6	64.4	38.4	16.0
2001	76.3	37.4	67.7	84.8	93.2	92.2	89.1	80.4	64.3	37.8	14.5
2002	75.2	34.7	62.8	82.1	91.6	91.8	88.9	80.7	64.3	39.3	14.6
2003	74.3	32.8	61.7	80.2	90.8	90.9	87.7	80.9	63.1	37.3	15.8
2004	74.2	32.1	58.9	80.2	91.0	91.1	87.9	80.1	64.5	37.1	16.7
2005	74.6	31.1	60.7	80.8	91.3	91.6	88.2	80.1	64.3	37.6	17.0
2006	74.5	30.9	57.9	80.1	91.9	91.8	88.0	80.6	64.1	38.3	17.3
2007	74.3	28.5	59.0	80.5	90.5	91.5	88.2	80.3	66.2	39.3	17.9
2008	73.2	24.4	55.1	78.7	90.7	91.1	86.4	79.3	66.0	40.3	17.9
2009	70.8	22.2	48.0	73.3	87.7	89.1	85.0	78.3	64.8	39.8	17.2
2010	69.4	16.9	43.2	71.3	86.0	88.0	84.1	78.9	62.8	43.4	17.5
2011	69.0	16.1	43.2	71.6	86.2	88.1	84.3	76.7	64.0	42.6	18.2
2012	69.7	19.1	45.9	72.2	86.9	88.9	84.8	79.9	64.2	43.2	18.5
2013	69.3	18.4	46.6	72.5	86.5	88.0	85.8	77.0	64.6	42.0	19.4
2014	69.4	20.5	44.9	70.4	87.2	89.0	85.1	78.1	66.5	42.2	19.4
2015	70.2	22.2	48.2	72.9	87.8	89.4	86.2	79.4	66.1	43.5	19.8
2016	70.1	22.2	48.1	74.1	88.2	90.0	86.1	78.1	67.5	44.2	20.0
2017	70.2	23.2	47.8	75.3	88.3	90.4	86.1	79.5	67.8	43.6	20.5
2018	69.9	21.8	46.3	73.6	88.8	90.1	87.3	80.1	68.2	43.2	20.0
Women											
1995	62.8	45.2	68.7	77.7	78.8	79.8	77.6	63.2	45.6	22.4	7.1
1996	63.2	42.5	69.2	79.5	78.9	79.5	78.4	65.4	46.9	23.0	7.1
1997	63.6	43.9	70.7	79.5	80.1	79.6	78.4	66.7	45.6	24.0	7.3
1998	63.7	44.1	68.2	79.4	80.1	80.0	78.6	66.3	46.2	23.8	7.8
1999	64.5	42.6	70.1	79.9	80.9	80.7	80.3	66.2	47.3	24.4	8.2
2000	64.3	42.3	69.0	80.2	80.9	80.5	79.5	65.7	47.0	23.9	8.2
2001	63.1	38.1	65.7	76.9	79.2	79.5	78.6	67.1	49.8	24.2	7.9
2002	62.3	34.3	62.8	74.9	77.2	78.4	78.7	69.1	50.0	27.8	7.4
2003	61.7	31.2	61.6	74.6	76.6	77.2	78.4	67.3	50.7	29.6	8.3
2004	61.5	33.1	60.7	73.7	75.6	77.4	77.5	68.2	50.3	28.7	9.0
2005	61.4	31.2	59.6	73.7	76.1	76.8	77.6	68.9	52.7	27.1	8.7
2006	61.6	30.9	58.7	73.7	76.9	76.9	77.9	68.8	53.0	29.5	9.3
2007	61.6	28.5	55.6	72.6	77.8	77.4	76.9	71.2	53.7	31.5	9.5
2008	61.3	24.8	55.4	73.2	77.3	76.7	77.3	70.1	55.0	30.1	10.3
2009	59.6	21.6	49.5	68.6	75.4	75.0	76.1	69.5	54.4	31.1	9.7
2010	58.5	18.7	44.5	66.9	74.3	74.7	74.4	69.1	54.2	31.6	9.6
2011	58.1	18.0	46.5	68.0	73.4	74.7	73.8	67.7	55.4	31.0	9.6
2012	58.4	20.7	48.3	68.1	74.3	73.8	74.3	69.4	54.8	32.2	10.6
2013	58.2	21.4	46.1	69.5	74.0	74.2	74.3	68.0	54.4	32.1	11.2
2014	58.3	20.2	48.5	69.6	73.8	75.1	74.1	68.3	54.7	33.7	11.2
2015	58.8	22.6	49.1	69.7	75.7	75.4	74.3	70.1	55.4	33.5	11.3
2016	59.0	25.0	50.0	71.3	77.4	75.5	74.8	69.0	55.0	32.4	12.1
2017	58.8	23.9	50.5	71.0	76.6	75.7	75.7	67.5	57.2	33.0	11.6
2018	59.4	22.9	52.4	72.7	77.6	75.9	76.5	68.9	56.2	35.6	12.6

Note: See notes and definitions for information on historical comparability.

Table 1-34. Persons with Work Experience During the Year, by Industry and Class of Worker of Job Held the Longest, 2005–2018

(Thousands of people.)

Industry and class of worker	2005	2006	2007	2008	2009	2010	2011	2012	2013	2014	2015	2016	2017	2018
TOTAL	155 127	157 352	158 468	158 317	154 772	153 141	154 330	157 050	157 878	159 881	163 169	164 435	166 045	167 261
Agriculture	2 344	2 332	2 407	2 382	2 581	2 383	2 470	2 176	2 497	2 748	2 890	2 591	2 715	2 344
Wage and salary workers	1 501	1 495	1 525	1 522	1 733	1 578	1 679	1 504	1 769	1 918	2 041	1 823	1 933	1 760
Self-employed workers	829	812	846	824	813	788	750	649	706	794	831	735	750	573
Unpaid family workers	14	25	36	37	35	17	42	22	22	36	19	33	32	11
Nonagricultural Industries	152 783	155 021	156 061	155 934	152 191	150 759	151 859	154 874	155 381	157 133	160 279	161 844	163 330	164 917
Wage and salary workers	143 002	145 152	146 485	146 521	142 946	141 686	142 962	145 787	146 688	148 247	151 029	152 914	154 158	156 139
Mining	696	758	746	840	778	771	890	1 146	1 173	1 114	1 000	814	777	817
Construction	10 423	10 989	10 547	10 234	9 443	8 633	8 607	8 445	8 589	9 015	9 173	9 467	9 844	9 921
Manufacturing	17 243	17 112	16 641	16 332	14 956	14 865	15 139	15 139	15 688	15 445	15 748	15 828	16 257	16 114
Durable goods	10 930	10 995	10 687	10 477	9 342	9 288	9 586	9 585	9 916	9 981	9 897	9 945	10 064	10 038
Nondurable goods	6 313	6 116	5 954	5 855	5 613	5 577	5 552	5 554	5 773	5 465	5 851	5 883	6 193	6 077
Wholesale and retail trade	22 479	21 822	21 837	21 838	21 210	20 854	20 685	20 485	21 353	21 352	21 339	21 557	20 896	20 683
Wholesale trade	4 517	4 395	4 017	4 016	3 849	3 921	3 601	3 606	3 738	3 840	3 761	3 566	3 810	3 429
Retail trade	17 962	17 427	17 820	17 822	17 361	16 933	17 084	16 879	17 615	17 512	17 578	17 991	17 086	17 254
Transportation and utilities	7 248	7 413	8 023	7 675	7 309	6 993	7 173	7 573	7 493	7 504	8 128	8 086	8 289	8 726
Transportation and warehousing	6 095	6 197	6 750	6 365	6 025	5 701	5 944	6 336	6 318	6 215	6 737	6 638	6 782	7 350
Utilities	1 153	1 216	1 273	1 310	1 284	1 292	1 229	1 237	1 175	1 290	1 392	1 448	1 507	1 377
Information	3 495	3 710	3 687	3 455	3 375	3 380	3 137	3 144	3 384	3 010	3 005	2 977	2 946	2 849
Financial activities	9 748	10 101	10 013	9 671	9 409	9 239	9 443	9 889	9 987	9 835	9 993	10 160	10 330	10 239
Finance and insurance	7 011	7 190	7 347	6 994	6 792	6 726	6 909	7 293	7 231	7 073	7 101	7 351	7 490	7 231
Real estate and rental and leasing	2 737	2 912	2 666	2 677	2 617	2 512	2 534	2 595	2 756	2 762	2 892	2 809	2 840	3 007
Professional and business services	13 537	14 412	14 659	14 868	14 633	15 094	15 339	15 924	15 923	16 375	16 949	17 346	17 309	18 482
Professional, scientific, and technical services	7 768	8 294	8 676	8 742	8 475	8 841	9 054	9 370	9 401	10 077	10 485	10 802	11 076	11 727
Management, administration, and waste management services	5 769	6 118	5 982	6 127	6 159	6 253	6 285	6 553	6 522	6 297	6 464	6 544	6 233	6 755
Education and health services	30 552	31 314	31 921	32 828	33 465	33 596	33 424	34 156	33 943	34 724	35 682	35 960	36 321	37 126
Education services	13 282	13 659	13 989	14 396	14 457	14 157	13 917	14 256	14 394	14 770	14 899	14 836	15 633	15 499
Health care and social assistance services	17 270	17 655	17 932	18 432	19 008	19 439	19 507	19 900	19 549	19 953	20 783	21 124	20 688	21 627
Leisure and hospitality	13 405	13 455	13 959	14 242	13 917	13 718	14 293	15 103	14 688	14 998	15 291	15 573	15 402	15 673
Arts, entertainment, and recreation	2 877	2 797	3 124	3 047	3 284	2 993	3 116	3 332	3 232	3 022	3 120	3 232	3 471	3 581
Accommodation and food services	10 528	10 658	10 835	11 195	10 633	10 725	11 177	11 771	11 457	11 976	12 171	12 340	11 931	12 092
Other services and private household	6 490	6 341	6 603	6 590	6 233	6 111	6 717	6 643	6 571	6 818	6 558	6 931	7 284	7 026
Private households	866	912	888	912	757	816	773	833	942	929	769	857	819	884
Public administration	6 917	7 076	7 095	7 121	7 332	7 597	7 270	7 333	7 094	7 245	7 398	7 565	7 723	7 781
Self-employed workers	9 658	9 733	9 451	9 332	9 121	8 962	8 778	8 955	8 605	8 786	9 122	8 836	9 079	8 680
Unpaid family workers	123	135	126	82	124	111	120	132	87	101	129	94	92	98

Note: See notes and definitions for information on historical comparability.

Table 1-35. Number of Persons with Work Experience During the Year, by Extent of Employment and Sex, 1995–2018

(Thousands of people.)

Sex and year	Total	Full-time workers				Part-time workers			
		Total	50 to 52 weeks	27 to 49 weeks	1 to 26 weeks	Total	50 to 52 weeks	27 to 49 weeks	1 to 26 weeks
Both Sexes									
1995	139 724	110 063	88 173	12 970	8 920	29 661	12 725	6 831	10 105
1996	142 201	112 313	90 252	12 997	9 064	29 888	13 382	6 643	9 863
1997	143 968	113 879	92 631	12 508	8 740	30 089	13 810	6 565	9 714
1998	145 566	116 412	95 772	12 156	8 484	29 155	13 538	6 480	9 137
1999	148 295	119 096	97 941	12 294	8 861	29 199	13 680	6 317	9 202
2000	149 361	120 591	100 349	12 071	8 171	28 770	13 865	6 161	8 744
2001	151 042	121 921	100 357	13 172	8 392	29 121	14 038	6 139	8 944
2002	151 546	121 726	100 659	12 544	8 523	29 819	14 635	6 184	9 000
2003	151 553	121 158	100 700	11 972	8 486	30 395	15 333	6 027	9 035
2004	153 024	122 404	102 427	11 862	8 115	30 621	15 552	6 077	8 992
2005	155 127	124 683	104 876	11 816	7 991	30 444	15 374	6 161	8 909
2006	157 352	127 340	107 734	11 736	7 870	30 012	15 131	6 223	8 657
2007	158 468	128 332	108 617	11 901	7 814	30 136	15 477	6 194	8 466
2008	158 317	125 937	104 023	13 421	8 493	32 380	16 562	6 630	9 188
2009	154 772	121 355	99 306	12 350	9 698	33 418	17 417	6 674	9 327
2010	153 141	119 940	99 250	11 705	8 985	33 201	17 122	6 582	9 497
2011	154 330	121 400	101 700	11 040	8 661	32 929	17 261	6 288	9 380
2012	157 050	123 229	103 078	11 708	8 442	33 821	17 494	6 681	9 646
2013	157 878	124 875	105 839	10 945	8 090	33 003	17 151	6 733	9 119
2014	159 881	127 353	108 687	11 297	7 369	32 528	17 144	6 539	8 845
2015	163 169	130 053	111 079	11 586	7 388	33 116	17 305	6 472	9 339
2016	164 435	131 340	113 306	10 842	7 192	33 095	17 447	6 611	9 037
2017	166 045	133 632	115 671	11 038	6 923	32 413	17 472	6 247	8 694
2018	167 261	135 277	117 957	10 743	6 578	31 984	17 381	6 383	8 220
Men									
1995	74 381	64 145	52 671	6 973	4 501	10 236	4 034	2 257	3 945
1996	75 760	65 356	53 795	6 891	4 670	10 404	4 321	2 136	3 947
1997	76 408	66 089	54 918	6 638	4 533	10 319	4 246	2 274	3 799
1998	76 918	67 250	56 953	6 208	4 089	9 669	4 197	2 090	3 382
1999	78 145	68 347	57 520	6 401	4 426	9 797	4 297	2 062	3 438
2000	78 804	68 925	58 756	6 094	4 075	9 879	4 485	1 957	3 437
2001	79 971	70 074	58 715	7 087	4 272	9 897	4 306	1 989	3 602
2002	80 282	70 132	58 765	6 804	4 563	10 151	4 519	2 042	3 590
2003	80 317	69 766	58 778	6 479	4 509	10 551	5 042	1 872	3 637
2004	81 261	70 780	60 096	6 428	4 256	10 482	4 987	1 992	3 503
2005	82 735	72 056	61 510	6 299	4 247	10 679	5 153	2 074	3 452
2006	83 767	73 578	63 058	6 373	4 147	10 189	4 747	2 046	3 396
2007	84 292	73 734	62 994	6 583	4 157	10 558	4 933	2 165	3 460
2008	83 889	72 204	59 869	7 645	4 690	11 685	5 425	2 457	3 803
2009	81 835	69 178	56 058	7 339	5 780	12 658	5 911	2 526	4 221
2010	81 076	68 402	56 416	6 760	5 225	12 674	5 883	2 523	4 267
2011	81 272	69 029	58 004	6 183	4 842	12 243	5 797	2 408	4 037
2012	82 910	70 181	59 022	6 547	4 611	12 729	6 199	2 481	4 049
2013	83 420	71 388	60 769	6 024	4 595	12 032	5 863	2 306	3 863
2014	84 358	72 398	62 445	6 016	3 937	11 960	6 018	2 313	3 628
2015	86 270	73 900	63 869	6 027	4 003	12 371	6 050	2 414	3 907
2016	86 768	74 574	64 970	5 723	3 882	12 194	6 129	2 339	3 726
2017	87 939	76 236	66 373	6 051	3 813	11 703	5 854	2 178	3 671
2018	87 956	76 305	67 185	5 627	3 493	11 651	6 018	2 275	3 358
Women									
1995	65 342	45 917	35 502	5 997	4 418	19 425	8 691	4 574	6 160
1996	66 439	46 955	36 457	6 105	4 393	19 484	9 061	4 507	5 916
1997	67 559	47 790	37 713	5 870	4 207	19 769	9 564	4 291	5 914
1998	68 648	49 162	38 819	5 948	4 395	19 486	9 341	4 390	5 755
1999	70 150	50 748	40 421	5 892	4 435	19 402	9 383	4 255	5 764
2000	70 556	51 665	41 593	5 977	4 095	18 891	9 380	4 204	5 307
2001	71 071	51 848	41 642	6 085	4 120	19 223	9 731	4 150	5 342
2002	71 263	51 593	41 893	5 741	3 959	19 671	10 117	4 143	5 411
2003	71 236	51 391	41 921	5 493	3 977	19 844	10 291	4 155	5 398
2004	71 763	51 624	42 331	5 434	3 859	20 139	10 565	4 085	5 489
2005	72 392	52 627	43 366	5 517	3 744	19 765	10 222	4 087	5 456
2006	73 585	53 762	44 676	5 364	3 723	19 823	10 384	4 178	5 261
2007	74 176	54 598	45 622	5 318	3 657	19 579	10 543	4 029	5 006
2008	74 428	53 733	44 154	5 776	3 803	20 695	11 137	4 172	5 385
2009	72 937	52 177	43 248	5 012	3 918	20 760	11 506	4 147	5 107
2010	72 066	51 538	42 834	4 944	3 760	20 528	11 239	4 058	5 230
2011	73 058	52 371	43 696	4 857	3 818	20 687	11 464	3 880	5 343
2012	74 140	53 048	44 055	5 161	3 831	21 092	11 295	4 200	5 597
2013	74 458	53 486	45 070	4 922	3 495	20 972	11 288	4 427	5 256
2014	75 523	54 955	46 241	5 281	3 432	20 568	11 125	4 226	5 217
2015	76 899	56 153	47 210	5 558	3 385	20 745	11 254	4 058	5 433
2016	77 667	56 766	48 337	5 119	3 310	20 901	11 318	4 272	5 311
2017	78 106	57 396	49 299	4 987	3 110	20 710	11 618	4 068	5 023
2018	79 305	58 972	50 771	5 116	3 084	20 333	11 364	4 107	4 862

Note: See notes and definitions for information on historical comparability.

Table 1-36. Percent Distribution of the Population with Work Experience During the Year, by Extent of Employment and Sex, 1995–2018

(Percent of total people with work experience.)

Sex and year	Total	Full-time workers				Part-time workers			
		Total	50 to 52 weeks	27 to 49 weeks	1 to 26 weeks	Total	50 to 52 weeks	27 to 49 weeks	1 to 26 weeks
Both Sexes									
1995	100.0	78.8	63.1	9.3	6.4	21.2	9.1	4.9	7.2
1996	100.0	79.0	63.5	9.1	6.4	21.0	9.4	4.7	6.9
1997	100.0	79.1	64.3	8.7	6.1	20.9	9.6	4.6	6.7
1998	100.1	80.0	65.8	8.4	5.8	20.1	9.3	4.5	6.3
1999	100.0	80.3	66.0	8.3	6.0	19.7	9.2	4.3	6.2
2000	100.1	80.8	67.2	8.1	5.5	19.3	9.3	4.1	5.9
2001	100.0	80.7	66.4	8.7	5.6	19.3	9.3	4.1	5.9
2002	100.0	80.3	66.4	8.3	5.6	19.7	9.7	4.1	5.9
2003	100.0	79.9	66.4	7.9	5.6	20.1	10.1	4.0	6.0
2004	100.1	80.0	66.9	7.8	5.3	20.1	10.2	4.0	5.9
2005	100.0	80.4	67.6	7.6	5.2	19.6	9.9	4.0	5.7
2006	100.0	80.9	68.5	7.5	5.0	19.1	9.6	4.0	5.5
2007	100.0	81.0	68.5	7.5	4.9	19.0	9.8	3.9	5.3
2008	100.0	79.5	65.7	8.5	5.4	20.5	10.5	4.2	5.8
2009	100.0	78.4	64.2	8.0	6.3	21.6	11.3	4.3	6.0
2010	100.0	78.3	64.8	7.6	5.9	21.7	11.2	4.3	6.2
2011	100.0	78.7	65.9	7.2	5.6	21.3	11.2	4.1	6.1
2012	100.0	78.5	65.6	7.5	5.4	21.5	11.1	4.3	6.1
2013	100.0	79.1	67.0	6.9	5.1	20.9	10.9	4.3	5.8
2014	100.0	79.7	68.0	7.1	4.6	20.3	10.7	4.1	5.5
2015	100.0	79.7	68.1	7.1	4.5	20.3	10.6	4.0	5.7
2016	100.0	79.9	68.9	6.6	4.4	20.1	10.6	4.0	5.5
2017	100.0	80.5	69.7	6.6	4.2	19.5	10.5	3.8	5.2
2018	100.0	80.9	70.5	6.4	3.9	19.1	10.4	3.8	4.9
Men									
1995	100.0	86.3	70.8	9.4	6.1	13.7	5.4	3.0	5.3
1996	100.0	86.3	71.0	9.1	6.2	13.7	5.7	2.8	5.2
1997	100.1	86.5	71.9	8.7	5.9	13.6	5.6	3.0	5.0
1998	100.0	87.4	74.0	8.1	5.3	12.6	5.5	2.7	4.4
1999	100.0	87.5	73.6	8.2	5.7	12.5	5.5	2.6	4.4
2000	100.1	87.5	74.6	7.7	5.2	12.6	5.7	2.5	4.4
2001	100.0	87.6	73.4	8.9	5.3	12.4	5.4	2.5	4.5
2002	100.0	87.4	73.2	8.5	5.7	12.6	5.6	2.5	4.5
2003	100.0	86.9	73.2	8.1	5.6	13.1	6.3	2.3	4.5
2004	100.0	87.1	74.0	7.9	5.2	12.9	6.1	2.5	4.3
2005	99.9	87.0	74.3	7.6	5.1	12.9	6.2	2.5	4.2
2006	100.0	87.8	75.3	7.6	5.0	12.2	5.7	2.4	4.1
2007	100.0	87.5	74.7	7.8	4.9	12.5	5.9	2.6	4.1
2008	100.0	86.1	71.4	9.1	5.6	13.9	6.5	2.9	4.5
2009	100.0	84.5	68.5	9.0	7.1	15.5	7.2	3.1	5.2
2010	100.0	84.4	69.6	8.3	6.4	15.6	7.3	3.1	5.3
2011	100.0	84.9	71.4	7.6	6.0	15.1	7.1	3.0	5.0
2012	100.0	84.6	71.2	7.9	5.6	15.4	7.5	3.0	4.9
2013	100.0	85.6	72.8	7.2	5.5	14.4	7.0	2.8	4.6
2014	100.0	85.8	74.0	7.1	4.7	14.2	7.1	2.7	4.3
2015	100.0	85.7	74.0	7.0	4.6	14.3	7.0	2.8	4.5
2016	100.0	85.9	74.9	6.6	4.5	14.1	7.1	2.7	4.3
2017	100.0	86.7	75.5	6.9	4.3	13.3	6.7	2.5	4.2
2018	100.0	86.8	76.4	6.4	4.0	13.2	6.8	2.6	3.8
Women									
1995	100.0	70.3	54.3	9.2	6.8	29.7	13.3	7.0	9.4
1996	100.0	70.7	54.9	9.2	6.6	29.3	13.6	6.8	8.9
1997	100.1	70.7	55.8	8.7	6.2	29.4	14.2	6.4	8.8
1998	100.0	71.6	56.5	8.7	6.4	28.4	13.6	6.4	8.4
1999	100.0	72.3	57.6	8.4	6.3	27.7	13.4	6.1	8.2
2000	100.0	73.2	58.9	8.5	5.8	26.8	13.3	6.0	7.5
2001	100.0	73.0	58.6	8.6	5.8	27.0	13.7	5.8	7.5
2002	100.1	72.5	58.8	8.1	5.6	27.6	14.2	5.8	7.6
2003	99.9	72.1	58.8	7.7	5.6	27.8	14.4	5.8	7.6
2004	100.0	72.0	59.0	7.6	5.4	28.0	14.7	5.7	7.6
2005	99.9	72.7	59.9	7.6	5.2	27.2	14.1	5.6	7.5
2006	100.0	73.1	60.7	7.3	5.1	26.9	14.1	5.7	7.1
2007	100.0	73.6	61.5	7.2	4.9	26.4	14.2	5.4	6.7
2008	100.0	72.2	59.3	7.8	5.1	27.8	15.0	5.6	7.2
2009	100.0	71.5	59.3	6.9	5.4	28.5	15.8	5.7	7.0
2010	100.0	71.5	59.4	6.9	5.2	28.5	15.6	5.6	7.3
2011	100.0	71.7	59.8	6.6	5.2	28.3	15.7	5.3	7.3
2012	100.0	71.6	59.4	7.0	5.2	28.4	15.2	5.7	7.5
2013	100.0	71.8	60.5	6.6	4.7	28.2	15.2	5.9	7.1
2014	100.0	72.8	61.2	7.0	4.5	27.2	14.7	5.6	6.9
2015	100.0	73.0	61.4	7.2	4.4	27.0	14.6	5.3	7.1
2016	100.0	73.1	62.2	6.6	4.3	26.9	14.6	5.5	6.8
2017	100.0	73.5	63.1	6.4	4.0	26.5	14.9	5.2	6.4
2018	100.0	74.4	64.0	6.5	3.9	25.6	14.3	5.2	6.1

Note: See notes and definitions for information on historical comparability.

Table 1-37. Extent of Unemployment During the Year, by Sex, 1995–2018

(Thousands of people, percent.)

Sex and extent of unemployment	1995	1996	1997	1998	1999	2000	2001	2002	2003	2004	2005	2006
BOTH SEXES												
Total Who Worked or Looked for Work	142 413	144 528	146 096	147 295	149 798	150 786	153 056	154 205	154 315	155 576	157 549	159 259
Percent with unemployment	12.7	11.6	10.7	9.5	8.7	8.1	10.4	10.9	10.7	9.7	9.2	9.1
Total with Unemployment	18 067	16 789	15 637	14 044	13 068	12 269	15 843	16 824	16 462	15 074	14 558	14 447
Did not work but looked for work	2 690	2 329	2 129	1 729	1 503	1 425	2 014	2 660	2 762	2 551	2 422	1 907
Worked during the year	15 377	14 460	13 508	12 316	11 566	10 845	13 829	14 164	13 699	12 522	12 136	12 540
Year-round workers with 1 or 2 weeks of unemployment	715	589	611	630	562	573	602	584	534	465	431	450
Part-year workers with unemployment	14 662	13 871	12 897	11 686	11 004	10 272	13 227	13 580	13 165	12 057	11 705	12 090
1 to 4 weeks	2 812	2 550	2 582	2 323	2 361	2 233	2 368	2 002	1 839	1 985	1 941	2 601
5 to 10 weeks	2 725	2 671	2 601	2 495	2 218	2 014	2 557	2 373	2 264	2 100	2 170	2 107
11 to 14 weeks	2 147	2 020	1 822	1 701	1 594	1 505	2 038	1 970	1 749	1 773	1 698	1 615
15 to 26 weeks	4 013	3 662	3 378	3 019	2 803	2 641	3 683	3 848	3 778	3 448	3 349	3 176
27 weeks or more	2 965	2 968	2 514	2 148	2 028	1 879	2 582	3 387	3 535	2 751	2 547	2 592
With 2 or more spells of unemployment	4 468	4 237	4 044	3 628	3 225	3 079	3 421	3 226	3 093	2 896	3 095	3 076
2 spells	1 963	1 982	1 853	1 650	1 449	1 397	1 643	1 556	1 585	1 344	1 477	1 564
3 or more spells	2 505	2 255	2 191	1 978	1 776	1 682	1 779	1 670	1 508	1 552	1 618	1 513
MEN												
Total Who Worked or Looked for Work	75 698	76 786	77 385	77 704	78 905	79 546	80 975	81 651	81 804	82 478	83 951	84 736
Percent with unemployment	13.2	11.9	11.1	9.4	9.0	8.6	11.0	11.8	11.4	10.0	9.7	9.6
Total with Unemployment	9 996	9 157	8 604	7 284	7 091	6 806	8 928	9 621	9 339	8 256	8 116	8 115
Did not work but looked for work	1 317	1 026	978	787	760	742	1 004	1 369	1 487	1 217	1 216	969
Worked during the year	8 679	8 130	7 626	6 497	6 332	6 064	7 924	8 252	7 854	7 039	6 899	7 146
Year-round workers with 1 or 2 weeks of unemployment	462	395	382	386	373	379	421	365	359	289	296	295
Part-year workers with unemployment	8 217	7 735	7 244	6 111	5 959	5 685	7 502	7 887	7 495	6 750	6 603	6 850
1 to 4 weeks	1 398	1 272	1 275	1 085	1 166	1 070	1 247	1 075	958	1 028	1 052	1 283
5 to 10 weeks	1 434	1 478	1 474	1 363	1 168	1 135	1 446	1 342	1 314	1 170	1 209	1 267
11 to 14 weeks	1 253	1 258	1 068	980	937	880	1 207	1 186	1 039	1 021	1 024	961
15 to 26 weeks	2 439	2 076	1 949	1 585	1 655	1 595	2 191	2 282	2 178	2 065	1 923	1 868
27 weeks or more	1 693	1 651	1 478	1 098	1 033	1 005	1 412	2 002	2 006	1 466	1 395	1 472
With 2 or more spells of unemployment	2 793	2 554	2 437	2 014	1 845	1 809	2 100	1 920	1 882	1 828	1 975	1 936
2 spells	1 110	1 109	1 078	880	787	804	1 002	914	946	808	940	945
3 or more spells	1 683	1 445	1 359	1 134	1 058	1 005	1 099	1 006	936	1 020	1 035	991
WOMEN												
Total Who Worked or Looked for Work	66 716	67 742	68 710	69 591	70 893	71 240	72 081	72 554	72 511	73 097	73 598	74 523
Percent with unemployment	12.1	11.3	10.2	9.7	8.4	7.7	9.6	9.9	9.8	9.3	8.8	8.5
Total with Unemployment	8 070	7 632	7 033	6 760	5 976	5 463	6 915	7 203	7 123	6 818	6 442	6 332
Did not work but looked for work	1 373	1 303	1 151	942	743	683	1 010	1 291	1 275	1 334	1 206	938
Worked during the year	6 696	6 330	5 882	5 816	5 234	4 779	5 905	5 913	5 848	5 484	5 236	5 394
Year-round workers with 1 or 2 weeks of unemployment	253	194	229	243	189	193	180	220	176	177	136	154
Part-year workers with unemployment	6 443	6 136	5 653	5 573	5 045	4 586	5 725	5 693	5 672	5 307	5 100	5 240
1 to 4 weeks	1 413	1 279	1 307	1 237	1 194	1 164	1 121	927	882	957	888	1 317
5 to 10 weeks	1 291	1 192	1 127	1 131	1 050	878	1 111	1 031	950	929	961	840
11 to 14 weeks	893	762	754	721	657	625	831	784	710	752	674	655
15 to 26 weeks	1 574	1 586	1 429	1 434	1 148	1 045	1 492	1 566	1 600	1 384	1 426	1 307
27 weeks or more	1 272	1 317	1 036	1 050	996	874	1 170	1 385	1 530	1 285	1 151	1 120
With 2 or more spells of unemployment	1 675	1 682	1 607	1 614	1 379	1 270	1 321	1 306	1 211	1 069	1 120	1 140
2 spells	853	872	775	770	662	593	641	642	639	537	537	619
3 or more spells	822	810	832	844	717	677	680	664	572	532	583	521

Table 1-37. Extent of Unemployment During the Year, by Sex, 1995–2018—*Continued*

(Thousands of people, percent.)

Sex and extent of unemployment	2007	2008	2009	2010	2011	2012	2013	2014	2015	2016	2017	2018
BOTH SEXES												
Total Who Worked or Looked for Work	160 565	161 506	160 624	159 706	160 545	162 574	162 706	163 582	166 339	167 021	168 420	169 476
Percent with unemployment	9.4	13.1	16.3	15.8	14.8	13.8	12.9	10.8	10.2	9.3	8.6	7.8
Total with Unemployment	15 130	21 231	26 151	25 262	23 752	22 460	20 908	17 731	16 940	15 583	14 476	13 185
Did not work but looked for work	2 097	3 189	5 851	6 564	6 216	5 525	4 828	3 701	3 170	2 586	2 375	2 215
Worked during the year	13 033	18 042	20 300	18 698	17 537	16 936	16 080	14 030	13 770	12 997	12 101	10 970
Year-round workers with 1 or 2 weeks of unemployment	500	763	693	591	417	465	462	392	392	480	426	456
Part-year workers with unemployment	12 533	17 279	19 607	18 107	17 119	16 470	15 618	13 638	13 378	12 517	11 675	10 514
1 to 4 weeks	2 593	2 794	2 528	2 267	2 211	2 252	2 395	2 372	2 621	2 557	2 772	2 357
5 to 10 weeks	2 090	2 944	2 562	2 397	2 276	2 351	2 176	2 001	2 104	2 085	1 905	1 651
11 to 14 weeks	1 888	2 438	2 414	2 302	2 064	2 176	2 032	1 889	1 917	1 560	1 587	1 430
15 to 26 weeks	3 373	4 859	5 698	5 116	4 949	4 715	4 487	3 864	3 572	3 288	2 851	2 795
27 weeks or more	2 589	4 244	6 405	6 025	5 619	4 976	4 528	3 512	3 164	3 027	2 560	2 281
With 2 or more spells of unemployment	3 108	3 991	4 152	3 875	3 527	3 763	3 325	2 873	2 975	2 877	2 441	2 382
2 spells	1 427	1 987	1 918	1 789	1 745	1 730	1 612	1 472	1 376	1 443	1 125	1 124
3 or more spells	1 681	2 004	2 234	2 086	1 782	2 033	1 713	1 401	1 599	1 434	1 316	1 258
MEN												
Total Who Worked or Looked for Work	85 368	85 563	85 161	84 738	84 486	85 778	85 863	86 320	87 904	88 075	89 152	89 158
Percent with unemployment	10.2	14.4	18.6	17.6	15.7	14.4	13.4	11.4	10.3	9.4	8.9	8.1
Total with Unemployment	8 698	12 331	15 877	14 900	13 273	12 388	11 548	9 807	9 076	8 312	7 932	7 215
Did not work but looked for work	1 076	1 674	3 325	3 662	3 214	2 868	2 443	1 962	1 634	1 307	1 213	1 202
Worked during the year	7 622	10 656	12 552	11 238	10 059	9 520	9 104	7 845	7 442	7 006	6 719	6 013
Year-round workers with 1 or 2 weeks of unemployment	365	484	458	379	271	310	259	286	245	280	265	291
Part-year workers with unemployment	7 257	10 172	12 093	10 859	9 788	9 210	8 845	7 559	7 197	6 726	6 454	5 722
1 to 4 weeks	1 367	1 523	1 466	1 186	1 170	1 189	1 235	1 234	1 370	1 263	1 414	1 098
5 to 10 weeks	1 214	1 701	1 594	1 423	1 240	1 364	1 238	1 170	1 162	1 075	1 073	888
11 to 14 weeks	1 163	1 467	1 558	1 441	1 277	1 243	1 126	1 095	993	846	906	783
15 to 26 weeks	2 058	3 035	3 564	3 233	2 941	2 719	2 607	2 133	2 000	1 894	1 571	1 621
27 weeks or more	1 455	2 445	3 911	3 577	3 159	2 696	2 640	1 928	1 672	1 648	1 490	1 333
With 2 or more spells of unemployment	1 992	2 623	2 865	2 623	2 450	2 328	2 070	1 789	1 766	1 639	1 484	1 421
2 spells	847	1 234	1 299	1 133	1 121	1 003	954	934	767	789	625	622
3 or more spells	1 145	1 389	1 566	1 491	1 329	1 325	1 117	855	998	851	858	798
WOMEN												
Total Who Worked or Looked for Work	75 197	75 943	75 463	74 968	76 060	76 797	76 843	77 263	78 435	78 945	79 267	80 318
Percent with unemployment	8.6	11.7	13.6	13.8	13.8	13.1	12.2	10.3	10.0	9.2	8.3	7.4
Total with Unemployment	6 432	8 900	10 274	10 362	10 479	10 073	9 361	7 924	7 864	7 270	6 544	5 970
Did not work but looked for work	1 021	1 514	2 526	2 903	3 002	2 657	2 385	1 740	1 536	1 278	1 162	1 014
Worked during the year	5 411	7 385	7 748	7 459	7 478	7 416	6 975	6 185	6 328	5 992	5 382	4 957
Year-round workers with 1 or 2 weeks of unemployment	135	279	235	211	147	155	203	106	147	199	160	165
Part-year workers with unemployment	5 276	7 106	7 513	7 248	7 331	7 261	6 773	5 344	6 181	5 792	5 222	4 792
1 to 4 weeks	1 226	1 270	1 061	1 081	1 041	1 064	1 160	1 138	1 251	1 294	1 358	1 259
5 to 10 weeks	876	1 243	968	974	1 036	987	938	831	943	1 010	832	763
11 to 14 weeks	725	971	857	861	787	933	907	794	924	715	682	647
15 to 26 weeks	1 316	1 823	2 134	1 883	2 008	1 997	1 881	1 731	1 571	1 394	1 280	1 175
27 weeks or more	1 134	1 800	2 494	2 448	2 459	2 280	1 887	849	1 492	1 380	1 070	948
With 2 or more spells of unemployment	1 116	1 368	1 287	1 252	1 077	1 435	1 254	1 084	1 210	1 237	957	962
2 spells	580	753	619	657	624	727	658	539	609	655	499	502
3 or more spells	536	616	668	595	453	707	596	546	601	583	458	460

Table 1-38. Percent Distribution of Persons with Unemployment During the Year, by Sex and Extent of Unemployment, 1990–2018

(Percent.)

Sex and extent of unemployment	1990	1991	1992	1993	1994	1995	1996	1997	1998	1999	2000	2001	2002	2003
BOTH SEXES														
Total with Unemployment Who Worked During the Year	100.0	100.0	100.0	100.0	100.0	100.0	100.0	100.0	100.0	100.0	100.0	100.0	100.0	100.0
Year-round workers with 1 or 2 weeks of unemployment	5.9	5.1	4.7	4.0	4.6	4.6	4.1	4.5	5.1	4.9	5.3	4.4	4.1	3.9
Part-year workers with unemployment	94.1	94.8	95.4	96.1	95.4	95.4	96.0	95.5	95.0	95.1	94.8	95.6	95.9	96.1
1 to 4 weeks	20.3	17.1	15.7	15.4	17.3	18.3	17.6	19.1	18.9	20.4	20.6	17.1	14.1	13.4
5 to 10 weeks	20.5	19.4	18.7	17.0	18.5	17.7	18.5	19.3	20.3	19.2	18.6	18.5	16.8	16.5
11 to 14 weeks	13.9	13.7	13.8	13.5	14.1	14.0	14.0	13.5	13.8	13.8	13.9	14.7	13.9	12.8
15 to 26 weeks	24.1	26.1	26.1	26.6	25.8	26.1	25.3	25.0	24.5	24.2	24.4	26.6	27.2	27.6
27 weeks or more	15.3	18.5	21.1	23.6	19.7	19.3	20.6	18.6	17.5	17.5	17.3	18.7	23.9	25.8
With 2 or more spells of unemployment	32.4	31.1	30.6	31.2	29.7	29.1	29.3	29.9	29.5	27.9	28.4	24.8	22.8	22.6
2 spells	15.9	14.5	14.4	15.0	13.7	12.8	13.7	13.7	13.4	12.5	12.9	11.9	11.0	11.6
3 or more spells	16.5	16.6	16.2	16.2	16.0	16.3	15.6	16.2	16.1	15.4	15.5	12.9	11.8	11.0
MEN														
Total with Unemployment Who Worked During the Year	100.0	100.0	100.0	100.0	100.0	100.0	100.0	100.0	100.0	100.0	100.0	100.0	100.0	100.0
Year-round workers with 1 or 2 weeks of unemployment	6.8	5.4	4.9	4.4	5.7	5.3	4.9	5.0	5.9	5.9	6.3	5.3	4.4	4.6
Part-year workers with unemployment	93.2	94.6	95.0	95.5	94.3	94.7	95.1	95.1	94.1	94.0	93.6	94.7	95.6	95.4
1 to 4 weeks	17.5	13.9	13.6	13.3	14.7	16.1	15.6	16.7	16.7	18.4	17.6	15.7	13.0	12.2
5 to 10 weeks	19.6	18.5	17.8	16.3	17.9	16.5	18.2	19.3	21.0	18.4	18.7	18.2	16.3	16.7
11 to 14 weeks	14.0	14.5	14.1	13.4	14.7	14.4	15.5	14.0	15.1	14.8	14.5	15.2	14.4	13.2
15 to 26 weeks	25.4	28.0	27.6	28.4	26.4	28.1	25.5	25.6	24.4	26.1	26.3	27.6	27.7	27.7
27 weeks or more	16.7	19.7	21.9	24.1	20.6	19.5	20.3	19.4	16.9	16.3	16.5	17.8	24.3	25.5
With 2 or more spells of unemployment	35.4	34.0	33.9	34.3	31.6	32.2	31.4	31.9	31.0	29.1	29.9	26.5	23.3	24.0
2 spells	16.1	15.2	15.5	15.7	13.6	12.8	13.6	14.1	13.5	12.4	13.3	12.6	11.1	12.1
3 or more spells	19.3	18.8	18.4	18.6	18.0	19.4	17.8	17.8	17.5	16.7	16.6	13.9	12.2	11.9
WOMEN														
Total With Unemployment Who Worked During the Year	100.0	100.0	100.0	100.0	100.0	100.0	100.0	100.0	100.0	100.0	100.0	100.0	100.0	100.0
Year-round workers with 1 or 2 weeks of unemployment	4.6	4.8	4.2	3.4	3.2	3.8	3.1	3.9	4.2	3.6	4.0	3.1	3.7	3.0
Part-year workers with unemployment	95.3	95.3	95.7	96.6	96.7	96.2	96.9	96.1	95.8	96.4	96.0	96.9	96.3	97.0
1 to 4 weeks	24.3	22.0	19.0	18.3	20.9	21.1	20.2	22.2	21.3	22.8	24.3	19.0	15.7	15.1
5 to 10 weeks	21.6	20.8	20.1	17.8	19.3	19.3	18.8	19.2	19.4	20.1	18.4	18.8	17.4	16.2
11 to 14 weeks	13.8	12.5	13.2	13.5	13.1	13.3	12.0	12.8	12.4	12.6	13.1	14.1	13.3	12.1
15 to 26 weeks	22.2	23.2	23.6	24.1	25.1	23.5	25.1	24.3	24.7	21.9	21.9	25.3	26.5	27.4
27 weeks or more	13.4	16.8	19.8	22.9	18.3	19.0	20.8	17.6	18.0	19.0	18.3	19.8	23.4	26.2
With 2 or more spells of unemployment	28.2	26.6	25.4	26.9	27.0	25.0	26.6	27.3	27.7	26.3	26.6	22.4	22.1	20.7
2 spells	15.7	13.4	12.6	14.1	13.8	12.7	13.8	13.2	13.2	12.6	12.4	10.9	10.9	10.9
3 or more spells	12.5	13.2	12.8	12.8	13.2	12.3	12.8	14.1	14.5	13.7	14.2	11.5	11.2	9.8

Table 1-38. Percent Distribution of Persons with Unemployment During the Year, by Sex and Extent of Unemployment, 1990–2018—*Continued*

(Percent.)

Sex and extent of unemployment	2004	2005	2006	2007	2008	2009	2010	2011	2012	2013	2014	2015	2016	2017	2018
BOTH SEXES															
Total with Unemployment Who Worked During the Year	100.0	100.0	100.0	100.0	100.0	100.0	100.0	100.0	100.0	100.0	100.0	100.0	100.0	100.0	100.0
Year-round workers with 1 or 2 weeks of unemployment	3.7	3.6	3.6	3.8	4.2	3.4	3.2	2.4	2.7	2.9	2.8	2.8	3.7	3.5	4.2
Part-year workers with unemployment	96.3	96.4	96.4	96.1	95.8	96.5	96.8	97.6	97.3	97.1	97.2	97.2	96.3	96.5	95.8
1 to 4 weeks	15.9	16.0	20.7	19.9	15.5	12.5	12.1	12.6	13.3	14.9	16.9	19.0	19.7	22.9	21.5
5 to 10 weeks	16.8	17.9	16.8	16.0	16.3	12.6	12.8	13.0	13.9	13.5	14.3	15.3	16.0	15.7	15.1
11 to 14 weeks	14.2	14.0	12.9	14.5	13.5	11.9	12.3	11.8	12.8	12.6	13.5	13.9	12.0	13.1	13.0
15 to 26 weeks	27.5	27.6	25.3	25.9	26.9	28.1	27.4	28.2	27.8	27.9	27.5	25.9	25.3	23.6	25.5
27 weeks or more	22.0	20.9	20.7	19.8	23.5	31.5	32.2	32.0	29.4	28.2	25.0	22.9	23.3	21.2	20.8
With 2 or more spells of unemployment	23.1	25.5	24.5	23.8	22.1	20.5	20.7	20.1	22.2	20.7	20.5	21.6	22.1	20.2	21.7
2 spells	10.7	12.2	12.5	10.9	11.0	9.4	9.6	10.0	10.2	10.0	10.5	10.0	11.1	9.3	10.2
3 or more spells	12.4	13.3	12.1	12.9	11.1	11.0	11.2	10.2	12.0	10.7	10.0	11.6	11.0	10.9	11.5
MEN															
Total with Unemployment Who Worked During the Year	100.0	100.0	100.0	100.0	100.0	100.0	100.0	100.0	100.0	100.0	100.0	100.0	100.0	100.0	100.0
Year-round workers with 1 or 2 weeks of unemployment	4.1	4.3	4.1	4.8	4.5	3.7	3.4	2.7	3.3	2.8	3.6	3.3	4.0	3.9	4.8
Part-year workers with unemployment	95.9	95.7	95.9	95.2	95.5	96.4	96.6	97.3	96.7	97.2	96.4	96.7	96.0	96.1	95.2
1 to 4 weeks	14.6	15.3	18.0	17.9	14.3	11.7	10.5	11.6	12.5	13.6	15.7	18.4	18.0	21.0	18.3
5 to 10 weeks	16.6	17.5	17.7	15.9	16.0	12.7	12.7	12.3	14.3	13.6	14.9	15.6	15.3	16.0	14.8
11 to 14 weeks	14.5	14.8	13.4	15.3	13.8	12.4	12.8	12.7	13.1	12.4	14.0	13.3	12.1	13.5	13.0
15 to 26 weeks	29.3	27.9	26.1	27.0	28.5	28.4	28.8	29.2	28.6	28.6	27.2	26.9	27.0	23.4	27.0
27 weeks or more	20.8	20.2	20.6	19.1	22.9	31.2	31.8	31.4	28.3	29.0	24.6	22.5	23.5	22.2	22.2
With 2 or more spells of unemployment	26.0	28.6	27.1	26.1	24.6	22.8	23.3	24.4	24.5	22.7	22.8	23.7	23.4	22.1	23.6
2 spells	11.5	13.6	13.2	11.1	11.6	10.3	10.1	11.1	10.5	10.5	11.9	10.3	11.3	9.3	10.4
3 or more spells	14.5	15.0	13.9	15.0	13.0	12.5	13.3	13.2	13.9	12.3	10.9	13.4	12.1	12.8	13.3
WOMEN															
Total With Unemployment Who Worked During the Year	100.0	100.0	100.0	100.0	100.0	100.0	100.0	100.0	100.0	100.0	100.0	100.0	100.0	100.0	100.0
Year-round workers with 1 or 2 weeks of unemployment	3.2	2.6	2.9	2.5	3.8	3.0	2.8	2.0	2.1	2.9	1.7	2.3	3.3	3.0	3.3
Part-year workers with unemployment	96.8	97.4	97.1	97.4	96.2	96.9	97.2	98.0	97.9	97.1	98.3	97.7	96.7	97.0	96.7
1 to 4 weeks	17.4	17.0	24.4	22.6	17.2	13.7	14.5	13.9	14.3	16.6	18.4	19.8	21.6	25.2	25.4
5 to 10 weeks	16.9	18.4	15.6	16.2	16.8	12.5	13.1	13.9	13.3	13.4	13.4	14.9	16.9	15.5	15.4
11 to 14 weeks	13.7	12.9	12.1	13.4	13.1	11.1	11.5	10.5	12.6	13.0	12.8	14.6	11.9	12.7	13.1
15 to 26 weeks	25.2	27.2	24.2	24.3	24.7	27.5	25.2	26.8	26.9	27.0	28.0	24.8	23.3	23.8	23.7
27 weeks or more	23.5	22.0	20.8	20.9	24.4	32.1	32.8	32.9	30.8	27.1	25.6	23.6	23.0	19.9	19.1
With 2 or more spells of unemployment	19.5	21.4	21.1	20.6	18.5	16.6	16.8	14.4	19.3	18.0	17.5	19.1	20.7	17.8	19.4
2 spells	9.8	10.3	11.5	10.7	10.2	8.0	8.8	8.3	9.8	9.4	8.7	9.6	10.9	9.3	10.1
3 or more spells	9.7	11.1	9.7	9.9	8.3	8.6	8.0	6.1	9.5	8.5	8.8	9.5	9.7	8.5	9.3

Table 1-39. Number and Median Annual Earnings of Year-Round, Full-Time Wage and Salary Workers, by Age, Sex, and Race, 1995–2018

(Thousands of people, dollars.)

Sex, age, and race	1995	1996	1997	1998	1999	2000	2001	2002	2003	2004	2005	2006
NUMBER												
Both Sexes, 16 Years and Over	83 407	85 611	86 905	89 748	91 722	94 359	94 531	94 526	94 731	96 098	98 632	101 353
16 to 24 years	6 892	6 809	7 063	7 618	7 631	8 384	7 989	7 903	7 631	7 702	7 956	8 113
25 to 44 years	48 695	49 225	49 513	50 264	50 532	51 159	49 939	49 120	48 343	48 421	49 149	50 056
25 to 34 years	23 310	23 071	23 186	23 048	22 952	23 044	22 744	22 657	22 512	22 405	22 808	23 613
35 to 44 years	25 385	26 154	26 327	27 216	27 580	28 115	27 195	26 463	25 831	26 016	26 341	26 443
45 to 54 years	18 436	19 714	20 109	21 274	22 375	23 307	23 855	23 999	24 507	25 074	25 661	26 338
55 to 64 years	8 122	8 455	8 901	9 273	9 594	9 870	10 948	11 584	12 207	12 812	13 605	14 340
65 years and over	1 263	1 408	1 318	1 318	1 590	1 639	1 800	1 921	2 042	2 090	2 262	2 507
Men, 16 Years and Over	49 334	50 407	50 772	52 509	53 132	54 477	54 630	54 420	54 575	55 610	57 020	58 533
16 to 24 years	4 094	3 942	4 021	4 479	4 347	4 602	4 605	4 570	4 421	4 493	4 663	4 812
25 to 44 years	28 940	29 282	29 453	29 763	29 738	30 080	29 271	28 855	28 499	28 763	29 151	29 589
25 to 34 years	13 844	13 817	13 735	13 612	13 471	13 497	13 386	13 400	13 288	13 430	13 629	13 933
35 to 44 years	15 096	15 465	15 718	16 151	16 267	16 583	15 885	15 455	15 211	15 333	15 522	15 655
45 to 54 years	10 589	11 372	11 388	12 030	12 546	13 045	13 363	13 330	13 616	13 975	14 382	14 758
55 to 64 years	4 884	4 908	5 133	5 438	5 498	5 693	6 253	6 502	6 872	7 165	7 489	7 905
65 years and over	827	903	775	801	1 003	1 057	1 138	1 163	1 165	1 213	1 334	1 469
Women, 16 Years and Over	34 073	35 203	36 133	37 239	38 591	39 887	39 901	40 106	40 156	40 488	41 613	42 820
16 to 24 years	2 798	2 867	3 041	3 140	3 285	3 782	3 384	3 333	3 210	3 209	3 293	3 301
25 to 44 years	19 755	19 942	20 060	20 503	20 794	21 081	20 668	20 264	19 844	19 656	19 997	20 467
25 to 34 years	9 467	9 254	9 451	9 437	9 481	9 548	9 358	9 257	9 224	8 974	9 179	9 679
35 to 44 years	10 288	10 688	10 609	11 066	11 313	11 533	11 310	11 007	10 620	10 682	10 818	10 788
45 to 54 years	7 847	8 343	8 721	9 244	9 829	10 263	10 493	10 669	10 891	11 099	11 279	11 580
55 to 64 years	3 238	3 547	3 767	3 836	4 096	4 178	4 695	5 082	5 335	5 647	6 116	6 434
65 years and over	436	505	543	517	586	583	662	758	877	877	927	1 038
White, 16 Years and Over	70 430	72 068	72 650	75 046	76 203	77 790	78 306	77 632	77 545	78 236	80 546	82 411
Men	42 608	43 554	43 429	44 901	45 211	46 105	46 373	45 823	45 816	46 317	47 790	48 897
Women	27 822	28 514	29 221	30 145	30 992	31 685	31 933	31 809	31 729	31 919	32 756	33 513
Black, 16 Years and Over	9 446	9 706	10 248	10 532	11 145	11 899	11 001	10 966	10 979	11 301	11 417	11 988
Men	4 686	4 682	5 026	5 202	5 411	5 636	5 281	5 150	5 196	5 470	5 402	5 679
Women	4 759	5 024	5 222	5 329	5 734	6 264	5 720	5 816	5 783	5 832	6 015	6 309
MEDIAN ANNUAL EARNINGS												
Both Sexes, 16 Years and Over	27 000	28 000	30 000	30 000	31 000	32 000	34 000	35 000	35 000	35 672	36 400	38 000
16 to 24 years	15 500	15 600	16 000	18 000	18 000	19 000	20 000	20 000	20 000	20 000	20 000	21 000
25 to 34 years	25 000	25 300	27 000	28 500	30 000	30 000	31 000	31 800	32 000	33 000	33 000	35 000
35 to 44 years	30 000	31 000	32 000	33 000	34 992	35 000	36 000	37 000	39 000	40 000	40 000	41 000
45 to 54 years	32 000	33 000	35 000	35 000	36 000	38 000	39 500	40 000	40 000	40 000	42 000	44 000
55 to 64 years	30 000	30 000	32 000	34 000	35 000	35 000	36 400	39 145	40 000	40 000	41 000	43 000
65 years and over	29 600	26 496	28 200	26 000	30 000	32 000	32 000	33 000	32 000	35 000	35 000	35 001
Men, 16 Years and Over	31 000	32 000	34 000	35 000	36 000	37 600	38 500	40 000	40 000	40 000	40 051	42 000
16 to 24 years	16 000	17 000	17 000	18 720	19 000	20 000	20 000	20 000	20 800	20 800	20 800	22 000
25 to 34 years	27 000	28 000	29 852	30 000	32 000	33 500	34 000	34 740	35 000	35 000	35 000	36 000
35 to 44 years	35 000	36 000	37 000	38 000	40 000	40 000	42 000	43 000	43 900	45 000	45 000	48 000
45 to 54 years	40 000	40 000	41 000	42 000	44 616	45 000	45 000	47 000	48 000	48 000	50 000	50 000
55 to 64 years	36 000	36 000	39 000	40 000	40 853	44 000	45 000	47 000	50 000	50 000	50 000	50 000
65 years and over	36 000	33 000	36 400	35 000	36 000	35 999	35 000	37 861	42 000	40 000	41 000	44 000
Women, 16 Years and Over	23 000	24 000	25 000	25 000	26 000	27 500	29 000	30 000	30 000	30 001	32 000	33 000
16 to 24 years	15 000	15 000	15 000	17 000	17 000	18 000	19 000	19 000	20 000	20 000	20 000	20 000
25 to 34 years	22 000	23 000	24 000	25 000	26 000	27 000	28 080	29 500	30 000	30 000	30 000	31 000
35 to 44 years	25 000	25 000	26 000	27 200	28 000	29 000	30 000	30 400	32 000	32 800	35 000	35 000
45 to 54 years	25 000	26 000	27 040	28 132	30 000	30 000	32 000	32 000	33 466	34 771	35 000	36 000
55 to 64 years	22 500	24 000	24 800	25 775	27 000	28 000	30 000	31 410	32 000	33 000	33 000	35 000
65 years and over	23 290	20 800	24 000	22 000	20 800	24 000	25 000	28 000	26 000	27 000	28 768	27 878
White, 16 Years and Over	28 000	29 000	30 000	31 000	32 000	34 000	35 000	35 000	36 000	37 000	38 000	40 000
Men	32 000	33 000	35 000	36 000	37 200	39 000	40 000	40 000	40 000	42 000	42 000	44 707
Women	23 000	24 000	25 000	26 000	27 000	28 000	30 000	30 000	31 000	31 800	32 000	34 000
Black, 16 Years and Over	22 000	23 784	24 000	25 000	25 760	26 000	28 500	29 000	30 000	30 000	30 000	31 000
Men	24 500	26 000	26 000	27 000	30 000	30 000	30 000	30 000	32 000	30 000	33 000	34 000
Women	20 000	21 000	22 000	23 000	24 000	25 000	26 000	26 000	27 000	28 000	29 141	30 000

Table 1-39. Number and Median Annual Earnings of Year-Round, Full-Time Wage and Salary Workers, by Age, Sex, and Race, 1995–2018—*Continued*

(Thousands of people, dollars.)

Sex, age, and race	2007	2008	2009	2010	2011	2012	2013	2014	2015	2016	2017	2018
NUMBER												
Both Sexes, 16 Years and Over	102 441	98 493	94 012	94 110	96 562	97 879	100 711	103 308	105 520	107 999	110 095	112 659
16 to 24 years	8 064	7 242	6 302	6 073	6 411	6 424	6 969	7 135	7 241	7 504	7 848	8 285
25 to 44 years	49 725	47 364	44 579	44 441	45 166	45 812	46 478	48 188	49 130	50 826	52 287	53 415
25 to 34 years	23 646	22 786	21 572	21 894	21 989	22 690	23 141	24 099	25 008	26 209	26 666	27 530
35 to 44 years	26 080	24 578	23 007	22 546	23 177	23 122	23 337	24 090	24 123	24 616	25 621	25 886
45 to 54 years	26 566	25 722	24 877	24 388	24 782	24 593	25 245	25 018	25 334	25 397	25 300	25 411
55 to 64 years	15 248	15 286	15 274	16 073	16 622	17 255	17 721	18 416	19 152	19 433	19 543	20 078
65 years and over	2 837	2 879	2 980	3 135	3 582	3 795	4 299	4 551	4 663	4 839	5 117	5 469
Men, 16 Years and Over	58 673	55 973	52 362	52 793	54 542	55 489	57 263	58 719	60 012	61 295	62 437	63 486
16 to 24 years	4 719	4 112	3 494	3 462	3 649	3 730	3 952	3 914	4 107	4 186	4 482	4 498
25 to 44 years	29 004	27 546	25 324	25 449	25 959	26 476	26 924	27 941	28 399	29 193	30 010	30 645
25 to 34 years	13 706	13 208	12 085	12 475	12 616	13 043	13 370	14 123	14 406	14 885	15 167	15 759
35 to 44 years	15 298	14 337	13 239	12 974	13 343	13 433	13 555	13 818	13 993	14 308	14 844	14 886
45 to 54 years	14 810	14 199	13 521	13 373	13 723	13 690	14 094	14 026	14 278	14 235	14 134	14 059
55 to 64 years	8 449	8 397	8 289	8 727	9 066	9 315	9 747	10 199	10 461	10 775	10 752	11 140
65 years and over	1 692	1 720	1 733	1 782	2 146	2 278	2 546	2 640	2 767	2 906	3 058	3 144
Women, 16 Years and Over	43 768	42 520	41 650	41 318	42 020	42 390	43 448	44 589	45 508	46 704	47 658	49 172
16 to 24 years	3 345	3 130	2 808	2 611	2 762	2 694	3 016	3 222	3 134	3 318	3 366	3 788
25 to 44 years	20 721	19 819	19 255	18 992	19 207	19 336	19 554	20 248	20 731	21 632	22 276	22 770
25 to 34 years	9 940	9 578	9 487	9 420	9 373	9 647	9 771	9 976	10 602	11 324	11 499	11 770
35 to 44 years	10 782	10 240	9 768	9 572	9 834	9 689	9 782	10 272	10 130	10 308	10 777	11 000
45 to 54 years	11 757	11 524	11 356	11 016	11 059	10 903	11 151	10 992	11 056	11 162	11 166	11 352
55 to 64 years	6 799	6 889	6 984	7 346	7 556	7 940	7 974	8 217	8 691	8 659	8 791	8 938
65 years and over	1 146	1 158	1 247	1 354	1 436	1 518	1 753	1 911	1 896	1 933	2 059	2 324
White, 16 Years and Over	83 139	79 980	76 470	76 557	77 669	78 266	80 188	81 557	82 879	84 303	85 613	87 180
Men	48 825	46 608	43 622	44 018	45 037	45 460	46 764	47 591	48 333	49 079	49 758	50 493
Women	34 314	33 372	32 848	32 540	32 632	32 806	33 424	33 966	34 546	35 224	35 855	36 687
Black, 16 Years and Over	11 987	11 424	10 716	10 676	11 009	11 193	11 865	12 370	12 754	13 419	13 832	14 384
Men	5 689	5 377	4 952	4 957	5 111	5 323	5 617	5 910	6 178	6 471	6 702	6 889
Women	6 299	6 046	5 764	5 719	5 898	5 870	6 248	6 460	6 577	6 948	7 129	7 495
MEDIAN ANNUAL EARNINGS												
Both Sexes, 16 Years and Over	40 000	40 000	41 000	42 000	42 000	44 000	44 000	45 000	45 000	47 500	48 000	50 000
16 to 24 years	22 421	24 000	23 532	23 000	22 650	23 000	24 570	25 000	25 000	26 000	27 000	29 000
25 to 34 years	35 000	36 500	38 000	37 815	38 000	39 000	40 000	40 000	40 000	40 023	42 000	44 847
35 to 44 years	43 000	45 000	45 000	45 000	45 000	48 000	48 000	48 000	50 000	52 000	52 002	55 000
45 to 54 years	45 000	45 000	46 000	48 000	48 000	50 000	49 920	50 000	50 000	52 000	54 000	56 000
55 to 64 years	45 000	46 000	48 000	49 000	50 000	50 000	50 000	50 000	51 000	52 000	52 000	55 000
65 years and over	40 000	42 000	42 000	45 000	44 200	48 000	48 000	50 000	50 000	54 167	54 000	54 000
Men, 16 Years and Over	45 000	46 000	48 000	48 000	48 000	50 000	50 000	50 000	50 000	51 000	52 000	55 000
16 to 24 years	23 000	25 000	25 000	24 000	24 000	24 480	25 000	26 000	25 000	28 000	28 000	30 000
25 to 34 years	38 000	40 000	40 000	40 000	40 000	40 000	40 000	42 000	43 000	45 000	45 000	48 000
35 to 44 years	50 000	50 000	50 000	50 000	51 000	52 000	52 000	52 000	55 132	58 000	60 000	60 000
45 to 54 years	50 000	52 000	53 004	55 000	55 000	57 000	56 000	60 000	60 000	60 000	60 000	63 000
55 to 64 years	52 000	54 000	55 000	55 000	57 000	55 000	57 998	58 000	60 000	60 000	60 000	63 000
65 years and over	44 000	50 000	49 000	50 002	50 000	53 700	55 000	60 000	60 000	65 000	60 000	60 000
Women, 16 Years and Over	35 000	35 000	36 000	37 000	37 000	38 000	39 000	40 000	40 000	41 000	42 000	45 000
16 to 24 years	22 000	22 000	22 000	20 816	22 000	22 000	23 000	22 880	24 000	25 000	25 000	26 400
25 to 34 years	33 000	34 000	35 000	35 000	35 000	35 002	37 000	36 000	38 000	38 000	40 000	40 000
35 to 44 years	36 000	38 000	38 000	40 000	40 000	40 000	40 000	42 000	45 000	46 000	46 000	50 000
45 to 54 years	37 163	38 000	40 000	40 000	40 000	40 000	40 000	42 000	43 000	45 000	46 000	50 000
55 to 64 years	37 100	39 000	40 000	40 000	40 000	41 000	41 161	41 000	44 000	45 000	45 000	48 000
65 years and over	31 000	34 193	36 000	40 000	37 000	38 000	40 000	40 000	42 500	42 000	48 000	47 000
White, 16 Years and Over	40 000	41 600	42 000	43 502	44 000	45 000	45 000	45 000	48 000	49 000	50 000	50 000
Men	45 000	48 000	49 000	50 000	50 000	50 000	50 000	50 000	52 000	53 000	54 200	56 000
Women	35 000	35 500	36 002	38 000	38 000	39 520	40 000	40 000	40 000	42 000	44 000	45 000
Black, 16 Years and Over	33 000	34 000	35 000	35 000	35 000	35 000	36 000	36 000	38 000	38 000	40 000	40 000
Men	35 000	37 500	38 000	36 000	39 000	38 000	40 000	40 000	40 000	40 000	42 000	44 000
Women	30 000	30 002	32 000	32 000	34 000	34 000	34 000	33 000	35 000	35 000	36 000	38 000

Table 1-40. Number and Median Annual Earnings of Year-Round, Full-Time Wage and Salary Workers, by Sex and Occupation of Job Held the Longest, 2005–2018

(Thousands of people, dollars.)

Sex and occupation	2005	2006	2007	2008	2009	2010	2011	2012	2013	2014	2015	2016	2017	2018
Both Sexes, Number of Workers														
Management, business, and financial operations	16 299	16 806	17 115	17 259	16 491	16 889	17 396	17 799	18 241	19 020	19 937	20 642	20 609	21 556
Management	11 685	11 866	12 191	12 256	11 733	11 804	12 140	12 548	12 646	13 240	13 928	14 370	14 215	14 958
Business and financial operations	4 613	4 941	4 924	5 003	4 758	5 085	5 256	5 251	5 595	5 780	6 009	6 272	6 395	6 597
Professional and related	20 093	21 268	21 939	21 748	21 831	21 966	22 165	22 751	23 251	24 109	24 721	25 883	26 797	27 234
Computer and mathematical	2 779	2 888	3 180	3 089	3 100	2 993	3 171	3 524	3 439	3 690	4 044	4 190	4 395	4 510
Architecture and engineering	2 361	2 491	2 467	2 360	2 133	2 409	2 451	2 398	2 302	2 362	2 602	2 776	2 868	3 045
Life, physical, and social sciences	1 096	1 142	1 026	1 044	1 054	993	991	1 050	1 075	1 090	1 085	1 172	1 245	1 184
Community and social services	1 728	1 835	1 791	1 754	1 827	1 905	1 784	1 846	1 982	1 947	2 002	1 974	2 157	2 148
Legal	1 093	1 168	1 159	1 228	1 230	1 255	1 226	1 350	1 350	1 360	1 271	1 319	1 408	1 327
Education, training, and library	4 894	5 195	5 482	5 478	5 500	5 510	5 390	5 285	5 588	5 683	5 546	5 956	6 188	6 181
Arts, design, entertainment, sports, and media	1 362	1 633	1 554	1 415	1 404	1 380	1 449	1 445	1 582	1 658	1 660	1 767	1 883	1 815
Health care practitioner and technical	4 780	4 916	5 278	5 380	5 583	5 521	5 703	5 852	5 932	6 319	6 512	6 731	6 653	7 024
Services	13 117	13 236	13 553	13 034	12 944	12 855	13 676	13 456	13 650	13 795	14 426	14 771	15 003	15 451
Health care support	2 027	2 081	2 027	2 019	2 135	2 008	2 236	2 037	2 307	2 144	2 261	2 309	2 511	2 425
Protective services	2 429	2 506	2 511	2 472	2 593	2 589	2 571	2 535	2 582	2 498	2 482	2 503	2 539	2 607
Food preparation and serving related	3 586	3 646	3 769	3 504	3 307	3 408	3 797	3 631	3 508	3 641	4 130	4 140	4 060	4 285
Building and grounds cleaning and maintenance	3 285	3 120	3 198	3 027	2 870	2 942	3 098	3 056	3 190	3 243	3 205	3 344	3 306	3 479
Personal care and services	1 790	1 883	2 048	2 012	2 038	1 908	1 974	2 196	2 062	2 269	2 348	2 474	2 588	2 654
Sales and office	24 010	24 467	24 472	23 058	22 320	21 859	21 949	22 121	22 841	22 843	22 520	22 571	22 598	23 056
Sales and related	10 251	10 497	10 301	9 763	9 275	9 187	9 191	9 312	10 010	9 937	9 757	9 929	10 026	10 172
Office and administrative support	13 758	13 970	14 171	13 294	13 045	12 671	12 758	12 810	12 831	12 906	12 763	12 642	12 571	12 883
Natural resources, construction, and maintenance	10 864	11 295	10 745	10 002	8 599	8 298	8 584	8 897	9 317	9 715	9 846	10 212	10 561	10 429
Farming, fishing, and forestry	556	585	607	581	555	532	562	539	621	631	768	737	730	708
Construction and extraction	6 145	6 484	5 885	5 158	4 172	4 029	4 283	4 329	4 604	5 077	5 081	5 303	5 664	5 795
Installation, maintenance, and repair	4 163	4 226	4 252	4 264	3 872	3 737	3 739	4 029	4 093	4 006	3 997	4 172	4 167	3 926
Production, transportation, and material moving	13 586	13 704	13 907	12 649	11 062	11 518	12 041	12 166	12 724	13 129	13 388	13 327	13 817	14 309
Production	7 623	7 762	7 589	6 652	5 834	6 226	6 574	6 410	6 723	6 904	7 080	6 946	6 966	7 291
Transportation and material moving	5 963	5 942	6 318	5 997	5 228	5 292	5 467	5 756	6 001	6 225	6 308	6 381	6 851	7 018
Armed forces	664	576	709	744	765	727	749	689	687	697	681	593	710	625
Both Sexes, Median Annual Earnings														
Management, business, and financial operations	57 000	60 000	60 000	60 800	60 000	64 000	65 000	65 000	65 000	65 000	70 000	70 000	72 000	75 000
Management	60 000	62 500	65 000	65 000	65 000	68 000	70 000	70 000	70 000	70 000	75 000	75 000	76 000	80 000
Business and financial operations	49 000	50 000	50 000	52 000	55 000	56 000	57 000	57 000	60 000	60 000	60 000	60 000	65 000	66 000
Professional and related	50 000	50 000	51 000	54 000	55 000	55 000	56 000	58 705	58 000	59 000	60 000	61 000	64 000	65 000
Computer and mathematical	62 400	68 000	70 000	70 000	72 000	70 000	73 000	75 000	75 000	80 000	80 000	80 000	87 000	86 000
Architecture and engineering	65 000	69 000	70 000	70 000	70 000	75 000	75 000	75 000	80 000	76 000	80 000	80 000	85 000	82 000
Life, physical, and social sciences	53 500	57 000	60 000	57 532	60 000	60 000	61 599	67 000	70 000	65 000	70 000	75 500	65 000	70 000
Community and social services	36 000	36 780	39 000	40 000	40 000	40 000	40 000	41 000	42 000	44 000	45 000	46 000	45 000	47 000
Legal	72 000	70 000	70 000	75 000	80 000	75 000	85 000	80 000	86 000	90 000	88 000	94 209	92 000	100 000
Education, training, and library	40 000	40 282	44 984	45 000	46 000	45 000	46 200	47 000	45 000	47 907	49 000	50 000	50 000	50 000
Arts, design, entertainment, sports, and media	42 000	45 000	44 297	47 000	49 000	48 000	50 000	50 000	50 000	52 000	52 000	54 000	60 000	58 908
Health care practitioner and technical	50 000	52 000	52 800	55 000	55 000	57 638	58 000	60 000	60 000	58 000	60 000	60 998	62 000	65 000
Services	23 000	24 000	25 000	25 000	26 000	26 000	26 000	27 000	26 255	27 040	29 044	30 000	30 000	30 000
Health care support	22 000	23 000	24 500	26 000	26 000	26 270	26 000	26 000	28 000	26 922	28 000	29 100	30 000	30 000
Protective services	42 000	45 000	45 000	45 000	46 000	48 000	50 000	50 000	50 000	50 000	50 000	50 000	52 000	55 000
Food preparation and serving related	19 656	19 000	20 000	20 800	20 000	20 800	21 000	21 840	22 000	22 607	25 000	25 000	24 960	25 000
Building and grounds cleaning and maintenance	21 000	23 000	23 000	24 000	24 024	25 000	24 002	25 000	24 000	25 301	28 000	27 560	30 000	30 000
Personal care and services	23 000	23 000	25 000	25 000	25 000	25 000	25 000	25 000	24 000	25 500	30 000	30 000	30 000	29 799
Sales and office	31 200	32 002	34 000	35 000	35 000	35 000	35 002	36 000	37 440	37 000	39 000	40 000	40 000	42 000
Sales and related	35 000	37 000	38 000	38 500	38 000	40 000	40 000	40 000	40 000	40 000	43 000	44 000	45 000	48 000
Office and administrative support	30 000	30 000	32 000	32 500	34 000	34 000	35 000	35 000	35 000	35 000	36 000	37 010	38 000	40 000
Natural resources, construction, and maintenance	35 000	35 000	36 000	40 000	40 000	40 000	40 000	40 000	40 000	40 000	41 000	43 000	42 000	45 000
Farming, fishing, and forestry	21 000	20 000	24 000	24 000	24 000	23 000	24 000	24 000	25 600	27 300	26 443	30 400	30 000	32 000
Construction and extraction	32 000	35 000	35 000	39 000	40 000	40 000	39 500	38 000	40 000	40 000	40 000	41 700	40 555	43 000
Installation, maintenance, and repair	40 000	40 000	40 000	42 000	44 192	43 981	44 018	44 000	45 000	45 000	46 000	46 000	45 002	50 000
Production, transportation, and material moving	30 200	30 000	33 000	34 000	34 000	34 000	35 000	36 000	35 761	36 000	37 000	38 000	40 000	40 000
Production	30 000	30 000	33 000	34 000	32 006	34 000	35 000	36 000	36 000	36 000	36 000	38 000	40 000	40 000
Transportation and material moving	30 800	30 000	33 800	34 000	35 000	33 000	35 000	36 000	35 000	35 000	38 000	38 000	40 000	40 000
Armed forces	39 000	40 000	42 000	45 000	47 000	47 000	45 000	45 000	47 000	48 000	50 000	50 156	50 000	52 000

Table 1-40. Number and Median Annual Earnings of Year-Round, Full-Time Wage and Salary Workers, by Sex and Occupation of Job Held the Longest, 2005–2018—*Continued*

(Thousands of people, dollars.)

Sex and occupation	2005	2006	2007	2008	2009	2010	2011	2012	2013	2014	2015	2016	2017	2018
Men, Number of Workers														
Management, business, and financial operations	9 496	9 519	9 784	9 836	9 418	9 569	9 886	9 917	10 137	10 773	11 084	11 513	11 388	11 885
Management	7 477	7 361	7 619	7 714	7 300	7 249	7 497	7 666	7 742	8 103	8 344	8 593	8 381	8 875
Business and financial operations	2 019	2 157	2 165	2 122	2 117	2 320	2 389	2 252	2 395	2 670	2 739	2 919	3 007	3 010
Professional and related	9 561	10 387	10 274	10 074	10 036	10 126	10 228	10 731	10 858	11 194	11 520	11 977	12 548	12 516
Computer and mathematical	2 060	2 159	2 378	2 348	2 227	2 244	2 329	2 564	2 636	2 821	3 100	3 125	3 372	3 383
Architecture and engineering	2 041	2 174	2 172	2 068	1 859	2 110	2 144	2 073	2 004	2 044	2 231	2 322	2 402	2 635
Life, physical, and social sciences	668	748	611	581	575	562	605	615	589	622	656	667	680	611
Community and social services	713	756	744	675	707	701	679	742	792	740	704	740	791	727
Legal	490	546	515	595	645	605	616	686	615	666	611	620	697	640
Education, training, and library	1 421	1 587	1 651	1 535	1 650	1 601	1 522	1 504	1 586	1 653	1 577	1 690	1 790	1 702
Arts, design, entertainment, sports, and media	789	953	790	782	829	839	860	824	989	937	940	1 013	1 083	979
Health care practitioner and technical	1 378	1 464	1 413	1 490	1 544	1 464	1 473	1 724	1 645	1 711	1 701	1 799	1 732	1 839
Services	6 658	6 715	6 871	6 389	6 379	6 426	6 923	7 040	6 931	6 922	7 323	7 417	7 471	7 465
Health care support	240	252	261	204	247	242	268	269	277	284	280	329	352	307
Protective services	1 919	1 998	2 000	1 930	2 026	2 070	2 108	2 041	2 087	2 054	1 998	2 008	2 065	2 077
Food preparation and serving related	1 873	1 991	1 985	1 816	1 744	1 743	2 050	2 068	1 880	1 896	2 309	2 286	2 116	2 255
Building and grounds cleaning and maintenance	2 153	1 939	2 048	1 911	1 832	1 862	1 974	2 055	2 069	2 057	2 050	2 171	2 220	2 104
Personal care and services	473	535	576	527	530	508	523	606	618	629	685	624	718	722
Sales and office	9 464	9 747	9 694	9 128	8 680	8 872	8 971	8 874	9 386	9 395	9 234	9 333	9 452	9 718
Sales and related	5 896	6 125	6 019	5 690	5 231	5 363	5 425	5 436	5 867	5 680	5 631	5 614	5 719	5 849
Office and administrative support	3 568	3 622	3 675	3 438	3 449	3 509	3 545	3 439	3 519	3 715	3 603	3 719	3 733	3 870
Natural resources, construction, and maintenance	10 503	10 904	10 343	9 627	8 225	7 936	8 274	8 550	8 996	9 330	9 456	9 820	10 117	9 949
Farming, fishing, and forestry	469	482	516	489	425	430	474	445	501	521	617	589	580	545
Construction and extraction	6 026	6 344	5 753	5 056	4 068	3 909	4 192	4 245	4 534	4 948	4 959	5 182	5 513	5 600
Installation, maintenance, and repair	4 008	4 078	4 074	4 081	3 732	3 597	3 608	3 860	3 961	3 861	3 880	4 049	4 024	3 805
Production, transportation, and material moving	10 747	10 733	11 047	10 226	8 921	9 214	9 583	9 754	10 331	10 490	10 775	10 710	10 818	11 357
Production	5 503	5 525	5 461	4 983	4 370	4 612	4 813	4 814	5 090	5 098	5 281	5 142	5 011	5 398
Transportation and material moving	5 244	5 208	5 585	5 242	4 552	4 602	4 770	4 940	5 241	5 392	5 495	5 568	5 806	5 959
Armed forces	591	528	660	696	703	649	677	622	625	616	620	525	644	596
Men, Median Annual Earnings														
Management, business, and financial operations	69 000	68 000	70 000	72 000	72 000	75 000	75 000	75 000	75 000	75 000	80 000	80 000	82 000	85 000
Management	70 000	70 000	75 000	75 000	75 000	78 000	80 000	75 056	77 975	78 000	82 000	83 000	85 000	90 000
Business and financial operations	60 000	60 000	60 000	65 000	65 000	67 000	65 000	67 500	70 000	68 000	70 000	72 000	75 000	75 000
Professional and related	60 000	61 000	62 000	67 000	65 000	67 000	70 000	70 000	71 000	70 000	75 000	75 000	78 000	80 000
Computer and mathematical	65 000	70 000	70 000	74 000	75 000	75 000	79 000	80 000	78 000	81 000	85 000	84 000	90 002	90 000
Architecture and engineering	66 921	70 000	72 000	74 000	72 000	77 000	75 000	79 002	80 000	78 000	80 000	80 000	90 000	85 000
Life, physical, and social sciences	62 000	61 000	65 000	65 000	65 000	64 000	65 000	72 000	76 000	70 000	75 000	84 152	68 797	76 000
Community and social services	40 000	39 000	40 000	44 085	45 000	42 002	42 000	42 000	42 640	45 000	50 000	50 000	45 000	50 000
Legal	108 000	100 000	104 146	130 000	120 000	120 000	120 000	100 000	125 000	127 000	120 000	133 125	135 000	140 000
Education, training, and library	50 000	50 000	50 000	54 000	52 000	53 000	55 000	55 000	56 000	55 000	56 000	60 000	60 000	60 000
Arts, design, entertainment, sports, and media	50 000	50 000	50 000	52 000	50 000	50 000	55 000	55 000	55 000	58 000	51 000	56 800	60 000	60 000
Health care practitioner and technical	70 000	72 000	75 000	75 000	74 000	75 000	75 000	75 000	78 000	75 000	85 000	80 000	78 893	88 000
Services	26 000	29 000	29 000	30 000	30 000	30 002	30 000	30 000	31 000	32 000	32 000	34 320	35 000	35 000
Health care support	22 880	25 000	25 000	28 000	30 000	34 000	29 904	30 000	35 000	30 000	30 000	32 170	35 000	39 700
Protective services	45 000	46 886	49 000	49 000	49 500	50 000	50 000	54 000	51 000	54 000	52 002	54 522	55 000	57 000
Food preparation and serving related	20 000	20 000	21 000	21 500	21 000	23 000	23 400	24 000	22 709	24 000	25 000	26 000	26 000	28 000
Building and grounds cleaning and maintenance	24 000	25 000	25 000	27 012	26 000	28 600	27 000	28 000	28 000	29 000	30 000	30 000	32 000	32 400
Personal care and services	30 000	30 000	30 000	30 500	30 000	30 000	32 000	32 000	30 000	32 000	35 000	35 000	40 000	33 000
Sales and office	40 000	40 000	42 000	40 000	42 002	42 000	43 000	45 000	44 400	45 000	48 000	49 000	48 000	50 000
Sales and related	42 000	45 000	45 000	48 000	48 002	48 000	50 000	49 000	50 000	50 000	51 000	52 000	52 000	57 000
Office and administrative support	34 000	35 000	36 000	35 000	37 400	37 000	37 000	40 000	40 000	40 000	40 000	40 000	40 000	42 000
Natural resources, construction, and maintenance	35 000	35 674	36 000	40 000	40 000	40 000	40 000	40 000	40 000	40 000	42 000	44 000	42 500	45 000
Farming, fishing, and forestry	22 500	20 000	24 000	24 000	25 000	23 400	25 000	25 000	28 705	29 900	28 000	32 000	32 517	35 000
Construction and extraction	32 000	35 000	35 000	40 000	40 000	40 000	40 000	39 000	40 000	40 000	40 000	42 000	40 560	44 000
Installation, maintenance, and repair	40 000	40 000	40 000	42 685	45 000	44 000	45 000	44 000	45 000	45 000	47 000	47 000	45 000	50 000
Production, transportation, and material moving	34 000	33 358	35 000	35 360	35 198	36 000	38 500	40 000	39 000	40 000	40 000	40 000	42 000	43 000
Production	35 000	35 000	36 000	36 000	36 000	36 944	40 000	40 000	40 000	40 000	40 000	42 000	44 120	45 000
Transportation and material moving	32 760	32 000	35 000	35 000	35 000	35 000	37 440	38 638	37 000	38 000	40 000	40 000	40 000	42 000
Armed forces	40 000	40 000	42 000	45 000	47 000	47 000	45 000	45 000	49 999	48 000	50 000	51 600	50 000	52 000

Table 1-40. Number and Median Annual Earnings of Year-Round, Full-Time Wage and Salary Workers, by Sex and Occupation of Job Held the Longest, 2005–2018—*Continued*

(Thousands of people, dollars.)

Sex and occupation	2005	2006	2007	2008	2009	2010	2011	2012	2013	2014	2015	2016	2017	2018
Women, Number of Workers														
Management, business, and financial operations	6 803	7 287	7 332	7 423	7 073	7 320	7 511	7 881	8 104	8 248	8 853	9 129	9 221	9 670
Management	4 209	4 504	4 573	4 542	4 432	4 555	4 643	4 882	4 904	5 137	5 584	5 776	5 834	6 083
Business and financial operations	2 594	2 783	2 759	2 881	2 641	2 765	2 867	2 999	3 200	3 110	3 269	3 353	3 388	3 587
Professional and related	10 532	10 881	11 664	11 675	11 795	11 840	11 937	12 020	12 394	12 915	13 202	13 906	14 249	14 718
Computer and mathematical	718	729	802	741	873	748	842	960	803	869	944	1 064	1 023	1 127
Architecture and engineering	320	317	295	293	274	299	307	325	298	318	371	454	466	410
Life, physical, and social sciences	428	394	415	462	479	431	386	435	486	468	429	505	565	574
Community and social services	1 015	1 079	1 047	1 079	1 119	1 204	1 105	1 104	1 190	1 208	1 298	1 233	1 366	1 421
Legal	603	622	645	633	585	650	610	664	735	694	660	699	711	688
Education, training, and library	3 473	3 608	3 831	3 944	3 850	3 909	3 868	3 781	4 001	4 030	3 969	4 266	4 398	4 479
Arts, design, entertainment, sports, and media	573	681	764	633	575	541	589	622	593	721	720	753	800	836
Health care practitioner and technical	3 403	3 452	3 865	3 890	4 039	4 057	4 230	4 129	4 287	4 608	4 811	4 932	4 920	5 184
Services	6 459	6 522	6 682	6 645	6 565	6 429	6 753	6 416	6 718	6 874	7 103	7 353	7 532	7 986
Health care support	1 787	1 829	1 766	1 815	1 888	1 766	1 969	1 768	2 030	1 860	1 980	1 980	2 159	2 118
Protective services	510	509	511	541	567	519	463	494	495	443	484	496	474	531
Food preparation and serving related	1 713	1 655	1 784	1 688	1 563	1 665	1 747	1 562	1 628	1 745	1 821	1 854	1 943	2 030
Building and grounds cleaning and maintenance	1 132	1 181	1 150	1 116	1 038	1 079	1 125	1 001	1 121	1 186	1 155	1 172	1 086	1 376
Personal care and services	1 317	1 349	1 471	1 485	1 508	1 400	1 451	1 590	1 444	1 640	1 663	1 851	1 870	1 932
Sales and office	14 546	14 720	14 778	13 930	13 640	12 986	12 979	13 247	13 455	13 448	13 285	13 238	13 146	13 338
Sales and related	4 355	4 372	4 282	4 073	4 044	3 824	3 766	3 876	4 143	4 256	4 126	4 315	4 307	4 324
Office and administrative support	10 191	10 348	10 496	9 856	9 596	9 162	9 213	9 371	9 313	9 191	9 159	8 923	8 839	9 014
Natural resources, construction, and maintenance	360	391	402	376	374	361	310	347	321	385	390	392	444	480
Farming, fishing, and forestry	87	104	92	91	130	102	87	94	120	110	151	148	150	163
Construction and extraction	119	140	132	101	104	120	91	85	70	130	122	121	151	195
Installation, maintenance, and repair	155	148	178	183	140	140	131	169	132	145	117	122	143	121
Production, transportation, and material moving	2 839	2 971	2 861	2 423	2 141	2 304	2 458	2 412	2 393	2 639	2 613	2 617	3 000	2 951
Production	2 120	2 237	2 128	1 668	1 464	1 614	1 761	1 596	1 633	1 806	1 800	1 804	1 955	1 893
Transportation and material moving	719	734	733	755	676	690	697	816	760	833	813	813	1 045	1 058
Armed forces	73	48	49	49	62	78	72	67	62	81	61	68	66	29
Women, Median Annual Earnings														
Management, business, and financial operations	46 000	50 000	50 000	50 000	50 000	52 779	52 000	54 000	55 000	56 000	59 000	60 000	60 000	63 000
Management	50 000	52 000	52 000	55 000	52 999	55 000	55 000	58 000	57 000	60 000	60 000	62 000	65 000	65 000
Business and financial operations	41 000	46 000	45 000	48 000	48 000	50 000	50 000	50 000	52 000	52 000	52 000	54 574	57 000	60 000
Professional and related	42 000	43 000	45 000	46 000	48 002	49 000	50 000	50 000	50 000	50 000	51 500	54 000	55 000	55 000
Computer and mathematical	57 000	60 000	60 000	62 000	65 000	65 000	65 000	66 002	71 000	73 000	70 000	70 000	80 000	75 000
Architecture and engineering	55 000	52 000	55 000	50 000	61 000	60 000	62 400	65 000	64 000	65 000	65 000	75 000	72 000	75 000
Life, physical, and social sciences	50 000	48 000	48 000	49 000	54 651	56 000	55 000	61 008	63 000	56 627	65 465	70 000	63 000	60 000
Community and social services	35 000	36 000	37 000	37 700	39 000	39 000	40 000	40 000	40 000	42 720	43 000	45 000	45 600	45 000
Legal	47 500	50 000	47 500	52 001	60 000	57 257	51 875	55 000	57 075	60 000	66 000	72 000	70 000	70 000
Education, training, and library	38 000	38 632	41 000	42 000	43 000	42 000	45 000	44 000	43 000	45 000	45 040	47 849	47 000	48 000
Arts, design, entertainment, sports, and media	35 000	38 000	40 000	40 000	45 000	42 000	43 000	45 000	48 000	49 000	53 000	50 000	55 000	55 000
Health care practitioner and technical	46 000	48 000	50 000	50 000	52 000	53 000	53 000	55 000	55 000	55 000	56 000	59 000	60 000	60 000
Services	20 000	20 500	22 000	23 516	24 000	23 000	23 000	24 000	24 000	24 000	25 000	26 000	26 000	28 000
Health care support	21 000	23 000	24 500	26 000	25 000	25 000	26 000	26 000	27 000	26 000	27 040	28 500	29 000	30 000
Protective services	34 344	37 896	35 000	35 000	38 000	38 500	42 000	42 000	43 419	38 000	39 800	39 915	45 000	47 454
Food preparation and serving related	18 000	18 000	19 000	20 000	19 000	19 000	20 000	20 000	22 000	20 000	24 000	23 000	22 000	25 000
Building and grounds cleaning and maintenance	18 000	19 000	19 500	20 000	20 000	20 000	20 020	20 000	20 000	21 000	22 000	22 000	23 000	25 000
Personal care and services	20 800	20 000	24 000	24 000	24 700	23 000	23 000	25 000	22 000	25 000	26 000	27 262	26 000	27 000
Sales and office	29 000	30 000	30 000	30 600	31 400	32 000	33 000	33 000	35 000	34 000	35 000	35 000	36 400	38 000
Sales and related	26 000	26 000	28 000	29 000	30 000	30 000	30 000	30 000	30 000	30 000	32 000	32 000	35 000	35 000
Office and administrative support	29 800	30 000	30 002	32 000	32 100	33 000	34 000	35 000	35 000	35 000	35 000	36 000	37 000	39 000
Natural resources, construction, and maintenance	30 200	27 000	37 025	30 000	30 000	30 000	30 000	32 000	30 000	30 000	30 000	30 000	38 000	33 218
Farming, fishing, and forestry	18 000	18 808	24 117	24 685	21 000	20 000	20 000	20 498	22 093	23 000	25 000	28 013	24 000	28 392
Construction and extraction	31 200	24 980	40 000	34 500	31 000	33 670	28 323	30 645	31 200	29 052	38 801	34 965	41 002	36 296
Installation, maintenance, and repair	36 000	40 000	42 000	33 913	38 139	41 888	35 000	43 889	43 000	37 000	38 639	37 000	48 000	38 000
Production, transportation, and material moving	23 000	23 000	25 000	25 000	25 000	25 000	25 000	27 560	28 000	27 000	29 000	30 000	30 000	30 000
Production	23 400	23 000	25 000	25 000	25 000	25 000	25 000	27 000	27 901	27 000	29 000	29 000	31 200	30 090
Transportation and material moving	21 000	24 000	27 000	24 000	25 000	25 000	26 000	28 000	28 000	27 000	29 000	30 000	28 000	30 000
Armed forces	32 652	32 000	41 000	32 000	43 600	50 000	52 000	48 000	39 000	45 000	50 121	47 860	48 000	55 648

Table 1-41. Distribution of Employed Wage and Salary Workers by Tenure with Current Employer, Age, Sex, Race, and Hispanic Origin, January 2018

(Thousands of people, percent.)

Characteristic	Number employed/ (in thousands)	Percent distribution by tenure with current employer								
		Total	12 months or less	13 to 23 months	2 years	3 to 4 years	5 to 9 years	10 to 14 years	15 to 19 years	20 years or more
Both Sexes										
16 years and over	137 442	100.0	22.3	6.9	5.6	17.6	18.8	11.6	6.9	10.3
16 to 19 years	4 597	100.0	74.0	11.9	7.4	6.2	0.4	-	-	-
20 years and over	132 845	100.0	20.5	6.7	5.5	18.0	19.5	12.1	7.2	10.6
20 to 24 years	13 455	100.0	53.6	12.6	11.0	18.3	4.5	0.1	-	-
25 to 34 years	32 512	100.0	27.7	9.5	7.9	26.2	21.8	6.3	0.7	-
35 to 44 years	29 110	100.0	17.1	6.0	4.8	18.5	23.8	17.3	8.8	3.8
45 to 54 years	28 528	100.0	11.9	4.7	3.5	14.5	20.5	15.9	11.9	17.2
55 to 64 years	22 367	100.0	9.2	3.5	3.2	11.5	18.5	14.9	11.9	27.4
65 years and over	6 872	100.0	8.4	4.0	2.9	11.5	18.8	15.4	10.4	28.6
Men										
16 years and over	71 178	100.0	21.8	6.6	5.5	17.5	19.1	11.8	6.9	10.9
16 to 19 years	2 217	100.0	72.9	12.2	6.5	8.0	0.4	-	-	-
20 years and over	68 960	100.0	20.2	6.4	5.5	17.8	19.7	12.1	7.1	11.2
20 to 24 years	6 838	100.0	52.2	12.0	11.3	19.9	4.5	0.2	-	-
25 to 34 years	17 374	100.0	27.2	9.1	7.6	25.0	23.6	6.9	0.6	-
35 to 44 years	15 334	100.0	16.2	6.0	4.8	18.2	23.4	17.8	9.3	4.3
45 to 54 years	14 673	100.0	12.2	4.0	3.4	14.2	19.4	16.0	12.2	18.6
55 to 64 years	11 202	100.0	9.5	3.5	3.0	11.4	18.8	13.3	10.9	29.7
65 years and over	3 539	100.0	7.9	3.7	3.3	11.5	18.2	16.6	9.7	29.1
Women										
16 years and over	66 264	100.0	22.8	7.1	5.7	17.7	18.6	11.5	7.0	9.6
16 to 19 years	2 380	100.0	75.1	11.6	8.3	4.6	0.3	-	-	-
20 years and over	63 884	100.0	20.9	7.0	5.6	18.2	19.3	12.0	7.2	9.9
20 to 24 years	6 617	100.0	55.0	13.1	10.8	16.6	4.5	-	-	-
25 to 34 years	15 138	100.0	28.4	9.9	8.2	27.6	19.7	5.5	0.7	-
35 to 44 years	13 776	100.0	18.1	5.9	4.7	18.9	24.3	16.8	8.1	3.2
45 to 54 years	13 856	100.0	11.6	5.4	3.7	14.8	21.7	15.7	11.5	15.7
55 to 64 years	11 165	100.0	8.9	3.4	3.4	11.6	18.2	16.5	12.9	25.1
65 years and over	3 333	100.0	8.9	4.4	2.4	11.6	19.3	14.2	11.1	28.1
White										
16 years and over	106 391	100.0	21.6	6.7	5.3	17.0	19.1	11.9	7.3	11.2
Men	56 112	100.0	20.9	6.4	5.2	17.0	19.4	12.0	7.2	11.9
Women	50 280	100.0	22.3	7.0	5.4	17.0	18.7	11.8	7.4	10.4
Black										
16 years and over	16 978	100.0	25.6	6.7	6.7	18.7	17.6	10.5	6.4	7.7
Men	7 764	100.0	26.8	6.8	7.0	17.5	17.4	10.5	6.6	7.3
Women	9 214	100.0	24.6	6.6	6.5	19.8	17.8	10.5	6.3	8.0
Asian										
16 years and over	8 941	100.0	20.4	7.7	6.1	20.6	20.3	12.6	5.7	6.6
Men	4 725	100.0	19.8	7.3	6.1	21.5	20.2	12.6	5.6	6.7
Women	4 216	100.0	21.1	8.1	6.1	19.6	20.4	12.6	5.7	6.5
Hispanic[1]										
16 years and over	23 720	100.0	25.6	5.9	7.5	19.1	19.4	10.4	5.7	6.5
Men	13 206	100.0	23.7	5.4	7.9	19.9	20.1	10.9	5.2	6.9
Women	10 514	100.0	28.0	6.5	6.9	18.0	18.5	9.8	6.2	6.0

[1]May be of any race.
- = Data represents or rounds to zero.

Table 1-42. Median Years of Tenure with Current Employer for Employed Wage and Salary Workers, 25 Years and Over, by Educational Attainment, Sex, and Age, January 2018

(Number of years.)

Year, sex, and age	Total employed	25 to 34 years	35 to 44 years	45 to 54 years	55 to 64 years	65 years and over
Both Sexes	5.0	2.8	4.9	7.6	10.1	10.2
Less than a high school diploma	4.6	2.6	4.2	5.3	7.7	9.8
High school graduates, no college	5.2	2.9	4.7	7.8	10.2	10.3
Some college, no degree	4.8	2.6	4.7	7.5	9.8	10.0
Associate degree	5.1	3.1	4.7	7.6	10.5	10.5
College graduates	5.1	2.8	5.3	8.0	10.3	10.3
Bachelor's degree	4.9	2.9	5.3	7.9	10.0	10.5
Master's degree	5.5	2.8	5.5	7.9	10.5	9.6
Doctoral or professional degree	5.3	2.0	4.5	8.9	12.4	14.6
Men	5.1	2.9	5.0	8.1	10.2	10.2
Less than a high school diploma	4.7	2.8	4.6	5.6	8.2	10.1
High school graduates, no college	5.2	3.1	4.9	8.0	10.2	11.5
Some college, no degree	4.9	2.7	4.8	8.4	9.8	9.6
Associate degree	5.4	3.1	5.4	9.4	10.3	10.9
College graduates	5.2	2.8	5.3	8.5	10.4	10.1
Bachelor's degree	5.1	2.9	5.7	8.3	10.1	10.1
Master's degree	5.4	2.8	5.1	8.5	10.4	9.5
Doctoral or professional degree	5.4	2.1	4.0	9.1	13.5	14.9
Women	4.9	2.7	4.7	7.1	10.1	10.1
Less than a high school diploma	4.2	2.4	3.3	5.1	6.3	9.1
High school graduates, no college	5.2	2.6	4.6	7.6	10.3	9.7
Some college, no degree	4.7	2.4	4.5	6.3	9.8	10.2
Associate degree	4.9	3.0	4.2	6.1	10.7	10.1
College graduates	5.0	2.8	5.2	7.6	10.2	10.8
Bachelor's degree	4.7	2.8	5.0	7.6	9.9	12.5
Master's degree	5.5	2.9	6.2	7.2	10.6	9.6
Doctoral or professional degree	5.2	2.0	4.8	8.8	11.6	11.0

Table 1-43. Median Years of Tenure with Current Employer for Employed Wage and Salary Workers, by Age and Sex, Selected Years, February 1998–January 2018

(Number of years.)

Sex and age	February 1998	February 2000	January 2002	January 2004	January 2006	January 2008	January 2010	January 2012	January 2014	January 2016	January 2018
Both Sexes											
16 years and over	3.6	3.5	3.7	4.0	4.0	4.1	4.4	4.6	4.6	4.2	4.2
16 to 17 years	0.6	0.6	0.7	0.7	0.6	0.7	0.7	0.7	0.7	0.6	0.6
18 to 19 years	0.7	0.7	0.8	0.8	0.7	0.8	1.0	0.8	0.8	0.8	0.8
20 to 24 years	1.1	1.1	1.2	1.3	1.3	1.3	1.5	1.3	1.3	1.3	1.2
25 years and over	4.7	4.7	4.7	4.9	4.9	5.1	5.2	5.4	5.5	5.1	5.0
25 to 34 years	2.7	2.6	2.7	2.9	2.9	2.7	3.1	3.2	3.0	2.8	2.8
35 to 44 years	5.0	4.8	4.6	4.9	4.9	4.9	5.1	5.3	5.2	4.9	4.9
45 to 54 years	8.1	8.2	7.6	7.7	7.3	7.6	7.8	7.8	7.9	7.9	7.6
55 to 64 years	10.1	10.0	9.9	9.6	9.3	9.9	10.0	10.3	10.4	10.1	10.1
65 years and over	7.8	9.4	8.6	9.0	8.8	10.2	9.9	10.3	10.3	10.3	10.2
Men											
16 years and over	3.8	3.8	3.9	4.1	4.1	4.2	4.6	4.7	4.7	4.3	4.3
16 to 17 years	0.6	0.6	0.8	0.7	0.7	0.7	0.7	0.6	0.7	0.6	0.5
18 to 19 years	0.7	0.7	0.8	0.8	0.7	0.8	1.0	0.8	0.9	0.8	0.8
20 to 24 years	1.2	1.2	1.4	1.3	1.4	1.4	1.6	1.4	1.4	1.3	1.3
25 years and over	4.9	4.9	4.9	5.1	5.0	5.2	5.3	5.5	5.5	5.2	5.1
25 to 34 years	2.8	2.7	2.8	3.0	2.9	2.8	3.2	3.2	3.1	2.9	2.9
35 to 44 years	5.5	5.3	5.0	5.2	5.1	5.2	5.3	5.4	5.4	5.0	5.0
45 to 54 years	9.4	9.5	9.1	9.6	8.1	8.2	8.5	8.5	8.2	8.4	8.1
55 to 64 years	11.2	10.2	10.2	9.8	9.5	10.1	10.4	10.7	10.7	10.2	10.2
65 years and over	7.1	9.0	8.1	8.2	8.3	10.4	9.7	10.2	10.0	10.2	10.2
Women											
16 years and over	3.4	3.3	3.4	3.8	3.9	3.9	4.2	4.6	4.5	4.0	4.0
16 to 17 years	0.6	0.6	0.7	0.6	0.6	0.6	0.7	0.7	0.7	0.6	0.7
18 to 19 years	0.7	0.7	0.8	0.8	0.7	0.8	1.0	0.8	0.8	0.8	0.8
20 to 24 years	1.1	1.0	1.1	1.3	1.2	1.3	1.5	1.3	1.3	1.2	1.2
25 years and over	4.4	4.4	4.4	4.7	4.8	4.9	5.1	5.4	5.4	5.0	4.9
25 to 34 years	2.5	2.5	2.5	2.8	2.8	2.6	3.0	3.1	2.9	2.6	2.7
35 to 44 years	4.5	4.3	4.2	4.5	4.6	4.7	4.9	5.2	5.1	4.8	4.7
45 to 54 years	7.2	7.3	6.5	6.4	6.7	7.0	7.1	7.3	7.6	7.5	7.1
55 to 64 years	9.6	9.9	9.6	9.2	9.2	9.8	9.7	10.0	10.2	10.0	10.1
65 years and over	8.7	9.7	9.4	9.6	9.5	9.9	10.1	10.5	10.5	10.4	10.1

Table 1-44. Median Years of Tenure with Current Employer for Employed Wage and Salary Workers, by Industry, Selected Years, February 2000–January 2018

(Number of years.)

Industry	February 2000	January 2002	January 2004	January 2006	January 2008	January 2010	January 2012	January 2014	January 2016	January 2018
TOTAL, 16 YEARS AND OVER	3.5	3.7	4.0	4.0	4.1	4.4	4.6	4.6	4.2	4.2
Private Sector	3.2	3.3	3.5	3.6	3.6	4.0	4.2	4.1	3.7	3.8
Agriculture and related industries	3.7	4.2	3.7	3.8	4.3	4.8	4.1	3.6	4.5	4.6
Nonagricultural industries	3.2	3.3	3.5	3.6	3.6	4.0	4.2	4.1	3.7	3.8
Mining	4.8	4.5	5.2	3.8	4.1	4.8	3.5	4.0	4.6	5.1
Construction	2.7	3.0	3.0	3.0	3.5	4.2	4.3	3.9	4.0	4.1
Manufacturing	4.9	5.4	5.8	5.5	5.9	6.1	6.0	5.9	5.3	5.0
Durable goods manufacturing	4.8	5.5	6.0	5.6	6.1	6.6	6.1	6.0	5.4	5.3
Nonmetallic mineral product	5.5	5.3	4.8	5.0	4.8	7.7	7.0	7.6	5.1	5.2
Primary metals and fabricated metal product	5.0	6.3	6.4	6.2	5.2	7.2	5.6	6.1	6.0	6.0
Machinery manufacturing	5.3	6.8	6.4	6.6	6.0	8.3	5.4	6.2	5.5	5.7
Computers and electronic product	3.9	4.7	5.2	5.9	6.7	5.9	7.7	5.1	5.3	5.8
Electrical equipment and appliances	5.0	5.5	9.8	6.2	6.2	5.0	5.9	5.8	4.7	4.5
Transportation equipment	6.4	7.0	7.7	7.2	7.8	8.3	7.1	7.1	6.1	5.7
Wood product	3.7	4.3	5.0	4.7	6.2	4.7	5.3	4.6	4.7	3.5
Furniture and fixtures	4.4	4.7	4.7	4.2	5.2	5.0	6.5	5.9	4.8	4.8
Miscellaneous manufacturing	3.7	4.5	4.6	3.9	4.7	5.4	4.8	5.1	5.0	4.8
Nondurable goods manufacturing	5.0	5.3	5.5	5.4	5.4	5.5	5.8	5.9	5.1	4.7
Food manufacturing	4.6	5.0	4.9	5.2	4.3	4.7	4.9	4.7	4.5	3.9
Beverage and tobacco product	5.5	4.6	8.0	5.4	6.9	8.1	6.4	4.8	4.3	4.1
Textiles, apparel, and leather	4.7	5.0	5.0	4.4	4.6	4.7	4.3	5.3	5.6	5.0
Paper and printing	5.1	6.2	6.9	6.3	5.5	6.8	9.7	9.7	5.3	5.4
Petroleum and coal product	9.5	9.8	11.4	5.0	4.3	5.1	6.4	6.1	6.6	5.0
Chemicals	6.0	5.7	5.3	6.1	7.6	7.3	6.1	7.1	5.3	4.7
Plastics and rubber product	4.6	5.3	5.7	5.0	5.3	7.4	6.1	6.5	5.3	5.0
Wholesale and retail trade	2.7	2.8	3.1	3.1	3.2	3.6	3.7	3.6	3.3	3.2
Wholesale trade	3.9	3.9	4.3	4.6	5.0	5.2	5.5	5.8	5.2	5.1
Retail trade	2.5	2.6	2.8	2.8	2.9	3.3	3.3	3.3	3.0	3.0
Transportation and utilities	4.7	4.9	5.3	4.9	5.1	5.3	5.6	5.1	4.6	4.8
Transportation and warehousing	4.0	4.3	4.7	4.3	4.6	5.0	5.3	4.7	4.4	4.2
Utilities	11.5	13.4	13.3	10.4	10.1	9.1	9.5	9.2	7.4	9.5
Information[1]	3.4	3.3	4.3	4.8	4.7	5.0	5.4	4.8	4.3	4.4
Publishing, except Internet	4.2	4.8	4.7	5.3	4.7	5.6	6.6	5.3	5.7	4.1
Motion picture and sound recording industries	1.6	2.3	2.2	1.9	1.9	3.8	2.6	2.4	2.4	2.9
Broadcasting, except Internet	3.6	3.1	4.0	4.6	3.4	4.3	4.9	4.1	3.6	5.0
Telecommunications	4.3	3.4	4.6	5.3	6.9	6.6	7.4	7.8	6.0	5.2
Financial activities	3.5	3.6	3.9	4.0	4.5	4.6	4.9	5.0	4.8	4.7
Finance and insurance	3.6	3.9	4.1	4.1	4.7	4.8	5.0	5.3	5.0	5.0
Finance	3.3	3.6	4.0	3.9	4.4	4.5	4.7	5.0	5.0	4.8
Insurance	4.4	4.5	4.4	4.7	5.2	5.5	5.7	6.0	5.2	5.4
Real estate and rental and leasing	3.1	3.0	3.3	3.4	3.7	3.9	4.5	4.4	3.8	3.6
Real estate	3.1	3.2	3.5	3.5	3.9	4.1	4.5	4.6	3.9	3.7
Rental and leasing services	3.0	2.2	2.9	3.1	3.0	3.3	4.2	3.5	3.4	3.4
Professional and business services	2.4	2.7	3.2	3.2	3.1	3.4	3.8	3.6	3.4	3.6
Professional and technical services	2.6	3.1	3.6	3.8	3.3	4.0	4.4	4.2	3.9	3.9
Management, administrative, and waste services[1]	2.0	2.1	2.6	2.5	2.5	2.9	3.1	3.1	2.8	3.3
Administrative and support services	1.8	1.9	2.4	2.4	2.4	2.8	3.0	3.0	2.6	3.1
Waste management and remediation services	3.6	4.3	3.4	4.1	4.1	2.9	4.4	4.7	4.6	5.8
Education and health services	3.4	3.5	3.6	4.0	4.1	4.1	4.4	4.5	3.9	3.9
Education services	3.2	3.6	3.8	4.0	4.3	4.4	4.3	4.8	4.0	4.2
Health care and social assistance	3.5	3.5	3.6	4.1	4.1	4.1	4.4	4.4	3.9	3.9
Hospitals	5.1	4.9	4.7	5.2	5.4	5.3	6.0	5.7	5.6	4.9
Health services, except hospitals	3.2	3.1	3.3	3.6	3.6	3.6	3.8	3.9	3.4	3.5
Social assistance	2.4	2.5	2.8	3.1	3.0	3.1	3.1	3.2	2.6	3.0
Leisure and hospitality	1.7	1.8	2.0	1.9	2.1	2.5	2.4	2.3	2.2	2.2
Arts, entertainment, and recreation	2.6	2.3	2.8	3.1	2.8	3.3	3.1	3.0	3.2	3.0
Accommodation and food services	1.5	1.6	1.9	1.6	1.9	2.3	2.3	2.1	2.0	2.1
Accommodation	2.8	2.7	3.1	2.5	3.1	3.3	3.8	3.5	3.0	3.1
Food services and drinking places	1.4	1.4	1.6	1.4	1.6	2.2	2.1	2.0	1.8	2.0
Other services	3.1	3.3	3.3	3.2	3.3	4.0	3.8	4.0	3.9	4.0
Other services, except private households	3.2	3.3	3.5	3.3	3.4	4.1	3.8	4.2	4.1	3.9
Repair and maintenance	3.0	3.0	3.2	2.9	3.0	4.0	3.7	4.0	3.5	3.3
Personal and laundry services	2.7	2.8	3.4	2.8	3.2	3.5	3.5	3.7	3.8	3.6
Membership associations and organizations	4.0	4.1	3.9	4.2	4.4	4.5	4.3	4.9	4.9	4.5
Other services, private households	3.0	2.7	2.3	2.8	2.8	3.4	3.3	3.0	3.3	4.5
Public Sector	7.1	6.7	6.9	6.9	7.2	7.2	7.8	7.8	7.7	6.8
Federal government	11.5	11.3	10.4	9.9	9.9	7.9	9.5	8.5	8.8	8.3
State government	5.5	5.4	6.4	6.3	6.5	6.4	6.4	7.4	5.8	5.9
Local government	6.7	6.2	6.4	6.6	7.1	7.5	8.1	7.9	8.3	6.9

[1]Includes other industries not shown separately.

Table 1-45. Employment Status of the Population, by Sex and Marital Status, March 1995–March 2019

(Thousands of people, percent.)

Marital status and year	Men						Women					
	Population	Labor force					Population	Labor force				
		Total		Employed	Unemployed			Total		Employed	Unemployed	
		Number	Percent of population		Number	Percent of labor force		Number	Percent of population		Number	Percent of labor force
Single												
1995	28 318	20 449	72.2	18 286	2 163	10.6	22 853	14 974	65.5	13 673	1 301	8.7
1996	28 695	20 561	71.7	18 097	2 464	12.0	23 632	15 417	65.2	14 084	1 333	8.6
1997	29 294	20 942	71.5	18 683	2 259	10.8	24 215	16 178	66.8	14 747	1 431	8.8
1998	29 558	21 255	71.9	19 124	2 131	10.0	24 808	16 885	68.1	15 626	1 259	7.5
1999	29 883	21 329	71.4	19 465	1 864	8.7	25 674	17 486	68.1	16 185	1 301	7.4
2000	30 232	21 641	71.6	19 823	1 818	8.4	25 863	17 749	68.6	16 446	1 303	7.3
2001	30 968	22 232	71.8	20 239	1 993	9.0	26 180	17 900	68.4	16 631	1 269	7.1
2002	32 220	22 761	70.6	20 066	2 695	11.8	26 942	18 079	67.1	16 499	1 580	8.7
2003	32 852	22 821	69.5	20 194	2 627	11.5	27 527	17 901	65.0	16 219	1 682	9.4
2004	33 786	23 212	68.7	20 434	2 778	12.0	28 033	18 089	64.5	16 506	1 583	8.8
2005	34 069	23 335	68.5	20 831	2 504	10.7	28 508	18 554	65.1	16 902	1 652	8.9
2006	34 906	24 369	69.8	21 961	2 408	9.9	29 357	18 989	64.7	17 444	1 545	8.1
2007	35 359	24 506	69.3	22 224	2 281	9.3	29 695	19 218	64.7	17 935	1 284	6.7
2008	36 522	25 229	69.1	22 695	2 534	10.0	30 772	19 889	64.6	18 369	1 520	7.6
2009	36 907	24 930	67.5	20 645	4 284	17.2	31 038	19 785	63.7	17 714	2 071	10.5
2010	38 110	25 663	67.3	21 038	4 626	18.0	32 085	19 973	62.3	17 517	2 457	12.3
2011	38 766	25 646	66.2	21 389	4 256	16.6	33 041	20 581	62.3	18 117	2 463	12.0
2012	38 933	25 615	65.8	21 838	3 778	14.7	34 241	21 417	62.5	18 895	2 523	11.8
2013	39 482	25 881	65.6	22 306	3 575	13.8	34 889	21 739	62.3	19 319	2 419	11.1
2014	40 338	26 602	65.9	23 220	3 382	12.7	35 288	22 174	62.8	19 974	2 200	9.9
2015	40 893	26 949	65.9	24 094	2 855	10.6	36 036	22 385	62.1	20 530	1 855	8.3
2016	41 933	27 894	66.5	25 275	2 619	9.4	37 035	23 216	62.7	21 359	1 856	8.0
2017	41 801	27 652	66.2	25 397	2 255	8.2	37 174	23 748	63.9	22 262	1 486	6.3
2018	42 654	28 755	67.4	26 516	2 239	7.8	37 786	24 390	64.5	23 031	1 359	5.6
2019	43 173	29 170	67.6	27 001	2 169	7.4	38 062	24 576	64.6	23 261	1 315	5.3
Married, Spouse Present												
1995	54 166	41 806	77.2	40 262	1 544	3.7	54 902	33 563	61.1	32 267	1 296	3.9
1996	53 996	41 837	77.5	40 356	1 481	3.5	54 640	33 382	61.1	32 258	1 124	3.4
1997	53 981	41 967	77.7	40 628	1 339	3.2	54 611	33 907	62.1	32 836	1 071	3.2
1998	54 685	42 288	77.3	41 039	1 249	3.0	55 241	34 136	61.8	33 028	1 108	3.2
1999	55 256	42 557	77.0	41 476	1 081	2.5	55 801	34 349	61.6	33 403	946	2.8
2000	55 897	43 254	77.4	42 261	993	2.3	56 432	34 959	61.9	33 998	961	2.7
2001	56 152	43 463	77.4	42 245	1 218	2.8	56 740	35 234	62.1	34 273	961	2.7
2002	57 325	44 271	77.2	42 508	1 763	4.0	57 883	35 624	61.5	34 295	1 329	3.7
2003	57 940	44 700	77.1	42 797	1 903	4.3	58 545	36 185	61.8	34 806	1 379	3.8
2004	58 395	44 860	76.8	43 247	1 613	3.6	59 008	35 918	60.9	34 582	1 336	3.7
2005	58 854	45 263	76.9	43 763	1 500	3.3	59 449	35 809	60.2	34 738	1 071	3.0
2006	58 850	45 082	76.6	43 877	1 205	2.7	59 476	36 192	60.9	35 185	1 007	2.8
2007	60 126	46 129	76.7	44 813	1 317	2.9	60 656	37 335	61.6	36 370	965	2.6
2008	59 455	45 451	76.4	43 958	1 493	3.3	60 108	37 074	61.7	35 919	1 155	3.1
2009	60 132	45 741	76.1	42 667	3 074	6.7	60 818	37 536	61.7	35 540	1 996	5.3
2010	59 694	45 110	75.6	41 762	3 348	7.4	60 339	37 201	61.7	34 964	2 237	6.0
2011	59 477	44 553	74.9	41 667	2 886	6.5	60 095	36 383	60.5	34 340	2 043	5.6
2012	60 346	44 915	74.4	42 387	2 528	5.6	61 011	36 363	59.6	34 423	1 940	5.3
2013	60 630	44 904	74.1	42 760	2 145	4.8	61 269	36 292	59.2	34 601	1 691	4.7
2014	61 224	44 874	73.3	43 091	1 784	4.0	61 917	36 257	58.6	34 759	1 499	4.1
2015	61 568	45 185	73.4	43 783	1 403	3.1	62 171	36 388	58.5	35 314	1 074	3.0
2016	61 973	45 348	73.2	44 021	1 327	2.9	62 577	36 858	58.9	35 731	1 127	3.1
2017	62 699	45 820	73.1	44 536	1 284	2.8	63 295	37 414	59.1	36 383	1 031	2.8
2018	63 026	45 855	72.8	44 759	1 096	2.4	63 683	37 136	58.3	36 176	960	2.6
2019	63 648	46 038	72.3	45 104	935	2.0	64 505	38 204	59.2	37 375	829	2.2
Widowed, Divorced, or Separated												
1995	12 410	8 315	67.0	7 632	683	8.2	25 373	12 001	47.3	11 308	693	5.8
1996	13 176	8 697	66.0	7 976	721	8.3	25 786	12 430	48.2	11 742	688	5.5
1997	14 113	9 420	66.7	8 715	705	7.5	26 301	12 814	48.7	12 071	743	5.8
1998	14 166	9 482	66.9	8 954	528	5.6	26 092	12 880	49.4	12 235	645	5.0
1999	14 225	9 449	66.4	8 971	478	5.1	26 199	12 951	49.4	12 307	644	5.0
2000	14 289	9 623	67.3	9 152	471	4.9	26 354	13 228	50.2	12 657	571	4.3
2001	14 392	9 421	65.5	8 927	494	5.2	26 747	13 454	50.3	12 887	567	4.2
2002	14 617	9 650	66.0	8 931	719	7.5	27 802	13 716	49.3	12 855	861	6.3
2003	15 180	9 855	64.9	9 020	835	8.5	28 240	14 154	50.1	13 240	914	6.5
2004	15 059	9 789	65.0	9 059	730	7.5	28 228	14 194	50.3	13 324	870	6.1
2005	15 779	10 256	65.0	9 569	687	6.7	28 576	14 233	49.8	13 472	761	5.3
2006	16 405	10 815	65.9	10 141	674	6.2	28 981	14 220	49.1	13 539	681	4.8
2007	16 247	10 799	66.5	10 150	650	6.0	28 950	14 320	49.5	13 620	700	4.9
2008	16 718	10 896	65.2	10 083	812	7.5	29 419	14 553	49.5	13 765	787	5.4
2009	16 719	10 687	63.9	9 224	1 463	13.7	29 471	14 449	49.0	13 169	1 281	8.9
2010	17 016	10 863	63.8	9 188	1 675	15.4	29 915	14 707	49.2	13 285	1 422	9.7
2011	17 744	11 095	62.5	9 676	1 420	12.8	29 876	14 610	48.9	13 221	1 389	9.5
2012	17 704	11 076	62.6	9 884	1 192	10.8	30 367	14 825	48.8	13 543	1 283	8.7
2013	18 090	11 045	61.1	9 968	1 077	10.8	30 633	14 688	47.9	13 494	1 193	8.1
2014	17 833	10 681	59.9	9 842	839	7.9	30 657	14 853	48.4	13 789	1 064	7.2
2015	18 277	10 973	60.0	10 110	864	7.9	31 135	14 607	46.9	13 792	815	5.6
2016	18 205	10 901	59.9	10 210	691	6.3	31 044	14 659	47.2	13 966	693	4.7
2017	18 445	10 883	59.0	10 333	549	5.0	31 000	14 375	46.4	13 643	731	5.1
2018	18 652	10 987	58.9	10 445	542	4.9	31 296	14 503	46.3	13 889	615	4.2
2019	18 206	10 540	57.9	10 029	511	4.8	30 932	14 181	45.8	13 647	534	3.8

Note: See notes and definitions for information on historical comparability.

Table 1-45. Employment Status of the Population, by Sex and Marital Status, March 1995–March 2019 —*Continued*

(Thousands of people, percent.)

Marital status and year	Men						Women					
		Labor force						Labor force				
	Population	Total		Employed	Unemployed		Population	Total		Employed	Unemployed	
		Number	Percent of population		Number	Percent of labor force		Number	Percent of population		Number	Percent of labor force
Widowed												
1995	2 282	496	21.7	469	27	5.4	11 080	1 941	17.5	1 844	97	5.0
1996	2 476	487	19.7	466	21	4.3	11 070	1 916	17.3	1 820	96	5.0
1997	2 686	559	20.8	529	30	5.4	11 058	2 018	18.2	1 926	92	4.6
1998	2 567	563	21.9	551	12	2.1	11 027	2 157	19.6	2 071	86	4.0
1999	2 540	562	22.1	532	30	5.3	10 943	2 039	18.6	1 942	97	4.8
2000	2 601	583	22.4	547	36	6.2	11 061	2 011	18.2	1 911	100	5.0
2001	2 638	568	21.5	546	22	3.9	11 182	2 137	19.1	2 045	92	4.3
2002	2 635	629	23.9	581	48	7.6	11 411	2 001	17.5	1 887	114	5.7
2003	2 694	628	23.3	588	40	6.4	11 295	2 087	18.5	1 991	96	4.6
2004	2 651	581	21.9	558	23	4.0	11 159	2 157	19.3	2 048	109	5.1
2005	2 729	618	22.6	590	28	4.5	11 125	2 111	19.0	2 005	106	5.0
2006	2 626	610	23.2	563	47	7.7	11 305	2 164	19.1	2 094	70	3.2
2007	2 697	631	23.4	588	43	6.8	11 220	2 058	18.3	1 971	87	4.2
2008	2 911	656	22.5	611	44	6.8	11 399	2 218	19.5	2 101	117	5.3
2009	2 813	632	22.5	543	90	14.2	11 446	2 174	19.0	2 032	143	6.6
2010	2 969	776	26.1	684	92	11.8	11 379	2 214	19.5	2 036	178	8.0
2011	2 931	698	23.8	648	50	7.1	11 310	2 291	20.3	2 118	173	7.6
2012	2 864	639	22.3	595	43	6.8	11 197	2 179	19.5	2 044	135	6.2
2013	3 122	686	22.0	631	55	8.1	11 234	2 132	19.0	1 987	145	6.8
2014	3 068	722	23.5	668	54	7.5	11 132	2 079	18.7	1 922	157	7.6
2015	3 271	782	23.9	746	36	4.6	11 333	2 153	19.0	2 035	119	5.5
2016	3 471	904	26.1	862	42	4.7	11 423	2 224	19.5	2 139	85	3.8
2017	3 280	810	24.7	758	52	6.5	11 684	2 369	20.3	2 244	125	5.3
2018	3 410	841	24.7	784	57	6.8	11 704	2 331	19.9	2 231	101	4.3
2019	3 471	828	23.8	801	26	3.2	11 433	2 123	18.6	2 041	81	3.8
Divorced												
1995	7 343	5 739	78.2	5 266	473	8.2	10 262	7 559	73.7	7 206	353	4.7
1996	7 734	5 954	77.0	5 468	486	8.2	10 508	7 829	74.5	7 468	361	4.6
1997	8 191	6 298	76.9	5 851	447	7.1	11 102	8 092	72.9	7 666	426	5.3
1998	8 307	6 378	76.8	6 045	333	5.2	11 065	8 038	72.6	7 687	351	4.4
1999	8 529	6 481	76.0	6 151	330	5.1	11 130	8 171	73.4	7 841	330	4.0
2000	8 532	6 583	77.2	6 279	304	4.6	11 061	8 505	76.9	8 217	288	3.4
2001	8 580	6 403	74.6	6 074	329	5.1	11 719	8 662	73.9	8 335	327	3.8
2002	8 643	6 519	75.4	6 053	466	7.1	12 227	8 902	72.8	8 416	486	5.5
2003	8 938	6 621	74.1	6 052	569	8.6	12 653	9 191	72.6	8 673	518	5.6
2004	8 942	6 622	74.1	6 104	518	7.8	12 817	9 246	72.1	8 706	540	5.8
2005	9 196	6 754	73.4	6 281	473	7.0	12 950	9 253	71.5	8 836	417	4.5
2006	9 646	7 065	73.2	6 631	434	6.1	13 107	9 188	70.1	8 799	389	4.2
2007	9 608	7 110	74.0	6 679	431	6.1	13 214	9 334	70.6	8 896	439	4.7
2008	9 767	7 106	72.8	6 607	499	7.0	13 551	9 387	69.3	8 938	449	4.8
2009	9 938	7 052	71.0	6 064	988	14.0	13 301	9 176	69.0	8 402	774	8.4
2010	9 944	7 018	70.6	5 888	1 131	16.1	13 758	9 394	68.3	8 510	885	9.4
2011	10 635	7 394	69.5	6 430	965	13.0	13 757	9 230	67.1	8 407	823	8.9
2012	10 662	7 394	69.3	6 572	822	11.1	14 210	9 416	66.3	8 620	797	8.5
2013	10 923	7 420	67.9	6 718	702	9.5	14 428	9 416	65.3	8 704	713	7.6
2014	10 630	7 044	66.3	6 456	588	8.3	14 633	9 615	65.7	9 020	596	6.2
2015	10 928	7 197	65.9	6 598	600	8.3	14 855	9 365	63.0	8 901	464	5.0
2016	10 689	7 117	66.6	6 671	446	6.3	14 835	9 358	63.1	8 923	435	4.7
2017	10 873	7 084	65.1	6 754	330	4.7	14 606	9 048	61.9	8 658	390	4.3
2018	11 031	7 188	65.2	6 845	343	4.8	14 830	9 143	61.6	8 822	321	3.5
2019	10 618	6 845	64.5	6 504	341	5.0	14 803	9 077	61.3	8 780	298	3.3
Separated												
1995	2 784	2 081	74.7	1 898	183	8.8	4 031	2 501	62.0	2 258	243	9.7
1996	2 966	2 255	76.0	2 041	214	9.5	4 209	2 684	63.8	2 453	231	8.6
1997	3 236	2 563	79.2	2 335	228	8.9	4 141	2 705	65.3	2 480	225	8.3
1998	3 293	2 542	77.2	2 358	184	7.2	4 000	2 683	67.1	2 476	207	7.7
1999	3 156	2 405	76.2	2 287	118	4.9	4 126	2 740	66.4	2 523	217	7.9
2000	3 157	2 456	77.8	2 326	130	5.3	4 012	2 711	67.6	2 528	183	6.8
2001	3 174	2 450	77.2	2 307	143	5.8	3 846	2 654	69.0	2 507	147	5.5
2002	3 339	2 502	74.9	2 297	205	8.2	4 164	2 812	67.5	2 551	261	9.3
2003	3 548	2 606	73.4	2 380	226	8.7	4 293	2 877	67.0	2 576	301	10.5
2004	3 466	2 586	74.6	2 397	189	7.3	4 251	2 791	65.7	2 569	222	8.0
2005	3 855	2 884	74.8	2 698	186	6.4	4 501	2 870	63.8	2 632	238	8.3
2006	4 132	3 141	76.0	2 947	194	6.2	4 569	2 869	62.8	2 647	222	7.7
2007	3 943	3 058	77.6	2 883	176	5.7	4 516	2 927	64.8	2 753	174	6.0
2008	4 040	3 134	77.6	2 865	269	8.6	4 469	2 947	65.9	2 726	221	7.5
2009	3 968	3 002	75.7	2 617	386	12.8	4 725	3 099	65.6	2 734	364	11.8
2010	4 103	3 069	74.8	2 616	452	14.7	4 778	3 099	64.8	2 739	359	11.6
2011	4 178	3 004	71.9	2 598	406	13.5	4 809	3 089	64.2	2 696	393	12.7
2012	4 177	3 044	72.9	2 717	327	10.7	4 960	3 230	65.1	2 879	351	10.9
2013	4 045	2 939	72.7	2 619	320	10.9	4 970	3 139	63.2	2 803	336	10.7
2014	4 134	2 915	70.5	2 718	197	6.8	4 892	3 159	64.6	2 848	311	9.9
2015	4 078	2 994	73.4	2 706	228	7.6	4 946	3 089	62.5	2 856	233	7.5
2016	4 045	2 879	71.2	2 677	202	7.0	4 786	3 077	64.3	2 905	172	5.6
2017	4 291	2 989	69.6	2 822	167	5.6	4 710	2 958	62.8	2 742	216	7.3
2018	4 211	2 958	70.2	2 816	142	4.8	4 762	3 029	63.6	2 836	193	6.4
2019	4 117	2 868	69.7	2 724	144	5.0	4 696	2 981	63.5	2 826	155	5.2

Note: See notes and definitions for information on historical comparability.

Table 1-46. Employment Status of All Women and Single Women, by Presence and Age of Children, March 1995–March 2019

(Thousands of women, percent.)

Presence and age of children and year	All women							Single women						
	Civilian labor force	Civilian labor force as percent of population	Employed			Unemployed		Civilian labor force	Civilian labor force as percent of population	Employed			Unemployed	
			Number	Percent full time	Percent part time	Number	Percent of labor force			Number	Percent full time	Percent part time	Number	Percent of labor force
Women with No Children Under 18 Years														
1995	35 843	52.9	34 054	72.9	27.1	1 789	5.0	12 870	67.1	11 919	64.5	35.5	951	7.4
1996	36 509	53.0	34 698	73.3	26.7	1 811	5.0	13 172	66.1	12 255	64.6	35.4	918	7.0
1997	37 295	53.6	35 572	73.7	26.3	1 723	4.6	13 405	66.5	12 442	64.0	36.0	964	7.2
1998	38 253	54.1	36 680	74.1	25.9	1 573	4.1	13 888	67.2	13 082	64.8	35.2	806	5.8
1999	39 316	54.3	37 589	74.6	25.4	1 727	4.4	14 435	67.1	13 491	65.6	34.4	944	6.5
2000	40 142	54.8	38 408	75.4	24.6	1 733	4.3	14 677	67.6	13 713	66.6	33.4	964	6.6
2001	40 836	54.9	39 219	75.7	24.3	1 617	4.0	14 877	67.4	13 993	67.3	32.7	884	5.9
2002	41 278	54.0	39 038	75.1	24.9	2 241	5.4	14 855	65.6	13 682	65.9	34.1	1 173	7.9
2003	42 039	54.1	39 667	74.8	25.2	2 372	5.6	14 678	63.5	13 430	65.1	34.9	1 249	8.5
2004	42 289	53.8	40 000	74.6	25.4	2 289	5.4	14 828	63.0	13 670	65.5	34.5	1 157	7.8
2005	42 039	54.1	39 667	74.8	25.2	2 372	5.6	14 678	63.5	13 430	65.1	34.9	1 249	8.5
2006	43 392	53.6	41 440	75.3	24.7	1 952	4.5	15 673	63.4	14 547	66.5	33.5	1 125	7.2
2007	44 039	53.9	42 279	75.3	24.7	1 760	4.0	15 704	63.4	14 801	66.4	33.6	903	5.7
2008	45 585	54.3	43 417	75.7	24.3	2 168	4.8	16 378	63.4	15 261	67.4	32.6	1 116	6.8
2009	45 649	53.8	42 343	73.3	26.7	3 306	7.2	16 112	62.1	14 607	64.9	35.1	1 506	9.3
2010	46 098	53.5	42 256	73.5	26.5	3 842	8.3	16 331	60.7	14 533	65.6	34.4	1 798	11.0
2011	46 198	53.0	42 569	73.3	26.7	3 629	7.9	16 758	60.8	15 016	65.2	34.8	1 743	10.4
2012	47 222	52.6	43 494	74.0	26.0	3 728	7.9	17 310	60.7	15 473	66.3	33.7	1 837	10.6
2013	47 607	52.3	44 294	73.6	26.4	3 313	7.0	17 650	60.5	15 915	65.5	34.5	1 735	9.8
2014	48 076	52.1	44 980	73.3	26.7	3 096	6.4	18 168	61.2	16 552	65.1	34.9	1 616	8.9
2015	48 273	51.7	45 794	74.4	25.6	2 479	5.1	18 199	60.2	16 873	67.9	32.1	1 326	7.3
2016	49 663	52.1	47 180	74.5	25.5	2 484	5.0	19 130	60.9	17 699	68.0	32.0	1 430	7.5
2017	50 675	52.5	48 541	74.7	25.3	2 134	4.2	19 711	62.2	18 603	68.6	31.4	1 108	5.6
2018	51 227	52.3	49 247	74.7	25.3	1 980	3.9	20 359	62.8	19 323	68.6	31.4	1 035	5.1
2019	52 068	52.5	50 244	75.4	24.6	1 824	3.5	20 692	62.9	19 682	70.3	29.7	1 010	4.9
Women with Children Under 18 Years														
1995	24 695	69.7	23 195	71.7	28.3	1 500	6.1	2 104	57.5	1 754	73.6	26.4	350	16.6
1996	24 720	70.2	23 386	72.6	27.4	1 334	5.4	2 245	60.5	1 829	73.5	26.5	416	18.5
1997	25 604	72.1	24 082	74.1	25.9	1 522	5.9	2 772	68.1	2 305	76.6	23.4	467	16.8
1998	25 647	72.3	24 209	74.0	26.0	1 438	5.6	2 997	72.5	2 544	75.6	24.4	453	15.1
1999	25 469	72.1	24 305	74.1	25.9	1 165	4.6	3 051	73.4	2 694	75.8	24.2	357	11.7
2000	25 795	72.9	24 693	74.6	25.4	1 102	4.3	3 073	73.9	2 734	79.7	20.3	339	11.0
2001	25 751	73.1	24 572	75.6	24.4	1 179	4.6	3 022	73.8	2 638	81.8	18.2	385	12.7
2002	26 140	72.2	24 612	74.8	25.2	1 529	5.8	3 224	75.3	2 818	79.1	20.9	406	12.6
2003	26 202	71.7	24 598	74.3	25.7	1 603	6.1	3 222	73.1	2 789	79.5	20.5	433	13.4
2004	25 913	70.7	24 413	74.2	25.8	1 501	5.8	3 262	72.6	2 836	76.8	23.2	426	13.1
2005	26 202	71.7	24 598	74.3	25.7	1 603	6.1	3 222	73.1	2 789	79.5	20.5	433	13.4
2006	26 009	70.6	24 728	75.6	24.4	1 281	4.9	3 317	71.5	2 896	77.8	22.2	420	12.7
2007	26 834	71.3	25 646	75.2	24.8	1 188	4.4	3 514	71.4	3 133	76.4	23.6	381	10.8
2008	25 930	71.2	24 637	75.7	24.3	1 294	5.0	3 511	71.0	3 108	78.0	22.0	403	11.5
2009	26 122	71.6	24 079	74.6	25.4	2 043	7.8	3 673	72.0	3 108	75.8	24.2	566	18.2
2010	25 783	71.3	23 510	73.7	26.3	2 273	8.8	3 642	70.1	2 984	71.9	28.1	659	18.1
2011	25 376	70.9	23 109	74.2	25.8	2 266	8.9	3 822	70.0	3 102	71.9	28.1	721	18.9
2012	25 384	70.9	23 366	75.4	24.6	2 018	7.9	4 108	71.5	3 422	73.2	26.8	686	16.7
2013	25 112	70.3	23 121	74.8	25.2	1 991	7.9	4 088	71.3	3 404	71.9	28.1	684	16.7
2014	25 209	70.8	23 542	75.6	24.4	1 667	6.6	4 007	71.4	3 423	74.8	25.2	584	14.6
2015	25 107	69.9	23 841	76.3	23.7	1 265	5.0	4 186	72.2	3 657	74.5	25.5	529	12.6
2016	25 070	70.8	23 877	76.4	23.6	1 193	4.8	4 086	72.8	3 660	73.3	26.7	426	10.4
2017	24 863	71.3	23 748	77.2	22.8	1 114	4.5	4 038	73.4	3 659	77.0	23.0	378	9.4
2018	24 802	71.4	23 849	77.9	22.1	953	3.8	4 031	75.0	3 708	77.8	22.2	324	8.0
2019	24 892	72.4	24 038	78.8	21.2	854	3.4	3 884	74.9	3 579	78.4	21.6	305	7.8
Women with Children Under 6 Years														
1995	10 395	62.3	9 587	67.5	32.5	809	7.8	1 328	53.0	1 069	68.6	31.4	259	19.5
1996	10 293	62.3	9 592	68.4	31.6	701	6.8	1 378	55.1	1 099	67.3	32.7	279	20.2
1997	10 610	65.0	9 800	70.5	29.5	810	7.6	1 755	65.1	1 424	71.6	28.4	330	18.8
1998	10 619	65.2	9 839	69.8	30.2	780	7.3	1 755	67.3	1 448	71.7	28.3	307	17.5
1999	10 322	64.4	9 674	69.0	31.0	648	6.3	1 811	68.1	1 565	71.0	29.0	246	13.6
2000	10 316	65.3	9 763	70.5	29.5	553	5.4	1 835	70.5	1 603	75.3	24.7	232	12.6
2001	10 200	64.9	9 618	71.2	28.8	582	5.7	1 783	69.7	1 542	79.1	20.9	242	13.6
2002	10 193	64.1	9 441	70.4	29.6	752	7.4	1 819	71.0	1 568	74.5	25.5	251	13.8
2003	10 209	62.9	9 433	70.0	30.0	776	7.6	1 893	70.2	1 614	75.2	24.8	279	14.7
2004	10 131	62.2	9 407	69.4	30.6	724	7.1	1 885	68.4	1 605	70.1	29.9	279	14.8
2005	10 209	62.9	9 433	70.0	30.0	776	7.6	1 893	70.2	1 614	75.2	24.8	279	14.7
2006	10 430	63.0	9 779	72.0	28.0	651	6.2	1 934	68.6	1 659	72.8	27.2	276	14.3
2007	10 894	63.5	10 305	71.9	28.1	589	5.4	2 066	67.4	1 827	72.7	27.3	239	11.6
2008	10 452	63.6	9 794	72.1	27.9	657	6.3	1 982	66.0	1 705	72.2	27.8	277	14.0
2009	10 497	63.6	9 517	71.8	28.2	980	9.3	2 137	67.8	1 754	70.3	29.7	383	17.9
2010	10 536	64.2	9 452	70.9	29.1	1 085	10.3	2 076	65.6	1 643	67.0	33.0	433	20.9
2011	10 403	64.2	9 268	71.3	28.7	1 135	10.9	2 177	65.8	1 678	65.5	34.5	499	22.9
2012	10 462	64.7	9 458	72.6	27.4	1 004	9.6	2 408	68.1	1 958	69.0	31.0	450	18.7
2013	10 171	64.7	9 212	72.8	27.2	958	9.4	2 305	68.2	1 864	66.7	33.3	441	19.1
2014	9 982	64.3	9 153	73.5	26.5	829	8.3	2 221	67.6	1 836	71.7	28.3	385	17.3
2015	10 048	63.9	9 405	73.4	26.6	643	6.4	2 333	68.5	1 993	68.9	31.1	340	14.6
2016	9 934	65.3	9 358	73.9	26.1	576	5.8	2 161	68.6	1 903	69.4	30.6	258	11.9
2017	9 783	65.1	9 268	74.5	25.5	515	5.3	2 088	68.9	1 852	72.4	27.6	236	11.3
2018	9 749	64.7	9 304	74.5	25.5	445	4.6	2 078	71.3	1 884	73.1	26.9	194	9.3
2019	9 920	66.4	9 513	75.9	24.1	407	4.1	2 003	70.9	1 816	75.0	25.0	187	9.3

Note: See notes and definitions for information on historical comparability.

Table 1-47. Employment Status of Ever-Married Women and Married Women, Spouse Present, by Presence and Age of Children, March 1995–March 2019

(Thousands of women, percent.)

Presence and age of children and year	Ever-married women[1]							Married women, spouse present						
	Civilian labor force	Civilian labor force as percent of population	Employed			Unemployed		Civilian labor force	Civilian labor force as percent of population	Employed			Unemployed	
			Number	Percent full time	Percent part time	Number	Percent of labor force			Number	Percent full time	Percent part time	Number	Percent of labor force
Women with No Children Under 18 Years														
1995	22 973	47.3	22 134	77.4	22.6	839	3.7	15 594	53.2	15 072	76.3	23.7	522	3.3
1996	23 337	47.7	22 444	78.1	21.9	893	3.8	15 628	53.4	15 123	76.8	23.2	506	3.2
1997	23 890	48.3	23 130	78.9	21.1	760	3.2	15 750	54.2	15 315	77.7	22.3	435	2.8
1998	24 366	48.7	23 598	79.3	20.7	767	3.1	16 007	54.1	15 581	78.3	21.7	426	2.7
1999	24 881	48.9	24 098	79.7	20.3	783	3.1	16 484	54.4	16 061	78.2	21.8	423	2.6
2000	25 465	49.4	24 695	80.3	19.7	769	3.0	16 786	54.7	16 357	79.1	20.9	429	2.6
2001	25 959	49.6	25 226	80.4	19.6	733	2.8	16 909	54.8	16 528	78.7	21.3	381	2.3
2002	26 423	49.1	25 356	80.0	20.0	1 068	4.0	17 353	54.8	16 780	78.4	21.6	573	3.3
2003	27 361	50.1	26 238	79.7	20.3	1 123	4.1	17 901	55.7	17 273	78.6	21.4	628	3.5
2004	27 461	49.8	26 329	79.3	20.7	1 131	4.1	17 965	55.0	17 367	78.6	21.4	598	3.3
2005	27 361	50.1	26 238	79.7	20.3	1 123	4.1	17 901	55.7	17 273	78.6	21.4	628	3.5
2006	27 719	49.3	26 893	80.1	19.9	827	3.0	18 124	54.8	17 691	79.3	20.7	434	2.4
2007	28 335	49.8	27 477	80.1	19.9	858	3.0	18 766	55.4	18 326	79.6	20.4	441	2.3
2008	29 207	50.3	28 156	80.2	19.8	1 052	3.6	19 188	55.9	18 650	79.8	20.2	539	2.8
2009	29 536	50.2	27 737	77.8	22.2	1 800	6.1	19 541	55.8	18 521	77.3	22.7	1 019	5.2
2010	29 767	50.2	27 723	77.7	22.3	2 044	6.9	19 579	55.8	18 454	77.3	22.7	1 125	5.7
2011	29 440	49.4	27 553	77.7	22.3	1 886	6.4	19 316	54.6	18 285	77.4	22.6	1 031	5.3
2012	29 912	48.8	28 021	78.2	21.8	1 891	6.3	19 617	53.6	18 536	77.8	22.2	1 081	5.5
2013	29 956	48.4	28 379	78.1	21.9	1 578	5.3	19 507	53.3	18 706	77.5	22.5	801	4.1
2014	29 908	47.8	28 428	78.0	22.0	1 480	4.9	19 350	52.0	18 582	77.5	22.5	768	4.1
2015	30 074	47.6	28 921	78.2	21.8	1 153	3.8	19 609	52.5	19 009	77.6	22.4	600	3.1
2016	30 534	47.8	29 481	78.3	21.7	1 053	3.4	19 977	52.6	19 392	78.2	21.8	584	2.9
2017	30 964	47.7	29 938	78.4	21.6	1 026	3.3	20 483	52.7	19 978	77.9	22.1	505	2.5
2018	30 868	47.0	29 924	78.6	21.4	945	3.1	20 227	51.6	19 698	78.5	21.5	529	2.6
2019	31 376	47.4	30 563	78.7	21.3	814	2.6	21 006	52.6	20 568	78.6	21.4	438	2.1
Women with Children Under 18 Years														
1995	22 591	71.1	21 441	71.5	28.5	1 150	5.1	17 969	70.2	17 195	68.8	31.2	774	4.3
1996	22 475	71.4	21 556	72.5	27.5	919	4.1	17 754	70.0	17 136	69.6	30.4	618	3.5
1997	22 831	72.6	21 777	73.9	26.1	1 054	4.6	18 157	71.1	17 521	71.6	28.4	636	3.5
1998	22 650	72.3	21 665	73.8	26.2	985	4.3	18 129	70.6	17 447	71.5	28.5	682	3.8
1999	22 419	71.9	21 611	73.9	26.1	808	3.6	17 865	70.1	17 342	71.5	28.5	523	2.9
2000	22 722	72.7	21 960	74.0	26.0	763	3.4	18 174	70.6	17 641	71.7	28.3	533	2.9
2001	22 729	73.0	21 934	74.9	25.1	795	3.5	18 325	70.8	17 745	72.6	27.4	580	3.2
2002	22 917	71.8	21 794	74.3	25.7	1 122	4.9	18 271	69.6	17 515	71.7	28.3	756	4.1
2003	22 979	71.5	21 809	73.7	26.3	1 170	5.1	18 284	69.2	17 533	71.0	29.0	751	4.1
2004	22 651	70.5	21 576	73.8	26.2	1 075	4.7	17 953	68.2	17 215	71.3	28.7	738	4.1
2005	22 979	71.5	21 809	73.7	26.3	1 170	5.1	18 284	69.2	17 533	71.0	29.0	751	4.1
2006	22 692	70.5	21 831	75.3	24.7	861	3.8	18 067	68.4	17 494	73.0	27.0	574	3.2
2007	23 320	71.3	22 513	75.0	25.0	807	3.5	18 569	69.3	18 045	72.6	27.4	524	2.8
2008	22 419	71.2	21 529	75.4	24.6	890	4.0	17 886	69.4	17 269	73.6	26.4	616	3.4
2009	22 449	71.5	20 972	74.5	25.5	1 477	6.6	17 995	69.8	17 018	73.1	26.9	977	5.4
2010	22 141	71.5	20 526	74.0	26.0	1 615	7.3	17 622	69.7	16 510	72.6	27.4	1 112	6.3
2011	21 553	71.1	20 008	74.6	25.4	1 546	7.2	17 067	69.1	16 055	73.1	26.9	1 012	5.9
2012	21 276	70.7	19 944	75.8	24.2	1 332	6.3	16 746	68.5	15 887	74.1	25.9	859	5.1
2013	21 024	70.1	19 717	75.3	24.7	1 306	6.2	16 786	68.1	15 896	74.1	25.9	890	5.3
2014	21 202	70.6	20 120	75.8	24.2	1 083	5.1	16 907	68.4	16 176	74.7	25.3	730	4.3
2015	20 921	69.5	20 185	76.7	23.3	736	3.5	16 779	67.6	16 305	75.3	24.7	474	2.8
2016	20 984	70.5	20 217	77.0	23.0	767	3.7	16 882	68.6	16 339	76.3	23.7	543	3.2
2017	20 825	70.9	20 089	77.2	22.8	736	3.5	16 931	69.3	16 406	76.2	23.8	525	3.1
2018	20 771	70.7	20 141	77.9	22.1	630	3.0	16 908	69.0	16 478	77.0	23.0	431	2.5
2019	21 008	71.9	20 459	78.9	21.1	549	2.6	17 197	70.1	16 807	77.9	22.1	390	2.3
Women with Children Under 6 Years														
1995	9 067	63.9	8 517	67.4	32.6	550	6.1	7 759	63.5	7 349	66.1	33.9	409	5.3
1996	8 915	63.6	8 493	68.6	31.4	422	4.7	7 590	62.7	7 297	66.5	33.5	293	3.9
1997	8 856	64.9	8 376	70.3	29.7	480	5.4	7 582	63.6	7 252	69.1	30.9	330	4.4
1998	8 864	64.8	8 391	69.5	30.5	473	5.3	7 655	63.7	7 309	68.1	31.9	346	4.5
1999	8 511	63.7	8 109	68.6	31.4	402	4.7	7 246	61.8	6 979	67.1	32.9	267	3.7
2000	8 481	64.3	8 159	69.5	30.5	321	3.8	7 341	62.8	7 087	68.1	31.9	254	3.5
2001	8 417	64.0	8 077	69.7	30.3	340	4.0	7 319	62.5	7 062	68.5	31.5	257	3.5
2002	8 373	62.8	7 873	69.6	30.4	501	6.0	7 166	60.8	6 804	67.7	32.3	363	5.1
2003	8 315	61.4	7 818	68.9	31.1	497	6.0	7 175	59.8	6 826	67.1	32.9	349	4.9
2004	8 246	61.0	7 801	69.3	30.7	445	5.4	7 107	59.3	6 774	68.1	31.9	332	4.7
2005	8 315	61.4	7 818	68.9	31.1	497	6.0	7 175	59.8	6 826	67.1	32.9	349	4.9
2006	8 496	61.9	8 121	71.8	28.2	375	4.4	7 366	60.3	7 092	70.6	29.4	274	3.7
2007	8 829	62.7	8 479	71.7	28.3	350	4.0	7 664	61.5	7 407	70.8	29.2	257	3.4
2008	8 470	63.0	8 089	72.1	27.9	381	4.5	7 285	61.6	6 999	70.9	29.1	285	3.9
2009	8 360	62.6	7 763	72.1	27.9	597	7.1	7 231	61.6	6 805	71.4	28.6	426	5.9
2010	8 460	63.8	7 809	71.7	28.3	651	7.7	7 227	62.5	6 741	71.5	28.5	486	6.7
2011	8 226	63.7	7 590	72.5	27.5	636	7.7	7 061	62.3	6 608	71.9	28.1	453	6.4
2012	8 054	63.7	7 501	73.5	26.5	554	6.9	6 878	62.3	6 491	72.7	27.3	387	5.6
2013	7 866	63.7	7 349	74.3	25.7	517	6.6	6 737	62.0	6 384	74.1	25.9	352	5.2
2014	7 761	63.4	7 317	73.9	26.1	444	5.7	6 663	61.5	6 326	73.7	26.3	336	5.0
2015	7 714	62.7	7 411	74.6	25.4	303	3.9	6 653	61.3	6 454	74.4	25.6	198	3.0
2016	7 773	64.4	7 455	75.0	25.0	318	4.1	6 715	62.9	6 483	74.6	25.4	232	3.4
2017	7 695	64.1	7 416	75.1	24.9	279	3.6	6 732	62.9	6 523	74.6	25.4	209	3.1
2018	7 671	63.1	7 420	74.8	25.2	251	3.3	6 789	61.8	6 596	74.2	25.8	193	2.8
2019	7 917	65.4	7 697	76.1	23.9	221	2.8	7 034	64.2	6 867	75.8	24.2	167	2.4

[1]Ever-married women are women who are, or have ever been, married.

Table 1-48. Employment Status of Women Who Maintain Families, by Marital Status and Presence and Age of Children, March 2000–March 2019

(Thousands of women, percent.)

Marital status, age of children, and year	Civilian noninstitutional population	Civilian labor force					Not in the labor force
		Number	Percent of the population	Employed	Unemployed		
					Number	Percent of the labor force	
Total, Women Who Maintain Families							
2000	13 145	9 226	70.2	8 592	634	6.9	3 918
2001	12 930	9 034	69.9	8 453	581	6.4	3 897
2002	13 489	9 523	70.6	8 755	768	8.1	3 966
2003	14 000	9 759	69.7	8 898	861	8.8	4 241
2004	14 165	9 869	69.7	9 054	815	8.3	4 297
2005	14 391	9 941	69.1	9 140	801	8.1	4 450
2006	14 485	9 966	68.8	9 227	739	7.4	4 520
2007	14 833	10 172	68.6	9 510	661	6.5	4 662
2008	14 820	10 166	68.6	9 447	719	7.1	4 654
2009	14 813	10 140	68.5	9 034	1 106	10.9	4 673
2010	15 214	10 206	67.1	9 027	1 179	11.6	5 008
2011	15 461	10 462	67.7	9 141	1 321	12.6	5 000
2012	16 122	11 009	68.3	9 807	1 202	10.9	5 113
2013	15 914	10 793	67.8	9 589	1 204	11.2	5 121
2014	15 612	10 505	67.3	9 511	994	9.5	5 107
2015	16 017	10 691	66.7	9 848	843	7.9	5 326
2016	16 003	10 695	66.8	9 988	707	6.6	5 308
2017	15 882	10 663	67.1	10 040	623	5.8	5 219
2018	15 700	10 460	66.6	9 875	585	5.6	5 241
2019	15 345	10 350	67.5	9 827	523	5.1	4 995
Women with No Children Under 18 Years							
2000	5 097	2 707	53.1	2 546	161	5.9	2 390
2001	5 185	2 772	53.5	2 668	104	3.8	2 413
2002	5 119	2 764	54.0	2 628	136	4.9	2 355
2003	5 457	2 934	53.8	2 728	206	7.0	2 522
2004	5 551	3 052	55.0	2 855	197	6.5	2 499
2005	5 692	3 095	54.4	2 961	134	4.3	2 597
2006	5 693	3 088	54.2	2 945	143	4.6	2 604
2007	5 823	3 124	53.7	2 990	134	4.3	2 699
2008	6 022	3 352	55.7	3 167	185	5.5	2 670
2009	6 068	3 332	54.9	3 075	258	7.7	2 735
2010	6 414	3 417	53.3	3 131	286	8.4	2 997
2011	6 403	3 455	54.0	3 131	324	9.4	2 948
2012	6 773	3 779	55.8	3 464	316	8.4	2 994
2013	6 822	3 790	55.5	3 466	324	8.5	3 032
2014	6 715	3 566	53.1	3 301	265	7.4	3 149
2015	6 977	3 732	53.5	3 521	211	5.7	3 246
2016	7 084	3 798	53.6	3 593	205	5.4	3 286
2017	7 317	4 034	55.1	3 860	173	4.3	3 284
2018	7 259	3 808	52.5	3 632	176	4.6	3 451
2019	7 335	3 952	53.9	3 798	154	3.9	3 383
Women with Children Under 18 Years							
2000	8 048	6 520	81.0	6 046	474	7.3	1 528
2001	7 746	6 261	80.8	5 785	476	7.6	1 484
2002	8 370	6 759	80.8	6 127	632	9.4	1 611
2003	8 543	6 825	79.9	6 170	655	9.6	1 718
2004	8 614	6 817	79.1	6 199	618	9.1	1 798
2005	8 699	6 846	78.7	6 179	667	9.7	1 853
2006	8 793	6 878	78.2	6 282	596	8.7	1 915
2007	9 010	7 047	78.2	6 520	527	7.5	1 963
2008	8 798	6 814	77.4	6 280	535	7.8	1 984
2009	8 745	6 807	77.8	5 959	848	12.5	1 938
2010	8 800	6 789	77.1	5 896	893	13.2	2 011
2011	9 059	7 007	77.4	6 009	998	14.2	2 052
2012	9 349	7 230	77.3	6 343	887	12.3	2 119
2013	9 092	7 003	77.0	6 123	880	12.6	2 089
2014	8 896	6 939	78.0	6 210	729	10.5	1 957
2015	9 040	6 959	77.0	6 327	632	9.1	2 081
2016	8 920	6 897	77.3	6 396	502	7.3	2 022
2017	8 565	6 630	77.4	6 180	450	6.8	1 935
2018	8 441	6 652	78.8	6 243	409	6.2	1 790
2019	8 010	6 398	79.9	6 029	369	5.8	1 612
Single Women with No Children Under 18 Years							
2000	1 004	720	71.7	642	78	10.8	284
2001	1 096	787	71.8	756	31	3.9	309
2002	1 154	796	69.0	747	49	6.2	358
2003	1 254	814	64.9	713	101	12.4	440
2004	1 381	977	70.7	887	90	9.2	404
2005	1 388	926	66.7	855	71	7.7	463
2006	1 370	933	68.1	861	72	7.7	437
2007	1 413	986	69.8	930	57	5.7	427
2008	1 515	1 057	69.8	989	68	6.5	458
2009	1 531	1 069	69.8	967	102	9.6	462
2010	1 718	1 166	67.9	1 041	125	10.7	552
2011	1 729	1 178	68.2	1 047	132	11.2	551

Note: See notes and definitions for information on historical comparability.

Table 1-48. Employment Status of Women Who Maintain Families, by Marital Status and Presence and Age of Children, March 2000–March 2019—*Continued*

(Thousands of women, percent.)

Marital status, age of children, and year	Civilian noninstitutional population	Civilian labor force					Not in the labor force
		Number	Percent of the population	Employed	Unemployed		
					Number	Percent of the labor force	
Single Women with No Children Under 18 Years—*Continued*							
2012	1 836	1 241	67.6	1 099	143	11.5	595
2013	1 933	1 322	68.4	1 178	144	10.9	611
2014	1 840	1 224	66.5	1 105	119	9.7	616
2015	2 008	1 288	64.1	1 203	85	6.6	720
2016	2 097	1 412	67.3	1 320	92	6.5	685
2017	2 301	1 579	68.6	1 493	87	5.5	722
2018	2 247	1 452	64.6	1 369	83	5.7	796
2019	2 323	1 622	69.8	1 551	71	4.4	701
Single Women with Children Under 18 Years							
2000	3 167	2 413	76.2	2 151	262	10.9	754
2001	3 097	2 351	75.9	2 055	296	12.6	745
2002	3 315	2 566	77.4	2 241	325	12.7	749
2003	3 421	2 584	75.5	2 272	312	12.1	837
2004	3 414	2 568	75.2	2 233	335	13.0	846
2005	3 591	2 708	75.4	2 325	383	14.1	882
2006	3 671	2 710	73.8	2 370	340	12.5	961
2007	3 748	2 782	74.2	2 491	291	10.4	966
2008	3 721	2 743	73.7	2 448	295	10.8	978
2009	3 872	2 877	74.3	2 448	429	14.9	995
2010	3 948	2 868	72.6	2 379	488	17.0	1 081
2011	4 193	3 072	73.3	2 522	550	17.9	1 120
2012	4 442	3 263	73.5	2 746	517	15.8	1 179
2013	4 403	3 220	73.1	2 698	522	16.2	1 183
2014	4 297	3 137	73.0	2 698	439	14.0	1 161
2015	4 438	3 296	74.3	2 889	407	12.4	1 142
2016	4 362	3 252	74.5	2 941	310	9.5	1 110
2017	4 278	3 201	74.8	2 928	273	8.5	1 078
2018	4 187	3 222	77.0	2 988	234	7.3	965
2019	4 002	3 074	76.8	2 830	244	7.9	928
Widowed, Divorced, or Separated Women with No Children Under 18 Years							
2000	4 093	1 987	48.5	1 904	83	4.2	2 106
2001	4 088	1 985	48.6	1 912	73	3.7	2 104
2002	3 964	1 968	49.6	1 882	86	4.4	1 997
2003	4 203	2 121	50.5	2 016	105	5.0	2 082
2004	4 170	2 075	49.8	1 968	107	5.2	2 095
2005	4 304	2 170	50.4	2 106	64	2.9	2 135
2006	4 323	2 156	49.9	2 084	72	3.3	2 168
2007	4 410	2 138	48.5	2 061	77	3.6	2 272
2008	4 507	2 295	50.9	2 178	117	5.1	2 213
2009	4 536	2 263	49.9	2 108	155	6.9	2 273
2010	4 696	2 251	47.9	2 090	161	7.1	2 445
2011	4 674	2 276	48.7	2 084	192	8.4	2 397
2012	4 937	2 538	51.4	2 365	173	6.8	2 399
2013	4 889	2 468	50.5	2 288	180	7.3	2 421
2014	4 875	2 342	48.0	2 196	146	6.2	2 533
2015	4 969	2 444	49.2	2 317	126	5.2	2 526
2016	4 987	2 386	47.8	2 273	113	4.7	2 601
2017	5 016	2 454	48.9	2 368	87	3.5	2 562
2018	5 012	2 356	47.0	2 263	93	4.0	2 655
2019	5 012	2 330	46.5	2 247	83	3.6	2 682
Widowed, Divorced, or Separated Women with Children Under 18 Years							
2000	4 881	4 107	84.1	3 895	212	5.2	774
2001	4 649	3 910	84.1	3 730	180	4.6	739
2002	5 056	4 193	82.9	3 886	307	7.3	862
2003	5 122	4 241	82.8	3 898	343	8.1	881
2004	5 201	4 249	81.7	3 966	283	6.7	952
2005	5 108	4 137	81.0	3 854	283	6.8	971
2006	5 121	4 167	81.4	3 912	255	6.1	955
2007	5 262	4 266	81.1	4 029	237	5.5	997
2008	5 077	4 071	80.2	3 832	239	5.9	1 006
2009	4 873	3 930	80.7	3 511	420	10.7	943
2010	4 852	3 922	80.8	3 517	405	10.3	931
2011	4 866	3 935	80.9	3 487	448	11.4	931
2012	4 907	3 966	80.8	3 597	370	9.3	940
2013	4 689	3 783	80.7	3 425	358	9.5	906
2014	4 599	3 802	82.7	3 512	290	7.6	797
2015	4 602	3 663	79.6	3 438	225	6.1	939
2016	4 558	3 646	80.0	3 455	191	5.2	912
2017	4 286	3 429	80.0	3 252	176	5.1	858
2018	4 255	3 430	80.6	3 255	175	5.1	825
2019	4 008	3 324	82.9	3 199	125	3.8	684

Note: See notes and definitions for information on historical comparability.

Table 1-49. Number and Age of Children in Families, by Type of Family and Labor Force Status of Mother, March 2000–March 2019

(Thousands of children.)

Age of children and year	Total children	Mother in labor force	Mother not in labor force	Married-couple families			Families maintained by women			Families maintained by men
				Total	Mother in labor force	Mother not in labor force	Total	Mother in labor force	Mother not in labor force	
Children Under 18 Years										
2000	65 601	44 188	18 674	48 902	33 149	15 753	13 960	11 039	2 921	2 739
2001	65 777	44 051	18 864	49 352	33 436	15 916	13 563	10 615	2 948	2 862
2002	65 978	43 821	19 243	48 836	32 673	16 163	14 228	11 149	3 079	2 914
2003	66 521	43 769	19 782	49 004	32 411	16 593	14 547	11 359	3 189	2 970
2004	66 386	43 144	20 229	48 656	31 892	16 764	14 717	11 252	3 465	3 014
2005	66 526	43 239	20 179	48 688	31 886	16 802	14 729	11 352	3 377	3 108
2006	66 883	43 278	20 440	48 853	31 946	16 908	14 865	11 332	3 532	3 165
2007	67 228	44 116	20 073	48 927	32 496	16 431	15 263	11 620	3 643	3 038
2008	67 153	43 798	19 966	48 303	32 110	16 193	15 461	11 688	3 773	3 388
2009	66 913	43 509	20 074	48 384	32 065	16 315	15 204	11 444	3 759	3 326
2010	66 811	43 335	19 913	47 730	31 686	16 044	15 518	11 649	3 869	3 563
2011	66 804	42 882	20 260	47 051	30 902	16 149	16 091	11 980	4 111	3 662
2012	66 472	42 643	19 885	45 989	30 228	15 761	16 539	12 414	4 125	3 944
2013	66 661	42 454	20 012	46 254	30 294	15 960	16 211	12 159	4 052	4 195
2014	66 137	42 447	19 718	46 428	30 471	15 958	15 737	11 977	3 760	3 972
2015	65 916	41 721	20 356	46 256	29 949	16 307	15 820	11 772	4 048	3 839
2016	66 124	42 427	19 675	46 198	30 450	15 748	15 903	11 976	3 927	4 022
2017	65 798	42 531	19 280	46 344	30 919	15 425	15 467	11 612	3 855	3 987
2018	65 979	42 506	19 275	46 563	30 666	15 897	15 218	11 840	3 378	4 198
2019	65 911	42 973	18 612	46 994	31 557	15 406	14 622	11 416	3 207	4 295
Children 6 to 17 Years Years										
2000	44 562	31 531	11 198	32 732	23 393	9 339	9 997	8 138	1 859	1 833
2001	44 458	31 411	11 153	32 957	23 599	9 358	9 608	7 813	1 795	1 894
2002	44 865	31 437	11 510	32 799	23 296	9 504	10 148	8 142	2 006	1 918
2003	45 273	31 559	11 635	32 782	23 160	9 622	10 412	8 399	2 013	2 080
2004	45 066	31 040	11 968	32 506	22 736	9 769	10 502	8 304	2 199	2 058
2005	45 027	30 930	11 995	32 412	22 565	9 847	10 514	8 366	2 148	2 102
2006	45 039	30 591	12 250	32 311	22 315	9 996	10 530	8 276	2 254	2 198
2007	45 155	31 252	11 855	32 417	22 788	9 629	10 690	8 464	2 226	2 048
2008	44 909	30 853	11 874	31 990	22 413	9 577	10 737	8 440	2 297	2 182
2009	44 595	30 600	11 811	31 966	22 425	9 537	10 449	8 175	2 274	2 180
2010	44 456	30 209	11 922	31 468	21 957	9 510	10 663	8 251	2 412	2 325
2011	44 471	29 904	12 244	31 072	21 365	9 707	11 076	8 539	2 537	2 323
2012	45 049	30 143	12 315	30 923	21 163	9 760	11 535	8 980	2 556	2 591
2013	45 492	30 091	12 694	31 411	21 352	10 058	11 375	8 738	2 636	2 707
2014	45 059	30 205	12 233	31 471	21 540	9 931	10 968	8 665	2 302	2 621
2015	44 817	29 490	12 830	31 359	21 090	10 269	10 961	8 400	2 560	2 498
2016	45 131	29 929	12 553	31 251	21 243	10 008	11 230	8 685	2 545	2 649
2017	44 756	30 136	12 002	31 118	21 617	9 500	11 021	8 519	2 502	2 618
2018	44 784	30 121	11 898	31 144	21 449	9 695	10 875	8 672	2 204	2 765
2019	44 815	30 341	11 554	31 460	21 939	9 504	10 451	8 401	2 050	2 903
Children Under 6 Years										
2000	21 039	12 657	7 476	16 170	9 757	6 413	3 963	2 901	1 062	906
2001	21 318	12 640	7 711	16 395	9 837	6 558	3 956	2 802	1 153	968
2002	21 113	12 384	7 733	16 037	9 377	6 660	4 080	3 007	1 073	996
2003	21 248	12 210	8 147	16 222	9 251	6 971	4 136	2 960	1 176	890
2004	21 321	12 104	8 261	16 151	9 156	6 995	4 214	2 948	1 266	956
2005	21 498	12 308	8 184	16 276	9 321	6 955	4 216	2 987	1 229	1 006
2006	21 844	12 687	8 190	16 542	9 631	6 911	4 335	3 057	1 278	968
2007	22 073	12 864	8 218	16 509	9 708	6 802	4 572	3 156	1 416	991
2008	22 244	12 946	8 092	16 313	9 697	6 616	4 724	3 248	1 476	1 207
2009	22 318	12 909	8 263	16 418	9 640	6 778	4 755	3 270	1 485	1 146
2010	22 355	13 127	7 991	16 262	9 729	6 533	4 855	3 398	1 457	1 237
2011	22 333	12 978	8 015	15 979	9 537	6 442	5 015	3 441	1 573	1 340
2012	21 423	12 500	7 570	15 066	9 065	6 001	5 004	3 435	1 569	1 353
2013	21 169	12 363	7 317	14 844	8 942	5 902	4 837	3 421	1 416	1 489
2014	21 078	12 242	7 484	14 958	8 931	6 027	4 769	3 312	1 457	1 351
2015	21 099	12 231	7 526	14 898	8 859	6 038	4 860	3 372	1 488	1 341
2016	20 993	12 498	7 121	14 947	9 207	5 739	4 673	3 291	1 382	1 373
2017	21 041	12 395	7 278	15 227	9 302	5 925	4 446	3 093	1 353	1 368
2018	21 195	12 385	7 377	15 419	9 217	6 202	4 343	3 168	1 174	1 434
2019	21 096	12 632	7 059	15 533	9 618	5 902	4 171	3 014	1 157	1 392

Note: See notes and definitions for information on historical comparability.

Table 1-50. Number of Families and Median Family Income, by Type of Family and Earner Status of Members, 1995–2018

(Thousands of families, dollars.)

Number and type of families and median family income	1995	1996	1997	1998	1999	2000	2001	2002	2003	2004	2005	2006
NUMBER OF FAMILIES												
Married-Couple Families, Total	53 621	53 654	54 362	54 829	55 352	55 650	56 798	57 362	57 767	58 180	58 225	59 050
No earners	7 276	7 145	7 286	7 257	7 160	7 297	7 662	7 803	8 043	7 998	8 017	8 091
One earner	11 708	11 493	11 700	12 246	12 290	12 450	12 852	13 503	14 061	14 385	14 301	14 562
Husband	8 792	8 611	8 770	9 173	9 062	9 319	9 573	10 121	10 478	10 853	10 611	10 706
Wife	2 251	2 207	2 298	2 411	2 585	2 545	2 689	2 821	3 027	2 993	3 097	3 264
Other family member	666	674	632	662	643	586	590	560	557	539	593	591
Two earners	27 180	27 260	27 712	27 593	28 010	28 329	28 779	28 891	28 693	28 806	28 802	29 216
Husband and wife	25 274	25 274	25 731	25 696	26 134	26 447	26 829	26 966	26 860	26 758	26 833	27 241
Husband and other family member	1 393	1 483	1 406	1 306	1 325	1 277	1 424	1 391	1 322	1 462	1 376	1 358
Husband not an earner	513	502	575	590	552	605	526	534	511	586	594	616
Three earners or more	7 456	7 756	7 664	7 733	7 892	7 575	7 504	7 165	6 970	6 991	7 104	7 181
Husband and wife	6 770	7 126	7 023	7 102	7 220	6 917	6 859	6 565	6 349	6 459	6 535	6 620
Husband, not wife	531	479	478	456	528	537	530	455	467	381	445	397
Husband not an earner	155	150	163	176	144	120	115	145	154	152	124	165
Families Maintained by Women, Total	13 007	13 277	13 115	13 206	13 164	12 950	13 517	14 033	14 196	14 404	14 505	14 852
No earners	2 664	2 574	2 332	2 143	1 883	1 786	2 076	2 228	2 451	2 610	2 616	2 627
One earner	6 815	7 027	7 091	7 351	7 441	7 462	7 693	8 153	8 012	8 074	8 052	8 303
Householder	5 590	5 817	5 841	6 167	6 127	6 132	6 436	6 832	6 725	6 788	6 724	6 904
Other family member	1 225	1 211	1 251	1 183	1 314	1 331	1 257	1 321	1 286	1 285	1 329	1 398
Two earners or more	3 527	3 675	3 692	3 712	3 840	3 702	3 748	3 652	3 733	3 720	3 836	3 923
Householder and other family member(s)	3 225	3 431	3 398	3 399	3 508	3 376	3 442	3 290	3 364	3 399	3 468	3 547
Householder not an earner	302	245	294	313	332	325	306	362	369	321	368	376
Families Maintained by Men, Total	3 557	3 924	3 982	4 041	4 086	4 316	4 499	4 747	4 778	4 953	5 193	5 119
No earners	357	359	344	381	376	380	461	466	530	492	537	555
One earner	1 800	1 972	2 104	2 027	2 044	2 223	2 319	2 434	2 466	2 573	2 661	2 584
Householder	1 548	1 667	1 791	1 725	1 721	1 879	1 911	2 026	2 053	2 152	2 196	2 155
Other family member	253	305	313	302	323	344	408	408	413	421	464	429
Two earners or more	1 400	1 593	1 534	1 634	1 666	1 713	1 719	1 847	1 782	1 888	1 995	1 979
Householder and other family member(s)	1 302	1 469	1 427	1 532	1 522	1 585	1 629	1 709	1 625	1 736	1 848	1 828
Householder not an earner	98	124	107	102	143	128	90	138	157	152	147	152
MEDIAN FAMILY INCOME												
Married-Couple Families, Total	47 000	49 614	51 475	54 043	56 792	59 200	60 100	61 000	62 388	63 627	65 586	69 300
No earners	21 888	22 622	23 782	24 525	25 262	25 356	25 900	25 954	26 312	26 798	28 376	30 000
One earner	35 100	36 468	39 140	40 519	41 261	44 424	44 400	45 000	46 546	47 749	50 000	50 400
Husband	36 052	38 150	40 300	42 000	44 200	47 010	47 500	48 004	48 948	50 000	52 000	53 360
Wife	32 098	30 301	34 050	35 625	35 546	36 458	36 140	39 072	41 180	41 000	43 505	45 000
Other family member	37 784	39 644	40 317	42 414	41 120	45 492	44 270	40 927	45 936	46 324	50 263	49 352
Two earners	53 500	56 000	58 020	61 300	64 007	67 500	69 543	71 282	73 309	75 100	76 960	81 500
Husband and wife	53 626	56 392	58 564	61 900	64 950	68 132	70 000	72 150	74 500	76 000	77 539	82 762
Husband and other family member	52 530	49 610	53 854	57 680	53 541	56 503	65 240	62 848	60 100	66 120	67 350	68 828
Husband not an earner	47 121	46 990	47 979	50 955	52 466	53 430	58 725	54 840	58 000	63 050	65 622	63 657
Three earners or more	68 996	70 400	75 593	78 973	81 940	83 990	86 090	88 632	93 000	94 212	98 000	103 803
Husband and wife	69 371	71 148	76 105	79 907	83 000	84 634	87 000	89 962	94 353	95 524	99 800	104 045
Husband, not wife	60 360	61 824	68 890	71 001	69 561	79 050	76 230	82 180	77 316	87 000	79 417	91 965
Husband not an earner	61 196	55 495	62 684	63 205	69 275	68 050	80 661	68 400	91 771	73 137	84 638	97 510
Families Maintained by Women, Total	19 306	19 416	20 470	21 875	23 100	25 000	25 064	26 000	26 000	26 400	27 000	28 218
No earners	7 440	7 092	7 476	7 737	8 010	8 988	8 160	8 808	8 344	8 400	8 228	8 657
One earner	18 824	18 500	19 000	20 000	20 092	22 306	23 008	24 597	24 752	25 040	25 308	26 393
Householder	17 890	18 000	18 000	18 800	19 000	21 400	22 001	23 760	23 832	24 801	24 505	25 381
Other family member	23 166	21 000	22 870	25 981	26 800	27 524	28 476	29 524	28 857	29 700	31 700	31 462
Two earners or more	35 000	36 400	39 275	40 000	41 144	43 035	45 244	46 580	47 576	48 549	50 000	52 400
Householder and other family member(s)	34 674	36 400	39 000	39 713	40 855	43 000	44 842	46 000	46 701	47 974	48 989	51 479
Householder not an earner	39 444	38 249	47 471	43 725	48 004	45 600	51 000	51 248	57 267	56 799	64 805	61 699
Families Maintained by Men, Total	30 000	31 500	32 984	35 000	37 000	37 040	36 000	37 440	37 914	40 000	40 293	41 130
No earners	12 240	12 030	14 252	15 468	13 752	14 946	12 840	15 200	15 408	14 167	13 950	15 462
One earner	25 337	26 100	26 897	29 125	31 038	30 160	30 800	30 139	32 097	35 000	35 001	35 100
Householder	25 069	25 874	27 000	29 125	30 483	30 816	30 500	30 014	31 355	35 000	35 075	35 011
Other family member	27 291	28 584	25 486	28 241	34 756	29 118	31 052	32 000	35 525	35 438	35 000	37 840
Two earners or more	43 100	44 275	49 900	51 288	51 040	55 010	55 024	55 000	57 840	57 600	60 024	61 000
Householder and other family member(s)	43 000	43 065	50 000	50 954	50 960	55 400	54 850	55 220	57 400	57 058	60 000	61 000
Householder not an earner	55 133	47 001	44 786	68 257	57 407	51 945	61 824	49 852	64 658	65 400	70 879	62 000

Note: See notes and definitions for information on historical comparability.

Table 1-50. Number of Families and Median Family Income, by Type of Family and Earner Status of Members, 1995–2018—*Continued*

(Thousands of families, dollars.)

Number and type of families and median family income	2007	2008	2009	2010	2011	2012	2013	2014	2015	2016	2017	2018
NUMBER OF FAMILIES												
Married-Couple Families, Total	58 490	59 181	58 521	58 135	59 071	59 327	59 795	60 091	60 338	60 912	61 348	61 692
No earners	7 914	8 083	8 467	8 626	9 152	9 101	9 556	9 437	9 380	9 814	9 944	10 039
One earner	14 272	14 625	15 046	15 421	15 981	15 841	15 828	15 642	15 653	15 496	15 895	15 600
Husband	10 396	10 567	10 570	10 895	11 308	11 276	11 370	11 246	11 185	11 057	11 394	10 925
Wife	3 267	3 437	3 854	3 935	4 016	3 894	3 788	3 776	3 739	3 744	3 841	3 976
Other family member	608	620	621	591	658	671	669	620	729	695	660	699
Two earners	29 256	29 466	28 371	27 821	27 661	27 902	27 978	28 255	28 505	28 754	28 469	29 159
Husband and wife	27 264	27 531	26 298	25 801	25 581	25 718	25 846	25 978	26 251	26 502	26 181	26 597
Husband and other family member	1 393	1 308	1 363	1 317	1 370	1 447	1 457	1 561	1 520	1 553	1 540	1 454
Husband not an earner	599	627	710	703	710	738	675	716	735	699	748	790
Three earners or more	7 048	7 008	6 638	6 267	6 277	6 482	6 434	6 756	6 800	6 848	7 040	6 894
Husband and wife	6 452	6 393	6 024	5 609	5 621	5 865	5 839	6 002	6 061	6 139	6 239	6 065
Husband, not wife	452	432	425	466	462	435	389	521	514	501	552	547
Husband not an earner	144	182	189	192	193	182	206	233	224	208	249	249
Families Maintained by Women, Total	14 846	14 842	15 236	15 491	16 154	15 949	15 632	16 055	16 038	15 913	15 716	15 360
No earners	2 502	2 678	3 076	3 297	3 373	3 300	3 143	3 173	3 022	2 821	2 921	2 703
One earner	8 418	8 381	8 475	8 638	8 790	8 621	8 537	8 702	8 672	8 618	8 388	8 103
Householder	7 020	6 978	6 941	7 158	7 303	7 170	6 998	7 158	7 076	6 924	6 785	6 445
Other family member	1 398	1 404	1 533	1 480	1 487	1 451	1 538	1 544	1 596	1 695	1 604	1 658
Two earners or more	3 925	3 783	3 685	3 555	3 991	4 028	3 953	4 180	4 344	4 473	4 407	4 554
Householder and other family member(s)	3 572	3 467	3 281	3 149	3 552	3 623	3 438	3 700	3 880	3 971	3 897	4 045
Householder not an earner	353	316	405	406	439	405	515	480	465	502	509	509
Families Maintained by Men, Total	5 181	5 301	5 630	5 649	5 975	6 308	6 384	6 236	6 386	6 526	6 485	6 567
No earners	532	611	539	775	838	883	824	817	802	765	781	755
One earner	2 703	2 636	2 801	2 911	3 106	3 242	3 311	3 230	3 236	3 262	3 291	3 265
Householder	2 297	2 199	2 261	2 389	2 535	2 698	2 715	2 664	2 634	2 622	2 732	2 650
Other family member	406	437	539	521	571	544	595	566	601	640	558	615
Two earners or more	1 947	2 054	2 030	1 963	2 031	2 183	2 249	2 190	2 348	2 500	2 413	2 548
Householder and other family member(s)	1 812	1 889	1 822	1 751	1 811	1 951	2 029	1 981	2 156	2 271	2 213	2 343
Householder not an earner	134	165	208	212	220	232	220	208	193	228	200	204
MEDIAN FAMILY INCOME												
Married-Couple Families, Total	72 802	72 805	71 464	72 224	73 678	75 002	76 000	80 234	84 076	86 508	90 000	93 041
No earners	30 134	31 164	32 093	32 350	33 756	33 584	35 948	36 748	37 678	39 378	41 656	44 737
One earner	52 686	53 865	53 087	55 000	56 609	58 415	57 000	60 009	63 015	65 333	68 000	70 000
Husband	55 350	56 000	55 333	56 533	59 842	60 002	59 748	60 381	64 490	69 174	70 008	72 000
Wife	47 000	47 015	47 550	50 150	52 007	52 517	52 000	57 189	59 914	58 595	61 139	65 030
Other family member	48 922	55 114	55 166	57 264	56 914	53 195	56 949	59 818	62 842	60 000	70 942	66 516
Two earners	85 012	85 500	86 361	88 500	90 001	91 651	94 100	98 023	102 256	104 247	109 302	112 235
Husband and wife	86 000	86 842	87 939	90 000	90 976	93 125	95 200	100 000	104 113	106 200	111 106	113 825
Husband and other family member	71 573	68 755	73 720	74 973	77 888	76 408	75 099	78 161	82 000	84 354	88 673	93 233
Husband not an earner	68 032	66 445	70 017	72 317	72 644	73 906	74 198	80 716	81 897	78 750	87 119	93 492
Three earners or more	106 747	105 618	107 000	107 542	111 000	114 201	118 408	123 850	127 000	130 249	136 207	144 064
Husband and wife	107 630	106 493	108 703	108 714	112 943	115 800	119 184	126 250	128 420	131 598	138 113	144 303
Husband, not wife	101 771	99 731	85 574	93 000	96 756	90 956	105 360	109 076	108 423	116 014	109 803	139 001
Husband not an earner	92 428	93 961	95 251	100 105	97 491	96 968	120 913	110 120	121 350	121 150	128 859	141 459
Families Maintained by Women, Total	30 000	29 698	29 025	28 774	29 848	30 000	30 500	30 816	33 405	36 003	36 800	39 714
No earners	8 873	9 404	10 037	9 600	9 600	10 299	10 224	10 205	10 736	10 200	11 904	11 382
One earner	27 795	28 060	29 000	29 009	28 912	29 558	30 000	29 740	30 205	33 259	33 895	35 987
Householder	26 644	27 000	27 928	27 924	27 488	28 077	28 000	28 000	29 402	31 308	32 002	34 036
Other family member	31 950	34 814	34 421	33 957	35 161	35 000	38 003	38 446	37 334	40 000	40 468	44 680
Two earners or more	55 749	54 369	54 500	55 047	56 000	58 694	58 535	59 008	63 651	67 001	69 086	71 898
Householder and other family member(s)	55 010	54 306	54 448	54 000	55 500	57 561	58 004	58 016	62 405	66 090	67 226	70 255
Householder not an earner	64 094	54 978	56 203	61 781	60 015	71 367	63 773	62 676	75 555	77 805	78 451	78 721
Families Maintained by Men, Total	44 001	43 050	41 000	42 500	43 000	42 000	44 394	47 159	49 000	50 936	52 407	53 628
No earners	12 921	15 557	15 653	16 176	17 945	18 006	16 440	15 828	17 107	18 810	17 865	16 920
One earner	37 716	36 806	35 116	37 707	38 000	35 500	38 300	40 754	40 989	45 000	45 000	46 111
Householder	37 720	37 569	35 117	37 990	38 069	36 000	39 185	40 530	42 000	45 039	45 000	47 005
Other family member	37 522	34 404	35 086	37 041	36 983	34 892	35 600	41 426	39 457	43 000	42 948	44 015
Two earners or more	63 600	64 077	64 747	66 000	67 301	65 017	69 505	71 997	77 729	77 000	80 000	79 610
Householder and other family member(s)	64 000	63 416	64 743	65 200	66 708	65 024	68 029	72 000	78 088	77 000	79 331	78 985
Householder not an earner	60 498	69 794	65 618	71 962	73 242	64 799	79 466	70 000	73 516	76 863	92 318	82 778

Note: See notes and definitions for information on historical comparability.

Table 1-51. Employment Status of the Foreign-Born and Native-Born Populations, by Selected Characteristics, 2017–2018

(Thousands of people, percent.)

Year and characteristic	Civilian noninstitutional population	Civilian labor force				
		Total	Participation rate	Employed	Unemployed	
					Number	Rate
2017						
TOTAL						
Both sexes, 16 years and over	255 079	160 320	62.9	153 337	6 982	4.4
Men	123 275	85 145	69.1	81 402	3 743	4.4
Women	131 804	75 175	57.0	71 936	3 239	4.3
FOREIGN BORN						
Both sexes, 16 years and over	41 500	27 373	66.0	26 254	1 119	4.1
Men	20 135	15 735	78.1	15 171	564	3.6
Women	21 365	11 638	54.5	11 083	555	4.8
Age						
16 to 24 years	3 547	1 886	53.2	1 727	159	8.4
25 to 34 years	7 820	5 898	75.4	5 656	242	4.1
35 to 44 years	9 189	7 299	79.4	7 043	256	3.5
45 to 54 years	8 481	6 826	80.5	6 592	234	3.4
55 to 64 years	6 146	4 209	68.5	4 040	169	4.0
65 years and over	6 317	1 256	19.9	1 196	60	4.8
Race and Hispanic Origin						
White, non-Hispanic	7 524	4 503	59.9	4 324	179	4.0
Black, non-Hispanic	3 599	2 575	71.5	2 430	145	5.6
Asian, non-Hispanic	10 738	6 903	64.3	6 684	220	3.2
Hispanic[1]	19 174	13 098	68.3	12 540	558	4.3
Educational Attainment						
Total, 25 years and over	37 953	25 488	67.2	24 527	961	3.8
Less than a high school diploma	9 510	5 566	58.5	5 309	257	4.6
High school graduate, no college[2]	9 697	6 412	66.1	6 160	252	3.9
Some college or associate's degree	6 070	4 273	70.4	4 116	156	3.7
Bachelor's degree or higher[3]	12 677	9 237	72.9	8 942	294	3.2
NATIVE BORN						
Both sexes, 16 years and over	213 579	132 946	62.2	127 083	5 863	4.4
Men	103 140	69 410	67.3	66 231	3 179	4.6
Women	110 439	63 536	57.5	60 852	2 684	4.2
Age						
16 to 24 years	34 603	19 275	55.7	17 479	1 796	9.3
25 to 34 years	36 138	30 187	83.5	28 782	1 405	4.7
35 to 44 years	30 763	25 735	83.7	24 849	886	3.4
45 to 54 years	33 306	26 737	80.3	25 911	827	3.1
55 to 64 years	35 544	22 690	63.8	22 024	666	2.9
65 years and over	43 225	8 321	19.3	8 038	283	3.4
Race and Hispanic Origin						
White, non-Hispanic or Latino	154 598	96 148	62.2	92 779	3 369	3.5
Black, non-Hispanic Latino	26 764	16 239	60.7	14 965	1 274	7.8
Asian, non-Hispanic Latino	4 219	2 614	62.0	2 515	99	3.8
Hispanic[1]	22 197	14 242	64.2	13 398	843	5.9
Educational Attainment						
Total, 25 years and over	178 976	113 672	63.5	109 604	4 067	3.6
Less than a high school diploma	13 128	4 776	36.4	4 359	417	8.7
High school graduates, no college[2]	52 496	29 462	56.1	28 050	1 412	4.8
Some college or associate's degree	51 191	33 424	65.3	32 166	1 257	3.8
Bachelor's degree or higher[3]	62 161	46 009	74.0	45 029	981	2.1

Note: Updated population controls are introduced annually with the release of January data.

[1]May be of any race.
[2]Includes persons with a high school diploma or equivalent.
[3]Includes persons with bachelor's, master's, professional, and doctoral degrees.

Table 1-51. Employment Status of the Foreign-Born and Native-Born Populations, by Selected Characteristics, 2017–2018—*Continued*

(Thousands of people, percent.)

Year and characteristic	Civilian noninstitutional population	Civilian labor force				
		Total	Participation rate	Employed	Unemployed	
					Number	Rate
2018						
TOTAL						
Both sexes, 16 years and over	257 791	162 075	62.9	155 761	6 314	3.9
Men	124 678	86 096	69.1	82 698	3 398	3.9
Women	133 112	75 978	57.1	73 063	2 916	3.8
FOREIGN BORN						
Both sexes, 16 years and over	42 898	28 202	65.7	27 217	986	3.5
Men	20 803	16 203	77.9	15 714	488	3.0
Women	22 095	12 000	54.3	11 502	497	4.1
Age						
16 to 24 years	3 443	1 761	51.2	1 638	124	7.0
25 to 34 years	7 946	6 092	76.7	5 877	215	3.5
35 to 44 years	9 499	7 520	79.2	7 302	219	2.9
45 to 54 years	8 715	7 044	80.8	6 844	200	2.8
55 to 64 years	6 542	4 425	67.6	4 255	170	3.8
65 years and over	6 754	1 360	20.1	1 301	58	4.3
Race and Hispanic Origin						
White, non-Hispanic	7 837	4 676	59.7	4 517	160	3.4
Black, non-Hispanic	3 786	2 682	70.8	2 560	122	4.6
Asian, non-Hispanic	11 118	7 082	63.7	6 895	187	2.6
Hispanic[1]	19 683	13 457	68.4	12 950	507	3.8
Educational Attainment						
Total, 25 years and over	39 455	26 441	67.0	25 579	862	3.3
Less than a high school diploma	9 616	5 607	58.3	5 378	229	4.1
High school graduates, no college[2]	10 127	6 629	65.5	6 415	214	3.2
Some college or associate degree	6 366	4 448	69.9	4 301	147	3.3
Bachelor's degree and higher[3]	13 347	9 758	73.1	9 485	273	2.8
NATIVE BORN						
Both sexes, 16 years and over	214 892	133 872	62.3	128 544	5 328	4.0
Men	103 875	69 894	67.3	66 984	2 910	4.2
Women	111 018	63 979	57.6	61 560	2 418	3.8
Age						
16 to 24 years	34 561	19 223	55.6	17 539	1 684	8.8
25 to 34 years	36 635	30 682	83.8	29 447	1 235	4.0
35 to 44 years	31 071	26 099	84.0	25 315	784	3.0
45 to 54 years	32 525	26 267	80.8	25 529	738	2.8
55 to 64 years	35 572	22 929	64.5	22 310	619	2.7
65 years and over	44 529	8 673	19.5	8 404	269	3.1
Race and Hispanic Origin						
White, non-Hispanic	154 396	95 991	62.2	92 952	3 038	3.2
Black, non-Hispanic	27 076	16 484	60.9	15 355	1 129	6.8
Asian, non-Hispanic	4 408	2 761	62.6	2 657	104	3.8
Hispanic[1]	23 051	14 879	64.5	14 063	816	5.5
Educational Attainment						
Total, 25 years and over	180 332	114 650	63.6	111 005	3 644	3.2
Less than a high school diploma	12 635	4 671	37.0	4 323	347	7.4
High school graduates, no college[2]	52 465	29 382	56.0	28 135	1 247	4.2
Some college or associate degree	51 038	33 138	64.9	32 036	1 101	3.3
Bachelor's degree or higher[3]	64 193	47 459	73.9	46 511	949	2.0

Note: Updated population controls are introduced annually with the release of January data.

[1]May be of any race.
[2]Includes persons with a high school diploma or equivalent.
[3]Includes persons with bachelor's, master's, professional, and doctoral degrees.

Table 1-52. Employment Status of the Foreign-Born and Native-Born Populations Age 16 Years and Over, by Sex and Presence and Age of Youngest Child, Annual Averages, 2017–2018

(Thousands of people, percent.)

Characteristic	2017			2018		
	Both sexes	Men	Women	Both sexes	Men	Women
FOREIGN BORN						
With Own Children Under 18 Years						
Civilian noninstitutional population	15 292	7 162	8 130	15 770	7 446	8 324
Civilian labor force	11 557	6 669	4 888	12 062	6 984	5 078
Participation rate	75.6	93.1	60.1	76.5	93.8	61.0
Employed	11 141	6 481	4 660	11 675	6 815	4 860
Employment-population ratio	72.9	90.5	57.3	74.0	91.5	58.4
Unemployed	416	187	228	387	168	219
Unemployment rate	3.6	2.8	4.7	3.2	2.4	4.3
With Own Children 6 to 17 Years, None Younger						
Civilian noninstitutional population	8 682	3 966	4 716	8 948	4 120	4 827
Civilian labor force	6 848	3 660	3 188	7 127	3 824	3 303
Participation rate	78.9	92.3	67.6	79.7	92.8	68.4
Employed	6 606	3 562	3 044	6 904	3 733	3 171
Employment-population ratio	76.1	89.8	64.5	77.2	90.6	65.7
Unemployed	243	99	144	223	91	132
Unemployment rate	3.5	2.7	4.5	3.1	2.4	4.0
With Own Children Under 6 Years						
Civilian noninstitutional population	6 609	3 196	3 414	6 823	3 326	3 497
Civilian labor force	4 709	3 008	1 700	4 935	3 160	1 775
Participation rate	71.2	94.1	49.8	72.3	95.0	50.8
Employed	4 536	2 920	1 616	4 771	3 082	1 689
Employment-population ratio	68.6	91.4	47.3	69.9	92.7	48.3
Unemployed	173	88	85	164	77	87
Unemployment rate	3.7	2.9	5.0	3.3	2.4	4.9
With Own Children Under 3 Years						
Civilian noninstitutional population	3 600	1 764	1 836	3 720	1 828	1 892
Civilian labor force	2 478	1 662	816	2 589	1 732	857
Participation rate	68.8	94.2	44.4	69.6	94.8	45.3
Employed	2 383	1 609	774	2 504	1 695	809
Employment-population ratio	66.2	91.2	42.2	67.3	92.7	42.8
Unemployed	95	53	42	85	37	48
Unemployment rate	3.8	3.2	5.1	3.3	2.2	5.6
With No Own Children Under 18 Years						
Civilian noninstitutional population	26 209	12 974	13 235	27 128	13 357	13 771
Civilian labor force	15 816	9 066	6 750	16 140	9 219	6 921
Participation rate	60.3	69.9	51.0	59.5	69.0	50.3
Employed	15 113	8 690	6 423	15 542	8 899	6 643
Employment-population ratio	57.7	67.0	48.5	57.3	66.6	48.2
Unemployed	704	377	327	599	320	279
Unemployment rate	4.4	4.2	4.8	3.7	3.5	4.0

Note: Updated population controls are introduced annually with the release of January data.

Table 1-52. Employment Status of the Foreign-Born and Native-Born Populations Age 16 Years and Over, by Sex and Presence and Age of Youngest Child, Annual Averages, 2017–2018—*Continued*

(Thousands of people, percent.)

Characteristic	2017			2018		
	Both sexes	Men	Women	Both sexes	Men	Women
NATIVE BORN						
With Own Children Under 18 Years						
Civilian noninstitutional population	48 896	21 578	27 318	48 464	21 467	26 998
Civilian labor force	40 318	19 993	20 325	40 144	19 984	20 161
Participation rate	82.5	92.7	74.4	82.8	93.1	74.7
Employed	38 895	19 438	19 457	38 915	19 501	19 414
Employment-population ratio	79.5	90.1	71.2	80.0	91.0	72.0
Unemployed	1 423	555	868	1 229	483	746
Unemployment rate	3.5	2.8	4.3	3.1	2.4	3.7
With Own Children 6 to 17 Years, None Younger						
Civilian noninstitutional population	27 604	12 187	15 416	26 933	11 874	15 059
Civilian labor force	23 212	11 152	12 060	22 810	10 929	11 880
Participation rate	84.1	91.5	78.2	84.7	92.0	78.9
Employed	22 458	10 866	11 591	22 193	10 696	11 497
Employment-population ratio	81.4	89.2	75.2	82.4	90.1	76.3
Unemployed	754	286	468	617	233	384
Unemployment rate	3.2	2.6	3.9	2.7	2.1	3.2
With Own Children Under 6 Years						
Civilian noninstitutional population	21 292	9 391	11 901	21 532	9 593	11 939
Civilian labor force	17 106	8 841	8 265	17 335	9 055	8 280
Participation rate	80.3	94.1	69.4	80.5	94.4	69.4
Employed	16 437	8 572	7 866	16 723	8 805	7 918
Employment-population ratio	77.2	91.3	66.1	77.7	91.8	66.3
Unemployed	669	269	399	612	249	363
Unemployment rate	3.9	3.0	4.8	3.5	2.8	4.4
With Own Children Under 3 Years						
Civilian noninstitutional population	12 690	5 649	7 041	12 556	5 623	6 933
Civilian labor force	10 060	5 348	4 712	9 932	5 328	4 605
Participation rate	79.3	94.7	66.9	79.1	94.8	66.4
Employed	9 661	5 185	4 476	9 576	5 174	4 401
Employment-population ratio	76.1	91.8	63.6	76.3	92.0	63.5
Unemployed	399	163	236	357	153	204
Unemployment rate	4.0	3.1	5.0	3.6	2.9	4.4
With No Own Children Under 18 Years						
Civilian noninstitutional population	164 683	81 562	83 121	166 428	82 408	84 020
Civilian labor force	92 629	49 417	43 211	93 728	49 910	43 818
Participation rate	56.2	60.6	52.0	56.3	60.6	52.2
Employed	88 188	46 793	41 395	89 629	47 483	42 146
Employment-population ratio	53.6	57.4	49.8	53.9	57.6	50.2
Unemployed	4 441	2 625	1 816	4 099	2 427	1 672
Unemployment rate	4.8	5.3	4.2	4.4	4.9	3.8

Note: Updated population controls are introduced annually with the release of January data.

Table 1-53. Employment Status of the Foreign-Born and Native-Born Populations Age 25 Years and Over, by Educational Attainment, Race, and Hispanic Origin, Annual Averages, 2017–2018

(Thousands of people, percent.)

Characteristic	2017				2018			
	Less than a high school diploma	High school graduate, no college[1]	Some college or associate's degree	Bachelor's degree or higher[2]	Less than a high school diploma	High school graduate, no college[1]	Some college or associate's degree	Bachelor's degree or higher[2]
FOREIGN BORN								
White, Non-Hispanic								
Civilian noninstitutional population	574	1 653	1 364	3 445	644	1 708	1 361	3 617
Civilian labor force	206	841	812	2 409	250	849	817	2 515
Participation rate	35.9	50.9	59.6	69.9	38.9	49.7	60.0	69.5
Employed	193	803	779	2 341	238	823	791	2 440
Employment-population ratio	33.7	48.6	57.1	68.0	36.9	48.2	58.1	67.5
Unemployed	13	39	33	68	12	26	27	75
Unemployment rate	6.3	4.6	4.1	2.8	4.9	3.1	3.3	3.0
Black, Non-Hispanic								
Civilian noninstitutional population	388	895	798	1 113	391	946	908	1 156
Civilian labor force	210	628	612	911	196	666	684	950
Participation rate	54.0	70.0	76.7	81.9	50.3	70.4	75.3	82.1
Employed	197	593	585	866	187	637	653	911
Employment-population ratio	50.7	66.3	73.2	77.8	47.8	67.4	71.9	78.8
Unemployed	14	35	27	45	10	28	31	38
Unemployment rate	6.5	5.5	4.5	5.0	4.9	4.2	4.5	4.0
Asian, Non-Hispanic								
Civilian noninstitutional population	1 052	1 932	1 381	5 515	1 015	1 955	1 402	5 844
Civilian labor force	421	1 185	940	3 983	403	1 145	934	4 257
Participation rate	40.0	61.3	68.1	72.0	39.7	58.6	66.7	72.8
Employed	404	1 154	909	3 864	393	1 121	910	4 152
Employment-population ratio	38.4	59.7	65.8	70.1	38.7	57.3	64.9	71.0
Unemployed	17	31	31	120	10	24	24	106
Unemployment rate	4.0	2.6	3.3	3.0	2.5	2.1	2.6	2.5
Hispanic[3]								
Civilian noninstitutional population	7 438	5 108	2 433	2 458	7 514	5 410	2 577	2 585
Civilian labor force	4 698	3 694	1 850	1 824	4 730	3 908	1 930	1 923
Participation rate	63.2	72.0	76.0	74.2	62.9	72.2	74.9	74.4
Employed	4 488	3 551	1 789	1 766	4 534	3 777	1 867	1 870
Employment-population ratio	60.3	69.5	73.5	71.8	60.3	69.8	72.4	72.4
Unemployed	210	143	61	58	196	131	63	53
Unemployment rate	4.5	3.9	3.3	3.2	4.1	3.4	3.2	2.7
NATIVE BORN								
White, Non-Hispanic								
Civilian noninstitutional population	7 804	38 295	37 581	50 848	7 423	37 857	37 328	52 012
Civilian labor force	2 713	20 767	23 817	37 050	2 641	20 379	23 507	37 817
Participation rate	34.8	54.2	63.4	72.9	35.6	53.8	63.0	72.7
Employed	2 524	19 959	23 057	36 326	2 479	19 670	22 855	37 117
Employment-population ratio	32.3	52.1	61.4	71.4	33.4	52.0	61.2	71.4
Unemployed	189	808	760	724	162	708	652	700
Unemployment rate	7.0	3.9	3.2	2.0	6.1	3.5	2.8	1.9
Black, Non-Hispanic								
Civilian noninstitutional population	2 486	7 507	6 754	5 065	2 427	7 487	6 713	5 555
Civilian labor force	785	4 355	4 632	3 888	782	4 340	4 571	4 259
Participation rate	31.6	58.0	68.6	76.8	32.2	58.0	68.1	76.7
Employed	663	3 998	4 352	3 766	684	4 029	4 324	4 146
Employment-population ratio	26.7	53.3	64.4	74.4	28.2	53.8	64.4	74.6
Unemployed	123	357	280	122	98	311	247	112
Unemployment rate	15.6	8.2	6.0	3.1	12.6	7.2	5.4	2.6
Asian, Non-Hispanic								
Civilian noninstitutional population	141	476	610	1 714	164	516	602	1 854
Civilian labor force	54	279	420	1 355	69	309	414	1 468
Participation rate	38.4	58.6	68.9	79.1	41.8	60.0	68.7	79.2
Employed	52	269	407	1 329	65	299	400	1 440
Employment-population ratio	36.8	56.6	66.8	77.5	39.7	58.0	66.4	77.7
Unemployed	2	10	13	26	4	10	14	28
Unemployment rate	4.3	3.5	3.1	1.9	5.1	3.4	3.3	1.9
Hispanic[3]								
Civilian noninstitutional population	2 291	4 904	4 787	3 422	2 223	5 227	4 903	3 613
Civilian labor force	1 057	3 273	3 556	2 837	1 023	3 531	3 624	2 989
Participation rate	46.1	66.7	74.3	82.9	46.0	67.6	73.9	82.7
Employed	974	3 091	3 407	2 759	954	3 369	3 487	2 900
Employment-population ratio	42.5	63.0	71.2	80.6	42.9	64.5	71.1	80.3
Unemployed	83	182	149	78	69	162	137	88
Unemployment rate	7.8	5.6	4.2	2.7	6.8	4.6	3.8	3.0

Note: Updated population controls are introduced annually with the release of January data.

[1]Includes persons with a high school diploma or equivalent.
[2]Includes persons with bachelor's, master's, professional, and doctoral degrees.
[3]May be of any race.

Table 1-54. Employed Foreign-Born and Native-Born Persons Age 16 Years and Over, by Occupation and Sex, Annual Averages, 2017–2018

(Thousands of people, percent.)

Occupation	2017					
	Foreign born			Native born		
	Both sexes	Male	Female	Both sexes	Male	Female
TOTAL EMPLOYED	26 254	15 171	11 083	127 083	66 231	60 852
Percent Employed	100.0	100.0	100.0	100.0	100.0	100.0
Management, professional, and related	32.3	30.7	34.3	41.3	37.5	45.4
Management, business, and financial operations	12.3	12.6	11.9	17.4	18.6	16.2
Management	8.6	9.6	7.4	12.2	14.0	10.3
Business and financial operations	3.7	3.0	4.6	5.2	4.6	5.9
Professional and related	20.0	18.2	22.4	23.8	18.9	29.2
Computer and mathematical	4.8	6.4	2.5	2.8	3.9	1.6
Architecture and engineering	2.3	3.2	1.0	2.1	3.3	0.7
Life, physical, and social sciences	1.3	1.2	1.4	0.9	0.9	0.9
Community and social services	0.9	0.6	1.2	1.9	1.2	2.6
Legal	0.5	0.4	0.8	1.3	1.2	1.4
Education, training, and library	3.7	2.2	5.7	6.5	3.3	10.0
Arts, design, entertainment, sports, and media	1.4	1.3	1.5	2.3	2.3	2.2
Health care practitioner and technical	5.2	2.9	8.4	6.1	2.8	9.7
Services	23.9	17.2	33.1	16.1	13.6	18.8
Health care support	2.8	0.6	5.8	2.2	0.5	4.0
Protective services	0.8	1.1	0.4	2.3	3.4	1.1
Food preparation and serving related	7.1	6.6	7.8	5.1	4.3	5.9
Building and grounds cleaning and maintenance	8.4	7.0	10.3	2.9	3.7	2.1
Personal care and services	4.8	1.8	8.8	3.7	1.7	5.8
Sales and office	15.0	11.1	20.4	23.3	17.0	30.1
Sales and related	7.5	6.7	8.7	10.9	10.6	11.2
Office and administrative support	7.5	4.4	11.8	12.4	6.4	18.9
Natural resources, construction, and maintenance	13.9	22.6	2.0	8.3	15.2	0.8
Farming, fishing, and forestry	1.7	2.1	1.2	0.6	0.9	0.2
Construction and extraction	9.3	15.6	0.5	4.4	8.2	0.3
Installation, maintenance, and repair	2.9	4.8	0.2	3.3	6.1	0.3
Production, transportation, and material moving	14.9	18.4	10.1	11.0	16.7	4.9
Production	7.5	7.9	7.0	5.1	7.3	2.7
Transportation and material moving	7.4	10.5	3.1	5.9	9.4	2.1

Occupation	2018					
	Foreign born			Native born		
	Both sexes	Male	Female	Both sexes	Male	Female
TOTAL EMPLOYED	27 217	15 714	11 502	128 544	66 984	61 560
Percent Employed	100.0	100.0	100.0	100.0	100.0	100.0
Management, professional, and related	32.7	30.7	35.5	41.6	38.0	45.6
Management, business, and financial operations	12.3	12.4	12.1	17.5	18.7	16.2
Management	8.5	9.3	7.5	12.4	14.2	10.5
Business and financial operations	3.7	3.1	4.6	5.1	4.5	5.8
Professional and related	20.5	18.4	23.4	24.1	19.3	29.4
Computer and mathematical	5.1	6.6	3.0	2.9	4.1	1.6
Architecture and engineering	2.2	3.2	0.9	2.1	3.4	0.7
Life, physical, and social sciences	1.2	1.1	1.2	0.9	0.9	0.9
Community and social services	0.9	0.6	1.3	1.9	1.2	2.6
Legal	0.6	0.4	0.8	1.4	1.3	1.4
Education, training, and library	3.7	2.2	5.7	6.5	3.2	10.0
Arts, design, entertainment, sports, and media	1.4	1.3	1.6	2.3	2.4	2.2
Health care practitioner and technical	5.4	2.9	8.8	6.2	2.8	9.8
Services	23.3	16.6	32.5	15.9	13.1	19.0
Health care support	2.7	0.6	5.5	2.3	0.6	4.1
Protective services	0.9	1.2	0.5	2.3	3.4	1.1
Food preparation and serving related	6.7	6.1	7.6	5.0	4.0	6.0
Building and grounds cleaning and maintenance	8.2	6.9	10.0	2.8	3.5	2.1
Personal care and services	4.8	1.8	8.9	3.6	1.6	5.8
Sales and office	14.9	11.2	19.9	22.9	16.8	29.5
Sales and related	7.7	6.9	8.7	10.7	10.3	11.1
Office and administrative support	7.2	4.3	11.2	12.2	6.5	18.4
Natural resources, construction, and maintenance	14.0	22.8	2.0	8.3	15.1	0.8
Farming, fishing, and forestry	1.6	2.0	1.1	0.5	0.8	0.2
Construction and extraction	9.5	15.9	0.7	4.5	8.3	0.3
Installation, maintenance, and repair	2.9	4.9	0.2	3.3	6.1	0.3
Production, transportation, and material moving	15.0	18.6	10.1	11.3	16.9	5.1
Production	7.4	7.9	6.7	5.1	7.3	2.8
Transportation and material moving	7.6	10.7	3.4	6.1	9.6	2.3

Note: Updated population controls are introduced annually with the release of January data.

Table 1-55. Median Usual Weekly Earnings of Full-Time Wage and Salary Workers for the Foreign-Born and Native-Born Populations, by Selected Characteristics, Annual Averages, 2017–2018

(Thousands of people, dollars, percent.)

Year and characteristic	Foreign born		Native born		Earnings of foreign born as a percent of earnings of native born[1]
	Number	Median weekly earnings	Number	Median weekly earnings	
2017					
Both Sexes, 16 Years and Over	19 914	730	93 358	885	82.5
Men	12 123	776	50 857	978	79.3
Women	7 791	660	42 501	788	83.8
Age					
16 to 24 years	1 065	506	9 216	521	97.1
25 to 34 years	4 610	701	23 586	786	89.2
35 to 44 years	5 560	790	20 102	1 003	78.8
45 to 54 years	5 009	760	20 642	1 019	74.6
55 to 64 years	2 958	765	16 199	1 007	76.0
65 years and over	712	721	3 615	937	76.9
Race and Hispanic Origin					
White, non-Hispanic	3 040	1 080	67 242	955	113.1
Black, non-Hispanic	1 885	682	11 669	683	99.9
Asian, non-Hispanic	5 189	1 076	1 943	1 007	106.9
Hispanic[2]	9 579	596	10 036	724	82.3
Educational Attainment					
Total, 25 years and over	18 848	751	84 142	937	80.1
Less than a high school diploma	4 113	506	2 925	560	90.4
High school graduate, no college[3]	4 539	619	21 472	734	84.3
Some college	3 003	727	24 384	808	90.0
Bachelor's degree or higher[4]	7 193	1 340	35 362	1 271	105.4
2018					
Both Sexes, 16 Years and Over	20 627	758	94 939	910	83.3
Men	12 469	815	51 673	1 007	80.9
Women	8 158	678	43 266	810	83.7
Age					
16 to 24 years	993	522	9 436	551	94.7
25 to 34 years	4 668	752	24 207	819	91.8
35 to 44 years	5 803	802	20 648	1 035	77.5
45 to 54 years	5 215	779	20 351	1 059	73.6
55 to 64 years	3 154	774	16 430	1 035	74.8
65 years and over	795	733	3 867	977	75.0
Race and Hispanic Origin					
White, non-Hispanic	3 135	1 083	67 771	986	109.8
Black, non-Hispanic	2 023	699	12 109	697	100.3
Asian, non-Hispanic	5 387	1 129	2 041	1 065	106.0
Hispanic[2]	9 852	621	10 445	741	83.8
Educational Attainment					
Total, 25 years and over	19 635	775	85 503	965	80.3
Less than a high school diploma	4 097	535	2 902	578	92.6
High school graduates, no college[3]	4 879	632	21 358	754	83.8
Some college	3 125	755	24 350	837	90.2
Bachelor's degree and higher[4]	7 534	1 362	36 893	1 309	104.0

Note: Updated population controls are introduced annually with the release of January data.

[1]These figures are computed using unrounded medians and may differ slightly from percentages computed using the rounded medians displayed in this table.
[2]May be of any race.
[3]Includes persons with a high school diploma or equivalent.
[4]Includes persons with bachelor's, master's, professional, and doctoral degrees.

Table 1-56. Percent Distribution of the Civilian Labor Force Age 25 to 64 Years, by Educational Attainment, Sex, and Race, March 1995–March 2019

(Thousands of people, percent.)

Sex, race, and year	Civilian labor force	Percent distribution				
		Total	Less than a high school diploma	4 years of high school only	1 to 3 years of college	4 or more years of college
Both Sexes						
1995	106 519	100.0	10.8	33.1	27.8	28.3
1996	108 037	100.0	10.9	32.9	27.7	28.5
1997	110 514	100.0	10.9	33.0	27.4	28.6
1998	111 857	100.0	10.7	32.8	27.4	29.1
1999	112 542	100.0	10.3	32.3	27.4	30.0
2000	114 052	100.0	9.8	31.8	27.9	30.4
2001	115 073	100.0	9.8	31.4	28.1	30.7
2002	117 738	100.0	10.1	30.6	27.7	31.6
2003	119 261	100.0	10.1	30.1	27.8	31.9
2004	119 392	100.0	9.7	30.1	27.8	32.4
2005	120 461	100.0	9.8	30.1	27.8	32.3
2006	122 541	100.0	9.8	29.6	28.0	32.6
2007	124 581	100.0	9.8	29.3	27.3	33.6
2008	125 493	100.0	9.0	28.8	27.9	34.4
2009	125 655	100.0	9.0	28.7	27.9	34.3
2010	126 363	100.0	8.8	29.1	27.5	34.5
2011	125 385	100.0	8.5	28.2	28.0	35.4
2012	125 726	100.0	8.6	27.5	27.9	36.0
2013	125 744	100.0	8.2	27.0	28.1	36.7
2014	125 847	100.0	8.4	26.9	27.8	37.0
2015	126 863	100.0	8.2	26.3	27.7	37.7
2016	128 660	100.0	7.9	25.8	27.6	38.8
2017	129 313	100.0	7.3	25.9	27.6	39.1
2018	130 447	100.0	7.2	25.5	26.8	40.5
2019	131 173	100.0	7.1	25.3	26.3	41.3
Men						
1995	57 454	100.0	12.2	32.3	25.7	29.7
1996	58 121	100.0	12.7	32.2	26.0	29.1
1997	59 268	100.0	12.8	32.2	25.8	29.2
1998	59 905	100.0	12.3	32.3	25.8	29.6
1999	60 030	100.0	11.7	32.0	25.8	30.5
2000	60 510	100.0	11.1	31.8	26.1	30.9
2001	61 091	100.0	11.0	31.6	26.3	31.1
2002	62 794	100.0	11.8	30.6	25.9	31.7
2003	63 466	100.0	12.0	30.1	25.8	32.1
2004	63 699	100.0	11.5	30.5	25.8	32.2
2005	64 562	100.0	11.6	31.4	25.4	31.6
2006	65 708	100.0	11.8	30.7	25.7	31.8
2007	66 742	100.0	11.7	30.6	25.1	32.7
2008	66 957	100.0	11.0	30.3	25.8	33.0
2009	66 843	100.0	10.8	30.4	26.0	32.8
2010	67 261	100.0	10.6	31.2	25.3	32.9
2011	66 801	100.0	10.2	30.4	25.5	33.9
2012	66 539	100.0	10.1	29.7	25.9	34.3
2013	66 594	100.0	9.9	29.1	26.2	34.8
2014	66 625	100.0	10.2	29.4	25.8	34.7
2015	67 578	100.0	10.0	29.1	25.8	35.1
2016	68 329	100.0	9.5	28.5	25.8	36.1
2017	68 312	100.0	8.8	28.9	25.9	36.3
2018	69 208	100.0	8.7	28.6	25.2	37.5
2019	69 463	100.0	8.7	28.3	25.0	38.0
Women						
1995	49 065	100.0	9.1	34.1	30.2	26.6
1996	49 916	100.0	8.8	33.7	29.7	27.8
1997	51 246	100.0	8.7	34.0	29.3	28.0
1998	51 953	100.0	8.8	33.3	29.3	28.6
1999	52 512	100.0	8.7	32.7	29.2	29.5
2000	53 541	100.0	8.4	31.8	30.0	29.8
2001	53 982	100.0	8.5	31.1	30.1	30.2
2002	54 944	100.0	8.2	30.6	29.7	31.5
2003	55 795	100.0	8.0	30.1	30.1	31.8
2004	55 693	100.0	7.7	29.6	30.2	32.5
2005	55 899	100.0	7.8	28.6	30.5	33.1
2006	56 833	100.0	7.6	28.2	30.6	33.6
2007	57 839	100.0	7.5	27.9	29.9	34.6
2008	58 536	100.0	6.7	27.0	30.4	35.9
2009	58 811	100.0	7.0	26.9	30.2	35.9
2010	59 102	100.0	6.8	26.8	30.1	36.3
2011	58 584	100.0	6.5	25.7	30.7	37.1
2012	59 187	100.0	6.8	25.1	30.2	37.9
2013	59 150	100.0	6.3	24.6	30.2	38.9
2014	59 222	100.0	6.4	24.1	30.0	39.6
2015	59 285	100.0	6.2	23.2	29.9	40.7
2016	60 331	100.0	6.1	22.6	29.6	41.7
2017	61 002	100.0	5.7	22.6	29.4	42.3
2018	61 239	100.0	5.5	22.1	28.5	43.9
2019	61 710	100.0	5.3	21.9	27.7	45.1

Table 1-56. Percent Distribution of the Civilian Labor Force Age 25 to 64 Years, by Educational Attainment, Sex, and Race, March 1995–March 2019—*Continued*

(Thousands of people, percent.)

Sex, race, and year	Civilian labor force	Percent distribution				
		Total	Less than a high school diploma	4 years of high school only	1 to 3 years of college	4 or more years of college
White[1]						
1995	90 192	100.0	10.0	32.8	27.8	29.3
1996	91 506	100.0	10.4	32.8	27.5	29.3
1997	93 179	100.0	10.4	32.8	27.3	29.5
1998	93 527	100.0	10.2	32.7	27.4	29.8
1999	94 216	100.0	9.8	32.2	27.2	30.8
2000	95 073	100.0	9.5	31.8	27.7	31.0
2001	95 562	100.0	9.5	31.0	28.0	31.4
2002	97 699	100.0	9.8	30.6	27.6	32.0
2003	98 241	100.0	9.9	30.0	27.7	32.4
2004	98 030	100.0	9.5	29.8	27.8	32.9
2005	98 581	100.0	9.7	29.8	27.8	32.7
2006	100 205	100.0	9.7	29.3	28.1	32.9
2007	101 548	100.0	9.7	29.1	27.3	33.9
2008	102 077	100.0	8.9	28.7	27.8	34.6
2009	102 261	100.0	9.1	28.6	27.7	34.6
2010	102 634	100.0	8.8	29.0	27.4	34.8
2011	101 707	100.0	8.4	27.8	27.9	35.8
2012	100 382	100.0	8.6	27.4	27.7	36.4
2013	99 964	100.0	8.2	27.0	27.9	36.9
2014	99 664	100.0	8.3	26.8	27.8	37.2
2015	99 813	100.0	8.4	26.3	27.5	37.9
2016	100 886	100.0	8.0	25.7	27.4	38.9
2017	100 794	100.0	7.4	25.9	27.5	39.2
2018	101 234	100.0	7.3	25.5	26.6	40.6
2019	101 321	100.0	7.2	25.4	26.1	41.3
Black[1]						
1995	11 695	100.0	14.1	38.6	29.6	17.7
1996	11 891	100.0	14.2	37.2	31.2	17.4
1997	12 253	100.0	14.3	37.8	31.3	16.6
1998	12 893	100.0	14.3	37.3	30.1	18.2
1999	12 945	100.0	13.0	37.2	30.4	19.5
2000	13 383	100.0	11.8	36.1	31.5	20.7
2001	13 617	100.0	12.0	37.1	31.1	19.8
2002	13 319	100.0	12.4	34.5	32.0	21.0
2003	13 315	100.0	11.3	35.6	31.5	21.6
2004	13 372	100.0	11.0	36.6	30.5	21.9
2005	13 635	100.0	11.2	37.3	29.9	21.6
2006	13 855	100.0	10.9	35.6	30.4	23.0
2007	14 186	100.0	10.1	35.4	31.4	23.1
2008	14 356	100.0	9.5	34.3	32.1	24.1
2009	14 325	100.0	8.5	35.1	33.0	23.5
2010	14 483	100.0	8.9	34.5	32.4	24.2
2011	14 377	100.0	8.5	33.8	33.1	24.6
2012	14 721	100.0	8.5	32.0	33.4	26.0
2013	14 869	100.0	8.5	31.4	33.4	26.7
2014	15 121	100.0	8.9	31.3	32.2	27.6
2015	15 415	100.0	7.1	31.2	34.1	27.5
2016	15 666	100.0	7.5	30.7	33.1	28.7
2017	16 108	100.0	6.9	30.3	33.5	29.3
2018	16 420	100.0	6.5	30.4	32.3	30.9
2019	16 687	100.0	6.7	29.5	31.8	32.0

[1]Beginning in 2003, persons who selected this race group only; persons who selected more than one race group are not included. Prior to 2003, persons who reported more than one race group were included in the group they identified as their main race.

Table 1-57. Labor Force Participation Rates of Persons Age 25 to 64 Years, by Educational Attainment, Sex, and Race, March 1995–March 2019

(Civilian labor force as a percent of the civilian noninstitutional population.)

Sex, race, and year	Participation rates				
	Total	Less than a high school diploma	4 years of high school only	1 to 3 years of college	4 or more years of college
Both Sexes					
1995	79.3	59.8	77.3	83.2	88.7
1996	79.4	60.2	77.9	83.7	87.8
1997	80.1	61.7	78.5	83.7	88.5
1998	80.2	63.0	78.4	83.5	88.0
1999	80.0	62.7	78.1	83.0	87.6
2000	80.3	62.7	78.4	83.2	87.8
2001	80.2	63.5	78.4	83.0	87.0
2002	79.7	63.5	77.7	82.1	86.7
2003	79.4	64.1	76.9	81.9	86.2
2004	78.8	63.2	76.1	81.2	85.9
2005	78.5	62.9	75.7	81.1	85.7
2006	78.7	63.2	75.9	81.0	85.9
2007	79.0	63.7	76.3	81.1	85.9
2008	79.0	62.5	76.0	80.9	86.1
2009	78.6	62.3	75.7	80.3	85.9
2010	78.7	62.7	76.2	79.7	85.7
2011	77.6	61.0	74.3	78.6	85.3
2012	77.4	61.7	73.2	78.5	85.5
2013	77.2	60.9	73.0	78.1	85.1
2014	76.7	61.3	72.3	77.3	84.9
2015	76.7	60.2	71.8	77.9	84.8
2016	77.2	61.6	71.9	77.3	85.6
2017	77.5	60.6	72.2	78.3	85.5
2018	77.7	60.8	72.4	77.8	85.7
2019	78.1	60.0	72.8	78.8	85.9
Men					
1995	87.4	72.0	86.9	90.1	93.8
1996	87.5	74.3	86.9	90.0	92.9
1997	87.7	75.2	86.4	90.6	93.5
1998	87.8	75.3	86.7	90.0	93.4
1999	87.5	74.4	86.6	89.4	93.0
2000	87.5	74.9	86.2	88.9	93.3
2001	87.4	75.4	85.8	89.1	92.9
2002	87.0	75.5	85.3	88.8	92.4
2003	86.4	76.1	84.3	87.5	92.2
2004	85.9	75.2	83.8	87.0	91.9
2005	86.0	75.7	83.7	87.5	91.7
2006	86.0	76.3	83.4	87.8	91.7
2007	86.2	75.7	83.9	87.2	92.4
2008	85.8	74.8	83.6	86.5	91.9
2009	85.1	73.7	82.3	86.0	91.9
2010	85.3	74.5	83.2	85.3	91.5
2011	84.0	73.3	81.8	83.2	91.1
2012	84.1	72.9	80.7	84.3	91.4
2013	84.0	72.7	80.5	83.8	91.4
2014	83.2	73.1	79.8	82.4	90.8
2015	83.6	73.4	80.0	83.7	90.6
2016	83.8	74.0	79.7	83.0	91.4
2017	83.8	72.3	79.7	83.6	91.2
2018	84.3	73.2	80.7	83.7	91.0
2019	84.6	72.6	80.5	85.0	91.2
Women					
1995	71.5	47.2	68.9	77.3	82.8
1996	71.8	45.7	69.8	78.1	82.3
1997	72.8	47.1	71.4	77.6	83.2
1998	73.0	49.8	70.9	77.8	82.3
1999	72.8	50.5	70.4	77.4	81.9
2000	73.5	50.4	71.2	78.3	82.0
2001	73.4	51.7	71.3	77.7	80.9
2002	72.7	50.4	70.4	76.4	81.0
2003	72.6	50.5	69.8	77.1	80.1
2004	72.0	49.7	68.6	76.2	80.0
2005	71.4	48.7	67.4	75.8	79.8
2006	71.7	48.3	68.2	75.3	80.4
2007	72.1	49.6	68.4	76.0	79.7
2008	72.5	47.9	68.2	76.1	80.9
2009	72.4	49.0	68.7	75.4	80.5
2010	72.3	48.9	68.6	75.0	80.4
2011	71.3	46.8	66.1	74.7	80.0
2012	71.1	49.2	65.2	73.5	80.3
2013	70.8	47.3	65.1	73.3	79.6
2014	70.6	47.6	64.1	72.9	79.8
2015	70.1	45.3	62.6	72.9	79.9
2016	70.8	47.6	63.2	72.4	80.5
2017	71.4	47.2	63.6	73.6	80.6
2018	71.3	46.8	63.0	72.7	81.1
2019	71.9	45.4	63.9	73.3	81.4

Table 1-57. Labor Force Participation Rates of Persons Age 25 to 64 Years, by Educational Attainment, Sex, and Race, March 1995–March 2019—*Continued*

(Civilian labor force as a percent of the civilian noninstitutional population.)

Sex, race, and year	Participation rates				
	Total	Less than a high school diploma	4 years of high school only	1 to 3 years of college	4 or more years of college
White[1]					
1995	80.1	61.6	77.9	83.4	88.8
1996	80.4	62.5	78.6	83.9	88.2
1997	81.0	63.8	79.2	83.9	89.0
1998	80.6	63.8	78.6	83.5	88.3
1999	80.6	64.2	78.5	83.3	87.9
2000	80.8	64.2	78.7	83.1	87.9
2001	80.7	64.5	78.7	83.1	87.2
2002	80.3	65.0	78.2	82.4	87.0
2003	80.1	65.7	77.5	82.3	86.5
2004	79.5	64.6	76.7	81.6	86.2
2005	79.2	63.8	76.4	81.5	86.1
2006	79.5	65.1	76.5	81.4	86.2
2007	79.6	65.1	77.2	81.4	86.1
2008	79.6	63.8	76.8	81.2	86.3
2009	79.4	64.7	76.4	80.7	86.2
2010	79.5	64.5	77.1	80.4	86.0
2011	78.5	62.9	75.3	79.3	85.5
2012	78.3	63.8	74.2	78.8	86.0
2013	78.0	63.0	73.9	78.5	85.6
2014	77.6	62.9	73.4	77.8	85.4
2015	77.5	62.4	72.8	78.1	85.4
2016	78.0	63.6	73.1	77.7	86.2
2017	78.2	62.6	73.1	78.5	86.0
2018	78.4	63.3	73.2	78.1	86.3
2019	78.8	61.7	73.8	78.9	86.5
Black[1]					
1995	74.2	51.0	74.5	82.8	90.9
1996	73.7	50.1	74.3	83.0	87.9
1997	74.9	52.9	75.0	83.8	89.0
1998	77.7	59.3	77.0	85.0	88.8
1999	76.5	55.1	76.5	82.9	88.6
2000	77.9	55.5	77.0	84.2	90.3
2001	78.1	58.7	76.8	83.0	90.5
2002	76.4	56.6	75.0	81.7	88.9
2003	75.8	55.4	73.9	81.2	88.2
2004	75.0	55.2	73.4	79.0	87.9
2005	75.2	58.2	72.6	79.5	87.2
2006	75.0	54.0	73.3	79.6	87.7
2007	75.6	55.3	72.5	80.7	88.0
2008	75.6	54.3	72.8	80.0	87.5
2009	74.4	50.0	72.6	78.7	86.2
2010	74.2	52.2	71.7	77.5	87.0
2011	72.4	49.0	69.6	76.3	85.5
2012	72.9	50.8	68.6	77.2	85.7
2013	73.0	50.2	69.2	77.7	84.2
2014	72.8	54.4	67.9	75.4	86.0
2015	72.8	49.0	66.6	78.1	85.4
2016	72.7	50.9	66.9	76.2	85.8
2017	73.9	50.9	67.7	78.1	86.0
2018	74.3	48.7	69.6	76.6	86.8
2019	74.9	50.0	68.8	78.8	86.7

[1]Beginning in 2003, persons who selected this race group only; persons who selected more than one race group are not included. Prior to 2003, persons who reported more than one race group were included in the group they identified as their main race.

Table 1-58. Unemployment Rates of Persons Age 25 to 64 Years, by Educational Attainment and Sex, March 1995–March 2019

(Unemployment as a percent of the civilian labor force.)

Sex, race, and year	Unemployment rates				
	Total	Less than a high school diploma	4 years of high school only	1 to 3 years of college	4 or more years of college
Both Sexes					
1995	4.8	10.0	5.2	4.5	2.5
1996	4.8	10.9	5.5	4.1	2.2
1997	4.4	10.4	5.1	3.8	2.0
1998	4.0	8.5	4.8	3.6	1.8
1999	3.5	7.7	4.0	3.1	1.9
2000	3.3	7.9	3.8	3.0	1.5
2001	3.5	8.1	4.2	2.9	2.0
2002	5.0	10.2	6.1	4.5	2.8
2003	5.3	9.9	6.4	5.2	3.0
2004	5.1	10.5	5.9	4.9	2.9
2005	4.4	9.0	5.5	4.1	2.3
2006	4.1	8.3	4.7	3.9	2.3
2007	3.9	8.5	4.7	3.7	1.8
2008	4.4	10.1	5.8	4.2	2.1
2009	8.1	15.8	10.4	8.0	4.3
2010	9.1	16.8	12.1	8.8	4.7
2011	8.3	16.2	10.9	8.1	4.4
2012	7.4	14.3	9.2	7.9	4.1
2013	6.6	12.7	8.7	6.5	3.8
2014	5.8	10.6	7.4	6.1	3.4
2015	4.7	9.2	6.2	4.9	2.4
2016	4.4	8.1	6.1	4.5	2.4
2017	3.9	8.3	5.2	3.8	2.3
2018	3.5	6.6	4.7	3.7	2.2
2019	3.2	6.5	4.0	3.5	1.9
Men					
1995	5.1	10.9	5.7	4.4	2.6
1996	5.3	11.0	6.4	4.5	2.3
1997	4.7	9.9	5.6	4.0	2.1
1998	4.1	8.0	5.1	3.7	1.7
1999	3.5	7.0	4.1	3.2	1.9
2000	3.3	7.1	3.9	3.1	1.6
2001	3.7	7.5	4.6	3.2	1.9
2002	5.5	9.9	6.7	4.9	3.0
2003	5.8	9.5	6.9	6.0	3.2
2004	5.4	9.4	6.6	5.4	3.0
2005	4.7	7.9	6.0	4.3	2.5
2006	4.3	7.6	5.0	4.2	2.4
2007	4.3	8.4	5.5	3.9	1.9
2008	4.9	10.9	6.3	4.2	2.0
2009	9.5	16.5	12.4	9.3	4.7
2010	10.5	17.8	13.8	10.2	5.1
2011	9.2	16.7	12.2	8.7	4.6
2012	8.0	13.6	10.1	8.2	4.3
2013	6.9	11.9	9.2	6.5	3.7
2014	5.9	9.4	7.8	5.9	3.4
2015	5.0	8.4	6.7	4.9	2.8
2016	4.5	7.5	6.3	4.7	2.3
2017	4.1	8.0	5.2	4.1	2.4
2018	3.7	6.0	5.0	3.8	2.2
2019	3.4	6.1	4.2	3.7	2.0
Women					
1995	4.4	8.6	4.6	4.5	2.4
1996	4.1	10.7	4.4	3.8	2.1
1997	4.1	11.3	4.5	3.6	2.0
1998	3.9	9.3	4.4	3.5	1.9
1999	3.5	8.8	3.9	3.0	1.9
2000	3.2	9.1	3.6	2.9	1.4
2001	3.3	8.9	3.8	2.6	2.0
2002	4.6	10.6	5.4	4.1	2.6
2003	4.8	10.6	5.9	4.4	2.8
2004	4.7	12.2	5.2	4.3	2.9
2005	4.2	10.9	4.8	4.0	2.2
2006	3.8	9.4	4.4	3.7	2.1
2007	3.4	8.5	3.8	3.6	1.8
2008	4.0	8.5	5.1	4.2	2.1
2009	6.6	14.5	7.9	6.7	4.0
2010	7.5	15.0	9.8	7.5	4.3
2011	7.2	15.2	9.1	7.5	4.3
2012	6.8	15.4	8.1	7.7	3.8
2013	6.3	14.1	8.1	6.4	3.8
2014	5.7	12.7	6.8	6.3	3.4
2015	4.3	10.6	5.6	5.0	2.1
2016	4.2	9.2	5.8	4.3	2.6
2017	3.7	8.7	5.3	3.5	2.3
2018	3.3	7.8	4.3	3.6	2.1
2019	2.9	7.2	3.7	3.3	1.8

Table 1-58. Unemployment Rates of Persons Age 25 to 64 Years, by Educational Attainment and Sex, March 1995–March 2019—*Continued*

(Unemployment as a percent of the civilian labor force.)

Sex, race, and year	Unemployment rates				
	Total	Less than a high school diploma	4 years of high school only	1 to 3 years of college	4 or more years of college
White[1]					
1995	4.3	9.2	4.6	4.2	2.3
1996	4.2	10.2	4.6	3.7	2.1
1997	3.9	9.4	4.6	3.4	1.8
1998	3.5	7.5	4.2	3.2	1.7
1999	3.1	7.0	3.4	2.8	1.7
2000	3.0	7.5	3.3	2.7	1.4
2001	3.1	7.2	3.6	2.7	1.8
2002	4.6	9.1	5.5	4.1	2.6
2003	4.7	9.0	5.7	4.5	2.7
2004	4.6	9.6	5.4	4.4	2.8
2005	3.9	7.7	4.9	3.6	2.2
2006	3.5	7.1	4.0	3.5	2.1
2007	3.5	7.8	4.2	3.3	1.7
2008	4.0	9.2	5.1	3.7	1.9
2009	7.6	15.2	9.9	7.4	4.0
2010	8.4	16.3	11.3	8.1	4.3
2011	7.5	15.1	9.9	7.2	4.0
2012	6.7	13.5	8.3	6.9	3.7
2013	5.9	11.2	7.7	5.7	3.5
2014	5.1	9.2	6.3	5.4	3.1
2015	4.1	8.2	5.3	4.2	2.3
2016	3.8	6.7	5.2	3.8	2.3
2017	3.5	7.3	4.6	3.3	2.1
2018	3.2	5.9	4.2	3.3	2.0
2019	2.8	5.4	3.5	3.1	1.8
Black[1]					
1995	7.7	13.7	8.4	6.3	4.1
1996	8.9	15.3	10.8	6.9	3.3
1997	8.1	16.6	8.2	6.1	4.4
1998	7.3	13.4	8.4	6.4	2.1
1999	6.3	12.0	6.7	5.2	3.3
2000	5.4	10.4	6.3	4.3	2.5
2001	6.5	14.0	7.7	4.3	3.3
2002	8.1	15.4	9.7	6.0	4.1
2003	9.0	14.7	9.9	8.9	4.7
2004	8.4	15.8	9.3	7.9	3.7
2005	8.3	17.9	8.6	7.5	3.6
2006	7.8	16.4	9.0	6.5	3.6
2007	6.5	14.0	7.7	5.7	2.5
2008	7.6	16.7	9.3	6.5	3.3
2009	12.1	22.0	14.0	11.2	7.2
2010	14.1	22.4	17.5	12.9	7.9
2011	13.9	25.0	16.6	12.7	7.7
2012	12.3	21.4	14.2	12.7	6.3
2013	11.4	22.8	14.2	10.0	6.1
2014	10.7	19.7	13.8	10.0	5.0
2015	8.8	17.6	10.8	8.6	4.3
2016	7.9	17.3	10.5	7.4	3.3
2017	6.7	16.4	8.5	5.9	3.4
2018	5.6	11.6	7.3	5.2	2.9
2019	5.4	15.0	6.6	5.3	2.5

[1]Beginning in 2003, persons who selected this race group only; persons who selected more than one race group are not included. Prior to 2003, persons who reported more than one race group were included in the group they identified as their main race.

Table 1-59. Workers Age 25 to 64 Years, by Educational Attainment, Occupation of Longest Job Held, and Sex, 2017–2018

(Thousands of people with work experience during the year.)

Year, sex, and occupation	Total	Less than a high school diploma	4 years of high school only	1 to 3 years of college	4 or more years of college
2017					
Both Sexes	132 630	9 462	33 721	35 780	53 667
Management, business, and financial operations	23 251	477	3 199	5 089	14 487
Management	16 080	427	2 508	3 650	9 495
Business and financial operations	7 171	50	691	1 439	4 991
Professional and related	32 933	181	2 088	6 482	24 182
Computer and mathematical	4 653	24	256	923	3 450
Architecture and engineering	2 971	2	201	502	2 266
Life, physical, and social sciences	1 401	1	46	115	1 239
Community and social services	2 437	19	195	412	1 811
Legal	1 552	9	88	221	1 234
Education, training, and library	8 852	59	535	1 129	7 130
Arts, design, entertainment, sports, and media	2 850	46	317	602	1 885
Health care practitioner and technical	8 216	21	451	2 578	5 167
Services	20 630	3 039	7 566	6 536	3 489
Health care support	3 138	187	978	1 484	489
Protective services	2 620	66	682	1 069	803
Food preparation and serving related	5 294	952	2 134	1 448	760
Building and grounds cleaning and maintenance	4 967	1 409	2 103	1 029	426
Personal care and services	4 611	426	1 669	1 505	1 011
Sales and office	26 379	1 018	7 699	9 384	8 279
Sales and related	11 891	590	3 277	3 719	4 305
Office and administrative support	14 488	428	4 422	5 664	3 974
Natural resources, construction, and maintenance	12 834	2 452	5 522	3 601	1 259
Farming, fishing, and forestry	1 068	443	339	180	106
Construction and extraction	7 409	1 573	3 389	1 797	650
Installation, maintenance, and repair	4 356	435	1 793	1 624	504
Production, transportation, and material moving	15 978	2 294	7 546	4 370	1 768
Production	7 565	1 138	3 520	2 116	792
Transportation and material moving	8 412	1 156	4 026	2 254	976
Armed forces	625	1	101	319	204
Men	70 242	5 999	19 918	17 950	26 374
Management, business, and financial operations	12 643	302	1 876	2 609	7 857
Management	9 439	280	1 623	2 120	5 416
Business and financial operations	3 204	22	253	489	2 441
Professional and related	13 982	71	859	2 462	10 590
Computer and mathematical	3 516	18	174	715	2 608
Architecture and engineering	2 470	1	156	452	1 861
Life, physical, and social sciences	726	1	31	66	628
Community and social services	779	5	91	135	548
Legal	690	. . .	17	22	651
Education, training, and library	2 354	11	96	248	1 998
Arts, design, entertainment, sports, and media	1 532	33	211	336	951
Health care practitioner and technical	1 915	1	82	487	1 344
Services	8 782	1 319	3 181	2 645	1 637
Health care support	362	9	87	147	119
Protective services	2 098	53	539	881	625
Food preparation and serving related	2 422	462	980	618	362
Building and grounds cleaning and maintenance	2 892	726	1 240	671	255
Personal care and services	1 008	69	335	328	277
Sales and office	10 092	418	2 791	3 181	3 702
Sales and related	6 223	231	1 630	1 857	2 506
Office and administrative support	3 869	188	1 161	1 324	1 197
Natural resources, construction, and maintenance	12 117	2 265	5 318	3 418	1 116
Farming, fishing, and forestry	767	301	263	127	77
Construction and extraction	7 180	1 544	3 310	1 726	600
Installation, maintenance, and repair	4 170	420	1 745	1 565	440
Production, transportation, and material moving	12 061	1 624	5 796	3 348	1 292
Production	5 244	704	2 510	1 535	495
Transportation and material moving	6 817	920	3 286	1 813	797
Armed forces	564	1	97	287	180
Women	62 388	3 463	13 803	17 830	27 292
Management, business, and financial operations	10 608	175	1 323	2 479	6 630
Management	6 641	147	885	1 530	4 080
Business and financial operations	3 966	28	438	950	2 550
Professional and related	18 951	111	1 230	4 019	13 591
Computer and mathematical	1 137	6	82	208	842
Architecture and engineering	500	1	45	50	405
Life, physical, and social sciences	675	. . .	15	49	611
Community and social services	1 658	15	104	276	1 263
Legal	862	9	70	200	583
Education, training, and library	6 499	48	439	881	5 131
Arts, design, entertainment, sports, and media	1 319	13	106	266	933
Health care practitioner and technical	6 301	20	369	2 090	3 822
Services	11 848	1 721	4 385	3 891	1 851
Health care support	2 776	178	891	1 337	370
Protective services	522	12	143	188	178
Food preparation and serving related	2 872	491	1 154	829	398
Building and grounds cleaning and maintenance	2 075	683	863	358	171
Personal care and services	3 602	357	1 334	1 177	733
Sales and office	16 287	600	4 908	6 203	4 577
Sales and related	5 668	360	1 647	1 863	1 799
Office and administrative support	10 619	240	3 261	4 341	2 777
Natural resources, construction, and maintenance	717	187	204	183	143
Farming, fishing, and forestry	301	142	76	53	29
Construction and extraction	229	29	80	71	50
Installation, maintenance, and repair	187	15	48	59	64
Production, transportation, and material moving	3 917	670	1 749	1 021	476
Production	2 321	434	1 010	581	297
Transportation and material moving	1 595	236	740	441	179
Armed forces	61	. . .	4	32	24

. . . = Not available.

Table 1-59. Workers Age 25 to 64 Years, by Educational Attainment, Occupation of Longest Job Held, and Sex, 2017–2018—*Continued*

(Thousands of people with work experience during the year.)

Year, sex, and occupation	Total	Less than a high school diploma	4 years of high school only	1 to 3 years of college	4 or more years of college
2018					
Both Sexes	133 412	9 326	33 677	35 394	55 015
Management, business, and financial operations	23 946	457	3 189	5 292	15 008
Management	16 673	405	2 548	3 809	9 911
Business and financial operations	7 272	52	640	1 483	5 097
Professional and related	32 863	129	2 137	6 015	24 582
Computer and mathematical	4 732	15	309	776	3 632
Architecture and engineering	3 037	9	241	544	2 243
Life, physical, and social sciences	1 353	. . .	68	105	1 181
Community and social services	2 379	22	185	351	1 822
Legal	1 492	. . .	87	194	1 211
Education, training, and library	8 610	47	509	1 040	7 014
Arts, design, entertainment, sports, and media	2 772	20	277	587	1 889
Health care practitioner and technical	8 488	16	462	2 419	5 591
Services	20 739	2 985	7 591	6 617	3 546
Health care support	3 012	164	952	1 416	480
Protective services	2 669	50	596	1 125	898
Food preparation and serving related	5 429	931	2 274	1 517	706
Building and grounds cleaning and maintenance	5 053	1 405	2 266	924	458
Personal care and services	4 577	435	1 504	1 634	1 004
Sales and office	26 658	1 062	7 738	9 232	8 626
Sales and related	12 115	597	3 371	3 668	4 479
Office and administrative support	14 542	464	4 367	5 564	4 147
Natural resources, construction, and maintenance	12 554	2 427	5 399	3 574	1 153
Farming, fishing, and forestry	982	449	315	148	70
Construction and extraction	7 481	1 616	3 358	1 804	703
Installation, maintenance, and repair	4 091	362	1 726	1 623	379
Production, transportation, and material moving	16 109	2 265	7 523	4 446	1 875
Production	7 657	1 126	3 511	2 227	794
Transportation and material moving	8 452	1 139	4 012	2 220	1 081
Armed forces	544	1	99	218	226
Men	70 580	5 967	19 978	17 858	26 777
Management, business, and financial operations	13 068	317	1 892	2 816	8 043
Management	9 802	289	1 639	2 296	5 578
Business and financial operations	3 266	28	253	520	2 465
Professional and related	13 725	49	886	2 167	10 623
Computer and mathematical	3 519	12	210	596	2 702
Architecture and engineering	2 586	9	191	492	1 894
Life, physical, and social sciences	644	. . .	44	49	551
Community and social services	741	10	80	109	541
Legal	676	. . .	13	15	648
Education, training, and library	2 164	13	92	186	1 872
Arts, design, entertainment, sports, and media	1 397	6	173	330	889
Health care practitioner and technical	1 999	. . .	83	389	1 526
Services	8 703	1 277	3 136	2 628	1 661
Health care support	364	9	117	136	102
Protective services	2 074	38	452	920	664
Food preparation and serving related	2 508	483	1 004	690	331
Building and grounds cleaning and maintenance	2 756	661	1 269	528	298
Personal care and services	1 001	86	293	355	267
Sales and office	10 343	474	2 910	3 169	3 790
Sales and related	6 333	249	1 663	1 817	2 604
Office and administrative support	4 010	225	1 247	1 352	1 186
Natural resources, construction, and maintenance	11 862	2 222	5 169	3 409	1 062
Farming, fishing, and forestry	707	323	227	111	47
Construction and extraction	7 220	1 558	3 274	1 733	655
Installation, maintenance, and repair	3 935	341	1 668	1 565	360
Production, transportation, and material moving	12 372	1 629	5 889	3 459	1 395
Production	5 435	694	2 541	1 670	530
Transportation and material moving	6 937	934	3 349	1 789	865
Armed forces	507	. . .	96	208	203
Women	62 832	3 358	13 699	17 537	28 238
Management, business, and financial operations	10 877	140	1 297	2 476	6 965
Management	6 871	117	909	1 512	4 333
Business and financial operations	4 006	24	387	963	2 632
Professional and related	19 138	79	1 251	3 848	13 959
Computer and mathematical	1 213	3	100	180	931
Architecture and engineering	451	. . .	50	52	350
Life, physical, and social sciences	709	. . .	24	55	630
Community and social services	1 639	12	104	241	1 281
Legal	816	. . .	74	179	563
Education, training, and library	6 446	34	417	854	5 141
Arts, design, entertainment, sports, and media	1 375	14	104	257	1 000
Health care practitioner and technical	6 489	16	379	2 030	4 064
Services	12 036	1 708	4 456	3 988	1 884
Health care support	2 649	155	835	1 280	379
Protective services	594	12	143	206	234
Food preparation and serving related	2 921	448	1 270	827	375
Building and grounds cleaning and maintenance	2 296	745	996	396	159
Personal care and services	3 576	349	1 211	1 279	737
Sales and office	16 315	588	4 828	6 063	4 836
Sales and related	5 782	348	1 708	1 851	1 875
Office and administrative support	10 532	239	3 120	4 212	2 961
Natural resources, construction, and maintenance	692	206	230	166	91
Farming, fishing, and forestry	275	126	89	37	23
Construction and extraction	261	58	84	71	49
Installation, maintenance, and repair	156	22	58	57	19
Production, transportation, and material moving	3 737	636	1 634	987	480
Production	2 222	432	970	557	264
Transportation and material moving	1 515	204	664	431	216
Armed forces	36	1	3	9	23

. . . = Not available.

Table 1-60. Percent Distribution of Workers Age 25 to 64 Years, by Educational Attainment, Occupation of Longest Job Held, and Sex, 2017–2018

(Percent of total workers in occupation.)

Year, sex, and occupation	Total	Less than a high school diploma	4 years of high school only	1 to 3 years of college	4 or more years of college
2017					
Both Sexes	100.0	7.1	25.4	27.0	40.5
Management, business, and financial operations	100.0	2.1	13.8	21.9	62.3
Management	100.0	2.7	15.6	22.7	59.0
Business and financial operations	100.0	0.7	9.6	20.1	69.6
Professional and related	100.0	0.6	6.3	19.7	73.4
Computer and mathematical	100.0	0.5	5.5	19.8	74.1
Architecture and engineering	100.0	0.1	6.8	16.9	76.3
Life, physical, and social sciences	100.0	0.1	3.3	8.2	88.4
Community and social services	100.0	0.8	8.0	16.9	74.3
Legal	100.0	0.6	5.6	14.3	79.5
Education, training, and library	100.0	0.7	6.0	12.8	80.5
Arts, design, entertainment, sports, and media	100.0	1.6	11.1	21.1	66.1
Health care practitioner and technical	100.0	0.3	5.5	31.4	62.9
Services	100.0	14.7	36.7	31.7	16.9
Health care support	100.0	6.0	31.2	47.3	15.6
Protective services	100.0	2.5	26.0	40.8	30.7
Food preparation and serving related	100.0	18.0	40.3	27.3	14.4
Building and grounds cleaning and maintenance	100.0	28.4	42.3	20.7	8.6
Personal care and services	100.0	9.2	36.2	32.6	21.9
Sales and office	100.0	3.9	29.2	35.6	31.4
Sales and related	100.0	5.0	27.6	31.3	36.2
Office and administrative support	100.0	3.0	30.5	39.1	27.4
Natural resources, construction, and maintenance	100.0	19.1	43.0	28.1	9.8
Farming, fishing, and forestry	100.0	41.5	31.7	16.9	9.9
Construction and extraction	100.0	21.2	45.7	24.3	8.8
Installation, maintenance, and repair	100.0	10.0	41.2	37.3	11.6
Production, transportation, and material moving	100.0	14.4	47.2	27.3	11.1
Production	100.0	15.0	46.5	28.0	10.5
Transportation and material moving	100.0	13.7	47.9	26.8	11.6
Armed forces	100.0	0.2	16.2	51.1	32.6
Men	100.0	8.5	28.4	25.6	37.5
Management, business, and financial operations	100.0	2.4	14.8	20.6	62.1
Management	100.0	3.0	17.2	22.5	57.4
Business and financial operations	100.0	0.7	7.9	15.3	76.2
Professional and related	100.0	0.5	6.1	17.6	75.7
Computer and mathematical	100.0	0.5	5.0	20.3	74.2
Architecture and engineering	100.0	0.0	6.3	18.3	75.3
Life, physical, and social sciences	100.0	0.2	4.3	9.1	86.4
Community and social services	100.0	0.6	11.7	17.4	70.4
Legal	100.0	. . .	2.5	3.2	94.3
Education, training, and library	100.0	0.5	4.1	10.5	84.9
Arts, design, entertainment, sports, and media	100.0	2.2	13.8	21.9	62.1
Health care practitioner and technical	100.0	0.1	4.3	25.5	70.2
Services	100.0	15.0	36.2	30.1	18.6
Health care support	100.0	2.5	24.1	40.6	32.8
Protective services	100.0	2.5	25.7	42.0	29.8
Food preparation and serving related	100.0	19.1	40.5	25.5	14.9
Building and grounds cleaning and maintenance	100.0	25.1	42.9	23.2	8.8
Personal care and services	100.0	6.8	33.2	32.5	27.5
Sales and office	100.0	4.1	27.7	31.5	36.7
Sales and related	100.0	3.7	26.2	29.8	40.3
Office and administrative support	100.0	4.8	30.0	34.2	30.9
Natural resources, construction, and maintenance	100.0	18.7	43.9	28.2	9.2
Farming, fishing, and forestry	100.0	39.2	34.3	16.6	10.0
Construction and extraction	100.0	21.5	46.1	24.0	8.4
Installation, maintenance, and repair	100.0	10.1	41.9	37.5	10.5
Production, transportation, and material moving	100.0	13.5	48.1	27.8	10.7
Production	100.0	13.4	47.9	29.3	9.4
Transportation and material moving	100.0	13.5	48.2	26.6	11.7
Armed forces	100.0	0.2	17.1	50.8	31.8
Women	100.0	5.6	22.1	28.6	43.7
Management, business, and financial operations	100.0	1.6	12.5	23.4	62.5
Management	100.0	2.2	13.3	23.0	61.4
Business and financial operations	100.0	0.7	11.0	23.9	64.3
Professional and related	100.0	0.6	6.5	21.2	71.7
Computer and mathematical	100.0	0.5	7.2	18.3	74.0
Architecture and engineering	100.0	0.2	8.9	9.9	80.9
Life, physical, and social sciences	100.0	. . .	2.2	7.3	90.6
Community and social services	100.0	0.9	6.3	16.7	76.2
Legal	100.0	1.1	8.1	23.1	67.7
Education, training, and library	100.0	0.7	6.8	13.5	79.0
Arts, design, entertainment, sports, and media	100.0	1.0	8.0	20.2	70.8
Health care practitioner and technical	100.0	0.3	5.9	33.2	60.7
Services	100.0	14.5	37.0	32.8	15.6
Health care support	100.0	6.4	32.1	48.2	13.3
Protective services	100.0	2.4	27.4	36.1	34.2
Food preparation and serving related	100.0	17.1	40.2	28.9	13.9
Building and grounds cleaning and maintenance	100.0	32.9	41.6	17.3	8.3
Personal care and services	100.0	9.9	37.0	32.7	20.4
Sales and office	100.0	3.7	30.1	38.1	28.1
Sales and related	100.0	6.3	29.1	32.9	31.7
Office and administrative support	100.0	2.3	30.7	40.9	26.2
Natural resources, construction, and maintenance	100.0	26.0	28.4	25.6	20.0
Farming, fishing, and forestry	100.0	47.4	25.2	17.7	9.7
Construction and extraction	100.0	12.7	34.7	30.9	21.7
Installation, maintenance, and repair	100.0	8.1	25.8	31.6	34.4
Production, transportation, and material moving	100.0	17.1	44.7	26.1	12.2
Production	100.0	18.7	43.5	25.0	12.8
Transportation and material moving	100.0	14.8	46.4	27.6	11.2
Armed forces	100.0	. . .	7.1	53.3	39.7

. . . = Not available.

Table 1-60. Percent Distribution of Workers Age 25 to 64 Years, by Educational Attainment, Occupation of Longest Job Held, and Sex, 2017–2018—*Continued*

(Percent of total workers in occupation.)

Year, sex, and occupation	Total	Less than a high school diploma	4 years of high school only	1 to 3 years of college	4 or more years of college
2018					
Both Sexes	100.0	7.0	25.2	26.5	41.2
Management, business, and financial operations	100.0	1.9	13.3	22.1	62.7
Management	100.0	2.4	15.3	22.8	59.4
Business and financial operations	100.0	0.7	8.8	20.4	70.1
Professional and related	100.0	0.4	6.5	18.3	74.8
Computer and mathematical	100.0	0.3	6.5	16.4	76.8
Architecture and engineering	100.0	0.3	7.9	17.9	73.9
Life, physical, and social sciences	100.0	. . .	5.0	7.7	87.3
Community and social services	100.0	0.9	7.8	14.7	76.6
Legal	100.0	. . .	5.8	13.0	81.2
Education, training, and library	100.0	0.6	5.9	12.1	81.5
Arts, design, entertainment, sports, and media	100.0	0.7	10.0	21.2	68.1
Health care practitioner and technical	100.0	0.2	5.4	28.5	65.9
Services	100.0	14.4	36.6	31.9	17.1
Health care support	100.0	5.4	31.6	47.0	15.9
Protective services	100.0	1.9	22.3	42.2	33.6
Food preparation and serving related	100.0	17.2	41.9	27.9	13.0
Building and grounds cleaning and maintenance	100.0	27.8	44.8	18.3	9.1
Personal care and services	100.0	9.5	32.9	35.7	21.9
Sales and office	100.0	4.0	29.0	34.6	32.4
Sales and related	100.0	4.9	27.8	30.3	37.0
Office and administrative support	100.0	3.2	30.0	38.3	28.5
Natural resources, construction, and maintenance	100.0	19.3	43.0	28.5	9.2
Farming, fishing, and forestry	100.0	45.7	32.1	15.1	7.2
Construction and extraction	100.0	21.6	44.9	24.1	9.4
Installation, maintenance, and repair	100.0	8.9	42.2	39.7	9.3
Production, transportation, and material moving	100.0	14.1	46.7	27.6	11.6
Production	100.0	14.7	45.9	29.1	10.4
Transportation and material moving	100.0	13.5	47.5	26.3	12.8
Armed forces	100.0	0.2	18.2	40.1	41.5
Men	100.0	8.5	28.3	25.3	37.9
Management, business, and financial operations	100.0	2.4	14.5	21.6	61.5
Management	100.0	2.9	16.7	23.4	56.9
Business and financial operations	100.0	0.9	7.7	15.9	75.5
Professional and related	100.0	0.4	6.5	15.8	77.4
Computer and mathematical	100.0	0.3	6.0	16.9	76.8
Architecture and engineering	100.0	0.3	7.4	19.0	73.2
Life, physical, and social sciences	100.0	. . .	6.8	7.7	85.5
Community and social services	100.0	1.3	10.8	14.8	73.1
Legal	100.0	. . .	1.9	2.3	95.8
Education, training, and library	100.0	0.6	4.3	8.6	86.5
Arts, design, entertainment, sports, and media	100.0	0.4	12.4	23.6	63.6
Health care practitioner and technical	100.0	. . .	4.1	19.5	76.4
Services	100.0	14.7	36.0	30.2	19.1
Health care support	100.0	2.4	32.2	37.5	27.9
Protective services	100.0	1.8	21.8	44.3	32.0
Food preparation and serving related	100.0	19.3	40.0	27.5	13.2
Building and grounds cleaning and maintenance	100.0	24.0	46.1	19.2	10.8
Personal care and services	100.0	8.6	29.3	35.4	26.7
Sales and office	100.0	4.6	28.1	30.6	36.6
Sales and related	100.0	3.9	26.3	28.7	41.1
Office and administrative support	100.0	5.6	31.1	33.7	29.6
Natural resources, construction, and maintenance	100.0	18.7	43.6	28.7	9.0
Farming, fishing, and forestry	100.0	45.6	32.0	15.6	6.7
Construction and extraction	100.0	21.6	45.3	24.0	9.1
Installation, maintenance, and repair	100.0	8.7	42.4	39.8	9.2
Production, transportation, and material moving	100.0	13.2	47.6	28.0	11.3
Production	100.0	12.8	46.7	30.7	9.7
Transportation and material moving	100.0	13.5	48.3	25.8	12.5
Armed forces	100.0	. . .	18.9	41.1	40.0
Women	100.0	5.3	21.8	27.9	44.9
Management, business, and financial operations	100.0	1.3	11.9	22.8	64.0
Management	100.0	1.7	13.2	22.0	63.1
Business and financial operations	100.0	0.6	9.7	24.0	65.7
Professional and related	100.0	0.4	6.5	20.1	72.9
Computer and mathematical	100.0	0.2	8.2	14.8	76.7
Architecture and engineering	100.0	. . .	11.0	11.4	77.5
Life, physical, and social sciences	100.0	. . .	3.4	7.8	88.8
Community and social services	100.0	0.7	6.4	14.7	78.2
Legal	100.0	. . .	9.1	21.9	69.0
Education, training, and library	100.0	0.5	6.5	13.2	79.8
Arts, design, entertainment, sports, and media	100.0	1.0	7.6	18.7	72.7
Health care practitioner and technical	100.0	0.3	5.8	31.3	62.6
Services	100.0	14.2	37.0	33.1	15.7
Health care support	100.0	5.9	31.5	48.3	14.3
Protective services	100.0	2.0	24.1	34.6	39.4
Food preparation and serving related	100.0	15.3	43.5	28.3	12.8
Building and grounds cleaning and maintenance	100.0	32.4	43.4	17.3	6.9
Personal care and services	100.0	9.8	33.9	35.8	20.6
Sales and office	100.0	3.6	29.6	37.2	29.6
Sales and related	100.0	6.0	29.5	32.0	32.4
Office and administrative support	100.0	2.3	29.6	40.0	28.1
Natural resources, construction, and maintenance	100.0	29.7	33.3	23.9	13.1
Farming, fishing, and forestry	100.0	45.9	32.2	13.6	8.3
Construction and extraction	100.0	22.2	32.1	27.2	18.6
Installation, maintenance, and repair	100.0	13.8	37.1	36.8	12.3
Production, transportation, and material moving	100.0	17.0	43.7	26.4	12.8
Production	100.0	19.4	43.7	25.0	11.9
Transportation and material moving	100.0	13.5	43.8	28.4	14.3
Armed forces	100.0	2.6	9.1	25.7	62.6

. . . = Not available.

Table 1-61. Median Annual Earnings of Year-Round, Full-Time Wage and Salary Workers Age 25 to 64 Years, by Educational Attainment and Sex, 2005–2018

(Thousands of workers, dollars.)

Year and sex	Total	Less than a high school diploma	4 years of high school only	1 to 3 years of college	4 or more years of college
2005					
Both Sexes					
Number of workers	88 415	7 758	26 023	24 623	30 012
Median annual earnings	39 768	22 880	31 000	38 000	55 000
Men					
Number of workers	51 022	5 376	15 451	13 199	16 996
Median annual earnings	44 000	25 000	35 360	45 000	65 000
Women					
Number of workers	37 393	2 381	10 571	11 424	13 016
Median annual earnings	33 644	18 200	26 000	32 000	46 700
2006					
Both Sexes					
Number of workers	90 733	7 951	26 233	24 737	31 812
Median annual earnings	40 000	23 000	32 000	39 482	57 588
Men					
Number of workers	52 252	5 485	15 525	13 204	18 038
Median annual earnings	45 000	25 000	36 665	45 000	68 000
Women					
Number of workers	38 481	2 466	10 708	11 533	13 774
Median annual earnings	35 000	19 000	26 800	33 000	49 000
2007					
Both Sexes					
Number of workers	91 540	7 123	25 925	25 574	32 918
Median annual earnings	41 000	24 000	33 000	40 000	60 000
Men					
Number of workers	52 262	4 902	15 390	13 655	18 316
Median annual earnings	47 000	25 000	38 000	45 188	70 000
Women					
Number of workers	39 277	2 221	10 535	11 919	14 603
Median annual earnings	35 000	19 200	27 120	35 000	50 000
2008					
Both Sexes					
Number of workers	88 373	6 600	24 531	24 887	32 355
Median annual earnings	42 000	24 000	34 000	40 000	60 000
Men					
Number of workers	50 141	4 503	14 480	13 283	17 876
Median annual earnings	49 564	27 000	39 040	47 000	72 000
Women					
Number of workers	38 231	2 097	10 051	11 604	14 479
Median annual earnings	36 000	19 567	28 000	35 000	50 000
2009					
Both Sexes					
Number of workers	84 730	5 847	23 277	23 515	32 091
Median annual earnings	43 000	24 000	34 320	40 000	60 000
Men					
Number of workers	47 135	3 809	13 620	12 283	17 424
Median annual earnings	50 000	26 000	40 000	49 000	71 000
Women					
Number of workers	37 595	2 037	9 657	11 233	14 667
Median annual earnings	38 000	20 000	29 000	35 000	52 000
2010					
Both Sexes					
Number of workers	84 902	5 548	22 768	23 725	32 861
Median annual earnings	44 217	24 000	35 000	40 000	60 000
Men					
Number of workers	47 549	3 653	13 526	12 405	17 965
Median annual earnings	50 000	26 500	40 000	48 000	72 000
Women					
Number of workers	37 353	1 895	9 241	11 321	14 896
Median annual earnings	38 000	20 000	30 000	35 000	51 000
2011					
Both Sexes					
Number of workers	86 570	5 858	22 921	23 947	33 843
Median annual earnings	45 000	25 000	35 000	41 000	62 000
Men					
Number of workers	48 748	3 971	13 750	12 705	18 322
Median annual earnings	50 000	27 819	40 000	50 000	75 000
Women					
Number of workers	37 822	1 887	9 171	11 243	15 521
Median annual earnings	39 000	20 000	30 000	35 000	52 000

Table 1-61. Median Annual Earnings of Year-Round, Full-Time Wage and Salary Workers Age 25 to 64 Years, by Educational Attainment and Sex, 2005–2018—*Continued*

(Thousands of workers, dollars.)

Year and sex	Total	Less than a high school diploma	4 years of high school only	1 to 3 years of college	4 or more years of college
2012					
Both Sexes					
Number of workers	87 660	5 671	22 628	24 217	35 144
Median annual earnings	45 000	24 750	35 000	41 500	63 000
Men					
Number of workers	49 481	3 874	13 629	13 051	18 927
Median annual earnings	50 000	26 000	40 000	49 000	75 000
Women					
Number of workers	38 179	1 797	8 999	11 165	16 217
Median annual earnings	40 000	20 000	30 000	35 395	54 000
2013					
Both Sexes					
Number of workers	89 443	6 100	23 427	24 477	35 440
Median annual earnings	45 000	25 000	35 000	42 000	65 000
Men					
Number of workers	50 765	4 260	14 338	13 201	18 965
Median annual earnings	50 000	28 000	40 000	49 999	75 000
Women					
Number of workers	38 678	1 840	9 089	11 275	16 475
Median annual earnings	40 000	20 800	30 000	35 340	55 000
2014					
Both Sexes					
Number of workers	91 622	6 280	23 537	24 967	36 837
Median annual earnings	46 000	25 000	35 000	41 600	65 000
Men					
Number of workers	52 165	4 377	14 649	13 402	19 736
Median annual earnings	50 000	29 000	40 000	49 000	75 000
Women					
Number of workers	39 456	1 903	8 888	11 565	17 101
Median annual earnings	40 000	20 800	30 000	35 000	55 000
2015					
Both Sexes					
Number of workers	93 616	6 208	23 376	25 747	38 284
Median annual earnings	48 000	27 000	36 000	43 000	68 000
Men					
Number of workers	53 137	4 313	14 495	13 830	20 499
Median annual earnings	53 000	30 000	40 000	50 000	80 000
Women					
Number of workers	40 478	1 895	8 881	11 917	17 785
Median annual earnings	41 600	20 800	30 000	37 000	57 747
2016					
Both Sexes					
Number of workers	95 656	5 916	23 927	26 180	39 632
Median annual earnings	50 000	30 000	37 010	45 000	69 507
Men					
Number of workers	54 203	4 067	15 038	14 138	20 960
Median annual earnings	54 000	32 000	42 000	50 000	80 000
Women					
Number of workers	41 453	1 849	8 889	12 042	18 672
Median annual earnings	44 000	24 000	31 000	38 000	60 000
2017					
Both Sexes					
Number of workers	97 130	5 920	24 030	25 853	41 327
Median annual earnings	50 000	30 000	39 000	45 000	70 000
Men					
Number of workers	54 897	4 067	15 157	13 997	21 676
Median annual earnings	55 000	32 000	42 500	51 000	80 000
Women					
Number of workers	42 233	1 853	8 873	11 856	19 651
Median annual earnings	45 000	24 002	32 000	38 000	60 000
2018					
Both Sexes					
Number of workers	98 904	5 920	24 601	25 630	42 753
Median annual earnings	51 000	30 000	40 000	47 466	71 000
Men					
Number of workers	55 844	4 075	15 548	13 991	22 230
Median annual earnings	58 000	34 000	45 000	54 000	84 000
Women					
Number of workers	43 060	1 845	9 053	11 639	20 523
Median annual earnings	45 760	24 000	32 000	40 000	60 000

Table 1-62. Employment Status of the Civilian Noninstitutional Population by Disability Status and Selected Characteristics, 2018 Annual Averages

(Thousands of people, percent.)

Characteristic	Civilian noninstitutional population	Civilian labor force						Not in labor force
		Total	Participation rate	Employed		Unemployed		
				Total	Percent	Total	Rate	
TOTAL								
Total, 16 Years and Over	257 791	162 075	62.9	155 761	60.4	6 314	3.9	95 716
Men	124 678	86 096	69.1	82 698	66.3	3 398	3.9	38 582
Women	133 112	75 978	57.1	73 063	54.9	2 916	3.8	57 134
PERSONS WITH A DISABILITY	30 136	6 266	20.8	5 767	19.1	499	8.0	23 870
Sex								
Men	13 997	3 389	24.2	3 122	22.3	267	7.9	10 608
Women	16 139	2 877	17.8	2 645	16.4	232	8.1	13 262
Age								
16 to 64 years	15 325	5 111	33.3	4 666	30.4	445	8.7	10 215
16 to 19 years	644	151	23.5	112	17.4	39	26.1	493
20 to 24 years	867	384	44.3	328	37.8	56	14.6	483
25 to 34 years	1 914	930	48.6	828	43.3	101	10.9	984
35 to 44 years	2 140	861	40.2	795	37.1	67	7.7	1 279
45 to 54 years	3 537	1 204	34.0	1 123	31.7	81	6.7	2 333
55 to 64 years	6 223	1 580	25.4	1 480	23.8	100	6.3	4 643
65 years and over	14 810	1 155	7.8	1 101	7.4	54	4.7	13 655
Race and Hispanic Origin								
White	23 987	5 043	21.0	4 676	19.5	367	7.3	18 944
Black or African American	4 151	763	18.4	677	16.3	85	11.2	3 388
Asian	878	162	18.4	150	17.1	12	7.1	716
Hispanic[1]	3 258	753	23.1	679	20.9	74	9.8	2 505
Educational Attainment								
Total, 25 years and over	28 625	5 731	20.0	5 327	18.6	403	7.0	22 894
Less than a high school diploma	5 250	581	11.1	513	9.8	68	11.7	4 668
High school graduates, no college[2]	10 326	1 748	16.9	1 609	15.6	139	7.9	8 578
Some college or associate degree	7 624	1 783	23.4	1 659	21.8	124	6.9	5 841
Bachelor's degree and higher[3]	5 425	1 619	29.8	1 546	28.5	73	4.5	3 806

[1]May be of any race.
[2]Includes persons with a high school diploma or equivalent.
[3]Includes persons with bachelor's, master's, professional, and doctoral degrees.

Table 1-63. Employed Full- and Part-Time Workers by Disability Status and Age, 2018 Annual Averages

(Thousands of people.)

Disability status and age	Employed			At work part-time for economic reasons[1]
	Total	Usually work full-time	Usually work part-time	
TOTAL				
Total, 16 Years and Over	155 761	128 572	27 189	4 778
16 to 64 years	146 056	122 605	23 450	4 535
65 years and over	9 705	5 967	3 739	243
Persons With a Disability				
16 years and over	5 767	3 956	1 811	243
16 to 64 years	4 666	3 406	1 259	208
65 years and over	1 101	550	551	35
Persons Without a Disability				
16 years and over	149 994	124 616	25 378	4 535
16 to 64 years	141 390	119 199	22 191	4 326
65 years and over	8 604	5 417	3 187	208

Note: Full time refers to persons who usually work 35 hours or more per week; part time refers to persons who usually work less than 35 hours per week.

[1]Refers to persons who, whether they usually work full or part time, worked 1 to 34 hours during the reference week for an economic reason such as slack work or unfavorable business conditions, inability to find full-time work, or seasonal declines in demand.

Table 1-64. Employed Persons by Disability Status, Occupation, and Sex, 2018 Annual Averages

(Number in thousands, percent.)

Occupation	Persons with a disability			Persons with no disability		
	Total	Men	Women	Total	Men	Women
TOTAL EMPLOYED	5 767	3 122	2 645	149 994	79 576	70 418
Occupation as a Percent of Total Employed						
Total	100.0	100.0	100.0	100.0	100.0	100.0
Management, professional, and related	33.7	31.0	37.0	40.3	36.8	44.3
Management, business, and financial operations	14.3	15.4	13.0	16.7	17.6	15.7
Management	10.5	12.5	8.2	11.8	13.3	10.1
Business and financial operations	3.8	2.9	4.8	4.9	4.3	5.6
Professional and related	19.4	15.6	24.0	23.6	19.3	28.6
Computer and mathematical	2.0	2.7	1.2	3.3	4.7	1.8
Architecture and engineering	1.6	2.4	0.5	2.1	3.4	0.7
Life, physical, and social science	0.7	0.7	0.8	1.0	1.0	1.0
Community and social services	2.3	1.6	3.2	1.7	1.1	2.4
Legal	1.3	1.4	1.2	1.2	1.1	1.3
Education, training, and library	5.3	2.9	8.2	6.0	3.0	9.4
Arts, design, entertainment, sports, and media	2.0	2.0	2.0	2.2	2.2	2.2
Healthcare practitioner and technical	4.2	2.0	6.9	6.1	2.9	9.8
Service	19.0	15.6	23.0	17.2	13.7	21.1
Healthcare support	2.2	0.6	4.1	2.3	0.6	4.3
Protective service	1.8	2.6	0.9	2.1	3.0	1.0
Food preparation and serving related	4.9	3.9	6.0	5.3	4.4	6.3
Building and grounds cleaning and maintenance	5.7	6.2	5.2	3.7	4.1	3.2
Personal care and service	4.4	2.3	6.9	3.8	1.6	6.2
Sales and office	23.1	16.2	31.2	21.4	15.7	27.9
Sales and related	10.5	9.4	11.7	10.1	9.7	10.6
Office and administrative support	12.6	6.7	19.5	11.3	6.0	17.2
Natural resources, construction, and maintenance	10.3	18.1	1.1	9.3	16.5	1.0
Farming, fishing, and forestry	0.9	1.4	0.3	0.7	1.0	0.4
Construction and extraction	5.0	8.9	0.5	5.4	9.8	0.4
Installation, maintenance, and repair	4.4	7.8	0.3	3.2	5.8	0.3
Production, transportation, and material moving	13.9	19.2	7.7	11.8	17.2	5.8
Production	6.0	7.4	4.3	5.5	7.4	3.4
Transportation and material moving	7.9	11.8	3.4	6.3	9.7	2.4

Table 1-65. Persons Not in the Labor Force by Disability Status, Age, and Sex, 2018 Annual Averages

(Thousands of people, percent distribution.)

Category	Total, 16 years and over	16 to 64 years			Total, 65 years and over
		Total	Men	Women	
Persons With a Disability					
Total not in the labor force	23 870	10 215	4 819	5 396	13 655
Persons who currently want a job	650	439	232	207	211
Marginally attached to the labor force[1]	162	127	76	51	35
Discouraged workers[2]	37	26	16	10	11
Other persons marginally attached to the labor force[3]	125	101	59	41	25
Persons Without a Disability					
Total not in the labor force	71 846	44 250	16 299	27 951	27 595
Persons who currently want a job	4 599	3 994	1 847	2 147	604
Marginally attached to the labor force[1]	1 355	1 224	655	569	131
Discouraged workers[2]	387	342	216	126	45
Other persons marginally attached to the labor force[3]	968	883	439	443	86

[1]Data refer to persons who want a job, have searched for work during the prior 12 months, and were available to take a job during the reference week, but had not looked for work in the past 4 weeks.
[2]Includes those who did not actively look for work in the prior 4 weeks for reasons such as thinks no work available, could not find work, lacks schooling or training, employer thinks too young or old, and other types of discrimination.
[3]Includes those who did not actively look for work in the prior 4 weeks for such reasons as school or family responsibilities, ill health, and transportation problems, as well as a number for whom reason for nonparticipation was not determined.

Table 1-66. Employment Status of Persons 18 Years and Over by Veteran Status, Period of Service, Sex, Race, and Hispanic or Latino Ethnicity, 2018

(Thousands of people, percent.)

Characteristic	Civilian noninstitutional population	Civilian labor force						Not in labor force
		Total	Percent of population	Employed		Unemployed		
				Total	Percent of population	Total	Percent of labor force	
TOTAL								
Total, 18 Years and Over	248 874	159 942	64.3	153 923	61.8	6 019	3.8	88 932
Veterans	19 201	9 453	49.2	9 127	47.5	326	3.5	9 748
Gulf War era, total	7 238	5 784	79.9	5 588	77.2	197	3.4	1 454
Gulf War era II	4 149	3 358	80.9	3 229	77.8	129	3.8	791
Gulf War era I	3 089	2 427	78.6	2 358	76.3	68	2.8	662
WW II, Korean War, and Vietnam era	7 626	1 594	20.9	1 537	20.2	57	3.6	6 033
Other service periods	4 336	2 075	47.9	2 002	46.2	73	3.5	2 261
Nonveterans	229 673	150 489	65.5	144 797	63.0	5 693	3.8	79 184
MEN								
Total, 18 Years and Over	120 152	85 094	70.8	81 852	68.1	3 242	3.8	35 058
Veterans	17 335	8 320	48.0	8 027	46.3	292	3.5	9 015
Gulf War era, total	6 043	4 919	81.4	4 748	78.6	171	3.5	1 124
Gulf War era II	3 444	2 853	82.8	2 742	79.6	111	3.9	592
Gulf War era I	2 599	2 066	79.5	2 005	77.2	61	2.9	533
WW II, Korean War, and Vietnam era	7 366	1 541	20.9	1 485	20.2	56	3.6	5 826
Other service periods	3 925	1 860	47.4	1 795	45.7	65	3.5	2 065
Nonveterans	102 817	76 774	74.7	73 824	71.8	2 950	3.8	26 043
WOMEN								
Total, 18 Years and Over	128 722	74 849	58.1	72 072	56.0	2 777	3.7	53 874
Veterans	1 866	1 133	60.7	1 099	58.9	34	3.0	732
Gulf War era, total	1 194	865	72.4	840	70.3	25	2.9	329
Gulf War era II	704	505	71.7	487	69.1	18	3.5	200
Gulf War era I	490	360	73.5	353	72.0	7	2.1	130
WW II, Korean War, and Vietnam era	260	53	20.3	52	19.9	1	1.7	207
Other service periods	412	215	52.3	208	50.5	8	3.6	196
Nonveterans	126 857	73 715	58.1	70 972	55.9	2 743	3.7	53 141
WHITE								
Total, 18 Years and Over	193 658	124 123	64.1	119 976	62.0	4 146	3.3	69 535
Veterans	15 819	7 580	47.9	7 328	46.3	252	3.3	8 239
Gulf War era, total	5 507	4 457	80.9	4 311	78.3	146	3.3	1 050
Gulf War era II	3 183	2 613	82.1	2 521	79.2	91	3.5	571
Gulf War era I	2 323	1 844	79.4	1 790	77.0	54	3.0	479
WW II, Korean War, and Vietnam era	6 702	1 413	21.1	1 364	20.4	49	3.5	5 288
Other service periods	3 610	1 710	47.4	1 653	45.8	57	3.3	1 901
Nonveterans	177 839	116 543	65.5	112 648	63.3	3 895	3.3	61 296
BLACK								
Total, 18 Years and Over	31 518	20 215	64.1	18 948	60.1	1 267	6.3	11 303
Veterans	2 433	1 323	54.4	1 266	52.0	57	4.3	1 110
Gulf War era, total	1 215	918	75.6	881	72.5	37	4.0	297
Gulf War era II	658	494	75.2	467	71.1	27	5.5	163
Gulf War era I	557	424	76.1	414	74.3	10	2.4	133
WW II, Korean War, and Vietnam era	644	117	18.2	112	17.4	5	4.6	527
Other service periods	574	287	50.0	273	47.5	14	5.0	287
Nonveterans	29 084	18 892	65.0	17 682	60.8	1 210	6.4	10 192
ASIAN								
Total, 18 Years and Over	15 412	10 027	65.1	9 729	63.1	298	3.0	5 384
Veterans	361	208	57.5	202	56.0	5	2.6	153
Gulf War era, total	204	153	74.8	148	72.4	5	3.2	52
Gulf War era II	127	100	78.7	96	75.6	4	3.9	27
Gulf War era I	77	52	68.2	51	66.9	1	1.9	24
WW II, Korean War, and Vietnam era	107	29	27.5	29	27.2	0	. . .	77
Other service periods	50	25	51.2	25	50.6	0	. . .	24
Nonveterans	15 051	9 820	65.2	9 527	63.3	293	3.0	5 231
HISPANIC[1]								
Total, 18 Years and Over	40 581	27 886	68.7	26 630	65.6	1 256	4.5	12 695
Veterans	1 345	849	63.1	817	60.7	33	3.8	496
Gulf War era, total	776	631	81.3	610	78.6	21	3.3	145
Gulf War era II	539	432	80.1	417	77.4	15	3.4	107
Gulf War era I	237	199	83.9	193	81.3	6	3.1	38
WW II, Korean War, and Vietnam era	338	86	25.5	82	24.3	4	5.0	252
Other service periods	231	132	57.2	125	54.0	7	5.5	99
Nonveterans	39 236	27 037	68.9	25 813	65.8	1 223	4.5	12 199

Note: Veterans are men and women who served in the U.S. Armed Forces during World War II, the Korean War, the Vietnam era, the Gulf War era, and all other service periods. Nonveterans are men and women who never served in the U.S. Armed Forces. Other service periods include the periods between World War II and the Korean War, between the Korean War and the Vietnam era, and between the Vietnam era and the Gulf War era. Estimates for the above race groups (White, Black, and Asian) do not sum to totals because data are not presented for all races.

[1]May be of any race.
. . . = Not available.

Table 1-67. Employment Status of Persons 18 Years and Over by Veteran Status, Age, Period of Service, and Sex, 2018 Annual Averages

(Thousands of people, percent.)

Veteran status, age, period of service, and sex	Civilian noninstitutional population	Civilian labor force						Not in labor force
		Total	Percent of population	Employed		Unemployed		
				Total	Percent of population	Total	Percent of labor force	
TOTAL VETERANS								
Total, 18 years and over	19 201	9 453	49.2	9 127	47.5	326	3.5	9 748
18 to 24 years	256	183	71.6	164	64.0	19	10.6	73
25 to 34 years	1 636	1 367	83.6	1 311	80.1	56	4.1	269
35 to 44 years	1 996	1 720	86.2	1 660	83.2	60	3.5	276
45 to 54 years	2 759	2 322	84.2	2 261	82.0	60	2.6	437
55 to 64 years	3 569	2 222	62.3	2 151	60.3	71	3.2	1 347
65 years and over	8 985	1 639	18.2	1 580	17.6	59	3.6	7 346
Gulf War Era, Total								
Total, 18 years and over	7 238	5 784	79.9	5 588	77.2	197	3.4	1 454
18 to 24 years	256	183	71.6	164	64.0	19	10.6	73
25 to 34 years	1 636	1 367	83.6	1 311	80.1	56	4.1	269
35 to 44 years	1 996	1 720	86.2	1 660	83.2	60	3.5	276
45 to 54 years	2 065	1 750	84.7	1 707	82.6	43	2.4	316
55 to 64 years	945	672	71.1	657	69.5	15	2.3	273
65 years and over	340	92	27.1	89	26.3	3	3.0	248
Gulf War Era II								
Total, 18 years and over	4 149	3 358	80.9	3 229	77.8	129	3.8	791
18 to 24 years	256	183	71.6	164	64.0	19	10.6	73
25 to 34 years	1 636	1 367	83.6	1 311	80.1	56	4.1	269
35 to 44 years	1 196	1 011	84.5	974	81.4	37	3.7	185
45 to 54 years	627	520	82.9	509	81.2	11	2.1	107
55 to 64 years	340	247	72.6	243	71.4	4	1.6	93
65 years and over	94	30	31.8	29	30.6	1	. . .	64
Gulf War Era I								
Total, 25 years and over	3 089	2 427	78.6	2 358	76.3	68	2.8	662
35 to 44 years	800	709	88.7	686	85.8	23	3.3	91
45 to 54 years	1 438	1 229	85.5	1 198	83.3	32	2.6	209
55 to 64 years	605	426	70.4	414	68.5	11	2.7	179
65 years and over	246	62	25.3	61	24.6	2	2.8	184
World War II, Korean War, Vietnam War								
Total, 55 years and over	7 626	1 594	20.9	1 537	20.2	57	3.6	6 033
55 to 64 years	659	288	43.7	280	42.5	8	2.8	371
65 years and over	6 967	1 305	18.7	1 257	18.0	49	3.7	5 662
Other Service Periods								
Total, 45 years and over	4 336	2 075	47.9	2 002	46.2	73	3.5	2 261
45 to 54 years	694	572	82.5	555	79.9	18	3.1	122
55 to 64 years	1 965	1 262	64.2	1 214	61.8	48	3.8	704
65 years and over	1 677	241	14.4	233	13.9	8	3.2	1 436
TOTAL NONVETERANS								
Total, 18 years and over	229 673	150 489	65.5	144 797	63.0	5 693	3.8	79 184
18 to 24 years	28 832	18 668	64.8	17 175	59.6	1 493	8.0	10 163
25 to 34 years	42 945	35 407	82.4	34 014	79.2	1 394	3.9	7 538
35 to 44 years	38 574	31 899	82.7	30 957	80.3	943	3.0	6 674
45 to 54 years	38 480	30 989	80.5	30 112	78.3	877	2.8	7 491
55 to 64 years	38 548	25 135	65.2	24 413	63.3	722	2.9	13 413
65 years and over	42 295	8 390	19.8	8 126	19.2	264	3.2	33 905

Note: Veterans are men and women who served in the U.S. Armed Forces during World War II, the Korean War, the Vietnam era, the Gulf War era, and all other service periods. Nonveterans are men and women who never served in the U.S. Armed Forces. Other service periods include the periods between World War II and the Korean War, between the Korean War and the Vietnam era, and between the Vietnam era and the Gulf War era.

. . . = Not available.

Table 1-67. Employment Status of Persons 18 Years and Over by Veteran Status, Age, Period of Service, and Sex, 2018 Annual Averages—*Continued*

(Thousands of people, percent.)

Veteran status, age, period of service, and sex	Civilian noninstitutional population	Civilian labor force						Not in labor force
		Total	Percent of population	Employed		Unemployed		
				Total	Percent of population	Total	Percent of labor force	
VETERANS, MEN								
Total, 18 years and over	17 335	8 320	48.0	8 027	46.3	292	3.5	9 015
18 to 24 years	210	155	73.8	137	65.2	18	11.6	55
25 to 34 years	1 314	1 133	86.2	1 086	82.6	47	4.1	181
35 to 44 years	1 626	1 430	88.0	1 378	84.8	52	3.6	196
45 to 54 years	2 359	2 022	85.7	1 968	83.4	54	2.7	337
55 to 64 years	3 161	1 996	63.1	1 932	61.1	64	3.2	1 165
65 years and over	8 664	1 584	18.3	1 526	17.6	58	3.7	7 080
Gulf War Era, Total								
Total, 18 years and over	6 043	4 919	81.4	4 748	78.6	171	3.5	1 124
18 to 24 years	210	155	73.8	137	65.2	18	11.6	55
25 to 34 years	1 314	1 133	86.2	1 086	82.6	47	4.1	181
35 to 44 years	1 626	1 430	88.0	1 378	84.8	52	3.6	196
45 to 54 years	1 763	1 522	86.4	1 484	84.2	39	2.5	240
55 to 64 years	821	594	72.4	581	70.8	13	2.3	227
65 years and over	309	84	27.2	81	26.3	3	3.3	225
Gulf War Era II								
Total, 18 years and over	3 444	2 853	82.8	2 742	79.6	111	3.9	592
18 to 24 years	210	155	73.8	137	65.2	18	11.6	55
25 to 34 years	1 314	1 133	86.2	1 086	82.6	47	4.1	181
35 to 44 years	988	852	86.3	820	83.0	32	3.7	136
45 to 54 years	549	466	84.9	456	83.1	10	2.1	83
55 to 64 years	299	220	73.7	217	72.7	3	1.4	79
65 years and over	84	26	31.0	25	29.8	1	. . .	58
Gulf War Era I								
Total, 25 years and over	2 599	2 066	79.5	2 005	77.2	61	2.9	533
35 to 44 years	638	578	90.6	558	87.4	20	3.5	60
45 to 54 years	1 213	1 056	87.0	1 028	84.7	29	2.7	157
55 to 64 years	522	374	71.6	364	69.6	10	2.8	148
65 years and over	225	58	25.7	56	25.0	2	3.0	167
World War II, Korean War, and Vietnam War								
Total, 55 years and over	7 366	1 541	20.9	1 485	20.2	56	3.6	5 826
55 to 64 years	605	269	44.5	261	43.1	8	3.0	336
65 years and over	6 761	1 272	18.8	1 224	18.1	48	3.8	5 490
Other Service Periods								
Total, 45 years and over	3 925	1 860	47.4	1 795	45.7	65	3.5	2 065
45 to 54 years	596	499	83.7	484	81.2	15	3.0	97
55 to 64 years	1 735	1 132	65.3	1 090	62.8	43	3.8	603
65 years and over	1 594	228	14.3	221	13.8	8	3.3	1 366
NONVETERANS, MEN								
Total, 18 years and over	102 817	76 774	74.7	73 824	71.8	2 950	3.8	26 043
18 to 24 years	14 396	9 538	66.3	8 693	60.4	844	8.9	4 858
25 to 34 years	20 890	18 656	89.3	17 940	85.9	716	3.8	2 234
35 to 44 years	18 307	16 693	91.2	16 230	88.7	463	2.8	1 614
45 to 54 years	17 797	15 506	87.1	15 070	84.7	436	2.8	2 291
55 to 64 years	17 105	12 444	72.7	12 069	70.6	375	3.0	4 661
65 years and over	14 321	3 938	27.5	3 822	26.7	116	2.9	10 383

Note: Veterans are men and women who served in the U.S. Armed Forces during World War II, the Korean War, the Vietnam era, the Gulf War era, and all other service periods. Nonveterans are men and women who never served in the U.S. Armed Forces. Other service periods include the periods between World War II and the Korean War, between the Korean War and the Vietnam era, and between the Vietnam era and the Gulf War era.

. . . = Not available.

Table 1-67. Employment Status of Persons 18 Years and Over by Veteran Status, Age, Period of Service, and Sex, 2018 Annual Averages—*Continued*

(Thousands of people, percent.)

Veteran status, age, period of service, and sex	Civilian noninstitutional population	Civilian labor force						Not in labor force
		Total	Percent of population	Employed		Unemployed		
				Total	Percent of population	Total	Percent of labor force	
VETERANS, WOMEN								
Total, 18 years and over	1 866	1 133	60.7	1 099	58.9	34	3.0	732
18 to 24 years	46	28	61.3	27	58.5	1	. . .	18
25 to 34 years	322	234	72.7	225	69.9	9	4.0	88
35 to 44 years	370	290	78.4	281	76.1	9	3.0	80
45 to 54 years	400	300	75.0	293	73.3	7	2.2	100
55 to 64 years	408	226	55.5	220	53.8	7	3.1	182
65 years and over	321	55	17.2	54	16.8	1	2.2	266
Gulf War Era, Total								
Total, 18 years and over	1 194	865	72.4	840	70.3	25	2.9	329
18 to 24 years	46	28	61.3	27	58.5	1	. . .	18
25 to 34 years	322	234	72.7	225	69.9	9	4.0	88
35 to 44 years	370	290	78.4	281	76.1	9	3.0	80
45 to 54 years	302	227	75.1	223	73.7	4	1.8	75
55 to 64 years	124	78	62.9	76	61.4	2	2.4	46
65 years and over	31	8	. . .	8	. . .	0	. . .	23
Gulf War Era II								
Total, 18 years and over	704	505	71.7	487	69.1	18	3.5	200
18 to 24 years	46	28	61.3	27	58.5	1	. . .	18
25 to 34 years	322	234	72.7	225	69.9	9	4.0	88
35 to 44 years	208	159	76.3	154	73.7	5	3.4	49
45 to 54 years	78	54	69.2	53	67.7	1	2.1	24
55 to 64 years	41	26	64.1	25	62.0	1	. . .	15
65 years and over	10	4	. . .	4	. . .	0	. . .	6
Gulf War Era I								
Total, 25 Years and over	490	360	73.5	353	72.0	7	2.1	130
35 to 44 years	161	131	81.2	128	79.1	3	2.5	30
45 to 54 years	225	173	77.2	170	75.8	3	1.8	51
55 to 64 years	83	52	62.4	51	61.1	1	2.0	31
65 years and over	21	4	. . .	4	. . .	0	. . .	17
World War II, Korean War, and Vietnam Era								
Total, 55 years and over	260	53	20.3	52	19.9	1	1.7	207
55 to 64 years	54	19	35.2	19	35.2	0	. . .	35
65 years and over	206	34	16.4	33	15.9	1	. . .	172
Other Service Periods								
Total, 45 years and over	412	215	52.3	208	50.5	8	3.6	196
45 to 54 years	97	73	74.7	70	72.1	2	3.4	25
55 to 64 years	230	130	56.2	124	54.0	5	3.9	101
65 years and over	84	13	15.7	13	15.4	0	. . .	70
NONVETERANS, WOMEN								
Total, 18 years and over	126 857	73 715	58.1	70 972	55.9	2 743	3.7	53 141
18 to 24 years	14 436	9 131	63.3	8 482	58.8	649	7.1	5 305
25 to 34 years	22 054	16 751	76.0	16 073	72.9	678	4.0	5 303
35 to 44 years	20 267	15 207	75.0	14 727	72.7	480	3.2	5 060
45 to 54 years	20 683	15 483	74.9	15 042	72.7	441	2.8	5 200
55 to 64 years	21 443	12 691	59.2	12 344	57.6	347	2.7	8 751
65 years and over	27 974	4 452	15.9	4 304	15.4	148	3.3	23 521

Note: Veterans are men and women who served in the U.S. Armed Forces during World War II, the Korean War, the Vietnam era, the Gulf War era, and all other service periods. Nonveterans are men and women who never served in the U.S. Armed Forces. Other service periods include the periods between World War II and the Korean War, between the Korean War and the Vietnam era, and between the Vietnam era and the Gulf War era.

. . . = Not available.

Table 1-68. Employment Status of Gulf War Era Veterans by Reserve or National Guard Status, August 2018, Not Seasonally Adjusted

(Thousands of people, percent.)

Reserve or National Guard status	Civilian noninstitutional population	Civilian labor force						Not in labor force
		Total	Percent of population	Employed		Unemployed		
				Total	Percent of population	Total	Percent of labor force	
GULF WAR ERA								
Total	7 258	5 863	80.8	5 627	77.5	236	4.0	1 395
Current or past member of Reserve or National Guard	2 371	1 965	82.9	1 899	80.1	66	3.4	406
Never a member of Reserve or National Guard	4 635	3 687	79.5	3 534	76.2	153	4.1	949
Reserve or National Guard membership not reported	251	212	84.2	195	77.5	17	7.9	40
GULF WAR ERA II								
Total	4 184	3 393	81.1	3 247	77.6	146	4.3	791
Current or past member of Reserve or National Guard	1 431	1 177	82.2	1 152	80.5	25	2.1	254
Never a member of Reserve or National Guard	2 588	2 063	79.7	1 958	75.7	105	5.1	526
Reserve or National Guard membership not reported	165	153	92.9	136	82.7	17	11.0	12
GULF WAR ERA I								
Total	3 074	2 470	80.4	2 381	77.5	90	3.6	603
Current or past member of Reserve or National Guard	940	788	83.8	746	79.4	41	5.3	152
Never a member of Reserve or National Guard	2 047	1 624	79.3	1 575	77.0	48	3.0	423
Reserve or National Guard membership not reported	87	59	67.7	59	67.7	0	-	28

Note: Veterans are men and women who served in the U.S. Armed Forces during World War II, the Korean War, the Vietnam era, the Gulf War era, and all other service periods. The Gulf War era began in August 1990 and continues to the present day. It is divided into two periods of service: Gulf War era II (September 2001–present) and Gulf War era I (August 1990–August 2001).

Table 1-69. Employed Persons 18 Years and Over by Occupation, Sex, Veteran Status, and Period of Service, 2018 Annual Averages

(Number in thousands, percent distribution.)

Occupation	Total veterans	Gulf War era			WWII, Korean War, and Vietnam War	Other services periods	Non-veteran
		Total	Gulf War era II	Gulf War era I			
TOTAL							
Total, 18 Years and Over	9 127	5 588	3 229	2 358	1 537	2 002	144 797
Percent	100.0	100.0	100.0	100.0	100.0	100.0	100.0
Management, professional, and related occupations	39.1	39.5	37.5	42.3	41.5	36.3	40.6
Management, business, and financial operations occupations	18.6	17.8	16.9	19.1	22.7	17.5	16.7
Professional and related occupations	20.6	21.7	20.6	23.2	18.8	18.7	23.9
Service occupations	14.2	15.4	17.0	13.2	11.7	13.0	17.1
Sales and office occupations	16.5	16.3	16.1	16.4	18.0	16.2	21.7
Sales and related occupations	8.4	7.2	6.8	7.8	11.8	8.9	10.1
Office and administrative support occupations	8.1	9.0	9.3	8.6	6.2	7.2	11.6
Natural resources, construction, and maintenance occupations	13.7	13.9	14.5	13.2	11.9	14.6	9.1
Farming, fishing, and forestry occupations	0.4	0.3	0.3	0.4	0.4	0.6	0.7
Construction and extraction occupations	6.1	5.5	5.6	5.4	6.5	7.6	5.3
Installation, maintenance, and repair occupations	7.2	8.1	8.6	7.3	5.0	6.4	3.0
Production, transportation, and material moving occupations	16.4	14.9	14.9	15.0	16.9	20.0	11.7
Production occupations	6.5	6.5	6.8	6.1	4.8	8.0	5.5
Transportation and material moving occupations	9.8	8.4	8.1	8.9	12.1	12.0	6.2
MEN							
Total, 18 Years and Over	8 027	4 748	2 742	2 005	1 485	1 795	73 824
Percent	100.0	100.0	100.0	100.0	100.0	100.0	100.0
Management, professional, and related occupations	37.7	37.8	36.4	39.9	41.1	34.5	36.8
Management, business, and financial operations occupations	18.5	17.6	17.0	18.3	22.7	17.4	17.6
Professional and related occupations	19.2	20.3	19.4	21.5	18.4	17.1	19.3
Service occupations	14.1	15.2	16.7	13.2	11.8	13.0	13.4
Sales and office occupations	15.0	14.1	13.9	14.4	17.5	15.0	15.7
Sales and related occupations	8.4	7.0	6.6	7.6	11.9	9.2	9.7
Office and administrative support occupations	6.5	7.1	7.3	6.8	5.6	5.9	6.0
Natural resources, construction, and maintenance occupations	15.4	16.1	16.7	15.3	12.3	16.2	16.8
Farming, fishing, and forestry occupations	0.4	0.4	0.3	0.4	0.4	0.6	1.0
Construction and extraction occupations	6.9	6.4	6.4	6.3	6.7	8.4	10.1
Installation, maintenance, and repair occupations	8.1	9.4	10.0	8.6	5.2	7.1	5.7
Production, transportation, and material moving occupations	17.9	16.7	16.4	17.2	17.3	21.3	17.2
Production occupations	7.2	7.3	7.6	6.9	4.9	8.6	7.5
Transportation and material moving occupations	10.7	9.4	8.8	10.2	12.4	12.7	9.7
WOMEN							
Total, 18 Years and Over	1 099	840	487	353	52	208	70 972
Percent	100.0	100.0	100.0	100.0	100.0	100.0	100.0
Management, professional, and related occupations	49.6	49.0	43.9	56.0	53.1	51.3	44.4
Management, business, and financial operations occupations	19.3	19.2	16.3	23.2	22.5	18.8	15.7
Professional and related occupations	30.3	29.8	27.6	32.8	30.6	32.5	28.7
Service occupations	15.4	16.3	18.7	13.1	9.1	13.4	20.8
Sales and office occupations	28.1	28.3	28.7	27.8	33.2	25.8	27.8
Sales and related occupations	8.2	8.5	8.1	9.1	9.3	6.8	10.4
Office and administrative support occupations	19.9	19.8	20.6	18.7	24.0	19.0	17.4
Natural resources, construction, and maintenance occupations	1.3	1.4	2.0	0.7	0.2	1.0	1.0
Farming, fishing, and forestry occupations	0.1	0.1	0.2	0.1	0.2	0.0	0.4
Construction and extraction occupations	0.7	0.6	0.8	0.4	0.0	0.9	0.4
Installation, maintenance, and repair occupations	0.5	0.7	0.9	0.3	0.0	0.0	0.3
Production, transportation, and material moving occupations	5.6	4.9	6.7	2.5	4.5	8.5	5.9
Production occupations	2.0	1.9	2.5	1.1	0.5	2.9	3.4
Transportation and material moving occupations	3.6	3.0	4.2	1.4	4.0	5.6	2.4

Note: Veterans are men and women who served in the U.S. Armed Forces during World War II, the Korean War, the Vietnam era, the Gulf War era, and all other service periods. Nonveterans are men and women who never served in the U.S. Armed Forces. Other service periods include the periods between World War II and the Korean War, between the Korean War and the Vietnam era, and between the Vietnam era and the Gulf War era.

Table 1-70. Employed Persons 18 Years and Over by Industry, Class of Worker, Sex, Veteran Status, and Period of Service, 2018 Annual Averages

(Number in thousands, percent distribution.)

Industry and class of worker	Total veterans	Gulf War era			WWII, Korean War, and Vietnam War	Other services periods	Non-veteran
		Total	Gulf War era II	Gulf War era I			
TOTAL							
Total, 18 Years and Over	9 127	5 588	3 229	2 358	1 537	2 002	144 797
Percent	100.0	100.0	100.0	100.0	100.0	100.0	100.0
Agriculture and related industries	1.8	0.8	0.6	1.0	5.0	2.1	1.5
Wage and salary workers	0.9	0.6	0.5	0.8	1.8	1.0	1.0
Self-employed workers	0.9	0.2	0.1	0.2	3.2	1.0	0.5
Nonagricultural industries	98.2	99.2	99.4	99.0	95.0	97.9	98.5
Wage and salary workers	92.2	95.7	96.5	94.7	81.0	90.9	92.7
Private industries	70.4	70.2	70.5	69.8	69.1	72.1	79.5
Mining	0.7	0.8	1.1	0.4	0.7	0.4	0.5
Construction	6.4	6.2	6.6	5.7	6.0	7.4	5.9
Manufacturing	11.7	11.6	10.8	12.6	8.8	14.4	9.7
Wholesale trade	2.6	2.5	2.4	2.5	2.7	2.7	2.3
Retail trade	8.4	7.6	8.3	6.6	10.7	8.9	10.1
Transportation and utilities	7.3	7.3	6.6	8.4	6.6	7.7	4.2
Information	2.0	2.2	1.6	3.0	1.5	1.5	1.7
Financial activities	4.3	4.3	3.6	5.4	5.1	3.7	6.4
Professional and business services	11.4	12.1	12.8	11.0	11.0	9.8	10.6
Education and health services	8.4	8.5	8.3	8.7	7.2	8.9	15.6
Leisure and hospitality	4.0	4.1	5.0	2.9	4.5	3.2	8.2
Other services	3.3	2.9	3.3	2.5	4.3	3.5	4.3
Government	21.7	25.5	26.0	24.8	11.9	18.8	13.1
Federal	10.0	13.2	14.3	11.6	2.8	6.8	2.0
State	4.7	5.1	4.9	5.2	3.3	5.0	4.6
Local	7.0	7.3	6.8	8.0	5.8	7.0	6.6
Self-employed workers	6.0	3.5	2.8	4.3	13.9	7.1	5.8
MEN							
Total, 18 Years and Over	8 027	4 748	2 742	2 005	1 485	1 795	73 824
Percent	100.0	100.0	100.0	100.0	100.0	100.0	100.0
Agriculture and related industries	1.9	0.8	0.6	1.1	5.1	2.2	2.2
Wage and salary workers	1.0	0.6	0.5	0.9	1.8	1.1	1.5
Self-employed workers	1.0	0.2	0.2	0.3	3.3	1.1	0.6
Nonagricultural industries	98.1	99.2	99.4	98.9	94.9	97.8	97.8
Wage and salary workers	91.8	95.8	96.7	94.6	80.6	90.6	91.2
Private industries	71.2	71.3	71.5	71.0	69.2	72.6	81.1
Mining	0.8	0.9	1.2	0.4	0.7	0.4	0.8
Construction	7.1	7.1	7.7	6.4	6.2	8.0	10.2
Manufacturing	12.7	13.0	12.1	14.2	8.9	15.3	13.2
Wholesale trade	2.7	2.7	2.6	2.8	2.7	2.9	3.1
Retail trade	8.5	7.6	8.2	6.7	10.8	8.9	9.9
Transportation and utilities	8.0	8.2	7.3	9.5	6.8	8.4	6.2
Information	2.1	2.4	1.8	3.3	1.6	1.6	2.0
Financial activities	4.0	3.8	3.1	4.8	5.0	3.6	5.7
Professional and business services	11.7	12.5	13.3	11.4	11.0	10.1	11.7
Education and health services	6.5	6.4	6.3	6.6	6.6	6.8	6.9
Leisure and hospitality	3.8	3.8	4.7	2.7	4.6	3.1	7.6
Other services	3.4	2.9	3.3	2.4	4.4	3.6	3.8
Government	20.6	24.5	25.2	23.6	11.4	18.1	10.1
Federal	9.3	12.6	13.7	11.0	2.5	6.3	1.8
State	4.3	4.6	4.5	4.7	3.1	4.7	3.4
Local	7.0	7.3	6.9	7.9	5.8	7.0	4.9
Self-employed workers	6.2	3.4	2.7	4.3	14.1	7.2	6.6
WOMEN							
Total, 18 Years and Over	1 099	840	487	353	52	208	70 972
Percent	100.0	100.0	100.0	100.0	100.0	100.0	100.0
Agriculture and related industries	0.5	0.4	0.5	0.4	0.6	0.9	0.9
Wage and salary workers	0.3	0.4	0.5	0.2	0.2	0.0	0.5
Self-employed workers	0.2	0.1	0.0	0.2	0.5	0.7	0.3
Nonagricultural industries	99.5	99.6	99.5	99.6	99.4	99.1	99.1
Wage and salary workers	94.9	95.6	95.8	95.3	91.2	92.9	94.2
Private industries	65.0	64.2	64.9	63.2	67.2	67.8	77.9
Mining	0.2	0.3	0.5	0.0	0.0	0.0	0.1
Construction	1.4	1.4	1.0	1.9	0.0	2.1	1.3
Manufacturing	4.5	3.9	3.8	3.9	5.6	7.1	6.1
Wholesale trade	1.4	1.3	1.6	0.9	3.4	1.3	1.4
Retail trade	8.0	7.6	8.5	6.5	7.3	9.4	10.3
Transportation and utilities	2.4	2.5	2.8	2.2	1.9	2.1	2.2
Information	1.1	1.3	0.9	1.8	0.5	0.6	1.3
Financial activities	6.7	7.2	6.1	8.9	6.5	4.3	7.2
Professional and business services	9.2	9.6	10.2	8.8	11.0	7.2	9.5
Education and health services	21.8	20.4	19.9	21.0	24.6	26.8	24.7
Leisure and hospitality	5.4	5.8	6.8	4.5	3.1	4.3	8.8
Other services	2.9	3.0	3.1	2.8	3.2	2.4	4.9
Government	29.9	31.4	30.8	32.1	24.0	25.2	16.3
Federal	15.4	16.7	17.7	15.4	11.0	11.2	2.1
State	7.6	7.6	7.4	8.0	8.3	7.1	5.8
Local	6.9	7.0	5.8	8.8	4.7	6.8	8.4
Self-employed workers	4.6	4.0	3.7	4.3	8.2	6.2	4.9

Note: Veterans are men and women who served in the U.S. Armed Forces during World War II, the Korean War, the Vietnam era, the Gulf War era, and all other service periods. Nonveterans are men and women who never served in the U.S. Armed Forces. Other service periods include the periods between World War II and the Korean War, between the Korean War and the Vietnam era, and between the Vietnam era and the Gulf War era.

Table 1-71. Employed Persons 18 Years and Over by Veteran Status, Presence of Service-Connected Disability, Period of Service, and Class of Worker, August 2018, Not Seasonally Adjusted

(Numbers in thousands, percent distribution.)

Veteran status, presence of disability, and period of service	Total employed (number)	Total employed (percent)	Agriculture and related industries	Nonagricultural industries: Wage and salary workers: Total	Nonagricultural industries: Wage and salary workers: Private sector	Nonagricultural industries: Wage and salary workers: Government: Total	Nonagricultural industries: Wage and salary workers: Government: Federal	Nonagricultural industries: Wage and salary workers: Government: State and local	Nonagricultural industries: Self-employed, unincorporated, and unpaid family workers
Veterans, Total[1]	8 949	100.0	1.7	98.3	70.4	21.7	11.0	10.7	6.2
With service-connected disability	2 156	100.0	1.2	98.8	61.6	32.0	21.5	10.5	5.2
Without service-connected disability	6 502	100.0	2.0	98.0	73.0	18.4	7.7	10.7	6.6
Gulf War Era, Total[1]	5 627	100.0	0.5	99.5	71.1	25.4	14.3	11.1	3.0
With service-connected disability	1 736	100.0	0.5	99.5	62.5	34.0	23.5	10.5	2.9
Without service-connected disability	3 670	100.0	0.5	99.5	74.7	21.6	10.3	11.2	3.2
Gulf War Era II[1]	3 247	100.0	0.2	99.8	71.3	26.4	14.5	11.8	2.1
With service-connected disability	1 190	100.0	0.3	99.7	65.9	32.1	21.1	11.0	1.7
Without service-connected disability	1 908	100.0	0.1	99.9	74.3	23.1	11.0	12.1	2.6
Gulf War Era I[1]	2 381	100.0	0.9	99.1	70.8	24.1	13.9	10.2	4.2
With service-connected disability	546	100.0	1.0	99.0	55.3	38.1	28.8	9.3	5.6
Without service-connected disability	1 761	100.0	1.0	99.0	75.2	19.9	9.6	10.3	3.9
WW II, Korean War, and Vietnam Era[1]	1 370	100.0	4.3	95.7	67.3	11.8	2.5	9.3	16.7
With service-connected disability	196	100.0	3.8	96.2	60.9	12.6	2.8	9.8	22.7
Without service-connected disability	1 142	100.0	4.5	95.5	68.2	11.8	2.4	9.5	15.4
Other Service Periods[1]	1 951	100.0	3.5	96.5	70.5	17.9	7.5	10.4	8.1
With service-connected disability	224	100.0	4.6	95.4	54.5	33.2	22.5	10.8	7.7
Without service-connected disability	1 690	100.0	3.4	96.6	72.6	16.1	5.7	10.5	7.9
Nonveterans	144 520	100.0	1.5	98.5	80.0	12.7	1.9	10.8	5.7

Note: Veterans are men and women who served in the U.S. Armed Forces during World War II, the Korean War, the Vietnam era, the Gulf War era, and all other service periods. Nonveterans are men and women who never served in the U.S. Armed Forces. Other service periods include the periods between World War II and the Korean War, between the Korean War and the Vietnam era, and between the Vietnam era and the Gulf War era.

[1]Includes veterans who did not report presence of disability.

Table 1-72. Long-Tenured Displaced Workers[1] by Age, Sex, Race, and Hispanic Origin, January 2018

(Numbers in thousands, percent.)

Characteristic	Total	Percent distribution by employment status			
		Total	Employed	Unemployed	Not in the labor force
TOTAL					
Total, 20 years and over	2 981	100.0	66.4	14.4	19.3
20 to 24 years	73	100.0	(2)	(2)	(2)
25 to 54 years	1 759	100.0	75.6	14.9	9.4
55 to 64 years	798	100.0	60.2	14.9	24.8
65 years and over	351	100.0	30.7	12.2	57.2
Men					
Total, 20 years and over	1 681	100.0	67.4	14.8	17.7
20 to 24 years	33	100.0	(2)	(2)	(2)
25 to 54 years	988	100.0	75.1	17.2	7.7
55 to 64 years	483	100.0	61.5	12.0	26.4
65 years and over	176	100.0	37.0	9.4	53.5
Women					
Total, 20 years and over	1 301	100.0	65.0	13.8	21.3
20 to 24 years	40	100.0	(2)	(2)	(2)
25 to 54 years	771	100.0	76.3	12.0	11.7
55 to 64 years	315	100.0	58.2	19.3	22.4
65 years and over	175	100.0	24.3	14.9	60.8
White					
Total, 20 years and over	2 435	100.0	65.3	14.3	20.4
Men	1 390	100.0	66.0	14.7	19.3
Women	1 045	100.0	64.4	13.6	22.0
Black					
Total, 20 years and over	285	100.0	65.9	21.2	12.9
Men	139	100.0	68.3	21.8	10.0
Women	146	100.0	63.7	20.7	15.6
Asian					
Total, 20 years and over	157	100.0	69.9	7.5	22.5
Men	83	100.0	78.2	5.8	16.0
Women	74	100.0	(2)	(2)	(2)
Hispanic[3]					
Total, 20 years and over	404	100.0	68.6	21.8	9.6
Men	238	100.0	72.1	18.1	9.9
Women	167	100.0	63.7	27.1	9.2

[1]Data refer to persons who had three or more years of tenure on a job that they had lost between January 2013 and December 2015 because of plant or company closings or moves, insufficient work, or the abolishment of their positions or skills.
[2]Data not shown where the base is less than 75,000.
[3]Persons of Hispanic origin may be of any race.

Table 1-73. Long-Tenured Displaced Workers[1] by Age, Sex, Race, and Hispanic Origin and Reason for Job Loss, January 2018

(Numbers in thousands, percent.)

Characteristic	Total	Percent distribution by reasons for job loss			
		Total	Plant or company closed down or moving	Insufficient work	Position or shift abolished
TOTAL					
Total, 20 years and over	2 981	100.0	36.7	26.3	37.0
20 to 24 years	73	100.0	(2)	(2)	(2)
25 to 54 years	1 759	100.0	36.4	28.6	35.0
55 to 64 years	798	100.0	35.9	20.3	43.8
65 years and over	351	100.0	37.1	28.9	33.9
Men					
Total, 20 years and over	1 681	100.0	33.0	31.8	35.2
20 to 24 years	33	100.0	(2)	(2)	(2)
25 to 54 years	988	100.0	31.9	35.3	32.8
55 to 64 years	483	100.0	37.1	22.2	40.6
65 years and over	176	100.0	32.1	35.9	32.0
Women					
Total, 20 years and over	1 301	100.0	41.4	19.4	39.3
20 to 24 years	40	100.0	(2)	(2)	(2)
25 to 54 years	771	100.0	42.1	20.0	37.9
55 to 64 years	315	100.0	34.1	17.3	48.6
65 years and over	175	100.0	42.2	21.9	35.9
White					
Total, 20 years and over	2 435	100.0	36.4	26.6	37.0
Men	1 390	100.0	33.3	32.1	34.7
Women	1 045	100.0	40.6	19.4	40.0
Black					
Total, 20 years and over	285	100.0	33.2	30.3	36.4
Men	139	100.0	26.2	33.1	40.6
Women	146	100.0	39.9	27.6	32.5
Asian					
Total, 20 years and over	157	100.0	46.5	14.2	39.3
Men	83	100.0	39.9	21.8	38.3
Women	74	100.0	(2)	(2)	(2)
Hispanic[3]					
Total, 20 years and over	404	100.0	52.0	28.0	20.0
Men	238	100.0	53.5	33.4	13.1
Women	167	100.0	49.8	20.3	29.9

[1]Data refer to persons who had three or more years of tenure on a job that they had lost between January 2013 and December 2015 because of plant or company closings or moves, insufficient work, or the abolishment of their positions or skills.
[2]Data not shown where the base is less than 75,000.
[3]Persons of Hispanic origin may be of any race.

Table 1-74. Long-Tenured Displaced Workers[1] by Whether they Received Written Advance Notice, Reason for Job Loss, and Employment Status, January 2018

(Numbers in thousands, percent.)

Characteristic	Total	Percent distribution by employment status			
		Total	Employed	Unemployed	Not in the labor force
TOTAL					
Total, 20 years and over[2]	2 981	100.0	66.4	14.4	19.3
Received written advance notice	1 272	100.0	65.9	14.2	19.9
Did not receive written advance notice	1 650	100.0	66.7	14.5	18.8
Plant or Company Closed Down or Moved					
Total, 20 years and over[2]	1 093	100.0	70.4	9.6	19.9
Received written advance notice	632	100.0	68.7	11.8	19.5
Did not receive written advance notice	432	100.0	73.3	6.2	20.6
Insufficient Work					
Total, 20 years and over[2]	786	100.0	66.1	14.2	19.7
Received written advance notice	206	100.0	60.1	15.5	24.4
Did not receive written advance notice	576	100.0	68.0	13.8	18.2
Position or Shift Abolished					
Total, 20 years and over[2]	1 103	100.0	62.5	19.2	18.2
Received written advance notice	435	100.0	64.6	17.0	18.3
Did not receive written advance notice	643	100.0	61.1	20.8	18.1

[1]Data refer to persons who had three or more years of tenure on a job that they had lost between January 2013 and December 2015 because of plant or company closings or moves, insufficient work, or the abolishment of their positions or skills.
[2]Includes a small number who did not report information on advance notice.

Table 1-75. Long-Tenured Displaced Workers[1] by Industry and Class of Worker of Lost Job and Employment Status, January 2018

(Numbers in thousands, percent.)

Industry of class of worker of lost job	Total	Percent distribution by employment status			
		Total	Employed	Unemployed	Not in the labor force
TOTAL, 20 YEARS AND OVER[2]	2 981	100.0	66.4	14.4	19.3
Agriculture and related industries wage and salary workers	35	100.0	(3)	(3)	(3)
Nonagricultural industries wage and salary workers	2 893	100.0	66.9	13.9	19.2
Private nonagricultural wage and salary workers	2 772	100.0	66.9	14.0	19.1
Mining, quarrying, and oil and gas extraction	96	100.0	54.1	13.4	32.5
Construction	165	100.0	60.9	15.5	23.6
Manufacturing	479	100.0	64.7	13.7	21.7
Durable goods manufacturing	313	100.0	67.5	8.6	23.9
Primary metals and fabricated metal products	48	100.0	(3)	(3)	(3)
Machinery manufacturing	67	100.0	(3)	(3)	(3)
Computers and electronic products	52	100.0	(3)	(3)	(3)
Electrical equipment and appliances	29	100.0	(3)	(3)	(3)
Transportation equipment	58	100.0	(3)	(3)	(3)
Miscellaneous manufacturing	49	100.0	(3)	(3)	(3)
Other durable goods industries	11	100.0	(3)	(3)	(3)
Nondurable goods manufacturing	166	100.0	59.3	23.3	17.4
Food manufacturing	46	100.0	(3)	(3)	(3)
Textiles, apparel, and leather	14	100.0	(3)	(3)	(3)
Paper and printing	32	100.0	(3)	(3)	(3)
Other nondurable goods industries	73	100.0	(3)	(3)	(3)
Wholesale and retail trade	479	100.0	67.7	10.6	21.7
Wholesale trade	122	100.0	67.4	11.7	20.9
Retail trade	357	100.0	67.9	10.2	21.9
Transportation and utilities	88	100.0	64.7	18.4	16.8
Transportation and warehousing	73	100.0	(3)	(3)	(3)
Information	98	100.0	47.3	38.9	13.8
Telecommunications	38	100.0	(3)	(3)	(3)
Financial activities	205	100.0	68.1	15.9	16.0
Finance and insurance	152	100.0	64.0	21.4	14.6
Finance	73	100.0	(3)	(3)	(3)
Insurance	80	100.0	51.6	29.5	18.9
Real estate and rental and leasing	53	100.0	(3)	(3)	(3)
Professional and business services	439	100.0	67.3	15.9	16.8
Professional and technical services	328	100.0	68.3	16.2	15.5
Management, administrative, and waste services	112	100.0	64.5	15.1	20.5
Education and health services	368	100.0	77.5	10.0	12.5
Educational services	98	100.0	67.5	19.1	13.4
Health care and social assistance	270	100.0	81.2	6.7	12.1
Hospitals	62	100.0	(3)	(3)	(3)
Health services, except hospitals	173	100.0	83.9	4.6	11.4
Leisure and hospitality	234	100.0	65.9	10.3	23.8
Accommodation and food services	188	100.0	65.8	11.7	22.6
Food services and drinking places	159	100.0	59.6	13.8	26.6
Other services	108	100.0	76.0	10.9	13.1
Government wage and salary workers	120	100.0	66.7	9.9	23.4

[1]Data refer to persons who had three or more years of tenure on a job that they had lost between January 2013 and December 2015 because of plant or company closings or moves, insufficient work, or the abolishment of their positions or skills.
[2]Total includes a small number of unpaid family workers and persons who did not report industry or class of worker, not shown separately.
[3]Data not shown where base is less than 75,000.

Table 1-76. Long-Tenured Displaced Workers[1] by Occupation of Lost Job and Employment Status, January 2018

(Numbers in thousands, percent.)

Occupation of lost job	Total	Percent distribution by employment status			
		Total	Employed	Unemployed	Not in the labor force
TOTAL, 20 YEARS AND OVER[2]	2 981	100.0	66.4	14.4	19.3
Management, professional, and related occupations	1 143	100.0	71.7	13.0	15.4
Management, business, and financial operations occupations	598	100.0	73.5	10.4	16.0
Professional and related occupations	545	100.0	69.6	15.8	14.6
Service occupations	293	100.0	63.9	16.5	19.6
Sales and office occupations	796	100.0	61.5	16.5	22.0
Sales and related occupations	343	100.0	67.8	13.2	19.0
Office and administrative support occupations	453	100.0	56.7	18.9	24.4
Natural resources, construction, and maintenance occupations	291	100.0	60.2	16.6	23.2
Farming, fishing, and forestry occupations	34	100.0	([3])	([3])	([3])
Construction and extraction occupations	169	100.0	60.4	14.1	25.5
Installation, maintenance, and repair occupations	88	100.0	62.1	18.5	19.4
Production, transportation, and material moving occupations	415	100.0	70.7	7.7	21.6
Production occupations	246	100.0	73.8	6.4	19.8
Transportation and material moving occupations	168	100.0	66.0	9.6	24.3

[1]Data refer to persons who had three or more years of tenure on a job that they had lost between January 2013 and December 2015 because of plant or company closings or moves, insufficient work, or the abolishment of their positions or skills.
[2]Includes a small number who did not report occupation.
[3]Data not shown where base is 75,000.

Table 1-77. Long-Tenured Displaced Workers[1] by Selected Characteristics and Area of Residence, January 2018

(Numbers in thousands.)

Characteristic	Total	New England	Middle Atlantic	East North Central	West North Central
Workers who Lost Jobs					
Total, 20 years and over	2 981	183	362	470	209
Men	1 681	82	242	241	131
Women	1 301	100	121	229	78
Reason for Loss					
Plant or company closed down or moved	1 093	74	85	162	63
Insufficient work	786	36	128	111	58
Position or shift abolished	1 103	73	149	197	87
Industry and Class of Worker who Lost Job[2]					
Agriculture and related industries wage and salary workers	35	8	-	-	3
Nonagricultural industries wage and salary workers	2 893	165	362	458	206
Private nonagricultural wage and salary	2 772	152	353	428	191
Mining, quarrying, and oil and gas extraction	96	-	4	-	3
Construction	165	4	18	17	13
Manufacturing	479	39	60	128	27
Durable goods	313	23	48	68	15
Nondurable goods	166	16	12	60	12
Wholesale and retail trade	479	28	43	80	44
Transportation and utilities	88	0	16	10	8
Information	98	1	32	18	10
Financial activities	205	17	10	37	17
Professional and business services	439	27	56	50	31
Education and health services	368	29	54	44	28
Leisure and hospitality	234	5	48	24	8
Other services	108	1	14	21	2
Government wage and salary workers	120	13	9	29	15
Employment Status in January 2014					
Employed	1 978	122	247	295	139
Unemployed	429	31	59	72	19
Not in the labor force	574	30	56	103	51

Characteristic	South Atlantic	East South Central	West South Central	Mountain	Pacific
Workers who Lost Jobs					
Total, 20 years and over	541	184	377	206	449
Men	298	103	236	117	231
Women	244	81	141	89	217
Reason for Loss					
Plant or company closed down or moved	211	98	146	67	186
Insufficient work	108	50	124	50	122
Position or shift abolished	222	36	108	89	141
Industry and Class of Worker who Lost Job[2]					
Agriculture and related industries wage and salary workers	4	-	1	1	19
Nonagricultural industries wage and salary workers	517	184	372	206	423
Private nonagricultural wage and salary	498	177	367	195	411
Mining, quarrying, and oil and gas extraction	8	8	44	28	1
Construction	37	12	22	18	25
Manufacturing	63	31	43	28	60
Durable goods	46	11	43	21	38
Nondurable goods	17	20	-	7	22
Wholesale and retail trade	63	61	61	21	78
Transportation and utilities	28	2	3	6	15
Information	9	-	12	5	11
Financial activities	63	16	25	1	18
Professional and business services	87	7	95	36	51
Education and health services	67	12	25	22	88
Leisure and hospitality	42	18	26	15	47
Other services	23	10	10	10	16
Government wage and salary workers	19	7	5	11	12
Employment Status in January 2014					
Employed	358	134	244	128	312
Unemployed	73	13	53	33	77
Not in the labor force	110	38	80	45	60

[1]Data refer to persons who had three or more years of tenure on a job that they had lost between January 2013 and December 2015 because of plant or company closings or moves, insufficient work, or the abolishment of their positions or skills.
[2]Total includes a small number of unpaid family workers and persons who did not report industry or class of worker, not shown separately.
- = Represents or rounds to zero.

Table 1-78. Long-Tenured Displaced Workers Who Lost Full-Time Wage and Salary Jobs and Were Reemployed in January 2018 by Industry of Lost Job and Characteristic of New Job

(Numbers in thousands.)

Industry and class of worker of lost job[1]	Reemployed in January 2016							
	Total	Wage and salary workers						Self-employed and unpaid family workers
		Part-time	Full-time					
			Total[2]	Earnings relative to those of lost job				
				20 percent or more below	Below, but within 20 percent	Equal or above, but within 20 percent	20 percent or more above	
TOTAL WHO LOST FULL-TIME WAGE AND SALARY JOBS[3]	1 755	185	1 430	326	259	340	278	139
Agriculture and related industries wage and salary workers	17	-	17	-	1	11	5	-
Nonagricultural industries wage and salary workers	1 720	185	1 395	321	258	325	264	139
Private nonagricultural wage and salary workers	1 655	174	1 346	303	248	317	253	135
Mining, quarrying, and oil and gas extraction	50	4	37	18	9	1	7	9
Construction	100	-	84	24	13	15	8	16
Manufacturing	299	29	252	65	35	73	38	19
Durable goods	206	14	179	44	24	57	29	14
Nondurable goods	93	15	73	22	11	16	9	5
Wholesale and retail trade	286	37	228	32	36	55	39	21
Transportation and utilities	53	10	43	10	14	3	8	-
Information	45	1	36	12	2	1	15	8
Financial activities	138	9	124	18	32	40	18	5
Professional and business services	269	14	233	49	50	65	49	21
Education and health services	233	38	185	55	40	32	41	10
Leisure and hospitality	103	19	67	19	8	18	2	18
Other services	71	14	49	0	3	13	27	8
Government wage and salary workers	65	11	49	18	10	7	11	5

Note: Dash represents or rounds to zero.

[1]Data refer to persons who had three or more years of tenure on a job that they had lost between January 2013 and December 2015 because of plant or company closings or moves, insufficient work, or the abolishment of their positions or skills.
[2]Includes about 330,000 persons who did not report earnings on lost job.
[3]Includes a small number who did not report industry.

Table 1-79. Total Displaced Workers by Selected Characteristics and Employment Status in January 2018

(Numbers in thousands, percent.)

Characteristic[1]	Total	Percent Distribution by Employment Status			
		Total	Employed	Unemployed	Not in the labor force
WORKERS WHO LOST JOBS					
Sex and Age					
Total, 20 years and over	6 825	100.0	67.8	16.1	16.1
20 to 24 years	717	100.0	73.1	12.3	14.7
25 to 54 years	4 377	100.0	73.0	16.6	10.5
55 to 64 years	1 236	100.0	60.8	17.1	22.1
65 years and over	494	100.0	31.5	15.0	53.5
Men, 20 years and over	4 025	100.0	68.9	16.7	14.4
20 to 24 years	439	100.0	73.3	13.3	13.4
25 to 54 years	2 549	100.0	73.2	18.4	8.4
55 to 64 years	772	100.0	62.9	14.8	22.3
65 years and over	264	100.0	38.0	11.1	50.8
Women, 20 years and over	2 800	100.0	66.1	15.2	18.6
20 to 24 years	278	100.0	72.7	10.5	16.7
25 to 54 years	1 828	100.0	72.7	14.0	13.4
55 to 64 years	464	100.0	57.3	21.0	21.7
65 years and over	230	100.0	24.0	19.4	56.6
Race and Hispanic Origin					
White	5 277	100.0	67.8	15.2	16.9
Black or African American	929	100.0	62.2	23.8	13.9
Asian	316	100.0	69.7	12.2	18.2
Hispanic[2]	1 135	100.0	64.4	22.3	13.3
Reason for Job Loss					
Plant or company closed down or moved	2 121	100.0	70.1	12.3	17.7
Insufficient work	2 616	100.0	67.3	17.0	15.7
Position or shift abolished	2 087	100.0	66.0	18.8	15.2
Occupation of Lost Job[3]					
Management, professional, and related occupations	2 209	100.0	73.5	13.1	13.4
Management, business, and financial operations occupations	1 134	100.0	73.5	15.1	11.4
Professional and related occupations	1 075	100.0	73.4	11.1	15.5
Service occupations	928	100.0	66.4	14.8	18.8
Sales and office occupations	1 626	100.0	63.4	18.9	17.7
Sales and related occupations	760	100.0	70.1	12.5	17.4
Office and administrative support occupations	866	100.0	57.5	24.5	18.0
Natural resources, construction, and maintenance occupations	803	100.0	70.0	15.2	14.9
Farming, fishing, and forestry occupations	71	100.0	-	-	-
Construction and extraction occupations	542	100.0	73.3	14.7	11.9
Installation, maintenance, and repair occupations	190	100.0	66.7	14.6	18.7
Production, transportation, and material moving occupations	1 012	100.0	65.6	15.1	19.3
Production occupations	554	100.0	70.7	13.4	15.9
Transportation and material moving occupations	459	100.0	59.4	17.1	23.5
Agriculture and related industries wage and salary workers	77	100.0	56.3	11.2	32.5
Nonagricultural industries wage and salary workers	6 508	100.0	68.3	15.7	16.1
Private nonagricultural wage and salary workers	6 287	100.0	68.2	15.7	16.1
Mining, quarrying, and oil and gas extraction	152	100.0	60.4	10.3	29.2
Construction	625	100.0	70.9	17.9	11.2
Manufacturing	924	100.0	67.2	16.5	16.3
Durable goods	603	100.0	68.9	14.2	17.0
Nondurable goods	322	100.0	64.0	20.9	15.1
Wholesale and retail trade	1 051	100.0	66.4	13.3	20.4
Transportation and utilities	249	100.0	70.7	16.6	12.7
Information	176	100.0	63.8	27.2	9.0
Financial activities	440	100.0	68.1	18.8	13.1
Professional and business services	1 044	100.0	65.0	19.3	15.8
Education and health services	722	100.0	71.8	13.1	15.1
Leisure and hospitality	641	100.0	69.9	10.6	19.5
Other services	238	100.0	76.0	11.3	12.8
Government wage and salary workers	221	100.0	70.7	14.2	15.1

Note: Dash represents or rounds to zero.

[1]Data refer to all persons (regardless of years of tenure on lost job) who had lost or left a job between January 2015 and December 2017 because of plant or company closings or moves, insufficient work, or the abolishment of their positions or shifts.
[2]Persons of Hispanic origin may be of any race.
[3]Total includes a small number of unpaid family workers and persons who did not report occupation, industry, or class of worker, not shown separately.

CHAPTER 2: EMPLOYMENT, HOURS, AND EARNINGS

HIGHLIGHTS

The employment, hours, and earnings data in this section are presented by industry and state and are derived from the Current Employment Statistics (CES) survey, which covers approximately 697,000 individual worksites and 145,000 business and government agencies. The employment numbers differ from those presented in from the household survey in Chapter 1 because of dissimilarities in methodology, concepts, definitions, and coverage. As the CES survey data are obtained from payroll records, they are consistent for industry classifications.

Figure 2-1. Percent Change in the Number of Employees by Selected Sector, 2005–2018

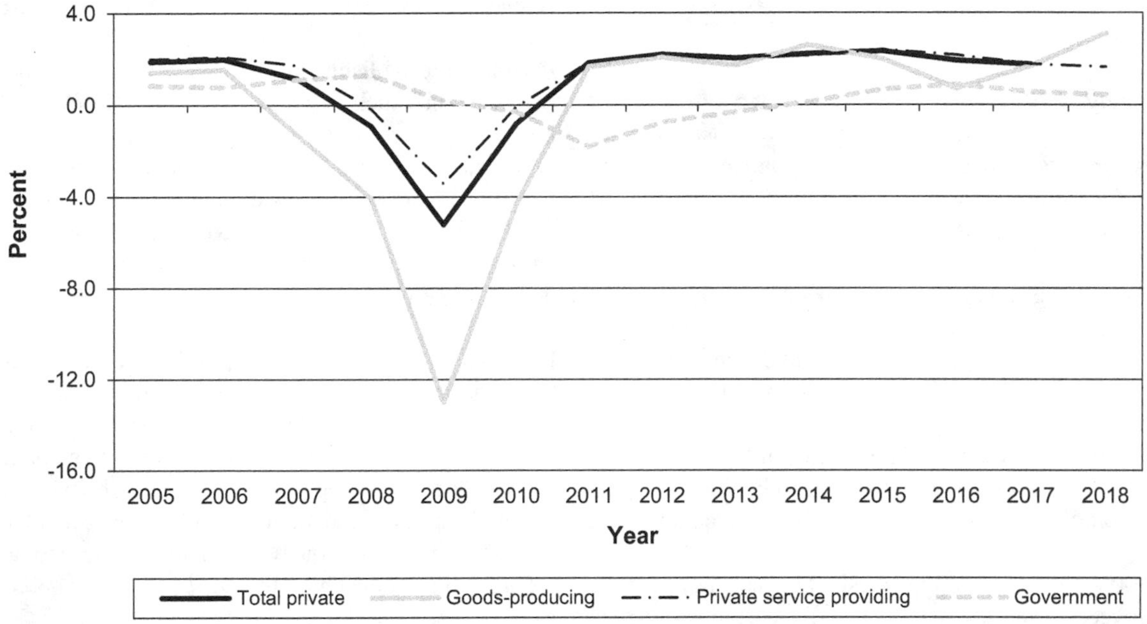

In 2018, total private employment increased for the eighth consecutive year after declining each year from 2008 to 2010. It increased 3.1 percent in the goods-producing sector and 1.7 percent in the private service-providing industry from 2017 to 2018. (See Table 2-1.)

OTHER HIGHLIGHTS:

- Employment increased in all major sectors in 2018 except in retail trade which experienced a small decrease and utilities which remained stable. Within retail trade, sporting goods, hobby, and bookstores experienced the largest decline at 5.0 percent followed by electronic and appliance stores at 3.0 percent. Although retail employment declined overall, employment in building material and garden supply stores increased 2.3 percent. (See Table 2-1.)

- From 2005 to 2018, the number of women employees on nonfarm payrolls increased nearly 14.0 percent. (See Table 2-2.)

- Average weekly hours of all employees on private nonfarm payrolls increased slightly to 34.5 hours in 2018. Employees in mining and logging worked the longest week (46.0 hours) followed by workers in utilities (42.1 hours) and manufacturing (40.9 hours). Workers in leisure and hospitality worked the shortest (26.1 hours). (See Table 2-6.)

NOTES AND DEFINITIONS

EMPLOYMENT, HOURS, AND EARNINGS

Collection and Coverage

The Bureau of Labor Statistics (BLS) conducts the Current Employment Statistics (CES), or establishment, survey. This survey collects monthly data on employment, hours, and earnings from a sample of nonfarm establishments (including government).

The CES sample includes about 145,000 businesses and government agencies and covers approximately 697,000 individual worksites. The reference period for the CES survey is the pay period which includes the 12th of the month.

The BLS publishes:

- Approximately 2,100 not seasonally adjusted employment series for all employees, production and nonsupervisory employees, and women employees are published monthly. The series for all employees include over 900 industries at various levels of aggregation.

- About 8,300 not seasonally adjusted special derivative series such as average weekly earnings, indexes, and constant dollar series for all employees and production and nonsupervisory employees are also published for over 600 industries.

- Approximately 5,600 seasonally adjusted employment, hours, and earnings series for all employees, production and nonsupervisory employees, and women employees are published.

- About 2,400 all employees and production and nonsupervisory employees series for average hourly earnings, average weekly hours, and, in manufacturing, average weekly overtime hours are published monthly on a not seasonally adjusted basis and cover over 600 industries.

Industry Classification

The CES survey completed a conversion from its original quota sample design to a probability-based sample survey design, and switched from the Standard Industrial Classification (SIC) system to the North American Industry Classification System (NAICS) in 2003. The industry-coding update included reconstruction of historical estimates in order to preserve time series for data users. The foundation of industrial classification with NAICS has changed how establishments are classified into industries and how businesses, as they exist today, are recognized. With the release of January 2008 data on February 1, 2008, the CES National Nonfarm Payroll series was updated to the 2007 North American Industry Classification System (NAICS) from the 2002 NAICS basis. In February 2012, the CES National Nonfarm Payroll series was updated again from the 2007 version to the 2012 version of NAICS with the release of January data.

Industry Employment

Employment data refer to persons on establishment payrolls who received pay for any part of the pay period containing the 12th day of the month. The data exclude proprietors, the self-employed, unpaid volunteer or family workers, farm workers, and domestic workers. Salaried officers of corporations are included. Government employment covers only civilian employees; military personnel are excluded. Employees of the Central Intelligence Agency, the National Security Agency, the National Imagery and Mapping Agency, and the Defense Intelligence Agency are also excluded.

Persons on establishment payrolls who were on paid sick leave (for cases in which pay is received directly from the firm), paid holiday, or vacation leave, or who work during part of the pay period despite being unemployed or on strike during the rest of the period were counted as employed. Not counted as employed were persons on layoff, on leave without pay, on strike for the entire period, or who had been hired but had not yet reported during to their new jobs.

Beginning with the June 2003 publication of May 2003 data, the CES national federal government employment series has been estimated from a sample of federal establishments and benchmarked annually to counts from unemployment insurance tax records. It reflects employee counts as of the pay period containing the 12th day of the month, which is consistent with other CES industry series. Previously, the national series was an end-of-month count produced by the Office of Personnel Management.

The exclusion of farm employment, self-employment, and domestic service employment accounts from the payroll survey accounts for the differences in employment figures between the household and payroll surveys. The payroll survey also excludes workers on leave without pay. (These workers are counted as employed in the household survey.) Persons who worked in more than one establishment during the reporting period are counted each time their names appear on payrolls; these persons are only counted once in the household survey.

Concepts and Definitions

Production and related workers. This category includes working supervisors and all nonsupervisory workers (including group leaders and trainees) engaged in fabricating, processing, assembling, inspecting, receiving, storing, handling, packing, warehousing, shipping, trucking, hauling, maintenance, repair, janitorial, guard services, product development, auxiliary production for plant's own use (such as a power plant), record-keeping, and other services closely associated with production operations.

Construction workers. This group includes the following employees in the construction division: working supervisors, qualified craft workers, mechanics, apprentices, helpers, and laborers engaged in new work, alterations, demolition, repair, maintenance, and the like, whether working at the site of construction or at jobs in shops or yards at jobs (such as precutting and pre-assembling) ordinarily performed by members of the construction trades.

Nonsupervisory workers. This category consists of employees such as office and clerical workers, repairers, salespersons, operators, drivers, physicians, lawyers, accountants, nurses, social workers, research aides, teachers, drafters, photographers, beauticians, musicians, restaurant workers, custodial workers, attendants, line installers and repairers, laborers, janitors, guards, and other employees at similar occupational levels whose services are closely associated with those of the employees listed. It excludes persons in executive, managerial, and supervisory positions.

Payroll. This refers to payments made to full- and part-time production, construction, or nonsupervisory workers who received pay for any part of the pay period containing the 12th day of the month. The payroll is reported before deductions of any kind, such as those for old age and unemployment insurance, group insurance, withholding tax, bonds, or union dues. Also included is pay for overtime, holidays, and vacation, as well as for sick leave paid directly by the firm. Bonuses (unless earned and paid regularly each pay period), other pay not earned in the pay period reported (such as retroactive pay), tips, and the value of free rent, fuel, meals, or other payment-in-kind are excluded. Employee benefits (such as health and other types of insurance and contributions to retirement, as paid by the employer) are also excluded.

Total hours. During the pay period, total hours include all hours worked (including overtime hours), hours paid for standby or reporting time, and equivalent hours for which employees received pay directly from the employer for sick leave, holidays, vacations, and other leave. Overtime and other premium pay hours are not converted to straight-time equivalent hours. The concept of total hours differs from those of scheduled hours and hours worked. The average weekly hours derived from paid total hours reflect the effects of such factors as unpaid absenteeism, labor turnover, part-time work, and work stoppages, as well as fluctuations in work schedules.

Average weekly hours. The workweek information relates to the average hours for which pay was received and is different from standard or scheduled hours. Such factors as unpaid absenteeism, labor turnover, part-time work, and work stoppages cause average weekly hours to be lower than scheduled hours of work for an establishment. Group averages further reflect changes in the workweeks of component industries.

Overtime hours. These are hours worked by production or related workers for which overtime premiums were paid because the hours were in excess of the number of hours of either the straight-time workday or the total workweek. Weekend and holiday hours are included only if overtime premiums were paid. Hours for which only shift differential, hazard, incentive, or other similar types of premiums were paid are excluded.

Average overtime hours. Overtime hours represent the portion of average weekly hours that exceeded regular hours and for which overtime premiums were paid. If an employee worked during a paid holiday at regular rates, receiving as total compensation his or her holiday pay plus straight-time pay for hours worked that day, no overtime hours would be reported.

Since overtime hours are premium hours by definition, weekly hours and overtime hours do not necessarily move in the same direction from month to month. Factors such as work stoppages, absenteeism, and labor turnover may not have the same influence on overtime hours as on average hours. Diverse trends at the industry group level may also be caused by a marked change in hours for a component industry in which little or no overtime was worked in both the previous and current months.

Industry hours and earnings. Average hours and earnings data are derived from reports of payrolls and hours for production and related workers in manufacturing and natural resources and mining, construction workers in construction, and nonsupervisory employees in private service-providing industries.

Average hourly earnings. Average hourly earnings are on a "gross" basis. They reflect not only changes in basic hourly and incentive wage rates, but also such variable factors as premium pay for overtime and late-shift work and changes in output of workers paid on an incentive plan. They also reflect shifts in the number of employees between relatively high-paid and low-paid work and changes in workers' earnings in individual establishments. Averages for groups and divisions further reflect changes in average hourly earnings for individual industries.

Averages of hourly earnings differ from wage rates. Earnings are the actual return to the worker for a stated period; rates are the amount stipulated for a given unit of work or time. The earnings series do not measure the level of total labor costs on the part of the employer because the following items are excluded: irregular bonuses, retroactive items, payroll taxes paid by employers, and earnings for those employees not covered under the definitions of production workers, construction workers, or nonsupervisory employees.

Average hourly earnings, excluding overtime-premium pay, are computed by dividing the total production worker payroll for the industry group by the sum of total production worker hours and one-half of total overtime hours. No adjustments are made for other premium payment provisions, such as holiday pay, late-shift premiums, and overtime rates other than time and one-half.

Average weekly earnings. These estimates are derived by multiplying average weekly hours estimates by average hourly earnings estimates. Therefore, weekly earnings are affected not only by changes in average hourly earnings but also by changes in the length of the workweek. Monthly variations in factors, such as the proportion of part-time workers, work stoppages, labor turnover during the survey period, and absenteeism for which employees are not paid may cause the average workweek to fluctuate.

Long-term trends of average weekly earnings can be affected by structural changes in the makeup of the workforce. For example, persistent long-term increases in the proportion of part-time workers in retail trade and many of the services industries have reduced average workweeks in these industries and have affected the average weekly earnings series.

These earnings are in constant dollars and are calculated from the earnings averages for the current month using a deflator derived from the Consumer Price Index for Urban Wage Earnings and Clerical Workers (CPI-W). The reference year for these series is 1982.

Seasonally adjustment removes the change in employment that is due to normal seasonal hiring or layoffs, thus leaving an over-the-month change that reflects only employment changes due to trend and irregular movements. Seasonally adjusted estimates of employment and other series are generated using the X-12 ARIMA program developed by the United States Census Bureau.

Data Revisions

CES revises published estimates to improve its data series by incorporating additional information that was not available at the time of the initial publication of the estimates. Each year, the CES incorporates a benchmark revision that re-anchors estimates to nearly complete employment counts available from Quarterly Census of Employment and Wages (QCEW) data, County Business Pattern data, and other state collected data. The benchmark helps to control for sampling error in the estimates. See more about the QCEW later in this chapter.

It can be nearly 2 years before not seasonally adjusted CES estimates are considered final. The first preliminary CES estimates of employment, hours, and earnings are published each month approximately 3 weeks after the reference period. Estimates are then revised twice before being held constant until the annual benchmark release. Second preliminary estimates for a given month are published the month following the initial release, and final sample-based estimates are published 2 months after the initial release. The annual benchmark revisions affect nearly 2 years of data, so most months are subject to revisions during 2 separate benchmark periods.

Sources of Additional Information

For further information on sampling, estimation methods, and data revisions for national data visit the Employment, Hours, and Earnings homepage on the BLS Web site at <http://www.bls.gov/ces>. For more information on state and area data, please visit the BLS Web site at <http://www.bls.gov/sae>.

Table 2-1. Employees on Nonfarm Payrolls, by Super Sector and Selected Component Groups, NAICS Basis, 2005–2018

(Thousands of people.)

Industry	2005	2006	2007	2008	2009	2010	2011	2012	2013	2014	2015	2016	2017	2018
TOTAL	134 051	136 453	137 999	137 241	131 313	130 362	131 932	134 175	136 381	138 958	141 843	144 352	146 624	149 074
Total Private	112 247	114 479	115 781	114 732	108 758	107 871	109 845	112 255	114 529	117 076	119 814	122 128	124 275	126 625
Goods-Producing	22 190	22 530	22 233	21 335	18 558	17 751	18 047	18 420	18 738	19 226	19 610	19 750	20 084	20 710
Mining and Logging	628	684	724	767	694	705	788	848	863	891	813	668	676	732
Mining	562	620	664	710	643	655	739	797	811	839	760	617	626	683
Logging	65	64	60	57	50	50	49	51	52	52	52	51	50	49
Construction	7 336	7 691	7 630	7 162	6 016	5 518	5 533	5 646	5 856	6 151	6 461	6 728	6 969	7 289
Construction of buildings	1 712	1 805	1 774	1 642	1 357	1 230	1 222	1 240	1 286	1 358	1 424	1 493	1 545	1 626
Heavy and civil engineering	951	985	1 005	965	851	825	837	868	885	912	938	952	996	1 052
Specialty trade contractors	4 673	4 901	4 850	4 556	3 808	3 463	3 474	3 537	3 684	3 881	4 100	4 283	4 427	4 612
Manufacturing	14 227	14 155	13 879	13 406	11 847	11 528	11 726	11 927	12 020	12 185	12 336	12 354	12 439	12 689
Durable goods	8 956	8 981	8 808	8 463	7 284	7 064	7 273	7 470	7 548	7 674	7 765	7 714	7 741	7 945
Wood product	561	561	517	458	360	342	337	339	353	372	383	393	397	406
Nonmetallic mineral product	505	510	501	465	394	371	367	365	373	384	398	406	410	415
Primary metals	466	464	456	442	362	362	388	402	395	399	394	375	371	378
Fabricated metal product	1 522	1 553	1 563	1 528	1 312	1 282	1 347	1 410	1 432	1 454	1 458	1 422	1 425	1 467
Machinery	1 166	1 183	1 187	1 188	1 029	996	1 056	1 099	1 105	1 127	1 121	1 077	1 079	1 120
Computer and electronic product	1 316	1 308	1 273	1 244	1 137	1 095	1 104	1 089	1 066	1 049	1 053	1 048	1 039	1 055
Electrical equipment and appliances	434	433	429	424	374	360	366	373	374	378	384	383	386	399
Transportation equipment	1 772	1 769	1 712	1 608	1 348	1 333	1 382	1 461	1 509	1 559	1 605	1 630	1 643	1 702
Furniture and related product	566	558	529	478	384	357	353	351	360	370	381	390	395	395
Miscellaneous manufacturing	647	644	642	629	584	567	574	580	581	582	590	591	595	608
Nondurable goods	5 271	5 174	5 071	4 943	4 564	4 464	4 453	4 457	4 472	4 512	4 571	4 640	4 699	4 743
Food manufacturing	1 478	1 479	1 484	1 481	1 456	1 451	1 459	1 469	1 474	1 484	1 512	1 557	1 598	1 620
Textile mills	218	195	170	151	124	119	120	119	117	117	117	115	113	113
Textile product mills	176	167	158	147	126	119	118	116	114	115	116	116	116	116
Apparel	251	232	215	199	168	157	152	148	145	140	137	131	119	113
Paper and paper product	484	471	458	445	407	395	387	380	378	373	373	371	366	367
Printing and related support activities	646	634	622	594	522	488	472	462	452	454	450	448	440	431
Petroleum and coal product	112	113	115	117	115	114	112	112	110	112	113	113	115	116
Chemicals	872	866	861	847	804	787	784	783	793	803	807	812	824	838
Plastics and rubber product	802	786	757	729	625	625	635	645	659	674	689	702	717	731
Private Service-Providing	90 057	91 949	93 548	93 398	90 201	90 121	91 798	93 835	95 791	97 850	100 204	102 379	104 191	105 916
Trade, Transportation, and Utilities	25 910	26 223	26 573	26 236	24 850	24 581	25 008	25 416	25 801	26 321	26 824	27 195	27 409	27 659
Wholesale Trade	5 706	5 842	5 948	5 875	5 521	5 387	5 475	5 595	5 660	5 740	5 780	5 787	5 814	5 853
Durable goods	3 119	3 203	3 257	3 191	2 944	2 848	2 905	2 978	3 013	3 056	3 080	3 083	3 108	3 153
Nondurable goods	2 109	2 134	2 161	2 148	2 063	2 026	2 041	2 071	2 092	2 121	2 137	2 145	2 153	2 152
Electronic markets, agents, and brokers	478	505	530	536	514	513	529	547	556	563	564	559	553	548
Retail Trade	15 285	15 359	15 526	15 289	14 528	14 446	14 674	14 847	15 085	15 363	15 611	15 832	15 846	15 833
Motor vehicle and parts dealers	1 919	1 910	1 908	1 831	1 638	1 629	1 691	1 737	1 793	1 862	1 929	1 980	2 005	2 021
Furniture and home furnishing stores	576	587	575	531	449	438	439	439	446	456	467	471	476	481
Electronic and appliance stores	586	581	583	570	516	523	528	508	497	498	523	522	503	488
Building material and garden supply stores	1 277	1 325	1 310	1 249	1 156	1 133	1 147	1 175	1 209	1 229	1 235	1 268	1 277	1 307
Food and beverage stores	2 818	2 821	2 844	2 862	2 830	2 808	2 823	2 861	2 930	3 004	3 062	3 090	3 086	3 087
Health and personal care stores	954	961	993	1 003	986	981	981	998	1 016	1 023	1 034	1 053	1 067	1 061
Gasoline stations	871	864	862	842	826	819	831	844	866	881	905	923	930	934
Clothing and clothing accessories stores	1 415	1 451	1 500	1 468	1 364	1 353	1 361	1 391	1 391	1 370	1 354	1 359	1 374	1 366
Sporting goods, hobby, and music stores	598	606	623	622	589	579	578	582	603	619	623	620	606	576
General merchandise stores	2 934	2 935	3 021	3 026	2 966	2 998	3 085	3 065	3 060	3 102	3 131	3 169	3 126	3 105
Miscellaneous store retailers	900	881	865	843	782	762	772	794	803	818	828	832	828	834
Nonstore retailers	438	437	442	442	425	425	438	452	472	501	519	543	567	573
Transportation and Warehousing	4 365	4 474	4 546	4 513	4 241	4 196	4 307	4 421	4 504	4 667	4 877	5 020	5 195	5 419
Air transportation	501	487	492	491	463	458	457	459	444	444	459	478	492	501
Rail transportation	228	228	234	231	218	216	228	231	231	236	241	217	215	214
Water transportation	61	63	66	67	63	62	61	64	65	67	66	66	65	65
Truck transportation	1 398	1 436	1 440	1 389	1 269	1 251	1 301	1 350	1 383	1 418	1 453	1 448	1 457	1 492
Transit and ground passenger transportation	389	399	412	423	422	430	440	440	449	467	478	484	489	488
Pipeline transportation	38	39	40	42	43	42	43	44	45	47	50	50	49	49
Scenic and sightseeing transportation	29	28	29	28	28	27	28	28	29	31	33	35	35	34
Support activities for transportation	552	571	584	592	549	543	562	580	598	626	652	667	690	712
Couriers and messengers	571	582	581	573	546	528	529	534	544	577	613	645	676	725
Warehousing and storage	599	643	670	677	642	638	658	692	716	755	834	932	1 027	1 140
Utilities	554	549	553	559	560	553	553	553	552	552	556	556	555	555

Table 2-1. Employees on Nonfarm Payrolls, by Super Sector and Selected Component Groups, NAICS Basis, 2005–2018—*Continued*

(Thousands of people.)

Industry	2005	2006	2007	2008	2009	2010	2011	2012	2013	2014	2015	2016	2017	2018
Information	3 061	3 038	3 032	2 984	2 804	2 707	2 674	2 676	2 706	2 726	2 750	2 794	2 814	2 828
Publishing industries, except Internet	904	902	901	880	796	759	749	740	733	727	727	730	729	733
Motion picture and sound recording industry	378	376	381	371	358	370	362	362	371	379	398	426	433	436
Broadcasting, except Internet	328	328	325	319	301	290	283	285	284	283	277	271	268	270
Internet publishing and broadcasting and web search portals	67	69	73	81	83	92	110	125	142	163	184	204	224	245
Telecommunications	1 071	1 048	1 031	1 019	966	903	874	857	853	839	811	801	781	751
Other information services	118	121	126	134	135	142	160	177	196	219	241	262	286	308
Financial Activities	8 197	8 367	8 348	8 206	7 838	7 695	7 697	7 784	7 886	7 977	8 123	8 287	8 451	8 569
Finance and insurance	6 063	6 194	6 179	6 076	5 844	5 761	5 769	5 828	5 886	5 931	6 035	6 148	6 262	6 314
Monetary authorities, central bank	21	21	22	22	21	20	18	18	18	18	18	19	19	20
Credit intermediation	2 869	2 925	2 866	2 733	2 590	2 550	2 554	2 583	2 614	2 564	2 571	2 610	2 645	2 647
Securities, commodity contracts, investments, and funds and trusts	834	869	900	916	862	850	860	859	865	883	908	927	938	957
Insurance carriers and related activities	2 339	2 379	2 392	2 405	2 371	2 341	2 336	2 368	2 389	2 466	2 538	2 593	2 660	2 690
Real estate and rental and leasing	2 134	2 173	2 169	2 130	1 994	1 934	1 927	1 955	2 000	2 046	2 088	2 139	2 189	2 255
Real estate	1 461	1 499	1 500	1 485	1 420	1 396	1 401	1 420	1 459	1 487	1 517	1 557	1 606	1 661
Rental and leasing services	646	646	640	617	547	514	502	511	518	535	548	558	560	571
Lessors of nonfinancial intangible assets	27	28	28	28	27	25	24	24	24	24	24	24	24	23
Professional and Business Services	17 003	17 619	17 998	17 792	16 634	16 783	17 389	17 992	18 575	19 124	19 695	20 114	20 508	20 999
Professional and technical services	7 065	7 399	7 705	7 845	7 553	7 486	7 713	7 941	8 170	8 386	8 658	8 881	9 058	9 300
Management and technical consulting services	853	917	985	1 035	1 027	1 031	1 098	1 152	1 215	1 268	1 318	1 394	1 433	1 483
Administrative and management consulting services	308	331	357	374	369	376	399	416	444	475	507	565	588	620
Waste management and remediation services	338	348	355	357	352	357	365	372	378	386	397	404	415	438
Education and Health Services	17 676	18 154	18 676	19 228	19 630	19 975	20 318	20 769	21 086	21 439	22 029	22 639	23 188	23 667
Education services	2 836	2 901	2 941	3 040	3 090	3 155	3 250	3 341	3 354	3 417	3 472	3 570	3 668	3 728
Health care and social assistance	14 840	15 253	15 735	16 188	16 540	16 820	17 069	17 428	17 731	18 022	18 557	19 069	19 520	19 939
Ambulatory health care services	5 114	5 286	5 474	5 647	5 793	5 975	6 136	6 307	6 477	6 632	6 856	7 080	7 297	7 499
Hospitals	4 345	4 423	4 515	4 627	4 667	4 679	4 722	4 779	4 786	4 787	4 896	5 015	5 072	5 145
Nursing and residential health facilities	2 855	2 893	2 958	3 016	3 082	3 124	3 168	3 196	3 229	3 258	3 291	3 318	3 348	3 362
Social assistance	2 527	2 651	2 788	2 898	2 997	3 043	3 043	3 147	3 240	3 346	3 515	3 655	3 803	3 933
Leisure and Hospitality	12 816	13 110	13 427	13 436	13 077	13 049	13 353	13 768	14 254	14 696	15 160	15 660	16 051	16 348
Arts, entertainment, and recreation	1 892	1 929	1 969	1 970	1 916	1 913	1 919	1 969	2 030	2 103	2 166	2 252	2 333	2 394
Performing arts and spectator sports	376	399	405	406	397	406	394	402	419	443	450	464	494	506
Museums, historical sites	121	124	130	132	129	128	133	136	140	147	153	160	166	170
Amusements, gambling, and recreation	1 395	1 406	1 434	1 433	1 389	1 379	1 392	1 430	1 470	1 513	1 563	1 628	1 674	1 717
Accommodation and food services	10 923	11 181	11 457	11 466	11 162	11 135	11 434	11 800	12 224	12 593	12 994	13 408	13 718	13 955
Accommodation	1 819	1 832	1 867	1 869	1 763	1 760	1 801	1 825	1 865	1 895	1 923	1 960	2 003	2 028
Food services and drinking places	9 104	9 349	9 590	9 598	9 399	9 376	9 633	9 975	10 359	10 698	11 071	11 448	11 715	11 926
Other Services	5 395	5 438	5 494	5 515	5 367	5 331	5 360	5 430	5 483	5 567	5 622	5 691	5 770	5 845
Repair and maintenance	1 236	1 249	1 253	1 227	1 150	1 139	1 169	1 194	1 217	1 242	1 277	1 293	1 311	1 329
Personal and laundry services	1 277	1 288	1 310	1 323	1 281	1 265	1 289	1 314	1 342	1 371	1 405	1 444	1 478	1 510
Membership associations and organizations	2 882	2 901	2 931	2 966	2 936	2 926	2 903	2 922	2 925	2 954	2 940	2 953	2 981	3 006
Government	21 804	21 974	22 218	22 509	22 555	22 490	22 086	21 920	21 853	21 882	22 029	22 224	22 350	22 449
Federal	2 732	2 732	2 734	2 762	2 832	2 977	2 859	2 820	2 769	2 733	2 757	2 795	2 805	2 796
Federal, excluding U.S. Postal Service	1 957	1 963	1 965	2 014	2 129	2 318	2 228	2 209	2 175	2 140	2 160	2 186	2 189	2 188
State	5 032	5 075	5 122	5 177	5 169	5 137	5 078	5 055	5 046	5 050	5 077	5 110	5 165	5 176
State, excluding education	2 772	2 782	2 804	2 823	2 809	2 764	2 704	2 666	2 653	2 661	2 676	2 681	2 686	2 690
Local	14 041	14 167	14 362	14 571	14 554	14 376	14 150	14 045	14 037	14 098	14 195	14 319	14 379	14 477
Local, excluding education	6 185	6 254	6 376	6 487	6 475	6 363	6 278	6 267	6 260	6 283	6 324	6 414	6 458	6 514

Table 2-2. Women Employees on Nonfarm Payrolls, by Super Sector and Selected Component Groups, NAICS Basis, 2005–2018

(Thousands of people.)

Industry	2005	2006	2007	2008	2009	2010	2011	2012	2013	2014	2015	2016	2017	2018
TOTAL NONFARM	64 997	65 821	67 134	67 452	65 618	65 087	65 444	66 375	67 429	68 570	69 981	71 518	72 623	74 016
Total Private	52 608	53 603	54 556	54 544	52 717	52 258	52 833	53 882	54 961	56 075	57 376	58 777	59 804	61 090
Goods-Producing	5 104	5 083	5 041	4 866	4 289	4 088	4 057	4 093	4 125	4 211	4 286	4 322	4 403	4 577
Mining and logging	79	82	93	101	98	98	105	113	116	119	114	98	91	93
Construction	890	944	947	916	801	723	711	724	746	780	813	841	881	935
Manufacturing	4 135	4 057	4 001	3 848	3 390	3 268	3 241	3 256	3 263	3 312	3 360	3 384	3 431	3 550
Private Service-Providing	47 505	48 520	49 515	49 678	48 428	48 169	48 777	49 790	50 836	51 864	53 090	54 455	55 401	56 513
Trade, transportation, and utilities	10 519	10 609	10 830	10 763	10 216	9 989	10 072	10 234	10 447	10 661	10 857	11 058	11 026	11 098
Wholesale trade	1 719	1 775	1 809	1 798	1 684	1 619	1 644	1 676	1 676	1 691	1 700	1 708	1 712	1 744
Retail trade	7 525	7 589	7 760	7 714	7 363	7 228	7 282	7 392	7 575	7 733	7 863	7 992	7 913	7 880
Transportation and warehousing	1 132	1 099	1 111	1 100	1 026	1 004	1 011	1 029	1 059	1 103	1 161	1 227	1 274	1 344
Utilities	143	146	150	151	143	139	135	137	136	134	133	131	128	129
Information	1 333	1 306	1 285	1 260	1 170	1 104	1 084	1 076	1 079	1 094	1 102	1 116	1 117	1 116
Financial activities	4 923	5 055	4 988	4 851	4 648	4 530	4 490	4 519	4 547	4 572	4 635	4 715	4 782	4 846
Professional and business services	7 590	7 797	8 026	7 964	7 490	7 472	7 706	7 954	8 267	8 522	8 755	9 006	9 220	9 506
Education and health services	13 661	14 037	14 478	14 904	15 218	15 435	15 637	15 964	16 202	16 469	16 948	17 444	17 861	18 249
Leisure and hospitality	6 708	6 903	7 054	7 056	6 861	6 819	6 964	7 190	7 421	7 636	7 858	8 133	8 349	8 592
Other services	2 772	2 814	2 854	2 880	2 824	2 820	2 823	2 852	2 874	2 912	2 935	2 984	3 046	3 106
Government	12 389	12 218	12 578	12 908	12 900	12 829	12 611	12 493	12 468	12 495	12 605	12 741	12 819	12 926
Federal	1 177	1 194	1 202	1 224	1 259	1 326	1 269	1 249	1 230	1 209	1 220	1 236	1 244	1 248
State	2 575	2 630	2 651	2 684	2 628	2 639	2 643	2 648	2 649	2 651	2 702	2 740	2 779	2 799
Local	8 637	8 395	8 725	9 000	9 014	8 864	8 700	8 596	8 589	8 635	8 683	8 766	8 796	8 879

Table 2-3. Production Workers on Private Nonfarm Payrolls, by Super Sector, NAICS Basis, 2005–2018

(Thousands of people.)

Industry	2005	2006	2007	2008	2009	2010	2011	2012	2013	2014	2015	2016	2017	2018
TOTAL PRIVATE	91 443	93 776	95 260	94 675	89 629	88 954	90 619	92 781	94 588	96 703	98 785	100 568	102 424	104 319
Goods-Producing	16 145	16 559	16 405	15 724	13 399	12 774	13 005	13 287	13 481	13 858	14 141	14 215	14 450	14 880
Mining and logging	473	519	547	574	510	525	594	641	636	653	592	471	490	544
Construction	5 611	5 903	5 883	5 521	4 567	4 172	4 184	4 246	4 423	4 640	4 866	5 074	5 230	5 438
Manufacturing	10 060	10 137	9 975	9 629	8 322	8 077	8 228	8 400	8 422	8 565	8 683	8 670	8 730	8 899
Private Service-Providing	75 298	77 217	78 855	78 951	76 231	76 180	77 614	79 494	81 108	82 845	84 644	86 354	87 975	89 439
Trade, transportation, and utilities	21 792	22 126	22 502	22 292	21 072	20 829	21 188	21 569	21 826	22 232	22 581	22 855	23 107	23 393
Wholesale trade	4 538	4 676	4 799	4 768	4 453	4 324	4 388	4 505	4 563	4 638	4 644	4 634	4 660	4 698
Retail trade	13 033	13 114	13 322	13 139	12 476	12 430	12 652	12 798	12 928	13 112	13 269	13 433	13 486	13 529
Transportation and warehousing	3 777	3 893	3 939	3 935	3 692	3 631	3 708	3 824	3 890	4 037	4 222	4 342	4 513	4 721
Utilities	443	443	444	450	451	444	441	441	445	446	447	447	447	445
Information	2 386	2 399	2 403	2 388	2 240	2 170	2 148	2 164	2 194	2 209	2 226	2 252	2 268	2 278
Financial activities	6 127	6 312	6 365	6 320	6 066	5 942	5 900	5 986	6 068	6 155	6 278	6 430	6 571	6 637
Professional and business services	13 892	14 487	14 828	14 631	13 565	13 744	14 298	14 851	15 352	15 818	16 183	16 455	16 751	17 123
Education and health services	15 401	15 832	16 318	16 842	17 240	17 531	17 818	18 230	18 505	18 827	19 337	19 859	20 365	20 788
Leisure and hospitality	11 263	11 568	11 861	11 873	11 560	11 507	11 772	12 154	12 590	12 968	13 360	13 782	14 139	14 382
Other services	4 438	4 494	4 578	4 606	4 488	4 458	4 491	4 541	4 573	4 637	4 678	4 720	4 775	4 839

Table 2-4. Production Workers on Manufacturing Payrolls, by Industry, NAICS Basis, 2005–2018

(Thousands of people.)

Industry	2005	2006	2007	2008	2009	2010	2011	2012	2013	2014	2015	2016	2017	2018
Total Manufacturing	10 060	10 137	9 975	9 629	8 322	8 077	8 228	8 400	8 422	8 565	8 683	8 670	8 730	8 899
Durable Goods	6 220	6 355	6 250	5 975	4 990	4 829	4 986	5 152	5 185	5 282	5 350	5 303	5 315	5 463
Wood products	454	451	407	358	278	269	269	272	283	298	306	309	311	319
Nometallic mineral products	387	391	384	363	303	284	278	273	275	280	297	306	305	310
Primary metals	363	363	358	348	273	275	301	317	306	310	307	293	292	294
Fabricated metal products	1 129	1 162	1 171	1 143	961	935	994	1 050	1 063	1 071	1 069	1 036	1 045	1 085
Machinery	749	770	774	772	641	616	662	700	699	716	711	686	691	718
Computer and electronic products	700	756	744	730	654	629	630	628	610	589	594	596	598	613
Electrical equipment and appliances	300	303	305	305	266	251	248	249	245	248	258	259	253	261
Transportation equipment	1 277	1 304	1 275	1 177	948	937	972	1 024	1 053	1 103	1 139	1 151	1 149	1 188
Furniture and related products	436	433	409	364	284	263	260	259	266	276	284	287	290	292
Miscellaneous manufacturing	424	423	425	416	382	370	373	380	386	390	384	382	381	384
Nondurable Goods	3 841	3 782	3 725	3 653	3 332	3 248	3 241	3 248	3 237	3 283	3 333	3 367	3 415	3 436
Food manufacturing	1 170	1 172	1 184	1 184	1 161	1 152	1 158	1 169	1 169	1 176	1 189	1 212	1 251	1 272
Textile mills	174	158	137	122	99	96	98	96	92	91	90	90	88	88
Textile products mills	143	135	123	115	98	92	89	85	83	86	88	89	89	86
Apparel	193	182	173	163	132	120	112	109	106	103	104	99	88	81
Paper and paper products	365	357	350	344	313	302	295	288	279	277	277	275	278	276
Printing and related support	447	447	443	424	369	342	327	316	310	312	310	312	305	295
Petroleum and coal products	75	72	73	77	70	70	70	72	70	72	74	76	80	77
Chemicals	510	508	504	512	479	474	480	491	490	497	507	516	525	548
Plastics and rubber products	620	608	592	572	476	472	482	487	497	518	532	536	543	548

Table 2-5. Total Employees on Manufacturing Payrolls, by Industry, NAICS Basis, 2005–2018

(Thousands of people.)

Industry	2005	2006	2007	2008	2009	2010	2011	2012	2013	2014	2015	2016	2017	2018
Total Manufacturing	14 227	14 155	13 879	13 406	11 847	11 528	11 726	11 927	12 020	12 185	12 336	12 354	12 439	12 689
Durable Goods	8 956	8 981	8 808	8 463	7 284	7 064	7 273	7 470	7 548	7 674	7 765	7 714	7 741	7 945
Wood products	561	561	517	458	360	342	337	339	353	372	383	393	397	406
Nometallic mineral products	505	510	501	465	394	371	367	365	373	384	398	406	410	415
Primary metals	466	464	456	442	362	362	388	402	395	399	394	375	371	378
Fabricated metal products	1 522	1 553	1 563	1 528	1 312	1 282	1 347	1 410	1 432	1 454	1 458	1 422	1 425	1 467
Machinery	1 166	1 183	1 187	1 188	1 029	996	1 056	1 099	1 105	1 127	1 121	1 077	1 079	1 120
Computer and electronic products	1 316	1 308	1 273	1 244	1 137	1 095	1 104	1 089	1 066	1 049	1 053	1 048	1 039	1 055
Electrical equipment and appliances	434	433	429	424	374	360	366	373	374	378	384	383	386	399
Transportation equipment	1 772	1 769	1 712	1 608	1 348	1 333	1 382	1 461	1 509	1 559	1 605	1 630	1 643	1 702
Furniture and related products	566	558	529	478	384	357	353	351	360	370	381	390	395	395
Miscellaneous manufacturing	647	644	642	629	584	567	574	580	581	582	590	591	595	608
Nondurable Goods	5 271	5 174	5 071	4 943	4 564	4 464	4 453	4 457	4 472	4 512	4 571	4 640	4 699	4 743
Food manufacturing	1 478	1 479	1 484	1 481	1 456	1 451	1 459	1 469	1 474	1 484	1 512	1 557	1 598	1 620
Textile mills	218	195	170	151	124	119	120	119	117	117	117	115	113	113
Textile products mills	176	167	158	147	126	119	118	116	114	115	116	116	116	116
Apparel	251	232	215	199	168	157	152	148	145	140	137	131	119	113
Paper and paper products	484	471	458	445	407	395	387	380	378	373	373	371	366	367
Printing and related support	646	634	622	594	522	488	472	462	452	454	450	448	440	431
Petroleum and coal products	112	113	115	117	115	114	112	112	110	112	113	113	115	116

Table 2-6. Average Weekly Hours of All Employees on Private Nonfarm Payrolls by NAICS Super Sector, 2010–2018

(Hours per week, seasonally adjusted.)

Year and month	Total private	Mining and logging	Construction	Manufacturing	Trade, transportation, and utilities				Information	Financial activities	Professional and business services	Education and health services	Leisure and hospitality	Other services
					Total	Wholesale trade	Retail trade	Utilities						
2010	34.1	43.4	37.8	40.2	34.2	38.1	31.4	41.1	36.5	36.9	35.4	32.7	25.7	31.6
2011	34.3	44.5	38.3	40.5	34.5	38.7	31.6	41.8	36.6	37.3	35.7	32.7	25.9	31.7
2012	34.5	44.0	38.7	40.7	34.6	38.7	31.7	41.8	36.6	37.4	36.0	32.8	26.1	31.6
2013	34.4	44.0	39.0	40.8	34.5	38.7	31.4	42.2	36.6	37.1	36.1	32.7	26.0	31.7
2014	34.5	44.8	39.0	41.0	34.5	38.9	31.3	42.4	36.8	37.3	36.3	32.7	26.2	31.8
2015	34.5	44.0	39.1	40.8	34.6	38.9	31.4	42.5	36.3	37.6	36.2	32.8	26.3	31.9
2016	34.4	43.3	39.1	40.7	34.3	38.8	31.0	42.3	35.9	37.4	36.0	32.8	26.1	31.9
2017	34.4	45.2	39.2	40.8	34.4	39.1	31.0	42.2	36.2	37.5	36.1	32.9	26.1	31.8
2018	34.5	46.0	39.3	40.9	34.5	39.1	31.0	42.1	36.1	37.6	36.2	32.9	26.1	31.8
2014														
January	34.4	44.4	38.6	40.7	34.4	38.8	31.2	42.3	36.7	37.1	36.2	32.7	26.0	31.7
February	34.3	44.8	38.3	40.7	34.3	38.7	31.0	42.4	36.8	37.2	36.1	32.6	25.8	31.7
March	34.5	45.1	39.2	41.0	34.5	38.9	31.3	42.3	36.9	37.2	36.3	32.7	26.2	31.9
April	34.5	45.0	38.9	40.9	34.5	38.8	31.4	42.3	36.8	37.1	36.3	32.7	26.2	31.9
May	34.5	44.5	38.9	41.1	34.5	38.9	31.3	42.4	36.7	37.2	36.3	32.7	26.1	31.8
June	34.5	45.1	39.0	41.1	34.4	38.9	31.3	42.4	36.6	37.2	36.3	32.7	26.1	31.7
July	34.5	44.8	39.2	40.9	34.5	38.9	31.3	42.5	36.6	37.1	36.2	32.6	26.1	31.7
August	34.6	45.0	39.1	41.0	34.6	39.0	31.4	42.4	36.7	37.3	36.2	32.8	26.3	31.8
September	34.5	44.7	39.1	41.0	34.5	39.0	31.3	42.3	36.8	37.3	36.2	32.7	26.2	31.8
October	34.6	44.9	39.0	41.0	34.6	38.9	31.4	42.5	36.7	37.3	36.3	32.8	26.2	31.8
November	34.6	44.9	39.1	41.1	34.6	39.0	31.4	42.6	36.6	37.4	36.3	32.8	26.2	31.8
December	34.6	45.1	39.1	41.0	34.6	38.9	31.4	42.2	36.5	37.4	36.3	32.8	26.3	31.8
2015														
January	34.5	44.9	38.9	40.9	34.5	38.9	31.3	42.3	36.5	37.5	36.2	32.8	26.3	31.9
February	34.6	44.4	39.5	41.0	34.6	38.9	31.4	42.7	36.4	37.4	36.2	32.8	26.2	31.9
March	34.5	44.0	39.2	40.9	34.6	38.8	31.4	42.8	36.4	37.5	36.1	32.8	26.2	31.9
April	34.5	43.8	38.9	40.8	34.6	38.8	31.4	42.6	36.3	37.6	36.1	32.8	26.2	31.8
May	34.5	43.6	38.9	40.7	34.7	38.9	31.5	42.5	36.3	37.6	36.2	32.8	26.2	31.8
June	34.5	43.6	39.2	40.7	34.5	38.8	31.3	42.3	36.3	37.7	36.2	32.8	26.3	31.8
July	34.5	43.9	39.1	40.8	34.6	38.9	31.4	42.6	36.3	37.6	36.2	32.8	26.2	31.9
August	34.6	43.7	39.3	40.9	34.7	38.8	31.5	42.7	36.3	37.6	36.2	32.9	26.2	31.8
September	34.5	44.1	38.9	40.6	34.8	38.8	31.8	42.5	36.1	37.7	36.1	32.8	26.3	31.9
October	34.6	44.0	39.7	40.7	34.6	38.9	31.4	42.5	36.1	37.6	36.3	32.8	26.3	31.9
November	34.5	44.2	39.1	40.7	34.6	38.9	31.4	42.6	36.1	37.6	36.1	32.8	26.1	31.9
December	34.5	44.3	39.7	40.7	34.6	39.0	31.2	42.5	36.0	37.7	36.2	32.8	26.3	31.9
2016														
January	34.6	43.8	39.3	40.7	34.6	39.0	31.3	42.6	36.3	37.8	36.3	32.9	26.2	32.0
February	34.4	43.2	39.2	40.7	34.5	38.9	31.2	41.7	36.0	37.6	36.1	32.8	26.2	31.9
March	34.4	42.7	38.9	40.7	34.3	38.8	31.0	41.8	36.0	37.6	36.1	32.8	26.1	31.9
April	34.4	42.9	39.1	40.8	34.4	38.9	31.1	42.4	36.0	37.7	36.2	32.8	26.1	31.9
May	34.4	43.0	39.0	40.8	34.3	38.7	31.0	42.4	36.1	37.5	36.1	32.8	26.1	31.9
June	34.4	43.0	39.0	40.7	34.3	38.8	31.0	42.3	36.0	37.5	36.0	32.9	26.1	31.9
July	34.4	43.2	39.1	40.7	34.3	38.9	31.0	42.4	36.1	37.6	36.1	32.9	26.1	32.0
August	34.3	43.7	38.9	40.6	34.2	38.8	30.9	42.3	35.9	37.5	36.0	32.9	26.0	31.9
September	34.4	43.7	39.0	40.7	34.3	39.0	30.9	42.1	35.9	37.5	36.1	32.9	26.2	31.9
October	34.4	43.8	39.2	40.7	34.3	39.0	30.9	42.9	35.9	37.4	36.1	32.9	26.0	32.0
November	34.3	43.8	39.1	40.6	34.2	38.9	30.8	41.8	36.0	37.4	36.0	32.9	26.1	31.9
December	34.4	43.7	38.9	40.7	34.4	38.9	31.1	42.5	36.1	37.4	36.0	32.9	26.0	31.9
2017														
January	34.4	44.0	39.2	40.8	34.3	38.9	30.9	42.5	36.6	37.2	36.2	32.9	26.0	31.8
February	34.3	44.4	39.0	40.7	34.2	38.9	30.7	42.1	36.3	37.4	36.1	32.9	25.9	31.8
March	34.3	45.0	38.9	40.6	34.2	39.0	30.8	42.3	36.2	37.3	36.0	32.9	26.0	31.8
April	34.4	45.3	39.2	40.8	34.5	39.0	31.2	41.9	36.3	37.4	36.1	32.9	26.1	31.8
May	34.4	45.4	39.1	40.7	34.4	39.0	31.0	42.1	36.3	37.4	36.1	32.8	26.0	31.8
June	34.4	45.1	39.1	40.8	34.4	39.0	31.0	42.3	36.3	37.6	36.1	32.9	26.1	31.8
July	34.4	45.5	39.0	40.9	34.4	39.1	31.0	42.3	36.2	37.4	36.1	32.9	26.1	31.7
August	34.4	45.1	38.9	40.8	34.4	39.1	30.9	41.7	36.0	37.5	36.0	32.9	26.1	31.7
September	34.3	45.3	38.9	40.8	34.3	39.0	30.9	42.3	36.2	37.5	36.0	32.8	26.0	31.7
October	34.4	45.4	39.1	40.9	34.4	39.0	31.0	42.1	36.1	37.5	36.0	32.9	26.1	31.7
November	34.5	45.5	39.2	41.0	34.7	39.2	31.3	42.2	35.9	37.6	36.1	32.9	26.1	31.7
December	34.5	45.7	39.3	40.8	34.5	39.3	31.1	42.0	36.2	37.6	36.0	33.0	26.2	31.7
2018														
January	34.4	45.2	39.1	40.8	34.5	39.0	31.1	41.9	35.8	37.6	35.9	32.9	26.0	31.7
February	34.5	45.9	39.3	41.0	34.5	39.0	31.1	41.9	36.0	37.6	36.2	33.0	26.1	31.7
March	34.5	45.7	39.3	40.9	34.5	39.1	31.1	42.1	36.0	37.5	36.2	32.9	26.1	31.7
April	34.5	45.9	39.4	41.0	34.5	39.0	31.0	42.2	36.1	37.6	36.1	33.0	26.0	31.8
May	34.5	46.1	39.5	40.8	34.5	39.1	31.0	42.0	36.0	37.6	36.2	33.0	26.1	31.7
June	34.5	46.4	39.2	40.9	34.6	39.1	31.2	42.0	35.8	37.7	36.2	33.0	26.1	31.8
July	34.5	45.9	39.4	41.0	34.6	39.0	31.1	41.9	36.0	37.5	36.2	32.9	26.1	31.8
August	34.5	46.1	39.2	41.0	34.5	39.1	30.9	42.0	36.1	37.6	36.1	33.0	26.1	31.8
September	34.5	46.0	39.1	40.9	34.4	39.0	30.9	42.2	36.3	37.5	36.1	32.9	26.0	31.8
October	34.5	46.1	38.8	40.8	34.4	38.9	30.8	42.1	36.2	37.8	36.2	32.9	26.1	31.9
November	34.4	45.9	38.7	40.8	34.5	39.0	30.9	42.4	36.1	37.6	36.1	32.9	25.9	31.9
December	34.5	46.2	39.5	40.9	34.3	39.0	30.6	42.4	36.3	37.6	36.1	33.0	26.0	31.9

Table 2-7. Average Weekly Hours of Production Workers on Private Nonfarm Payrolls, by Super Sector, NAICS Basis, 2005–2018

(Hours.)

Industry	2005	2006	2007	2008	2009	2010	2011	2012	2013	2014	2015	2016	2017	2018
TOTAL PRIVATE	33.8	33.9	33.8	33.6	33.1	33.4	33.6	33.7	33.7	33.7	33.7	33.6	33.7	33.8
Goods-Producing	40.1	40.5	40.6	40.2	39.2	40.4	40.9	41.1	41.3	41.5	41.2	41.2	41.3	41.5
Mining and logging	45.6	45.6	45.9	45.1	43.2	44.6	46.7	46.6	45.9	47.3	45.8	45.3	46.1	46.8
Construction	38.6	39.0	39.0	38.5	37.6	38.4	39.0	39.3	39.6	39.6	39.6	39.7	39.7	40.0
Manufacturing	40.7	41.1	41.2	40.8	39.8	41.1	41.4	41.7	41.8	42.0	41.8	41.9	41.9	42.2
Private Service-Providing	32.4	32.4	32.4	32.3	32.1	32.2	32.4	32.5	32.4	32.4	32.4	32.3	32.4	32.4
Trade, transportation, and utilities	33.4	33.4	33.3	33.2	32.9	33.3	33.7	33.8	33.7	33.6	33.7	33.5	33.8	33.9
Wholesale trade	37.7	38.0	38.2	38.3	37.7	37.9	38.5	38.7	38.7	38.6	38.6	38.6	39.0	38.9
Retail trade	30.6	30.5	30.2	30.0	29.9	30.2	30.5	30.6	30.2	30.0	30.1	29.7	30.2	30.4
Transportation and warehousing	37.0	36.9	37.0	36.4	36.0	37.1	37.8	38.0	38.5	38.5	38.8	38.8	38.4	38.4
Utilities	41.1	41.4	42.4	42.7	42.0	42.0	42.1	41.1	41.7	42.3	42.4	42.5	42.5	42.7
Information	36.5	36.6	36.5	36.7	36.6	36.3	36.2	36.0	35.9	35.9	35.7	35.5	35.8	35.6
Financial activities	36.0	35.8	35.9	35.9	36.1	36.2	36.4	36.8	36.7	36.7	37.1	36.9	37.0	37.0
Professional and business services	34.2	34.6	34.8	34.8	34.7	35.1	35.2	35.3	35.4	35.6	35.5	35.4	35.4	35.4
Education and health services	32.6	32.5	32.5	32.4	32.2	32.0	32.2	32.3	32.1	32.0	32.1	32.2	32.2	32.2
Leisure and hospitality	25.7	25.7	25.5	25.2	24.8	24.8	24.8	25.0	25.0	25.1	25.1	24.9	24.9	24.9
Other services	30.9	30.9	30.9	30.8	30.5	30.7	30.8	30.7	30.8	30.7	30.7	30.8	30.7	30.8

Table 2-8. Employees on Total Nonfarm Payrolls, by State and Selected Territory, 1975–2018

(Thousands of people.)

State	1975	1976	1977	1978	1979	1980	1981	1982	1983	1984	1985	1986	1987	1988	1989	1990
UNITED STATES	77 069	79 502	82 593	86 826	89 933	90 533	91 297	89 689	90 295	94 548	97 532	99 500	102 116	105 378	108 051	109 527
Alabama	1 155	1 207	1 269	1 337	1 362	1 356	1 348	1 313	1 329	1 388	1 427	1 463	1 508	1 559	1 601	1 645
Alaska	162	172	163	164	167	169	186	200	214	226	231	221	210	214	227	238
Arizona	729	759	809	895	980	1 014	1 041	1 030	1 078	1 182	1 279	1 338	1 386	1 419	1 455	1 483
Arkansas	624	660	696	733	750	742	740	720	741	780	797	814	837	865	893	923
California	7 847	8 154	8 600	9 200	9 666	9 853	9 993	9 822	9 933	10 408	10 792	11 111	11 501	11 944	12 274	12 540
Colorado	964	1 003	1 058	1 150	1 218	1 251	1 295	1 317	1 327	1 402	1 419	1 408	1 413	1 436	1 482	1 521
Connecticut	1 223	1 240	1 282	1 346	1 398	1 427	1 438	1 429	1 444	1 517	1 558	1 598	1 638	1 667	1 666	1 625
Delaware	230	237	239	248	257	259	259	259	266	280	293	303	321	334	345	348
District of Columbia	577	576	579	596	613	616	611	598	597	614	629	640	656	674	681	687
Florida	2 746	2 784	2 933	3 181	3 381	3 576	3 736	3 762	3 905	4 204	4 410	4 599	4 848	5 067	5 261	5 363
Georgia	1 756	1 839	1 927	2 050	2 128	2 159	2 199	2 202	2 280	2 449	2 570	2 672	2 782	2 876	2 941	3 027
Hawaii	343	349	359	377	394	404	405	399	406	413	426	439	460	478	506	528
Idaho	273	291	307	331	338	330	328	312	318	331	336	328	333	349	366	385
Illinois	4 419	4 565	4 656	4 789	4 880	4 850	4 732	4 593	4 531	4 672	4 755	4 791	4 928	5 098	5 214	5 288
Indiana	1 942	2 024	2 114	2 206	2 236	2 130	2 115	2 028	2 030	2 122	2 169	2 222	2 305	2 396	2 479	2 522
Iowa	999	1 037	1 079	1 119	1 132	1 110	1 089	1 042	1 040	1 075	1 074	1 074	1 109	1 156	1 200	1 226
Kansas	801	835	871	913	947	945	950	921	922	961	968	985	1 005	1 035	1 064	1 092
Kentucky	1 058	1 103	1 148	1 210	1 245	1 210	1 196	1 161	1 152	1 214	1 250	1 274	1 328	1 382	1 433	1 460
Louisiana	1 250	1 314	1 365	1 464	1 517	1 579	1 631	1 607	1 565	1 602	1 591	1 519	1 484	1 512	1 539	1 590
Maine	357	375	388	406	416	418	419	416	425	446	458	477	501	527	542	535
Maryland	1 479	1 498	1 546	1 626	1 691	1 712	1 716	1 676	1 724	1 814	1 888	1 952	2 028	2 102	2 155	2 178
Massachusetts	2 273	2 324	2 416	2 526	2 604	2 654	2 672	2 642	2 697	2 856	2 931	2 992	3 071	3 138	3 118	2 988
Michigan	3 137	3 283	3 442	3 609	3 637	3 443	3 364	3 193	3 223	3 381	3 562	3 657	3 736	3 819	3 922	3 944
Minnesota	1 474	1 521	1 597	1 689	1 767	1 770	1 761	1 707	1 718	1 820	1 866	1 893	1 963	2 028	2 087	2 136
Mississippi	692	728	766	814	838	829	819	791	793	821	839	848	864	896	919	938
Missouri	1 741	1 798	1 862	1 953	2 011	1 970	1 957	1 923	1 937	2 033	2 095	2 143	2 198	2 259	2 315	2 345
Montana	238	251	265	280	284	280	282	274	276	281	279	275	274	283	291	297
Nebraska	558	572	594	610	631	628	623	610	611	635	651	653	667	688	708	731
Nevada	263	280	308	350	384	400	411	401	403	426	446	468	500	538	581	621
New Hampshire	293	313	337	360	379	385	395	394	410	442	466	490	513	529	529	508
New Jersey	2 700	2 754	2 837	2 962	3 027	3 060	3 099	3 093	3 165	3 329	3 414	3 488	3 576	3 651	3 690	3 635
New Mexico	370	390	415	444	461	465	476	474	480	503	520	526	529	548	562	580
New York	6 830	6 790	6 858	7 045	7 179	7 207	7 287	7 255	7 313	7 570	7 751	7 908	8 059	8 187	8 247	8 203
North Carolina	1 980	2 083	2 171	2 278	2 373	2 380	2 392	2 347	2 419	2 565	2 651	2 744	2 863	2 987	3 074	3 124
North Dakota	204	215	221	234	244	245	249	250	251	253	252	250	252	257	260	266
Ohio	4 016	4 095	4 230	4 395	4 485	4 367	4 318	4 124	4 093	4 260	4 373	4 472	4 583	4 701	4 818	4 882
Oklahoma	900	931	972	1 036	1 088	1 138	1 201	1 217	1 171	1 180	1 165	1 124	1 109	1 132	1 164	1 210
Oregon	837	879	937	1 009	1 056	1 045	1 019	961	967	1 007	1 030	1 059	1 100	1 153	1 206	1 256
Pennsylvania	4 436	4 513	4 565	4 716	4 806	4 753	4 729	4 580	4 524	4 655	4 730	4 791	4 915	5 042	5 139	5 173
Rhode Island	349	367	382	396	400	398	401	391	396	416	429	443	452	459	462	454
South Carolina	983	1 038	1 082	1 138	1 176	1 189	1 197	1 162	1 189	1 263	1 296	1 338	1 392	1 449	1 500	1 528
South Dakota	209	219	227	237	241	238	236	230	235	247	249	252	257	266	276	288
Tennessee	1 506	1 575	1 648	1 737	1 777	1 747	1 755	1 703	1 719	1 812	1 868	1 930	2 012	2 092	2 167	2 196
Texas	4 463	4 684	4 907	5 272	5 602	5 851	6 180	6 263	6 194	6 492	6 663	6 564	6 517	6 678	6 840	7 126
Utah	440	463	489	525	548	551	558	561	567	601	624	634	640	660	691	726
Vermont	162	168	178	191	198	200	204	203	206	215	225	234	246	256	262	258
Virginia	1 779	1 848	1 930	2 034	2 115	2 157	2 161	2 146	2 207	2 333	2 455	2 558	2 680	2 773	2 862	2 896
Washington	1 226	1 283	1 367	1 485	1 581	1 608	1 612	1 569	1 586	1 660	1 710	1 770	1 852	1 942	2 048	2 148
West Virginia	575	596	612	633	659	646	629	608	582	597	597	598	599	610	615	613
Wisconsin	1 677	1 726	1 799	1 887	1 960	1 938	1 923	1 867	1 867	1 949	1 983	2 024	2 090	2 169	2 236	2 291
Wyoming	146	157	171	187	201	210	224	218	203	204	207	196	183	189	193	198
Puerto Rico	. . .	. . .	. . .	. . .	. . .	693	680	642	646	684	693	728	764	818	837	846
Virgin Islands	33	31	32	34	36	37	38	37	36	37	37	38	40	42	42	43

. . . = Not available.

Table 2-8. Employees on Total Nonfarm Payrolls, by State and Selected Territory, 1975–2018—*Continued*

(Thousands of people.)

State	1991	1992	1993	1994	1995	1996	1997	1998	1999	2000	2001	2002	2003	2004
UNITED STATES	108 427	108 802	110 935	114 399	117 407	119 836	122 951	126 157	129 240	132 024	132 087	130 649	130 347	131 787
Alabama	1 651	1 684	1 727	1 770	1 815	1 841	1 879	1 912	1 934	1 947	1 924	1 898	1 891	1 917
Alaska	243	247	253	259	262	264	269	275	279	284	289	295	299	304
Arizona	1 491	1 517	1 585	1 692	1 793	1 892	1 985	2 075	2 163	2 243	2 266	2 268	2 299	2 385
Arkansas	935	962	993	1 033	1 069	1 087	1 104	1 122	1 141	1 158	1 153	1 146	1 144	1 157
California	12 407	12 208	12 096	12 213	12 478	12 806	13 202	13 689	14 094	14 587	14 720	14 601	14 576	14 749
Colorado	1 545	1 597	1 670	1 756	1 834	1 900	1 980	2 057	2 132	2 213	2 226	2 183	2 152	2 179
Connecticut	1 563	1 533	1 536	1 549	1 567	1 587	1 612	1 648	1 674	1 698	1 686	1 669	1 649	1 656
Delaware	342	341	349	356	366	376	388	400	413	421	420	415	416	425
District of Columbia	678	674	671	659	643	623	619	614	628	650	654	664	666	674
Florida	5 274	5 337	5 549	5 777	5 973	6 159	6 395	6 611	6 801	7 054	7 145	7 154	7 235	7 483
Georgia	2 976	3 029	3 144	3 300	3 435	3 560	3 646	3 771	3 885	3 979	3 971	3 897	3 870	3 923
Hawaii	539	543	539	536	533	531	532	531	535	551	555	557	568	583
Idaho	398	415	434	459	476	489	506	522	539	560	568	569	572	588
Illinois	5 233	5 235	5 330	5 462	5 591	5 681	5 766	5 894	5 956	6 042	5 993	5 883	5 810	5 816
Indiana	2 508	2 555	2 628	2 714	2 788	2 817	2 861	2 920	2 973	3 004	2 937	2 907	2 902	2 934
Iowa	1 238	1 253	1 279	1 320	1 358	1 383	1 407	1 443	1 469	1 479	1 466	1 447	1 440	1 457
Kansas	1 097	1 116	1 135	1 167	1 200	1 228	1 270	1 314	1 328	1 346	1 349	1 336	1 313	1 325
Kentucky	1 464	1 498	1 537	1 587	1 632	1 661	1 701	1 742	1 785	1 817	1 795	1 779	1 773	1 789
Louisiana	1 613	1 627	1 659	1 722	1 772	1 810	1 850	1 890	1 896	1 920	1 918	1 898	1 908	1 920
Maine	514	512	520	532	538	543	554	570	587	604	608	607	607	612
Maryland	2 108	2 088	2 109	2 153	2 191	2 221	2 276	2 332	2 394	2 457	2 473	2 482	2 489	2 517
Massachusetts	2 825	2 799	2 844	2 908	2 982	3 042	3 117	3 187	3 250	3 338	3 350	3 272	3 214	3 213
Michigan	3 883	3 917	3 997	4 139	4 267	4 351	4 438	4 513	4 584	4 676	4 564	4 487	4 416	4 399
Minnesota	2 146	2 194	2 252	2 320	2 387	2 442	2 499	2 564	2 621	2 683	2 688	2 663	2 658	2 679
Mississippi	939	962	1 004	1 057	1 076	1 090	1 109	1 135	1 155	1 155	1 131	1 125	1 116	1 126
Missouri	2 310	2 335	2 396	2 472	2 523	2 570	2 642	2 687	2 730	2 753	2 735	2 704	2 687	2 701
Montana	304	317	326	340	352	362	367	376	384	391	391	396	400	411
Nebraska	741	752	770	799	820	839	858	880	896	913	919	911	914	921
Nevada	628	639	671	738	786	843	891	926	983	1 027	1 051	1 052	1 088	1 153
New Hampshire	482	487	502	523	540	554	570	589	606	622	627	618	617	627
New Jersey	3 497	3 455	3 489	3 548	3 594	3 632	3 716	3 797	3 897	3 989	3 991	3 978	3 971	3 991
New Mexico	585	602	626	657	682	695	709	720	730	745	757	766	776	790
New York	7 878	7 721	7 750	7 822	7 882	7 929	8 057	8 227	8 446	8 625	8 581	8 448	8 396	8 451
North Carolina	3 077	3 141	3 243	3 352	3 451	3 535	3 651	3 756	3 846	3 911	3 889	3 834	3 785	3 831
North Dakota	271	277	285	295	302	309	314	320	324	328	330	330	333	338
Ohio	4 819	4 848	4 918	5 076	5 221	5 296	5 392	5 482	5 564	5 625	5 543	5 445	5 397	5 408
Oklahoma	1 225	1 236	1 261	1 294	1 330	1 367	1 407	1 454	1 475	1 502	1 520	1 499	1 471	1 487
Oregon	1 253	1 277	1 318	1 373	1 428	1 485	1 537	1 562	1 586	1 618	1 605	1 585	1 574	1 606
Pennsylvania	5 086	5 078	5 125	5 195	5 256	5 309	5 409	5 498	5 588	5 693	5 684	5 642	5 613	5 645
Rhode Island	424	424	430	434	439	441	450	458	466	477	478	479	484	488
South Carolina	1 497	1 512	1 553	1 592	1 636	1 670	1 719	1 780	1 826	1 854	1 815	1 795	1 799	1 827
South Dakota	296	308	318	331	342	347	353	360	370	378	379	378	378	384
Tennessee	2 186	2 248	2 331	2 426	2 503	2 537	2 588	2 642	2 689	2 733	2 688	2 664	2 663	2 706
Texas	7 204	7 301	7 515	7 786	8 059	8 292	8 643	8 974	9 190	9 462	9 545	9 447	9 401	9 529
Utah	748	771	812	862	910	956	994	1 023	1 049	1 076	1 081	1 074	1 074	1 104
Vermont	249	251	257	264	270	275	279	285	292	299	302	299	299	303
Virginia	2 830	2 849	2 920	3 004	3 072	3 138	3 235	3 321	3 414	3 520	3 523	3 500	3 502	3 587
Washington	2 182	2 228	2 267	2 317	2 361	2 431	2 536	2 622	2 679	2 746	2 735	2 694	2 702	2 740
West Virginia	611	621	634	655	667	676	682	692	697	705	704	702	696	706
Wisconsin	2 302	2 358	2 412	2 490	2 558	2 600	2 655	2 717	2 783	2 832	2 812	2 780	2 772	2 802
Wyoming	203	206	210	217	219	221	225	228	233	239	245	248	250	255
Puerto Rico	838	858	872	898	930	973	989	997	1 011	1 025	1 009	1 005	1 024	1 050
Virgin Islands	44	45	49	45	42	41	42	42	41	42	44	43	42	43

Table 2-8. Employees on Total Nonfarm Payrolls, by State and Selected Territory, 1975–2018—*Continued*

(Thousands of people.)

State	2005	2006	2007	2008	2009	2010	2011	2012	2013	2014	2015	2016	2017	2018
UNITED STATES	134 051	136 453	137 999	137 241	131 313	130 362	131 932	134 175	136 381	138 958	141 843	144 352	146 624	149 074
Alabama	1 961	1 996	2 023	2 010	1 905	1 890	1 890	1 906	1 924	1 944	1 971	1 997	2 019	2 042
Alaska	310	315	318	322	321	325	330	335	337	338	339	334	329	327
Arizona	2 513	2 639	2 679	2 623	2 433	2 386	2 411	2 462	2 520	2 570	2 636	2 709	2 777	2 856
Arkansas	1 177	1 198	1 204	1 203	1 165	1 163	1 170	1 177	1 178	1 190	1 213	1 233	1 249	1 262
California	15 046	15 326	15 462	15 300	14 439	14 283	14 435	14 762	15 151	15 576	16 052	16 481	16 837	17 175
Colorado	2 225	2 278	2 330	2 349	2 244	2 221	2 257	2 312	2 381	2 464	2 541	2 602	2 660	2 725
Connecticut	1 668	1 689	1 701	1 704	1 631	1 612	1 628	1 642	1 655	1 666	1 679	1 684	1 687	1 689
Delaware	433	438	439	437	417	414	417	420	429	438	448	453	457	461
District of Columbia	682	688	694	704	702	712	726	733	743	748	764	777	785	792
Florida	7 783	7 985	8 001	7 717	7 235	7 175	7 255	7 400	7 586	7 828	8 111	8 388	8 573	8 782
Georgia	4 024	4 111	4 167	4 122	3 900	3 860	3 900	3 954	4 032	4 145	4 262	4 372	4 454	4 540
Hawaii	602	617	625	619	592	587	593	606	619	627	638	646	653	657
Idaho	611	638	655	649	610	603	610	622	637	654	672	694	715	737
Illinois	5 862	5 931	5 977	5 946	5 655	5 610	5 675	5 750	5 804	5 879	5 968	6 019	6 063	6 117
Indiana	2 960	2 979	2 991	2 963	2 791	2 799	2 845	2 902	2 937	2 979	3 035	3 077	3 113	3 144
Iowa	1 481	1 504	1 519	1 524	1 479	1 469	1 486	1 509	1 528	1 547	1 561	1 571	1 573	1 584
Kansas	1 334	1 355	1 381	1 392	1 345	1 330	1 340	1 358	1 372	1 391	1 400	1 404	1 404	1 416
Kentucky	1 814	1 837	1 857	1 842	1 760	1 760	1 784	1 811	1 831	1 858	1 886	1 909	1 921	1 932
Louisiana	1 894	1 856	1 918	1 940	1 904	1 888	1 906	1 930	1 957	1 987	1 996	1 975	1 973	1 982
Maine	612	615	618	618	597	593	595	599	602	606	611	619	624	629
Maryland	2 557	2 591	2 611	2 603	2 526	2 522	2 548	2 578	2 603	2 625	2 665	2 697	2 725	2 744
Massachusetts	3 231	3 267	3 305	3 318	3 211	3 223	3 259	3 310	3 365	3 432	3 499	3 565	3 612	3 643
Michigan	4 390	4 327	4 268	4 162	3 871	3 864	3 952	4 034	4 110	4 182	4 243	4 320	4 369	4 419
Minnesota	2 721	2 756	2 769	2 760	2 652	2 638	2 683	2 725	2 773	2 811	2 855	2 894	2 932	2 954
Mississippi	1 132	1 143	1 154	1 149	1 098	1 093	1 093	1 102	1 111	1 121	1 134	1 146	1 152	1 155
Missouri	2 743	2 783	2 804	2 800	2 697	2 666	2 675	2 694	2 720	2 748	2 806	2 848	2 874	2 887
Montana	420	434	444	445	429	428	431	440	449	453	462	468	472	478
Nebraska	934	946	962	969	950	945	953	969	980	993	1 007	1 015	1 019	1 023
Nevada	1 223	1 279	1 292	1 264	1 148	1 118	1 126	1 145	1 174	1 216	1 259	1 299	1 341	1 387
New Hampshire	636	642	647	649	628	624	627	634	639	646	656	668	676	681
New Jersey	4 031	4 062	4 068	4 039	3 885	3 839	3 837	3 880	3 924	3 956	4 000	4 060	4 117	4 155
New Mexico	809	832	844	847	812	803	802	805	812	820	827	828	832	842
New York	8 523	8 604	8 719	8 777	8 540	8 544	8 692	8 820	8 957	9 123	9 291	9 435	9 560	9 670
North Carolina	3 909	4 034	4 139	4 129	3 902	3 868	3 915	3 985	4 057	4 140	4 240	4 340	4 411	4 488
North Dakota	345	352	358	367	367	376	397	429	445	461	454	434	431	433
Ohio	5 427	5 435	5 427	5 362	5 072	5 036	5 108	5 202	5 267	5 344	5 424	5 481	5 526	5 560
Oklahoma	1 525	1 566	1 595	1 618	1 568	1 556	1 578	1 614	1 635	1 656	1 668	1 654	1 663	1 687
Oregon	1 654	1 703	1 731	1 718	1 612	1 602	1 620	1 640	1 674	1 722	1 781	1 834	1 875	1 910
Pennsylvania	5 703	5 757	5 799	5 800	5 617	5 622	5 686	5 726	5 741	5 789	5 835	5 883	5 941	6 006
Rhode Island	491	493	492	481	459	458	461	465	471	479	485	490	493	496
South Carolina	1 863	1 906	1 945	1 926	1 814	1 811	1 833	1 864	1 901	1 951	2 007	2 055	2 095	2 145
South Dakota	390	399	407	411	404	403	408	414	418	424	429	432	434	439
Tennessee	2 743	2 783	2 797	2 775	2 620	2 615	2 661	2 715	2 760	2 822	2 894	2 965	3 011	3 060
Texas	9 773	10 099	10 429	10 643	10 342	10 376	10 606	10 915	11 241	11 594	11 866	12 014	12 228	12 503
Utah	1 148	1 204	1 253	1 252	1 189	1 183	1 208	1 250	1 291	1 328	1 379	1 427	1 469	1 517
Vermont	306	308	308	307	297	298	301	305	307	310	312	313	315	316
Virginia	3 667	3 732	3 771	3 772	3 652	3 646	3 693	3 736	3 762	3 783	3 859	3 915	3 956	4 001
Washington	2 813	2 894	2 968	2 994	2 863	2 836	2 873	2 920	2 984	3 057	3 145	3 243	3 321	3 406
West Virginia	715	726	726	731	715	717	725	734	732	729	726	717	716	726
Wisconsin	2 836	2 859	2 876	2 868	2 741	2 725	2 752	2 781	2 809	2 852	2 892	2 926	2 948	2 972
Wyoming	264	278	290	299	287	284	289	293	294	298	297	286	284	286
Puerto Rico	1 051	1 045	1 032	1 014	965	932	924	940	926	910	901	894	871	861
Virgin Islands	44	46	46	46	44	44	44	40	39	38	38	38	37	33

Table 2-9. Employees on Total Private Payrolls, by State and Selected Territory, 2005–2018

(Thousands of people.)

State	2005	2006	2007	2008	2009	2010	2011	2012	2013	2014	2015	2016	2017	2018
UNITED STATES	112 247	114 479	115 781	114 732	108 758	107 871	109 845	112 255	114 529	117 076	119 814	122 128	124 275	126 625
Alabama	1 595	1 623	1 643	1 622	1 518	1 499	1 504	1 524	1 543	1 563	1 590	1 615	1 634	1 656
Alaska	229	234	237	240	237	240	245	251	254	256	257	252	248	247
Arizona	2 110	2 231	2 258	2 190	2 010	1 970	2 004	2 054	2 111	2 160	2 227	2 298	2 364	2 441
Arkansas	974	991	994	989	948	945	953	961	963	977	1 001	1 021	1 038	1 050
California	12 626	12 874	12 967	12 781	11 960	11 835	12 030	12 386	12 777	13 162	13 589	13 965	14 273	14 588
Colorado	1 863	1 911	1 956	1 966	1 854	1 828	1 865	1 917	1 977	2 056	2 125	2 174	2 224	2 280
Connecticut	1 416	1 432	1 447	1 444	1 376	1 362	1 381	1 397	1 410	1 421	1 435	1 443	1 449	1 452
Delaware	373	377	377	374	354	350	354	356	365	374	383	387	391	395
District of Columbia	448	454	462	469	461	465	479	489	503	513	526	536	544	554
Florida	6 700	6 884	6 876	6 588	6 118	6 061	6 159	6 317	6 506	6 751	7 026	7 291	7 467	7 669
Georgia	3 358	3 431	3 474	3 411	3 191	3 161	3 213	3 268	3 351	3 467	3 583	3 690	3 767	3 846
Hawaii	482	496	503	494	466	462	469	481	494	501	511	520	528	531
Idaho	496	522	538	529	490	485	493	505	520	536	553	573	592	612
Illinois	5 016	5 085	5 130	5 092	4 799	4 757	4 839	4 919	4 975	5 053	5 140	5 191	5 236	5 291
Indiana	2 534	2 553	2 560	2 522	2 353	2 361	2 415	2 474	2 513	2 554	2 608	2 651	2 685	2 714
Iowa	1 235	1 257	1 269	1 271	1 224	1 216	1 233	1 255	1 274	1 292	1 306	1 313	1 313	1 323
Kansas	1 083	1 100	1 123	1 132	1 083	1 068	1 080	1 099	1 115	1 134	1 144	1 148	1 147	1 158
Kentucky	1 513	1 532	1 547	1 532	1 449	1 443	1 463	1 488	1 507	1 535	1 567	1 593	1 605	1 618
Louisiana	1 518	1 505	1 560	1 573	1 533	1 519	1 546	1 578	1 615	1 655	1 667	1 646	1 644	1 654
Maine	507	511	514	513	493	489	493	497	502	506	511	519	524	528
Maryland	2 091	2 120	2 132	2 114	2 032	2 020	2 043	2 075	2 100	2 123	2 161	2 194	2 221	2 240
Massachusetts	2 806	2 838	2 873	2 881	2 773	2 783	2 825	2 873	2 922	2 981	3 048	3 111	3 159	3 188
Michigan	3 716	3 662	3 612	3 512	3 224	3 228	3 335	3 425	3 511	3 586	3 649	3 720	3 765	3 812
Minnesota	2 306	2 340	2 354	2 342	2 235	2 221	2 273	2 313	2 360	2 392	2 437	2 475	2 509	2 529
Mississippi	891	903	910	901	848	844	847	856	866	876	890	902	909	914
Missouri	2 313	2 349	2 364	2 354	2 245	2 218	2 236	2 255	2 284	2 316	2 372	2 414	2 439	2 454
Montana	334	346	357	357	339	336	341	351	359	363	372	377	381	387
Nebraska	773	783	799	806	781	775	785	800	812	823	836	842	846	850
Nevada	1 080	1 130	1 136	1 102	991	964	976	995	1 023	1 064	1 104	1 141	1 181	1 226
New Hampshire	545	550	554	553	531	528	535	542	548	555	566	578	586	591
New Jersey	3 395	3 420	3 427	3 397	3 239	3 206	3 226	3 272	3 317	3 348	3 398	3 459	3 516	3 554
New Mexico	608	635	649	649	613	604	608	612	620	629	637	639	644	655
New York	7 033	7 119	7 218	7 262	7 016	7 033	7 186	7 336	7 487	7 659	7 823	7 958	8 077	8 181
North Carolina	3 239	3 347	3 436	3 408	3 178	3 147	3 202	3 273	3 341	3 425	3 521	3 614	3 682	3 755
North Dakota	270	277	283	291	289	296	317	350	365	381	372	351	348	351
Ohio	4 627	4 635	4 629	4 563	4 280	4 250	4 333	4 428	4 501	4 578	4 653	4 706	4 746	4 781
Oklahoma	1 204	1 236	1 261	1 281	1 219	1 208	1 234	1 267	1 287	1 308	1 317	1 301	1 313	1 340
Oregon	1 369	1 417	1 441	1 420	1 313	1 302	1 325	1 349	1 385	1 428	1 480	1 527	1 566	1 614
Pennsylvania	4 949	5 002	5 044	5 041	4 849	4 852	4 935	4 994	5 020	5 077	5 131	5 180	5 238	5 303
Rhode Island	426	428	427	417	397	396	400	405	411	418	425	429	433	435
South Carolina	1 527	1 566	1 599	1 571	1 459	1 456	1 484	1 513	1 548	1 595	1 647	1 692	1 729	1 776
South Dakota	315	323	331	335	326	325	330	337	341	346	351	354	355	359
Tennessee	2 333	2 369	2 379	2 350	2 194	2 185	2 236	2 293	2 337	2 398	2 469	2 537	2 581	2 625
Texas	8 061	8 364	8 666	8 835	8 491	8 485	8 751	9 088	9 399	9 733	9 981	10 093	10 288	10 552
Utah	946	999	1 046	1 041	974	965	988	1 027	1 065	1 098	1 145	1 187	1 225	1 269
Vermont	253	254	255	253	243	243	246	249	251	254	256	257	259	259
Virginia	3 005	3 057	3 086	3 077	2 949	2 940	2 980	3 022	3 050	3 073	3 148	3 200	3 239	3 278
Washington	2 286	2 364	2 435	2 448	2 313	2 286	2 329	2 378	2 441	2 507	2 583	2 667	2 735	2 819
West Virginia	572	580	582	584	565	563	573	580	578	577	573	561	562	573
Wisconsin	2 421	2 444	2 460	2 446	2 320	2 305	2 337	2 370	2 400	2 440	2 483	2 515	2 541	2 564
Wyoming	199	212	222	230	217	213	217	221	222	227	226	215	214	217
Puerto Rico	747	744	734	714	676	664	665	681	681	675	670	667	654	654
Virgin Islands	32	33	33	33	31	31	31	29	28	27	27	28	26	23

Table 2-10. Employees on Manufacturing Payrolls, by State and Selected Territory, NAICS Basis, 2005–2018

(Thousands of people.)

State	2005	2006	2007	2008	2009	2010	2011	2012	2013	2014	2015	2016	2017	2018
UNITED STATES	14 227	14 155	13 879	13 406	11 847	11 528	11 726	11 927	12 020	12 185	12 336	12 354	12 439	12 689
Alabama	299	303	296	284	247	236	238	244	249	253	258	261	264	267
Alaska	13	13	13	13	13	13	14	14	14	15	14	14	13	13
Arizona	182	186	182	173	154	148	150	155	155	157	158	160	164	170
Arkansas	202	200	191	184	164	160	159	155	153	154	155	155	157	161
California	1 506	1 491	1 466	1 429	1 286	1 248	1 255	1 260	1 263	1 280	1 303	1 309	1 311	1 325
Colorado	148	147	145	142	128	124	128	131	133	137	141	143	144	148
Connecticut	193	191	188	185	168	163	163	162	160	157	157	157	159	160
Delaware	33	34	33	32	28	26	26	26	25	25	26	26	26	27
District of Columbia	2	2	2	2	1	1	1	1	1	1	1	1	1	1
Florida	416	417	399	371	324	309	313	318	323	332	344	356	363	372
Georgia	451	449	433	411	360	347	353	357	360	370	381	392	400	408
Hawaii	15	15	15	15	14	13	13	13	14	14	14	14	14	14
Idaho	64	66	66	63	55	53	55	57	60	61	62	64	66	68
Illinois	689	684	676	658	577	561	574	583	580	581	582	575	576	588
Indiana	570	565	549	520	441	446	463	481	491	506	518	523	532	542
Iowa	229	231	230	228	203	201	206	211	215	217	216	214	216	223
Kansas	179	182	185	185	165	158	159	161	161	162	161	160	162	165
Kentucky	262	261	256	245	213	209	213	223	229	235	241	248	251	252
Louisiana	152	153	157	153	142	138	140	142	145	148	144	136	135	135
Maine	61	60	59	59	52	51	51	51	50	50	51	51	51	52
Maryland	141	137	134	130	121	117	115	112	108	106	106	106	107	108
Massachusetts	305	299	294	286	258	252	252	251	249	249	248	245	244	244
Michigan	668	638	608	563	455	466	502	531	549	575	592	606	616	630
Minnesota	347	346	342	336	300	293	301	306	307	312	318	318	318	321
Mississippi	178	176	170	160	141	136	135	137	137	140	142	143	144	145
Missouri	312	310	304	293	257	246	250	252	253	257	262	264	267	273
Montana	20	20	21	20	17	17	17	18	18	19	19	20	20	21
Nebraska	101	102	101	101	93	92	93	95	97	98	97	97	98	100
Nevada	48	50	50	48	40	38	38	39	41	42	42	44	48	56
New Hampshire	80	78	78	76	68	66	67	66	66	66	67	68	69	71
New Jersey	328	321	308	295	261	252	247	241	239	239	239	242	245	247
New Mexico	36	38	37	35	30	29	30	30	29	28	28	27	26	27
New York	580	567	552	532	476	457	459	459	456	454	455	451	445	443
North Carolina	565	554	539	516	448	433	434	441	443	450	462	466	469	474
North Dakota	26	26	26	26	24	23	24	25	25	26	26	25	25	26
Ohio	813	797	772	740	630	621	639	657	664	676	688	686	687	699
Oklahoma	152	156	158	157	136	130	137	142	142	145	143	134	134	138
Oregon	204	207	204	195	167	164	168	172	175	180	186	188	190	195
Pennsylvania	680	671	660	644	575	561	566	568	566	569	569	561	563	569
Rhode Island	55	53	51	48	42	40	40	40	40	41	41	40	40	40
South Carolina	260	252	249	241	213	207	215	219	223	228	234	236	241	248
South Dakota	40	42	42	43	38	37	39	41	42	42	43	42	43	44
Tennessee	406	397	378	359	307	297	302	311	316	323	331	342	346	351
Texas	901	928	939	929	843	817	842	870	876	888	879	847	853	881
Utah	119	124	128	126	113	111	114	117	119	121	124	126	129	133
Vermont	37	36	36	35	31	31	31	32	32	31	31	30	30	30
Virginia	296	288	278	265	240	231	231	232	231	232	234	233	235	240
Washington	273	286	294	292	266	259	269	281	287	289	292	290	284	288
West Virginia	62	61	59	57	51	49	50	49	48	48	48	47	47	47
Wisconsin	505	506	501	493	437	431	445	456	458	465	467	465	467	476
Wyoming	10	10	10	10	9	9	9	9	10	10	10	9	9	10
Puerto Rico	115	110	107	101	92	87	84	82	77	75	74	74	71	72
Virgin Islands	2	2	2	2	2	2	2	1	1	1	1	1	1	1

Table 2-11. Employees on Government Payrolls, by State and Selected Territory, NAICS Basis, 2005–2018

(Thousands of people.)

State	2005	2006	2007	2008	2009	2010	2011	2012	2013	2014	2015	2016	2017	2018
UNITED STATES	21 804	21 974	22 218	22 509	22 555	22 490	22 086	21 920	21 853	21 882	22 029	22 224	22 350	22 449
Alabama	366	374	380	387	388	391	386	381	381	382	381	382	385	386
Alaska	81	81	81	82	84	85	85	84	83	82	82	82	81	80
Arizona	403	409	421	432	423	416	407	409	409	410	410	411	413	415
Arkansas	203	207	211	214	217	218	216	216	215	213	212	212	211	212
California	2 420	2 452	2 495	2 519	2 480	2 448	2 405	2 376	2 374	2 414	2 463	2 516	2 564	2 587
Colorado	362	367	374	384	390	393	392	394	403	408	417	428	437	445
Connecticut	252	257	254	260	255	251	247	246	245	245	244	241	239	237
Delaware	60	61	62	63	63	64	64	64	64	65	65	66	66	66
District of Columbia	234	233	232	235	241	247	248	244	241	236	238	241	241	239
Florida	1 084	1 102	1 125	1 130	1 117	1 115	1 096	1 082	1 079	1 077	1 085	1 098	1 106	1 113
Georgia	667	680	693	711	709	699	687	686	682	678	679	683	688	694
Hawaii	120	121	122	125	126	125	125	126	125	126	126	126	126	126
Idaho	115	116	117	119	120	119	117	117	117	118	119	121	123	125
Illinois	846	846	848	854	856	852	836	831	828	826	828	829	828	826
Indiana	426	426	431	441	438	437	430	428	425	425	427	426	428	430
Iowa	245	247	250	253	255	253	253	254	255	255	256	258	260	261
Kansas	251	255	258	260	261	262	260	259	257	257	257	256	256	258
Kentucky	301	305	310	310	311	317	321	324	324	323	318	316	316	314
Louisiana	376	350	358	367	372	369	360	352	341	332	330	329	328	328
Maine	105	104	104	104	104	104	102	102	101	100	100	100	100	100
Maryland	466	471	480	489	495	502	504	503	503	502	503	503	504	505
Massachusetts	425	429	433	437	438	439	435	437	443	452	451	454	453	455
Michigan	674	665	656	650	647	636	617	609	599	596	594	599	604	607
Minnesota	415	416	415	419	417	417	410	412	413	419	419	419	424	426
Mississippi	241	239	244	248	250	249	246	246	245	244	243	244	243	241
Missouri	429	434	440	446	452	448	439	438	435	432	434	434	435	434
Montana	86	88	87	88	90	92	90	90	90	90	90	91	91	90
Nebraska	161	162	162	164	169	170	168	168	169	170	171	173	173	174
Nevada	143	149	156	161	157	154	150	149	151	153	155	158	161	161
New Hampshire	91	92	93	95	97	96	92	92	90	91	90	91	90	90
New Jersey	636	641	641	643	645	633	611	608	607	608	602	601	602	601
New Mexico	201	198	195	198	199	200	195	193	191	191	189	189	187	187
New York	1 489	1 485	1 501	1 516	1 524	1 511	1 505	1 483	1 470	1 464	1 468	1 477	1 484	1 489
North Carolina	671	687	703	721	724	721	713	713	716	715	720	726	730	733
North Dakota	75	76	76	76	78	80	79	79	80	80	81	83	83	83
Ohio	800	800	798	799	792	786	775	773	765	766	771	775	780	779
Oklahoma	321	330	334	337	348	349	344	347	349	348	351	352	349	348
Oregon	285	286	290	298	300	300	295	291	289	294	301	307	310	295
Pennsylvania	754	755	755	760	768	771	751	732	721	711	705	703	703	703
Rhode Island	65	65	64	64	62	62	61	60	60	60	60	60	61	61
South Carolina	336	340	346	356	355	355	348	352	353	356	360	363	366	369
South Dakota	75	75	76	76	78	79	78	78	77	78	78	78	79	80
Tennessee	410	414	419	425	426	431	426	422	423	424	425	428	430	436
Texas	1 712	1 735	1 764	1 809	1 852	1 891	1 854	1 827	1 842	1 861	1 885	1 921	1 940	1 952
Utah	202	205	207	212	215	218	220	223	225	230	234	239	244	248
Vermont	53	54	54	54	55	55	55	55	55	56	56	56	56	56
Virginia	661	675	685	695	703	707	713	714	713	711	711	714	717	723
Washington	527	530	534	546	550	550	544	541	543	551	562	576	586	587
West Virginia	143	146	144	148	150	154	152	154	154	153	153	156	154	153
Wisconsin	415	415	416	422	421	420	415	411	409	412	409	412	407	408
Wyoming	65	65	67	69	70	71	72	72	72	71	71	71	70	69
Puerto Rico	305	300	297	299	289	268	259	259	245	235	231	228	217	207
Virgin Islands	12	13	13	13	13	13	13	12	11	11	11	11	11	11

EARNINGS

Figure 2-2. Average Hourly Earnings of All Employees on Nonfarm Payrolls by Industry, 2018

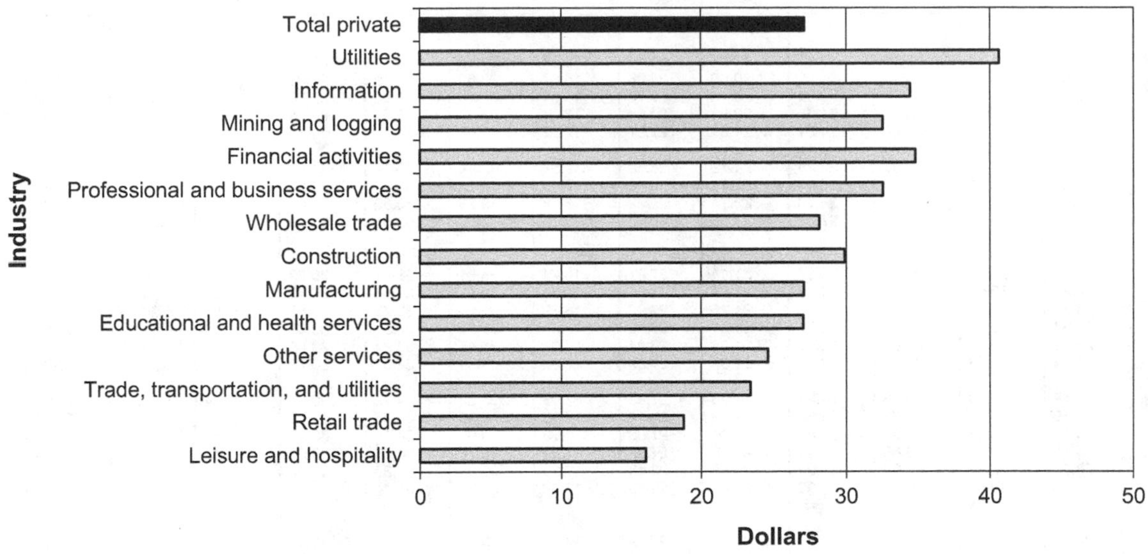

Average hourly earnings increased in all super sectors in 2018. While they $27.11 in all super sectors in 2018, workers in utilities had the highest average hourly earnings at $40.63 followed by those in information ($40.01), financial activities ($34.79), and professional and business services ($32.57). (See Table 2-12.)

OTHER HIGHLIGHTS

- Average hourly earnings for all employees also varied significantly by state and region in 2018. Earnings were highest in the District of Columbia ($43.06) followed by Massachusetts ($33.19), Washington ($32.74), and Connecticut ($32.05). Mississippi had the lowest average hourly earnings ($20.34) followed by Arkansas ($21.15) and New Mexico ($21.88). (See Table 2-13.)

- In 2018, average weekly earnings increased 3.3 percent for all employees on nonfarm payrolls. When adjusted for inflation, average weekly earnings increased 0.8 percent. Average weekly earnings of all employees on nonfarm payrolls ranged from $416.88 in leisure and hospitality to $1,709.64 utilities. (See Table 2-15.)

- From 2017 to 2018, average weekly earnings increased in each state in the United States except in Mississippi and New Hampshire where average weekly earnings declined -0.6 and -0.4 percent respectively. Wyoming (8.6 percent), West Virginia (5.7 percent), Colorado (5.4 percent), Hawaii (5.0 percent) and District of Columbia (5.0 percent) experienced the highest increases. (See Table 2-17.)

Table 2-12. Average Hourly Earnings of All Employees on Total Private Payrolls by NAICS Super Sector, 2010–2018

(Dollars, seasonally adjusted.)

Year and month	Total private	Mining and logging	Construction	Manufacturing	Trade, transportation, and utilities				Information	Financial activities	Professional and business services	Education and health services	Leisure and hospitality	Other services
					Total	Wholesale trade	Retail trade	Utilities						
2010	22.56	27.39	25.19	23.31	19.61	26.04	15.57	32.55	30.53	27.21	27.27	22.76	13.08	20.16
2011	23.03	28.10	25.41	23.69	20.00	26.28	15.87	33.62	31.59	27.91	27.79	23.42	13.23	20.50
2012	23.49	28.76	25.73	23.92	20.46	26.79	16.31	34.25	31.83	29.26	28.16	24.01	13.37	20.85
2013	23.96	29.72	26.12	24.35	20.93	27.54	16.64	35.17	32.91	30.15	28.58	24.42	13.50	21.40
2014	24.47	30.79	26.69	24.81	21.34	27.97	17.01	35.60	34.07	30.76	29.32	24.72	13.91	21.97
2015	25.02	31.15	27.37	25.25	21.79	28.53	17.52	37.14	35.14	31.52	30.11	25.24	14.32	22.48
2016	25.64	31.91	28.12	26.00	22.28	29.36	17.88	38.32	36.67	32.29	30.82	25.74	14.87	23.05
2017	26.33	32.05	28.90	26.60	22.74	29.92	18.18	39.25	38.30	33.24	31.67	26.32	15.47	23.85
2018	27.11	32.54	29.89	27.05	23.35	30.48	18.78	40.63	40.01	34.79	32.57	27.02	15.98	24.56
2014														
January	24.21	30.50	26.41	24.68	21.14	27.81	16.76	35.61	33.41	30.32	28.92	24.58	13.69	21.75
February	24.32	30.60	26.76	24.73	21.22	27.84	16.82	35.81	33.44	30.43	29.08	24.60	13.73	21.80
March	24.31	30.56	26.48	24.73	21.26	27.90	16.89	35.60	33.73	30.55	29.06	24.59	13.75	21.73
April	24.34	30.82	26.56	24.71	21.31	27.93	16.97	35.23	33.91	30.56	29.12	24.60	13.76	21.85
May	24.40	30.91	26.61	24.75	21.35	27.94	17.01	35.46	33.94	30.58	29.23	24.65	13.83	21.87
June	24.44	30.86	26.67	24.83	21.33	27.83	17.03	35.54	34.01	30.72	29.27	24.67	13.90	21.96
July	24.48	30.90	26.66	24.84	21.35	27.85	17.07	35.35	34.29	30.77	29.34	24.72	13.93	22.01
August	24.55	30.93	26.73	24.88	21.43	28.14	17.08	35.50	34.35	30.88	29.45	24.79	13.98	22.07
September	24.56	30.88	26.81	24.83	21.40	27.98	17.09	35.66	34.54	30.90	29.42	24.80	14.03	22.08
October	24.58	30.80	26.86	24.91	21.38	27.95	17.10	35.79	34.26	30.90	29.47	24.83	14.08	22.10
November	24.65	30.82	26.92	24.94	21.49	28.13	17.20	35.96	34.38	31.00	29.56	24.89	14.11	22.17
December	24.65	30.82	26.87	24.92	21.41	28.13	17.07	36.02	34.44	31.04	29.61	24.93	14.13	22.19
2015														
January	24.74	30.51	27.06	25.01	21.57	28.19	17.34	36.12	34.55	31.07	29.74	25.00	14.15	22.18
February	24.79	30.73	27.12	25.04	21.62	28.26	17.34	36.63	34.64	31.18	29.77	25.03	14.18	22.29
March	24.85	30.87	27.24	25.10	21.61	28.28	17.29	36.89	34.75	31.25	29.87	25.12	14.22	22.33
April	24.89	30.69	27.28	25.11	21.67	28.35	17.39	36.93	34.76	31.37	29.97	25.10	14.25	22.32
May	24.97	31.13	27.31	25.15	21.74	28.58	17.43	37.05	34.88	31.54	30.05	25.22	14.30	22.43
June	24.99	31.03	27.34	25.14	21.74	28.55	17.47	36.96	34.96	31.59	30.07	25.24	14.30	22.55
July	25.01	31.20	27.36	25.23	21.79	28.51	17.53	37.30	35.05	31.50	30.11	25.22	14.31	22.47
August	25.09	31.36	27.43	25.37	21.82	28.54	17.58	37.60	35.35	31.55	30.19	25.31	14.34	22.57
September	25.12	31.54	27.35	25.40	21.85	28.63	17.67	37.35	35.47	31.67	30.29	25.34	14.38	22.61
October	25.20	31.43	27.52	25.44	21.96	28.76	17.71	37.57	35.51	31.71	30.35	25.41	14.42	22.64
November	25.25	31.88	27.66	25.51	21.97	28.70	17.72	37.95	35.75	31.71	30.41	25.45	14.46	22.67
December	25.26	31.49	27.63	25.54	21.99	28.71	17.75	37.76	35.87	31.81	30.33	25.49	14.51	22.72
2016														
January	25.37	31.78	27.64	25.64	22.04	28.88	17.74	37.93	36.06	32.03	30.51	25.56	14.59	22.78
February	25.39	31.73	27.77	25.66	22.07	28.93	17.79	37.75	36.24	32.03	30.56	25.59	14.62	22.78
March	25.46	31.90	27.87	25.75	22.17	29.21	17.84	37.99	36.12	32.17	30.58	25.62	14.67	22.85
April	25.54	31.98	27.98	25.86	22.20	29.29	17.83	38.22	36.29	32.17	30.70	25.67	14.74	22.91
May	25.57	32.12	28.08	25.96	22.22	29.37	17.87	38.37	36.56	32.18	30.78	25.64	14.78	22.97
June	25.64	32.11	28.14	25.98	22.33	29.38	17.96	38.52	36.54	32.21	30.89	25.68	14.86	23.03
July	25.70	32.03	28.19	26.02	22.34	29.52	17.90	38.40	36.67	32.41	30.93	25.73	14.93	23.09
August	25.73	31.65	28.20	26.13	22.38	29.59	17.92	38.33	36.82	32.49	30.95	25.69	14.97	23.15
September	25.78	31.90	28.23	26.12	22.38	29.53	17.92	38.31	37.05	32.57	30.99	25.83	15.02	23.17
October	25.87	32.04	28.41	26.27	22.46	29.61	17.97	38.86	37.33	32.47	31.10	25.89	15.08	23.32
November	25.91	31.93	28.34	26.25	22.52	29.64	18.09	38.36	37.42	32.67	31.13	25.93	15.13	23.32
December	25.93	32.10	28.40	26.31	22.45	29.70	17.94	38.81	37.54	32.69	31.21	25.97	15.16	23.38
2017														
January	25.98	32.16	28.50	26.33	22.55	29.80	18.02	39.06	37.51	32.61	31.20	25.99	15.22	23.51
February	26.08	32.10	28.50	26.40	22.58	29.83	18.03	38.80	37.59	32.85	31.36	26.10	15.29	23.62
March	26.11	31.98	28.60	26.40	22.59	29.79	18.05	38.89	37.63	32.75	31.53	26.11	15.35	23.61
April	26.17	31.80	28.61	26.55	22.60	29.84	18.07	39.23	38.00	32.89	31.58	26.20	15.38	23.66
May	26.22	31.80	28.73	26.53	22.67	29.85	18.13	38.97	38.19	32.89	31.53	26.25	15.50	23.69
June	26.28	31.90	28.91	26.56	22.75	29.92	18.18	39.14	38.51	33.08	31.55	26.25	15.46	23.75
July	26.36	32.19	28.94	26.68	22.79	30.00	18.20	39.26	38.69	33.24	31.64	26.36	15.47	23.85
August	26.39	32.04	29.00	26.61	22.80	29.95	18.26	38.83	38.66	33.35	31.70	26.40	15.54	23.93
September	26.51	32.01	29.18	26.70	22.86	30.02	18.26	39.45	38.58	33.47	31.89	26.52	15.62	24.06
October	26.47	32.09	29.12	26.73	22.79	29.78	18.24	39.66	38.42	33.72	31.82	26.44	15.59	24.09
November	26.55	32.15	29.23	26.73	22.88	30.08	18.28	39.46	38.65	33.74	31.91	26.54	15.65	24.16
December	26.64	32.21	29.32	26.79	22.96	30.12	18.33	39.54	38.84	34.03	32.03	26.61	15.71	24.21
2018														
January	26.71	32.29	29.36	26.84	22.98	30.07	18.42	39.53	39.06	34.23	32.10	26.69	15.74	24.25
February	26.75	32.19	29.53	26.84	23.04	30.13	18.47	39.98	39.15	34.25	32.10	26.71	15.75	24.25
March	26.84	32.39	29.47	26.89	23.09	30.15	18.49	40.28	39.30	34.39	32.25	26.85	15.81	24.41
April	26.90	32.36	29.67	26.95	23.13	30.11	18.60	40.16	39.46	34.46	32.28	26.84	15.86	24.46
May	26.99	32.26	29.72	26.97	23.24	30.31	18.70	40.25	39.55	34.67	32.40	26.95	15.89	24.51
June	27.05	32.53	29.79	27.03	23.27	30.51	18.68	40.36	39.73	34.68	32.50	27.00	15.95	24.52
July	27.11	32.49	29.92	27.03	23.32	30.47	18.76	40.81	39.75	34.81	32.61	27.05	16.00	24.55
August	27.23	32.67	30.02	27.11	23.46	30.59	18.87	40.92	40.04	34.92	32.82	27.13	16.05	24.59
September	27.30	32.94	30.15	27.14	23.51	30.70	18.92	41.06	40.50	35.02	32.82	27.15	16.08	24.68
October	27.35	32.72	30.23	27.16	23.58	30.73	19.02	40.97	40.68	34.96	32.89	27.22	16.14	24.74
November	27.43	32.84	30.26	27.24	23.63	30.82	19.07	41.13	41.02	35.31	32.93	27.27	16.21	24.80
December	27.53	32.77	30.42	27.33	23.79	30.92	19.23	41.68	41.29	35.37	32.99	27.32	16.27	24.88

Table 2-13. Average Hourly Earnings of All Employees on Total Private Payrolls, by State, NAICS Basis, 2007–2018

(Dollars.)

State	2007	2008	2009	2010	2011	2012	2013	2014	2015	2016	2017	2018
UNITED STATES	20.92	21.56	22.17	22.56	23.03	23.49	23.96	24.47	25.02	25.64	26.33	27.11
Alabama	19.37	19.56	19.67	19.85	20.14	20.21	20.17	20.73	21.02	21.85	22.59	23.38
Alaska	24.70	25.01	24.80	23.90	24.49	25.58	26.74	27.15	27.89	28.22	28.28	28.78
Arizona	19.84	20.69	22.03	22.16	22.56	22.60	23.00	22.90	23.13	23.99	25.26	25.63
Arkansas	16.27	17.21	17.97	18.08	18.36	18.57	19.28	19.54	19.51	20.07	20.62	21.15
California	24.69	24.72	25.48	26.36	26.91	26.90	27.25	27.53	28.06	28.90	30.00	30.92
Colorado	23.13	23.79	23.78	23.79	23.95	24.61	25.64	26.29	26.85	27.07	27.60	28.92
Connecticut	26.59	27.71	27.81	28.08	28.23	28.14	27.96	28.16	29.14	30.43	31.16	32.05
Delaware	21.98	22.73	22.30	22.71	22.32	22.01	22.12	21.70	22.63	24.40	26.22	26.20
District of Columbia	33.54	32.37	31.37	34.18	35.44	36.84	38.31	38.89	38.27	38.40	40.65	43.06
Florida	20.57	21.00	21.61	21.44	21.46	21.62	21.95	22.19	22.63	23.31	24.04	24.81
Georgia	20.43	20.77	21.08	21.57	21.83	21.75	22.47	23.34	23.84	24.48	25.91	26.61
Hawaii	20.68	20.80	21.11	21.65	22.16	22.72	23.74	24.33	24.63	25.42	26.17	27.74
Idaho	16.52	17.53	19.26	21.04	20.79	21.04	21.20	21.37	22.08	22.39	22.50	22.85
Illinois	22.94	22.67	23.06	23.15	23.58	24.32	24.82	25.40	25.98	26.58	26.82	27.76
Indiana	19.93	20.30	20.56	20.57	20.65	21.38	22.08	22.61	22.85	23.52	24.45	24.91
Iowa	18.01	18.35	20.01	20.38	20.22	20.87	21.57	21.88	22.55	23.23	23.42	24.16
Kansas	19.64	20.12	20.17	20.07	20.51	21.02	21.45	22.09	22.57	22.88	23.25	24.10
Kentucky	17.73	18.07	18.82	19.40	19.80	20.06	20.15	20.53	21.08	21.26	21.82	22.11
Louisiana	18.74	19.22	19.46	19.55	20.63	21.37	21.98	22.11	22.19	22.65	22.99	23.49
Maine	18.74	18.96	19.16	19.45	19.95	20.96	21.01	21.33	21.85	22.25	23.22	23.86
Maryland	24.04	24.56	25.41	26.17	25.80	25.94	26.66	27.35	27.31	27.27	28.34	29.57
Massachusetts	26.08	26.39	26.86	27.15	27.65	28.16	28.93	29.54	30.46	31.25	32.14	33.19
Michigan	21.55	21.61	21.89	22.26	22.35	22.45	22.94	23.58	24.05	24.09	24.65	25.65
Minnesota	23.13	23.23	23.41	23.85	24.54	24.95	25.64	25.79	26.06	27.11	28.42	29.06
Mississippi	16.46	16.89	17.87	18.05	18.13	18.83	19.43	19.39	19.71	19.97	20.41	20.34
Missouri	19.79	20.57	20.94	21.19	20.79	21.48	21.87	21.99	22.09	22.54	23.91	24.73
Montana	17.80	18.44	19.86	20.19	20.67	20.70	20.96	21.42	22.05	22.38	23.10	23.83
Nebraska	19.92	19.79	20.19	20.89	20.84	20.95	20.92	21.36	22.18	22.98	24.11	24.78
Nevada	19.64	19.75	19.56	19.13	19.35	19.83	20.21	20.95	21.95	22.15	22.52	23.34
New Hampshire	22.06	22.66	22.70	22.98	23.00	23.71	24.31	24.33	24.90	25.72	26.30	26.59
New Jersey	24.84	25.32	25.92	25.95	25.63	26.45	26.80	26.91	27.78	28.11	29.18	29.75
New Mexico	18.57	18.73	18.92	19.57	19.70	19.82	20.19	20.49	20.47	20.60	21.21	21.88
New York	25.27	25.49	25.71	26.07	26.48	27.18	27.81	28.15	28.78	29.24	30.08	31.15
North Carolina	19.26	19.92	20.61	20.63	20.92	21.71	21.68	21.85	22.31	23.41	24.12	24.97
North Dakota	18.34	18.75	19.21	20.19	21.45	22.77	23.88	24.87	25.29	25.77	26.06	26.60
Ohio	20.22	20.11	19.95	20.22	21.07	22.01	22.25	22.16	22.68	23.40	24.04	24.82
Oklahoma	17.35	17.44	18.09	19.21	20.36	20.91	21.23	21.54	21.82	22.03	22.87	23.69
Oregon	20.61	20.93	21.33	21.56	21.75	22.23	22.52	22.91	23.53	24.72	25.66	26.22
Pennsylvania	20.08	20.44	20.75	21.22	21.86	22.63	23.29	23.73	24.22	24.68	25.10	25.74
Rhode Island	22.17	22.50	22.52	22.67	23.73	25.00	25.42	25.10	24.94	25.99	26.97	27.68
South Carolina	18.76	18.80	19.18	19.89	20.58	20.09	20.52	21.05	21.42	22.11	22.89	23.96
South Dakota	16.47	16.53	17.94	18.55	19.05	19.42	19.62	20.17	20.98	21.37	21.95	22.62
Tennessee	19.02	19.41	19.53	19.94	20.20	20.14	20.29	20.76	20.91	21.80	22.66	23.40
Texas	21.07	21.30	21.40	21.36	21.97	22.21	22.91	23.86	24.46	24.58	25.39	25.91
Utah	21.41	21.10	22.48	24.31	23.11	22.28	23.00	23.59	24.17	24.42	25.13	25.80
Vermont	20.42	21.35	22.41	23.01	23.03	22.79	22.77	23.17	24.06	24.34	24.43	25.39
Virginia	22.46	22.31	22.58	23.54	24.66	24.98	25.23	25.34	26.14	26.96	27.57	28.39
Washington	24.18	25.21	26.31	26.94	27.25	27.32	27.70	28.45	29.63	30.33	31.39	32.74
West Virginia	17.12	17.78	18.17	18.71	19.00	19.62	20.43	20.60	20.80	20.98	21.76	23.01
Wisconsin	20.46	20.68	21.13	21.35	21.85	22.38	23.11	23.24	23.46	24.03	24.73	25.93
Wyoming	20.04	20.82	21.05	21.43	22.15	22.52	22.91	23.17	23.11	23.22	23.86	25.39

. . . = Not available.

Table 2-14. Average Hourly Earnings of Production Workers on Private Nonfarm Payrolls, by Super Sector, NAICS Basis, 2005–2018

(Dollars.)

Industry	2005	2006	2007	2008	2009	2010	2011	2012	2013	2014	2015	2016	2017	2018
TOTAL PRIVATE	16.12	16.75	17.42	18.06	18.61	19.05	19.44	19.74	20.13	20.61	21.03	21.54	22.06	22.71
Goods-Producing	17.60	18.02	18.67	19.33	19.90	20.28	20.67	20.94	21.24	21.59	21.96	22.58	23.18	24.00
Mining and logging	18.72	19.90	20.97	22.50	23.29	23.82	24.50	25.79	26.80	26.84	26.48	26.97	27.44	28.30
Construction	19.46	20.02	20.95	21.87	22.66	23.22	23.65	23.97	24.22	24.67	25.20	25.97	26.74	27.74
Manufacturing	16.56	16.81	17.26	17.75	18.24	18.61	18.93	19.08	19.30	19.56	19.91	20.44	20.90	21.54
Private Service-Providing	15.73	16.40	17.09	17.75	18.33	18.78	19.18	19.48	19.90	20.40	20.84	21.32	21.82	22.44
Trade, transportation, and utilities	14.91	15.37	15.76	16.14	16.46	16.80	17.12	17.39	17.71	18.23	18.63	18.95	19.31	19.90
Wholesale trade	18.13	18.87	19.54	20.08	20.78	21.46	21.88	22.13	22.52	23.14	23.52	24.07	24.58	25.18
Retail trade	12.36	12.58	12.76	12.87	13.02	13.25	13.52	13.82	14.03	14.40	14.83	15.05	15.33	15.91
Transportation and warehousing	16.71	17.28	17.73	18.42	18.81	19.17	19.50	19.55	19.82	20.52	20.75	20.91	21.30	21.84
Utilities	26.68	27.40	27.88	28.83	29.48	30.04	30.82	31.61	32.27	32.86	34.02	35.33	36.22	36.77
Information	22.06	23.23	23.96	24.78	25.45	25.87	26.62	27.04	27.98	28.70	29.05	30.05	30.74	31.93
Financial activities	17.98	18.83	19.67	20.32	20.90	21.55	21.93	22.82	23.87	24.71	25.34	26.12	26.57	26.94
Professional and business services	18.09	19.14	20.16	21.19	22.36	22.80	23.14	23.31	23.74	24.31	24.81	25.43	26.05	26.81
Education and health services	16.62	17.28	17.99	18.73	19.34	19.95	20.60	20.91	21.29	21.64	22.09	22.52	23.03	23.65
Leisure and hospitality	9.38	9.75	10.41	10.84	11.12	11.31	11.45	11.62	11.78	12.09	12.41	12.85	13.38	13.87
Other services	14.34	14.77	15.42	16.09	16.59	17.06	17.32	17.59	18.00	18.51	19.01	19.36	20.10	20.78

Table 2-15. Average Weekly Earnings of All Employees on Nonfarm Payrolls, by Industry, in Current and 1982–1984 Dollars, NAICS Basis, 2010–2018

(Dollars.)

Industry	2010	2011	2012	2013	2014	2015	2016	2017	2018
TOTAL PRIVATE									
Current dollars	769.63	790.85	809.57	825.02	844.91	864.21	881.20	906.30	936.06
1982–1984 dollars	352.95	351.58	352.61	354.15	356.90	364.62	367.16	369.74	372.77
Goods-Producing									
Current dollars	952.07	976.16	994.38	1 016.09	1 041.52	1 057.13	1 083.74	1 113.61	1 145.06
1982–1984 dollars	436.62	433.97	433.10	436.17	439.95	446.01	451.55	454.31	456.00
Mining and logging									
Current dollars	1 189.32	1 250.91	1 263.98	1 306.16	1 380.77	1 371.13	1 383.16	1 448.75	1 495.98
1982–1984 dollars	545.42	556.11	550.53	560.69	583.25	578.49	576.30	591.04	595.75
Construction									
Current dollars	952.78	973.85	997.01	1 018.01	1 040.85	1 070.93	1 100.94	1 131.76	1 174.46
1982–1984 dollars	436.94	432.94	434.25	436.99	439.67	451.84	458.71	461.72	467.71
Manufacturing									
Current dollars	937.34	958.84	973.96	994.30	1 016.42	1 029.68	1 057.77	1 084.86	1 107.47
1982–1984 dollars	429.86	426.27	424.21	426.82	429.35	434.43	440.72	442.58	441.04
Private Service-Providing									
Current dollars	733.23	754.68	773.81	787.85	806.31	826.61	842.05	866.24	895.06
1982–1984 dollars	336.26	335.50	337.03	338.20	340.59	348.76	350.84	353.39	356.45
Trade, transportation, and utilities									
Current dollars	671.38	690.95	707.71	721.85	736.63	754.66	764.95	782.61	805.61
1982–1984 dollars	307.89	307.17	308.24	309.86	311.16	318.40	318.72	319.28	320.82
Wholesale trade									
Current dollars	991.59	1 015.85	1 038.30	1 066.81	1 088.33	1 109.79	1 140.05	1 169.15	1 190.39
1982–1984 dollars	454.74	451.61	452.23	457.94	459.72	468.23	475.01	476.97	474.06
Retail trade									
Current dollars	488.08	501.04	516.10	522.57	532.88	550.74	554.27	563.80	582.00
1982–1984 dollars	223.83	222.74	224.79	224.32	225.09	232.36	230.94	230.01	231.77
Transportation and warehousing									
Current dollars	804.30	835.10	844.95	865.28	883.33	891.80	901.67	925.13	949.68
1982–1984 dollars	368.85	371.26	368.02	371.43	373.13	376.26	375.68	377.42	378.20
Utilities									
Current dollars	1 338.50	1 404.36	1 432.93	1 484.54	1 508.94	1 580.30	1 620.24	1 655.22	1 709.64
1982–1984 dollars	613.83	624.33	624.11	637.26	637.39	666.75	675.08	675.27	680.84
Information									
Current dollars	1 114.65	1 156.56	1 166.45	1 206.05	1 252.44	1 274.99	1 315.74	1 388.30	1 444.58
1982–1984 dollars	511.18	514.17	508.05	517.71	529.05	537.93	548.21	566.38	575.28
Financial activities									
Current dollars	1 004.14	1 039.70	1 093.00	1 119.71	1 146.22	1 185.77	1 207.93	1 246.39	1 309.68
1982–1984 dollars	460.50	462.21	476.06	480.65	484.18	500.29	503.29	508.48	521.56
Professional and business services									
Current dollars	964.63	992.94	1 014.67	1 031.57	1 063.77	1 089.87	1 110.34	1 142.52	1 178.42
1982–1984 dollars	442.38	441.43	441.94	442.82	449.35	459.83	462.63	466.11	469.29
Education and health services									
Current dollars	743.41	766.88	787.43	798.73	809.11	828.36	844.80	865.65	889.97
1982–1984 dollars	340.93	340.93	342.97	342.87	341.78	349.49	351.99	353.15	354.42
Leisure and hospitality									
Current dollars	336.83	342.67	349.12	350.95	364.07	376.20	387.80	403.77	416.68
1982–1984 dollars	154.47	152.34	152.06	150.65	153.79	158.72	161.58	164.72	165.94
Other services									
Current dollars	637.65	649.87	659.49	679.43	698.41	716.17	734.90	757.95	781.44
1982–1984 dollars	292.42	288.91	287.24	291.65	295.02	302.16	306.20	309.22	311.20

Table 2-16. Average Weekly Earnings of Production Workers on Nonfarm Payrolls, by Industry, in Current and 1982–1984 Dollars, NAICS Basis, 2005–2018

(Dollars.)

Industry	2005	2006	2007	2008	2009	2010	2011	2012	2013	2014	2015	2016	2017	2018
TOTAL PRIVATE														
Current dollars	544.02	567.09	589.18	607.42	615.96	636.19	652.89	665.65	677.70	694.85	708.90	723.31	742.62	767.08
1982–1984 dollars	284.83	287.72	290.57	287.80	293.83	297.33	294.66	294.24	295.52	298.51	305.81	309.01	310.65	312.91
Goods-Producing														
Current dollars	705.28	730.16	757.50	776.63	779.68	818.96	844.89	861.39	877.09	895.09	905.43	930.34	956.83	996.75
1982–1984 dollars	369.26	370.45	373.58	367.98	371.93	382.75	381.31	380.76	382.47	384.54	390.59	397.45	400.26	406.59
Mining and logging														
Current dollars	853.87	907.95	962.63	1 014.69	1 006.67	1 063.11	1 144.64	1 201.69	1 229.70	1 270.91	1 211.91	1 221.69	1 265.92	1 323.22
1982–1984 dollars	447.05	460.65	474.75	480.77	480.21	496.86	516.59	531.18	536.23	545.99	522.80	521.92	529.56	539.77
Construction														
Current dollars	750.37	781.59	816.23	842.61	851.76	891.83	921.84	942.14	958.72	977.11	998.02	1 031.88	1 061.98	1 108.49
1982–1984 dollars	392.86	396.54	402.55	399.24	406.32	416.81	416.04	416.45	418.06	419.77	430.53	440.83	444.25	452.18
Manufacturing														
Current dollars	673.30	690.88	711.53	724.46	726.12	765.18	784.29	794.67	807.37	822.03	832.25	855.77	876.10	908.08
1982–1984 dollars	352.51	350.52	350.91	343.26	346.38	357.62	353.96	351.27	352.07	353.15	359.02	365.59	366.49	370.42
Private Service-Providing														
Current dollars	509.26	532.19	554.18	573.29	587.56	605.07	620.97	633.06	645.00	661.61	676.08	689.29	707.18	728.11
1982–1984 dollars	266.63	270.01	273.31	271.63	280.28	282.79	280.25	279.83	281.26	284.23	291.65	294.47	295.83	297.01
Trade, transportation, and utilities														
Current dollars	497.82	513.90	525.41	535.18	541.12	558.75	576.56	587.68	596.13	612.45	627.45	634.80	652.76	675.21
1982–1984 dollars	260.64	260.73	259.12	253.58	258.13	261.14	260.21	259.77	259.95	263.11	270.67	271.19	273.06	275.43
Wholesale trade														
Current dollars	683.99	717.42	747.08	768.14	782.62	814.04	842.06	857.06	871.89	894.06	907.72	929.09	957.95	980.54
1982–1984 dollars	358.11	363.99	368.44	363.96	373.33	380.45	380.03	378.85	380.20	384.09	391.58	396.92	400.73	399.98
Retail trade														
Current dollars	377.58	383.25	385.18	386.44	388.74	400.38	412.29	422.35	423.44	431.97	446.01	447.69	463.10	482.90
1982–1984 dollars	197.69	194.44	189.96	183.10	185.44	187.12	186.07	186.69	184.65	185.58	192.40	191.26	193.72	196.98
Transportation and warehousing														
Current dollars	618.70	637.10	655.29	670.46	677.80	711.22	737.38	742.71	762.57	789.61	804.95	810.89	817.13	838.89
1982–1984 dollars	323.93	323.24	323.17	317.67	323.33	332.40	332.79	328.30	332.53	339.22	347.25	346.42	341.82	342.20
Utilities														
Current dollars	1 095.91	1 135.57	1 182.65	1 230.65	1 239.34	1 262.89	1 296.92	1 298.23	1 344.70	1 388.91	1 444.03	1 502.09	1 540.27	1 569.90
1982–1984 dollars	573.77	576.14	583.26	583.10	591.20	590.23	585.32	573.86	586.38	596.69	622.94	641.71	644.33	640.39
Information														
Current dollars	805.11	850.64	874.45	908.78	931.08	939.85	964.85	973.52	1 003.65	1 030.17	1 038.10	1 068.23	1 100.03	1 137.84
1982–1984 dollars	421.52	431.58	431.26	430.59	444.15	439.25	435.45	430.33	437.66	442.57	447.82	456.36	460.17	464.15
Financial activities														
Current dollars	646.48	673.63	706.52	729.64	754.90	780.19	798.68	840.04	875.04	908.19	939.68	962.95	982.50	997.43
1982–1984 dollars	338.47	341.77	348.44	345.71	360.11	364.63	360.46	371.32	381.57	390.16	405.37	411.38	411.00	406.87
Professional and business services														
Current dollars	619.49	662.80	701.39	738.31	776.30	799.24	814.52	823.34	839.86	865.25	879.66	899.58	922.51	948.85
1982–1984 dollars	324.34	336.28	345.91	349.82	370.32	373.53	367.60	363.94	366.23	371.72	379.47	384.31	385.91	387.06
Education and health services														
Current dollars	541.40	561.02	585.44	607.82	622.30	639.37	663.04	674.48	683.24	692.56	709.25	723.91	741.55	762.32
1982–1984 dollars	283.46	284.64	288.73	287.99	296.86	298.82	299.24	298.14	297.94	297.53	305.96	309.26	310.21	310.97
Leisure and hospitality														
Current dollars	241.36	250.34	265.54	273.39	275.95	280.87	283.82	290.54	294.31	303.81	311.32	319.67	332.54	345.04
1982–1984 dollars	126.37	127.01	130.96	129.54	131.64	131.27	128.09	128.43	128.34	130.52	134.30	136.57	139.11	140.75
Other services														
Current dollars	443.40	456.50	477.06	495.57	506.26	523.70	532.63	539.46	553.77	568.92	583.54	595.68	617.91	640.38
1982–1984 dollars	232.15	231.61	235.27	234.81	241.50	244.76	240.38	238.46	241.48	244.41	251.73	254.48	258.48	261.22

Table 2-17. Average Weekly Earnings of All Employees on Total Private Payrolls, by State, NAICS Basis, 2007–2018

(Dollars.)

State	2007	2008	2009	2010	2011	2012	2013	2014	2015	2016	2017	2018
UNITED STATES	719.85	739.02	749.98	769.63	790.85	809.57	825.02	844.91	864.21	881.20	906.30	936.06
Alabama	708.94	704.16	684.52	696.74	708.93	727.56	728.14	735.92	746.21	777.86	797.43	825.31
Alaska	876.85	882.85	868.00	843.67	884.09	905.53	943.92	939.39	967.78	970.77	992.63	1 010.18
Arizona	698.37	720.01	766.64	780.03	789.60	791.00	800.40	790.05	802.61	822.86	879.05	894.49
Arkansas	571.08	605.79	621.76	630.99	642.60	648.09	672.87	681.95	673.10	686.39	717.58	744.48
California	851.81	845.42	861.22	896.24	925.70	925.36	937.40	949.79	970.88	994.16	1 035.00	1 066.74
Colorado	807.24	827.89	815.65	816.00	826.28	861.35	892.27	907.01	912.90	906.85	924.60	974.60
Connecticut	912.04	939.37	917.73	935.06	957.00	956.76	939.46	946.18	976.19	1 022.45	1 050.09	1 086.50
Delaware	753.91	768.27	729.21	735.80	738.79	726.33	718.90	713.93	751.32	810.08	862.64	864.60
District of Columbia	1 217.50	1 158.85	1 135.59	1 203.14	1 258.12	1 318.87	1 379.16	1 407.82	1 362.41	1 367.04	1 443.08	1 515.71
Florida	728.18	739.20	756.35	761.12	746.81	741.57	755.08	763.34	776.21	792.54	824.57	863.39
Georgia	727.31	733.18	729.37	748.48	757.50	761.25	790.94	821.57	836.78	851.90	899.08	928.69
Hawaii	674.17	678.08	686.08	710.12	740.14	770.21	788.17	817.49	820.18	831.23	866.23	909.87
Idaho	566.64	594.27	647.14	704.84	704.78	706.94	708.08	713.76	737.47	736.63	756.00	774.62
Illinois	789.14	777.58	793.26	796.36	815.87	843.90	856.29	873.76	891.11	906.38	917.24	949.39
Indiana	707.52	710.50	711.38	722.01	722.75	741.89	763.97	789.09	797.47	816.14	858.20	874.34
Iowa	615.94	620.23	666.33	694.96	687.48	715.84	744.17	767.99	782.49	801.44	805.65	831.10
Kansas	681.51	700.18	687.80	684.39	707.60	733.60	742.17	764.31	774.15	773.34	792.83	826.63
Kentucky	652.46	654.13	666.23	684.82	693.00	696.08	699.21	716.50	744.12	746.23	765.88	773.85
Louisiana	670.89	701.53	702.51	713.58	748.87	773.59	786.88	802.59	796.62	795.02	816.15	847.99
Maine	640.91	650.33	638.03	657.41	678.30	714.74	714.34	725.22	749.46	754.28	789.48	816.01
Maryland	836.59	852.23	876.65	892.40	887.52	881.96	903.77	932.64	936.73	935.36	974.90	1 011.29
Massachusetts	873.68	886.70	902.50	912.24	915.22	929.28	960.48	983.68	1 020.41	1 046.88	1 076.69	1 108.55
Michigan	752.10	739.06	728.94	750.16	764.37	767.79	784.55	811.15	827.32	826.29	855.36	890.06
Minnesota	781.79	778.21	763.17	787.05	817.18	838.32	864.07	876.86	886.04	921.74	969.12	988.04
Mississippi	587.62	601.28	632.60	648.00	652.68	670.35	687.82	694.16	685.91	692.96	710.27	705.80
Missouri	680.78	709.67	709.87	718.34	721.41	743.21	752.33	752.06	748.85	752.84	800.99	833.40
Montana	633.68	595.61	619.63	658.19	680.04	687.24	697.97	702.58	718.83	731.83	759.99	795.92
Nebraska	667.32	666.92	680.40	712.35	710.64	712.30	715.46	728.38	756.34	776.72	824.56	837.56
Nevada	732.57	730.75	700.25	659.99	665.64	674.22	677.04	699.73	737.52	750.89	767.93	795.89
New Hampshire	734.60	743.25	742.29	760.64	763.60	784.80	814.39	812.62	836.64	869.34	891.57	888.11
New Jersey	844.56	850.75	870.91	877.11	868.86	888.72	900.48	906.87	938.96	958.55	992.12	1 014.48
New Mexico	642.52	663.04	664.09	684.95	691.47	687.75	702.61	711.00	700.07	690.10	714.78	741.73
New York	861.71	869.21	866.43	883.77	902.97	924.12	939.98	948.66	969.89	979.54	1 004.67	1 037.30
North Carolina	670.25	683.26	696.62	703.48	717.56	749.00	747.96	758.20	769.70	802.96	832.14	861.47
North Dakota	605.22	607.50	614.72	660.21	731.45	799.23	850.13	890.35	887.68	886.49	906.89	936.32
Ohio	687.48	681.73	658.35	677.37	710.06	750.54	760.95	757.87	775.66	802.62	826.98	853.81
Oklahoma	608.99	619.12	634.96	683.88	722.78	742.31	745.17	758.21	759.34	771.05	811.89	843.36
Oregon	704.86	707.43	708.16	724.42	735.15	751.37	758.92	776.65	800.02	842.95	875.01	894.10
Pennsylvania	678.70	690.87	684.75	706.63	732.31	751.32	780.22	799.70	823.48	834.18	848.38	880.31
Rhode Island	742.70	767.25	763.43	768.51	783.09	827.50	836.32	828.30	825.51	849.87	887.31	921.74
South Carolina	675.36	669.28	665.55	692.17	716.18	705.16	716.15	726.23	743.27	762.80	791.99	829.02
South Dakota	543.51	543.84	597.40	626.99	645.80	673.87	676.89	693.85	713.32	726.58	739.72	762.29
Tennessee	669.50	683.23	687.46	703.88	709.02	712.96	716.24	732.83	736.03	773.90	802.16	828.36
Texas	769.06	773.19	753.28	766.82	808.50	808.44	831.63	870.89	883.01	877.51	911.50	935.35
Utah	747.21	730.06	804.78	863.01	808.85	784.26	805.00	830.37	841.12	847.37	882.06	900.42
Vermont	696.32	734.44	764.18	786.94	776.11	768.02	769.63	773.88	801.20	812.96	818.41	848.03
Virginia	790.59	780.85	781.27	833.32	872.96	874.30	870.44	879.30	917.51	940.90	953.92	982.29
Washington	851.14	872.27	902.43	918.65	940.13	942.54	950.11	972.99	1 019.27	1 049.42	1 092.37	1 139.35
West Virginia	604.34	627.63	626.87	654.85	657.40	676.89	706.88	718.94	723.84	736.40	772.48	816.86
Wisconsin	673.13	682.44	680.39	700.28	723.24	749.73	774.19	785.51	790.60	805.01	833.40	871.25
Wyoming	725.45	764.09	747.28	769.34	799.62	817.48	822.47	824.85	811.16	770.90	816.01	886.11

NOTES AND DEFINITIONS

QUARTERLY CENSUS OF EMPLOYMENT AND WAGES

The Quarterly Census of Employment and Wages (QCEW), often referred to as the ES-202 program, is a cooperative endeavor of the Bureau of Labor Statistics (BLS) and the State Employment Security Agencies (SESAs). Using quarterly data submitted by the agencies, BLS summarizes the employment and wage data for workers covered by state unemployment insurance laws and civilian workers covered by the Unemployment Compensation for Federal Employees (UCFE) program.

Since the introduction of 2001 data, the QCEW data have been coded according to the North American Classification System, either NAICS 2002, which was used for the data up through 2006; NAICS 2007, which was used for data from 2007 through 2010; or NAICS 2012 which was introduced with the release of first quarter data in 2011. As a result of the revision, approximately 8 percent of establishments, 11 percent of employment, and 6 percent of total wages were reclassified into different industries within private industry.

NAICS is the statistical classification standard underlying all establishment-based federal economic statistics classified by industry. Before 2001, QCEW data were coded according to the Standard Industrial Classification (SIC) system. Due to the differences in the classification systems, data coded according to NAICS are often not directly comparable to SIC coded data.

The QCEW data series is the most complete universe of employment and wage information by industry, county, and state. It includes 98 percent of all wage and salary civilian employment. These data serve as the basic source of benchmark information for employment by industry in the Current Employment Statistics (CES) survey, which is described in the first section of notes in this chapter. Therefore, the entire employment series is not presented here. The wage series is presented because the CES only provides earnings only for production and nonsupervisory employees. The QCEW is more comprehensive. BLS aggregates the data by industry and ownership; these aggregations are available at the national, state, county, and metropolitan statistical area (MSA) levels.

Collection and Coverage

Employment data under the QCEW program represent the number of covered workers who worked during, or received pay for, the pay period including the 12th of the month. Excluded are members of the armed forces, the self-employed, proprietors, domestic workers, unpaid family workers, and railroad workers covered by the railroad unemployment insurance system. Wages represent total compensation paid during the calendar quarter, regardless of when services were performed. Included in wages are pay for vacation and other paid leave, bonuses, stock options, tips, the cash value of meals and lodging, and in some states, contributions to deferred compensation plans (such as 401(k) plans). The QCEW program does provide partial information on agricultural industries and employees in private households.

Data from the QCEW program serve as an important input to many BLS programs. The QCEW data are used as the benchmark source for employment by the Current Employment Statistics program and the Occupational employment statistics program. The UI administrative records collected under the QCEW program serve as a sampling frame for BLS establishment surveys.

In addition, data from the QCEW program serve as an input to other federal and state programs. The Bureau of Economic Analysis (BEA) of the Department of Commerce uses QCEW data as the base for developing the wage and salary component of personal income. The Employment and Training Administration (ETA) of the Department of Labor and the SESAs use QCEW data to administer the employment security program. The QCEW data accurately reflect the extent of coverage of the state UI laws and are used to measure UI revenues; national, state and local area employment; and total and UI taxable wage trends.

Sources of Additional Information

Additional information is available on the BLS Web site at <http://www.bls.gov/cew>.

Table 2-18. Employment and Average Annual Pay for Covered Workers,[1] by Industry, NAICS Basis, 2013–2018

(Number, dollars.)

Industry	2013		2014		2015	
	Employment	Average annual pay	Employment	Average annual pay	Employment	Average annual pay
Total Private	112 958 334	49 701	115 568 686	51 296	118 307 717	52 876
Natural resources and mining	2 023 732	57 070	2 073 041	59 660	2 001 103	58 461
Agriculture, forestry, fishing, and hunting	1 210 474	29 447	1 231 162	30 614	1 249 192	31 977
Construction	5 819 950	53 181	6 108 673	55 037	6 423 866	57 009
Manufacturing	11 994 922	61 102	12 156 537	62 976	12 291 676	64 305
Wholesale trade	5 739 082	68 580	5 815 992	71 043	5 874 282	73 363
Retail trade	15 073 504	28 008	15 343 711	28 742	15 642 116	29 742
Transportation and warehousing	4 246 329	47 444	4 391 274	48 708	4 600 012	49 931
Utilities	547 807	95 157	548 993	98 123	553 685	101 445
Information	2 703 250	86 787	2 732 191	90 823	2 754 109	95 098
Financial activities	7 616 922	80 731	7 674 037	85 267	7 828 679	87 915
Professional and business services	18 478 164	64 623	19 074 275	66 668	19 607 372	69 270
Education and health services	20 204 352	44 976	20 573 137	45 950	21 080 792	47 383
Leisure and hospitality	14 195 179	20 413	14 626 556	20 995	15 100 935	21 807
Other services	4 149 819	32 844	4 235 390	33 936	4 308 880	35 116
Total Government	21 010 100	50 380	21 044 923	51 733	21 183 982	53 309
Federal	2 770 831	72 903	2 729 603	75 797	2 756 434	77 900
State	4 525 213	52 544	4 545 441	54 179	4 566 622	55 878
Local	13 714 056	45 115	13 769 879	46 155	13 860 926	47 573

Industry	2016		2017		2018	
	Employment	Average annual pay	Employment	Average annual pay	Employment	Average annual pay
Total Private	120 504 622	53 515	122 386 565	55 338	124 551 838	57 198
Natural resources and mining	1 872 879	56 115	1 885 246	56 859	1 937 219	59 628
Agriculture, forestry, fishing, and hunting	1 259 490	33 287	1 261 312	34 464	1 263 676	35 841
Construction	6 686 142	58 647	6 919 107	60 735	7 225 870	62 727
Manufacturing	12 296 697	64 870	12 406 757	66 840	12 647 900	68 525
Wholesale trade	5 859 605	73 710	5 898 637	75 904	5 855 477	77 870
Retail trade	15 824 396	30 299	15 854 454	31 217	15 791 102	31 217
Transportation and warehousing	4 765 869	50 459	4 947 369	51 726	5 208 134	53 197
Utilities	553 007	102 868	551 935	107 194	551 920	109 957
Information	2 796 947	98 458	2 793 429	105 722	2 815 363	113 781
Financial activities	7 953 761	88 841	8 088 405	92 923	8 187 308	95 561
Professional and business services	20 024 917	69 992	20 339 284	72 525	20 872 036	75 169
Education and health services	21 654 265	48 058	22 146 912	49 201	22 632 823	50 444
Leisure and hospitality	15 556 625	22 445	15 900 633	23 188	16 196 857	24 087
Other services	4 387 613	35 921	4 434 678	37 320	4 501 913	38 464
Total Government	21 365 445	54 221	21 473 291	55 686	21 579 916	57 658
Federal	2 792 987	78 379	2 802 583	80 432	2 795 195	83 657
State	4 569 606	57 168	4 628 557	58 802	4 624 977	83 657
Local	14 002 852	48 440	14 042 151	49 720	14 159 744	60 751

[1]Includes workers covered by unemployment insurance (UI) and Unemployment Compensation for Federal Employees (UCFE) programs.

Table 2-19. Employment and Average Annual Pay for Covered Workers,[1] by State and Selected Territory, 2010–2018

(Number, dollars.)

State	2010		2011		2012		2013		2014	
	Employment	Average annual pay	Employment	Average annual pay	Employment	Average annual pay	Employment	Average annual pay	Employment	Average annual pay
UNITED STATES	127 820 442	46 751	129 411 095	48 043	131 696 378	49 289	133 968 434	49 808	136 613 609	51 364
Alabama	1 813 155	40 289	1 813 497	41 186	1 828 248	41 990	1 845 086	42 276	1 863 561	43 287
Alaska	316 691	48 230	322 084	49 383	327 378	50 614	328 716	51 566	330 105	53 418
Arizona	2 356 789	43 299	2 378 248	44 581	2 431 788	45 593	2 488 009	45 921	2 539 253	46 919
Arkansas	1 134 071	36 254	1 139 682	37 280	1 146 811	38 226	1 146 274	38 941	1 157 630	39 975
California	14 414 461	53 285	14 567 128	55 013	14 959 808	56 784	15 378 962	57 111	15 809 082	59 042
Colorado	2 176 986	47 868	2 213 059	49 082	2 266 503	50 563	2 335 803	50 873	2 417 735	52 724
Connecticut	1 595 713	59 465	1 612 292	61 145	1 627 748	62 085	1 640 333	62 357	1 653 573	63 919
Delaware	399 078	48 669	402 959	50 499	405 646	51 734	413 825	52 040	423 598	53 212
District of Columbia	693 274	80 200	707 359	81 529	714 930	82 783	724 270	83 054	729 349	85 877
Florida	7 109 630	41 581	7 195 232	42 313	7 341 002	43 211	7 518 448	43 649	7 755 371	44 803
Georgia	3 753 934	43 899	3 792 209	45 090	3 841 767	46 267	3 918 085	46 760	4 032 488	48 138
Hawaii	586 772	41 709	593 668	42 473	605 240	43 385	618 195	43 845	626 146	45 210
Idaho	605 571	34 900	607 504	35 626	614 463	36 152	630 328	36 836	646 305	37 982
Illinois	5 502 322	49 497	5 566 648	50 840	5 636 918	52 194	5 687 541	52 590	5 762 156	54 106
Indiana	2 709 831	39 256	2 755 826	40 248	2 812 347	41 240	2 849 311	41 660	2 890 758	42 553
Iowa	1 436 340	38 146	1 452 769	39 204	1 475 884	40 343	1 496 426	41 107	1 515 822	42 538
Kansas	1 297 779	38 936	1 303 799	39 989	1 320 285	41 118	1 336 948	41 548	1 357 090	42 716
Kentucky	1 712 178	38 720	1 734 503	39 646	1 761 043	40 451	1 779 777	40 793	1 807 068	41 941
Louisiana	1 832 357	41 461	1 848 399	42 375	1 871 037	43 300	1 893 823	44 008	1 923 745	45 336
Maine	577 790	37 338	579 838	38 020	583 196	38 606	586 525	39 279	590 377	40 442
Maryland	2 453 197	51 739	2 478 505	53 008	2 511 669	54 035	2 531 656	54 052	2 552 623	55 389
Massachusetts	3 149 169	57 770	3 189 753	59 671	3 242 273	60 898	3 295 647	61 790	3 360 035	64 103
Michigan	3 770 225	44 439	3 854 837	45 828	3 935 694	46 720	4 018 602	47 131	4 090 009	48 487
Minnesota	2 558 310	46 787	2 602 988	47 858	2 644 408	49 349	2 691 832	50 116	2 730 301	51 602
Mississippi	1 074 617	34 343	1 076 488	34 976	1 085 748	35 875	1 093 581	36 455	1 102 603	37 111
Missouri	2 573 703	40 679	2 585 009	41 461	2 607 420	42 695	2 637 273	43 066	2 667 996	44 258
Montana	419 231	34 595	422 726	35 791	430 315	37 096	436 867	37 575	440 198	38 878
Nebraska	896 936	37 324	901 584	38 269	920 295	39 268	932 768	39 965	946 110	41 185
Nevada	1 108 238	42 512	1 115 062	43 102	1 132 140	43 667	1 160 115	44 119	1 202 475	44 727
New Hampshire	600 697	45 957	605 853	47 281	612 419	48 272	618 781	48 963	626 566	51 165
New Jersey	3 735 703	56 382	3 734 660	57 546	3 768 935	58 644	3 812 940	59 467	3 841 854	60 597
New Mexico	781 694	39 264	781 226	40 032	785 455	40 698	791 804	40 809	798 912	41 925
New York	8 340 732	60 291	8 444 791	61 792	8 563 125	62 669	8 685 758	63 089	8 846 774	65 880
North Carolina	3 788 581	41 119	3 838 300	42 121	3 907 085	43 110	3 974 937	43 795	4 057 439	44 973
North Dakota	358 635	38 128	379 432	41 778	411 709	45 909	427 108	47 779	444 652	50 855
Ohio	4 908 571	41 788	4 968 724	42 972	5 048 166	44 244	5 110 011	44 671	5 183 462	46 000
Oklahoma	1 485 400	38 237	1 507 558	40 108	1 540 292	41 633	1 560 799	42 457	1 582 712	43 773
Oregon	1 598 173	41 675	1 616 634	43 090	1 642 434	44 258	1 678 726	45 019	1 725 906	46 529
Pennsylvania	5 472 171	45 733	5 535 283	47 035	5 578 414	48 397	5 596 841	49 077	5 644 443	50 567
Rhode Island	447 408	44 645	448 570	45 705	450 711	46 716	456 112	47 732	463 303	49 297
South Carolina	1 758 204	37 553	1 780 690	38 427	1 810 150	39 286	1 846 621	39 792	1 895 420	40 797
South Dakota	389 198	34 331	393 744	35 413	400 475	36 534	404 652	37 225	410 929	38 690
Tennessee	2 558 438	41 572	2 602 604	42 454	2 653 392	43 961	2 694 288	44 091	2 750 032	45 202
Texas	10 182 150	46 952	10 422 295	48 735	10 727 642	50 579	11 031 907	51 201	11 379 184	53 218
Utah	1 150 737	39 389	1 176 530	40 279	1 215 983	41 301	1 254 582	41 792	1 291 859	42 942
Vermont	293 058	39 434	295 512	40 293	299 519	40 967	301 586	42 043	304 472	43 025
Virginia	3 536 676	49 651	3 578 848	50 657	3 619 176	51 646	3 640 209	51 918	3 654 831	52 929
Washington	2 808 698	48 516	2 844 622	50 256	2 894 703	51 962	2 960 123	53 050	3 043 562	55 016
West Virginia	692 448	37 675	701 905	39 092	710 590	39 727	703 916	40 201	700 846	41 201
Wisconsin	2 633 572	39 966	2 664 920	41 003	2 695 404	41 966	2 721 960	42 777	2 758 496	43 829
Wyoming	271 151	41 963	274 743	43 394	278 595	44 580	279 748	44 972	284 394	46 492

[1]Includes workers covered by the unemployment insurance (UI) and Unemployment Compensation for Federal Employees (UCFE) programs.

Table 2-19. Employment and Average Annual Pay for Covered Workers,[1] by State and Selected Territory, 2010–2018—*Continued*

(Number, dollars.)

State	2015		2016		2017		2018	
	Employment	Average annual pay	Employment	Average annual pay	Employment	Average annual pay	Employment	Average annual pay
UNITED STATES	139 491 699	52 942	141 870 066	53 621	143 859 855	55 390	146 131 754	57 266
Alabama	1 890 340	44 273	1 915 306	44 832	1 936 819	45 997	1 961 625	47 414
Alaska	331 681	54 755	326 295	53 605	322 136	53 714	321 078	55 668
Arizona	2 609 770	47 933	2 680 065	48 523	2 747 638	50 146	2 826 095	51 865
Arkansas	1 177 884	40 895	1 191 763	41 571	1 200 542	42 959	1 211 021	43 950
California	16 295 204	61 698	16 718 647	62 964	17 019 702	65 857	17 355 855	68 478
Colorado	2 494 450	54 182	2 552 503	54 664	2 609 770	56 914	2 674 030	58 941
Connecticut	1 662 825	65 530	1 666 554	65 870	1 669 616	66 636	1 673 925	67 742
Delaware	433 748	53 991	438 238	53 765	441 873	55 828	447 075	56 814
District of Columbia	743 596	88 159	756 646	89 481	763 847	92 544	771 750	95 909
Florida	8 039 635	46 260	8 309 351	47 035	8 494 623	48 455	8 700 654	50 094
Georgia	4 151 011	49 551	4 262 937	50 676	4 346 453	52 189	4 430 136	53 496
Hawaii	637 854	46 919	647 545	48 178	654 185	49 671	658 341	50 977
Idaho	664 792	38 857	687 919	39 637	706 820	41 345	730 716	42 882
Illinois	5 848 451	55 989	5 895 633	56 447	5 934 549	57 971	5 973 316	59 941
Indiana	2 941 991	43 903	2 987 091	44 590	3 018 177	46 192	3 051 879	47 590
Iowa	1 530 234	44 095	1 539 752	44 910	1 540 435	46 074	1 549 958	47 511
Kansas	1 367 329	43 878	1 370 665	44 142	1 371 633	45 116	1 383 119	46 607
Kentucky	1 835 550	43 365	1 861 063	44 099	1 874 455	45 166	1 884 653	46 302
Louisiana	1 930 688	45 928	1 908 397	45 622	1 907 721	46 500	1 921 498	48 116
Maine	595 889	41 791	603 785	42 596	609 271	43 911	615 271	45 370
Maryland	2 591 189	57 176	2 627 172	58 106	2 653 569	59 603	2 679 064	61 151
Massachusetts	3 428 020	66 692	3 494 553	67 432	3 543 383	69 929	3 586 034	72 606
Michigan	4 161 641	50 063	4 242 537	50 943	4 294 711	52 487	4 340 045	53 803
Minnesota	2 776 684	53 527	2 815 248	54 297	2 856 105	56 140	2 882 944	58 007
Mississippi	1 114 379	37 642	1 124 854	38 144	1 128 498	38 788	1 130 786	39 762
Missouri	2 715 579	45 565	2 755 477	46 122	2 781 242	47 364	2 794 483	49 053
Montana	448 688	40 056	454 819	40 716	459 431	42 045	464 818	43 407
Nebraska	959 176	42 854	968 601	43 597	972 764	44 851	978 066	46 262
Nevada	1 244 635	45 739	1 283 642	47 114	1 326 151	48 126	1 371 030	50 041
New Hampshire	636 806	52 553	647 347	53 563	653 487	55 138	658 836	56 782
New Jersey	3 889 975	62 365	3 953 972	62 777	4 006 799	64 042	4 043 517	65 727
New Mexico	806 762	42 555	807 387	42 599	810 516	43 535	822 351	45 167
New York	9 014 385	67 521	9 154 025	67 940	9 276 868	70 682	9 432 830	72 900
North Carolina	4 161 654	46 530	4 259 276	47 269	4 330 606	48 920	4 410 791	50 756
North Dakota	437 072	50 696	417 119	48 873	414 038	50 313	417 578	52 356
Ohio	5 257 971	47 146	5 319 679	47 700	5 364 626	49 153	5 405 891	50 573
Oklahoma	1 594 011	44 306	1 575 978	43 906	1 581 198	45 121	1 605 887	46 727
Oregon	1 787 398	48 328	1 840 874	49 474	1 883 407	51 118	1 920 804	53 053
Pennsylvania	5 691 613	52 187	5 737 759	52 460	5 799 123	54 000	5 867 783	55 628
Rhode Island	469 981	50 651	473 406	51 453	477 362	52 840	481 569	53 736
South Carolina	1 949 881	42 002	1 996 297	42 881	2 035 341	44 177	2 091 683	44 729
South Dakota	416 020	40 181	420 460	41 178	422 489	42 432	426 927	43 694
Tennessee	2 820 198	46 742	2 887 754	47 403	2 930 932	48 820	2 976 889	50 450
Texas	11 655 919	54 281	11 805 698	54 333	12 014 802	55 795	12 302 358	57 747
Utah	1 340 591	44 318	1 388 878	45 255	1 430 588	46 575	1 478 493	48 513
Vermont	307 058	44 234	308 044	45 030	309 442	46 186	310 334	47 640
Virginia	3 735 713	54 276	3 789 744	54 836	3 838 368	56 503	3 893 254	58 239
Washington	3 122 749	56 661	3 215 014	59 024	3 290 209	62 041	3 372 533	66 119
West Virginia	696 195	41 727	684 322	41 665	683 807	43 419	693 478	46 120
Wisconsin	2 794 170	45 365	2 828 166	46 008	2 850 145	47 238	2 876 534	48 872
Wyoming	282 667	46 306	271 813	44 974	269 586	46 270	272 171	48 059

[1]Includes workers covered by the unemployment insurance (UI) and Unemployment Compensation for Federal Employees (UCFE) programs.

BUSINESS EMPLOYMENT DYNAMICS

Figure 2-3. Private Sector Gross Job Gains and Gross Job Losses, Seasonally Adjusted, March 2000–December 2018

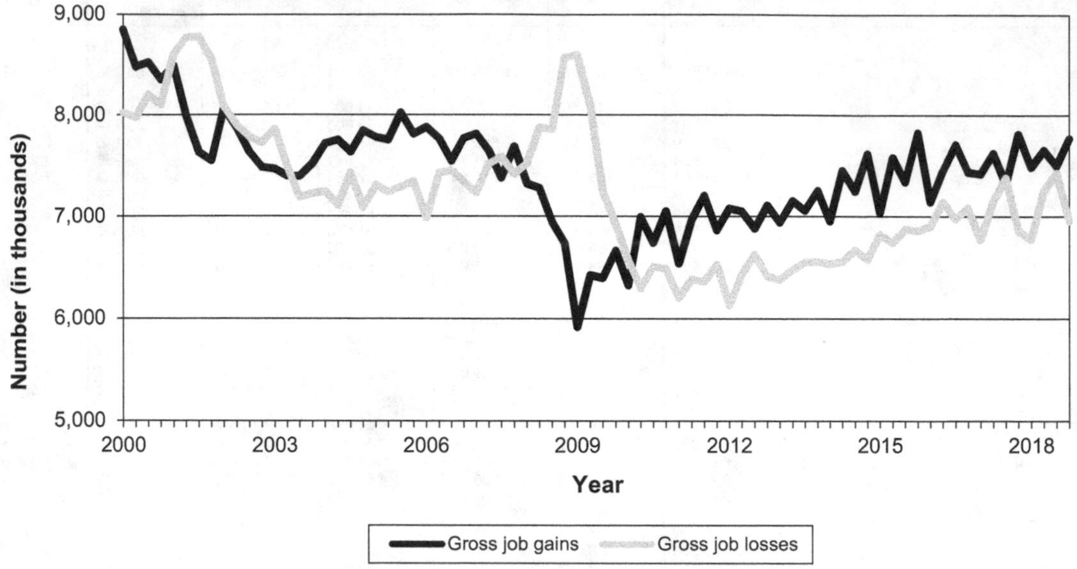

The change in the number of jobs is the net result of the gross increase in the number of jobs from expanding and opening establishments and the gross decrease in jobs from contracting and closing establishments. The net gain of over 800,000 jobs in the fourth quarter of 2018 resulted from 7.768 million gross job gains and 6.957 million gross job losses. There was a net gain of jobs in 29 consecutive quarters from June 2010 to June 2017. In September 2017, there was a net loss of 68,000 jobs. However just three months later in December 2017 there was a net gain of 955,000 jobs. This was the highest net gain since December 2015. (See Table 2-20.)

OTHER HIGHLIGHTS

- Of the nearly 6.9 million jobs that were lost in the fourth quarter of 2018, 80.9 percent resulted from contracting establishments while 19.1 percent were the result of establishments closing. (See Table 2-20.)

- The service-providing industries experienced a net job gain of 414,000 in the first quarter of 2019. Within the service-providing industry, education and health services experienced the greatest net job gain at 152,000. In the utilities sector, gross job losses actually exceeded gross job gains by 1,000. (See Table 2-22.)

- In construction, gross job gains exceeded gross job losses by 84,000 in the first quarter of 2019—more than in any other goods-producing sector. In natural resources and mining, gross job gains only exceeded gross job losses by 1,000. (See Table 2-22.)

- Job losses exceeded job gains in nine states. Connecticut experienced the highest net loss in jobs at nearly 7,000 followed by Mississippi at 4,600 and Iowa at over 4,500. Meanwhile, New York experienced the highest net gain in jobs during the same period with 51,000. (See Table 2-23.)

NOTES AND DEFINITIONS

BUSINESS EMPLOYMENT DYNAMICS (BED)

The Business Employment Dynamics (BED) data are a set of statistics generated from the federal-state cooperative program known as the Quarterly Census of Employment and Wages (QCEW), or the ES-202 program. These quarterly data series consist of gross job gains and gross job losses statistics from 1992 forward.

The Bureau of Labor Statistics (BLS) compiles the BED data from existing quarterly state unemployment insurance (UI) records. Most employers in the United States are required to file quarterly reports on the employment and wages of workers covered by UI laws and to pay quarterly UI taxes. The quarterly UI reports are sent by the State Workforce Agencies (SWAs) to BLS. These reports form the basis of the BLS establishment universe-sampling frame.

In the BED program, the quarterly UI records are linked across quarters to provide a longitudinal history for each establishment. The linkage process allows the tracking of net employment changes at the establishment level, which in turn allows estimations of jobs gained at opening and expanding establishments and of jobs lost at closing and contracting establishments. BLS publishes three different establishment-based employment measures for every given quarter. Each of these measures—the Current Employment Statistics (CES) survey, the QCEW program, and the BED data each make use of the quarterly UI employment reports. However, each measure has somewhat different types of universal coverage, estimation procedures, and publication products. (See the notes and corresponding tables for CES and QCEW in earlier sections of this chapter.)

Concepts and Definitions

The BED data measure the net change in employment at the establishment level. These changes can come about in four different ways. A net increase in employment can come from either opening establishments or expanding establishments. A net decrease in employment can come from either closing establishments or contracting establishments.

Gross job gains include the sum of all jobs added at either opening or expanding establishments.

Gross job losses include the sum of all jobs lost in either closing or contracting establishments. The net change in employment is the difference between gross job gains and gross job losses.

Openings consist of establishments with positive third-month employment for the first time in the current quarter, with no links to the prior quarter, or with positive third-month employment in the current quarter, following zero employment in the previous quarter.

Expansions include establishments with positive employment in the third month in both the previous and current quarters, with a net increase in employment over this period.

Closings consist of establishments with positive third-month employment in the previous quarter, with no employment or zero employment reported in the current quarter.

Contractions include establishments with positive employment in the third month in both the previous and current quarters, with a net decrease in employment over this period.

Sources of Additional Information

For additional information, see BLS news release 19-1865 "Business Employment Dynamics: First Quarter 2019."

Table 2-20. Private Sector Gross Job Gains and Job Losses, Seasonally Adjusted, March 2006–December 2018

(Thousands of jobs.)

Year and month	Net change[1]	Gross job gains			Gross job losses		
		Total	Expanding establishments	Opening establishments	Total	Contracting establishments	Closing establishments
2006							
March	896	7 880	6 383	1 497	6 984	5 661	1 323
June	342	7 766	6 228	1 538	7 424	6 026	1 398
September	92	7 545	6 076	1 469	7 453	6 067	1 386
December	431	7 770	6 226	1 544	7 339	5 964	1 375
2007							
March	584	7 815	6 331	1 484	7 231	5 894	1 337
June	132	7 647	6 205	1 442	7 515	6 084	1 431
September	-209	7 376	5 870	1 506	7 585	6 190	1 395
December	268	7 687	6 181	1 506	7 419	6 040	1 379
2008							
March	-199	7 320	5 860	1 460	7 519	6 111	1 408
June	-593	7 281	5 833	1 448	7 874	6 363	1 511
September	-913	6 944	5 535	1 409	7 857	6 436	1 421
December	-1 838	6 738	5 345	1 393	8 576	7 056	1 520
2009							
March	-2 680	5 918	4 675	1 243	8 598	7 142	1 456
June	-1 667	6 425	5 080	1 345	8 092	6 674	1 418
September	-849	6 399	5 139	1 260	7 248	5 854	1 394
December	-264	6 665	5 308	1 357	6 929	5 605	1 324
2010							
March	-247	6 325	5 108	1 217	6 572	5 324	1 248
June	698	6 995	5 674	1 321	6 297	5 090	1 207
September	237	6 741	5 438	1 303	6 504	5 231	1 273
December	566	7 052	5 639	1 413	6 486	5 219	1 267
2011							
March	334	6 540	5 322	1 218	6 206	5 025	1 181
June	582	6 966	5 625	1 341	6 384	5 115	1 269
September	841	7 205	5 810	1 395	6 364	5 172	1 192
December	335	6 865	5 503	1 362	6 530	5 273	1 257
2012							
March	948	7 080	5 746	1 334	6 132	5 005	1 127
June	616	7 051	5 724	1 327	6 435	5 266	1 169
September	252	6 881	5 571	1 310	6 629	5 430	1 199
December	695	7 110	5 753	1 357	6 415	5 225	1 190
2013							
March	558	6 941	5 705	1 236	6 383	5 201	1 182
June	674	7 152	5 830	1 322	6 478	5 271	1 207
September	507	7 058	5 719	1 339	6 551	5 408	1 143
December	700	7 255	5 926	1 329	6 555	5 353	1 202
2014							
March	419	6 953	5 687	1 266	6 534	5 380	1 154
June	895	7 454	6 114	1 340	6 559	5 342	1 217
September	577	7 247	5 918	1 329	6 670	5 487	1 183
December	1 038	7 617	6 248	1 369	6 579	5 346	1 233
2015							
March	216	7 040	5 727	1 313	6 824	5 622	1 202
June	838	7 580	6 236	1 344	6 742	5 550	1 192
September	466	7 340	5 977	1 363	6 874	5 665	1 209
December	968	7 827	6 367	1 460	6 859	5 594	1 265
2016							
March	242	7 144	5 860	1 284	6 902	5 699	1 203
June	305	7 448	6 077	1 371	7 143	5 836	1 307
September	734	7 709	6 249	1 460	6 975	5 730	1 245
December	351	7 436	6 021	1 415	7 085	5 784	1 301
2017							
March	649	7 420	6 086	1 334	6 771	5 588	1 183
June	473	7 623	6 255	1 368	7 150	5 878	1 272
September	-68	7 317	5 964	1 353	7 385	6 088	1 297
December	955	7 814	6 374	1 440	6 859	5 561	1 298
2018							
March	707	7 484	6 135	1 349	6 777	5 587	1 190
June	401	7 655	6 257	1 398	7 254	5 967	1 287
September	67	7 499	6 122	1 377	7 432	6 113	1 319
December	811	7 768	6 318	1 450	6 957	5 626	1 331

[1]Net change is the difference between total gross job gains and total gross job losses.

Table 2-21. Private Sector Gross Job Gains and Job Losses, as a Percent of Employment,[1] Seasonally Adjusted, March 2006–December 2018

(Percent.)

Year and month	Net change[2]	Gross job gains			Gross job losses		
		Total	Expanding establishments	Opening establishments	Total	Contracting establishments	Closing establishments
2006							
March	0.8	7.0	5.7	1.3	6.2	5.0	1.2
June	0.4	6.9	5.5	1.4	6.5	5.3	1.2
September	0.1	6.7	5.4	1.3	6.6	5.4	1.2
December	0.4	6.9	5.5	1.4	6.5	5.3	1.2
2007							
March	0.5	6.9	5.6	1.3	6.4	5.2	1.2
June	0.1	6.7	5.4	1.3	6.6	5.3	1.3
September	-0.2	6.4	5.1	1.3	6.6	5.4	1.2
December	0.2	6.7	5.4	1.3	6.5	5.3	1.2
2008							
March	-0.1	6.4	5.1	1.3	6.5	5.3	1.2
June	-0.5	6.4	5.1	1.3	6.9	5.6	1.3
September	-0.9	6.1	4.9	1.2	7.0	5.7	1.3
December	-1.7	6.0	4.8	1.2	7.7	6.3	1.4
2009							
March	-2.4	5.4	4.3	1.1	7.8	6.5	1.3
June	-1.5	6.0	4.7	1.3	7.5	6.2	1.3
September	-0.8	6.0	4.8	1.2	6.8	5.5	1.3
December	-0.3	6.3	5.0	1.3	6.6	5.3	1.3
2010							
March	-0.2	6.0	4.8	1.2	6.2	5.0	1.2
June	0.7	6.6	5.4	1.2	5.9	4.8	1.1
September	0.2	6.3	5.1	1.2	6.1	4.9	1.2
December	0.5	6.6	5.3	1.3	6.1	4.9	1.2
2011							
March	0.3	6.1	5.0	1.1	5.8	4.7	1.1
June	0.5	6.4	5.2	1.2	5.9	4.7	1.2
September	0.8	6.7	5.4	1.3	5.9	4.8	1.1
December	0.4	6.4	5.1	1.3	6.0	4.8	1.2
2012							
March	0.8	6.4	5.2	1.2	5.6	4.6	1.0
June	0.5	6.4	5.2	1.2	5.9	4.8	1.1
September	0.2	6.2	5.0	1.2	6.0	4.9	1.1
December	0.6	6.4	5.2	1.2	5.8	4.7	1.1
2013							
March	0.5	6.2	5.1	1.1	5.7	4.6	1.1
June	0.6	6.4	5.2	1.2	5.8	4.7	1.1
September	0.5	6.3	5.1	1.2	5.8	4.8	1.0
December	0.6	6.4	5.2	1.2	5.8	4.7	1.1
2014							
March	0.4	6.1	5.0	1.1	5.7	4.7	1.0
June	0.8	6.5	5.3	1.2	5.7	4.6	1.1
September	0.5	6.2	5.1	1.1	5.7	4.7	1.0
December	0.9	6.6	5.4	1.2	5.7	4.6	1.1
2015							
March	0.2	6.0	4.9	1.1	5.8	4.8	1.0
June	0.7	6.4	5.3	1.1	5.7	4.7	1.0
September	0.5	6.3	5.1	1.2	5.8	4.8	1.0
December	0.8	6.6	5.4	1.2	5.8	4.7	1.1
2016							
March	0.2	6.0	4.9	1.1	5.8	4.8	1.0
June	0.2	6.2	5.1	1.1	6.0	4.9	1.1
September	0.6	6.4	5.2	1.2	5.8	4.8	1.0
December	0.3	6.2	5.0	1.2	5.9	4.8	1.1
2017							
March	0.5	6.1	5.0	1.1	5.6	4.6	1.0
June	0.4	6.2	5.1	1.1	5.8	4.8	1.0
September	-0.1	6.0	4.9	1.1	6.1	5.0	1.1
December	0.8	6.4	5.2	1.2	5.6	4.5	1.1
2018							
March	0.6	6.1	5.0	1.1	5.5	4.5	1.0
June	0.3	6.1	5.0	1.1	5.8	4.8	1.0
September	0.0	6.0	4.9	1.1	6.0	4.9	1.1
December	0.7	6.3	5.1	1.2	5.6	4.5	1.1

[1]The rates measure gross job gains and job losses as a percentage of the average of the previous and current employment.
[2]Net change is the difference between total gross job gains and total gross job losses.

Table 2-22. Three-Month Private Sector Job Gains and Losses, by Industry, Seasonally Adjusted, March 2018–March 2019

(Thousands of jobs.)

Industry	Gross job gains and job losses (3 months ended)					Gross job gains and losses as a percent of employment (3 months ended)				
	March 2018	June 2018	September 2018	December 2018	March 2019	March 2018	June 2018	September 2018	December 2018	March 2019
TOTAL PRIVATE[1]										
Gross job gains	7 484	7 655	7 499	7 768	7 375	6.1	6.1	6.0	6.3	5.9
Gross job losses	6 777	7 254	7 432	6 957	6 850	5.5	5.8	6.0	5.6	5.5
Net employment change	707	401	67	811	525	0.6	0.3	0.0	0.7	0.4
Goods-Producing										
Gross job gains	1 413	1 410	1 314	1 406	1 343	6.6	6.5	6.0	6.4	6.1
Gross job losses	1 197	1 271	1 316	1 255	1 232	5.6	5.8	6.0	5.7	5.5
Net employment change	216	139	-2	151	111	1.0	0.7	0.0	0.7	0.6
Natural Resources and Mining										
Gross job gains	259	275	240	246	243	13.4	14.2	12.5	12.6	12.4
Gross job losses	242	249	247	256	242	12.6	12.8	12.8	13.2	12.4
Net employment change	17	26	-7	-10	1	0.8	1.4	-0.3	-0.6	0.0
Construction										
Gross job gains	730	695	651	695	698	10.2	9.6	9.0	9.6	9.3
Gross job losses	595	643	657	621	614	8.3	8.9	9.1	8.6	8.2
Net employment change	135	52	-6	74	84	1.9	0.7	-0.1	1.0	1.1
Manufacturing										
Gross job gains	424	440	423	465	402	3.4	3.5	3.3	3.6	3.2
Gross job losses	360	379	412	378	376	2.8	3.0	3.3	3.0	2.9
Net employment change	64	61	11	87	26	0.6	0.5	0.0	0.6	0.3
Service-Providing[1]										
Gross job gains	6 071	6 245	6 185	6 362	6 032	5.9	6.1	6.1	6.2	5.8
Gross job losses	5 580	5 983	6 116	5 702	5 618	5.5	5.9	6.0	5.5	5.4
Net employment change	491	262	69	660	414	0.4	0.2	0.1	0.7	0.4
Wholesale Trade										
Gross job gains	270	277	275	279	258	4.6	4.7	4.7	4.8	4.3
Gross job losses	249	251	269	245	243	4.2	4.2	4.6	4.1	4.2
Net employment change	21	26	6	34	15	0.4	0.5	0.1	0.7	0.1
Retail Trade										
Gross job gains	945	909	918	847	905	5.9	5.7	5.8	5.4	5.7
Gross job losses	861	961	1 002	918	863	5.5	6.1	6.3	5.8	5.5
Net employment change	84	-52	-84	-71	42	0.4	-0.4	-0.5	-0.4	0.2
Transportation and Warehousing										
Gross job gains	267	286	313	421	281	5.2	5.5	6.0	7.8	5.2
Gross job losses	327	254	256	239	346	6.4	4.9	4.9	4.5	6.3
Net employment change	-60	32	57	182	-65	-1.2	0.6	1.1	3.3	-1.1
Utilities										
Gross job gains	11	13	12	12	12	2.0	2.4	2.2	2.2	2.2
Gross job losses	11	15	13	14	13	2.0	2.7	2.4	2.6	2.4
Net employment change	0	-2	-1	-2	-1	0.0	-0.3	-0.2	-0.4	-0.2
Information										
Gross job gains	156	160	150	145	175	5.6	5.7	5.3	5.1	6.2
Gross job losses	148	167	156	150	145	5.3	5.9	5.6	5.3	5.2
Net employment change	8	-7	-6	-5	30	0.3	-0.2	-0.3	-0.2	1.0
Financial Activities										
Gross job gains	360	395	381	394	362	4.4	4.8	4.6	4.8	4.4
Gross job losses	350	357	387	376	343	4.3	4.4	4.8	4.6	4.2
Net employment change	10	38	-6	18	19	0.1	0.4	-0.2	0.2	0.2
Professional and Business Services										
Gross job gains	1 357	1 471	1 438	1 508	1 318	6.5	7.0	6.8	7.2	6.3
Gross job losses	1 279	1 374	1 368	1 352	1 318	6.2	6.6	6.6	6.4	6.2
Net employment change	78	97	70	156	0	0.3	0.4	0.2	0.8	0.1
Education and Health Services										
Gross job gains	998	1 015	1 014	1 004	1 003	4.4	4.5	4.5	4.4	4.4
Gross job losses	843	934	917	868	851	3.7	4.2	4.1	3.8	3.7
Net employment change	155	81	97	136	152	0.7	0.3	0.4	0.6	0.7
Leisure and Hospitality										
Gross job gains	1 360	1 353	1 344	1 406	1 338	8.4	8.4	8.3	8.6	8.2
Gross job losses	1 208	1 364	1 418	1 230	1 198	7.5	8.4	8.7	7.6	7.3
Net employment change	152	-11	-74	176	140	0.9	0.0	-0.4	1.0	0.9
Other Services										
Gross job gains	299	318	301	304	299	7.1	7.5	7.1	7.2	7.0
Gross job losses	279	286	308	291	276	6.7	6.8	7.3	6.9	6.5
Net employment change	20	32	-7	13	23	0.4	0.7	-0.2	0.3	0.5

[1]Includes unclassified sector, not shown separately.

Table 2-23. Private Sector Gross Job Gains and Losses, by State and Selected Territory, Seasonally Adjusted, March 2018–March 2019

(Number.)

State	Gross job gains (3 months ended)					Gross job losses (3 months ended)				
	March 2018	June 2018	September 2018	December 2018	March 2019	March 2018	June 2018	September 2018	December 2018	March 2019
UNITED STATES	7 484 000	7 655 000	7 499 000	7 768 000	7 375 000	6 777 000	7 254 000	7 432 000	6 957 000	6 850 000
Alabama	96 243	93 553	95 605	100 816	96 841	85 683	90 394	94 075	85 914	88 823
Alaska	24 717	26 848	21 838	27 051	24 748	21 909	26 274	26 246	24 029	22 229
Arizona	144 367	143 473	159 941	154 406	139 196	127 341	141 803	123 519	126 130	136 405
Arkansas	55 048	51 191	61 294	59 915	53 605	52 471	57 719	56 723	50 421	51 893
California	950 953	993 961	966 144	1 019 583	958 690	889 271	954 808	915 540	893 290	918 099
Colorado	152 407	153 001	149 713	155 491	150 523	133 492	137 876	152 379	137 868	143 527
Connecticut	74 217	83 110	76 246	76 068	74 499	76 379	73 433	81 586	71 454	81 433
Delaware	27 064	24 680	21 797	25 620	24 839	22 591	23 081	24 936	21 770	21 612
District of Columbia	32 187	29 647	28 183	29 712	29 198	25 882	29 812	29 027	27 027	25 795
Florida	469 018	489 717	519 828	494 076	470 398	420 317	461 536	440 722	466 878	428 898
Georgia	244 706	236 132	253 968	239 126	257 662	214 883	240 777	231 723	217 509	218 890
Hawaii	27 534	28 398	27 332	30 742	28 766	25 410	29 123	29 198	27 198	31 811
Idaho	47 951	44 622	41 300	45 579	46 481	36 726	41 477	41 911	38 775	38 110
Illinois	296 252	291 805	288 877	286 588	273 000	268 957	289 244	297 620	288 063	268 937
Indiana	151 082	145 966	139 987	148 866	156 880	134 571	146 896	141 825	133 677	129 593
Iowa	73 382	75 164	69 079	75 879	67 346	69 343	71 924	74 868	69 658	71 892
Kansas	59 788	65 217	66 704	69 531	62 736	62 522	63 441	64 414	62 125	64 959
Kentucky	98 385	94 540	90 984	97 782	92 536	93 740	90 495	96 148	87 327	88 220
Louisiana	107 755	98 870	101 284	99 438	95 919	94 088	104 991	100 616	92 940	94 705
Maine	35 900	41 729	31 809	37 301	37 368	36 356	36 986	38 866	34 444	33 681
Maryland	136 993	133 457	137 468	146 421	139 079	125 341	126 397	144 563	138 449	125 036
Massachusetts	178 032	191 451	175 065	182 975	180 711	163 557	173 457	192 871	167 127	164 915
Michigan	212 391	210 759	191 034	212 257	193 954	171 633	196 604	231 163	196 309	175 917
Minnesota	133 777	142 600	135 956	142 627	129 422	125 177	130 507	142 031	135 392	128 720
Mississippi	49 284	51 745	52 579	58 977	50 681	53 389	54 204	52 352	47 947	55 297
Missouri	130 075	136 499	142 095	137 961	129 371	125 766	135 700	142 563	128 093	126 018
Montana	29 884	30 525	27 396	34 407	29 494	27 084	29 704	30 117	27 518	31 004
Nebraska	46 781	47 822	47 885	47 835	46 491	45 895	47 343	48 225	46 760	45 655
Nevada	78 192	74 364	81 913	80 193	74 485	64 990	70 770	68 777	67 175	66 481
New Hampshire	34 968	38 372	32 249	37 886	36 640	34 105	35 862	38 996	32 781	32 983
New Jersey	198 889	226 662	208 014	223 239	201 365	209 536	202 305	221 513	199 050	198 569
New Mexico	41 085	42 557	41 563	43 809	41 983	36 544	40 031	40 829	39 424	38 022
New York	496 300	502 371	486 928	504 548	485 292	451 254	461 346	506 220	460 838	433 874
North Carolina	228 106	228 178	209 963	248 759	237 488	193 957	212 847	236 976	197 480	188 107
North Dakota	24 307	23 387	23 039	23 548	24 826	21 801	21 570	22 667	21 746	22 437
Ohio	262 472	263 954	250 824	261 361	258 396	238 635	253 449	271 299	245 446	241 765
Oklahoma	78 908	81 937	86 152	84 052	74 976	72 500	81 082	78 486	78 597	75 282
Oregon	128 621	102 489	101 862	110 386	105 038	94 400	103 335	102 384	98 153	95 104
Pennsylvania	274 495	277 509	277 395	277 414	266 704	255 248	267 878	271 106	249 012	249 431
Rhode Island	26 899	26 383	26 185	26 789	24 678	25 668	25 787	27 144	24 229	23 887
South Carolina	106 531	129 611	100 477	128 913	113 237	88 225	117 324	112 911	93 825	106 262
South Dakota	22 742	21 371	21 218	22 202	20 396	20 815	21 480	20 331	20 696	22 444
Tennessee	130 419	141 283	149 585	148 634	138 640	125 868	135 300	135 764	127 807	124 279
Texas	604 297	612 249	621 424	652 219	584 029	530 142	548 504	565 749	537 389	541 312
Utah	92 762	85 338	91 311	87 692	92 927	74 864	80 041	80 280	78 369	78 342
Vermont	16 748	18 662	17 596	18 863	17 446	18 260	18 380	19 550	17 285	16 200
Virginia	187 420	195 880	178 662	199 472	201 989	171 487	184 766	198 599	176 271	175 654
Washington	201 233	204 847	172 644	182 294	176 059	172 808	180 137	181 187	160 020	160 092
West Virginia	37 853	38 056	39 104	35 422	33 504	32 593	35 348	35 779	36 511	36 947
Wisconsin	140 206	136 299	126 775	134 830	127 951	116 847	138 290	145 097	122 971	120 014
Wyoming	17 713	17 365	17 117	20 839	18 347	16 402	17 344	17 393	16 307	16 590
Puerto Rico	55 317	52 276	48 405	40 125	47 891	44 701	41 342	38 736	45 122	34 491
Virgin Islands	2 974	2 978	3 030	1 934	2 987	4 166	1 575	1 410	1 736	1 853

Table 2-24. Private Sector Gross Job Gains and Losses as a Percent of Total Employment, by State and Selected Territory, Seasonally Adjusted, March 2018–March 2019

(Percent.)

State	Gross job gains (3 months ended)					Gross job losses (3 months ended)				
	March 2018	June 2018	September 2018	December 2018	March 2019	March 2018	June 2018	September 2018	December 2018	March 2019
UNITED STATES	6.1	6.1	6.0	6.3	5.9	5.5	5.8	6.0	5.6	5.5
Alabama	6.1	5.8	6.0	6.3	6.0	5.4	5.7	5.9	5.3	5.5
Alaska	10.1	10.9	8.9	11.0	10.0	8.9	10.7	10.7	9.8	9.0
Arizona	6.0	6.0	6.6	6.2	5.6	5.3	5.9	5.1	5.1	5.5
Arkansas	5.4	5.0	6.1	5.9	5.2	5.2	5.7	5.6	5.0	5.1
California	6.4	6.7	6.5	6.9	6.3	6.0	6.4	6.2	5.9	6.2
Colorado	6.8	6.8	6.6	6.8	6.6	6.0	6.1	6.8	6.0	6.3
Connecticut	5.1	5.8	5.3	5.3	5.2	5.3	5.1	5.7	4.9	5.7
Delaware	7.1	6.4	5.7	6.6	6.4	5.9	6.0	6.5	5.6	5.5
District of Columbia	6.0	5.6	5.3	5.6	5.4	4.9	5.6	5.5	5.1	4.9
Florida	6.2	6.4	6.8	6.4	6.1	5.5	6.1	5.8	6.1	5.6
Georgia	6.5	6.3	6.7	6.3	6.8	5.7	6.4	6.1	5.8	5.7
Hawaii	5.1	5.3	5.1	5.8	5.4	4.7	5.4	5.4	5.1	5.9
Idaho	7.9	7.3	6.8	7.4	7.5	6.1	6.8	6.9	6.3	6.1
Illinois	5.7	5.6	5.5	5.5	5.2	5.2	5.6	5.8	5.6	5.1
Indiana	5.7	5.5	5.2	5.6	5.9	5.1	5.5	5.4	5.0	4.8
Iowa	5.6	5.7	5.3	5.8	5.1	5.3	5.4	5.7	5.3	5.4
Kansas	5.3	5.7	5.9	6.1	5.4	5.4	5.6	5.7	5.4	5.7
Kentucky	6.2	5.9	5.8	6.1	5.8	5.9	5.7	6.0	5.4	5.5
Louisiana	6.7	6.2	6.3	6.2	5.9	5.9	6.5	6.3	5.8	5.9
Maine	7.0	8.0	6.1	7.3	7.2	7.0	7.1	7.5	6.7	6.4
Maryland	6.3	6.1	6.3	6.8	6.4	5.8	5.8	6.6	6.4	5.7
Massachusetts	5.7	6.1	5.6	5.8	5.7	5.2	5.5	6.1	5.3	5.2
Michigan	5.6	5.5	5.0	5.6	5.1	4.6	5.2	6.2	5.2	4.6
Minnesota	5.4	5.8	5.5	5.7	5.2	5.1	5.2	5.7	5.4	5.1
Mississippi	5.5	5.7	5.9	6.5	5.7	6.0	6.0	5.9	5.3	6.2
Missouri	5.5	5.7	5.9	5.8	5.4	5.2	5.7	6.0	5.4	5.3
Montana	7.9	8.0	7.2	8.9	7.6	7.1	7.8	7.9	7.2	8.0
Nebraska	5.8	5.8	5.9	5.9	5.7	5.6	5.8	5.9	5.7	5.6
Nevada	6.5	6.1	6.7	6.6	6.0	5.5	5.8	5.7	5.5	5.4
New Hampshire	6.1	6.7	5.7	6.6	6.3	6.0	6.2	6.8	5.7	5.7
New Jersey	5.7	6.5	6.0	6.4	5.7	6.1	5.8	6.4	5.7	5.6
New Mexico	6.5	6.7	6.4	6.8	6.4	5.7	6.2	6.4	6.1	5.8
New York	6.3	6.3	6.1	6.3	6.0	5.6	5.8	6.4	5.7	5.3
North Carolina	6.2	6.1	5.7	6.7	6.3	5.3	5.7	6.4	5.3	5.1
North Dakota	7.1	6.7	6.6	6.8	7.1	6.3	6.2	6.6	6.2	6.4
Ohio	5.6	5.6	5.4	5.6	5.5	5.1	5.4	5.8	5.3	5.1
Oklahoma	6.2	6.4	6.7	6.5	5.8	5.7	6.3	6.1	6.1	5.8
Oregon	8.0	6.2	6.2	6.7	6.3	5.8	6.3	6.3	6.0	5.8
Pennsylvania	5.3	5.3	5.4	5.3	5.1	4.9	5.1	5.2	4.8	4.8
Rhode Island	6.4	6.3	6.2	6.4	5.8	6.1	6.1	6.4	5.7	5.6
South Carolina	6.3	7.5	5.8	7.4	6.4	5.1	6.7	6.5	5.4	6.0
South Dakota	6.4	6.1	6.0	6.3	5.7	5.9	6.1	5.7	5.8	6.4
Tennessee	5.1	5.5	5.8	5.8	5.4	4.9	5.3	5.3	4.9	4.8
Texas	5.9	5.9	6.0	6.2	5.5	5.1	5.3	5.4	5.2	5.2
Utah	7.5	6.9	7.3	6.9	7.3	6.0	6.4	6.4	6.2	6.2
Vermont	6.5	7.2	6.9	7.4	6.7	7.0	7.1	7.6	6.8	6.3
Virginia	6.0	6.2	5.7	6.3	6.4	5.4	5.8	6.3	5.6	5.5
Washington	7.2	7.3	6.2	6.4	6.2	6.2	6.5	6.5	5.6	5.6
West Virginia	6.9	6.8	7.0	6.3	6.0	6.0	6.4	6.4	6.5	6.6
Wisconsin	5.6	5.5	5.1	5.4	5.1	4.7	5.5	5.9	5.0	4.8
Wyoming	8.6	8.4	8.3	10.0	8.6	8.0	8.4	8.4	7.8	7.8
Puerto Rico	8.5	7.9	7.2	6.0	7.1	6.9	6.2	5.8	6.8	5.1
Virgin Islands	13.3	13.2	12.8	7.9	11.9	18.6	7.0	5.9	7.1	7.4

CHAPTER 3: OCCUPATIONAL EMPLOYMENT AND WAGES

HIGHLIGHTS

This chapter presents employment and wage statistics from the Bureau of Labor Statistics Occupational Employment Statistics (OES) program.

Figure 3-1. Highest and Lowest Mean Annual Wages by Major Occupational Group, 2018

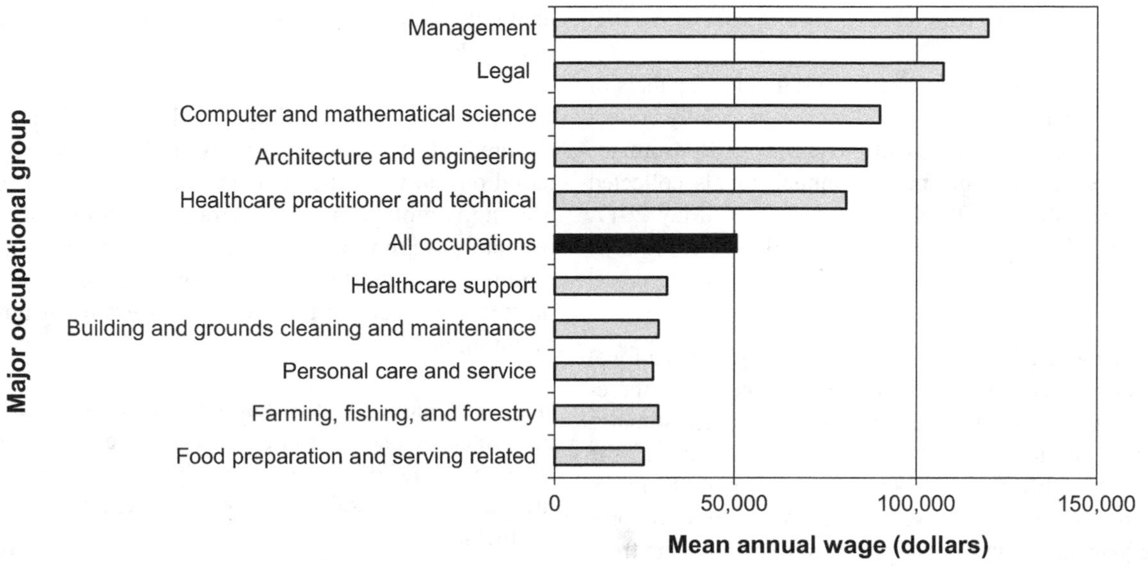

Workers in management continued to have the highest mean annual wage ($121,560) followed by those in legal occupations ($108,690), and computer and mathematical science occupations ($91,530) in 2018. Meanwhile, workers in food preparation and serving related workers ($25,580) and farming, fishing, and forestry ($30,140) had the lowest mean annual wages. (See Table 3-1.)

OTHER HIGHLIGHTS

- Most of the largest occupations were relatively low paying. Food preparation and serving related occupations, which employed over 13 million people, had a mean annual wage of $25,580 in 2018. Likewise, office and administrative support occupations employed nearly 22 million people and had a mean annual wage of $38,990 in 2018. Registered nurses ($75,510) and operations managers ($123,880) were the largest occupations with above-average wages. (See Table 3-1.)

- Within business and financial operations occupations, personal financial advisors had the highest salary at $121,770 while tax preparers had the lowest at $46,860. (See Table 3-2.)

- The highest paying education, training, and library occupations were all postsecondary teaching occupations, including postsecondary law teachers ($130,710) and postsecondary health specialties teachers ($122,320). (See Table 3-2.)

- STEM occupations had an annual mean wage of $93,070, compared with $49,170 for non-STEM occupations. Ninety-three of the 99 STEM occupations had mean wages significantly above the all-occupations average of $51,960. (See Table 3-2.)

NOTES AND DEFINITIONS

Collection and Coverage

The Occupational Employment Statistics (OES) survey is a federal-state cooperative program conducted by the Bureau of Labor Statistics (BLS) and the State Workforce Agencies (SWAs). The OES program collects data on wage and salary workers in nonfarm establishments in order to produce employment and wage estimates for over 810 occupations. The survey does not include the self-employed, owners and partners in unincorporated firms, household workers, or unpaid family workers. BLS funds the survey and provides procedural and technical support, while the SWAs collect the necessary data.

Every six months, forms are mailed to two semiannual panels of between 180,000 and 200,000 taking three years to fully collect a sample of 1.2 million establishments. The May 2018 estimates are based on responses from six semiannual panels collected over a 3-year period: May 2018, November 2017, May 2017, November 2016, May 2016, and November 2015.

Scope of the Survey

Prior to 1996, the OES program collected only occupational employment data for selected industries in each year of the three-year survey cycle, and produced only industry-specific estimates of occupational employment. The 1996 survey round was the first year that the OES program began collecting occupational employment and wage data in every state. In addition, the program's three-year survey cycle was modified to collect data from all covered industries each year. In 1997, the OES program began producing estimates of cross-industry as well as industry-specific occupational employment and wages.

In 1999, the OES survey began using the Standard Occupational Classification (SOC) system. The SOC system is the first occupational classification system for federal agencies required by the Office of Management and Budget (OMB). The May 2012 estimates are the first estimates based on the 2010 Standard Occupational Classification (SOC) system. In addition to 22 major occupational groups and 821 detailed occupations, employment and wage estimates for 94 minor groups and 458 broad occupations are available for the first time.

In 2002, the OES survey switched from the Standard Industrial Classification System (SIC) to the North American Industry Classification System (NAICS). In 2008, the OES survey switched to the 2007 NAICS from the 2002 NAICS. The most significant revisions were in the information sector, particularly within the telecommunications area. The May 2018 OES estimates use the 2017 North American Industry Classification System (NAICS). More information about NAICS can be found on the BLS Web site at <https://www.bls.gov/bls/naics.htm >.

Concepts and Definitions

Employment is the estimate of total wage and salary employment in an occupation across the industries in which it was reported. The OES survey defines employment as the number of workers who can be classified as full-time or part-time employees, including workers on paid vacations or other types of leave; workers on unpaid short-term absences; employees who are salaried officers, executives, or staff members of incorporated firms; employees temporarily assigned to other units; and employees for whom the reporting unit is their permanent duty station regardless of whether that unit prepares their paycheck.

Occupations are classified based on work performed and required skills. Employees are assigned to an occupation based on the work they perform and not on their education or training. Employees who perform the duties of two or more occupations are reported as being in either the occupation that requires the highest level of skill or the occupation in which the most time is spent (if there is no measurable difference in skill requirements).

Wages are money that is paid or received for work or services performed in a specified period. Base rate, cost-of-living allowances, guaranteed pay, hazardous-duty pay, incentive pay (including commissions and production bonuses), tips, and on-call pay are included.

Mean wage refers to an average wage; an occupational mean wage estimate is calculated by summing the wages of all the employees in a given occupation and then dividing the total wages by the number of employees.

An *establishment* is defined as an economic unit that processes goods or provides services, such as a factory, store, or mine. The establishment is generally at a single physical location and is primarily engaged in one type of economic activity.

An *industry* is a group of establishments that produce similar products or provide similar services. A given industry, or even a particular establishment in that industry, might have employees in dozens of occupations. The North American Industry Classification System (NAICS) groups similar establishments into industries.

Additional Information

For additional data including area data, see BLS news release USDL 19-0493 "Occupational Employment and Wages, May 2018," and special reports on the BLS Web site at < https://www.bls.gov/OES/>.

Table 3-1. Employment and Wages, by Major Occupational Group, May 2015–May 2018

(Number, percent, dollars.)

Occupation	May 2015				May 2016			
	Employment		Mean hourly wage	Mean annual wage[1]	Employment		Mean hourly wage	Mean annual wage[1]
	Number	Percent			Number	Percent		
All Occupations	137 896 660	100.0	23.23	48 320	140 400 040	100.0	23.86	49 630
Management	6 936 990	5.0	55.30	115 020	7 090 790	5.1	56.74	118 020
Business and financial operations	7 032 560	5.1	35.48	73 800	7 281 190	5.2	36.09	75 070
Computer and mathematical sciences	4 005 250	2.9	41.43	86 170	4 165 140	3.0	42.25	87 880
Architecture and engineering	2 475 390	1.8	39.89	82 980	2 499 050	1.8	40.53	84 300
Life, physical, and social sciences	1 146 110	0.8	34.24	71 220	1 152 840	0.8	35.06	72 930
Community and social services	1 972 140	1.4	22.19	46 160	2 019 250	1.4	22.69	47 200
Legal	1 062 370	0.8	49.74	103 460	1 075 520	0.8	50.95	105 980
Education, training, and library	8 542 670	6.2	25.48	53 000	8 636 430	6.2	26.21	54 520
Arts, design, entertainment, sports, and media	1 843 600	1.3	27.39	56 980	1 902 970	1.4	28.07	58 390
Health care practitioner and technical	8 021 800	5.8	37.40	77 800	8 318 500	5.9	38.06	79 160
Health care support	3 989 910	2.9	14.19	29 520	4 043 480	2.9	14.65	30 470
Protective services	3 351 620	2.4	21.45	44 610	3 386 360	2.4	22.03	45 810
Food preparation and serving related	12 577 080	9.1	10.30	22 850	12 981 720	9.2	11.47	23 850
Building and grounds cleaning and maintenance	4 407 050	3.2	13.02	27 080	4 426 090	3.2	13.47	28 010
Personal care and services	4 307 500	3.1	12.33	25 650	4 514 960	3.2	12.74	26 510
Sales and related	14 462 120	10.5	18.90	39 320	14 536 530	10.4	19.50	40 560
Office and administrative support	21 846 420	15.8	17.47	36 330	22 026 080	15.7	17.91	37 260
Farming, fishing, and forestry	454 230	0.3	24.38	26 360	463 640	0.3	13.37	27 810
Construction and extraction	5 477 820	4.0	22.88	26 360	5 585 420	4.0	23.51	48 900
Installation, maintenance, and repair	5 374 150	3.9	22.11	45 990	5 456 640	3.9	22.45	46 690
Production	9 073 290	6.6	17.41	36 220	9 105 650	6.5	17.88	37 190
Transportation and material moving	9 536 610	6.9	16.90	35 160	9 731 790	6.9	17.34	36 070

Occupation	May 2017				May 2018			
	Employment		Mean hourly wage	Mean annual wage[1]	Employment		Mean hourly wage	Mean annual wage[1]
	Number	Percent			Number	Percent		
All Occupations	142 549 250	100.0	24.34	50 620	144 733 270	100.0	24.98	51 960
Management	7 280 330	5.1	57.65	119 910	7 616 650	5.3	58.44	121 560
Business and financial operations	7 472 750	5.2	36.70	76 330	7 721 300	5.3	36.98	76 910
Computer and mathematical sciences	4 261 460	3.0	43.18	89 810	4 384 300	3.0	44.01	91 530
Architecture and engineering	2 516 780	1.8	41.44	86 190	2 556 220	1.8	42.01	87 370
Life, physical, and social sciences	1 148 300	0.8	35.76	74 370	1 171 910	0.8	36.62	76 160
Community and social services	2 096 740	1.5	23.10	48 050	2 171 820	1.5	23.69	49 280
Legal	1 095 770	0.8	51.62	107 370	1 127 900	0.8	52.25	108 690
Education, training, and library	8 727 710	6.1	26.67	55 470	8 779 780	6.1	27.22	56 620
Arts, design, entertainment, sports, and media	1 925 140	1.4	28.34	58 950	1 951 170	1.3	28.74	59 780
Health care practitioner and technical	8 506 740	6.0	38.83	80 760	8 646 730	6.0	39.42	82 000
Health care support	4 113 410	2.9	15.05	31 310	4 117 450	2.8	15.57	32 380
Protective services	3 408 680	2.4	22.69	47 190	3 437 410	2.4	23.36	48 580
Food preparation and serving related	13 193 090	9.3	11.88	24 710	13 374 620	9.2	12.30	25 580
Building and grounds cleaning and maintenance	4 424 440	3.1	13.91	28 930	4 421 980	3.1	14.43	30 020
Personal care and services	5 159 100	3.6	13.11	27 270	5 451 330	3.8	13.51	28 090
Sales and related	14 522 580	10.2	19.56	40 680	14 542 290	10.0	20.09	41 790
Office and administrative support	21 965 480	15.4	18.24	37 950	21 828 990	15.1	18.75	38 990
Farming, fishing, and forestry	470 920	0.3	13.87	28 840	480 130	0.3	14.49	30 140
Construction and extraction	5 728 460	4.0	24.01	49 930	5 962 640	4.1	24.62	51 220
Installation, maintenance, and repair	5 528 390	3.9	17.82	47 870	5 628 880	3.9	23.54	48 960
Production	9 024 560	6.3	18.30	38 070	9 115 530	6.3	18.84	39 190
Transportation and material moving	9 978 390	7.0	17.82	37 070	10 244 260	7.1	18.41	38 290

[1]The annual wage has been calculated by multiplying the hourly mean wage by a "year-round, full-time" hours figure of 2,080 hours; for occupations with no published hourly mean wage, the annual wage has been directly calculated from the reported survey data.

Table 3-2. Employment and Wages, by Occupation, May 2018

(Number of people, dollars.)

Occupation	May 2018			
	Employment	Mean hourly wage	Mean annual wage[1]	Median hourly wage
All Occupations	144 733 270	24.98	51 960	18.58
Management Occupations	7 616 650	58.44	121 560	50.11
Top Executives	2 535 640	61.66	128 240	49.73
Chief Executives	195 530	96.22	200 140	91.15
General and Operations Managers	2 289 770	59.56	123 880	48.52
Legislators	50 330	(2)	47 620	(2)
Advertising, Marketing, Promotions, Public Relations, and Sales Managers	717 220	68.03	141 500	60.70
Advertising and Promotions Managers	25 260	63.99	133 090	56.31
Marketing and Sales Managers	619 500	68.75	143 000	61.59
Marketing Managers	240 440	70.79	147 240	64.56
Sales Managers	379 050	67.46	140 320	59.72
Public Relations and Fundraising Managers	72 460	63.26	131 570	55.19
Operations Specialties Managers	1 853 660	63.79	132 680	57.01
Administrative Services Managers	283 570	50.99	106 050	46.24
Computer and Information Systems Managers	391 430	73.49	152 860	68.53
Financial Managers	608 120	70.59	146 830	61.53
Industrial Production Managers	181 310	54.51	113 370	49.70
Purchasing Managers	69 490	60.40	125 630	57.18
Transportation, Storage, and Distribution Managers	124 810	49.45	102 850	45.54
Compensation and Benefits Managers	15 660	63.87	132 860	58.18
Human Resources Managers	143 580	60.91	126 700	54.47
Training and Development Managers	35 690	58.53	121 730	53.53
Other Management Occupations	2 510 140	48.51	100 900	43.33
Farmers, Ranchers, and Other Agricultural Managers	4 770	38.43	79 940	32.67
Construction Managers	278 460	49.57	103 110	44.89
Education Administrators	498 200	46.65	97 030	43.30
Education Administrators, Preschool and Childcare Center/Program	50 650	25.96	53 990	23.05
Education Administrators, Elementary and Secondary School	263 120	(2)	98 750	(2)
Education Administrators, Postsecondary	143 430	53.47	111 210	45.36
Education Administrators, All Other	41 000	43.06	89 570	39.83
Architectural and Engineering Managers	188 290	71.62	148 970	67.67
Food Service Managers	219 160	28.35	58 960	26.08
Funeral Service Managers	8 400	45.11	93 820	38.07
Gaming Managers	4 300	40.99	85 260	35.91
Lodging Managers	37 050	29.94	62 270	25.67
Medical and Health Services Managers	372 670	54.68	113 730	47.95
Natural Sciences Managers	60 260	67.16	139 680	59.55
Postmasters and Mail Superintendents	13 770	37.04	77 040	36.52
Property, Real Estate, and Community Association Managers	202 550	34.49	71 730	28.05
Social and Community Service Managers	149 870	34.46	71 670	31.41
Emergency Management Directors	9 550	39.70	82 570	35.78
Miscellaneous Managers	462 840	55.57	115 590	51.67
Managers, All Other	462 840	55.57	115 590	51.67
Business and Financial Operations Occupations	7 721 300	36.98	76 910	32.86
Business Operations Specialists	5 022 640	35.52	73 890	32.27
Agents and Business Managers of Artists, Performers, and Athletes	14 830	43.72	90 930	31.75
Buyers and Purchasing Agents	407 410	32.47	67 530	30.17
Claims Adjusters, Appraisers, Examiners, and Investigators	302 930	32.42	67 440	31.57
Insurance Appraisers, Auto Damage	15 200	31.50	65 510	30.06
Compliance Officers	300 900	34.86	72 520	33.10
Cost Estimators	211 600	33.52	69 710	30.79
Human Resources Workers	671 140	32.32	67 240	29.52
Farm Labor Contractors	200	25.45	52 930	22.19
Labor Relations Specialists	77 140	34.01	70 730	32.59
Logisticians	169 820	37.85	78 730	35.86
Management Analysts	684 470	45.38	94 390	40.20
Meeting, Convention, and Event Planners	110 120	25.83	53 730	23.74
Fundraisers	75 700	29.62	61 610	27.38
Compensation, Benefits, and Job Analysis Specialists	83 550	32.65	67 910	30.29
Training and Development Specialists	291 380	31.31	65 120	29.26
Market Research Analysts and Marketing Specialists	638 200	34.11	70 960	30.35
Miscellaneous Business Operations Specialists	1 060 580	37.00	76 960	33.91
Business Operations Specialists, All Other	1 060 580	37.00	76 960	33.91
Financial Specialists	2 698 660	39.69	82 550	34.02
Accountants and Auditors	1 259 930	37.89	78 820	33.89
Appraisers and Assessors of Real Estate	57 900	29.75	61 870	26.43
Budget Analysts	52 810	38.38	79 830	36.65
Credit Analysts	74 820	39.57	82 300	34.38
Financial Analysts and Advisors	602 500	50.03	104 050	39.84
Financial Analysts	306 200	48.55	100 990	41.18
Personal Financial Advisors	200 260	58.54	121 770	42.73
Insurance Underwriters	96 040	36.96	76 880	33.36
Financial Examiners	58 590	43.42	90 310	38.55

[1]Annual wages have been calculated by multiplying the hourly mean wage by a "year-round, full-time" hours figure of 2,080 hours; for occupations with no published hourly mean wage, the annual wage has been directly calculated from the reported survey data.
[2]Wages for some occupations that do not generally entail year-round, full-time employment are reported as either hourly wages or annual salaries (depending on how employees are typically paid).

Table 3-2. Employment and Wages, by Occupation, May 2018—*Continued*

(Number of people, dollars.)

Occupation	May 2018			
	Employment	Mean hourly wage	Mean annual wage[1]	Median hourly wage
Business and Financial Operations Occupations—*Continued*				
Credit Counselors and Loan Officers	340 690	35.33	73 490	29.11
Credit Counselors	35 740	23.95	49 820	21.72
Loan Officers	304 950	36.67	76 270	30.31
Tax Examiners, Collectors and Preparers, and Revenue Agents	122 640	25.45	52 930	22.92
Tax Examiners and Collectors, and Revenue Agents	54 550	29.09	60 500	26.17
Tax Preparers	68 090	22.53	46 860	18.94
Miscellaneous Financial Specialists	128 760	37.30	77 580	33.79
Financial Specialists, All Other	128 760	37.30	77 580	33.79
Computer and Mathematical Occupations	4 384 300	44.01	91 530	41.51
Computer Occupations	4 214 820	43.98	91 480	41.50
Computer and Information Research Scientists	30 070	59.54	123 850	56.91
Computer and Information Analysts	696 030	45.67	94 990	43.31
Computer Systems Analysts	587 970	45.01	93 610	42.66
Information Security Analysts	108 060	49.26	102 470	47.28
Software Developers and Programmers	1 666 270	50.23	104 480	48.04
Computer Programmers	230 470	43.07	89 580	40.52
Software Developers, Applications	903 160	51.96	108 080	49.82
Software Developers, Systems Software	405 330	54.81	114 000	52.89
Web Developers	127 300	36.34	75 580	33.38
Database and Systems Administrators and Network Architects	629 020	45.09	93 780	42.79
Database Administrators	110 090	44.25	92 030	43.31
Network and Computer Systems Administrators	366 250	41.86	87 070	39.45
Computer Network Architects	152 670	53.43	111 130	52.41
Computer Support Specialists	812 060	27.86	57 950	25.70
Computer User Support Specialists	630 700	26.46	55 050	24.51
Computer Network Support Specialists	181 360	32.72	68 050	30.18
Miscellaneous Computer Occupations	381 380	44.88	93 350	43.40
Computer Occupations, All Other	381 380	44.88	93 350	43.40
Mathematical Science Occupations	169 480	44.63	92 830	41.68
Actuaries	20 760	55.89	116 250	49.46
Mathematicians	2 580	50.42	104 870	48.99
Operations Research Analysts	104 200	42.48	88 350	40.09
Statisticians	39 920	44.52	92 600	42.20
Miscellaneous Mathematical Science Occupations	2 010	34.80	72 390	27.50
Architecture and Engineering Occupations	2 556 220	42.01	87 370	38.55
Architects, Surveyors, and Cartographers	179 380	38.61	80 300	35.20
Architects, Except Naval	123 020	41.58	86 480	37.37
Architects, Except Landscape and Naval	104 360	42.72	88 860	38.16
Landscape Architects	18 660	35.17	73 160	32.80
Surveyors, Cartographers, and Photogrammetrists	56 360	32.12	66 810	30.27
Cartographers and Photogrammetrists	11 050	32.86	68 340	30.98
Surveyors	45 310	31.94	66 440	30.09
Engineers	1 700 880	47.71	99 230	44.75
Aerospace Engineers	63 960	56.30	117 100	55.39
Agricultural Engineers	1 630	38.03	79 090	37.07
Biomedical Engineers	18 970	45.72	95 090	42.57
Chemical Engineers	32 060	55.03	114 470	50.44
Civil Engineers	306 030	45.06	93 720	41.65
Computer Hardware Engineers	60 750	56.66	117 840	55.10
Electrical and Electronics Engineers	320 610	50.12	104 250	47.63
Electrical Engineers	186 490	48.85	101 600	46.46
Electronics Engineers, Except Computer	134 110	51.89	107 930	49.37
Environmental Engineers	53 070	44.54	92 640	42.13
Industrial Engineers, Including Health and Safety	305 780	44.14	91 800	41.92
Health and Safety Engineers, Except Mining Safety Engineers and Inspectors	26 230	45.01	93 630	42.85
Industrial Engineers	279 550	44.05	91 630	41.84
Marine Engineers and Naval Architects	11 350	47.58	98 970	44.50
Materials Engineers	26 930	46.60	96 930	44.42
Mechanical Engineers	303 440	44.62	92 800	42.00
Mining and Geological Engineers, Including Mining Safety Engineers	5 780	47.32	98 420	44.35
Nuclear Engineers	15 980	53.26	110 790	51.73
Petroleum Engineers	32 510	75.18	156 370	65.95
Miscellaneous Engineers	142 030	47.80	99 410	46.62
Engineers, All Other	142 030	47.80	99 410	46.62
Drafters, Engineering Technicians, and Mapping Technicians	675 960	28.56	59 410	27.32
Drafters	193 260	27.97	58 180	26.71
Architectural and Civil Drafters	97 610	27.26	56 700	26.40
Electrical and Electronics Drafters	24 900	30.96	64 400	28.88
Mechanical Drafters	56 170	28.37	59 010	26.89
Drafters, All Other	14 580	26.08	54 240	24.93
Engineering Technicians, Except Drafters	430 400	29.51	61 380	28.37
Aerospace Engineering and Operations Technicians	10 110	33.16	68 970	32.22
Civil Engineering Technicians	71 150	26.29	54 670	25.28
Electrical and Electronics Engineering Technicians	126 950	31.27	65 050	30.93
Electro-Mechanical Technicians	13 520	28.96	60 240	27.78

[1]Annual wages have been calculated by multiplying the hourly mean wage by a "year-round, full-time" hours figure of 2,080 hours; for occupations with no published hourly mean wage, the annual wage has been directly calculated from the reported survey data.

Table 3-2. Employment and Wages, by Occupation, May 2018—*Continued*

(Number of people, dollars.)

Occupation	May 2018			
	Employment	Mean hourly wage	Mean annual wage[1]	Median hourly wage
Architecture and Engineering Occupations—*Continued*				
Environmental Engineering Technicians	17 310	26.34	54 800	24.31
Industrial Engineering Technicians	66 540	28.30	58 860	26.66
Mechanical Engineering Technicians	41 460	28.00	58 240	27.04
Engineering Technicians, Except Drafters, All Other	83 360	31.60	65 720	30.38
Surveying and Mapping Technicians	52 300	22.93	47 690	21.34
Life, Physical, and Social Science Occupations	1 171 910	36.62	76 160	31.77
Life Scientists	304 750	41.56	86 450	36.47
Agricultural and Food Scientists	30 880	34.24	71 230	30.78
Animal Scientists	2 530	32.54	67 690	28.07
Food Scientists and Technologists	13 330	34.89	72 570	31.39
Soil and Plant Scientists	15 010	33.96	70 630	30.74
Biological Scientists	109 040	41.54	86 390	37.29
Biochemists and Biophysicists	28 500	50.93	105 940	44.85
Microbiologists	20 030	39.02	81 150	34.45
Zoologists and Wildlife Biologists	17 860	32.58	67 760	30.49
Biological Scientists, All Other	42 640	40.19	83 600	38.27
Conservation Scientists and Foresters	30 600	31.12	64 720	29.49
Conservation Scientists	22 200	31.40	65 320	29.48
Foresters	8 410	30.36	63 150	29.53
Medical Scientists	127 380	45.80	95 270	40.16
Epidemiologists	7 060	36.39	75 690	33.49
Medical Scientists, Except Epidemiologists	120 320	46.36	96 420	40.77
Miscellaneous Life Scientists	6 850	42.86	89 150	37.59
Life Scientists, All Other	6 850	42.86	89 150	37.59
Physical Scientists	254 790	43.49	90 470	38.89
Astronomers and Physicists	19 770	59.48	123 730	57.49
Astronomers	2 160	53.41	111 090	50.81
Physicists	17 620	60.23	125 280	58.15
Atmospheric and Space Scientists	9 310	45.95	95 580	45.25
Chemists and Materials Scientists	92 300	41.06	85 400	37.66
Chemists	84 560	40.31	83 850	36.97
Materials Scientists	7 730	49.25	102 450	47.98
Environmental Scientists and Geoscientists	116 020	41.10	85 480	36.34
Environmental Scientists and Specialists, Including Health	80 480	37.30	77 580	34.20
Geoscientists, Except Hydrologists and Geographers	29 260	51.83	107 800	43.81
Hydrologists	6 290	39.81	82 790	38.16
Miscellaneous Physical Scientists	17 380	52.93	110 090	51.55
Physical Scientists, All Other	17 380	52.93	110 090	51.55
Social Scientists and Related Workers	247 290	41.30	85 900	37.81
Economists	18 650	55.78	116 020	50.16
Survey Researchers	11 690	30.40	63 240	27.74
Psychologists	124 750	41.63	86 600	37.99
Clinical, Counseling, and School Psychologists	110 490	41.03	85 340	37.01
Industrial-Organizational Psychologists	780	52.42	109 030	46.76
Psychologists, All Other	13 480	45.97	95 610	48.45
Sociologists	2 710	43.41	90 290	39.45
Urban and Regional Planners	37 840	36.65	76 240	35.12
Miscellaneous Social Scientists and Related Workers	51 640	41.02	85 320	38.68
Anthropologists and Archeologists	6 020	31.40	65 310	30.01
Geographers	1 390	38.72	80 530	38.60
Historians	3 040	31.91	66 380	29.40
Political Scientists	5 660	55.43	115 300	56.52
Social Scientists and Related Workers, All Other	35 530	41.22	85 750	39.11
Life, Physical, and Social Science Technicians	365 080	24.52	50 990	22.47
Agricultural and Food Science Technicians	21 290	21.24	44 170	19.65
Biological Technicians	77 450	23.10	48 060	21.39
Chemical Technicians	65 500	24.84	51 670	23.15
Geological and Petroleum Technicians	15 060	30.23	62 890	25.62
Nuclear Technicians	7 230	38.45	79 970	38.05
Social Science Research Assistants	34 550	24.24	50 420	22.42
Miscellaneous Life, Physical, and Social Science Technicians	144 010	24.38	50 720	22.54
Environmental Science and Protection Technicians, Including Health	32 600	24.21	50 350	22.20
Forensic Science Technicians	15 970	30.05	62 490	27.99
Forest and Conservation Technicians	30 220	19.28	40 110	17.88
Life, Physical, and Social Science Technicians, All Other	65 220	25.45	52 940	23.88
Community and Social Service Occupations	2 171 820	23.69	49 280	21.62
Counselors, Social Workers, and Other Community and Social Service Specialists	2 090 700	23.69	49 270	21.62
Counselors	735 100	24.96	51 920	22.98
Educational, Guidance, School, and Vocational Counselors	285 460	28.93	60 160	27.07
Marriage and Family Therapists	48 520	26.03	54 150	24.08
Rehabilitation Counselors	106 860	19.20	39 930	17.13
Substance Abuse, Behavioral Disorder, and Mental Health Counselors	267 730	23.04	47 920	21.46
Counselors, All Other	26 530	22.95	47 740	20.26
Social Workers	662 550	25.51	53 060	23.79
Child, Family, and School Social Workers	320 170	23.92	49 760	22.24
Healthcare Social Workers	168 190	28.11	58 470	27.02

[1]Annual wages have been calculated by multiplying the hourly mean wage by a "year-round, full-time" hours figure of 2,080 hours; for occupations with no published hourly mean wage, the annual wage has been directly calculated from the reported survey data.

Table 3-2. Employment and Wages, by Occupation, May 2018—*Continued*

(Number of people, dollars.)

Occupation	May 2018			
	Employment	Mean hourly wage	Mean annual wage[1]	Median hourly wage
Community and Social Service Occupations—*Continued*				
Mental Health and Substance Abuse Social Workers	116 750	23.86	49 630	21.56
Social Workers, All Other	57 440	30.12	62 660	30.35
Miscellaneous Community and Social Service Specialists	693 040	20.59	42 820	18.35
Health Educators	58 780	28.68	59 660	26.07
Probation Officers and Correctional Treatment Specialists	87 660	28.27	58 790	25.49
Social and Human Service Assistants	392 300	17.22	35 830	16.22
Community Health Workers	56 130	20.90	43 480	19.01
Community and Social Service Specialists, All Other	98 170	22.14	46 050	20.49
Religious Workers	81 120	23.94	49 790	21.62
Clergy	50 960	25.62	53 290	23.55
Directors, Religious Activities and Education	21 700	22.59	46 980	19.62
Miscellaneous Religious Workers	8 460	17.24	35 860	14.33
Religious Workers, All Other	8 460	17.24	35 860	14.33
Legal Occupations	1 127 900	52.25	108 690	38.85
Lawyers, Judges, and Related Workers	708 140	67.23	139 850	56.68
Lawyers and Judicial Law Clerks	659 090	68.33	142 130	57.00
Lawyers	642 750	69.34	144 230	58.13
Judicial Law Clerks	16 350	28.63	59 540	25.74
Judges, Magistrates, and Other Judicial Workers	49 040	52.49	109 170	52.05
Administrative Law Judges, Adjudicators, and Hearing Officers	14 280	48.66	101 210	48.00
Arbitrators, Mediators, and Conciliators	6 240	34.98	72 760	29.94
Judges, Magistrate Judges, and Magistrates	28 520	58.23	121 130	64.39
Legal Support Workers	419 770	26.98	56 130	24.72
Paralegals and Legal Assistants	309 940	26.20	54 500	24.49
Miscellaneous Legal Support Workers	109 820	29.19	60 710	25.40
Court Reporters	14 490	30.00	62 390	27.48
Title Examiners, Abstractors, and Searchers	52 180	24.70	51 380	22.66
Legal Support Workers, All Other	43 150	34.34	71 420	28.33
Education, Training, and Library Occupations	8 779 780	27.22	56 620	23.89
Postsecondary Teachers	1 517 100	(2)	85 190	(2)
Business Teachers, Postsecondary	84 230	(2)	103 330	(2)
Math and Computer Teachers, Postsecondary	83 690	(2)	90 650	(2)
Computer Science Teachers, Postsecondary	32 430	(2)	96 200	(2)
Mathematical Science Teachers, Postsecondary	51 250	(2)	87 140	(2)
Engineering and Architecture Teachers, Postsecondary	44 420	(2)	111 450	(2)
Architecture Teachers, Postsecondary	6 880	(2)	99 320	(2)
Engineering Teachers, Postsecondary	37 530	(2)	113 680	(2)
Life Sciences Teachers, Postsecondary	64 660	(2)	96 110	(2)
Agricultural Sciences Teachers, Postsecondary	10 810	(2)	90 890	(2)
Biological Science Teachers, Postsecondary	51 770	(2)	97 340	(2)
Forestry and Conservation Science Teachers, Postsecondary	2 070	(2)	92 550	(2)
Physical Sciences Teachers, Postsecondary	52 160	(2)	97 280	(2)
Atmospheric, Earth, Marine, and Space Sciences Teachers, Postsecondary	11 020	(2)	101 890	(2)
Chemistry Teachers, Postsecondary	21 370	(2)	92 360	(2)
Environmental Science Teachers, Postsecondary	6 040	(2)	91 330	(2)
Physics Teachers, Postsecondary	13 730	(2)	103 830	(2)
Social Sciences Teachers, Postsecondary	117 510	(2)	92 440	(2)
Anthropology and Archeology Teachers, Postsecondary	5 890	(2)	94 080	(2)
Area, Ethnic, and Cultural Studies Teachers, Postsecondary	9 850	(2)	85 450	(2)
Economics Teachers, Postsecondary	12 750	(2)	117 180	(2)
Geography Teachers, Postsecondary	3 960	(2)	88 950	(2)
Political Science Teachers, Postsecondary	15 890	(2)	99 480	(2)
Psychology Teachers, Postsecondary	37 630	(2)	88 490	(2)
Sociology Teachers, Postsecondary	13 870	(2)	83 310	(2)
Social Sciences Teachers, Postsecondary, All Other	17 670	(2)	87 950	(2)
Health Teachers, Postsecondary	255 190	(2)	113 370	(2)
Health Specialties Teachers, Postsecondary	199 480	(2)	122 320	(2)
Nursing Instructors and Teachers, Postsecondary	55 710	(2)	81 350	(2)
Education and Library Science Teachers, Postsecondary	65 570	(2)	73 800	(2)
Education Teachers, Postsecondary	60 930	(2)	73 680	(2)
Library Science Teachers, Postsecondary	4 650	(2)	75 450	(2)
Law, Criminal Justice, and Social Work Teachers, Postsecondary	44 500	(2)	96 110	(2)
Criminal Justice and Law Enforcement Teachers, Postsecondary	14 890	(2)	72 390	(2)
Law Teachers, Postsecondary	16 990	(2)	130 710	(2)
Social Work Teachers, Postsecondary	12 620	(2)	77 520	(2)
Arts, Communications, and Humanities Teachers, Postsecondary	260 960	(2)	80 670	(2)
Art, Drama, and Music Teachers, Postsecondary	94 310	(2)	82 560	(2)
Communications Teachers, Postsecondary	29 100	(2)	78 090	(2)
English Language and Literature Teachers, Postsecondary	68 360	(2)	78 150	(2)
Foreign Language and Literature Teachers, Postsecondary	25 590	(2)	79 160	(2)
History Teachers, Postsecondary	20 510	(2)	83 990	(2)
Philosophy and Religion Teachers, Postsecondary	23 100	(2)	82 420	(2)
Miscellaneous Postsecondary Teachers	444 210	(2)	60 200	(2)
Graduate Teaching Assistants	131 490	(2)	36 390	(2)

[1]Annual wages have been calculated by multiplying the hourly mean wage by a "year-round, full-time" hours figure of 2,080 hours; for occupations with no published hourly mean wage, the annual wage has been directly calculated from the reported survey data.
[2]Wages for some occupations that do not generally entail year-round, full-time employment are reported as either hourly wages or annual salaries (depending on how employees are typically paid).

Table 3-2. Employment and Wages, by Occupation, May 2018—*Continued*

(Number of people, dollars.)

Occupation	May 2018			
	Employment	Mean hourly wage	Mean annual wage[1]	Median hourly wage
Education, Training, and Library Occupations—*Continued*				
Home Economics Teachers, Postsecondary	2 080	(2)	77 170	(2)
Recreation and Fitness Studies Teachers, Postsecondary	16 490	(2)	72 190	(2)
Vocational Education Teachers, Postsecondary	110 400	28.14	58 520	25.54
Postsecondary Teachers, All Other	183 750	(2)	76 990	(2)
Preschool, Primary, Secondary, and Special Education School Teachers	4 193 290	(2)	59 980	(2)
Preschool and Kindergarten Teachers	555 680	19.26	40 070	16.33
Preschool Teachers, Except Special Education	424 520	16.54	34 410	14.32
Kindergarten Teachers, Except Special Education	131 160	(2)	58 370	(2)
Elementary and Middle School Teachers	2 032 880	(2)	62 150	(2)
Elementary School Teachers, Except Special Education	1 410 970	(2)	62 200	(2)
Middle School Teachers, Except Special and Career/Technical Education	609 970	(2)	62 030	(2)
Career/Technical Education Teachers, Middle School	11 940	(2)	62 570	(2)
Secondary School Teachers	1 129 040	(2)	64 230	(2)
Secondary School Teachers, Except Special and Career/Technical Education	1 051 570	(2)	64 340	(2)
Career/Technical Education Teachers, Secondary School	77 460	(2)	62 810	(2)
Special Education Teachers	475 700	(2)	63 890	(2)
Special Education Teachers, Preschool	23 480	(2)	61 610	(2)
Special Education Teachers, Kindergarten and Elementary School	185 190	(2)	63 110	(2)
Special Education Teachers, Middle School	87 870	(2)	64 390	(2)
Special Education Teachers, Secondary School	142 360	(2)	65 320	(2)
Special Education Teachers, All Other	36 800	(2)	62 500	(2)
Other Teachers and Instructors	1 203 570	19.35	40 250	15.89
Adult Basic and Secondary Education and Literacy Teachers and Instructors	57 750	27.94	58 110	25.79
Self-Enrichment Education Teachers	243 080	21.62	44 960	18.62
Miscellaneous Teachers and Instructors	902 740	18.19	37 840	14.83
Teachers and Instructors, All Other, Except Substitute Teachers	315 510	(2)	48 040	(2)
Substitute Teachers	587 240	15.56	32 360	13.79
Librarians, Curators, and Archivists	246 200	24.66	51 290	23.08
Archivists, Curators, and Museum Technicians	31 760	25.61	53 280	23.27
Archivists	6 370	27.12	56 400	25.11
Curators	12 280	28.12	58 490	25.86
Museum Technicians and Conservators	13 100	22.53	46 870	20.68
Librarians	125 750	29.58	61 530	28.39
Library Technicians	88 690	17.34	36 080	16.37
Other Education, Training, and Library Occupations	1 619 610	(2)	34 110	(2)
Audio-Visual and Multimedia Collections Specialists	9 540	25.13	52 270	23.85
Farm and Home Management Advisors	8 020	25.33	52 700	23.96
Instructional Coordinators	163 900	32.45	67 490	30.98
Teacher Assistants	1 331 560	(2)	28 750	(2)
Miscellaneous Education, Training, and Library Workers	106 590	22.44	46 680	20.23
Education, Training, and Library Workers, All Other	106 590	22.44	46 680	20.23
Arts, Design, Entertainment, Sports, and Media Occupations	1 951 170	28.74	59 780	23.70
Art and Design Workers	610 180	26.55	55 230	22.43
Artists and Related Workers	90 990	40.83	84 930	36.34
Art Directors	40 210	50.29	104 590	44.60
Craft Artists	3 980	19.47	40 490	16.46
Fine Artists, Including Painters, Sculptors, and Illustrators	11 620	28.06	58 370	23.74
Multimedia Artists and Animators	28 560	37.61	78 230	34.87
Artists and Related Workers, All Other	6 620	32.55	67 700	31.44
Designers	519 180	24.05	50 020	20.66
Commercial and Industrial Designers	33 200	34.34	71 430	32.01
Fashion Designers	19 750	42.12	87 610	34.96
Floral Designers	43 360	13.90	28 900	13.08
Graphic Designers	217 810	26.29	54 680	24.21
Interior Designers	57 070	28.42	59 120	25.66
Merchandise Displayers and Window Trimmers	128 960	15.31	31 850	13.68
Set and Exhibit Designers	10 590	29.34	61 020	26.09
Designers, All Other	8 450	32.99	68 610	29.12
Entertainers and Performers, Sports and Related Workers	515 310	28.80	59 900	20.64
Actors, Producers, and Directors	166 060	39.24	81 610	29.40
Actors	47 430	29.34	(2)	17.54
Producers and Directors	118 630	43.19	89 840	34.46
Athletes, Coaches, Umpires, and Related Workers	266 860	(2)	45 080	(2)
Athletes and Sports Competitors	10 800	(2)	87 030	(2)
Coaches and Scouts	236 970	(2)	43 870	(2)
Umpires, Referees, and Other Sports Officials	19 090	(2)	36 440	(2)
Dancers and Choreographers	14 810	22.44	46 670	18.17
Dancers	9 720	20.70	(2)	16.31
Choreographers	5 090	25.75	53 560	22.98
Musicians, Singers, and Related Workers	53 840	35.53	(2)	26.84
Music Directors and Composers	12 160	28.75	59 790	23.86
Musicians and Singers	41 680	37.51	(2)	28.15
Miscellaneous Entertainers and Performers, Sports and Related Workers	13 740	21.53	(2)	15.94
Entertainers and Performers, Sports and Related Workers, All Other	13 740	21.53	(2)	15.94
Media and Communication Workers	586 190	31.72	65 980	27.66
Announcers	35 260	23.54	48 960	15.38
Radio and Television Announcers	27 780	24.82	51 630	15.97

[1]Annual wages have been calculated by multiplying the hourly mean wage by a "year-round, full-time" hours figure of 2,080 hours; for occupations with no published hourly mean wage, the annual wage has been directly calculated from the reported survey data.
[2]Wages for some occupations that do not generally entail year-round, full-time employment are reported as either hourly wages or annual salaries (depending on how employees are typically paid).

Table 3-2. Employment and Wages, by Occupation, May 2018—*Continued*

(Number of people, dollars.)

Occupation	May 2018			
	Employment	Mean hourly wage	Mean annual wage[1]	Median hourly wage
Arts, Design, Entertainment, Sports, and Media Occupations—*Continued*				
Public Address System and Other Announcers	7 480	18.77	39 040	13.33
News Analysts, Reporters and Correspondents	43 030	29.10	60 530	20.91
Broadcast News Analysts	5 890	44.23	91 990	32.15
Reporters and Correspondents	37 140	26.70	55 530	19.84
Public Relations Specialists	239 030	32.90	68 440	28.85
Writers and Editors	191 320	34.58	71 920	30.53
Editors	95 750	33.41	69 480	28.60
Technical Writers	50 350	36.30	75 500	34.54
Writers and Authors	45 210	35.14	73 090	29.89
Miscellaneous Media and Communication Workers	77 560	26.20	54 490	23.84
Interpreters and Translators	57 140	26.55	55 230	24.00
Media and Communication Workers, All Other	20 420	25.21	52 430	23.24
Media and Communication Equipment Workers	239 490	26.91	55 970	22.24
Broadcast and Sound Engineering Technicians and Radio Operators	121 890	24.02	49 960	20.98
Audio and Video Equipment Technicians	75 940	23.53	48 940	21.04
Broadcast Technicians	31 580	22.48	46 770	19.27
Radio Operators	870	21.49	44 710	20.30
Sound Engineering Technicians	13 510	30.53	63 500	25.19
Photographers	49 560	20.56	42 770	16.35
Television, Video, and Motion Picture Camera Operators and Editors	49 240	36.58	76 090	28.36
Camera Operators, Television, Video, and Motion Picture	21 080	29.69	61 750	26.24
Film and Video Editors	28 160	41.75	86 830	30.12
Miscellaneous Media and Communication Equipment Workers	18 790	37.06	77 080	38.26
Media and Communication Equipment Workers, All Other	18 790	37.06	77 080	38.26
Healthcare Practitioners and Technical Occupations	8 646 730	39.42	82 000	31.94
Health Diagnosing and Treating Practitioners	5 367 930	49.02	101 960	38.94
Chiropractors	34 740	41.28	85 870	34.33
Dentists	128 060	86.82	180 590	75.12
Dentists, General	113 000	84.54	175 840	73.00
Oral and Maxillofacial Surgeons	4 830	116.52	242 370	(3)
Orthodontists	5 350	108.54	225 760	(3)
Prosthodontists	380	92.02	191 400	84.88
Dentists, All Other Specialists	4 490	85.96	178 800	70.66
Dietitians and Nutritionists	64 670	29.43	61 210	29.02
Optometrists	37 220	57.68	119 980	53.75
Pharmacists	309 550	59.45	123 670	60.64
Physicians and Surgeons	679 280	101.43	210 980	(3)
Anesthesiologists	31 060	128.38	267 020	(3)
Family and General Practitioners	114 130	101.82	211 780	96.68
Internists, General	37 820	94.47	196 490	93.51
Obstetricians and Gynecologists	18 590	114.58	238 320	(3)
Pediatricians, General	28 490	88.10	183 240	82.00
Psychiatrists	25 630	105.95	220 380	(3)
Surgeons	34 390	122.65	255 110	(3)
Physicians and Surgeons, All Other	389 180	98.02	203 880	96.58
Physician Assistants	114 710	52.13	108 430	52.22
Podiatrists	9 500	71.26	148 220	62.28
Therapists	687 790	38.24	79 530	37.23
Occupational Therapists	126 900	41.04	85 350	40.51
Physical Therapists	228 600	42.73	88 880	42.27
Radiation Therapists	18 260	41.70	86 730	39.58
Recreational Therapists	18 840	24.34	50 640	23.01
Respiratory Therapists	129 600	30.05	62 500	28.98
Speech-Language Pathologists	146 900	38.80	80 700	37.26
Exercise Physiologists	6 740	26.33	54 760	23.69
Therapists, All Other	11 950	27.73	57 680	24.51
Veterinarians	71 060	50.59	105 240	45.11
Registered Nurses	2 951 960	36.30	75 510	34.48
Nurse Anesthetists	43 520	84.03	174 790	80.75
Nurse Midwives	6 250	51.40	106 910	49.89
Nurse Practitioners	179 650	52.90	110 030	51.46
Audiologists	13 300	39.52	82 210	36.50
Miscellaneous Health Diagnosing and Treating Practitioners	36 680	41.16	85 600	35.56
Health Diagnosing and Treating Practitioners, All Other	36 680	41.16	85 600	35.56
Health Technologists and Technicians	3 110 180	23.26	48 380	21.49
Clinical Laboratory Technologists and Technicians	321 220	25.91	53 880	25.16
Dental Hygienists	215 150	36.30	75 500	35.97
Diagnostic Related Technologists and Technicians	390 630	31.38	65 260	30.60
Cardiovascular Technologists and Technicians	56 560	28.24	58 730	27.33
Diagnostic Medical Sonographers	71 130	35.51	73 860	34.86
Nuclear Medicine Technologists	18 810	37.92	78 870	36.93
Radiologic Technologists	205 590	29.59	61 540	28.62
Magnetic Resonance Imaging Technologists	38 540	34.73	72 230	34.46
Emergency Medical Technicians and Paramedics	257 210	18.15	37 760	16.50
Health Practitioner Support Technologists and Technicians	801 590	17.76	36 930	16.70

[1]Annual wages have been calculated by multiplying the hourly mean wage by a "year-round, full-time" hours figure of 2,080 hours; for occupations with no published hourly mean wage, the annual wage has been directly calculated from the reported survey data.
[3]Median hourly wage is equal to or greater than $100.00 per hour.

Table 3-2. Employment and Wages, by Occupation, May 2018—*Continued*

(Number of people, dollars.)

Occupation	May 2018			
	Employment	Mean hourly wage	Mean annual wage[1]	Median hourly wage
Healthcare Practitioners and Technical Occupations—*Continued*				
Dietetic Technicians	33 540	14.49	30 130	13.05
Pharmacy Technicians	417 860	16.35	34 020	15.72
Psychiatric Technicians	71 360	18.15	37 760	15.80
Respiratory Therapy Technicians	9 090	24.70	51 380	24.62
Surgical Technologists	110 160	23.58	49 040	22.74
Veterinary Technologists and Technicians	106 680	17.10	35 560	16.55
Ophthalmic Medical Technicians	52 890	18.38	38 220	17.56
Licensed Practical and Licensed Vocational Nurses	701 690	22.62	47 050	22.23
Medical Records and Health Information Technicians	208 650	21.16	44 010	19.40
Opticians, Dispensing	72 250	19.20	39 930	17.80
Miscellaneous Health Technologists and Technicians	141 790	23.82	49 540	21.43
Orthotists and Prosthetists	8 830	35.51	73 860	33.23
Hearing Aid Specialists	7 680	26.75	55 650	25.37
Health Technologists and Technicians, All Other	125 270	22.81	47 450	20.63
Other Healthcare Practitioners and Technical Occupations	168 630	32.01	66 590	30.01
Occupational Health and Safety Specialists and Technicians	106 410	34.43	71 610	33.35
Occupational Health and Safety Specialists	88 390	36.03	74 940	35.11
Occupational Health and Safety Technicians	18 020	26.57	55 270	24.41
Miscellaneous Health Practitioners and Technical Workers	62 210	27.89	58 000	24.35
Athletic Trainers	26 890	([2])	49 280	([2])
Genetic Counselors	2 640	38.88	80 860	38.64
Healthcare Practitioners and Technical Workers, All Other	32 680	30.45	63 340	26.26
Healthcare Support Occupations	4 117 450	15.57	32 380	14.30
Nursing, Psychiatric, and Home Health Aides	2 355 640	13.55	28 180	12.89
Home Health Aides	797 670	12.18	25 330	11.63
Psychiatric Aides	56 910	14.95	31 090	14.03
Nursing Assistants	1 450 960	14.22	29 580	13.72
Orderlies	50 100	14.35	29 840	13.49
Occupational Therapy and Physical Therapist Assistants and Aides	191 870	24.10	50 130	24.86
Occupational Therapy Assistants and Aides	50 360	27.00	56 150	27.70
Occupational Therapy Assistants	42 660	29.04	60 410	28.95
Occupational Therapy Aides	7 700	15.66	32 580	13.54
Physical Therapist Assistants and Aides	141 510	23.07	47 980	23.12
Physical Therapist Assistants	94 250	27.77	57 750	27.91
Physical Therapist Aides	47 260	13.70	28 500	12.62
Other Healthcare Support Occupations	1 569 940	17.55	36 500	16.75
Massage Therapists	105 160	22.06	45 880	19.92
Miscellaneous Healthcare Support Occupations	1 464 780	17.23	35 830	16.63
Dental Assistants	341 060	19.12	39 770	18.59
Medical Assistants	673 660	16.61	34 540	16.16
Medical Equipment Preparers	55 610	18.27	37 990	17.42
Medical Transcriptionists	53 730	17.48	36 350	16.72
Pharmacy Aides	36 970	14.03	29 190	12.72
Veterinary Assistants and Laboratory Animal Caretakers	89 480	13.79	28 690	13.24
Phlebotomists	125 280	17.10	35 560	16.58
Healthcare Support Workers, All Other	88 990	18.80	39 110	18.19
Protective Service Occupations	3 437 410	23.36	48 580	19.54
Supervisors of Protective Service Workers	304 940	36.72	76 380	33.92
First-Line Supervisors of Law Enforcement Workers	160 410	41.51	86 350	39.35
First-Line Supervisors of Correctional Officers	43 760	32.86	68 350	30.45
First-Line Supervisors of Police and Detectives	116 660	44.76	93 100	42.80
First-Line Supervisors of Fire Fighting and Prevention Workers	65 920	38.61	80 310	36.70
Miscellaneous First-Line Supervisors, Protective Service Workers	78 610	25.35	52 730	23.87
First-Line Supervisors of Protective Service Workers, All Other	78 610	25.35	52 730	23.87
Fire Fighting and Prevention Workers	336 230	25.78	53 630	24.04
Firefighters	321 570	25.60	53 240	23.85
Fire Inspectors	14 660	29.82	62 030	28.94
Fire Inspectors and Investigators	12 530	30.84	64 140	30.05
Forest Fire Inspectors and Prevention Specialists	2 130	23.85	49 610	19.04
Law Enforcement Workers	1 217 260	29.42	61 190	26.81
Bailiffs, Correctional Officers, and Jailers	433 900	23.71	49 320	21.35
Bailiffs	18 900	23.97	49 870	22.00
Correctional Officers and Jailers	415 000	23.70	49 300	21.31
Detectives and Criminal Investigators	103 450	40.88	85 020	39.38
Fish and Game Wardens	6 040	28.49	59 260	27.75
Parking Enforcement Workers	8 070	20.29	42 200	19.15
Police Officers	665 800	31.47	65 460	29.56
Police and Sheriff's Patrol Officers	661 330	31.44	65 400	29.51
Transit and Railroad Police	4 470	35.79	74 450	35.59
Other Protective Service Workers	1 578 980	15.59	32 430	13.76
Animal Control Workers	12 080	18.51	38 490	17.47
Private Detectives and Investigators	30 990	27.31	56 810	24.08

[1]Annual wages have been calculated by multiplying the hourly mean wage by a "year-round, full-time" hours figure of 2,080 hours; for occupations with no published hourly mean wage, the annual wage has been directly calculated from the reported survey data.
[2]Wages for some occupations that do not generally entail year-round, full-time employment are reported as either hourly wages or annual salaries (depending on how employees are typically paid).

Table 3-2. Employment and Wages, by Occupation, May 2018—*Continued*

(Number of people, dollars.)

Occupation	May 2018			
	Employment	Mean hourly wage	Mean annual wage[1]	Median hourly wage
Protective Service Occupations—*Continued*				
Security Guards and Gaming Surveillance Officers	1 124 610	15.43	32 090	13.72
Gaming Surveillance Officers and Gaming Investigators	10 230	17.41	36 200	15.71
Security Guards	1 114 380	15.41	32 050	13.70
Miscellaneous Protective Service Workers	411 300	15.06	31 330	13.22
Crossing Guards	79 880	15.37	31 970	13.92
Lifeguards, Ski Patrol, and Other Recreational Protective Service Workers	144 370	11.74	24 420	10.77
Transportation Security Screeners	45 250	20.13	41 860	19.95
Protective Service Workers, All Other	141 790	16.66	34 650	14.77
Food Preparation and Serving Related Occupations	13 374 620	12.30	25 580	11.09
Supervisors of Food Preparation and Serving Workers	1 093 000	18.30	38 070	16.30
Chefs and Head Cooks	128 600	25.08	52 160	23.30
First-Line Supervisors of Food Preparation and Serving Workers	964 400	17.40	36 190	15.60
Cooks and Food Preparation Workers	3 218 110	12.56	26 120	11.91
Cooks	2 403 510	12.77	26 560	12.12
Cooks, Fast Food	487 510	10.89	22 650	10.74
Cooks, Institution and Cafeteria	400 320	13.60	28 290	12.91
Cooks, Private Household	460	19.83	41 240	18.07
Cooks, Restaurant	1 340 810	13.26	27 580	12.76
Cooks, Short Order	155 840	12.09	25 140	11.44
Cooks, All Other	18 570	14.60	30 360	13.78
Food Preparation Workers	814 600	11.94	24 830	11.41
Food and Beverage Serving Workers	7 630 110	11.51	23 940	10.43
Bartenders	631 480	12.88	26 780	10.84
Fast Food and Counter Workers	4 150 030	10.70	22 260	10.32
Combined Food Preparation and Serving Workers, Including Fast Food	3 676 180	10.64	22 140	10.22
Counter Attendants, Cafeteria, Food Concession, and Coffee Shop	473 860	11.17	23 240	10.74
Waiters and Waitresses	2 582 410	12.42	25 830	10.47
Food Servers, Nonrestaurant	266 190	12.01	24 980	11.20
Other Food Preparation and Serving Related Workers	1 433 400	11.32	23 540	10.81
Dining Room and Cafeteria Attendants and Bartender Helpers	455 700	11.52	23 950	10.71
Dishwashers	504 770	11.15	23 190	10.93
Hosts and Hostesses, Restaurant, Lounge, and Coffee Shop	416 950	11.18	23 260	10.65
Miscellaneous Food Preparation and Serving Related Workers	55 980	12.23	25 430	11.47
Food Preparation and Serving Related Workers, All Other	55 980	12.23	25 430	11.47
Building and Grounds Cleaning and Maintenance Occupations	4 421 980	14.43	30 020	12.91
Supervisors of Building and Grounds Cleaning and Maintenance Workers	255 580	22.30	46 380	20.82
First-Line Supervisors of Building and Grounds Cleaning and Maintenance Workers	255 580	22.30	46 380	20.82
First-Line Supervisors of Housekeeping and Janitorial Workers	154 180	20.75	43 150	19.20
First-Line Supervisors of Landscaping, Lawn Service, and Groundskeeping Workers	101 390	24.66	51 280	23.18
Building Cleaning and Pest Control Workers	3 171 520	13.56	28 200	12.17
Building Cleaning Workers	3 094 210	13.44	27 960	12.10
Janitors and Cleaners, Except Maids and Housekeeping Cleaners	2 156 270	13.92	28 950	12.55
Maids and Housekeeping Cleaners	924 290	12.30	25 570	11.43
Building Cleaning Workers, All Other	13 650	15.73	32 710	14.07
Pest Control Workers	77 300	18.24	37 950	17.12
Grounds Maintenance Workers	994 880	15.19	31 600	14.13
Landscaping and Groundskeeping Workers	913 480	14.88	30 940	13.94
Pesticide Handlers, Sprayers, and Applicators, Vegetation	24 500	18.37	38 210	16.98
Tree Trimmers and Pruners	42 440	19.47	40 510	18.36
Grounds Maintenance Workers, All Other	14 470	17.17	35 710	14.63
Personal Care and Service Occupations	5 451 330	13.51	28 090	11.74
Supervisors of Personal Care and Service Workers	258 960	20.53	42 710	18.92
First-Line Supervisors of Gaming Workers	30 330	24.16	50 250	23.76
First-Line Supervisors of Personal Service Workers	228 620	20.05	41 710	18.46
Animal Care and Service Workers	214 680	12.76	26 540	11.51
Animal Trainers	14 830	16.95	35 260	14.08
Nonfarm Animal Caretakers	199 850	12.45	25 890	11.42
Entertainment Attendants and Related Workers	601 890	11.56	24 050	10.66
Gaming Services Workers	113 640	11.65	24 240	10.07
Gaming Dealers	92 530	11.09	23 070	9.68
Gaming and Sports Book Writers and Runners	11 150	13.29	27 640	11.74
Gaming Service Workers, All Other	9 950	15.03	31 260	13.24
Motion Picture Projectionists	4 840	12.42	25 820	10.94
Ushers, Lobby Attendants, and Ticket Takers	133 970	11.35	23 610	10.70
Miscellaneous Entertainment Attendants and Related Workers	349 440	11.61	24 140	10.78
Amusement and Recreation Attendants	319 890	11.28	23 460	10.70
Costume Attendants	6 460	22.12	46 010	19.80
Locker Room, Coatroom, and Dressing Room Attendants	17 610	12.84	26 720	11.55
Entertainment Attendants and Related Workers, All Other	5 480	14.27	29 690	11.68
Funeral Service Workers	65 150	19.77	41 130	16.30
Embalmers	4 070	22.42	46 640	21.27
Funeral Attendants	35 340	13.69	28 480	12.69
Morticians, Undertakers, and Funeral Directors	25 740	27.70	57 620	25.31
Personal Appearance Workers	575 110	14.44	30 040	11.94
Barbers, Hairdressers, Hairstylists and Cosmetologists	397 350	14.59	30 340	11.94
Barbers	20 130	15.97	33 220	13.44

[1]Annual wages have been calculated by multiplying the hourly mean wage by a "year-round, full-time" hours figure of 2,080 hours; for occupations with no published hourly mean wage, the annual wage has been directly calculated from the reported survey data.

Table 3-2. Employment and Wages, by Occupation, May 2018—*Continued*

(Number of people, dollars.)

Occupation	May 2018			
	Employment	Mean hourly wage	Mean annual wage[1]	Median hourly wage
Personal Care and Service Occupations—*Continued*				
Hairdressers, Hairstylists, and Cosmetologists	377 210	14.51	30 190	11.89
Miscellaneous Personal Appearance Workers	177 770	14.13	29 380	11.94
Makeup Artists, Theatrical and Performance	3 140	34.63	72 030	30.89
Manicurists and Pedicurists	110 170	12.43	25 860	11.70
Shampooers	13 720	10.65	22 160	10.40
Skincare Specialists	50 740	17.48	36 350	15.05
Baggage Porters, Bellhops, and Concierges	79 840	14.46	30 070	12.91
Baggage Porters and Bellhops	42 350	12.98	26 990	11.64
Concierges	37 490	16.13	33 550	14.61
Tour and Travel Guides	49 740	14.25	29 630	12.77
Other Personal Care and Service Workers	3 605 950	13.07	27 190	11.70
Childcare Workers	564 630	11.83	24 610	11.17
Personal Care Aides	2 211 950	12.06	25 090	11.55
Recreation and Fitness Workers	662 040	17.25	35 890	14.14
Fitness Trainers and Aerobics Instructors	308 470	21.43	44 580	19.15
Recreation Workers	353 570	13.61	28 310	12.05
Residential Advisors	108 380	14.41	29 970	13.39
Miscellaneous Personal Care and Service Workers	58 970	13.59	28 270	12.59
Personal Care and Service Workers, All Other	58 970	13.59	28 270	12.59
Sales and Related Occupations	14 542 290	20.09	41 790	13.55
Supervisors of Sales Workers	1 429 100	24.97	51 930	20.84
First-Line Supervisors of Sales Workers	1 429 100	24.97	51 930	20.84
First-Line Supervisors of Retail Sales Workers	1 181 530	21.67	45 080	19.05
First-Line Supervisors of Non-Retail Sales Workers	247 570	40.67	84 600	35.29
Retail Sales Workers	8 787 270	12.75	26 520	11.33
Cashiers	3 657 570	11.19	23 270	10.79
Gaming Change Persons and Booth Cashiers	22 020	13.09	27 220	11.96
Counter and Rental Clerks and Parts Salespersons	681 580	15.52	32 280	13.68
Counter and Rental Clerks	426 700	15.00	31 200	13.12
Parts Salespersons	254 870	16.39	34 080	14.63
Retail Salespersons	4 448 120	13.61	28 310	11.63
Sales Representatives, Services	2 046 120	34.37	71 490	26.13
Advertising Sales Agents	133 110	30.46	63 360	24.87
Insurance Sales Agents	393 830	32.64	67 890	24.33
Securities, Commodities, and Financial Services Sales Agents	415 890	47.49	98 770	30.83
Travel Agents	69 480	20.54	42 720	18.61
Miscellaneous Sales Representatives, Services	1 033 820	31.18	64 860	26.23
Sales Representatives, Services, All Other	1 033 820	31.18	64 860	26.23
Sales Representatives, Wholesale and Manufacturing	1 663 160	35.43	73 680	29.64
Sales Representatives, Wholesale and Manufacturing, Technical and Scientific Products	312 980	44.15	91 830	38.31
Sales Representatives, Wholesale and Manufacturing, Except Technical and Scientific Products	1 350 180	33.40	69 480	28.13
Other Sales and Related Workers	616 650	24.70	51 380	17.17
Models, Demonstrators, and Product Promoters	84 560	15.96	33 200	13.85
Demonstrators and Product Promoters	81 250	15.99	33 260	13.92
Models	3 310	15.18	31 570	11.43
Real Estate Brokers and Sales Agents	197 080	31.37	65 240	24.18
Real Estate Brokers	40 320	37.95	78 940	27.99
Real Estate Sales Agents	156 760	29.67	61 720	23.41
Sales Engineers	65 720	52.22	108 610	48.76
Telemarketers	164 160	13.72	28 550	12.14
Miscellaneous Sales and Related Workers	105 120	19.19	39 910	15.60
Door-to-Door Sales Workers, News and Street Vendors, and Related Workers	9 430	16.40	34 120	12.71
Sales and Related Workers, All Other	95 690	19.46	40 480	15.97
Office and Administrative Support Occupations	21 828 990	18.75	38 990	17.19
Supervisors of Office and Administrative Support Workers	1 477 560	28.53	59 340	26.83
First-Line Supervisors of Office and Administrative Support Workers	1 477 560	28.53	59 340	26.83
Communications Equipment Operators	78 860	15.45	32 140	14.36
Switchboard Operators, Including Answering Service	71 600	15.04	31 290	14.14
Telephone Operators	5 160	18.93	39 360	17.91
Miscellaneous Communications Equipment Operators	2 100	20.87	43 410	19.74
Communications Equipment Operators, All Other	2 100	20.87	43 410	19.74
Financial Clerks	2 978 640	19.07	39 660	18.02
Bill and Account Collectors	251 330	18.38	38 220	17.32
Billing and Posting Clerks	469 250	19.00	39 520	18.17
Bookkeeping, Accounting, and Auditing Clerks	1 530 430	20.25	42 110	19.35
Gaming Cage Workers	16 020	13.93	28 980	13.22
Payroll and Timekeeping Clerks	144 030	22.17	46 110	21.66
Procurement Clerks	68 100	20.76	43 180	20.51
Tellers	468 470	14.49	30 140	14.16
Miscellaneous Financial Clerks	31 010	21.00	43 670	19.72
Financial Clerks, All Other	31 010	21.00	43 670	19.72
Information and Record Clerks	5 773 540	17.19	35 750	15.91
Brokerage Clerks	55 100	25.93	53 940	24.71
Correspondence Clerks	5 460	18.75	38 990	17.93

[1]Annual wages have been calculated by multiplying the hourly mean wage by a "year-round, full-time" hours figure of 2,080 hours; for occupations with no published hourly mean wage, the annual wage has been directly calculated from the reported survey data.

Table 3-2. Employment and Wages, by Occupation, May 2018—*Continued*

(Number of people, dollars.)

Occupation	May 2018			
	Employment	Mean hourly wage	Mean annual wage[1]	Median hourly wage
Office and Administrative Support Occupations—*Continued*				
Court, Municipal, and License Clerks	142 350	19.76	41 100	18.48
Credit Authorizers, Checkers, and Clerks	29 980	19.55	40 670	18.63
Customer Service Representatives	2 871 400	17.53	36 470	16.23
Eligibility Interviewers, Government Programs	137 830	22.34	46 480	22.12
File Clerks	110 020	16.25	33 810	15.24
Hotel, Motel, and Resort Desk Clerks	260 780	12.08	25 130	11.39
Interviewers, Except Eligibility and Loan	192 820	17.08	35 520	16.38
Library Assistants, Clerical	88 970	13.92	28 960	12.74
Loan Interviewers and Clerks	222 620	19.86	41 310	19.18
New Accounts Clerks	41 500	17.79	37 000	17.21
Order Clerks	159 210	17.21	35 790	16.09
Human Resources Assistants, Except Payroll and Timekeeping	124 600	20.01	41 620	19.42
Receptionists and Information Clerks	1 043 630	14.59	30 350	14.01
Reservation and Transportation Ticket Agents and Travel Clerks	132 050	20.06	41 730	17.90
Miscellaneous Information and Record Clerks	155 220	20.15	41 900	19.69
Information and Record Clerks, All Other	155 220	20.15	41 900	19.69
Material Recording, Scheduling, Dispatching, and Distributing Workers	4 149 140	17.28	35 950	15.45
Cargo and Freight Agents	92 280	22.15	46 070	20.77
Couriers and Messengers	75 720	14.72	30 620	13.81
Dispatchers	294 900	20.70	43 050	19.17
Police, Fire, and Ambulance Dispatchers	95 020	20.81	43 290	19.55
Dispatchers, Except Police, Fire, and Ambulance	199 880	20.64	42 940	18.98
Meter Readers, Utilities	33 570	21.46	44 640	19.40
Postal Service Workers	525 070	24.78	51 540	28.25
Postal Service Clerks	78 830	24.45	50 860	26.58
Postal Service Mail Carriers	342 410	24.89	51 780	26.54
Postal Service Mail Sorters, Processors, and Processing Machine Operators	103 830	24.64	51 250	28.26
Production, Planning, and Expediting Clerks	350 150	24.05	50 020	22.88
Shipping, Receiving, and Traffic Clerks	655 590	16.82	34 980	15.88
Stock Clerks and Order Fillers	2 056 030	13.71	28 520	12.36
Weighers, Measurers, Checkers, and Samplers, Recordkeeping	65 830	16.39	34 100	15.53
Secretaries and Administrative Assistants	3 498 120	20.34	42 320	18.69
Executive Secretaries and Executive Administrative Assistants	570 530	29.59	61 550	28.53
Legal Secretaries	176 880	24.06	50 040	22.29
Medical Secretaries	585 410	17.83	37 090	17.19
Secretaries and Administrative Assistants, Except Legal, Medical, and Executive	2 165 310	18.28	38 030	17.61
Other Office and Administrative Support Workers	3 873 130	17.28	35 940	16.16
Computer Operators	34 700	22.47	46 750	22.04
Data Entry and Information Processing Workers	228 060	17.05	35 470	16.24
Data Entry Keyers	174 930	16.22	33 740	15.47
Word Processors and Typists	53 130	19.79	41 160	19.11
Desktop Publishers	10 740	22.47	46 750	20.63
Insurance Claims and Policy Processing Clerks	274 560	20.26	42 150	19.07
Mail Clerks and Mail Machine Operators, Except Postal Service	86 150	15.41	32 040	14.63
Office Clerks, General	2 972 930	16.92	35 200	15.74
Office Machine Operators, Except Computer	48 580	16.60	34 530	15.76
Proofreaders and Copy Markers	9 820	20.17	41 950	18.82
Statistical Assistants	11 010	24.09	50 110	23.24
Miscellaneous Office and Administrative Support Workers	196 570	18.02	37 480	16.76
Office and Administrative Support Workers, All Other	196 570	18.02	37 480	16.76
Farming, Fishing, and Forestry Occupations	480 130	14.49	30 140	12.20
Supervisors of Farming, Fishing, and Forestry Workers	21 800	24.42	50 790	22.57
First-Line Supervisors of Farming, Fishing, and Forestry Workers	21 800	24.42	50 790	22.57
Agricultural Workers	411 460	13.42	27 910	11.89
Agricultural Inspectors	13 240	22.10	45 970	21.22
Animal Breeders	2 160	20.71	43 080	17.82
Graders and Sorters, Agricultural Products	38 210	12.74	26 510	11.75
Miscellaneous Agricultural Workers	357 850	13.12	27 290	11.83
Agricultural Equipment Operators	26 060	15.68	32 620	14.99
Farmworkers and Laborers, Crop, Nursery, and Greenhouse	287 420	12.72	26 450	11.69
Farmworkers, Farm, Ranch, and Aquacultural Animals	37 780	13.87	28 840	12.77
Agricultural Workers, All Other	6 600	16.51	34 340	14.18
Forest, Conservation, and Logging Workers	44 910	19.47	40 500	18.64
Forest and Conservation Workers	7 510	15.06	31 320	13.20
Logging Workers	37 400	20.36	42 340	19.54
Fallers	4 680	23.33	48 520	21.19
Logging Equipment Operators	25 730	20.12	41 840	19.48
Log Graders and Scalers	3 330	18.78	39 060	18.38
Logging Workers, All Other	3 670	19.68	40 940	19.11
Construction and Extraction Occupations	5 962 640	24.62	51 220	22.12
Supervisors of Construction and Extraction Workers	598 210	33.91	70 540	31.36
First-Line Supervisors of Construction Trades and Extraction Workers	598 210	33.91	70 540	31.36
Construction Trades Workers	4 497 490	23.97	49 850	21.54
Boilermakers	13 870	30.41	63 240	29.88
Brickmasons, Blockmasons, and Stonemasons	76 240	25.39	52 810	23.78

[1]Annual wages have been calculated by multiplying the hourly mean wage by a "year-round, full-time" hours figure of 2,080 hours; for occupations with no published hourly mean wage, the annual wage has been directly calculated from the reported survey data.

Table 3-2. Employment and Wages, by Occupation, May 2018—*Continued*

(Number of people, dollars.)

Occupation	May 2018			
	Employment	Mean hourly wage	Mean annual wage[1]	Median hourly wage
Construction and Extraction Occupations—*Continued*				
Brickmasons and Blockmasons	63 930	26.17	54 430	24.49
Stonemasons	12 310	21.33	44 370	19.82
Carpenters	718 730	24.58	51 120	22.40
Carpet, Floor, and Tile Installers and Finishers	83 740	21.79	45 330	19.63
Carpet Installers	26 100	21.42	44 550	18.92
Floor Layers, Except Carpet, Wood, and Hard Tiles	14 050	22.48	46 760	20.56
Floor Sanders and Finishers	4 460	19.18	39 890	18.04
Tile and Marble Setters	39 130	22.09	45 950	20.12
Cement Masons, Concrete Finishers, and Terrazzo Workers	189 130	22.76	47 340	20.67
Cement Masons and Concrete Finishers	186 400	22.76	47 350	20.67
Terrazzo Workers and Finishers	2 730	22.71	47 230	20.43
Construction Laborers	1 001 470	19.40	40 350	17.21
Construction Equipment Operators	433 690	25.09	52 190	22.59
Paving, Surfacing, and Tamping Equipment Operators	46 760	21.32	44 360	19.13
Pile-Driver Operators	3 450	30.94	64 360	28.21
Operating Engineers and Other Construction Equipment Operators	383 480	25.50	53 030	22.98
Drywall Installers, Ceiling Tile Installers, and Tapers	120 220	24.24	50 420	21.72
Drywall and Ceiling Tile Installers	101 900	23.64	49 170	21.03
Tapers	18 320	27.57	57 340	26.48
Electricians	655 840	28.46	59 190	26.53
Glaziers	50 940	23.38	48 620	20.94
Insulation Workers	56 440	22.55	46 910	20.15
Insulation Workers, Floor, Ceiling, and Wall	31 840	20.23	42 070	18.50
Insulation Workers, Mechanical	24 610	25.57	53 180	22.95
Painters and Paperhangers	231 200	20.69	43 030	18.72
Painters, Construction and Maintenance	228 420	20.70	43 050	18.72
Paperhangers	2 780	19.64	40 840	18.31
Pipelayers, Plumbers, Pipefitters, and Steamfitters	476 140	27.39	56 980	25.33
Pipelayers	38 070	20.91	43 500	18.54
Plumbers, Pipefitters, and Steamfitters	438 070	27.96	58 150	25.92
Plasterers and Stucco Masons	24 870	22.89	47 610	20.93
Reinforcing Iron and Rebar Workers	18 360	26.28	54 670	23.23
Roofers	128 680	21.09	43 870	19.22
Sheet Metal Workers	131 570	25.34	52 710	23.30
Structural Iron and Steel Workers	77 410	27.97	58 170	25.95
Solar Photovoltaic Installers	8 950	22.12	46 010	20.52
Helpers, Construction Trades	233 580	15.82	32 900	15.00
Helpers–Brickmasons, Blockmasons, Stonemasons, and Tile and Marble Setters	24 340	17.50	36 390	16.05
Helpers–Carpenters	33 020	15.32	31 850	14.85
Helpers–Electricians	75 970	15.84	32 960	15.10
Helpers–Painters, Paperhangers, Plasterers, and Stucco Masons	10 600	15.25	31 720	14.40
Helpers–Pipelayers, Plumbers, Pipefitters, and Steamfitters	54 710	15.66	32 570	14.89
Helpers–Roofers	8 630	15.26	31 740	14.61
Helpers, Construction Trades, All Other	26 320	15.56	32 370	14.67
Other Construction and Related Workers	422 540	24.15	50 240	21.72
Construction and Building Inspectors	104 090	30.36	63 150	28.70
Elevator Installers and Repairers	26 830	38.16	79 370	38.36
Fence Erectors	23 530	18.10	37 650	16.73
Hazardous Materials Removal Workers	44 000	22.62	47 050	20.21
Highway Maintenance Workers	149 260	19.92	41 440	19.08
Rail-Track Laying and Maintenance Equipment Operators	14 410	27.46	57 120	27.37
Septic Tank Servicers and Sewer Pipe Cleaners	27 090	19.97	41 530	18.74
Miscellaneous Construction and Related Workers	33 340	20.68	43 000	18.68
Extraction Workers	210 820	22.96	47 760	21.34
Derrick, Rotary Drill, and Service Unit Operators, Oil, Gas, and Mining	79 030	25.46	52 950	23.36
Derrick Operators, Oil and Gas	11 310	22.90	47 630	22.17
Rotary Drill Operators, Oil and Gas	18 010	27.28	56 740	25.86
Service Unit Operators, Oil, Gas, and Mining	49 710	25.38	52 780	23.01
Earth Drillers, Except Oil and Gas	18 270	22.87	47 570	21.36
Explosives Workers, Ordnance Handling Experts, and Blasters	5 640	25.38	52 780	23.97
Mining Machine Operators	22 910	25.53	53 090	25.34
Continuous Mining Machine Operators	14 710	26.19	54 470	26.21
Mine Cutting and Channeling Machine Operators	4 920	23.59	49 080	22.68
Mining Machine Operators, All Other	3 280	25.44	52 920	24.76
Rock Splitters, Quarry	4 870	17.19	35 760	16.71
Roof Bolters, Mining	3 250	28.41	59 090	28.20
Roustabouts, Oil and Gas	54 810	19.34	40 220	18.07
Helpers–Extraction Workers	15 930	18.10	37 660	17.48
Miscellaneous Extraction Workers	6 110	26.10	54 300	26.37
Installation, Maintenance, and Repair Occupations	5 628 880	23.54	48 960	21.89
Supervisors of Installation, Maintenance, and Repair Workers	471 820	33.33	69 320	31.80
First-Line Supervisors of Mechanics, Installers, and Repairers	471 820	33.33	69 320	31.80
Electrical and Electronic Equipment Mechanics, Installers, and Repairers	583 310	25.57	53 190	24.53
Computer, Automated Teller, and Office Machine Repairers	102 810	19.65	40 880	18.50
Radio and Telecommunications Equipment Installers and Repairers	243 820	27.42	57 030	26.93

[1]Annual wages have been calculated by multiplying the hourly mean wage by a "year-round, full-time" hours figure of 2,080 hours; for occupations with no published hourly mean wage, the annual wage has been directly calculated from the reported survey data.

Table 3-2. Employment and Wages, by Occupation, May 2018—*Continued*

(Number of people, dollars.)

Occupation	May 2018			
	Employment	Mean hourly wage	Mean annual wage[1]	Median hourly wage
Installation, Maintenance, and Repair Occupations—*Continued*				
Radio, Cellular, and Tower Equipment Installers and Repairers	13 930	27.09	56 340	26.39
Telecommunications Equipment Installers and Repairers, Except Line Installers	229 890	27.44	57 080	26.97
Miscellaneous Electrical and Electronic Equipment Mechanics, Installers, and Repairers	236 690	26.23	54 570	25.27
Avionics Technicians	18 860	31.41	65 330	30.84
Electric Motor, Power Tool, and Related Repairers	15 800	22.00	45 770	20.60
Electrical and Electronics Installers and Repairers, Transportation Equipment	11 680	29.55	61 460	29.01
Electrical and Electronics Repairers, Commercial and Industrial Equipment	59 520	28.47	59 210	27.94
Electrical and Electronics Repairers, Powerhouse, Substation, and Relay	22 980	38.48	80 040	38.56
Electronic Equipment Installers and Repairers, Motor Vehicles	10 880	17.67	36 750	17.11
Electronic Home Entertainment Equipment Installers and Repairers	26 070	19.13	39 800	18.35
Security and Fire Alarm Systems Installers	70 900	23.34	48 540	22.69
Vehicle and Mobile Equipment Mechanics, Installers, and Repairers	1 614 070	22.21	46 200	20.83
Aircraft Mechanics and Service Technicians	131 690	31.36	65 230	30.25
Automotive Technicians and Repairers	809 740	21.17	44 030	19.63
Automotive Body and Related Repairers	142 060	22.34	46 460	20.55
Automotive Glass Installers and Repairers	19 640	17.49	36 370	16.43
Automotive Service Technicians and Mechanics	648 050	21.02	43 730	19.57
Bus and Truck Mechanics and Diesel Engine Specialists	264 860	23.63	49 150	22.76
Heavy Vehicle and Mobile Equipment Service Technicians and Mechanics	199 280	24.89	51 780	24.19
Farm Equipment Mechanics and Service Technicians	34 300	20.29	42 190	19.54
Mobile Heavy Equipment Mechanics, Except Engines	140 260	25.66	53 370	24.96
Rail Car Repairers	24 720	26.93	56 020	27.03
Small Engine Mechanics	69 130	18.84	39 180	17.82
Motorboat Mechanics and Service Technicians	22 280	20.35	42 330	19.32
Motorcycle Mechanics	15 090	18.87	39 260	17.69
Outdoor Power Equipment and Other Small Engine Mechanics	31 760	17.76	36 940	17.02
Miscellaneous Vehicle and Mobile Equipment Mechanics, Installers, and Repairers	139 370	14.80	30 780	13.84
Bicycle Repairers	12 200	14.56	30 290	13.92
Recreational Vehicle Service Technicians	15 560	19.28	40 090	18.35
Tire Repairers and Changers	111 620	14.20	29 530	13.41
Other Installation, Maintenance, and Repair Occupations	2 959 670	22.30	46 380	20.68
Control and Valve Installers and Repairers	74 400	25.70	53 460	23.89
Mechanical Door Repairers	22 670	20.84	43 350	19.71
Control and Valve Installers and Repairers, Except Mechanical Door	51 730	27.83	57 890	26.96
Heating, Air Conditioning, and Refrigeration Mechanics and Installers	324 310	24.12	50 160	22.89
Home Appliance Repairers	31 130	19.72	41 020	18.88
Industrial Machinery Installation, Repair, and Maintenance Workers	487 640	25.64	53 330	24.82
Industrial Machinery Mechanics	362 440	25.96	54 000	25.16
Maintenance Workers, Machinery	80 270	23.42	48 720	22.63
Millwrights	43 810	27.04	56 250	26.47
Refractory Materials Repairers, Except Brickmasons	1 120	25.24	52 510	25.09
Line Installers and Repairers	233 010	31.03	64 540	31.67
Electrical Power-Line Installers and Repairers	114 800	33.77	70 240	34.09
Telecommunications Line Installers and Repairers	118 200	28.36	59 000	28.02
Precision Instrument and Equipment Repairers	72 010	24.58	51 120	23.13
Camera and Photographic Equipment Repairers	3 690	20.45	42 540	19.53
Medical Equipment Repairers	46 320	25.34	52 710	23.66
Musical Instrument Repairers and Tuners	8 450	18.81	39 110	17.47
Watch Repairers	2 610	21.55	44 830	19.19
Precision Instrument and Equipment Repairers, All Other	10 930	27.91	58 060	27.70
Maintenance and Repair Workers, General	1 384 240	19.72	41 020	18.42
Wind Turbine Service Technicians	5 580	27.88	58 000	26.14
Miscellaneous Installation, Maintenance, and Repair Workers	347 350	19.25	40 040	17.39
Coin, Vending, and Amusement Machine Servicers and Repairers	32 920	17.49	36 390	16.61
Commercial Divers	3 380	28.59	59 470	23.63
Fabric Menders, Except Garment	400	16.13	33 550	14.77
Locksmiths and Safe Repairers	16 970	21.03	43 740	19.93
Manufactured Building and Mobile Home Installers	2 920	15.82	32 910	15.40
Riggers	20 970	24.68	51 330	24.22
Signal and Track Switch Repairers	7 730	32.60	67 800	33.89
Helpers–Installation, Maintenance, and Repair Workers	105 040	15.09	31 390	14.16
Installation, Maintenance, and Repair Workers, All Other	157 030	20.70	43 050	18.90
Production Occupations	9 115 530	18.84	39 190	16.86
Supervisors of Production Workers	622 790	30.93	64 340	29.05
First-Line Supervisors of Production and Operating Workers	622 790	30.93	64 340	29.05
Assemblers and Fabricators	1 831 200	17.14	35 650	15.78
Aircraft Structure, Surfaces, Rigging, and Systems Assemblers	43 150	26.70	55 530	25.64
Electrical, Electronics, and Electromechanical Assemblers	287 630	17.26	35 910	16.20
Coil Winders, Tapers, and Finishers	12 190	17.60	36 610	16.54
Electrical, Electronic, and Electromechanical Assemblers, Except Coil Winders, Tapers, and Finishers	275 450	17.25	35 880	16.18
Engine and Other Machine Assemblers	48 200	21.79	45 330	21.34
Structural Metal Fabricators and Fitters	76 090	20.02	41 640	18.89
Miscellaneous Assemblers and Fabricators	1 376 130	16.49	34 300	15.19

[1]Annual wages have been calculated by multiplying the hourly mean wage by a "year-round, full-time" hours figure of 2,080 hours; for occupations with no published hourly mean wage, the annual wage has been directly calculated from the reported survey data.

Table 3-2. Employment and Wages, by Occupation, May 2018—*Continued*

(Number of people, dollars.)

Occupation	May 2018			
	Employment	Mean hourly wage	Mean annual wage[1]	Median hourly wage
Production Occupations—*Continued*				
Fiberglass Laminators and Fabricators	21 190	17.39	36 170	16.59
Timing Device Assemblers and Adjusters	780	18.01	37 460	16.66
Assemblers and Fabricators, All Other, Including Team Assemblers	1 354 150	16.48	34 270	15.16
Food Processing Workers	801 770	14.46	30 090	13.58
Bakers	180 010	13.78	28 660	12.75
Butchers and Other Meat, Poultry, and Fish Processing Workers	365 660	14.38	29 910	13.69
Butchers and Meat Cutters	133 670	15.97	33 210	15.18
Meat, Poultry, and Fish Cutters and Trimmers	156 440	13.36	27 790	12.96
Slaughterers and Meat Packers	75 550	13.68	28 450	13.59
Miscellaneous Food Processing Workers	256 100	15.07	31 340	13.99
Food and Tobacco Roasting, Baking, and Drying Machine Operators and Tenders	21 060	15.74	32 730	14.83
Food Batchmakers	160 160	15.43	32 090	14.29
Food Cooking Machine Operators and Tenders	32 260	15.23	31 690	14.48
Food Processing Workers, All Other	42 620	13.26	27 590	12.44
Metal Workers and Plastic Workers	1 940 370	19.94	41 480	18.70
Computer Control Programmers and Operators	171 920	21.13	43 940	19.95
Computer-Controlled Machine Tool Operators, Metal and Plastic	148 150	20.17	41 960	19.26
Computer Numerically Controlled Machine Tool Programmers, Metal and Plastic	23 770	27.07	56 300	25.57
Forming Machine Setters, Operators, and Tenders, Metal and Plastic	120 630	18.35	38 170	17.52
Extruding and Drawing Machine Setters, Operators, and Tenders, Metal and Plastic	75 610	17.61	36 620	16.90
Forging Machine Setters, Operators, and Tenders, Metal and Plastic	18 330	19.60	40 770	18.70
Rolling Machine Setters, Operators, and Tenders, Metal and Plastic	26 700	19.61	40 790	18.58
Machine Tool Cutting Setters, Operators, and Tenders, Metal and Plastic	318 860	18.00	37 450	17.05
Cutting, Punching, and Press Machine Setters, Operators, and Tenders, Metal and Plastic	186 640	17.40	36 180	16.57
Drilling and Boring Machine Tool Setters, Operators, and Tenders, Metal and Plastic	11 400	19.95	41 490	18.28
Grinding, Lapping, Polishing, and Buffing Machine Tool Setters, Operators, and Tenders, Metal and Plastic	71 870	17.64	36 690	16.76
Lathe and Turning Machine Tool Setters, Operators, and Tenders, Metal and Plastic	29 510	19.76	41 090	18.84
Milling and Planing Machine Setters, Operators, and Tenders, Metal and Plastic	19 440	21.39	44 490	20.95
Machinists	384 350	21.75	45 250	20.97
Metal Furnace Operators, Tenders, Pourers, and Casters	25 520	19.79	41 160	19.18
Metal-Refining Furnace Operators and Tenders	17 670	20.10	41 810	19.82
Pourers and Casters, Metal	7 850	19.07	39 670	18.14
Model Makers and Patternmakers, Metal and Plastic	8 090	25.69	53 430	24.88
Model Makers, Metal and Plastic	5 210	27.36	56 920	26.98
Patternmakers, Metal and Plastic	2 880	22.66	47 130	22.04
Molders and Molding Machine Setters, Operators, and Tenders, Metal and Plastic	179 710	16.44	34 200	15.30
Foundry Mold and Coremakers	15 600	17.70	36 820	17.04
Molding, Coremaking, and Casting Machine Setters, Operators, and Tenders, Metal and Plastic	164 110	16.32	33 950	15.13
Multiple Machine Tool Setters, Operators, and Tenders, Metal and Plastic	133 840	18.03	37 510	17.01
Tool and Die Makers	72 700	25.79	53 650	25.36
Welding, Soldering, and Brazing Workers	424 270	21.12	43 930	19.71
Welders, Cutters, Solderers, and Brazers	389 190	21.33	44 360	19.89
Welding, Soldering, and Brazing Machine Setters, Operators, and Tenders	35 080	18.83	39 160	18.11
Miscellaneous Metal Workers and Plastic Workers	100 470	18.24	37 940	17.14
Heat Treating Equipment Setters, Operators, and Tenders, Metal and Plastic	19 690	18.77	39 050	18.04
Layout Workers, Metal and Plastic	8 170	22.78	47 380	23.03
Plating and Coating Machine Setters, Operators, and Tenders, Metal and Plastic	40 070	16.74	34 830	15.58
Tool Grinders, Filers, and Sharpeners	7 070	19.66	40 890	18.34
Metal Workers and Plastic Workers, All Other	25 470	18.34	38 140	17.27
Printing Workers	249 140	18.39	38 260	17.36
Prepress Technicians and Workers	29 990	20.31	42 240	19.43
Printing Press Operators	173 470	18.49	38 470	17.41
Print Binding and Finishing Workers	45 690	16.76	34 850	15.81
Textile, Apparel, and Furnishings Workers	574 130	13.31	27 690	12.11
Laundry and Dry-Cleaning Workers	213 350	11.77	24 480	11.16
Pressers, Textile, Garment, and Related Materials	38 320	11.57	24 060	11.23
Sewing Machine Operators	136 450	12.98	26 990	12.03
Shoe and Leather Workers	12 450	14.37	29 900	14.09
Shoe and Leather Workers and Repairers	8 640	14.33	29 800	13.87
Shoe Machine Operators and Tenders	3 810	14.47	30 110	14.63
Tailors, Dressmakers, and Sewers	26 500	16.04	33 350	14.59
Sewers, Hand	5 350	14.19	29 510	13.78
Tailors, Dressmakers, and Custom Sewers	21 150	16.50	34 330	14.90
Textile Machine Setters, Operators, and Tenders	75 490	14.37	29 880	13.88
Textile Bleaching and Dyeing Machine Operators and Tenders	9 330	14.39	29 930	13.84
Textile Cutting Machine Setters, Operators, and Tenders	13 310	14.16	29 440	13.57
Textile Knitting and Weaving Machine Setters, Operators, and Tenders	21 190	14.65	30 470	14.02
Textile Winding, Twisting, and Drawing Out Machine Setters, Operators, and Tenders	31 650	14.26	29 660	13.90
Miscellaneous Textile, Apparel, and Furnishings Workers	71 570	17.18	35 740	15.99
Extruding and Forming Machine Setters, Operators, and Tenders, Synthetic and Glass Fibers	18 130	17.07	35 500	16.44
Fabric and Apparel Patternmakers	5 220	23.65	49 180	19.50
Upholsterers	32 870	17.27	35 920	16.58
Textile, Apparel, and Furnishings Workers, All Other	15 360	14.94	31 070	13.34
Woodworkers	257 840	16.19	33 680	15.19
Cabinetmakers and Bench Carpenters	102 100	17.59	36 580	16.70

[1]Annual wages have been calculated by multiplying the hourly mean wage by a "year-round, full-time" hours figure of 2,080 hours; for occupations with no published hourly mean wage, the annual wage has been directly calculated from the reported survey data.

Table 3-2. Employment and Wages, by Occupation, May 2018—*Continued*

(Number of people, dollars.)

Occupation	May 2018			
	Employment	Mean hourly wage	Mean annual wage[1]	Median hourly wage
Production Occupations—*Continued*				
Furniture Finishers	17 250	16.27	33 850	15.36
Model Makers and Patternmakers, Wood	1 280	26.70	55 540	27.07
Model Makers, Wood	740	25.29	52 590	25.53
Patternmakers, Wood	530	28.68	59 650	29.30
Woodworking Machine Setters, Operators, and Tenders	131 240	14.98	31 150	14.25
Sawing Machine Setters, Operators, and Tenders, Wood	52 260	15.00	31 200	14.18
Woodworking Machine Setters, Operators, and Tenders, Except Sawing	78 980	14.96	31 110	14.29
Miscellaneous Woodworkers	5 970	16.60	34 530	14.98
Woodworkers, All Other	5 970	16.60	34 530	14.98
Plant and System Operators	301 200	29.72	61 820	28.42
Power Plant Operators, Distributors, and Dispatchers	51 820	39.31	81 760	39.92
Nuclear Power Reactor Operators	6 280	45.82	95 310	45.36
Power Distributors and Dispatchers	11 620	41.03	85 340	41.54
Power Plant Operators	33 920	37.51	78 030	38.27
Stationary Engineers and Boiler Operators	31 710	30.62	63 690	29.06
Water and Wastewater Treatment Plant and System Operators	123 650	23.79	49 490	22.49
Miscellaneous Plant and System Operators	94 010	31.94	66 430	31.85
Chemical Plant and System Operators	28 190	29.60	61 570	29.84
Gas Plant Operators	14 620	34.36	71 470	34.17
Petroleum Pump System Operators, Refinery Operators, and Gaugers	38 930	33.96	70 630	34.07
Plant and System Operators, All Other	12 270	28.03	58 300	27.45
Other Production Occupations	2 537 090	17.92	37 270	16.35
Chemical Processing Machine Setters, Operators, and Tenders	132 660	23.30	48 470	21.97
Chemical Equipment Operators and Tenders	82 880	24.55	51 070	23.45
Separating, Filtering, Clarifying, Precipitating, and Still Machine Setters, Operators, and Tenders	49 770	21.22	44 140	19.62
Crushing, Grinding, Polishing, Mixing, and Blending Workers	190 770	18.25	37 960	17.25
Crushing, Grinding, and Polishing Machine Setters, Operators, and Tenders	31 890	18.30	38 060	17.50
Grinding and Polishing Workers, Hand	30 280	15.34	31 900	14.21
Mixing and Blending Machine Setters, Operators, and Tenders	128 600	18.92	39 360	17.89
Cutting Workers	71 420	16.87	35 090	16.26
Cutters and Trimmers, Hand	10 580	15.19	31 600	14.13
Cutting and Slicing Machine Setters, Operators, and Tenders	60 840	17.16	35 700	16.64
Extruding, Forming, Pressing, and Compacting Machine Setters, Operators, and Tenders	72 870	17.69	36 800	16.89
Furnace, Kiln, Oven, Drier, and Kettle Operators and Tenders	17 730	19.52	40 610	18.83
Inspectors, Testers, Sorters, Samplers, and Weighers	557 510	20.20	42 010	18.39
Jewelers and Precious Stone and Metal Workers	25 910	20.95	43 570	18.96
Medical, Dental, and Ophthalmic Laboratory Technicians	77 110	19.15	39 840	17.64
Dental Laboratory Technicians	34 480	20.76	43 180	19.44
Medical Appliance Technicians	14 670	20.28	42 180	18.84
Ophthalmic Laboratory Technicians	27 960	16.58	34 490	15.30
Packaging and Filling Machine Operators and Tenders	395 330	15.74	32 740	14.50
Painting Workers	156 470	19.16	39 850	17.70
Coating, Painting, and Spraying Machine Setters, Operators, and Tenders	88 560	17.55	36 510	16.73
Painters, Transportation Equipment	55 710	22.34	46 460	20.33
Painting, Coating, and Decorating Workers	12 200	16.33	33 960	14.93
Semiconductor Processors	25 730	19.14	39 810	17.92
Photographic Process Workers and Processing Machine Operators	16 680	16.78	34 910	14.03
Miscellaneous Production Workers	796 900	16.02	33 320	14.53
Adhesive Bonding Machine Operators and Tenders	16 310	17.23	35 850	16.26
Cleaning, Washing, and Metal Pickling Equipment Operators and Tenders	17 630	15.91	33 090	14.80
Cooling and Freezing Equipment Operators and Tenders	8 820	16.60	34 520	15.58
Etchers and Engravers	8 600	16.61	34 550	15.06
Molders, Shapers, and Casters, Except Metal and Plastic	42 500	16.92	35 190	16.03
Paper Goods Machine Setters, Operators, and Tenders	97 960	19.38	40 320	18.62
Tire Builders	23 920	21.89	45 530	22.42
Helpers–Production Workers	350 410	14.12	29 380	13.33
Production Workers, All Other	230 760	16.58	34 490	14.50
Transportation and Material Moving Occupations	10 244 260	18.41	38 290	15.74
Supervisors of Transportation and Material Moving Workers	419 980	27.92	58 070	26.67
Aircraft Cargo Handling Supervisors	8 920	26.49	55 110	23.37
First-Line Supervisors of Transportation and Material Moving Workers, Except Aircraft Cargo Handling Supervisors	411 060	27.95	58 140	26.73
Air Transportation Workers	271 890	(2)	101 910	(2)
Aircraft Pilots and Flight Engineers	120 760	(2)	146 660	(2)
Airline Pilots, Copilots, and Flight Engineers	82 890	(2)	169 560	(2)
Commercial Pilots	37 870	(2)	96 530	(2)
Air Traffic Controllers and Airfield Operations Specialists	32 360	48.61	101 100	46.11
Air Traffic Controllers	22 390	58.09	120 830	59.87
Airfield Operations Specialists	9 960	27.29	56 760	25.10

[1]Annual wages have been calculated by multiplying the hourly mean wage by a "year-round, full-time" hours figure of 2,080 hours; for occupations with no published hourly mean wage, the annual wage has been directly calculated from the reported survey data.
[2]Wages for some occupations that do not generally entail year-round, full-time employment are reported as either hourly wages or annual salaries (depending on how employees are typically paid).

Table 3-2. Employment and Wages, by Occupation, May 2018—*Continued*

(Number of people, dollars.)

Occupation	May 2018			
	Employment	Mean hourly wage	Mean annual wage[1]	Median hourly wage
Transportation Occupations—*Continued*				
Flight Attendants	118 770	(2)	56 630	(2)
Motor Vehicle Operators	4 088 870	18.94	39 400	17.85
Ambulance Drivers and Attendants, Except Emergency Medical Technicians	15 380	13.95	29 010	12.38
Bus Drivers	678 260	17.44	36 280	16.56
Bus Drivers, Transit and Intercity	174 110	21.47	44 650	20.23
Bus Drivers, School or Special Client	504 150	16.05	33 390	15.58
Driver/Sales Workers and Truck Drivers	3 130 500	19.68	40 920	18.66
Driver/Sales Workers	414 860	14.24	29 610	11.88
Heavy and Tractor-Trailer Truck Drivers	1 800 330	21.91	45 570	21.00
Light Truck or Delivery Services Drivers	915 310	17.75	36 920	15.78
Taxi Drivers and Chauffeurs	207 920	13.68	28 450	12.49
Miscellaneous Motor Vehicle Operators	56 810	17.14	35 640	14.60
Motor Vehicle Operators, All Other	56 810	17.14	35 640	14.60
Rail Transportation Workers	109 460	30.95	64 380	29.69
Locomotive Engineers and Operators	41 090	31.37	65 240	29.41
Locomotive Engineers	34 850	32.17	66 920	29.86
Locomotive Firers	560	33.19	69 030	30.69
Rail Yard Engineers, Dinkey Operators, and Hostlers	5 690	26.27	54 640	25.30
Railroad Brake, Signal, and Switch Operators	14 270	28.31	58 890	27.53
Railroad Conductors and Yardmasters	42 360	31.77	66 080	30.26
Subway and Streetcar Operators	8 850	30.28	62 970	32.78
Miscellaneous Rail Transportation Workers	2 890	28.12	58 490	26.64
Water Transportation Workers	79 860	31.75	66 040	26.16
Sailors and Marine Oilers	32 220	22.20	46 180	19.66
Ship and Boat Captains and Operators	38 910	38.61	80 310	32.40
Captains, Mates, and Pilots of Water Vessels	36 390	39.61	82 380	33.26
Motorboat Operators	2 510	24.21	50 350	24.18
Ship Engineers	8 740	36.40	75 710	34.20
Other Transportation Workers	363 130	15.61	32 460	12.23
Bridge and Lock Tenders	3 170	22.91	47 660	24.19
Parking Lot Attendants	145 900	12.08	25 130	11.47
Automotive and Watercraft Service Attendants	113 760	12.47	25 940	11.64
Traffic Technicians	7 290	24.38	50 700	22.39
Transportation Inspectors	29 990	36.22	75 330	35.47
Transportation Attendants, Except Flight Attendants	25 460	14.73	30 640	12.87
Miscellaneous Transportation Workers	37 560	20.61	42 870	18.03
Transportation Workers, All Other	37 560	20.61	42 870	18.03
Material Moving Workers	4 911 060	15.17	31 560	13.74
Conveyor Operators and Tenders	23 390	16.88	35 110	15.86
Crane and Tower Operators	44 410	27.96	58 160	26.03
Dredge, Excavating, and Loading Machine Operators	49 780	23.46	48 790	21.44
Dredge Operators	1 190	22.84	47 500	21.76
Excavating and Loading Machine and Dragline Operators	46 090	23.40	48 680	21.28
Loading Machine Operators, Underground Mining	2 500	24.73	51 450	24.60
Hoist and Winch Operators	3 180	27.11	56 390	21.87
Industrial Truck and Tractor Operators	604 130	17.54	36 480	16.71
Laborers and Material Movers, Hand	4 002 390	14.32	29 790	13.02
Cleaners of Vehicles and Equipment	378 850	12.93	26 900	11.79
Laborers and Freight, Stock, and Material Movers, Hand	2 893 180	14.85	30 890	13.59
Machine Feeders and Offbearers	66 380	15.24	31 710	14.21
Packers and Packagers, Hand	663 970	12.74	26 490	11.82
Pumping Station Operators	27 560	25.24	52 510	24.47
Gas Compressor and Gas Pumping Station Operators	3 460	30.24	62 900	31.35
Pump Operators, Except Wellhead Pumpers	10 820	22.84	47 510	21.34
Wellhead Pumpers	13 280	25.90	53 870	25.72
Refuse and Recyclable Material Collectors	118 520	19.50	40 560	17.92
Mine Shuttle Car Operators	1 690	26.99	56 150	27.09
Tank Car, Truck, and Ship Loaders	9 000	20.35	42 330	18.38
Miscellaneous Material Moving Workers	27 010	16.83	35 000	14.14

[1]Annual wages have been calculated by multiplying the hourly mean wage by a "year-round, full-time" hours figure of 2,080 hours; for occupations with no published hourly mean wage, the annual wage has been directly calculated from the reported survey data.
[2]Wages for some occupations that do not generally entail year-round, full-time employment are reported as either hourly wages or annual salaries (depending on how employees are typically paid).

CHAPTER 4: LABOR FORCE AND EMPLOYMENT PROJECTIONS BY INDUSTRY AND OCCUPATION

HIGHLIGHTS

Every two years, the Bureau of Labor Statistics (BLS) develops decade-long projections for industry output, employment, and occupations. This chapter presents the employment outlook for the 2018–2028 period. The projections are based on a set of explicit assumptions and an application of a model of economic relationships.

Figure 4-1. Percent Distribution of Population by Age, 16 Years and Over, 1996 and 2026

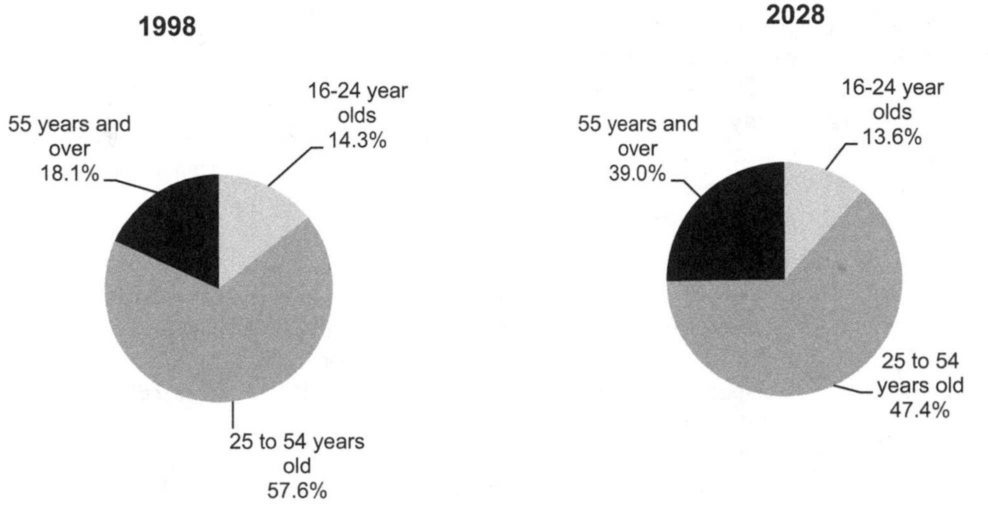

From 2018 to 2028, the civilian non-institutional population is projected to grow at an annual rate of 0.8 percent. The number of Hispanics is expected to grow at a much faster rate than the general population, increasing at a rate of 2.4 percent per year. In contrast, the number of White non-Hispanics is expected to increase at a rate of 0.1 percent. (See Table 4-1.)

OTHER HIGHLIGHTS

- It is projected that there will also be significant variation in growth rates by age group. While the number of persons 75 years and over is expected to increase by 4.0 percent, the number of those aged 55 to 64 is expected to decline 0.6 percent while the 16 to 19 age population is expected to decline 0.1 percent. (See Table 4-1.)

- The number of jobs in the healthcare and social assistance sector is projected to grow rapidly between 2018 and 2028. Of the 30 fastest growing occupations, 18 are in healthcare and related occupations. Increased demand for healthcare services from an aging population and people with chronic conditions will drive much of the expected population growth. (See Table 4-8)

- Meanwhile, employment is expected to decline for several occupations such as mail carriers, administrative assistants, and data entry workers due to advances in technology and automation. (See Table 4-4)

- The labor force continues to age. The median age of the labor force was 38.8 in 1998, 41.2 in 2008, 41.9 in 2018, and is projected to be 42.5 in 2028. (See Table 4-7.)

NOTES AND DEFINITIONS

The Bureau of Labor Statistics (BLS) develops long-term projections of likely employment patterns in the U.S. economy. Since the early 1970s, projections have been prepared on a 2-year cycle. The last projections were released in September 2019. The projections cover the future size and composition of the labor force, aggregate economic growth, detailed estimates of industry production, and industry and occupational employment. The resulting data serve a variety of users who need information about expected patterns of economic growth and the effects these patterns are expected to have on employment. For example, information about future employment opportunities by occupation is used by counselors, educators, and others helping people choose a career and by officials who plan education and training programs.

The labor force projections are a function of two components—projections of the population and projections of labor force participation rates. Population projections are provided by the Census Bureau for detailed age, sex, race, and ethnicity groupings. BLS extrapolates participation rates for these same categories by applying well-specified smoothing and time series techniques to historical time series for the detailed participation rates.

Concepts and Definitions

Economic dependency ratio. This ratio is measured *by* measured by estimating the number of persons in the total population (including all Armed Forces personnel overseas and children) who are *not* in the labor force per hundred of those who are.

Employment. In the employment projections survey, employment is defined as a count of jobs, not a count of individual workers.

Employment change. The numerical change in employment measures the projected number of job gains or losses.

Employment change, percent. The percent change in employment measures the projected rate of change of employment in an occupation. A rapidly growing occupation usually indicates favorable prospects for employment. However, even modest employment growth in a large occupation can result in many more job openings due to growth than can rapid employment growth in a small occupation.

Job openings due to growth and replacement needs. Estimates of the projected number of net entrants into an occupation. For occupations that require training, the data may be used to assess the minimum number of workers who will need to be trained. The number of openings due to growth is the positive employment change from 2018 to 2028. If employment declines, then there are no job openings due to growth. The number of openings due to replacement needs is the net number of workers leaving an occupation who will need to be replaced.

On-the-Job Training Terms:

Apprenticeship. An apprenticeship is a formal relationship between a worker and sponsor that combines technical instruction and on-the-job training. The typical programs provides at least 2,000 hours of on-the-job training per year over a 3-to-5 year period and 144 hours of technical instruction. Apprenticeship programs are sponsored by individual employers, joint employer-and-labor groups, and employer associations.

Internship/residency. An internship or residency typically involves supervised training in a professional setting such as a classroom or hospital. Internships and/or residency programs are often required for certification or to obtain a license in fields such as architecture, counseling, medicine, and teaching. This does not include internships that are recommended for advancement.

Moderate-term on-the-job training. Skills needed for a worker to become fully qualified can be acquired during 1 to 12 months of combined on-the-job experience and informal training. Examples include heavy and tractor-trailer truck drivers and medical secretaries.

Short-term on-the-job training. Skills needed for a worker to become fully qualified can be acquired during a short demonstration of job duties or during 1 month or less of on-the-job experience or instruction. Examples include retail salespersons and waiters and waitresses.

Long-term on-the-job training. More than 12 months of on-the-job training or, alternatively, combined work experience and formal classroom instruction are needed for workers to develop the skills to become fully qualified. This category includes formal or informal apprenticeships that may last up to 5 years. Long-term on-the-job training also includes intensive occupation-specific, employer-sponsored programs that workers must complete. Such programs include those offered by fire and police academies and schools for air traffic controllers and flight attendants. Individuals undergoing training usually are considered to be employed in the occupation. Also included in this category is the development of some natural ability.

Sources of Additional Information

A complete presentation of the projections, including analysis of results and additional tables and a comprehensive description of the methodology, can be found in the October 2019 edition of the *Monthly Labor Review* which is available on the BLS Web site at https://www.bls.gov/mlr/. In addition, more information on employment projections can be found on the BLS Web site at < https://www.bls.gov/emp/home.htm />.

Table 4-1. Civilian Noninstitutional Population, by Age, Sex, Race, and Hispanic Origin, 1998, 2008, 2018, and Projected 2028

(Numbers in thousands, percent.)

Age, sex, race, and Hispanic origin	Level				Change		
	1998	2008	2018	2028	1998–2008	2008–2018	2018–2028
Both Sexes, 16 Years and Over	205 220	233 788	257 791	279 454	28 568	24 003	21 663
16 to 24 years	33 237	37 484	38 005	38 109	4 247	521	104
16 to 19 years	15 644	17 075	16 766	16 628	1 431	-309	-138
20 to 24 years	17 593	20 409	21 239	21 481	2 816	830	242
25 to 54 years	117 450	125 652	126 389	132 472	8 202	737	6 083
25 to 34 years	38 778	39 993	44 581	45 257	1 215	4 588	676
35 to 44 years	44 299	41 699	40 569	46 516	-2 600	-1 130	5 947
45 to 54 years	34 373	43 960	41 239	40 699	9 587	-2 721	-540
55 years and over	54 533	70 652	93 397	108 873	16 119	22 745	15 476
55 to 64 years	22 296	33 491	42 113	39 758	11 196	8 622	-2 355
65 to 74 years	17 947	19 881	30 354	38 130	1 934	10 473	7 776
75 years and over	14 290	17 281	20 930	30 985	2 991	3 649	10 055
Men, 16 Years and Over	98 758	113 113	124 680	135 542	14 355	11 567	10 862
16 to 24 years	16 772	18 909	19 133	19 145	2 137	224	12
16 to 19 years	7 968	8 660	8 494	8 426	692	-166	-68
20 to 24 years	8 804	10 249	10 639	10 719	1 445	390	80
25 to 54 years	57 724	62 078	62 294	65 860	4 354	216	3 566
25 to 34 years	19 094	19 999	22 205	22 647	905	2 206	442
35 to 44 years	21 857	20 567	19 932	23 237	-1 290	-635	3 305
45 to 54 years	16 773	21 512	20 157	19 976	4 739	-1 355	-181
55 years and over	24 262	32 125	43 253	50 537	7 863	11 128	7 284
55 to 64 years	10 649	16 123	20 263	19 249	5 474	4 140	-1 014
65 to 74 years	8 074	9 158	14 165	17 872	1 084	5 007	3 707
75 years and over	5 539	6 844	8 825	13 417	1 305	1 981	4 592
Women, 16 Years and Over	106 462	120 675	133 111	143 912	14 213	12 436	10 801
16 to 24 years	16 466	18 575	18 872	18 964	2 109	297	92
16 to 19 years	7 676	8 415	8 272	8 202	739	-143	-70
20 to 24 years	8 790	10 160	10 600	10 762	1 370	440	162
25 to 54 years	59 725	63 574	64 095	66 612	3 849	521	2 517
25 to 34 years	19 683	19 994	22 376	22 610	311	2 382	234
35 to 44 years	22 442	21 132	20 637	23 279	-1 310	-495	2 642
45 to 54 years	17 600	22 448	21 082	20 723	4 848	-1 366	-359
55 years and over	30 271	38 527	50 144	58 336	8 256	11 617	8 192
55 to 64 years	11 646	17 367	21 850	20 509	5 721	4 483	-1 341
65 to 74 years	9 873	10 723	16 189	20 258	850	5 466	4 069
75 years and over	8 752	10 437	12 105	17 569	1 686	1 668	5 464
White, 16 Years and Over	171 478	189 540	200 221	211 474	18 062	10 681	11 253
Men	83 352	92 725	97 933	103 714	9 373	5 208	5 781
Women	88 126	96 814	102 288	107 761	8 688	5 474	5 473
Black, 16 Years and Over	24 373	27 843	32 762	36 644	3 470	4 919	3 882
Men	10 927	12 516	14 965	16 916	1 589	2 449	1 951
Women	13 446	15 328	17 797	19 728	1 882	2 469	1 931
Asian, 16 Years and Over	9 369	10 751	15 961	19 831	1 382	5 210	3 870
Men	4 479	5 112	7 471	9 268	633	2 359	1 797
Women	4 890	5 639	8 491	10 564	749	2 852	2 073
All Other Groups,[1] 16 Years and Over	. . .	5 654	8 848	11 504	. . .	3 194	2 656
Men	. . .	2 760	4 310	5 645	. . .	1 550	1 335
Women	. . .	2 895	4 536	5 859	. . .	1 641	1 323
Hispanic,[2] 16 Years and Over	21 070	32 141	42 734	54 292	11 072	10 593	11 558
Men	10 734	16 524	21 286	27 153	5 790	4 762	5 867
Women	10 336	15 616	21 446	27 139	5 281	5 830	5 693
Non-Hispanic, 16 Years and Over	184 150	201 647	215 057	225 162	17 497	13 410	10 105
Men	88 023	96 589	103 394	108 389	8 566	6 805	4 995
Women	96 127	105 059	111 665	116 773	8 932	6 606	5 108
White Non-Hispanic, 16 Years and Over	151 406	159 674	162 232	163 429	8 268	2 558	1 197
Men	73 100	77 317	78 970	79 635	4 217	1 653	665
Women	78 305	82 357	83 262	83 794	4 052	905	532

[1]The "All other groups" category includes respondents who reported the racial categories of "American Indian and Alaska Native" or "Native Hawaiian and Other Pacific Islander," as well as those who reported two or more races. This category was not defined prior to 2003.
[2]May be of any race.
. . . = Not available.

Table 4-1. Civilian Noninstitutional Population, by Age, Sex, Race, and Hispanic Origin, 1998, 2008, 2018, and Projected 2028—*Continued*

(Numbers in thousands, percent.)

Age, sex, race, and Hispanic origin	Percent distribution				Annual growth rate (percent)		
	1998	2008	2018	2028	1998–2008	2008–2018	2018–2028
Both Sexes, 16 Years and Over	100.0	100.0	100.0	100.0	1.3	1.0	0.8
16 to 24 years	16.2	16.0	14.7	13.6	1.2	0.1	0.0
16 to 19 years	7.6	7.3	6.5	6.0	0.9	-0.2	-0.1
20 to 24 years	8.6	8.7	8.2	7.7	1.5	0.4	0.1
25 to 54 years	57.2	53.7	49.0	47.4	0.7	0.1	0.5
25 to 34 years	18.9	17.1	17.3	16.2	0.3	1.1	0.2
35 to 44 years	21.6	17.8	15.7	16.6	-0.6	-0.3	1.4
45 to 54 years	16.7	18.8	16.0	14.6	2.5	-0.6	-0.1
55 years and over	26.6	30.2	36.2	39.0	2.6	2.8	1.5
55 to 64 years	10.9	14.3	16.3	14.2	4.2	2.3	-0.6
65 to 74 years	8.7	8.5	11.8	13.6	1.0	4.3	2.3
75 years and over	7.0	7.4	8.1	11.1	1.9	1.9	4.0
Men, 16 Years and Over	48.1	48.4	48.4	48.5	1.4	1.0	0.8
16 to 24 years	8.2	8.1	7.4	6.9	1.2	0.1	0.0
16 to 19 years	3.9	3.7	3.3	3.0	0.8	-0.2	-0.1
20 to 24 years	4.3	4.4	4.1	3.8	1.5	0.4	0.1
25 to 54 years	28.1	26.6	24.2	23.6	0.7	0.0	0.6
25 to 34 years	9.3	8.6	8.6	8.1	0.5	1.1	0.2
35 to 44 years	10.7	8.8	7.7	8.3	-0.6	-0.3	1.5
45 to 54 years	8.2	9.2	7.8	7.1	2.5	-0.6	-0.1
55 years and over	11.8	13.7	16.8	18.1	2.8	3.0	1.6
55 to 64 years	5.2	6.9	7.9	6.9	4.2	2.3	-0.5
65 to 74 years	3.9	3.9	5.5	6.4	1.3	4.5	2.4
75 years and over	2.7	2.9	3.4	4.8	2.1	2.6	4.3
Women, 16 Years and Over	51.9	51.6	51.6	51.5	1.3	1.0	0.8
16 to 24 years	8.0	7.9	7.3	6.8	1.2	0.2	0.0
16 to 19 years	3.7	3.6	3.2	2.9	0.9	-0.2	-0.1
20 to 24 years	4.3	4.3	4.1	3.9	1.5	0.4	0.2
25 to 54 years	29.1	27.2	24.9	23.8	0.6	0.1	0.4
25 to 34 years	9.6	8.6	8.7	8.1	0.2	1.1	0.1
35 to 44 years	10.9	9.0	8.0	8.3	-0.6	-0.2	1.2
45 to 54 years	8.6	9.6	8.2	7.4	2.5	-0.6	-0.2
55 years and over	14.8	16.5	19.5	20.9	2.4	2.7	1.5
55 to 64 years	5.7	7.4	8.5	7.3	4.1	2.3	-0.6
65 to 74 years	4.8	4.6	6.3	7.2	0.8	4.2	2.3
75 years and over	4.3	4.5	4.7	6.3	1.8	1.5	3.8
White, 16 Years and Over	83.6	81.1	77.7	75.7	1.0	0.5	0.5
Men	40.6	39.7	38.0	37.1	1.1	0.5	0.6
Women	42.9	41.4	39.7	38.6	0.9	0.6	0.5
Black, 16 Years and Over	11.9	11.9	12.7	13.1	1.3	1.6	1.1
Men	5.3	5.4	5.8	6.1	1.4	1.8	1.2
Women	6.6	6.6	6.9	7.1	1.3	1.5	1.0
Asian, 16 Years and Over	4.6	4.6	6.2	7.1	1.4	4.0	2.2
Men	2.2	2.2	2.9	3.3	1.3	3.9	2.2
Women	2.4	2.4	3.3	3.8	1.4	4.2	2.2
All Other Groups,[1] 16 Years and Over	. . .	2.2	3.4	4.1	. . .	4.6	2.7
Men	. . .	1.1	1.7	2.0	. . .	4.6	2.7
Women	. . .	1.1	1.8	2.1	. . .	4.6	2.6
Hispanic,[2] 16 Years and Over	10.3	13.7	16.6	19.4	4.3	2.9	2.4
Men	5.2	7.1	8.3	9.7	4.4	2.6	2.5
Women	5.0	6.7	8.3	9.7	4.2	3.2	2.4
Non-Hispanic, 16 Years and Over	89.7	86.3	83.4	80.6	0.9	0.6	0.5
Men	42.9	41.3	40.1	38.8	0.9	0.7	0.5
Women	46.8	44.9	43.3	41.8	0.9	0.6	0.4
White Non-Hispanic, 16 Years and Over	73.8	68.3	62.9	58.5	0.5	0.2	0.1
Men	35.6	33.1	30.6	28.5	0.6	0.2	0.1
Women	38.2	35.2	32.3	30.0	0.5	0.1	0.1

[1]The "All other groups" category includes respondents who reported the racial categories of "American Indian and Alaska Native" or "Native Hawaiian and Other Pacific Islander," as well as those who reported two or more races. This category was not defined prior to 2003.
[2]May be of any race.
. . . = Not available.

Table 4-2. Fastest-Growing Occupations, 2018 and Projected 2028

(Numbers in thousands, percent.)

Occupation	Employment		Change, 2018–2028		Mean annual wage, 2018
	2018	2028	Number	Percent	
TOTAL, ALL OCCUPATIONS	161 037.7	169 435.9	8 398.1	5.2	38 640
Solar photovoltaic installers	9.7	15.8	6.1	63.3	42 680
Wind turbine service technicians	6.6	10.3	3.8	56.9	54 370
Home health aides	831.8	1 136.6	304.8	36.6	24 200
Personal care aides	2 421.2	3 302.1	881.0	36.4	24 020
Occupational therapy assistants	43.8	58.3	14.5	33.1	60 220
Information security analysts	112.3	147.7	35.5	31.6	98 350
Physician assistants	118.8	155.7	37.0	31.1	108 610
Statisticians	44.4	58.0	13.6	30.7	87 780
Nurse practicioners	189.1	242.4	53.3	28.2	107 030
Speech language pathologists	153.7	195.6	41.9	27.3	77 510
Physical therapy assistants	98.4	125.0	26.7	27.1	58 040
Genetic counselors	3.0	3.8	0.8	27.0	80 370
Mathematicians	2.9	3.6	0.8	26.0	101 900
Operations research analysts	109.7	137.9	28.1	25.6	83 390
Software developers, applications	944.2	1 185.7	241.5	25.6	103 620
Forest fire inspectors and prevention specialists	2.2	2.8	0.5	24.1	39 600
Health specialists teachers, postsecondary	254.8	313.9	59.1	23.2	97 370
Phlebotomists	128.3	157.8	29.5	23.0	34 480
Physical therapist aides	49.8	61.2	11.3	22.8	26 240
Medical assistants	686.6	841.5	154.9	22.6	33 610
Substance abuse, behavioral disorder, and mental health counselors	304.5	373.1	68.5	22.5	44 630
Marriage and family counselors	55.3	67.7	12.3	22.3	50 090
Massage therapists	159.8	195.2	35.4	22.2	41 420
Cooks, restaurant	1 362.3	1 661.3	299.0	21.9	26 530
Physical therapists	247.7	301.9	54.2	21.9	87 930
Respiratory therapists	134.0	162.0	27.9	20.8	60 280
Market research analysts and marketing specialists	681.9	821.1	139.2	20.4	63 120
Actuaries	25.0	30.0	5.0	20.1	102 880
Computer numerically controlled machine tool programmers, metal and plastic	24.3	29.2	4.9	20.0	53 190
Nursing instructors and teachers, postsecondary	69.0	82.8	13.8	20.0	73 490

Table 4-3. Occupations with the Largest Job Growth, 2018–2028

(Numbers in thousands, percent.)

Occupation	Employment		Change, 2018–2028		Mean annual wage, 2018
	2018	2028	Number	Percent	
TOTAL, ALL OCCUPATIONS	161 037.7	169 435.9	8 398.1	5.2	38 640
Personal care aides	2 421.2	3 302.1	881.0	36.4	24 020
Combined food preparation and serving workers, including fast food	3 704.2	4 344.3	640.1	17.3	21 250
Registered nurses	3 059.8	3 431.3	371.5	12.1	71 730
Home health aides	831.8	1 136.6	304.8	36.6	24 200
Cooks, restaurants	1 362.3	1 661.3	299.0	21.9	26 530
Software developers, applications	944.2	1 185.7	241.5	25.6	103 620
Waiters and waitresses	2 634.6	2 804.8	170.2	6.5	21 780
General and operation managers	2 376.4	2 541.4	165.0	6.9	100 930
Janitors and cleaners, except maids and housekeeping cleaners	2 404.4	2 564.2	159.8	6.6	26 110
Medical assistants	686.6	841.5	154.9	22.6	33 610
Construction laborers	1 405.0	1 553.1	148.1	10.5	35 800
Laborers and freight, stock, and material movers, hand	2 953.8	3 097.9	144.0	4.9	28 260
Market research analysts and marketing specialists	681.9	821.1	139.2	20.4	63 120
Nursing assistants	1 513.2	1 648.6	135.4	8.9	28 540
Management analysts	876.3	994.6	118.3	13.5	83 610
First-line supervisors of food preparation and serving workers	988.9	1 096.1	107.2	10.8	32 450
Landscaping and groundskeeping workers	1 205.2	1 311.6	106.4	8.8	29 000
Financial managers	653.6	758.3	104.7	16.0	127 990
Heavy and tractor-trailer truck drivers	1 958.8	2 058.5	99.7	5.1	43 680
Medical secretaries	601.7	698.1	96.4	16.0	35 760
Accountants and auditors	1 424.0	1 514.7	90.7	6.4	70 500
Maintenance and repair workers, general	1 488.0	1 573.4	85.4	5.7	38 300
Carpenters	1 006.5	1 086.6	80.1	8.0	46 590
Licensed practical and licensed vocational nurses	728.9	807.0	78.1	10.7	46 240
Sales representatives, services, all other	1 060.6	1 137.0	76.4	7.2	54 550
Electricians	715.4	789.5	74.1	10.4	55 190
Taxi drivers and chauffeurs	370.4	442.8	72.4	19.5	25 980
Medical and health services managers	406.1	477.6	71.6	17.6	99 730
Business operations specialists, all other	1 135.7	1 207.0	71.3	6.3	70 530
Computer user support specialists	671.8	742.7	70.9	10.6	50 980

Table 4-4. Fastest Declining Occupations, 2018 and Projected 2028

(Numbers in thousands, percent, dollars.)

Occupation	2018	2028	Number	Percent	Median annual wage
TOTAL, ALL OCCUPATIONS	161 037.7	169 435.9	8 398.1	5.2	38 640
Locomotive firers	0.5	0.2	-0.4	-68.3	63 820
Respiratory therapy technicians	9.3	3.9	-5.3	-57.5	51 210
Parking enforcement workers	8.6	5.4	-3.1	-36.7	39 840
Word processors and typists	60.4	40.0	-20.4	-33.8	39 750
Watch repairers	3.0	2.1	-0.9	-29.6	39 910
Electronic equipment installers and repairers, motor vehicles	11.0	7.9	-3.1	-28.6	35 590
Telephone operators	5.7	4.1	-1.6	-28.4	37 240
Cutters and trimmers, hand	10.7	7.7	-3.0	-28.4	29 390
Postmasters and mail superintendents	13.3	9.6	-3.7	-27.5	75 970
Mine shuttle car operators	1.7	1.3	-0.4	-25.3	56 340
Computer operators	36.8	28.0	-8.9	-24.1	45 840
Switchboard operators, including answering service	73.4	55.9	-17.5	-23.8	29 420
Postal service mail sorters, processors, and processing machine operators	99.7	76.0	-23.7	-23.8	58 770
Data entry keyers	187.3	143.9	-43.4	-23.2	32 170
Aircraft structure, surfaces, rigging, and systems assemblers	45.1	35.2	-9.9	-22.0	53 340
Coil winders, tapers, and finishers	12.3	9.7	-2.7	-21.6	34 400
Photographic process workers and processing machine operators	17.1	13.4	-3.6	-21.3	29 180
Pressers, textile, garment, and related materials	39.9	31.4	-8.5	-21.2	23 350
Legal secretaries	180.1	142.5	-37.6	-20.9	46 360
Pressers, textile, garment, and related materials	29.9	23.7	-6.2	-20.8	40 410
Milling and planing machine setters, operators, and tenders, metal and plastic	19.8	15.7	-4.1	-20.7	43 590
Drilling and boring machine tool setters, operators, and tenders, metal and plastic	11.6	9.2	-2.4	-20.5	38 020
Postal service clerks	75.7	60.7	-15.0	-19.8	55 280
Postal service mail carriers	328.7	263.7	-65.1	-19.8	55 210
Executive secretaries and executive administrative assistants	622.5	499.4	-123.0	-19.8	59 340
Forging machine setters, operators, and tenders, metal and plastic	18.6	15.0	-3.6	-19.5	38 900
Textile bleaching and dyeing machine operators and tenders	9.7	7.9	-1.9	-19.4	28 780
Timing device assemblers and adjusters	0.8	0.6	-0.2	-19.3	34 650
Grinding and polishing workers, hand	30.7	24.8	-5.9	-19.2	29 550
Textile knitting and weaving machine setters, operators, and tenders	22.1	17.9	-4.2	-18.9	29 160

Table 4-5. Economic Dependency Ratio, 1998, 2008, 2018, and Projected 2028

(Number.)

Group	1998	2008	2018	2028
TOTAL POPULATION	94.2	95.1	100.6	103.5
Under age 16	44.6	41.8	40.0	38.8
Ages 16 to 64	28.7	33.4	35.5	34.2
Ages 65 and older	21.9	20.9	26.0	31.4

Table 4-6. Industries with the Largest Wage and Salary Employment Growth and Declines, 2018–2028

(Number in thousands, percent.)

Industry	Sector	Employment		Change, 2018–2028	Annual rate of change, 2018–2028
		2018	2028		
Largest Growth					
Food services and drinking places	Leisure and hospitality	11 926.3	13 315.8	1 389.5	1.1
Construction	Construction	7 289.3	8 096.8	807.5	1.1
Individual and family services	Health care and social assistance	2 464.2	3 255.7	791.5	2.8
Home health care services	Health care and social assistance	1 472.7	2 186.4	713.7	4.0
Computer systems design and related services	Professional and business services	2 121.6	2 642.3	520.7	2.2
Offices of physicians	Health care and social assistance	2 620.6	2 970.5	349.9	1.3
Nursing and reidential care facilities	Health care and social assistance	3 362.2	3 698.7	336.5	1.0
Outpatient care centers	Health care and social assistance	934.4	1 265.4	331.0	3.1
Hospitals	Health care and social assistance	5 145.1	5 467.8	322.7	0.6
Management, scientific, and technical consulting services	Professional and business services	1 483.2	1 776.0	292.8	1.8
Largest Declines					
Wired telecommunications carriers	Information	547.3	420.1	-127.2	-2.6
Postal service	Federal government	608.6	482.1	-126.5	-2.3
Wholesale trade	Wholesale trade	5 852.5	5 754.0	-98.5	-0.2
All other retail	Retail trade	7 619.9	7 531.2	-88.7	-0.1
Printing and related support activities	Manufacturing	430.9	346.4	-84.5	-2.2
Newspaper, periodical, book, and directory publishers	Information	324.7	247.9	-76.8	-2.7
Private households	Other services	777.8	702.2	-75.6	-1.0
General merchandise stores	Retail trade	3 104.9	3 035.0	-69.9	-0.2
Textile mills and textile product mills	Manufacturing	228.9	188.6	-40.3	-1.9
Apparel, leather, and allied product manufacturing	Manufacturing	139.6	99.5	-40.1	-3.3

Table 4-7. Median Age of the Labor Force, by Sex, Race, and Ethnicity, 1998, 2008, 2018, and Projected 2028

(Number.)

	1998	2008	2018	2028
TOTAL	38.8	41.2	41.9	42.5
Sex				
Men	38.8	41.0	41.9	42.4
Women	38.7	41.4	41.9	42.7
Race				
White	39.1	41.7	42.7	43.3
Black	36.9	39.1	39.5	40.6
Asian	37.8	40.6	41.3	42.9
Ethnicity				
Hispanic origin[1]	34.2	36.2	38.0	39.5
White non-Hispanic	39.7	43.0	44.1	44.6

[1]May be of any race.

Table 4-8. Employment and Output, by Industry, 2008, 2018, and Projected 2028

(Number, percent, dollars.)

Industry	Employment							Output				
	Number of jobs (thousands)			Change		Average annual rate of change (percent)		Billions of chained (2005) dollars			Average annual rate of change (percent)	
	2008	2018	2028	2008–2018	2018–2028	2008–2018	2018–2028	2008	2018	2028	2008–2018	2018–2028
Total[1,2]	149 276	161 038	169 436	11 762	8 398	0.8	0.5	28 910	33 242	40 045	1.4	1.9
Nonagriculture Wage and Salary	137 991	149 804	157 662	11 813	7 858	0.8	0.5	28 459	32 729	39 428	1.4	1.9
Mining	710	683	728	-27	45	-0.4	0.6	508	607	844	1.8	3.4
Oil and gas extraction	161	145	129	-15	-17	-1.0	-1.2	260	466	692	6.0	4.0
Mining, except oil and gas	226	192	191	-34	-1	-1.6	-0.1	138	111	121	-2.1	0.9
Coal mining	81	52	45	-29	-7.0	-4.4	-1.3	59	44	46	-2.7	0.4
Metal ore mining	40	41	44	1	3.0	0.3	0.6	38	43	47	1.2	1.0
Nonmetallic mineral mining and quarrying	105	99	102	-6	3	-0.6	0.3	41	26	29	-4.4	1.2
Support activities for mining	323	346	408	23.0	62	0.7	1.7	118	65	85	-5.7	2.6
Utilities	559	555	537	-4	-17	-0.1	-0.3	514	464	526	-1.0	1.2
Electric power generation, transmission and distribution	404	393	386	-11	-6	-0.3	-0.2	408	357	411	-1.3	1.4
Natural gas distribution	107	110	96	3	-14	0.3	-1.4	93	98	103	0.5	0.5
Water, sewage and other systems	48.0	52.0	55.0	4.0	3.0	0.8	0.6	16.0	11.0	12.0	-3.5	1.2
Construction	7 163	7 289	8 097	127	808	0.2	1.1	1 329	1 427	1 581	0.7	1.0
Manufacturing	13 406	12 689	12 048	-717	-641	-0.5	-0.5	5 989	6 134	7 165	0.2	1.6
Food manufacturing	1 481	1 620	1 624	139	4	0.9	0.0	713	821	978	1.4	1.8
Animal food manufacturing	52	63	66	12	3.0	2.0	0.4	50	65	79	2.6	2.0
Grain and oilseed milling	62	60	57	-2	-3	-0.3	-0.5	82	137	165	5.3	1.9
Sugar and confectionery product manufacturing	73	76	76	4	-1	0.5	-0.1	37	36	41	-0.1	1.3
Fruit and vegetable preserving and specialty food manufacturing	173	172	160	-1	-12	0.0	-0.7	71	66	77	-0.6	1.5
Dairy product manufacturing	129	149	151	20	2	1.4	0.1	102	122	150	1.8	2.1
Animal slaughtering and processing	510	521	528	11	7	0.2	0.1	206	224	267	0.9	1.8
Seafood product preparation and packaging	39	37	33	-1	-5	-0.3	-1.3	12	11	11	-1.0	0.3
Bakeries and tortilla manufacturing	281	313	312	32	0	1.1	0.0	64	66	77	0.2	1.6
Other food manufacturing	163	228	241	65	13	3.4	0.5	91	97	115	0.6	1.8
Beverage and tobacco product	198	273	285	74	12	3.2	0.4	178	169	172	-0.5	0.2
Beverage manufacturing	177	261	278	84	17	4.0	0.6	108	122	144	1.2	1.7
Tobacco manufacturing	22	12	7	-10	-4	-5.9	-4.6	70	48	33	-3.8	-3.6
Textile mills and textile product mills	298	229	189	-70	-40	-2.6	-1.9	63	51	60	-2.1	1.5
Apparel, leather and allied product manufacturing	232	140	100	-93	-40	-5.0	-3.3	28	28	28	-0.1	0.0
Wood product manufacturing	458	406	388	-51	-19	-1.2	-0.5	94	95	107	0.1	1.2
Sawmills and wood preservation	102	93	90	-10	-3	-1.0	-0.3	25	27	31	0.5	1.3
Veneer, plywood, and engineered wood product manufacturing	90	81	80	-9	-1.0	-1.1	-0.1	21	19	22	-0.8	1.5
Other wood product manufacturing, including wood tv, radio and sewing machine cabinet manufacturing	265	233	217	-33	-15	-1.3	-0.7	48	49	54	0.4	0.9
Paper manufacturing	445	367	326	-78	-41	-1.9	-1.2	191	172	180	-1.0	0.5
Pulp, paper, and paperboard mills	126	95	76	-31	-19	-2.8	-2.2	86	78	83	-0.9	0.6
Converted paper product manufacturing	319	272	249	-47	-23	-1.6	-0.9	105	94	97	-1.1	0.3
Printing and related support activities	594	431	346	-163	-85	-3.2	-2.2	101	77	83	-2.7	0.8
Petroleum and coal products manufacturing	117	116	106	-2	-10	-0.2	-0.9	843	856	1 036	0.1	1.9
Chemical manufacturing	847	838	808	-9	-30	-0.1	-0.4	836	814	951	-0.3	1.6
Basic chemical manufacturing	152	153	142	1.0	-11	0.0	-0.7	260	310	351	1.7	1.3
Resin, synthetic rubber, and artificial synthetic fibers and filaments manufacturing	104	94	87	-9	-8	-0.9	-0.8	113	112	116	-0.1	0.3
Pesticide, fertilizer, and other agricultural chemical manufacturing	37	36	32	-1	-4	-0.1	-1.2	28	49	54	5.8	1.0
Pharmaceutical and medicine manufacturing	291	296	296	5	0	0.2	0.0	256	185	250	-3.2	3.0
Paint, coating, and adhesive manufacturing	62	65	62	2	-3	0.3	-0.4	40	36	37	-1.3	0.4
Soap, cleaning compound, and toilet preparation manufacturing	107	110	115	4	5	0.3	0.4	89	82	91	-0.9	1.1
Other chemical product and preparation manufacturing	95	85	75	-11	-9	-1.2	-1.1	51	45	46	-1.1	0.2
Plastics and rubber products manufacturing	729	731	691	2	-40	0.0	-0.6	224	223	234	-0.1	0.5
Plastics product manufacturing	585	593	571	8	-23	0.1	-0.4	180	175	181	-0.2	0.3
Rubber product manufacturing	145	138	121	-7	-17	-0.5	-1.3	45	48	54	0.6	1.2
Nonmetallic mineral product manufacturing	465	415	386	-50	-29	-1.1	-0.7	122	118	128	-0.3	0.8
Clay product and refractory manufacturing	52	39	34	-13	-5	-2.8	-1.3	9	9	11	0.1	1.7
Glass and glass product manufacturing	97	87	79	-10	-8	-1.1	-0.9	23	28	29	1.8	0.4
Cement and concrete product manufacturing	220	192	175	-28	-18	-1.4	-1.0	56	48	53	-1.5	0.9
Lime, gypsum and other nonmetallic mineral product manufacturing	96	97	99	1	2	0.1	0.2	32	33	35	0.1	0.8
Primary metal manufacturing	442	378	332	-64	-46	-1.5	-1.3	272	238	278	-1.3	1.6
Iron and steel mills and ferroalloy manufacturing	99	83	70	-16	-13	-1.8	-1.6	104	97	108	-0.7	1.1

[1]Employment data for wage and salary workers are from the BLS Current Employment Statistics (CES) Survey, which counts jobs, whereas data for self-employed, unpaid family workers, and agriculture, forestry, fishing, and hunting workers are from the Current Population Survey (CPS, or household, survey), which counts workers.
[2]Output subcategories do not necessarily add to higher categories as a by-product of chain weighting.

Table 4-8. Employment and Output, by Industry, 2008, 2018, and Projected 2028—*Continued*

(Number, percent, dollars.)

Industry	Employment							Output				
	Number of jobs (thousands)			Change		Average annual rate of change (percent)		Billions of chained (2005) dollars			Average annual rate of change (percent)	
	2008	2018	2028	2008–2018	2018–2028	2008–2018	2018–2028	2008	2018	2028	2008–2018	2018–2028
Manufacturing—*Continued*												
Steel product manufacturing from purchased steel	61	57	54	-4	-3	-0.6	-0.6	24	21	27	-1.5	2.5
Alumina and aluminum production and processing	66	58	53	-8	-5	-1.3	-1.0	38	30	37	-2.4	2.0
Nonferrous metal (except aluminum) production and processing	67	60	54	-7	-6	-1.1	-1.1	67	59	74	-1.3	2.4
Foundries	148	120	101	-29	-19	-2.1	-1.7	38	31	32	-2.1	0.3
Fabricated metal product manufacturing	1 527	1 467	1 428	-61	-38	-0.4	-0.3	382	352	404	-0.8	1.4
Forging and stamping	107	100	94	-7	-6	-0.7	-0.6	36	38	43	0.5	1.3
Cutlery and handtool manufacturing	49	37	33	-12	-4	-2.7	-1.2	13	10	12	-2.3	1.7
Architectural and structural metals manufacturing	406	390	389	-16	-1	-0.4	0.0	93	79	90	-1.7	1.3
Boiler, tank, and shipping container manufacturing	97	91	88	-6	-3	-0.7	-0.3	35	36	43	0.1	1.9
Hardware manufacturing	30	25	23	-4	-2	-1.6	-0.8	10	7	6	-3.0	-1.4
Spring and wire product manufacturing	52	44	40	-8	-4	-1.7	-1.0	10	9	11	-1.0	1.8
Machine shops; turned product; and screw, nut, and bolt manufacturing	361	362	363	1.0	2	0.0	0.0	69	71	74	0.3	0.3
Coating, engraving, heat treating, and allied activities	144	140	133	-4	-8.0	-0.3	-0.6	30	28	31	-0.7	1.3
Other fabricated metal product manufacturing	281	277	265	-4	-12	-0.2	-0.4	87	75	94	-1.4	2.3
Machinery manufacturing	1 188	1 120	1 058	-68	-63	-0.6	-0.6	380	358	414	-0.6	1.5
Agriculture, construction, and mining machinery manufacturing	242	220	215	-22	-6	-1.0	-0.3	96	98	107	0.2	0.9
Industrial machinery manufacturing	121	120	110	-2	-10	-0.1	-0.8	38	29	38	-2.6	2.5
Commercial and service industry machinery manufacturing, including digital camera manufacturing	105	95	88	-10	-6	-1.0	-0.7	27	25	27	-0.9	0.9
Ventilation, heating, air-conditioning, and commercial refrigeration equipment manufacturing	150	133	118	-17	-15	-1.2	-1.2	43	43	47	0.0	0.8
Metalworking machinery manufacturing	191	182	174	-9	-7	-0.5	-0.4	30	28	29	-0.8	0.7
Engine, turbine, and power transmission equipment manufacturing	105	99	96	-6	-3	-0.5	-0.3	48	50	57	0.4	1.3
Other general purpose machinery manufacturing	274	272	257	-2	-15	-0.1	-0.6	98	86	109	-1.3	2.4
Computer and electronic product manufacturing	1 244	1 055	933	-189	-123	-1.6	-1.2	394	373	447	-0.6	1.8
Computer and peripheral equipment manufacturing, excluding digital camera manufacturing	183	156	137	-27	-20	-1.6	-1.3	50	42	60	-1.7	3.5
Communications equipment manufacturing	127	86	62	-42	-24	-3.9	-3.2	71	59	71	-1.9	1.9
Audio and video equipment manufacturing	27	20	18	-7	-2	-3.1	-1.0	11	4	4	-9.4	0.5
Semiconductor and other electronic component manufacturing	432	369	330	-63	-39	-1.6	-1.1	106	121	123	1.3	0.2
Navigational, measuring, electromedical, and control instruments manufacturing	441	410	375	-31	-35	-0.7	-0.9	150	145	186	-0.4	2.5
Manufacturing and reproducing magnetic and optical media	34	14	11	-20	-4	-8.4	-2.8	5	3	3	-4.7	0.2
Electrical equipment, appliance, and component manufacturing	424	399	380	-25	-19	-0.6	-0.5	137	127	147	-0.7	1.5
Electric lighting equipment manufacturing	57	50	46	-8	-4	-1.4	-0.8	14	17	17	1.5	0.5
Household appliance manufacturing	71	63	54	-8	-10	-1.2	-1.6	24	20	25	-1.7	2.5
Electrical equipment manufacturing	159	141	133	-18	-8	-1.2	-0.6	45	38	43	-1.8	1.3
Other electrical equipment and component manufacturing	137	145	148	9	3	0.6	0.2	54	53	62	-0.2	1.6
Transportation equipment manufacturing	1 608	1 702	1 692	94	-10	0.6	-0.1	756	1 023	1 244	3.1	2.0
Motor vehicle manufacturing	192	234	260	42	26	2.0	1.1	237	360	484	4.3	3.0
Motor vehicle body and trailer manufacturing	140	165	165	25	0	1.7	0.0	31	44	51	3.7	1.5
Motor vehicle parts manufacturing	544	597	609	53	12	0.9	0.2	188	327	328	5.7	0.0
Aerospace product and parts manufacturing	507	509	473	3	-37	0.1	-0.7	222	229	299	0.3	2.7
Railroad rolling stock manufacturing	29	22	22	-6	-1.0	-2.4	-0.3	14	16	19	1.3	1.8
Ship and boat building	156	139	132	-16	-8	-1.1	-0.6	35	29	37	-1.7	2.4
Other transportation equipment manufacturing	42	35	33	-6	-2	-1.6	-0.7	31	20	26	-4.2	2.6
Furniture and related product manufacturing	478	395	374	-83	-20	-1.9	-0.5	83	70	86	-1.6	2.0
Household and institutional furniture and kitchen cabinet manufacturing, excluding wood tv, radio and sewing maching cabinet manufacturing	305	249	233	-56	-17	-2.0	-0.7	46	35	42	-2.6	1.7
Office furniture (including fixtures) manufacturing	129	109	108	-20	-1.0	-1.7	-0.1	27	25	31	-0.9	2.3
Other furniture related product manufacturing	44	36	33	-8	-3.0	-1.9	-0.8	10	11	13	0.5	2.2
Miscellaneous manufacturing	629	608	603	-21	-5	-0.3	-0.1	179	164	207	-0.8	2.3
Medical equipment and supplies manufacturing	311	317	321	6	4	0.2	0.1	95	99	133	0.5	2.9
Other miscellaneous manufacturing	318	291	282	-27	-9	-0.9	-0.3	84	65	74	-2.6	1.3
Wholesale Trade	5 875	5 853	5 754	-23	-99	0.0	-0.2	1 470	1 846	2 406	2.3	2.7
Retail Trade	15 289	15 833	15 679	544	-154	0.4	-0.1	1 357	1 785	2 191	2.8	2.1
Motor vehicle and parts dealers	1 831	2 021	2 056	190	35	1.0	0.2	200	349	420	5.7	1.9
Food and beverage stores	2 862	3 087	3 057	225	-30	0.8	-0.1	211	208	228	-0.2	0.9
General Merchandise stores	3 026	3 105	3 035	79	-70	0.3	-0.2	224	256	313	1.4	2.0
All other retail	7 570	7 620	7 531	50	-89	0.1	-0.1	723	980	1 240	3.1	2.4

Table 4-8. Employment and Output, by Industry, 2008, 2018, and Projected 2028—*Continued*

(Number, percent, dollars.)

Industry	Employment							Output				
	Number of jobs (thousands)			Change		Average annual rate of change (percent)		Billions of chained (2005) dollars			Average annual rate of change (percent)	
	2008	2018	2028	2008–2018	2018–2028	2008–2018	2018–2028	2008	2018	2028	2008–2018	2018–2028
Transportation and Warehousing	4 514	5 419	5 741	906	322	1.8	0.6	1 063	1 061	1 263	0.0	1.8
Air transportation	491	501	526	11	25.0	0.2	0.5	192	213	256	1.1	1.9
Rail transportation	231	214	208	-17	-6	-0.8	-0.3	77	71	74	-0.8	0.3
Water transportation	67	65	61	-2	-4	-0.3	-0.6	57	48	62	-1.6	2.5
Truck transportation	1 389	1 492	1 548	103	56	0.7	0.4	302	317	399	0.5	2.3
Transit and ground passenger transportation	423	488	510	64	23	1.4	0.5	48	70	88	3.8	2.3
Pipeline transportation	42	49	50	7	1.0	1.5	0.2	45	41	49	-0.8	1.8
Scenic and sightseeing transportation and support activities for transportation	620	746	787	126	41	1.9	0.5	108	124	141	1.4	1.3
Postal Service	747	609	482	-139	-127	-2.0	-2.3	80	52	43	-4.3	-1.7
Couriers and messengers	573	725	743	152	18	2.4	0.2	101	75	84	-2.9	1.1
Warehousing and storage	677	1 140	1 309	463.0	169	5.3	1.4	137	103	116	-2.8	1.2
Information	2 984	2 828	2 834	-156	6	-0.5	0.0	1 268	1 834	2 424	3.8	2.8
Publishing industries	881	733	737	-148	4	-1.8	0.1	320	374	550	1.6	3.9
Newspaper, periodical, book, and directory publishers	617	325	248	-292	-77	-6.2	-2.7	165	134	149	-2.1	1.1
Software publishers	264	408	489	144	81	4.5	1.8	156	240	410	4.4	5.5
Motion picture, video, and sound recording industries	371	436	456	65	20	1.6	0.5	146	130	136	-1.1	0.4
Broadcasting (except Internet)	319	271	257	-48	-14	-1.6	-0.5	131	187	231	3.6	2.1
Radio and television broadcasting	233	217	213	-16	-4	-0.7	-0.2	67	92	114	3.3	2.1
Cable and other subscription programming	86	54	44	-32	-10	-4.6	-2.1	64	95	118	4.0	2.2
Telecommunications	1 020	751	599	-268	-152	-3.0	-2.2	534	743	957	3.4	2.6
Wired telecommunications carriers	666	547	420	-119	-127	-1.9	-2.6	342	346	434	0.1	2.3
Wireless telecommunications carriers (except satellite)	201	114	108	-86	-6	-5.5	-0.5	162	359	479	8.3	2.9
Satellite, telecommunications resellers, and all other telecommunications	153	90	71	-63	-19.0	-5.2	-2.4	34	49	62	3.7	2.4
Data processing, hosting, and related services	260	330	391	70	62	2.4	1.7	88	206	280	8.9	3.1
Other information services	134	308	394	174	86	8.7	2.5	51	198	280	14.5	3.5
Finance and Insurance	6 077	6 314	6 482	237	168	0.4	0.3	2 125	2 343	2 900	1.0	2.2
Monetary authorities, credit intermediation, and related activities	2 755	2 667	2 685	-89	18	-0.3	0.1	733	668	875	-0.9	2.7
Securities, commodity contracts, funds, trusts and other financial investments and related activities	916	957	996	41	39	0.4	0.4	619	573	677	-0.8	1.7
Insurance carriers and related activities	2 405	2 690	2 802	285	111	1.1	0.4	774	1 130	1 379	3.9	2.0
Insurance carriers	1 475	1 522	1 523	46	2	0.3	0.0	584	713	879	2.0	2.1
Agencies, brokerages, and other insurance related activities	930	1 169	1 278	239	110	2.3	0.9	194	418	500	8.0	1.8
Real estate, rental, and leasing	2 130	2 255	2 367	125	112	0.6	0.5	1 590	1 895	2 402	1.8	2.4
Real estate	1 485	1 661	1 764	176	103	1.1	0.6	1 285	1 565	1 983	2.0	2.4
Rental and leasing services and lessors of intangible assets	645	594	604	-51	10	-0.8	0.2	306	327	415	0.7	2.4
Automotive equipment rental and leasing	193	220	232	27	13	1.3	0.6	55	60	75	0.8	2.2
Consumer goods rental and general rental centers	297	183	167	-114	-16	-4.7	-0.9	34	32	40	-0.5	2.4
Commercial and industrial machinery and equipment rental and leasing	128	168	183	41	15	2.8	0.9	64	66	81	0.3	2.1
Lessors of nonfinancial intangible assets (except copyrighted works)	28	23	21	-4	-2	-1.7	-0.8	153	170	220	1.0	2.6
Professional, Scientific, and Technical Services	7 846	9 300	10 385	1 455	1 085	1.7	1.1	1 718	2 213	2 717	2.6	2.1
Legal services	1 162	1 141	1 148	-21	7	-0.2	0.1	328	330	356	0.1	0.8
Accounting, tax preparation, bookkeeping, and payroll services	952	1 014	1 045	62	32	0.6	0.3	164	182	204	1.1	1.1
Architectural, engineering, and related services	1 440	1 476	1 544	36	68	0.2	0.5	303	346	429	1.4	2.2
Specialized design services	141	144	151	3	7	0.2	0.4	30	34	43	1.2	2.4
Computer systems design and related services	1 446	2 122	2 642	675	521	3.9	2.2	268	498	672	6.4	3.0
Management, scientific, and technical consulting services	1 035	1 483	1 776	448	293	3.7	1.8	202	323	409	4.8	2.4
Scientific research and development services	623	693	734	70	41	1.1	0.6	178	219	263	2.1	1.9
Advertising and related services	463	490	500	26	11	0.6	0.2	132	141	181	0.7	2.5
Other professional, scientific, and technical services	584	739	845	154	107	2.4	1.4	120	149	186	2.2	2.3
Management of companies and enterprises	1 910	2 372	2 482	462	110	2.2	0.5	451	421	503	-0.7	1.8
Administrative and support and waste management and remediation services	8 037	9 328	9 795	1 291	468	1.5	0.5	711	984	1 228	3.3	2.2
Administrative and support services	7 680	8 890	9 323	1 210	433	1.5	0.5	625	890	1 125	3.6	2.4
Office administrative services	403	515	608	112	93	2.5	1.7	48	69	90	3.7	2.7
Facilities support services	133	153	162	20	9	1.4	0.6	28	36	46	2.6	2.3
Employment services	3 134	3 679	3 712	545	33	1.6	0.1	197	330	418	5.3	2.4
Business support services	834	899	954	65	55	0.7	0.6	73	93	117	2.5	2.3
Travel arrangement and reservation services	223	219	196	-4	-23	-0.2	-1.1	43	55	68	2.4	2.2
Investigation and security services	806	945	1 007	139	61	1.6	0.6	47	68	85	3.8	2.2
Services to buildings and dwellings	1 840	2 153	2 351	313	198	1.6	0.9	147	186	242	2.4	2.7
Other support services	307	326	333	19	7	0.6	0.2	43	54	61	2.3	1.2

Table 4-8. Employment and Output, by Industry, 2008, 2018, and Projected 2028—*Continued*

(Number, percent, dollars.)

Industry	Employment							Output				
	Number of jobs (thousands)			Change		Average annual rate of change (percent)		Billions of chained (2005) dollars			Average annual rate of change (percent)	
	2008	2018	2028	2008–2018	2018–2028	2008–2018	2018–2028	2008	2018	2028	2008–2018	2018–2028
Professional, Scientific, and Technical Services—*Continued*												
Waste management and remediation services	357	438	473	81	35	2.1	0.8	86	95	104	0.9	1.0
Education services	3 040	3 728	4 201	688	474	2.1	1.2	312	305	346	-0.2	1.3
Elementary and secondary schools	858	1 083	1 220	226	137	2.4	1.2	42	35	37	-1.6	0.4
Junior colleges, colleges, universities, and professional schools	1 599	1 864	2 085	264	222	1.5	1.1	202	201	231	-0.1	1.4
Other educational services	583	781	895	198	115	3.0	1.4	68	70	79	0.2	1.2
Health care and social assistance	16 189	19 939	23 335	3 751	3 396	2.1	1.6	1 788	2 360	3 135	2.8	2.9
Ambulatory health care services	5 647	7 499	9 383	1 852.0	1 884	2.9	2.3	802	1 060	1 411	2.8	2.9
Offices of physicians	2 205	2 621	2 971	416	350	1.7	1.3	397	526	723	2.9	3.2
Offices of dentists	818	956	1 053	138	98	1.6	1.0	114	119	135	0.5	1.3
Offices of other health practitioners	627	930	1 185	303	255	4.0	2.4	74	102	142	3.2	3.3
Outpatient care centers	581	934	1 265	354	331	4.9	3.1	84	119	159	3.6	2.9
Medical and diagnostic laboratories	217	278	350	61	72	2.5	2.3	41	69	91	5.3	2.8
Home health care services	961	1 473	2 186	511	714	4.4	4.0	57	86	115	4.3	2.9
Other ambulatory health care services	238	308	372	70	65	2.6	1.9	36	39	51	0.8	2.7
Hospitals	4 627	5 145	5 468	518	323	1.1	0.6	632	871	1 166	3.3	3.0
Nursing and residential care facilities	3 016	3 362	3 699	346	337	1.1	1.0	195	235	304	1.9	2.6
Social assistance	2 899	3 933	4 786	1 035	853	3.1	2.0	159	195	255	2.1	2.7
Individual and family services	1 502	2 464	3 256	962	792	5.1	2.8	71	99	134	3.4	3.1
Community, and vocational rehabilitation services	537	505	496	-32	-9	-0.6	-0.2	41	48	62	1.5	2.7
Child day care services	859	964	1 035	105	71	1.2	0.7	47	48	59	0.2	2.1
Arts, entertainment, and recreation	1 970	2 394	2 552	424	158	2.0	0.6	263	319	398	1.9	2.2
Performing arts, spectator sports, and related industries	406	506	529	100	23	2.2	0.4	128	158	200	2.2	2.4
Performing arts companies	118	126	121	8	-5	0.6	-0.4	22	26	34	2.0	2.7
Spectator sports	131	153	160	23	6	1.6	0.4	39	43	52	1.2	1.9
Promoters of events, and agents and managers	108	177	197	69	20	5.0	1.1	33	44	57	3.0	2.7
Independent artists, writers, and performers	49	50	52	1	2	0.2	0.4	35	45	57	2.6	2.4
Museums, historical sites, and similar institutions	132	170	189	39	19	2.6	1.1	13	17	23	3.1	2.8
Amusement, gambling, and recreation industries	1 433	1 718	1 834	285	116	1.8	0.7	123	143	176	1.5	2.0
Amusement parks and arcades	155	211	224	57	13	3.2	0.6	21	17	21	-2.4	2.4
Gambling industries (except casino hotels)	141	120	101	-20	-20	-1.5	-1.8	32	38	44	1.8	1.5
Other amusement and recreation industries	1 138	1 386	1 509	249	123	2.0	0.9	71	89	111	2.4	2.2
Accomodation and food services	11 466	13 955	15 353	2 489	1 398	2.0	1.0	795	989	1 185	2.2	1.8
Accomodation	1 869	2 028	2 037	160	9	0.8	0.0	206	251	319	2.0	2.4
Food services and drinking places	9 598	11 926	13 316	2 329	1 390	2.2	1.1	589	738	867	2.3	1.6
Other services	6 321	6 622	6 717	302	94	0.5	0.1	605	637	750	0.5	1.6
Repair and mantenance	1 227	1 329	1 367	102	37	0.8	0.3	202	212	239	0.5	1.2
Automotive repair and maintenance	856	938	967	81	29	0.9	0.3	124	128	137	0.3	0.7
Electronic and precision equipment repair and maintenance	103	103	99	0	-4	0.0	-0.4	19	26	33	2.9	2.6
Commercial and industrial machinery and equipment (except automotive and electronic) repair and maintenance	192	211	223	19.0	12	0.9	0.6	34	39	49	1.2	2.4
Personal and household goods repair and maintenance	75	78	78	3	0	0.3	0.0	24	20	21	-1.7	0.4
Personal and laundry services	1 323	1 510	1 608	187	98	1.3	0.6	176	187	217	0.6	1.5
Personal care services	616	728	811	112	84	1.7	1.1	68	77	92	1.2	1.8
Death care services	135	136	137	1	1	0.1	0.0	21	23	23	0.7	0.2
Drycleaning and laundry services	332	297	273	-35	-25	-1.1	-0.9	29	29	32	-0.1	1.1
Other personal services	239	348	387	109	39	3.8	1.1	58	59	69	0.2	1.6
Religious, grantmaking, civic, professional, and similar organizatons	2 966	3 006	3 040	40	34	0.1	0.1	208	221	274	0.6	2.2
Religious organizations	1 687	1 720	1 747	33	27	0.2	0.2	86	87	103	0.1	1.7
Grantmaking and giving services and social advocacy organizations	352	417	442	64	25	1.7	0.6	49	49	62	0.1	2.3
Civic, social, professional, and similar organizations	926	869	851	-57	-18	-0.6	-0.2	73	85	109	1.6	2.5
Private households	805	778	702	-27	-76.0	-0.3	-1.0	19	17	20	-1.1	1.5
Federal Government	2 762	2 796	2 670	34	-126	0.1	-0.5	1 075	1 114	1 099	0.4	-0.1
Postal Service	747	609	482	-139	-127	-2.0	-2.3	80	52	43	-4.3	-1.7
Federal electric utilities	24	15	10	-9	-5	-4.7	-3.5	14	17	17	1.9	0.5
Federal enterprises except the Postal Service and electric utilities	84	76	74	-8	-3	-0.9	-0.4	20	21	26	0.6	2.4
Federal defense government compensation	496	528	522	33	-6	0.6	-0.1	228	231	224	0.2	-0.3
Federal defense government consumption of fixed capital	0	0	0	0	0	0.0	0.0	146	151	146	0.4	-0.3
Federal defense government except compensation and consumption of fixed capital	0	0	0	0	0	0.0	0.0	254	249	246	-0.2	-0.2
Federal non-defense government compensation - except enterprises	1 411	1 568	1 582	157	14	1.1	0.1	148	160	154	0.8	-0.3
Federal non-defense government consumption of fixed capital	0	0	0	0	0	0.0	0.0	85	107	103	2.3	-0.3
Federal non-defense government except compensation and consumption of fixed capital	0	0	0	0	0	0.0	0.0	101	128	141	2.4	1.0
Federal government except enterprises	1 907	2 096	2 104	189	8	1.0	0.0	962	1 026	1 013	0.6	-0.1

Table 4-8. Employment and Output, by Industry, 2008, 2018, and Projected 2028—*Continued*

(Number, percent, dollars.)

Industry	Employment							Output				
	Number of jobs (thousands)			Change		Average annual rate of change (percent)		Billions of chained (2005) dollars			Average annual rate of change (percent)	
	2008	2018	2028	2008–2018	2018–2028	2008–2018	2018–2028	2008	2018	2028	2008–2018	2018–2028
State and Local Government	19 747	19 653	19 904	-94	251	0.0	0.1	2 279	2 445	2 686	0.7	0.9
Local government passenger transit	268	288	300	20	12	0.7	0.4	15	16	20	0.7	2.2
Local government enterprises except passenger transit	1 331	1 337	1 381	6	45	0.0	0.3	171	194	218	1.2	1.2
Local government hospitals - compensation	659	675	679	16	4.0	0.2	0.1	64	62	65	-0.4	0.4
Local government educational services - compensation	8 084	7 963	7 973	-121	9	-0.2	0.0	437	417	434	-0.5	0.4
Local government excluding enterprises, educational services, and hospitals - compensation	4 229	4 214	4 336	-14	121	0.0	0.3	345	344	359	0.0	0.4
State government enterprises	535	494	469	-41	-24	-0.8	-0.5	85	94	107	1.1	1.2
State government hospitals - compensation	361	381	403	20	22	0.6	0.6	45	39	40	-1.3	0.2
State government educational services - compensation	2 354	2 486	2 563	131.0	77	0.5	0.3	126	141	157	1.1	1.1
State government, other compensation	1 927	1 816	1 800	-112	-15.0	-0.6	-0.1	181	167	165	-0.8	-0.1
State and local government capital services	0	0	0	0	0	0.0	0.0	167	192	200	1.4	0.4
General state and local government except compensation and capital services	0	0	0	0	0	0.0	0.0	643	791	943	2.1	1.8
Owner-Occupied Dwellings	0	0	0	0	0	0.0	0.0	1 269	1 515	1 700	1.8	1.2
Agriculture, Forestry, Fishing, and Hunting[3]	2 071	2 310	2 321	239	11	1.1	0.0	448	510	613	1.3	1.9
Crop production	941	1 210	1 239	269	29	2.5	0.2	207	274	319	2.8	1.6
Animal production	845	794	772	-51	-22	-0.6	-0.3	191	192	241	0.0	2.3
Forestry	17	11	12	-7	2	-4.7	1.6	6	4	5	-3.6	1.6
Logging	81	72	57	-9	-15	-1.1	-2.4	15	13	14	-0.9	0.5
Fishing, hunting and trapping	47	53	50	6	-2	1.2	-0.4	7	9	11	2.1	2.0
Support activities for agriculture and forestry	140	170	190	30	20	2.0	1.1	22	23	26	0.5	1.4
Nonagriculture Self-Employed[4]	9 214	8 924	9 453	-290.0	529	-0.3	0.6	. . .	. . .	. . .	0.0	0.0

[3]Includes agriculture, forestry, fishing, and hunting wage and salary, and self-employed data from the Current Population Survey, except logging, which is from Current Employment Statistics survey.
[4]Comparable estimate of output growth is not available.
. . . = Not available.

Table 4-9. Employment and Wages by Typical Entry Level Education, Projected 2018–2028

(Numbers in thousands, percent, dollars.)

Education, work experience, and on-the-job training	2018 Employment		Employment changes, 2018–2028 (percent)	Median annual wage, 2018
	Number	Percent distribution		
TOTAL, ALL OCCUPATIONS	161 038	100.0	5.2	38 640
Doctoral or professional degree	4 383	2.7	9.0	105 700
Master's degree	2 685	1.7	13.7	73 580
Bachelor's degree	35 479	22.0	7.7	73 960
Associate's degree	3 573	2.2	7.9	53 700
Postsecondary nondegree award	9 993	6.2	8.2	38 640
Some college, no degree	4 106	2.5	1.4	35 820
High school diploma or equivalent	62 427	38.8	2.9	37 020
No formal educational credential	38 392	23.8	5.0	24 430

Table 4-10. Employment in STEM Occupations 2018 and Projected 2028

(Numbers, percent, dollars.)

Education, work experience, and on-the-job training	Employment		Change 2018–2028		Median annual wage, 2018[1]
	2018	2028	Number	Percent	
TOTAL, ALL OCCUPATIONS	161 038	169 436	8 398	5.2	38 640
STEM Occupations[2]	9 708	10 567	858	8.8	84 880
Non-STEM occupations	151 329	158 869	7 540	5.0	37 020

[1]Science, technology, engineering, and math (STEM) occupations include computer and mathematical, architecture and engineering, and life and physical science occupations, as well as managerial and postsecondary teaching
occupations related to these functional areas and sales occupations requiring scientific or technical knowledge at the postsecondary level.
[2]Wage data cover non-farm wage and salary workers and do not cover the self-employed, owners and partners in unincorporated firms, or household workers.

CHAPTER 5: PRODUCTIVITY AND COSTS

HIGHLIGHTS

This chapter covers two kinds of productivity measures produced by the Bureau of Labor Statistics (BLS): output per hour (or labor productivity) and multifactor productivity. Multifactor productivity is designed to combine the joint influence of technological change, efficiency improvements, returns to scale, and other factors on economic growth.

Figure 5-1. Percent Change in Labor Productivity for Business, Nonfinancial Corporations, and Manufacturing Industries, 2000–2018

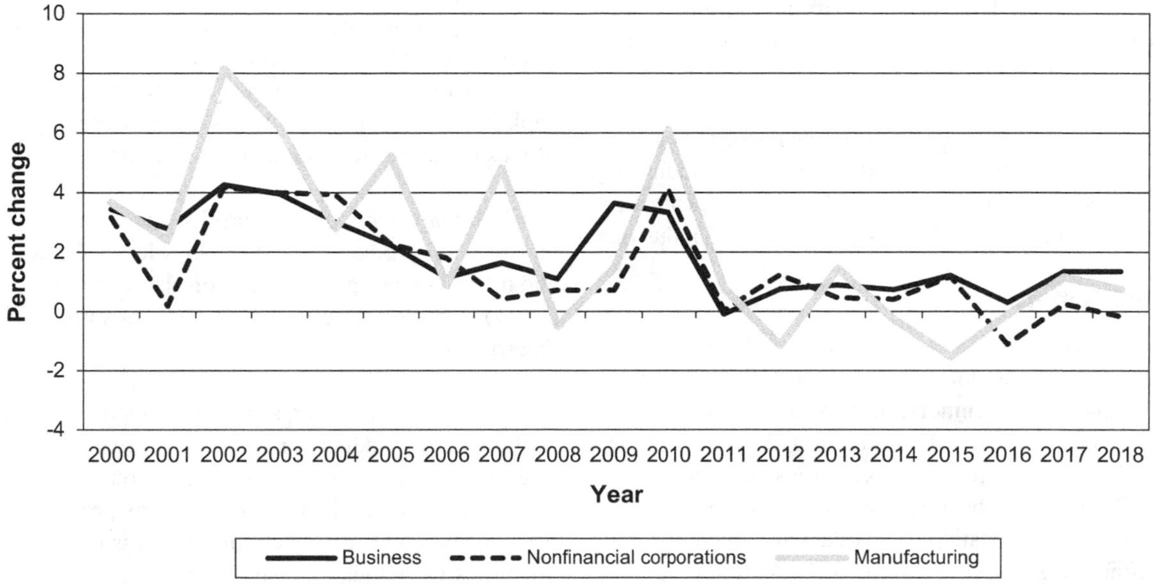

In 2018, labor productivity increased in all major sectors except for nonfinancial corporations which experienced a slight decline of 0.2 percent. It increased 1.3 percent in business, 1.2 percent in nonfarm business, and 0.7 percent in manufacturing. (See Table 5-1.)

OTHER HIGHLIGHTS:

- Labor productivity grew rapidly among wireless telecommunications carries and software publishers, increasing at average annual rate of 11.9 percent and 10.8 percent respectively from 1987 through 2017. (See Table 5-2.)

- During the 1987–2018 period, unit labor costs increased in 77 of the 86 NAICS 4-digit manufacturing industries. All 4 mining industries saw an increase in unit labor costs. (See Table 5-2.)

- Productivity grew on average 2.7 percent in wholesale trade while hours worked increased 0.3 percent from 1987 through 2018. In retail trade, productivity grew 2.9 percent while hours worked increased 0.5 percent. Productivity was significantly slower in food services and drinking places only increasing 0.5 percent while hours worked increased 1.8 percent. (See Table 5-3.)

- From 1987 to 2018, unit labor costs increased on average 3.0 percent in food services and drinking places, increased 0.9 percent in wholesale trade, and remained unchanged in retail trade. (See Table 5-3.)

- Multifactor productivity increased again in 2018 in both private business and private nonfarm business after declining in 2016. (See Table 5-4.)

NOTES AND DEFINITIONS

PRODUCTIVITY AND COSTS

The Bureau of Labor Statistics (BLS) produces labor productivity and costs (LPC) measures for sectors of the U.S. economy. Productivity is a measure of economic efficiency that shows how effectively economic inputs are converted into output. The Major Sector Productivity program develops quarterly labor productivity measures for the major U.S. economic sectors including the business sector, the nonfarm business sector, nonfinancial corporations, and manufacturing, along with subsectors of durable and nondurable goods manufacturing. The Industry Productivity program develops annual labor productivity and unit labor cost measures for U.S. industries. In addition, the BLS produces multifactor productivity measures.

Quarterly labor productivity measures are available for business and nonfarm business sectors, nonfinancial corporations and Manufacturing sector. Annual labor productivity measures are available for selected 2-, 3-, 4-, 5-, and 6-digit NAICS industries.

Concepts and Definitions

Business sector output is an annual-weighted index constructed after excluding from gross domestic product (GDP) the following outputs: General government, nonprofit institutions, paid employees of private households, and the rental value of owner-occupied dwellings. Corresponding exclusions also are made in labor inputs. The nonfarm business sector output also excludes the farm sector. Gross domestic product data are prepared by the Bureau of Economic Analysis of the U.S. Department of Commerce as part of the National Income and Product Accounts.

Hourly compensation costs are defined as the sum of wage and salary accruals and supplements to wages and salaries. Wage and salary accruals consist of the monetary remuneration of employees, including the compensation of corporate officers; commissions, tips, and bonuses; voluntary employee contributions to certain deferred compensation plans, such as 401(k) plans; employee gains from exercising nonqualified stock options; and receipts in kind that represent income. Supplements to wages and salaries consist of employer contributions for social insurance and employer payments (including payments in kind) to private pension and profit-sharing plans, group health and life insurance plans, privately administered workers' compensation plans. For employees (wage and salary workers), hourly compensation is measured relative to hours at work and includes payments made by employers for time not at work, such as vacation, holiday, and sick pay. Because compensation costs for the business and nonfarm business sectors would otherwise be severely understated, an estimate of the hourly compensation of proprietors of unincorporated businesses is made by assuming that their hourly compensation is equal to that of employees in the same sector.

Hours at work include paid time working, traveling between job sites, coffee breaks, and machine downtime. Hours at work, however, exclude hours for which employees are paid but not at work.

The *Nonfarm business sector* is a subset of the domestic economy and excludes the economic activities of the following: general government, private households, nonprofit organizations serving individuals, and farms.

Nonfinancial corporations are a subset of the domestic economy and excludes the economic activities of the following: general government, private households, nonprofit organizations serving individuals, and those corporations classified as offices of bank holding companies, offices of other holding companies, or offices in the finance and insurance sector.

Nonlabor payments include profits, consumption of fixed capital, taxes on production and imports less subsidies, net interest and miscellaneous payments, business current transfer payments, rental income of persons, and the current surplus of government enterprises.

Output is measured as an annual-weighted index of the changes in the various products or services (in real terms) provided for sale outside the industry. Real industry output is usually derived by deflating nominal sales or values of production using BLS price indexes, but for some industries it is measured by physical quantities of output. Industry output measures are constructed primarily using data from the economic censuses and annual surveys of the U.S. Census Bureau, U.S. Department of Commerce, together with information on price changes primarily from BLS. Output measures for some mining and utilities industries are based on physical quantity data from the Energy Information Administration, U.S. Department of Energy, while output measures for some transportation industries are based on physical quantity data from the Bureau of Transportation Statistics, U.S. Department of Transportation. Other data sources for some industries include the U.S. Geological Survey, U.S. Department of the Interior; the U.S. Postal Service; the Federal Deposit Insurance Corporation; and the Postal Rate Commission.

Productivity measures describe the relationship between industry output and the labor time involved in its production. They show the changes from period to period in the amount of goods and services produced per hour. Although the labor productivity measures relate output to hours of employees or all persons in an industry, they do not measure the specific contribution of labor or any other factor of production. Rather, they reflect the joint effects of many influences, including changes in technology; capital investment; utilization of capacity, energy, and materials; the use of purchased services inputs, including contract employment services; the organization of production; managerial skill; and the characteristics and effort of the workforce.

Unit labor costs show the growth in compensation relative to that of real output. These costs are calculated by dividing total labor compensation by real output. Changes in unit labor costs can be approximated by subtracting the change in productivity from the change in hourly compensation.

Multifactor Productivity Concepts and Definitions

For the private business and private nonfarm business sectors, the growth rate of multifactor productivity is measured as the growth rate of output less the growth rate of combined inputs of labor and capital. Labor is measured by a weighted average of the number of hours worked classified by education, work experience, and gender. Capital services measure the flow of services from the stocks of equipment and software, structures, land, and inventories. For the manufacturing sector, multifactor productivity is the growth rate of output less the combined inputs of labor, capital, and intermediate purchases. Labor is measured by the number of hours worked. Capital services measure the flow of services from the stocks of equipment and software, structures, land, and inventories. Intermediate purchases are composed of materials, fuels, electricity, and purchased services.

Sectoral output is defined as gross output excluding intra-industry transactions. This measure defines output as deliveries to consumers outside the sector, in an effort to avoid the problem of double-counting that occurs when one establishment provides materials used by other establishments in the same industry.

Value-added output is defined as gross output (sales or receipts and other income, plus inventory change) minus intermediate inputs (goods and service inputs purchased from other domestic industries and foreign sources).

Sources of Additional Information

Productivity concepts and methodology are described in the *BLS Handbook of Methods*. More information on productivity can be found in BLS news releases on the BLS Web site at <http://www.bls.gov/lpc/>. More information can be found in BLS new release USDL19-1343 "Productivity and Costs by Industry: Wholesale Trade, Retail Trade, and Food Services and Drinking Places Industries, 2018" as well as BLS new release 19-0858 "Productivity and Costs by Industry: Selected Service-Providing Industries, 2018."

Table 5-1. Indexes of Productivity and Related Data, 1947–2018

(2012 = 100.)

Year	Business											
	Output per hour	Output	Hours	Hourly compen-sation	Real hourly compen-sation	Unit labor costs	Unit nonlabor payments	Implicit price deflator	Employment	Output per job	Compen-sation in current dollars	Nonlabor payments in current dollars
1947	20.4	11.2	54.8	3.6	33.9	17.7	11.8	15.1	47.2	23.7	2.0	1.3
1948	21.3	11.7	55.2	3.9	34.0	18.4	13.0	16.0	47.7	24.6	2.2	1.5
1949	21.8	11.6	53.4	4.0	34.9	18.2	12.9	15.9	46.6	24.9	2.1	1.5
1950	23.5	12.7	54.1	4.2	36.9	18.0	13.5	16.1	47.1	27.1	2.3	1.7
1951	24.3	13.6	55.9	4.6	37.5	19.2	14.9	17.3	48.3	28.0	2.6	2.0
1952	25.0	14.0	56.0	4.9	39.0	19.8	14.6	17.5	48.6	28.8	2.8	2.0
1953	25.9	14.7	56.7	5.2	41.2	20.2	14.3	17.6	49.2	29.8	3.0	2.1
1954	26.5	14.5	54.8	5.4	42.2	20.4	14.2	17.7	48.0	30.2	3.0	2.1
1955	27.6	15.7	56.8	5.6	43.4	20.1	15.2	18.0	49.4	31.8	3.2	2.4
1956	27.7	16.0	57.7	5.9	45.6	21.4	14.9	18.5	50.4	31.7	3.4	2.4
1957	28.6	16.3	56.9	6.3	47.0	22.1	15.4	19.1	50.3	32.3	3.6	2.5
1958	29.4	16.0	54.3	6.6	47.8	22.4	15.7	19.5	48.4	33.0	3.6	2.5
1959	30.5	17.2	56.6	6.8	49.4	22.5	16.1	19.7	49.9	34.5	3.9	2.8
1960	31.0	17.6	56.7	7.1	50.6	23.0	15.9	19.9	50.2	35.0	4.0	2.8
1961	32.1	17.9	55.8	7.4	52.0	23.1	16.2	20.1	49.7	36.1	4.1	2.9
1962	33.6	19.1	56.8	7.7	53.7	23.0	16.6	20.2	50.3	38.0	4.4	3.2
1963	34.9	20.0	57.2	8.0	54.9	23.0	17.0	20.4	50.6	39.5	4.6	3.4
1964	36.0	21.2	58.9	8.3	56.2	23.1	17.4	20.6	51.5	41.2	4.9	3.7
1965	37.3	22.7	60.9	8.6	57.4	23.1	18.1	20.9	53.0	42.9	5.3	4.1
1966	38.9	24.3	62.5	9.2	59.6	23.7	18.6	21.4	54.6	44.5	5.8	4.5
1967	39.8	24.8	62.3	9.7	61.0	24.5	18.9	22.0	55.3	44.8	6.1	4.7
1968	41.2	26.0	63.3	10.5	63.2	25.5	19.5	22.9	56.4	46.2	6.6	5.1
1969	41.4	26.8	64.9	11.2	64.1	27.1	19.8	23.9	58.2	46.2	7.3	5.3
1970	42.2	26.8	63.6	12.1	65.2	28.6	20.3	24.9	58.0	46.3	7.7	5.4
1971	43.9	27.9	63.4	12.8	66.2	29.1	22.0	26.0	58.1	47.9	8.1	6.1
1972	45.4	29.7	65.3	13.6	68.2	30.0	23.0	26.9	59.8	49.6	8.9	6.8
1973	46.8	31.7	67.9	14.7	69.3	31.4	24.3	28.3	62.4	50.8	10.0	7.7
1974	46.0	31.2	68.0	16.0	68.2	34.9	26.1	31.1	63.4	49.3	10.9	8.2
1975	47.6	31.0	65.0	17.8	69.2	37.3	29.8	34.1	61.5	50.4	11.6	9.2
1976	49.2	33.0	67.2	19.2	70.7	39.0	31.8	35.8	63.4	52.2	12.9	10.5
1977	50.1	34.9	69.8	20.7	71.7	41.4	33.6	38.0	66.1	52.8	14.5	11.7
1978	50.7	37.2	73.3	22.5	72.6	44.3	35.8	40.6	69.7	53.3	16.5	13.3
1979	50.7	38.5	75.8	24.6	72.8	48.6	38.1	44.0	72.4	53.1	18.7	14.7
1980	50.7	38.1	75.2	27.3	72.4	53.8	40.3	47.9	72.6	52.5	20.5	15.4
1981	51.8	39.2	75.7	29.8	72.4	57.6	45.5	52.3	73.4	53.5	22.6	17.9
1982	51.6	38.1	73.9	32.1	73.4	62.2	46.4	55.3	72.2	52.8	23.7	17.7
1983	53.3	40.1	75.3	33.5	73.5	62.8	50.1	57.3	72.8	55.1	25.2	20.1
1984	54.8	43.7	79.7	35.0	73.7	63.8	52.6	58.9	76.5	57.1	27.9	23.0
1985	56.1	45.7	81.5	36.8	74.9	65.5	53.9	60.4	78.4	58.4	30.0	24.6
1986	57.7	47.4	82.2	38.8	77.8	67.4	53.4	61.3	79.7	59.5	31.9	25.3
1987	58.0	49.1	84.6	40.3	78.0	69.5	53.3	62.4	81.8	60.0	34.1	26.2
1988	58.9	51.2	87.0	42.4	79.3	72.1	54.5	64.4	84.3	60.7	36.9	27.9
1989	59.6	53.2	89.3	43.7	78.3	73.4	58.2	66.8	86.2	61.7	39.0	31.0
1990	60.8	54.0	88.9	46.5	79.3	76.5	59.3	69.0	86.7	62.3	41.3	32.1
1991	61.7	53.7	87.0	48.6	80.0	78.8	61.0	71.0	85.4	62.9	42.3	32.7
1992	64.6	56.0	86.6	51.6	82.9	79.9	62.2	72.1	84.9	65.9	44.7	34.8
1993	64.7	57.6	89.0	52.4	82.0	81.0	64.5	73.8	86.7	66.4	46.6	37.1
1994	65.0	60.3	92.8	52.8	80.9	81.1	67.4	75.1	89.7	67.3	48.9	40.7
1995	65.5	62.2	94.9	54.0	81.0	82.5	68.7	76.5	92.2	67.4	51.3	42.7
1996	67.1	65.1	97.0	56.0	81.7	83.4	70.3	77.7	94.2	69.0	54.3	45.7
1997	68.6	68.5	99.9	58.2	83.2	84.9	71.0	78.8	96.8	70.8	58.2	48.6
1998	70.7	72.0	101.9	61.7	86.9	87.2	69.0	79.3	98.8	72.9	62.8	49.7
1999	73.5	76.1	103.5	64.6	89.2	87.9	69.3	79.8	100.4	75.8	66.9	52.7
2000	76.1	79.8	104.9	69.1	92.3	90.9	68.2	81.0	102.1	78.1	72.5	54.4
2001	78.2	80.4	102.8	72.3	93.8	92.5	69.2	82.3	101.4	79.3	74.3	55.6
2002	81.5	81.8	100.3	73.9	94.4	90.7	72.9	82.9	99.2	82.5	74.2	59.6
2003	84.7	84.5	99.7	76.7	95.8	90.5	75.5	83.9	99.0	85.3	76.5	63.8
2004	87.3	88.1	100.9	80.3	97.6	92.0	78.5	86.1	100.3	87.8	81.0	69.1
2005	89.2	91.5	102.6	83.2	97.9	93.2	82.9	88.7	102.1	89.6	85.3	75.9
2006	90.3	94.6	104.8	86.4	98.4	95.7	85.2	91.1	104.1	90.9	90.6	80.6
2007	91.7	96.8	105.5	90.3	100.0	98.4	86.6	93.2	105.0	92.2	95.2	83.8
2008	92.7	95.8	103.3	92.8	99.0	100.0	87.8	94.7	103.5	92.6	95.8	84.1
2009	96.1	92.3	96.0	93.6	100.2	97.4	91.7	94.9	97.7	94.5	89.8	84.6
2010	99.3	95.2	95.9	95.3	100.4	95.9	96.1	96.0	96.5	98.6	91.3	91.5
2011	99.2	97.1	97.8	97.3	99.4	98.1	98.3	98.2	98.1	99.0	95.2	95.4
2012	100.0	100.0	100.0	100.0	100.0	100.0	100.0	100.0	100.0	100.0	100.0	100.0
2013	100.9	102.4	101.5	101.5	100.0	100.6	102.6	101.5	101.7	100.8	103.0	105.1
2014	101.6	105.6	103.9	104.1	100.9	102.5	104.0	103.1	103.8	101.8	108.2	109.9
2015	102.9	109.4	106.3	107.1	103.6	104.1	103.2	103.7	106.3	102.9	113.9	112.8
2016	103.2	111.3	107.9	108.3	103.4	105.0	103.9	104.5	108.2	102.9	116.8	115.7
2017	104.6	114.4	109.4	112.1	104.8	107.2	105.2	106.3	109.8	104.2	122.7	120.4
2018	106.0	118.3	111.7	115.7	105.6	109.2	108.1	108.7	111.9	105.7	129.2	127.9

Table 5-1. Indexes of Productivity and Related Data, 1947–2018—*Continued*

(2012 = 100.)

Year	Nonfarm business											
	Output per hour	Output	Hours	Hourly compensation	Real hourly compensation	Unit labor costs	Unit nonlabor payments	Implicit price deflator	Employment	Output per job	Compensation in current dollars	Nonlabor payments in current dollars
1947	23.5	10.9	46.5	3.9	36.2	16.4	11.3	14.2	39.6	27.6	1.8	1.2
1948	24.1	11.4	47.2	4.2	36.4	17.4	12.2	15.1	40.4	28.2	2.0	1.4
1949	24.9	11.3	45.4	4.3	38.0	17.3	12.5	15.2	39.3	28.8	2.0	1.4
1950	26.5	12.4	46.9	4.6	39.7	17.2	13.1	15.4	40.2	30.9	2.1	1.6
1951	27.2	13.4	49.1	5.0	40.0	18.2	14.1	16.4	42.0	31.8	2.4	1.9
1952	27.8	13.8	49.6	5.2	41.4	18.9	14.0	16.8	42.5	32.4	2.6	1.9
1953	28.4	14.5	50.9	5.5	43.4	19.5	14.0	17.1	43.8	33.0	2.8	2.0
1954	29.0	14.2	49.1	5.7	44.5	19.7	14.0	17.2	42.6	33.4	2.8	2.0
1955	30.2	15.4	51.1	5.9	46.3	19.6	14.9	17.5	43.9	35.2	3.0	2.3
1956	30.0	15.7	52.4	6.3	48.4	20.9	14.6	18.2	45.2	34.8	3.3	2.3
1957	30.8	16.1	52.1	6.6	49.5	21.5	15.1	18.7	45.4	35.3	3.5	2.4
1958	31.5	15.7	49.9	6.9	50.1	21.9	15.3	19.0	43.8	35.9	3.4	2.4
1959	32.6	17.0	52.2	7.2	51.6	22.0	15.9	19.3	45.4	37.5	3.7	2.7
1960	33.0	17.3	52.5	7.5	53.0	22.6	15.5	19.5	45.9	37.8	3.9	2.7
1961	34.1	17.7	51.9	7.7	54.2	22.6	15.8	19.7	45.5	38.9	4.0	2.8
1962	35.7	18.9	53.1	8.0	55.8	22.5	16.4	19.9	46.4	40.8	4.3	3.1
1963	36.9	19.8	53.7	8.3	56.9	22.5	16.8	20.0	46.9	42.2	4.5	3.3
1964	37.9	21.1	55.7	8.6	57.9	22.6	17.3	20.3	48.1	44.0	4.8	3.7
1965	39.1	22.6	57.9	8.9	58.9	22.6	17.9	20.5	49.7	45.5	5.1	4.0
1966	40.6	24.3	59.9	9.4	60.6	23.1	18.3	21.0	51.7	46.9	5.6	4.4
1967	41.3	24.7	59.8	9.9	62.3	24.0	18.6	21.7	52.6	47.0	5.9	4.6
1968	42.8	26.0	60.9	10.7	64.3	24.9	19.3	22.5	53.8	48.4	6.5	5.0
1969	42.8	26.8	62.6	11.4	65.1	26.6	19.5	23.5	55.7	48.2	7.1	5.2
1970	43.5	26.8	61.7	12.2	65.9	28.0	20.0	24.5	55.8	48.1	7.5	5.4
1971	45.2	27.8	61.5	12.9	67.0	28.6	21.7	25.6	55.9	49.7	8.0	6.0
1972	46.8	29.7	63.5	13.8	69.1	29.5	22.4	26.4	57.6	51.5	8.7	6.6
1973	48.2	31.8	66.1	14.8	70.0	30.8	22.8	27.3	60.2	52.9	9.8	7.3
1974	47.4	31.4	66.1	16.2	69.0	34.2	24.8	30.2	61.2	51.3	10.7	7.8
1975	48.7	30.9	63.3	17.9	69.9	36.8	28.9	33.4	59.4	51.9	11.4	8.9
1976	50.4	33.1	65.6	19.3	71.2	38.4	31.0	35.2	61.4	53.8	12.7	10.3
1977	51.3	35.0	68.2	20.9	72.4	40.8	32.9	37.4	64.2	54.4	14.3	11.5
1978	52.0	37.3	71.7	22.7	73.4	43.7	34.8	39.8	67.8	55.0	16.3	13.0
1979	51.9	38.6	74.3	24.9	73.5	47.9	36.9	43.1	70.7	54.5	18.5	14.2
1980	51.9	38.2	73.7	27.6	73.2	53.1	39.6	47.2	70.9	53.9	20.3	15.1
1981	52.7	39.1	74.3	30.2	73.3	57.4	44.5	51.8	71.7	54.5	22.4	17.4
1982	52.2	37.9	72.5	32.4	74.2	62.1	45.7	55.0	70.6	53.7	23.5	17.3
1983	54.4	40.3	74.0	33.9	74.3	62.3	49.8	56.9	71.3	56.5	25.1	20.1
1984	55.6	43.7	78.5	35.3	74.4	63.6	51.8	58.5	75.1	58.1	27.7	22.6
1985	56.6	45.6	80.6	37.1	75.5	65.5	53.4	60.2	77.2	59.0	29.9	24.3
1986	58.3	47.3	81.2	39.2	78.5	67.3	53.0	61.1	78.6	60.2	31.8	25.1
1987	58.6	49.0	83.7	40.7	78.7	69.4	52.9	62.2	80.8	60.7	34.0	25.9
1988	59.5	51.3	86.1	42.8	79.9	71.8	54.1	64.1	83.4	61.5	36.8	27.7
1989	60.1	53.1	88.4	44.0	78.8	73.2	57.7	66.5	85.2	62.3	38.9	30.6
1990	61.1	53.9	88.3	46.7	79.6	76.3	58.9	68.7	85.9	62.8	41.2	31.7
1991	62.1	53.6	86.3	48.9	80.4	78.7	60.7	70.9	84.5	63.5	42.2	32.6
1992	64.9	55.8	85.9	51.9	83.4	80.0	61.8	72.1	84.0	66.4	44.6	34.5
1993	65.0	57.5	88.5	52.6	82.3	80.9	64.5	73.8	86.0	66.8	46.5	37.1
1994	65.4	60.1	91.9	53.1	81.4	81.1	67.3	75.1	88.8	67.7	48.8	40.5
1995	66.1	62.2	94.0	54.4	81.5	82.2	68.9	76.5	91.4	68.1	51.2	42.9
1996	67.5	65.0	96.2	56.3	82.1	83.3	70.0	77.5	93.5	69.5	54.2	45.5
1997	68.8	68.4	99.3	58.5	83.5	84.9	71.0	78.9	96.2	71.1	58.0	48.5
1998	71.0	72.0	101.4	61.9	87.2	87.2	69.3	79.4	98.3	73.2	62.7	49.9
1999	73.7	76.1	103.3	64.7	89.3	87.9	69.8	80.0	100.1	76.0	66.8	53.1
2000	76.1	79.7	104.7	69.3	92.4	91.0	68.7	81.3	101.9	78.2	72.5	54.7
2001	78.2	80.3	102.7	72.3	93.8	92.4	69.7	82.6	101.3	79.3	74.2	56.0
2002	81.6	81.7	100.1	74.0	94.5	90.7	73.7	83.3	99.0	82.5	74.1	60.2
2003	84.7	84.3	99.6	76.7	95.8	90.6	75.9	84.2	98.9	85.2	76.4	64.0
2004	87.1	87.9	100.9	80.2	97.6	92.1	78.6	86.2	100.3	87.6	80.9	69.0
2005	89.0	91.3	102.6	83.1	97.8	93.4	83.4	89.1	102.2	89.4	85.3	76.2
2006	90.0	94.4	104.9	86.3	98.4	95.9	85.9	91.6	104.2	90.7	90.6	81.1
2007	91.6	96.7	105.6	90.1	99.8	98.4	86.9	93.4	105.1	92.0	95.2	84.1
2008	92.6	95.7	103.4	92.7	98.9	100.1	88.1	94.9	103.6	92.4	95.8	84.3
2009	95.9	92.0	96.0	93.5	100.2	97.5	92.5	95.4	97.7	94.2	89.8	85.2
2010	99.2	95.0	95.8	95.3	100.4	96.1	96.6	96.3	96.5	98.5	91.4	91.8
2011	99.2	96.9	97.8	97.4	99.5	98.2	98.1	98.2	98.0	98.9	95.2	95.1
2012	100.0	100.0	100.0	100.0	100.0	100.0	100.0	100.0	100.0	100.0	100.0	100.0
2013	100.5	102.2	101.7	101.3	99.8	100.8	102.3	101.5	101.8	100.4	103.0	104.6
2014	101.4	105.4	104.0	104.1	100.9	102.7	104.0	103.3	103.9	101.5	108.3	109.7
2015	102.7	109.1	106.2	107.3	103.8	104.5	103.6	104.1	106.2	102.7	114.0	113.1
2016	103.0	111.0	107.8	108.5	103.6	105.4	104.8	105.1	108.1	102.7	117.0	116.4
2017	104.4	114.2	109.4	112.3	105.0	107.6	105.9	106.9	109.8	104.0	122.8	120.9
2018	105.7	118.1	111.8	115.8	105.7	109.5	109.1	109.3	112.0	105.5	129.4	128.9

Table 5-1. Indexes of Productivity and Related Data, 1947–2018—*Continued*

(2012 = 100.)

Year	Nonfinancial corporations												
	Output per hour	Output	Hours	Hourly compen-sation	Real hourly compen-sation	Unit labor costs	Unit nonlabor costs	Unit profits	Implicit price deflator	Employment	Output per job	Compen-sation in current dollars	Nonlabor payments in current dollars
1947	22.5	8.8	38.9	4.4	19.5	19.5	10.9	21.3	17.3	33.6	26.0	1.7	1.3
1948	24.0	9.4	39.3	4.8	20.1	20.1	11.5	25.4	18.4	34.2	27.6	1.9	1.5
1949	25.3	9.3	37.0	5.0	19.7	19.7	12.4	23.1	18.1	32.6	28.7	1.8	1.5
1950	27.2	10.6	38.9	5.3	19.4	19.4	11.8	26.1	18.2	33.8	31.2	2.0	1.8
1951	26.9	11.1	41.4	5.8	21.4	21.4	12.4	28.0	19.8	36.0	31.0	2.4	2.0
1952	27.5	11.6	42.0	6.1	22.1	22.1	13.0	25.3	19.9	36.5	31.7	2.6	2.0
1953	28.7	12.4	43.3	6.4	22.4	22.4	12.9	23.7	19.9	37.8	32.9	2.8	2.1
1954	29.9	12.3	41.1	6.6	22.2	22.2	13.3	23.1	19.8	36.3	33.9	2.7	2.0
1955	31.7	13.8	43.5	6.9	21.7	21.7	12.9	26.9	19.9	37.9	36.4	3.0	2.4
1956	31.9	14.3	44.7	7.3	23.0	23.0	13.7	25.2	20.7	39.2	36.3	3.3	2.5
1957	32.6	14.4	44.3	7.8	23.8	23.8	14.8	24.2	21.3	39.3	36.7	3.4	2.6
1958	33.3	13.9	41.8	8.1	24.2	24.2	16.2	22.0	21.6	37.4	37.2	3.4	2.5
1959	34.9	15.5	44.3	8.4	24.0	24.0	15.6	25.5	21.8	39.1	39.5	3.7	2.9
1960	35.5	16.0	45.0	8.7	24.5	24.5	16.0	23.5	21.9	40.0	40.0	3.9	3.0
1961	36.7	16.4	44.6	9.0	24.5	24.5	16.3	23.6	22.0	39.7	41.2	4.0	3.1
1962	38.3	17.8	46.4	9.3	24.4	24.4	16.1	25.3	22.1	41.0	43.3	4.3	3.4
1963	39.7	18.8	47.4	9.6	24.2	24.2	16.0	26.8	22.2	41.9	45.0	4.6	3.7
1964	40.3	20.2	50.0	9.8	24.3	24.3	16.0	27.8	22.4	43.4	46.5	4.9	4.0
1965	41.4	21.9	52.8	10.1	24.4	24.4	15.9	29.9	22.7	45.7	47.9	5.3	4.5
1966	42.2	23.5	55.6	10.6	25.2	25.2	16.0	30.0	23.3	48.2	48.7	5.9	4.8
1967	43.0	24.2	56.2	11.2	26.2	26.2	16.9	28.1	23.8	49.6	48.7	6.3	5.0
1968	44.5	25.7	57.8	12.1	27.1	27.1	18.1	28.1	24.7	51.4	50.1	7.0	5.5
1969	44.6	26.7	60.0	12.9	28.9	28.9	19.6	25.4	25.7	53.7	49.8	7.7	5.8
1970	44.9	26.5	59.1	13.7	30.6	30.6	22.1	20.9	26.8	53.8	49.3	8.1	5.8
1971	46.7	27.6	59.0	14.6	31.2	31.2	23.2	23.7	27.8	53.9	51.1	8.6	6.4
1972	47.7	29.6	62.2	15.3	32.2	32.2	23.1	25.9	28.7	56.7	52.3	9.5	7.1
1973	48.1	31.5	65.4	16.4	34.2	34.2	24.4	26.8	30.3	59.8	52.6	10.7	7.9
1974	47.2	31.0	65.6	17.9	38.0	38.0	28.0	24.5	33.2	61.0	50.8	11.8	8.3
1975	49.0	30.5	62.3	19.8	40.4	40.4	32.0	29.6	36.5	58.7	52.1	12.3	9.5
1976	50.7	33.1	65.2	21.3	42.0	42.0	31.8	34.9	38.1	61.3	53.9	13.9	10.9
1977	52.1	35.5	68.2	23.0	44.2	44.2	33.0	37.9	40.1	64.4	55.1	15.7	12.3
1978	52.7	37.8	71.7	25.1	47.6	47.6	34.4	40.4	42.8	68.0	55.6	18.0	13.7
1979	52.3	39.0	74.6	27.4	52.4	52.4	37.2	38.7	46.1	71.2	54.8	20.5	14.7
1980	52.2	38.6	74.1	30.2	57.9	57.9	43.7	35.0	50.6	71.4	54.1	22.4	15.8
1981	53.5	40.2	75.2	32.9	61.5	61.5	49.7	41.0	55.2	72.7	55.3	24.7	18.8
1982	53.8	39.3	73.1	35.1	65.3	65.3	55.1	38.2	58.5	71.0	55.4	25.7	19.5
1983	55.6	41.3	74.2	36.6	65.8	65.8	55.4	44.3	59.7	71.4	57.8	27.1	21.3
1984	56.9	44.9	79.0	38.1	67.0	67.0	55.1	51.9	61.5	75.5	59.5	30.1	24.3
1985	58.2	47.0	80.7	40.0	68.8	68.8	56.3	50.1	62.5	77.7	60.5	32.3	25.5
1986	59.5	48.2	81.0	42.3	71.0	71.0	59.2	41.4	63.4	78.8	61.2	34.2	25.7
1987	60.8	50.8	83.5	43.8	72.0	72.0	59.7	44.3	64.6	81.0	62.7	36.6	27.7
1988	62.5	53.9	86.2	46.0	73.5	73.5	60.9	47.3	66.2	83.7	64.4	39.6	30.4
1989	61.8	54.9	88.8	47.3	76.4	76.4	64.3	43.3	68.2	85.8	64.0	42.0	31.4
1990	62.3	55.7	89.4	49.5	79.4	79.4	67.2	40.9	70.4	87.3	63.8	44.2	32.5
1991	63.7	55.4	87.0	51.7	81.1	81.1	70.0	42.0	72.3	85.4	64.9	44.9	33.6
1992	65.5	57.1	87.1	54.5	83.2	83.2	68.6	43.6	73.3	85.4	66.9	47.5	34.4
1993	65.5	58.5	89.3	55.2	84.2	84.2	68.5	50.7	74.9	87.1	67.2	49.3	36.6
1994	66.6	62.1	93.3	55.8	83.8	83.8	68.9	60.5	76.2	90.3	68.8	52.1	41.1
1995	67.7	65.1	96.2	56.9	84.1	84.1	69.1	64.1	77.0	93.6	69.6	54.8	43.9
1996	70.0	68.9	98.5	58.8	84.0	84.0	68.3	68.7	77.3	95.9	71.9	57.9	47.2
1997	72.1	73.6	102.0	60.9	84.4	84.4	67.9	70.4	77.7	99.0	74.3	62.1	50.6
1998	74.4	77.6	104.2	64.4	86.6	86.6	68.3	62.9	78.0	101.4	76.5	67.1	51.6
1999	76.8	81.5	106.1	67.7	88.1	88.1	69.9	58.6	78.7	103.5	78.8	71.8	53.9
2000	79.3	85.4	107.8	72.4	91.4	91.4	72.8	49.2	80.1	105.6	80.9	78.1	55.5
2001	79.4	83.3	104.9	74.1	93.3	93.3	78.2	40.2	81.4	104.3	79.9	77.7	54.6
2002	82.7	84.2	101.7	75.5	91.3	91.3	78.7	49.2	81.7	101.3	83.1	76.8	57.9
2003	86.0	86.0	100.0	78.0	90.7	90.7	77.9	59.5	82.6	100.0	86.0	78.0	61.7
2004	89.4	90.2	100.9	80.9	90.4	90.4	77.4	72.6	84.2	100.8	89.5	81.6	68.4
2005	91.4	93.5	102.3	83.4	91.2	91.2	81.1	82.5	87.0	102.4	91.3	85.3	76.2
2006	93.1	97.1	104.3	85.9	92.2	92.2	82.8	91.8	89.5	104.1	93.3	89.6	83.3
2007	93.5	98.0	104.8	89.2	95.4	95.4	88.1	82.3	91.4	104.7	93.6	93.5	84.4
2008	94.1	96.9	102.9	92.0	97.7	97.7	94.2	73.8	93.3	103.3	93.8	94.7	84.7
2009	94.8	90.0	94.9	93.6	98.7	98.7	99.7	68.1	94.6	96.7	93.1	88.9	80.3
2010	98.7	93.9	95.1	95.1	96.3	96.3	97.9	89.1	95.7	95.7	98.1	90.4	89.2
2011	98.8	96.5	97.7	97.2	98.4	98.4	99.3	93.6	98.0	97.7	98.7	94.9	94.0
2012	100.0	100.0	100.0	100.0	100.0	100.0	100.0	100.0	100.0	100.0	100.0	100.0	100.0
2013	100.5	102.5	102.0	101.4	100.9	100.9	101.2	103.3	101.4	102.1	100.4	103.5	104.5
2014	100.9	105.8	104.8	104.0	103.1	103.1	102.5	104.2	103.1	104.7	101.0	109.1	109.0
2015	102.1	109.3	107.1	107.2	105.0	105.0	103.4	99.3	103.7	107.2	102.0	114.8	111.5
2016	100.9	109.7	108.7	108.4	107.3	107.3	104.5	93.0	104.5	109.1	100.5	117.8	110.4
2017	101.2	111.9	110.5	111.9	110.6	110.6	106.8	90.3	106.6	110.9	100.8	123.7	113.3
2018	101.0	114.0	112.9	115.5	114.3	114.3	110.0	89.3	109.5	113.1	100.8	130.4	117.5

Table 5-1. Indexes of Productivity and Related Data, 1947–2018—*Continued*

(2012 = 100.)

Year	Manufacturing											
	Output per hour	Output	Hours	Hourly compen-sation	Real hourly compen-sation	Unit labor costs	Unit nonlabor payments	Implicit price deflator	Employment	Output per job	Compen-sation in current dollars	Nonlabor payments in current dollars
1947	. . .	. . .	. . .	. . .	. . .	. . .	. . .	. . .	. . .	. . .	. . .	. . .
1948	. . .	. . .	. . .	. . .	. . .	. . .	. . .	. . .	. . .	. . .	. . .	. . .
1949	. . .	. . .	. . .	. . .	. . .	. . .	. . .	. . .	. . .	. . .	. . .	. . .
1950	. . .	. . .	. . .	. . .	. . .	. . .	. . .	. . .	. . .	. . .	. . .	. . .
1951	. . .	. . .	. . .	. . .	. . .	. . .	. . .	. . .	. . .	. . .	. . .	. . .
1952	. . .	. . .	. . .	. . .	. . .	. . .	. . .	. . .	. . .	. . .	. . .	. . .
1953	. . .	. . .	. . .	. . .	. . .	. . .	. . .	. . .	. . .	. . .	. . .	. . .
1954	. . .	. . .	. . .	. . .	. . .	. . .	. . .	. . .	. . .	. . .	. . .	. . .
1955	. . .	. . .	. . .	. . .	. . .	. . .	. . .	. . .	. . .	. . .	. . .	. . .
1956	. . .	. . .	. . .	. . .	. . .	. . .	. . .	. . .	. . .	. . .	. . .	. . .
1957	. . .	. . .	. . .	. . .	. . .	. . .	. . .	. . .	. . .	. . .	. . .	. . .
1958	. . .	. . .	. . .	. . .	. . .	. . .	. . .	. . .	. . .	. . .	. . .	. . .
1959	. . .	. . .	. . .	. . .	. . .	. . .	. . .	. . .	. . .	. . .	. . .	. . .
1960	. . .	. . .	. . .	. . .	. . .	. . .	. . .	. . .	. . .	. . .	. . .	. . .
1961	. . .	. . .	. . .	. . .	. . .	. . .	. . .	. . .	. . .	. . .	. . .	. . .
1962	. . .	. . .	. . .	. . .	. . .	. . .	. . .	. . .	. . .	. . .	. . .	. . .
1963	. . .	. . .	. . .	. . .	. . .	. . .	. . .	. . .	. . .	. . .	. . .	. . .
1964	. . .	. . .	. . .	. . .	. . .	. . .	. . .	. . .	. . .	. . .	. . .	. . .
1965	. . .	. . .	. . .	. . .	. . .	. . .	. . .	. . .	. . .	. . .	. . .	. . .
1966	. . .	. . .	. . .	. . .	. . .	. . .	. . .	. . .	. . .	. . .	. . .	. . .
1967	. . .	. . .	. . .	. . .	. . .	. . .	. . .	. . .	. . .	. . .	. . .	. . .
1968	. . .	. . .	. . .	. . .	. . .	. . .	. . .	. . .	. . .	. . .	. . .	. . .
1969	. . .	. . .	. . .	. . .	. . .	. . .	. . .	. . .	. . .	. . .	. . .	. . .
1970	. . .	. . .	. . .	. . .	. . .	. . .	. . .	. . .	. . .	. . .	. . .	. . .
1971	. . .	. . .	. . .	. . .	. . .	. . .	. . .	. . .	. . .	. . .	. . .	. . .
1972	. . .	. . .	. . .	. . .	. . .	. . .	. . .	. . .	. . .	. . .	. . .	. . .
1973	. . .	. . .	. . .	. . .	. . .	. . .	. . .	. . .	. . .	. . .	. . .	. . .
1974	. . .	. . .	. . .	. . .	. . .	. . .	. . .	. . .	. . .	. . .	. . .	. . .
1975	. . .	. . .	. . .	. . .	. . .	. . .	. . .	. . .	. . .	. . .	. . .	. . .
1976	. . .	. . .	. . .	. . .	. . .	. . .	. . .	. . .	. . .	. . .	. . .	. . .
1977	. . .	. . .	. . .	. . .	. . .	. . .	. . .	. . .	. . .	. . .	. . .	. . .
1978	. . .	. . .	. . .	. . .	. . .	. . .	. . .	. . .	. . .	. . .	. . .	. . .
1979	. . .	. . .	. . .	. . .	. . .	. . .	. . .	. . .	. . .	. . .	. . .	. . .
1980	. . .	. . .	. . .	. . .	. . .	. . .	. . .	. . .	. . .	. . .	. . .	. . .
1981	. . .	. . .	. . .	. . .	. . .	. . .	. . .	. . .	. . .	. . .	. . .	. . .
1982	. . .	. . .	. . .	. . .	. . .	. . .	. . .	. . .	. . .	. . .	. . .	. . .
1983	. . .	. . .	. . .	. . .	. . .	. . .	. . .	. . .	. . .	. . .	. . .	. . .
1984	. . .	. . .	. . .	. . .	. . .	. . .	. . .	. . .	. . .	. . .	. . .	. . .
1985	. . .	. . .	. . .	. . .	. . .	. . .	. . .	. . .	. . .	. . .	. . .	. . .
1986	. . .	. . .	. . .	. . .	. . .	. . .	. . .	. . .	. . .	. . .	. . .	. . .
1987	45.3	64.7	142.8	42.6	82.4	93.9	52.8	62.3	146.8	44.1	60.8	34.2
1988	45.8	67.4	147.1	44.3	82.7	96.7	55.3	64.8	149.4	45.1	65.1	37.2
1989	46.0	68.1	148.0	45.8	81.9	99.5	58.0	67.6	150.2	45.3	67.7	39.5
1990	47.6	68.3	143.4	48.2	82.3	101.3	59.6	69.3	148.0	46.1	69.2	40.7
1991	48.6	67.0	138.0	50.6	83.2	104.1	59.1	69.5	142.8	46.9	69.8	39.6
1992	51.4	70.3	136.8	53.4	85.7	103.9	59.5	69.8	140.4	50.1	73.0	41.8
1993	52.6	72.8	138.4	54.1	84.7	102.8	60.4	70.2	140.5	51.8	74.9	44.0
1994	54.0	76.7	142.0	54.9	84.2	101.6	61.8	71.0	142.3	53.9	78.0	47.4
1995	55.9	79.9	142.9	56.3	84.4	100.8	64.5	72.9	144.3	55.3	80.5	51.5
1996	58.3	83.2	142.8	57.9	84.4	99.3	64.9	72.9	144.2	57.7	82.6	54.0
1997	61.0	88.9	145.7	58.9	84.1	96.5	65.0	72.3	145.4	61.1	85.8	57.7
1998	63.7	93.1	146.2	62.1	87.5	97.5	62.0	70.2	146.7	63.5	90.7	57.7
1999	67.2	96.7	143.8	65.6	90.6	97.6	61.7	70.0	144.4	67.0	94.4	59.6
2000	69.7	99.5	142.7	69.9	93.3	100.3	62.6	71.3	144.0	69.1	99.7	62.3
2001	71.4	95.3	133.5	71.9	93.4	100.8	61.7	70.7	137.3	69.4	96.0	58.8
2002	77.2	95.7	124.0	74.3	94.9	96.3	62.1	70.0	127.4	75.1	92.1	59.5
2003	81.9	96.6	117.9	78.3	97.8	95.5	64.0	71.3	121.4	79.6	92.3	61.9
2004	84.2	98.7	117.2	81.2	98.8	96.4	68.6	75.0	119.7	82.5	95.2	67.7
2005	88.6	102.7	115.9	84.3	99.1	95.1	75.3	79.9	119.1	86.2	97.6	77.3
2006	89.4	104.4	116.8	86.2	98.3	96.5	79.1	83.1	118.4	88.2	100.7	82.7
2007	93.7	107.6	114.8	89.7	99.4	95.7	83.4	86.3	116.4	92.4	103.0	89.8
2008	93.2	102.6	110.0	92.3	98.5	99.0	90.4	92.4	112.3	91.4	101.5	92.7
2009	94.6	90.7	95.9	95.3	102.1	100.8	82.3	86.5	99.6	91.0	91.4	74.6
2010	100.4	96.2	95.8	96.6	101.7	96.2	89.1	90.8	96.8	99.3	92.5	85.7
2011	101.2	98.8	97.7	98.3	100.4	97.2	98.7	98.4	98.1	100.7	96.1	97.6
2012	100.0	100.0	100.0	100.0	100.0	100.0	100.0	100.0	100.0	100.0	100.0	100.0
2013	101.5	102.2	100.8	100.6	99.1	99.1	100.5	100.2	100.6	101.6	101.3	102.8
2014	101.2	103.6	102.4	103.3	100.1	102.1	99.2	99.9	102.0	101.6	105.8	102.8
2015	99.6	103.0	103.4	105.9	102.4	106.3	90.4	94.1	103.2	99.8	109.5	93.1
2016	99.5	102.9	103.4	106.5	101.7	107.0	87.9	92.3	103.3	99.7	110.1	. . .
2017	100.7	105.2	104.5	110.2	103.0	109.5	. . .	. . .	104.2	100.9	115.1	. . .
2018	101.4	108.0	106.5	112.6	102.8	111.0	. . .	. . .	105.9	102.0	119.9	. . .

. . . = Not available.

Table 5-2. Average Annual Percent Change in Output Per Hour and Related Series, Selected Industries, 1987–2017

(Number, percent.)

Industry	NAICS code	2017 employment (thousands)	Average annual percent change, 1987–2017				
			Labor productivity	Unit labor costs	Output	Hours worked	Labor compensation
Utilities							
Utilities	22	555	2.0	1.6	1.3	-0.7	2.9
Power generation and supply	2211	393	2.8	0.8	1.9	-0.9	2.7
Natural gas distribution	2212	112	0.7	3.6	-0.3	-1.0	3.3
Water, sewage and other systems	2213	51	-1.8	4.7	0.7	2.5	5.4
Transportation and Warehousing							
Air transportation	481	468	3.0	0.9	2.7	-0.3	3.6
Line-haul railroads	482111	168	3.6	-0.4	1.8	-1.7	1.4
Truck transportation	484	1 667	0.7	1.0	2.0	1.3	3.0
General freight trucking	4841	1 195	1.1	1.0	2.3	1.2	3.4
General freight trucking, local	48411	318	2.7	0.2	3.7	1.0	3.9
General freight trucking, long-distance	48412	877	1.3	0.5	2.2	0.9	2.8
Specialized freight trucking	4842	472	0.8	1.9	1.9	1.1	3.8
Used household and office goods moving	48421	101	-0.4	2.6	-0.1	0.3	2.5
Other specialized trucking, local	48422	234	0.3	2.3	1.7	1.4	4.1
Other specialized trucking, long distance	48423	138	1.1	1.3	3.2	2.0	4.6
Postal service	491	615	0.4	2.9	-0.6	-1.0	2.3
Couriers and messengers	492	711	-1.9	3.2	0.6	2.6	3.9
Warehousing and storage	493	1 038	1.4	0.3	5.6	4.1	5.8
General warehousing and storage	49311	915	2.5	-0.5	6.9	4.3	6.4
Refrigerated warehousing and storage	49312	62	-0.2	1.5	2.9	3.1	4.4
Information							
Publishing	511	760	3.8	1.6	3.3	-0.5	5.0
Newspaper, book, and directory publishers	5111	379	0.1	4.0	-2.5	-2.6	1.3
Newspaper publishers	51111	169	-0.6	4.0	-4.2	-3.7	-0.5
Periodical publishers	51112	102	-0.4	4.7	-1.6	-1.2	3.0
Book publishers	51113	66	-0.2	4.7	-0.9	-0.7	3.7
Software publishers	5112	382	10.8	-5.2	17.2	5.8	11.1
Motion picture and video exhibition	51213	149	1.4	2.0	1.8	0.4	3.8
Broadcasting, except Internet	515	276	3.0	1.7	2.9	-0.1	4.6
Radio and television broadcasting	5151	222	2.2	1.7	1.8	-0.4	3.5
Radio broadcasting	51511	88	3.7	1.1	2.5	-1.2	3.6
Cable and other subscription programming	5152	54	5.2	2.9	6.4	1.2	9.5
Wired telecommunications carriers	5171	587	3.6	-0.7	2.6	-0.9	1.9
Wireless telecommunications carriers	5172	120	11.9	-6.9	18.5	5.9	10.4
Finance and Insurance							
Commercial banking	52211	1 324	3.0	2.0	3.0	0.0	5.0
Real Estate and Rental and Leasing							
Passenger car rental	532111	122	2.1	1.4	3.1	1.0	4.6
Truck, trailer, and RV rental and leasing	53212	80	1.9	1.1	2.7	0.7	3.8
Video tape and disc rental	53223	10	6.7	-2.3	-2.3	-8.4	-4.6
Professional and Technical Services							
Accounting and bookkeeping services	5412	1 152	2.6	1.0	3.3	0.6	4.4
Offices of certified public accountants	541211	490	2.0	2.1	3.0	1.0	5.2
Tax preparation services	541213	137	0.5	2.1	2.0	1.5	4.2
Other accounting services	541219	353	4.6	-1.8	4.7	0.1	2.8
Architectural services	54131	209	1.4	1.9	2.6	1.2	4.5
Engineering services	54133	994	1.2	2.7	2.8	1.6	5.6
Advertising agencies	54181	219	1.9	2.1	2.4	0.5	4.6
Photography studios, portrait	541921	58	0.3	1.7	1.2	1.0	2.9
Veterinary services	54194	386	-0.2	3.4	2.3	2.6	5.8
Administrative and Waste Services							
Employment placement and executive search	56131	303	4.3	0.0	5.3	1.0	5.3
Travel arrangement and reservation services	5615	246	6.0	-1.0	4.1	-1.8	3.0
Travel agencies	56151	108	5.6	-0.7	4.6	-0.9	3.8
Janitorial services	56172	1 466	1.7	1.8	3.4	1.8	5.3
Health Care and Social Assistance							
Medical and diagnostic laboratories	6215	282	1.9	0.5	5.0	3.0	5.5
Medical laboratories	621511	201	1.9	0.5	5.0	3.0	5.5
Diagnostic imaging centers	621512	81	2.1	0.8	5.0	2.8	5.8

Table 5-2. Average Annual Percent Change in Output Per Hour and Related Series, Selected Industries, 1987–2017—*Continued*

(Number, percent.)

Industry	NAICS code	2017 employment (thousands)	Average annual percent change, 1987–2017				
			Labor productivity	Unit labor costs	Output	Hours worked	Labor compensation
Hospitals, except psychiatric and substance abuse hospitals	6221	4 886	0.5	3.2	2.0	1.5	5.3
Arts, Entertainment, and Recreation							
Amusement parks and arcades	7131	211	-1.4	5.3	-0.7	0.8	4.6
Amusement and theme parks	71311	182	-0.5	4.0	1.8	2.3	5.9
Gambling industries	7132	131	2.1	2.0	2.1	0.0	4.2
Golf courses and country clubs	71391	395	-1.2	4.1	0.1	1.3	4.2
Fitness and recreational sports centers	71394	658	3.7	-0.7	4.4	0.7	3.7
Bowling centers	71395	69	0.7	3.0	-1.1	-1.7	1.9
Accommodation and Food Services							
Accommodation and food services	72	13 979	0.8	2.7	2.3	1.6	5.1
Accommodation	721	2 027	1.9	1.8	2.7	0.8	4.6
Traveler accommodation	7211	1 934	2.0	1.8	2.8	0.8	4.6
Hotels and motels, except casino hotels	72111	1 624	1.4	2.5	2.2	0.8	4.7
Food services and drinking places	722	11 952	0.4	3.0	2.2	1.8	5.3
Special food services	7223	843	1.2	1.5	2.5	1.2	4.0
Drinking places, alcoholic beverages	7224	406	-0.3	3.1	-0.1	0.2	3.0
Restaurants and other eating places	72251	10 703	0.4	3.2	2.3	1.9	5.6
Full-service restaurants	722511	5 482	0.5	3.6	2.3	1.7	6.0
Limited-service eating places	722513	5 220	0.4	2.8	2.4	2.0	5.2
Other Services							
Automotive repair and maintenance	8111	1 129	1.1	2.1	1.5	0.4	3.7
Reupholstery and furniture repair	81142	21	-0.9	3.8	-2.8	-2.0	0.8
Personal care services	8121	1 263	2.2	1.7	3.4	1.2	5.2
Hair, nail, and skin care services	81211	1 037	2.0	1.8	3.0	1.0	4.9
Funeral homes and funeral services	81221	110	-0.2	3.9	-0.3	0.0	3.6
Drycleaning and laundry services	8123	314	2.0	1.5	1.1	-0.9	2.6
Coin-operated laundries and drycleaners	81231	43	2.3	1.8	0.4	-1.9	2.3
Drycleaning and laundry services	81232	138	0.8	2.2	-1.2	-1.9	1.0
Linen and uniform supply	81233	133	2.3	0.9	3.1	0.8	4.1
Photofinishing	81292	10	3.4	1.7	-4.0	-7.1	-2.4

Table 5-3. Average Annual Percent Change in Output Per Hour and Related Series, Wholesale Trade, Retail Trade, Food Service, and Drinking Places, 1987–2018

(Number, percent.)

Industry	NAICS code	2018 employment (thousands)	Average annual percent change, 1987–2018				
			Labor productivity	Unit labor costs	Output	Hours worked	Labor compensation
Wholesale Trade							
Wholesale trade	42	5 977	2.7	0.9	3.1	0.3	4.0
Durable goods	423	3 215	4.3	-0.4	4.5	0.2	4.0
Motor vehicles and parts	4231	353	3.4	0.3	3.2	-0.2	3.6
Furniture and furnishings	4232	120	1.6	2.2	1.7	0.1	3.9
Lumber and construction supplies	4233	247	0.9	1.7	1.6	0.7	3.4
Commercial equipment	4234	692	11.4	-6.6	11.6	0.2	4.3
Metals and minerals	4235	137	-0.4	3.8	0.0	0.3	3.8
Appliance and electric goods	4236	360	7.4	-2.9	7.2	-0.2	4.1
Hardware and plumbing	4237	281	1.5	2.0	2.4	0.9	4.5
Machinery and supplies	4238	704	1.9	1.9	2.0	0.1	4.0
Miscellaneous durable goods	4239	322	1.0	2.6	1.6	0.6	4.2
Nondurable goods	424	2 206	1.0	2.8	1.3	0.2	4.1
Paper and paper products	4241	131	0.8	2.4	0.3	-0.5	2.7
Druggists' goods	4242	237	2.3	3.5	3.5	1.2	7.2
Apparel and piece goods	4243	156	2.0	1.4	1.6	-0.4	3.0
Grocery and related products	4244	812	0.9	2.4	1.6	0.7	4.1
Farm product raw materials	4245	72	1.3	3.9	-0.5	-1.8	3.4
Chemicals	4246	151	0.2	3.3	0.7	0.6	4.1
Petroleum	4247	104	2.2	2.4	0.9	-1.3	3.3
Alcoholic beverages	4248	201	0.3	2.8	2.1	1.8	4.9
Miscellaneous nondurable goods	4249	342	0.0	3.3	-0.4	-0.4	2.9
Electronic markets and agents and brokers	425	556	1.6	0.6	3.3	1.7	3.9
Retail Trade							
Retail trade	44-45	16 680	2.9	0.0	3.3	0.5	3.3
Motor vehicle and parts dealers	441	2 075	2.2	0.6	3.0	0.8	3.6
Automobile dealers	4411	1 332	2.3	0.5	3.1	0.8	3.7
Other motor vehicle dealers	4412	170	2.5	1.0	3.7	1.2	4.8
Auto parts, accessories, and tire stores	4413	573	1.1	1.3	1.8	0.7	3.1
Furniture and home furnishings stores	442	527	3.8	-0.9	3.8	0.0	2.8
Furniture stores	4421	245	3.3	-0.8	3.4	0.0	2.6
Home furnishings stores	4422	282	4.4	-1.2	4.4	0.0	3.2
Electronics and appliance stores	443	510	10.7	-7.2	11.1	0.4	3.1
Building material and garden supply stores	444	1 336	2.6	-0.1	3.3	0.7	3.2
Building material and supplies dealers	4441	1 166	2.5	0.0	3.3	0.8	3.4
Lawn and garden equipment and supplies stores	4442	171	3.0	-0.6	2.9	0.0	2.3
Food and beverage stores	445	3 166	0.7	2.1	0.7	0.0	2.8
Grocery stores	4451	2 724	0.6	2.3	0.6	0.1	3.0
Specialty food stores	4452	263	0.1	2.0	-0.3	-0.4	1.7
Beer, wine and liquor stores	4453	179	2.2	0.6	1.5	-0.6	2.2
Health and personal care stores	446	1 114	1.6	1.6	2.7	1.1	4.3
Gasoline stations	447	942	1.4	1.6	1.1	-0.2	2.7
Clothing and clothing accessories stores	448	1 476	3.9	-1.1	3.7	-0.2	2.5
Clothing stores	4481	1 095	4.3	-1.3	4.1	-0.1	2.7
Shoe stores	4482	207	2.9	-0.7	2.5	-0.3	1.8
Jewelry, luggage, and leather goods stores	4483	173	3.3	-0.2	2.7	-0.6	2.5
Sports, hobby, book, and music stores	451	633	3.5	-0.6	3.7	0.2	3.0
Sporting goods and musical instrument stores	4511	547	4.0	-1.1	4.5	0.5	3.4
Book stores and news dealers	4512	86	1.9	1.0	0.3	-1.6	1.3
General merchandise stores	452	3 114	2.9	-0.7	4.2	1.3	3.5
Department stores	4521	1 164	0.6	0.9	0.5	-0.1	1.4
Other general merchandise stores	4529	1 951	4.9	-1.8	7.4	2.3	5.5
Miscellaneous store retailers	453	988	3.3	-0.8	3.1	-0.2	2.3
Florists	4531	77	3.3	-0.1	0.1	-3.1	0.0
Office supplies, stationery and gift stores	4532	262	5.6	-2.5	3.8	-1.7	1.2
Used merchandise stores	4533	223	4.7	-2.0	5.9	1.1	3.8
Other miscellaneous store retailers	4539	426	0.9	0.6	2.4	1.5	3.1
Nonstore retailers	454	799	8.1	-3.6	8.9	0.7	5.0
Electronic shopping and mail-order houses	4541	496	9.9	-4.6	14.1	3.8	8.8
Vending machine operators	4542	47	0.5	3.0	-1.9	-2.4	1.0
Direct selling establishments	4543	256	2.4	0.3	1.0	-1.3	1.4
Food Services and Drinking Places							
Food services and drinking places	722	12 163	0.5	3.0	2.3	1.8	5.3
Special food services	7223	864	1.2	1.4	2.6	1.4	4.1
Drinking places, alcoholic beverages	7224	407	-0.3	3.1	0.0	0.3	3.0
Restaurants and other eating places	7225	10 892	0.5	3.2	2.4	1.9	5.6

Table 5-4. Indexes of Multifactor Productivity and Related Measures, 1995–2018

(2012 =100 for private business and private nonfarm business, 2009 =100 for manufacturing.)

Sector	1995	1996	1997	1998	1999	2000	2001	2002	2003	2004	2005	2006
PRIVATE BUSINESS												
Productivity												
Labor productivity	64.8	66.4	67.7	69.9	72.7	75.2	77.6	81.0	84.3	86.9	88.8	89.9
Output per unit of capital services	112.3	112.3	112.1	111.2	110.4	108.9	104.8	103.3	103.9	105.5	106.0	105.6
Multifactor productivity	82.1	83.2	84.0	85.3	87.2	88.7	89.2	91.0	93.4	95.5	97.0	97.4
Real value-added output	61.7	64.6	67.9	71.5	75.6	79.2	79.9	81.3	84.0	87.6	91.1	94.3
Inputs												
Labor input	88.6	90.9	94.0	96.3	98.2	99.8	97.9	96.0	95.8	97.2	99.0	101.5
Capital services	55.0	57.5	60.6	64.3	68.5	72.8	76.3	78.7	80.9	83.1	86.0	89.2
Combined input quantity	75.2	77.7	80.9	83.8	86.7	89.4	89.6	89.3	90.0	91.7	93.9	96.7
PRIVATE NONFARM BUSINESS												
Productivity												
Labor productivity	65.4	66.8	68.0	70.1	72.8	75.3	77.6	81.1	84.2	86.7	88.6	89.7
Output per unit of capital services	114.1	113.8	113.3	112.3	111.3	109.5	105.3	103.6	104.0	105.5	106.1	105.8
Multifactor productivity	82.9	83.7	84.4	85.7	87.4	88.8	89.3	91.1	93.3	95.4	96.9	97.3
Real value-added output	61.7	64.5	67.8	71.5	75.5	79.1	79.8	81.2	83.9	87.4	90.9	94.1
Inputs												
Labor input	87.7	90.2	93.4	95.9	97.9	99.5	97.7	95.7	95.6	97.1	98.9	101.5
Capital services	54.1	56.7	59.9	63.6	67.9	72.3	75.8	78.4	80.6	82.8	85.7	88.9
Combined input quantity	74.5	77.1	80.3	83.4	86.4	89.1	89.4	89.1	89.9	91.6	93.8	96.7
MANUFACTURING												
Productivity												
Labor productivity	55.6	57.8	60.6	63.3	66.9	69.4	71.0	77.0	82.0	84.2	88.5	89.4
Output per unit of capital services	117.8	117.4	119.8	119.6	119.7	118.8	110.9	110.2	110.6	112.6	115.5	115.5
Sector output	79.8	82.9	88.6	92.8	96.7	99.1	94.8	95.6	96.8	98.8	102.7	104.3
Combined inputs	98.8	101.7	104.5	108.6	110.6	109.8	106.7	105.0	101.4	100.8	104.0	103.2
Energy	106.1	102.8	105.2	105.6	152.8	178.3	207.2	137.4	113.7	114.0	134.6	108.9
Materials	94.7	100.4	100.1	106.2	107.2	102.1	94.0	103.0	95.3	100.6	105.7	101.4
Capital services	67.8	70.6	73.9	77.7	80.8	83.5	85.5	86.8	87.5	87.8	88.9	90.3
Purchased services	109.2	110.1	118.1	123.8	125.0	122.0	124.1	117.7	119.5	102.9	110.2	115.8

Sector	2007	2008	2009	2010	2011	2012	2013	2014	2015	2016	2017	2018
PRIVATE BUSINESS												
Productivity												
Labor productivity	91.5	92.6	96.4	99.5	99.3	100.0	100.9	101.6	102.8	102.9	104.1	105.5
Output per unit of capital services	104.8	101.0	96.5	98.9	99.0	100.0	99.9	100.3	100.9	99.7	99.5	100.1
Multifactor productivity	97.9	96.8	97.2	99.7	99.4	100.0	100.4	100.8	101.7	101.1	101.5	102.5
Real value-added output	96.5	95.5	92.2	95.2	97.0	100.0	102.5	105.7	109.5	111.3	114.2	118.1
Inputs												
Labor input	102.6	101.2	94.4	95.0	97.3	100.0	101.9	104.5	107.2	109.1	111.1	113.6
Capital services	92.1	94.6	95.5	96.3	98.0	100.0	102.5	105.4	108.4	111.6	114.8	118.0
Combined input quantity	98.5	98.7	94.9	95.5	97.6	100.0	102.1	104.9	107.7	110.1	112.5	115.3
PRIVATE NONFARM BUSINESS												
Productivity												
Labor productivity	91.3	92.4	96.1	99.4	99.2	100.0	100.5	101.3	102.6	102.8	103.9	105.3
Output per unit of capital services	105.0	100.9	96.2	98.6	98.9	100.0	99.7	100.0	100.5	99.1	98.9	99.6
Multifactor productivity	97.9	96.7	96.9	99.5	99.3	100.0	100.0	100.5	101.4	100.8	101.2	102.1
Real value-added output	96.4	95.4	92.0	95.0	96.9	100.0	102.3	105.5	109.2	111.0	114.0	118.0
Inputs												
Labor input	102.6	101.2	94.4	94.9	97.3	100.0	102.0	104.6	107.1	109.0	111.1	113.8
Capital services	91.9	94.6	95.6	96.4	98.0	100.0	102.5	105.4	108.7	111.9	115.2	118.5
Combined input quantity	98.6	98.7	94.9	95.5	97.6	100.0	102.2	104.9	107.7	110.1	112.6	115.5
MANUFACTURING												
Productivity												
Labor productivity	93.5	93.1	94.2	100.1	100.9	100.0	101.1	100.6	98.8	98.4	98.2	95.6
Output per unit of capital services	116.3	107.6	93.6	98.8	100.2	100.0	99.9	98.8	96.0	94.0	93.1	91.1
Sector output	107.5	102.6	90.3	96.1	98.7	100.0	101.9	103.1	102.2	102.0	102.6	101.9
Combined inputs	105.6	100.7	92.0	94.1	97.1	100.0	102.0	102.0	102.2	104.3	104.6	104.9
Energy	120.3	126.4	92.9	89.9	98.8	100.0	103.5	95.2	76.6	70.2	67.9	65.2
Materials	105.7	98.6	86.0	89.7	96.4	100.0	103.1	101.4	104.0	107.2	99.0	98.1
Capital services	92.4	95.3	96.5	97.3	98.5	100.0	102.1	104.3	106.4	108.5	110.2	111.8
Purchased services	118.4	98.4	96.2	99.7	95.8	100.0	100.2	99.5	90.9	94.9	111.8	109.6

. . . = Not available.

CHAPTER 6: COMPENSATION OF EMPLOYEES

HIGHLIGHTS

This chapter discusses the Employment Cost Index (ECI), which covers changes in wages and salaries and benefits; the Employer Costs for Employee Compensation (ECEC); and employee participation in various benefit plans.

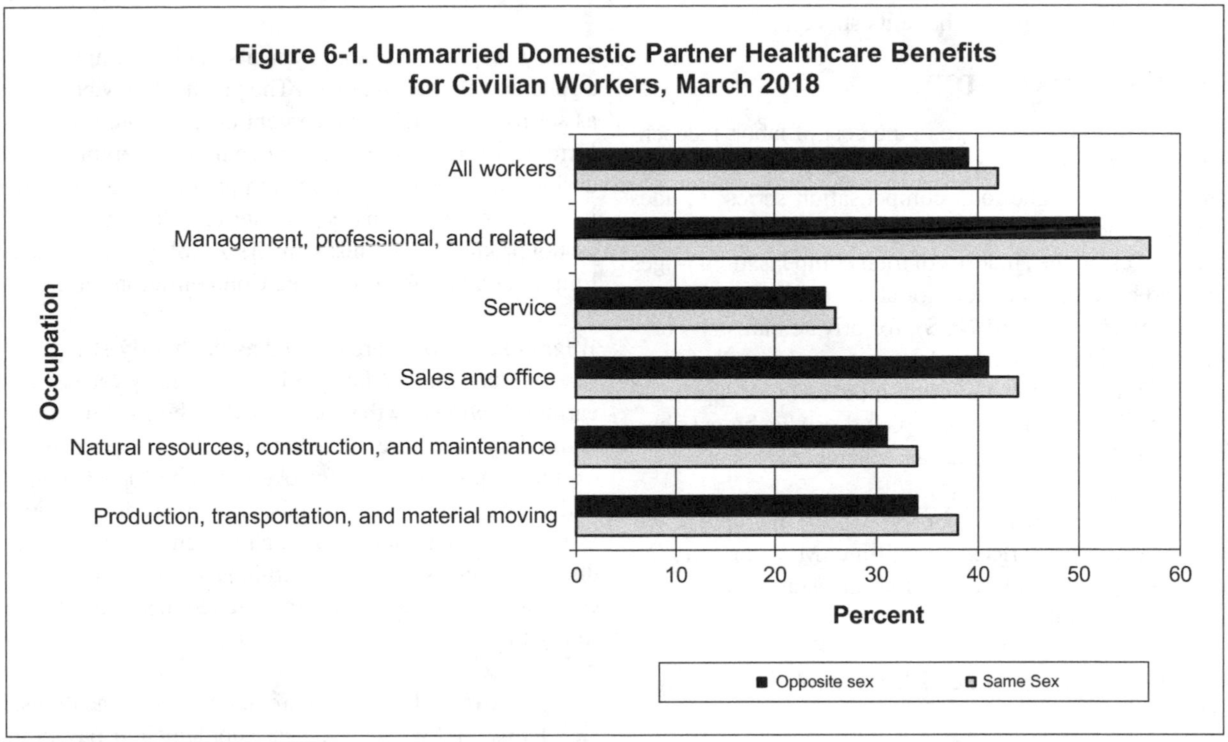

In March 2019, state and local government workers were far more likely to have access to benefits than those in the private sector. Eighty-nine percent of state and local government workers had access to medical benefits compared while just 69 percent of private industry workers. (See Table 6-10.)

OTHER HIGHLIGHTS

- State and local government workers were also far more likely to have access to life insurance benefits than those in the private industry. In March 2019, 81 percent of state and local government workers had access to life insurance benefits compared with only 56 percent of workers in private industry did. (See Table 6-13.)

- Belonging to a union also increased the chances that an individual would have access to benefits. In March 2019, 94 percent of civilian worked who belonged to a union had access to retirement benefits compared with only 67 percent of nonunion civilian workers. Similarly, 94 percent of civilian union members had access to medical benefits compared with only 68 percent of non-union civilian workers. (See Tables 6-9 and 6-10.)

- The Employment Cost Index (ECI) for total compensation for private industry workers increased 3.0 percent from December 2017 to December 2018 which was the largest increase since 2007. (See Table 6-1.)

- Many companies now offer nontraditional benefits in order to entice workers. In March 2019, 54 percent of civilian workers had access to employee assistance programs, 44 percent of civilian workers had access to wellness programs, and 11 percent had access to childcare. (Table 6-16.)

NOTES AND DEFINITIONS

NATIONAL COMPENSATION SURVEY

The National Compensation Survey (NCS) is an establishment survey conducted by the Office of Compensation Levels and Trends (OCLT) at the Bureau of Labor Statistics (BLS). It provides data for the Employment Cost Index (ECI), the Employer Costs for Employee Compensation (ECEC), the occupational earnings series, and the employee benefits survey.

EMPLOYMENT COST INDEX

The ECI is a measure of the change in the cost of labor, independent of the influence of employment shifts among occupations and industry categories. The total compensation series includes changes in wages and salaries and in employer costs for employee benefits. The ECI calculates indexes of total compensation, wages and salaries, and benefits separately for all civilian workers in the United States (as defined by the NCS), for private industry workers, and for workers in state and local government. For all of these categories, the ECI calculates the same indexes by occupational group, worker attribute, industry group, and establishment characteristic. Seasonally adjusted series are calculated as well.

It was developed in the mid 1970s in response to the rapid acceleration of both wages and prices at that time. Monetary and fiscal policymakers needed a more accurate measure of the actual changes in employers' labor costs.

Beginning with estimates for March 2006, the following changes were introduced to the ECI:

- The Standard Industrial Classification (SIC) System was replaced by the North American Industry Classification System for classifying establishments by industry.
- The Occupational Classification System (OCS) Manual was replaced by the Standard Occupational Classification Manual for classifying occupations.
- Estimates were weighted to 2002 fixed employment counts until December 2013. For March 1995 through December 2005, ECI estimates were weighted on 1990 fixed employment counts.
- The ECI base was changed to December 2005=100. Prior to this, the base was June 1989=100, which was used from March 1990 through December 2005.

Concepts and Definitions

Compensation is a term used to encompass the entire range of wages and benefits, both current and deferred, that employees receive in return for their work. In the Employment Cost Index (ECI), compensation includes the employer's cost of wages and salaries, plus the employer's cost of providing employee benefits.

Lump-sum payments are payments made to employees in lieu of a general wage rate increase. The payment may be a fixed amount as set forth in a labor agreement or an amount determined by a formula—for example, 2.5 percent of an employee's earnings during the prior year. Lump-sum payments are not incorporated into an employee's base pay rate or salary, but are considered as nonproduction bonuses in the Employment Cost Index and Employer Costs for Employee Compensation series.

Wages and salaries are defined as the hourly straight-time wage rate or, for workers not paid on an hourly basis, straight-time earnings divided by the corresponding hours. Straight-time wage and salary rates are total earnings before payroll deductions, excluding premium pay for overtime and for work on weekends and holidays, shift differentials, and nonproduction bonuses such as lump-sum payments provided in lieu of wage increases. Production bonuses, incentive earnings, commission payments, and cost-of-living adjustments are included in straight-time wage and salary rates.

Benefits covered by the ECI are: paid leave—vacations, holidays, sick leave, and personal leave; supplemental pay-premium pay for work in addition to the regular work schedule (such as overtime, weekends, and holidays), shift differentials, and nonproduction bonuses (such as referral bonuses and attendance bonuses); insurance benefits—life, health, short-term disability, and long-term disability; retirement and savings benefits—defined benefit and defined contribution plans; and legally required benefits—Social Security, Medicare, federal and state unemployment insurance, and workers' compensation.

Sources of Additional Information

Additional information on ECI methodology and more tables are available in the *BLS Handbook of Methods* and BLS new releases. The BLS publication *Compensation and Working Conditions* contains articles on all aspects of the NCS. All of these resources are on the BLS Web site at < https://www.bls.gov/ncs/ect/ />.

Table 6-1. Employment Cost Index, Private Industry Workers, Total Compensation[1] and Wages and Salaries, by Selected Industry and Occupation, 2001–2019

(December 2005 = 100.)

Characteristic and year	Total compensation					Wages and salaries				
	Indexes				Percent change for 12 months (ended December)	Indexes				Percent change for 12 months (ended December)
	March	June	September	December		March	June	September	December	
WORKERS BY INDUSTRY										
Total Private										
2001	85.0	85.8	86.7	87.3	4.1	87.6	88.4	89.2	89.9	3.8
2002	88.2	89.2	89.7	90.0	3.1	90.7	91.6	92.0	92.2	2.6
2003	91.4	92.3	93.2	93.6	4.0	93.3	94.0	94.8	95.1	3.1
2004	94.9	95.9	96.7	97.2	3.8	95.7	96.5	97.3	97.6	2.6
2005	98.2	98.9	99.5	100.0	2.9	98.3	98.9	99.5	100.0	2.5
2006	100.8	101.7	102.5	103.2	3.2	100.7	101.7	102.5	103.2	3.2
2007	104.0	104.9	105.7	106.3	3.0	104.3	105.1	106.0	106.6	3.3
2008	107.3	108.0	108.7	108.9	2.4	107.6	108.4	109.1	109.4	2.6
2009	109.3	109.6	110.0	110.2	1.2	109.8	110.1	110.6	110.8	1.3
2010	111.1	111.7	112.2	112.5	2.1	111.4	111.9	112.4	112.8	1.8
2011	113.3	114.3	114.6	115.0	2.2	113.2	113.8	114.3	114.6	1.6
2012	115.7	116.4	116.8	117.1	1.8	115.3	115.9	116.4	116.6	1.7
2013	117.9	118.6	119.0	119.4	2.0	117.3	118.1	118.5	119.0	2.1
2014	119.9	121.0	121.7	122.2	2.3	119.3	120.3	121.2	121.6	2.2
2015	123.2	123.3	124.0	124.5	1.9	122.6	122.9	123.7	124.2	2.1
2016	125.4	126.2	126.8	127.2	2.2	125.1	126.1	126.7	127.1	2.3
2017	128.3	129.2	130.0	130.5	2.6	128.3	129.1	130.0	130.6	2.8
2018	131.9	132.9	133.8	134.4	3.0	132.0	132.9	134.0	134.7	3.1
2019	135.6	136.4	137.4	. . .	. . .	135.9	136.9	138.0	. . .	. . .
Goods-Producing[2]										
2001	83.9	84.7	85.3	86.0	3.6	87.9	88.8	89.3	90.0	3.6
2002	87.0	87.7	88.2	89.0	3.5	90.7	91.4	91.9	92.6	2.9
2003	90.5	91.5	92.1	92.6	4.0	93.3	94.1	94.6	94.9	2.5
2004	94.5	95.4	96.5	96.9	4.6	95.6	96.2	97.2	97.2	2.4
2005	98.0	99.0	99.8	100.0	3.2	97.9	98.7	99.5	100.0	2.9
2006	100.3	101.3	102.0	102.5	2.5	100.7	101.8	102.3	102.9	2.9
2007	102.9	103.9	104.4	105.0	2.4	103.9	104.7	105.4	106.0	3.0
2008	106.1	106.8	107.2	107.5	2.4	107.1	108.0	108.6	109.0	2.8
2009	107.9	108.2	108.4	108.6	1.0	109.2	109.5	109.8	110.0	0.9
2010	109.7	110.3	111.0	111.1	2.3	110.5	110.9	111.5	111.6	1.5
2011	112.0	113.2	113.4	113.8	2.4	112.2	112.7	113.2	113.5	1.7
2012	114.1	114.7	115.3	115.6	1.6	114.0	114.5	115.1	115.4	1.7
2013	116.4	117.0	117.5	117.7	1.8	116.1	116.8	117.4	117.6	1.9
2014	118.5	119.1	119.9	120.3	2.2	118.2	119.0	119.6	120.1	2.1
2015	121.0	121.9	122.5	123.2	2.4	120.8	121.8	122.5	123.2	2.6
2016	123.8	124.7	125.2	125.8	2.1	123.9	124.9	125.5	126.2	2.4
2017	126.5	127.3	128.4	128.9	2.5	127.1	127.9	128.8	129.3	2.5
2018	129.9	130.9	131.2	131.9	2.3	130.4	131.4	132.2	133.0	2.9
2019	133.1	134.1	135.1	. . .	. . .	134.2	135.3	136.5	. . .	. . .
Service-Providing[3]										
2001	85.4	86.2	87.1	87.8	4.4	87.4	88.3	89.2	89.8	3.8
2002	88.7	89.7	90.2	90.4	3.0	90.7	91.7	92.0	92.1	2.6
2003	91.7	92.5	93.6	94.0	4.0	93.3	93.9	94.9	95.2	3.4
2004	95.1	96.1	96.8	97.3	3.5	95.8	96.6	97.3	97.7	2.6
2005	98.3	98.9	99.5	100.0	2.8	98.4	99.0	99.5	100.0	2.4
2006	101.0	101.8	102.7	103.4	3.4	100.8	101.7	102.6	103.3	3.3
2007	104.3	105.2	106.1	106.7	3.2	104.4	105.3	106.1	106.8	3.4
2008	107.7	108.5	109.1	109.4	2.5	107.7	108.6	109.3	109.6	2.6
2009	109.8	110.1	110.5	110.8	1.3	110.0	110.3	110.8	111.1	1.4
2010	111.6	112.1	112.6	113.0	2.0	111.7	112.3	112.7	113.1	1.8
2011	113.8	114.6	115.0	115.3	2.0	113.5	114.1	114.6	114.9	1.6
2012	116.3	117.0	117.3	117.6	2.0	115.6	116.3	116.7	117.0	1.8
2013	118.4	119.1	119.6	120.0	2.0	117.7	118.4	118.9	119.4	2.1
2014	120.4	121.6	122.3	122.8	2.3	119.7	120.7	121.6	122.1	2.3
2015	123.8	123.8	124.5	124.9	1.7	123.1	123.3	124.1	124.5	2.0
2016	125.9	126.7	127.3	127.7	2.2	125.5	126.5	127.1	127.4	2.3
2017	128.9	129.8	130.6	131.0	2.6	128.6	129.5	130.4	131.0	2.8
2018	132.6	133.5	134.6	135.2	3.2	132.5	133.3	134.5	135.2	3.2
2019	136.3	137.1	138.1	. . .	. . .	136.4	137.3	138.4	. . .	. . .

[1]Includes wages, salaries, and employer costs for employee benefits.
[2]Includes mining, construction, and manufacturing.
[3]Includes the following industries: wholesale trade; retail trade; transportation and warehousing; utilities; information; finance and insurance; real estate and rental and leasing; professional, scientific, and technical services; management of companies and enterprises; administrative and support and waste management and remediation services; education services; health care and social assistance; arts, entertainment, and recreation; accommodation and food services; and other services, except public administration.
. . . = Not available.

Table 6-1. Employment Cost Index, Private Industry Workers, Total Compensation[1] and Wages and Salaries, by Selected Industry and Occupation, 2001–2019—*Continued*

(December 2005 = 100.)

Characteristic and year	Total compensation					Wages and salaries				
	Indexes				Percent change for 12 months (ended December)	Indexes				Percent change for 12 months (ended December)
	March	June	September	December		March	June	September	December	
WORKERS BY OCCUPATION										
Management, Professional, and Related										
2001	85.2	86.1	87.1	87.7	4.8	86.7	87.7	88.7	89.3	4.3
2002	88.6	89.5	89.8	90.1	2.7	90.2	91.1	91.4	91.5	2.5
2003	91.9	92.6	93.6	94.2	4.6	93.2	93.8	94.8	95.3	4.2
2004	95.2	96.0	96.8	97.4	3.4	96.0	96.5	97.4	97.9	2.7
2005	98.6	99.1	99.5	100.0	2.7	98.7	99.2	99.6	100.0	2.1
2006	101.3	102.2	103.2	103.8	3.8	101.1	102.0	103.1	103.7	3.7
2007	105.0	105.9	106.8	107.3	3.4	105.0	105.9	106.8	107.4	3.6
2008	108.5	109.3	110.2	110.6	3.1	108.6	109.4	110.3	110.8	3.2
2009	111.1	111.2	111.4	111.6	0.9	111.4	111.5	111.7	111.9	1.0
2010	112.5	112.9	113.4	113.7	1.9	112.8	113.2	113.7	114.1	2.0
2011	114.8	115.4	115.7	116.0	2.0	114.8	115.2	115.6	115.8	1.5
2012	117.0	117.7	118.0	118.3	2.0	116.6	117.3	117.5	118.0	1.9
2013	119.0	120.0	120.5	120.9	2.2	118.6	119.6	120.1	120.5	2.1
2014	121.3	122.6	123.3	123.7	2.3	120.9	122.0	122.9	123.2	2.2
2015	124.5	124.7	125.5	125.9	1.8	123.7	124.5	125.4	125.9	2.2
2016	126.6	127.0	127.7	128.0	1.7	126.7	127.1	127.9	128.3	1.9
2017	129.1	130.2	130.7	131.1	2.4	129.2	130.3	130.9	131.4	2.4
2018	132.4	133.2	134.1	134.6	2.7	132.6	133.3	134.4	134.9	2.7
2019	135.4	136.3	137.1	. . .	. . .	135.6	136.6	137.5	. . .	. . .
Management, Business, and Financial										
2001	86.1	87.1	87.8	88.5	4.4	87.3	88.3	89.1	89.8	4.1
2002	89.5	90.7	90.7	90.6	2.4	90.8	92.2	92.4	92.1	2.6
2003	93.3	93.9	94.9	95.4	5.3	94.8	95.5	96.4	96.7	5.0
2004	95.9	96.8	97.3	97.9	2.6	96.8	97.5	98.1	98.5	1.9
2005	99.1	99.6	99.7	100.0	2.1	99.2	99.7	99.5	100.0	1.5
2006	101.3	102.0	102.7	103.1	3.1	101.3	102.2	102.8	103.1	3.1
2007	104.3	105.1	106.0	106.3	3.1	104.7	105.5	106.3	106.6	3.4
2008	108.0	108.7	109.3	109.5	3.0	108.2	109.0	109.7	110.0	3.2
2009	109.6	109.7	109.7	109.9	0.4	110.3	110.3	110.4	110.8	0.7
2010	111.3	111.7	112.0	112.3	2.2	112.0	112.6	112.8	113.2	2.2
2011	113.6	114.5	114.8	115.0	2.4	113.9	114.4	114.9	115.0	1.6
2012	116.0	116.9	116.9	117.1	1.8	115.7	116.7	116.7	116.9	1.7
2013	118.0	119.3	119.6	119.9	2.4	117.9	119.3	119.4	119.8	2.5
2014	120.3	122.1	123.0	123.0	2.6	120.2	121.7	122.8	122.7	2.4
2015	123.9	124.2	125.4	125.7	2.2	123.4	124.2	125.7	126.2	2.9
2016	126.5	126.8	127.7	128.4	2.1	127.1	127.3	128.4	129.2	2.4
2017	129.5	130.6	131.3	131.7	2.6	129.9	131.0	131.8	132.3	2.4
2018	133.2	133.9	134.7	135.2	2.7	133.7	134.2	135.3	135.8	2.6
2019	136.2	137.3	138.1	. . .	. . .	136.8	137.9	138.9	. . .	. . .
Professional and Related										
2001	84.1	85.0	86.0	86.5	4.7	86.9	87.8	88.7	89.3	4.1
2002	87.3	87.9	88.5	89.1	3.0	90.1	90.5	91.0	91.4	2.4
2003	90.3	91.0	92.0	92.6	3.9	92.1	92.7	93.6	94.2	3.1
2004	94.1	94.8	95.8	96.5	4.2	95.3	95.7	96.7	97.2	3.2
2005	98.0	98.8	99.5	100.0	3.6	98.2	98.8	99.6	100.0	2.9
2006	101.0	101.8	103.1	103.9	3.9	100.9	101.8	103.1	104.0	4.0
2007	104.9	105.9	106.7	107.3	3.3	105.1	106.0	107.0	107.6	3.5
2008	108.3	109.0	109.9	110.3	2.8	108.7	109.5	110.4	110.9	3.1
2009	111.0	111.1	111.4	111.4	1.0	111.6	111.8	112.1	112.1	1.1
2010	112.2	112.6	113.3	113.5	1.9	112.8	113.2	113.9	114.1	1.8
2011	114.6	115.1	115.4	115.7	1.9	114.8	115.2	115.6	115.9	1.6
2012	116.8	117.3	117.7	118.2	2.2	116.7	117.2	117.7	118.2	2.0
2013	118.9	119.5	120.2	120.5	1.9	118.8	119.5	120.2	120.5	1.9
2014	121.0	121.9	122.5	122.9	2.0	120.9	121.7	122.3	122.8	1.9
2015	123.7	124.1	124.5	124.9	1.6	123.4	124.2	124.7	125.2	2.0
2016	125.7	126.2	126.7	126.7	1.4	126.0	126.6	127.2	127.2	1.6
2017	127.8	128.7	129.1	129.6	2.3	128.2	129.3	129.6	130.2	2.4
2018	130.8	131.6	132.3	132.8	2.5	131.3	132.1	133.2	133.7	2.7
2019	133.7	134.4	135.1	. . .	. . .	134.4	135.2	136.0	. . .	. . .

[1]Includes wages, salaries, and employer costs for employee benefits.
[2]Includes mining, construction, and manufacturing.
[3]Includes the following industries: wholesale trade; retail trade; transportation and warehousing; utilities; information; finance and insurance; real estate and rental and leasing; professional, scientific, and technical services; management of companies and enterprises; administrative and support and waste management and remediation services; education services; health care and social assistance; arts, entertainment, and recreation; accommodation and food services; and other services, except public administration.
. . . = Not available.

Table 6-1. Employment Cost Index, Private Industry Workers, Total Compensation[1] and Wages and Salaries, by Selected Industry and Occupation, 2001–2019—*Continued*

(December 2005 = 100.)

Characteristic and year	Total compensation					Wages and salaries				
	Indexes				Percent change for 12 months (ended December)	Indexes				Percent change for 12 months (ended December)
	March	June	September	December		March	June	September	December	
Office and Administrative Support										
2001	84.2	84.9	85.9	86.6	4.6	87.0	87.7	88.8	89.4	4.2
2002	87.9	88.6	89.3	89.9	3.8	90.7	91.3	91.8	92.4	3.4
2003	91.0	92.0	92.8	93.3	3.8	93.1	93.9	94.4	94.7	2.5
2004	94.7	95.8	96.5	97.2	4.2	95.6	96.4	97.1	97.6	3.1
2005	98.1	98.9	99.5	100.0	2.9	98.2	99.0	99.4	100.0	2.5
2006	100.9	101.9	102.7	103.4	3.4	100.9	101.9	102.6	103.3	3.3
2007	104.5	105.4	106.0	106.7	3.2	104.5	105.4	106.0	106.7	3.3
2008	107.8	108.5	109.2	109.6	2.7	107.7	108.5	109.2	109.7	2.8
2009	110.5	110.9	111.3	111.6	1.8	110.6	111.1	111.4	111.8	1.9
2010	112.6	113.1	113.7	114.0	2.2	112.2	112.6	113.3	113.6	1.6
2011	115.1	115.8	116.2	116.5	2.2	114.4	114.8	115.4	115.7	1.8
2012	117.5	118.1	118.4	118.7	1.9	116.4	117.0	117.4	117.7	1.7
2013	119.7	120.4	120.7	121.1	2.0	118.6	119.3	119.7	120.1	2.0
2014	121.8	122.9	123.3	123.8	2.2	120.8	121.5	122.0	122.5	2.0
2015	124.6	125.4	125.9	126.6	2.3	123.3	124.2	124.8	125.6	2.5
2016	128.1	129.0	129.6	130.2	2.8	127.1	128.0	128.7	129.5	3.1
2017	131.4	132.1	132.8	133.3	2.4	130.7	131.4	132.2	132.9	2.6
2018	135.0	136.5	137.3	138.0	3.5	134.5	135.9	136.8	137.6	3.5
2019	139.5	140.5	141.4	. . .	. . .	139.2	140.2	141.4	. . .	. . .
Natural Resources, Construction, and Maintenance										
2001	84.3	85.0	86.4	86.6	4.0	87.6	88.4	89.9	90.0	3.8
2002	87.4	88.5	89.3	89.7	3.6	90.5	91.7	92.3	92.6	2.9
2003	90.8	92.0	92.8	93.3	4.0	93.2	94.1	94.8	95.2	2.8
2004	94.8	96.1	96.5	97.1	4.1	95.8	96.7	97.1	97.5	2.4
2005	97.9	98.9	99.5	100.0	3.0	97.8	98.7	99.4	100.0	2.6
2006	100.8	102.1	103.0	103.6	3.6	100.7	101.8	102.8	103.4	3.4
2007	104.0	105.0	105.9	106.7	3.0	104.2	105.1	106.2	107.1	3.6
2008	107.6	108.3	109.0	109.6	2.7	108.1	109.0	109.8	110.5	3.2
2009	109.9	110.3	110.8	111.2	1.5	110.6	111.0	111.6	112.0	1.4
2010	112.2	112.7	113.1	113.3	1.9	112.5	112.8	113.1	113.3	1.2
2011	113.8	114.9	115.5	115.8	2.2	113.7	114.4	115.2	115.4	1.9
2012	116.3	117.0	117.7	117.8	1.7	115.6	116.0	116.6	116.7	1.1
2013	118.6	119.1	119.9	120.1	2.0	117.2	117.6	118.5	118.8	1.8
2014	120.8	122.0	122.8	123.2	2.6	119.3	120.0	120.9	121.4	2.2
2015	123.6	124.1	124.6	124.9	1.4	121.7	122.7	123.2	123.5	1.7
2016	125.7	126.6	127.1	127.7	2.2	124.3	125.5	126.0	126.7	2.6
2017	128.5	129.7	130.6	131.2	2.7	127.5	128.8	129.8	130.4	2.9
2018	131.8	133.4	133.9	134.5	2.5	130.9	132.0	132.6	133.4	2.3
2019	135.3	136.2	137.3	. . .	. . .	134.1	135.4	136.6	. . .	. . .
Construction, Extraction, Farming, Fishing, and Forestry										
2001	84.2	85.1	86.2	86.4	3.8	87.8	88.9	89.8	90.0	3.6
2002	87.3	88.1	88.8	89.5	3.6	90.6	91.3	91.9	92.4	2.7
2003	90.3	91.6	92.5	93.1	4.0	92.7	93.7	94.6	94.9	2.7
2004	94.7	95.8	96.4	97.2	4.4	95.8	96.6	96.9	97.5	2.7
2005	97.7	98.7	99.5	100.0	2.9	97.8	98.5	99.3	100.0	2.6
2006	100.7	102.2	103.1	103.7	3.7	100.7	102.0	103.0	103.7	3.7
2007	104.4	105.7	106.5	107.4	3.6	104.7	105.8	106.7	107.8	4.0
2008	108.6	109.7	110.3	110.8	3.2	109.2	110.1	110.8	111.5	3.4
2009	110.9	111.5	112.0	112.4	1.4	111.4	111.7	112.3	112.7	1.1
2010	113.1	113.6	114.3	114.4	1.8	112.9	113.3	113.9	114.0	1.2
2011	114.8	115.5	116.0	116.5	1.8	114.5	114.9	115.4	115.7	1.5
2012	116.6	117.1	117.8	117.9	1.2	115.7	116.0	116.8	116.7	0.9
2013	118.6	118.9	119.9	120.3	2.0	117.1	117.3	118.2	118.5	1.5
2014	120.7	121.4	122.1	122.9	2.2	118.7	119.6	120.3	121.1	2.2
2015	123.1	124.0	124.6	125.1	1.8	121.2	122.0	122.6	123.1	1.7
2016	125.8	127.1	127.3	128.4	2.6	124.0	125.5	125.6	126.9	3.1
2017	129.2	130.2	131.1	131.6	2.5	127.9	128.8	129.9	130.4	2.8
2018	132.2	133.4	133.8	134.4	2.1	131.1	132.3	132.9	133.6	2.5
2019	135.5	136.7	137.9	. . .	. . .	134.6	136.0	137.1	. . .	. . .

[1]Includes wages, salaries, and employer costs for employee benefits.
[2]Includes mining, construction, and manufacturing.
[3]Includes the following industries: wholesale trade; retail trade; transportation and warehousing; utilities; information; finance and insurance; real estate and rental and leasing; professional, scientific, and technical services; management of companies and enterprises; administrative and support and waste management and remediation services; education services; health care and social assistance; arts, entertainment, and recreation; accommodation and food services; and other services, except public administration.
. . . = Not available.

Table 6-1. Employment Cost Index, Private Industry Workers, Total Compensation[1] and Wages and Salaries, by Selected Industry and Occupation, 2001–2019—*Continued*

(December 2005 = 100.)

Characteristic and year	Total compensation					Wages and salaries				
	Indexes				Percent change for 12 months (ended December)	Indexes				Percent change for 12 months (ended December)
	March	June	September	December		March	June	September	December	
Installation, Maintenance, and Repair										
2001	84.4	84.9	86.8	86.8	4.1	87.4	87.9	90.1	90.1	4.3
2002	87.4	89.1	90.0	90.1	3.8	90.4	92.2	92.9	92.9	3.1
2003	91.4	92.5	93.1	93.6	3.9	93.8	94.6	95.1	95.5	2.8
2004	95.0	96.3	96.7	97.0	3.6	95.9	96.8	97.3	97.4	2.0
2005	98.1	99.3	99.6	100.0	3.1	97.8	99.1	99.5	100.0	2.7
2006	100.9	102.1	103.0	103.4	3.4	100.7	101.6	102.6	103.0	3.0
2007	103.5	104.1	105.2	105.8	2.3	103.7	104.2	105.6	106.1	3.0
2008	106.3	106.6	107.4	108.1	2.2	106.8	107.6	108.5	109.3	3.0
2009	108.6	108.9	109.4	109.8	1.6	109.7	110.2	110.7	111.2	1.7
2010	111.1	111.5	111.6	111.9	1.9	112.1	112.1	112.1	112.5	1.2
2011	112.6	114.2	114.9	115.0	2.8	112.7	113.9	115.0	115.0	2.2
2012	116.1	116.8	117.5	117.8	2.4	115.5	115.9	116.4	116.7	1.5
2013	118.6	119.3	119.9	119.9	1.8	117.5	118.0	119.0	119.2	2.1
2014	121.0	122.6	123.5	123.5	3.0	120.1	120.6	121.6	121.7	2.1
2015	124.1	124.2	124.6	124.8	1.1	122.3	123.4	123.9	124.1	2.0
2016	125.6	126.1	126.9	127.1	1.8	124.8	125.5	126.4	126.6	2.0
2017	127.7	129.2	130.2	130.9	3.0	127.2	128.8	129.7	130.5	3.1
2018	131.3	133.4	133.9	134.6	2.8	130.8	131.8	132.4	133.1	2.0
2019	135.1	135.6	136.7	. . .	. . .	133.5	134.9	136.3	. . .	. . .
Production, Transportation, and Material Moving										
2001	85.3	85.8	86.7	87.4	3.6	88.7	89.4	90.2	91.0	3.9
2002	88.4	89.1	89.7	90.3	3.3	91.9	92.4	92.8	93.3	2.5
2003	91.5	92.4	93.2	93.6	3.7	94.0	94.6	95.1	95.4	2.3
2004	95.5	96.5	97.4	97.8	4.5	96.0	96.7	97.6	97.8	2.5
2005	98.5	99.0	99.7	100.0	2.2	98.3	98.9	99.6	100.0	2.2
2006	100.4	101.1	101.7	102.3	2.3	100.6	101.2	101.8	102.4	2.4
2007	102.5	103.3	103.9	104.5	2.2	103.1	103.8	104.5	105.0	2.5
2008	105.5	106.0	106.6	106.9	2.3	106.0	106.8	107.5	107.8	2.7
2009	107.7	108.1	108.6	108.9	1.9	108.3	108.8	109.4	109.6	1.7
2010	109.9	110.5	111.3	111.5	2.4	109.8	110.3	111.1	111.3	1.6
2011	112.2	113.5	113.8	114.2	2.4	111.6	112.0	112.5	112.8	1.3
2012	114.5	115.1	115.7	116.0	1.6	113.7	114.0	114.7	115.1	2.0
2013	116.7	117.2	117.5	118.0	1.7	115.8	116.2	116.7	117.2	1.8
2014	118.9	119.5	120.3	120.6	2.2	118.0	118.7	119.6	119.9	2.3
2015	121.7	122.5	123.1	123.7	2.6	120.8	121.5	122.2	122.8	2.4
2016	124.7	125.6	126.4	127.0	2.7	123.9	124.9	125.9	126.6	3.1
2017	128.3	129.0	130.4	131.0	3.1	128.0	128.8	130.1	130.7	3.2
2018	132.5	133.2	134.1	134.7	2.8	132.3	133.2	134.4	135.1	3.4
2019	136.4	137.2	138.1	. . .	. . .	137.1	137.9	139.1	. . .	. . .
Production										
2001	84.9	85.2	86.0	86.7	3.2	88.4	89.1	89.7	90.5	3.7
2002	87.7	88.3	88.8	89.4	3.1	91.3	91.8	92.3	92.8	2.5
2003	91.0	91.7	92.5	93.0	4.0	93.6	94.1	94.8	95.1	2.5
2004	95.3	96.4	97.4	97.7	5.1	95.6	96.5	97.4	97.5	2.5
2005	98.6	99.1	99.6	100.0	2.4	98.3	98.9	99.5	100.0	2.6
2006	100.4	101.0	101.6	102.0	2.0	100.7	101.2	101.7	102.2	2.2
2007	102.1	102.8	103.2	104.0	2.0	103.1	103.6	104.2	104.6	2.3
2008	104.8	105.2	105.8	106.1	2.0	105.6	106.4	107.2	107.4	2.7
2009	107.1	107.6	108.0	108.2	2.0	108.1	108.5	109.0	109.3	1.8
2010	109.5	110.0	110.7	110.8	2.4	109.6	110.0	110.5	110.5	1.1
2011	111.7	113.2	113.4	113.8	2.7	111.1	111.5	112.0	112.3	1.6
2012	113.8	114.4	114.8	115.0	1.1	113.2	113.5	113.9	114.2	1.7
2013	115.7	116.1	116.3	116.7	1.5	115.0	115.5	116.0	116.4	1.9
2014	117.8	118.1	118.8	119.4	2.3	117.4	117.8	118.6	119.1	2.3
2015	120.4	121.0	121.7	122.5	2.6	119.9	120.5	121.2	122.0	2.4
2016	123.4	124.2	125.0	125.5	2.4	123.0	123.9	124.8	125.4	2.8
2017	126.5	127.2	128.6	129.2	2.9	126.5	127.4	128.6	129.3	3.1
2018	130.2	131.1	131.5	132.3	2.4	130.4	131.4	132.2	133.1	2.9
2019	133.5	134.4	135.1	. . .	. . .	134.4	135.4	136.2	. . .	. . .

[1]Includes wages, salaries, and employer costs for employee benefits.
[2]Includes mining, construction, and manufacturing.
[3]Includes the following industries: wholesale trade; retail trade; transportation and warehousing; utilities; information; finance and insurance; real estate and rental and leasing; professional, scientific, and technical services; management of companies and enterprises; administrative and support and waste management and remediation services; education services; health care and social assistance; arts, entertainment, and recreation; accommodation and food services; and other services, except public administration.
. . . = Not available.

Table 6-1. Employment Cost Index, Private Industry Workers, Total Compensation[1] and Wages and Salaries, by Selected Industry and Occupation, 2001–2019—*Continued*

(December 2005 = 100.)

Characteristic and year	Total compensation					Wages and salaries				
	Indexes				Percent change for 12 months (ended December)	Indexes				Percent change for 12 months (ended December)
	March	June	September	December		March	June	September	December	
Transportation and Material Moving										
2001	85.8	86.7	87.7	88.5	4.2	89.0	89.9	90.8	91.6	4.1
2002	89.5	90.2	90.9	91.4	3.3	92.6	93.1	93.6	94.0	2.6
2003	92.4	93.4	94.0	94.4	3.3	94.7	95.3	95.6	95.8	1.9
2004	95.7	96.7	97.5	97.9	3.7	96.4	97.1	97.9	98.2	2.5
2005	98.3	99.0	99.8	100.0	2.1	98.5	98.9	99.7	100.0	1.8
2006	100.4	101.2	102.0	102.6	2.6	100.4	101.2	102.0	102.6	2.6
2007	103.1	104.1	104.9	105.3	2.6	103.2	104.1	105.0	105.4	2.7
2008	106.4	107.2	107.7	107.9	2.5	106.5	107.4	108.0	108.3	2.8
2009	108.4	108.9	109.6	109.7	1.7	108.5	109.2	109.9	110.1	1.7
2010	110.4	111.2	112.2	112.5	2.6	110.2	110.8	111.8	112.2	1.9
2011	113.0	114.0	114.4	114.9	2.1	112.2	112.8	113.2	113.6	1.2
2012	115.5	116.0	117.0	117.6	2.3	114.4	114.8	115.7	116.3	2.4
2013	118.2	118.6	119.2	119.7	1.8	116.9	117.0	117.7	118.2	1.6
2014	120.4	121.4	122.3	122.4	2.3	118.9	119.9	121.0	120.9	2.3
2015	123.5	124.4	125.1	125.3	2.4	121.9	122.8	123.4	123.8	2.4
2016	126.6	127.5	128.4	129.1	3.0	125.1	126.3	127.2	128.1	3.5
2017	130.6	131.4	133.0	133.4	3.3	129.7	130.4	132.1	132.6	3.5
2018	135.4	136.0	137.4	137.8	3.3	134.7	135.3	137.0	137.5	3.7
2019	140.1	140.7	142.0	. . .	. . .	140.3	140.8	142.6	. . .	. . .
Service										
2001	87.1	87.7	88.2	89.4	3.8	89.7	90.2	90.6	91.7	3.4
2002	90.2	90.6	91.5	92.0	2.9	92.5	92.8	93.4	93.9	2.4
2003	93.0	93.4	94.4	95.0	3.3	94.5	94.8	95.6	96.1	2.3
2004	95.9	96.7	97.2	97.7	2.8	96.4	96.9	97.4	97.9	1.9
2005	98.5	99.0	99.5	100.0	2.4	98.6	99.0	99.6	100.0	2.1
2006	100.8	101.5	102.3	103.1	3.1	100.6	101.3	102.0	102.9	2.9
2007	104.5	105.2	106.4	107.0	3.8	104.6	105.3	106.5	107.1	4.1
2008	107.8	108.7	109.4	109.8	2.6	107.9	108.8	109.7	110.1	2.8
2009	110.7	110.9	111.7	111.8	1.8	111.0	111.2	112.1	112.3	2.0
2010	112.4	112.7	113.3	113.5	1.5	112.6	112.7	113.3	113.5	1.1
2011	114.5	114.7	115.0	115.4	1.7	114.2	114.2	114.6	115.1	1.4
2012	116.0	116.4	116.8	117.4	1.7	115.4	115.8	116.2	116.8	1.5
2013	117.9	118.3	118.4	119.0	1.4	117.2	117.6	117.6	118.3	1.3
2014	119.2	119.6	120.5	121.1	1.8	118.5	119.0	120.1	120.7	2.0
2015	122.0	122.1	122.6	123.2	1.7	121.6	121.6	122.2	122.8	1.7
2016	124.4	125.5	126.5	127.2	3.2	124.0	125.2	126.4	127.1	3.5
2017	128.6	129.2	130.0	130.9	2.9	128.6	129.3	130.2	131.3	3.3
2018	132.7	133.5	134.5	135.6	3.6	133.0	134.0	135.2	136.4	3.9
2019	137.2	138.5	139.2	. . .	. . .	138.3	139.7	140.5	. . .	. . .

[1]Includes wages, salaries, and employer costs for employee benefits.
[2]Includes mining, construction, and manufacturing.
[3]Includes the following industries: wholesale trade; retail trade; transportation and warehousing; utilities; information; finance and insurance; real estate and rental and leasing; professional, scientific, and technical services; management of companies and enterprises; administrative and support and waste management and remediation services; education services; health care and social assistance; arts, entertainment, and recreation; accommodation and food services; and other services, except public administration.
. . . = Not available.

Table 6-2. Employment Cost Index, Private Industry Workers, Total Compensation[1] and Wages and Salaries, by Bargaining Status and Selected Industry, 2001–2019

(December 2005 = 100.)

Characteristic and year	Total compensation					Wages and salaries				
	Indexes				Percent change for 12 months (ended December)	Indexes				Percent change for 12 months (ended December)
	March	June	September	December		March	June	September	December	
WORKERS BY BARGAINING STATUS AND INDUSTRY										
Union Workers										
2001	82.0	82.9	83.7	84.8	4.2	86.5	87.4	88.3	89.6	4.3
2002	85.7	86.5	87.5	88.2	4.0	90.2	91.1	91.9	92.6	3.3
2003	89.5	90.7	91.6	92.3	4.6	93.0	93.8	94.4	94.9	2.5
2004	94.5	95.9	96.7	97.3	5.4	95.6	96.4	97.1	97.6	2.8
2005	97.9	98.8	99.6	100.0	2.8	97.9	98.7	99.5	100.0	2.5
2006	100.5	101.8	102.4	103.0	3.0	100.3	101.2	101.7	102.3	2.3
2007	102.7	103.9	104.4	105.1	2.0	102.8	103.7	104.4	104.7	2.3
2008	105.9	106.7	107.4	108.0	2.8	105.5	106.7	107.4	108.1	3.2
2009	109.1	109.8	110.5	111.1	2.9	108.8	109.6	110.2	110.9	2.6
2010	112.8	113.7	114.6	114.8	3.3	111.5	112.1	112.7	112.9	1.8
2011	115.6	117.1	117.4	117.9	2.7	113.6	114.0	114.6	114.9	1.8
2012	118.3	119.3	120.2	120.5	2.2	115.6	116.2	116.9	117.4	2.2
2013	121.5	122.1	122.5	122.6	1.7	118.4	119.0	119.6	119.8	2.0
2014	123.5	125.0	125.8	126.7	3.3	120.5	121.2	122.1	123.1	2.8
2015	127.4	127.5	128.0	128.7	1.6	123.7	124.5	124.8	125.5	1.9
2016	129.6	130.0	130.4	130.6	1.5	126.4	126.8	127.2	127.3	1.4
2017	131.9	132.7	133.7	134.5	3.0	128.6	129.2	129.9	130.9	2.8
2018	135.4	137.4	137.8	138.8	3.2	131.6	132.7	133.5	134.6	2.8
2019	140.0	140.8	141.4	. . .	. . .	135.7	137.0	138.1	. . .	. . .
Union Workers, Goods-Producing[2]										
2001	81.9	82.7	83.4	84.0	2.9	87.2	88.2	88.9	89.5	3.5
2002	84.8	85.5	86.4	87.1	3.7	90.0	90.9	91.7	92.4	3.2
2003	88.9	90.2	90.9	91.7	5.3	92.9	94.0	94.5	95.0	2.8
2004	94.6	95.9	96.7	97.2	6.0	95.4	96.3	96.9	97.1	2.2
2005	97.7	98.8	99.6	100.0	2.9	97.5	98.5	99.2	100.0	3.0
2006	99.9	101.2	101.8	102.2	2.2	100.5	101.6	101.9	102.3	2.3
2007	101.5	102.8	103.1	104.0	1.8	102.7	103.6	104.3	104.3	2.0
2008	104.6	105.6	106.2	106.9	2.8	105.2	106.4	107.1	107.7	3.3
2009	108.0	108.9	109.5	110.0	2.9	108.2	108.8	109.5	109.8	1.9
2010	111.9	112.6	113.8	113.9	3.5	110.2	110.7	111.1	111.2	1.3
2011	114.3	116.4	116.3	116.9	2.6	111.7	112.1	112.8	112.9	1.5
2012	115.8	116.6	117.7	118.0	0.9	113.5	113.8	114.4	115.0	1.9
2013	118.6	118.8	119.2	119.6	1.4	115.7	115.9	116.8	117.0	1.7
2014	120.6	120.9	121.9	122.4	2.3	117.7	118.2	119.0	119.5	2.1
2015	123.0	123.9	124.5	125.4	2.5	119.9	120.7	121.2	121.9	2.0
2016	125.9	126.8	127.1	128.0	2.1	122.3	123.3	123.7	124.7	2.3
2017	128.4	129.4	131.2	131.8	3.0	125.2	126.1	126.8	127.6	2.3
2018	132.3	133.3	132.7	133.2	1.1	127.9	129.1	129.6	130.2	2.0
2019	134.1	135.4	136.3	. . .	. . .	130.9	132.3	133.1	. . .	. . .
Union Workers, Manufacturing										
2001	81.1	81.4	82.0	83.0	2.7	87.3	88.1	88.8	89.7	3.7
2002	84.1	84.7	85.4	86.5	4.2	90.3	90.8	91.6	92.5	3.1
2003	88.6	89.5	90.1	91.0	5.2	93.3	94.2	94.5	95.0	2.7
2004	95.6	96.7	97.5	97.8	7.5	95.5	96.2	97.0	97.1	2.2
2005	98.3	99.1	99.7	100.0	2.2	97.6	98.3	99.0	100.0	3.0
2006	99.3	100.1	100.5	100.8	0.8	100.6	101.2	101.4	101.7	1.7
2007	99.2	100.0	100.0	101.0	0.2	102.0	102.5	102.9	102.6	0.9
2008	101.4	101.7	102.1	102.8	1.8	103.4	104.4	104.9	105.5	2.8
2009	104.4	104.8	105.3	105.8	2.9	106.0	106.4	107.0	107.3	1.7
2010	108.6	109.1	110.5	110.5	4.4	107.8	108.2	108.6	108.7	1.3
2011	110.9	113.8	113.2	113.8	3.0	109.4	109.8	110.6	110.7	1.8
2012	112.1	112.8	113.6	113.7	-0.1	111.5	111.8	112.1	112.5	1.6
2013	113.9	114.1	113.8	114.2	0.4	113.5	113.9	114.4	114.8	2.0
2014	115.4	115.9	116.8	117.4	2.8	115.6	116.2	116.7	116.9	1.8
2015	118.1	118.6	119.3	120.4	2.6	117.8	118.5	118.8	119.6	2.3
2016	121.1	121.7	121.9	122.8	2.0	120.2	120.8	121.4	122.3	2.3
2017	122.9	123.9	126.8	127.2	3.6	122.7	123.6	124.5	125.2	2.4
2018	127.8	128.2	126.5	126.9	-0.2	125.7	126.3	126.9	127.5	1.8
2019	127.7	128.3	129.1	. . .	. . .	128.0	128.6	129.6	. . .	. . .

[1]Includes wages, salaries, and employer costs for employee benefits.
[2]Includes mining, construction, and manufacturing.
[3]Includes the following industries: wholesale trade; retail trade; transportation and warehousing; utilities; information; finance and insurance; real estate and rental and leasing; professional, scientific, and technical services; management of companies and enterprises; administrative and support and waste management and remediation services; education services; health care and social assistance; arts, entertainment, and recreation; accommodation and food services; and other services, except public administration.
. . . = Not available.

Table 6-2. Employment Cost Index, Private Industry Workers, Total Compensation[1] and Wages and Salaries, by Bargaining Status and Selected Industry, 2001–2019—*Continued*

(December 2005 = 100.)

Characteristic and year	Total compensation					Wages and salaries				
	Indexes				Percent change for 12 months (ended December)	Indexes				Percent change for 12 months (ended December)
	March	June	September	December		March	June	September	December	
Union Workers, Service-Providing[3]										
2001	82.0	83.0	84.0	85.5	5.2	85.9	86.8	87.8	89.6	4.9
2002	86.4	87.3	88.4	89.1	4.2	90.3	91.2	92.0	92.7	3.5
2003	90.1	91.1	92.3	92.8	4.2	93.1	93.6	94.4	94.8	2.3
2004	94.4	95.8	96.6	97.3	4.8	95.7	96.5	97.3	98.0	3.4
2005	98.1	98.8	99.6	100.0	2.8	98.2	99.0	99.7	100.0	2.0
2006	101.0	102.2	102.9	103.6	3.6	100.1	100.9	101.6	102.2	2.2
2007	103.7	104.7	105.4	106.0	2.3	102.9	103.8	104.6	104.9	2.6
2008	107.0	107.5	108.3	108.8	2.6	105.8	106.9	107.7	108.3	3.2
2009	109.9	110.6	111.3	111.9	2.8	109.2	110.1	110.8	111.6	3.0
2010	113.4	114.5	115.2	115.5	3.2	112.4	113.1	113.8	114.2	2.3
2011	116.8	117.7	118.3	118.8	2.9	115.0	115.3	115.8	116.3	1.8
2012	120.4	121.5	122.2	122.6	3.2	117.0	117.9	118.7	119.1	2.4
2013	123.9	124.9	125.2	125.2	2.1	120.4	121.3	121.7	121.8	2.3
2014	126.0	128.3	129.0	130.0	3.8	122.6	123.4	124.4	125.6	3.1
2015	130.8	130.4	130.8	131.4	1.1	126.3	127.2	127.3	128.0	1.9
2016	132.7	132.7	133.2	133.1	1.3	129.1	129.2	129.8	129.4	1.1
2017	134.8	135.5	136.1	137.1	3.0	131.0	131.5	132.2	133.3	3.0
2018	138.2	140.7	141.6	142.8	4.2	134.2	135.3	136.2	137.5	3.2
2019	144.1	144.7	145.2	. . .	. . .	138.9	140.1	141.4	. . .	. . .
Nonunion Workers										
2001	85.5	86.3	87.2	87.8	4.2	87.7	88.6	89.3	89.9	3.7
2002	88.7	89.6	90.0	90.3	2.8	90.8	91.7	92.0	92.2	2.6
2003	91.8	92.5	93.5	93.9	4.0	93.3	94.0	94.9	95.1	3.1
2004	95.0	95.9	96.7	97.2	3.5	95.8	96.5	97.3	97.6	2.6
2005	98.3	98.9	99.5	100.0	2.9	98.3	98.9	99.5	100.0	2.5
2006	100.9	101.7	102.6	103.2	3.2	100.8	101.8	102.7	103.3	3.3
2007	104.2	105.1	105.9	106.5	3.2	104.5	105.3	106.2	106.9	3.5
2008	107.5	108.3	108.9	109.1	2.4	107.9	108.7	109.4	109.6	2.5
2009	109.4	109.6	109.9	110.1	0.9	110.0	110.2	110.6	110.9	1.2
2010	110.9	111.4	111.8	112.1	1.8	111.4	111.9	112.4	112.7	1.6
2011	113.0	113.8	114.2	114.5	2.1	113.2	113.8	114.3	114.6	1.7
2012	115.3	116.0	116.3	116.6	1.8	115.2	115.9	116.3	116.5	1.7
2013	117.3	118.0	118.5	119.0	2.1	117.2	117.9	118.4	118.9	2.1
2014	119.4	120.4	121.1	121.5	2.1	119.2	120.2	121.0	121.5	2.2
2015	122.5	122.7	123.4	123.8	1.9	122.4	122.7	123.6	124.0	2.1
2016	124.7	125.7	126.3	126.6	2.3	125.0	126.0	126.6	127.1	2.5
2017	127.8	128.6	129.5	129.9	2.6	128.2	129.1	130.0	130.6	2.8
2018	131.4	132.2	133.2	133.7	2.9	132.1	132.9	134.1	134.7	3.1
2019	134.9	135.8	136.8	. . .	. . .	136.0	136.9	138.0	. . .	. . .
Nonunion, Goods-Producing[2]										
2001	84.7	85.5	86.0	86.7	3.8	88.1	89.0	89.5	90.1	3.6
2002	87.8	88.5	88.8	89.7	3.5	91.0	91.6	91.9	92.7	2.9
2003	91.1	91.9	92.6	92.9	3.6	93.4	94.1	94.6	94.9	2.4
2004	94.5	95.2	96.4	96.8	4.2	95.6	96.2	97.3	97.3	2.5
2005	98.1	99.0	99.9	100.0	3.3	98.0	98.7	99.6	100.0	2.8
2006	100.5	101.4	102.0	102.5	2.5	100.7	101.9	102.4	103.0	3.0
2007	103.3	104.2	104.8	105.4	2.8	104.2	105.0	105.8	106.4	3.3
2008	106.5	107.1	107.6	107.7	2.2	107.7	108.4	109.0	109.3	2.7
2009	107.9	108.0	108.0	108.2	0.5	109.5	109.7	109.9	110.1	0.7
2010	109.1	109.5	110.1	110.2	1.8	110.6	111.0	111.6	111.7	1.5
2011	111.3	112.2	112.5	112.9	2.5	112.3	112.9	113.3	113.7	1.8
2012	113.5	114.1	114.6	114.9	1.8	114.2	114.7	115.3	115.5	1.6
2013	115.7	116.4	116.9	117.2	2.0	116.2	117.0	117.5	117.8	2.0
2014	117.9	118.6	119.2	119.7	2.1	118.3	119.2	119.8	120.3	2.1
2015	120.4	121.3	121.8	122.5	2.3	121.1	122.1	122.8	123.5	2.7
2016	123.2	124.1	124.6	125.1	2.1	124.3	125.3	125.9	126.6	2.5
2017	125.9	126.6	127.6	128.1	2.4	127.5	128.3	129.3	129.8	2.5
2018	129.2	130.2	130.7	131.4	2.6	131.0	132.0	132.8	133.6	2.9
2019	132.6	133.6	134.7	. . .	. . .	134.9	136.0	137.3	. . .	. . .

[1]Includes wages, salaries, and employer costs for employee benefits.
[2]Includes mining, construction, and manufacturing.
[3]Includes the following industries: wholesale trade; retail trade; transportation and warehousing; utilities; information; finance and insurance; real estate and rental and leasing; professional, scientific, and technical services; management of companies and enterprises; administrative and support and waste management and remediation services; education services; health care and social assistance; arts, entertainment, and recreation; accommodation and food services; and other services, except public administration.
. . . = Not available.

Table 6-2. Employment Cost Index, Private Industry Workers, Total Compensation[1] and Wages and Salaries, by Bargaining Status and Selected Industry, 2001–2019—*Continued*

(December 2005 = 100.)

Characteristic and year	Total compensation					Wages and salaries				
	Indexes				Percent change for 12 months (ended December)	Indexes				Percent change for 12 months (ended December)
	March	June	September	December		March	June	September	December	
Nonunion Workers, Manufacturing										
2001	84.5	85.3	85.8	86.3	3.6	88.5	89.4	89.8	90.3	3.4
2002	87.6	88.4	88.7	89.4	3.6	91.4	92.0	92.4	92.9	2.9
2003	91.2	91.9	92.6	92.8	3.8	93.9	94.5	94.9	95.2	2.5
2004	94.4	95.3	96.4	96.6	4.1	95.8	96.5	97.5	97.5	2.4
2005	98.2	99.1	99.8	100.0	3.5	98.4	99.0	99.8	100.0	2.6
2006	100.3	101.3	101.7	102.1	2.1	100.7	101.8	102.0	102.5	2.5
2007	102.8	103.7	104.1	104.6	2.4	103.6	104.2	104.9	105.5	2.9
2008	105.6	106.2	106.6	106.8	2.1	106.6	107.3	108.0	108.2	2.6
2009	107.1	107.3	107.3	107.5	0.7	108.6	108.9	109.1	109.3	1.0
2010	108.5	109.2	109.9	110.0	2.3	109.8	110.5	111.1	111.2	1.7
2011	111.6	112.5	112.8	113.0	2.7	112.1	112.6	113.0	113.3	1.9
2012	113.9	114.4	115.0	115.3	2.0	114.1	114.6	115.2	115.4	1.9
2013	116.3	117.0	117.5	117.8	2.2	116.2	117.1	117.5	117.8	2.1
2014	118.8	119.5	120.1	120.6	2.4	118.7	119.6	120.0	120.5	2.3
2015	121.6	122.5	122.9	123.5	2.4	121.5	122.5	123.2	123.8	2.7
2016	124.4	125.3	126.0	126.3	2.3	124.8	125.9	126.6	127.1	2.7
2017	127.3	128.0	129.0	129.5	2.5	128.1	128.9	129.7	130.3	2.5
2018	130.7	131.5	132.0	132.7	2.5	131.4	132.4	133.1	134.0	2.8
2019	134.2	135.1	135.8	. . .	. . .	135.5	136.5	137.4	. . .	. . .
Nonunion, Service-Providing[3]										
2001	85.7	86.5	87.5	88.0	4.1	87.6	88.5	89.3	89.9	3.8
2002	88.9	89.9	90.4	90.5	2.8	90.8	91.7	92.0	92.1	2.4
2003	91.9	92.7	93.7	94.1	4.0	93.3	94.0	94.9	95.2	3.4
2004	95.2	96.1	96.9	97.3	3.4	95.8	96.6	97.3	97.7	2.6
2005	98.3	98.9	99.4	100.0	2.8	98.4	99.0	99.5	100.0	2.4
2006	101.0	101.8	102.7	103.4	3.4	100.8	101.7	102.7	103.4	3.4
2007	104.4	105.3	106.2	106.8	3.3	104.6	105.4	106.3	107.0	3.5
2008	107.7	108.6	109.2	109.4	2.4	107.9	108.8	109.4	109.7	2.5
2009	109.8	110.0	110.4	110.6	1.1	110.1	110.3	110.8	111.0	1.2
2010	111.3	111.9	112.3	112.7	1.9	111.6	112.2	112.6	113.0	1.8
2011	113.5	114.3	114.7	115.0	2.0	113.4	114.0	114.5	114.8	1.6
2012	115.8	116.5	116.8	117.1	1.8	115.5	116.2	116.5	116.8	1.7
2013	117.8	118.5	119.0	119.4	2.0	117.4	118.2	118.6	119.2	2.1
2014	119.8	120.9	121.6	122.0	2.2	119.4	120.5	121.3	121.7	2.1
2015	123.1	123.1	123.9	124.2	1.8	122.8	122.9	123.8	124.2	2.1
2016	125.2	126.1	126.7	127.1	2.3	125.1	126.2	126.8	127.3	2.5
2017	128.2	129.2	130.0	130.4	2.6	128.4	129.3	130.3	130.8	2.7
2018	132.0	132.8	133.8	134.4	3.1	132.4	133.1	134.4	135.0	3.2
2019	135.5	136.4	137.3	. . .	. . .	136.2	137.1	138.2	. . .	. . .

[1]Includes wages, salaries, and employer costs for employee benefits.
[2]Includes mining, construction, and manufacturing.
[3]Includes the following industries: wholesale trade; retail trade; transportation and warehousing; utilities; information; finance and insurance; real estate and rental and leasing; professional, scientific, and technical services; management of companies and enterprises; administrative and support and waste management and remediation services; education services; health care and social assistance; arts, entertainment, and recreation; accommodation and food services; and other services, except public administration.
. . . = Not available.

Table 6-3. Employment Cost Index, Private Industry Workers, Total Compensation[1] and Wages and Salaries, by Region, and Metropolitan Area Status, 2001–2019

(December 2005 = 100.)

Geography type and year	Total compensation					Wages and salaries				
	Indexes				Percent change for 12 months (ended December)	Indexes				Percent change for 12 months (ended December)
	March	June	September	December		March	June	September	December	
CENSUS REGIONS AND DIVISIONS										
Northeast										
2001	84.3	85.3	86.2	86.7	3.8	86.8	87.8	88.6	89.2	3.8
2002	87.7	88.6	88.9	89.3	3.0	90.2	91.0	91.1	91.5	2.6
2003	90.6	91.4	92.4	92.9	4.0	92.4	93.2	94.1	94.5	3.3
2004	94.2	95.5	96.3	96.6	4.0	95.3	96.3	97.1	97.2	2.9
2005	97.6	98.5	99.2	100.0	3.5	97.8	98.6	99.2	100.0	2.9
2006	100.9	101.8	102.5	103.3	3.3	100.8	101.7	102.5	103.1	3.1
2007	104.0	105.1	106.2	106.8	3.4	104.0	105.0	106.1	106.6	3.4
2008	107.4	108.1	108.7	109.5	2.5	107.5	108.2	108.7	109.6	2.8
2009	109.8	110.2	110.7	111.0	1.4	109.9	110.3	110.8	111.1	1.4
2010	111.8	112.7	113.1	113.6	2.3	111.7	112.6	112.9	113.4	2.1
2011	114.4	115.3	115.7	116.1	2.2	113.7	114.6	114.9	115.3	1.7
2012	116.5	117.1	117.6	117.8	1.5	115.8	116.4	116.7	117.0	1.5
2013	118.7	119.4	119.7	120.1	2.0	117.6	118.4	118.7	119.1	1.8
2014	120.5	121.8	122.7	123.2	2.6	119.4	120.6	121.7	122.2	2.6
2015	125.3	124.3	125.1	125.6	1.9	124.7	123.2	124.2	124.7	2.0
2016	127.3	127.7	128.2	128.7	2.5	126.9	127.2	127.7	128.3	2.9
2017	130.2	131.2	131.8	132.0	2.6	129.7	130.7	131.5	131.7	2.7
2018	133.7	134.7	135.9	136.5	3.4	133.4	133.9	135.3	136.0	3.3
2019	138.1	139.0	140.0	. . .	. . .	137.6	138.8	139.8	. . .	. . .
New England										
2006	100.7	101.4	102.1	103.1	3.1	100.7	101.5	102.3	103.1	3.1
2007	103.6	104.8	105.4	106.1	2.9	103.6	104.8	105.7	106.3	3.1
2008	106.7	107.1	107.8	109.5	3.2	107.1	107.6	108.3	110.3	3.8
2009	109.9	110.2	111.2	111.5	1.8	110.5	110.6	111.7	112.1	1.6
2010	112.3	113.1	113.4	114.1	2.3	112.6	113.4	113.5	114.3	2.0
2011	114.8	116.0	116.2	116.3	1.9	114.5	115.9	116.0	116.0	1.5
2012	116.9	117.4	118.0	118.5	1.9	116.6	117.2	117.8	118.2	1.9
2013	118.9	120.0	120.5	121.6	2.6	118.6	119.8	120.5	121.8	3.0
2014	121.5	123.4	125.2	124.8	2.6	121.4	123.5	126.0	125.3	2.9
2015	130.6	125.3	127.6	127.7	2.3	133.1	125.5	128.5	128.4	2.5
2016	131.2	131.3	130.2	131.1	2.7	132.9	132.8	131.1	132.1	2.9
2017	132.7	133.8	134.9	135.3	3.2	134.1	135.2	136.4	136.8	3.6
2018	136.5	136.6	139.7	139.9	3.4	138.0	137.4	141.3	141.5	3.4
2019	141.1	142.0	143.4	. . .	. . .	142.8	143.7	145.4	. . .	. . .
Middle Atlantic										
2006	100.9	101.9	102.6	103.3	3.3	100.8	101.7	102.5	103.1	3.1
2007	104.2	105.3	106.5	107.1	3.7	104.2	105.1	106.4	106.7	3.5
2008	107.8	108.6	109.1	109.5	2.2	107.6	108.4	109.0	109.4	2.5
2009	109.8	110.2	110.6	110.8	1.2	109.7	110.1	110.4	110.7	1.2
2010	111.6	112.5	113.0	113.4	2.3	111.3	112.3	112.7	113.1	2.2
2011	114.3	115.1	115.5	116.0	2.3	113.4	114.0	114.5	115.0	1.7
2012	116.4	117.0	117.4	117.6	1.4	115.4	116.1	116.4	116.5	1.3
2013	118.6	119.2	119.5	119.6	1.7	117.3	117.9	118.0	118.1	1.4
2014	120.1	121.2	121.8	122.6	2.5	118.6	119.4	120.1	120.9	2.4
2015	123.4	123.9	124.2	124.8	1.8	121.6	122.3	122.6	123.3	2.0
2016	125.9	126.3	127.4	127.8	2.4	124.6	125.2	126.3	126.9	2.9
2017	129.3	130.2	130.7	130.9	2.4	128.0	129.1	129.6	129.8	2.3
2018	132.7	134.0	134.5	135.4	3.4	131.7	132.5	133.1	134.0	3.2
2019	137.1	138.0	138.8	. . .	. . .	135.7	136.9	137.8	. . .	. . .
South										
2001	86.4	87.2	88.1	88.7	4.2	88.9	89.7	90.5	91.0	3.6
2002	89.5	90.5	91.2	91.2	2.8	91.8	92.7	93.3	93.2	2.4
2003	92.0	92.7	93.6	93.9	3.0	93.5	94.1	94.9	95.0	1.9
2004	95.2	96.2	97.1	97.7	4.0	95.8	96.7	97.5	98.0	3.2
2005	98.9	99.3	99.7	100.0	2.4	98.9	99.3	99.7	100.0	2.0
2006	101.0	101.6	102.8	103.5	3.5	101.0	101.6	102.9	103.6	3.6
2007	104.3	105.3	106.1	106.7	3.1	104.6	105.6	106.5	107.0	3.3
2008	107.8	108.5	109.1	109.3	2.4	108.1	109.1	109.8	110.0	2.8
2009	109.8	110.1	110.6	110.7	1.3	110.4	110.7	111.3	111.5	1.4
2010	111.5	112.0	112.5	112.8	1.9	111.9	112.4	112.9	113.4	1.7
2011	113.4	114.3	114.7	115.0	2.0	113.7	114.4	115.0	115.2	1.6
2012	116.0	116.8	117.2	117.7	2.3	116.0	116.7	117.3	117.8	2.3
2013	118.6	119.3	119.7	120.1	2.0	118.7	119.3	119.7	120.2	2.0
2014	120.6	121.7	122.3	122.7	2.2	120.7	121.7	122.4	122.8	2.2
2015	123.2	123.9	124.3	124.6	1.5	123.3	124.2	124.7	125.0	1.8
2016	125.1	125.9	126.2	126.2	1.3	125.4	126.5	126.8	126.7	1.4
2017	127.1	127.9	128.7	129.2	2.4	127.7	128.6	129.5	130.1	2.7
2018	130.4	131.4	132.0	132.5	2.6	131.3	132.3	133.0	133.6	2.7
2019	133.3	134.2	135.3	. . .	. . .	134.4	135.5	136.7	. . .	. . .

[1]Includes wages, salaries, and employer costs for employee benefits.
. . . = Not available.

Table 6-3. Employment Cost Index, Private Industry Workers, Total Compensation[1] and Wages and Salaries, by Region, and Metropolitan Area Status, 2001–2019—*Continued*

(December 2005 = 100.)

Geography type and year	Total compensation					Wages and salaries				
	Indexes				Percent change for 12 months (ended December)	Indexes				Percent change for 12 months (ended December)
	March	June	September	December		March	June	September	December	
South Atlantic										
2006	101.2	101.9	103.1	103.8	3.8	101.3	101.9	103.2	103.9	3.9
2007	104.9	106.0	106.8	107.3	3.4	105.0	106.1	106.9	107.5	3.5
2008	108.5	109.1	109.7	109.8	2.3	108.6	109.5	110.2	110.3	2.6
2009	110.3	110.7	111.3	111.5	1.5	110.8	111.3	111.9	112.2	1.7
2010	112.2	112.6	113.0	113.3	1.6	112.5	112.9	113.3	113.7	1.3
2011	113.8	114.6	115.1	115.4	1.9	114.0	114.6	115.4	115.6	1.7
2012	116.4	117.3	117.8	118.3	2.5	116.4	117.3	118.0	118.5	2.5
2013	119.1	119.8	120.2	120.6	1.9	119.2	120.0	120.2	120.7	1.9
2014	121.3	122.4	122.9	123.4	2.3	121.3	122.3	122.9	123.4	2.2
2015	124.2	124.6	125.3	125.6	1.8	124.1	124.7	125.6	126.0	2.1
2016	126.0	127.4	127.4	127.8	1.8	126.4	128.0	127.9	128.3	1.8
2017	128.7	129.7	130.4	131.1	2.6	129.2	130.3	131.1	132.0	2.9
2018	132.3	133.5	134.0	134.8	2.8	133.3	134.5	135.1	135.9	3.0
2019	135.6	136.5	137.5	. . .	. . .	136.7	137.9	139.1	. . .	. . .
East South Central										
2006	100.7	100.9	101.5	102.3	2.3	100.7	101.5	102.1	103.1	3.1
2007	103.3	103.8	104.8	105.4	3.0	104.2	104.5	105.6	106.3	3.1
2008	106.5	107.2	108.0	108.0	2.5	107.2	107.9	109.0	109.0	2.5
2009	108.5	108.7	109.2	109.3	1.2	109.2	109.5	110.1	110.2	1.1
2010	110.0	110.8	111.0	110.9	1.5	110.8	111.4	111.6	111.5	1.2
2011	112.1	112.7	113.0	113.2	2.1	112.6	112.9	113.4	113.5	1.8
2012	114.0	115.1	115.3	115.8	2.3	114.1	114.8	114.9	115.4	1.7
2013	116.8	116.9	117.5	117.8	1.7	116.3	116.4	116.8	117.3	1.6
2014	118.4	119.1	119.3	119.8	1.7	117.8	118.5	118.8	119.4	1.8
2015	120.7	121.3	121.7	122.4	2.2	120.2	121.2	121.7	122.5	2.6
2016	123.1	124.7	125.1	125.5	2.5	123.0	124.7	125.2	125.5	2.4
2017	126.5	127.0	128.8	128.4	2.3	126.7	127.2	129.1	128.6	2.5
2018	130.0	130.2	131.1	131.3	2.3	130.3	130.6	131.5	131.7	2.4
2019	132.1	132.9	134.9	. . .	. . .	132.4	133.4	135.6	. . .	. . .
West South Central										
2006	100.7	101.4	102.7	103.4	3.4	100.6	101.2	102.7	103.4	3.4
2007	103.7	104.8	105.6	106.1	2.6	104.1	105.3	106.1	106.6	3.1
2008	107.3	108.2	108.7	109.0	2.7	107.8	108.8	109.4	109.8	3.0
2009	109.4	109.5	109.9	109.9	0.8	110.1	110.2	110.8	110.9	1.0
2010	110.8	111.4	112.2	112.7	2.5	111.3	111.9	112.8	113.5	2.3
2011	113.2	114.4	114.7	115.0	2.0	113.7	114.5	115.0	115.2	1.5
2012	116.2	116.8	117.0	117.6	2.3	116.1	116.6	117.1	117.7	2.2
2013	118.5	119.3	119.8	120.2	2.2	118.7	119.5	120.0	120.6	2.5
2014	120.3	121.7	122.4	122.6	2.0	120.8	121.9	122.9	123.1	2.1
2015	122.6	123.7	123.6	123.6	0.8	123.2	124.5	124.4	124.3	1.0
2016	124.1	123.9	124.6	123.8	0.2	124.8	124.5	125.5	124.5	0.2
2017	124.4	125.3	125.9	126.4	2.1	125.4	126.3	127.1	127.5	2.4
2018	127.4	128.3	129.0	129.2	2.2	128.5	129.4	130.2	130.4	2.3
2019	130.0	130.9	131.8	. . .	. . .	131.3	132.2	133.2	. . .	. . .
Midwest										
2001	84.8	85.4	86.1	86.7	3.5	86.8	87.6	88.3	88.9	3.3
2002	88.0	88.7	89.0	89.5	3.2	90.3	91.0	91.3	91.7	3.1
2003	92.1	92.8	93.6	94.0	5.0	94.2	94.7	95.2	95.5	4.1
2004	95.0	95.9	96.6	96.9	3.1	95.6	96.1	96.9	97.1	1.7
2005	97.8	98.4	99.5	100.0	3.2	97.8	98.2	99.4	100.0	3.0
2006	100.7	101.7	102.3	102.8	2.8	100.4	101.4	102.0	102.6	2.6
2007	103.3	104.2	104.6	105.3	2.4	103.6	104.4	105.0	105.6	2.9
2008	106.0	107.0	107.4	107.6	2.2	106.3	107.5	107.9	108.0	2.3
2009	107.9	108.1	108.4	108.6	0.9	108.4	108.6	108.9	109.2	1.1
2010	109.9	110.4	111.0	111.3	2.5	109.9	110.4	110.9	111.2	1.8
2011	112.2	113.3	113.6	113.9	2.3	111.8	112.2	112.7	112.9	1.5
2012	114.7	115.3	115.6	115.9	1.8	113.8	114.3	114.7	115.0	1.9
2013	116.4	117.0	117.4	117.8	1.6	115.5	116.0	116.6	117.1	1.8
2014	118.4	119.5	120.0	120.3	2.1	117.4	118.3	118.9	119.1	1.7
2015	121.2	121.4	122.1	122.5	1.8	119.8	120.6	121.4	121.8	2.3
2016	123.4	124.5	125.3	125.7	2.6	122.5	123.9	124.8	125.3	2.9
2017	126.8	127.4	128.0	128.5	2.2	126.4	126.9	127.5	128.1	2.2
2018	129.8	130.6	131.6	132.3	3.0	129.4	130.1	131.4	132.3	3.3
2019	133.5	134.1	135.0	. . .	. . .	133.5	134.0	135.0	. . .	. . .

[1]Includes wages, salaries, and employer costs for employee benefits.
. . . = Not available.

Table 6-3. Employment Cost Index, Private Industry Workers, Total Compensation[1] and Wages and Salaries, by Region, and Metropolitan Area Status, 2001–2019—*Continued*

(December 2005 = 100.)

Geography type and year	Total compensation					Wages and salaries				
	Indexes				Percent change for 12 months (ended December)	Indexes				Percent change for 12 months (ended December)
	March	June	September	December		March	June	September	December	
East North Central										
2006	100.7	101.7	102.3	102.8	2.8	100.3	101.4	101.9	102.5	2.5
2007	103.2	104.1	104.4	105.0	2.1	103.6	104.4	104.7	105.3	2.7
2008	105.5	106.5	106.9	107.0	1.9	105.8	107.0	107.3	107.4	2.0
2009	107.0	107.3	107.5	107.8	0.7	107.5	107.7	108.0	108.3	0.8
2010	109.2	109.8	110.3	110.5	2.5	109.1	109.7	110.1	110.3	1.8
2011	111.6	112.7	113.1	113.2	2.4	110.9	111.3	111.8	111.9	1.5
2012	113.9	114.5	114.6	114.8	1.4	112.7	113.1	113.4	113.5	1.4
2013	115.4	116.0	116.4	116.7	1.7	114.1	114.7	115.3	115.7	1.9
2014	117.3	118.4	118.8	119.1	2.1	116.0	116.8	117.2	117.5	1.6
2015	120.2	120.4	120.8	121.1	1.7	118.4	119.4	119.8	120.1	2.2
2016	121.9	123.0	123.6	124.1	2.5	120.8	122.1	122.8	123.4	2.7
2017	125.2	126.0	126.5	127.0	2.3	124.5	125.3	125.9	126.5	2.5
2018	128.4	129.0	130.2	130.9	3.1	127.9	128.3	129.7	130.7	3.3
2019	132.3	132.7	133.5	. . .	. . .	132.1	132.4	133.4	. . .	. . .
West North Central										
2006	100.6	101.5	102.4	102.7	2.7	100.6	101.5	102.4	102.7	2.7
2007	103.5	104.3	105.3	105.9	3.1	103.8	104.5	105.6	106.3	3.5
2008	107.3	108.4	108.8	109.0	2.9	107.9	108.9	109.5	109.7	3.2
2009	109.9	110.2	110.6	110.7	1.6	110.7	110.8	111.2	111.4	1.5
2010	111.6	112.0	112.8	113.2	2.3	111.9	112.4	113.1	113.5	1.9
2011	113.9	114.8	115.0	115.6	2.1	114.0	114.5	114.9	115.4	1.7
2012	116.9	117.5	118.2	118.7	2.7	116.5	117.1	118.0	118.5	2.7
2013	119.1	119.4	119.9	120.6	1.6	119.0	119.2	119.8	120.7	1.9
2014	121.0	122.3	123.0	123.3	2.2	120.7	122.0	122.8	123.1	2.0
2015	123.7	123.8	125.3	125.8	2.0	123.1	123.5	125.3	125.8	2.2
2016	126.9	128.4	129.5	129.8	3.2	126.5	128.2	129.4	129.8	3.2
2017	130.8	130.9	131.7	132.1	1.8	131.0	130.7	131.6	132.1	1.8
2018	133.3	134.4	135.2	135.8	2.8	133.2	134.4	135.4	136.1	3.0
2019	136.6	137.6	138.7	. . .	. . .	136.9	137.9	139.1	. . .	. . .
West										
2001	84.1	85.0	85.9	86.9	5.2	87.4	88.3	89.2	90.2	4.8
2002	87.4	88.5	89.1	89.8	3.3	90.4	91.5	92.0	92.4	2.4
2003	90.9	92.0	93.2	93.8	4.5	93.0	93.9	95.1	95.5	3.4
2004	95.3	96.2	96.9	97.4	3.8	96.4	97.0	97.7	98.0	2.6
2005	98.4	99.3	99.7	100.0	2.7	98.4	99.3	99.6	100.0	2.0
2006	100.6	101.8	102.5	103.0	3.0	100.7	102.1	102.7	103.2	3.2
2007	104.2	104.9	105.7	106.5	3.4	104.8	105.4	106.2	107.0	3.7
2008	107.8	108.4	109.3	109.4	2.7	108.3	108.9	109.9	110.1	2.9
2009	109.9	110.0	110.3	110.6	1.1	110.5	110.8	111.2	111.6	1.4
2010	111.3	111.7	112.3	112.5	1.7	112.0	112.4	112.9	113.0	1.3
2011	113.5	114.3	114.6	115.1	2.3	113.6	114.1	114.5	114.9	1.7
2012	115.7	116.3	116.8	116.8	1.5	115.4	116.1	116.5	116.4	1.3
2013	117.6	118.5	119.2	119.6	2.4	117.1	118.1	118.8	119.2	2.4
2014	120.1	120.9	121.9	122.5	2.4	119.5	120.4	121.5	122.2	2.5
2015	123.1	123.8	124.6	125.3	2.3	122.6	123.4	124.4	125.2	2.5
2016	126.2	127.2	127.9	128.6	2.6	125.8	127.0	127.9	128.7	2.8
2017	129.9	131.0	132.3	132.9	3.3	129.8	130.9	132.2	132.9	3.3
2018	134.6	135.7	136.6	137.2	3.2	134.6	135.8	137.1	137.8	3.7
2019	138.5	139.5	140.4	. . .	. . .	139.3	140.2	141.4	. . .	. . .
Mountain										
2006	101.0	101.8	102.7	103.1	3.1	100.6	101.7	102.8	103.2	3.2
2007	105.2	105.2	106.6	107.5	4.3	105.3	105.5	106.7	107.8	4.5
2008	108.4	109.4	110.3	110.4	2.7	108.9	109.9	110.8	111.0	3.0
2009	110.5	110.6	110.9	111.0	0.5	111.1	111.4	111.9	111.9	0.8
2010	111.3	112.3	113.0	112.8	1.6	112.3	113.2	114.1	113.7	1.6
2011	113.4	113.9	114.8	115.3	2.2	113.7	114.1	115.0	115.2	1.3
2012	115.4	116.0	116.5	115.7	0.3	115.2	115.7	116.3	115.2	0.0
2013	116.6	118.1	118.7	119.2	3.0	116.0	117.8	118.3	118.8	3.1
2014	119.5	119.8	120.1	120.6	1.2	119.0	120.5	120.8	121.5	2.3
2015	121.9	122.5	123.4	124.0	2.8	122.5	123.0	124.1	124.9	2.8
2016	124.1	125.4	125.8	126.4	1.9	124.4	125.9	126.4	127.0	1.7
2017	127.5	128.7	129.4	130.0	2.8	128.0	129.3	130.0	130.8	3.0
2018	131.7	132.5	133.2	134.1	3.2	132.5	133.4	134.2	135.2	3.4
2019	135.3	136.6	137.8	. . .	. . .	136.3	137.5	139.0	. . .	. . .
Pacific										
2006	100.5	101.8	102.5	103.0	3.0	100.8	102.2	102.7	103.3	3.3
2007	103.9	104.8	105.4	106.1	3.0	104.6	105.3	106.0	106.8	3.4
2008	107.6	108.1	108.9	109.1	2.8	108.1	108.6	109.6	109.8	2.8
2009	109.7	109.9	110.1	110.5	1.3	110.3	110.6	110.9	111.5	1.5
2010	111.4	111.5	112.0	112.4	1.7	112.0	112.1	112.4	112.8	1.2
2011	113.6	114.5	114.6	115.1	2.4	113.6	114.1	114.4	114.9	1.9
2012	115.9	116.5	117.0	117.4	2.0	115.5	116.3	116.7	117.0	1.8
2013	118.1	118.7	119.5	119.9	2.1	117.6	118.3	119.1	119.5	2.1
2014	120.5	121.4	122.7	123.3	2.8	119.8	120.5	121.8	122.5	2.5
2015	123.7	124.4	125.2	125.9	2.1	122.7	123.7	124.6	125.4	2.4
2016	127.1	128.0	128.8	129.6	2.9	126.5	127.5	128.6	129.5	3.3
2017	130.9	132.0	133.6	134.2	3.5	130.7	131.7	133.2	133.8	3.3
2018	135.9	137.1	138.0	138.5	3.2	135.5	136.8	138.4	138.9	3.8
2019	139.9	140.7	141.6	. . .	. . .	140.7	141.4	142.5	. . .	. . .

[1]Includes wages, salaries, and employer costs for employee benefits.
. . . = Not available.

Table 6-4. Employment Cost Index, Benefits, by Industry and Occupation, 2002–2019

(December 2005 = 100.)

Characteristic and year	Indexes				Percent change for 3 months (ended December)
	March	June	September	December	
Civilian Workers[1]					
2002	81.5	82.5	83.5	84.6	1.3
2003	86.3	87.5	88.9	90.0	1.2
2004	92.1	93.7	94.8	95.9	1.2
2005	97.5	98.4	99.4	100.2	0.8
2006	100.8	101.7	102.7	103.7	1.0
2007	104.0	105.2	106.0	107.0	0.9
2008	107.5	108.1	108.8	109.3	0.5
2009	109.6	109.9	110.4	110.9	0.5
2010	112.0	112.7	113.5	114.1	0.5
2011	115.4	116.8	117.1	117.7	0.5
2012	118.5	119.3	119.9	120.5	0.5
2013	121.3	121.9	122.6	123.2	0.5
2014	123.8	125.1	125.7	126.4	0.6
2015	127.1	127.2	127.8	128.7	0.7
2016	129.3	129.9	130.7	131.3	0.5
2017	132.2	133.0	134.0	134.7	0.5
2018	135.7	136.9	137.5	138.4	0.7
2019	139.3	140.0	140.8	. . .	. . .
Total Private					
2002	82.3	83.3	84.1	85.0	1.1
2003	87.0	88.1	89.4	90.5	1.2
2004	92.9	94.4	95.4	96.5	1.2
2005	98.0	98.8	99.7	100.3	0.6
2006	100.8	101.6	102.5	103.4	0.9
2007	103.1	104.2	105.0	105.9	0.9
2008	106.4	106.9	107.5	107.9	0.4
2009	108.1	108.2	108.6	109.1	0.5
2010	110.3	110.9	111.6	112.1	0.4
2011	113.6	115.2	115.4	116.1	0.6
2012	116.8	117.5	117.9	118.5	0.5
2013	119.1	119.6	120.3	120.8	0.4
2014	121.3	122.5	123.2	123.8	0.5
2015	124.5	124.2	124.8	125.3	0.4
2016	125.9	126.3	127.0	127.5	0.4
2017	128.3	129.1	130.0	130.5	0.4
2018	131.5	132.7	133.2	133.9	0.5
2019	134.6	135.1	135.8	. . .	. . .
State and Local Government Workers					
2002	78.8	79.9	81.4	82.9	1.8
2003	84.1	85.4	86.9	88.0	1.3
2004	89.5	91.1	92.5	93.9	1.5
2005	95.6	96.8	98.4	99.9	1.5
2006	100.8	102.0	103.5	105.1	1.5
2007	107.1	108.7	109.7	110.9	1.1
2008	111.4	112.4	113.3	114.1	0.7
2009	115.3	116.2	116.8	117.7	0.8
2010	118.1	119.1	120.2	121.2	0.8
2011	122.0	122.5	123.2	123.7	0.4
2012	124.7	125.8	127.1	127.9	0.6
2013	129.1	129.9	130.9	132.1	0.9
2014	133.0	134.2	134.8	135.8	0.7
2015	136.7	137.8	138.9	140.5	1.2
2016	141.5	142.4	144.0	144.8	0.6
2017	146.0	147.0	148.2	149.6	0.9
2018	150.3	151.7	152.8	154.2	0.9
2019	155.8	157.2	158.1	. . .	. . .
WORKERS BY OCCUPATION					
Management, Professional, and Related					
2002	82.7	83.7	84.2	85.2	1.2
2003	87.1	88.0	89.5	90.7	1.3
2004	91.9	93.4	94.5	95.9	1.5
2005	97.9	98.8	99.8	100.4	0.6
2006	101.0	101.7	102.8	103.8	1.0
2007	103.5	104.8	105.5	106.4	0.9
2008	107.1	107.8	108.5	109.0	0.5
2009	108.5	108.7	108.9	109.2	0.3
2010	110.0	110.3	110.9	111.7	0.7
2011	113.2	114.6	114.7	115.6	0.8
2012	116.6	117.1	117.7	118.3	0.5
2013	118.5	119.3	120.2	120.7	0.4
2014	120.9	122.4	123.1	123.8	0.6
2015	124.6	123.9	124.3	124.9	0.5
2016	124.9	125.2	125.8	126.4	0.5
2017	127.2	128.0	129.0	129.6	0.5
2018	130.4	131.4	131.7	132.6	0.7
2019	133.0	133.6	134.5	. . .	. . .

[1]Includes workers in the private nonfarm economy, except those in private households, and workers in the public sector, except those in the federal government.
. . . = Not available.

Table 6-4. Employment Cost Index, Benefits, by Industry and Occupation, 2002–2019—*Continued*

(December 2005 = 100.)

Characteristic and year	Indexes				Percent change for 3 months (ended December)
	March	June	September	December	
Sales and Office					
2002	81.8	83.2	84.2	85.1	1.1
2003	86.6	88.0	89.3	90.4	1.2
2004	92.5	94.2	95.2	96.1	0.9
2005	97.5	98.4	99.3	100.2	0.9
2006	100.7	101.5	102.1	103.0	0.9
2007	103.3	104.2	105.2	106.1	0.9
2008	106.5	106.9	107.6	108.0	0.4
2009	108.0	108.0	108.6	108.9	0.3
2010	110.1	110.9	111.6	112.1	0.4
2011	113.3	114.9	115.3	115.8	0.4
2012	116.6	117.4	117.4	117.9	0.4
2013	118.9	119.3	120.1	120.9	0.7
2014	121.2	122.5	123.0	123.8	0.7
2015	123.7	123.9	124.6	125.5	0.7
2016	126.7	127.4	128.2	128.8	0.5
2017	129.2	129.9	130.7	131.3	0.5
2018	132.3	133.8	134.7	135.8	0.8
2019	136.2	136.9	137.4	. . .	. . .
Natural Resources, Construction, and Maintenance					
2002	81.2	82.1	83.3	84.6	1.6
2003	86.0	87.6	88.7	90.3	1.8
2004	92.9	94.5	95.4	96.9	1.6
2005	98.0	98.9	99.7	100.4	0.7
2006	101.1	102.4	103.4	104.4	1.0
2007	103.5	104.5	105.2	106.3	1.0
2008	106.6	106.7	107.4	108.0	0.6
2009	108.3	108.5	109.1	109.8	0.6
2010	111.6	112.1	112.8	113.5	0.6
2011	114.2	115.6	116.1	117.1	0.9
2012	117.9	118.8	119.9	120.6	0.6
2013	121.6	122.0	122.6	123.2	0.5
2014	124.0	126.0	126.7	127.4	0.6
2015	127.7	126.9	127.5	128.2	0.5
2016	128.6	128.9	129.4	130.1	0.5
2017	130.6	131.5	132.3	133.1	0.6
2018	133.6	136.0	136.4	137.1	0.5
2019	138.0	137.5	138.5	. . .	. . .
Production, Transportation, and Material Moving					
2002	81.8	82.7	83.7	84.8	1.3
2003	86.7	88.1	89.4	90.4	1.1
2004	94.4	96.0	97.1	98.0	0.9
2005	98.7	99.2	99.9	100.1	0.2
2006	100.0	100.8	101.6	102.3	0.7
2007	101.1	102.3	102.7	103.9	1.2
2008	104.4	104.4	104.8	105.3	0.5
2009	106.4	106.7	107.1	107.5	0.4
2010	109.9	110.7	111.7	112.2	0.4
2011	113.5	116.4	116.3	117.1	0.7
2012	116.1	117.0	117.6	118.1	0.4
2013	118.7	119.0	119.1	119.7	0.5
2014	120.5	120.9	121.6	122.3	0.6
2015	123.5	124.2	124.9	125.5	0.5
2016	126.3	126.7	127.4	128.0	0.5
2017	128.7	129.5	131.0	131.6	0.5
2018	132.6	133.3	133.4	134.0	0.4
2019	134.9	135.7	136.1	. . .	. . .
Service					
2002	83.5	84.4	86.0	86.8	0.9
2003	88.5	89.4	90.8	92.0	1.3
2004	94.3	95.9	96.7	97.3	0.6
2005	98.0	98.8	99.5	100.3	0.8
2006	101.3	102.1	103.0	103.9	0.9
2007	104.0	105.0	106.0	107.0	0.9
2008	107.4	108.3	108.7	109.2	0.5
2009	109.5	109.8	110.4	110.9	0.5
2010	111.5	112.3	113.3	113.8	0.4
2011	115.2	115.9	116.0	116.7	0.6
2012	117.8	118.2	118.8	119.4	0.5
2013	119.7	120.3	120.8	121.2	0.3
2014	120.9	121.1	121.7	122.4	0.6
2015	122.9	123.3	123.9	124.5	0.5
2016	125.2	126.0	126.7	127.3	0.5
2017	128.0	128.6	129.3	129.9	0.5
2018	131.0	131.5	132.4	133.0	0.5
2019	133.3	134.5	134.9	. . .	. . .

. . . = Not available.

Table 6-4. Employment Cost Index, Benefits, by Industry and Occupation, 2002–2019—*Continued*

(December 2005 = 100.)

Characteristic and year	Indexes				Percent change for 3 months (ended December)
	March	June	September	December	
WORKERS BY INDUSTRY					
Goods-Producing Industries[2]					
2002	79.9	80.6	81.2	82.5	1.6
2003	85.2	86.5	87.5	88.4	1.0
2004	92.4	93.8	95.0	96.5	1.6
2005	98.3	99.5	100.3	100.2	-0.1
2006	99.4	100.3	101.3	102.0	0.7
2007	100.9	102.1	102.4	103.4	1.0
2008	104.0	104.3	104.6	105.0	0.4
2009	105.4	105.5	105.6	106.2	0.6
2010	108.4	108.9	110.0	110.2	0.2
2011	111.7	114.1	113.8	114.5	0.6
2012	114.2	114.8	115.7	116.1	0.3
2013	117.0	117.3	117.6	118.1	0.4
2014	119.2	119.4	120.3	120.8	0.4
2015	121.4	122.1	122.3	123.2	0.7
2016	123.6	124.2	124.5	124.9	0.3
2017	125.4	126.0	127.5	128.0	0.4
2018	129.0	129.7	129.2	129.6	0.3
2019	130.8	131.6	132.2	...	...
Manufacturing					
2002	78.8	79.7	80.3	81.5	1.5
2003	84.7	85.7	86.8	87.5	0.8
2004	92.7	94.1	95.4	96.1	0.7
2005	98.2	99.4	100.1	100.1	0.0
2006	98.6	99.6	100.7	101.1	0.4
2007	99.4	100.8	100.9	101.9	1.0
2008	102.2	102.0	102.4	102.8	0.4
2009	103.4	103.4	103.4	104.0	0.6
2010	106.6	107.4	108.7	108.9	0.2
2011	111.0	113.9	113.4	114.0	0.5
2012	113.2	113.9	114.7	115.1	0.3
2013	115.7	116.1	116.4	116.7	0.3
2014	118.1	118.2	119.3	119.9	0.5
2015	120.8	121.5	121.6	122.5	0.7
2016	123.1	123.7	124.0	124.4	0.3
2017	125.0	125.6	127.6	128.1	0.4
2018	129.1	129.7	128.8	129.2	0.3
2019	130.4	131.1	131.6	...	...
Service-Providing[3]					
2002	83.2	84.4	85.2	86.0	0.9
2003	87.7	88.8	90.2	91.4	1.3
2004	93.0	94.6	95.5	96.5	1.0
2005	97.9	98.6	99.4	100.3	0.9
2006	101.3	102.2	103.0	104.0	1.0
2007	104.0	105.1	106.0	106.9	0.8
2008	107.4	108.0	108.7	109.1	0.4
2009	109.2	109.3	109.9	110.2	0.3
2010	111.1	111.7	112.3	112.9	0.5
2011	114.4	115.7	116.0	116.7	0.6
2012	117.8	118.5	118.8	119.4	0.5
2013	120.0	120.6	121.4	121.9	0.4
2014	122.2	123.8	124.3	125.0	0.6
2015	125.7	125.1	125.8	126.3	0.4
2016	126.9	127.3	128.0	128.6	0.5
2017	129.5	130.3	131.0	131.6	0.5
2018	132.6	133.9	134.7	135.5	0.6
2019	136.0	136.5	137.2	...	...

[2]Includes mining, construction, and manufacturing.
[3]Includes the following industries: wholesale trade; retail trade; transportation and warehousing; utilities; information; finance and insurance; real estate and rental and leasing; professional, scientific, and technical services; management of companies and enterprises; administrative and support and waste management and remediation services; education services; health care and social assistance; arts, entertainment, and recreation; accommodation and food services; and other services, except public administration.
. . . = Not available.

NOTES AND DEFINITIONS

EMPLOYER COSTS FOR EMPLOYEE COMPENSATION (ECEC)

The ECEC series measures the average cost to employers for wages and salaries, and for benefits, per employee hour worked. The series provides quarterly data on employer costs per hour worked for total compensation, wages and salaries, total benefits, and the following benefits: paid leave—vacations, holidays, sick leave, and personal leave; supplemental pay—premium pay for work in addition to the regular work schedule (such as overtime, weekend, and holiday work) and for shift differentials, and non-production bonuses (such as yearend, referral, and attendance bonuses); insurance benefits—life, health, short-term disability, and long-term disability insurance; retirement and savings benefits—defined benefit and defined contribution plans; and legally required benefits—Social Security, Medicare, federal and state unemployment insurance, and workers' compensation. Cost data are presented both in dollar amounts and as percentages of total compensation. The ECEC uses current employment weights to reflect the composition of today's labor force.

Differences in the estimates for the state and local government and private industry sectors stem from factors such as variation in work activities and in occupational structures. Manufacturing and sales, for example, make up a large part of private industry work activities but are rare in state and local government. In contrast, professional and administrative support occupations (including teachers) account for two-thirds of the state and local government workforce but less than one-half of private industry.

Data for the September 2019 reference period were collected from a probability sample of approximately 26,300 occupational observations selected from a sample of about 6,400 private industry establishments and approximately 7,900 occupational observations selected from a sample of about 1,400 state and local government establishments that provided data at the initial interview.

ECEC includes the civilian economy, which includes data from both private industry and state and local government. Excluded from private industry are the self-employed and farm and private household workers. Federal government workers are excluded from the public sector. The private industry series and the state and local government series provide data for the two sectors separately.

Sources of Additional Information

Additional information may be obtained from BLS news release 19-2195 "Employer Costs for Employee Compensation—September 2019," and Chapter 8 of *the Handbook of Methods*.

Table 6-5. Employer Costs for Employee Compensation by Ownership, September 2019

(Dollars, percent of total cost.)

Compensation component	Civilian workers[1]		Private industry workers		State and local governmnet workers	
	Cost	Percent	Cost	Percent	Cost	Percent
TOTAL COMPENSATION[2]	37.03	100.0	34.77	100.0	51.66	100.0
Wages and Salaries	25.43	68.7	24.38	70.1	32.19	62.3
Total Benefits	11.60	31.3	10.38	29.9	19.47	37.7
Paid leave	2.68	7.2	2.50	7.2	3.87	7.5
Vacation	1.31	3.5	1.29	3.7	1.47	2.8
Holiday	0.79	2.1	0.75	2.2	1.10	2.1
Sick	0.41	1.1	0.32	0.9	1.00	1.9
Personal	0.16	0.4	0.14	0.4	0.31	0.6
Supplemental pay	1.04	2.8	1.12	3.2	0.51	1.0
Overtime and premium pay[3]	0.29	0.8	0.30	0.9	0.22	0.4
Shift differentials	0.08	0.2	0.08	0.2	0.05	0.1
Nonproduction bonuses	0.67	1.8	0.74	2.1	0.24	0.5
Insurance	3.22	8.7	2.78	8.0	6.07	11.7
Life insurance	0.05	0.1	0.04	0.1	0.07	0.1
Health insurance	3.06	8.3	2.62	7.5	5.92	11.5
Short-term disability	0.06	0.2	0.07	0.2	0.03	0.1
Long-term disability	0.04	0.1	0.04	0.1	0.05	0.1
Retirement and savings	1.96	5.3	1.31	3.8	6.17	11.9
Defined benefit plans	1.21	3.3	0.52	1.5	5.74	11.1
Defined contribution plans	0.74	2.0	0.79	2.3	0.43	0.8
Legally required benefits	2.70	7.3	2.68	7.7	2.85	5.5
Social Security and Medicare	2.08	5.6	2.05	5.9	2.22	4.3
Social Security[4]	1.65	4.5	1.65	4.7	1.70	3.3
Medicare	0.42	1.1	0.40	1.2	0.53	1.0
Federal unemployment insurance	0.02	0.1	0.03	0.1	(5)	(6)
State unemployment insurance	0.13	0.4	0.14	0.4	0.06	0.1
Workers' compensation	0.47	1.3	0.45	1.3	0.56	1.1

[1]Includes workers in the private nonfarm economy except those in private households, and workers in the public sector, except the federal government.
[2]Includes costs for wages and salaries and benefits.
[3]Includes premium pay for work (such as overtime, weekends, and holidays) in addition to the regular work schedule.
[4]Social Security refers to the Old-Age, Survivors, and Disability Insurance (OASDI) program.
[5]Cost per hour worked is $0.01 or less.
[6]Less than .05 percent.

Table 6-6. Employer Costs for Employee Compensation for Civilian Workers by Occupational and Industry Group, September 2019

(Dollars, percent of total costs.)

Compensation component	Total compensation[1]		Wages and salaries		Total benefits		Paid leave	
	Cost	Percent	Cost	Percent	Cost	Percent	Cost	Percent
Civilian Workers[2]	37.03	100.0	25.43	68.7	11.60	31.3	2.68	7.2
Occupational Group								
Management, professional, and related	61.11	100.0	41.79	68.4	19.32	31.6	5.19	8.5
Management, business, and financial	68.28	100.0	46.70	68.4	21.58	31.6	6.40	9.4
Professional and related	57.89	100.0	39.59	68.4	18.30	31.6	4.64	8.0
Teachers[3]	63.93	100.0	43.68	68.3	20.25	31.7	3.32	5.2
Prmary, secondary, and special education school teachers	63.76	100.0	42.55	66.7	21.21	33.3	2.99	4.7
Registered nurses	57.12	100.0	37.36	65.4	19.75	34.6	5.46	9.6
Sales and office	27.43	100.0	19.25	70.2	8.18	29.8	1.87	6.8
Sales and related	25.83	100.0	19.50	75.5	6.33	24.5	1.52	5.9
Office and administrative support	28.38	100.0	19.10	67.3	9.28	32.7	2.08	7.3
Service	19.75	100.0	14.11	71.4	5.65	28.6	1.03	5.2
Natural resources, construction, and maintenance	36.76	100.0	24.66	67.1	12.10	32.9	1.95	5.3
Construction, extraction, farming, fishing, and forestry	37.69	100.0	24.99	66.3	12.69	33.7	1.57	4.2
Installation, maintenance, and repair	35.76	100.0	24.30	68.0	11.46	32.0	2.37	6.6
Production, transportation, and material moving	29.30	100.0	19.29	65.8	10.01	34.2	1.74	5.9
Production	28.37	100.0	18.76	66.1	9.62	33.9	1.75	6.2
Transportation and material moving	30.16	100.0	19.79	65.6	10.38	34.4	1.74	5.8
Industry Group								
Education and health services	43.08	100.0	29.26	67.9	13.82	32.1	3.27	7.6
Educational services	53.80	100.0	35.76	66.5	18.04	33.5	3.47	6.4
Elementary and secondaty schools	52.73	100.0	34.66	65.7	18.06	34.3	2.84	5.4
Junior colleges, colleges, and universities	59.96	100.0	39.99	66.7	19.97	33.3	5.26	8.8
Health care and social assistance	36.93	100.0	25.53	69.1	11.40	30.9	3.15	8.5
Hospitals	50.50	100.0	32.58	64.5	17.92	35.5	4.91	9.7

Compensation component	Supplemental pay		Insurance		Retirement and savings		Legally required benefits	
	Cost	Percent	Cost	Percent	Cost	Percent	Cost	Percent
Civilian Workers[2]	1.04	2.8	3.22	8.7	1.96	5.3	2.70	7.3
Occupational Group								
Management, professional, and related	1.68	2.7	4.89	8.0	3.76	6.1	3.80	6.2
Management, business, and financial	2.60	3.8	4.76	7.0	3.53	5.2	4.29	6.3
Professional and related	1.27	2.2	4.95	8.6	3.86	6.7	3.58	6.2
Teachers[3]	0.24	0.4	6.31	9.9	7.08	11.1	3.31	5.2
Prmary, secondary, and special education school teachers	0.21	0.3	6.93	10.9	8.02	12.6	3.06	4.8
Registered nurses	2.08	3.6	5.32	9.3	3.09	5.4	3.80	6.6
Sales and office	0.69	2.5	2.61	9.5	1.01	3.7	2.00	7.3
Sales and related	0.63	2.4	1.59	6.2	0.63	2.4	1.96	7.6
Office and administrative support	0.72	2.5	3.21	11.3	1.24	4.4	2.03	7.1
Service	0.41	2.1	1.64	8.3	0.86	4.4	1.70	8.6
Natural resources, construction, and maintenance	1.21	3.3	3.35	9.1	2.12	5.8	3.47	9.4
Construction, extraction, farming, fishing, and forestry	1.24	3.3	3.38	9.0	2.65	7.0	3.85	10.2
Installation, maintenance, and repair	1.17	3.3	3.31	9.3	1.55	4.3	3.05	8.5
Production, transportation, and material moving	1.19	4.0	3.09	10.6	1.35	4.6	2.64	9.0
Production	1.39	4.9	3.08	10.9	0.98	3.4	2.43	8.5
Transportation and material moving	1.00	3.3	3.11	10.3	1.69	5.6	2.84	9.4
Industry Group								
Education and health services	0.65	1.5	4.23	9.8	2.99	6.9	2.68	6.2
Educational services	0.25	0.5	5.80	10.8	5.63	10.5	2.88	5.4
Elementary and secondaty schools	0.20	0.4	6.06	11.5	6.31	12.0	2.66	5.0
Junior colleges, colleges, and universities	0.37	0.6	5.92	9.9	4.97	8.3	3.45	5.7
Health care and social assistance	0.88	2.4	3.33	9.0	1.47	4.0	2.57	7.0
Hospitals	1.78	3.5	5.30	10.5	2.69	5.3	3.24	6.4

[1]Includes costs for wages and salaries and benefits.
[2]Includes workers in the private nonfarm economy except those in private households, and workers in the public sector, except the federal government.
[3]Includes postsecondary teachers; primary, secondary, and special education teachers; and other teachers and instructors.

Table 6-7. Employer Compensation Costs Per Hour Worked for Employee Compensation and Costs as a Percent of Total Compensation: State and Local Government, by Major Occupational and Industry Group, September 2019

(Dollars, percent of total compensation.)

Characteristic	Total compensation	Wages and salaries	Benefit costs					
			Total	Paid leave	Supplemental pay	Insurance	Retirement and savings	Legally required benefits
COSTS PER HOUR WORKED								
State and Local Government Workers	51.66	32.19	19.47	3.87	0.51	6.07	6.17	2.85
Occupational Group								
Management, professional, and related	62.08	40.06	22.02	4.37	0.41	6.64	7.40	3.21
Professional and related	60.26	39.19	21.06	3.87	0.37	6.60	7.12	3.09
Teachers[1]	68.22	45.64	22.58	3.40	0.24	7.15	8.50	3.28
Primary, secondary, and special education school teachers	68.15	44.97	23.17	3.09	0.23	7.64	9.08	3.13
Sales and office	35.85	20.68	15.16	3.14	0.32	5.69	3.88	2.15
Office and administrative support	36.02	20.74	15.28	3.15	0.32	5.76	3.91	2.14
Service	37.97	21.81	16.16	3.21	0.81	4.81	5.00	2.34
Industry Group								
Education and health services	54.10	34.97	19.13	3.56	0.34	6.24	6.21	2.78
Education services	55.56	36.18	19.39	3.41	0.25	6.36	6.58	2.79
Elementary and secondary schools	54.06	35.22	18.84	2.81	0.21	6.39	6.79	2.64
Junior colleges, colleges, and universities	59.91	39.02	20.89	5.22	0.34	6.18	5.92	3.23
Health care and social assistance	45.80	28.11	17.69	4.42	0.88	5.59	4.05	2.76
Hospitals	48.39	30.27	18.12	4.68	1.05	5.55	3.93	2.91
Public administration	49.71	28.76	20.95	4.63	0.78	5.98	6.55	3.01
PERCENT OF TOTAL COMPENSATION								
State and Local Government Workers	100.0	62.3	37.7	7.5	1.0	11.7	11.9	5.5
Occupational Group								
Management, professional, and related	100.0	64.5	35.5	7.0	0.7	10.7	11.9	5.2
Professional and related	100.0	65.0	35.0	6.4	0.6	11.0	11.8	5.1
Teachers[1]	100.0	66.9	33.1	5.0	0.4	10.5	12.5	4.8
Primary, secondary, and special education school teachers	100.0	66.0	34.0	4.5	0.3	11.2	13.3	4.6
Sales and office	100.0	57.7	42.3	8.7	0.9	15.9	10.8	6.0
Office and administrative support	100.0	57.6	42.4	8.7	0.9	16.0	10.9	6.0
Service	100.0	57.4	42.6	8.5	2.1	12.7	13.2	6.2
Industry Group								
Education and health services	100.0	64.6	35.4	6.6	0.6	11.5	11.5	5.1
Education services	100.0	65.1	34.9	6.1	0.5	11.4	11.9	5.0
Elementary and secondary schools	100.0	65.1	34.9	5.2	0.4	11.8	12.6	4.9
Junior colleges, colleges, and universities	100.0	65.1	34.9	8.7	0.6	10.3	9.9	5.4
Health care and social assistance	100.0	61.4	38.6	9.6	1.9	12.2	8.8	6.0
Hospitals	100.0	62.6	37.4	9.7	2.2	11.5	8.1	6.0
Public administration	100.0	57.9	42.1	9.3	1.6	12.0	13.2	6.0

Note: Individual items may not sum to totals due to rounding.

[1]Includes postsecondary teachers; primary, secondary, and special education teachers; and other teachers and instructors.

Table 6-8. Employer Costs Per Hour Worked for Employee Compensation and Costs as a Percent of Total Compensation: Private Industry Workers, by Occupational Group and Industry, September 2019

(Dollars, percent.)

Compensation component	Total compensation		Wages and salaries		Total benefits		Paid leave	
	Cost	Percent	Cost	Percent	Cost	Percent	Cost	Percent
Private Industry Workers	34.77	100.0	24.38	70.1	10.38	29.9	2.50	7.2
Occupational Group								
Management, professional, and related	60.79	100.0	42.36	69.7	18.43	30.3	5.50	9.0
Management, business, and financial	67.69	100.0	46.90	69.3	20.78	30.7	6.30	9.3
Professional and related	56.86	100.0	39.77	69.9	17.09	30.1	5.00	8.8
Sales and office	26.69	100.0	19.12	71.6	7.57	28.4	1.80	6.6
Sales and related	25.80	100.0	19.51	75.6	6.29	24.4	1.50	5.9
Office and adminsitrative support	27.29	100.0	18.87	69.1	8.43	30.9	1.90	7.1
Service	17.24	100.0	13.04	75.7	4.20	24.3	0.70	4.2
Natural resources, construction, and maintenance	36.18	100.0	24.56	67.9	11.61	32.1	1.80	5.0
Construction, extraction, farming, fishing, and forestry	37.23	100.0	24.97	67.1	12.27	32.9	1.40	3.7
Installation, maintenance, and repair	35.05	100.0	24.13	68.8	10.92	31.2	2.20	6.4
Production, transportation, and material moving	28.88	100.0	19.14	66.3	9.74	33.7	1.70	5.9
Production	28.11	100.0	18.64	66.3	9.47	33.7	1.70	6.1
Transportation and material moving	29.63	100.0	19.64	66.3	10.00	33.7	1.70	5.7
Industry Group								
Goods-producting	40.50	100.0	27.06	66.8	13.44	33.2	2.60	6.4
Construction	40.45	100.0	28.05	69.4	12.40	30.6	1.80	4.4
Manufacturing	40.01	100.0	26.19	65.5	13.81	34.5	3.00	7.6
Aircraft manufacturing	71.69	100.0	43.49	60.7	28.20	39.3	6.40	8.9
Service-providing	33.58	100.0	23.83	71.0	9.75	29.0	2.50	7.4
Trade, transportation, and utlities	28.82	100.0	20.30	70.4	8.53	29.6	1.80	6.2
Wholesale trade	37.80	100.0	26.71	70.7	11.08	29.3	2.80	7.3
Retail trade[4]	20.54	100.0	15.54	75.6	5.00	24.4	1.00	4.8
Transportation and warehousing	39.14	100.0	25.24	64.5	13.89	35.5	2.70	6.9
Utilities	63.68	100.0	38.47	60.4	25.21	39.6	5.40	8.5
Information	58.32	100.0	39.22	67.2	19.10	32.8	5.40	9.2
Financial activities	47.97	100.0	32.20	67.1	15.77	32.9	4.20	8.7
Financial and insurance	53.61	100.0	35.48	66.2	18.13	33.8	4.90	9.1
Credit intermediation and related activities	45.63	100.0	30.49	66.8	15.15	33.2	4.20	9.2
Insurance carriers and related activities[4]	52.02	100.0	34.07	65.5	17.95	34.5	4.60	8.9
Real estate and rental and leasing	32.06	100.0	22.96	71.6	9.11	28.4	2.20	6.8

Compensation component	Supplemental pay		Insurance		retirement and savings		Legally required benfits	
	Cost	Percent	Cost	Percent	Cost	Percent	Cost	Percent
Private Industry Workers	1.12	3.2	2.78	8.0	1.31	3.8	2.68	7.7
Occupational Group								
Management, professional, and related	2.10	3.4	4.32	7.1	2.56	4.2	4.00	6.6
Management, business, and financial	2.86	4.2	4.48	6.6	2.81	4.1	4.35	6.4
Professional and related	1.66	2.9	4.23	7.4	2.43	4.3	3.80	6.7
Sales and office	0.72	2.7	2.34	8.8	0.76	2.9	1.99	7.5
Sales and related	0.63	2.4	1.58	6.1	0.61	2.4	1.96	7.6
Office and adminsitrative support	0.78	2.9	2.85	10.4	0.86	3.2	2.01	7.4
Service	0.35	2.0	1.21	7.0	0.29	1.7	1.62	9.4
Natural resources, construction, and maintenance	1.24	3.4	3.14	8.7	1.93	5.3	3.51	9.7
Construction, extraction, farming, fishing, and forestry	1.29	3.5	3.16	8.5	2.49	6.7	3.93	10.6
Installation, maintenance, and repair	1.19	3.4	3.11	8.9	1.32	3.8	3.06	8.7
Production, transportation, and material moving	1.20	4.2	2.99	10.3	1.22	4.2	2.64	9.1
Production	1.39	4.9	3.03	10.8	0.91	3.2	2.42	8.6
Transportation and material moving	1.01	3.4	2.94	9.9	1.52	5.1	2.84	9.6
Industry Group								
Goods-producting	1.74	4.3	3.74	9.2	1.96	4.8	3.39	8.4
Construction	1.31	3.2	3.26	8.1	2.08	5.2	3.97	9.8
Manufacturing	1.97	4.9	3.99	10.0	1.78	4.4	3.04	7.6
Aircraft manufacturing	4.94	6.9	6.97	9.7	5.33	7.4	4.55	6.4
Service-providing	1.00	3.0	2.58	7.7	1.18	3.5	2.53	7.5
Trade, transportation, and utlities	0.82	2.8	2.38	8.3	1.15	4.0	2.38	8.3
Wholesale trade	1.20	3.2	2.92	7.7	1.32	3.5	2.89	7.6
Retail trade[4]	0.46	2.2	1.40	6.8	0.41	2.0	1.75	8.5
Transportation and warehousing	1.28	3.3	4.10	10.5	2.43	6.2	3.39	8.7
Utilities	2.26	3.5	6.30	9.9	6.77	10.6	4.46	7.0
Information	2.60	4.5	5.09	8.7	2.25	3.9	3.80	6.5
Financial activities	2.61	5.4	4.15	8.7	1.76	3.7	3.08	6.4
Financial and insurance	3.20	6.0	4.65	8.7	2.14	4.0	3.28	6.1
Credit intermediation and related activities	2.20	4.8	4.22	9.2	1.64	3.6	2.90	6.4
Insurance carriers and related activities[4]	3.03	5.8	4.70	9.0	2.36	4.5	3.24	6.2
Real estate and rental and leasing	0.94	2.9	2.76	8.6	0.70	2.2	2.54	7.9

[4]Comprises the Old-Age, Survivors, and Disability Insurance (OASDI) program.

NOTES AND DEFINITIONS

EMPLOYEE BENEFITS SURVEY

The Employee Benefits Survey provides data on the incidence and provisions of selected employee benefit plans.

Coverage

Data in this section are from the National Compensation Survey (NCS), conducted by the Bureau of Labor Statistics (BLS). This release contains March 2018 data on employer-provided benefits offered to civilian, private industry, and state and local government workers in the United States. Excluded are federal government workers, the military, agricultural workers, private household workers, and the self-employed.

Definitions

Access to a benefit is determined on an occupational basis within an establishment. An employee is considered to have access to a benefit if it is available for his or her use.

Participation refers to the proportion of employees covered by a benefit. There will be cases where employees with access to a plan will not participate. For example, some employees may decline to participate in a health insurance plan if there is an employee cost involved.

A *private establishment* is an economic unit that produces goods or services, a central administrative office, or an auxiliary unit providing support services to a company. For private industries, the establishment is usually at a single physical location. For state and local governments, an establishment is defined as an agency or entity such as a school district, college, university, hospital, nursing home, administrative body, court, police department, fire department, health or social service operation, highway maintenance operation, urban transit operation, or other governmental unit. It provides services under the authority of a specific state or local government organization within a defined geographic area or jurisdiction.

Take-up rates are the percentage of workers with access to a plan who participate in the plan. They are computed by using the number of workers participating in a plan divided by the number of workers with access to the plan, times 100 and rounded to the nearest one percent. Since the computation of take-up rates is based on the number of workers collected, rather the rounded percentage estimates, the take-up rates in the tables may not equal the ratio of participation to access estimates.

An employee is considered to be a *union worker* when all the following conditions are met: 1.) a labor organization is recognized as the bargaining agent for all workers in the occupation. 2.) wage and salary rates are determined through collective bargaining or negotiations. 3.) settlement terms, which must include earnings provisions and may include benefit provisions, are embodied in a signed, mutually binding collective bargaining agreement.

Sources of Additional Information

For more information, see Bureau of Labor Statistics (BLS) news release 19-1650 "Employee Benefits in the United States in the United States–March 2019" which is available on the BLS Web site at <http://www.bls.gov/ncs/ebs/>.

Table 6-9. Retirement Benefits:[1] Access, Participation, and Take-Up Rates, Civilian Workers[2] March 2019

(Percent.)

Characteristic	Civilian[3]			Private industry			State and local government		
	Access	Participation	Take-up rate	Access	Participation	Take-up rate	Access	Participation	Take-up rate
ALL WORKERS	71	56	79	67	52	77	91	83	91
Worker Characteristics									
Management, professional, and related	86	75	87	84	72	86	93	84	90
Management, business, and financial	88	78	89	87	77	89	-	-	-
Professional and related	85	74	87	82	69	85	93	84	90
Teachers	87	77	89	-	-	-	94	85	90
Primary, secondary, and special education school teachers	95	85	90	-	-	-	99	90	91
Registered nurses	89	79	88	-	-	-	-	-	-
Service	48	32	66	43	25	58	84	78	93
Protective service	78	66	85	61	39	64	92	88	96
Sales and office	74	56	76	72	54	74	91	82	90
Sales and related	68	44	65	68	44	65	-	-	-
Office and administrative support	77	63	82	75	60	80	92	83	90
Natural resources, construction, and maintenance	64	50	78	61	47	76	97	90	93
Construction, extraction, farming, fishing, and forestry	60	48	79	57	44	77	-	-	-
Installation, maintenance, and repair	67	52	77	65	49	75	-	-	-
Production, transportation, and material moving	72	56	77	72	55	77	90	81	90
Production	74	58	79	73	58	79	-	-	-
Transportation and material moving	71	54	76	70	52	74	-	-	-
Full-time workers	80	66	82	77	61	80	99	90	91
Part-time workers	40	24	60	39	22	57	45	39	87
Union workers	94	85	90	91	82	90	97	88	91
Nonunion workers	67	51	77	65	49	75	86	78	91
Average Wage Within the Following Percentiles[4]									
Lowest 25 percent	46	27	58	43	23	54	78	70	90
Lowest 10 percent	32	16	48	31	13	43	69	60	88
Second 25 percent	70	54	77	67	49	73	94	86	91
Third 25 percent	84	70	84	80	66	82	98	89	91
Highest 25 percent	90	80	90	87	77	89	97	87	91
Highest 10 percent	90	81	90	88	79	90	95	85	90
Establishment Characteristics									
Goods-producing industries	76	61	80	76	61	80	-	-	-
Service-providing industries	70	55	79	66	50	76	91	83	91
Education and health services	79	66	84	72	57	80	93	83	89
Educational services	88	78	89	73	61	84	93	83	90
Elementary and secondary schools	91	82	90	-	-	-	93	85	91
Junior colleges, colleges, and universities	91	79	87	89	81	91	92	79	86
Health care and social assistance	74	59	80	72	57	79	93	81	87
Hospitals	93	81	87	-	-	-	93	79	85
Public administration	91	85	94	-	-	-	91	85	94
Number of Workers									
1 to 99 workers	56	41	73	54	38	71	87	82	94
1 to 49 workers	51	38	74	50	36	72	85	80	95
50 to 99 workers	70	51	73	67	46	69	90	84	93
100 workers or more	86	71	83	84	68	81	93	83	90
100 to 499 workers	81	64	78	80	61	76	91	85	93
500 workers or more	90	79	88	89	78	88	93	82	88
Geographic Areas[5]									
Northeast	71	59	83	67	55	81	91	84	92
New England	72	60	83	70	57	82	85	75	88
Middle Atlantic	70	59	84	66	54	81	93	86	93
South	70	52	75	66	47	71	94	84	90
South Atlantic	70	53	75	67	48	72	91	81	89
East South Central	71	52	73	67	46	69	94	86	92
West South Central	68	52	77	62	45	73	97	88	91
Midwest	72	57	79	70	54	78	90	79	89
East North Central	71	57	80	69	54	79	89	78	88
West North Central	74	58	78	71	54	75	92	82	89
West	71	58	82	68	54	79	89	83	93
Mountain	75	63	84	73	60	82	86	82	95
Pacific	69	56	80	66	51	78	91	84	92

[1]Includes defined benefit pension plans and defined contribution retirement plans. Workers are considered as having access or as participating if they have access to or participate in at least one of these plan types.
[2]The take-up rate is an estimate of the percentage of workers with access to a plan who participate in the plan, rounded for presentation.
[3]Includes workers in the private nonfarm economy except those in private households, and workers in the public sector, except the federal government.
[4]The percentile groupings are based on the average wage for each occupation surveyed, which may include workers both above and below the threshold.
[5]The states that comprise the Census divisions are: New England—Connecticut, Maine, Massachusetts, New Hampshire, Rhode Island, and Vermont; Middle Atlantic—New Jersey, New York, and Pennsylvania; South Atlantic—Delaware, District of Columbia, Florida, Georgia, Maryland, North Carolina, South Carolina, Virginia, and West Virginia; East South Central—Alabama, Kentucky, Mississippi, and Tennessee; West South Central—Arkansas, Louisiana, Oklahoma, and Texas; East North Central—Illinois, Indiana, Michigan, Ohio, and Wisconsin; West North Central—Iowa, Kansas, Minnesota, Missouri, Nebraska, North Dakota, and South Dakota; Mountain—Arizona, Colorado, Idaho, Montana, Nevada, New Mexico, Utah, and Wyoming; and Pacific—Alaska, California, Hawaii, Oregon, and Washington.
\- = No workers in this area or data does not meet standards of reliability or precision.

Table 6-10. Medical Care Benefits: Access, Participation, and Take-Up Rates,[1] March 2019

(Percent.)

Characteristic	Civilian[2]			Private industry			State and local government		
	Access	Participation	Take-up rate	Access	Participation	Take-up rate	Access	Participation	Take-up rate
ALL WORKERS	71	52	73	69	49	71	89	70	78
Worker Characteristics									
Management, professional, and related	88	67	76	86	65	75	92	71	78
Management, business, and financial	94	71	75	94	70	75	-	-	-
Professional and related	85	65	76	82	62	76	91	70	77
Teachers	85	64	75	-	-	-	92	70	76
Primary, secondary, and special education school teachers	95	71	75	-	-	-	99	75	76
Registered nurses	88	64	73	-	-	-	-	-	-
Service	48	30	63	43	26	59	81	63	77
Protective service	74	52	70	55	30	55	90	69	77
Sales and office	69	49	71	67	47	70	89	72	81
Sales and related	54	35	65	54	35	65	-	-	-
Office and administrative support	78	57	73	76	54	72	90	73	82
Natural resources, construction, and maintenance	74	58	78	72	56	77	95	78	82
Construction, extraction, farming, fishing, and forestry	70	55	78	68	53	77	-	-	-
Installation, maintenance, and repair	78	61	78	77	59	77	-	-	-
Production, transportation, and material moving	76	56	73	76	55	73	84	66	78
Production	81	60	75	81	60	74	-	-	-
Transportation and material moving	72	52	71	72	51	71	-	-	-
Full-time workers	87	64	74	84	61	73	99	78	79
Part-time workers	22	12	56	21	12	55	26	19	71
Union workers	94	75	80	94	76	82	95	73	77
Nonunion workers	68	48	71	66	46	70	84	66	79
Average Wage Within the Following Percentiles[3]									
Lowest 25 percent	40	24	61	36	21	59	72	56	78
Lowest 10 percent	26	15	57	24	13	55	61	48	78
Second 25 percent	74	52	70	70	48	68	93	73	78
Third 25 percent	88	67	76	86	65	75	97	77	79
Highest 25 percent	93	71	77	91	70	77	95	74	78
Highest 10 percent	94	73	78	94	72	77	93	74	80
Establishment Characteristics									
Goods-producing industries	85	65	77	85	65	76	-	-	-
Service-providing industries	69	50	72	65	46	70	89	69	78
Education and health services	77	56	72	71	49	69	90	70	77
Educational services	86	66	76	74	53	72	90	69	77
Elementary and secondary schools	88	66	75	-	-	-	90	68	76
Junior colleges, colleges, and universities	90	71	79	91	68	75	89	72	81
Health care and social assistance	72	50	70	70	48	69	91	73	81
Hospitals	91	66	73	-	-	-	91	73	80
Public administration	90	72	80	-	-	-	90	72	80
Number of Workers									
1 to 99 workers	57	40	71	55	38	70	85	67	79
1 to 49 workers	52	37	71	51	36	70	82	66	81
50 to 99 workers	72	50	69	69	47	68	88	69	78
100 workers or more	86	63	74	85	62	73	90	70	78
100 to 499 workers	82	59	72	81	58	71	87	69	80
500 workers or more	90	68	76	89	67	75	92	71	77
Geographic Areas[4]									
Northeast	71	51	72	69	49	71	87	66	76
New England	73	53	72	71	51	72	88	63	72
Middle Atlantic	70	51	72	68	48	71	86	67	78
South	71	51	71	67	47	69	92	74	80
South Atlantic	70	50	71	67	46	69	91	72	79
East South Central	73	53	72	70	48	69	92	78	85
West South Central	72	51	71	68	47	69	96	74	78
Midwest	70	50	71	67	48	71	86	65	75
East North Central	69	50	72	67	48	72	85	65	77
West North Central	71	49	70	68	47	69	88	63	72
West	74	56	76	72	54	75	88	70	80
Mountain	74	54	74	72	53	74	86	64	74
Pacific	74	57	76	72	54	75	89	74	83

[1]The take-up rate is an estimate of the percentage of workers with access to a plan who participate in the plan, rounded for presentation.
[2]Includes workers in the private nonfarm economy except those in private households, and workers in the public sector, except the federal government.
[3]The percentile groupings are based on the average wage for each occupation surveyed, which may include workers both above and below the threshold.
[4]The states that comprise the Census divisions are: New England—Connecticut, Maine, Massachusetts, New Hampshire, Rhode Island, and Vermont; Middle Atlantic—New Jersey, New York, and Pennsylvania; South Atlantic—Delaware, District of Columbia, Florida, Georgia, Maryland, North Carolina, South Carolina, Virginia, and West Virginia; East South Central—Alabama, Kentucky, Mississippi, and Tennessee; West South Central—Arkansas, Louisiana, Oklahoma, and Texas; East North Central—Illinois, Indiana, Michigan, Ohio, and Wisconsin; West North Central—Iowa, Kansas, Minnesota, Missouri, Nebraska, North Dakota, and South Dakota; Mountain—Arizona, Colorado, Idaho, Montana, Nevada, New Mexico, Utah, and Wyoming; and Pacific—Alaska, California, Hawaii, Oregon, and Washington.
- = No workers in this area or data does not meet standards of reliability or precision.

Table 6-11. Medical Plans: Share of Premiums Paid by Employer and Employee for Single Coverage, March 2019

(Percent.)

Characteristic	Civilian[1]		Private industry		State and local government	
	Employer share of premium	Employee share of premium	Employer share of premium	Employee share of premium	Employer share of premium	Employee share of premium
ALL WORKERS	80	20	79	21	86	14
Worker Characteristics						
Management, professional, and related	81	19	80	20	85	15
Management, business, and financial	79	21	78	22	-	-
Professional and related	82	18	81	19	85	15
Teachers	83	17	-	-	84	16
Primary, secondary, and special education school teachers	83	17	-	-	84	16
Registered nurses	83	17	-	-	-	-
Service	80	20	78	22	87	13
Protective service	86	14	79	21	88	12
Sales and office	79	21	78	22	88	12
Sales and related	76	24	76	24	-	-
Office and administrative support	80	20	79	21	88	12
Natural resources, construction, and maintenance	79	21	78	22	89	11
Construction, extraction, farming, fishing, and forestry	79	21	78	22	-	-
Installation, maintenance, and repair	79	21	78	22	-	-
Production, transportation, and material moving	79	21	79	21	86	14
Production	80	20	79	21	-	-
Transportation and material moving	79	21	78	22	-	-
Full-time workers	80	20	79	21	86	14
Part-time workers	79	21	78	22	86	14
Union workers	86	14	87	13	86	14
Nonunion workers	79	21	78	22	87	13
Average Wage Within the Following Percentiles[2]						
Lowest 25 percent	77	23	76	24	87	13
Lowest 10 percent	76	24	75	25	87	13
Second 25 percent	79	21	78	22	87	13
Third 25 percent	80	20	79	21	86	14
Highest 25 percent	82	18	81	19	85	15
Highest 10 percent	81	19	80	20	84	16
Establishment Characteristics						
Goods-producing industries	80	20	79	21	-	-
Service-providing industries	80	20	79	21	86	14
Education and health services	82	18	80	20	85	15
Educational services	84	16	79	21	85	15
Elementary and secondary schools	84	16	-	-	84	16
Junior colleges, colleges, and universities	84	16	80	20	86	14
Health care and social assistance	81	19	81	19	87	13
Hospitals	84	16	-	-	87	13
Public administration	88	12	-	-	88	12
Number of Workers						
1 to 99 workers	79	21	78	22	87	13
1 to 49 workers	79	21	78	22	88	12
50 to 99 workers	79	21	78	22	85	15
100 workers or more	81	19	79	21	86	14
100 to 499 workers	80	20	78	22	87	13
500 workers or more	82	18	81	19	86	14
Geographic Areas[3]						
Northeast	81	19	81	19	85	15
New England	78	22	78	22	77	23
Middle Atlantic	82	18	81	19	87	13
South	79	21	77	23	86	14
South Atlantic	79	21	77	23	86	14
East South Central	79	21	77	23	88	12
West South Central	80	20	78	22	87	13
Midwest	79	21	78	22	87	13
East North Central	79	21	78	22	85	15
West North Central	81	19	78	22	91	9
West	81	19	80	20	86	14
Mountain	79	21	77	23	87	13
Pacific	82	18	82	18	86	14

[1]Includes workers in the private nonfarm economy except those in private households, and workers in the public sector, except the federal government.
[2]The percentile groupings are based on the average wage for each occupation surveyed, which may include workers both above and below the threshold.
[3]The states that comprise the Census divisions are: New England—Connecticut, Maine, Massachusetts, New Hampshire, Rhode Island, and Vermont; Middle Atlantic—New Jersey, New York, and Pennsylvania; South Atlantic—Delaware, District of Columbia, Florida, Georgia, Maryland, North Carolina, South Carolina, Virginia, and West Virginia; East South Central—Alabama, Kentucky, Mississippi, and Tennessee; West South Central—Arkansas, Louisiana, Oklahoma, and Texas; East North Central—Illinois, Indiana, Michigan, Ohio, and Wisconsin; West North Central—Iowa, Kansas, Minnesota, Missouri, Nebraska, North Dakota, and South Dakota; Mountain—Arizona, Colorado, Idaho, Montana, Nevada, New Mexico, Utah, and Wyoming; and Pacific—Alaska, California, Hawaii, Oregon, and Washington.
- = No workers in this area or data does not meet standards of reliability or precision.

Table 6-12. Medical Plans: Share of Premiums Paid by Employer and Employee for Family Coverage, March 2019

(Percent.)

Characteristic	Civilian[1]		Private industry		State and local government	
	Employer share of premium	Employee share of premium	Employer share of premium	Employee share of premium	Employer share of premium	Employee share of premium
ALL WORKERS	67	33	66	34	71	29
Worker Characteristics						
Management, professional, and related	68	32	68	32	70	30
Management, business, and financial	69	31	68	32	-	-
Professional and related	68	32	67	33	69	31
Teachers	66	34	-	-	66	34
Primary, secondary, and special education school teachers	64	36	-	-	65	35
Registered nurses	72	28	-	-	-	-
Service	63	37	60	40	72	28
Protective service	74	26	67	33	77	23
Sales and office	66	34	65	35	73	27
Sales and related	63	37	63	37	-	-
Office and administrative support	67	33	65	35	73	27
Natural resources, construction, and maintenance	68	32	67	33	76	24
Construction, extraction, farming, fishing, and forestry	67	33	66	34	-	-
Installation, maintenance, and repair	68	32	67	33	-	-
Production, transportation, and material moving	70	30	70	30	71	29
Production	72	28	72	28	-	-
Transportation and material moving	69	31	68	32	-	-
Full-time workers	67	33	67	33	71	29
Part-time workers	63	37	62	38	71	29
Union workers	80	20	84	16	76	24
Nonunion workers	64	36	64	36	67	33
Average Wage Within the Following Percentiles[2]						
Lowest 25 percent	59	41	58	42	67	33
Lowest 10 percent	60	40	60	40	61	39
Second 25 percent	66	34	63	37	74	26
Third 25 percent	68	32	67	33	69	31
Highest 25 percent	71	29	71	29	75	25
Highest 10 percent	72	28	71	29	76	24
Establishment Characteristics						
Goods-producing industries	71	29	71	29	-	-
Service-providing industries	66	34	65	35	71	29
Education and health services	66	34	64	36	68	32
Educational services	67	33	65	35	67	33
Elementary and secondary schools	65	35	-	-	65	35
Junior colleges, colleges, and universities	71	29	71	29	72	28
Health care and social assistance	65	35	63	37	75	25
Hospitals	75	25	-	-	74	26
Public administration	77	23	-	-	77	23
Number of Workers						
1 to 99 workers	62	38	61	39	73	27
1 to 49 workers	62	38	61	39	74	26
50 to 99 workers	63	37	61	39	73	27
100 workers or more	70	30	70	30	71	29
100 to 499 workers	67	33	66	34	72	28
500 workers or more	74	26	76	24	70	30
Geographic Areas[3]						
Northeast	74	26	72	28	83	17
New England	72	28	71	29	77	23
Middle Atlantic	74	26	72	28	85	15
South	63	37	63	37	63	37
South Atlantic	64	36	63	37	66	34
East South Central	64	36	64	36	62	38
West South Central	61	39	61	39	58	42
Midwest	69	31	68	32	74	26
East North Central	70	30	69	31	76	24
West North Central	67	33	66	34	71	29
West	67	33	66	34	75	25
Mountain	66	34	65	35	72	28
Pacific	68	32	66	34	76	24

[1]Includes workers in the private nonfarm economy except those in private households, and workers in the public sector, except the federal government.
[2]The percentile groupings are based on the average wage for each occupation surveyed, which may include workers both above and below the threshold.
[3]The states that comprise the Census divisions are: New England—Connecticut, Maine, Massachusetts, New Hampshire, Rhode Island, and Vermont; Middle Atlantic—New Jersey, New York, and Pennsylvania; South Atlantic—Delaware, District of Columbia, Florida, Georgia, Maryland, North Carolina, South Carolina, Virginia, and West Virginia; East South Central—Alabama, Kentucky, Mississippi, and Tennessee; West South Central—Arkansas, Louisiana, Oklahoma, and Texas; East North Central—Illinois, Indiana, Michigan, Ohio, and Wisconsin; West North Central—Iowa, Kansas, Minnesota, Missouri, Nebraska, North Dakota, and South Dakota; Mountain—Arizona, Colorado, Idaho, Montana, Nevada, New Mexico, Utah, and Wyoming; and Pacific—Alaska, California, Hawaii, Oregon, and Washington.
- = No workers in this area or data does not meet standards of reliability or precision.

Table 6-13. Life Insurance Benefits: Access, Participation, and Take-Up Rates, National Compensation Survey, March 2019

(Percent.)

Characteristic	Civilian[1]			Private industry			State and local government		
	Access	Participation	Take-up rates[2]	Access	Participation	Take-up rates[2]	Access	Participation	Take-up rates[2]
ALL WORKERS	60	58	98	56	55	98	81	79	98
Worker Characteristics									
Management, professional, and related	79	78	99	77	76	99	83	81	97
Management, business, and financial	83	82	99	82	81	99	-	-	-
Professional and related	77	76	98	74	74	99	82	80	97
Teachers	77	75	98	-	-	-	82	80	97
Primary, secondary, and special education school teachers	83	82	98	-	-	-	87	85	98
Registered nurses	83	82	99	-	-	-	-	-	-
Service	36	34	96	30	29	95	76	74	97
Protective service	63	61	98	34	33	97	86	84	98
Sales and office	57	56	98	54	53	98	82	80	98
Sales and related	40	39	98	40	39	98	-	-	-
Office and administrative support	66	65	99	64	63	99	83	81	98
Natural resources, construction, and maintenance	55	54	98	52	51	98	89	88	99
Construction, extraction, farming, fishing, and forestry	47	46	99	44	43	98	-	-	-
Installation, maintenance, and repair	63	61	98	60	59	98	-	-	-
Production, transportation, and material moving	64	63	98	64	62	98	80	79	98
Production	69	68	99	68	68	99	-	-	-
Transportation and material moving	60	58	97	59	57	97	-	-	-
Full-time workers	73	72	98	70	69	99	91	89	98
Part-time workers	15	14	91	14	13	91	24	23	93
Union workers	85	83	97	83	80	97	89	87	98
Nonunion workers	55	54	98	54	53	98	75	73	97
Average Wage Within the Following Percentiles[3]									
Lowest 25 percent	28	26	95	24	23	95	65	63	97
Lowest 10 percent	16	15	93	15	14	92	53	51	97
Second 25 percent	60	58	98	56	55	98	87	85	98
Third 25 percent	76	75	99	72	71	99	87	86	98
Highest 25 percent	83	83	99	82	81	99	88	86	97
Highest 10 percent	86	85	99	85	85	99	85	82	97
Establishment Characteristics									
Goods-producing industries	70	69	99	70	69	99	-	-	-
Service-providing industries	58	57	98	53	52	98	82	79	98
Education and health services	69	68	98	62	61	99	82	80	97
Educational services	78	76	98	67	66	99	81	79	97
Elementary and secondary schools	78	76	98	-	-	-	79	77	98
Junior colleges, colleges, and universities	86	84	97	87	86	99	86	83	96
Health care and social assistance	64	62	98	62	61	98	87	84	96
Hospitals	90	88	99	-	-	-	87	83	95
Public administration	84	82	98	-	-	-	84	82	98
Number of Workers									
1 to 99 workers	42	42	98	40	40	98	75	73	98
1 to 49 workers	37	37	99	36	35	99	69	68	99
50 to 99 workers	57	56	98	54	52	97	80	79	98
100 workers or more	77	75	98	75	74	98	84	81	97
100 to 499 workers	70	69	98	69	68	98	78	76	97
500 workers or more	84	82	98	84	82	98	86	84	97
Geographic Areas[4]									
Northeast	58	57	98	54	53	99	82	79	97
New England	63	61	97	60	58	98	82	74	90
Middle Atlantic	56	55	99	52	51	99	81	81	99
South	59	58	98	55	54	98	82	80	97
South Atlantic	60	59	98	56	55	98	85	82	97
East South Central	58	56	98	54	53	98	74	72	96
West South Central	59	58	98	55	54	98	83	81	98
Midwest	62	60	97	59	57	97	81	79	97
East North Central	62	61	98	59	58	98	81	78	96
West North Central	61	59	97	58	56	97	81	80	100
West	60	59	99	56	56	99	81	80	99
Mountain	64	63	99	61	60	99	82	82	100
Pacific	58	57	99	54	54	99	80	79	99

[1]Includes workers in the private nonfarm economy except those in private households, and workers in the public sector, except the federal government.
[2]The take-up rate is an estimate of the percentage of workers with access to a plan who participate in the plan, rounded for presentation.
[3]The percentile groupings are based on the average wage for each occupation surveyed, which may include workers both above and below the threshold.
[4]The states that comprise the Census divisions are: New England—Connecticut, Maine, Massachusetts, New Hampshire, Rhode Island, and Vermont; Middle Atlantic—New Jersey, New York, and Pennsylvania; South Atlantic—Delaware, District of Columbia, Florida, Georgia, Maryland, North Carolina, South Carolina, Virginia, and West Virginia; East South Central—Alabama, Kentucky, Mississippi, and Tennessee; West South Central—Arkansas, Louisiana, Oklahoma, and Texas; East North Central—Illinois, Indiana, Michigan, Ohio, and Wisconsin; West North Central—Iowa, Kansas, Minnesota, Missouri, Nebraska, North Dakota, and South Dakota; Mountain—Arizona, Colorado, Idaho, Montana, Nevada, New Mexico, Utah, and Wyoming; and Pacific—Alaska, California, Hawaii, Oregon, and Washington.
- = No workers in this area or data does not meet standards of reliability or precision.

Table 6-14. Life Insurance Plans: Employee Contribution Requirement, Civilian Workers,[1] March 2019

(Percent.)

Characteristic	Employee contribution required	Employee contribution not required
ALL WORKERS	5	95
Worker Characteristics		
Management, professional, and related	5	95
Management, business, and financial	3	97
Professional and related	5	95
Teachers	10	90
Primary, secondary, and special education school teachers	9	91
Registered nurses	3	97
Service	5	95
Sales and office	5	95
Sales and related	7	93
Office and administrative support	4	96
Natural resources, construction, and maintenance	5	95
Construction, extraction, farming, fishing, and forestry	5	95
Installation, maintenance, and repair	5	95
Production, transportation, and material moving	5	95
Production	4	96
Transportation and material moving	6	94
Full-time workers	5	95
Part-time workers	4	96
Union workers	6	94
Nonunion workers	5	95
Average Wage Within the Following Percentiles[2]		
Lowest 25 percent	6	94
Lowest 10 percent	8	92
Second 25 percent	6	94
Third 25 percent	4	96
Highest 25 percent	5	95
Highest 10 percent	5	95
Establishment Characteristics		
Service-providing industries	5	95
Education and health services	5	95
Educational services	10	90
Elementary and secondary schools	10	90
Junior colleges, colleges, and universities	10	90
Health care and social assistance	2	98
Hospitals	3	97
Public administration	7	93
Number of Workers		
1 to 99 workers	5	95
1 to 49 workers	6	94
50 to 99 workers	4	96
100 workers or more	5	95
100 to 499 workers	4	96
500 workers or more	6	94
Geographic Areas[3]		
Northeast	6	94
New England	11	89
Middle Atlantic	4	96
South	6	94
South Atlantic	5	95
East South Central	6	94
West South Central	7	93
Midwest	5	95
East North Central	5	95
West North Central	5	95
West	4	96
Mountain	5	95
Pacific	3	97

[1]Includes workers in the private nonfarm economy except those in private households, and workers in the public sector, except the federal government.
[2]The percentile groupings are based on the average wage for each occupation surveyed, which may include workers both above and below the threshold.
[3]The states that comprise the Census divisions are: New England—Connecticut, Maine, Massachusetts, New Hampshire, Rhode Island, and Vermont; Middle Atlantic—New Jersey, New York, and Pennsylvania; South Atlantic—Delaware, District of Columbia, Florida, Georgia, Maryland, North Carolina, South Carolina, Virginia, and West Virginia; East South Central—Alabama, Kentucky, Mississippi, and Tennessee; West South Central—Arkansas, Louisiana, Oklahoma, and Texas; East North Central—Illinois, Indiana, Michigan, Ohio, and Wisconsin; West North Central—Iowa, Kansas, Minnesota, Missouri, Nebraska, North Dakota, and South Dakota; Mountain—Arizona, Colorado, Idaho, Montana, Nevada, New Mexico, Utah, and Wyoming; and Pacific—Alaska, California, Hawaii, Oregon, and Washington.

Table 6-15. Access to Paid Leave Benefits, March 2019

(Percent.)

Characteristic	Civilian[1]			Private industry			State and local government		
	Paid sick leave	Paid vacation	Paid holidays	Paid sick leave	Paid vacation	Paid holidays	Paid sick leave	Paid vacation	Paid holidays
ALL WORKERS	76	76	78	73	79	79	91	61	68
Worker Characteristics									
Management, professional, and related	91	79	82	90	90	91	93	47	57
Management, business, and financial	94	95	95	94	96	96	-	-	-
Professional and related	90	72	77	88	86	88	93	40	52
Teachers	87	20	35	-	-	-	93	14	31
Primary, secondary, and special education school teachers	96	18	31	-	-	-	99	12	27
Registered nurses	90	89	91	-	-	-	-	-	-
Service	61	62	59	58	60	56	85	75	79
Protective service	83	83	82	74	76	73	91	89	90
Sales and office	76	81	84	75	80	83	92	86	88
Sales and related	64	70	75	64	70	75	-	-	-
Office and administrative support	83	87	89	82	87	89	93	87	88
Natural resources, construction, and maintenance	68	78	80	66	77	79	96	96	95
Construction, extraction, farming, fishing, and forestry	59	67	70	56	64	68	-	-	-
Installation, maintenance, and repair	77	90	90	76	90	89	-	-	-
Production, transportation, and material moving	70	84	85	69	84	86	90	62	73
Production	68	88	91	68	88	91	-	-	-
Transportation and material moving	72	79	80	71	81	81	-	-	-
Full-time workers	86	87	87	83	91	90	99	67	74
Part-time workers	43	41	46	43	42	47	45	23	33
Union workers	91	75	81	86	89	91	97	58	69
Nonunion workers	73	76	77	72	78	78	86	63	67
Average Wage Within the Following Percentiles[2]									
Lowest 25 percent	51	56	58	47	55	56	79	59	65
Lowest 10 percent	31	42	43	30	42	41	67	45	53
Second 25 percent	79	82	82	77	82	82	95	86	89
Third 25 percent	88	90	91	86	91	91	97	61	69
Highest 25 percent	92	81	84	90	92	93	96	42	53
Highest 10 percent	94	82	85	93	94	94	94	37	49
Establishment Characteristics									
Goods-producing industries	72	88	89	72	88	89	-	-	-
Service-providing industries	76	74	76	73	77	77	91	60	67
Education and health services	87	70	74	84	84	84	92	44	55
Educational services	90	41	52	79	56	63	92	37	49
Elementary and secondary schools	93	27	39	-	-	-	93	25	38
Junior colleges, colleges, and universities	89	71	82	87	73	86	90	69	81
Health care and social assistance	85	88	87	85	88	87	92	92	92
Hospitals	94	93	94	-	-	-	91	92	91
Public administration	92	90	91	-	-	-	92	90	91
Number of Workers									
1 to 99 workers	66	70	71	65	71	72	89	54	61
1 to 49 workers	64	69	70	64	70	70	85	62	68
50 to 99 workers	71	71	73	68	75	76	92	46	56
100 workers or more	85	82	84	84	88	88	92	63	70
100 to 499 workers	81	82	83	80	85	85	90	62	70
500 workers or more	91	83	85	89	92	92	93	63	70
Geographic Areas[3]									
Northeast	78	74	77	76	77	79	90	57	64
New England	82	73	75	81	76	77	90	55	60
Middle Atlantic	77	74	78	75	77	80	90	57	65
South	72	76	78	68	79	79	92	62	69
South Atlantic	71	77	78	68	78	78	91	66	77
East South Central	67	75	79	62	78	80	90	61	71
West South Central	74	76	76	71	79	80	94	56	56
Midwest	69	74	75	66	77	77	89	55	66
East North Central	67	75	75	65	77	76	88	55	68
West North Central	73	74	76	70	77	78	91	56	60
West	87	80	80	86	82	82	93	67	72
Mountain	77	80	80	75	83	82	89	61	66
Pacific	91	80	80	91	81	81	96	70	74

[1]Includes workers in the private nonfarm economy except those in private households, and workers in the public sector, except the federal government.
[2]The percentile groupings are based on the average wage for each occupation surveyed, which may include workers both above and below the threshold.
[3]The states that comprise the Census divisions are: New England—Connecticut, Maine, Massachusetts, New Hampshire, Rhode Island, and Vermont; Middle Atlantic—New Jersey, New York, and Pennsylvania; South Atlantic—Delaware, District of Columbia, Florida, Georgia, Maryland, North Carolina, South Carolina, Virginia, and West Virginia; East South Central—Alabama, Kentucky, Mississippi, and Tennessee; West South Central—Arkansas, Louisiana, Oklahoma, and Texas; East North Central—Illinois, Indiana, Michigan, Ohio, and Wisconsin; West North Central—Iowa, Kansas, Minnesota, Missouri, Nebraska, North Dakota, and South Dakota; Mountain—Arizona, Colorado, Idaho, Montana, Nevada, New Mexico, Utah, and Wyoming; and Pacific—Alaska, California, Hawaii, Oregon, and Washington.
- = No workers in this area or data does not meet standards of reliability or precision.

Table 6-16. Quality of Life Benefits:[1] Access for Civilian Workers, March 2019

(Percent.)

Characteristic	Childcare[2]	Flexible workplace	Subsidized commuting	Wellness programs	Employee assistance programs
ALL WORKERS	11	7	8	44	54
Worker Characteristics					
Management, professional, and related	17	14	13	59	70
Management, business, and financial	18	22	15	60	69
Professional and related	17	11	13	58	70
Teachers	13	3	7	54	66
Primary, secondary, and special education school teachers	9	2	3	52	65
Registered nurses	24	4	13	81	88
Service	8	1	6	28	38
Protective service	10	2	7	41	57
Sales and office	9	7	7	44	56
Sales and related	5	5	4	39	53
Office and administrative support	10	8	9	48	58
Natural resources, construction, and maintenance	7	2	4	29	37
Construction, extraction, farming, fishing, and forestry	6	1	4	24	28
Installation, maintenance, and repair	8	2	5	35	45
Production, transportation, and material moving	5	2	3	43	54
Production	7	3	3	46	52
Transportation and material moving	3	2	4	41	55
Full-time workers	12	8	9	49	60
Part-time workers	5	2	4	26	36
Union workers	16	3	12	57	78
Nonunion workers	10	7	7	42	50
Average Wage Within the Following Percentiles[3]					
Lowest 25 percent	4	1	3	27	36
Lowest 10 percent	4	1	3	19	27
Second 25 percent	8	4	6	40	51
Third 25 percent	12	7	10	50	61
Highest 25 percent	20	16	14	62	73
Highest 10 percent	22	21	18	64	77
Establishment Characteristics					
Goods-producing industries	9	6	4	45	51
Service-providing industries	11	7	9	44	55
Education and health services	15	4	9	52	65
Educational services	14	4	8	58	72
Elementary and secondary schools	9	2	3	52	67
Junior colleges, colleges, and universities	27	8	20	77	90
Health care and social assistance	16	4	10	49	61
Hospitals	35	3	18	83	95
Public administration	17	6	17	64	81
Number of Workers					
1 to 99 workers	5	6	5	26	33
1 to 49 workers	4	6	6	21	29
50 to 99 workers	8	5	5	38	47
100 workers or more	16	8	10	62	75
100 to 499 workers	9	7	7	53	67
500 workers or more	24	10	14	73	85
Geographic Areas[4]					
Northeast	15	7	10	42	55
New England	17	9	12	47	59
Middle Atlantic	14	6	9	41	54
South	10	7	6	48	54
South Atlantic	12	8	7	49	56
East South Central	6	5	3	46	55
West South Central	10	7	6	47	50
Midwest	9	7	5	43	55
East North Central	9	7	5	42	53
West North Central	8	5	6	44	58
West	10	6	12	40	54
Mountain	9	8	9	41	54
Pacific	10	6	13	39	53

[1]Includes workers in the private nonfarm economy except those in private households, and workers in the public sector, except the federal government.
[2]A workplace program that provides for either the full or partial cost of caring for an employee's children in a nursery, day care center, or a baby sitter in facilities either on or off the employer's premises.
[3]The categories are based on the average wage for each occupation surveyed, which may include workers with earnings both above and below the threshold.
[4]The states that comprise the Census divisions are: New England—Connecticut, Maine, Massachusetts, New Hampshire, Rhode Island, and Vermont; Middle Atlantic—New Jersey, New York, and Pennsylvania; South Atlantic—Delaware, District of Columbia, Florida, Georgia, Maryland, North Carolina, South Carolina, Virginia, and West Virginia; East South Central—Alabama, Kentucky, Mississippi, and Tennessee; West South Central—Arkansas, Louisiana, Oklahoma, and Texas; East North Central—Illinois, Indiana, Michigan, Ohio, and Wisconsin; West North Central—Iowa, Kansas, Minnesota, Missouri, Nebraska, North Dakota, and South Dakota; Mountain—Arizona, Colorado, Idaho, Montana, Nevada, New Mexico, Utah, and Wyoming; and Pacific—Alaska, California, Hawaii, Oregon, and Washington.

Table 6-17. Financial Benefits: Access for Civilian Workers, March 2019

(Percent.)

Characteristic	Health savings account	Section 125 cafeteria benefits			Savings plans with no employer contribution[1]	Financial planning
		Flexible benefits	Dependent care flexible spending account	Healthcare flexible spending account		
ALL WORKERS	31	17	42	45	22	21
Worker Characteristics						
Management, professional, and related	45	26	61	65	32	28
Management, business, and financial	50	24	64	67	25	31
Professional and related	42	27	59	64	34	27
Teachers	36	35	54	61	53	22
Primary, secondary, and special education school teachers	36	37	53	62	55	20
Registered nurses	43	35	77	79	33	29
Service	15	10	25	26	15	11
Protective service	22	23	43	49	38	19
Sales and office	34	14	39	42	17	24
Sales and related	28	7	29	30	9	23
Office and administrative support	37	19	45	49	22	24
Natural resources, construction, and maintenance	22	12	27	30	17	14
Construction, extraction, farming, fishing, and forestry	17	10	18	21	15	10
Installation, maintenance, and repair	28	14	36	39	19	18
Production, transportation, and material moving	25	15	42	42	22	18
Production	28	17	42	43	20	22
Transportation and material moving	23	14	42	42	24	15
Full-time workers	37	21	50	53	25	24
Part-time workers	12	5	18	17	12	11
Union workers	29	21	58	64	45	26
Nonunion workers	31	16	39	42	18	20
Average Wage Within Following Percentiles:[2]						
Lowest 25 percent	15	8	21	20	12	12
Lowest 10 percent	8	7	14	13	8	6
Second 25 percent	29	14	38	41	19	18
Third 25 percent	37	21	51	55	26	24
Highest 25 percent	46	27	64	68	33	31
Highest 10 percent	51	25	67	73	33	32
Establishment Characteristics						
Goods-producing industries	31	17	40	41	15	23
Service-providing industries	31	17	43	45	23	20
Education and health services	32	26	52	57	34	21
Educational services	38	35	59	65	55	24
Elementary and secondary schools	34	37	53	61	55	20
Junior colleges, colleges, and universities	50	35	79	83	64	36
Health care and social assistance	29	21	47	52	22	19
Hospitals	46	39	81	86	32	38
Public administration	35	35	65	70	65	30
Number of Workers						
1 to 99 workers	20	9	25	27	14	10
1 to 49 workers	18	7	21	22	12	8
50 to 99 workers	26	15	36	39	19	15
100 workers or more	41	25	60	63	30	31
100 to 499 workers	38	20	49	50	22	29
500 workers or more	45	31	72	76	39	34
Geographic Areas[3]						
Northeast	25	13	42	46	23	21
New England	30	12	49	54	21	23
Middle Atlantic	24	13	39	43	24	20
South	30	22	42	44	22	22
South Atlantic	30	20	43	44	22	22
East South Central	29	25	40	40	24	24
West South Central	31	24	42	45	20	20
Midwest	34	17	43	45	22	21
East North Central	32	16	42	44	24	22
West North Central	37	19	47	48	19	19
West	33	13	42	44	20	19
Mountain	32	15	44	47	20	19
Pacific	33	12	40	43	20	18

[1]Savings plans established by the employer on behalf of the employee, but with no employer contribution. These are cash or deferred arrangement plans or individual retirement accounts used to fund savings and retirement plans authorized by section 401(k), 403(b), or 457 of the Internal Revenue Code. The employees' contributions can be pre- and post-tax. Employees may authorize a payroll deduction by the employer to fund the established plan.
[2]Surveyed occupations are classified into wage categories based on the average wage for the occupation, which may include workers with earnings both above and below the threshold. The categories were formed using percentile estimates generated using ECEC data for March 2016.
[3]The states that comprise the Census divisions are: New England—Connecticut, Maine, Massachusetts, New Hampshire, Rhode Island, and Vermont; Middle Atlantic—New Jersey, New York, and Pennsylvania; South Atlantic—Delaware, District of Columbia, Florida, Georgia, Maryland, North Carolina, South Carolina, Virginia, and West Virginia; East South Central—Alabama, Kentucky, Mississippi, and Tennessee; West South Central—Arkansas, Louisiana, Oklahoma, and Texas; East North Central—Illinois, Indiana, Michigan, Ohio, and Wisconsin; West North Central—Iowa, Kansas, Minnesota, Missouri, Nebraska, North Dakota, and South Dakota; Mountain—Arizona, Colorado, Idaho, Montana, Nevada, New Mexico, Utah, and Wyoming; and Pacific—Alaska, California, Hawaii, Oregon, and Washington.

Table 6-18 Nonproduction Bonuses: Access for Civilian Workers,[1] March 2019

(Percent.)

Characteristic	All nonproduction bonuses[2]	Cash-profit sharing bonus	Employee recognition bonus	End-of-year-bonus	Holiday bonus	Payment in lieu of benefits bonus	Longevity bonus	Referral bonus	Other bonus[3]
ALL WORKERS	39	6	3	10	6	6	2	5	10
Worker Characteristics									
Management, professional, and related	45	5	5	11	3	9	2	6	13
Management, business, and financial	54	8	7	16	4	7	2	8	15
Professional and related	41	4	4	9	3	11	3	5	11
Teachers	29	-	2	1	-	17	4	(4)	10
Primary, secondary, and special education school teachers	32	-	2	1	-	20	5	-	12
Registered nurses	45	-	4	5	-	10	1	12	17
Service	26	1	2	7	5	4	3	4	5
Protective service	37	1	3	4	1	14	9	-	12
Sales and office	42	9	3	10	6	5	1	5	8
Sales and related	36	13	1	8	6	3	1	4	5
Office and administrative support	46	7	4	11	7	6	2	6	10
Natural resources, construction, and maintenance	42	6	2	14	11	3	1	3	9
Construction, extraction, farming, fishing, and forestry	40	5	1	15	13	2	1	1	7
Installation, maintenance, and repair	43	7	3	13	9	5	1	5	11
Production, transportation, and material moving	40	8	1	8	6	4	1	5	15
Production	45	11	2	12	6	3	1	4	16
Transportation and material moving	36	4	1	5	5	5	1	6	13
Full-time workers	44	6	4	11	6	7	2	6	12
Part-time workers	22	4	1	5	4	1	1	4	3
Union workers	39	4	4	2	1	19	4	2	15
Nonunion workers	39	6	3	11	6	4	2	6	9
Average Wage Within the Following Percentiles[5]									
Lowest 25 percent	26	5	1	6	5	2	2	5	4
Lowest 10 percent	21	1	-	7	5	1	(4)	3	3
Second 25 percent	40	5	2	10	8	4	1	4	10
Third 25 percent	46	6	4	12	6	8	2	5	12
Highest 25 percent	48	7	6	12	4	11	2	7	14
Highest 10 percent	50	8	6	13	3	13	2	8	14
Establishment Characteristics									
Goods-producing industries	49	11	2	16	8	3	1	3	14
Service-providing industries	37	5	3	9	5	6	2	5	9
Education and health services	34	1	3	5	5	10	3	5	9
Educational services	28	-	2	1	-	16	4	(4)	9
Elementary and secondary schools	30	-	1	1	-	19	5	-	10
Junior colleges, colleges, and universities	27	-	5	-	1	13	4	1	5
Health care and social assistance	37	1	3	8	8	7	3	8	9
Hospitals	38	2	3	4	-	9	1	10	15
Public administration	45	-	6	2	1	22	9	-	13
Number of Workers									
1 to 99 workers	36	3	2	12	8	4	1	4	6
1 to 49 workers	36	3	2	13	9	3	1	3	6
50 to 99 workers	38	4	2	10	6	4	2	6	8
100 workers or more	42	8	4	7	3	8	3	6	13
100 to 499 workers	41	9	3	7	4	6	3	7	11
500 workers or more	42	8	5	7	1	10	3	5	17
Geographic Areas[6]									
Northeast	41	4	3	12	3	11	2	5	10
New England	42	3	2	16	2	8	2	4	8
Middle Atlantic	41	4	3	10	4	12	1	5	11
South	42	6	4	11	7	3	2	5	11
South Atlantic	44	6	5	11	8	3	2	6	13
East South Central	42	7	2	8	7	2	3	6	13
West South Central	39	7	3	12	7	2	2	3	9
Midwest	39	6	2	9	5	6	2	6	10
East North Central	41	7	2	9	6	6	2	6	11
West North Central	35	6	1	8	4	5	3	6	9
West	33	6	3	7	5	7	2	4	6
Mountain	34	5	2	8	7	2	1	4	9
Pacific	32	6	3	6	4	9	3	5	5

[1]Includes workers in the private nonfarm economy except those in private households, and workers in the public sector, except the federal government.
[2]The sum of the individual components may be greater than the total because some employees may have access to more than one type of stock option.
[3]Includes all other bonuses provided to employees and not published separately.
[4]Less than 0.5.
[5]The categories are based on the average wage for each occupation surveyed, which may include workers with earnings both above and below the threshold.
[6]The states that comprise the Census divisions are: New England—Connecticut, Maine, Massachusetts, New Hampshire, Rhode Island, and Vermont; Middle Atlantic—New Jersey, New York, and Pennsylvania; South Atlantic—Delaware, District of Columbia, Florida, Georgia, Maryland, North Carolina, South Carolina, Virginia, and West Virginia; East South Central—Alabama, Kentucky, Mississippi, and Tennessee; West South Central—Arkansas, Louisiana, Oklahoma, and Texas; East North Central—Illinois, Indiana, Michigan, Ohio, and Wisconsin; West North Central—Iowa, Kansas, Minnesota, Missouri, Nebraska, North Dakota, and South Dakota; Mountain—Arizona, Colorado, Idaho, Montana, Nevada, New Mexico, Utah, and Wyoming; and Pacific—Alaska, California, Hawaii, Oregon, and Washington.

Table 6-19 Unmarried Domestic Partner Benefits: Access[1] for Civilian Workers,[2] March 2019

(Percent.)

Characteristic	Defined benefit retirement survivor benefits		Healthcare benefits	
	Same sex	Opposite sex	Same sex	Opposite sex
ALL WORKERS	17	16	42	39
Worker Characteristics				
Management, professional, and related	27	26	57	52
Management, business, and financial	23	23	65	60
Professional and related	28	28	54	49
Teachers	48	47	46	41
Primary, secondary, and special education school teachers	55	54	47	44
Registered nurses	22	23	52	50
Service	10	10	26	25
Protective service	33	33	42	38
Sales and office	14	13	44	41
Sales and related	6	6	35	33
Office and administrative support	18	18	49	45
Natural resources, construction, and maintenance	12	10	34	31
Construction, extraction, farming, fishing, and forestry	9	9	29	28
Installation, maintenance, and repair	14	12	40	35
Production, transportation, and material moving	13	12	38	34
Production	9	7	35	31
Transportation and material moving	17	17	40	37
Full-time workers	20	19	50	46
Part-time workers	7	7	17	17
Union workers	48	44	64	56
Nonunion workers	12	12	39	36
Average Wage Within the Following Percentiles[3]				
Lowest 25 percent	5	5	21	20
Lowest 10 percent	2	2	13	12
Second 25 percent	13	12	40	38
Third 25 percent	20	19	50	46
Highest 25 percent	32	31	64	57
Highest 10 percent	31	31	72	63
Establishment Characteristics				
Goods-producing industries	10	9	39	37
Service-providing industries	18	17	43	40
Education and health services	27	26	45	42
Educational services	50	49	49	44
Elementary and secondary schools	57	55	46	42
Junior colleges, colleges, and universities	42	42	58	50
Health care and social assistance	13	12	42	40
Hospitals	27	27	58	54
Public administration	55	55	50	46
Number of Workers				
1 to 99 workers	8	8	30	29
1 to 49 workers	6	6	27	26
50 to 99 workers	13	13	39	38
100 workers or more	25	25	54	49
100 to 499 workers	16	16	48	45
500 workers or more	36	34	62	55
Geographic Areas[4]				
Northeast	22	21	49	45
New England	16	15	46	43
Middle Atlantic	24	23	49	46
South	16	16	34	32
South Atlantic	15	15	35	32
East South Central	16	14	31	28
West South Central	17	17	35	34
Midwest	10	9	32	28
East North Central	10	8	33	27
West North Central	11	11	30	29
West	20	20	60	57
Mountain	17	17	53	48
Pacific	21	22	63	61

[1]The percentage of workers with access to the benefit reflects both the availability of the benefit and the employer's policy on providing the benefit to unmarried domestic partners.
[2]Includes workers in the private nonfarm economy except those in private households, and workers in the public sector, except the federal government.
[3]The categories are based on the average wage for each occupation surveyed, which may include workers with earnings both above and below the threshold.
[4]The states that comprise the Census divisions are: New England—Connecticut, Maine, Massachusetts, New Hampshire, Rhode Island, and Vermont; Middle Atlantic—New Jersey, New York, and Pennsylvania; South Atlantic—Delaware, District of Columbia, Florida, Georgia, Maryland, North Carolina, South Carolina, Virginia, and West Virginia; East South Central—Alabama, Kentucky, Mississippi, and Tennessee; West South Central—Arkansas, Louisiana, Oklahoma, and Texas; East North Central—Illinois, Indiana, Michigan, Ohio, and Wisconsin; West North Central—Iowa, Kansas, Minnesota, Missouri, Nebraska, North Dakota, and South Dakota; Mountain—Arizona, Colorado, Idaho, Montana, Nevada, New Mexico, Utah, and Wyoming; and Pacific—Alaska, California, Hawaii, Oregon, and Washington.

CHAPTER 7: RECENT TRENDS IN THE LABOR MARKET

HIGHLIGHTS

This chapter contains information on local area unemployment statistics, movement of work, job openings, hires, and separations.

Figure 7-1. Metropolitan Statistical Areas with the Highest and Lowest Unemployment Rates, November 2019

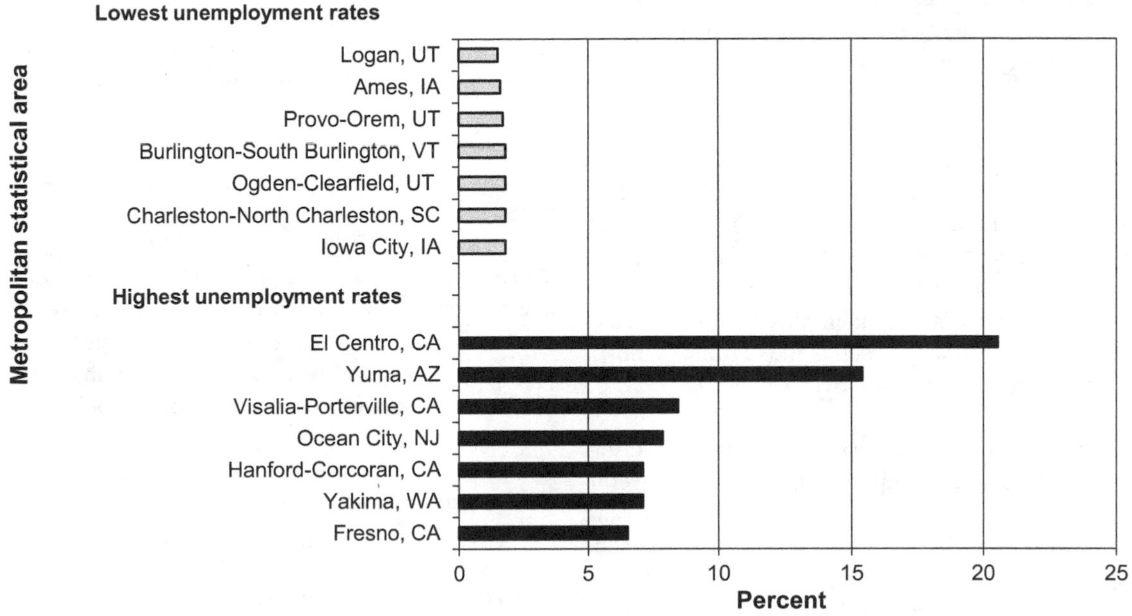

El Centro, CA again had the highest unemployment rate at 20.6 percent among all metropolitan areas in November 2019 followed by Yuma, AZ at 15.4 percent and Visalia-Porterville, CA at 8.5 percent. Logan, UT-ID had the lowest unemployment rate at 1.5 percent. From November 2018 to November 2019, unemployment rates declined in 223 of the 389 metropolitan areas. Among metropolitan areas with a 2010 Census population of one million or more, New Orleans-Metairie, LA had the highest unemployment rate of 4.4 percent while Salt Lake City, UT, had the lowest at 1.9 percent. (See Table 7-3.)

OTHER HIGHLIGHTS

- In November 2019, 51 metropolitan areas had over-the-year increases in nonfarm payroll employment and 338 were essentially unchanged. The largest over-the-year employment increases occurred in Dallas-Fort Worth-Arlington, TX (+120,700), New York-Newark-Jersey City, NY-NJ-PA (+99,400), and Los Angeles-Long Beach-Anaheim, CA (+96,000). (See Table 7-1.)

- The number of job openings decreased from nearly 7.6 million in October 2018 to nearly 7.4 million in October 2019. While the number of job openings decreased in most industries during this time period, they increased in government and construction. (See Table 7-4.)

- In October 2019, there were nearly 1.8 million layoffs and discharges. Construction had the highest rate of layoffs and discharges at 3.4 percent followed by arts, entertainment at 3.2 percent, and professional and business services at 1.9 percent. (See Table 7-8.)

NOTES AND DEFINITIONS

LOCAL AREA UNEMPLOYMENT STATISTICS

Collection and Coverage

The LAUS program provides monthly and annual average estimates for labor force, employment, unemployment, and the unemployment rate for over 7,500 areas. The areas include census regions and divisions, states, metropolitan areas, metropolitan divisions, micropolitan areas, combined areas, small labor market areas, counties and county equivalents, cities with a population of 25,000 and over, and all cities and towns in New England regardless of population.

The labor force and unemployment data are based on the same concepts and definitions as those used for the official national estimates obtained from the Current Population Survey (CPS), a sample survey of households that is conducted for the Bureau of Labor Statistics (BLS) by the U.S. Census Bureau. More information on the CPS can be found in Chapter 1. The LAUS program measures employment and unemployment on a place-of-residence basis. The universe for each is the civilian noninstitutional population 16 years of age and over.

The estimates presented in this chapter are based on sample surveys, administrative data, and modeling and, thus, are subject to sampling and other types of errors. *Sampling error* is a measure of sampling variability—that is, variation that occurs by chance because a sample rather than the entire population is surveyed. Survey data also are subject to *nonsampling errors*, such as those which can be introduced into the data collection and processing operations. Estimates not directly derived from sample surveys are subject to additional errors resulting from the specific estimation processes used.

Concepts and Definitions

Employed persons are those who did any work at all for pay or profit in the reference week (the week including the 12th of the month) or worked 15 hours or more without pay in a family business or farm, plus those not working who had a job from which they were temporarily absent, whether or not paid, for such reasons as labor management dispute, illness, or vacation.

The e*mployment-population ratio* is the proportion of the civilian noninstitutional population 16 years of age and over that is employed.

The *labor force* is the sum of employed and unemployed persons.

Unemployed persons are those who were not employed during the reference week (based on the definition above), had actively looked for a job sometime in the 4-week period ending with the reference week, and were currently available for work; persons on layoff expecting recall need not be looking for work to be counted as unemployed.

The *unemployment rate* is the number of unemployed expressed as a percent of the labor force.

Sources of Additional Information

For more extensive information on Local Area Unemployment Statistics, please see https://www.bls.gov/lau/ and BLS news release USDL 20-0001 "Metropolitan Area Employment and Unemployment—November 2019".

Table 7-1. Employees on Nonfarm Payrolls by State and Selected Metropolitan Areas, October 2018–November 2019

(Number in thousands, percent.)

State and area	October		November		Change from November 2018 to November 2019	
	2018	2019	2018	2019	Number	Percent
Alabama	2 059.9	2 105.7	2 064.4	2 114.8	50.4	2.4
Anniston-Oxford-Jacksonville	46.8	47.4	47.2	47.5	0.3	0.6
Auburn-Opelika	66.9	68.8	67.3	69.3	2.0	3.0
Birmingham-Hoover	541.9	551.3	544.1	553.6	9.5	1.7
Daphne-Fairhope-Foley	76.5	79.4	76.5	79.4	2.9	3.8
Decatur	56.5	57.5	56.8	58.0	1.2	2.1
Dothan	58.9	59.3	58.8	59.6	0.8	1.4
Florence-Muscle Shoals	57.6	58.2	57.9	58.3	0.4	0.7
Gadsden	38.4	38.9	38.2	39.1	0.9	2.4
Huntsville	240.5	247.2	242.3	248.1	5.8	2.4
Mobile	186.3	189.1	186.7	189.7	3.0	1.6
Montgomery	176.6	179.9	177.2	180.1	2.9	1.6
Tuscaloosa	112.0	114.7	111.9	114.7	2.8	2.5
Alaska	323.6	323.5	313.8	314.9	1.1	0.4
Anchorage	175.8	175.4	173.4	174.6	1.2	0.7
Fairbanks	37.9	37.6	36.7	36.8	0.1	0.3
Arizona	2 903.6	2 974.0	2 936.5	3 008.2	71.7	2.4
Flagstaff	70.0	70.4	69.0	70.0	1.0	1.4
Lake Havasu-City-Kingman	52.0	53.1	52.2	53.8	1.6	3.1
Phoenix-Mesa-Scottsdale	2 145.1	2 203.0	2 169.3	2 225.8	56.5	2.6
Prescott	66.4	67.3	67.0	67.8	0.8	1.2
Sierra Vista-Douglas	33.4	34.4	34.1	34.6	0.5	1.5
Tucson	387.2	393.8	391.7	398.3	6.6	1.7
Yuma	56.8	56.8	58.3	57.8	-0.5	-0.9
Arkansas	1 273.2	1 291.8	1 276.7	1 292.3	15.6	1.2
Fayetteville-Springdale-Rogers	261.1	271.3	262.5	271.9	9.4	3.6
Fort Smith	113.8	113.5	114.4	114.2	-0.2	-0.2
Hot Springs	38.8	39.3	38.7	39.2	0.5	1.3
Jonesboro	59.1	60.6	59.4	61.0	1.6	2.7
Little Rock-North Little Rock-Conway	364.7	368.3	366.0	369.5	3.5	1.0
Pine Bluff	33.6	33.1	33.6	33.0	-0.6	-1.8
California	17 344.3	17 660.6	17 440.7	17 766.9	326.2	1.9
Bakersfield	270.3	275.8	272.6	278.4	5.8	2.1
Chico	84.8	86.0	84.5	86.0	1.5	1.8
El Centro	52.1	53.1	53.3	53.8	0.5	0.9
Fresno	358.3	367.7	361.7	369.3	7.6	2.1
Hanford-Corcoran	41.3	41.7	41.1	41.8	0.7	1.7
Los Angeles-Long Beach-Anaheim	6 217.4	6 302.2	6 247.2	6 343.2	9.6	1.5
Madera	39.2	40.1	39.2	40.1	0.9	2.3
Merced	70.1	72.9	68.8	72.1	3.3	4.8
Modesto	179.4	182.5	179.2	182.7	3.5	2.0
Napa	75.9	76.7	74.9	75.9	1.0	1.3
Oxnard-Thousand Oaks-Ventura	310.3	313.2	312.5	315.2	2.7	0.9
Redding	67.7	68.8	67.4	68.8	1.4	2.1
Riverside-San Bernardino-Ontario	1 518.8	1 550.6	1 538.9	1 571.9	33.0	2.1
Sacramento—Roseville—Arden-Arcade	1 009.4	1 024.8	1 017.0	1 033.5	16.5	1.6
Salinas	145.7	150.1	146.2	150.9	4.7	3.2
San Diego-Carlsbad	1 495.4	1 528.0	1 503.8	1 538.1	34.3	2.3
San Francisco-Oakland-Hayward	2 461.0	2 528.0	2 479.2	2 538.7	59.5	2.4
San Jose-Sunnyvale-Santa Clara	1 132.9	1 166.1	1 141.9	1 174.4	32.5	2.8
San Luis Obispo-Paso Robles-Arroyo	119.5	121.5	120.2	122.3	2.1	1.7
Grande Santa Cruz-Watsonville	104.4	105.9	103.9	105.6	1.7	1.6
Santa Maria-Santa Barbara	186.0	190.0	187.4	191.0	3.6	1.9
Santa Rosa	211.2	213.9	209.7	213.4	3.7	1.8
Stockton-Lodi	245.4	244.6	245.6	246.1	0.5	0.2
Vallejo-Fairfield	142.2	142.5	142.6	143.0	0.4	0.3
Visalia-Porterville	126.9	130.2	128.9	130.6	1.7	1.3
Yuba City	45.1	45.9	45.4	47.2	1.8	4.0
Colorado	2 744.8	2 798.6	2 750.4	2 808.5	58.1	2.1
Boulder	197.4	202.4	198.5	202.9	4.4	2.2
Colorado Springs	297.1	305.4	297.2	307.2	10.0	3.4
Denver-Aurora-Lakewood	1 513.5	1 544.1	1 510.1	1 546.0	35.9	2.4
Fort Collins	172.3	178.1	173.4	178.6	5.2	3.0
Grand Junction	65.3	66.7	65.7	66.4	0.7	1.1
Greeley	112.0	114.6	110.4	114.2	3.8	3.4
Pueblo	62.9	63.2	62.9	63.7	0.8	1.3

Table 7-1. Employees on Nonfarm Payrolls by State and Selected Metropolitan Areas, October 2018–November 2019—*Continued*

(Number in thousands, percent.)

State and area	October		November		Change from November 2018 to November 2019	
	2018	2019	2018	2019	Number	Percent
Connecticut	1 704.3	1 709.8	1 714.2	1 717.7	3.5	0.2
Bridgeport-Stamford-Norwalk	408.9	412.5	413.0	413.4	0.4	0.1
Danbury	77.9	78.1	78.6	78.7	0.1	0.1
Hartford-West Hartford-East Hartford	588.4	586.6	591.8	589.6	-2.2	-0.4
New Haven	290.6	292.7	290.7	292.5	1.8	0.6
Norwich-New London-Westerly	129.9	130.1	130.3	130.6	0.3	0.2
Waterbury	69.3	69.9	69.9	70.3	0.4	0.6
Delaware	464.1	471.4	466.6	473.7	7.1	1.5
Dover	70.0	71.3	70.3	71.5	1.2	1.7
Salisbury	161.7	161.8	159.9	159.9	0.0	0.0
District of Columbia	797.6	805.1	795.4	807.9	12.5	1.6
Washington-Arlington-Alexandria	3 313.2	3 363.7	3 323.8	3 384.9	61.1	1.8
Florida	8 855.3	9 089.2	8 954.8	9 174.8	220.0	2.5
Cape Coral-Fort Myers	272.1	283.2	278.2	287.4	9.2	3.3
Crestview-Fort Walton Beach-Destin	115.2	119.0	115.9	118.9	3.0	2.6
Deltona-Daytona Beach-Ormond Beach	205.4	207.3	206.5	209.7	3.2	1.5
Gainesville	148.1	149.0	148.6	150.0	1.4	0.9
Homosassa Springs	33.8	34.3	34.0	34.4	0.4	1.2
Jacksonville	710.2	735.0	713.7	738.1	24.4	3.4
Lakeland-Winter Haven	232.6	234.6	234.0	237.9	3.9	1.7
Miami-Fort Lauderdale-West Palm Beach	2 705.6	2 755.3	2 735.0	2 775.1	40.1	1.5
Naples-Immokalee-Marco Island	150.7	155.3	153.8	159.7	5.9	3.8
North Port-Sarasota-Bradenton	307.3	312.8	310.6	318.6	8.0	2.6
Ocala	105.5	108.2	106.2	108.9	2.7	2.5
Orlando-Kissimmee-Sanford	1 311.9	1 354.9	1 328.2	1 364.9	36.7	2.8
Palm Bay-Melbourne-Titusville	225.6	233.0	227.4	235.1	7.7	3.4
Panama City	84.6	83.8	83.0	83.4	0.4	0.5
Pensacola-Ferry Pass-Brent	184.0	185.1	185.1	186.5	1.4	0.8
Port St Lucie	154.1	157.4	156.1	159.0	2.9	1.9
Punta Gorda	49.0	50.4	49.6	51.6	2.0	4.0
Sebastian-Vero Beach	53.5	55.4	54.9	56.9	2.0	3.6
Sebring	25.6	26.0	26.1	26.6	0.5	1.9
Tallahassee	187.4	193.0	189.4	194.4	5.0	2.6
Tampa-St Petersburg-Clearwater	1 363.8	1 394.3	1 373.9	1 404.7	30.8	2.2
The Villages	29.9	30.8	30.2	31.3	1.1	3.6
Georgia	4 588.2	4 659.7	4 611.1	4 680.8	69.7	1.5
Albany	63.3	63.4	63.8	63.7	-0.1	-0.2
Athens-Clarke County	100.8	101.6	101.5	101.9	0.4	0.4
Atlanta-Sandy Springs-Roswell	2 815.7	2 873.5	2 826.7	2 887.9	61.2	2.2
Augusta-Richmond County	241.9	244.6	242.7	246.6	3.9	1.6
Brunswick	44.8	45.7	45.1	45.9	0.8	1.8
Columbus	123.4	123.1	124.3	123.8	-0.5	-0.4
Dalton	68.4	69.2	68.5	69.0	0.5	0.7
Gainesville	94.8	98.0	95.2	98.6	3.4	3.6
Hinesville	20.8	21.1	20.8	21.1	0.3	1.4
Macon	103.5	104.4	104.6	105.4	0.8	0.8
Rome	41.8	42.9	41.9	43.1	1.2	2.9
Savannah	184.6	186.4	185.2	188.3	3.1	1.7
Valdosta	56.9	57.8	57.3	58.1	0.8	1.4
Warner Robins	76.3	77.4	76.6	77.7	1.1	1.4
Hawaii	658.7	664.5	664.8	669.1	4.3	0.6
Kahului-Wailuku-Lahaina	76.7	78.0	77.3	78.4	1.1	1.4
Urban Honolulu	481.2	485.6	485.0	489.7	4.7	1.0
Idaho	748.5	765.1	745.0	764.7	19.7	2.6
Boise City	336.7	345.1	337.2	346.7	9.5	2.8
Coeur d'Alene	66.2	67.8	65.5	66.5	1.0	1.5
Idaho Falls	69.0	71.6	69.2	72.3	3.1	4.5
Lewiston	28.7	29.4	28.8	29.3	0.5	1.7
Pocatello	37.2	38.3	37.2	38.4	1.2	3.2
Twin Falls	47.2	48.1	46.9	47.7	0.8	1.7
Illinois	6 197.8	6 262.2	6 205.9	6 243.4	37.5	0.6
Bloomington	93.6	93.9	93.5	93.5	0.0	0.0
Carbondale-Marion	59.6	61.1	59.8	61.3	1.5	2.5
Champaign-Urbana	112.9	116.9	112.6	116.4	3.8	3.4
Chicago-Naperville-Elgin	4 806.1	4 860.4	4 820.0	4 848.6	28.6	0.6

Table 7-1. Employees on Nonfarm Payrolls by State and Selected Metropolitan Areas, October 2018–November 2019—*Continued*

(Number in thousands, percent.)

State and area	October		November		Change from November 2018 to November 2019	
	2018	2019	2018	2019	Number	Percent
Illinois— *Continued*						
Danville	27.8	27.8	27.8	27.7	-0.1	-0.4
Davenport-Moline-Rock Island	188.4	187.9	189.2	186.9	-2.3	-1.2
Decatur	52.3	53.0	52.3	53.1	0.8	1.5
Kankakee	46.8	47.6	47.2	47.3	0.1	0.2
Peoria	177.8	176.8	178.2	175.1	-3.1	-1.7
Rockford	154.4	155.4	155.0	154.6	-0.4	-0.3
Springfield	115.2	116.6	115.5	116.5	1.0	0.9
Indiana	3 177.3	3 192.6	3 188.6	3 196.8	8.2	0.3
Bloomington	79.9	80.1	80.6	80.5	-0.1	-0.1
Columbus	53.9	54.9	54.4	55.0	0.6	1.1
Elkhart-Goshen	143.0	143.6	142.9	144.0	1.1	0.8
Evansville	165.1	165.5	166.1	165.8	-0.3	-0.2
Fort Wayne	228.4	228.8	228.4	231.2	2.8	1.2
Indianapolis-Carmel-Anderson	1 081.6	1 089.4	1 084.3	1 090.9	6.6	0.6
Kokomo	41.1	41.9	41.7	42.0	0.3	0.7
Lafayette-West Lafayette	107.7	105.4	107.5	105.2	-2.3	-2.1
Michigan City-La Porte	41.4	41.5	41.8	41.6	-0.2	-0.5
Muncie	51.8	52.1	51.9	52.6	0.7	1.3
South Bend-Mishawaka	145.7	146.2	146.1	146.0	-0.1	-0.1
Terre Haute	71.4	71.5	71.7	71.8	0.1	0.1
Iowa	1 603.5	1 613.2	1 606.7	1 612.6	5.9	0.4
Ames	56.0	57.3	56.1	57.3	1.2	2.1
Cedar Rapids	145.2	146.2	145.8	147.5	1.7	1.2
Des Moines-West Des Moines	374.3	384.6	375.7	383.8	8.1	2.2
Dubuque	61.6	61.9	61.8	62.3	0.5	0.8
Iowa City	102.1	101.2	102.3	101.3	-1.0	-1.0
Sioux City	90.7	90.5	90.9	91.2	0.3	0.3
Waterloo-Cedar Falls	93.0	92.7	93.3	92.4	-0.9	-1.0
Kansas	1 434.1	1 453.7	1 440.3	1 457.8	17.5	1.2
Lawrence	55.0	55.3	55.1	55.4	0.3	0.5
Manhattan	44.6	44.8	44.8	44.7	-0.1	-0.2
Topeka	113.2	116.4	113.2	115.8	2.6	2.3
Wichita	301.8	304.6	303.6	306.1	2.5	0.8
Kentucky	1 940.5	1 973.8	1 959.1	1 983.8	24.7	1.3
Bowling Green	77.0	77.9	77.8	78.9	1.1	1.4
Elizabethtown-Fort Knox	57.0	57.4	57.5	57.6	0.1	0.2
Lexington-Fayette	278.6	285.5	281.4	285.8	4.4	1.6
Louisville/Jefferson County	668.5	681.2	676.0	684.9	8.9	1.3
Owensboro	54.1	54.3	54.1	54.2	0.1	0.2
Louisiana	1 998.2	2 000.5	2 001.7	2 011.0	9.3	0.5
Alexandria	61.5	61.3	61.4	61.5	0.1	0.2
Baton Rouge	412.6	417.2	415.1	419.9	4.8	1.2
Hammond	45.9	46.9	45.9	47.2	1.3	2.8
Houma-Thibodaux	86.3	84.7	86.1	84.5	-1.6	-1.9
Lafayette	204.5	205.9	204.9	205.5	0.6	0.3
Lake Charles	118.9	119.1	118.9	118.2	-0.7	-0.6
Monroe	78.8	78.0	79.2	78.9	-0.3	-0.4
New Orleans-Metairie	584.4	592.8	585.6	599.9	14.3	2.4
Shreveport-Bossier City	180.8	179.4	181.1	181.0	-0.1	-0.1
Maine	634.7	640.7	628.7	633.1	4.4	0.7
Bangor	68.7	69.1	68.4	69.0	0.6	0.9
Lewiston-Auburn	51.8	51.8	51.3	51.6	0.3	0.6
Portland-South Portland	210.7	212.6	210.6	211.2	0.6	0.3
Maryland	2 758.7	2 786.8	2 771.2	2 802.6	31.4	1.1
Baltimore-Columbia-Towson	1 424.6	1 447.7	1 433.3	1 456.9	23.6	1.6
California-Lexington Park	46.0	46.5	46.1	46.6	0.5	1.1
Cumberland	39.7	39.7	39.9	39.7	-0.2	-0.5
Hagerstown-Martinsburg	106.5	108.7	108.5	111.3	2.8	2.6
Massachusetts	3 679.6	3 730.4	3 678.0	3 727.3	49.3	1.3
Barnstable Town	106.8	108.2	103.8	104.1	0.3	0.3
Boston-Cambridge-Nashua	2 793.9	2 834.9	2 796.5	2 835.5	39.0	1.4
Leominster-Gardner	55.1	55.7	55.6	56.4	0.8	1.4
New Bedford	67.4	67.8	67.9	68.2	0.3	0.4
Pittsfield	41.0	41.4	41.0	41.3	0.3	0.7
Springfield	343.6	351.6	344.5	352.7	8.2	2.4
Worcester	288.8	288.9	290.5	289.6	-0.9	-0.3

Table 7-1. Employees on Nonfarm Payrolls by State and Selected Metropolitan Areas, October 2018–November 2019—*Continued*

(Number in thousands, percent.)

State and area	October		November		Change from November 2018 to November 2019	
	2018	2019	2018	2019	Number	Percent
Michigan	4 470.2	4 465.4	4 468.3	4 485.7	17.4	0.4
Ann Arbor	227.2	230.2	228.0	231.1	3.1	1.4
Battle Creek	58.8	58.4	59.1	58.7	-0.4	-0.7
Bay City	35.8	34.9	35.8	35.1	-0.7	-2.0
Detroit-Warren-Dearborn	2 050.9	2 041.8	2 052.7	2 046.1	-6.6	-0.3
Flint	142.8	137.9	143.1	145.1	2.0	1.4
Grand Rapids-Wyoming	568.0	569.1	570.0	568.7	-1.3	-0.2
Jackson	59.2	58.8	59.2	59.2	0.0	0.0
Kalamazoo-Portage	152.1	152.9	152.0	152.6	0.6	0.4
Lansing-East Lansing	241.5	240.4	241.6	244.9	3.3	1.4
Midland	38.1	37.8	38.0	38.0	0.0	0.0
Monroe	42.8	42.7	42.6	42.8	0.2	0.5
Muskegon	65.5	66.8	65.9	67.0	1.1	1.7
Niles-Benton Harbor	62.6	63.7	62.5	63.6	1.1	1.8
Saginaw	88.6	86.8	89.5	88.9	-0.6	-0.7
Minnesota	2 987.0	2 996.1	2 975.9	2 981.8	5.9	0.2
Duluth	138.6	139.5	138.6	138.4	-0.2	-0.1
Mankato-North Mankato	60.3	60.9	59.6	61.1	1.5	2.5
Minneapolis-St Paul-Bloomington	2 031.1	2 029.3	2 027.4	2 021.3	-6.1	-0.3
Rochester	123.7	124.9	122.7	124.0	1.3	1.1
St. Cloud	112.0	113.1	111.5	112.4	0.9	0.8
Mississippi	1 165.8	1 177.8	1 173.6	1 181.3	7.7	0.7
Gulfport-Biloxi-Pascagoula	155.1	158.9	155.7	159.9	4.2	2.7
Hattiesburg	66.6	68.4	67.4	69.3	1.9	2.8
Jackson	282.1	285.3	283.0	285.5	2.5	0.9
Missouri	2 912.9	2 944.1	2 911.5	2 948.3	36.8	1.3
Cape Girardeau	45.5	46.0	45.8	46.1	0.3	0.7
Columbia	102.0	102.3	102.1	102.3	0.2	0.2
Jefferson City	77.2	77.6	76.9	77.9	1.0	1.3
Joplin	81.8	82.2	82.2	82.6	0.4	0.5
Kansas City	1 109.4	1 124.6	1 110.8	1 126.9	16.1	1.4
St. Joseph	63.4	63.2	63.4	63.1	-0.3	-0.5
St. Louis	1 396.8	1 421.4	1 399.6	1 421.5	21.9	1.6
Springfield	217.9	219.7	220.0	221.1	1.1	0.5
Montana	481.9	488.0	478.7	485.7	7.0	1.5
Billings	85.3	85.9	84.9	85.4	0.5	0.6
Great Falls	36.1	36.3	36.1	36.3	0.2	0.6
Missoula	63.5	65.0	62.9	64.2	1.3	2.1
Nebraska	1 028.3	1 043.7	1 031.0	1 045.6	14.6	1.4
Grand Island	42.2	42.6	42.2	42.3	0.1	0.2
Lincoln	192.9	194.0	193.2	196.3	3.1	1.6
Omaha-Council Bluffs	505.7	522.8	508.4	523.6	15.2	3.0
Nevada	1 413.5	1 445.8	1 416.8	1 454.7	37.9	2.7
Carson City	30.5	31.6	30.5	31.5	1.0	3.3
Las Vegas-Henderson-Paradise	1 026.1	1 043.1	1 023.0	1 052.2	29.2	2.9
Reno	251.2	262.2	254.5	264.5	10.0	3.9
New Hampshire	687.5	694.4	686.7	690.6	3.9	0.6
Dover-Durham	54.8	55.2	55.2	54.9	-0.3	-0.5
Manchester	116.0	116.8	116.0	117.4	1.4	1.2
Portsmouth	94.8	95.6	94.0	95.1	1.1	1.2
New Jersey	4 192.3	4 224.0	4 212.6	4 245.6	33.0	0.8
Atlantic City-Hammonton	134.5	134.6	133.6	133.4	-0.2	-0.1
Ocean City	42.0	44.0	38.8	41.5	2.7	7.0
Trenton	275.6	279.9	278.1	281.7	3.6	1.3
Vineland-Bridgeton	59.5	60.7	59.7	61.2	1.5	2.5
New Mexico	850.6	865.7	851.6	867.8	16.2	1.9
Albuquerque	395.6	398.5	397.0	400.1	3.1	0.8
Farmington	48.1	48.4	48.3	48.3	0.0	0.0
Las Cruces	74.7	75.7	75.2	75.7	0.5	0.7
Santa Fe	64.1	63.8	63.9	64.0	0.1	0.2
New York	9 780.5	9 889.4	9 810.1	9 926.8	116.7	1.2
Albany-Schenectady-Troy	480.3	479.1	481.2	483.4	2.2	0.5
Binghamton	105.8	105.6	105.6	105.1	-0.5	-0.5
Buffalo-Cheektowaga-Niagara Falls	572.7	576.3	571.6	575.7	4.1	0.7
Elmira	37.0	37.2	37.5	37.3	-0.2	-0.5
Glens Falls	55.7	55.6	54.9	54.7	-0.2	-0.4

Table 7-1. Employees on Nonfarm Payrolls by State and Selected Metropolitan Areas, October 2018–November 2019—*Continued*

(Number in thousands, percent.)

State and area	October		November		Change from November 2018 to November 2019	
	2018	2019	2018	2019	Number	Percent
New York—*Continued*						
Ithaca	66.9	68.7	66.8	68.4	1.6	2.4
Kingston	64.8	65.5	64.0	64.8	0.8	1.3
New York-Newark-Jersey City	9 923.1	10 017.1	9 980.7	10 080.1	99.4	1.0
Rochester	547.1	552.6	545.6	553.5	7.9	1.4
Syracuse	325.8	330.7	325.9	330.5	4.6	1.4
Utica-Rome	129.5	129.2	129.7	129.4	-0.3	-0.2
Watertown-Fort Drum	42.3	42.7	42.1	42.3	0.2	0.5
North Carolina	4 527.9	4 617.5	4 540.4	4 629.5	89.1	2.0
Asheville	198.1	206.0	198.1	205.1	7.0	3.5
Burlington	63.4	64.3	63.9	64.4	0.5	0.8
Charlotte-Concord-Gastonia	1 221.2	1 249.6	1 224.0	1 252.8	28.8	2.4
Durham-Chapel Hill	315.8	320.5	316.9	320.8	3.9	1.2
Fayetteville	131.2	132.3	132.5	133.4	0.9	0.7
Goldsboro	42.0	41.7	41.9	42.1	0.2	0.5
Greensboro-High Point	363.8	366.4	363.4	368.1	4.7	1.3
Greenville	80.7	81.9	81.0	82.7	1.7	2.1
Hickory-Lenoir-Morganton	156.3	155.8	157.6	157.4	-0.2	-0.1
Jacksonville	49.0	49.6	49.3	49.9	0.6	1.2
New Bern	44.6	45.1	45.0	45.3	0.3	0.7
Raleigh	635.5	657.2	636.5	660.7	24.2	3.8
Rocky Mount	57.0	56.6	57.6	57.2	-0.4	-0.7
Wilmington	128.9	134.7	130.2	135.4	5.2	4.0
Winston-Salem	268.4	276.1	269.8	275.0	5.2	1.9
North Dakota	441.8	442.6	438.1	441.4	3.3	0.8
Bismarck	73.3	73.5	72.7	73.5	0.8	1.1
Fargo	144.8	145.6	143.7	146.0	2.3	1.6
Grand Forks	56.6	56.8	56.5	56.7	0.2	0.4
Ohio	5 614.8	5 632.4	5 617.1	5 639.4	22.3	0.4
Akron	344.8	341.7	344.9	342.4	-2.5	-0.7
Canton-Massillon	177.0	177.9	177.1	177.8	0.7	0.4
Cincinnati	1 121.9	1 140.7	1 122.3	1 142.2	19.9	1.8
Cleveland-Elyria	1 075.9	1 083.2	1 076.2	1 089.8	13.6	1.3
Columbus	1 113.5	1 124.3	1 114.5	1 132.2	17.7	1.6
Dayton	391.4	396.2	393.5	397.2	3.7	0.9
Lima	53.7	53.6	53.8	53.8	0.0	0.0
Mansfield	53.1	53.0	53.0	53.6	0.6	1.1
Springfield	50.8	50.9	50.6	50.9	0.3	0.6
Toledo	312.4	312.4	313.7	313.4	-0.3	-0.1
Weirton-Steubenville	40.6	39.8	40.5	39.6	-0.9	-2.2
Youngstown-Warren-Boardman	220.1	216.5	220.7	216.1	-4.6	-2.1
Oklahoma	1 705.0	1 708.3	1 711.8	1 707.4	-4.4	-0.3
Enid	25.7	25.4	25.6	25.4	-0.2	-0.8
Lawton	45.2	45.7	45.3	46.2	0.9	2.0
Oklahoma City	659.0	666.6	661.4	666.4	5.0	0.8
Tulsa	457.4	460.2	461.5	460.5	-1.0	-0.2
Oregon	1 931.6	1 965.4	1 931.2	1 968.4	37.2	1.9
Albany	46.1	47.1	46.5	47.5	1.0	2.2
Bend-Redmond	85.7	88.3	85.3	87.8	2.5	2.9
Corvallis	44.6	45.1	44.5	45.1	0.6	1.3
Eugene	162.3	164.5	162.3	165.1	2.8	1.7
Grants Pass	27.5	28.2	27.4	28.3	0.9	3.3
Medford	90.3	93.0	90.2	93.3	3.1	3.4
Portland-Vancouver-Hillsboro	1 209.8	1 231.6	1 213.4	1 233.9	20.5	1.7
Salem	171.4	172.7	171.8	172.1	0.3	0.2
Pennsylvania	6 087.0	6 119.0	6 085.9	6 136.9	51.0	0.8
Allentown-Bethlehem-Easton	380.8	383.2	379.3	385.8	6.5	1.7
Altoona	61.2	62.0	61.6	62.0	0.4	0.6
Bloomsburg-Berwick	43.5	43.9	43.4	43.9	0.5	1.2
Chambersburg-Waynesboro	62.5	63.6	62.9	64.0	1.1	1.7
East Stroudsburg	58.7	59.5	59.0	59.8	0.8	1.4
Erie	130.1	130.1	129.9	130.2	0.3	0.2
Gettysburg	35.6	35.9	35.5	35.7	0.2	0.6
Harrisburg-Carlisle	348.7	348.5	349.2	351.7	2.5	0.7
Johnstown	55.3	55.6	55.1	55.5	0.4	0.7
Lancaster	259.6	259.6	258.0	261.0	3.0	1.2

Table 7-1. Employees on Nonfarm Payrolls by State and Selected Metropolitan Areas, October 2018–November 2019—*Continued*

(Number in thousands, percent.)

State and area	October		November		Change from November 2018 to November 2019	
	2018	2019	2018	2019	Number	Percent
Pennsylvania—*Continued*						
Lebanon	53.8	55.1	53.9	55.1	1.2	2.2
Philadelphia-Camden-Wilmington	2 975.4	3 002.6	2 982.3	3 011.3	29.0	1.0
Pittsburgh	1 201.8	1 200.2	1 205.3	1 200.7	-4.6	-0.4
Reading	181.5	183.8	182.3	184.5	2.2	1.2
Scranton—Wilkes-Barre—Hazleton	266.2	266.6	268.7	266.6	-2.1	-0.8
State College	83.6	84.7	84.3	85.2	0.9	1.1
Williamsport	53.7	54.1	53.4	54.1	0.7	1.3
York-Hanover	188.6	188.7	189.0	189.8	0.8	0.4
Rhode Island	503.0	512.3	500.7	511.8	11.1	2.2
Providence-Warwick	600.6	609.6	598.9	611.8	12.9	2.2
South Carolina	2 158.5	2 189.8	2 168.0	2 201.5	33.5	1.5
Charleston-North Charleston	370.2	371.4	372.2	374.2	2.0	0.5
Columbia	404.2	404.6	403.7	407.7	4.0	1.0
Florence	91.7	92.4	92.4	93.1	0.7	0.8
Greenville-Anderson-Mauldin	426.8	432.7	429.1	433.2	4.1	1.0
Hilton Head Island-Bluffton-Beaufort	82.1	85.9	82.1	85.6	3.5	4.3
Myrtle Beach-Conway-North Myrtle Beach	172.3	181.0	170.6	179.3	8.7	5.1
Spartanburg	159.6	163.6	160.1	164.1	4.0	2.5
Sumter	40.7	40.9	40.9	41.1	0.2	0.5
South Dakota	443.3	452.1	443.3	449.7	6.4	1.4
Rapid City	69.4	70.0	68.8	69.0	0.2	0.3
Sioux Falls	159.2	164.2	159.5	163.7	4.2	2.6
Tennessee	3 102.8	3 148.0	3 126.2	3 174.6	48.4	1.5
Chattanooga	265.1	268.3	265.3	269.3	4.0	1.5
Clarksville	93.3	95.3	94.7	95.6	0.9	1.0
Cleveland	47.1	47.6	48.9	48.6	-0.3	-0.6
Jackson	70.0	71.2	70.1	71.4	1.3	1.9
Johnson City	82.3	82.5	82.2	83.1	0.9	1.1
Kingsport-Bristol-Bristol	122.2	124.9	123.8	125.8	2.0	1.6
Knoxville	403.4	412.1	406.4	415.1	8.7	2.1
Memphis	655.7	660.0	665.0	667.1	2.1	0.3
Morristown	46.8	47.3	46.7	47.5	0.8	1.7
Nashville-Davidson—Murfreesboro—Franklin	1 028.4	1 045.2	1 038.7	1 055.5	16.8	1.6
Texas	12 651.0	12 966.8	12 704.1	13 047.1	343.0	2.7
Abilene	70.3	71.0	70.6	71.6	1.0	1.4
Amarillo	120.5	121.3	121.4	122.0	0.6	0.5
Austin-Round Rock	1 079.9	1 108.4	1 083.2	1 112.2	29.0	2.7
Beaumont-Port Arthur	169.0	170.0	168.2	169.3	1.1	0.7
Brownsville-Harlingen	141.4	142.4	142.2	143.0	0.8	0.6
College Station-Bryan	124.2	126.3	124.4	127.1	2.7	2.2
Corpus Christi	193.9	197.1	195.7	197.7	2.0	1.0
Dallas-Fort Worth-Arlington	3 729.9	3 837.2	3 749.7	3 870.4	120.7	3.2
El Paso	320.4	324.5	321.0	327.5	6.5	2.0
Houston-The Woodlands-Sugar Land	3 121.7	3 204.1	3 137.6	3 223.1	85.5	2.7
Killeen-Temple	143.6	147.4	144.9	149.2	4.3	3.0
Laredo	105.4	107.1	106.2	107.8	1.6	1.5
Longview	98.5	97.8	98.8	97.8	-1.0	-1.0
Lubbock	149.7	151.9	150.3	152.6	2.3	1.5
McAllen-Edinburg-Mission	266.3	274.6	268.5	275.4	6.9	2.6
Midland	111.5	111.8	111.7	112.3	0.6	0.5
Odessa	82.7	83.5	82.8	83.2	0.4	0.5
San Angelo	50.2	50.6	50.4	50.7	0.3	0.6
San Antonio-New Braunfels	1 063.2	1 098.4	1 068.5	1 102.2	33.7	3.2
Sherman-Denison	48.3	49.1	48.8	49.3	0.5	1.0
Texarkana	60.4	60.5	60.8	61.2	0.4	0.7
Tyler	107.2	108.3	107.6	108.7	1.1	1.0
Victoria	42.2	41.7	42.6	42.1	-0.5	-1.2
Waco	121.9	123.0	122.5	124.1	1.6	1.3
Wichita Falls	60.0	60.0	60.2	60.4	0.2	0.3
Utah	1 542.0	1 592.8	1 544.2	1 595.8	51.6	3.3
Logan	65.1	66.7	65.5	66.8	1.3	2.0
Ogden-Clearfield	265.0	276.6	265.0	276.0	11.0	4.2
Provo-Orem	269.6	278.0	269.7	279.0	9.3	3.4
St. George	70.3	72.8	70.4	72.9	2.5	3.6
Salt Lake City	742.1	760.2	745.5	762.2	16.7	2.2
Vermont	319.5	319.6	319.3	318.2	-1.1	-0.3
Burlington-South Burlington	127.4	129.5	127.4	128.6	1.2	0.9

Table 7-1. Employees on Nonfarm Payrolls by State and Selected Metropolitan Areas, October 2018–November 2019—*Continued*

(Number in thousands, percent.)

State and area	October		November		Change from November 2018 to November 2019	
	2018	2019	2018	2019	Number	Percent
Virginia	4 018.1	4 045.6	4 035.7	4 077.9	42.2	1.0
Blacksburg-Christiansburg-Radford	78.3	75.5	78.6	79.0	0.4	0.5
Charlottesville	119.1	120.6	119.5	121.0	1.5	1.3
Harrisonburg	69.4	70.6	69.5	70.7	1.2	1.7
Lynchburg	106.0	107.0	106.6	107.1	0.5	0.5
Richmond	681.5	687.9	683.0	695.2	12.2	1.8
Roanoke	162.6	165.1	162.4	166.0	3.6	2.2
Staunton-Waynesboro	51.2	52.1	51.5	52.3	0.8	1.6
Virginia Beach-Norfolk-Newport News	789.8	794.3	791.1	798.3	7.2	0.9
Winchester	65.3	66.9	65.2	67.2	2.0	3.1
Washington	3 449.2	3 526.2	3 446.5	3 532.7	86.2	2.5
Bellingham	97.3	98.5	97.5	98.0	0.5	0.5
Bremerton-Silverdale	94.0	96.4	93.9	96.9	3.0	3.2
Kennewick-Richland	117.5	121.2	117.2	121.0	3.8	3.2
Longview	40.4	40.8	40.4	40.9	0.5	1.2
Mount Vernon-Anacortes	52.2	52.4	52.2	52.5	0.3	0.6
Olympia-Tumwate	121.7	124.5	121.5	124.7	3.2	2.6
Seattle-Tacoma-Bellevue	2 067.2	2 128.3	2 073.7	2 132.9	59.2	2.9
Spokane-Spokane Valley	255.1	260.8	255.4	259.6	4.2	1.6
Walla Walla	29.0	29.4	29.1	29.6	0.5	1.7
Wenatchee	47.1	47.6	46.2	47.3	1.1	2.4
Yakima	88.3	89.1	87.3	88.6	1.3	1.5
West Virginia	740.3	742.8	740.5	740.5	0.0	0.0
Beckley	44.7	44.8	44.0	44.2	0.2	0.5
Charleston	110.6	110.2	110.5	110.1	-0.4	-0.4
Huntington-Ashland	136.0	135.6	136.5	136.2	-0.3	-0.2
Morgantown	72.0	71.2	72.0	71.6	-0.4	-0.6
Parkersburg-Vienna	38.3	38.6	38.4	38.6	0.2	0.5
Wheeling	70.1	69.9	70.3	69.8	-0.5	-0.7
Wisconsin	2 992.5	3 011.6	2 999.7	3 005.9	6.2	0.2
Appleton	125.8	126.4	126.4	126.8	0.4	0.3
Eau Claire	87.8	88.9	88.5	88.6	0.1	0.1
Fond du Lac	49.4	49.4	49.4	49.5	0.1	0.2
Green Bay	183.3	186.2	184.0	186.5	2.5	1.4
Janesville-Beloit	69.8	71.1	70.1	71.9	1.8	2.6
La Crosse-Onalaska	79.7	81.3	80.2	82.0	1.8	2.2
Madison	406.0	412.0	408.4	414.4	6.0	1.5
Milwaukee-Waukesha-West Allis	879.0	890.3	878.9	893.2	14.3	1.6
Oshkosh-Neenah	98.5	99.3	98.6	99.7	1.1	1.1
Racine	79.1	79.4	79.2	78.9	-0.3	-0.4
Sheboygan	63.7	64.8	63.3	64.4	1.1	1.7
Wausau	73.3	74.5	73.5	74.7	1.2	1.6
Wyoming	289.0	288.9	285.0	283.9	-1.1	-0.4
Casper	39.4	39.6	39.1	39.3	0.2	0.5
Cheyenne	47.1	47.6	46.8	47.2	0.4	0.9

Table 7-2. Civilian Labor Force by State and Selected Metropolitan Areas, October 2018–November 2019

(Number in thousands, percent.)

State and area	October		November	
	2018	2019	2018	2019
Alabama	2 212 503	2 269 499	2 205 363	2 259 373
Anniston-Oxford-Jacksonville	45 795	46 702	45 801	46 428
Auburn-Opelika	76 149	78 443	76 282	78 483
Birmingham-Hoover	548 653	562 703	548 078	561 598
Daphne-Fairhope-Foley	93 506	97 082	92 774	96 415
Decatur	71 190	73 390	71 190	73 253
Dothan	63 152	64 021	62 325	63 677
Florence-Muscle Shoals	66 258	67 307	65 949	66 917
Gadsden	43 394	44 402	43 063	44 201
Huntsville	224 628	232 480	224 908	231 907
Mobile	188 386	192 647	187 958	192 046
Montgomery	172 359	176 740	171 846	175 730
Tuscaloosa	117 409	121 337	117 080	120 788
Alaska	354 262	344 026	353 278	342 571
Anchorage	199 196	193 150	201 422	195 479
Fairbanks	46 270	44 631	46 182	44 398
Arizona	3 491 620	3 599 850	3 512 594	3 622 661
Flagstaff	78 808	80 225	77 887	79 453
Lake Havasu-City-Kingman	86 465	89 061	86 525	89 749
Phoenix-Mesa-Scottsdale	2 440 085	2 527 808	2 459 584	2 545 071
Prescott	107 103	109 304	107 496	110 144
Sierra Vista-Douglas	50 156	51 811	50 734	51 968
Tucson	491 259	504 239	495 039	508 946
Yuma	104 775	102 415	103 119	102 582
Arkansas	1 355 060	1 371 482	1 351 062	1 368 523
Fayetteville-Springdale-Rogers	276 369	286 907	275 869	286 326
Fort Smith	118 933	118 795	118 675	118 861
Hot Springs	40 404	40 985	40 099	40 662
Jonesboro	64 667	66 146	64 643	66 130
Little Rock-North Little Rock-Conway	355 560	360 122	353 968	359 984
Pine Bluff	35 546	35 246	35 338	34 907
California	19 542 699	19 588 210	19 562 413	19 616 666
Bakersfield	392 498	393 210	388 958	389 849
Chico	104 924	104 426	103 625	103 395
El Centro	72 081	74 108	72 596	74 280
Fresno	447 143	450 299	449 306	451 121
Hanford-Corcoran	57 747	57 914	57 493	57 885
Los Angeles-Long Beach-Anaheim	6 806 284	6 797 275	6 817 785	6 833 846
Madera	61 415	61 537	60 846	61 012
Merced	116 860	118 254	114 185	116 352
Modesto	243 913	243 933	242 704	242 768
Napa	75 762	75 414	73 517	73 636
Oxnard-Thousand Oaks-Ventura	427 355	423 843	428 472	424 712
Redding	75 087	74 764	74 406	74 080
Riverside-San Bernardino-Ontario	2 071 476	2 078 795	2 086 173	2 092 615
Sacramento—Roseville—Arden-Arcade	1 104 825	1 103 783	1 108 474	1 106 907
Salinas	226 619	228 088	221 037	222 561
San Diego-Carlsbad	1 604 579	1 611 237	1 607 105	1 613 206
San Francisco-Oakland-Hayward	2 608 606	2 633 310	2 617 117	2 630 977
San Jose-Sunnyvale-Santa Clara	1 086 645	1 101 952	1 090 373	1 103 362
San Luis Obispo-Paso Robles-Arroyo	142 915	142 963	142 702	142 509
Grande Santa Cruz-Watsonville	144 629	144 394	142 585	142 339
Santa Maria-Santa Barbara	218 635	219 350	218 589	218 707
Santa Rosa	265 201	264 425	261 752	261 799
Stockton-Lodi	329 029	326 961	326 746	324 747
Vallejo-Fairfield	210 499	208 941	210 504	208 465
Visalia-Porterville	201 854	202 693	203 862	203 535
Yuba City	74 629	74 678	74 294	75 352
Colorado	3 135 286	3 178 231	3 133 401	3 181 397
Boulder	197 284	199 825	196 896	199 892
Colorado Springs	356 469	361 924	356 109	363 747
Denver-Aurora-Lakewood	1 666 651	1 687 201	1 659 436	1 688 087
Fort Collins	206 009	211 608	206 475	211 506
Grand Junction	77 589	78 346	77 634	77 993
Greeley	169 734	173 988	168 221	172 731
Pueblo	76 607	76 350	76 703	76 897

Table 7-2. Civilian Labor Force by State and Selected Metropolitan Areas, October 2018–November 2019—*Continued*

(Number in thousands, percent.)

State and area	October		November	
	2018	2019	2018	2019
Connecticut	1 915 336	1 929 565	1 920 441	1 934 041
Bridgeport-Stamford-Norwalk	466 514	471 753	470 566	473 847
Danbury	106 623	107 736	107 558	108 310
Hartford-West Hartford-East Hartford	630 843	632 683	631 538	634 231
New Haven	330 043	332 945	329 597	332 942
Norwich-New London-Westerly	142 468	143 035	142 507	143 530
Waterbury	112 797	113 439	113 033	113 807
Delaware	481 871	490 529	482 804	493 066
Dover	78 126	80 094	78 215	80 169
Salisbury	189 219	190 816	187 353	189 123
District of Columbia	402 446	408 339	402 811	415 088
Washington-Arlington-Alexandria	3 393 284	3 487 666	3 385 124	3 492 075
Florida	10 305 265	10 566 507	10 293 133	10 479 146
Cape Coral-Fort Myers	343 976	356 370	346 877	356 213
Crestview-Fort Walton Beach-Destin	126 655	130 198	125 952	128 376
Deltona-Daytona Beach-Ormond Beach	302 842	306 739	301 176	305 407
Gainesville	147 079	147 623	145 611	146 363
Homosassa Springs	48 201	48 568	47 863	48 116
Jacksonville	775 655	800 072	769 881	792 056
Lakeland-Winter Haven	304 059	306 181	302 265	305 445
Miami-Fort Lauderdale-West Palm Beach	3 163 808	3 270 402	3 168 158	3 221 968
Naples-Immokalee-Marco Island	176 782	181 170	179 149	183 849
North Port-Sarasota-Bradenton	365 580	370 882	365 866	372 749
Ocala	136 819	139 549	136 236	138 467
Orlando-Kissimmee-Sanford	1 355 177	1 395 626	1 353 797	1 385 303
Palm Bay-Melbourne-Titusville	279 292	287 068	277 669	285 519
Panama City	94 288	93 348	95 413	91 719
Pensacola-Ferry Pass-Brent	228 630	229 930	227 183	228 240
Port St Lucie	219 745	223 359	219 678	222 195
Punta Gorda	71 114	72 667	71 476	73 100
Sebastian-Vero Beach	65 536	67 312	66 266	67 818
Sebring	35 682	35 920	36 158	36 277
Tallahassee	196 582	202 052	196 231	200 427
Tampa-St Petersburg-Clearwater	1 543 442	1 572 438	1 536 852	1 562 597
The Villages	31 324	32 127	31 335	32 097
Georgia	5 112 773	5 132 608	5 111 058	5 124 821
Albany	67 416	66 773	68 204	66 712
Athens-Clarke County	103 341	102 735	103 622	102 378
Atlanta-Sandy Springs-Roswell	3 073 624	3 098 361	3 066 497	3 093 261
Augusta-Richmond County	266 838	268 468	266 171	268 091
Brunswick	53 382	53 603	53 430	53 524
Columbus	124 934	123 569	124 888	123 115
Dalton	61 094	61 253	60 942	60 534
Gainesville	103 346	104 994	103 495	105 044
Hinesville	33 697	33 831	33 634	33 754
Macon	104 212	103 651	104 859	103 931
Rome	44 214	44 712	44 113	44 682
Savannah	188 232	187 966	187 340	188 546
Valdosta	64 938	64 945	65 291	65 045
Warner Robins	86 457	86 015	86 877	85 677
Hawaii	673 215	663 422	678 100	668 035
Kahului-Wailuku-Lahaina	84 790	83 939	85 147	84 260
Urban Honolulu	462 290	456 535	466 316	459 950
Idaho	862 938	888 317	861 411	887 360
Boise City	361 662	373 204	365 395	377 621
Coeur d'Alene	77 092	79 313	77 644	79 169
Idaho Falls	70 883	74 007	71 129	74 627
Lewiston	31 125	31 976	31 433	32 265
Pocatello	41 812	43 336	42 426	43 789
Twin Falls	53 047	54 351	52 998	54 311
Illinois	6 477 162	6 487 355	6 468 774	6 447 310
Bloomington	96 188	96 249	95 626	95 238
Carbondale-Marion	61 427	62 494	61 426	62 365
Champaign-Urbana	122 180	125 578	121 100	124 048
Chicago-Naperville-Elgin	4 877 420	4 873 069	4 873 710	4 852 539

Table 7-2. Civilian Labor Force by State and Selected Metropolitan Areas, October 2018–November 2019—*Continued*

(Number in thousands, percent.)

State and area	October		November	
	2018	2019	2018	2019
Illinois— *Continued*				
Danville	33 416	33 417	33 218	33 036
Davenport-Moline-Rock Island	193 286	196 472	191 934	194 044
Decatur	50 130	50 585	49 898	50 176
Kankakee	56 192	56 785	56 305	56 435
Peoria	181 323	180 216	181 127	177 301
Rockford	167 798	168 985	171 319	168 016
Springfield	111 527	112 484	111 458	111 781
Indiana	3 393 074	3 377 838	3 387 893	3 365 352
Bloomington	80 893	80 214	80 789	80 031
Columbus	45 399	45 602	45 671	45 730
Elkhart-Goshen	116 099	115 956	115 736	115 691
Evansville	165 713	164 507	165 658	164 475
Fort Wayne	219 048	221 972	217 697	218 994
Indianapolis-Carmel-Anderson	1 066 591	1 061 054	1 063 148	1 059 419
Kokomo	37 350	37 713	39 569	37 561
Lafayette-West Lafayette	113 795	110 440	112 984	109 718
Michigan City-La Porte	47 608	47 221	47 787	47 162
Muncie	54 782	54 526	54 518	54 745
South Bend-Mishawaka	162 196	161 321	161 687	161 126
Terre Haute	77 549	76 499	77 361	76 418
Iowa	1 695 446	1 774 385	1 691 018	1 768 820
Ames	59 957	63 552	59 610	63 092
Cedar Rapids	143 332	149 807	142 484	149 974
Des Moines-West Des Moines	355 900	379 149	353 450	375 574
Dubuque	55 766	58 299	55 433	58 194
Iowa City	97 784	100 820	97 193	100 275
Sioux City	93 462	96 315	93 244	96 877
Waterloo-Cedar Falls	90 152	93 647	89 642	92 709
Kansas	1 488 086	1 502 927	1 490 418	1 504 743
Lawrence	66 491	67 012	66 643	67 306
Manhattan	49 305	49 434	49 471	49 454
Topeka	120 026	122 632	119 877	122 399
Wichita	309 637	311 349	310 890	313 687
Kentucky	2 050 539	2 074 332	2 054 178	2 088 173
Bowling Green	83 503	85 337	83 633	85 354
Elizabethtown-Fort Knox	67 085	67 535	67 239	67 826
Lexington-Fayette	271 383	277 046	272 920	278 339
Louisville/Jefferson County	664 268	672 615	666 983	676 072
Owensboro	55 735	55 593	55 542	55 831
Louisiana	2 105 178	2 101 385	2 098 944	2 109 952
Alexandria	62 872	62 306	62 595	62 275
Baton Rouge	419 725	421 133	419 997	423 482
Hammond	54 306	54 937	54 174	55 245
Houma-Thibodaux	87 597	85 399	86 786	84 925
Lafayette	212 434	212 318	211 594	211 512
Lake Charles	114 405	113 891	113 932	113 302
Monroe	79 544	78 325	79 585	79 153
New Orleans-Metairie	598 756	601 544	596 750	607 415
Shreveport-Bossier City	186 718	183 900	186 258	185 583
Maine	699 745	692 566	693 756	687 881
Bangor	72 269	71 764	71 476	71 587
Lewiston-Auburn	56 399	55 858	55 925	55 682
Portland-South Portland	209 715	208 723	208 589	207 544
Maryland	3 198 764	3 297 387	3 191 352	3 292 061
Baltimore-Columbia-Towson	1 496 052	1 547 824	1 495 407	1 545 363
California-Lexington Park	55 244	56 626	54 961	56 420
Cumberland	44 515	45 768	44 339	45 370
Hagerstown-Martinsburg	131 799	136 278	132 392	137 341
Massachusetts	3 817 350	3 840 687	3 823 218	3 837 116
Barnstable Town	127 539	127 842	124 516	123 533
Boston-Cambridge-Nashua	2 821 289	2 844 515	2 827 796	2 844 941
Leominster-Gardner	82 000	82 429	82 856	82 991
New Bedford	86 114	86 299	86 990	86 898
Pittsfield	43 365	43 242	43 319	43 164
Springfield	384 172	389 514	385 892	390 230
Worcester	362 453	361 317	364 388	361 837

Table 7-2. Civilian Labor Force by State and Selected Metropolitan Areas, October 2018–November 2019—*Continued*

(Number in thousands, percent.)

State and area	October		November	
	2018	2019	2018	2019
Michigan	4 909 341	4 938 576	4 893 580	4 934 862
Ann Arbor	195 442	195 853	196 725	199 308
Battle Creek	62 506	61 982	63 021	62 912
Bay City	49 815	49 338	50 164	49 857
Detroit-Warren-Dearborn	2 149 643	2 175 085	2 129 400	2 148 174
Flint	180 469	183 267	181 767	184 491
Grand Rapids-Wyoming	575 240	573 670	578 696	580 641
Jackson	73 850	73 356	74 347	74 749
Kalamazoo-Portage	168 725	168 748	168 969	170 354
Lansing-East Lansing	249 413	253 187	251 305	254 591
Midland	40 098	39 688	40 274	40 358
Monroe	76 181	75 156	76 390	76 354
Muskegon	77 167	77 846	77 669	79 216
Niles-Benton Harbor	72 430	73 052	72 828	73 810
Saginaw	86 163	85 777	87 094	87 437
Minnesota	3 077 928	3 138 147	3 073 359	3 129 485
Duluth	142 608	145 204	143 339	145 571
Mankato-North Mankato	62 681	64 496	61 952	64 315
Minneapolis-St Paul-Bloomington	2 003 584	2 032 710	2 005 563	2 032 283
Rochester	123 772	127 239	122 834	126 030
St. Cloud	112 734	115 833	112 343	115 111
Mississippi	1 270 344	1 283 688	1 274 959	1 284 175
Gulfport-Biloxi-Pascagoula	162 291	166 060	162 915	166 323
Hattiesburg	69 102	70 913	69 997	71 592
Jackson	269 116	272 560	270 220	271 635
Missouri	3 045 583	3 141 604	3 039 341	3 128 004
Cape Girardeau	47 736	49 358	47 942	49 295
Columbia	98 061	100 325	97 940	100 132
Jefferson City	73 192	75 018	72 897	74 757
Joplin	83 833	86 192	83 847	86 116
Kansas City	1 134 437	1 162 766	1 131 451	1 161 907
St. Joseph	63 085	64 177	63 040	63 598
St. Louis	1 455 409	1 501 286	1 452 805	1 496 955
Springfield	230 389	237 403	231 420	238 243
Montana	528 418	534 388	527 399	537 146
Billings	86 558	86 947	86 316	87 374
Great Falls	37 765	38 002	37 827	38 255
Missoula	63 595	64 892	63 291	64 951
Nebraska	1 022 354	1 045 946	1 020 931	1 046 220
Grand Island	43 288	44 580	43 231	43 914
Lincoln	183 949	186 605	182 547	187 143
Omaha-Council Bluffs	488 718	509 532	486 576	506 412
Nevada	1 516 177	1 567 125	1 518 855	1 572 315
Carson City	25 709	26 903	25 759	26 853
Las Vegas-Henderson-Paradise	1 110 177	1 139 764	1 108 053	1 145 579
Reno	256 884	271 567	260 367	272 715
New Hampshire	759 725	774 283	761 578	775 060
Dover-Durham	85 611	86 862	85 912	86 786
Manchester	120 021	122 210	120 902	123 211
Portsmouth	77 403	78 521	77 128	78 369
New Jersey	4 412 319	4 557 721	4 409 867	4 563 111
Atlantic City-Hammonton	119 829	123 706	118 704	122 463
Ocean City	43 479	46 362	41 888	45 355
Trenton	196 542	205 039	197 184	205 574
Vineland-Bridgeton	64 062	67 429	64 269	67 573
New Mexico	948 513	967 324	952 647	970 731
Albuquerque	433 428	442 134	436 153	444 243
Farmington	53 202	54 262	53 171	53 756
Las Cruces	97 751	99 635	98 138	99 907
Santa Fe	74 709	74 456	75 162	75 486
New York	9 603 222	9 583 705	9 576 358	9 511 374
Albany-Schenectady-Troy	455 703	450 192	453 576	450 885
Binghamton	108 095	106 792	107 389	105 918
Buffalo-Cheektowaga-Niagara Falls	546 329	546 830	542 340	541 404
Elmira	35 258	34 995	35 394	34 747
Glens Falls	59 607	58 890	59 462	58 492

Table 7-2. Civilian Labor Force by State and Selected Metropolitan Areas, October 2018–November 2019—*Continued*

(Number in thousands, percent.)

State and area	October		November	
	2018	2019	2018	2019
New York—*Continued*				
Ithaca	51 467	52 287	51 313	51 775
Kingston	89 936	89 805	89 005	88 809
New York-Newark-Jersey City	9 937 952	10 027 732	9 916 030	9 978 678
Rochester	526 171	527 410	523 910	524 957
Syracuse	309 179	311 209	308 308	309 043
Utica-Rome	129 561	128 471	129 908	128 168
Watertown-Fort Drum	44 263	44 323	44 450	44 186
North Carolina	5 007 407	5 153 426	4 992 016	5 109 338
Asheville	236 145	247 607	235 217	244 234
Burlington	81 364	83 169	81 337	82 388
Charlotte-Concord-Gastonia	1 347 774	1 390 489	1 343 343	1 378 010
Durham-Chapel Hill	299 396	307 411	298 863	304 153
Fayetteville	148 334	150 831	148 750	150 016
Goldsboro	52 831	52 844	52 416	53 185
Greensboro-High Point	370 424	377 189	368 821	374 071
Greenville	89 516	91 853	89 483	91 362
Hickory-Lenoir-Morganton	175 686	177 416	176 130	176 695
Jacksonville	64 242	65 191	64 041	64 753
New Bern	51 437	52 061	51 323	51 761
Raleigh	714 682	742 595	711 827	735 911
Rocky Mount	65 370	65 522	65 596	65 393
Wilmington	149 297	156 333	149 949	155 563
Winston-Salem	328 455	339 506	328 237	334 497
North Dakota	402 879	404 174	398 404	402 076
Bismarck	66 733	67 218	66 201	67 380
Fargo	136 045	138 130	135 217	138 588
Grand Forks	54 312	55 032	54 111	54 816
Ohio	5 774 153	5 826 663	5 754 616	5 822 254
Akron	359 552	359 555	358 174	359 485
Canton-Massillon	200 307	202 151	199 757	201 861
Cincinnati	1 123 610	1 145 341	1 117 245	1 143 717
Cleveland-Elyria	1 035 215	1 033 425	1 030 378	1 037 709
Columbus	1 089 855	1 105 977	1 085 672	1 109 726
Dayton	386 105	393 175	385 780	392 168
Lima	48 034	48 269	47 843	48 330
Mansfield	52 608	52 944	52 471	53 495
Springfield	63 368	64 668	63 182	64 062
Toledo	302 636	305 030	302 741	303 197
Weirton-Steubenville	50 272	50 572	49 874	50 087
Youngstown-Warren-Boardman	240 096	238 388	239 635	237 398
Oklahoma	1 844 742	1 856 199	1 845 292	1 841 383
Enid	27 276	27 026	27 183	26 805
Lawton	51 024	51 351	51 118	51 228
Oklahoma City	684 926	689 733	684 831	684 701
Tulsa	478 148	480 273	480 197	476 306
Oregon	2 117 663	2 119 417	2 117 387	2 109 609
Albany	58 855	59 176	58 968	58 830
Bend-Redmond	95 831	97 296	96 098	96 530
Corvallis	49 013	48 966	49 307	49 151
Eugene	182 153	181 773	182 036	181 396
Grants Pass	36 382	36 501	36 131	36 179
Medford	106 374	106 829	105 973	106 454
Portland-Vancouver-Hillsboro	1 323 190	1 336 179	1 329 266	1 337 907
Salem	203 005	201 962	202 927	200 139
Pennsylvania	6 444 551	6 570 222	6 437 401	6 542 425
Allentown-Bethlehem-Easton	439 216	447 869	436 483	447 560
Altoona	58 745	60 475	59 220	60 346
Bloomsburg-Berwick	42 701	43 572	42 568	43 279
Chambersburg-Waynesboro	76 976	79 518	77 501	79 510
East Stroudsburg	81 761	83 782	81 791	83 596
Erie	129 549	131 296	129 319	130 807
Gettysburg	55 105	56 027	54 921	55 512
Harrisburg-Carlisle	296 672	300 768	296 465	300 750
Johnstown	58 404	59 548	58 204	59 254
Lancaster	281 454	285 656	279 701	284 655

Table 7-2. Civilian Labor Force by State and Selected Metropolitan Areas, October 2018–November 2019—*Continued*

(Number in thousands, percent.)

State and area	October		November	
	2018	2019	2018	2019
Pennsylvania—*Continued*				
Lebanon	70 870	73 280	71 018	72 892
Philadelphia-Camden-Wilmington	3 096 866	3 173 357	3 093 266	3 164 985
Pittsburgh	1 208 178	1 223 415	1 208 177	1 217 254
Reading	212 363	218 185	212 784	217 231
Scranton—Wilkes-Barre—Hazleton	276 991	281 092	278 639	279 906
State College	82 361	84 535	82 865	84 411
Williamsport	56 607	57 812	56 381	57 587
York-Hanover	233 944	237 502	234 006	237 194
Rhode Island	556 208	558 149	558 933	563 424
Providence-Warwick	691 368	694 592	694 124	700 131
South Carolina	2 330 794	2 380 158	2 318 289	2 368 727
Charleston-North Charleston	385 901	390 273	384 176	389 305
Columbia	399 763	403 810	396 103	403 000
Florence	96 054	97 356	95 928	97 230
Greenville-Anderson-Mauldin	425 543	434 168	423 423	430 751
Hilton Head Island-Bluffton-Beaufort	87 369	91 486	86 788	90 476
Myrtle Beach-Conway-North Myrtle Beach	197 538	207 486	194 464	203 876
Spartanburg	160 137	165 121	158 999	164 071
Sumter	44 164	44 657	44 107	44 503
South Dakota	461 575	470 707	461 667	471 210
Rapid City	74 560	75 789	74 378	75 429
Sioux Falls	153 741	159 205	154 167	159 825
Tennessee	3 259 609	3 354 882	3 255 813	3 355 085
Chattanooga	272 203	276 883	269 455	275 964
Clarksville	115 031	118 995	115 539	118 607
Cleveland	57 630	58 870	58 783	59 824
Jackson	64 416	66 360	63 908	66 272
Johnson City	91 597	93 448	90 880	93 495
Kingsport-Bristol-Bristol	136 856	142 222	137 301	142 202
Knoxville	422 838	437 611	421 738	437 679
Memphis	636 392	646 723	639 381	649 688
Morristown	51 558	53 145	51 356	53 266
Nashville-Davidson—Murfreesboro—Franklin	1 052 647	1 088 325	1 052 145	1 086 288
Texas	13 901 088	14 190 783	13 961 940	14 265 562
Abilene	77 153	77 637	77 284	78 039
Amarillo	132 132	132 970	132 672	133 364
Austin-Round Rock	1 203 065	1 230 534	1 207 111	1 234 797
Beaumont-Port Arthur	177 316	178 164	176 834	177 867
Brownsville-Harlingen	163 865	164 651	164 708	165 593
College Station-Bryan	136 391	138 796	136 390	139 222
Corpus Christi	207 479	209 883	209 039	210 576
Dallas-Fort Worth-Arlington	3 928 885	4 030 421	3 948 427	4 061 740
El Paso	362 407	365 865	362 747	368 879
Houston-The Woodlands-Sugar Land	3 403 759	3 476 436	3 420 558	3 500 133
Killeen-Temple	176 049	180 120	177 549	181 634
Laredo	116 413	118 108	117 309	118 898
Longview	98 232	97 523	98 464	97 592
Lubbock	162 976	165 275	163 408	165 689
McAllen-Edinburg-Mission	345 285	355 574	348 987	358 376
Midland	107 454	108 004	107 736	108 457
Odessa	86 853	87 734	86 910	87 863
San Angelo	55 893	56 220	56 098	56 278
San Antonio-New Braunfels	1 191 437	1 226 439	1 196 835	1 230 340
Sherman-Denison	63 863	64 870	64 302	65 221
Texarkana	65 123	64 953	65 391	65 217
Tyler	108 396	108 909	108 817	109 526
Victoria	46 701	46 310	47 058	46 679
Waco	125 360	126 507	125 969	127 299
Wichita Falls	65 741	65 935	66 105	66 229
Utah	1 581 739	1 620 475	1 584 804	1 633 726
Logan	71 851	73 373	71 918	73 570
Ogden-Clearfield	327 041	337 431	327 254	339 781
Provo-Orem	310 095	318 181	310 416	321 523
St. George	75 372	77 507	75 364	78 100
Salt Lake City	655 548	668 907	658 694	675 387
Vermont	344 338	339 228	344 435	339 907
Burlington-South Burlington	125 505	126 186	125 252	125 995

Table 7-2. Civilian Labor Force by State and Selected Metropolitan Areas, October 2018–November 2019—*Continued*

(Number in thousands, percent.)

State and area	October		November	
	2018	2019	2018	2019
Virginia	4 332 241	4 444 585	4 319 915	4 442 397
Blacksburg-Christiansburg-Radford	90 553	89 414	90 375	92 206
Charlottesville	119 483	122 880	119 530	122 957
Harrisonburg	66 412	68 771	66 543	68 337
Lynchburg	122 491	125 865	122 469	125 143
Richmond	676 836	693 313	673 149	694 760
Roanoke	156 853	161 738	155 643	161 305
Staunton-Waynesboro	59 746	61 615	59 718	61 415
Virginia Beach-Norfolk-Newport News	845 987	863 369	840 941	860 647
Winchester	72 448	75 367	72 119	75 032
Washington	3 829 284	3 959 290	3 828 288	3 971 745
Bellingham	113 257	118 133	114 478	118 627
Bremerton-Silverdale	124 369	130 523	125 449	132 292
Kennewick-Richland	141 665	148 341	140 632	147 318
Longview	46 206	47 907	46 663	48 468
Mount Vernon-Anacortes	61 595	63 716	61 408	63 905
Olympia-Tumwate	139 676	146 659	140 936	148 329
Seattle-Tacoma-Bellevue	2 117 874	2 188 523	2 127 070	2 203 712
Spokane-Spokane Valley	271 270	283 806	274 118	285 890
Walla Walla	32 843	33 816	32 513	33 723
Wenatchee	69 274	70 064	64 855	67 083
Yakima	134 495	136 906	126 242	129 077
West Virginia	788 391	810 483	781 723	803 798
Beckley	45 610	46 930	44 627	46 080
Charleston	92 340	93 983	91 279	93 361
Huntington-Ashland	145 452	147 127	144 570	146 846
Morgantown	69 548	70 594	68 955	70 202
Parkersburg-Vienna	37 962	39 217	37 726	39 002
Wheeling	67 715	69 393	67 457	69 066
Wisconsin	3 121 149	3 112 283	3 116 247	3 102 020
Appleton	130 174	129 077	130 308	128 992
Eau Claire	92 637	92 378	92 945	91 782
Fond du Lac	57 705	56 922	57 564	56 714
Green Bay	175 833	176 186	176 011	175 631
Janesville-Beloit	84 514	85 428	85 503	85 804
La Crosse-Onalaska	77 662	78 490	77 926	78 626
Madison	386 487	387 071	387 637	387 083
Milwaukee-Waukesha-West Allis	822 019	824 356	819 065	823 180
Oshkosh-Neenah	92 273	91 911	92 209	91 918
Racine	98 681	98 417	98 565	97 942
Sheboygan	62 531	62 688	62 262	62 184
Wausau	73 579	73 555	73 764	73 394
Wyoming	289 628	293 236	289 088	294 329
Casper	39 013	39 291	39 147	39 687
Cheyenne	47 340	48 206	47 773	48 555

Table 7-3. Unemployment Number and Rate by State and Selected Metropolitan Area October 2018–November 2019

(Number, rate.)

State and area	October		November		October		November	
	2018	2019	2018	2019	2018	2019	2018	2019
Alabama	81 676	54 941	73 717	55 794	3.7	2.4	3.3	2.5
Anniston-Oxford-Jacksonville	2 001	1 330	1 819	1 355	4.4	2.8	4.0	2.9
Auburn-Opelika	2 539	1 668	2 299	1 722	3.3	2.1	3.0	2.2
Birmingham-Hoover	18 447	12 306	16 618	12 490	3.4	2.2	3.0	2.2
Daphne-Fairhope-Foley	3 228	2 122	2 934	2 195	3.5	2.2	3.2	2.3
Decatur	2 359	1 607	2 147	1 637	3.3	2.2	3.0	2.2
Dothan	2 469	1 544	2 193	1 604	3.9	2.4	3.5	2.5
Florence-Muscle Shoals	2 615	1 819	2 346	1 836	3.9	2.7	3.6	2.7
Gadsden	1 669	1 239	1 523	1 186	3.8	2.8	3.5	2.7
Huntsville	7 441	4 764	6 598	4 799	3.3	2.0	2.9	2.1
Mobile	8 147	5 722	7 367	5 793	4.3	3.0	3.9	3.0
Montgomery	6 430	4 295	5 773	4 333	3.7	2.4	3.4	2.5
Tuscaloosa	3 945	2 699	3 640	2 801	3.4	2.2	3.1	2.3
Alaska	21 539	19 289	22 657	20 638	6.1	5.6	6.4	6.0
Anchorage	11 106	9 721	11 379	10 228	5.6	5.0	5.6	5.2
Fairbanks	2 433	2 180	2 573	2 356	5.3	4.9	5.6	5.3
Arizona	170 174	155 340	166 722	157 057	4.9	4.3	4.7	4.3
Flagstaff	4 152	3 783	4 115	3 779	5.3	4.7	5.3	4.8
Lake Havasu-City-Kingman	4 915	4 657	4 997	4 798	5.7	5.2	5.8	5.3
Phoenix-Mesa-Scottsdale	102 079	93 956	102 136	95 656	4.2	3.7	4.2	3.8
Prescott	4 754	4 400	4 882	4 575	4.4	4.0	4.5	4.2
Sierra Vista-Douglas	2 805	2 631	2 844	2 761	5.6	5.1	5.6	5.3
Tucson	21 941	20 638	22 132	20 950	4.5	4.1	4.5	4.1
Yuma	19 431	16 458	16 107	15 762	18.5	16.1	15.6	15.4
Arkansas	44 065	43 551	43 405	43 732	3.3	3.2	3.2	3.2
Fayetteville-Springdale-Rogers	6 889	6 492	6 644	6 400	2.5	2.3	2.4	2.2
Fort Smith	4 093	4 122	3 890	4 056	3.4	3.5	3.3	3.4
Hot Springs	1 514	1 420	1 463	1 386	3.7	3.5	3.6	3.4
Jonesboro	1 794	1 694	1 749	1 669	2.8	2.6	2.7	2.5
Little Rock-North Little Rock-Conway	10 672	10 735	10 347	10 702	3.0	3.0	2.9	3.0
Pine Bluff	1 602	1 645	1 603	1 696	4.5	4.7	4.5	4.9
California	772 789	719 195	760 287	719 250	4.0	3.7	3.9	3.7
Bakersfield	25 417	23 993	25 161	24 843	6.5	6.1	6.5	6.4
Chico	4 418	3 992	4 503	4 100	4.2	3.8	4.3	4.0
El Centro	14 209	15 642	13 455	15 309	19.7	21.1	18.5	20.6
Fresno	28 434	26 273	30 606	29 498	6.4	5.8	6.8	6.5
Hanford-Corcoran	3 604	3 632	3 951	4 085	6.2	6.3	6.9	7.1
Los Angeles-Long Beach-Anaheim	286 727	275 353	278 806	261 949	4.2	4.1	4.1	3.8
Madera	3 571	3 318	3 726	3 703	5.8	5.4	6.1	6.1
Merced	7 272	6 805	7 808	7 581	6.2	5.8	6.8	6.5
Modesto	13 201	11 844	13 668	12 677	5.4	4.9	5.6	5.2
Napa	1 927	1 748	1 934	1 893	2.5	2.3	2.6	2.6
Oxnard-Thousand Oaks-Ventura	15 761	13 914	15 726	14 476	3.7	3.3	3.7	3.4
Redding	3 247	2 827	3 235	2 925	4.3	3.8	4.3	3.9
Riverside-San Bernardino-Ontario	85 350	77 097	80 930	75 864	4.1	3.7	3.9	3.6
Sacramento—Roseville—Arden-Arcade	38 370	34 585	37 570	35 235	3.5	3.1	3.4	3.2
Salinas	9 263	8 380	10 618	10 070	4.1	3.7	4.8	4.5
San Diego-Carlsbad	51 942	45 952	50 138	46 119	3.2	2.9	3.1	2.9
San Francisco-Oakland-Hayward	68 309	61 088	65 402	60 963	2.6	2.3	2.5	2.3
San Jose-Sunnyvale-Santa Clara	27 599	25 273	26 422	25 485	2.5	2.3	2.4	2.3
San Luis Obispo-Paso Robles-Arroyo	3 937	3 480	3 817	3 571	2.8	2.4	2.7	2.5
Grande Santa Cruz-Watsonville	5 164	4 809	5 837	5 618	3.6	3.3	4.1	3.9
Santa Maria-Santa Barbara	7 312	6 585	7 329	6 878	3.3	3.0	3.4	3.1
Santa Rosa	6 687	6 035	6 502	6 209	2.5	2.3	2.5	2.4
Stockton-Lodi	17 168	16 229	17 860	17 246	5.2	5.0	5.5	5.3
Vallejo-Fairfield	7 601	6 800	7 475	6 926	3.6	3.3	3.6	3.3
Visalia-Porterville	16 931	16 226	17 396	17 303	8.4	8.0	8.5	8.5
Yuba City	4 233	3 852	4 627	4 288	5.7	5.2	6.2	5.7
Colorado	106 223	75 810	111 166	79 586	3.4	2.4	3.5	2.5
Boulder	5 897	4 155	5 905	4 197	3.0	2.1	3.0	2.1
Colorado Springs	14 362	10 112	15 008	10 630	4.0	2.8	4.2	2.9
Denver-Aurora-Lakewood	54 623	39 396	56 732	40 641	3.3	2.3	3.4	2.4
Fort Collins	6 069	4 237	6 222	4 389	2.9	2.0	3.0	2.1
Grand Junction	3 022	2 173	3 253	2 300	3.9	2.8	4.2	2.9
Greeley	5 233	3 818	5 352	3 992	3.1	2.2	3.2	2.3
Pueblo	3 846	2 695	4 045	2 890	5.0	3.5	5.3	3.8

Table 7-3. Unemployment Number and Rate by State and Selected Metropolitan Area October 2018–November 2019—*Continued*

(Number, rate.)

State and area	October		November		October		November	
	2018	2019	2018	2019	2018	2019	2018	2019
Connecticut	66 683	67 229	60 478	63 780	3.5	3.5	3.1	3.3
Bridgeport-Stamford-Norwalk	16 515	16 644	14 932	15 824	3.5	3.5	3.2	3.3
Danbury	3 056	3 077	2 775	2 971	2.9	2.9	2.6	2.7
Hartford-West Hartford-East Hartford	21 802	22 334	19 784	21 055	3.5	3.5	3.1	3.3
New Haven	11 324	11 378	10 176	10 683	3.4	3.4	3.1	3.2
Norwich-New London-Westerly	4 754	4 761	4 508	4 656	3.3	3.3	3.2	3.2
Waterbury	4 924	4 849	4 563	4 623	4.4	4.3	4.0	4.1
Delaware	16 101	18 760	14 349	18 110	3.3	3.8	3.0	3.7
Dover	2 796	3 402	2 451	3 182	3.6	4.2	3.1	4.0
Salisbury	7 764	7 655	8 390	8 946	4.1	4.0	4.5	4.7
District of Columbia	21 315	21 835	20 563	20 558	5.3	5.3	5.1	5.0
Washington-Arlington-Alexandria	104 742	98 416	98 787	96 779	3.1	2.8	2.9	2.8
Florida	340 078	307 598	335 916	287 779	3.3	2.9	3.3	2.7
Cape Coral-Fort Myers	10 996	9 996	10 902	9 432	3.2	2.8	3.1	2.6
Crestview-Fort Walton Beach-Destin	3 433	3 021	3 539	2 998	2.7	2.3	2.8	2.3
Deltona-Daytona Beach-Ormond Beach	10 685	9 734	10 604	9 317	3.5	3.2	3.5	3.1
Gainesville	4 466	4 077	4 352	3 725	3.0	2.8	3.0	2.5
Homosassa Springs	2 307	2 006	2 317	1 966	4.8	4.1	4.8	4.1
Jacksonville	24 420	22 443	23 986	20 946	3.1	2.8	3.1	2.6
Lakeland-Winter Haven	11 390	10 414	11 074	9 662	3.7	3.4	3.7	3.2
Miami-Fort Lauderdale-West Palm Beach	107 396	94 652	101 211	87 410	3.4	2.9	3.2	2.7
Naples-Immokalee-Marco Island	5 881	5 326	5 661	4 925	3.3	2.9	3.2	2.7
North Port-Sarasota-Bradenton	11 592	10 407	11 603	9 975	3.2	2.8	3.2	2.7
Ocala	5 368	4 745	5 365	4 562	3.9	3.4	3.9	3.3
Orlando-Kissimmee-Sanford	40 714	37 790	40 219	35 144	3.0	2.7	3.0	2.5
Palm Bay-Melbourne-Titusville	9 001	8 387	8 991	7 937	3.2	2.9	3.2	2.8
Panama City	2 839	2 760	6 687	2 606	3.0	3.0	7.0	2.8
Pensacola-Ferry Pass-Brent	7 115	6 542	7 121	6 214	3.1	2.8	3.1	2.7
Port St Lucie	8 150	7 407	7 992	6 945	3.7	3.3	3.6	3.1
Punta Gorda	2 685	2 378	2 710	2 326	3.8	3.3	3.8	3.2
Sebastian-Vero Beach	2 586	2 296	2 529	2 152	3.9	3.4	3.8	3.2
Sebring	1 631	1 468	1 636	1 406	4.6	4.1	4.5	3.9
Tallahassee	6 228	5 771	6 216	5 266	3.2	2.9	3.2	2.6
Tampa-St Petersburg-Clearwater	49 462	45 318	49 015	42 767	3.2	2.9	3.2	2.7
The Villages	1 443	1 271	1 508	1 324	4.6	4.0	4.8	4.1
Georgia	191 762	156 277	176 023	139 294	3.8	3.0	3.4	2.7
Albany	3 062	2 447	3 019	2 262	4.5	3.7	4.4	3.4
Athens-Clarke County	3 704	2 888	3 259	2 490	3.6	2.8	3.1	2.4
Atlanta-Sandy Springs-Roswell	109 747	89 284	100 086	79 695	3.6	2.9	3.3	2.6
Augusta-Richmond County	10 426	8 147	9 545	7 527	3.9	3.0	3.6	2.8
Brunswick	1 980	1 638	1 784	1 416	3.7	3.1	3.3	2.6
Columbus	5 439	4 317	4 942	3 934	4.4	3.5	4.0	3.2
Dalton	2 809	2 705	2 619	2 194	4.6	4.4	4.3	3.6
Gainesville	3 166	2 497	2 812	2 195	3.1	2.4	2.7	2.1
Hinesville	1 346	1 160	1 232	1 041	4.0	3.4	3.7	3.1
Macon	4 465	3 439	4 162	3 049	4.3	3.3	4.0	2.9
Rome	1 850	1 471	1 673	1 389	4.2	3.3	3.8	3.1
Savannah	6 639	5 491	5 963	4 845	3.5	2.9	3.2	2.6
Valdosta	2 564	2 054	2 266	1 873	3.9	3.2	3.5	2.9
Warner Robins	3 918	2 747	3 844	2 314	4.5	3.2	4.4	2.7
Hawaii	17 405	17 488	18 287	16 956	2.6	2.6	2.7	2.5
Kahului-Wailuku-Lahaina	2 274	2 280	2 297	2 121	2.7	2.7	2.7	2.5
Urban Honolulu	10 977	11 087	12 004	10 880	2.4	2.4	2.6	2.4
Idaho	19 220	20 718	22 900	25 151	2.2	2.3	2.7	2.8
Boise City	7 968	8 743	9 259	10 562	2.2	2.3	2.5	2.8
Coeur d'Alene	2 027	2 197	2 520	2 555	2.6	2.8	3.2	3.2
Idaho Falls	1 323	1 429	1 538	1 720	1.9	1.9	2.2	2.3
Lewiston	849	905	1 015	995	2.7	2.8	3.2	3.1
Pocatello	922	1 003	1 098	1 169	2.2	2.3	2.6	2.7
Twin Falls	1 125	1 191	1 306	1 501	2.1	2.2	2.5	2.8
Illinois	263 231	235 472	259 018	218 259	4.1	3.6	4.0	3.4
Bloomington	4 142	3 353	3 949	2 984	4.3	3.5	4.1	3.1
Carbondale-Marion	2 893	2 339	2 817	2 097	4.7	3.7	4.6	3.4
Champaign-Urbana	5 553	4 432	5 205	3 902	4.5	3.5	4.3	3.1
Chicago-Naperville-Elgin	182 549	168 980	172 179	158 665	3.7	3.5	3.5	3.3

Table 7-3. Unemployment Number and Rate by State and Selected Metropolitan Area October 2018–November 2019—*Continued*

(Number, rate.)

State and area	October		November		October		November	
	2018	2019	2018	2019	2018	2019	2018	2019
Illinois— *Continued*								
Danville	1 956	1 627	1 914	1 516	5.9	4.9	5.8	4.6
Davenport-Moline-Rock Island	7 701	7 586	7 129	7 577	4.0	3.9	3.7	3.9
Decatur	2 764	2 453	2 762	2 261	5.5	4.8	5.5	4.5
Kankakee	2 874	2 458	2 914	2 620	5.1	4.3	5.2	4.6
Peoria	8 920	7 574	8 694	7 071	4.9	4.2	4.8	4.0
Rockford	9 039	8 527	16 052	8 529	5.4	5.0	9.4	5.1
Springfield	4 715	3 926	4 646	3 597	4.2	3.5	4.2	3.2
Indiana	112 491	101 447	111 876	106 202	3.3	3.0	3.3	3.2
Bloomington	2 973	2 492	2 747	2 568	3.7	3.1	3.4	3.2
Columbus	1 106	986	1 115	1 052	2.4	2.2	2.4	2.3
Elkhart-Goshen	3 172	3 214	3 181	3 294	2.7	2.8	2.7	2.8
Evansville	5 143	4 673	4 912	4 926	3.1	2.8	3.0	3.0
Fort Wayne	6 646	7 209	6 327	6 881	3.0	3.2	2.9	3.1
Indianapolis-Carmel-Anderson	33 614	29 085	32 520	30 552	3.2	2.7	3.1	2.9
Kokomo	1 350	1 204	3 161	1 265	3.6	3.2	8.0	3.4
Lafayette-West Lafayette	3 574	3 076	3 353	3 198	3.1	2.8	3.0	2.9
Michigan City-La Porte	1 892	1 679	1 935	1 829	4.0	3.6	4.0	3.9
Muncie	2 127	1 939	2 074	2 033	3.9	3.6	3.8	3.7
South Bend-Mishawaka	5 641	5 525	5 419	5 579	3.5	3.4	3.4	3.5
Terre Haute	3 306	2 759	3 183	2 994	4.3	3.6	4.1	3.9
Iowa	31 524	38 168	31 556	41 064	1.9	2.2	1.9	2.3
Ames	634	856	717	995	1.1	1.3	1.2	1.6
Cedar Rapids	2 988	3 612	3 102	3 945	2.1	2.4	2.2	2.6
Des Moines-West Des Moines	6 693	7 945	6 602	8 485	1.9	2.1	1.9	2.3
Dubuque	891	1 130	981	1 292	1.6	1.9	1.8	2.2
Iowa City	1 426	1 616	1 476	1 813	1.5	1.6	1.5	1.8
Sioux City	1 790	2 310	1 859	2 469	1.9	2.4	2.0	2.5
Waterloo-Cedar Falls	1 693	2 347	1 696	2 470	1.9	2.5	1.9	2.7
Kansas	44 868	42 682	44 166	42 884	3.0	2.8	3.0	2.8
Lawrence	1 765	1 742	1 767	1 752	2.7	2.6	2.7	2.6
Manhattan	1 235	1 207	1 273	1 233	2.5	2.4	2.6	2.5
Topeka	3 842	3 516	3 712	3 598	3.2	2.9	3.1	2.9
Wichita	10 347	9 790	10 140	9 893	3.3	3.1	3.3	3.2
Kentucky	79 263	77 635	72 305	80 388	3.9	3.7	3.5	3.8
Bowling Green	2 947	3 044	2 630	3 001	3.5	3.6	3.1	3.5
Elizabethtown-Fort Knox	2 557	2 472	2 310	2 570	3.8	3.7	3.4	3.8
Lexington-Fayette	8 521	8 126	7 455	8 411	3.1	2.9	2.7	3.0
Louisville/Jefferson County	23 668	21 991	21 900	22 732	3.6	3.3	3.3	3.4
Owensboro	1 997	1 852	1 807	1 906	3.6	3.3	3.3	3.4
Louisiana	97 073	98 917	90 359	102 329	4.6	4.7	4.3	4.8
Alexandria	3 221	3 127	3 053	3 306	5.1	5.0	4.9	5.3
Baton Rouge	17 505	18 141	16 093	18 655	4.2	4.3	3.8	4.4
Hammond	2 757	2 866	2 615	2 976	5.1	5.2	4.8	5.4
Houma-Thibodaux	4 060	3 935	3 747	4 038	4.6	4.6	4.3	4.8
Lafayette	9 781	9 852	9 135	10 188	4.6	4.6	4.3	4.8
Lake Charles	4 061	4 332	3 781	4 583	3.5	3.8	3.3	4.0
Monroe	4 056	4 199	3 837	4 399	5.1	5.4	4.8	5.6
New Orleans-Metairie	26 182	26 310	24 191	26 808	4.4	4.4	4.1	4.4
Shreveport-Bossier City	9 269	9 467	8 654	9 815	5.0	5.1	4.6	5.3
Maine	20 500	16 386	23 036	18 444	2.9	2.4	3.3	2.7
Bangor	2 208	1 739	2 359	1 871	3.1	2.4	3.3	2.6
Lewiston-Auburn	1 653	1 370	1 814	1 452	2.9	2.5	3.2	2.6
Portland-South Portland	5 248	4 260	5 820	4 623	2.5	2.0	2.8	2.2
Maryland	115 284	106 455	109 903	105 249	3.6	3.2	3.4	3.2
Baltimore-Columbia-Towson	54 728	50 710	51 551	49 510	3.7	3.3	3.4	3.2
California-Lexington Park	1 856	1 662	1 776	1 622	3.4	2.9	3.2	2.9
Cumberland	2 068	2 285	2 034	2 257	4.6	5.0	4.6	5.0
Hagerstown-Martinsburg	5 027	4 442	4 808	4 346	3.8	3.3	3.6	3.2
Massachusetts	104 354	94 594	98 823	88 675	2.7	2.5	2.6	2.3
Barnstable Town	3 680	3 411	4 012	3 708	2.9	2.7	3.2	3.0
Boston-Cambridge-Nashua	71 261	65 300	66 984	60 618	2.5	2.3	2.4	2.1
Leominster-Gardner	2 513	2 273	2 369	2 198	3.1	2.8	2.9	2.6
New Bedford	3 452	3 185	3 277	3 029	4.0	3.7	3.8	3.5
Pittsfield	1 396	1 242	1 462	1 257	3.2	2.9	3.4	2.9
Springfield	12 769	11 879	12 003	11 059	3.3	3.0	3.1	2.8
Worcester	10 906	9 992	10 166	9 368	3.0	2.8	2.8	2.6

Table 7-3. Unemployment Number and Rate by State and Selected Metropolitan Area October 2018–November 2019—*Continued*

(Number, rate.)

State and area	October		November		October		November	
	2018	2019	2018	2019	2018	2019	2018	2019
Michigan	181 296	174 052	166 773	157 495	3.7	3.5	3.4	3.2
Ann Arbor	5 517	4 988	4 947	4 436	2.8	2.5	2.5	2.2
Battle Creek	2 174	2 183	2 109	2 026	3.5	3.5	3.3	3.2
Bay City	1 788	2 030	1 754	1 833	3.6	4.1	3.5	3.7
Detroit-Warren-Dearborn	93 159	81 502	78 916	72 550	4.3	3.7	3.7	3.4
Flint	7 110	8 840	6 935	7 020	3.9	4.8	3.8	3.8
Grand Rapids-Wyoming	14 604	14 206	13 815	13 481	2.5	2.5	2.4	2.3
Jackson	2 372	2 411	2 310	2 238	3.2	3.3	3.1	3.0
Kalamazoo-Portage	5 069	5 195	4 929	4 808	3.0	3.1	2.9	2.8
Lansing-East Lansing	7 109	9 104	7 526	6 466	2.9	3.6	3.0	2.5
Midland	1 252	1 246	1 212	1 220	3.1	3.1	3.0	3.0
Monroe	2 971	2 209	2 794	2 190	3.9	2.9	3.7	2.9
Muskegon	2 906	2 801	2 759	2 823	3.8	3.6	3.6	3.6
Niles-Benton Harbor	2 489	2 281	2 452	2 307	3.4	3.1	3.4	3.1
Saginaw	3 255	4 119	3 224	3 388	3.8	4.8	3.7	3.9
Minnesota	68 733	79 870	69 288	89 398	2.2	2.5	2.3	2.9
Duluth	3 945	4 579	4 386	5 639	2.8	3.2	3.1	3.9
Mankato-North Mankato	1 147	1 293	1 052	1 298	1.8	2.0	1.7	2.0
Minneapolis-St Paul-Bloomington	43 886	51 492	41 742	54 157	2.2	2.5	2.1	2.7
Rochester	2 328	2 653	2 314	2 940	1.9	2.1	1.9	2.3
St. Cloud	2 441	2 690	2 548	3 158	2.2	2.3	2.3	2.7
Mississippi	54 552	66 490	53 790	70 042	4.3	5.2	4.2	5.5
Gulfport-Biloxi-Pascagoula	7 300	8 631	7 248	9 150	4.5	5.2	4.4	5.5
Hattiesburg	2 568	3 120	2 518	3 260	3.7	4.4	3.6	4.6
Jackson	10 237	12 330	10 015	12 973	3.8	4.5	3.7	4.8
Missouri	70 459	79 156	75 593	93 595	2.3	2.5	2.5	3.0
Cape Girardeau	1 056	1 232	1 143	1 513	2.2	2.5	2.4	3.1
Columbia	1 549	1 719	1 730	2 172	1.6	1.7	1.8	2.2
Jefferson City	1 352	1 435	1 470	1 863	1.8	1.9	2.0	2.5
Joplin	1 751	2 066	1 897	2 477	2.1	2.4	2.3	2.9
Kansas City	30 859	31 028	31 057	33 093	2.7	2.7	2.7	2.8
St. Joseph	1 369	1 474	1 463	1 666	2.2	2.3	2.3	2.6
St. Louis	41 198	40 959	42 518	44 233	2.8	2.7	2.9	3.0
Springfield	4 475	5 263	4 895	6 606	1.9	2.2	2.1	2.8
Montana	17 784	16 680	18 980	18 309	3.4	3.1	3.6	3.4
Billings	2 698	2 531	2 753	2 684	3.1	2.9	3.2	3.1
Great Falls	1 249	1 190	1 281	1 226	3.3	3.1	3.4	3.2
Missoula	1 898	1 812	2 011	1 989	3.0	2.8	3.2	3.1
Nebraska	25 751	30 541	23 458	28 999	2.5	2.9	2.3	2.8
Grand Island	1 116	1 863	1 067	1 249	2.6	4.2	2.5	2.8
Lincoln	4 350	5 031	3 825	4 926	2.4	2.7	2.1	2.6
Omaha-Council Bluffs	12 330	13 934	11 586	13 689	2.5	2.7	2.4	2.7
Nevada	64 664	58 495	64 041	54 471	4.3	3.7	4.2	3.5
Carson City	1 062	924	1 079	890	4.1	3.4	4.2	3.3
Las Vegas-Henderson-Paradise	50 049	45 267	49 415	41 951	4.5	4.0	4.5	3.7
Reno	8 518	7 766	8 447	7 297	3.3	2.9	3.2	2.7
New Hampshire	15 191	17 913	16 449	17 697	2.0	2.3	2.2	2.3
Dover-Durham	1 603	1 833	1 750	1 827	1.9	2.1	2.0	2.1
Manchester	2 333	2 715	2 484	2 709	1.9	2.2	2.1	2.2
Portsmouth	1 529	1 650	1 655	1 610	2.0	2.1	2.1	2.1
New Jersey	154 190	149 755	145 777	150 539	3.5	3.3	3.3	3.3
Atlantic City-Hammonton	5 558	5 631	5 504	5 778	4.6	4.6	4.6	4.7
Ocean City	2 485	2 371	3 601	3 604	5.7	5.1	8.6	7.9
Trenton	6 125	6 094	5 698	5 989	3.1	3.0	2.9	2.9
Vineland-Bridgeton	3 179	3 231	3 200	3 349	5.0	4.8	5.0	5.0
New Mexico	46 182	43 970	46 012	44 575	4.9	4.5	4.8	4.6
Albuquerque	20 466	19 351	19 947	19 148	4.7	4.4	4.6	4.3
Farmington	2 944	2 853	2 926	2 948	5.5	5.3	5.5	5.5
Las Cruces	5 163	4 956	5 291	5 242	5.3	5.0	5.4	5.2
Santa Fe	3 114	2 750	3 068	2 736	4.2	3.7	4.1	3.6
New York	347 452	373 274	339 417	345 862	3.6	3.9	3.5	3.6
Albany-Schenectady-Troy	14 368	15 466	14 178	14 409	3.2	3.4	3.1	3.2
Binghamton	4 063	4 446	4 036	4 233	3.8	4.2	3.8	4.0
Buffalo-Cheektowaga-Niagara Falls	19 978	21 931	20 485	21 349	3.7	4.0	3.8	3.9
Elmira	1 368	1 407	1 286	1 283	3.9	4.0	3.6	3.7
Glens Falls	1 972	2 124	2 272	2 337	3.3	3.6	3.8	4.0

Table 7-3. Unemployment Number and Rate by State and Selected Metropolitan Area October 2018–November 2019—*Continued*

(Number, rate.)

State and area	October		November		October		November	
	2018	2019	2018	2019	2018	2019	2018	2019
New York—*Continued*								
Ithaca	1 593	1 820	1 539	1 564	3.1	3.5	3.0	3.0
Kingston	2 874	3 064	2 804	2 874	3.2	3.4	3.2	3.2
New York-Newark-Jersey City	356 047	368 011	337 329	342 886	3.6	3.7	3.4	3.4
Rochester	18 247	20 214	18 382	19 409	3.5	3.8	3.5	3.7
Syracuse	10 697	12 096	11 044	11 509	3.5	3.9	3.6	3.7
Utica-Rome	4 698	5 052	4 910	4 999	3.6	3.9	3.8	3.9
Watertown-Fort Drum	1 834	2 150	2 179	2 446	4.1	4.9	4.9	5.5
North Carolina	181 089	185 225	180 250	173 571	3.6	3.6	3.6	3.4
Asheville	6 727	7 059	6 747	6 432	2.8	2.9	2.9	2.6
Burlington	2 697	2 878	2 712	2 651	3.3	3.5	3.3	3.2
Charlotte-Concord-Gastonia	44 938	44 880	44 468	43 178	3.3	3.2	3.3	3.1
Durham-Chapel Hill	9 517	9 845	9 521	8 998	3.2	3.2	3.2	3.0
Fayetteville	7 173	7 230	7 185	6 841	4.8	4.8	4.8	4.6
Goldsboro	2 104	2 076	2 123	1 923	4.0	3.9	4.1	3.6
Greensboro-High Point	13 763	14 299	14 077	13 342	3.7	3.8	3.8	3.6
Greenville	3 469	3 630	3 446	3 398	3.9	4.0	3.9	3.7
Hickory-Lenoir-Morganton	5 733	6 187	5 863	5 731	3.3	3.5	3.3	3.2
Jacksonville	3 221	2 871	2 942	2 618	5.0	4.4	4.6	4.0
New Bern	2 242	1 925	2 146	1 807	4.4	3.7	4.2	3.5
Raleigh	22 561	23 310	22 460	21 718	3.2	3.1	3.2	3.0
Rocky Mount	3 248	3 210	3 177	2 976	5.0	4.9	4.8	4.6
Wilmington	5 842	5 080	5 511	4 755	3.9	3.2	3.7	3.1
Winston-Salem	11 258	11 618	11 196	10 857	3.4	3.4	3.4	3.2
North Dakota	7 157	6 958	8 348	8 417	1.8	1.7	2.1	2.1
Bismarck	1 272	1 235	1 539	1 527	1.9	1.8	2.3	2.3
Fargo	2 338	2 266	2 522	2 632	1.7	1.6	1.9	1.9
Grand Forks	964	1 007	1 108	1 180	1.8	1.8	2.0	2.2
Ohio	246 996	227 937	243 308	220 841	4.3	3.9	4.2	3.8
Akron	15 539	14 823	15 524	14 371	4.3	4.1	4.3	4.0
Canton-Massillon	9 099	8 785	9 122	8 860	4.5	4.3	4.6	4.4
Cincinnati	42 602	40 864	40 452	39 000	3.8	3.6	3.6	3.4
Cleveland-Elyria	46 825	33 512	45 012	34 193	4.5	3.2	4.4	3.3
Columbus	40 923	38 993	39 665	37 130	3.8	3.5	3.7	3.3
Dayton	16 357	16 373	15 893	14 826	4.2	4.2	4.1	3.8
Lima	1 999	1 935	1 922	1 851	4.2	4.0	4.0	3.8
Mansfield	2 359	2 263	2 433	2 339	4.5	4.3	4.6	4.4
Springfield	2 770	3 245	2 703	2 748	4.4	5.0	4.3	4.3
Toledo	14 240	12 838	14 287	12 223	4.7	4.2	4.7	4.0
Weirton-Steubenville	2 730	2 888	2 719	2 792	5.4	5.7	5.5	5.6
Youngstown-Warren-Boardman	13 085	13 118	12 986	13 181	5.4	5.5	5.4	5.6
Oklahoma	56 342	61 944	53 190	63 239	3.1	3.3	2.9	3.4
Enid	737	795	704	862	2.7	2.9	2.6	3.2
Lawton	1 897	1 877	1 774	1 899	3.7	3.7	3.5	3.7
Oklahoma City	19 361	20 425	18 145	21 373	2.8	3.0	2.6	3.1
Tulsa	15 072	17 053	14 250	16 614	3.2	3.6	3.0	3.5
Oregon	83 429	74 476	85 731	65 040	3.9	3.5	4.0	3.1
Albany	2 640	2 391	2 779	2 100	4.5	4.0	4.7	3.6
Bend-Redmond	3 689	3 270	4 002	2 982	3.8	3.4	4.2	3.1
Corvallis	1 556	1 334	1 495	1 097	3.2	2.7	3.0	2.2
Eugene	7 904	6 987	7 932	6 059	4.3	3.8	4.4	3.3
Grants Pass	1 846	1 635	1 948	1 467	5.1	4.5	5.4	4.1
Medford	4 591	3 882	4 778	3 408	4.3	3.6	4.5	3.2
Portland-Vancouver-Hillsboro	49 507	46 922	49 963	41 809	3.7	3.5	3.8	3.1
Salem	8 332	7 545	8 566	6 519	4.1	3.7	4.2	3.3
Pennsylvania	248 016	285 827	233 777	278 771	3.8	4.4	3.6	4.3
Allentown-Bethlehem-Easton	17 811	19 275	16 519	18 455	4.1	4.3	3.8	4.1
Altoona	2 210	2 703	2 136	2 697	3.8	4.5	3.6	4.5
Bloomsburg-Berwick	1 568	1 787	1 512	1 752	3.7	4.1	3.6	4.0
Chambersburg-Waynesboro	2 540	3 014	2 390	2 913	3.3	3.8	3.1	3.7
East Stroudsburg	3 964	4 504	3 823	4 463	4.8	5.4	4.7	5.3
Erie	5 191	5 745	4 967	5 850	4.0	4.4	3.8	4.5
Gettysburg	1 677	1 805	1 481	1 727	3.0	3.2	2.7	3.1
Harrisburg-Carlisle	9 960	11 652	9 410	10 971	3.4	3.9	3.2	3.6
Johnstown	2 556	2 898	2 478	3 028	4.4	4.9	4.3	5.1
Lancaster	8 674	9 979	8 078	9 394	3.1	3.5	2.9	3.3

Table 7-3. Unemployment Number and Rate by State and Selected Metropolitan Area October 2018–November 2019—*Continued*

(Number, rate.)

State and area	October		November		October		November	
	2018	2019	2018	2019	2018	2019	2018	2019
Pennsylvania—*Continued*								
Lebanon	2 445	2 852	2 279	2 747	3.4	3.9	3.2	3.8
Philadelphia-Camden-Wilmington	118 481	131 058	109 302	125 591	3.8	4.1	3.5	4.0
Pittsburgh	44 687	52 321	42 483	51 801	3.7	4.3	3.5	4.3
Reading	8 138	9 517	7 618	9 202	3.8	4.4	3.6	4.2
Scranton—Wilkes-Barre—Hazleton	12 575	14 506	12 079	14 513	4.5	5.2	4.3	5.2
State College	2 367	2 784	2 138	2 638	2.9	3.3	2.6	3.1
Williamsport	2 292	2 626	2 290	2 655	4.0	4.5	4.1	4.6
York-Hanover	8 178	9 235	7 627	8 802	3.5	3.9	3.3	3.7
Rhode Island	19 182	16 205	21 567	18 006	3.4	2.9	3.9	3.2
Providence-Warwick	23 416	20 280	25 470	21 580	3.4	2.9	3.7	3.1
South Carolina	75 373	50 186	68 439	50 489	3.2	2.1	3.0	2.1
Charleston-North Charleston	10 462	6 898	9 499	6 942	2.7	1.8	2.5	1.8
Columbia	12 397	7 981	11 276	8 087	3.1	2.0	2.8	2.0
Florence	3 476	2 236	3 156	2 241	3.6	2.3	3.3	2.3
Greenville-Anderson-Mauldin	12 545	8 402	11 322	8 480	2.9	1.9	2.7	2.0
Hilton Head Island-Bluffton-Beaufort	2 648	1 735	2 378	1 695	3.0	1.9	2.7	1.9
Myrtle Beach-Conway-North Myrtle Beach	8 343	6 163	7 916	6 162	4.2	3.0	4.1	3.0
Spartanburg	4 772	3 193	4 274	3 251	3.0	1.9	2.7	2.0
Sumter	1 638	1 115	1 502	1 146	3.7	2.5	3.4	2.6
South Dakota	12 065	13 387	12 749	14 944	2.6	2.8	2.8	3.2
Rapid City	2 129	2 288	2 272	2 591	2.9	3.0	3.1	3.4
Sioux Falls	3 363	3 787	3 502	4 211	2.2	2.4	2.3	2.6
Tennessee	106 795	105 783	98 204	103 165	3.3	3.2	3.0	3.1
Chattanooga	9 317	8 333	8 140	8 091	3.4	3.0	3.0	2.9
Clarksville	4 434	4 824	4 047	4 444	3.9	4.1	3.5	3.7
Cleveland	1 982	1 880	1 841	1 890	3.4	3.2	3.1	3.2
Jackson	2 275	2 182	2 043	2 112	3.5	3.3	3.2	3.2
Johnson City	3 218	3 048	2 999	3 098	3.5	3.3	3.3	3.3
Kingsport-Bristol-Bristol	4 554	4 608	4 269	4 554	3.3	3.2	3.1	3.2
Knoxville	13 058	12 629	12 123	12 549	3.1	2.9	2.9	2.9
Memphis	24 943	24 725	22 951	25 246	3.9	3.8	3.6	3.9
Morristown	1 783	1 842	1 698	1 829	3.5	3.5	3.3	3.4
Nashville-Davidson—Murfreesboro—Franklin	27 312	27 780	25 305	26 127	2.6	2.6	2.4	2.4
Texas	489 204	467 680	485 960	477 021	3.5	3.3	3.5	3.3
Abilene	2 397	2 245	2 355	2 276	3.1	2.9	3.0	2.9
Amarillo	3 397	3 242	3 390	3 283	2.6	2.4	2.6	2.5
Austin-Round Rock	33 376	31 388	32 915	31 359	2.8	2.6	2.7	2.5
Beaumont-Port Arthur	9 074	8 827	9 150	9 214	5.1	5.0	5.2	5.2
Brownsville-Harlingen	8 705	8 458	8 793	8 938	5.3	5.1	5.3	5.4
College Station-Bryan	3 670	3 615	3 607	3 603	2.7	2.6	2.6	2.6
Corpus Christi	8 945	8 230	8 937	8 517	4.3	3.9	4.3	4.0
Dallas-Fort Worth-Arlington	128 366	123 844	126 608	123 322	3.3	3.1	3.2	3.0
El Paso	14 312	13 541	14 047	13 634	3.9	3.7	3.9	3.7
Houston-The Woodlands-Sugar Land	131 468	123 023	130 454	126 404	3.9	3.5	3.8	3.6
Killeen-Temple	6 956	6 337	6 849	6 435	4.0	3.5	3.9	3.5
Laredo	4 068	4 043	4 047	4 191	3.5	3.4	3.4	3.5
Longview	3 761	3 507	3 691	3 601	3.8	3.6	3.7	3.7
Lubbock	4 587	4 371	4 493	4 332	2.8	2.6	2.7	2.6
McAllen-Edinburg-Mission	19 020	19 778	20 259	21 905	5.5	5.6	5.8	6.1
Midland	2 106	2 243	2 083	2 313	2.0	2.1	1.9	2.1
Odessa	2 057	2 369	2 043	2 522	2.4	2.7	2.4	2.9
San Angelo	1 683	1 611	1 692	1 634	3.0	2.9	3.0	2.9
San Antonio-New Braunfels	37 225	35 679	36 813	35 968	3.1	2.9	3.1	2.9
Sherman-Denison	1 942	1 877	1 923	1 921	3.0	2.9	3.0	2.9
Texarkana	3 149	2 584	3 065	2 568	4.8	4.0	4.7	3.9
Tyler	3 797	3 412	3 743	3 483	3.5	3.1	3.4	3.2
Victoria	1 597	1 527	1 610	1 639	3.4	3.3	3.4	3.5
Waco	4 108	3 944	4 095	3 944	3.3	3.1	3.3	3.1
Wichita Falls	2 029	1 928	2 060	1 942	3.1	2.9	3.1	2.9
Utah	45 535	29 957	44 023	30 819	2.9	1.8	2.8	1.9
Logan	1 715	1 117	1 692	1 126	2.4	1.5	2.4	1.5
Ogden-Clearfield	9 649	6 085	9 180	6 252	3.0	1.8	2.8	1.8
Provo-Orem	8 153	5 392	7 738	5 438	2.6	1.7	2.5	1.7
St. George	2 337	1 600	2 322	1 649	3.1	2.1	3.1	2.1
Salt Lake City	18 720	12 439	18 030	12 706	2.9	1.9	2.7	1.9
Vermont	6 419	5 434	8 218	7 328	1.9	1.6	2.4	2.2
Burlington-South Burlington	2 050	1 689	2 489	2 235	1.6	1.3	2.0	1.8

Table 7-3. Unemployment Number and Rate by State and Selected Metropolitan Area October 2018–November 2019—*Continued*

(Number, rate.)

State and area	October		November		October		November	
	2018	2019	2018	2019	2018	2019	2018	2019
Virginia	115 281	106 915	108 524	109 049	2.7	2.4	2.5	2.5
Blacksburg-Christiansburg-Radford	2 479	2 300	2 409	2 366	2.7	2.6	2.7	2.6
Charlottesville	2 917	2 619	2 752	2 718	2.4	2.1	2.3	2.2
Harrisonburg	1 732	1 485	1 659	1 526	2.6	2.2	2.5	2.2
Lynchburg	3 632	3 449	3 433	3 542	3.0	2.7	2.8	2.8
Richmond	19 220	17 831	17 975	18 041	2.8	2.6	2.7	2.6
Roanoke	4 071	3 915	3 808	4 018	2.6	2.4	2.4	2.5
Staunton-Waynesboro	1 506	1 389	1 410	1 379	2.5	2.3	2.4	2.2
Virginia Beach-Norfolk-Newport News	25 012	23 350	23 747	23 611	3.0	2.7	2.8	2.7
Winchester	1 868	1 706	1 768	1 749	2.6	2.3	2.5	2.3
Washington	156 123	159 682	169 864	157 780	4.1	4.0	4.4	4.0
Bellingham	4 834	5 732	5 228	5 887	4.3	4.9	4.6	5.0
Bremerton-Silverdale	5 309	5 797	5 586	5 756	4.3	4.4	4.5	4.4
Kennewick-Richland	6 416	7 176	7 326	7 964	4.5	4.8	5.2	5.4
Longview	2 435	2 831	2 621	2 864	5.3	5.9	5.6	5.9
Mount Vernon-Anacortes	2 895	3 344	3 085	3 526	4.7	5.2	5.0	5.5
Olympia-Tumwater	6 002	6 978	6 477	7 034	4.3	4.8	4.6	4.7
Seattle-Tacoma-Bellevue	77 856	71 157	83 265	63 848	3.7	3.3	3.9	2.9
Spokane-Spokane Valley	12 474	13 913	13 546	14 475	4.6	4.9	4.9	5.1
Walla Walla	1 318	1 512	1 407	1 529	4.0	4.5	4.3	4.5
Wenatchee	2 662	2 920	3 166	3 457	3.8	4.2	4.9	5.2
Yakima	6 590	7 249	8 394	9 111	4.9	5.3	6.6	7.1
West Virginia	35 784	36 518	35 750	38 960	4.5	4.5	4.6	4.8
Beckley	2 227	2 188	2 310	2 397	4.9	4.7	5.2	5.2
Charleston	4 409	4 173	4 333	4 430	4.8	4.4	4.7	4.7
Huntington-Ashland	7 014	6 695	6 752	6 806	4.8	4.6	4.7	4.6
Morgantown	2 724	2 467	2 621	2 557	3.9	3.5	3.8	3.6
Parkersburg-Vienna	1 814	1 930	1 847	2 064	4.8	4.9	4.9	5.3
Wheeling	2 885	3 588	2 845	3 765	4.3	5.2	4.2	5.5
Wisconsin	74 734	85 913	77 545	90 771	2.4	2.8	2.5	2.9
Appleton	2 863	3 101	2 912	3 232	2.2	2.4	2.2	2.5
Eau Claire	2 035	2 366	2 102	2 467	2.2	2.6	2.3	2.7
Fond du Lac	1 180	1 401	1 185	1 397	2.0	2.5	2.1	2.5
Green Bay	3 879	4 505	3 910	4 718	2.2	2.6	2.2	2.7
Janesville-Beloit	2 154	2 723	2 837	2 926	2.5	3.2	3.3	3.4
La Crosse-Onalaska	1 588	1 784	1 606	1 838	2.0	2.3	2.1	2.3
Madison	7 515	8 329	7 445	8 512	1.9	2.2	1.9	2.2
Milwaukee-Waukesha-West Allis	22 348	25 671	22 596	26 353	2.7	3.1	2.8	3.2
Oshkosh-Neenah	2 068	2 382	2 040	2 440	2.2	2.6	2.2	2.7
Racine	2 876	3 507	2 909	3 628	2.9	3.6	3.0	3.7
Sheboygan	1 290	1 497	1 325	1 591	2.1	2.4	2.1	2.6
Wausau	1 560	1 777	1 539	1 813	2.1	2.4	2.1	2.5
Wyoming	10 831	9 580	11 587	10 524	3.7	3.3	4.0	3.6
Casper	1 734	1 447	1 719	1 535	4.4	3.7	4.4	3.9
Cheyenne	1 756	1 577	1 784	1 609	3.7	3.3	3.7	3.3

Table 7-4. Job Openings Levels and Rates, by Industry, 2008–October 2019

(Seasonally adjusted, levels in thousands, rates per 100.)

Year and month	Level											
	Total nonfarm[1]	Total private[1]	Construction	Manufacturing	Trade, transportation, and utilities[2]	Retail trade	Professional and business services	Education and health services	Leisure and hospitality[3]	Accommodation and food services	Government[4]	State and local government
2008												
January	4 604	4 202	145	288	779	450	988	748	574	517	401	364
February	4 233	3 806	121	263	654	390	967	802	552	486	427	382
March	4 205	3 772	108	245	641	409	920	789	583	509	434	375
April	4 124	3 693	122	290	653	427	838	723	549	488	431	386
May	4 237	3 787	189	285	707	450	821	738	555	483	450	398
June	3 849	3 408	145	245	608	376	736	758	471	417	441	387
July	3 800	3 391	132	260	636	398	665	764	440	385	409	352
August	3 709	3 318	88	259	667	441	659	707	431	354	391	343
September	3 240	2 856	115	220	482	273	631	606	410	354	383	352
October	3 403	3 022	71	246	651	455	577	670	409	355	381	336
November	3 158	2 785	52	162	582	417	527	669	349	295	373	329
December	3 059	2 742	46	137	520	388	578	618	348	298	317	279
2009												
January	2 731	2 382	38	112	504	376	536	590	241	206	349	291
February	2 838	2 470	73	130	452	323	533	551	326	296	368	306
March	2 521	2 152	48	111	442	297	452	507	263	239	369	264
April	2 343	1 976	29	103	341	219	438	521	273	247	367	315
May	2 574	2 294	51	99	547	406	446	531	296	268	280	253
June	2 517	2 188	67	107	451	299	405	523	283	264	329	286
July	2 264	1 980	50	110	303	196	449	536	259	223	284	233
August	2 365	2 058	65	123	426	281	420	546	198	173	307	275
September	2 481	2 199	66	131	381	261	464	537	286	260	282	226
October	2 422	2 045	54	132	339	215	413	531	261	244	377	274
November	2 435	2 096	49	127	365	241	435	508	279	251	338	250
December	2 487	2 169	55	152	410	299	432	543	258	239	318	247
2010												
January	2 833	2 437	54	142	451	332	457	623	279	257	396	249
February	2 651	2 303	65	157	468	343	430	521	266	239	348	220
March	2 679	2 257	86	153	500	348	390	528	239	211	422	261
April	3 217	2 587	101	191	448	294	513	521	283	255	631	256
May	3 019	2 622	88	190	486	323	603	510	312	260	398	246
June	2 813	2 511	83	210	474	314	582	458	329	267	301	220
July	3 127	2 806	113	241	483	324	621	543	323	285	321	239
August	3 025	2 674	59	188	451	284	641	497	364	319	351	246
September	2 912	2 582	78	189	440	255	634	512	317	283	330	253
October	3 256	2 911	67	198	513	333	652	630	417	382	345	275
November	3 134	2 810	66	207	490	327	700	551	319	291	324	257
December	2 969	2 584	32	171	506	325	579	546	352	312	385	293
2011												
January	3 100	2 770	61	217	557	353	538	552	366	331	330	269
February	3 213	2 894	45	209	643	397	610	571	389	342	319	256
March	3 253	2 921	67	211	568	351	641	600	393	352	332	272
April	3 337	2 985	91	247	628	401	590	610	331	289	352	298
May	3 207	2 901	124	220	640	431	585	587	319	279	306	240
June	3 467	3 103	77	217	668	451	676	616	406	325	364	307
July	3 676	3 348	94	250	679	437	790	642	363	288	328	260
August	3 358	3 026	111	234	570	396	669	650	392	343	332	279
September	3 763	3 371	87	254	637	392	891	608	428	362	392	333
October	3 650	3 283	82	233	687	410	708	635	429	366	367	294
November	3 485	3 142	63	200	739	497	667	637	434	380	342	287
December	3 662	3 311	56	215	666	442	847	628	441	402	351	284
2012												
January	3 904	3 565	85	246	666	403	948	684	453	380	339	275
February	3 605	3 203	61	237	651	389	747	677	379	320	403	323
March	3 976	3 566	94	312	695	448	837	689	447	398	409	321
April	3 878	3 497	134	265	640	384	772	686	481	404	381	300
May	3 861	3 455	105	306	624	372	750	727	458	393	405	336
June	3 916	3 524	70	308	631	377	774	760	483	411	393	319
July	3 790	3 417	95	287	671	416	740	693	489	424	373	311
August	3 839	3 417	134	268	747	483	730	665	423	364	422	327
September	3 861	3 482	92	252	780	496	694	709	422	368	379	309
October	3 808	3 428	107	278	553	305	755	705	483	429	380	315
November	3 787	3 439	73	220	679	469	749	731	499	442	348	298
December	3 840	3 446	93	223	775	507	697	705	481	415	393	320
2013												
January	3 915	3 477	116	251	751	473	776	632	470	415	438	353
February	3 981	3 553	121	276	651	402	757	687	520	468	428	356
March	4 080	3 672	121	260	732	472	750	710	514	451	408	345
April	4 078	3 635	133	257	804	534	761	721	478	430	442	356
May	4 173	3 755	137	253	817	558	788	689	469	422	418	369
June	4 166	3 756	146	223	888	634	749	682	489	438	410	362
July	3 946	3 576	111	254	727	488	696	657	503	451	370	321
August	4 112	3 718	129	286	769	484	809	755	523	429	393	352
September	4 105	3 711	121	270	815	530	751	669	550	482	394	343
October	4 268	3 873	141	302	793	530	819	684	540	450	395	352
November	4 002	3 616	117	272	793	508	745	657	543	462	386	332
December	3 996	3 662	86	265	799	525	774	613	585	504	334	292

[1]Includes natural resources and mining, information, financial activities, and other services, not shown separately.
[2]Includes wholesale trade and transportation, warehousing, and utilities, not shown separately.
[3]Includes arts, entertainment, and recreation, not shown separately.
[4]Includes federal government, not shown separately.

Table 7-4. Job Openings Levels and Rates, by Industry, 2008–October 2019—*Continued*

(Seasonally adjusted, levels in thousands, rates per 100.)

Year and month	Rate											
	Total[1]	Total private[1]	Construction	Manufacturing	Trade, transportation, and utilities[2]	Retail trade	Professional and business services	Education and health services	Leisure and hospitality[3]	Accommodation and food services	Government[4]	State and local government
2008												
January	3.2	3.5	1.9	2.1	2.8	2.8	5.2	3.8	4.1	4.3	1.8	1.8
February	3.0	3.2	1.6	1.9	2.4	2.4	5.1	4.0	3.9	4.0	1.9	1.9
March	3.0	3.2	1.4	1.8	2.4	2.6	4.9	4.0	4.1	4.2	1.9	1.9
April	2.9	3.1	1.6	2.1	2.4	2.7	4.5	3.6	3.9	4.1	1.9	1.9
May	3.0	3.2	2.5	2.1	2.6	2.8	4.4	3.7	3.9	4.0	2.0	2.0
June	2.7	2.9	2.0	1.8	2.3	2.4	3.9	3.8	3.4	3.5	1.9	1.9
July	2.7	2.9	1.8	1.9	2.4	2.5	3.6	3.8	3.2	3.2	1.8	1.7
August	2.6	2.8	1.2	1.9	2.5	2.8	3.6	3.5	3.1	3.0	1.7	1.7
September	2.3	2.4	1.6	1.6	1.8	1.8	3.4	3.0	3.0	3.0	1.7	1.7
October	2.4	2.6	1.0	1.8	2.4	2.9	3.2	3.3	3.0	3.0	1.7	1.7
November	2.3	2.4	0.8	1.2	2.2	2.7	2.9	3.3	2.6	2.5	1.6	1.6
December	2.2	2.4	0.7	1.1	2.0	2.5	3.2	3.1	2.6	2.6	1.4	1.4
2009												
January	2.0	2.1	0.6	0.9	1.9	2.5	3.0	2.9	1.8	1.8	1.5	1.4
February	2.1	2.2	1.1	1.0	1.8	2.1	3.1	2.7	2.4	2.6	1.6	1.5
March	1.9	1.9	0.8	0.9	1.7	2.0	2.6	2.5	2.0	2.1	1.6	1.3
April	1.7	1.8	0.5	0.8	1.3	1.5	2.6	2.6	2.0	2.2	1.6	1.6
May	1.9	2.1	0.8	0.8	2.2	2.7	2.6	2.6	2.2	2.3	1.2	1.3
June	1.9	2.0	1.1	0.9	1.8	2.0	2.4	2.6	2.1	2.3	1.4	1.4
July	1.7	1.8	0.8	0.9	1.2	1.3	2.7	2.7	1.9	2.0	1.2	1.2
August	1.8	1.9	1.1	1.0	1.7	1.9	2.5	2.7	1.5	1.5	1.3	1.4
September	1.9	2.0	1.1	1.1	1.5	1.8	2.7	2.7	2.1	2.3	1.2	1.1
October	1.8	1.9	0.9	1.1	1.4	1.5	2.4	2.6	2.0	2.2	1.6	1.4
November	1.8	1.9	0.8	1.1	1.5	1.7	2.6	2.5	2.1	2.2	1.5	1.3
December	1.9	2.0	1.0	1.3	1.6	2.0	2.5	2.7	2.0	2.1	1.4	1.2
2010												
January	2.1	2.2	1.0	1.2	1.8	2.3	2.7	3.0	2.1	2.3	1.7	1.3
February	2.0	2.1	1.2	1.3	1.9	2.3	2.5	2.6	2.0	2.1	1.5	1.1
March	2.0	2.1	1.5	1.3	2.0	2.3	2.3	2.6	1.8	1.9	1.8	1.3
April	2.4	2.3	1.8	1.6	1.8	2.0	3.0	2.6	2.1	2.3	2.7	1.3
May	2.3	2.4	1.6	1.6	1.9	2.2	3.5	2.5	2.3	2.3	1.7	1.2
June	2.1	2.3	1.5	1.8	1.9	2.1	3.4	2.2	2.5	2.3	1.3	1.1
July	2.3	2.5	2.0	2.0	1.9	2.2	3.6	2.6	2.4	2.5	1.4	1.2
August	2.3	2.4	1.0	1.6	1.8	1.9	3.7	2.4	2.7	2.8	1.5	1.2
September	2.2	2.3	1.4	1.6	1.8	1.7	3.6	2.5	2.4	2.5	1.5	1.3
October	2.4	2.6	1.2	1.7	2.0	2.2	3.7	3.0	3.1	3.3	1.5	1.4
November	2.3	2.5	1.2	1.8	1.9	2.2	4.0	2.7	2.4	2.5	1.4	1.3
December	2.2	2.3	0.6	1.5	2.0	2.2	3.3	2.6	2.6	2.7	1.7	1.5
2011												
January	2.3	2.5	1.1	1.8	2.2	2.4	3.1	2.7	2.7	2.9	1.5	1.4
February	2.4	2.6	0.8	1.8	2.5	2.7	3.4	2.8	2.9	2.9	1.4	1.3
March	2.4	2.6	1.2	1.8	2.2	2.3	3.6	2.9	2.9	3.0	1.5	1.4
April	2.5	2.7	1.6	2.1	2.5	2.7	3.3	2.9	2.4	2.5	1.6	1.5
May	2.4	2.6	2.2	1.8	2.5	2.9	3.3	2.8	2.3	2.4	1.4	1.2
June	2.6	2.7	1.4	1.8	2.6	3.0	3.8	2.9	3.0	2.8	1.6	1.6
July	2.7	3.0	1.7	2.1	2.6	2.9	4.3	3.1	2.6	2.5	1.5	1.3
August	2.5	2.7	2.0	1.9	2.2	2.6	3.7	3.1	2.8	2.9	1.5	1.4
September	2.8	3.0	1.5	2.1	2.5	2.6	4.8	2.9	3.1	3.1	1.8	1.7
October	2.7	2.9	1.4	1.9	2.7	2.7	3.9	3.0	3.1	3.1	1.6	1.5
November	2.6	2.8	1.1	1.7	2.9	3.3	3.7	3.0	3.1	3.2	1.5	1.5
December	2.7	2.9	1.0	1.8	2.6	2.9	4.6	3.0	3.2	3.3	1.6	1.5
2012												
January	2.8	3.1	1.5	2.0	2.6	2.7	5.1	3.2	3.2	3.2	1.5	1.4
February	2.6	2.8	1.1	2.0	2.5	2.6	4.0	3.2	2.7	2.7	1.8	1.7
March	2.9	3.1	1.6	2.6	2.7	2.9	4.5	3.2	3.2	3.3	1.8	1.7
April	2.8	3.0	2.3	2.2	2.5	2.5	4.1	3.2	3.4	3.3	1.7	1.5
May	2.8	3.0	1.8	2.5	2.4	2.4	4.0	3.4	3.2	3.2	1.8	1.7
June	2.8	3.0	1.2	2.5	2.4	2.5	4.1	3.5	3.4	3.4	1.8	1.6
July	2.7	3.0	1.7	2.3	2.6	2.7	3.9	3.2	3.4	3.5	1.7	1.6
August	2.8	2.9	2.3	2.2	2.9	3.2	3.9	3.1	3.0	3.0	1.9	1.7
September	2.8	3.0	1.6	2.1	3.0	3.2	3.7	3.3	3.0	3.0	1.7	1.6
October	2.7	2.9	1.9	2.3	2.1	2.0	4.0	3.3	3.4	3.5	1.7	1.6
November	2.7	3.0	1.3	1.8	2.6	3.0	4.0	3.4	3.5	3.6	1.6	1.5
December	2.8	3.0	1.6	1.8	2.9	3.3	3.7	3.3	3.3	3.3	1.8	1.6
2013												
January	2.8	3.0	2.0	2.0	2.8	3.1	4.1	2.9	3.2	3.3	2.0	1.8
February	2.9	3.0	2.0	2.2	2.5	2.6	4.0	3.2	3.6	3.7	1.9	1.8
March	2.9	3.1	2.0	2.1	2.8	3.1	3.9	3.3	3.5	3.6	1.8	1.8
April	2.9	3.1	2.2	2.1	3.0	3.4	4.0	3.3	3.3	3.4	2.0	1.8
May	3.0	3.2	2.3	2.1	3.1	3.6	4.1	3.2	3.2	3.4	1.9	1.9
June	3.0	3.2	2.4	1.8	3.3	4.0	3.9	3.1	3.3	3.5	1.8	1.9
July	2.8	3.0	1.9	2.1	2.7	3.1	3.6	3.0	3.4	3.5	1.7	1.7
August	2.9	3.1	2.2	2.3	2.9	3.1	4.2	3.4	3.5	3.4	1.8	1.8
September	2.9	3.1	2.0	2.2	3.0	3.4	3.9	3.1	3.7	3.8	1.8	1.8
October	3.0	3.3	2.3	2.4	3.0	3.4	4.2	3.1	3.6	3.5	1.8	1.8
November	2.8	3.0	1.9	2.2	3.0	3.2	3.8	3.0	3.6	3.6	1.7	1.7
December	2.8	3.1	1.4	2.1	3.0	3.3	4.0	2.8	3.9	3.9	1.5	1.5

[1]Includes natural resources and mining, information, financial activities, and other services, not shown separately.
[2]Includes wholesale trade and transportation, warehousing, and utilities, not shown separately.
[3]Includes arts, entertainment, and recreation, not shown separately.
[4]Includes federal government, not shown separately.

Table 7-4. Job Openings Levels and Rates, by Industry, 2008–October 2019—*Continued*

(Seasonally adjusted, levels in thousands, rates per 100.)

Year and month	Level											
	Total nonfarm[1]	Total private[1]	Construction	Manufacturing	Trade, transportation, and utilities[2]	Retail trade	Professional and business services	Education and health services	Leisure and hospitality[3]	Accommodation and food services	Government[4]	State and local government
2014												
January	4 131	3 756	152	261	829	528	713	709	596	505	375	327
February	4 347	3 939	122	279	879	630	848	728	558	485	409	350
March	4 388	3 949	130	284	937	665	773	756	571	518	439	372
April	4 662	4 204	137	288	962	652	842	728	662	570	458	391
May	4 775	4 326	137	301	939	625	857	818	710	621	449	381
June	4 999	4 473	171	320	947	634	916	847	674	598	526	460
July	4 919	4 450	158	330	939	601	908	883	630	566	469	410
August	5 383	4 946	148	327	1 183	840	967	931	705	621	437	363
September	4 876	4 412	105	312	923	589	941	876	708	632	464	395
October	5 066	4 635	156	301	970	598	956	893	671	604	431	363
November	4 719	4 270	104	285	871	508	970	796	631	573	449	374
December	4 981	4 499	100	281	870	544	1 041	937	707	621	482	411
2015												
January	5 377	4 876	150	326	997	609	1 034	923	806	718	501	422
February	5 410	4 877	146	301	1 037	666	1 072	928	748	652	533	432
March	5 223	4 707	177	323	903	533	1 101	900	733	632	516	424
April	5 726	5 176	179	332	1 012	598	1 224	1 015	725	647	550	444
May	5 587	5 055	184	334	1 011	548	1 233	978	701	630	532	453
June	5 259	4 778	160	294	953	575	1 112	1 014	659	601	481	392
July	6 147	5 604	156	379	1 264	827	1 165	1 169	751	685	544	447
August	5 517	5 031	168	315	1 056	679	1 092	1 045	689	635	487	398
September	5 450	4 982	106	315	1 071	697	1 105	1 075	701	634	468	397
October	5 846	5 328	145	322	1 123	672	1 208	1 068	790	712	519	436
November	5 564	5 064	89	258	1 001	560	1 283	1 099	764	678	500	403
December	5 678	5 157	115	304	998	642	1 199	1 050	750	674	521	427
2016												
January	5 977	5 482	161	321	1 075	715	1 301	1 178	751	662	495	405
February	5 747	5 246	188	318	1 046	702	1 244	1 024	762	684	500	390
March	6 151	5 644	219	337	1 052	702	1 488	1 080	827	707	507	410
April	5 872	5 344	196	399	1 097	665	1 054	1 123	754	651	528	424
May	5 775	5 230	188	362	1 068	712	1 163	1 090	742	654	545	446
June	5 778	5 276	186	374	1 077	714	1 139	1 084	792	695	502	415
July	6 088	5 513	244	379	1 090	700	1 268	1 120	753	650	575	479
August	5 720	5 223	205	333	1 046	658	1 103	1 053	793	701	498	399
September	5 828	5 306	240	320	1 042	706	1 205	1 100	738	664	521	413
October	5 616	5 126	221	298	1 034	670	972	1 221	765	655	491	408
November	5 862	5 311	176	316	980	625	1 213	1 187	777	667	551	464
December	5 831	5 293	138	338	1 052	692	1 055	1 188	763	661	538	389
2017												
January	5 624	5 149	150	371	984	635	1 007	1 155	735	649	475	402
February	5 875	5 354	179	360	1 012	638	997	1 232	887	798	521	436
March	5 848	5 318	186	400	1 083	684	1 031	1 139	752	655	530	442
April	6 157	5 593	229	388	1 031	624	1 037	1 134	847	763	564	470
May	5 821	5 264	184	349	1 042	675	1 008	1 091	842	780	557	443
June	6 371	5 788	220	406	1 112	675	1 238	1 204	847	731	582	480
July	6 349	5 805	247	394	1 177	701	1 134	1 157	856	748	544	442
August	6 352	5 820	226	423	1 279	798	1 118	1 177	877	782	532	451
September	6 256	5 701	178	427	1 208	736	1 127	1 122	774	672	555	466
October	6 405	5 861	203	423	1 169	763	1 297	1 116	829	736	544	461
November	6 163	5 655	212	417	1 263	911	1 026	1 102	886	798	509	431
December	6 204	5 644	180	377	1 406	970	924	1 137	906	806	560	475
2018												
January	6 591	6 025	245	436	1 367	873	1 124	1 175	926	832	566	452
February	6 530	5 925	198	436	1 292	827	1 138	1 173	905	789	605	532
March	6 894	6 236	234	426	1 399	900	1 213	1 253	935	840	659	547
April	7 106	6 497	258	451	1 571	1 032	1 232	1 249	974	868	609	526
May	7 126	6 525	279	470	1 526	973	1 238	1 246	974	860	600	491
June	7 393	6 752	323	475	1 505	1 003	1 271	1 321	1 071	910	641	526
July	7 442	6 764	314	488	1 533	1 020	1 276	1 293	1 024	931	678	558
August	7 342	6 611	315	501	1 341	876	1 341	1 286	994	885	730	610
September	7 392	6 771	299	469	1 554	978	1 352	1 282	1 074	974	621	538
October	7 593	6 956	278	500	1 558	1 080	1 363	1 285	1 039	944	637	536
November	7 626	6 962	279	501	1 642	1 103	1 313	1 324	1 050	948	665	554
December	7 479	6 860	299	435	1 482	986	1 391	1 348	1 102	948	619	532
2019												
January	7 625	6 929	313	458	1 454	881	1 472	1 372	1 077	969	696	576
February	7 142	6 437	287	480	1 340	861	1 424	1 212	988	882	705	575
March	7 474	6 772	364	461	1 385	825	1 413	1 355	1 035	929	702	585
April	7 372	6 635	434	496	1 435	818	1 260	1 254	1 022	917	737	587
May	7 384	6 680	376	503	1 352	815	1 313	1 329	1 027	916	704	595
June	7 248	6 560	331	515	1 390	863	1 292	1 322	913	809	688	578
July	7 174	6 462	360	513	1 256	793	1 238	1 287	959	858	712	585
August	7 301	6 562	384	470	1 337	816	1 305	1 330	929	809	739	618
September	7 032	6 314	327	462	1 285	741	1 241	1 205	992	838	719	608
October	7 361	6 600	326	447	1 487	884	1 236	1 277	996	858	761	641

[1]Includes natural resources and mining, information, financial activities, and other services, not shown separately.
[2]Includes wholesale trade and transportation, warehousing, and utilities, not shown separately.
[3]Includes arts, entertainment, and recreation, not shown separately.
[4]Includes federal government, not shown separately.

Table 7-4. Job Openings Levels and Rates, by Industry, 2008–October 2019—*Continued*

(Seasonally adjusted, levels in thousands, rates per 100.)

Year and month	Rate											
	Total[1]	Total private[1]	Construction	Manufacturing	Trade, transportation, and utilities[2]	Retail trade	Professional and business services	Education and health services	Leisure and hospitality[3]	Accommodation and food services	Government[4]	State and local government
2014												
January	2.9	3.1	2.5	2.1	3.1	3.3	3.6	3.2	4.0	3.9	1.7	1.7
February	3.1	3.3	2.0	2.3	3.3	4.0	4.3	3.3	3.7	3.8	1.8	1.8
March	3.1	3.3	2.1	2.3	3.5	4.2	3.9	3.4	3.8	4.0	2.0	1.9
April	3.3	3.5	2.2	2.3	3.5	4.1	4.2	3.3	4.3	4.4	2.1	2.0
May	3.3	3.6	2.2	2.4	3.5	3.9	4.3	3.7	4.6	4.7	2.0	2.0
June	3.5	3.7	2.7	2.6	3.5	4.0	4.6	3.8	4.4	4.5	2.3	2.3
July	3.4	3.7	2.5	2.6	3.4	3.8	4.5	4.0	4.1	4.3	2.1	2.1
August	3.7	4.0	2.3	2.6	4.3	5.2	4.8	4.2	4.6	4.7	2.0	1.9
September	3.4	3.6	1.7	2.5	3.4	3.7	4.7	3.9	4.6	4.8	2.1	2.0
October	3.5	3.8	2.4	2.4	3.5	3.7	4.7	4.0	4.3	4.5	1.9	1.9
November	3.3	3.5	1.6	2.3	3.2	3.2	4.8	3.5	4.1	4.3	2.0	1.9
December	3.4	3.7	1.6	2.2	3.2	3.4	5.1	4.1	4.5	4.6	2.1	2.1
2015												
January	3.7	3.9	2.3	2.6	3.6	3.8	5.1	4.1	5.1	5.3	2.2	2.1
February	3.7	3.9	2.2	2.4	3.7	4.1	5.2	4.1	4.8	4.8	2.4	2.2
March	3.6	3.8	2.7	2.6	3.3	3.3	5.3	4.0	4.7	4.7	2.3	2.2
April	3.9	4.2	2.7	2.6	3.6	3.7	5.9	4.4	4.6	4.8	2.4	2.3
May	3.8	4.1	2.8	2.6	3.6	3.4	5.9	4.3	4.4	4.6	2.4	2.3
June	3.6	3.8	2.4	2.3	3.4	3.6	5.3	4.4	4.2	4.4	2.1	2.0
July	4.1	4.5	2.4	3.0	4.5	5.0	5.6	5.0	4.7	5.0	2.4	2.3
August	3.7	4.0	2.5	2.5	3.8	4.2	5.2	4.5	4.3	4.6	2.2	2.0
September	3.7	4.0	1.6	2.5	3.8	4.3	5.3	4.6	4.4	4.6	2.1	2.0
October	3.9	4.2	2.2	2.5	4.0	4.1	5.7	4.6	4.9	5.1	2.3	2.2
November	3.7	4.0	1.3	2.0	3.6	3.4	6.1	4.7	4.7	4.9	2.2	2.0
December	3.8	4.1	1.7	2.4	3.6	3.9	5.7	4.5	4.6	4.9	2.3	2.2
2016												
January	4.3	4.3	2.4	2.5	3.8	4.3	6.1	5.0	4.6	4.8	2.2	2.1
February	4.1	4.1	2.8	2.5	3.7	4.3	5.9	4.4	4.7	4.9	2.2	2.0
March	4.4	4.4	3.2	2.7	3.7	4.3	6.9	4.6	5.1	5.0	2.2	2.1
April	4.2	4.2	2.8	3.1	3.9	4.0	5.0	4.8	4.6	4.7	2.3	2.1
May	4.1	4.1	2.7	2.9	3.8	4.3	5.5	4.6	4.5	4.7	2.4	2.2
June	4.1	4.1	2.7	2.9	3.8	4.3	5.4	4.6	4.8	4.9	2.2	2.1
July	4.3	4.3	3.5	3.0	3.9	4.2	5.9	4.7	4.6	4.6	2.5	2.4
August	4.1	4.1	3.0	2.6	3.7	4.0	5.2	4.4	4.8	5.0	2.2	2.0
September	4.1	4.1	3.4	2.5	3.7	4.3	5.6	4.6	4.5	4.7	2.3	2.1
October	4.0	4.0	3.1	2.4	3.6	4.0	4.6	5.1	4.6	4.6	2.2	2.0
November	4.1	4.1	2.5	2.5	3.5	3.8	5.7	4.9	4.7	4.7	2.4	2.3
December	4.1	4.1	2.0	2.7	3.7	4.2	4.9	4.9	4.6	4.6	2.4	2.0
2017												
January	3.7	4.0	2.1	2.9	3.5	3.8	4.7	4.8	4.4	4.6	2.1	2.0
February	3.9	4.2	2.5	2.8	3.6	3.9	4.7	5.1	5.3	5.5	2.3	2.2
March	3.9	4.1	2.6	3.1	3.8	4.1	4.8	4.7	4.5	4.6	2.3	2.2
April	4.0	4.3	3.2	3.0	3.6	3.8	4.8	4.7	5.0	5.3	2.5	2.3
May	3.8	4.1	2.6	2.7	3.7	4.1	4.7	4.5	5.0	5.4	2.4	2.2
June	4.2	4.5	3.1	3.2	3.9	4.1	5.7	4.9	5.0	5.1	2.5	2.4
July	4.1	4.5	3.4	3.1	4.1	4.2	5.2	4.7	5.0	5.2	2.4	2.2
August	4.1	4.5	3.1	3.3	4.5	4.8	5.2	4.8	5.2	5.4	2.3	2.3
September	4.1	4.4	2.5	3.3	4.2	4.5	5.2	4.6	4.6	4.7	2.4	2.3
October	4.2	4.5	2.8	3.3	4.1	4.6	5.9	4.6	4.9	5.1	2.4	2.3
November	4.0	4.3	2.9	3.2	4.4	5.4	4.7	4.5	5.2	5.5	2.2	2.2
December	4.0	4.3	2.5	2.9	4.9	5.8	4.3	4.6	5.3	5.5	2.4	2.4
2018												
January	4.3	4.6	3.3	3.4	4.7	5.2	5.1	4.8	5.4	5.7	2.5	2.3
February	4.2	4.5	2.7	3.3	4.5	5.0	5.2	4.8	5.3	5.4	2.6	2.6
March	4.4	4.7	3.2	3.3	4.8	5.4	5.5	5.1	5.4	5.7	2.9	2.7
April	4.6	4.9	3.4	3.4	5.4	6.1	5.6	5.0	5.6	5.9	2.6	2.6
May	4.6	4.9	3.7	3.6	5.2	5.8	5.6	5.0	5.6	5.8	2.6	2.4
June	4.7	5.1	4.2	3.6	5.2	6.0	5.7	5.3	6.1	6.1	2.8	2.6
July	4.8	5.1	4.1	3.7	5.3	6.1	5.7	5.2	5.9	6.2	2.9	2.8
August	4.7	4.9	4.1	3.8	4.6	5.2	6.0	5.1	5.7	5.9	3.1	3.0
September	4.7	5.1	3.9	3.6	5.3	5.8	6.0	5.1	6.2	6.5	2.7	2.7
October	4.8	5.2	3.6	3.8	5.3	6.4	6.0	5.1	5.9	6.3	2.8	2.6
November	4.8	5.2	3.6	3.8	5.6	6.5	5.8	5.3	6.0	6.3	2.9	2.7
December	4.7	5.1	3.9	3.3	5.1	5.9	6.1	5.3	6.2	6.3	2.7	2.6
2019												
January	4.8	5.1	4.0	3.4	5.0	5.3	6.5	5.4	6.1	6.4	3.0	2.8
February	4.5	4.8	3.7	3.6	4.6	5.2	6.3	4.8	5.6	5.9	3.0	2.8
March	4.7	5.0	4.7	3.5	4.7	5.0	6.2	5.3	5.8	6.1	3.0	2.9
April	4.7	4.9	5.5	3.7	4.9	4.9	5.6	4.9	5.8	6.1	3.2	2.9
May	4.7	4.9	4.8	3.8	4.6	4.9	5.8	5.2	5.8	6.0	3.0	2.9
June	4.6	4.8	4.2	3.9	4.8	5.2	5.7	5.2	5.2	5.4	3.0	2.8
July	4.5	4.8	4.6	3.8	4.3	4.8	5.4	5.0	5.4	5.7	3.1	2.9
August	4.6	4.8	4.9	3.5	4.6	4.9	5.7	5.2	5.3	5.4	3.2	3.0
September	4.4	4.7	4.2	3.5	4.4	4.5	5.4	4.7	5.6	5.5	3.1	3.0
October	4.6	4.9	4.2	3.4	5.1	5.3	5.4	5.0	5.6	5.6	3.3	3.1

[1]Includes natural resources and mining, information, financial activities, and other services, not shown separately.
[2]Includes wholesale trade and transportation, warehousing, and utilities, not shown separately.
[3]Includes arts, entertainment, and recreation, not shown separately.
[4]Includes federal government, not shown separately.

Table 7-5. Hires Levels[1] and Rates,[2] by Industry, 2008–October 2019

(Seasonally adjusted, levels in thousands, rates per 100.)

Year and month	Level[3]											
	Total[4]	Total private[4]	Construction	Manufacturing	Trade, transportation, and utilities[5]	Retail trade	Professional and business services	Education and health services	Leisure and hospitality[6]	Accommodation and food services	Government[7]	State and local government
2008												
January	5 071	4 762	383	333	1 058	749	1 016	574	848	708	309	129
February	5 077	4 755	384	318	1 065	748	975	571	920	758	322	135
March	4 924	4 592	396	317	1 035	733	922	568	844	707	332	155
April	4 948	4 645	399	347	1 025	714	909	576	848	729	303	129
May	4 691	4 371	364	321	925	643	802	549	907	767	321	150
June	4 893	4 562	379	313	1 056	741	986	538	802	681	331	150
July	4 637	4 332	391	255	1 007	719	847	552	807	696	304	146
August	4 682	4 390	403	283	1 000	701	849	540	838	680	292	119
September	4 499	4 217	333	303	931	655	857	509	795	683	281	130
October	4 548	4 248	396	303	944	658	831	542	773	650	300	135
November	4 104	3 830	357	243	834	594	784	508	706	611	274	120
December	4 348	4 076	350	264	865	625	900	513	738	613	272	118
2009												
January	4 095	3 800	368	207	827	567	711	524	715	598	295	136
February	4 061	3 789	343	254	791	549	731	532	692	591	271	125
March	3 858	3 605	328	239	807	537	680	497	632	559	253	111
April	3 888	3 515	331	210	818	593	668	491	617	531	374	105
May	3 758	3 496	324	178	805	546	643	484	678	587	262	119
June	3 639	3 375	277	195	727	506	611	501	630	537	263	140
July	3 857	3 601	323	247	744	507	722	512	615	514	256	63
August	3 810	3 529	264	240	768	538	665	532	653	533	281	133
September	3 944	3 710	319	277	844	579	711	527	630	518	234	95
October	3 838	3 510	317	237	727	503	692	513	614	512	328	175
November	4 024	3 736	316	245	817	533	783	503	685	568	288	141
December	4 004	3 753	347	246	769	527	783	500	651	555	251	113
2010												
January	3 904	3 615	305	225	790	565	770	453	663	564	289	129
February	3 864	3 580	282	256	786	549	767	475	613	532	284	126
March	4 302	3 959	416	257	915	669	771	522	676	570	344	126
April	4 159	3 820	361	278	815	563	806	474	678	550	338	120
May	4 420	3 686	307	254	803	549	791	469	641	527	735	133
June	4 111	3 833	279	261	860	584	867	505	637	508	278	137
July	4 163	3 882	336	272	855	585	815	540	668	537	281	119
August	4 046	3 780	338	270	776	556	879	465	643	527	266	117
September	4 034	3 784	315	261	838	569	791	507	668	558	250	111
October	4 173	3 865	358	267	822	583	811	505	659	559	309	166
November	4 182	3 903	337	284	833	566	838	529	657	560	279	131
December	4 299	4 013	378	274	794	508	971	506	670	565	285	142
2011												
January	4 000	3 714	280	262	824	588	860	452	641	543	286	151
February	4 231	4 003	345	270	901	608	905	479	666	567	227	88
March	4 430	4 179	378	268	887	620	990	471	771	640	251	122
April	4 296	4 028	372	267	871	612	932	502	679	564	268	141
May	4 261	4 022	392	270	855	590	964	475	655	537	239	109
June	4 366	4 075	396	256	887	605	848	515	733	610	291	167
July	4 261	4 020	337	257	860	608	914	492	723	600	242	83
August	4 298	4 057	339	262	832	565	941	508	729	603	241	106
September	4 429	4 159	381	245	856	598	965	503	749	612	270	119
October	4 370	4 101	333	247	852	569	962	489	739	605	269	129
November	4 365	4 093	321	227	847	581	926	520	791	634	272	131
December	4 356	4 062	322	268	824	522	909	520	750	613	294	132
2012												
January	4 457	4 172	332	267	873	588	944	537	776	620	285	138
February	4 560	4 260	345	264	859	578	1 012	564	771	612	300	140
March	4 575	4 279	315	277	887	588	945	528	860	702	296	135
April	4 389	4 098	279	262	892	587	914	494	758	618	291	149
May	4 533	4 228	324	253	894	591	987	550	737	606	306	144
June	4 440	4 121	356	274	892	590	906	524	722	599	319	138
July	4 327	4 032	370	248	864	584	868	515	752	626	295	130
August	4 450	4 136	337	233	929	617	825	514	802	667	315	144
September	4 302	4 022	366	229	882	612	845	508	722	617	280	127
October	4 389	4 120	319	250	907	604	882	522	762	636	269	105
November	4 489	4 213	388	247	893	617	920	512	720	598	276	120
December	4 452	4 162	320	234	894	593	907	532	814	654	290	128
2013												
January	4 487	4 204	337	247	901	615	879	540	805	678	283	114
February	4 571	4 275	378	246	957	668	862	520	792	667	296	135
March	4 369	4 100	355	221	820	562	870	547	805	679	270	122
April	4 572	4 282	294	244	905	630	928	571	859	729	290	127
May	4 663	4 376	339	275	917	645	916	580	811	674	288	136
June	4 440	4 196	340	235	882	620	956	479	810	665	244	117
July	4 561	4 291	307	235	913	634	968	554	792	663	270	132
August	4 730	4 430	303	266	991	700	1 011	588	772	650	299	152
September	4 726	4 433	319	261	981	679	963	555	826	686	293	137
October	4 518	4 237	372	231	969	691	863	516	803	667	281	134
November	4 622	4 326	311	259	1 014	713	949	538	789	652	296	135
December	4 614	4 333	270	248	1 008	750	960	551	800	652	280	131

[1]Hires are the number of hires during the entire month.
[2]The hires rate is the number of hires during the entire month as a percent of total employment.
[3]Detail will not necessarily add to totals because of the independent seasonal adjustment of the various series.
[4]Includes natural resources and mining, information, financial activities, and other services, not shown separately.
[5]Includes wholesale trade and transportation, warehousing, and utilities, not shown separately.
[6]Includes arts, entertainment, and recreation, not shown separately.
[7]Includes federal government, not shown separately.
. . . = Not available.

Table 7-5. Hires Levels[1] and Rates,[2] by Industry, 2008–October 2019—*Continued*

(Seasonally adjusted, levels in thousands, rates per 100.)

Year and month	Rate											
	Total[4]	Total private[4]	Construction	Manufacturing	Trade, transportation, and utilities[5]	Retail trade	Professional and business services	Education and health services	Leisure and hospitality[6]	Accommodation and food services	Government[7]	State and local government
2008												
January	3.7	4.1	5.1	2.4	4.0	4.8	5.6	3.0	6.3	6.1	1.4	1.4
February	3.7	4.1	5.2	2.3	4.0	4.8	5.4	3.0	6.8	6.6	1.4	1.4
March	3.6	4.0	5.3	2.3	3.9	4.7	5.1	3.0	6.2	6.1	1.5	1.5
April	3.6	4.0	5.5	2.5	3.9	4.6	5.1	3.0	6.3	6.3	1.3	1.4
May	3.4	3.8	5.0	2.4	3.5	4.2	4.5	2.9	6.7	6.7	1.4	1.5
June	3.6	4.0	5.2	2.3	4.0	4.8	5.5	2.8	5.9	5.9	1.5	1.5
July	3.4	3.8	5.5	1.9	3.8	4.7	4.8	2.9	6.0	6.0	1.3	1.4
August	3.4	3.8	5.7	2.1	3.8	4.6	4.8	2.8	6.2	5.9	1.3	1.4
September	3.3	3.7	4.7	2.3	3.6	4.3	4.8	2.6	5.9	6.0	1.2	1.3
October	3.3	3.7	5.7	2.3	3.6	4.4	4.7	2.8	5.8	5.7	1.3	1.4
November	3.0	3.4	5.2	1.9	3.2	4.0	4.5	2.6	5.3	5.4	1.2	1.2
December	3.2	3.6	5.2	2.1	3.4	4.2	5.2	2.6	5.6	5.4	1.2	1.3
2009												
January	3.1	3.4	5.6	1.7	3.3	3.8	4.2	2.7	5.4	5.3	1.3	1.3
February	3.0	3.4	5.3	2.1	3.1	3.7	4.3	2.7	5.2	5.3	1.2	1.2
March	2.9	3.3	5.2	2.0	3.2	3.7	4.1	2.5	4.8	5.0	1.1	1.2
April	2.9	3.2	5.4	1.7	3.3	4.1	4.0	2.5	4.7	4.8	1.6	1.2
May	2.9	3.2	5.3	1.5	3.2	3.8	3.9	2.5	5.2	5.2	1.2	1.2
June	2.8	3.1	4.6	1.7	2.9	3.5	3.7	2.6	4.8	4.8	1.2	1.2
July	3.0	3.3	5.4	2.1	3.0	3.5	4.4	2.6	4.7	4.6	1.1	1.1
August	2.9	3.3	4.5	2.1	3.1	3.7	4.0	2.7	5.0	4.8	1.2	1.3
September	3.0	3.4	5.5	2.4	3.4	4.0	4.3	2.7	4.8	4.7	1.0	1.1
October	3.0	3.3	5.5	2.1	3.0	3.5	4.2	2.6	4.7	4.6	1.5	1.5
November	3.1	3.5	5.6	2.1	3.3	3.7	4.7	2.5	5.3	5.1	1.3	1.3
December	3.1	3.5	6.1	2.1	3.1	3.7	4.7	2.5	5.0	5.0	1.1	1.2
2010												
January	3.0	3.4	5.5	2.0	3.2	3.9	4.6	2.3	5.1	5.1	1.3	1.2
February	3.0	3.3	5.1	2.2	3.2	3.8	4.6	2.4	4.7	4.8	1.3	1.2
March	3.3	3.7	7.5	2.2	3.7	4.6	4.7	2.6	5.2	5.1	1.5	1.3
April	3.2	3.6	6.5	2.4	3.3	3.9	4.8	2.4	5.2	5.0	1.5	1.2
May	3.4	3.4	5.6	2.2	3.3	3.8	4.7	2.4	4.9	4.7	3.2	1.2
June	3.1	3.6	5.1	2.3	3.5	4.0	5.2	2.5	4.9	4.6	1.2	1.1
July	3.2	3.6	6.1	2.4	3.5	4.1	4.9	2.7	5.1	4.8	1.2	1.2
August	3.1	3.5	6.1	2.3	3.2	3.8	5.2	2.3	4.9	4.7	1.2	1.1
September	3.1	3.5	5.7	2.3	3.4	3.9	4.7	2.5	5.1	5.0	1.1	1.1
October	3.2	3.6	6.5	2.3	3.3	4.0	4.8	2.5	5.0	5.0	1.4	1.4
November	3.2	3.6	6.1	2.5	3.4	3.9	4.9	2.6	5.0	5.0	1.3	1.3
December	3.3	3.7	6.9	2.4	3.2	3.5	5.7	2.5	5.1	5.0	1.3	1.3
2011												
January	3.1	3.4	5.2	2.3	3.3	4.0	5.0	2.2	4.9	4.8	1.3	1.3
February	3.2	3.7	6.3	2.3	3.6	4.2	5.3	2.4	5.1	5.0	1.0	1.0
March	3.4	3.8	6.9	2.3	3.6	4.3	5.7	2.3	5.8	5.6	1.1	1.2
April	3.3	3.7	6.8	2.3	3.5	4.2	5.4	2.5	5.1	5.0	1.2	1.3
May	3.2	3.7	7.1	2.3	3.4	4.0	5.6	2.3	4.9	4.7	1.1	1.1
June	3.3	3.7	7.2	2.2	3.5	4.1	4.9	2.5	5.5	5.3	1.3	1.4
July	3.2	3.7	6.1	2.2	3.4	4.1	5.3	2.4	5.4	5.2	1.1	1.1
August	3.3	3.7	6.1	2.2	3.3	3.8	5.4	2.5	5.4	5.3	1.1	1.2
September	3.3	3.8	6.8	2.1	3.4	4.1	5.5	2.5	5.6	5.3	1.2	1.3
October	3.3	3.7	6.0	2.1	3.4	3.9	5.5	2.4	5.5	5.2	1.2	1.3
November	3.3	3.7	5.7	1.9	3.4	3.9	5.3	2.5	5.9	5.5	1.2	1.3
December	3.3	3.7	5.7	2.3	3.3	3.5	5.1	2.5	5.5	5.3	1.3	1.4
2012												
January	3.3	3.7	5.9	2.3	3.5	4.0	5.3	2.6	5.7	5.3	1.3	1.4
February	3.4	3.8	6.1	2.2	3.4	3.9	5.7	2.7	5.7	5.2	1.4	1.4
March	3.4	3.8	5.6	2.3	3.5	4.0	5.3	2.6	6.3	6.0	1.3	1.4
April	3.3	3.7	5.0	2.2	3.5	4.0	5.1	2.4	5.5	5.3	1.3	1.4
May	3.4	3.8	5.8	2.1	3.5	4.0	5.5	2.7	5.4	5.2	1.4	1.4
June	3.3	3.7	6.3	2.3	3.5	4.0	5.0	2.5	5.3	5.1	1.5	1.5
July	3.2	3.6	6.6	2.1	3.4	3.9	4.8	2.5	5.5	5.3	1.3	1.4
August	3.3	3.7	6.0	1.9	3.7	4.2	4.6	2.5	5.8	5.6	1.4	1.5
September	3.2	3.6	6.5	1.9	3.5	4.1	4.7	2.4	5.2	5.2	1.3	1.3
October	3.3	3.7	5.6	2.1	3.6	4.1	4.9	2.5	5.5	5.3	1.2	1.3
November	3.3	3.7	6.8	2.1	3.5	4.1	5.1	2.5	5.2	5.0	1.3	1.3
December	3.3	3.7	5.6	2.0	3.5	4.0	5.0	2.5	5.8	5.5	1.3	1.4
2013												
January	3.3	3.7	5.9	2.1	3.5	4.1	4.8	2.6	5.7	5.6	1.3	1.3
February	3.4	3.8	6.5	2.0	3.7	4.5	4.7	2.5	5.6	5.5	1.4	1.4
March	3.2	3.6	6.1	1.8	3.2	3.8	4.7	2.6	5.7	5.6	1.2	1.3
April	3.4	3.8	5.1	2.0	3.5	4.2	5.0	2.7	6.1	6.0	1.3	1.4
May	3.4	3.8	5.8	2.3	3.6	4.3	4.9	2.8	5.7	5.5	1.3	1.4
June	3.3	3.7	5.8	2.0	3.4	4.1	5.1	2.3	5.7	5.4	1.1	1.1
July	3.3	3.7	5.2	2.0	3.5	4.2	5.2	2.6	5.5	5.4	1.2	1.3
August	3.5	3.9	5.1	2.2	3.8	4.6	5.4	2.8	5.4	5.3	1.4	1.4
September	3.5	3.9	5.4	2.2	3.8	4.5	5.2	2.6	5.8	5.6	1.3	1.4
October	3.3	3.7	6.3	1.9	3.7	4.5	4.6	2.4	5.6	5.4	1.3	1.3
November	3.4	3.7	5.2	2.1	3.9	4.7	5.0	2.5	5.5	5.3	1.4	1.4
December	3.4	3.7	4.6	2.1	3.9	4.9	5.1	2.6	5.5	5.3	1.3	1.3

[1]Hires are the number of hires during the entire month.
[2]The hires rate is the number of hires during the entire month as a percent of total employment.
[3]Detail will not necessarily add to totals because of the independent seasonal adjustment of the various series.
[4]Includes natural resources and mining, information, financial activities, and other services, not shown separately.
[5]Includes wholesale trade and transportation, warehousing, and utilities, not shown separately.
[6]Includes arts, entertainment, and recreation, not shown separately.
[7]Includes federal government, not shown separately.
. . . = Not available.

Table 7-5. Hires Levels[1] and Rates,[2] by Industry, 2008–October 2019—*Continued*

(Seasonally adjusted, levels in thousands, rates per 100.)

Year and month	Level[3]											
	Total[4]	Total private[4]	Construction	Manufacturing	Trade, transportation, and utilities[5]	Retail trade	Professional and business services	Education and health services	Leisure and hospitality[6]	Accommodation and food services	Government[7]	State and local government
2014												
January	4 626	4 336	285	243	945	620	985	563	834	693	289	125
February	4 696	4 405	282	241	1 014	718	992	541	853	711	291	127
March	4 763	4 456	270	257	1 016	709	1 004	583	833	713	307	141
April	4 880	4 582	299	252	1 115	793	1 000	580	864	711	298	136
May	4 808	4 522	319	251	1 089	754	927	548	902	739	285	99
June	4 925	4 600	284	266	1 089	749	1 026	551	909	764	326	158
July	5 008	4 721	334	267	1 092	758	1 055	584	876	726	287	131
August	4 810	4 542	340	243	1 030	712	1 071	515	847	702	267	101
September	5 149	4 815	296	288	1 058	726	1 094	667	919	766	334	168
October	5 111	4 806	328	296	1 134	780	1 079	600	893	740	306	133
November	4 978	4 682	322	263	1 103	760	933	577	910	758	296	122
December	5 192	4 874	399	276	1 119	783	1 041	603	936	781	318	132
2015												
January	5 071	4 756	353	257	1 085	761	1 034	605	910	745	315	133
February	5 096	4 774	326	263	1 058	728	1 084	625	920	757	322	146
March	5 138	4 813	321	269	1 107	765	1 082	609	925	768	326	137
April	5 205	4 853	347	262	1 077	749	1 090	608	957	807	352	151
May	5 166	4 838	314	257	1 108	771	1 073	611	970	797	328	146
June	5 127	4 795	345	267	1 106	765	1 045	584	923	790	332	145
July	5 170	4 812	306	266	1 113	761	1 017	630	958	824	358	164
August	5 183	4 837	327	265	1 061	749	1 034	617	1 035	891	347	161
September	5 260	4 943	339	285	1 067	740	1 068	647	1 013	859	317	134
October	5 321	4 968	338	286	1 074	755	1 071	660	1 006	848	353	162
November	5 341	4 990	346	276	1 087	767	1 108	671	1 005	849	351	167
December	5 546	5 181	333	274	1 110	779	1 233	648	1 032	864	365	172
2016												
January	5 214	4 856	285	283	1 054	759	1 186	593	943	783	358	174
February	5 493	5 148	345	288	1 174	851	1 118	650	1 053	896	344	145
March	5 369	4 996	354	259	1 068	736	1 118	621	1 031	863	373	174
April	5 304	4 959	363	277	1 080	719	1 095	636	1 001	870	345	154
May	5 228	4 869	327	272	1 028	704	1 103	649	1 031	873	359	163
June	5 288	4 930	284	280	1 063	730	1 070	657	1 051	878	357	160
July	5 427	5 033	348	278	1 085	755	1 184	638	1 042	871	394	195
August	5 321	4 973	342	261	1 089	729	1 099	648	1 054	881	348	137
September	5 273	4 906	322	283	1 106	761	1 093	649	960	827	366	166
October	5 177	4 849	356	285	1 080	740	1 035	640	971	812	328	117
November	5 320	4 995	341	286	1 019	666	1 112	655	1 062	899	326	135
December	5 408	5 082	454	304	1 028	697	1 119	643	1 028	857	326	142
2017												
January	5 528	5 177	395	309	1 055	707	1 151	639	1 037	877	352	163
February	5 313	4 963	361	296	1 100	757	1 052	628	1 005	838	349	157
March	5 389	5 048	383	329	1 073	739	1 051	669	1 007	879	341	155
April	5 292	4 955	397	322	1 000	675	1 011	671	1 018	841	337	152
May	5 469	5 123	390	333	1 063	730	1 097	680	1 000	839	346	151
June	5 652	5 304	379	339	1 108	759	1 244	646	1 051	869	348	135
July	5 510	5 173	370	329	1 015	678	1 170	684	1 033	830	337	149
August	5 548	5 205	391	365	1 016	681	1 155	698	1 010	841	343	149
September	5 395	5 049	405	330	1 028	673	1 145	646	984	820	346	142
October	5 587	5 241	402	345	1 030	686	1 155	675	1 043	860	346	160
November	5 486	5 122	360	346	1 070	721	1 115	700	1 012	839	364	167
December	5 488	5 133	327	353	1 098	697	1 091	681	1 014	855	355	167
2018												
January	5 525	5 194	354	365	1 132	763	1 092	693	1 014	840	330	149
February	5 594	5 243	391	371	1 087	718	1 171	668	1 040	856	351	163
March	5 625	5 282	362	364	1 106	742	1 175	701	1 040	848	344	153
April	5 694	5 334	367	367	1 136	772	1 157	680	1 070	880	359	158
May	5 862	5 510	397	374	1 133	753	1 175	679	1 114	921	352	157
June	5 833	5 460	378	370	1 140	765	1 212	695	1 078	888	373	175
July	5 833	5 443	387	393	1 141	779	1 162	688	1 136	944	390	169
August	5 826	5 435	386	368	1 232	819	1 117	683	1 081	897	391	196
September	5 670	5 327	378	336	1 158	797	1 129	669	1 086	909	343	158
October	5 877	5 515	363	382	1 225	785	1 200	715	1 114	923	362	170
November	5 821	5 447	393	368	1 183	744	1 136	692	1 085	905	375	178
December	5 717	5 353	399	351	1 176	802	1 144	717	1 037	883	364	176
2019												
January	5 829	5 434	433	377	1 127	748	1 120	724	1 116	935	395	184
February	5 695	5 333	367	351	1 143	744	1 175	715	1 079	901	362	169
March	5 697	5 345	364	357	1 094	725	1 173	720	1 106	935	352	170
April	5 991	5 613	420	367	1 146	756	1 253	726	1 129	968	379	171
May	5 760	5 398	387	340	1 161	770	1 172	675	1 100	933	361	171
June	5 716	5 377	413	336	1 177	798	1 112	676	1 114	986	339	166
July	5 978	5 620	374	338	1 233	804	1 180	750	1 150	995	358	172
August	5 884	5 489	414	337	1 173	782	1 163	686	1 135	973	396	169
September	5 951	5 596	451	338	1 197	788	1 209	719	1 150	984	355	154
October	5 782	5 426	488	321	1 114	712	1 143	712	1 098	937	356	157

[1]Hires are the number of hires during the entire month.
[2]The hires rate is the number of hires during the entire month as a percent of total employment.
[3]Detail will not necessarily add to totals because of the independent seasonal adjustment of the various series.
[4]Includes natural resources and mining, information, financial activities, and other services, not shown separately.
[5]Includes wholesale trade and transportation, warehousing, and utilities, not shown separately.
[6]Includes arts, entertainment, and recreation, not shown separately.
[7]Includes federal government, not shown separately.
. . . = Not available.

Table 7-5. Hires Levels[1] and Rates,[2] by Industry, 2008–October 2019—*Continued*

(Seasonally adjusted, levels in thousands, rates per 100.)

Year and month	Rate											
	Total[4]	Total private[4]	Construction	Manufacturing	Trade, transportation, and utilities[5]	Retail trade	Professional and business services	Education and health services	Leisure and hospitality[6]	Accommodation and food services	Government[7]	State and local government
2014												
January	3.4	3.7	4.8	2.0	3.6	4.1	5.2	2.7	5.8	5.6	1.3	1.4
February	3.4	3.8	4.7	2.0	3.9	4.7	5.2	2.5	5.9	5.7	1.3	1.4
March	3.5	3.8	4.5	2.1	3.9	4.6	5.3	2.7	5.7	5.7	1.4	1.5
April	3.5	3.9	4.9	2.1	4.3	5.2	5.3	2.7	5.9	5.7	1.4	1.4
May	3.5	3.9	5.2	2.1	4.2	4.9	4.9	2.6	6.1	5.9	1.3	1.3
June	3.5	3.9	4.6	2.2	4.1	4.9	5.4	2.6	6.2	6.1	1.5	1.5
July	3.6	4.0	5.4	2.2	4.1	4.9	5.5	2.7	6.0	5.8	1.3	1.4
August	3.5	3.9	5.5	2.0	3.9	4.6	5.6	2.4	5.8	5.6	1.2	1.3
September	3.7	4.1	4.7	2.4	4.0	4.7	5.7	3.1	6.2	6.1	1.5	1.6
October	3.7	4.1	5.2	2.4	4.3	5.0	5.6	2.8	6.0	5.8	1.4	1.4
November	3.6	4.0	5.1	2.1	4.2	4.9	4.8	2.7	6.1	6.0	1.4	1.4
December	3.7	4.1	6.3	2.2	4.2	5.0	5.4	2.8	6.3	6.1	1.4	1.5
2015												
January	3.6	4.0	5.6	2.1	4.1	4.9	5.3	2.8	6.1	5.8	1.4	1.5
February	3.6	4.0	5.1	2.1	4.0	4.7	5.6	2.9	6.1	5.9	1.5	1.5
March	3.6	4.0	5.1	2.2	4.1	4.9	5.5	2.8	6.2	6.0	1.5	1.5
April	3.7	4.1	5.4	2.1	4.0	4.8	5.6	2.8	6.4	6.3	1.6	1.6
May	3.6	4.0	4.9	2.1	4.1	4.9	5.5	2.8	6.4	6.2	1.5	1.5
June	3.6	4.0	5.4	2.2	4.1	4.9	5.3	2.7	6.1	6.1	1.5	1.6
July	3.6	4.0	4.7	2.2	4.1	4.9	5.2	2.9	6.3	6.3	1.6	1.7
August	3.6	4.0	5.0	2.2	3.9	4.8	5.2	2.8	6.8	6.8	1.6	1.6
September	3.7	4.1	5.2	2.3	4.0	4.7	5.4	2.9	6.6	6.6	1.4	1.5
October	3.7	4.1	5.2	2.3	4.0	4.8	5.4	3.0	6.6	6.5	1.6	1.7
November	3.7	4.1	5.2	2.2	4.0	4.9	5.6	3.0	6.5	6.4	1.6	1.6
December	3.9	4.3	5.0	2.2	4.1	5.0	6.2	2.9	6.7	6.5	1.7	1.7
2016												
January	3.6	4.0	4.3	2.3	3.9	4.8	5.9	2.7	6.1	5.9	1.6	1.7
February	3.8	4.2	5.2	2.3	4.3	5.4	5.6	2.9	6.8	6.7	1.6	1.6
March	3.7	4.1	5.3	2.1	3.9	4.7	5.6	2.8	6.6	6.5	1.7	1.7
April	3.7	4.1	5.4	2.2	4.0	4.5	5.5	2.8	6.4	6.5	1.6	1.6
May	3.6	4.0	4.9	2.2	3.8	4.5	5.5	2.9	6.6	6.5	1.6	1.7
June	3.7	4.0	4.2	2.3	3.9	4.6	5.3	2.9	6.7	6.6	1.6	1.7
July	3.8	4.1	5.2	2.2	4.0	4.8	5.9	2.8	6.6	6.5	1.8	1.9
August	3.7	4.1	5.1	2.1	4.0	4.6	5.5	2.9	6.7	6.6	1.6	1.6
September	3.6	4.0	4.8	2.3	4.1	4.8	5.4	2.9	6.1	6.1	1.6	1.7
October	3.6	3.9	5.2	2.3	4.0	4.7	5.1	2.8	6.2	6.0	1.5	1.5
November	3.7	4.1	5.0	2.3	3.7	4.2	5.5	2.9	6.7	6.6	1.5	1.5
December	3.7	4.1	6.6	2.5	3.8	4.4	5.5	2.8	6.5	6.3	1.5	1.5
2017												
January	3.8	4.2	5.8	2.5	3.9	4.4	5.7	2.8	6.5	6.5	1.6	1.6
February	3.6	4.0	5.2	2.4	4.0	4.8	5.2	2.7	6.3	6.2	1.6	1.6
March	3.7	4.1	5.5	2.7	3.9	4.7	5.2	2.9	6.3	6.4	1.5	1.6
April	3.6	4.0	5.7	2.6	3.7	4.3	5.0	2.9	6.4	6.1	1.5	1.6
May	3.7	4.1	5.6	2.7	3.9	4.6	5.4	2.9	6.2	6.1	1.6	1.6
June	3.9	4.3	5.4	2.7	4.0	4.8	6.1	2.8	6.5	6.3	1.6	1.6
July	3.8	4.2	5.3	2.6	3.7	4.3	5.7	2.9	6.4	6.0	1.5	1.6
August	3.8	4.2	5.6	2.9	3.7	4.3	5.6	3.0	6.3	6.1	1.5	1.6
September	3.7	4.1	5.8	2.6	3.7	4.3	5.6	2.8	6.1	6.0	1.5	1.6
October	3.8	4.2	5.7	2.8	3.8	4.3	5.6	2.9	6.5	6.2	1.5	1.6
November	3.7	4.1	5.1	2.8	3.9	4.6	5.4	3.0	6.3	6.1	1.6	1.7
December	3.7	4.1	4.6	2.8	4.0	4.4	5.3	2.9	6.3	6.2	1.6	1.7
2018												
January	3.7	4.1	5.0	2.9	4.1	4.8	5.3	3.0	6.3	6.1	1.5	1.5
February	3.8	4.2	5.4	2.9	3.9	4.5	5.6	2.8	6.4	6.2	1.6	1.6
March	3.8	4.2	5.0	2.9	4.0	4.7	5.6	3.0	6.4	6.1	1.5	1.6
April	3.8	4.2	5.1	2.9	4.1	4.9	5.5	2.9	6.6	6.3	1.6	1.6
May	3.9	4.4	5.5	3.0	4.1	4.8	5.6	2.9	6.8	6.6	1.6	1.7
June	3.9	4.3	5.2	2.9	4.1	4.8	5.8	2.9	6.6	6.4	1.7	1.7
July	3.9	4.3	5.3	3.1	4.1	4.9	5.5	2.9	6.9	6.7	1.7	1.8
August	3.9	4.3	5.3	2.9	4.4	5.2	5.3	2.9	6.6	6.4	1.7	1.8
September	3.8	4.2	5.1	2.6	4.2	5.0	5.3	2.8	6.6	6.5	1.5	1.6
October	3.9	4.3	4.9	3.0	4.4	5.0	5.7	3.0	6.8	6.6	1.6	1.7
November	3.9	4.3	5.3	2.9	4.3	4.7	5.4	2.9	6.6	6.4	1.7	1.7
December	3.8	4.2	5.4	2.7	4.2	5.1	5.4	3.0	6.3	6.3	1.6	1.7
2019												
January	3.9	4.2	5.8	2.9	4.0	4.7	5.3	3.0	6.7	6.6	1.8	1.8
February	3.8	4.2	4.9	2.7	4.1	4.7	5.5	3.0	6.5	6.4	1.6	1.7
March	3.8	4.2	4.9	2.8	3.9	4.6	5.5	3.0	6.6	6.6	1.6	1.6
April	4.0	4.4	5.6	2.9	4.1	4.8	5.9	3.0	6.8	6.8	1.7	1.7
May	3.8	4.2	5.2	2.6	4.2	4.9	5.5	2.8	6.6	6.6	1.6	1.7
June	3.8	4.2	5.5	2.6	4.2	5.1	5.2	2.8	6.7	6.9	1.5	1.6
July	3.9	4.4	5.0	2.6	4.4	5.1	5.5	3.1	6.9	7.0	1.6	1.6
August	3.9	4.3	5.5	2.6	4.2	5.0	5.4	2.8	6.8	6.8	1.7	1.6
September	3.9	4.3	6.0	2.6	4.3	5.0	5.6	2.9	6.9	6.9	1.6	1.6
October	3.8	4.2	6.5	2.5	4.0	4.5	5.3	2.9	6.5	6.5	1.6	1.6

1Hires are the number of hires during the entire month.
2The hires rate is the number of hires during the entire month as a percent of total employment.
3Detail will not necessarily add to totals because of the independent seasonal adjustment of the various series.
4Includes natural resources and mining, information, financial activities, and other services, not shown separately.
5Includes wholesale trade and transportation, warehousing, and utilities, not shown separately.
6Includes arts, entertainment, and recreation, not shown separately.
7Includes federal government, not shown separately.
. . . = Not available.

Table 7-6. Separations Levels[1] and Rates,[2] by Industry, 2008–October 2019

(Seasonally adjusted, levels in thousands, rates per 100.)

Year and month	Level[3]											
	Total[4]	Total private[4]	Construction	Manufacturing	Trade, transportation, and utilities[5]	Retail trade	Professional and business services	Education and health services	Leisure and hospitality[6]	Accommodation and food services	Government[7]	State and local government
2008												
January	5 194	4 889	420	367	1 120	780	1 022	524	880	737	305	259
February	5 184	4 894	403	361	1 084	761	1 045	531	936	783	290	256
March	4 910	4 616	423	362	1 028	731	934	521	837	701	294	270
April	5 182	4 878	475	407	1 095	779	973	520	847	725	304	279
May	4 840	4 556	407	359	1 017	718	862	492	890	744	284	262
June	5 043	4 760	450	384	1 115	796	1 002	486	831	703	283	260
July	4 868	4 606	462	324	1 079	762	899	500	833	713	263	244
August	5 014	4 714	450	336	1 107	775	938	506	877	710	300	279
September	4 901	4 613	400	381	1 051	725	922	479	845	713	288	268
October	4 977	4 676	466	399	1 065	732	935	509	795	683	300	270
November	4 787	4 513	494	368	1 005	704	954	455	742	652	274	251
December	4 879	4 607	445	412	1 049	715	961	481	767	645	272	246
2009												
January	4 925	4 644	502	487	1 002	651	875	495	742	627	281	260
February	4 824	4 529	454	429	934	624	943	509	733	636	294	277
March	4 693	4 427	474	427	970	625	818	486	700	613	266	244
April	4 695	4 419	476	403	985	677	858	484	697	589	275	254
May	4 184	3 859	383	370	874	571	705	404	641	564	326	242
June	4 226	3 908	388	355	786	536	734	478	690	562	319	244
July	4 256	3 959	423	309	858	562	739	494	645	528	297	271
August	3 992	3 725	336	283	793	535	685	502	681	560	267	242
September	4 123	3 820	386	305	917	618	697	491	606	528	303	282
October	4 003	3 740	381	284	829	567	682	469	636	516	263	225
November	3 983	3 702	332	259	822	535	746	458	685	573	281	246
December	4 103	3 813	374	250	877	567	714	470	676	568	290	256
2010												
January	3 989	3 703	393	245	757	504	757	451	675	566	286	264
February	3 978	3 675	355	267	801	552	761	458	620	549	303	272
March	4 072	3 769	361	263	863	636	760	459	644	537	303	268
April	3 948	3 641	350	246	801	573	738	467	639	535	307	260
May	3 911	3 600	347	221	778	536	759	422	622	522	311	254
June	4 308	3 756	297	245	826	586	798	489	658	508	552	274
July	4 299	3 859	347	259	841	579	797	507	706	529	440	256
August	4 067	3 642	334	271	756	540	837	453	603	490	425	280
September	4 047	3 643	335	242	791	540	775	498	618	513	404	297
October	3 883	3 622	346	264	763	539	754	430	647	525	262	222
November	4 041	3 746	329	258	821	581	771	474	663	558	295	267
December	4 143	3 844	393	261	781	524	877	492	626	528	299	273
2011												
January	4 045	3 759	325	245	815	527	849	449	649	533	286	258
February	4 014	3 742	317	243	825	576	836	469	629	548	272	247
March	4 109	3 835	337	249	826	593	903	443	689	566	274	249
April	3 994	3 700	371	242	762	550	869	445	623	522	294	263
May	4 179	3 877	366	258	836	590	903	451	675	547	302	275
June	4 168	3 899	412	241	811	569	840	484	693	578	270	237
July	4 180	3 866	327	238	807	559	893	451	711	589	314	288
August	4 189	3 897	341	240	827	583	888	488	705	579	293	263
September	4 213	3 927	347	232	831	581	907	428	734	590	286	256
October	4 147	3 887	319	235	821	553	930	455	661	542	260	234
November	4 237	3 933	317	236	814	567	919	472	747	599	305	272
December	4 090	3 769	296	237	820	540	785	480	720	589	320	292
2012												
January	4 195	3 901	324	241	821	546	843	514	717	580	294	267
February	4 322	4 017	336	245	818	576	961	489	735	585	305	274
March	4 257	3 947	310	239	839	563	900	480	759	615	310	283
April	4 329	4 013	292	248	864	574	873	488	742	599	316	283
May	4 430	4 099	338	232	855	592	955	506	737	603	331	300
June	4 383	4 086	358	265	885	607	861	541	729	613	297	269
July	4 178	3 880	369	228	849	585	810	470	727	612	298	265
August	4 338	4 034	328	235	922	629	803	510	731	612	304	276
September	4 100	3 834	352	225	862	587	827	440	671	564	266	236
October	4 260	3 958	296	240	879	586	842	496	731	606	302	270
November	4 303	4 011	372	249	816	544	894	495	693	578	292	257
December	4 117	3 827	273	227	872	617	807	476	741	597	290	256
2013												
January	4 381	4 082	332	235	921	630	819	530	755	640	298	268
February	4 257	3 966	331	236	889	617	772	524	744	629	291	260
March	4 215	3 918	336	217	843	580	811	484	756	639	296	267
April	4 424	4 127	305	248	867	613	882	538	810	679	297	270
May	4 433	4 136	296	267	880	605	873	567	754	624	297	259
June	4 313	4 027	330	236	812	575	921	502	754	629	287	258
July	4 459	4 168	303	265	898	594	890	544	761	625	291	261
August	4 522	4 249	282	235	933	666	997	532	732	609	273	240
September	4 521	4 236	286	234	917	654	928	537	826	684	285	257
October	4 354	4 060	340	207	952	663	849	503	757	639	294	256
November	4 332	4 049	281	230	958	693	905	493	748	613	283	259
December	4 387	4 087	290	235	894	648	905	538	757	630	299	269

[1]Total separations are the number of separations during the entire month.
[2]The total separations rate is the number of total separations during the entire month as a percent of total employment.
[3]Detail will not necessarily add to totals because of the independent seasonal adjustment of the various series.
[4]Includes natural resources and mining, information, financial activities, and other services, not shown separately.
[5]Includes wholesale trade and transportation, warehousing, and utilities, not shown separately.
[6]Includes arts, entertainment, and recreation, not shown separately.
[7]Includes federal government, not shown separately.

Table 7-6. Separations Levels[1] and Rates,[2] by Industry, 2008–October 2019—*Continued*

(Seasonally adjusted, levels in thousands, rates per 100.)

Year and month	Rate											
	Total[4]	Total private[4]	Construction	Manufacturing	Trade, transportation, and utilities[5]	Retail trade	Professional and business services	Education and health services	Leisure and hospitality[6]	Accommodation and food services	Government[7]	State and local government
2008												
January	3.8	4.2	5.6	2.7	4.2	5.0	5.7	2.8	6.5	6.4	1.4	1.3
February	3.7	4.2	5.4	2.6	4.1	4.9	5.8	2.8	6.9	6.8	1.3	1.3
March	3.6	4.0	5.7	2.7	3.9	4.7	5.2	2.7	6.2	6.1	1.3	1.4
April	3.8	4.2	6.5	3.0	4.1	5.0	5.4	2.7	6.3	6.3	1.4	1.4
May	3.5	3.9	5.6	2.6	3.9	4.7	4.8	2.6	6.6	6.5	1.3	1.3
June	3.7	4.1	6.2	2.8	4.2	5.2	5.6	2.5	6.2	6.1	1.3	1.3
July	3.5	4.0	6.5	2.4	4.1	5.0	5.0	2.6	6.2	6.2	1.2	1.2
August	3.7	4.1	6.3	2.5	4.2	5.1	5.3	2.6	6.5	6.2	1.3	1.4
September	3.6	4.0	5.7	2.9	4.0	4.8	5.2	2.5	6.3	6.2	1.3	1.4
October	3.7	4.1	6.7	3.0	4.1	4.8	5.3	2.6	6.0	6.0	1.3	1.4
November	3.5	4.0	7.2	2.8	3.9	4.7	5.5	2.3	5.6	5.7	1.2	1.3
December	3.6	4.1	6.6	3.2	4.1	4.8	5.6	2.5	5.8	5.7	1.2	1.2
2009												
January	3.7	4.2	7.7	3.9	3.9	4.4	5.1	2.5	5.6	5.6	1.2	1.3
February	3.6	4.1	7.0	3.5	3.7	4.2	5.6	2.6	5.6	5.7	1.3	1.4
March	3.5	4.0	7.5	3.5	3.9	4.3	4.9	2.5	5.3	5.5	1.2	1.2
April	3.6	4.0	7.7	3.3	3.9	4.7	5.2	2.5	5.3	5.3	1.2	1.3
May	3.2	3.5	6.3	3.1	3.5	3.9	4.2	2.1	4.9	5.0	1.4	1.2
June	3.2	3.6	6.4	3.0	3.2	3.7	4.4	2.4	5.3	5.0	1.4	1.2
July	3.3	3.7	7.1	2.7	3.5	3.9	4.5	2.5	4.9	4.7	1.3	1.4
August	3.1	3.5	5.7	2.4	3.2	3.7	4.2	2.5	5.2	5.0	1.2	1.2
September	3.2	3.5	6.7	2.6	3.7	4.3	4.2	2.5	4.6	4.7	1.3	1.4
October	3.1	3.5	6.7	2.5	3.4	3.9	4.1	2.4	4.9	4.7	1.2	1.1
November	3.1	3.4	5.8	2.3	3.4	3.7	4.5	2.3	5.3	5.2	1.2	1.2
December	3.2	3.6	6.6	2.2	3.6	4.0	4.3	2.4	5.2	5.1	1.3	1.3
2010												
January	3.1	3.5	7.0	2.1	3.1	3.5	4.6	2.3	5.2	5.1	1.3	1.3
February	3.1	3.4	6.5	2.3	3.3	3.8	4.6	2.3	4.8	5.0	1.3	1.4
March	3.1	3.5	6.5	2.3	3.5	4.4	4.6	2.3	5.0	4.9	1.3	1.4
April	3.0	3.4	6.3	2.1	3.3	4.0	4.4	2.3	4.9	4.8	1.4	1.3
May	3.0	3.3	6.3	1.9	3.2	3.7	4.5	2.1	4.8	4.7	1.4	1.3
June	3.3	3.5	5.4	2.1	3.4	4.1	4.8	2.5	5.0	4.6	2.4	1.4
July	3.3	3.6	6.3	2.2	3.4	4.0	4.8	2.5	5.4	4.8	2.0	1.3
August	3.1	3.4	6.1	2.3	3.1	3.7	5.0	2.3	4.6	4.4	1.9	1.4
September	3.1	3.4	6.1	2.1	3.2	3.7	4.6	2.5	4.7	4.6	1.8	1.5
October	3.0	3.3	6.3	2.3	3.1	3.7	4.5	2.1	4.9	4.7	1.2	1.1
November	3.1	3.5	6.0	2.2	3.3	4.0	4.5	2.4	5.1	5.0	1.3	1.4
December	3.2	3.5	7.2	2.2	3.2	3.6	5.1	2.4	4.8	4.7	1.3	1.4
2011												
January	3.1	3.5	6.0	2.1	3.3	3.6	5.0	2.2	4.9	4.7	1.3	1.3
February	3.1	3.4	5.8	2.1	3.3	4.0	4.9	2.3	4.8	4.9	1.2	1.3
March	3.1	3.5	6.2	2.1	3.3	4.1	5.2	2.2	5.2	5.0	1.2	1.3
April	3.0	3.4	6.8	2.1	3.1	3.8	5.0	2.2	4.7	4.6	1.3	1.4
May	3.2	3.5	6.6	2.2	3.3	4.0	5.2	2.2	5.1	4.8	1.4	1.4
June	3.2	3.6	7.4	2.1	3.2	3.9	4.8	2.4	5.2	5.1	1.2	1.2
July	3.2	3.5	5.9	2.0	3.2	3.8	5.1	2.2	5.3	5.2	1.4	1.5
August	3.2	3.5	6.1	2.0	3.3	4.0	5.1	2.4	5.3	5.1	1.3	1.4
September	3.2	3.6	6.2	2.0	3.3	3.9	5.2	2.1	5.5	5.1	1.3	1.3
October	3.1	3.5	5.7	2.0	3.3	3.8	5.3	2.2	4.9	4.7	1.2	1.2
November	3.2	3.6	5.7	2.0	3.2	3.8	5.2	2.3	5.5	5.2	1.4	1.4
December	3.1	3.4	5.3	2.0	3.3	3.7	4.4	2.3	5.3	5.1	1.5	1.5
2012												
January	3.1	3.5	5.8	2.0	3.2	3.7	4.8	2.5	5.3	5.0	1.3	1.4
February	3.2	3.6	6.0	2.1	3.2	3.9	5.4	2.4	5.4	5.0	1.4	1.4
March	3.2	3.5	5.5	2.0	3.3	3.8	5.0	2.3	5.5	5.2	1.4	1.5
April	3.2	3.6	5.2	2.1	3.4	3.9	4.9	2.4	5.4	5.1	1.4	1.5
May	3.3	3.7	6.0	1.9	3.4	4.0	5.3	2.4	5.4	5.1	1.5	1.6
June	3.3	3.6	6.4	2.2	3.5	4.1	4.8	2.6	5.3	5.2	1.4	1.4
July	3.1	3.5	6.6	1.9	3.3	3.9	4.5	2.3	5.3	5.2	1.4	1.4
August	3.2	3.6	5.8	2.0	3.6	4.2	4.4	2.5	5.3	5.2	1.4	1.4
September	3.0	3.4	6.2	1.9	3.4	3.9	4.6	2.1	4.8	4.7	1.2	1.2
October	3.2	3.5	5.2	2.0	3.4	3.9	4.6	2.4	5.3	5.1	1.4	1.4
November	3.2	3.6	6.5	2.1	3.2	3.6	4.9	2.4	5.0	4.8	1.3	1.3
December	3.0	3.4	4.8	1.9	3.4	4.1	4.4	2.3	5.3	5.0	1.3	1.3
2013												
January	3.2	3.6	5.8	2.0	3.6	4.2	4.5	2.5	5.4	5.3	1.4	1.4
February	3.1	3.5	5.7	2.0	3.5	4.1	4.2	2.5	5.3	5.2	1.3	1.4
March	3.1	3.4	5.8	1.8	3.3	3.9	4.4	2.3	5.4	5.3	1.4	1.4
April	3.3	3.6	5.3	2.1	3.4	4.1	4.8	2.6	5.7	5.6	1.4	1.4
May	3.3	3.6	5.1	2.2	3.4	4.0	4.7	2.7	5.3	5.1	1.4	1.4
June	3.2	3.5	5.6	2.0	3.2	3.8	5.0	2.4	5.3	5.1	1.3	1.4
July	3.3	3.6	5.2	2.2	3.5	3.9	4.8	2.6	5.3	5.1	1.3	1.4
August	3.3	3.7	4.8	2.0	3.6	4.4	5.3	2.5	5.1	5.0	1.3	1.3
September	3.3	3.7	4.8	1.9	3.5	4.3	5.0	2.5	5.8	5.6	1.3	1.3
October	3.2	3.5	5.7	1.7	3.7	4.4	4.5	2.4	5.3	5.2	1.3	1.3
November	3.2	3.5	4.7	1.9	3.7	4.6	4.8	2.3	5.2	5.0	1.3	1.4
December	3.2	3.5	4.9	1.9	3.4	4.2	4.8	2.5	5.2	5.1	1.4	1.4

[1]Total separations are the number of separations during the entire month.
[2]The total separations rate is the number of total separations during the entire month as a percent of total employment.
[3]Detail will not necessarily add to totals because of the independent seasonal adjustment of the various series.
[4]Includes natural resources and mining, information, financial activities, and other services, not shown separately.
[5]Includes wholesale trade and transportation, warehousing, and utilities, not shown separately.
[6]Includes arts, entertainment, and recreation, not shown separately.
[7]Includes federal government, not shown separately.

Table 7-6. Separations Levels[1] and Rates,[2] by Industry, 2008–October 2019—*Continued*

(Seasonally adjusted, levels in thousands, rates per 100.)

Year and month	Level[3]											
	Total[4]	Total private[4]	Construc-tion	Manufac-turing	Trade, transpor-tation, and utilities[5]	Retail trade	Profes-sional and business services	Education and health services	Leisure and hospitality[6]	Accommo-dation and food services	Govern-ment[7]	State and local govern-ment
2014												
January	4 464	4 172	247	256	952	661	915	540	800	671	292	265
February	4 511	4 223	255	218	970	690	945	511	841	699	288	256
March	4 498	4 193	242	246	999	717	956	528	765	636	305	277
April	4 584	4 304	252	245	1 030	746	952	568	809	666	280	254
May	4 569	4 271	282	233	1 029	723	911	509	820	682	298	270
June	4 617	4 346	263	245	1 023	721	962	527	878	741	272	241
July	4 786	4 506	285	250	1 068	744	995	531	869	729	280	255
August	4 654	4 349	306	223	994	688	1 018	499	842	680	305	284
September	4 861	4 563	262	262	1 023	713	1 038	589	890	744	298	269
October	4 941	4 643	308	265	1 067	741	1 096	574	867	722	298	271
November	4 642	4 362	306	224	1 040	729	905	518	861	709	280	252
December	4 815	4 505	360	266	1 056	753	898	552	885	743	310	283
2015												
January	4 874	4 567	321	265	1 081	770	987	539	894	729	307	277
February	4 827	4 513	300	256	971	669	1 033	581	880	715	314	287
March	5 057	4 717	341	261	1 095	763	1 055	553	908	752	339	307
April	4 943	4 626	284	264	1 031	720	1 060	543	924	780	317	289
May	4 835	4 515	267	236	1 054	739	1 028	565	863	736	320	273
June	5 010	4 666	348	270	1 067	748	985	567	907	762	343	311
July	4 885	4 566	278	255	1 092	751	965	573	896	790	319	286
August	5 058	4 733	306	269	1 061	757	999	586	998	853	325	293
September	5 104	4 774	322	271	1 072	741	1 051	579	949	814	330	298
October	5 036	4 692	295	278	1 027	718	1 037	588	961	801	344	311
November	5 065	4 734	298	270	1 043	757	1 100	619	930	791	331	301
December	5 208	4 863	291	263	1 060	751	1 128	601	1 003	837	345	315
2016												
January	5 112	4 773	289	266	1 079	753	1 141	573	923	765	339	303
February	5 258	4 923	333	312	1 071	754	1 086	595	1 011	878	335	304
March	5 130	4 795	316	285	1 026	704	1 092	566	980	830	336	305
April	5 125	4 785	340	278	1 018	698	1 086	587	979	849	340	306
May	5 150	4 806	331	290	1 014	703	1 138	589	975	821	344	312
June	5 058	4 703	286	266	1 038	701	1 021	609	982	838	354	324
July	5 118	4 813	314	262	1 076	755	1 129	597	998	856	304	274
August	5 188	4 823	340	271	1 046	706	1 086	605	1 021	840	365	336
September	4 978	4 641	287	286	1 087	760	1 019	573	928	782	337	307
October	5 127	4 798	336	291	1 057	749	1 061	585	990	830	329	297
November	5 108	4 772	320	284	1 013	698	1 083	616	998	854	336	303
December	5 115	4 808	414	291	957	643	1 059	590	1 017	834	306	284
2017												
January	5 289	4 950	374	299	1 035	686	1 068	623	1 023	881	339	300
February	5 132	4 780	320	283	1 090	778	1 023	567	975	828	353	320
March	5 264	4 939	367	323	1 097	769	1 018	626	980	842	325	291
April	5 107	4 772	375	316	975	681	1 008	616	954	808	334	298
May	5 285	4 936	378	322	1 051	744	1 074	636	949	797	349	323
June	5 453	5 124	370	326	1 085	752	1 198	620	1 007	837	329	295
July	5 356	5 024	373	328	1 023	691	1 127	622	995	771	333	301
August	5 367	5 028	362	299	1 008	678	1 112	658	1 015	842	339	305
September	5 339	5 003	391	323	992	678	1 136	613	1 037	864	337	304
October	5 349	5 020	391	324	992	692	1 133	652	967	811	329	295
November	5 225	4 878	320	326	1 052	729	1 083	651	984	814	347	312
December	5 283	4 930	294	343	1 054	681	1 042	660	996	841	354	320
2018												
January	5 317	4 983	329	347	1 103	736	1 028	626	1 019	850	334	304
February	5 270	4 930	318	348	1 016	682	1 101	643	1 011	840	341	305
March	5 446	5 108	358	351	1 087	753	1 139	675	999	816	338	306
April	5 467	5 128	330	346	1 121	767	1 102	643	1 037	854	339	304
May	5 502	5 166	354	345	1 077	726	1 144	626	1 037	863	336	306
June	5 565	5 210	370	342	1 127	779	1 151	641	1 018	823	355	323
July	5 675	5 281	365	364	1 124	782	1 129	647	1 106	915	394	356
August	5 600	5 257	349	339	1 216	842	1 055	633	1 081	903	343	309
September	5 558	5 216	361	320	1 174	838	1 079	628	1 097	932	342	306
October	5 642	5 279	344	352	1 195	801	1 161	663	1 079	904	363	332
November	5 597	5 230	380	361	1 141	741	1 092	651	1 056	879	367	332
December	5 469	5 122	369	342	1 134	765	1 116	652	1 007	853	347	304
2019												
January	5 532	5 146	387	355	1 098	735	1 085	662	1 043	892	386	353
February	5 576	5 206	364	347	1 114	720	1 122	710	1 044	878	370	335
March	5 508	5 171	350	364	1 115	738	1 150	683	1 014	882	337	297
April	5 687	5 335	405	357	1 137	781	1 174	637	1 067	919	353	321
May	5 557	5 208	390	334	1 134	768	1 139	622	1 047	874	349	315
June	5 513	5 174	407	331	1 118	767	1 059	611	1 096	960	339	306
July	5 810	5 473	376	326	1 217	807	1 148	682	1 144	994	336	300
August	5 732	5 385	415	320	1 202	817	1 145	633	1 110	951	347	307
September	5 798	5 454	428	349	1 204	801	1 168	655	1 125	972	344	304
October	5 652	5 282	456	324	1 086	708	1 099	662	1 097	923	370	316

[1]Total separations are the number of separations during the entire month.
[2]The total separations rate is the number of total separations during the entire month as a percent of total employment.
[3]Detail will not necessarily add to totals because of the independent seasonal adjustment of the various series.
[4]Includes natural resources and mining, information, financial activities, and other services, not shown separately.
[5]Includes wholesale trade and transportation, warehousing, and utilities, not shown separately.
[6]Includes arts, entertainment, and recreation, not shown separately.
[7]Includes federal government, not shown separately.

Table 7-6. Separations Levels[1] and Rates,[2] by Industry, 2008–October 2019—*Continued*

(Seasonally adjusted, levels in thousands, rates per 100.)

Year and month	Rate											
	Total[4]	Total private[4]	Construction	Manufacturing	Trade, transportation, and utilities[5]	Retail trade	Professional and business services	Education and health services	Leisure and hospitality[6]	Accommodation and food services	Government[7]	State and local government
2014												
January	3.2	3.6	4.1	2.1	3.6	4.3	4.9	2.5	5.5	5.4	1.3	1.4
February	3.3	3.6	4.3	1.8	3.7	4.5	5.0	2.4	5.8	5.6	1.3	1.3
March	3.3	3.6	4.0	2.0	3.8	4.7	5.0	2.5	5.3	5.1	1.4	1.5
April	3.3	3.7	4.1	2.0	3.9	4.9	5.0	2.7	5.5	5.3	1.3	1.3
May	3.3	3.7	4.6	1.9	3.9	4.7	4.8	2.4	5.6	5.4	1.4	1.4
June	3.3	3.7	4.3	2.0	3.9	4.7	5.0	2.5	6.0	5.9	1.2	1.3
July	3.4	3.8	4.6	2.1	4.1	4.8	5.2	2.5	5.9	5.8	1.3	1.3
August	3.3	3.7	4.9	1.8	3.8	4.5	5.3	2.3	5.7	5.4	1.4	1.5
September	3.5	3.9	4.2	2.1	3.9	4.6	5.4	2.7	6.0	5.9	1.4	1.4
October	3.5	3.9	4.9	2.2	4.0	4.8	5.7	2.7	5.9	5.7	1.4	1.4
November	3.3	3.7	4.9	1.8	3.9	4.7	4.7	2.4	5.8	5.6	1.3	1.3
December	3.4	3.8	5.7	2.2	4.0	4.9	4.6	2.5	5.9	5.8	1.4	1.5
2015												
January	3.5	3.8	5.1	2.2	4.1	5.0	5.1	2.5	6.0	5.7	1.4	1.4
February	3.4	3.8	4.7	2.1	3.6	4.3	5.3	2.7	5.9	5.6	1.4	1.5
March	3.6	4.0	5.4	2.1	4.1	4.9	5.4	2.5	6.1	5.8	1.5	1.6
April	3.5	3.9	4.4	2.1	3.9	4.6	5.4	2.5	6.1	6.1	1.4	1.5
May	3.4	3.8	4.1	1.9	3.9	4.7	5.2	2.6	5.7	5.7	1.5	1.4
June	3.5	3.9	5.4	2.2	4.0	4.8	5.0	2.6	6.0	5.9	1.6	1.6
July	3.4	3.8	4.3	2.1	4.1	4.8	4.9	2.6	5.9	6.1	1.4	1.5
August	3.6	3.9	4.7	2.2	3.9	4.8	5.1	2.7	6.6	6.5	1.5	1.5
September	3.6	4.0	4.9	2.2	4.0	4.7	5.3	2.6	6.2	6.2	1.5	1.5
October	3.5	3.9	4.5	2.2	3.8	4.6	5.2	2.6	6.3	6.1	1.6	1.6
November	3.5	3.9	4.5	2.2	3.9	4.8	5.5	2.8	6.0	6.0	1.5	1.6
December	3.6	4.0	4.4	2.1	3.9	4.8	5.7	2.7	6.5	6.3	1.6	1.6
2016												
January	3.6	3.9	4.4	2.2	4.0	4.8	5.7	2.6	6.0	5.8	1.5	1.6
February	3.7	4.1	5.0	2.5	4.0	4.8	5.4	2.7	6.5	6.6	1.5	1.6
March	3.6	3.9	4.7	2.3	3.8	4.5	5.5	2.5	6.3	6.2	1.5	1.6
April	3.6	3.9	5.1	2.3	3.8	4.4	5.4	2.6	6.3	6.4	1.5	1.6
May	3.6	3.9	4.9	2.3	3.7	4.4	5.7	2.6	6.3	6.1	1.6	1.6
June	3.5	3.9	4.3	2.2	3.8	4.4	5.1	2.7	6.3	6.3	1.6	1.7
July	3.5	3.9	4.7	2.1	4.0	4.8	5.6	2.6	6.4	6.4	1.4	1.4
August	3.6	3.9	5.1	2.2	3.8	4.4	5.4	2.7	6.5	6.2	1.6	1.7
September	3.4	3.8	4.2	2.3	4.0	4.8	5.0	2.5	5.9	5.8	1.5	1.6
October	3.5	3.9	4.9	2.4	3.9	4.7	5.2	2.6	6.3	6.1	1.5	1.5
November	3.5	3.9	4.7	2.3	3.7	4.4	5.3	2.7	6.3	6.3	1.5	1.6
December	3.5	3.9	6.1	2.4	3.5	4.0	5.2	2.6	6.4	6.1	1.4	1.5
2017												
January	3.6	4.0	5.4	2.4	3.8	4.3	5.3	2.7	6.4	6.5	1.5	1.5
February	3.5	3.9	4.7	2.3	4.0	4.9	5.0	2.5	6.1	6.1	1.6	1.6
March	3.6	4.0	5.3	2.6	4.0	4.8	5.0	2.7	6.1	6.2	1.5	1.5
April	3.5	3.9	5.4	2.5	3.6	4.3	4.9	2.7	6.0	5.9	1.5	1.5
May	3.6	4.0	5.5	2.6	3.8	4.7	5.2	2.7	5.9	5.8	1.6	1.7
June	3.7	4.1	5.3	2.6	4.0	4.8	5.8	2.7	6.3	6.1	1.5	1.5
July	3.7	4.0	5.4	2.6	3.7	4.4	5.5	2.7	6.2	5.6	1.5	1.5
August	3.7	4.0	5.2	2.4	3.7	4.3	5.4	2.8	6.3	6.1	1.5	1.6
September	3.6	4.0	5.6	2.6	3.6	4.3	5.5	2.6	6.5	6.3	1.5	1.6
October	3.6	4.0	5.6	2.6	3.6	4.4	5.5	2.8	6.0	5.9	1.5	1.5
November	3.5	3.9	4.5	2.6	3.8	4.6	5.2	2.8	6.1	5.9	1.5	1.6
December	3.6	3.9	4.1	2.7	3.8	4.3	5.0	2.8	6.1	6.1	1.6	1.6
2018												
January	3.6	4.0	4.6	2.8	4.0	4.7	5.0	2.7	6.3	6.1	1.5	1.6
February	3.6	3.9	4.4	2.8	3.7	4.3	5.3	2.7	6.2	6.1	1.5	1.6
March	3.7	4.1	5.0	2.8	3.9	4.8	5.5	2.9	6.2	5.9	1.5	1.6
April	3.7	4.1	4.6	2.7	4.1	4.8	5.3	2.7	6.4	6.1	1.5	1.5
May	3.7	4.1	4.9	2.7	3.9	4.6	5.5	2.7	6.4	6.2	1.5	1.6
June	3.7	4.1	5.1	2.7	4.1	4.9	5.5	2.7	6.2	5.9	1.6	1.6
July	3.8	4.2	5.0	2.9	4.1	4.9	5.4	2.7	6.8	6.5	1.8	1.8
August	3.7	4.1	4.8	2.7	4.4	5.3	5.0	2.7	6.6	6.4	1.5	1.6
September	3.7	4.1	4.9	2.5	4.2	5.3	5.1	2.6	6.7	6.7	1.5	1.6
October	3.8	4.1	4.7	2.8	4.3	5.1	5.5	2.8	6.6	6.4	1.6	1.7
November	3.7	4.1	5.2	2.8	4.1	4.7	5.1	2.7	6.4	6.3	1.6	1.7
December	3.6	4.0	5.0	2.7	4.1	4.8	5.3	2.7	6.1	6.0	1.5	1.5
2019												
January	3.7	4.0	5.2	2.8	3.9	4.6	5.1	2.8	6.3	6.3	1.7	1.8
February	3.7	4.1	4.9	2.7	4.0	4.6	5.3	3.0	6.3	6.2	1.6	1.7
March	3.7	4.0	4.7	2.8	4.0	4.7	5.4	2.8	6.1	6.2	1.5	1.5
April	3.8	4.2	5.4	2.8	4.1	4.9	5.5	2.6	6.4	6.5	1.6	1.6
May	3.7	4.1	5.2	2.6	4.1	4.9	5.3	2.6	6.3	6.1	1.5	1.6
June	3.6	4.0	5.4	2.6	4.0	4.9	4.9	2.5	6.6	6.7	1.5	1.6
July	3.8	4.2	5.0	2.5	4.4	5.1	5.3	2.8	6.9	7.0	1.5	1.5
August	3.8	4.2	5.5	2.5	4.3	5.2	5.3	2.6	6.6	6.7	1.5	1.6
September	3.8	4.2	5.7	2.7	4.3	5.1	5.4	2.7	6.7	6.8	1.5	1.5
October	3.7	4.1	6.1	2.5	3.9	4.5	5.1	2.7	6.5	6.4	1.6	1.6

[1]Total separations are the number of separations during the entire month.
[2]The total separations rate is the number of total separations during the entire month as a percent of total employment.
[3]Detail will not necessarily add to totals because of the independent seasonal adjustment of the various series.
[4]Includes natural resources and mining, information, financial activities, and other services, not shown separately.
[5]Includes wholesale trade and transportation, warehousing, and utilities, not shown separately.
[6]Includes arts, entertainment, and recreation, not shown separately.
[7]Includes federal government, not shown separately.

NOTES AND DEFINITIONS

JOB OPENINGS AND LABOR TURNOVER SURVEY

Data from a sample of approximately 16,000 businesses for the Job Openings and Labor Turnover Survey (JOLTS) are collected and compiled monthly from a sample of business establishments by the Bureau of Labor Statistics (BLS). Each month, data are collected in a survey of business establishments for total employment, job openings, hires, quits, layoffs and discharges, and other separations. Data collection methods include computer-assisted telephone interviewing, touchtone data entry, fax, and mail.

Concepts and Definitions

The JOLTS program covers all private nonfarm establishments such as factories, offices, and stores, as well as federal, state, and local government entities in the 50 states and the District of Columbia.

Employment includes persons on the payroll who worked or received pay for the pay period that includes the 12th day of the reference month. Full-time, part-time, permanent, short-term, seasonal, salaried, and hourly employees are included, as are employees on paid vacations or other paid leave. Proprietors or partners of unincorporated businesses, unpaid family workers, or persons on leave without pay or on strike for the entire pay period, are not counted as employed. Employees of temporary help agencies, employee leasing companies, outside contractors, and consultants are counted by their employer of record, not by the establishment where they are working.

Job openings information is submitted by establishments for the last business day of the reference month. A job opening requires that: 1) a specific position exists and there is work available for that position, 2) work could start within 30 days regardless of whether a suitable candidate is found, and 3) the employer is actively recruiting from outside the establishment to fill the position. Included are full-time, part-time, permanent, short-term, and seasonal openings. Active recruiting means that the establishment is taking steps to fill a position by advertising in newspapers or on the Internet, posting help-wanted signs, accepting applications, or using other similar methods.

Jobs to be filled only by internal transfers, promotions, demotions, or recall from layoffs are excluded. Also excluded are jobs with start dates more than 30 days in the future, jobs for which employees have been hired but have not yet reported for work, and jobs to be filled by employees of temporary help agencies, employee leasing companies, outside contractors, or consultants. The job openings rate is computed by dividing the number of job openings by the sum of employment and job openings and multiplying that quotient by 100.

Hires are the total number of additions to the payroll occurring at any time during the reference month, including both new and rehired employees, full-time and part-time, permanent, short-term and seasonal employees, employees recalled to the location after a layoff lasting more than 7 days, on-call or intermittent employees who returned to work after having been formally separated, and transfers from other locations. The hires count does not include transfers or promotions within the reporting site, employees returning from strike, employees of temporary help agencies or employee leasing companies, outside contractors, or consultants. The hires rate is computed by dividing the number of hires by employment and multiplying that quotient by 100.

Separations are the total number of terminations of employment occurring at any time during the reference month, and are reported by type of separation—quits, layoffs and discharges, and other separations. Quits are voluntary separations by employees (except for retirements, which are reported as other separations). Layoffs and discharges are involuntary separations initiated by the employer and include layoffs with no intent to rehire, formal layoffs lasting or expected to last more than 7 days, discharges resulting from mergers, downsizing, or closings, firings or other discharges for cause, terminations of permanent or short-term employees, and terminations of seasonal employees. Other separations include retirements, transfers to other locations, deaths, and separations due to disability. Separations do not include transfers within the same location or employees on strike.

The separations rate is computed by dividing the number of separations by employment and multiplying that quotient by 100. The quits, layoffs and discharges, and other separations rates are computed similarly, dividing the number by employment and multiplying by 100.

The JOLTS annual level estimates for hires, quits, layoffs and discharges, other separations, and total separations are the sum of the 12 published monthly levels. The annual rate estimates are computed by dividing the annual level by the Current Employment Statistics (CES) annual average employment level, and multiplying that quotient by 100. This figure will be approximately equal to the sum of the 12 monthly rates.

Annual estimates are not calculated for job openings because job openings are a stock, or point-in-time, measurement for the last business day of each month. Only jobs still open on the last day of the month are counted. For the same reason job openings cannot be cumulated throughout each month, annual figures for job openings cannot be created by summing the monthly estimates. Hires and separations are flow measures and are cumulated over the month with a total reported for the month. Therefore, the annual figures can be created by summing the monthly estimates.

Sources of Additional Information

For more extensive information see the Job Openings and Labor Turnover Survey (JOLTS) page on the BLS Web site at <http://www.bls.gov/jlt/>.

Table 7-7. Quits Levels[1] and Rates,[2] by Industry, 2008–October 2019

(Seasonally adjusted, levels in thousands, rates per 100.)

Year and month	Level[3]											
	Total[4]	Total private[4]	Construction	Manufacturing	Trade, transportation, and utilities[5]	Retail trade	Professional and business services	Education and health services	Leisure and hospitality[6]	Accommodation and food services	Government[7]	State and local government
2008												
January	2 851	2 703	146	191	652	487	460	316	588	527	149	135
February	2 866	2 717	158	189	609	429	585	308	560	504	149	137
March	2 652	2 514	128	186	579	414	467	316	554	510	139	130
April	2 840	2 693	161	184	633	470	526	335	548	499	147	139
May	2 609	2 473	134	162	605	436	440	261	579	518	136	129
June	2 597	2 462	137	164	548	399	500	283	547	491	135	129
July	2 495	2 366	192	135	552	400	422	293	528	470	128	123
August	2 452	2 304	162	139	574	438	384	283	504	463	149	141
September	2 477	2 340	120	145	568	420	424	286	520	465	137	130
October	2 352	2 222	113	143	530	375	397	291	494	455	130	121
November	2 148	2 031	104	123	483	360	397	253	452	427	117	110
December	2 081	1 955	91	101	508	379	351	258	426	396	126	117
2009												
January	1 978	1 873	87	112	465	344	346	256	404	371	105	100
February	1 945	1 842	97	99	402	307	308	260	417	385	102	99
March	1 829	1 721	92	86	434	318	279	240	384	353	108	103
April	1 713	1 609	60	78	375	274	285	231	367	325	104	100
May	1 684	1 580	82	87	356	262	294	235	345	302	104	95
June	1 686	1 586	76	88	366	283	275	257	353	305	100	93
July	1 689	1 582	64	92	391	285	268	240	337	311	107	103
August	1 561	1 460	39	86	336	243	250	241	345	313	101	92
September	1 631	1 530	73	90	364	263	265	261	300	285	100	93
October	1 663	1 567	61	80	379	280	272	259	331	297	96	90
November	1 803	1 691	92	72	410	284	278	262	371	335	112	104
December	1 758	1 646	84	70	396	295	296	254	372	339	112	101
2010												
January	1 744	1 640	100	82	343	256	329	231	379	324	104	98
February	1 834	1 718	83	105	419	328	322	239	374	341	116	106
March	1 853	1 744	83	86	409	307	340	243	367	337	110	100
April	1 898	1 793	64	89	430	326	352	286	365	324	105	96
May	1 814	1 715	60	85	421	324	337	239	357	321	98	88
June	1 911	1 778	62	98	422	318	374	263	327	297	133	105
July	1 789	1 677	69	84	425	328	325	241	336	304	112	92
August	1 852	1 739	79	107	404	302	381	240	336	300	114	99
September	1 901	1 774	83	97	416	317	363	247	356	315	127	113
October	1 848	1 741	81	99	393	308	360	249	362	306	108	99
November	1 881	1 777	70	94	420	320	355	266	364	322	105	96
December	1 968	1 856	90	105	396	295	395	251	385	342	112	104
2011												
January	1 833	1 710	70	102	367	248	369	227	375	336	123	113
February	1 952	1 841	72	96	440	310	410	244	371	331	111	104
March	2 028	1 919	80	112	440	333	451	254	382	338	109	101
April	1 883	1 775	94	103	404	310	369	244	372	328	108	99
May	1 966	1 836	84	108	449	334	369	258	367	328	129	122
June	1 923	1 822	79	111	430	329	368	245	392	354	101	91
July	1 990	1 860	74	103	419	312	410	234	381	333	130	122
August	2 043	1 918	67	100	443	330	396	275	419	370	125	116
September	2 045	1 929	86	94	440	323	442	248	401	348	116	106
October	2 000	1 892	81	108	445	323	442	245	339	302	107	98
November	2 031	1 909	116	118	398	283	434	247	378	336	122	113
December	1 975	1 832	82	107	445	336	315	265	406	352	143	134
2012												
January	2 032	1 902	78	103	417	308	405	274	402	358	130	120
February	2 123	1 984	81	108	456	342	409	305	414	362	139	127
March	2 163	2 030	91	110	460	330	410	288	444	396	133	124
April	2 136	1 996	72	113	468	341	376	280	437	390	140	130
May	2 140	2 001	79	110	463	334	407	280	437	387	139	126
June	2 151	2 027	90	112	480	343	363	277	454	405	124	116
July	2 075	1 949	81	102	476	339	348	274	431	382	126	116
August	2 080	1 952	66	110	479	328	344	288	388	340	129	120
September	1 957	1 838	74	107	438	325	351	253	389	355	118	109
October	2 037	1 904	101	105	474	327	319	263	413	367	133	123
November	2 070	1 931	104	106	445	322	355	287	411	370	139	128
December	2 045	1 915	75	109	434	324	384	281	420	381	130	120
2013												
January	2 281	2 150	134	100	537	394	353	313	456	404	131	124
February	2 281	2 152	107	108	497	356	383	300	484	428	129	119
March	2 118	1 994	93	97	453	330	385	289	447	388	124	113
April	2 297	2 144	90	117	496	362	452	301	449	406	153	143
May	2 237	2 103	91	118	455	321	441	293	446	399	134	124
June	2 203	2 076	99	109	455	331	460	294	429	381	127	117
July	2 367	2 233	103	118	467	349	527	316	452	401	134	122
August	2 331	2 205	93	105	537	414	458	299	424	374	127	114
September	2 307	2 184	92	114	535	405	433	310	444	396	123	114
October	2 374	2 244	92	106	525	389	454	322	522	475	130	118
November	2 384	2 257	80	121	548	406	487	299	483	426	127	119
December	2 281	2 143	78	114	481	356	469	322	456	403	138	126

[1]Quits are the number of quits during the entire month.
[2]The quits rate is the number of quits during the entire month as a percent of total employment.
[3]Detail will not necessarily add to totals because of the independent seasonal adjustment of the various series.
[4]Includes natural resources and mining, information, financial activities, and other services, not shown separately.
[5]Includes wholesale trade and transportation, warehousing, and utilities, not shown separately.
[6]Includes arts, entertainment, and recreation, not shown separately.
[7]Includes federal government, not shown separately.

Table 7-7. Quits Levels[1] and Rates,[2] by Industry, 2008–October 2019—*Continued*

(Seasonally adjusted, levels in thousands, rates per 100.)

Year and month	Rate											
	Total[4]	Total private[4]	Construction	Manufacturing	Trade, transportation, and utilities[5]	Retail trade	Professional and business services	Education and health services	Leisure and hospitality[6]	Accommodation and food services	Government[7]	State and local government
2008												
January	2.1	2.3	1.9	1.4	2.4	3.1	2.5	1.7	4.3	4.6	0.7	0.7
February	2.1	2.3	2.1	1.4	2.3	2.8	3.2	1.6	4.1	4.4	0.7	0.7
March	1.9	2.2	1.7	1.4	2.2	2.7	2.6	1.7	4.1	4.4	0.6	0.7
April	2.1	2.3	2.2	1.4	2.4	3.0	2.9	1.8	4.1	4.3	0.7	0.7
May	1.9	2.1	1.8	1.2	2.3	2.8	2.5	1.4	4.3	4.5	0.6	0.7
June	1.9	2.1	1.9	1.2	2.1	2.6	2.8	1.5	4.1	4.3	0.6	0.7
July	1.8	2.1	2.7	1.0	2.1	2.6	2.4	1.5	3.9	4.1	0.6	0.6
August	1.8	2.0	2.3	1.0	2.2	2.9	2.2	1.5	3.7	4.0	0.7	0.7
September	1.8	2.0	1.7	1.1	2.2	2.8	2.4	1.5	3.9	4.1	0.6	0.7
October	1.7	2.0	1.6	1.1	2.0	2.5	2.3	1.5	3.7	4.0	0.6	0.6
November	1.6	1.8	1.5	0.9	1.9	2.4	2.3	1.3	3.4	3.8	0.5	0.6
December	1.5	1.7	1.4	0.8	2.0	2.5	2.0	1.3	3.2	3.5	0.6	0.6
2009												
January	1.5	1.7	1.3	0.9	1.8	2.3	2.0	1.3	3.1	3.3	0.5	0.5
February	1.5	1.7	1.5	0.8	1.6	2.1	1.8	1.3	3.2	3.4	0.5	0.5
March	1.4	1.6	1.5	0.7	1.7	2.2	1.7	1.2	2.9	3.2	0.5	0.5
April	1.3	1.5	1.0	0.6	1.5	1.9	1.7	1.2	2.8	2.9	0.5	0.5
May	1.3	1.5	1.3	0.7	1.4	1.8	1.8	1.2	2.6	2.7	0.5	0.5
June	1.3	1.5	1.3	0.7	1.5	1.9	1.7	1.3	2.7	2.7	0.4	0.5
July	1.3	1.5	1.1	0.8	1.6	2.0	1.6	1.2	2.6	2.8	0.5	0.5
August	1.2	1.4	0.7	0.7	1.4	1.7	1.5	1.2	2.6	2.8	0.4	0.5
September	1.3	1.4	1.3	0.8	1.5	1.8	1.6	1.3	2.3	2.6	0.4	0.5
October	1.3	1.5	1.1	0.7	1.5	1.9	1.6	1.3	2.5	2.7	0.4	0.5
November	1.4	1.6	1.6	0.6	1.7	2.0	1.7	1.3	2.9	3.0	0.5	0.5
December	1.4	1.5	1.5	0.6	1.6	2.1	1.8	1.3	2.9	3.1	0.5	0.5
2010												
January	1.3	1.5	1.8	0.7	1.4	1.8	2.0	1.2	2.9	2.9	0.5	0.5
February	1.4	1.6	1.5	0.9	1.7	2.3	1.9	1.2	2.9	3.1	0.5	0.5
March	1.4	1.6	1.5	0.8	1.7	2.1	2.1	1.2	2.8	3.1	0.5	0.5
April	1.5	1.7	1.1	0.8	1.8	2.3	2.1	1.4	2.8	2.9	0.5	0.5
May	1.4	1.6	1.1	0.7	1.7	2.2	2.0	1.2	2.7	2.9	0.4	0.4
June	1.5	1.6	1.1	0.8	1.7	2.2	2.2	1.3	2.5	2.7	0.6	0.5
July	1.4	1.6	1.3	0.7	1.7	2.3	1.9	1.2	2.6	2.7	0.5	0.5
August	1.4	1.6	1.4	0.9	1.6	2.1	2.3	1.2	2.6	2.7	0.5	0.5
September	1.5	1.6	1.5	0.8	1.7	2.2	2.2	1.2	2.7	2.8	0.6	0.6
October	1.4	1.6	1.5	0.9	1.6	2.1	2.1	1.2	2.8	2.7	0.5	0.5
November	1.4	1.6	1.3	0.8	1.7	2.2	2.1	1.3	2.8	2.9	0.5	0.5
December	1.5	1.7	1.6	0.9	1.6	2.0	2.3	1.2	2.9	3.0	0.5	0.5
2011												
January	1.4	1.6	1.3	0.9	1.5	1.7	2.2	1.1	2.9	3.0	0.6	0.6
February	1.5	1.7	1.3	0.8	1.8	2.1	2.4	1.2	2.8	2.9	0.5	0.5
March	1.5	1.8	1.5	1.0	1.8	2.3	2.6	1.3	2.9	3.0	0.5	0.5
April	1.4	1.6	1.7	0.9	1.6	2.1	2.1	1.2	2.8	2.9	0.5	0.5
May	1.5	1.7	1.5	0.9	1.8	2.3	2.1	1.3	2.8	2.9	0.6	0.6
June	1.5	1.7	1.4	0.9	1.7	2.2	2.1	1.2	2.9	3.1	0.5	0.5
July	1.5	1.7	1.3	0.9	1.7	2.1	2.4	1.2	2.8	2.9	0.6	0.6
August	1.5	1.7	1.2	0.9	1.8	2.2	2.3	1.4	3.1	3.2	0.6	0.6
September	1.5	1.7	1.5	0.8	1.8	2.2	2.5	1.2	3.0	3.0	0.5	0.6
October	1.5	1.7	1.5	0.9	1.8	2.2	2.5	1.2	2.5	2.6	0.5	0.5
November	1.5	1.7	2.1	1.0	1.6	1.9	2.5	1.2	2.8	2.9	0.6	0.6
December	1.5	1.7	1.5	0.9	1.8	2.3	1.8	1.3	3.0	3.0	0.7	0.7
2012												
January	1.5	1.7	1.4	0.9	1.6	2.1	2.3	1.3	3.0	3.1	0.6	0.6
February	1.6	1.8	1.4	0.9	1.8	2.3	2.3	1.5	3.0	3.1	0.6	0.7
March	1.6	1.8	1.6	0.9	1.8	2.2	2.3	1.4	3.2	3.4	0.6	0.6
April	1.6	1.8	1.3	0.9	1.8	2.3	2.1	1.4	3.2	3.3	0.6	0.7
May	1.6	1.8	1.4	0.9	1.8	2.2	2.3	1.4	3.2	3.3	0.6	0.7
June	1.6	1.8	1.6	0.9	1.9	2.3	2.0	1.3	3.3	3.4	0.6	0.6
July	1.5	1.7	1.4	0.9	1.9	2.3	1.9	1.3	3.1	3.2	0.6	0.6
August	1.5	1.7	1.2	0.9	1.9	2.2	1.9	1.4	2.8	2.9	0.6	0.6
September	1.5	1.6	1.3	0.9	1.7	2.2	1.9	1.2	2.8	3.0	0.5	0.6
October	1.5	1.7	1.8	0.9	1.9	2.2	1.8	1.3	3.0	3.1	0.6	0.6
November	1.5	1.7	1.8	0.9	1.7	2.2	2.0	1.4	3.0	3.1	0.6	0.7
December	1.5	1.7	1.3	0.9	1.7	2.2	2.1	1.3	3.0	3.2	0.6	0.6
2013												
January	1.7	1.9	1.4	0.8	2.1	2.6	1.9	1.5	3.3	3.4	0.6	0.6
February	1.7	1.9	1.4	0.9	1.9	2.4	2.1	1.4	3.4	3.5	0.6	0.6
March	1.6	1.8	1.6	0.8	1.8	2.2	2.1	1.4	3.2	3.2	0.6	0.6
April	1.7	1.9	1.3	1.0	1.9	2.4	2.4	1.4	3.2	3.3	0.7	0.8
May	1.6	1.8	1.4	1.0	1.8	2.1	2.4	1.4	3.1	3.3	0.6	0.6
June	1.6	1.8	1.6	0.9	1.8	2.2	2.5	1.4	3.0	3.1	0.6	0.6
July	1.7	1.9	1.4	1.0	1.8	2.3	2.8	1.5	3.2	3.3	0.6	0.6
August	1.7	1.9	1.2	0.9	2.1	2.7	2.5	1.4	3.0	3.0	0.6	0.6
September	1.7	1.9	1.3	1.0	2.1	2.7	2.3	1.5	3.1	3.2	0.6	0.6
October	1.7	1.9	1.8	0.9	2.0	2.6	2.4	1.5	3.6	3.9	0.6	0.6
November	1.7	2.0	1.8	1.0	2.1	2.7	2.6	1.4	3.3	3.4	0.6	0.6
December	1.7	1.9	1.3	0.9	1.8	2.3	2.5	1.5	3.2	3.3	0.6	0.7

[1]Quits are the number of quits during the entire month.
[2]The quits rate is the number of quits during the entire month as a percent of total employment.
[3]Detail will not necessarily add to totals because of the independent seasonal adjustment of the various series.
[4]Includes natural resources and mining, information, financial activities, and other services, not shown separately.
[5]Includes wholesale trade and transportation, warehousing, and utilities, not shown separately.
[6]Includes arts, entertainment, and recreation, not shown separately.
[7]Includes federal government, not shown separately.

Table 7-7. Quits Levels[1] and Rates,[2] by Industry, 2008–October 2019—*Continued*

(Seasonally adjusted, levels in thousands, rates per 100.)

Year and month	Level[3]											
	Total[4]	Total private[4]	Construction	Manufacturing	Trade, transportation, and utilities[5]	Retail trade	Professional and business services	Education and health services	Leisure and hospitality[6]	Accommodation and food services	Government[7]	State and local government
2014												
January	2 312	2 181	96	114	537	404	449	303	464	417	132	122
February	2 401	2 267	97	110	553	410	433	309	529	483	135	125
March	2 441	2 304	93	121	560	410	520	274	497	440	137	127
April	2 476	2 334	106	107	571	422	480	321	506	461	141	130
May	2 486	2 344	123	117	611	436	458	322	459	411	141	131
June	2 506	2 388	116	108	589	436	506	327	513	456	118	107
July	2 637	2 497	110	132	612	456	505	346	517	461	140	132
August	2 564	2 412	127	115	558	412	493	297	544	488	152	147
September	2 737	2 577	108	135	589	421	555	347	549	502	160	148
October	2 721	2 568	108	131	603	447	512	361	586	518	152	142
November	2 588	2 452	93	108	613	442	455	343	565	502	136	125
December	2 543	2 403	118	131	607	440	412	336	553	499	141	129
2015												
January	2 754	2 609	110	143	610	451	543	360	584	525	144	132
February	2 729	2 578	112	125	567	411	561	382	546	497	151	141
March	2 754	2 596	112	124	621	462	547	359	572	534	157	147
April	2 709	2 561	122	140	610	440	512	349	545	494	148	139
May	2 750	2 600	115	125	624	451	555	365	536	479	150	134
June	2 757	2 592	112	140	620	462	505	354	598	538	165	153
July	2 776	2 621	107	124	609	433	513	379	616	559	154	142
August	2 900	2 739	100	137	623	454	561	394	665	598	161	149
September	2 786	2 636	123	144	634	456	508	354	609	554	150	138
October	2 821	2 655	97	144	622	454	539	380	598	543	167	154
November	2 886	2 733	121	137	630	486	563	418	611	561	154	144
December	3 012	2 845	127	133	672	491	571	403	638	583	167	156
2016												
January	2 883	2 716	96	146	656	481	566	340	633	570	166	153
February	2 982	2 820	104	154	643	474	587	392	648	579	162	150
March	2 908	2 744	139	143	655	479	544	370	625	575	164	152
April	2 952	2 791	112	139	646	463	583	388	650	589	161	148
May	3 023	2 857	119	137	601	453	675	394	671	600	166	154
June	2 982	2 796	117	138	641	456	543	405	655	592	186	173
July	2 988	2 825	127	142	629	460	620	396	661	595	163	150
August	3 009	2 826	147	148	644	470	596	382	662	598	183	171
September	3 038	2 867	112	152	670	467	619	403	669	592	171	159
October	3 105	2 934	133	173	669	497	618	384	686	611	171	159
November	3 006	2 846	151	159	646	463	591	380	683	609	159	145
December	2 963	2 799	133	159	592	412	603	390	675	598	164	155
2017												
January	3 154	2 976	154	168	663	479	625	423	645	576	178	160
February	3 076	2 902	157	176	699	514	559	391	637	563	174	159
March	3 148	2 965	161	188	689	513	593	421	645	568	183	168
April	3 030	2 871	153	183	598	435	581	409	658	579	159	145
May	3 138	2 972	146	203	669	491	582	411	665	601	166	154
June	3 151	2 989	138	201	653	468	621	423	658	591	162	146
July	3 134	2 971	149	194	671	463	612	391	628	568	163	150
August	3 147	2 983	154	184	644	455	657	386	637	577	165	149
September	3 210	3 041	178	194	637	443	667	404	657	606	169	155
October	3 209	3 045	184	200	648	456	655	426	628	570	164	149
November	3 156	2 975	135	195	637	437	681	416	647	580	181	166
December	3 189	3 015	143	211	668	460	624	418	668	596	174	160
2018												
January	3 022	2 853	155	208	650	451	550	377	615	544	169	156
February	3 176	3 012	153	214	649	450	625	401	685	609	165	151
March	3 300	3 131	156	217	674	463	644	414	692	614	168	155
April	3 339	3 154	164	205	692	485	678	423	702	634	185	169
May	3 342	3 154	163	197	731	510	636	420	698	625	188	173
June	3 354	3 160	177	205	746	544	658	413	691	614	194	180
July	3 443	3 262	201	213	724	529	645	407	748	671	181	165
August	3 473	3 303	177	206	761	531	607	437	763	683	170	155
September	3 393	3 223	170	202	763	569	605	411	739	658	170	152
October	3 469	3 287	180	205	732	514	673	461	732	643	182	166
November	3 379	3 184	174	226	706	480	625	451	686	615	195	178
December	3 391	3 205	185	211	715	493	649	448	706	650	186	166
2019												
January	3 483	3 282	185	212	727	512	664	433	753	679	201	187
February	3 447	3 259	184	211	729	494	645	461	748	668	188	171
March	3 461	3 278	149	222	738	500	656	467	735	653	184	162
April	3 516	3 327	145	224	744	524	647	425	773	691	190	175
May	3 478	3 277	168	203	784	543	619	406	761	688	202	186
June	3 462	3 278	186	203	745	540	621	412	782	705	183	170
July	3 668	3 487	177	195	771	545	679	485	822	742	181	164
August	3 601	3 419	182	197	777	554	646	459	831	748	181	164
September	3 471	3 288	187	214	731	522	654	442	754	677	182	165
October	3 497	3 317	184	198	663	465	626	462	802	712	180	162

[1]Quits are the number of quits during the entire month.
[2]The quits rate is the number of quits during the entire month as a percent of total employment.
[3]Detail will not necessarily add to totals because of the independent seasonal adjustment of the various series.
[4]Includes natural resources and mining, information, financial activities, and other services, not shown separately.
[5]Includes wholesale trade and transportation, warehousing, and utilities, not shown separately.
[6]Includes arts, entertainment, and recreation, not shown separately.
[7]Includes federal government, not shown separately.

Table 7-7. Quits Levels[1] and Rates,[2] by Industry, 2008–October 2019—*Continued*

(Seasonally adjusted, levels in thousands, rates per 100.)

Year and month	Rate											
	Total[4]	Total private[4]	Construction	Manufacturing	Trade, transportation, and utilities[5]	Retail trade	Professional and business services	Education and health services	Leisure and hospitality[6]	Accommodation and food services	Government[7]	State and local government
2014												
January	1.7	1.9	1.6	0.9	2.1	2.6	2.4	1.4	3.2	3.4	0.6	0.6
February	1.7	2.0	1.6	0.9	2.1	2.7	2.3	1.5	3.6	3.9	0.6	0.7
March	1.8	2.0	1.5	1.0	2.1	2.7	2.7	1.3	3.4	3.5	0.6	0.7
April	1.8	2.0	1.7	0.9	2.2	2.8	2.5	1.5	3.5	3.7	0.6	0.7
May	1.8	2.0	2.0	1.0	2.3	2.8	2.4	1.5	3.1	3.3	0.6	0.7
June	1.8	2.0	1.9	0.9	2.2	2.8	2.6	1.5	3.5	3.6	0.5	0.6
July	1.9	2.1	1.8	1.1	2.3	3.0	2.6	1.6	3.5	3.7	0.6	0.7
August	1.8	2.1	2.0	0.9	2.1	2.7	2.6	1.4	3.7	3.9	0.7	0.8
September	2.0	2.2	1.7	1.1	2.2	2.7	2.9	1.6	3.7	4.0	0.7	0.8
October	1.9	2.2	1.7	1.1	2.3	2.9	2.7	1.7	4.0	4.1	0.7	0.7
November	1.8	2.1	1.5	0.9	2.3	2.9	2.4	1.6	3.8	3.9	0.6	0.7
December	1.8	2.0	1.9	1.1	2.3	2.8	2.1	1.5	3.7	3.9	0.6	0.7
2015												
January	2.0	2.2	1.7	1.2	2.3	2.9	2.8	1.7	3.9	4.1	0.7	0.7
February	1.9	2.2	1.8	1.0	2.1	2.6	2.9	1.8	3.6	3.9	0.7	0.7
March	2.0	2.2	1.8	1.0	2.3	3.0	2.8	1.6	3.8	4.2	0.7	0.8
April	1.9	2.1	1.9	1.1	2.3	2.8	2.6	1.6	3.6	3.8	0.7	0.7
May	1.9	2.2	1.8	1.0	2.3	2.9	2.8	1.7	3.5	3.7	0.7	0.7
June	1.9	2.2	1.7	1.1	2.3	3.0	2.6	1.6	4.0	4.2	0.7	0.8
July	2.0	2.2	1.7	1.0	2.3	2.8	2.6	1.7	4.1	4.3	0.7	0.7
August	2.0	2.3	1.5	1.1	2.3	2.9	2.8	1.8	4.4	4.6	0.7	0.8
September	2.0	2.2	1.9	1.2	2.4	2.9	2.6	1.6	4.0	4.2	0.7	0.7
October	2.0	2.2	1.5	1.2	2.3	2.9	2.7	1.7	3.9	4.1	0.8	0.8
November	2.0	2.3	1.8	1.1	2.3	3.1	2.8	1.9	4.0	4.3	0.7	0.7
December	2.1	2.4	1.9	1.1	2.5	3.1	2.9	1.8	4.1	4.4	0.8	0.8
2016												
January	2.0	2.2	1.4	1.2	2.4	3.1	2.8	1.5	4.1	4.3	0.8	0.8
February	2.1	2.3	1.6	1.2	2.4	3.0	2.9	1.8	4.2	4.4	0.7	0.8
March	2.0	2.3	2.1	1.2	2.4	3.0	2.7	1.6	4.0	4.3	0.7	0.8
April	2.1	2.3	1.7	1.1	2.4	2.9	2.9	1.7	4.2	4.4	0.7	0.8
May	2.1	2.3	1.8	1.1	2.2	2.9	3.4	1.7	4.3	4.5	0.7	0.8
June	2.1	2.3	1.7	1.1	2.4	2.9	2.7	1.8	4.2	4.4	0.8	0.9
July	2.1	2.3	1.9	1.1	2.3	2.9	3.1	1.7	4.2	4.4	0.7	0.8
August	2.1	2.3	2.2	1.2	2.4	3.0	3.0	1.7	4.2	4.5	0.8	0.9
September	2.1	2.3	1.7	1.2	2.5	2.9	3.1	1.8	4.2	4.4	0.8	0.8
October	2.1	2.4	2.0	1.4	2.5	3.1	3.1	1.7	4.4	4.5	0.8	0.8
November	2.1	2.3	2.2	1.3	2.4	2.9	2.9	1.7	4.3	4.5	0.7	0.7
December	2.0	2.3	1.9	1.3	2.2	2.6	3.0	1.7	4.3	4.4	0.7	0.8
2017												
January	2.2	2.4	2.2	1.4	2.4	3.0	3.1	1.8	4.1	4.2	0.8	0.8
February	2.1	2.3	2.3	1.4	2.6	3.2	2.7	1.7	4.0	4.1	0.8	0.8
March	2.2	2.4	2.3	1.5	2.5	3.2	2.9	1.8	4.0	4.2	0.8	0.9
April	2.1	2.3	2.2	1.5	2.2	2.7	2.8	1.8	4.1	4.2	0.7	0.7
May	2.1	2.4	2.1	1.6	2.4	3.1	2.8	1.8	4.2	4.4	0.7	0.8
June	2.2	2.4	2.0	1.6	2.4	3.0	3.0	1.8	4.1	4.3	0.7	0.7
July	2.1	2.4	2.1	1.6	2.5	2.9	3.0	1.7	3.9	4.1	0.7	0.8
August	2.1	2.4	2.2	1.5	2.4	2.9	3.2	1.7	4.0	4.2	0.7	0.8
September	2.2	2.4	2.5	1.6	2.3	2.8	3.2	1.7	4.1	4.4	0.8	0.8
October	2.2	2.4	2.6	1.6	2.4	2.9	3.2	1.8	3.9	4.1	0.7	0.8
November	2.1	2.4	1.9	1.6	2.3	2.8	3.3	1.8	4.0	4.2	0.8	0.8
December	2.2	2.4	2.0	1.7	2.4	2.9	3.0	1.8	4.1	4.3	0.8	0.8
2018												
January	2.0	2.3	2.2	1.7	2.4	2.9	2.7	1.6	3.8	3.9	0.8	0.8
February	2.1	2.4	2.1	1.7	2.4	2.8	3.0	1.7	4.2	4.4	0.7	0.8
March	2.2	2.5	2.2	1.7	2.4	2.9	3.1	1.8	4.3	4.4	0.8	0.8
April	2.2	2.5	2.3	1.6	2.5	3.1	3.2	1.8	4.3	4.6	0.8	0.9
May	2.2	2.5	2.2	1.6	2.6	3.2	3.0	1.8	4.3	4.5	0.8	0.9
June	2.3	2.5	2.4	1.6	2.7	3.4	3.1	1.7	4.2	4.4	0.9	0.9
July	2.3	2.6	2.8	1.7	2.6	3.3	3.1	1.7	4.6	4.8	0.8	0.8
August	2.3	2.6	2.4	1.6	2.7	3.4	2.9	1.8	4.7	4.9	0.8	0.8
September	2.3	2.5	2.3	1.6	2.8	3.6	2.9	1.7	4.5	4.7	0.8	0.8
October	2.3	2.6	2.4	1.6	2.6	3.3	3.2	1.9	4.4	4.6	0.8	0.8
November	2.3	2.5	2.4	1.8	2.5	3.0	2.9	1.9	4.2	4.4	0.9	0.9
December	2.3	2.5	2.5	1.7	2.6	3.1	3.1	1.9	4.3	4.6	0.8	0.8
2019												
January	2.3	2.6	2.5	1.6	2.6	3.2	3.1	1.8	4.5	4.8	0.9	0.9
February	2.3	2.5	2.5	1.6	2.6	3.1	3.0	1.9	4.5	4.7	0.8	0.9
March	2.3	2.6	2.0	1.7	2.7	3.2	3.1	1.9	4.4	4.6	0.8	0.8
April	2.3	2.6	1.9	1.7	2.7	3.3	3.0	1.8	4.6	4.9	0.8	0.9
May	2.3	2.5	2.2	1.6	2.8	3.4	2.9	1.7	4.6	4.8	0.9	0.9
June	2.3	2.5	2.5	1.6	2.7	3.4	2.9	1.7	4.7	4.9	0.8	0.9
July	2.4	2.7	2.4	1.5	2.8	3.5	3.2	2.0	4.9	5.2	0.8	0.8
August	2.4	2.7	2.4	1.5	2.8	3.5	3.0	1.9	5.0	5.3	0.8	0.8
September	2.3	2.5	2.5	1.7	2.6	3.3	3.0	1.8	4.5	4.7	0.8	0.8
October	2.3	2.6	2.4	1.5	2.4	2.9	2.9	1.9	4.8	5.0	0.8	0.8

[1]Quits are the number of quits during the entire month.
[2]The quits rate is the number of quits during the entire month as a percent of total employment.
[3]Detail will not necessarily add to totals because of the independent seasonal adjustment of the various series.
[4]Includes natural resources and mining, information, financial activities, and other services, not shown separately.
[5]Includes wholesale trade and transportation, warehousing, and utilities, not shown separately.
[6]Includes arts, entertainment, and recreation, not shown separately.
[7]Includes federal government, not shown separately.

Table 7-8. Layoffs and Discharges Levels[1] and Rates,[2] by Industry, 2008–October 2019

(Not seasonally adjusted, levels in thousands, rates per 100.)

Year and month	Level												
	Total	Total private	Mining and logging	Construction	Manufacturing	Durable goods	Non-durable goods	Trade, transportation, and utilities	Wholesale trade	Retail trade	Transportation, warehousing, and utilities	Information	Financial activities
2010	22 562	20 465	102	3 109	1 673	936	738	3 848	754	2 443	655	326	768
2011	22 134	20 794	83	2 893	1 393	768	622	3 830	632	2 517	679	280	656
2012	22 023	20 747	148	2 812	1 332	802	529	3 827	678	2 438	709	288	690
2013	20 959	19 783	150	2 426	1 243	776	466	3 810	554	2 504	755	405	748
2014	21 147	20 074	141	1 986	1 213	716	497	4 061	615	2 629	814	454	666
2015	21 777	20 434	241	2 136	1 278	791	487	4 014	572	2 586	862	344	706
2016	21 243	19 903	172	2 241	1 295	802	494	3 688	493	2 304	891	307	707
2017	21 581	20 242	129	2 245	1 252	702	550	3 730	488	2 300	945	397	685
2018	21 888	20 581	141	2 016	1 387	750	638	4 190	493	2 681	1 017	430	711
2008													
January	2 010	1 906	9	256	149	100	49	400	95	246	59	25	85
February	1 990	1 902	15	233	146	83	62	395	59	269	67	22	78
March	1 906	1 802	8	275	136	84	52	366	53	252	62	35	80
April	1 957	1 852	11	277	196	117	79	363	70	228	65	28	105
May	1 948	1 846	8	257	175	108	67	358	56	244	57	19	77
June	2 153	2 053	12	295	197	121	76	497	82	349	66	37	83
July	2 076	1 986	12	263	164	119	45	458	55	323	80	18	106
August	2 185	2 083	8	272	174	126	49	444	79	285	80	20	101
September	2 087	1 988	8	269	207	126	80	404	69	261	74	40	96
October	2 253	2 141	12	332	219	138	81	460	85	311	64	52	71
November	2 289	2 176	16	369	221	140	80	442	81	289	72	43	94
December	2 497	2 395	15	334	291	196	95	473	116	295	62	42	93
2009													
January	2 614	2 482	16	392	354	252	102	456	130	256	70	37	139
February	2 590	2 439	19	349	310	209	101	477	94	280	103	38	132
March	2 560	2 446	23	373	314	218	96	451	83	257	112	39	128
April	2 651	2 523	17	398	303	220	83	526	92	345	89	47	111
May	2 228	2 050	22	296	258	171	87	445	88	260	97	41	118
June	2 242	2 067	18	304	235	155	79	367	70	212	84	37	116
July	2 274	2 140	20	348	199	112	88	396	82	230	84	46	119
August	2 113	1 994	11	291	175	95	80	391	81	240	70	34	95
September	2 195	2 045	16	306	187	106	81	479	68	306	105	28	76
October	2 028	1 930	16	314	186	110	76	362	64	234	64	40	91
November	1 911	1 796	11	232	172	99	72	362	67	214	81	33	53
December	2 045	1 926	13	270	158	96	63	417	80	228	109	45	87
2010													
January	1 902	1 770	9	267	140	93	47	338	83	211	45	36	60
February	1 817	1 694	8	256	147	83	64	300	67	173	60	23	66
March	1 916	1 781	8	259	153	83	71	401	52	303	47	24	70
April	1 744	1 610	7	262	135	71	64	315	57	208	50	23	65
May	1 761	1 611	9	278	115	70	45	292	66	167	59	34	84
June	2 061	1 708	7	225	130	63	68	334	47	222	64	24	49
July	2 173	1 910	7	263	153	85	68	347	83	212	52	27	74
August	1 886	1 646	8	249	144	77	66	264	50	174	40	26	50
September	1 834	1 627	9	238	130	72	58	304	69	185	50	29	52
October	1 746	1 647	8	240	141	79	63	309	56	188	65	22	76
November	1 848	1 712	10	246	146	77	68	335	59	222	54	23	64
December	1 865	1 737	9	300	130	73	58	322	65	191	66	30	67
2011													
January	1 846	1 743	8	244	124	64	60	371	72	236	63	24	66
February	1 748	1 639	3	238	126	71	55	317	46	227	44	21	66
March	1 787	1 679	3	243	116	62	55	322	48	226	48	29	42
April	1 787	1 660	8	260	119	58	61	286	39	201	46	20	38
May	1 903	1 795	7	270	131	72	59	309	63	209	36	26	44
June	1 926	1 818	8	323	109	65	43	307	64	195	48	25	63
July	1 850	1 728	6	236	111	64	46	301	49	197	55	24	44
August	1 842	1 728	9	264	119	66	53	313	34	222	57	20	49
September	1 875	1 755	8	247	119	67	53	319	50	218	51	21	66
October	1 796	1 704	5	222	102	56	46	298	50	181	67	21	52
November	1 911	1 798	8	191	104	62	42	344	47	241	57	22	64
December	1 811	1 700	8	204	111	60	52	315	70	170	76	26	61
2012													
January	1 817	1 713	10	228	114	63	51	329	89	187	53	24	42
February	1 896	1 788	11	248	109	62	47	290	38	194	58	29	72
March	1 775	1 660	13	210	104	57	46	299	58	183	57	28	52
April	1 868	1 755	12	206	111	63	48	314	60	187	67	26	70
May	1 968	1 831	15	252	100	55	45	322	47	215	60	26	68
June	1 883	1 772	14	257	138	91	48	322	39	215	68	20	63
July	1 729	1 623	8	273	106	62	44	296	44	196	56	20	52
August	1 889	1 775	15	247	101	64	38	372	52	255	65	38	55
September	1 808	1 720	13	269	102	68	34	348	68	209	71	24	39
October	1 897	1 793	13	193	119	78	41	332	66	216	51	18	62
November	1 920	1 827	13	259	125	72	53	290	55	177	58	20	82
December	1 708	1 614	13	191	99	65	34	346	62	219	65	20	54
2013													
January	1 690	1 593	13	185	108	71	37	306	56	192	57	22	69
February	1 655	1 559	13	216	108	66	42	303	38	200	65	24	56
March	1 780	1 657	9	239	102	71	31	306	37	207	62	12	50
April	1 786	1 699	12	203	109	74	35	305	31	202	72	26	45
May	1 833	1 730	10	191	121	80	41	356	50	236	70	29	66
June	1 755	1 661	10	222	103	66	37	287	36	199	52	42	52
July	1 731	1 634	17	191	114	66	47	348	81	195	73	45	68
August	1 814	1 725	10	170	109	64	45	309	40	192	77	58	63
September	1 892	1 781	14	179	99	60	38	306	47	198	61	44	91
October	1 681	1 573	16	242	85	55	30	343	52	223	68	43	61
November	1 630	1 538	11	194	91	49	43	328	40	223	65	23	60
December	1 774	1 679	13	204	99	58	41	344	46	238	60	43	63

[1]Layoffs and discharges are the number of layoffs and discharges during the entire month.
[2]The layoffs and discharges rate is the number of layoffs and discharges during the entire month as a percent of total employment.

Table 7-8. Layoffs and Discharges Levels[1] and Rates,[2] by Industry, 2008–October 2019 —*Continued*

(Not seasonally adjusted, levels in thousands, rates per 100.)

Year and month	Level												
	Finance and insurance	Real estate and rental and leasing	Profes-sional and business services	Education and health services	Educa-tional services	Health care and social assistance	Leisure and hospitality	Arts, enter-tainment, and recreation	Accommo-dation and food services	Other services	Govern-ment	Federal	State and local govern-ment
2010	473	299	4 540	2 206	421	1 784	3 069	811	2 257	825	2 096	746	1 350
2011	364	295	5 144	1 988	410	1 576	3 442	949	2 492	1 085	1 340	117	1 221
2012	375	313	5 214	2 067	445	1 624	3 367	961	2 407	1 007	1 275	125	1 150
2013	427	321	4 751	2 036	465	1 571	3 326	895	2 429	893	1 177	118	1 058
2014	423	243	5 216	2 039	424	1 617	3 535	1 044	2 489	762	1 072	92	979
2015	416	288	5 210	1 825	400	1 424	3 714	1 064	2 648	970	1 344	128	1 213
2016	419	288	5 199	1 977	395	1 580	3 471	987	2 484	848	1 341	121	1 222
2017	381	302	4 887	2 062	425	1 639	3 841	1 145	2 696	1 011	1 338	118	1 221
2018	497	216	4 936	2 087	469	1 616	3 762	1 134	2 631	921	1 308	92	1 213
2008													
January	52	32	496	175	35	140	251	77	174	60	104	23	81
February	44	34	402	179	30	149	363	96	267	69	88	12	76
March	54	26	395	168	29	139	264	91	173	75	104	9	96
April	70	36	401	142	43	99	269	72	197	59	106	11	95
May	42	35	374	191	31	160	280	83	197	108	102	8	94
June	58	25	450	174	33	141	254	70	185	54	100	10	90
July	68	38	422	176	34	143	272	59	213	94	90	8	82
August	65	36	454	173	34	139	351	122	229	84	102	7	95
September	61	35	440	158	26	131	304	71	233	62	99	6	93
October	39	32	468	169	39	130	277	71	206	80	112	11	102
November	57	37	502	155	46	109	269	61	208	65	112	9	104
December	59	34	548	189	38	151	329	90	239	80	103	11	92
2009													
January	89	50	476	191	32	159	319	77	243	102	132	10	121
February	84	47	563	199	42	157	291	64	226	62	150	10	141
March	75	53	511	195	36	159	297	52	244	117	114	11	103
April	68	44	496	215	44	171	317	65	251	95	127	13	115
May	80	37	365	141	44	98	271	34	237	93	177	68	109
June	69	47	412	165	33	133	306	78	228	107	175	63	113
July	74	45	419	222	51	171	284	86	198	87	134	12	122
August	41	54	392	205	46	160	308	85	223	92	119	7	113
September	34	42	394	191	41	150	276	60	216	93	150	7	143
October	42	49	369	185	36	149	286	82	204	81	98	8	91
November	31	22	396	175	25	150	297	72	226	64	115	20	95
December	46	41	377	176	29	146	288	75	213	94	120	10	110
2010													
January	34	26	383	179	29	150	274	50	223	83	132	9	124
February	36	30	388	188	25	162	226	35	191	92	123	11	112
March	39	31	363	176	36	140	260	76	184	66	135	16	119
April	38	28	344	154	27	127	251	62	190	54	134	24	110
May	43	41	329	156	29	127	240	61	179	73	151	40	111
June	29	20	373	181	37	144	312	117	195	73	354	242	112
July	38	36	428	224	36	189	326	141	186	59	263	154	109
August	34	15	411	178	43	135	237	72	164	79	240	122	118
September	43	9	364	220	47	173	232	62	170	49	208	84	124
October	53	24	361	150	22	128	261	63	198	78	99	21	77
November	39	25	366	178	36	142	265	62	203	79	136	11	124
December	43	24	432	192	37	156	218	52	166	36	127	10	118
2011													
January	36	30	431	149	33	116	247	72	175	78	103	7	95
February	38	29	376	168	50	119	234	39	195	89	108	8	101
March	27	15	408	148	35	113	296	77	219	72	108	9	99
April	14	24	448	155	30	125	226	55	171	101	126	12	114
May	28	16	481	156	34	121	289	86	203	84	108	10	97
June	33	30	428	190	35	156	284	76	208	81	108	11	97
July	26	18	436	171	38	134	295	72	223	104	123	9	114
August	24	25	439	175	27	148	261	75	186	78	114	12	101
September	43	23	413	149	34	116	311	89	221	101	120	11	109
October	23	29	418	167	35	132	304	81	223	114	92	9	84
November	41	23	436	196	42	154	341	104	237	92	113	10	102
December	33	28	430	160	30	130	298	76	222	87	112	5	106
2012													
January	23	19	377	201	59	142	302	92	210	86	104	10	94
February	25	47	512	143	27	116	299	96	203	74	108	9	99
March	20	32	431	153	27	126	300	96	204	71	115	8	107
April	49	21	444	180	41	139	279	94	186	113	113	10	104
May	39	29	488	187	43	144	273	82	190	100	137	9	128
June	34	29	437	217	40	177	244	65	178	59	111	9	102
July	24	27	392	163	36	127	258	65	193	54	106	12	94
August	30	25	413	157	26	131	311	69	242	67	114	13	102
September	26	13	426	142	23	119	257	70	187	99	88	11	77
October	34	28	464	197	55	142	289	76	213	106	103	11	92
November	55	26	493	167	34	132	269	73	196	110	93	10	83
December	25	29	372	150	38	112	297	104	193	73	93	10	83
2013													
January	38	31	421	156	32	125	259	61	199	54	97	8	89
February	38	18	351	193	46	147	244	57	187	50	97	9	88
March	26	25	379	154	39	115	283	56	228	122	123	8	115
April	27	18	386	175	41	134	329	86	243	109	87	9	78
May	34	32	398	199	32	167	272	80	193	89	103	14	89
June	23	29	415	158	35	123	287	74	212	86	95	10	85
July	42	27	325	167	35	131	279	81	198	79	97	8	89
August	36	26	480	181	50	132	281	68	212	65	88	9	79
September	53	38	454	179	48	131	354	89	265	64	111	10	101
October	33	28	361	152	31	121	211	67	144	60	108	15	93
November	38	22	375	164	42	122	235	75	159	57	91	7	84
December	37	26	387	170	45	126	277	71	206	77	96	9	87

[1]Layoffs and discharges are the number of layoffs and discharges during the entire month.
[2]The layoffs and discharges rate is the number of layoffs and discharges during the entire month as a percent of total employment.

Table 7-8. Layoffs and Discharges Levels[1] and Rates,[2] by Industry, 2008–October 2019 —*Continued*

(Not seasonally adjusted, levels in thousands, rates per 100.)

Year and month	Rate												
	Total	Total private	Mining and logging	Construction	Manufacturing	Durable goods	Nondurable goods	Trade, transportation, and utilities	Wholesale trade	Retail trade	Transportation, warehousing, and utilities	Information	Financial activities
2010	17.3	19.0	14.5	56.3	14.5	13.3	16.5	15.7	14.0	16.9	13.8	12.0	10.0
2011	16.8	18.9	10.5	52.3	11.9	10.6	14.0	15.3	11.5	17.2	14.0	10.5	8.5
2012	16.4	18.5	17.5	49.8	11.2	10.7	11.9	15.1	12.1	16.4	14.3	10.8	8.9
2013	15.4	17.3	17.4	41.4	10.3	10.3	10.4	14.8	9.8	16.6	14.9	15.0	9.5
2014	15.2	17.1	15.8	32.3	10.0	9.3	11.0	15.4	10.7	17.1	15.6	16.7	8.3
2015	15.4	17.1	29.6	33.1	10.4	10.2	10.6	15.0	9.9	16.6	15.9	12.5	8.7
2016	14.7	16.3	25.7	33.3	10.5	10.4	10.6	13.6	8.5	14.6	16.0	11.0	8.5
2017	14.7	16.3	19.1	32.2	10.1	9.1	11.7	13.6	8.4	14.5	16.4	14.1	8.1
2018	14.7	16.3	19.3	27.7	10.9	9.4	13.5	15.1	8.4	16.9	17.0	15.2	8.3
2008													
January	1.5	1.6	1.2	3.4	1.1	1.1	1.0	1.5	1.6	1.6	1.1	0.8	1.0
February	1.4	1.6	2.0	3.1	1.1	1.0	1.2	1.5	1.0	1.7	1.3	0.7	0.9
March	1.4	1.6	1.1	3.7	1.0	1.0	1.0	1.4	0.9	1.6	1.2	1.2	1.0
April	1.4	1.6	1.4	3.8	1.4	1.4	1.6	1.4	1.2	1.5	1.3	0.9	1.3
May	1.4	1.6	1.0	3.5	1.3	1.3	1.4	1.4	1.0	1.6	1.1	0.6	0.9
June	1.6	1.8	1.5	4.1	1.5	1.4	1.5	1.9	1.4	2.3	1.3	1.2	1.0
July	1.5	1.7	1.5	3.7	1.2	1.4	0.9	1.7	0.9	2.1	1.6	0.6	1.3
August	1.6	1.8	1.1	3.8	1.3	1.5	1.0	1.7	1.4	1.9	1.6	0.7	1.2
September	1.5	1.7	1.1	3.8	1.6	1.5	1.6	1.6	1.2	1.7	1.5	1.4	1.2
October	1.7	1.9	1.5	4.8	1.7	1.7	1.7	1.8	1.5	2.1	1.3	1.8	0.9
November	1.7	1.9	2.0	5.4	1.7	1.7	1.7	1.7	1.4	1.9	1.5	1.5	1.2
December	1.9	2.1	1.9	5.0	2.3	2.4	2.0	1.9	2.0	2.0	1.3	1.5	1.1
2009													
January	1.9	2.2	2.1	6.0	2.8	3.2	2.2	1.8	2.3	1.7	1.4	1.3	1.7
February	1.9	2.2	2.5	5.4	2.5	2.7	2.2	1.9	1.7	1.9	2.1	1.3	1.7
March	1.9	2.2	3.2	5.9	2.6	2.9	2.1	1.8	1.5	1.8	2.3	1.4	1.6
April	2.0	2.3	2.3	6.5	2.5	3.0	1.8	2.1	1.7	2.4	1.8	1.7	1.4
May	1.7	1.9	3.2	4.8	2.2	2.3	1.9	1.8	1.6	1.8	2.0	1.5	1.5
June	1.7	1.9	2.6	5.1	2.0	2.2	1.7	1.5	1.3	1.5	1.8	1.3	1.5
July	1.7	2.0	2.9	5.9	1.7	1.6	1.9	1.6	1.5	1.6	1.8	1.6	1.5
August	1.6	1.8	1.7	5.0	1.5	1.3	1.8	1.6	1.5	1.7	1.5	1.2	1.2
September	1.7	1.9	2.4	5.3	1.6	1.5	1.8	1.9	1.3	2.1	2.2	1.0	1.0
October	1.6	1.8	2.5	5.5	1.6	1.6	1.7	1.5	1.2	1.6	1.4	1.5	1.2
November	1.5	1.7	1.7	4.1	1.5	1.4	1.6	1.5	1.2	1.5	1.7	1.2	0.7
December	1.6	1.8	2.0	4.8	1.4	1.4	1.4	1.7	1.5	1.6	2.3	1.6	1.1
2010													
January	1.5	1.6	1.4	4.8	1.2	1.3	1.0	1.4	1.5	1.5	0.9	1.3	0.8
February	1.4	1.6	1.2	4.6	1.3	1.2	1.4	1.2	1.3	1.2	1.3	0.8	0.9
March	1.5	1.7	1.2	4.7	1.3	1.2	1.6	1.6	1.0	2.1	1.0	0.9	0.9
April	1.3	1.5	1.1	4.7	1.2	1.0	1.4	1.3	1.1	1.4	1.1	0.8	0.8
May	1.3	1.5	1.3	5.0	1.0	1.0	1.0	1.2	1.2	1.2	1.3	1.3	1.1
June	1.6	1.6	1.0	4.1	1.1	0.9	1.5	1.4	0.9	1.5	1.4	0.9	0.6
July	1.7	1.8	1.0	4.8	1.3	1.2	1.5	1.4	1.5	1.5	1.1	1.0	1.0
August	1.4	1.5	1.2	4.5	1.2	1.1	1.5	1.1	0.9	1.2	0.8	0.9	0.6
September	1.4	1.5	1.2	4.3	1.1	1.0	1.3	1.2	1.3	1.3	1.0	1.1	0.7
October	1.3	1.5	1.1	4.4	1.2	1.1	1.4	1.3	1.0	1.3	1.4	0.8	1.0
November	1.4	1.6	1.3	4.5	1.3	1.1	1.5	1.4	1.1	1.5	1.1	0.8	0.8
December	1.4	1.6	1.3	5.5	1.1	1.0	1.3	1.3	1.2	1.3	1.4	1.1	0.9
2011													
January	1.4	1.6	1.2	4.5	1.1	0.9	1.3	1.5	1.3	1.6	1.3	0.9	0.9
February	1.3	1.5	0.4	4.4	1.1	1.0	1.2	1.3	0.8	1.6	0.9	0.8	0.9
March	1.4	1.5	0.4	4.4	1.0	0.9	1.2	1.3	0.9	1.5	1.0	1.1	0.5
April	1.4	1.5	1.1	4.7	1.0	0.8	1.4	1.1	0.7	1.4	1.0	0.7	0.5
May	1.4	1.6	0.9	4.9	1.1	1.0	1.3	1.2	1.2	1.4	0.7	1.0	0.6
June	1.5	1.7	1.1	5.8	0.9	0.9	1.0	1.2	1.2	1.3	1.0	0.9	0.8
July	1.4	1.6	0.8	4.2	0.9	0.9	1.0	1.2	0.9	1.3	1.1	0.9	0.6
August	1.4	1.6	1.1	4.8	1.0	0.9	1.2	1.2	0.6	1.5	1.2	0.7	0.6
September	1.4	1.6	1.0	4.4	1.0	0.9	1.2	1.3	0.9	1.5	1.0	0.8	0.9
October	1.4	1.5	0.7	4.0	0.9	0.8	1.0	1.2	0.9	1.2	1.4	0.8	0.7
November	1.4	1.6	1.0	3.4	0.9	0.8	1.0	1.4	0.9	1.6	1.2	0.8	0.8
December	1.4	1.5	0.9	3.6	0.9	0.8	1.2	1.2	1.3	1.1	1.5	1.0	0.8
2012													
January	1.4	1.5	1.2	4.1	1.0	0.8	1.2	1.3	1.6	1.3	1.1	0.9	0.5
February	1.4	1.6	1.3	4.4	0.9	0.8	1.1	1.1	0.7	1.3	1.2	1.1	0.9
March	1.3	1.5	1.5	3.7	0.9	0.8	1.0	1.2	1.0	1.2	1.2	1.0	0.7
April	1.4	1.6	1.4	3.7	0.9	0.8	1.1	1.2	1.1	1.3	1.4	1.0	0.9
May	1.5	1.6	1.7	4.5	0.8	0.7	1.0	1.3	0.8	1.5	1.2	1.0	0.9
June	1.4	1.6	1.7	4.6	1.2	1.2	1.1	1.3	0.7	1.5	1.4	0.7	0.8
July	1.3	1.4	1.0	4.9	0.9	0.8	1.0	1.2	0.8	1.3	1.1	0.8	0.7
August	1.4	1.6	1.7	4.4	0.8	0.9	0.8	1.5	0.9	1.7	1.3	1.4	0.7
September	1.3	1.5	1.5	4.8	0.9	0.9	0.8	1.4	1.2	1.4	1.4	0.9	0.5
October	1.4	1.6	1.6	3.4	1.0	1.0	0.9	1.3	1.2	1.4	1.0	0.7	0.8
November	1.4	1.6	1.5	4.6	1.0	1.0	1.2	1.1	1.0	1.2	1.2	0.7	1.0
December	1.3	1.4	1.5	3.3	0.8	0.9	0.8	1.4	1.1	1.5	1.3	0.7	0.7
2013													
January	1.2	1.4	1.6	3.2	0.9	0.9	0.8	1.2	1.0	1.3	1.1	0.8	0.9
February	1.2	1.4	1.6	3.7	0.9	0.9	0.9	1.2	0.7	1.3	1.3	0.9	0.7
March	1.3	1.5	1.1	4.1	0.9	0.9	0.7	1.2	0.7	1.4	1.2	0.4	0.6
April	1.3	1.5	1.4	3.5	0.9	1.0	0.8	1.2	0.5	1.4	1.4	0.9	0.6
May	1.3	1.5	1.1	3.3	1.0	1.1	0.9	1.4	0.9	1.6	1.4	1.1	0.8
June	1.3	1.5	1.1	3.8	0.9	0.9	0.8	1.1	0.6	1.3	1.0	1.5	0.7
July	1.3	1.4	1.9	3.3	0.9	0.9	1.1	1.4	1.4	1.3	1.4	1.7	0.9
August	1.3	1.5	1.1	2.9	0.9	0.8	1.0	1.2	0.7	1.3	1.5	2.2	0.8
September	1.4	1.5	1.6	3.0	0.8	0.8	0.9	1.2	0.8	1.3	1.2	1.6	1.1
October	1.2	1.4	1.8	4.1	0.7	0.7	0.7	1.3	0.9	1.5	1.3	1.6	0.8
November	1.2	1.3	1.3	3.3	0.8	0.6	0.9	1.3	0.7	1.5	1.3	0.8	0.8
December	1.3	1.5	1.5	3.4	0.8	0.8	0.9	1.3	0.8	1.6	1.2	1.6	0.8

[1]Layoffs and discharges are the number of layoffs and discharges during the entire month.
[2]The layoffs and discharges rate is the number of layoffs and discharges during the entire month as a percent of total employment.

Table 7-8. Layoffs and Discharges Levels[1] and Rates,[2] by Industry, 2008–October 2019 —*Continued*

(Not seasonally adjusted, levels in thousands, rates per 100.)

Year and month	Rate												
	Finance and insurance	Real estate and rental and leasing	Professional and business services	Education and health services	Educational services	Health care and social assistance	Leisure and hospitality	Arts, entertainment, and recreation	Accommodation and food services	Other services	Government	Federal	State and local government
2010	8.2	15.5	27.1	11.0	13.3	10.6	23.5	42.4	20.3	15.5	9.3	25.1	6.9
2011	6.3	15.3	29.6	9.8	12.6	9.2	25.8	49.5	21.8	20.2	6.1	4.1	6.3
2012	6.4	16.0	29.0	10.0	13.3	9.3	24.5	48.8	20.4	18.5	5.8	4.4	6.0
2013	7.3	16.1	25.6	9.7	13.9	8.9	23.3	44.1	19.9	16.3	5.4	4.3	5.5
2014	7.1	11.9	27.3	9.5	12.4	9.0	24.1	49.6	19.8	13.7	4.9	3.4	5.1
2015	6.9	13.8	26.5	8.3	11.5	7.7	24.5	49.1	20.4	17.3	6.1	4.6	6.3
2016	6.8	13.5	25.8	8.7	11.1	8.3	22.2	43.8	18.5	14.9	6.0	4.3	6.3
2017	6.1	13.8	23.8	8.9	11.6	8.4	23.9	49.1	19.7	17.5	6.0	4.2	6.2
2018	7.9	9.6	23.5	8.8	12.6	8.1	23.0	47.4	18.9	15.8	5.8	3.3	6.2
2008													
January	0.9	1.5	2.7	0.9	1.2	0.9	1.9	3.9	1.5	1.1	0.5	0.8	0.4
February	0.7	1.6	2.2	0.9	1.0	0.9	2.7	4.8	2.3	1.2	0.4	0.4	0.4
March	0.9	1.2	2.2	0.9	1.0	0.9	2.0	4.6	1.5	1.4	0.5	0.3	0.5
April	1.1	1.7	2.2	0.7	1.4	0.6	2.0	3.6	1.7	1.1	0.5	0.4	0.5
May	0.7	1.6	2.1	1.0	1.0	1.0	2.1	4.2	1.7	1.9	0.5	0.3	0.5
June	0.9	1.2	2.5	0.9	1.1	0.9	1.9	3.5	1.6	1.0	0.4	0.4	0.5
July	1.1	1.8	2.4	0.9	1.1	0.9	2.0	3.0	1.9	1.7	0.4	0.3	0.4
August	1.1	1.7	2.6	0.9	1.1	0.9	2.6	6.2	2.0	1.5	0.5	0.3	0.5
September	1.0	1.6	2.5	0.8	0.9	0.8	2.3	3.6	2.0	1.1	0.4	0.2	0.5
October	0.6	1.5	2.7	0.9	1.3	0.8	2.1	3.6	1.8	1.5	0.5	0.4	0.5
November	0.9	1.8	2.9	0.8	1.5	0.7	2.0	3.1	1.8	1.2	0.5	0.3	0.5
December	1.0	1.6	3.2	1.0	1.2	0.9	2.5	4.6	2.1	1.5	0.5	0.4	0.5
2009													
January	1.5	2.4	2.8	1.0	1.0	1.0	2.4	3.9	2.2	1.9	0.6	0.4	0.6
February	1.4	2.3	3.3	1.0	1.4	1.0	2.2	3.3	2.0	1.1	0.7	0.3	0.7
March	1.3	2.6	3.0	1.0	1.2	1.0	2.3	2.7	2.2	2.2	0.5	0.4	0.5
April	1.2	2.2	3.0	1.1	1.4	1.0	2.4	3.4	2.3	1.8	0.6	0.4	0.6
May	1.4	1.9	2.2	0.7	1.4	0.6	2.1	1.8	2.1	1.7	0.8	2.4	0.6
June	1.2	2.4	2.5	0.8	1.1	0.8	2.3	4.1	2.0	2.0	0.8	2.2	0.6
July	1.3	2.3	2.5	1.1	1.7	1.0	2.2	4.5	1.8	1.6	0.6	0.4	0.6
August	0.7	2.7	2.4	1.0	1.5	1.0	2.4	4.5	2.0	1.7	0.5	0.2	0.6
September	0.6	2.1	2.4	1.0	1.3	0.9	2.1	3.1	1.9	1.7	0.7	0.2	0.7
October	0.7	2.5	2.2	0.9	1.2	0.9	2.2	4.3	1.8	1.5	0.4	0.3	0.5
November	0.5	1.1	2.4	0.9	0.8	0.9	2.3	3.8	2.0	1.2	0.5	0.7	0.5
December	0.8	2.1	2.3	0.9	0.9	0.9	2.2	4.0	1.9	1.8	0.5	0.4	0.6
2010													
January	0.6	1.3	2.3	0.9	0.9	0.9	2.1	2.7	2.0	1.6	0.6	0.3	0.6
February	0.6	1.5	2.3	0.9	0.8	1.0	1.7	1.8	1.7	1.7	0.5	0.4	0.6
March	0.7	1.6	2.2	0.9	1.1	0.8	2.0	4.0	1.7	1.2	0.6	0.6	0.6
April	0.7	1.4	2.1	0.8	0.9	0.8	1.9	3.2	1.7	1.0	0.6	0.8	0.6
May	0.7	2.1	2.0	0.8	0.9	0.8	1.8	3.2	1.6	1.4	0.7	1.2	0.6
June	0.5	1.0	2.2	0.9	1.2	0.9	2.4	6.1	1.8	1.4	1.6	7.6	0.6
July	0.7	1.9	2.6	1.1	1.1	1.1	2.5	7.3	1.7	1.1	1.2	5.1	0.6
August	0.6	0.8	2.4	0.9	1.4	0.8	1.8	3.8	1.5	1.5	1.1	4.1	0.6
September	0.7	0.5	2.2	1.1	1.5	1.0	1.8	3.2	1.5	0.9	0.9	2.9	0.6
October	0.9	1.2	2.1	0.7	0.7	0.8	2.0	3.3	1.8	1.5	0.4	0.7	0.4
November	0.7	1.3	2.2	0.9	1.1	0.8	2.0	3.3	1.8	1.5	0.6	0.4	0.6
December	0.7	1.2	2.5	1.0	1.1	0.9	1.7	2.7	1.5	0.7	0.6	0.3	0.6
2011													
January	0.6	1.6	2.5	0.7	1.0	0.7	1.9	3.8	1.6	1.5	0.5	0.3	0.5
February	0.7	1.5	2.2	0.8	1.5	0.7	1.8	2.0	1.7	1.7	0.5	0.3	0.5
March	0.5	0.8	2.4	0.7	1.1	0.7	2.2	4.0	1.9	1.3	0.5	0.3	0.5
April	0.2	1.3	2.6	0.8	0.9	0.7	1.7	2.9	1.5	1.9	0.6	0.4	0.6
May	0.5	0.8	2.8	0.8	1.1	0.7	2.2	4.5	1.8	1.6	0.5	0.4	0.5
June	0.6	1.5	2.5	0.9	1.1	0.9	2.1	3.9	1.8	1.5	0.5	0.4	0.5
July	0.5	0.9	2.5	0.8	1.2	0.8	2.2	3.7	1.9	1.9	0.6	0.3	0.6
August	0.4	1.3	2.5	0.9	0.8	0.9	1.9	3.9	1.6	1.5	0.5	0.4	0.5
September	0.7	1.2	2.4	0.7	1.0	0.7	2.3	4.6	1.9	1.9	0.5	0.4	0.6
October	0.4	1.5	2.4	0.8	1.1	0.8	2.3	4.2	1.9	2.1	0.4	0.3	0.4
November	0.7	1.2	2.5	1.0	1.3	0.9	2.5	5.4	2.0	1.7	0.5	0.4	0.5
December	0.6	1.5	2.4	0.8	0.9	0.8	2.2	3.9	1.9	1.6	0.5	0.2	0.6
2012													
January	0.4	1.0	2.1	1.0	1.8	0.8	2.2	4.7	1.8	1.6	0.5	0.4	0.5
February	0.4	2.4	2.9	0.7	0.8	0.7	2.2	4.9	1.7	1.4	0.5	0.3	0.5
March	0.3	1.6	2.4	0.7	0.8	0.7	2.2	4.8	1.7	1.3	0.5	0.3	0.6
April	0.8	1.1	2.5	0.9	1.2	0.8	2.0	4.8	1.6	2.1	0.5	0.3	0.5
May	0.7	1.5	2.7	0.9	1.3	0.8	2.0	4.2	1.6	1.9	0.6	0.3	0.7
June	0.6	1.5	2.4	1.0	1.2	1.0	1.8	3.3	1.5	1.1	0.5	0.3	0.5
July	0.4	1.4	2.2	0.8	1.1	0.7	1.9	3.3	1.6	1.0	0.5	0.4	0.5
August	0.5	1.3	2.3	0.8	0.8	0.8	2.3	3.5	2.0	1.2	0.5	0.4	0.5
September	0.4	0.7	2.4	0.7	0.7	0.7	1.9	3.5	1.6	1.8	0.4	0.4	0.4
October	0.6	1.4	2.6	0.9	1.7	0.8	2.1	3.8	1.8	1.9	0.5	0.4	0.5
November	0.9	1.3	2.7	0.8	1.0	0.8	1.9	3.7	1.6	2.0	0.4	0.4	0.4
December	0.4	1.5	2.0	0.7	1.1	0.6	2.1	5.2	1.6	1.3	0.4	0.4	0.4
2013													
January	0.6	1.6	2.3	0.7	1.0	0.7	1.8	3.0	1.7	1.0	0.4	0.3	0.5
February	0.7	0.9	1.9	0.9	1.4	0.8	1.7	2.8	1.5	0.9	0.4	0.3	0.5
March	0.4	1.3	2.1	0.7	1.2	0.7	2.0	2.8	1.9	2.2	0.6	0.3	0.6
April	0.5	0.9	2.1	0.8	1.2	0.8	2.3	4.3	2.0	2.0	0.4	0.3	0.4
May	0.6	1.6	2.1	0.9	1.0	0.9	1.9	3.9	1.6	1.6	0.5	0.5	0.5
June	0.4	1.4	2.2	0.7	1.0	0.7	2.0	3.7	1.7	1.6	0.4	0.3	0.4
July	0.7	1.3	1.7	0.8	1.1	0.7	2.0	4.0	1.6	1.4	0.4	0.3	0.5
August	0.6	1.3	2.6	0.9	1.5	0.7	2.0	3.4	1.7	1.2	0.4	0.3	0.4
September	0.9	1.9	2.4	0.8	1.4	0.7	2.5	4.4	2.2	1.2	0.5	0.4	0.5
October	0.6	1.4	1.9	0.7	0.9	0.7	1.5	3.3	1.2	1.1	0.5	0.6	0.5
November	0.6	1.1	2.0	0.8	1.2	0.7	1.6	3.7	1.3	1.0	0.4	0.3	0.4
December	0.6	1.3	2.1	0.8	1.3	0.7	1.9	3.5	1.7	1.4	0.4	0.3	0.5

[1]Layoffs and discharges are the number of layoffs and discharges during the entire month.
[2]The layoffs and discharges rate is the number of layoffs and discharges during the entire month as a percent of total employment.

Table 7-8. Layoffs and Discharges Levels[1] and Rates,[2] by Industry, 2008–October 2019 —*Continued*

(Not seasonally adjusted, levels in thousands, rates per 100.)

Year and month	Level												
	Total	Total private	Mining and logging	Construction	Manufacturing	Durable goods	Non-durable goods	Trade, transportation, and utilities	Wholesale trade	Retail trade	Transportation, warehousing, and utilities	Information	Financial activities
2014													
January	1 815	1 722	10	144	114	76	38	353	50	222	81	40	65
February	1 758	1 668	9	144	79	52	27	330	37	219	73	55	65
March	1 697	1 594	13	144	94	43	51	329	30	223	75	47	64
April	1 752	1 670	8	141	117	76	42	363	46	252	65	39	62
May	1 706	1 620	17	148	94	55	39	317	39	216	62	30	66
June	1 753	1 653	10	135	112	61	51	328	57	214	58	28	57
July	1 801	1 718	11	169	89	57	32	366	78	220	67	47	46
August	1 698	1 615	10	156	83	43	40	344	72	214	58	26	47
September	1 716	1 636	14	147	107	62	45	325	45	212	68	33	39
October	1 844	1 763	13	183	108	62	45	349	57	212	80	40	42
November	1 727	1 636	14	204	101	64	37	333	53	214	67	39	55
December	1 860	1 749	15	229	114	68	46	326	51	213	61	32	64
2015													
January	1 772	1 666	21	206	100	57	43	369	64	234	71	30	51
February	1 743	1 641	20	180	109	71	38	307	49	188	70	28	40
March	1 951	1 832	23	209	113	69	44	380	64	229	87	30	65
April	1 848	1 738	25	144	100	64	36	331	30	224	77	37	71
May	1 711	1 602	18	138	89	52	37	328	26	221	82	27	57
June	1 829	1 708	10	225	107	61	45	353	74	216	64	31	57
July	1 712	1 609	23	153	110	73	37	370	66	234	70	26	65
August	1 765	1 661	23	185	110	68	42	327	42	221	64	27	70
September	1 951	1 834	20	190	110	68	42	324	26	207	91	26	67
October	1 845	1 727	18	188	113	68	44	322	49	206	67	30	43
November	1 792	1 672	18	167	111	71	40	311	44	193	74	32	58
December	1 836	1 715	19	155	104	68	36	304	38	201	64	20	58
2016													
January	1 806	1 689	16	182	99	63	36	326	51	204	71	27	54
February	1 913	1 794	21	216	132	92	39	316	45	191	80	29	61
March	1 863	1 744	27	161	112	72	40	279	47	160	71	24	68
April	1 783	1 660	16	215	112	67	45	279	46	171	61	32	60
May	1 795	1 670	13	199	130	88	42	329	59	191	79	34	51
June	1 738	1 638	16	158	106	67	40	319	40	188	91	28	49
July	1 777	1 686	9	166	95	59	36	364	36	240	88	29	47
August	1 825	1 701	13	177	105	65	40	312	47	179	86	25	57
September	1 593	1 482	10	157	107	61	46	329	31	243	56	14	56
October	1 637	1 538	12	186	96	57	39	273	34	171	69	19	77
November	1 772	1 649	9	150	104	60	44	287	29	186	72	27	56
December	1 769	1 679	6	257	102	57	45	275	28	174	73	19	68
2017													
January	1 735	1 634	12	185	107	61	46	307	47	164	96	29	48
February	1 687	1 569	12	141	81	49	32	310	49	212	49	22	72
March	1 745	1 660	9	194	111	69	42	325	54	203	67	30	69
April	1 719	1 608	8	212	111	54	58	289	35	183	71	28	47
May	1 796	1 671	12	219	98	56	42	295	44	186	66	43	49
June	1 958	1 847	10	218	101	64	38	342	41	221	80	39	61
July	1 886	1 771	10	216	113	59	54	275	43	172	60	26	66
August	1 849	1 733	9	197	95	62	34	308	44	187	76	32	64
September	1 817	1 713	7	206	106	59	47	281	32	178	71	43	43
October	1 803	1 695	11	187	105	53	51	275	34	185	57	38	74
November	1 738	1 636	14	174	112	56	56	345	31	242	72	24	49
December	1 787	1 663	11	133	107	59	47	329	34	188	107	43	49
2018													
January	1 934	1 829	8	167	111	67	44	373	52	232	89	41	69
February	1 763	1 646	7	161	116	60	56	301	43	184	74	35	45
March	1 771	1 663	10	182	111	55	55	313	28	216	70	35	41
April	1 788	1 697	14	155	121	68	53	357	41	236	80	42	73
May	1 811	1 720	15	174	127	65	62	278	23	171	84	38	84
June	1 843	1 746	14	179	117	60	57	308	37	195	76	39	74
July	1 859	1 708	15	155	129	61	68	327	35	214	78	30	58
August	1 809	1 693	14	162	113	60	53	396	39	272	86	38	57
September	1 818	1 701	14	180	101	59	41	360	42	231	87	46	56
October	1 855	1 731	10	148	130	83	47	409	58	256	96	21	34
November	1 889	1 780	13	192	109	60	49	366	50	221	94	24	64
December	1 751	1 653	10	164	111	51	60	360	45	230	85	38	58
2019													
January	1 695	1 562	11	181	123	52	70	305	43	179	82	32	57
February	1 784	1 664	14	169	118	61	56	324	42	190	92	30	48
March	1 693	1 601	15	181	122	76	46	326	30	207	88	24	32
April	1 830	1 726	11	240	111	64	47	351	36	234	80	33	54
May	1 773	1 683	8	211	112	61	51	297	34	194	70	28	65
June	1 711	1 615	8	211	109	55	54	313	56	184	73	28	63
July	1 788	1 698	12	183	112	63	49	372	63	216	93	42	63
August	1 812	1 709	10	218	104	57	48	368	54	227	88	38	59
September	1 971	1 871	12	218	112	65	48	400	77	235	88	36	62
October	1 795	1 674	13	254	106	64	43	355	66	200	89	38	43

[1]Layoffs and discharges are the number of layoffs and discharges during the entire month.
[2]The layoffs and discharges rate is the number of layoffs and discharges during the entire month as a percent of total employment.

Table 7-8. Layoffs and Discharges Levels[1] and Rates,[2] by Industry, 2008–October 2019 —*Continued*

(Not seasonally adjusted, levels in thousands, rates per 100.)

Year and month	Level												
	Finance and insurance	Real estate and rental and leasing	Professional and business services	Education and health services	Educational services	Health care and social assistance	Leisure and hospitality	Arts, entertainment, and recreation	Accommodation and food services	Other services	Government	Federal	State and local government
2014													
January	47	17	420	194	49	145	314	81	234	68	93	8	85
February	37	27	457	162	34	128	291	95	196	75	90	9	82
March	44	20	401	205	49	156	246	71	176	52	103	6	97
April	38	25	431	192	29	163	276	96	180	40	83	6	77
May	20	46	401	155	33	122	334	88	245	60	87	8	79
June	36	20	417	160	32	127	337	74	264	68	101	10	90
July	25	21	440	151	35	116	318	80	239	81	83	9	75
August	31	17	472	155	35	120	258	102	156	64	83	8	76
September	25	14	421	190	43	147	305	94	211	54	80	9	71
October	31	11	531	178	32	146	257	75	182	63	80	8	73
November	33	22	396	143	27	116	277	84	193	74	91	8	84
December	51	14	436	168	32	136	304	84	220	61	111	6	105
2015													
January	24	27	400	131	32	99	287	103	184	72	106	9	96
February	18	22	411	156	30	125	315	115	199	76	103	9	94
March	42	23	456	155	30	125	317	117	200	84	119	13	106
April	44	27	463	142	30	112	362	92	271	62	111	11	99
May	34	22	419	155	33	123	310	67	243	61	109	18	91
June	34	23	401	152	39	113	274	81	193	98	122	11	111
July	46	20	403	143	24	119	236	44	192	80	103	10	93
August	41	29	370	143	39	104	313	74	239	93	104	8	96
September	39	28	485	180	37	142	316	77	238	116	116	11	106
October	24	19	443	158	46	112	333	101	232	79	118	12	106
November	31	27	461	162	38	124	302	85	217	49	120	11	109
December	38	20	481	156	20	136	338	110	228	79	121	11	110
2016													
January	32	22	507	165	34	131	255	92	163	58	117	12	105
February	39	22	448	170	55	115	335	61	273	67	119	10	109
March	46	22	492	168	38	130	326	98	227	88	118	11	107
April	34	26	438	152	40	112	290	66	224	66	123	12	110
May	33	18	401	164	38	126	272	81	191	77	125	12	112
June	27	22	428	166	36	130	301	79	222	67	99	11	89
July	24	22	451	158	35	123	307	74	234	60	91	9	82
August	37	20	436	185	27	158	324	113	211	66	124	10	114
September	33	24	348	133	19	113	238	68	170	89	112	9	103
October	44	34	389	163	23	140	273	83	190	50	99	11	88
November	34	22	450	204	26	178	282	68	213	80	123	11	113
December	33	35	406	153	25	128	311	105	206	82	90	5	85
2017													
January	28	20	381	128	29	99	354	69	286	84	100	10	91
February	45	27	396	146	16	130	309	70	239	80	118	10	108
March	30	39	366	158	32	126	307	60	247	89	86	10	76
April	22	25	376	171	38	132	265	65	200	100	112	13	98
May	24	26	440	190	41	148	253	84	169	72	125	8	117
June	42	19	523	158	36	122	333	101	233	62	111	9	102
July	30	36	460	176	31	145	347	163	184	81	115	10	105
August	33	31	394	213	32	181	343	106	238	77	116	11	106
September	19	24	436	164	35	129	353	118	235	73	104	10	94
October	48	25	406	175	45	130	318	96	222	106	108	9	99
November	32	16	330	189	39	150	317	97	220	81	102	11	91
December	29	21	383	189	45	144	298	80	218	122	124	9	115
2018													
January	48	21	418	185	40	146	382	96	286	75	106	9	96
February	31	15	425	181	44	138	308	91	217	66	117	10	107
March	23	17	426	224	40	184	287	100	186	35	108	8	100
April	53	20	360	175	33	143	317	113	204	84	91	7	84
May	60	25	430	159	38	121	321	97	224	94	91	7	84
June	52	22	432	183	30	153	300	114	186	101	97	7	90
July	42	16	384	196	52	145	334	112	222	80	151	11	140
August	41	15	410	143	46	97	286	92	194	74	115	7	108
September	43	13	399	162	37	125	314	75	239	69	117	7	110
October	20	14	418	165	28	136	320	85	236	75	125	7	118
November	44	20	426	166	45	121	329	100	230	89	110	5	104
December	44	14	406	155	42	112	279	96	183	73	98	9	89
2019													
January	33	24	358	175	42	133	263	74	189	59	132	10	122
February	31	17	423	193	46	147	274	84	189	72	120	6	114
March	22	10	422	164	38	126	262	48	214	54	92	7	86
April	31	23	451	170	35	135	263	63	201	43	104	6	97
May	35	30	469	170	36	134	257	97	160	65	90	7	83
June	31	31	376	164	30	134	272	57	215	71	97	8	89
July	27	36	410	159	26	133	296	67	229	49	91	7	84
August	33	26	441	137	36	100	257	71	186	76	102	10	93
September	25	37	456	178	33	145	335	72	263	62	100	9	91
October	18	25	416	165	29	136	249	79	170	35	121	25	96

[1]Layoffs and discharges are the number of layoffs and discharges during the entire month.
[2]The layoffs and discharges rate is the number of layoffs and discharges during the entire month as a percent of total employment.

Table 7-8. Layoffs and Discharges Levels[1] and Rates,[2] by Industry, 2008–October 2019 —*Continued*

(Not seasonally adjusted, levels in thousands, rates per 100.)

Year and month	Rate												
	Total	Total private	Mining and logging	Construction	Manufacturing	Durable goods	Nondurable goods	Trade, transportation, and utilities	Wholesale trade	Retail trade	Transportation, warehousing, and utilities	Information	Financial activities
2014													
January	1.3	1.5	1.1	2.4	0.9	1.0	0.8	1.4	0.9	1.5	1.6	1.5	0.8
February	1.3	1.4	1.1	2.4	0.7	0.7	0.6	1.3	0.7	1.4	1.4	2.0	0.8
March	1.2	1.4	1.4	2.4	0.8	0.6	1.1	1.3	0.5	1.5	1.5	1.7	0.8
April	1.3	1.4	0.9	2.3	1.0	1.0	0.9	1.4	0.8	1.6	1.3	1.4	0.8
May	1.2	1.4	1.9	2.4	0.8	0.7	0.9	1.2	0.7	1.4	1.2	1.1	0.8
June	1.3	1.4	1.1	2.2	0.9	0.8	1.1	1.2	1.0	1.4	1.1	1.0	0.7
July	1.3	1.5	1.2	2.7	0.7	0.7	0.7	1.4	1.4	1.4	1.3	1.7	0.6
August	1.2	1.4	1.1	2.5	0.7	0.6	0.9	1.3	1.3	1.4	1.1	1.0	0.6
September	1.2	1.4	1.5	2.4	0.9	0.8	1.0	1.2	0.8	1.4	1.3	1.2	0.5
October	1.3	1.5	1.4	2.9	0.9	0.8	1.0	1.3	1.0	1.4	1.5	1.5	0.5
November	1.2	1.4	1.6	3.2	0.8	0.8	0.8	1.3	0.9	1.4	1.3	1.4	0.7
December	1.3	1.5	1.7	3.6	0.9	0.9	1.0	1.2	0.9	1.4	1.1	1.2	0.8
2015													
January	1.3	1.4	2.3	3.3	0.8	0.7	1.0	1.4	1.1	1.5	1.3	1.1	0.6
February	1.2	1.4	2.3	2.8	0.9	0.9	0.8	1.2	0.8	1.2	1.3	1.0	0.5
March	1.4	1.5	2.6	3.3	0.9	0.9	1.0	1.4	1.1	1.5	1.6	1.1	0.8
April	1.3	1.5	3.0	2.2	0.8	0.8	0.8	1.2	0.5	1.4	1.4	1.3	0.9
May	1.2	1.3	2.2	2.1	0.7	0.7	0.8	1.2	0.4	1.4	1.5	1.0	0.7
June	1.3	1.4	1.3	3.5	0.9	0.8	1.0	1.3	1.3	1.4	1.2	1.1	0.7
July	1.2	1.3	2.8	2.4	0.9	0.9	0.8	1.4	1.1	1.5	1.3	0.9	0.8
August	1.2	1.4	2.9	2.8	0.9	0.9	0.9	1.2	0.7	1.4	1.2	1.0	0.9
September	1.4	1.5	2.6	2.9	0.9	0.9	0.9	1.2	0.4	1.3	1.7	0.9	0.8
October	1.3	1.4	2.4	2.9	0.9	0.9	1.0	1.2	0.9	1.3	1.2	1.1	0.5
November	1.3	1.4	2.4	2.5	0.9	0.9	0.9	1.2	0.8	1.2	1.4	1.2	0.7
December	1.3	1.4	2.6	2.3	0.8	0.9	0.8	1.1	0.7	1.3	1.2	0.7	0.7
2016													
January	1.3	1.4	2.3	2.7	0.8	0.8	0.8	1.2	0.9	1.3	1.3	1.0	0.7
February	1.3	1.5	2.9	3.3	1.1	1.2	0.9	1.2	0.8	1.2	1.5	1.0	0.7
March	1.3	1.4	4.0	2.4	0.9	0.9	0.9	1.0	0.8	1.0	1.3	0.8	0.8
April	1.2	1.4	2.3	3.2	0.9	0.9	1.0	1.0	0.8	1.1	1.1	1.1	0.7
May	1.2	1.4	1.9	3.0	1.1	1.1	0.9	1.2	1.0	1.2	1.4	1.2	0.6
June	1.2	1.3	2.4	2.4	0.9	0.9	0.9	1.2	0.7	1.2	1.6	1.0	0.6
July	1.2	1.4	1.4	2.5	0.8	0.8	0.8	1.3	0.6	1.5	1.6	1.0	0.6
August	1.3	1.4	2.1	2.6	0.9	0.8	0.9	1.1	0.8	1.1	1.5	0.9	0.7
September	1.1	1.2	1.5	2.3	0.9	0.8	1.0	1.2	0.5	1.5	1.0	0.5	0.7
October	1.1	1.3	1.8	2.7	0.8	0.7	0.8	1.0	0.6	1.1	1.2	0.7	0.9
November	1.2	1.3	1.5	2.2	0.8	0.8	0.9	1.1	0.5	1.2	1.3	1.0	0.7
December	1.2	1.4	0.9	3.8	0.8	0.7	1.0	1.0	0.5	1.1	1.3	0.7	0.8
2017													
January	1.2	1.3	1.8	2.7	0.9	0.8	1.0	1.1	0.8	1.0	1.7	1.0	0.6
February	1.2	1.3	1.8	2.0	0.7	0.6	0.7	1.1	0.8	1.3	0.9	0.8	0.9
March	1.2	1.3	1.4	2.8	0.9	0.9	0.9	1.2	0.9	1.3	1.2	1.1	0.8
April	1.2	1.3	1.2	3.1	0.9	0.7	1.2	1.1	0.6	1.2	1.3	1.0	0.6
May	1.2	1.3	1.7	3.2	0.8	0.7	0.9	1.1	0.8	1.2	1.1	1.5	0.6
June	1.3	1.5	1.4	3.1	0.8	0.8	0.8	1.2	0.7	1.4	1.4	1.4	0.7
July	1.3	1.4	1.4	3.1	0.9	0.8	1.2	1.0	0.7	1.1	1.0	0.9	0.8
August	1.3	1.4	1.3	2.8	0.8	0.8	0.7	1.1	0.8	1.2	1.3	1.1	0.8
September	1.2	1.4	1.0	2.9	0.8	0.8	1.0	1.0	0.6	1.1	1.2	1.5	0.5
October	1.2	1.4	1.6	2.7	0.8	0.7	1.1	1.0	0.6	1.2	1.0	1.4	0.9
November	1.2	1.3	2.1	2.5	0.9	0.7	1.2	1.3	0.5	1.5	1.2	0.9	0.6
December	1.2	1.3	1.6	1.9	0.8	0.8	1.0	1.2	0.6	1.2	1.8	1.5	0.6
2018													
January	1.3	1.5	1.1	2.3	0.9	0.9	0.9	1.4	0.9	1.5	1.5	1.5	0.8
February	1.2	1.3	1.0	2.2	0.9	0.8	1.2	1.1	0.7	1.2	1.3	1.3	0.5
March	1.2	1.3	1.4	2.5	0.9	0.7	1.2	1.1	0.5	1.4	1.2	1.3	0.5
April	1.2	1.3	1.9	2.1	1.0	0.9	1.1	1.3	0.7	1.5	1.3	1.5	0.9
May	1.2	1.4	2.1	2.4	1.0	0.8	1.3	1.0	0.4	1.1	1.4	1.4	1.0
June	1.2	1.4	1.9	2.5	0.9	0.8	1.2	1.1	0.6	1.2	1.3	1.4	0.9
July	1.2	1.3	2.0	2.1	1.0	0.8	1.4	1.2	0.6	1.3	1.3	1.1	0.7
August	1.2	1.3	1.9	2.2	0.9	0.7	1.1	1.4	0.7	1.7	1.4	1.4	0.7
September	1.2	1.3	1.9	2.4	0.8	0.7	0.9	1.3	0.7	1.5	1.4	1.6	0.7
October	1.2	1.4	1.3	2.0	1.0	1.0	1.0	1.5	1.0	1.6	1.6	0.7	0.4
November	1.3	1.4	1.8	2.6	0.9	0.7	1.0	1.3	0.9	1.4	1.6	0.9	0.7
December	1.2	1.3	1.3	2.2	0.9	0.6	1.3	1.3	0.8	1.5	1.4	1.3	0.7
2019													
January	1.1	1.2	1.4	2.4	1.0	0.6	1.5	1.1	0.7	1.1	1.4	1.1	0.7
February	1.2	1.3	1.8	2.3	0.9	0.8	1.2	1.2	0.7	1.2	1.5	1.1	0.6
March	1.1	1.2	1.9	2.4	0.9	0.9	1.0	1.2	0.5	1.3	1.4	0.8	0.4
April	1.2	1.3	1.5	3.2	0.9	0.8	1.0	1.3	0.6	1.5	1.3	1.2	0.6
May	1.2	1.3	1.1	2.8	0.9	0.8	1.1	1.1	0.6	1.2	1.1	1.0	0.8
June	1.1	1.3	1.0	2.8	0.8	0.7	1.1	1.1	0.9	1.2	1.2	1.0	0.7
July	1.2	1.3	1.6	2.4	0.9	0.8	1.0	1.3	1.1	1.4	1.5	1.5	0.7
August	1.2	1.3	1.4	2.9	0.8	0.7	1.0	1.3	0.9	1.4	1.4	1.4	0.7
September	1.3	1.4	1.6	2.9	0.9	0.8	1.0	1.4	1.3	1.5	1.4	1.3	0.7
October	1.2	1.3	1.7	3.4	0.8	0.8	0.9	1.3	1.1	1.3	1.5	1.3	0.5

[1]Layoffs and discharges are the number of layoffs and discharges during the entire month.
[2]The layoffs and discharges rate is the number of layoffs and discharges during the entire month as a percent of total employment.

Table 7-8. Layoffs and Discharges Levels[1] and Rates,[2] by Industry, 2008–October 2019 —*Continued*

(Not seasonally adjusted, levels in thousands, rates per 100.)

Year and month	Rate												
	Finance and insurance	Real estate and rental and leasing	Professional and business services	Education and health services	Educational services	Health care and social assistance	Leisure and hospitality	Arts, entertainment, and recreation	Accommodation and food services	Other services	Government	Federal	State and local government
2014													
January	0.8	0.9	2.2	0.9	1.4	0.8	2.2	3.9	1.9	1.2	0.4	0.3	0.4
February	0.6	1.3	2.4	0.8	1.0	0.7	2.0	4.5	1.6	1.4	0.4	0.3	0.4
March	0.7	1.0	2.1	1.0	1.4	0.9	1.7	3.4	1.4	0.9	0.5	0.2	0.5
April	0.6	1.2	2.3	0.9	0.9	0.9	1.9	4.6	1.4	0.7	0.4	0.2	0.4
May	0.3	2.2	2.1	0.7	1.0	0.7	2.3	4.2	2.0	1.1	0.4	0.3	0.4
June	0.6	1.0	2.2	0.7	0.9	0.7	2.3	3.5	2.1	1.2	0.5	0.4	0.5
July	0.4	1.0	2.3	0.7	1.0	0.6	2.2	3.8	1.9	1.5	0.4	0.3	0.4
August	0.5	0.8	2.5	0.7	1.0	0.7	1.8	4.9	1.2	1.1	0.4	0.3	0.4
September	0.4	0.7	2.2	0.9	1.3	0.8	2.1	4.5	1.7	1.0	0.4	0.3	0.4
October	0.5	0.6	2.8	0.8	0.9	0.8	1.7	3.5	1.4	1.1	0.4	0.3	0.4
November	0.5	1.1	2.0	0.7	0.8	0.6	1.9	3.9	1.5	1.3	0.4	0.3	0.4
December	0.8	0.7	2.2	0.8	0.9	0.7	2.0	3.9	1.7	1.1	0.5	0.2	0.5
2015													
January	0.4	1.3	2.1	0.6	0.9	0.5	1.9	4.8	1.4	1.3	0.5	0.3	0.5
February	0.3	1.1	2.1	0.7	0.9	0.7	2.1	5.4	1.6	1.4	0.5	0.3	0.5
March	0.7	1.1	2.3	0.7	0.9	0.7	2.1	5.5	1.6	1.5	0.5	0.5	0.6
April	0.7	1.3	2.4	0.7	0.9	0.6	2.4	4.3	2.1	1.1	0.5	0.4	0.5
May	0.6	1.1	2.1	0.7	0.9	0.7	2.0	3.1	1.9	1.1	0.5	0.7	0.5
June	0.6	1.1	2.0	0.7	1.1	0.6	1.8	3.8	1.5	1.7	0.6	0.4	0.6
July	0.8	0.9	2.0	0.6	0.7	0.6	1.6	2.1	1.5	1.4	0.5	0.4	0.5
August	0.7	1.4	1.9	0.6	1.1	0.6	2.1	3.4	1.8	1.7	0.5	0.3	0.5
September	0.6	1.3	2.5	0.8	1.1	0.8	2.1	3.5	1.8	2.1	0.5	0.4	0.5
October	0.4	0.9	2.2	0.7	1.3	0.6	2.2	4.6	1.8	1.4	0.5	0.4	0.6
November	0.5	1.3	2.3	0.7	1.1	0.7	2.0	3.9	1.6	0.9	0.5	0.4	0.6
December	0.6	1.0	2.4	0.7	0.6	0.7	2.2	5.0	1.7	1.4	0.5	0.4	0.6
2016													
January	0.5	1.0	2.5	0.7	1.0	0.7	1.7	4.2	1.2	1.0	0.5	0.4	0.5
February	0.6	1.0	2.2	0.8	1.6	0.6	2.2	2.8	2.1	1.2	0.5	0.4	0.6
March	0.8	1.0	2.5	0.7	1.1	0.7	2.1	4.4	1.7	1.6	0.5	0.4	0.6
April	0.6	1.2	2.2	0.7	1.1	0.6	1.9	3.0	1.7	1.2	0.6	0.4	0.6
May	0.5	0.8	2.0	0.7	1.1	0.7	1.7	3.6	1.4	1.4	0.6	0.4	0.6
June	0.4	1.0	2.1	0.7	1.0	0.7	1.9	3.5	1.7	1.2	0.4	0.4	0.5
July	0.4	1.0	2.2	0.7	1.0	0.6	2.0	3.2	1.7	1.1	0.4	0.3	0.4
August	0.6	0.9	2.2	0.8	0.8	0.8	2.1	5.0	1.6	1.2	0.6	0.4	0.6
September	0.5	1.1	1.7	0.6	0.5	0.6	1.5	3.0	1.3	1.6	0.5	0.3	0.5
October	0.7	1.6	1.9	0.7	0.6	0.7	1.7	3.7	1.4	0.9	0.4	0.4	0.5
November	0.5	1.0	2.2	0.9	0.7	0.9	1.8	3.0	1.6	1.4	0.6	0.4	0.6
December	0.5	1.6	2.0	0.7	0.7	0.7	2.0	4.6	1.5	1.4	0.4	0.2	0.4
2017													
January	0.5	0.9	1.9	0.6	0.8	0.5	2.2	3.0	2.1	1.5	0.4	0.3	0.5
February	0.7	1.2	1.9	0.6	0.4	0.7	1.9	3.0	1.8	1.4	0.5	0.4	0.6
March	0.5	1.8	1.8	0.7	0.9	0.7	1.9	2.6	1.8	1.6	0.4	0.4	0.4
April	0.4	1.2	1.8	0.7	1.1	0.7	1.7	2.8	1.5	1.7	0.5	0.5	0.5
May	0.4	1.2	2.1	0.8	1.1	0.8	1.6	3.6	1.2	1.2	0.6	0.3	0.6
June	0.7	0.9	2.6	0.7	1.0	0.6	2.1	4.3	1.7	1.1	0.5	0.3	0.5
July	0.5	1.6	2.2	0.8	0.8	0.7	2.2	6.9	1.3	1.4	0.5	0.4	0.5
August	0.5	1.4	1.9	0.9	0.9	0.9	2.1	4.5	1.7	1.3	0.5	0.4	0.5
September	0.3	1.1	2.1	0.7	0.9	0.7	2.2	5.1	1.7	1.3	0.5	0.3	0.5
October	0.8	1.2	2.0	0.7	1.2	0.7	2.0	4.1	1.6	1.8	0.5	0.3	0.5
November	0.5	0.7	1.6	0.8	1.1	0.8	2.0	4.1	1.6	1.4	0.5	0.4	0.5
December	0.5	0.9	1.8	0.8	1.2	0.7	1.8	3.4	1.6	2.1	0.6	0.3	0.6
2018													
January	0.8	0.9	2.0	0.8	1.1	0.7	2.4	4.0	2.1	1.3	0.5	0.3	0.5
February	0.5	0.7	2.0	0.8	1.2	0.7	1.9	3.9	1.6	1.1	0.5	0.4	0.5
March	0.4	0.8	2.0	1.0	1.1	0.9	1.8	4.2	1.3	0.6	0.5	0.3	0.5
April	0.8	0.9	1.7	0.7	0.9	0.7	1.9	4.7	1.5	1.4	0.4	0.2	0.4
May	0.9	1.1	2.1	0.7	1.0	0.6	2.0	4.1	1.6	1.6	0.4	0.2	0.4
June	0.8	1.0	2.1	0.8	0.8	0.8	1.8	4.8	1.3	1.7	0.4	0.2	0.5
July	0.7	0.7	1.8	0.8	1.4	0.7	2.0	4.7	1.6	1.4	0.7	0.4	0.7
August	0.7	0.7	1.9	0.6	1.2	0.5	1.7	3.8	1.4	1.3	0.5	0.3	0.5
September	0.7	0.6	1.9	0.7	1.0	0.6	1.9	3.1	1.7	1.2	0.5	0.2	0.6
October	0.3	0.6	2.0	0.7	0.8	0.7	1.9	3.5	1.7	1.3	0.6	0.2	0.6
November	0.7	0.9	2.0	0.7	1.2	0.6	2.0	4.1	1.6	1.5	0.5	0.2	0.5
December	0.7	0.6	1.9	0.6	1.1	0.6	1.7	3.9	1.3	1.2	0.4	0.3	0.5
2019													
January	0.5	1.0	1.7	0.7	1.1	0.7	1.6	3.0	1.3	1.0	0.6	0.3	0.6
February	0.5	0.7	2.0	0.8	1.2	0.7	1.6	3.4	1.3	1.2	0.5	0.2	0.6
March	0.4	0.4	2.0	0.7	1.0	0.6	1.6	1.9	1.5	0.9	0.4	0.2	0.4
April	0.5	1.0	2.1	0.7	0.9	0.7	1.6	2.5	1.4	0.7	0.5	0.2	0.5
May	0.5	1.3	2.2	0.7	1.0	0.7	1.5	4.0	1.1	1.1	0.4	0.3	0.4
June	0.5	1.3	1.8	0.7	0.8	0.7	1.6	2.3	1.5	1.2	0.4	0.3	0.5
July	0.4	1.5	1.9	0.7	0.7	0.7	1.8	2.8	1.6	0.8	0.4	0.2	0.4
August	0.5	1.1	2.1	0.6	1.0	0.5	1.5	2.9	1.3	1.3	0.5	0.3	0.5
September	0.4	1.6	2.1	0.7	0.9	0.7	2.0	2.9	1.8	1.0	0.4	0.3	0.5
October	0.3	1.1	1.9	0.7	0.8	0.7	1.5	3.2	1.2	0.6	0.5	0.9	0.5

[1]Layoffs and discharges are the number of layoffs and discharges during the entire month.
[2]The layoffs and discharges rate is the number of layoffs and discharges during the entire month as a percent of total employment.

CHAPTER 8: LABOR-MANAGEMENT RELATIONS

HIGHLIGHTS

This chapter contains information on historical trends in union membership, earnings, and work stoppages.

Figure 8-1. Number of Work Stoppages Involving 1,000 Workers or More, 1947–2018

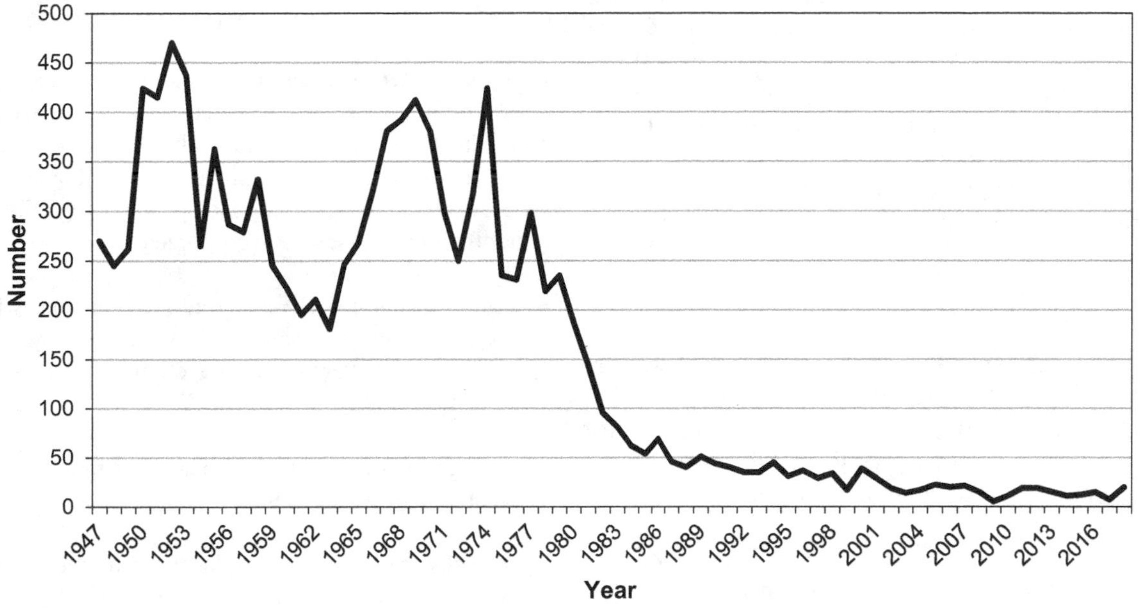

In 2018, the number of work stoppages involving 1,000 employees or more increased to 20—the highest level since 2007 but still far lower than the high of 470 in 1952. The number of workers involved (485,000) was the highest since 1986. In comparison, in 2017, only 25,000 workers were involved in a work stoppage. (See Table 8-1.)

OTHER HIGHLIGHTS

- Union membership continued to be higher for men (11.1 percent) than for women (9.9 percent) in 2018. According to race, Blacks had the highest rate of union membership at 12.5 percent, followed by Whites at 10.4 percent, Hispanics at 9.1 percent and Asians at 8.4 percent. (See Table 8-2.)

- The number of workers in a union or employee association declined in 2018 to 14.7 million after increasing in 2017. This number has been gradually declining since 1983 when a high of 17.7 million workers were involved in a union or employee association. The percentage of workers belonging to a union decreased from 10.7 in 2017 to 10.5 percent in 2018. (See Table 8-5.)

- Workers in the public sector were far more likely to be in a union than those in the private sector (33.9 percent compared with 6.4 percent). In the private sector, workers in utilities had the highest unionization rate at 20.5 percent while those in food services and drinking places had the lowest rate at 1.7 percent. (See Table 8-3.)

- Hawaii had the highest rate of union membership at 23.1 percent surpassing New York at 22.3 percent and Washington at 19.8 percent. The South continued to have low rates of union membership. South Carolina (2.7 percent), North Carolina (2.7 percent), and Utah (4.1 percent) had the lowest rates of union membership in the country. (See Table 8-6.)

NOTES AND DEFINITIONS

WORK STOPPAGES

Collection and Coverage

Data on work stoppages measure the number and duration of major strikes or lockouts (involving 1,000 workers or more) during the year, the number of workers involved in these stoppages, and the amount of time lost due to these stoppages.

Information on work stoppages is obtained from reports issued by the Federal Mediation and Conciliation Service, state labor market information offices, Bureau of Labor Statistics (BLS) Strike Reports from the Office of Employment and Unemployment Statistics, and media sources such as the Daily Labor Report and the Wall Street Journal. One or both parties involved in the work stoppage (employer and/or union) is contacted to verify the duration of the stoppage and number of workers idled by the stoppage.

Concepts and Definitions

Days of idleness is calculated by taking the number of workers involved in the strike or lockout and multiplying it by the number of days workers are off the job. The number of working days lost for every major work stoppage is based on a 5-day workweek (Monday through Friday), excluding federal holidays.

Major work stoppage includes both worker-initiated strikes and employer-initiated lockouts involving 1,000 workers or more. BLS does not distinguish between lockouts and strikes in its statistics.

Workers involved consists of workers directly involved in the stoppage. This category does not measure the indirect or secondary effect of stoppages on other establishments whose employees are idle from material shortages or lack of service.

Sources of Additional Information

Additional information is available in BLS news release USDL 19-0189, "Major Work Stoppages in 2018". More information on measures and methods used to calculate the information in this chapter can be found on the BLS Web site at https://www.bls.gov/opub/hom/home.htm.

UNION MEMBERSHIP

Collection and Coverage

The estimates of union membership are obtained from the Current Population Survey (CPS), which provides basic information on the labor force, employment, and unemployment. The survey is conducted monthly for the Bureau of Labor Statistics by the U.S. Census Bureau from a scientifically selected national sample of about 60,000 households. The union membership and earnings data are tabulated from one-quarter of the CPS monthly sample and are limited to wage and salary workers. All self-employed workers are excluded. The data in these tables are annual averages.

Beginning in January of each year, data reflect revised population controls used in the CPS.

Concepts and Definitions

Full-time workers are workers who usually work 35 hours or more per week at their sole or principal job.

Part-time workers are workers who usually work fewer than 35 hours per week at their sole or principal job.

Wage and salary workers are workers who receive wages, salaries, commissions, tips, payment in kind, or piece rates. The group includes employees in both the private and public sectors, but, for the purposes of the union membership and earnings series, excludes all self-employed persons, regardless of whether or not their businesses are incorporated.

Hispanic or Latino ethnicity refers to persons who identified themselves in the enumeration process as being Spanish, Hispanic, or Latino. Persons whose ethnicity is identified as Hispanic or Latino may be of any race.

Union members are members of a labor union or an employee association similar to a union.

Represented by unions refers to union members, as well as to workers who have no union affiliation but whose jobs are covered by a union contract.

Median earnings is the amount which divides a given earnings distribution into two equal groups, one having earnings above the median and the other having earnings below the median. The estimating procedure places each reported or calculated weekly earnings value into $50-wide intervals which are centered around multiples of $50. The actual value is estimated through the linear interpolation of the interval in which the median lies.

Usual weekly earnings represent earnings before taxes and other deductions and include any overtime pay, commissions, or tips usually received (at the main job in the case of multiple jobholders). Prior to 1994, respondents were asked how much they usually earned per week. Since January 1994, respondents have been asked to identify the easiest way for them to report earnings (hourly, weekly, biweekly, twice monthly, monthly, annually, other) and how much they usually earn in the reported time period. Earnings reported on a basis other than weekly are converted to a weekly equivalent. The term "usual" is as perceived by the respondent. If the respondent asks for a definition of "usual," interviewers are instructed to define the term as more than half of the weeks worked during the past 4 or 5 months.

Sources of Additional Information

For additional information see BLS news release USDL 19-0079, "Union Members–2018".

Table 8-1. Work Stoppages Involving 1,000 Workers or More, 1947–2018

(Number, percent.)

Year	Stoppages beginning during the year		Days idle during the year[1]	
	Number	Workers involved (thousands)[2]	Number (thousands)	Percent of estimated total working time[3]
1947	270	1 629	25 720	. . .
1948	245	1 435	26 127	0.22
1949	262	2 537	43 420	0.38
1950	424	1 698	30 390	0.26
1951	415	1 462	15 070	0.12
1952	470	2 746	48 820	0.38
1953	437	1 623	18 130	0.14
1954	265	1 075	16 630	0.13
1955	363	2 055	21 180	0.16
1956	287	1 370	26 840	0.20
1957	279	887	10 340	0.07
1958	332	1 587	17 900	0.13
1959	245	1 381	60 850	0.43
1960	222	896	13 260	0.09
1961	195	1 031	10 140	0.07
1962	211	793	11 760	0.08
1963	181	512	10 020	0.07
1964	246	1 183	16 220	0.11
1965	268	999	15 140	0.10
1966	321	1 300	16 000	0.10
1967	381	2 192	31 320	0.18
1968	392	1 855	35 367	0.20
1969	412	1 576	29 397	0.16
1970	381	2 468	52 761	0.29
1971	298	2 516	35 538	0.19
1972	250	975	16 764	0.09
1973	317	1 400	16 260	0.08
1974	424	1 796	31 809	0.16
1975	235	965	17 563	0.09
1976	231	1 519	23 962	0.12
1977	298	1 212	21 258	0.10
1978	219	1 006	23 774	0.11
1979	235	1 021	20 409	0.09
1980	187	795	20 844	0.09
1981	145	729	16 908	0.07
1982	96	656	9 061	0.04
1983	81	909	17 461	0.08
1984	62	376	8 499	0.04
1985	54	324	7 079	0.03
1986	69	533	11 861	0.05
1987	46	174	4 481	0.02
1988	40	118	4 381	0.02
1989	51	452	16 996	0.07
1990	44	185	5 926	0.02
1991	40	392	4 584	0.02
1992	35	364	3 989	0.01
1993	35	182	3 981	0.01
1994	45	322	5 021	0.02
1995	31	192	5 771	0.02
1996	37	273	4 889	0.02
1997	29	339	4 497	0.01
1998	34	387	5 116	0.02
1999	17	73	1 996	0.01
2000	39	394	20 419	0.06
2001	29	99	1 151	(4)
2002	19	46	660	(4)
2003	14	129	4 091	0.01
2004	17	171	3 344	0.01
2005	22	100	1 736	0.01
2006	20	70	2 688	0.01
2007	21	189	1 265	(4)
2008	15	72	1 954	0.01
2009	5	13	124	(4)
2010	11	45	302	(4)
2011	19	113	1 020	(4)
2012	19	148	1 131	(4)
2013	15	55	290	(4)
2014	11	34	200	(4)
2015	12	47	740	(4)
2016	15	99	1 543	(4)
2017	7	25	439	(4)
2018	20	485	2 815	0.01

[1]Days idle include all stoppages in effect during the reference period. For work stoppages that are still ongoing at the end of the calendar year, only those days of idleness during the calendar year are counted.
[2]Workers are counted more than once if involved in more than one stoppage during the reference period.
[3]Agricultural and government workers are included in the calculation of estimated working time; private household, forestry, and fishery workers are excluded.
[4]Less than 0.005 percent.
. . . = Not available.

Table 8-2. Union Affiliation of Employed Wage and Salary Workers, by Selected Characteristics, 2013–2018

(Numbers in thousands, percent.)

Characteristic	2013					2014					2015				
	Total employed	Member of union[1]		Represented by union[2]		Total employed	Member of union[1]		Represented by union[2]		Total employed	Member of union[1]		Represented by union[2]	
		Total	Percent of employed	Total	Percent of employed		Total	Percent of employed	Total	Percent of employed		Total	Percent of employed	Total	Percent of employed
SEX AND AGE															
Both Sexes, 16 Years and Over	129 110	14 528	11.3	16 028	12.4	131 431	14 576	11.1	16 152	12.3	133 743	14 795	11.1	16 441	12.3
16 to 24 years	17 647	745	4.2	854	4.8	18 019	804	4.5	956	5.3	18 311	800	4.4	967	5.3
25 years and over	111 463	13 783	12.4	15 174	13.6	113 412	13 772	12.1	15 196	13.4	115 431	13 995	12.1	15 474	13.4
25 to 34 years	29 404	2 886	9.8	3 228	11.0	30 158	2 879	9.5	3 205	10.6	30 870	2 985	9.7	3 363	10.9
35 to 44 years	27 631	3 458	12.5	3 790	13.7	27 948	3 460	12.4	3 823	13.7	28 101	3 457	12.3	3 785	13.5
45 to 54 years	28 498	3 990	14.0	4 377	15.4	28 540	3 927	13.8	4 286	15.0	28 764	3 909	13.6	4 306	15.0
55 to 64 years	20 207	2 899	14.3	3 176	15.7	20 781	2 924	14.1	3 229	15.5	21 288	3 035	14.3	3 329	15.6
65 years and over	5 723	549	9.6	603	10.5	5 985	582	9.7	653	10.9	6 408	610	9.5	691	10.8
Men, 16 Years and Over	66 794	7 955	11.9	8 688	13.0	68 048	7 939	11.7	8 717	12.8	69 298	7 963	11.5	8 760	12.6
16 to 24 years	8 918	434	4.9	488	5.5	9 141	462	5.1	540	5.9	9 250	485	5.2	563	6.1
25 years and over	57 876	7 522	13.0	8 200	14.2	58 907	7 476	12.7	8 177	13.9	60 048	7 478	12.5	8 197	13.7
25 to 34 years	15 755	1 635	10.4	1 807	11.5	16 172	1 611	10.0	1 773	11.0	16 550	1 639	9.9	1 825	11.0
35 to 44 years	14 667	1 940	13.2	2 104	14.3	14 769	1 913	13.0	2 108	14.3	14 844	1 857	12.5	2 023	13.6
45 to 54 years	14 466	2 157	14.9	2 347	16.2	14 508	2 085	14.4	2 256	15.6	14 696	2 079	14.1	2 281	15.5
55 to 64 years	10 033	1 513	15.1	1 640	16.3	10 419	1 553	14.9	1 689	16.2	10 698	1 588	14.8	1 717	16.0
65 years and over	2 954	277	9.4	302	10.2	3 040	315	10.4	351	11.5	3 259	315	9.7	352	10.8
Women, 16 Years and Over	62 316	6 573	10.5	7 340	11.8	63 383	6 638	10.5	7 434	11.7	64 445	6 833	10.6	7 681	11.9
16 to 24 years	8 729	311	3.6	366	4.2	8 879	342	3.8	416	4.7	9 061	315	3.5	405	4.5
25 years and over	53 587	6 261	11.7	6 974	13.0	54 505	6 296	11.6	7 019	12.9	55 384	6 518	11.8	7 277	13.1
25 to 34 years	13 649	1 251	9.2	1 420	10.4	13 985	1 268	9.1	1 431	10.2	14 320	1 346	9.4	1 538	10.7
35 to 44 years	12 964	1 518	11.7	1 686	13.0	13 180	1 548	11.7	1 715	13.0	13 257	1 600	12.1	1 762	13.3
45 to 54 years	14 032	1 834	13.1	2 030	14.5	14 032	1 842	13.1	2 030	14.5	14 068	1 830	13.0	2 025	14.4
55 to 64 years	10 175	1 386	13.6	1 536	15.1	10 362	1 371	13.2	1 541	14.9	10 590	1 447	13.7	1 613	15.2
65 years and over	2 768	273	9.8	302	10.9	2 946	267	9.1	302	10.2	3 149	294	9.3	339	10.8
RACE, HISPANIC ORIGIN, AND SEX															
White, 16 Years and Over[3]	102 670	11 324	11.0	12 507	12.2	104 065	11 274	10.8	12 503	12.0	104 991	11 301	10.8	12 627	12.0
Men	54 017	6 320	11.7	6 897	12.8	54 747	6 295	11.5	6 900	12.6	55 402	6 222	11.2	6 875	12.4
Women	48 653	5 004	10.3	5 609	11.5	49 318	4 979	10.1	5 602	11.4	49 590	5 079	10.2	5 752	11.6
Black, 16 Years and Over[3]	15 274	2 081	13.6	2 294	15.0	15 830	2 097	13.2	2 303	14.6	16 552	2 246	13.6	2 427	14.7
Men	6 965	1 031	14.8	1 129	16.2	7 243	1 047	14.5	1 147	15.8	7 558	1 097	14.5	1 174	15.5
Women	8 310	1 049	12.6	1 165	14.0	8 586	1 050	12.2	1 156	13.5	8 995	1 149	12.8	1 253	13.9
Asian, 16 Years and Over[3]	7 271	683	9.4	758	10.4	7 476	779	10.4	866	11.6	7 883	770	9.8	860	10.9
Men	3 786	338	8.9	380	10.0	3 921	361	9.2	416	10.6	4 113	367	8.9	416	10.1
Women	3 485	346	9.9	377	10.8	3 555	418	11.8	450	12.6	3 770	403	10.7	444	11.8
Hispanic, 16 Years and Over[4]	20 730	1 952	9.4	2 141	10.3	21 571	1 978	9.2	2 220	10.3	22 351	2 104	9.4	2 365	10.6
Men	11 903	1 121	9.4	1 218	10.2	12 339	1 155	9.4	1 286	10.4	12 670	1 211	9.6	1 346	10.6
Women	8 827	831	9.4	923	10.5	9 232	823	8.9	933	10.1	9 681	892	9.0	1 019	10.5
FULL- OR PART-TIME STATUS[5]															
Full-time workers	104 262	13 020	12.5	14 341	13.8	106 526	13 132	12.3	14 491	13.6	109 080	13 340	12.0	14 768	13.5
Part-time workers	24 664	1 483	6.0	1 662	6.7	24 707	1 424	5.8	1 636	6.6	24 445	1 431	6.0	1 646	6.7

[1]Data refer to members of a labor union or to an employee association similar to a union.
[2]Data refer to members of a labor union or to an employee association similar to a union, as well as to workers who report no union affiliation but whose jobs are covered by a union or an employee association contract.
[3]Beginning in 2003, persons who selected this race group only; persons who selected more than one race group are not included. Prior to 2003, persons who reported more than one race group were included in the group they identified as their main race. Additionally, estimates for the above race groups (White, Black, and Asian) do not sum to totals because data are not presented for all races.
[4]May be of any race.
[5]The distinction between full- and part-time workers is based on hours usually worked. Data will not sum to totals because full- or part-time status on the principal job is not identifiable for a small number of multiple job holders.

Table 8-2. Union Affiliation of Employed Wage and Salary Workers, by Selected Characteristics, 2013–2018 —*Continued*

(Numbers in thousands, percent.)

Characteristic	2016					2017					2018				
	Total employed	Member of union[1]		Represented by union[2]		Total employed	Member of union[1]		Represented by union[2]		Total employed	Member of union[1]		Represented by union[2]	
		Total	Percent of employed	Total	Percent of employed		Total	Percent of employed	Total	Percent of employed		Total	Percent of employed	Total	Percent of employed
SEX AND AGE															
Both Sexes, 16 Years and Over	136 101	14 555	10.7	16 271	12.0	137 890	14 817	10.7	16 444	11.9	140 099	14 744	10.5	16 380	11.7
16 to 24 years	18 556	816	4.4	988	5.3	18 757	877	4.7	1 014	5.4	18 698	823	4.4	966	5.2
25 years and over	117 545	13 739	11.7	15 283	13.0	119 133	13 940	11.7	15 430	13.0	121 401	13 921	11.5	15 415	12.7
25 to 34 years	31 750	2 924	9.2	3 296	10.4	32 407	3 061	9.4	3 426	10.6	33 232	3 084	9.3	3 452	10.4
35 to 44 years	28 515	3 423	12.0	3 782	13.3	28 729	3 421	11.9	3 806	13.2	29 433	3 445	11.7	3 802	12.9
45 to 54 years	28 807	3 846	13.3	4 269	14.8	28 655	3 771	13.2	4 145	14.5	28 525	3 664	12.8	4 029	14.1
55 to 64 years	21 778	2 903	13.3	3 209	14.7	22 382	3 032	13.5	3 329	14.9	22 839	3 041	13.3	3 355	14.7
65 years and over	6 696	643	9.6	726	10.8	6 960	655	9.4	723	10.4	7 372	687	9.3	777	10.5
Men, 16 Years and Over	70 589	7 888	11.2	8 704	12.3	71 469	8 166	11.4	8 930	12.5	72 632	8 082	11.1	8 868	12.2
16 to 24 years	9 412	484	5.1	568	6.0	9 486	529	5.6	609	6.4	9 366	513	5.5	587	6.3
25 years and over	61 177	7 404	12.1	8 136	13.3	61 983	7 637	12.3	8 321	13.4	63 266	7 569	12.0	8 281	13.1
25 to 34 years	16 930	1 640	9.7	1 833	10.8	17 199	1 755	10.2	1 940	11.3	17 710	1 781	10.1	1 957	11.0
35 to 44 years	15 102	1 881	12.5	2 051	13.6	15 220	1 900	12.5	2 088	13.7	15 617	1 884	12.1	2 057	13.2
45 to 54 years	14 775	2 048	13.9	2 253	15.3	14 693	2 040	13.9	2 189	14.9	14 593	1 934	13.3	2 109	14.5
55 to 64 years	10 957	1 511	13.8	1 633	14.9	11 318	1 617	14.3	1 745	15.4	11 575	1 611	13.9	1 752	15.1
65 years and over	3 412	323	9.5	365	10.7	3 554	324	9.1	359	10.1	3 771	360	9.5	405	10.8
Women, 16 Years and Over	65 512	6 667	10.2	7 567	11.6	66 421	6 651	10.0	7 514	11.3	67 467	6 662	9.9	7 512	11.1
16 to 24 years	9 143	332	3.6	420	4.6	9 271	348	3.8	405	4.4	9 332	310	3.3	379	4.1
25 years and over	56 368	6 335	11.2	7 147	12.7	57 150	6 303	11.0	7 109	12.4	58 135	6 352	10.9	7 134	12.3
25 to 34 years	14 820	1 284	8.7	1 463	9.9	15 208	1 306	8.6	1 486	9.8	15 521	1 303	8.4	1 495	9.6
35 to 44 years	13 412	1 542	11.5	1 731	12.9	13 509	1 521	11.3	1 718	12.7	13 817	1 561	11.3	1 744	12.6
45 to 54 years	14 032	1 797	12.8	2 016	14.4	13 962	1 731	12.4	1 956	14.0	13 932	1 730	12.4	1 920	13.8
55 to 64 years	10 820	1 392	12.9	1 576	14.6	11 065	1 415	12.8	1 584	14.3	11 264	1 430	12.7	1 603	14.2
65 years and over	3 283	320	9.8	361	11.0	3 406	330	9.7	364	10.7	3 601	327	9.1	372	10.3
RACE, HISPANIC ORIGIN, AND SEX															
White, 16 Years and Over[3]	106 160	11 120	10.5	12 436	11.7	107 121	11 358	10.6	12 589	11.8	108 164	11 215	10.4	12 471	11.5
Men	56 007	6 153	11.0	6 769	12.1	56 545	6 432	11.4	7 025	12.4	57 132	6 311	11.0	6 920	12.1
Women	50 153	4 967	9.9	5 667	11.3	50 576	4 926	9.7	5 564	11.0	51 032	4 904	9.6	5 551	10.9
Black, 16 Years and Over[3]	17 014	2 209	13.0	2 475	14.5	17 498	2 210	12.6	2 459	14.1	17 994	2 258	12.5	2 487	13.8
Men	7 852	1 104	14.1	1 229	15.7	8 042	1 101	13.7	1 205	15.0	8 330	1 111	13.3	1 221	14.7
Women	9 163	1 105	12.1	1 245	13.6	9 456	1 109	11.7	1 254	13.3	9 664	1 147	11.9	1 266	13.1
Asian, 16 Years and Over[3]	8 340	752	9.0	839	10.1	8 561	763	8.9	843	9.8	8 973	758	8.4	855	9.5
Men	4 368	355	8.1	404	9.3	4 457	365	8.2	402	9.0	4 652	375	8.1	416	8.9
Women	3 972	397	10.0	435	10.9	4 105	398	9.7	441	10.7	4 321	383	8.9	439	10.2
Hispanic, 16 Years and Over[4]	23 085	2 032	8.8	2 308	10.0	23 656	2 201	9.3	2 476	10.5	24 591	2 239	9.1	2 482	10.1
Men	13 125	1 209	9.2	1 348	10.3	13 342	1 261	9.5	1 410	10.6	13 775	1 304	9.5	1 443	10.5
Women	9 960	823	8.3	960	9.6	10 315	940	9.1	1 067	10.3	10 815	934	8.6	1 039	9.6
FULL- OR PART-TIME STATUS[5]															
Full-time workers	111 091	13 119	11.8	14 593	13.1	113 272	13 396	11.8	14 812	13.1	115 567	13 415	11.6	14 844	12.8
Part-time workers	24 832	1 415	5.7	1 655	6.7	24 433	1 403	5.7	1 611	6.6	24 346	1 313	5.4	1 518	6.2

[1]Data refer to members of a labor union or to an employee association similar to a union.
[2]Data refer to members of a labor union or to an employee association similar to a union, as well as to workers who report no union affiliation but whose jobs are covered by a union or an employee association contract.
[3]Beginning in 2003, persons who selected this race group only; persons who selected more than one race group are not included. Prior to 2003, persons who reported more than one race group were included in the group they identified as their main race. Additionally, estimates for the above race groups (White, Black, and Asian) do not sum to totals because data are not presented for all races.
[4]May be of any race.
[5]The distinction between full- and part-time workers is based on hours usually worked. Data will not sum to totals because full- or part-time status on the principal job is not identifiable for a small number of multiple job holders.

Table 8-3. Union Affiliation of Wage and Salary Workers, by Occupation and Industry, 2017–2018

(Thousands of people, percent.)

Occupation and industry	2017					2018				
	Total employed	Member of union[1]		Represented by union[2]		Total employed	Member of union[1]		Represented by union[2]	
		Total	Percent of employed	Total	Percent of employed		Total	Percent of employed	Total	Percent of employed
OCCUPATION										
Management, professional, and related	53 442	6 155	11.5	6 972	13.0	55 258	6 183	11.2	7 069	12.8
Management, business, and financial operations	20 617	902	4.4	1 097	5.3	21 196	916	4.3	1 130	5.3
Management	13 894	596	4.3	727	5.2	14 299	607	4.2	750	5.2
Business and financial operations	6 723	307	4.6	370	5.5	6 897	309	4.5	379	5.5
Professional and related	32 824	5 253	16.0	5 876	17.9	34 062	5 267	15.5	5 939	17.4
Computer and mathematical	4 544	178	3.9	225	4.9	4 937	181	3.7	227	4.6
Architecture and engineering	3 053	220	7.2	250	8.2	3 124	232	7.4	263	8.4
Life, physical, and social science	1 360	138	10.2	154	11.3	1 436	141	9.8	160	11.1
Community and social service	2 555	392	15.3	426	16.7	2 614	360	13.8	395	15.1
Legal	1 500	119	7.9	134	8.9	1 585	94	6.0	121	7.6
Education, training, and library	8 949	2 996	33.5	3 327	37.2	9 140	3 089	33.8	3 435	37.6
Arts, design, entertainment, sports, and media	2 314	157	6.8	173	7.5	2 417	161	6.6	187	7.7
Health care practitioner and technical	8 548	1 054	12.3	1 186	13.9	8 810	1 008	11.4	1 152	13.1
Services	24 207	2 392	9.9	2 623	10.8	24 320	2 389	9.8	2 613	10.7
Health care support	3 412	286	8.4	314	9.2	3 507	284	8.1	314	8.9
Protective service	3 119	1 082	34.7	1 152	37.0	3 193	1 081	33.9	1 135	35.5
Food preparation and serving related	8 220	314	3.8	359	4.4	8 052	314	3.9	373	4.6
Building and grounds cleaning and maintenance	4 864	441	9.1	492	10.1	4 990	453	9.1	510	10.2
Personal care and service	4 592	268	5.8	305	6.6	4 577	256	5.6	282	6.2
Sales and office	31 018	1 944	6.3	2 207	7.1	30 767	1 993	6.5	2 223	7.2
Sales and related	13 682	432	3.2	513	3.7	13 694	455	3.3	538	3.9
Office and administrative support	17 337	1 511	8.7	1 694	9.8	17 073	1 538	9.0	1 685	9.9
Natural resources, construction, and maintenance	12 238	2 015	16.5	2 129	17.4	12 319	1 865	15.1	1 978	16.1
Farming, fishing, and forestry	1 090	37	3.4	42	3.8	1 024	24	2.4	31	3.0
Construction and extraction	6 529	1 262	19.3	1 318	20.2	6 776	1 158	17.1	1 217	18.0
Installation, maintenance, and repair	4 619	716	15.5	770	16.7	4 518	682	15.1	730	16.2
Production, transportation, and material moving	16 985	2 311	13.6	2 514	14.8	17 435	2 315	13.3	2 497	14.3
Production	8 143	1 006	12.4	1 092	13.4	8 272	985	11.9	1 062	12.8
Transportation and material moving	8 842	1 304	14.8	1 422	16.1	9 163	1 330	14.5	1 435	15.7
INDUSTRY										
Private sector	116 935	7 601	6.5	8 494	7.3	118 968	7 578	6.4	8 512	7.2
Agriculture and related industries	1 337	28	2.1	30	2.3	1 344	29	2.2	35	2.6
Nonagricultural industries	115 598	7 573	6.6	8 463	7.3	117 624	7 548	6.4	8 477	7.2
Mining	735	32	4.4	35	4.8	721	34	4.7	38	5.3
Construction	7 844	1 102	14.0	1 156	14.7	8 169	1 048	12.8	1 125	13.8
Manufacturing	14 670	1 328	9.1	1 461	10.0	14 861	1 340	9.0	1 444	9.7
Durable goods	9 194	836	9.1	913	9.9	9 401	850	9.0	917	9.8
Nondurable goods	5 477	492	9.0	548	10.0	5 460	490	9.0	527	9.6
Wholesale and retail trade	18 778	839	4.5	940	5.0	18 736	805	4.3	928	5.0
Wholesale trade	3 291	147	4.5	160	4.9	3 351	137	4.1	158	4.7
Retail trade	15 487	692	4.5	780	5.0	15 385	669	4.3	769	5.0
Transportation and utilities	6 232	1 139	18.3	1 225	19.7	6 467	1 116	17.3	1 185	18.3
Transportation and warehousing	5 205	903	17.3	978	18.8	5 410	904	16.7	968	17.9
Utilities	1 028	237	23.0	247	24.1	1 057	212	20.1	217	20.5
Information[3]	2 464	242	9.8	264	10.7	2 536	244	9.6	260	10.3
Publishing, except Internet	458	17	3.6	19	4.1	437	17	3.9	18	4.2
Motion pictures and sound recording	379	43	11.4	45	11.8	395	49	12.5	50	12.6
Broadcasting, except Internet	544	42	7.8	47	8.7	526	41	7.7	45	8.6
Telecommunications	814	131	16.1	138	17.0	851	131	15.4	138	16.2
Financial activities	9 067	217	2.4	278	3.1	9 148	192	2.1	253	2.8
Finance and insurance	6 720	101	1.5	142	2.1	6 770	99	1.5	137	2.0
Finance	4 156	46	1.1	67	1.6	4 244	55	1.3	81	1.9
Insurance	2 563	55	2.1	76	2.9	2 526	43	1.7	56	2.2
Real estate and rental and leasing	2 348	117	5.0	135	5.8	2 379	94	3.9	115	4.8
Professional and business services	14 739	335	2.3	407	2.8	15 228	390	2.6	481	3.2
Professional and technical services	9 328	162	1.7	210	2.2	9 718	148	1.5	203	2.1
Management, administrative, and waste services	5 412	173	3.2	198	3.7	5 510	242	4.4	278	5.0
Education and health services	22 324	1 798	8.1	2 077	9.3	22 982	1 853	8.1	2 144	9.3
Education services	4 600	526	11.4	621	13.5	4 828	632	13.1	748	15.5
Health care and social assistance	17 724	1 272	7.2	1 456	8.2	18 154	1 221	6.7	1 396	7.7
Leisure and hospitality	12 748	374	2.9	428	3.4	12 582	367	2.9	436	3.5
Arts, entertainment, and recreation	2 424	144	5.9	157	6.5	2 390	136	5.7	159	6.6
Accommodation and food services	10 324	230	2.2	271	2.6	10 193	231	2.3	277	2.7
Accommodation	1 454	106	7.3	114	7.8	1 369	113	8.3	127	9.3
Food services and drinking places	8 870	124	1.4	158	1.8	8 823	118	1.3	150	1.7
Other services[3]	5 994	167	2.8	192	3.2	6 192	159	2.6	184	3.0
Other services, except private households	5 390	164	3.0	186	3.5	5 431	155	2.9	179	3.3
Public sector	20 956	7 216	34.4	7 951	37.9	21 131	7 167	33.9	7 868	37.2
Federal government	3 652	972	26.6	1 131	31.0	3 707	977	26.4	1 128	30.4
State government	7 103	2 153	30.3	2 371	33.4	7 109	2 035	28.6	2 259	31.8
Local government	10 201	4 091	40.1	4 449	43.6	10 315	4 155	40.3	4 481	43.4

Note: Updated population controls are introduced annually with the release of January data. Data refer to the sole or principal job of full- and part-time workers. Excluded are all self-employed workers, regardless of whether or not their businesses are incorporated.

[1]Data refer to members of a labor union or an employee association similar to a union.
[2]Data refer to members of a labor union or an employee association similar to a union, as well as to workers who report no union affiliation but whose jobs are covered by a union or an employee association contract.
[3]Includes other industries, not shown separately.

Table 8-4. Median Weekly Earnings of Full-Time Wage and Salary Workers, by Union Affiliation, Occupation, and Industry, 2017–2018

(Dollars.)

Occupation and industry	2017 Total	2017 Member of union[1]	2017 Represented by union[2]	2017 Non-union	2018 Total	2018 Member of union[1]	2018 Represented by union[2]	2018 Non-union
OCCUPATION								
Management, professional, and related	1 224	1 215	1 206	1 227	1 246	1 229	1 222	1 250
Management, business, and financial operations	1 327	1 276	1 276	1 329	1 355	1 318	1 334	1 356
Management	1 392	1 349	1 361	1 395	1 429	1 401	1 425	1 430
Business and financial operations	1 174	1 188	1 163	1 174	1 216	1 159	1 164	1 221
Professional and related	1 160	1 199	1 187	1 154	1 176	1 210	1 193	1 173
Computer and mathematical	1 465	1 375	1 371	1 473	1 539	1 458	1 460	1 543
Architecture and engineering	1 478	1 479	1 473	1 479	1 484	1 516	1 529	1 479
Life, physical, and social science	1 286	1 297	1 338	1 276	1 270	1 331	1 323	1 262
Community and social service	900	1 035	1 035	866	913	1 076	1 083	880
Legal	1 443	1 550	1 577	1 428	1 467	1 593	1 503	1 464
Education, training, and library	1 002	1 157	1 144	900	1 002	1 151	1 136	909
Arts, design, entertainment, sports, and media	1 066	1 354	1 334	1 041	1 086	1 277	1 205	1 074
Health care practitioner and technical	1 124	1 244	1 239	1 103	1 140	1 292	1 288	1 122
Services	544	792	774	518	569	802	781	541
Health care support	542	577	573	539	561	618	618	552
Protective service	852	1 163	1 146	713	848	1 137	1 132	715
Food preparation and serving related	484	594	583	479	501	609	598	496
Building and grounds cleaning and maintenance	522	638	629	511	551	679	670	533
Personal care and service	520	624	609	516	544	590	587	541
Sales and office	718	829	814	710	742	835	828	735
Sales and related	763	806	813	761	798	774	766	800
Office and administrative support	701	834	815	688	717	850	843	703
Natural resources, construction, and maintenance	801	1 146	1 132	750	824	1 181	1 176	782
Farming, fishing, and forestry	539	(3)	(3)	533	581	(3)	(3)	581
Construction and extraction	796	1 136	1 124	734	808	1 178	1 172	759
Installation, maintenance, and repair	878	1 187	1 176	822	934	1 208	1 204	891
Production, transportation, and material moving	692	922	902	662	707	924	913	680
Production	701	895	878	678	723	935	923	699
Transportation and material moving	681	949	926	640	689	913	902	657
INDUSTRY								
Private sector	829	984	971	816	861	999	989	848
Agriculture and related industries	599	(3)	(3)	599	619	(3)	(3)	619
Nonagricultural industries	833	986	974	820	865	1 001	991	853
Mining	1 257	(3)	(3)	1 263	1 291	(3)	(3)	1 269
Construction	840	1 163	1 155	797	868	1 220	1 210	819
Manufacturing	884	943	927	878	917	992	992	908
Durable goods	910	968	955	904	951	1 025	1 023	941
Nondurable goods	837	892	871	830	858	923	931	843
Wholesale and retail trade	705	758	753	702	722	759	743	721
Wholesale trade	903	979	986	899	917	896	917	917
Retail trade	656	721	714	653	671	719	700	669
Transportation and utilities	888	1 147	1 121	828	901	1 106	1 091	864
Transportation and warehousing	815	1 053	1 016	781	838	1 024	1 014	808
Utilities	1 325	1 432	1 432	1 254	1 292	1 329	1 327	1 271
Information[4]	1 154	1 344	1 330	1 142	1 169	1 355	1 336	1 157
Publishing, except Internet	1 171	(3)	(3)	1 167	1 153	(3)	(3)	1 151
Motion pictures and sound recording	1 189	(3)	(3)	1 134	1 114	(3)	(3)	1 027
Broadcasting, except Internet	973	(3)	(3)	959	1 056	(3)	(3)	1 051
Telecommunications	1 197	1 195	1 201	1 195	1 170	1 331	1 325	1 150
Financial activities	1 009	943	945	1 012	1 047	937	940	1 052
Finance and insurance	1 076	980	964	1 081	1 130	909	948	1 134
Finance	1 125	(3)	1 010	1 126	1 155	914	940	1 159
Insurance	1 027	(3)	931	1 032	1 071	(3)	953	1 078
Real estate and rental and leasing	839	918	931	833	897	979	921	896
Professional and business services	1 037	1 005	1 016	1 038	1 094	888	906	1 105
Professional and technical services	1 347	1 231	1 252	1 349	1 364	1 264	1 205	1 367
Management, administrative, and waste services	629	873	842	622	664	711	711	661
Education and health services	843	978	964	831	860	984	978	845
Education services	957	1 026	1 018	942	985	1 068	1 053	968
Health care and social assistance	810	928	914	800	822	920	921	813
Leisure and hospitality	547	676	669	538	584	700	695	579
Arts, entertainment, and recreation	716	750	766	710	732	772	791	726
Accommodation and food services	513	636	620	510	551	666	655	546
Accommodation	598	685	678	588	615	715	702	604
Food services and drinking places	501	586	564	500	536	621	619	535
Other services[4]	705	913	874	699	735	1 165	1 186	725
Other services, except private households	722	924	890	717	764	1 171	1 195	754
Public sector	986	1 104	1 096	917	999	1 099	1 094	936
Federal government	1 176	1 138	1 146	1 213	1 166	1 076	1 112	1 228
State government	955	1 061	1 050	907	967	1 074	1 058	916
Local government	949	1 121	1 106	832	969	1 114	1 106	859

Note: Updated population controls are introduced annually with the release of January data. Data refer to the sole or principal job of full- and part-time workers. Excluded are all self-employed workers, regardless of whether or not their businesses are incorporated.

[1]Data refer to members of a labor union or an employee association similar to a union.
[2]Data refer to members of a labor union or an employee association similar to a union, as well as to workers who report no union affiliation but whose jobs are covered by a union or an employee association contract.
[3]Data not shown where base is less than 50,000.
[4]Includes other industries, not shown separately.

Table 8-5. Union or Employee Association Members Among Wage and Salary Employees, 1977–2018

(Numbers in thousands, percent.)

Year	Total wage and salary employment	Union or employee association member	Union or association members as a percent of total wage and salary employment
1977	81 334	19 335	23.8
1978	84 968	19 548	23.0
1979	87 117	20 986	24.1
1980	87 480	20 095	23.0
1983[1]	88 290	17 717	20.1
1984	92 194	17 340	18.8
1985	94 521	16 996	18.0
1986	96 903	16 975	17.5
1987	99 303	16 913	17.0
1988	101 407	17 002	16.8
1989	103 480	16 980	16.4
1990	103 905	16 740	16.1
1991	102 786	16 568	16.1
1992	103 688	16 390	15.8
1993	105 087	16 598	15.8
1994[2]	107 989	16 748	15.5
1995	110 038	16 360	14.9
1996	111 960	16 269	14.5
1997	114 533	16 110	14.1
1998	116 730	16 211	13.9
1999	118 963	16 477	13.9
2000	120 786	16 258	13.5
2001	122 482	16 387	13.4
2002	121 826	16 145	13.3
2003	122 358	15 776	12.9
2004	123 554	15 472	12.5
2005	125 889	15 685	12.5
2006	128 237	15 359	12.0
2007	129 767	15 670	12.1
2008	129 377	16 098	12.4
2009	124 490	15 327	12.3
2010	124 073	14 715	11.9
2011	125 187	14 764	13.0
2012	127 577	14 366	11.3
2013	129 110	14 528	11.3
2014	131 431	14 576	11.1
2015	133 743	14 795	11.1
2016	136 101	14 555	10.7
2017	137 890	14 817	10.7
2018	140 099	14 744	10.5

[1]Annual average data beginning in 1983 are not directly comparable with the data for 1977–1980.
[2]Data beginning in 1994 are not strictly comparable with data for 1993 and earlier years because of the introduction of a major redesign of the Current Population Survey questionnaire and collection methodology and the introduction of 1990 census–based population controls.
. . . = Not available.

Table 8-6. Union Affiliation of Employed Wage and Salary Workers, by State, 2017–2018

(Numbers in thousands, percent.)

State	2017					2018				
	Total employed	Member of union[1]		Represented by union[2]		Total employed	Member of union[1]		Represented by union[2]	
		Total	Percent of employed	Total	Percent of employed		Total	Percent of employed	Total	Percent of employed
UNITED STATES	137 890	14 817	10.7	16 444	11.9	140 099	14 744	10.5	16 380	11.7
Alabama	1 869	138	7.4	152	8.1	1 950	180	9.2	196	10.1
Alaska	304	55	18.1	59	19.4	299	55	18.5	60	20.0
Arizona	2 805	111	4.0	145	5.2	2 943	156	5.3	191	6.5
Arkansas	1 209	62	5.1	74	6.1	1 176	56	4.8	62	5.3
California	16 064	2 491	15.5	2 708	16.9	16 399	2 405	14.7	2 587	15.8
Colorado	2 494	238	9.6	273	11.0	2 564	281	11.0	307	12.0
Connecticut	1 645	278	16.9	295	17.9	1 677	268	16.0	280	16.7
Delaware	425	45	10.7	48	11.2	434	45	10.3	47	10.8
District of Columbia	347	34	9.8	40	11.5	354	35	9.9	41	11.6
Florida	8 573	480	5.6	570	6.6	8 702	484	5.6	588	6.8
Georgia	4 342	173	4.0	217	5.0	4 466	201	4.5	249	5.6
Hawaii	605	129	21.3	139	22.9	601	139	23.1	146	24.3
Idaho	723	35	4.8	42	5.8	733	34	4.7	41	5.6
Illinois	5 516	827	15.0	872	15.8	5 694	786	13.8	839	14.7
Indiana	2 987	266	8.9	289	9.7	3 049	269	8.8	283	9.3
Iowa	1 475	104	7.0	127	8.6	1 461	113	7.7	129	8.8
Kansas	1 296	101	7.8	131	10.1	1 283	90	7.0	129	10.1
Kentucky	1 810	174	9.6	232	12.8	1 812	161	8.9	207	11.4
Louisiana	1 780	78	4.4	96	5.4	1 785	89	5.0	104	5.8
Maine	576	66	11.4	81	14.0	573	74	12.9	85	14.8
Maryland	2 772	299	10.8	326	11.8	2 784	307	11.0	336	12.1
Massachusetts	3 231	401	12.4	431	13.3	3 397	464	13.7	493	14.5
Michigan	4 230	658	15.6	711	16.8	4 320	625	14.5	663	15.4
Minnesota	2 693	411	15.2	428	15.9	2 634	395	15.0	421	16.0
Mississippi	1 106	59	5.3	77	7.0	1 121	58	5.1	80	7.1
Missouri	2 613	226	8.7	265	10.1	2 675	251	9.4	283	10.6
Montana	419	50	11.9	57	13.6	427	50	11.8	60	14.0
Nebraska	858	70	8.2	78	9.1	882	59	6.6	71	8.0
Nevada	1 290	164	12.7	189	14.6	1 376	191	13.9	216	15.7
New Hampshire	642	72	11.3	83	13.0	664	68	10.2	77	11.6
New Jersey	3 898	630	16.2	665	17.1	3 935	587	14.9	639	16.2
New Mexico	769	52	6.7	63	8.3	812	56	6.8	67	8.2
New York	8 472	2 017	23.8	2 148	25.3	8 404	1 872	22.3	2 027	24.1
North Carolina	4 305	145	3.4	171	4.0	4 331	118	2.7	174	4.0
North Dakota	356	18	5.1	24	6.8	343	18	5.2	23	6.7
Ohio	5 062	635	12.5	688	13.6	5 054	639	12.6	722	14.3
Oklahoma	1 536	84	5.5	108	7.1	1 583	90	5.7	117	7.4
Oregon	1 763	262	14.9	277	15.7	1 738	242	13.9	256	14.7
Pennsylvania	5 543	665	12.0	723	13.0	5 575	701	12.6	748	13.4
Rhode Island	486	78	16.1	84	17.2	479	83	17.4	89	18.5
South Carolina	1 986	52	2.6	78	3.9	2 016	55	2.7	72	3.6
South Dakota	380	20	5.4	25	6.7	387	22	5.6	28	7.1
Tennessee	2 728	155	5.7	176	6.4	2 816	155	5.5	179	6.4
Texas	11 626	543	4.7	669	5.8	11 989	512	4.3	653	5.4
Utah	1 375	54	3.9	74	5.4	1 343	56	4.1	76	5.7
Vermont	288	32	11.0	35	12.1	291	31	10.5	34	11.6
Virginia	3 801	176	4.6	222	5.8	3 875	168	4.3	213	5.5
Washington	3 112	584	18.8	630	20.2	3 270	649	19.8	671	20.5
West Virginia	683	75	11.0	82	11.9	684	68	10.0	74	10.8
Wisconsin	2 778	230	8.3	250	9.0	2 700	219	8.1	233	8.6
Wyoming	243	15	6.0	16	6.7	235	15	6.5	18	7.7

Note: Updated population controls are introduced annually with the release of January data. Data refer to the sole or principal job of full- and part-time workers. Excluded are all self-employed workers, regardless of whether or not their businesses are incorporated.

[1]Data refer to members of a labor union or an employee association similar to a union.
[2]Data refer to members of a labor union or an employee association similar to a union, as well as to workers who report no union affiliation but whose jobs are covered by a union or an employee association contract.

CHAPTER 9: PRICES

HIGHLIGHTS

This chapter examines the movement of prices, which is one of the most important indicators of the state of the economy. Several indexes are covered: the Producer Price Index (PPI), which gives information about prices received by producers; the Consumer Price Index (CPI), which gives information about prices paid by consumers; and the Import Price Index (MPI) and the Export Price Index (XPI), which give information about prices involved in various foreign trade, export, and import price indexes.

Figure 9-1. Consumer Price Indexes by Selected Commodity Groups, 1990–2018

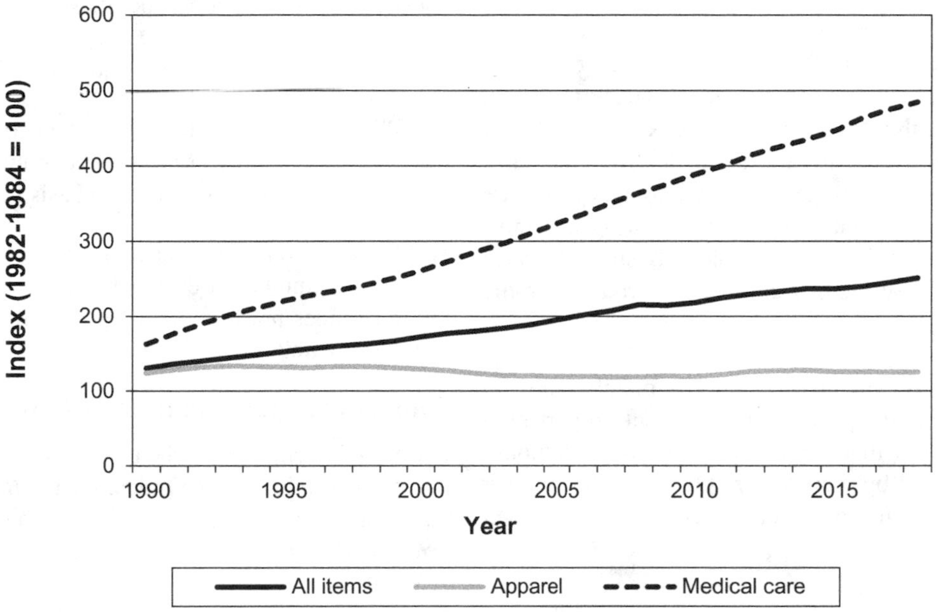

The CPI-U rose for all major groups listed in Table 9-2. It increased 2.4 percent for all items while growing 4.5 percent for transportation and 2.9 percent for housing. The CPI for education and communication grew at a much slower rate than average, increasing only 0.2 percent. (See Table 9-2.)

OTHER HIGHLIGHTS

- From 2000 to 2018, the producer price index increased 52.2 percent. Chemicals and related products grew the fastest during this period at 95.4 percent followed by fuels and related products and power at 75.5 percent and metal and metal products at 74.6 percent. (See Table 9-1.)

- The PPI for all items increased in 2018 for the second consecutive year after decreasing in 2015 and 2016. From 2010 to 2014, the PPI for all commodities increased each year. (See Table 9-1.)

- Among all expenditure categories listed in Table 9-6, the CPI for fuel oil and other fuels experienced the highest increase from 2017 to 2018 at 15.2 percent followed by motor fuel at 13.7 percent and gasoline at 13.6 percent. Meanwhile, computers, peripherals, and smart home assisted devices experienced the greatest decline at 4.2 percent. (Table 9-6.)

- Among selected metropolitan statistical areas listed in Table 9-8, the CPI for Phoenix-Mesa-Scottsdale, AZ grew the fastest at 4.2 percent followed by San Francisco-Oakland-Hayward, CA at 3.9 percent and Los Angeles-Long Beach-Anaheim, CA at 3.8 percent. The CPI for Philadelphia-Camden-Wilmington, PA-NJ-DE-MD grew the slowest at 1.3 percent. (See Table 9-8.)

NOTES AND DEFINITIONS

PRODUCER PRICE INDEX

Coverage

The *Producer Price Index (PPI)* measures average changes in prices received by domestic producers of goods and services. PPIs measure price change from the perspective of the seller. This contrasts with other measures, such as the Consumer Price Index (CPI). CPIs measure price change from the purchaser's perspective. Sellers' and purchasers' prices can differ due to government subsidies, sales and excise taxes, and distribution costs.

The PPI is the oldest continuous series of the federal government. When first published in 1902, it covered the years from 1890 through 1901 and was named the Wholesale Price Index (WPI). It was renamed the Producer Price Index in 1978. Many major commodity-based indexes are available from the early 1900s. Indexes for the major stage-of-processing categories are available from 1947 to present. Most manufacturing and mining industry indexes, however, are available only since the early 1980s; most indexes for services began being introduced in the mid 2000s.

Over 25,000 establishments provide approximately 100,000 price quotations per month today. Establishments report selling prices on the Tuesday that includes the 13th of each month and they usually respond by mail or fax. Over 10,000 PPIs for individual products and groups of products are released each month.

PPIs are typically organized into one of three main structures: (1) industry classification, (2) commodity classification, and (3) commodity-based final demand-intermediate demand (FD-ID) system. The PPI publishes approximately 535 industry price indexes in combination with over 4,000 specific product line and product category sub-indexes, as well as, roughly 500 indexes for groupings of industries. The commodity classification structure of the PPI organizes products and services by similarity or material composition, regardless of the industry classification of the producing establishment. Commodity-based FD-ID price indexes regroup commodity indexes for goods, services, and construction at the subproduct class (six-digit) level, according to the type of buyer and the amount of physical processing or assembling the products have undergone.

The PPI is widely used in many aspects of business and government. It is commonly used as an economic indicator, a deflator of other economic series, and as a basis for contract escalation.

A PPI may go out of publication if there is not cooperation from a minimum number of establishments or if in any given month, the index does not have actual prices from a minimum number of reporting units.

Sources of Additional Information

For more information on the underlying concepts and methodology of the Producer Price Index, see the *BLS Handbook of Methods,* which is available on the BLS Web site at https://www.bls.gov/opub/hom/.

Table 9-1. Producer Price Indexes, by Commodity Group, 1913–2018

(1982 = 100.)

Year	All commodities	Farm products	Processed foods and feeds	Industrial commodities: Total	Textile products and apparel	Hides, leather, and related products	Fuels and related products and power	Chemicals and related products	Rubber and plastics products	Lumber and wood products	Pulp, paper, and allied products	Metals and metal products	Machinery and equipment	Furniture and household durables	Nonmetallic mineral products	Transportation equipment	Miscellaneous products
1913	12.0	18.0	. . .	11.9	. . .	. . .	. . .	. . .	. . .	. . .	. . .	. . .	. . .	. . .	. . .	. . .	. . .
1914	11.8	17.9	. . .	11.3	. . .	. . .	. . .	. . .	. . .	. . .	. . .	. . .	. . .	. . .	. . .	. . .	. . .
1915	12.0	18.0	. . .	11.6	. . .	. . .	. . .	. . .	. . .	. . .	. . .	. . .	. . .	. . .	. . .	. . .	. . .
1916	14.7	21.3	. . .	15.0	. . .	. . .	. . .	. . .	. . .	. . .	. . .	. . .	. . .	. . .	. . .	. . .	. . .
1917	20.2	32.6	. . .	19.5	. . .	. . .	. . .	. . .	. . .	. . .	. . .	. . .	. . .	. . .	. . .	. . .	. . .
1918	22.6	37.4	. . .	21.1	. . .	. . .	. . .	. . .	. . .	. . .	. . .	. . .	. . .	. . .	. . .	. . .	. . .
1919	23.9	39.8	. . .	22.0	. . .	. . .	. . .	. . .	. . .	. . .	. . .	. . .	. . .	. . .	. . .	. . .	. . .
1920	26.6	38.0	. . .	27.4	. . .	. . .	. . .	. . .	. . .	. . .	. . .	. . .	. . .	. . .	. . .	. . .	. . .
1921	16.8	22.3	. . .	17.8	. . .	. . .	. . .	. . .	. . .	. . .	. . .	. . .	. . .	. . .	. . .	. . .	. . .
1922	16.7	23.7	. . .	17.4	. . .	. . .	. . .	. . .	. . .	. . .	. . .	. . .	. . .	. . .	. . .	. . .	. . .
1923	17.3	24.9	. . .	17.8	. . .	. . .	. . .	. . .	. . .	. . .	. . .	. . .	. . .	. . .	. . .	. . .	. . .
1924	16.9	25.2	. . .	17.0	. . .	. . .	. . .	. . .	. . .	. . .	. . .	. . .	. . .	. . .	. . .	. . .	. . .
1925	17.8	27.7	. . .	17.5	. . .	. . .	. . .	. . .	. . .	. . .	. . .	. . .	. . .	. . .	. . .	. . .	. . .
1926	17.2	25.3	. . .	17.0	. . .	17.1	10.3	. . .	47.1	9.3	. . .	13.7	. . .	28.6	16.4	. . .	. . .
1927	16.5	25.1	. . .	16.0	. . .	18.4	9.1	. . .	35.7	8.8	. . .	12.9	. . .	27.9	15.7	. . .	. . .
1928	16.7	26.7	. . .	15.8	. . .	20.7	8.7	. . .	28.3	8.5	. . .	12.9	. . .	27.2	16.2	. . .	. . .
1929	16.4	26.4	. . .	15.6	. . .	18.6	8.6	. . .	24.6	8.8	. . .	13.3	. . .	27.0	16.0	. . .	. . .
1930	14.9	22.4	. . .	14.5	. . .	17.1	8.1	. . .	21.5	8.0	. . .	12.0	. . .	26.5	15.9	. . .	. . .
1931	12.6	16.4	. . .	12.8	. . .	14.7	7.0	. . .	18.3	6.5	. . .	10.8	. . .	24.4	14.9	. . .	. . .
1932	11.2	12.2	. . .	11.9	. . .	12.5	7.3	. . .	15.9	5.6	. . .	9.9	. . .	21.5	13.9	. . .	. . .
1933	11.4	13.0	. . .	12.1	. . .	13.8	6.9	16.2	16.7	6.7	. . .	10.2	. . .	21.6	14.7	. . .	. . .
1934	12.9	16.5	. . .	13.3	. . .	14.8	7.6	17.0	19.5	7.8	. . .	11.2	. . .	23.4	15.7	. . .	. . .
1935	13.8	19.8	. . .	13.3	. . .	15.3	7.6	17.7	19.6	7.5	. . .	11.2	. . .	23.2	15.7	. . .	. . .
1936	13.9	20.4	. . .	13.5	. . .	16.3	7.9	17.8	21.1	7.9	. . .	11.4	. . .	23.6	15.8	. . .	. . .
1937	14.9	21.8	. . .	14.5	. . .	17.9	8.0	18.6	24.9	9.3	. . .	13.1	. . .	26.1	16.1	. . .	. . .
1938	13.5	17.3	. . .	13.9	. . .	15.8	7.9	17.7	24.4	8.5	. . .	12.6	. . .	25.5	15.6	. . .	. . .
1939	13.3	16.5	. . .	13.9	. . .	16.3	7.5	17.6	25.4	8.7	. . .	12.5	14.8	25.4	15.3	. . .	. . .
1940	13.5	17.1	. . .	14.1	. . .	17.2	7.4	17.9	23.7	9.6	. . .	12.5	14.9	26.0	15.3	. . .	. . .
1941	15.1	20.8	. . .	15.1	. . .	18.4	7.9	19.5	25.5	11.5	. . .	12.8	15.1	27.6	15.7	. . .	. . .
1942	17.0	26.7	. . .	16.2	. . .	20.1	8.1	21.7	29.7	12.5	. . .	13.0	15.4	29.9	16.3	. . .	. . .
1943	17.8	30.9	. . .	16.5	. . .	20.1	8.3	21.9	30.5	13.2	. . .	12.9	15.2	29.7	16.4	. . .	. . .
1944	17.9	31.2	. . .	16.7	. . .	19.9	8.6	22.2	30.1	14.3	. . .	12.9	15.1	30.5	16.7	. . .	. . .
1945	18.2	32.4	. . .	17.0	. . .	20.1	8.7	22.3	29.2	14.5	. . .	13.1	15.1	30.5	17.4	. . .	. . .
1946	20.8	37.5	. . .	18.6	. . .	23.3	9.3	24.1	29.3	16.6	. . .	14.7	16.6	32.4	18.5	. . .	. . .
1947	25.6	45.1	33.0	22.7	50.6	31.7	11.1	32.1	29.2	25.8	25.1	18.2	19.3	37.2	20.7	. . .	26.6
1948	27.7	48.5	35.3	24.6	52.8	32.1	13.1	32.8	30.2	29.5	26.2	20.7	20.9	39.4	22.4	. . .	27.7
1949	26.3	41.9	32.1	24.1	48.3	30.4	12.4	30.0	29.2	27.3	25.1	20.9	21.9	40.1	23.0	. . .	28.2
1950	27.3	44.0	33.2	25.0	50.2	32.9	12.6	30.4	35.6	31.4	25.7	22.0	22.6	40.9	23.5	. . .	28.6
1951	30.4	51.2	36.9	27.6	56.0	37.7	13.0	34.8	43.7	34.1	30.5	24.5	25.3	44.4	25.0	. . .	30.3
1952	29.6	48.4	36.4	26.9	50.5	30.5	13.0	33.0	39.6	33.2	29.7	24.5	25.3	43.5	25.0	. . .	30.2
1953	29.2	43.8	34.8	27.2	49.3	31.0	13.4	33.4	36.9	33.1	29.6	25.3	25.9	44.4	26.0	. . .	31.0
1954	29.3	43.2	35.4	27.2	48.2	29.5	13.2	33.8	37.5	32.5	29.6	25.5	26.3	44.9	26.6	. . .	31.3
1955	29.3	40.5	33.8	27.8	48.2	29.4	13.2	33.7	42.4	34.1	30.4	27.2	27.2	45.1	27.3	. . .	31.3
1956	30.3	40.0	33.8	29.1	48.2	31.2	13.6	33.9	43.0	34.6	32.4	29.6	29.3	46.3	28.5	. . .	31.7
1957	31.2	41.1	34.8	29.9	48.3	31.2	14.3	34.6	42.8	32.8	33.0	30.2	31.4	47.5	29.6	. . .	32.6
1958	31.6	42.9	36.5	30.0	47.4	31.6	13.7	34.9	42.8	32.5	33.4	30.0	32.1	47.9	29.9	. . .	33.3
1959	31.7	40.2	35.6	30.5	48.1	35.9	13.7	34.8	42.6	34.7	33.7	30.6	32.8	48.0	30.3	. . .	33.4
1960	31.7	40.1	35.6	30.5	48.6	34.6	13.9	34.8	42.7	33.5	34.0	30.6	33.0	47.8	30.4	. . .	33.6
1961	31.6	39.7	36.2	30.4	47.8	34.9	14.0	34.5	41.1	32.0	33.0	30.5	33.0	47.5	30.5	. . .	33.7
1962	31.7	40.4	36.5	30.4	48.2	35.3	14.0	33.9	39.9	32.2	33.4	30.2	33.0	47.2	30.5	. . .	33.9
1963	31.6	39.6	36.8	30.3	48.2	34.3	13.9	33.5	40.1	32.8	33.1	30.3	33.1	46.9	30.3	. . .	34.2
1964	31.6	39.0	36.7	30.5	48.5	34.4	13.5	33.6	39.6	33.5	33.0	31.1	33.3	47.1	30.4	. . .	34.4

. . . = Not available.

Table 9-1. Producer Price Indexes, by Commodity Group, 1913–2018—*Continued*

(1982 = 100.)

Year	All commodities	Farm products	Processed foods and feeds	Industrial commodities													
				Total	Textile products and apparel	Hides, leather, and related products	Fuels and related products and power	Chemicals and related products	Rubber and plastics products	Lumber and wood products	Pulp, paper, and allied products	Metals and metal products	Machinery and equipment	Furniture and household durables	Nonmetallic mineral products	Transportation equipment	Miscellaneous products
1965	32.3	40.7	38.0	30.9	48.8	35.9	13.8	33.9	39.7	33.7	33.3	32.0	33.7	46.8	30.4	. . .	34.7
1966	33.3	43.7	40.2	31.5	48.9	39.4	14.1	34.0	40.5	35.2	34.2	32.8	34.7	47.4	30.7	. . .	35.3
1967	33.4	41.3	39.8	32.0	48.9	38.1	14.4	34.2	41.4	35.1	34.6	33.2	35.9	48.3	31.2	. . .	36.2
1968	34.2	42.3	40.6	32.8	50.7	39.3	14.3	34.1	42.8	39.8	35.0	34.0	37.0	49.7	32.4	. . .	37.0
1969	35.6	45.0	42.7	33.9	51.8	41.5	14.6	34.2	43.6	44.0	36.0	36.0	38.2	50.7	33.6	40.4	38.1
1970	36.9	45.8	44.6	35.2	52.4	42.0	15.3	35.0	44.9	39.9	37.5	38.7	40.0	51.9	35.3	41.9	39.8
1971	38.1	46.6	45.5	36.5	53.3	43.4	16.6	35.6	45.2	44.7	38.1	39.4	41.4	53.1	38.2	44.2	40.8
1972	39.8	51.6	48.0	37.8	55.5	50.0	17.1	35.6	45.3	50.7	39.3	40.9	42.3	53.8	39.4	45.5	41.5
1973	45.0	72.7	58.9	40.3	60.5	54.5	19.4	37.6	46.6	62.2	42.3	44.0	43.7	55.7	40.7	46.1	43.3
1974	53.5	77.4	68.0	49.2	68.0	55.2	30.1	50.2	56.4	64.5	52.5	57.0	50.0	61.8	47.8	50.3	48.1
1975	58.4	77.0	72.6	54.9	67.4	56.5	35.4	62.0	62.2	62.1	59.0	61.5	57.9	67.5	54.4	56.7	53.4
1976	61.1	78.8	70.8	58.4	72.4	63.9	38.3	64.0	66.0	72.2	62.1	65.0	61.3	70.3	58.2	60.5	55.6
1977	64.9	79.4	74.0	62.5	75.3	68.3	43.6	65.9	69.4	83.0	64.6	69.3	65.2	73.2	62.6	64.6	59.4
1978	69.9	87.7	80.6	67.0	78.1	76.1	46.5	68.0	72.4	96.9	67.7	75.3	70.3	77.5	69.6	69.5	66.7
1979	78.7	99.6	88.5	75.7	82.5	96.1	58.9	76.0	80.5	105.5	75.9	86.0	76.7	82.8	77.6	75.3	75.5
1980	89.8	102.9	95.9	88.0	89.7	94.7	82.8	89.0	90.1	101.5	86.3	95.0	86.0	90.7	88.4	82.9	93.6
1981	98.0	105.2	98.9	97.4	97.6	99.3	100.2	98.4	96.4	102.8	94.8	99.6	94.4	95.9	96.7	94.3	96.1
1982	100.0	100.0	100.0	100.0	100.0	100.0	100.0	100.0	100.0	100.0	100.0	100.0	100.0	100.0	100.0	100.0	100.0
1983	101.3	102.4	101.8	101.1	100.3	103.2	95.9	100.3	100.8	107.9	103.3	101.8	102.7	103.4	101.6	102.8	104.8
1984	103.7	105.5	105.4	103.3	102.7	109.0	94.8	102.9	102.3	108.0	110.3	104.8	105.1	105.7	105.4	105.2	107.0
1985	103.2	95.1	103.5	103.7	102.9	108.9	91.4	103.7	101.9	106.6	113.3	104.4	107.2	107.1	108.6	107.9	109.4
1986	100.2	92.9	105.4	100.0	103.2	113.0	69.8	102.6	101.9	107.2	116.1	103.2	108.8	108.2	110.0	110.5	111.6
1987	102.8	95.5	107.9	102.6	105.1	120.4	70.2	106.4	103.0	112.8	121.8	107.1	110.4	109.9	110.0	112.5	114.9
1988	106.9	104.9	112.7	106.3	109.2	131.4	66.7	116.3	109.3	118.9	130.4	118.7	113.2	113.1	111.2	114.3	120.2
1989	112.2	110.9	117.8	111.6	112.3	136.3	72.9	123.0	112.6	126.7	137.8	124.1	117.4	116.9	112.6	117.7	126.5
1990	116.3	112.2	121.9	115.8	115.0	141.7	82.3	123.6	113.6	129.7	141.2	122.9	120.7	119.2	114.7	121.5	134.2
1991	116.5	105.7	121.9	116.5	116.3	138.9	81.2	125.6	115.1	132.1	142.9	120.2	123.0	121.2	117.2	126.4	140.8
1992	117.2	103.6	122.1	117.4	117.8	140.4	80.4	125.9	115.1	146.6	145.2	119.2	123.4	122.2	117.3	130.4	145.3
1993	118.9	107.1	124.0	119.0	118.0	143.7	80.0	128.2	116.0	174.0	147.3	119.2	124.0	123.7	120.0	133.7	145.4
1994	120.4	106.3	125.5	120.7	118.3	148.5	77.8	132.1	117.6	180.0	152.5	124.8	125.1	126.1	124.2	137.2	141.9
1995	124.7	107.4	127.0	125.5	120.8	153.7	78.0	142.5	124.3	178.1	172.2	134.5	126.6	128.2	129.0	139.7	145.4
1996	127.7	122.4	133.3	127.3	122.4	150.5	85.8	142.1	123.8	176.1	168.7	131.0	126.5	130.4	131.0	141.7	147.7
1997	127.6	112.9	134.0	127.7	122.6	154.2	86.1	143.6	123.2	183.8	167.9	131.8	125.9	130.8	133.2	141.6	150.9
1998	124.4	104.6	131.6	124.8	122.9	148.0	75.3	143.9	122.6	179.1	171.7	127.8	124.9	131.3	135.4	141.2	156.0
1999	125.5	98.4	131.1	126.5	121.1	146.0	80.5	144.2	122.5	183.6	174.1	124.6	124.3	131.7	138.9	141.8	166.6
2000	132.7	99.5	133.1	134.8	121.4	151.5	103.5	151.0	125.5	178.2	183.7	128.1	124.0	132.6	142.5	143.8	170.8
2001	134.2	103.8	137.3	135.7	121.3	158.4	105.3	151.8	127.2	174.4	184.8	125.4	123.7	133.2	144.3	145.2	181.3
2002	131.1	99.0	136.2	132.4	119.9	157.6	93.2	151.9	126.8	173.3	185.9	125.9	122.9	133.5	146.2	144.6	182.4
2003	138.1	111.5	143.4	139.1	119.8	162.3	112.9	161.8	130.1	177.4	190.0	129.2	121.9	133.9	148.2	145.7	179.6
2004	146.7	123.3	151.2	147.6	121.0	164.5	126.9	174.4	133.8	195.6	195.7	149.6	122.1	135.1	153.2	148.6	183.2
2005	157.4	118.5	153.1	160.2	122.8	165.4	156.4	192.0	143.8	196.5	202.6	160.8	123.7	139.4	164.2	151.0	195.1
2006	164.7	117.0	153.8	168.8	124.5	168.4	166.7	205.8	153.8	194.4	209.8	181.6	126.2	142.6	179.9	152.6	205.6
2007	172.6	143.4	165.1	175.1	125.8	173.6	177.6	214.8	155.0	192.4	216.9	193.5	127.3	144.7	186.2	155.0	210.3
2008	189.6	161.3	180.5	192.3	128.9	173.1	214.6	245.5	165.9	191.3	226.8	213.0	129.7	148.9	197.1	158.6	216.6
2009	172.9	134.6	176.2	174.8	129.5	157.0	158.7	229.4	165.2	182.8	225.6	186.8	131.3	153.1	202.4	162.2	217.5
2010	184.7	151.0	182.3	187.0	131.7	181.4	185.8	246.6	170.7	192.7	236.9	207.6	131.1	153.2	201.8	163.4	221.5
2011	201.0	186.7	197.5	202.0	141.7	199.9	215.9	275.1	182.7	194.7	245.1	225.9	132.7	156.4	205.0	166.1	229.2
2012	202.2	192.5	205.2	202.1	142.2	202.3	212.1	276.6	186.9	201.6	244.2	219.9	134.2	160.6	211.0	169.8	235.6
2013	203.4	195.3	208.3	203.0	143.4	217.9	211.8	279.2	189.0	214.9	248.8	213.5	135.2	161.1	216.9	171.8	239.5
2014	205.3	197.4	216.5	204.1	145.5	229.1	209.8	280.9	190.2	224.2	250.5	215.0	136.2	163.2	223.7	174.1	243.0
2015	190.4	173.8	209.1	188.8	144.1	210.4	160.5	266.0	187.0	221.9	248.8	200.3	136.9	164.7	228.9	176.5	247.4
2016	185.4	157.0	203.5	184.6	143.3	195.1	145.9	265.1	184.6	222.7	247.7	194.3	136.9	165.1	233.3	177.4	252.1
2017	193.5	161.8	205.4	193.7	145.1	192.1	163.7	280.8	189.0	230.4	254.6	207.8	137.9	166.9	238.6	179.0	257.6
2018	202.0	160.9	206.1	203.7	149.3	180.4	181.6	295.1	195.1	243.9	260.0	223.6	140.3	171.6	247.3	181.2	264.0

. . . = Not available.

NOTES AND DEFINITIONS

CONSUMER PRICE INDEX

The Consumer Price Index (CPI) is a measure of the average change over time in the prices of consumer items—goods and services that people buy for day-to-day living. The CPI is a complex construct that combines economic theory with sampling and other statistical techniques and uses data from several surveys to produce a timely and precise measure of average price change for the consumption sector of the American economy.

The Bureau of Labor Statistics (BLS) publishes CPIs for the following population groups: (1) the CPI for Urban Wage Earners and Clerical Workers (CPI-W), which covers households of wage earners and clerical workers that comprise approximately 29 percent of the total population and (2) the CPI for All Urban Consumers (CPI-U) which covers approximately 93 percent of the population and includes in addition to wage earners and clerical worker households, groups such as professional, managerial, and technical workers, the self-employed, short-term workers, the unemployed, and retirees and others not in the labor force. BLS began publishing the CPI-U in January 1978, but did not begin publishing the Chained CPI-U for All Urban Consumers (C-CPI-U) until August 2002 with data beginning in January 2000. The CPI-W is much older than either the CPI-U or C-CPI-U.

The CPIs are based on prices of food, clothing, shelter, and fuels, transportation fares, charges for doctors' and dentists' services, drugs, and other goods and services that people buy for day-to-day living. Prices are collected each month in 75 urban areas across the country from about 23,000 retail and service establishments. Data on rents are collected from about 50,000 landlords or tenants. All taxes directly associated with the purchase and use of items are included in the index.

Various indexes have been devised to measure different aspects of inflation. The CPI measures inflation as experienced by consumers in their day-to-day living expenses; the Producer Price Index (PPI), as described earlier in this chapter, measures inflation at earlier stages of the production process; the Employment Cost Index (ECI), as described in Chapter 6, measures it in the labor market; the BLS International Price Program measures it for imports and exports; and the Gross Domestic Product Deflator (GDP Deflator) measures inflation experienced by both consumers themselves as well as governments and other institutions providing goods and services to consumers. Finally, there are specialized measures, such as measures of interest rates. The CPI is generally the best measure for adjusting payments to consumers when the intent is to allow consumers to purchase at today's prices, a market basket of goods and services equivalent to one that they could purchase in an earlier period.

The CPI does have some limitation, however. The CPI may not be applicable to all population groups. For example, the CPI-U is designed to measure inflation for the U.S. urban population and thus may not accurately reflect the experience of people living in rural areas. In addition, the CPI does not produce official estimates for the rate of inflation experienced by subgroups of the population, such as the elderly or the poor.

The Consumer Price Index Research Series Using Current Methods (CPI-U-RS), shown in Table 9-10 provides estimates for the period since 1977 of what the CPI would have been had the most current methods been in effect. Each time there are new methods introduced into the CPI, the CPI-U-RS is revised from 1978 forward.

The CPI-U-RS provides an annual inflation series that adjusts only for specified changes in BLS methodology. It does not incorporate all possible research results on past inflation.

Sources of Additional Information

An extensive description of the methodology is available in the updated version of Chapter 17 in the *BLS Handbook of Methods*. Additional detailed data can be found in the *Consumer Price Index Detailed Report* and in special reports. These resources can be found on the BLS Web site at <https://www.bls.gov>.

Table 9-2. Consumer Price Indexes, All Urban Consumers (CPI-U): U.S. City Average, Major Groups, 1913–2018

(1982–1984 = 100, unless otherwise specified.)

Year	All items	Food and beverages	Housing	Apparel	Transportation	Medical care	Recreation[1]	Education and communication[1]	Other goods and services
1913	9.9	...	...	14.9	...	...	...	...	...
1914	10.0	...	...	15.0	...	...	...	...	...
1915	10.1	...	...	15.3	...	...	...	...	...
1916	10.9	...	...	16.8	...	...	...	...	...
1917	12.8	...	...	20.2	...	...	...	...	...
1918	15.1	...	...	27.3	...	...	...	...	...
1919	17.3	...	...	36.2	...	...	...	...	...
1920	20.0	...	...	43.1	...	...	...	...	...
1921	17.9	...	...	33.2	...	...	...	...	...
1922	16.8	...	...	27.0	...	...	...	...	...
1923	17.1	...	...	27.1	...	...	...	...	...
1924	17.1	...	...	26.8	...	...	...	...	...
1925	17.5	...	...	26.3	...	...	...	...	...
1926	17.7	...	...	25.9	...	...	...	...	...
1927	17.4	...	...	25.3	...	...	...	...	...
1928	17.1	...	...	25.0	...	...	...	...	...
1929	17.1	...	...	24.7	...	...	...	...	...
1930	16.7	...	...	24.2	...	...	...	...	...
1931	15.2	...	...	22.0	...	...	...	...	...
1932	13.7	...	...	19.5	...	...	...	...	...
1933	13.0	...	...	18.8	...	...	...	...	...
1934	13.4	...	...	20.6	...	...	...	...	...
1935	13.7	...	...	20.8	14.2	10.2	...	...	...
1936	13.9	...	...	21.0	14.3	10.2	...	...	...
1937	14.4	...	...	22.0	14.5	10.3	...	...	...
1938	14.1	...	...	21.9	14.6	10.3	...	...	...
1939	13.9	...	...	21.6	14.3	10.3	...	...	...
1940	14.0	...	...	21.8	14.2	10.4	...	...	...
1941	14.7	...	...	22.8	14.7	10.4	...	...	...
1942	16.3	...	...	26.7	16.0	10.7	...	...	...
1943	17.3	...	...	27.8	15.9	11.2	...	...	...
1944	17.6	...	...	29.8	15.9	11.6	...	...	...
1945	18.0	...	...	31.4	15.9	11.9	...	...	...
1946	19.5	...	...	34.4	16.7	12.5	...	...	...
1947	22.3	...	...	39.9	18.5	13.5	...	...	...
1948	24.1	...	...	42.5	20.6	14.4	...	...	...
1949	23.8	...	...	40.8	22.1	14.8	...	...	...
1950	24.1	...	...	40.3	22.7	15.1	...	...	...
1951	26.0	...	...	43.9	24.1	15.9	...	...	...
1952	26.5	...	...	43.5	25.7	16.7	...	...	...
1953	26.7	...	...	43.1	26.5	17.3	...	...	...
1954	26.9	...	...	43.1	26.1	17.8	...	...	...
1955	26.8	...	...	42.9	25.8	18.2	...	...	...
1956	27.2	...	...	43.7	26.2	18.9	...	...	...
1957	28.1	...	...	44.5	27.7	19.7	...	...	...
1958	28.9	...	...	44.6	28.6	20.6	...	...	...
1959	29.1	...	...	45.0	29.8	21.5	...	...	...
1960	29.6	...	...	45.7	29.8	22.3	...	...	...
1961	29.9	...	...	46.1	30.1	22.9	...	...	...
1962	30.2	...	...	46.3	30.8	23.5	...	...	...
1963	30.6	...	...	46.9	30.9	24.1	...	...	...
1964	31.0	...	...	47.3	31.4	24.6	...	...	...
1965	31.5	...	...	47.8	31.9	25.2	...	...	...
1966	32.4	...	...	49.0	32.3	26.3	...	...	...
1967	33.4	35.0	30.8	51.0	33.3	28.2	...	...	35.1
1968	34.8	36.2	32.0	53.7	34.3	29.9	...	...	36.9
1969	36.7	38.1	34.0	56.8	35.7	31.9	...	...	38.7
1970	38.8	40.1	36.4	59.2	37.5	34.0	...	...	40.9
1971	40.5	41.4	38.0	61.1	39.5	36.1	...	...	42.9
1972	41.8	43.1	39.4	62.3	39.9	37.3	...	...	44.7
1973	44.4	48.8	41.2	64.6	41.2	38.8	...	...	46.4
1974	49.3	55.5	45.8	69.4	45.8	42.4	...	...	49.8
1975	53.8	60.2	50.7	72.5	50.1	47.5	...	...	53.9
1976	56.9	62.1	53.8	75.2	55.1	52.0	...	...	57.0
1977	60.6	65.8	57.4	78.6	59.0	57.0	...	...	60.4
1978	65.2	72.2	62.4	81.4	61.7	61.8	...	...	64.3
1979	72.6	79.9	70.1	84.9	70.5	67.5	...	...	68.9
1980	82.4	86.7	81.1	90.9	83.1	74.9	...	...	75.2
1981	90.9	93.5	90.4	95.3	93.2	82.9	...	...	82.6
1982	96.5	97.3	96.9	97.8	97.0	92.5	...	...	91.1
1983	99.6	99.5	99.5	100.2	99.3	100.6	...	...	101.1

See footnotes at end of table.

Table 9-2. Consumer Price Indexes, All Urban Consumers (CPI-U): U.S. City Average, Major Groups, 1913–2018—*Continued*

(1982–1984 = 100, unless otherwise specified.)

Year	All items	Food and beverages	Housing	Apparel	Transportation	Medical care	Recreation[1]	Education and communication[1]	Other goods and services
1984	103.9	103.2	103.6	102.1	103.7	106.8	. . .	. . .	107.9
1985	107.6	105.6	107.7	105.0	106.4	113.5	. . .	. . .	114.5
1986	109.6	109.1	110.9	105.9	102.3	122.0	. . .	. . .	121.4
1987	113.6	113.5	114.2	110.6	105.4	130.1	. . .	. . .	128.5
1988	118.3	118.2	118.5	115.4	108.7	138.6	. . .	. . .	137.0
1989	124.0	124.9	123.0	118.6	114.1	149.3	. . .	. . .	147.7
1990	130.7	132.1	128.5	124.1	120.5	162.8	. . .	. . .	159.0
1991	136.2	136.8	133.6	128.7	123.8	177.0	. . .	. . .	171.6
1992	140.3	138.7	137.5	131.9	126.5	190.1	. . .	. . .	183.3
1993	144.5	141.6	141.2	133.7	130.4	201.4	90.7	85.5	192.9
1994	148.2	144.9	144.8	133.4	134.3	211.0	92.7	88.8	198.5
1995	152.4	148.9	148.5	132.0	139.1	220.5	94.5	92.2	206.9
1996	156.9	153.7	152.8	131.7	143.0	228.2	97.4	95.3	215.4
1997	160.5	157.7	156.8	132.9	144.3	234.6	99.6	98.4	224.8
1998	163.0	161.1	160.4	133.0	141.6	242.1	101.1	100.3	237.7
1999	166.6	164.6	163.9	131.3	144.4	250.6	102.0	101.2	258.3
2000	172.2	168.4	169.6	129.6	153.3	260.8	103.3	102.5	271.1
2001	177.1	173.6	176.4	127.3	154.3	272.8	104.9	105.2	282.6
2002	179.9	176.8	180.3	124.0	152.9	285.6	106.2	107.9	293.2
2003	184.0	180.5	184.8	120.9	157.6	297.1	107.5	109.8	298.7
2004	188.9	186.6	189.5	120.4	163.1	310.1	108.6	111.6	304.7
2005	195.3	191.2	195.7	119.5	173.9	323.2	109.4	113.7	313.4
2006	201.6	195.7	203.2	119.5	180.9	336.2	110.9	116.8	321.7
2007	207.3	203.3	209.6	119.0	184.7	351.1	111.4	119.6	333.3
2008	215.3	214.2	216.3	118.9	195.5	364.1	113.3	123.6	345.4
2009	214.5	218.2	217.1	120.1	179.3	375.6	114.3	127.4	368.6
2010	218.1	220.0	216.3	119.5	193.4	388.4	113.3	129.9	381.3
2011	224.9	227.9	219.1	122.1	212.4	400.3	113.4	131.5	387.2
2012	229.6	233.7	222.7	126.3	217.3	414.9	114.7	133.8	394.4
2013	233.0	237.0	227.4	127.4	217.4	425.1	115.3	135.9	401.0
2014	236.7	242.4	233.2	127.5	215.9	435.3	115.5	137.5	408.1
2015	237.0	246.8	238.1	125.9	199.1	446.8	115.9	138.2	414.9
2016	240.0	247.7	244.0	126.0	194.9	463.7	117.0	139.1	423.1
2017	245.1	249.8	251.2	125.6	201.6	475.3	118.5	136.5	432.6
2018	251.1	253.3	258.5	125.7	210.7	484.7	119.1	136.8	442.3

[1]December 1997 = 100.
. . . = Not available.

Table 9-3. Consumer Price Indexes, All Urban Consumers (CPI-U): U.S. City Average, Commodity, Service, and Special Groups, 1957–2018

(1982–1984 = 100, unless otherwise specified.)

Year	All items less food	All items less shelter	All items less medical care	All items less energy	All items less food and energy	Commodities	Commodities less food and beverages	Commodities less food and energy	Energy commodities	Nondurables	Nondurables less food	Nondurables less food and apparel
1957	28.0	29.7	28.7	28.9	28.9	32.6	. . .	37.4	21.6	30.9	32.9	28.5
1958	28.6	30.6	29.5	29.7	29.6	33.3	. . .	37.9	21.3	31.7	33.1	28.8
1959	29.2	30.8	29.8	29.9	30.2	33.3	. . .	38.4	21.5	31.5	33.5	29.2
1960	29.7	31.3	30.2	30.4	30.6	33.6	. . .	38.5	21.9	32.0	34.1	29.7
1961	30.0	31.7	30.5	30.7	31.0	33.8	. . .	38.6	21.9	32.2	34.3	29.8
1962	30.3	32.0	30.8	31.1	31.4	34.1	. . .	38.9	22.0	32.5	34.5	30.1
1963	30.7	32.4	31.1	31.5	31.8	34.4	. . .	39.2	22.1	32.9	34.8	30.4
1964	31.1	32.8	31.5	32.0	32.3	34.8	. . .	39.6	21.9	33.2	35.1	30.6
1965	31.6	33.3	32.0	32.5	32.7	35.2	. . .	39.8	22.6	33.8	35.6	31.2
1966	32.3	34.3	33.0	33.5	33.5	36.1	. . .	40.3	23.2	35.1	36.4	31.8
1967	33.4	35.2	33.7	34.4	34.7	36.8	38.3	41.3	23.9	35.7	37.6	32.6
1968	34.9	36.7	35.1	35.9	36.3	38.1	39.7	42.9	24.4	37.1	39.1	33.7
1969	36.8	38.4	37.0	38.0	38.4	39.9	41.4	44.7	25.2	38.9	40.9	34.9
1970	39.0	40.3	39.2	40.3	40.8	41.7	43.1	46.7	25.6	40.8	42.5	36.3
1971	40.8	42.0	40.8	42.0	42.7	43.2	44.7	48.5	26.1	42.1	44.0	37.6
1972	42.0	43.3	42.1	43.4	44.0	44.5	45.8	49.7	26.4	43.5	45.0	38.6
1973	43.7	46.2	44.8	46.1	45.6	47.8	47.3	51.1	29.1	47.5	46.9	40.3
1974	48.0	51.4	49.8	50.6	49.4	53.5	52.4	55.0	40.4	54.0	52.9	46.9
1975	52.5	56.0	54.3	55.1	53.9	58.2	57.3	60.1	43.4	58.3	57.0	51.5
1976	56.0	59.3	57.2	58.2	57.4	60.7	60.2	63.2	45.4	60.5	59.5	54.1
1977	59.6	63.1	60.8	61.9	61.0	64.2	63.6	66.5	48.7	64.0	62.5	57.2
1978	63.9	67.4	65.4	66.7	65.5	68.8	67.3	70.5	51.0	68.6	65.5	60.4
1979	71.2	74.2	72.9	73.4	71.9	76.6	75.2	76.4	68.7	77.2	74.6	71.2
1980	81.5	82.9	82.8	81.9	80.8	86.0	85.7	83.5	95.2	87.6	88.4	87.1
1981	90.4	91.0	91.4	90.1	89.2	93.2	93.1	90.0	107.6	95.2	96.7	96.8
1982	96.3	96.2	96.8	96.1	95.8	97.0	96.9	95.3	102.9	97.8	98.3	98.2
1983	99.7	99.8	99.6	99.6	99.6	99.8	100.0	100.2	99.0	99.7	100.0	100.0
1984	104.0	103.9	103.7	104.3	104.6	103.2	103.1	104.4	98.1	102.5	101.7	101.8
1985	108.0	107.0	107.2	108.4	109.1	105.4	105.2	107.1	98.2	104.8	104.1	104.1
1986	109.8	108.0	108.8	112.6	113.5	104.4	101.4	108.6	77.2	103.5	98.5	96.9
1987	113.6	111.6	112.6	117.2	118.2	107.7	104.0	111.8	80.2	107.5	101.8	100.3
1988	118.3	115.9	117.0	122.3	123.4	111.5	107.3	115.8	80.8	111.8	105.8	104.0
1989	123.7	121.6	122.4	128.1	129.0	116.7	111.6	119.6	87.9	118.2	111.7	111.3
1990	130.3	128.2	128.8	134.7	135.5	122.8	117.0	123.6	101.2	126.0	119.9	120.9
1991	136.1	133.5	133.8	140.9	142.1	126.6	120.4	128.8	99.1	130.3	124.5	125.7
1992	140.8	137.3	137.5	145.4	147.3	129.1	123.2	132.5	98.3	132.8	127.6	128.9
1993	145.1	141.4	141.2	150.0	152.2	131.5	125.3	135.2	97.3	135.1	129.3	130.7
1994	149.0	144.8	144.7	154.1	156.5	133.8	126.9	137.1	97.6	136.8	129.7	131.6
1995	153.1	148.6	148.6	158.7	161.2	136.4	128.9	139.3	98.8	139.3	130.9	134.1
1996	157.5	152.8	152.8	163.1	165.6	139.9	131.5	141.3	105.7	143.5	134.5	139.5
1997	161.1	155.9	156.3	167.1	169.5	141.8	132.2	142.3	105.7	146.4	136.3	141.8
1998	163.4	157.2	158.6	170.9	173.4	141.9	130.5	143.2	92.1	146.9	134.6	139.2
1999	167.0	160.2	162.0	174.4	177.0	144.4	132.5	144.1	100.0	151.2	139.4	147.5
2000	173.0	165.7	167.3	178.6	181.3	149.2	137.7	144.9	129.5	158.2	149.1	162.9
2001	177.8	169.7	171.9	183.5	186.1	150.7	137.2	145.3	125.2	160.6	149.1	164.1
2002	180.5	170.8	174.3	187.7	190.5	149.7	134.2	143.7	117.1	161.1	147.4	163.3
2003	184.7	174.6	178.1	190.6	193.2	151.2	134.5	140.9	136.7	165.3	151.9	172.1
2004	189.4	179.3	182.7	194.4	196.6	154.7	136.7	139.6	161.2	172.2	159.3	183.8
2005	196.0	186.1	188.7	198.7	200.9	160.2	142.5	140.3	197.4	180.2	170.1	201.2
2006	202.7	191.9	194.7	203.7	205.9	164.0	145.9	140.6	223.0	186.7	178.2	213.9
2007	208.1	196.6	200.1	208.9	210.7	167.5	147.5	140.1	241.0	193.5	184.0	223.4
2008	215.5	205.5	207.8	214.8	215.6	174.8	153.0	140.2	284.4	205.9	197.3	244.4
2009	214.0	203.3	206.6	218.4	219.2	169.7	144.4	142.0	205.3	198.5	181.5	218.7
2010	217.8	208.6	209.7	220.5	221.3	174.6	150.4	143.6	242.6	205.3	191.9	235.6
2011	224.5	217.0	216.3	224.8	225.0	183.9	159.9	145.5	306.4	219.0	209.6	262.1
2012	229.0	221.4	220.6	229.7	229.8	187.6	162.7	147.3	316.0	224.6	215.0	268.2
2013	232.3	223.8	223.6	233.6	233.8	187.7	161.5	147.3	307.4	225.3	213.6	265.4
2014	235.8	226.2	227.1	238.0	237.9	187.9	159.6	146.8	296.9	226.7	211.7	262.3
2015	235.4	223.3	226.9	242.3	242.2	181.7	149.2	146.1	216.7	217.6	192.3	232.7
2016	238.8	223.8	229.3	247.0	247.6	179.2	145.4	145.4	191.6	215.0	187.2	224.5
2017	244.3	227.2	234.1	251.2	252.2	181.2	147.2	144.4	216.3	219.6	193.8	235.0
2018	250.7	231.8	239.9	256.3	257.6	184.6	150.3	144.1	246.2	225.8	201.9	247.8

. . . = Not available.

Table 9-3. Consumer Price Indexes, All Urban Consumers (CPI-U): U.S. City Average, Commodity, Service, and Special Groups, 1957–2018—*Continued*

(1982–1984 = 100, unless otherwise specified.)

Year	Total services[1]	Rent of shelter[2]	Gasoline, all types	Transportation services	Medical care services	Other services	Services less medical care	Energy	Services less energy
1957	21.8	. . .	23.8	24.1	17.0	. . .	22.8	21.5	21.9
1958	22.6	. . .	23.5	25.6	17.9	. . .	23.6	21.5	22.7
1959	23.3	. . .	23.7	26.5	18.7	. . .	24.2	21.9	23.4
1960	24.1	. . .	24.4	27.2	19.5	. . .	25.0	22.4	24.2
1961	24.5	. . .	24.1	27.8	20.2	. . .	25.4	22.5	24.7
1962	25.0	. . .	24.3	28.3	20.9	. . .	25.9	22.6	25.2
1963	25.5	. . .	24.2	28.6	21.5	. . .	26.3	22.6	25.7
1964	26.0	. . .	24.1	29.2	22.0	. . .	26.8	22.5	26.2
1965	26.6	. . .	25.1	30.3	22.7	. . .	27.4	22.9	26.9
1966	27.6	. . .	25.6	31.6	23.9	. . .	28.3	23.3	28.0
1967	28.8	. . .	26.4	32.6	26.0	36.0	29.3	23.8	29.3
1968	30.3	. . .	26.8	33.9	27.9	38.1	30.8	24.2	30.9
1969	32.4	. . .	27.7	36.3	30.2	40.0	32.9	24.8	33.2
1970	35.0	. . .	27.9	40.2	32.3	42.2	35.6	25.5	36.0
1971	37.0	. . .	28.1	43.4	34.7	44.4	37.5	26.5	38.0
1972	38.4	. . .	28.4	44.4	35.9	45.6	38.9	27.2	39.4
1973	40.1	. . .	31.2	44.7	37.5	47.7	40.6	29.4	41.1
1974	43.8	. . .	42.2	46.3	41.4	51.3	44.3	38.1	44.8
1975	48.0	. . .	45.1	49.8	46.6	55.1	48.3	42.1	48.8
1976	52.0	. . .	47.0	56.9	51.3	58.4	52.2	45.1	52.7
1977	56.0	. . .	49.7	61.5	56.4	62.1	55.9	49.4	56.5
1978	60.8	. . .	51.8	64.4	61.2	66.4	60.7	52.5	61.3
1979	67.5	. . .	70.2	69.5	67.2	71.9	67.5	65.7	68.2
1980	77.9	. . .	97.5	79.2	74.8	78.7	78.2	86.0	78.5
1981	88.1	. . .	108.5	88.6	82.8	86.1	88.7	97.7	88.7
1982	96.0	. . .	102.8	96.1	92.6	93.5	96.4	99.2	96.3
1983	99.4	102.7	99.4	99.1	100.7	100.0	99.2	99.9	99.2
1984	104.6	107.7	97.8	104.8	106.7	106.5	104.4	100.9	104.5
1985	109.9	113.9	98.6	110.0	113.2	113.0	109.6	101.6	110.2
1986	115.4	120.2	77.0	116.3	121.9	119.4	114.6	88.2	116.5
1987	120.2	125.9	80.1	121.9	130.0	125.7	119.1	88.6	122.0
1988	125.7	132.0	80.8	128.0	138.3	132.6	124.3	89.3	127.9
1989	131.9	138.0	88.5	135.6	148.9	140.9	130.1	94.3	134.4
1990	139.2	145.5	101.0	144.2	162.7	150.2	136.8	102.1	142.3
1991	146.3	152.1	99.2	151.2	177.1	159.8	143.3	102.5	149.8
1992	152.0	157.3	99.0	155.7	190.5	168.5	148.4	103.0	155.9
1993	157.9	162.0	97.7	162.9	202.9	177.0	153.6	104.2	161.9
1994	163.1	167.0	98.2	168.6	213.4	185.4	158.4	104.6	167.6
1995	168.7	172.4	99.8	175.9	224.2	193.3	163.5	105.2	173.7
1996	174.1	178.0	105.9	180.5	232.4	201.4	168.7	110.1	179.4
1997	179.4	183.4	105.8	185.0	239.1	209.6	173.9	111.5	185.0
1998	184.2	189.6	91.6	187.9	246.8	216.9	178.4	102.9	190.6
1999	188.8	195.0	100.1	190.7	255.1	223.1	182.7	106.6	195.7
2000	195.3	201.3	128.6	196.1	266.0	229.9	188.9	124.6	202.1
2001	203.4	208.9	124.0	201.9	278.8	238.0	196.6	129.3	209.6
2002	209.8	216.7	116.0	209.1	292.9	246.4	202.5	121.7	217.5
2003	216.5	221.9	135.1	216.3	306.0	254.4	208.7	136.5	223.8
2004	222.8	227.9	159.7	220.6	321.3	261.3	214.5	151.4	230.2
2005	230.1	233.7	194.7	225.7	336.7	268.4	221.2	177.1	236.6
2006	238.9	241.9	219.9	230.8	350.6	277.5	229.6	196.9	244.7
2007	246.8	250.8	238.0	233.7	369.3	285.6	236.8	207.7	253.1
2008	255.5	257.2	277.5	244.1	384.9	295.8	245.0	236.7	261.0
2009	259.2	259.9	201.6	251.0	397.3	304.0	248.1	193.1	265.9
2010	261.3	258.8	238.6	259.8	411.2	309.6	249.6	211.4	268.3
2011	265.8	262.2	301.7	268.0	423.8	314.4	253.6	243.9	273.1
2012	271.4	267.8	311.5	272.9	440.3	322.3	258.5	246.1	279.7
2013	277.9	274.0	302.6	280.0	454.0	328.7	264.5	244.4	286.4
2014	285.1	281.8	290.9	285.3	464.8	334.4	271.5	243.6	293.5
2015	291.7	290.4	212.0	291.0	476.2	339.4	277.7	202.9	301.1
2016	299.9	300.3	187.6	299.4	494.8	346.0	285.2	189.5	310.4
2017	308.1	310.3	211.8	309.9	506.8	347.8	293.0	204.5	318.7
2018	316.6	320.7	240.6	321.8	517.8	352.7	301.3	219.9	328.0

[1]Includes tenants, household insurance, water, sewer, trash, and household operations services, not shown separately.
[2]December 1982 = 100.
. . . = Not available.

Table 9-4. Consumer Price Indexes, All Urban Consumers (CPI-U): U.S. City Average, Selected Groups and Purchasing Power of the Consumer Dollar, 1913–2018

(1982–1984 = 100, unless otherwise specified.)

Year	All items	Food	Rent of primary residence	Owners' equivalent of primary residence[1]	Apparel	Purchasing power of the consumer dollar
1913	9.9	10.0	21.0	...	14.9	1 007.7
1914	10.0	10.2	21.0	...	15.0	994.2
1915	10.1	10.0	21.1	...	15.3	984.3
1916	10.9	11.3	21.3	...	16.8	915.2
1917	12.8	14.5	21.2	...	20.2	779.3
1918	15.1	16.7	21.5	...	27.3	663.5
1919	17.3	18.6	23.3	...	36.2	577.9
1920	20.0	21.0	27.4	...	43.1	498.9
1921	17.9	15.9	31.5	...	33.2	558.5
1922	16.8	14.9	32.4	...	27.0	596.2
1923	17.1	15.4	33.2	...	27.1	585.7
1924	17.1	15.2	34.4	...	26.8	584.5
1925	17.5	16.5	34.6	...	26.3	570.1
1926	17.7	17.0	34.2	...	25.9	564.7
1927	17.4	16.4	33.7	...	25.3	575.5
1928	17.1	16.3	32.9	...	25.0	583.3
1929	17.1	16.5	32.1	...	24.7	583.3
1930	16.7	15.6	31.2	...	24.2	598.6
1931	15.2	12.9	29.6	...	22.0	656.3
1932	13.7	10.7	26.5	...	19.5	731.7
1933	13.0	10.4	22.9	...	18.8	771.2
1934	13.4	11.6	21.4	...	20.6	746.4
1935	13.7	12.4	21.4	...	20.8	728.1
1936	13.9	12.6	21.9	...	21.0	721.3
1937	14.4	13.1	22.9	...	22.0	696.1
1938	14.1	12.1	23.7	...	21.9	709.3
1939	13.9	11.8	23.7	...	21.6	719.5
1940	14.0	12.0	23.7	...	21.8	712.6
1941	14.7	13.1	24.2	...	22.8	678.8
1942	16.3	15.4	24.7	...	26.7	613.2
1943	17.3	17.1	24.7	...	27.8	577.9
1944	17.6	16.9	24.8	...	29.8	568.0
1945	18.0	17.3	24.8	...	31.4	555.2
1946	19.5	19.8	25.0	...	34.4	511.5
1947	22.3	24.1	25.8	...	39.9	447.4
1948	24.1	26.1	27.5	...	42.5	415.1
1949	23.8	25.0	28.7	...	40.8	419.3
1950	24.1	25.4	29.7	...	40.3	415.1
1951	26.0	28.2	30.9	...	43.9	384.6
1952	26.5	28.7	32.2	...	43.5	376.5
1953	26.7	28.3	33.9	...	43.1	373.5
1954	26.9	28.2	35.1	...	43.1	371.7
1955	26.8	27.8	35.6	...	42.9	373.2
1956	27.2	28.0	36.3	...	43.7	367.8
1957	28.1	28.9	37.0	...	44.5	354.9
1958	28.9	30.2	37.6	...	44.6	345.7
1959	29.1	29.7	38.2	...	45.0	342.7
1960	29.6	30.0	38.7	...	45.7	337.3
1961	29.9	30.4	39.2	...	46.1	334.0
1962	30.2	30.6	39.7	...	46.3	330.4
1963	30.6	31.1	40.1	...	46.9	326.5
1964	31.0	31.5	40.5	...	47.3	322.0
1965	31.5	32.2	40.9	...	47.8	316.6
1966	32.4	33.8	41.5	...	49.0	308.0
1967	33.4	34.1	42.2	...	51.0	299.3
1968	34.8	35.3	43.3	...	53.7	287.3
1969	36.7	37.1	44.7	...	56.8	272.6
1970	38.8	39.2	46.5	...	59.2	257.4
1971	40.5	40.4	48.7	...	61.1	246.6
1972	41.8	42.1	50.4	...	62.3	239.1
1973	44.4	48.2	52.5	...	64.6	225.1
1974	49.3	55.1	55.2	...	69.4	202.9
1975	53.8	59.8	58.0	...	72.5	185.9
1976	56.9	61.6	61.1	...	75.2	175.7
1977	60.6	65.5	64.8	...	78.6	164.9
1978	65.2	72.0	69.3	...	81.4	153.2
1979	72.6	79.9	74.3	...	84.9	138.0

[1]December 1982 = 100.
. . . = Not available.

Table 9-4. Consumer Price Indexes, All Urban Consumers (CPI-U): U.S. City Average, Selected Groups and Purchasing Power of the Consumer Dollar, 1913–2018—*Continued*

(1982–1984 = 100, unless otherwise specified.)

Year	All items	Food	Rent of primary residence	Owners' equivalent of primary residence[1]	Apparel	Purchasing power of the consumer dollar
1980	82.4	86.8	80.9	...	90.9	121.5
1981	90.9	93.6	87.9	...	95.3	109.8
1982	96.5	97.4	94.6	...	97.8	103.5
1983	99.6	99.4	100.1	102.5	100.2	100.3
1984	103.9	103.2	105.3	107.3	102.1	96.1
1985	107.6	105.6	111.8	113.2	105.0	92.8
1986	109.6	109.0	118.3	119.4	105.9	91.3
1987	113.6	113.5	123.1	124.8	110.6	88.0
1988	118.3	118.2	127.8	131.1	115.4	84.6
1989	124.0	125.1	132.8	137.4	118.6	80.7
1990	130.7	132.4	138.4	144.8	124.1	76.6
1991	136.2	136.3	143.3	150.4	128.7	73.4
1992	140.3	137.9	146.9	155.5	131.9	71.3
1993	144.5	140.9	150.3	160.5	133.7	69.2
1994	148.2	144.3	154.0	165.8	133.4	67.5
1995	152.4	148.4	157.8	171.3	132.0	65.6
1996	156.9	153.3	162.0	176.8	131.7	63.8
1997	160.5	157.3	166.7	181.9	132.9	62.3
1998	163.0	160.7	172.1	187.8	133.0	61.4
1999	166.6	164.1	177.5	192.9	131.3	60.0
2000	172.2	167.8	183.9	198.7	129.6	58.1
2001	177.1	173.1	192.1	206.3	127.3	56.5
2002	179.9	176.2	199.7	214.7	124.0	55.6
2003	184.0	180.0	205.5	219.9	120.9	54.4
2004	188.9	186.2	211.0	224.9	120.4	53.0
2005	195.3	190.7	217.3	230.2	119.5	51.2
2006	201.6	195.2	225.1	238.2	119.5	49.6
2007	207.3	202.9	234.7	246.2	119.0	48.2
2008	215.3	214.1	243.3	252.4	118.9	46.5
2009	214.5	218.0	248.8	256.6	120.1	46.6
2010	218.1	219.6	249.4	256.6	119.5	45.9
2011	224.9	227.8	253.6	259.6	122.1	44.5
2012	229.6	233.8	260.4	264.8	126.3	43.6
2013	233.0	237.0	267.7	270.7	127.4	42.9
2014	236.7	242.7	276.2	277.8	127.5	42.2
2015	237.0	247.2	286.0	285.9	125.9	42.2
2016	240.0	247.9	296.8	295.4	126.0	41.7
2017	245.1	250.1	308.1	305.1	125.6	40.8
2018	251.1	253.6	319.3	315.2	125.7	39.8

[1]December 1982 = 100.
. . . = Not available.

Table 9-5. Consumer Price Indexes, Urban Wage Earners and Clerical Workers (CPI-W): U.S. City Average, Major Groups, 1950–2018

(1982–1984 = 100, unless otherwise specified.)

Year	All items	Food and beverages	Housing	Apparel	Transportation	Medical care	Recreation[1]	Education and communication[1]	Other goods and services
1950	24.2	. . .	. . .	40.5	22.6	15.2	. . .	. . .	. . .
1951	26.1	. . .	. . .	44.1	24.0	15.9	. . .	. . .	. . .
1952	26.7	. . .	. . .	43.7	25.6	16.8	. . .	. . .	. . .
1953	26.9	. . .	. . .	43.3	26.3	17.4	. . .	. . .	. . .
1954	27.0	. . .	. . .	43.3	25.9	17.9	. . .	. . .	. . .
1955	26.9	. . .	. . .	43.1	25.6	18.3	. . .	. . .	. . .
1956	27.3	. . .	. . .	44.0	26.1	19.0	. . .	. . .	. . .
1957	28.3	. . .	. . .	44.7	27.6	19.8	. . .	. . .	. . .
1958	29.1	. . .	. . .	44.8	28.4	20.7	. . .	. . .	. . .
1959	29.3	. . .	. . .	45.2	29.6	21.6	. . .	. . .	. . .
1960	29.8	. . .	. . .	45.9	29.6	22.4	. . .	. . .	. . .
1961	30.1	. . .	. . .	46.3	30.0	23.0	. . .	. . .	. . .
1962	30.4	. . .	. . .	46.6	30.6	23.6	. . .	. . .	. . .
1963	30.8	. . .	. . .	47.1	30.8	24.2	. . .	. . .	. . .
1964	31.2	. . .	. . .	47.5	31.2	24.7	. . .	. . .	. . .
1965	31.7	. . .	. . .	48.0	31.7	25.3	. . .	. . .	. . .
1966	32.6	. . .	. . .	49.2	32.2	26.4	. . .	. . .	. . .
1967	33.6	35.0	31.1	51.2	33.1	28.3	. . .	. . .	35.4
1968	35.0	36.2	32.3	54.0	34.1	30.0	. . .	. . .	37.2
1969	36.9	38.0	34.3	57.1	35.5	32.1	. . .	. . .	39.1
1970	39.0	40.1	36.7	59.5	37.3	34.1	. . .	. . .	41.3
1971	40.7	41.3	38.3	61.4	39.2	36.3	. . .	. . .	43.3
1972	42.1	43.1	39.8	62.7	39.7	37.5	. . .	. . .	45.1
1973	44.7	48.8	41.5	65.0	41.0	39.0	. . .	. . .	46.9
1974	49.6	55.5	46.2	69.8	45.5	42.6	. . .	. . .	50.2
1975	54.1	60.2	51.1	72.9	49.8	47.7	. . .	. . .	54.4
1976	57.2	62.0	54.2	75.6	54.7	52.3	. . .	. . .	57.6
1977	60.9	65.7	57.9	79.0	58.6	57.3	. . .	. . .	60.9
1978	65.6	72.1	62.9	81.7	61.5	62.1	. . .	. . .	64.8
1979	73.1	79.9	70.7	85.2	70.4	68.0	. . .	. . .	69.4
1980	82.9	86.9	81.7	90.9	82.9	75.6	. . .	. . .	75.6
1981	91.4	93.6	91.1	95.6	93.0	83.5	. . .	. . .	82.5
1982	96.9	97.3	97.7	97.8	97.0	92.5	. . .	. . .	90.9
1983	99.8	99.5	100.0	100.2	99.2	100.5	. . .	. . .	101.3
1984	103.3	103.2	102.2	102.0	103.8	106.9	. . .	. . .	107.9
1985	106.9	105.5	106.6	105.0	106.4	113.6	. . .	. . .	114.2
1986	108.6	108.9	109.7	105.8	101.7	122.0	. . .	. . .	120.9
1987	112.5	113.3	112.8	110.4	105.1	130.2	. . .	. . .	127.8
1988	117.0	117.9	116.8	114.9	108.3	139.0	. . .	. . .	136.5
1989	122.6	124.6	121.2	117.9	113.9	149.6	. . .	. . .	147.4
1990	129.0	131.8	126.4	123.1	120.1	162.7	. . .	. . .	158.9
1991	134.3	136.5	131.2	127.4	123.1	176.5	. . .	. . .	171.7
1992	138.2	138.3	135.0	130.7	125.8	189.6	. . .	. . .	183.3
1993	142.1	141.2	138.5	132.4	129.4	200.9	91.2	86.0	192.2
1994	145.6	144.4	142.0	132.2	133.4	210.4	93.0	89.1	196.4
1995	149.8	148.3	145.4	130.9	138.8	219.8	94.7	92.3	204.2
1996	154.1	153.2	149.6	130.9	142.8	227.6	97.5	95.4	212.2
1997	157.6	157.2	153.4	132.1	143.6	234.0	99.7	98.5	221.6
1998	159.7	160.4	156.7	131.6	140.5	241.4	100.9	100.4	236.1
1999	163.2	163.8	160.0	130.1	143.4	249.7	101.3	101.5	261.9
2000	168.9	167.7	165.4	128.3	152.8	259.9	102.4	102.7	276.5
2001	173.5	173.0	172.1	126.1	153.6	271.8	103.6	105.3	289.5
2002	175.9	176.1	175.7	123.1	151.8	284.6	104.6	107.6	302.0
2003	179.8	179.9	180.4	120.0	156.3	296.3	105.5	109.0	307.0
2004	184.5	186.2	185.0	120.0	161.5	309.5	106.3	110.0	312.6
2005	191.0	190.5	191.2	119.1	173.0	322.8	106.8	111.4	322.2
2006	197.1	194.9	198.5	119.1	180.3	335.7	108.2	113.9	330.9
2007	202.8	202.5	204.8	118.5	184.3	350.9	108.6	116.3	344.0
2008	211.1	213.5	211.8	118.7	195.7	364.2	110.1	119.8	357.9
2009	209.6	217.5	213.1	119.8	176.7	376.1	111.0	123.0	391.6
2010	214.0	219.2	212.9	118.7	192.6	389.8	109.8	124.9	409.3
2011	221.6	227.3	215.8	121.3	213.3	402.2	109.9	125.5	416.9
2012	226.2	233.1	219.3	125.8	218.7	417.8	111.1	127.3	424.7
2013	229.3	236.3	224.0	126.8	218.3	428.3	111.7	128.7	432.6
2014	232.8	241.9	229.9	126.6	216.4	438.3	111.8	129.7	440.9
2015	231.8	246.3	234.5	125.3	197.8	449.6	111.8	129.5	449.5
2016	234.1	246.9	240.2	125.3	192.9	467.7	112.6	129.8	459.5
2017	239.1	248.9	247.4	124.9	200.2	479.8	114.0	125.8	471.5
2018	245.1	252.3	254.6	125.4	210.5	488.6	114.3	125.4	482.4

[1]December 1997 = 100.
. . . = Not available.

Table 9-6. Consumer Price Indexes, All Urban Consumers (CPI-U): U.S. City Average, by Expenditure Category, 1995–2018

(1982–1984 = 100, unless otherwise specified.)

Expenditure category	1995	1996	1997	1998	1999	2000	2001	2002	2003	2004	2005	2006
ALL ITEMS	152.4	156.9	160.5	163.0	166.6	172.2	177.1	179.9	184.0	188.9	195.3	201.6
Food and Beverages	148.9	153.7	157.7	161.1	164.6	168.4	173.6	176.8	180.5	186.6	191.2	195.7
Food	148.4	153.3	157.3	160.7	164.1	167.8	173.1	176.2	180.0	186.2	190.7	195.2
Food at home	148.8	154.3	158.1	161.1	164.2	167.9	173.4	175.6	179.4	186.2	189.8	193.1
Cereals and bakery product	167.5	174.0	177.6	181.1	185.0	188.3	193.8	198.0	202.8	206.0	209.0	212.8
Meats, poultry, fish, and eggs	138.8	144.8	148.5	147.3	147.9	154.5	161.3	162.1	169.3	181.7	184.7	186.6
Dairy and related product	132.8	142.1	145.5	150.8	159.6	160.7	167.1	168.1	167.9	180.2	182.4	181.4
Fruits and vegetables	177.7	183.9	187.5	198.2	203.1	204.6	212.2	220.9	225.9	232.7	241.4	252.9
Nonalcoholic beverages and beverage materials	131.7	128.6	133.4	133.0	134.3	137.8	139.2	139.2	139.8	140.4	144.4	147.4
Other food at home	140.8	142.9	147.3	150.8	153.5	155.6	159.6	160.8	162.6	164.9	167.0	169.6
Sugar and sweets	137.5	143.7	147.8	150.2	152.3	154.0	155.7	159.0	162.0	163.2	165.2	171.5
Fats and oils	137.3	140.5	141.7	146.9	148.3	147.4	155.7	155.4	157.4	167.8	167.7	168.0
Other food	151.1	156.2	161.2	165.5	168.9	172.2	176.0	177.1	178.8	179.7	182.5	185.0
Other miscellaneous food[1]	. . .	. . .	. . .	102.6	104.9	107.5	108.9	109.2	110.3	110.4	111.3	113.9
Food away from home	149.0	152.7	157.0	161.1	165.1	169.0	173.9	178.3	182.1	187.5	193.4	199.4
Other food away from home[1]	. . .	. . .	. . .	101.6	105.2	109.0	113.4	117.7	121.3	125.3	131.3	136.6
Alcoholic beverages	153.9	158.5	162.8	165.7	169.7	174.7	179.3	183.6	187.2	192.1	195.9	200.7
Housing	148.5	152.8	156.8	160.4	163.9	169.6	176.4	180.3	184.8	189.5	195.7	203.2
Shelter	165.7	171.0	176.3	182.1	187.3	193.4	200.6	208.1	213.1	218.8	224.4	232.1
Rent of primary residence	157.8	162.0	166.7	172.1	177.5	183.9	192.1	199.7	205.5	211.0	217.3	225.1
Lodging away from home[1]	. . .	. . .	. . .	109.0	112.3	117.5	118.6	118.3	119.3	125.9	130.3	136.0
Owners' equivalent rent of primary residence[2]	171.3	176.8	181.9	187.8	192.9	198.7	206.3	214.7	219.9	224.9	230.2	238.2
Tenants' and household insurance[1]	. . .	. . .	. . .	99.8	101.3	103.7	106.2	108.7	114.8	116.2	117.6	116.5
Fuels and utilities	123.7	127.5	130.8	128.5	128.8	137.9	150.2	143.6	154.5	161.9	179.0	194.7
Household energy	111.5	115.2	117.9	113.7	113.5	122.8	135.4	127.2	138.2	144.4	161.6	177.1
Fuel oil and other fuels	88.1	99.2	99.8	90.0	91.4	129.7	129.3	115.5	139.5	160.5	208.6	234.9
Energy services	119.2	122.1	125.1	121.2	120.9	128.0	142.4	134.4	145.0	150.6	166.5	182.1
Water, sewer, and trash collection services[1]	. . .	. . .	. . .	101.6	104.0	106.5	109.6	113.0	117.2	124.0	130.3	136.8
Household furnishings and operations	123.0	124.7	125.4	126.6	126.7	128.2	129.1	128.3	126.1	125.5	126.1	127.0
Household operations[1]	. . .	. . .	. . .	101.5	104.5	110.5	115.6	119.0	121.8	125.0	130.3	136.6
Apparel	132.0	131.7	132.9	133.0	131.3	129.6	127.3	124.0	120.9	120.4	119.5	119.5
Men's and boys' apparel	126.2	127.7	130.1	131.8	131.1	129.7	125.7	121.7	118.0	117.5	116.1	114.1
Women's and girls' apparel	126.9	124.7	126.1	126.0	123.3	121.5	119.3	115.8	113.1	113.0	110.8	110.7
Infants' and toddlers' apparel	127.2	129.7	129.0	126.1	129.0	130.6	129.2	126.4	122.1	118.5	116.7	116.5
Footwear	125.4	126.6	127.6	128.0	125.7	123.8	123.0	121.4	119.6	119.3	122.6	123.5
Transportation	139.1	143.0	144.3	141.6	144.4	153.3	154.3	152.9	157.6	163.1	173.9	180.9
Private transportation	136.3	140.0	141.0	137.9	140.5	149.1	150.0	148.8	153.6	159.4	170.2	177.0
New and used motor vehicles[1]	99.4	101.0	100.5	100.1	100.1	100.8	101.3	99.2	96.5	94.2	95.6	95.6
New vehicles	141.0	143.7	144.3	143.4	142.9	142.8	142.1	140.0	137.9	137.1	137.9	137.6
Used cars and trucks	156.5	157.0	151.1	150.6	152.0	155.8	158.7	152.0	142.9	133.3	139.4	140.0
Motor fuel	100.0	106.3	106.2	92.2	100.7	129.3	124.7	116.6	135.8	160.4	195.7	221.0
Gasoline (all types)	99.8	105.9	105.8	91.6	100.1	128.6	124.0	116.0	135.1	159.7	194.7	219.9
Motor vehicle parts and equipment	102.1	102.2	101.9	101.1	100.5	101.5	104.8	106.9	107.8	108.7	111.9	117.3
Motor vehicle maintenance and repair	154.0	158.4	162.7	167.1	171.9	177.3	183.5	190.2	195.6	200.2	206.9	215.6
Public transportation	175.9	181.9	186.7	190.3	197.7	209.6	210.6	207.4	209.3	209.1	217.3	226.6
Medical Care	220.5	228.2	234.6	242.1	250.6	260.8	272.8	285.6	297.1	310.1	323.2	336.2
Medical care commodities	204.5	210.4	215.3	221.8	230.7	238.1	247.6	256.4	262.8	269.3	276.0	285.9
Medical care services	224.2	232.4	239.1	246.8	255.1	266.0	278.8	292.9	306.0	321.3	336.7	350.6
Professional services	201.0	208.3	215.4	222.2	229.2	237.7	246.5	253.9	261.2	271.5	281.7	289.3
Hospital and related services	257.8	269.5	278.4	287.5	299.5	317.3	338.3	367.8	394.8	417.9	439.9	468.1
Recreation[1]	94.5	97.4	99.6	101.1	102.0	103.3	104.9	106.2	107.5	108.6	109.4	110.9
Video and audio[1]	95.1	96.6	99.4	101.1	100.7	101.0	101.5	102.8	103.6	104.2	104.2	104.6
Education and Communication[1]	92.2	95.3	98.4	100.3	101.2	102.5	105.2	107.9	109.8	111.6	113.7	116.8
Education[1]	88.0	92.7	97.3	102.1	107.0	112.5	118.5	126.0	134.4	143.7	152.7	162.1
Educational books and supplies	214.4	226.9	238.4	250.8	261.7	279.9	295.9	317.6	335.4	351.0	365.6	388.9
Tuition, other school fees, and childcare	253.8	267.1	280.4	294.2	308.4	324.0	341.1	362.1	386.7	414.3	440.9	468.1
Communication[1]	98.8	99.6	100.3	98.7	96.0	93.6	93.3	92.3	89.7	86.7	84.7	84.1
Information and information processing[1]	98.7	99.5	100.4	98.5	95.5	92.8	92.3	90.8	87.8	84.6	82.6	81.7
Telephone services[1]	. . .	. . .	. . .	100.7	100.1	98.5	99.3	99.7	98.3	95.8	94.9	95.8
Information technology, hardware, and services[3]	63.8	57.2	50.1	39.9	30.5	25.9	21.3	18.3	16.1	14.8	13.6	12.5
Computers, peripherals, and smart home assistant devices[1]	. . .	. . .	. . .	875.1	598.7	459.9	330.1	248.4	196.9	171.2	143.2	120.9
Other Goods and Services	206.9	215.4	224.8	237.7	258.3	271.1	282.6	293.2	298.7	304.7	313.4	321.7
Tobacco and smoking product	225.7	232.8	243.7	274.8	355.8	394.9	425.2	461.5	469.0	478.0	502.8	519.9
Personal care	147.1	150.1	152.7	156.7	161.1	165.6	170.5	174.7	178.0	181.7	185.6	190.2
Personal care product	143.1	144.3	144.2	148.3	151.8	153.7	155.1	154.7	153.5	153.9	154.4	155.8
Personal care services	151.5	156.6	162.4	166.0	171.4	178.1	184.3	188.4	193.2	197.6	203.9	209.7
Miscellaneous personal services	205.9	215.6	226.1	234.7	243.0	252.3	263.1	274.4	283.5	293.9	303.0	313.6

[1]December 1997 = 100.
[2]December 1982 = 100.
[3]December 1988 = 100.
. . . = Not available.

Table 9-6. Consumer Price Indexes, All Urban Consumers (CPI-U): U.S. City Average, by Expenditure Category, 1995–2018—*Continued*

(1982–1984 = 100, unless otherwise specified.)

Expenditure category	2007	2008	2009	2010	2011	2012	2013	2014	2015	2016	2017	2018
ALL ITEMS	207.3	215.3	214.5	218.1	224.9	229.6	233.0	236.7	237.0	240.0	245.1	251.1
Food and Beverages	203.3	214.2	218.2	220.0	227.9	233.7	237.0	242.4	246.8	247.7	249.8	253.3
Food	202.9	214.1	218.0	219.6	227.8	233.8	237.0	242.7	247.2	247.9	250.1	253.6
Food at home	201.2	214.1	215.1	215.8	226.2	231.8	233.9	239.5	242.3	239.1	238.6	239.7
Cereals and bakery product	222.1	244.9	252.6	250.4	260.3	267.7	270.4	271.1	274.1	273.1	271.7	272.8
Meats, poultry, fish, and eggs	195.6	204.7	203.8	207.7	223.2	231.0	236.0	253.0	260.3	247.7	245.8	248.9
Dairy and related product	194.8	210.4	197.0	199.2	212.7	217.3	217.6	225.3	222.4	217.3	217.5	216.5
Fruits and vegetables	262.6	278.9	272.9	273.5	284.7	282.8	290.0	294.4	293.8	296.3	295.7	297.8
Nonalcoholic beverages and beverage materials	153.4	160.0	163.0	161.6	166.8	168.6	166.9	166.0	167.9	167.3	167.6	167.6
Other food at home	173.3	184.2	191.2	191.1	197.4	204.8	204.8	206.2	209.3	209.5	209.9	210.2
Sugar and sweets	176.8	186.6	196.9	201.2	207.8	214.7	211.0	209.3	216.1	215.3	215.1	215.9
Fats and oils	172.9	196.8	201.2	200.6	219.2	232.6	229.3	229.7	227.3	225.9	227.7	228.0
Other food	188.2	198.1	205.5	204.6	209.3	216.6	217.7	219.9	223.4	224.1	224.4	224.7
Other miscellaneous food[1]	115.1	119.9	122.4	121.7	124.0	128.3	129.2	130.4	131.8	131.6	131.9	131.5
Food away from home	206.7	215.8	223.3	226.1	231.4	238.0	243.1	249.0	256.1	262.7	268.8	275.9
Other food away from home[1]	144.1	150.6	155.9	159.3	162.8	166.5	169.6	173.8	179.6	182.7	184.5	191.8
Alcoholic beverages	207.0	214.5	220.8	223.3	226.7	230.8	234.6	237.3	239.5	242.5	245.4	249.1
Housing	209.6	216.3	217.1	216.3	219.1	222.7	227.4	233.2	238.1	244.0	251.2	258.5
Shelter	240.6	246.7	249.4	248.4	251.6	257.1	263.1	270.5	278.8	288.2	297.8	307.7
Rent of primary residence	234.7	243.3	248.8	249.4	253.6	260.4	267.7	276.2	286.0	296.8	308.1	319.3
Lodging away from home[1]	142.8	143.7	134.2	133.7	137.4	140.5	142.4	148.5	153.0	158.1	159.4	161.1
Owners' equivalent rent of primary residence[2]	246.2	252.4	256.6	256.6	259.6	264.8	270.7	277.8	285.9	295.4	305.1	315.2
Tenants' and household insurance[1]	117.0	118.8	121.5	125.7	127.4	131.3	135.4	141.9	146.4	147.7	148.8	150.7
Fuels and utilities	200.6	220.0	210.7	214.2	220.4	219.0	225.2	234.6	230.1	228.9	237.3	241.6
Household energy	181.7	200.8	188.1	189.3	193.6	189.3	193.8	202.2	194.7	191.1	198.3	200.8
Fuel oil and other fuels	251.5	334.4	239.8	275.1	337.1	335.9	332.0	338.9	256.2	226.3	254.4	293.0
Energy services	186.3	202.2	193.6	192.9	194.4	189.7	194.8	203.4	198.7	196.1	202.7	203.8
Water, sewer, and trash collection services[1]	143.7	152.1	161.1	170.9	179.6	189.3	197.6	204.9	214.0	221.7	229.1	237.1
Household furnishings and operations	126.9	127.8	128.7	125.5	124.9	125.7	124.8	123.1	122.6	121.6	120.7	121.6
Household operations[1]	140.6	147.5	150.3	150.3	151.8	155.2	157.6	161.6	166.9	171.6	176.3	186.0
Apparel	119.0	118.9	120.1	119.5	122.1	126.3	127.4	127.5	125.9	126.0	125.6	125.7
Men's and boys' apparel	112.4	113.0	113.6	111.9	114.7	119.5	121.6	120.6	119.6	118.8	117.2	118.1
Women's and girls' apparel	110.3	107.5	108.1	107.1	109.2	113.0	113.3	114.4	111.2	111.2	111.0	110.4
Infants' and toddlers' apparel	113.9	113.8	114.5	114.2	113.6	119.7	116.5	117.6	119.7	115.9	114.9	120.3
Footwear	122.4	124.2	126.9	128.0	128.5	131.8	135.0	135.5	136.8	137.3	136.7	136.1
Transportation	184.7	195.5	179.3	193.4	212.4	217.3	217.4	215.9	199.1	194.9	201.6	210.7
Private transportation	180.8	191.0	174.8	188.7	207.6	212.8	212.4	211.0	193.7	189.5	196.6	206.4
New and used motor vehicles[1]	94.3	93.3	93.5	97.1	99.8	100.6	100.9	100.8	100.8	100.2	98.9	99.1
New vehicles	136.3	134.2	135.6	138.0	141.9	144.2	145.8	146.3	147.1	147.4	147.0	146.3
Used cars and trucks	135.7	134.0	127.0	143.1	149.0	150.3	149.9	149.1	147.1	143.5	138.3	138.4
Motor fuel	239.1	279.7	202.0	239.2	302.6	312.7	303.9	292.4	213.1	188.4	212.7	241.9
Gasoline (all types)	238.0	277.5	201.6	238.6	301.7	311.5	302.6	290.9	212.0	187.6	211.8	240.6
Motor vehicle parts and equipment	121.6	128.7	134.1	137.0	143.9	148.6	146.4	144.8	144.2	143.6	143.0	143.7
Motor vehicle maintenance and repair	223.0	233.9	243.3	248.0	253.1	257.6	261.6	266.0	270.7	275.4	280.8	286.4
Public transportation	230.0	250.5	236.3	251.4	269.4	271.4	278.9	276.4	268.7	265.4	263.1	258.8
Medical Care	351.1	364.1	375.6	388.4	400.3	414.9	425.1	435.3	446.8	463.7	475.3	484.7
Medical care commodities	290.0	296.0	305.1	314.7	324.1	333.6	335.1	343.4	354.6	366.8	377.0	381.4
Medical care services	369.3	384.9	397.3	411.2	423.8	440.3	454.0	464.8	476.2	494.8	506.8	517.8
Professional services	300.8	311.0	319.4	328.2	335.7	342.0	349.5	355.2	361.5	371.5	375.1	378.4
Hospital and related services	498.9	534.0	567.9	607.7	641.5	672.1	701.3	733.8	761.9	795.1	831.7	866.9
Recreation[1]	111.4	113.3	114.3	113.3	113.4	114.7	115.3	115.5	115.9	117.0	118.5	119.1
Video and audio[1]	102.9	102.6	101.3	99.1	98.4	99.4	99.7	99.8	99.6	100.9	104.2	104.2
Education and Communication[1]	119.6	123.6	127.4	129.9	131.5	133.8	135.9	137.5	138.2	139.1	136.5	136.8
Education[1]	171.4	181.3	190.9	199.3	207.8	216.3	224.5	231.9	240.5	247.5	253.2	258.8
Educational books and supplies	420.4	450.2	482.1	505.6	529.5	562.6	594.7	615.4	648.2	678.8	689.5	696.1
Tuition, other school fees, and childcare	494.1	522.1	549.0	573.2	597.2	621.0	643.7	664.8	688.8	708.1	724.7	741.3
Communication[1]	83.4	84.2	85.0	84.7	83.3	83.1	82.6	82.1	80.2	79.2	75.0	73.9
Information and information processing[1]	80.7	81.4	81.9	81.5	80.0	79.5	78.9	78.2	76.4	75.4	71.1	70.0
Telephone services[1]	98.2	100.5	102.4	102.4	101.2	101.7	101.6	101.1	99.3	98.8	91.8	90.4
Information technology, hardware, and services[3]	10.6	10.1	9.7	9.4	9.0	8.7	8.5	8.4	8.1	7.8	7.6	7.5
Computers, peripherals, and smart home assistant devices[1]	108.4	94.9	82.3	76.4	68.9	62.3	56.8	52.6	47.9	44.4	42.6	40.8
Other Goods and Services	333.3	345.4	368.6	381.3	387.2	394.4	401.0	408.1	414.9	423.1	432.6	442.3
Tobacco and smoking product	554.2	588.7	730.3	807.3	834.8	853.5	876.8	903.3	930.8	963.4	1 022.8	1 063.5
Personal care	195.6	201.3	204.6	206.6	208.6	212.1	215.0	218.0	220.8	224.3	227.0	231.1
Personal care product	158.3	159.3	162.6	161.1	160.5	162.2	161.8	163.4	163.3	163.1	161.7	161.5
Personal care services	216.6	223.7	227.6	229.6	230.8	234.2	238.8	242.0	247.2	252.9	257.4	264.2
Miscellaneous personal services	325.0	338.9	344.5	354.1	362.9	372.7	381.9	389.7	399.3	411.8	424.0	439.8

[1]December 1997 = 100.
[2]December 1982 = 100.
[3]December 1988 = 100.

Table 9-7. Relative Importance of Components in the Consumer Price Index: U.S. City Average, Selected Groups, December 1997–December 2018

(Percent distribution.)

Index and year	All items	Food and beverages	Housing	Apparel	Transportation	Medical care	Recreation	Education and communication	Other goods and services
ALL URBAN CONSUMERS (CPI-U)									
December 1997	100.0	16.3	39.6	4.9	17.6	5.6	6.1	5.5	4.3
December 1998	100.0	16.4	39.8	4.8	17.0	5.7	6.1	5.5	4.6
December 1999	100.0	16.3	39.6	4.7	17.5	5.8	6.0	5.4	4.7
December 2000	100.0	16.2	40.0	4.4	17.6	5.8	5.9	5.3	4.8
December 2001[1]	100.0	16.4	40.5	4.2	16.6	6.0	5.9	5.4	4.9
December 2001[2]	100.0	15.7	40.9	4.4	17.1	5.8	6.0	5.8	4.3
December 2002	100.0	15.6	40.9	4.2	17.3	6.0	5.9	5.8	4.4
December 2003	100.0	15.4	42.1	4.0	16.9	6.1	5.9	5.9	3.8
December 2004	100.0	15.3	42.0	3.8	17.4	6.1	5.7	5.8	3.8
December 2005	100.0	15.1	42.2	3.7	17.7	6.2	5.6	5.8	3.7
December 2006	100.0	15.0	42.7	3.7	17.2	6.3	5.6	6.0	3.5
December 2007	100.0	14.9	42.4	3.7	17.7	6.2	5.6	6.1	3.3
December 2008	100.0	15.8	43.4	3.7	15.3	6.4	5.7	6.3	3.4
December 2009	100.0	14.8	42.0	3.7	16.7	6.5	6.4	6.4	3.5
December 2010	100.0	14.8	42.0	3.7	16.7	6.5	6.4	3.0	3.5
December 2011	100.0	15.3	41.0	3.6	16.9	7.1	6.0	6.8	3.4
December 2012	100.0	15.3	41.0	3.6	16.8	7.2	6.0	6.8	3.4
December 2013	100.0	15.2	41.3	3.5	16.7	7.2	5.9	6.8	3.4
December 2014	100.0	15.3	42.2	3.3	15.3	7.7	5.8	7.1	3.4
December 2015	100.0	15.3	42.7	3.3	14.6	7.9	5.7	7.1	3.4
December 2016	100.0	14.6	42.6	3.0	15.3	8.5	5.7	7.0	3.2
December 2017	100.0	14.4	41.8	3.0	16.5	8.7	5.7	6.7	3.2
December 2018	100.0	14.3	42.2	3.0	16.3	8.7	5.7	6.6	3.2
URBAN WAGE EARNERS AND WORKERS (CPI-W)									
December 1997	100.0	17.9	36.5	5.3	19.8	4.6	6.0	5.4	4.5
December 1998	100.0	18.0	36.7	5.2	19.2	4.7	5.9	5.4	5.0
December 1999	100.0	17.9	36.5	5.0	19.7	4.7	5.8	5.3	5.1
December 2000	100.0	17.8	36.8	4.8	19.9	4.7	5.7	5.2	5.2
December 2001[1]	100.0	18.0	37.3	4.6	18.8	4.9	5.7	5.3	5.4
December 2001[2]	100.0	17.2	38.1	4.8	19.4	4.6	5.6	5.6	4.5
December 2002	100.0	17.1	38.1	4.6	19.7	4.7	5.6	5.6	4.6
December 2003	100.0	17.2	39.1	4.4	19.1	5.0	5.7	5.6	3.9
December 2004	100.0	17.0	39.0	4.2	19.8	5.0	5.5	5.5	3.9
December 2005	100.0	16.8	39.2	4.0	20.1	5.1	5.4	5.4	3.9
December 2006	100.0	16.5	40.5	4.0	19.5	5.2	5.0	5.6	3.7
December 2007	100.0	15.9	40.0	4.0	20.1	5.2	5.3	6.0	3.5
December 2008	100.0	16.9	41.3	4.0	17.1	5.4	5.5	6.2	3.7
December 2009	100.0	16.4	39.8	3.8	18.6	5.3	6.0	6.2	3.9
December 2010	100.0	16.4	39.8	3.8	18.6	5.3	6.0	6.2	3.9
December 2011	100.0	15.9	39.8	3.6	19.0	5.7	5.6	6.8	3.5
December 2012	100.0	15.9	39.9	3.6	19.0	5.8	5.5	6.8	3.5
December 2013	100.0	15.9	40.2	3.6	18.8	5.8	5.5	6.7	3.5
December 2014	100.0	16.0	40.5	3.6	18.0	6.3	5.1	6.9	3.6
December 2015	100.0	16.1	41.1	3.5	17.1	6.5	5.1	6.9	3.7
December 2016	100.0	15.8	41.1	3.2	17.1	7.2	5.2	6.8	3.5
December 2017	100.0	15.7	39.8	3.1	18.7	7.5	5.2	6.6	3.4
December 2018	100.0	15.7	40.3	3.1	18.5	7.5	5.1	6.4	3.4

[1]1993–1995 weights.
[2]1999–2000 weights.

Table 9-8. Consumer Price Indexes, All Urban Consumers (CPI-U), All Items: Selected Metropolitan Statistical Areas, Selected Years, 1985–2018

(1982–1984 = 100, unless otherwise specified.)

Area	1985	1990	1991	1992	1993	1994	1995	1996	1997	1998	1999	2000	2001	2002	2003
NORTHEAST															
Boston-Cambridge-Newton, MA-NH	109.4	138.9	145.0	148.6	152.9	154.9	158.6	163.3	167.9	171.7	176.0	183.6	191.5	196.5	203.9
New York-Newark-New Jersey NY-NJ-PA	108.7	138.5	144.8	150.0	154.5	158.2	162.2	166.9	170.8	173.6	177.0	182.5	187.1	191.9	197.8
Philadelphia-Camden-Wilmington, PA-NJ-DE-MD	108.8	135.8	142.2	146.6	150.2	154.6	158.7	162.8	166.5	168.2	171.9	176.5	181.3	184.9	188.8
NORTH CENTRAL															
Chicago-Naperville-Elgin, IL-IN-WI	107.7	131.7	137.0	141.1	145.4	148.6	153.3	157.4	161.7	165.0	168.4	173.8	178.3	181.2	184.5
Detroit-Warren-Dearborn, MI	106.8	128.6	133.1	135.9	139.6	144.0	148.6	152.5	156.3	159.8	163.9	169.8	174.4	178.9	182.5
Minneapolis-St. Paul-Bloomington, MN-WI	107.0	127.0	130.4	135.0	139.2	143.6	147.0	151.9	155.4	158.3	163.3	170.1	176.5	179.6	182.7
St. Louis, MO-IL	107.1	128.1	132.1	134.7	137.5	141.3	145.2	149.6	152.9	154.5	157.6	163.1	167.3	169.1	173.4
SOUTH															
Atlanta-Sandy Springs-Roswell GA	108.9	131.7	135.9	138.5	143.4	146.7	150.9	156.0	158.9	161.2	164.8	170.6	176.2	178.2	180.8
Dallas-Fort Worth-Arlington, TX	108.2	125.1	130.8	133.9	137.3	141.2	144.9	148.8	151.4	153.6	158.0	164.7	170.4	172.7	176.2
Houston-The Woodlands-Sugar Land TX	104.9	120.6	125.1	129.1	133.4	137.9	139.8	142.7	145.4	146.8	148.7	154.2	158.8	159.2	163.7
Miami-Fort Lauderdale-West Palm Beach FL	106.5	128.0	132.3	134.5	139.1	143.6	148.9	153.7	158.4	160.5	162.4	167.8	173.0	175.5	180.6
Tampa-St. Petersburg-Clearwater, FL[1]	. . .	111.7	116.4	119.2	124.0	126.5	129.7	131.6	134.0	137.5	140.6	145.7	148.8	153.9	158.1
Washington-Arlington-Alexandria, DC-VA-MD-WV	109.0	135.6	141.2	144.7	149.3	152.2	155.3	159.6	162.4	. . .	. . .	. . .	. . .	. . .	. . .
Baltimore-Columbia-Towson, MD	108.2	130.8	136.4	140.1	143.1	146.9	150.7	154.2	156.4	. . .	. . .	. . .	. . .	. . .	. . .
WEST															
Urban Alaska, AK	105.8	118.6	124.0	128.2	132.2	135.0	138.9	142.7	144.8	146.9	148.4	150.9	155.2	158.2	162.5
Denver-Aurora-Lakewood, CO	107.1	120.9	125.6	130.3	135.8	141.8	147.9	153.1	158.1	161.9	166.6	173.2	181.3	184.8	186.8
Urban Hawaii, HI	106.8	138.1	148.0	155.1	160.1	164.5	168.1	170.7	171.9	171.5	173.3	176.3	178.4	180.3	184.5
Los Angeles-Long Beach-Anaheim, CA	108.4	135.9	141.4	146.5	150.3	152.3	154.6	157.5	160.0	162.3	166.1	171.6	177.3	182.2	187.0
Phoenix-Mesa-Scottsdale, AZ	. . .	. . .	. . .	. . .	. . .	. . .	. . .	. . .	. . .	. . .	. . .	. . .	. . .	101.2	103.3
San Diego-Carlsbad, CA	110.4	138.4	143.4	147.4	150.6	154.5	156.8	160.9	163.7	166.9	172.8	182.8	191.2	197.9	205.3
San Francisco-Oakland-Hayward, CA	108.4	132.1	137.9	142.5	146.3	148.7	151.6	155.1	160.4	165.5	172.5	180.2	189.9	193.0	196.4
Seattle-Tacoma-Bellevue, WA	105.6	126.8	134.1	139.0	142.9	147.8	152.3	157.5	163.0	167.7	172.8	179.2	185.7	189.3	192.3

Area	2004	2005	2006	2007	2008	2009	2010	2011	2012	2013	2014	2015	2016	2017	2018
NORTHEAST															
Boston-Cambridge-Newton, MA-NH	209.5	216.4	223.1	227.4	235.4	233.8	237.4	243.9	247.7	251.1	255.2	256.7	260.5	267.0	275.8
New York-Newark-New Jersey NY-NJ-PA	204.8	212.7	220.7	226.9	235.8	236.8	240.9	247.7	252.6	256.8	260.2	260.6	263.4	268.5	273.6
Philadelphia-Camden-Wilmington, PA-NJ-DE-MD	196.5	204.2	212.1	216.7	224.1	223.3	227.7	233.8	238.1	240.9	244.1	243.9	245.3	248.4	251.6
NORTH CENTRAL															
Chicago-Naperville-Elgin, IL-IN-WI	188.6	194.3	198.3	204.8	212.5	210.0	212.9	218.7	222.0	224.5	228.5	227.8	229.3	233.6	237.7
Detroit-Warren-Dearborn, MI	185.4	190.8	196.6	200.1	204.7	203.5	205.1	211.8	216.1	219.5	221.8	218.7	222.2	226.9	232.3
Minneapolis-St. Paul-Bloomington, MN-WI	187.9	193.1	196.2	201.2	209.0	207.9	211.7	219.3	224.5	228.8	232.0	230.6	234.1	239.2	245.0
St. Louis, MO-IL	180.3	186.2	189.5	193.2	198.7	198.5	203.2	209.8	214.8	218.0	220.2	219.3	221.1	224.7	228.9
SOUTH															
Atlanta-Sandy Springs-Roswell GA	183.2	188.9	193.8	200.0	206.5	201.0	203.5	209.1	212.8	216.3	221.0	221.6	225.5	232.9	238.6
Dallas-Fort Worth-Arlington, TX	178.7	184.7	190.1	193.2	201.8	200.5	201.6	207.9	212.2	216.0	218.4	217.5	220.7	226.1	232.8
Houston-The Woodlands-Sugar Land TX	169.5	175.6	180.6	183.8	190.0	190.5	194.2	200.5	204.2	207.6	213.4	213.0	216.4	220.7	225.9
Miami-Fort Lauderdale-West Palm Beach FL	185.6	194.3	203.9	212.4	222.1	221.4	223.1	230.9	235.2	238.2	243.1	245.4	249.8	256.7	265.1
Tampa-St. Petersburg-Clearwater, FL[1]	162.0	168.5	175.2	184.3	190.1	189.9	193.5	198.9	203.6	206.8	210.8	211.6	214.0	219.5	224.3
Washington-Arlington-Alexandria, DC-VA-MD-WV	. . .	. . .	. . .	. . .	. . .	. . .	. . .	. . .	. . .	. . .	. . .	250.7	253.4	256.2	261.4
Baltimore-Columbia-Towson, MD	. . .	. . .	. . .	. . .	. . .	. . .	. . .	. . .	. . .	. . .	. . .	240.7	244.0	248.6	253.4
WEST															
Urban Alaska, AK	166.7	171.8	177.3	181.2	189.5	191.7	195.1	201.4	205.9	212.4	215.8	216.9	217.8	218.9	225.5
Denver-Aurora-Lakewood, CO	187.0	190.9	197.7	202.0	209.9	208.5	212.4	220.3	224.6	230.8	237.2	240.0	246.6	255.0	262.0
Urban Hawaii, HI	190.6	197.8	209.4	219.5	228.9	230.0	234.9	243.6	249.5	253.9	257.6	260.2	265.3	272.0	277.1
Los Angeles-Long Beach-Anaheim, CA	193.2	201.8	210.4	217.3	225.0	223.2	225.9	231.9	236.6	239.2	242.4	244.6	249.2	256.2	266.0
Phoenix-Mesa-Scottsdale, AZ	105.2	108.3	111.5	115.3	119.3	117.6	118.2	121.5	124.2	125.8	127.8	128.0	130.1	133.3	138.9
San Diego-Carlsbad, CA	212.8	220.6	228.1	233.3	242.3	242.3	245.5	252.9	257.0	260.3	265.1	269.4	274.7	283.0	292.5
San Francisco-Oakland-Hayward, CA	198.8	202.7	209.2	216.0	222.8	224.4	227.5	233.4	239.7	245.0	252.0	258.6	266.3	274.9	285.6
Seattle-Tacoma-Bellevue, WA	194.7	200.2	207.6	215.7	224.7	226.0	226.7	232.8	238.7	241.6	246.0	249.4	254.9	262.7	271.1

[1] 1987 = 100.
. . . = Not available.

Table 9-9. Consumer Price Index Research Series, Using Current Methods (CPI-U-RS), by Month and Annual Average, 1977–2018

(December 1977 = 100.)

Year	January	February	March	April	May	June	July	August	September	October	November	December	Annual average
1977	. . .	. . .	. . .	. . .	. . .	. . .	. . .	. . .	. . .	. . .	. . .	100.0	. . .
1978	100.5	101.1	101.8	102.7	103.6	104.5	105.0	105.5	106.1	106.7	107.3	107.8	104.4
1979	108.7	109.7	110.7	111.8	113.0	114.1	115.1	116.0	117.1	117.9	118.5	119.5	114.3
1980	120.8	122.4	123.8	124.7	125.7	126.7	127.5	128.6	129.9	130.7	131.5	132.4	127.1
1981	133.6	135.2	136.3	137.1	137.9	138.7	139.7	140.7	141.8	142.4	142.9	143.4	139.1
1982	144.2	144.7	144.9	145.0	146.1	147.5	148.5	148.8	149.5	150.2	150.5	150.6	147.5
1983	151.0	151.1	151.2	152.4	153.2	153.7	154.3	154.8	155.6	156.0	156.2	156.4	153.8
1984	157.2	158.0	158.3	159.1	159.5	160.0	160.5	161.1	161.8	162.2	162.2	162.4	160.2
1985	162.6	163.2	164.0	164.6	165.3	165.7	166.0	166.4	166.9	167.3	167.9	168.2	165.7
1986	168.7	168.3	167.5	167.1	167.6	168.4	168.4	168.7	169.6	169.7	169.7	169.9	168.6
1987	170.9	171.5	172.3	173.1	173.6	174.3	174.6	175.5	176.4	176.7	176.9	176.7	174.4
1988	177.2	177.5	178.3	179.1	179.7	180.4	181.1	181.8	183.0	183.4	183.6	183.7	180.7
1989	184.5	185.2	186.2	187.4	188.4	188.8	189.3	189.4	190.1	190.9	191.2	191.4	188.6
1990	193.3	194.1	195.2	195.5	195.8	196.8	197.6	199.3	200.9	202.0	202.3	202.3	197.9
1991	203.2	203.4	203.6	203.8	204.4	204.8	205.0	205.5	206.4	206.5	207.0	207.1	205.1
1992	207.5	208.1	208.9	209.3	209.6	210.1	210.4	210.9	211.5	212.1	212.4	212.3	210.2
1993	212.9	213.6	214.3	214.9	215.3	215.5	215.6	216.1	216.3	217.1	217.2	217.0	215.5
1994	217.4	218.0	218.7	219.0	219.2	219.8	220.3	221.1	221.4	221.6	221.8	221.7	220.0
1995	222.5	223.2	223.9	224.6	225.0	225.5	225.6	226.0	226.5	227.0	226.9	226.7	225.3
1996	227.8	228.6	229.8	230.6	231.1	231.3	231.6	231.9	232.7	233.3	233.7	233.7	231.3
1997	234.4	235.1	235.6	235.8	235.8	236.1	236.2	236.7	237.4	237.8	237.8	237.3	236.3
1998	237.8	238.1	238.5	239.0	239.3	239.5	239.7	240.1	240.4	240.9	240.8	240.6	239.5
1999	241.3	241.6	242.3	244.0	244.0	244.1	244.7	245.4	246.5	247.1	247.2	247.2	244.6
2000	248.0	249.4	251.4	251.6	251.8	253.2	253.7	253.8	255.1	255.5	255.7	255.5	252.9
2001	257.2	258.2	258.9	259.8	260.9	261.5	260.7	260.8	261.8	261.0	260.5	259.5	260.1
2002	260.2	261.2	262.6	264.1	264.0	264.2	264.5	265.4	265.8	266.3	266.3	265.7	264.2
2003	266.9	269.0	270.6	269.9	269.5	269.9	270.2	271.2	272.0	271.8	271.0	270.7	270.2
2004	272.1	273.6	275.3	276.2	277.7	278.6	278.3	278.4	278.9	280.4	280.6	279.6	277.5
2005	280.1	281.7	283.9	285.8	285.6	285.7	287.0	288.5	292.0	292.6	290.3	289.0	286.9
2006	291.3	291.9	293.6	296.0	297.4	298.1	298.9	299.6	298.1	296.5	296.0	296.5	296.2
2007	297.4	299.0	301.7	303.6	305.5	306.1	306.0	305.5	306.3	306.9	308.8	308.6	304.6
2008	310.1	311.0	313.7	315.6	318.2	321.5	323.2	321.9	321.4	318.2	312.1	308.8	316.3
2009	310.2	311.7	312.5	313.3	314.2	316.9	316.4	317.1	317.3	317.6	317.8	317.3	315.2
2010	318.3	318.4	319.7	320.3	320.5	320.2	320.3	320.7	320.9	321.3	321.5	322.0	320.4
2011	323.6	325.2	328.3	330.5	332.0	331.7	332.0	332.9	333.4	332.7	332.4	331.6	330.5
2012	333.1	334.6	337.1	338.1	337.7	337.3	336.7	338.6	340.1	340.0	338.4	337.5	337.5
2013	338.6	341.4	342.2	341.9	342.5	343.3	343.5	343.9	344.3	343.4	342.8	342.8	342.5
2014	344.1	345.4	347.6	348.7	350.0	350.7	350.5	349.9	350.2	349.3	347.5	345.6	348.3
2015	344.0	345.5	347.5	348.3	350.0	351.3	351.3	350.8	350.3	350.2	349.4	348.3	348.9
2016	348.8	349.1	350.6	352.3	353.7	354.9	354.3	354.7	355.5	356.0	355.4	355.5	353.4
2017	357.6	358.7	359.0	360.1	360.4	360.7	360.5	361.6	363.5	363.2	363.3	363.1	361.0
2018	365.0	366.7	367.5	369.0	370.5	371.1	371.1	371.3	371.8	372.4	371.2	370.0	369.8

. . . = Not available.

NOTES AND DEFINITIONS

IMPORT AND EXPORT PRICE INDEXES

Collection and Coverage

The International Price Program (IPP) at the Bureau of Labor Statistics (BLS) produces Import/Export Price Indexes (MXP) which contain data on changes in the prices of goods and services traded between the U.S. and the rest of the world. Price indexes are available for nearly all merchandise categories. Military goods, works of art, used items, charity donations, railroad equipment, items leased for less than a year, rebuilt and repaired items, and selected exports are not included in the IPP program.

The (IPP) selects sample establishments based upon their relative trade value in imports and exports during the course of a year. After an establishment is selected for inclusion, a BLS field economist visits the establishment to enlist cooperation and to select the exact items that will be priced on a monthly basis. All information provided by the establishment is protected under BLS confidentiality rules.

The MXP are primarily used to deflate foreign trade statistics produced by the U.S. government. The MXP are also a valuable input into the processes of measuring inflation, formulating fiscal and monetary policy, forecasting future prices, conducting elasticity studies, measuring U.S. industrial competitiveness, analyzing exchange rates, negotiating trade contracts, and analyzing import prices by locality of origin. The IPP collects prices as close as possible to the first day of each reference month.

The formula used to calculate the MXP is a modified form of the Laspeyres index. A Laspeyres index uses fixed base period quantities to aggregate prices. This means that the quality of goods and services is fixed; new goods do not appear, and the prices of goods that disappear must be observable. Because these implications are not consistent with the actually workings of the economy, adjustments must be made to the index. All MXP data are not seasonally adjusted.

Items are classified by end use for the Bureau of Economic Analysis System, by industry according to the North American Industry Classification System (NAICS), and product category according to the Harmonized System (HS). While classification by end use and product category are self-explanatory, a couple of notes are in order for classifying items by industry. In the NAICS tables, for both imports and exports, items are classified by output industry, not input industry. As an example, NAICS import index 326 (plastics and rubber products) includes outputs such as manufactured plastic rather than inputs such as petroleum. The NAICS classification structure also matches the classification system used by the PPI to produce the NAICS primary products indexes.

Although import and export transaction prices are used to calculate the MXP, the IPP does not publish price information. For this reason, the MXP cannot be used to measure differences in price levels among different products and services or among different localities of origin.

Sources of Additional Information

Concepts and methodology are described in Chapter 15 of the *BLS Handbook of Methods* and in monthly BLS press releases. These resources are available on the BLS Web site at <https://www.bls.gov>.

Table 9-10. U.S. Export Price Indexes for Selected Categories of Goods, by End Use, 2007–2018

(2000 = 100, unless otherwise indicated.)

Commodity	2007				2008				2009			
	March	June	September	December	March	June	September	December	March	June	September	December
ALL COMMODITIES	114.7	116.0	116.7	119.3	123.8	126.1	124.9	115.8	115.5	117.8	117.9	119.7
Foods, Feeds, and Beverages	146.9	148.6	157.8	171.1	196.9	198.0	190.4	155.1	156.7	174.8	158.2	165.1
Agricultural foods, feeds, and beverages excluding distilled beverages	149.2	151.0	160.8	175.2	202.6	204.0	195.6	156.6	158.3	178.6	160.7	167.9
Nonagricultural foods (fish, distilled beverages)	128.0	128.5	133.0	136.1	148.3	146.1	145.5	143.5	144.4	141.5	137.3	140.9
Industrial Supplies and Materials	145.5	149.0	148.8	154.1	165.5	173.2	169.4	139.6	136.5	140.4	143.9	150.1
Industrial supplies and materials, durable	160.2	160.9	155.5	159.2	172.7	172.9	167.1	141.5	143.4	144.0	150.7	157.7
Industrial supplies and materials, nondurable	137.6	142.8	145.5	151.9	162.0	174.2	171.6	139.1	133.1	139.0	140.5	146.2
Agricultural industrial supplies and materials	127.3	128.7	140.0	144.7	159.3	158.0	157.4	126.1	122.9	131.0	142.2	152.5
Fuels and lubricants	188.8	201.1	200.9	222.8	249.5	297.2	267.2	166.8	146.9	175.2	171.9	189.6
Nonagricultural supplies and materials excluding fuels and building materials	143.5	146.1	145.0	148.5	158.2	161.6	160.8	138.8	138.2	138.5	142.7	147.3
Selected building materials	112.7	113.9	114.4	113.7	114.2	113.8	115.4	115.1	114.0	113.0	114.0	113.5
Capital Goods	99.2	99.6	99.9	100.6	101.2	102.0	101.8	101.5	102.3	103.1	103.5	103.3
Electrical generating equipment	106.0	106.5	106.7	107.5	108.6	108.9	109.5	109.0	106.8	107.2	107.4	109.3
Nonelectrical machinery	92.8	92.9	93.1	93.6	93.7	94.2	93.9	93.3	93.8	94.4	94.9	94.5
Transportation equipment excluding motor vehicles[1]	121.1	122.3	123.4	125.0	128.1	130.3	130.7	131.5	135.1	137.3	137.2	136.5
Automotive Vehicles, Parts, and Engines	105.9	106.1	106.3	106.7	107.1	107.4	107.9	108.0	108.2	108.0	108.0	108.2
Consumer Goods, Excluding Automotives	104.8	105.8	106.2	107.3	108.0	108.2	109.3	109.0	108.5	108.4	109.2	109.4
Nondurables, manufactured	105.0	106.7	107.0	108.2	109.3	110.1	109.0	107.2	107.1	108.5	109.4	110.0
Durables, manufactured	103.4	103.7	104.2	105.2	105.4	105.2	108.7	109.7	109.9	108.1	109.5	109.2
Agricultural Commodities	145.0	146.7	156.8	169.3	194.3	195.2	188.3	150.8	151.6	169.7	156.9	164.7
Nonagricultural Commodities	112.6	113.8	113.8	115.7	118.8	121.2	120.4	113.2	112.9	114.1	115.1	116.5

Commodity	2010				2011				2012			
	March	June	September	December	March	June	September	December	March	June	September	December
ALL COMMODITIES	121.2	122.2	123.7	127.5	132.7	134.5	135.3	132.1	134.1	131.7	134.5	133.6
Foods, Feeds, and Beverages	163.4	164.5	174.6	191.1	206.9	210.6	213.8	199.0	206.0	205.8	231.6	229.3
Agricultural foods, feeds, and beverages excluding distilled beverages	165.7	166.7	177.6	194.6	212.1	214.6	217.3	201.2	208.6	208.0	235.9	233.8
Nonagricultural foods (fish, distilled beverages)	145.9	147.2	149.4	161.1	157.9	174.6	184.6	183.8	186.2	190.1	193.0	187.9
Industrial Supplies and Materials	155.1	159.8	162.6	172.6	188.3	191.8	192.8	184.6	188.2	178.4	183.6	180.6
Industrial supplies and materials, durable	160.4	165.5	167.0	174.8	186.1	190.3	196.6	188.2	191.1	183.5	183.4	186.1
Industrial supplies and materials, nondurable	152.6	157.2	160.8	172.2	190.4	193.6	191.7	183.4	187.4	176.3	184.5	178.4
Agricultural industrial supplies and materials	155.7	162.5	173.2	223.0	258.9	234.8	212.5	200.7	201.4	189.2	201.2	196.3
Fuels and lubricants	197.0	208.0	213.1	233.9	276.4	284.0	284.6	270.6	280.4	248.3	272.9	253.8
Nonagricultural supplies and materials excluding fuels and building materials	152.2	155.8	158.0	164.4	173.8	178.5	181.2	173.8	176.3	171.0	171.6	172.4
Selected building materials	116.0	118.7	117.1	116.2	116.3	116.2	115.8	115.6	117.2	118.1	118.8	117.9
Capital Goods	103.8	103.5	103.5	103.9	104.0	104.6	104.6	104.6	105.9	105.8	105.6	105.7
Electrical generating equipment	109.8	109.3	108.7	109.8	111.1	113.6	114.1	112.8	113.1	114.3	113.9	114.3
Nonelectrical machinery	94.7	94.3	94.3	94.4	93.9	94.2	94.2	94.3	95.3	95.0	94.8	94.9
Transportation equipment excluding motor vehicles[1]	139.1	139.5	140.1	141.6	144.5	145.3	144.9	145.6	148.6	149.1	149.2	149.0
Automotive Vehicles, Parts, and Engines	108.6	108.5	108.7	109.1	109.7	110.3	111.4	111.9	112.5	112.9	112.9	112.9
Consumer Goods, Excluding Automotives	110.2	110.4	111.8	112.7	113.9	116.3	117.4	116.6	116.8	117.0	116.7	116.4
Nondurables, manufactured	111.9	111.5	112.9	114.0	113.4	114.1	114.7	113.9	114.9	114.9	115.3	115.6
Durables, manufactured	107.7	108.2	109.9	110.9	112.9	112.7	113.6	113.3	114.3	114.9	114.9	113.9
Agricultural Commodities	163.3	165.3	176.1	198.5	218.8	217.2	216.0	200.5	206.9	204.5	229.9	227.4
Nonagricultural Commodities	118.1	119.1	120.0	122.4	126.5	128.6	129.5	127.3	128.9	126.5	127.6	126.9

[1]December 2001 = 100.

Table 9-10. U.S. Export Price Indexes for Selected Categories of Goods, by End Use, 2007–2018—*Continued*

(2000 = 100, unless otherwise indicated.)

Commodity	2013				2014				2015			
	March	June	September	December	March	June	September	December	March	June	September	December
ALL COMMODITIES	134.4	132.8	132.4	132.3	134.9	133.0	131.9	128.3	125.9	125.3	122.3	119.8
Foods, Feeds, and Beverages	225.5	223.8	215.2	213.2	220.9	222.5	210.0	204.1	193.6	184.6	179.6	177.2
Agricultural foods, feeds, and beverages excluding distilled beverages	229.4	228.8	218.8	216.2	224.7	226.5	212.4	206.1	192.9	185.8	180.4	177.5
Nonagricultural foods (fish, distilled beverages)	191.2	178.3	184.3	189.6	187.6	185.7	192.5	190.1	210.0	179.3	177.8	182.2
Industrial Supplies and Materials	183.1	177.6	178.4	178.0	185.9	177.0	175.3	162.6	155.6	155.8	145.7	137.4
Industrial supplies and materials, durable	182.8	175.5	172.5	170.8	171.6	170.3	170.2	165.0	160.8	159.6	152.8	147.7
Industrial supplies and materials, nondurable	184.1	179.5	182.5	182.9	194.5	181.5	179.0	162.1	153.7	154.5	142.7	132.7
Agricultural industrial supplies and materials	205.1	203.8	202.1	199.6	210.0	198.8	185.6	182.5	188.1	180.4	174.7	169.9
Fuels and lubricants	264.5	250.7	261.4	265.3	294.4	257.1	250.5	204.2	183.6	186.3	157.9	136.9
Nonagricultural supplies and materials excluding fuels and building materials	172.4	168.2	166.4	164.8	167.0	165.8	166.4	161.6	157.8	157.7	152.3	146.9
Selected building materials	120.7	122.5	125.1	126.5	128.8	125.7	121.6	121.3	119.2	115.8	112.9	114.5
Capital Goods	106.7	106.5	106.5	106.5	107.1	107.5	107.3	107.4	107.8	107.5	107.4	106.9
Electrical generating equipment	114.9	114.5	115.1	114.6	115.2	115.9	116.0	115.4	114.8	114.3	113.3	112.3
Nonelectrical machinery	95.6	95.4	95.4	95.3	95.5	95.7	95.5	95.4	95.6	95.1	94.9	94.5
Transportation equipment excluding motor vehicles[1]	151.6	151.6	151.9	152.0	155.7	156.3	156.6	158.4	160.6	161.4	162.2	161.9
Automotive Vehicles, Parts, and Engines	113.5	113.4	113.3	113.6	113.5	114.1	114.0	114.1	113.9	114.0	113.8	113.5
Consumer Goods, Excluding Automotives	115.8	115.2	114.5	115.0	114.8	115.0	115.2	114.3	112.9	113.0	112.0	111.5
Nondurables, manufactured	115.0	114.9	113.9	114.2	111.0	111.0	112.2	111.6	108.8	108.8	107.7	107.2
Durables, manufactured	112.3	111.5	111.7	111.8	112.2	112.3	111.6	111.1	110.9	111.1	110.1	109.5
Agricultural Commodities	224.9	224.2	215.4	212.8	221.7	221.4	207.5	201.8	191.4	184.3	178.9	175.7
Nonagricultural Commodities	127.9	126.2	126.4	126.4	128.6	126.6	126.3	122.9	121.1	120.9	118.0	115.6

Commodity	2016				2017				2018			
	March	June	September	December	March	June	September	December	March	June	September	December
ALL COMMODITIES	118.1	120.9	120.5	121.3	122.1	121.6	123.9	124.7	126.3	128.0	127.3	126.1
Foods, Feeds, and Beverages	172.6	184.1	175.0	176.5	182.0	176.5	179.3	180.5	187.2	185.0	175.0	185.2
Agricultural foods, feeds, and beverages excluding distilled beverages	172.4	184.7	174.2	176.2	181.5	175.9	178.3	179.3	185.4	183.9	172.8	183.6
Nonagricultural foods (fish, distilled beverages)	182.9	184.9	193.0	187.8	197.7	192.5	201.9	204.8	221.2	208.5	216.8	215.7
Industrial Supplies and Materials	132.5	140.8	141.9	145.8	147.0	145.4	153.0	154.6	158.0	164.2	163.5	156.0
Industrial supplies and materials, durable	150.1	151.7	154.8	154.4	159.3	157.3	162.6	162.1	167.4	168.9	162.2	162.8
Industrial supplies and materials, nondurable	124.0	135.8	135.8	141.9	141.4	140.0	148.7	151.3	153.9	162.3	164.4	153.1
Agricultural industrial supplies and materials	167.6	170.0	172.8	173.6	177.7	174.2	174.0	178.9	189.9	192.0	182.4	181.5
Fuels and lubricants	117.0	147.9	148.3	164.6	160.7	160.8	181.9	184.6	185.2	204.5	210.4	182.8
Nonagricultural supplies and materials excluding fuels and building materials	146.5	148.1	149.4	149.5	152.6	150.2	154.1	155.2	160.0	161.8	158.9	158.4
Selected building materials	113.6	115.4	116.8	117.5	119.1	119.7	121.5	123.7	123.3	125.0	123.0	120.7
Capital Goods	107.0	107.1	106.8	106.9	107.5	107.7	108.0	108.7	109.0	109.8	110.1	110.1
Electrical generating equipment	112.4	112.5	112.0	111.8	112.7	112.6	113.2	116.0	115.5	117.4	117.6	117.1
Nonelectrical machinery	94.2	94.2	93.8	93.6	93.7	93.7	94.0	94.3	94.3	94.8	95.0	94.9
Transportation equipment excluding motor vehicles[1]	163.6	164.4	164.9	166.7	169.6	170.5	171.2	172.3	174.7	176.4	177.0	177.7
Automotive Vehicles, Parts, and Engines	113.1	113.2	112.7	112.5	113.1	113.2	113.4	113.2	114.0	114.2	114.2	114.0
Consumer Goods, Excluding Automotives	110.4	110.1	110.6	108.8	107.9	108.5	109.2	109.5	109.8	109.8	109.8	109.8
Nondurables, manufactured	105.4	106.0	106.7	105.3	103.4	104.3	105.3	105.8	106.6	106.4	106.5	106.3
Durables, manufactured	108.8	107.8	108.0	107.0	106.8	107.2	107.8	107.7	107.6	107.7	107.5	107.6
Agricultural Commodities	171.0	181.9	173.3	175.1	180.2	174.9	176.9	178.5	185.2	184.2	173.2	182.6
Nonagricultural Commodities	114.1	116.3	116.5	117.2	117.7	117.5	119.8	120.5	121.8	123.7	123.8	121.7

[1]December 2001 = 100.

Table 9-11. U.S. Import Price Indexes for Selected Categories of Goods, by End Use, 2007–2018

(2000 = 100, unless otherwise indicated.)

Commodity	2007				2008				2009			
	March	June	September	December	March	June	September	December	March	June	September	December
ALL COMMODITIES	115.9	120.0	121.8	127.3	133.5	145.5	137.8	114.5	113.6	120.0	121.3	124.4
Foods, Feeds, and Beverages	124.6	127.8	131.8	134.4	141.8	147.7	147.9	142.3	137.0	139.8	140.6	143.7
Agricultural foods, feeds, and beverages, excluding distilled beverages	135.1	139.5	144.4	148.3	157.3	165.1	165.1	159.4	151.3	155.5	156.8	160.8
Nonagricultural foods (fish and distilled beverages)	101.3	101.5	103.5	103.0	106.8	108.4	109.1	103.8	104.8	104.4	104.1	104.9
Industrial Supplies and Materials	169.8	185.6	190.7	211.3	234.5	283.0	248.9	150.4	149.3	177.3	183.0	196.2
Fuels and lubricants	209.6	238.2	250.0	290.3	329.0	423.7	346.3	153.9	162.3	222.1	228.5	249.7
Paper and paper base stocks	111.5	110.8	111.2	109.2	114.1	117.3	119.9	113.2	106.6	101.8	99.1	103.1
Materials associated with nondurable supplies and materials	124.0	125.4	128.2	135.3	147.8	152.9	162.4	148.5	136.7	137.5	134.8	140.6
Selected building materials	111.4	113.1	116.9	116.0	114.1	119.2	122.7	118.1	116.2	116.0	118.9	120.9
Unfinished metals related to durable goods	202.9	219.7	209.1	217.2	241.5	273.2	255.4	185.7	171.6	178.3	204.0	221.5
Finished metals related to durable goods	125.4	133.7	134.8	135.0	145.8	158.7	159.9	140.8	132.7	133.2	137.1	140.4
Nonmetals related to durable goods	101.8	101.6	102.5	103.8	105.2	107.6	111.4	109.0	105.2	103.0	104.3	105.4
Industrial Supplies and Materials, Durable	141.0	148.4	146.3	149.1	158.9	173.5	169.7	141.8	134.7	136.0	145.7	152.5
Industrial Supplies and Materials, Excluding Fuels[1]	146.2	151.6	151.2	155.4	166.8	178.8	179.5	155.1	145.5	146.5	151.7	158.6
Industrial Supplies and Materials, Excluding Petroleum	139.3	144.6	141.0	147.5	159.4	173.7	167.4	146.0	133.1	132.1	134.4	145.2
Industrial Supplies and Materials, Nondurable, Excluding Petroleum	136.3	139.1	133.6	144.5	159.3	173.0	163.5	150.8	131.0	127.4	121.0	136.3
Capital Goods	91.1	91.3	91.9	92.2	92.2	93.2	93.3	92.7	91.8	91.9	91.9	91.9
Electric generating equipment	104.3	105.7	106.5	107.9	109.3	112.0	112.9	111.4	109.4	110.0	110.3	111.3
Nonelectrical machinery	87.2	87.2	87.7	87.7	87.5	88.2	88.2	87.5	86.6	86.5	86.5	86.4
Transportation equipment, excluding motor vehicles[1]	110.1	111.0	113.4	114.7	115.3	117.7	118.2	120.2	120.6	122.4	123.2	122.6
Automotive Parts and Accessories	103.5	103.3	103.6	104.8	106.2	106.7	107.4	108.8	108.9	108.5	109.2	110.0
Consumer Goods, Excluding Automotive	101.3	101.4	102.1	102.6	104.0	104.9	105.1	104.4	103.9	104.3	104.1	104.3
Nondurables, manufactured	104.1	104.3	105.0	105.5	107.5	107.9	108.2	108.2	108.4	108.1	107.8	107.9
Nonmanufactured consumer goods	102.2	102.6	103.4	103.8	104.3	106.6	106.6	103.6	101.2	101.4	101.2	102.1
All Imports, Excluding Fuels	108.4	109.5	110.1	111.4	113.9	116.5	116.8	112.7	110.7	111.2	111.9	113.0
All Imports, Excluding Petroleum	105.9	107.1	107.1	108.9	111.6	114.9	114.0	109.9	107.3	107.4	107.9	109.7

Commodity	2010				2011				2012			
	March	June	September	December	March	June	September	December	March	June	September	December
ALL COMMODITIES	126.3	125.2	125.7	131.0	139.3	142.2	141.7	142.2	144.2	138.7	140.8	139.4
Foods, Feeds, and Beverages	147.4	148.7	153.3	162.7	174.9	174.8	174.7	172.4	174.4	171.8	171.6	169.1
Agricultural foods, feeds, and beverages, excluding distilled beverages	165.8	166.1	171.1	182.6	198.9	197.0	196.5	194.0	196.3	193.4	194.4	190.7
Nonagricultural foods (fish and distilled beverages)	105.6	109.2	113.0	117.4	120.7	124.5	125.3	123.7	124.7	122.9	120.1	120.4
Industrial Supplies and Materials	205.0	199.5	200.1	222.6	256.3	266.1	262.5	263.6	272.0	245.5	255.8	249.3
Fuels and lubricants	262.4	245.8	247.1	285.2	343.7	359.0	348.2	356.3	371.0	317.7	343.1	328.2
Paper and paper base stocks	107.6	115.5	117.5	117.5	116.3	119.4	117.1	114.8	114.0	114.1	112.6	111.5
Materials associated with nondurable supplies and materials	144.6	146.2	147.7	157.0	165.8	173.0	175.9	175.1	177.7	183.3	176.0	175.6
Selected building materials	127.6	131.9	124.6	127.0	131.5	129.3	131.2	130.7	134.4	138.1	141.3	143.6
Unfinished metals related to durable goods	233.4	244.6	244.2	266.0	290.2	297.0	304.9	277.8	283.9	263.5	257.1	263.8
Finished metals related to durable goods	142.4	146.5	147.7	152.7	157.4	161.1	165.6	162.1	163.9	161.8	161.6	161.7
Nonmetals related to durable goods	107.1	107.2	107.7	108.7	112.1	114.3	116.3	115.2	115.4	115.0	114.2	114.4
Industrial Supplies and Materials, Durable	158.4	163.7	162.5	171.2	181.4	184.7	189.3	179.9	183.4	176.7	174.9	177.4
Industrial Supplies and Materials, Excluding Fuels[1]	164.3	168.9	168.9	178.0	187.8	192.8	196.6	190.0	192.9	191.1	187.1	188.4
Industrial Supplies and Materials, Excluding Petroleum	149.7	151.6	151.0	159.4	168.4	172.5	174.5	167.8	167.6	165.3	163.1	167.8
Industrial Supplies and Materials, Nondurable, Excluding Petroleum	139.4	137.5	137.5	145.5	153.1	158.2	157.4	153.5	149.5	151.7	149.1	155.9
Capital Goods	91.4	91.5	91.8	92.0	92.6	92.7	92.9	93.1	93.5	93.2	93.4	93.2
Electric generating equipment	111.0	111.4	112.7	113.7	115.6	117.1	118.4	118.4	118.9	118.8	119.5	119.7
Nonelectrical machinery	85.9	86.0	86.1	86.2	86.5	86.4	86.4	86.4	86.6	86.2	86.4	86.0
Transportation equipment, excluding motor vehicles[1]	121.5	121.3	121.6	121.9	124.8	126.1	126.4	130.0	133.1	133.8	133.8	134.8
Automotive Parts and Accessories	109.9	110.2	111.5	112.0	113.7	115.7	116.6	117.0	117.6	118.3	118.9	118.6
Consumer Goods, Excluding Automotive	104.5	104.4	104.2	104.2	104.7	105.8	106.6	107.7	107.6	107.6	107.3	107.6
Nondurables, manufactured	109.0	109.3	110.0	110.4	110.3	111.6	112.8	114.4	114.5	114.8	114.7	115.3
Nonmanufactured consumer goods	102.5	102.4	103.0	103.7	107.8	111.8	114.9	119.3	118.0	119.3	115.5	115.3
All Imports, Excluding Fuels	113.7	114.4	114.7	116.4	118.7	120.1	120.9	120.4	121.1	120.8	120.4	120.4
All Imports, Excluding Petroleum	110.3	110.7	111.0	112.6	115.0	116.4	117.0	116.4	116.7	116.3	116.0	116.5

[1]December 2001 = 100.

Table 9-11. U.S. Import Price Indexes for Selected Categories of Goods, by End Use, 2007–2018—*Continued*

(2000 = 100, unless otherwise indicated.)

Commodity	2013				2014				2015			
	March	June	September	December	March	June	September	December	March	June	September	December
ALL COMMODITIES	141.2	138.8	139.8	137.8	140.5	140.5	137.9	130.1	125.3	126.6	121.9	119.3
Foods, Feeds, and Beverages	173.7	172.2	174.9	175.9	182.1	176.6	180.1	182.1	178.0	175.5	174.7	172.4
Agricultural foods, feeds, and beverages, excluding distilled beverages	194.5	190.0	191.1	192.1	198.9	193.6	197.4	201.5	196.0	195.0	193.5	190.1
Nonagricultural foods (fish and distilled beverages)	126.4	131.9	138.1	138.9	143.9	138.0	140.7	137.9	137.2	131.1	132.1	132.3
Industrial Supplies and Materials	257.7	247.2	253.2	242.3	254.8	254.7	241.4	199.4	175.9	185.9	160.2	148.2
Fuels and lubricants	346.5	329.9	347.3	324.3	349.8	350.3	320.0	230.0	183.0	209.7	157.5	135.7
Paper and paper base stocks	112.7	113.2	113.3	113.9	112.7	113.6	113.2	112.8	111.6	110.3	109.9	108.4
Materials associated with nondurable supplies and materials	175.0	173.4	168.3	168.0	171.4	169.8	168.3	167.9	161.2	161.1	156.4	151.8
Selected building materials	148.9	143.6	141.5	142.4	143.0	141.6	142.5	140.6	138.3	136.6	133.2	134.3
Unfinished metals related to durable goods	263.7	243.6	238.9	235.6	239.2	239.6	242.3	228.9	214.8	207.1	189.8	177.1
Finished metals related to durable goods	160.6	158.3	156.1	155.8	157.4	157.9	158.5	156.9	154.1	152.7	149.0	145.5
Nonmetals related to durable goods	114.4	113.7	112.2	112.3	111.5	112.0	112.3	111.5	110.2	109.8	109.1	108.4
Industrial Supplies and Materials, Durable	178.0	170.1	167.3	166.8	168.0	168.2	169.3	164.1	158.4	155.2	148.2	143.5
Industrial Supplies and Materials, Excluding Fuels[1]	188.6	182.9	179.2	178.5	180.6	180.2	180.4	176.9	170.5	168.4	162.0	157.2
Industrial Supplies and Materials, Excluding Petroleum	167.1	163.4	157.3	160.1	167.4	161.6	160.3	158.2	150.8	148.4	143.2	138.4
Industrial Supplies and Materials, Nondurable, Excluding Petroleum	153.9	154.8	145.3	151.7	165.8	153.2	149.1	150.5	141.3	139.8	136.7	131.8
Capital Goods	93.0	92.6	92.4	92.5	92.3	92.6	92.4	92.1	91.4	90.9	90.4	89.8
Electric generating equipment	119.5	119.5	119.5	119.3	119.0	120.0	120.4	120.1	119.2	118.2	117.7	116.6
Nonelectrical machinery	85.8	85.3	85.1	85.2	85.0	85.2	84.9	84.6	83.9	83.4	82.9	82.3
Transportation equipment, excluding motor vehicles[1]	135.8	135.8	136.0	136.0	136.2	135.8	136.7	136.8	136.8	137.0	136.9	137.0
Automotive Parts and Accessories	118.6	117.1	115.6	115.5	115.8	116.1	115.6	115.4	113.2	112.0	111.5	111.0
Consumer Goods, Excluding Automotive	107.7	107.6	107.3	107.2	108.1	108.4	108.3	107.9	107.5	107.4	107.2	107.2
Nondurables, manufactured	115.8	116.0	116.1	116.3	117.9	118.5	118.8	119.1	119.1	119.1	119.2	119.3
Nonmanufactured consumer goods	116.4	116.4	116.4	117.1	120.4	121.3	121.1	119.1	118.1	118.4	116.7	120.3
All Imports, Excluding Fuels	120.6	119.6	119.0	119.0	119.7	119.6	119.5	119.0	117.5	116.9	115.9	114.9
All Imports, Excluding Petroleum	116.5	115.7	114.8	115.2	116.5	115.8	115.6	115.1	113.5	112.8	111.9	110.8

Commodity	2016				2017				2018			
	March	June	September	December	March	June	September	December	March	June	September	December
ALL COMMODITIES	117.7	120.7	120.6	121.6	122.5	122.4	123.9	125.5	126.5	128.2	127.7	124.4
Foods, Feeds, and Beverages	170.4	172.3	180.8	179.3	177.9	182.1	185.4	181.0	182.7	178.0	179.7	180.3
Agricultural foods, feeds, and beverages, excluding distilled beverages	186.1	187.4	198.9	196.4	194.0	199.8	205.2	199.1	200.2	194.7	196.5	198.1
Nonagricultural foods (fish and distilled beverages)	135.0	138.6	139.9	140.8	141.9	142.0	140.2	139.9	143.3	140.2	142.1	139.9
Industrial Supplies and Materials	139.9	158.1	156.7	163.6	169.2	166.6	174.5	185.8	188.5	201.0	197.0	177.7
Fuels and lubricants	115.8	158.4	151.7	169.2	174.8	166.4	181.1	206.1	203.5	230.5	227.4	179.0
Paper and paper base stocks	107.5	107.4	105.8	105.6	105.0	107.3	107.6	109.7	113.2	118.6	122.7	124.9
Materials associated with nondurable supplies and materials	148.5	149.2	149.0	150.3	154.2	153.9	153.7	159.1	162.4	163.2	162.5	162.6
Selected building materials	134.3	137.4	137.4	137.3	142.0	145.8	149.4	151.3	157.5	162.7	152.7	144.5
Unfinished metals related to durable goods	180.1	189.3	200.1	198.9	214.3	214.2	226.1	223.5	238.8	245.5	230.6	232.7
Finished metals related to durable goods	145.1	145.0	145.4	144.6	146.4	150.4	155.2	157.6	162.3	163.4	160.7	160.0
Nonmetals related to durable goods	108.7	108.7	108.0	107.8	109.2	109.2	109.9	110.4	111.6	113.1	114.7	113.9
Industrial Supplies and Materials, Durable	144.4	147.9	151.2	150.6	157.0	158.6	164.2	164.3	171.7	175.4	168.6	167.3
Industrial Supplies and Materials, Excluding Fuels[1]	156.5	159.0	161.0	161.1	166.7	167.8	171.4	173.7	180.0	183.1	178.6	177.9
Industrial Supplies and Materials, Excluding Petroleum	136.8	138.8	142.1	142.7	147.1	148.1	150.1	153.7	158.3	159.8	156.2	160.6
Industrial Supplies and Materials, Nondurable, Excluding Petroleum	127.3	127.4	130.6	132.7	134.7	135.0	132.5	140.3	141.6	140.1	140.5	152.3
Capital Goods	89.4	89.0	89.0	88.7	88.7	89.0	89.3	89.3	89.7	89.4	89.3	89.1
Electric generating equipment	116.4	115.9	115.9	116.2	116.5	116.3	117.0	117.0	117.7	117.9	118.1	118.0
Nonelectrical machinery	81.8	81.5	81.5	81.1	81.1	81.5	81.8	81.8	82.2	81.9	81.7	81.5
Transportation equipment, excluding motor vehicles[1]	137.4	136.6	136.3	136.6	136.5	134.5	134.4	135.0	135.6	134.9	134.6	134.7
Automotive Parts and Accessories	110.2	111.0	111.1	111.0	109.9	109.9	110.4	110.4	110.2	110.2	110.1	110.3
Consumer Goods, Excluding Automotive	107.2	106.9	106.6	106.5	106.9	106.9	106.9	106.7	107.3	107.3	107.5	107.4
Nondurables, manufactured	119.9	119.8	119.3	119.9	121.5	121.7	121.5	121.4	122.1	122.7	123.6	123.2
Nonmanufactured consumer goods	118.8	119.0	118.5	115.3	114.9	115.0	114.6	114.8	115.8	114.9	115.3	117.7
All Imports, Excluding Fuels	114.6	114.8	115.2	115.1	115.6	116.1	116.7	116.6	117.8	117.8	117.4	117.3
All Imports, Excluding Petroleum	110.4	110.5	111.2	111.1	111.6	112.0	112.5	112.6	113.7	113.5	113.2	113.7

[1]December 2001 = 100.

CHAPTER 10: THE WORKING POOR

HIGHLIGHTS

This chapter includes information on the working poor which was collected in the Annual Social and Economic Supplement (ASEC) to the Current Population Survey (CPS) For more information about the CPS, please see Chapter 1.

Figure 10-1. Poverty Status by Educational Attainment, 2017

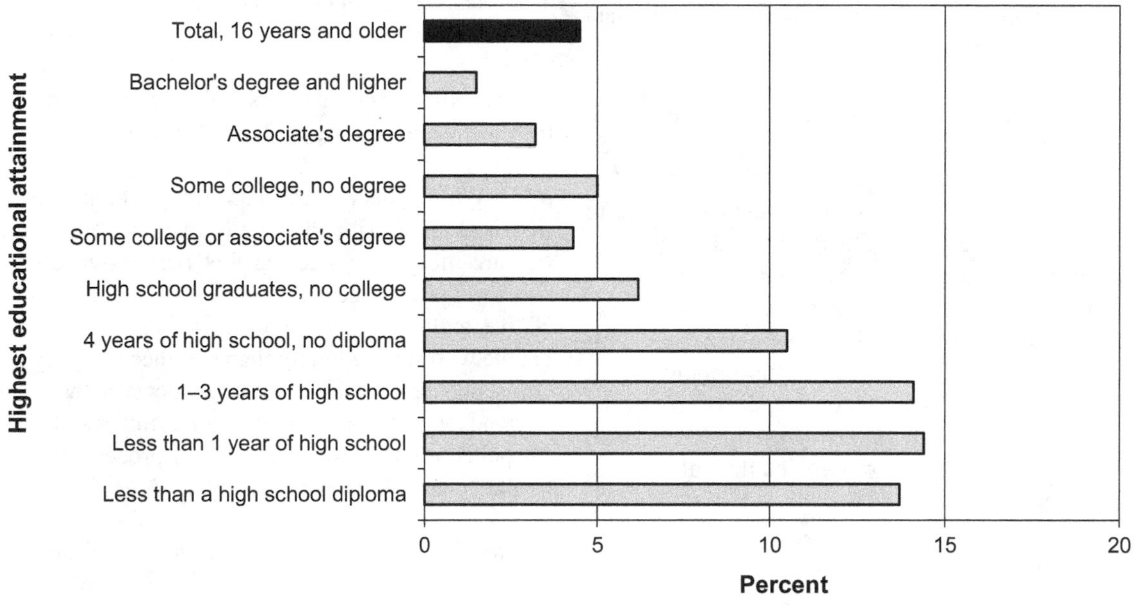

Poverty rates declined as educational attainment levels increased. In 2017, the poverty rate of those with less than a high school diploma was 13.7 percent. For high school graduates, the poverty rates declined to 6.2 percent. Those with a bachelor's degree or higher had the lowest poverty rate at 1.5 percent. (See Table 10-3.)

OTHER HIGHLIGHTS

- Nearly four million families lived in poverty in 2017 despite having at least one member of the family in the labor force for a half the year or more in 2017. (See Table 10-1.)

- Full-time workers continued to be much less likely to be among the working poor than were part-time workers. Among persons in the labor force for 27 weeks or more, 2.9 percent of those usually employed full-time were classified as working poor, compared with 10.9 percent of part-time workers. (See Table 10-2.)

- Women were more likely than men to be among the working poor. In 2017, 5.3 percent of women who were in the labor force for 27 weeks or more were in poverty compared with 3.8 percent of men. Blacks and Hispanics continued to be far more likely than Whites and Asians to be among the working poor. (See Table 10-3.)

- Younger people in the labor force had a much higher rate of poverty than older workers. In 2017, 30.9 percent of unrelated individuals aged 16 to 19 in the labor force for 27 weeks or more were in poverty compared with 5.8 percent of those aged 25 to 64 years. (See Table 10-6.)

NOTES AND DEFINITIONS

Collection and Coverage

The data presented in this chapter were collected in the Annual Social and Economic Supplement (ASEC) to the Current Population Survey (CPS). Conducted by the U.S. Census Bureau for the Bureau of Labor Statistics, the CPS is a monthly sample survey of about 60,000 eligible households. Data from the CPS are used to obtain monthly estimates of the nation's employment and unemployment levels. The ASEC, conducted in the months of February through April, includes questions about work activity and income during the previous calendar year. For instance, data collected in 2018 are for the 2017 calendar year.

The estimates presented in this report are based on a sample and, consequently, may differ from estimates that would have been obtained from a complete count using the same questionnaire and procedures. Sampling variability may be relatively large in cases where the numbers are small. Thus, both small estimates and small differences between estimates should be interpreted with caution. For a detailed explanation of the ASEC supplement to the CPS, its sampling variability, more extensive definitions than those provided here, and additional information about income and poverty measures, see "Income and Poverty in the United States: 2017 *Current Population Reports*, p60-263 (U.S. Census Bureau, September 2018). For more detailed information on the CPS, please see Chapter 1.

Concepts and Definitions

Family. A family is defined as a group of two or more people residing together who are related by birth, marriage, or adoption. The count of families used in this report includes only primary families. A primary family consists of the reference person (the householder) and all people living in the household who are related to the reference person. Families are classified either as married-couple families or as those maintained by men or women without spouses present. Family status is determined at the time of the survey interview and, thus, may be different from that of the previous year.

Income. Data on income are limited to money income—before personal income taxes and payroll deductions—received in the calendar year preceding the CPS supplement. Data on income do not include the value of noncash benefits, such as food stamps, Medicare, Medicaid, public housing, and employer-provided benefits.

Hispanic or Latino ethnicity. This term refers to people who identified themselves in the CPS enumeration process as being of Hispanic, Latino, or Spanish ethnicity. People whose ethnicity is identified as Hispanic or Latino may be of any race.

Involuntary part-time workers. These are people who, during at least 1 week of the year, worked fewer than 35 hours because of slack work or unfavorable business conditions or because they could not find full-time work. The number of weeks of involuntary part-time work is accumulated over the year.

Labor force. People in the labor force are those who worked or looked for work sometime during the calendar year. The number of weeks in the labor force is accumulated over the entire year. The focus in this report is on people who were in the labor force for 27 weeks or more.

Occupation. This term refers to the job in which a person worked the most weeks during the calendar year.

Race. White, Black or African American, and Asian are categories used to describe the race of people. People in these categories are those who selected that race group only. Data for the two remaining race categories—American Indian and Alaska Native, and Native Hawaiian and Other Pacific Islander—and for people who selected more than one race category are included in totals, but are not shown separately because the number of survey respondents is too small to develop estimates of sufficient quality for publication. In the enumeration process, race is determined by the household respondent.

Related children. Related children are children under age 18 (including sons, daughters, stepchildren, and adopted children) of the husband, wife, or person maintaining the family, as well as other children related to the householder by birth, marriage, or adoption.

Unrelated individuals. These are people who are not living with anyone related to them by birth, marriage, or adoption. Such individuals may live alone, reside in a nonrelated family household, or live in group quarters with other unrelated individuals.

Unemployed. Unemployed people are those who looked for work while not employed or those who were on layoff from a job and were expecting to be recalled to that job. The number of weeks unemployed is accumulated over the entire year.

Unemployed. Unemployed people are those who looked for work while not employed or those who were on layoff from a job and were expecting to be recalled to that job. The number of weeks unemployed is accumulated over the entire year.

Unrelated individuals. These are people who are not living with anyone related to them by birth, marriage, or adoption. Such individuals may live alone, reside in a nonrelated family household, or live in group quarters with other unrelated individuals.

Working poor. The working poor are people who spent at least 27 weeks in the labor force (that is, working or looking for work) but whose incomes still fell below the official poverty level.

Working-poor rate. This rate is the number of individuals in the labor force for at least 27 weeks whose incomes still fell below the official poverty level, as a percentage of all people who were in the labor force for at least 27 weeks during the calendar year.

Sources of Additional Information

Additional information on the working poor can be found in BLS report 1079 "A Profile of the Working Poor".

Table 10-1. Poverty Status of People and Primary Families in the Labor Force for 27 Weeks or More, 2007–2017

(Number in thousands, percent.)

Characteristic	2007	2008	2009	2010	2011	2012	2013	2014	2015	2016	2017
Total in the Labor Force[1]	146 567	147 838	147 902	146 859	147 475	148 735	149 483	150 319	152 230	153 364	154 762
In poverty	7 521	8 883	10 391	10 512	10 382	10 612	10 450	9 487	8 560	7 572	6 946
Working-poor rate	5.1	6.0	7.0	7.2	7.0	7.1	7.0	6.3	5.6	4.9	4.5
Unrelated individuals	33 226	32 785	33 798	34 099	33 731	34 810	35 061	35 018	35 953	35 789	36 959
In poverty	2 558	3 275	3 947	3 947	3 621	3 851	4 141	3 395	3 137	2 792	2 524
Working-poor rate	7.7	10.0	11.7	11.6	10.7	11.1	11.8	9.7	8.7	7.8	6.8
Primary families[2]	65 158	65 907	65 467	64 931	66 225	66 541	66 462	66 732	67 193	67 628	67 588
In poverty	4 169	4 538	5 193	5 269	5 469	5 478	5 137	5 108	4 607	4 082	3 854
Working-poor rate	6.4	6.9	7.9	8.1	8.3	8.2	7.7	7.7	6.9	6.0	5.7

[1]Includes individuals in families, not shown separately.
[2]Primary families with at least one member in the labor force for more than half the year.

Table 10-2. People in the Labor Force: Poverty Status and Work Experience, by Weeks in the Labor Force, 2017

(Number in thousands, percent.)

Characteristic	Total in labor force	27 weeks or more in the labor force	
		Total	50 to 52 weeks
Total			
Total in the labor force	167 538	154 762	141 425
Did not work during the year	2 375	1 067	907
Worked during the year	165 163	153 694	140 519
Usual full-time workers	132 784	128 271	120 513
Usual part-time workers	32 379	25 424	20 006
Involuntary part-time workers	6 144	5 282	4 446
Voluntary part-time workers	26 235	20 141	15 560
At or Above Poverty Level			
Total in the labor force	158 195	147 816	135 730
Did not work during the year	1 529	661	551
Worked during the year	156 666	147 155	135 178
Usual full-time workers	128 244	124 494	117 309
Usual part-time workers	28 422	22 661	17 869
Involuntary part-time workers	4 916	4 311	3 631
Voluntary part-time workers	23 506	18 350	14 238
Below Poverty Level			
Total in the labor force	9 343	6 946	5 696
Did not work during the year	846	407	355
Worked during the year	8 497	6 539	5 340
Usual full-time workers	4 540	3 777	3 204
Usual part-time workers	3 957	2 762	2 137
Involuntary part-time workers	1 228	971	816
Voluntary part-time workers	2 729	1 791	1 321
Rate[1]			
Total in the labor force	5.6	4.5	4.0
Did not work during the year	35.6	38.1	39.2
Worked during the year	5.1	4.3	3.8
Usual full-time workers	3.4	2.9	2.7
Usual part-time workers	12.2	10.9	10.7
Involuntary part-time workers	20.0	18.4	18.3
Voluntary part-time workers	10.4	8.9	8.5

[1]Number below the poverty level as a percentage of the total in the labor force.

Table 10-3. People in the Labor Force for 27 Weeks or More: Poverty Status by Educational Attainment, Race, Hispanic or Latino Ethnicity, and Gender, 2017

(Number in thousands, rate.)

Characteristic	Total	Men	Women	Below poverty level			Rate[1]		
				Total	Men	Women	Total	Men	Women
Total, 16 Years and Older	154 762	82 562	72 199	6 946	3 132	3 814	4.5	3.8	5.3
Less than a high school diploma	12 013	7 488	4 525	1 640	925	715	13.7	12.4	15.8
Less than 1 year of high school	3 792	2 496	1 296	548	351	197	14.4	14.0	15.2
1–3 years of high school	6 398	3 822	2 576	901	457	444	14.1	12.0	17.2
4 years of high school, no diploma	1 823	1 169	654	192	117	75	10.5	10.0	11.4
High school graduates, no college[2]	40 550	24 017	16 534	2 531	1 076	1 455	6.2	4.5	8.8
Some college or associate's degree	43 673	21 789	21 885	1 888	690	1 198	4.3	3.2	5.5
Some college, no degree	27 236	14 142	13 094	1 370	534	836	5.0	3.8	6.4
Associate's degree	16 437	7 647	8 790	518	156	362	3.2	2.0	4.1
Bachelor's degree and higher[3]	58 524	29 269	29 255	886	441	445	1.5	1.5	1.5
White, 16 Years and Older	120 750	65 721	55 030	4 754	2 291	2 463	3.9	3.5	4.5
Less than a high school diploma	9 482	6 164	3 318	1 185	715	471	12.5	11.6	14.2
Less than 1 year of high school	3 150	2 170	980	442	291	150	14.0	13.4	15.3
1–3 years of high school	4 992	3 097	1 895	614	328	286	12.3	10.6	15.1
4 years of high school, no diploma	1 339	896	443	130	95	34	9.7	10.6	7.8
High school graduates, no college[2]	31 517	19 023	12 493	1 697	775	922	5.4	4.1	7.4
Some college or associate's degree	33 806	17 287	16 519	1 216	473	743	3.6	2.7	4.5
Some college, no degree	20 737	11 051	9 686	863	352	511	4.2	3.2	5.3
Associate's degree	13 069	6 236	6 833	353	121	232	2.7	1.9	3.4
Bachelor's degree and higher[3]	45 946	23 247	22 699	655	328	327	1.4	1.4	1.4
Black or African American, 16 Years and Older	19 225	9 047	10 178	1 518	503	1 015	7.9	5.6	10.0
Less than a high school diploma	1 344	676	668	296	121	174	22.0	17.9	26.1
Less than 1 year of high school	220	94	126	36	14	22	16.4	15.0	17.5
1–3 years of high school	801	413	388	214	92	123	26.8	22.3	31.6
4 years of high school, no diploma	323	169	154	45	15	30	14.0	9.0	19.4
High school graduates, no college[2]	6 026	3 284	2 742	609	185	424	10.1	5.6	15.4
Some college or associate's degree	6 402	2 808	3 595	489	145	343	7.6	5.2	9.5
Some college, no degree	4 283	1 977	2 306	380	126	254	8.9	6.4	11.0
Associate's degree	2 119	831	1 288	109	19	89	5.1	2.3	6.9
Bachelor's degree and higher[3]	5 453	2 279	3 174	124	51	74	2.3	2.2	2.3
Asian, 16 Years and Older	9 699	5 202	4 497	279	166	113	2.9	3.2	2.5
Less than a high school diploma	564	279	285	59	34	25	10.4	12.2	8.6
Less than 1 year of high school	236	109	127	38	22	16	16.1	20.4	12.5
1–3 years of high school	238	114	124	16	8	8	6.7	7.2	6.2
4 years of high school, no diploma	91	56	35	5	4	1	5.3	. . .	. . .
High school graduates, no college[2]	1 551	870	681	86	52	34	5.6	6.0	5.1
Some college or associate's degree	1 727	872	855	56	28	28	3.3	3.2	3.3
Some college, no degree	1 041	551	490	33	19	14	3.2	3.5	2.8
Associate's degree	687	321	365	23	9	14	3.4	2.8	3.9
Bachelor's degree and higher[3]	5 857	3 181	2 676	78	52	26	1.3	1.6	1.0
Hispanic or Latino Ethnicity, 16 Years and Older	26 371	15 085	11 286	2 082	1 051	1 032	7.9	7.0	9.1
Less than a high school diploma	5 987	4 008	1 979	893	553	340	14.9	13.8	17.2
Less than 1 year of high school	2 851	1 954	897	405	260	145	14.2	13.3	16.2
1–3 years of high school	2 428	1 542	887	401	225	177	16.5	14.6	20.0
4 years of high school, no diploma	708	513	195	87	69	18	12.3	13.5	9.3
High school graduates, no college	8 411	5 164	3 247	676	322	354	8.0	6.2	10.9
Some college or associate's degree	7 003	3 512	3 491	368	112	256	5.3	3.2	7.3
Some college, no degree	4 695	2 448	2 246	277	85	191	5.9	3.5	8.5
Associate's degree	2 309	1 064	1 244	91	27	64	4.0	2.5	5.2
Bachelor's degree and higher	4 970	2 401	2 569	145	63	82	2.9	2.6	3.2

[1]Number below the poverty level as a percentage of the total in the labor force for 27 weeks or more.
[2]Includes people with a high school diploma or equivalent.
[3]Includes people with bachelor's, master's, professional, and doctoral degrees.
. . . = Not available.

Table 10-4. Primary Families: Poverty Status, Presence of Related Children, and Work Experience of Family Members in the Labor Force for 27 Weeks or More, 2017

(Number in thousands.)

Year	Total families	At or above poverty level	Below poverty level	Rate[1]
Total Primary Families	67 588	63 734	3 854	5.7
With related children under 18 years	34 759	31 547	3 212	9.2
Without children	32 829	32 187	642	2.0
With one member in the labor force	29 212	25 803	3 410	11.7
With two or more members in the labor force	38 376	37 932	444	1.2
With two members	31 792	31 372	420	1.3
With three or more members	6 584	6 560	24	0.4
Married-Couple Families[2]	49 945	48 422	1 523	3.0
With related children under 18 years	24 275	23 063	1 212	5.0
Without children	25 670	25 359	311	1.2
With one member in the labor force	17 497	16 253	1 243	7.1
Husband	12 463	11 489	973	7.8
Wife	4 326	4 100	226	5.2
Relative	708	664	44	6.2
With two or more members in the labor force	32 448	32 169	280	0.9
With two members	27 210	26 942	268	1.0
With three or more members	5 239	5 227	12	0.2
Families Maintained by Women[3]	12 140	10 199	1 941	16.0
With related children under 18 years	7 665	5 951	1 714	22.4
Without children	4 474	4 247	227	5.1
With one member in the labor force	8 368	6 567	1 801	21.5
Householder	6 734	5 170	1 564	23.2
Relative	1 634	1 397	236	14.5
With two or more members in the labor force	3 772	3 631	140	3.7
Families Maintained by Men[3]	5 503	5 114	390	7.1
With related children under 18 years	2 819	2 533	286	10.1
Without children	2 685	2 581	104	3.9
With one member in the labor force	3 348	2 982	366	10.9
Householder	2 744	2 465	279	10.2
Relative	603	517	86	14.3
With two or more members in the labor force	2 156	2 132	24	1.1

[1]Number below the poverty level as a percentage of the total in the labor force for 27 weeks or more who worked during the year.
[2]Refers to opposite-sex married-couple families only.
[3]No opposite-sex spouse present.

Table 10-5. People in Families and Unrelated Individuals: Poverty Status and Work Experience, 2017

(Numbers in thousands, rate.)

Poverty status and work experience	Total people	In married-couple families[1]				In families maintained by women[2]			In families maintained by men[2]			Unrelated individuals
		Husbands	Wives	Related children under 18 years	Other relatives	Househol-der	Related children under 18 years	Other relatives	Househol-der	Related children under 18 years	Other relatives	
Total												
All people	257 097	60 550	61 186	5 663	22 032	15 410	2 202	14 792	6 394	662	6 910	61 297
With labor force activity	167 538	45 465	37 355	1 497	14 062	10 668	474	9 067	4 950	173	4 390	39 438
1 to 26 weeks	12 776	1 512	2 626	827	2 526	660	269	1 097	281	96	403	2 479
27 weeks or more	154 762	43 953	34 729	671	11 536	10 008	205	7 969	4 668	77	3 987	36 959
With no labor force activity	89 559	15 085	23 832	4 165	7 970	4 741	1 728	5 725	1 444	489	2 520	21 859
At or Above the Poverty Level												
All people	228 963	57 564	58 183	5 321	21 217	11 453	1 516	12 618	5 604	567	6 336	48 583
With labor force activity	158 195	44 038	36 676	1 456	13 871	8 642	363	8 428	4 556	159	4 220	35 785
1 to 26 weeks	10 379	1 325	2 417	795	2 460	318	199	886	189	85	356	1 350
27 weeks or more	147 816	42 714	34 259	661	11 411	8 324	164	7 542	4 367	75	3 864	34 435
With no labor force activity	70 768	13 525	21 507	3 865	7 346	2 811	1 153	4 191	1 048	408	2 116	12 798
Below Poverty Line												
All people	28 134	2 986	3 003	341	815	3 957	686	2 174	790	94	574	12 714
With labor force activity	9 343	1 426	678	41	190	2 027	111	639	394	13	170	3 652
1 to 26 weeks	2 397	187	209	32	66	342	70	211	92	11	47	1 129
27 weeks or more	6 946	1 239	469	9	124	1 684	41	427	302	2	123	2 524
With no labor force activity	18 791	1 560	2 325	300	624	1 930	575	1 535	396	81	404	9 062
Rate[3]												
All people	10.9	4.9	4.9	6.0	3.7	25.7	31.1	14.7	12.4	14.3	8.3	20.7
With labor force activity	5.6	3.1	1.8	2.8	1.4	19.0	23.4	7.0	8.0	7.7	3.9	9.3
1 to 26 weeks	18.8	12.4	8.0	3.9	2.6	51.9	25.9	19.3	32.8	11.6	11.7	45.5
27 weeks or more	4.5	2.8	1.4	1.4	1.1	16.8	20.1	5.4	6.5	2.9	3.1	6.8
With no labor force activity	21.0	10.3	9.8	7.2	7.8	40.7	33.3	26.8	27.4	16.6	16.0	41.5

[1]Refers to opposite-sex married-couple families only.
[2]No opposite-sex spouse present.
[3]Number below the poverty level as a percentage of the total.
- = Represents zero, rounds to zero, or indicates that base is less than 80,000.

Table 10-6. Unrelated Individuals in the Labor Force for 27 Weeks or More: Poverty Status by Age, Gender, Race, Hispanic or Latino Ethnicity and Living Arrangement, 2017

(Number in thousands, percent.)

Characteristic	Total	At or Above the Poverty Level	Below the Poverty Level	Rate[1]
AGE AND GENDER				
Total Unrelated Individuals	36 959	34 435	2 524	6.8
16 to 19 years	413	285	127	30.9
20 to 24 years	4 360	3 728	632	14.5
25 to 64 years	29 302	27 588	1 714	5.8
65 Years and Older	2 885	2 834	51	1.8
Men	20 206	18 945	1 261	6.2
Women	16 753	15 490	1 263	7.5
Race and Hispanic or Latino Ethnicity				
White	28 482	26 717	1 765	6.2
Men	15 760	14 862	898	5.7
Women	12 722	11 855	867	6.8
Black or African American	5 432	4 912	520	9.6
Men	2 793	2 548	245	8.8
Women	2 639	2 364	275	10.4
Asian	1 762	1 681	82	4.6
Men	971	934	37	3.8
Women	792	747	45	5.7
Hispanic or Latino, ethnicity	5 030	4 531	499	9.9
Men	3 198	2 928	270	8.4
Women	1 832	1 603	229	12.5
Living Arrangement				
Living alone	18 503	17 521	982	5.3
Living with others	18 456	16 915	1 541	8.4

[1]Number below the poverty level as a percentage of the total in the labor force for 27 weeks or more.

Table 10-7. People in the Labor Force for 27 Weeks or More: Poverty Status and Labor Market Problems of Full-Time Wage and Salary Workers, 2017

(Number in thousands, percent.)

Characteristic	Total	At or above the poverty level	Below poverty level	Rate[1]
Total, Full-Time Wage and Salary Workers	121 997	118 683	3 314	2.7
No unemployment, involuntary part-time employment, or low earnings[2]	104 625	103 966	659	0.6
Workers Experiencing One Labor Market Problem				
Unemployment only	5 000	4 720	280	5.6
Involuntary part-time employment only	2 602	2 540	61	2.4
Low earnings only	6 936	5 451	1 485	21.4
Workers Experiencing Multiple Labor Market Problems				
Unemployment and involuntary part-time employment	828	742	86	10.4
Unemployment and low earnings	1 097	659	438	39.9
Involuntary part-time employment and low earnings	600	405	195	32.5
Unemployment, involuntary part-time employment, and low earnings	310	199	111	35.7
Workers Experiencing Each Labor Market Problem				
Unemployment (alone or with other problems)	7 235	6 320	915	12.6
Involuntary part-time employment (alone or with other problems)	4 340	3 887	453	10.4
Low earnings (alone or with other problems)	8 943	6 714	2 228	24.9

[1]Number below the poverty level as a percentage of the total in the labor force for 27 weeks or more.
[2]The low-earnings threshold in 2016 was $353.25 per week.

CHAPTER 11: CONSUMER EXPENDITURES

HIGHLIGHTS

The principal objective of the Consumer Expenditure (CE) Survey is to collect information about the buying habits of American households. The survey breaks down expenditures for different demographic categories, such as income, age, family size, and geographic location. These data are used in a variety of government, business, and academic research projects and provide important weights for the periodic revisions of the Consumer Price Index (CPI).

Figure 11-1. Consumer Expenditures, Average Annual Percent Change, 2016–2017 and 2017–2018

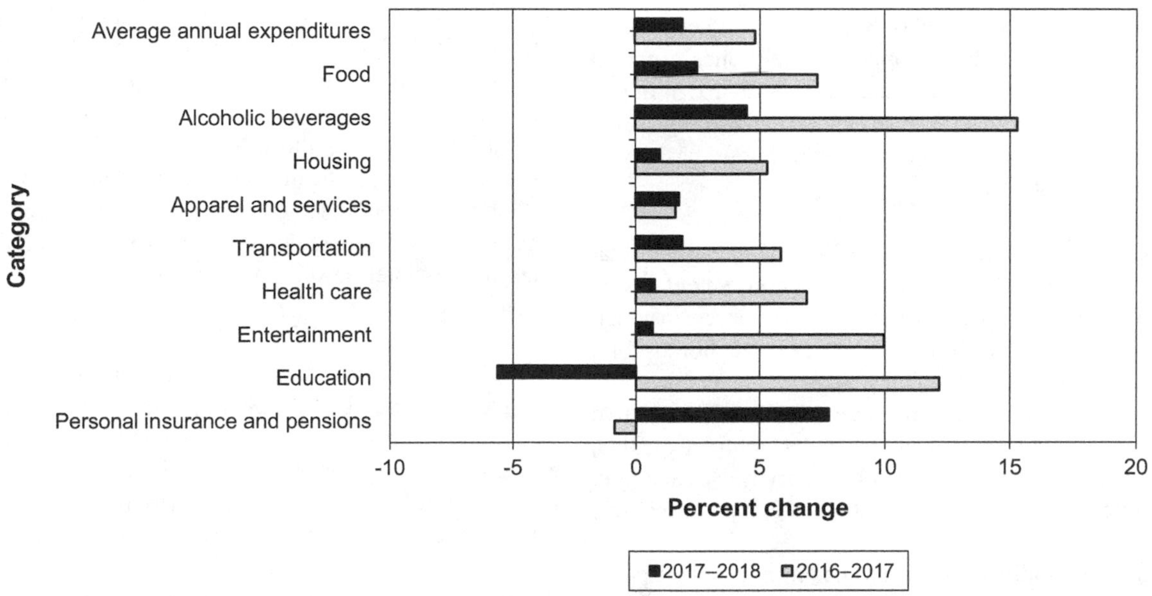

In 2018, average annual expenditures increased 1.9 percent after increasing 4.8 percent the previous year. They increased for all major categories except for reading, education, and miscellaneous expenditures. (See Table 11-1.)

OTHER HIGHLIGHTS

- Average annual consumer expenditures varied substantially by age group. Older age groups typically spend more in health care while those in younger age groups spent more on education. In 2018, persons 65 years and older had $6,802 in annual expenditures for healthcare while those under 30 years of age had only $1,994 in annual expenditures. (See Table 11-10.)

- As educational attainment increased, so did average annual expenditures. Those with less than a high school diploma had average annual expenditures of $30,285 while those with a master's, professional, or doctoral degree had average annual expenditures of $95,446. (See Table 11-13.)

- Cities in the South and the Midwest typically had lower average annual expenditures than those in the North or the West. Among the selected cities list in Table 11-15, Miami had the lowest average annual expenditures at $57,555 followed by Chicago at $63,726. Meanwhile, Seattle had the highest average annual expenditures at $84,864. (See Table 11-15.)

NOTES AND DEFINITIONS

Purpose, Collection, and Coverage

The buying habits of American consumers change over time because of changes in relative prices, real income, family size and composition, and other determinants of tastes and preferences. The introduction of new products into the marketplace and the emergence of new concepts in retailing also influence consumer buying habits. Data from the Consumer Expenditure Survey (CE), the only national survey that relates family expenditures to demographic characteristics, are of great importance to researchers. The survey data are also used to revise the Consumer Price Index market baskets and item samples.

Until the 1970s, the Bureau of Labor Statistics (BLS) conducted surveys of consumer expenditures approximately once every 10 years. The last such survey was conducted in 1972–1973. In late 1979, in a significant departure from previous methodology, BLS initiated a survey to be conducted on a continuous basis with rotating panels of respondents.

The current CE is similar to its 1972–1973 predecessor in that it consists of two separate components. Each component has its own questionnaire and sample: (1) the Interview Survey, in which an interviewer visits each consumer unit every three months for a twelve-month period; and (2) the Diary Survey, a record-keeping survey completed by other consumer units for two consecutive one-week periods. The Census Bureau, under contract to BLS, collects the data for both components of the survey. Beginning in 1999, the sample was increased from 5,000 to 7,500 households.

In 2003, the survey modified the questions on race and Hispanic origin to comply with the new standards for maintaining, collecting, and presenting federal data on race and ethnicity for federal statistical agencies. Beginning with the data collected in 2003, the CE tables use data collected from the new race and ethnicity questions. A number of new classifications were made with publication of the 2003 data.

Beginning with the publication of the 2004 tables, the CE has been implementing multiple imputations of income data. Prior to 2004, the CE only published income data collected from complete income reporters. The introduction of multiply imputed income data affects the published CE tables in several ways, because income data are now published for all consumer units (instead of for complete reporters only). The most obvious result of this change is seen on the tables showing expenditures categorized by income before taxes, including income by quintile. Starting with the 2004 data, columns describing income, expenditures, and characteristics for "total complete reporting" and "incomplete reporting of income" no longer appear in these tables, and the column entitled "all consumer units" appears on all income tables. Due to the implementation of income imputation, data for 2004 are not strictly comparable to those of prior years, especially for the income tables. Averages for demographic characteristics and annual expenditures will change due to differences between the incomplete and complete income reporters in these categories. Furthermore, certain expenditures (such as personal insurance and pensions) are computed using income data. As a result of imputation, average annual values for these expenditures may be substantially different in the 2004 CE tables than in tables for previous years. The regular flow of data resulting from this design substantially enhances the usefulness of the survey by providing more timely information on consumption patterns within different kinds of consumer units.

The Quarterly *Interview Survey* is designed to collect data on the types of expenditures that respondents can be expected to recall after a period of three months or longer. These include relatively large expenditures (such as those for property, travel, automobiles, and major appliances) and expenditures that occur on a regular basis (such as those for rent, utilities, insurance premiums, and clothing). The interview also obtains "global estimates" for food and other selected items. The survey collects data for approximately 95 percent of total expenditures. Each sample household is interviewed once per quarter, for five consecutive quarters.

The *Diary Survey* is designed to collect data on expenditures for frequently purchased items that are more difficult to recall over longer periods of time. Respondents complete a diary of expenses for two consecutive 1-week periods. Expenditures for tobacco, drugs (including nonprescription drugs), and personal care supplies and services are also collected in the Diary Survey.

Participants in both surveys record dollar amounts for goods and services purchased during the reporting period, regardless of whether payment was made at the time of purchase. Excluded from both surveys are business-related expenditures and expenditures for which the family is reimbursed. Information is collected on demographic and family characteristics at the initial interview for each survey.

The tables in this chapter present integrated data from the Diary Survey and the Interview Survey and provide a complete accounting of consumer expenditures and income, which neither survey component is designed to do alone. Data for some expenditure items are only collected in one of the surveys. For example, the Diary Survey does not collect data for expenditures on overnight travel or information on reimbursements, while the Interview Survey records these purchases. Examples of expenditures for which reimbursements are netted out include those for medical care, auto repair, and construction, repairs, alterations, and maintenance of property.

For items unique to one survey or the other, the choice of which survey to use as the source of data is obvious. However, there is considerable overlap in coverage between the two surveys.

Integrating the data thus presents the problem of determining the appropriate survey component. When data are available from both survey sources, the more reliable of the two (as determined by statistical methods) is selected. As a result, some items are selected from the Interview Survey and others are selected from the Diary Survey.

Data Included in This Edition

Data for single characteristics are for calendar year 2018 and data for two cross-classified characteristics are for an average of calendar years 2017 and 2018. Income values from the survey are derived from "complete income reporters" only. Complete income reporters are defined as consumer units that provide values for at least one of the major sources of their income: wages and salaries, self-employment income, retirement income, dividends and interest, and welfare benefits. Some consumer units are defined as complete income reporters, even though they may not have provided a full accounting of all income from all sources.

Consumer units are classified by quintiles of income before taxes, age of reference person, size of consumer unit, region, composition of consumer unit, number of earners in consumer unit, housing tenure, race, type of area (urban or rural), and occupation.

Concepts and Definitions

A *consumer unit* comprises either (1) all members of a particular household related by blood, marriage, adoption, or other legal arrangements; (2) a person living alone, sharing a household with others, living as a roomer in a private home or lodging house or in permanent living quarters in a hotel or motel, but who is financially independent; or (3) two or more persons living together who pool their income to make joint expenditure decisions. Financial independence is determined by the three major expense categories: housing, food, and other living expenses. To be considered financially independent, at least two of the three major expense categories have to be provided by the respondent. The terms "family," "household," and "consumer unit" are used interchangeably in descriptions of the CE.

An *earner* is a consumer unit member, 14 years of age or older, who reported having worked at least 1 week during the 12 months prior to the interview date.

The *education of reference person* refers to the number of years of formal education of the reference person, on the basis of the highest grade completed. If enrolled at time of the interview, the interviewer records the grade currently attended. Persons not reporting the extent of their education are classified under no school or not reported.

The *householder* or *reference person* is the first member of the consumer unit mentioned by the respondent as owner or renter of the premises at the time of the initial interview.

Housing tenure refers to the family's principal place of residence during the survey. "Owner" includes families living in their own homes, cooperatives or condominium apartments, or townhouses. "Renter" includes families paying rent, as well as families living rent-free in lieu of wages.

Quintiles of income before taxes refers to the ranking of complete income reporters in ascending order, according to the level of total before-tax income reported by the consumer unit. The ranking is then divided into five equal groups. Incomplete income reporters are not ranked and are shown separately.

Total expenditures include the transaction costs, including excise and sales taxes of goods and services acquired during the interview period. Estimates include expenditures for gifts and contributions and payments for pensions and personal insurance.

Sources of Additional Information

More extensive descriptions and tables can be found in an updated version of *BLS Handbook of Methods* and in an anthology of articles relating to consumer expenditures. These resources can be found on the BLS Web site at <https://www.bls.gov>.

Table 11-1. Consumer Expenditures, Annual Average of All Consumer Units, 2005–2018

(Number, dollar, percent.)

Item	2005	2006	2007	2008	2009	2010	2011	2012	2013	2014	2015	2016	2017	2018
NUMBER OF CONSUMER UNITS (THOUSANDS)	117 356	118 843	120 171	120 770	120 847	121 107	122 287	124 416	125 670	127 006	128 437	129 549	130 001	131 439
CONSUMER UNIT CHARACTERISTICS														
Income Before Taxes	58 712	60 533	63 091	63 563	62 857	62 481	63 685	65 596	63 784	66 877	69 627	74 664	73 573	78 635
Age of Reference Person	48.6	48.7	48.8	49.1	49.4	49.4	49.7	50.0	50.1	50.3	50.5	50.9	50.9	51.1
Average Number in Consumer Unit														
All persons	2.5	2.5	2.5	2.5	2.5	2.5	2.5	2.5	2.5	2.5	2.5	2.5	2.5	2.5
Children under 18 years	0.6	0.6	0.6	0.6	0.6	0.6	0.6	0.6	0.6	0.6	0.6	0.6	0.6	0.6
Persons 65 years and over	0.3	0.3	0.3	0.3	0.3	0.3	0.3	0.3	0.3	0.4	0.4	0.4	0.4	0.4
Earners	1.3	1.3	1.3	1.3	1.3	1.3	1.3	1.3	1.3	1.3	1.3	1.3	1.3	1.3
Vehicles	2.0	1.9	1.9	2.0	2.0	1.9	1.9	1.9	1.9	1.9	1.9	1.9	1.9	1.9
Percent Homeowner	67	67	67	66	66	66	65	64	64	63	62	62	63	63
With mortgage	43	43	43	42	41	41	40	39	37	37	35	36	36	37
Without mortgage	25	24	23	24	25	25	25	26	26	26	27	27	27	26
AVERAGE ANNUAL EXPENDITURES	46 409	48 398	49 638	50 486	49 067	48 109	49 705	51 442	51 100	53 495	55 978	57 311	60 060	61 224
Food	5 931	6 111	6 133	6 443	6 372	6 129	6 458	6 599	6 602	6 759	7 023	7 203	7 729	7 923
Food at home	3 297	3 417	3 465	3 744	3 753	3 624	3 838	3 921	3 977	3 971	4 015	4 049	4 363	4 464
Cereals and bakery products	445	446	460	507	506	502	531	538	544	519	518	524	564	569
Meats, poultry, fish, and eggs	764	797	777	846	841	784	832	852	856	892	896	890	944	961
Dairy products	378	368	387	430	406	380	407	419	414	423	413	410	450	449
Fruits and vegetables	552	592	600	657	656	679	715	731	751	756	769	783	837	858
Other food at home	1 158	1 212	1 241	1 305	1 343	1 278	1 353	1 380	1 412	1 382	1 419	1 442	1 568	1 627
Food away from home	2 634	2 694	2 668	2 698	2 619	2 505	2 620	2 678	2 625	2 787	3 008	3 154	3 365	3 459
Alcoholic Beverages	426	497	457	444	435	412	456	451	445	463	515	484	558	583
Housing	15 167	16 366	16 920	17 109	16 895	16 557	16 803	16 887	17 148	17 798	18 409	18 886	19 884	20 091
Shelter	8 805	9 673	10 023	10 183	10 075	9 812	9 825	9 891	10 080	10 491	10 742	11 128	11 895	11 747
Owned dwellings	5 958	6 516	6 730	6 760	6 543	6 277	6 148	6 056	6 108	6 149	6 210	6 295	6 947	6 678
Rented dwellings	2 345	2 590	2 602	2 724	2 860	2 900	3 029	3 186	3 324	3 631	3 802	4 035	4 167	4 249
Other lodging	502	567	691	698	672	635	648	649	649	710	730	798	782	821
Utilities, fuels, and public services	3 183	3 397	3 477	3 649	3 645	3 660	3 727	3 648	3 737	3 921	3 885	3 884	3 836	4 049
Household operations	801	948	984	998	1 011	1 007	1 122	1 159	1 144	1 174	1 309	1 384	1 412	1 522
Housekeeping supplies	611	640	639	654	659	612	615	610	645	632	655	660	755	747
Household furnishings and equipment	1 767	1 708	1 797	1 624	1 506	1 467	1 514	1 580	1 542	1 581	1 818	1 829	1 987	2 025
Apparel and Services	1 886	1 874	1 881	1 801	1 725	1 700	1 740	1 736	1 604	1 786	1 846	1 803	1 833	1 866
Transportation	8 344	8 508	8 758	8 604	7 658	7 677	8 293	8 998	9 004	9 073	9 503	9 049	9 576	9 761
Vehicle purchases (net outlay)	3 544	3 421	3 244	2 755	2 657	2 588	2 669	3 210	3 271	3 301	3 997	3 634	4 054	3 975
Gasoline and motor oil	2 013	2 227	2 384	2 715	1 986	2 132	2 655	2 756	2 611	2 468	2 090	1 909	1 968	2 109
Other vehicle expenses	2 339	2 355	2 592	2 621	2 536	2 464	2 454	2 490	2 584	2 723	2 756	2 884	2 842	2 859
Public and other transportation	448	505	538	513	479	493	516	542	537	581	661	623	712	818
Health Care	2 664	2 766	2 853	2 976	3 126	3 157	3 313	3 556	3 631	4 290	4 342	4 612	4 928	4 968
Health insurance	1 361	1 465	1 545	1 653	1 785	1 831	1 922	2 061	2 229	2 868	2 977	3 160	3 414	3 405
Medical services	677	670	709	727	736	722	768	839	796	790	791	838	872	909
Drugs	521	514	481	482	486	485	489	515	470	486	425	463	486	483
Medical supplies	105	117	118	114	119	119	134	142	135	146	149	151	156	172
Entertainment	2 388	2 376	2 698	2 835	2 693	2 504	2 572	2 605	2 482	2 728	2 842	2 913	3 203	3 226
Personal Care Products and Services	541	585	588	616	596	582	634	628	608	645	683	707	762	768
Reading	126	117	118	116	110	100	115	109	102	103	114	118	110	108
Education	940	888	945	1 046	1 068	1 074	1 051	1 207	1 138	1 236	1 315	1 329	1 491	1 407
Tobacco Products and Smoking Supplies	319	327	323	317	380	362	351	332	330	319	349	337	332	347
Miscellaneous	808	846	808	840	816	849	775	829	645	782	871	959	1 010	993
Cash Contributions	1 663	1 869	1 821	1 737	1 723	1 633	1 721	1 913	1 834	1 788	1 819	2 081	1 873	1 888
Personal Insurance and Pensions	5 204	5 270	5 336	5 605	5 471	5 373	5 424	5 591	5 528	5 726	6 349	6 831	6 771	7 296
Life and other personal insurance	381	322	309	317	309	318	317	353	319	327	333	322	418	465
Pensions and Social Security	4 823	4 948	5 027	5 288	5 162	5 054	5 106	5 238	5 209	5 399	6 016	6 509	6 353	6 831

Table 11-2. Consumer Expenditures, Deciles of Income, 2018

(Number, dollar, percent.)

Item	All consumer units	Lowest 10 percent	Second 10 percent	Third 10 percent	Fourth 10 percent	Fifth 10 percent	Sixth 10 percent	Seventh 10 percent	Eighth 10 percent	Ninth 10 percent	Highest 10 percent
NUMBER OF CONSUMER UNITS (THOUSANDS)	131 439	13 169	13 164	13 156	13 159	13 117	13 079	13 124	13 097	13 207	13 167
CONSUMER UNIT CHARACTERISTICS											
Income Before Taxes	78 635	5 724	16 848	26 306	36 167	47 738	62 083	79 250	101 729	138 383	271 773
Income After Taxes	67 241	5 947	17 445	26 592	35 805	45 489	56 950	71 072	88 835	117 022	207 024
Age of Reference Person	51.1	48.0	59.4	56.6	53.7	51.0	48.8	48.1	47.7	48.4	49.4
Average Number in Consumer Unit											
All persons	2.5	1.6	1.7	2.0	2.3	2.4	2.5	2.8	2.9	3.1	3.2
Children under 18 years	0.6	0.3	0.3	0.4	0.5	0.5	0.6	0.8	0.7	0.8	0.8
Persons 65 years and over	0.4	0.3	0.6	0.6	0.6	0.5	0.4	0.3	0.3	0.2	0.2
Earners	1.3	0.5	0.5	0.7	0.9	1.2	1.4	1.7	1.9	2.1	2.1
Vehicles	1.9	0.9	1.1	1.5	1.7	1.8	2.0	2.2	2.4	2.7	2.8
Percent Distribution											
Male	47	40	34	44	44	47	49	51	52	54	58
Female	53	60	66	56	56	53	51	49	48	46	42
Percent Homeowner	63	32	50	54	58	60	62	69	75	84	90
With mortgage	37	11	14	17	23	32	36	48	55	63	71
Without mortgage	26	21	36	38	35	28	26	21	20	21	19
AVERAGE ANNUAL EXPENDITURES	61 224	25 309	27 488	37 164	42 771	49 241	54 223	64 029	74 236	95 056	142 554
Food	7 923	4 175	4 045	5 753	5 927	6 697	7 219	8 677	10 026	11 184	15 508
Food at home	4 464	2 673	2 746	3 656	3 584	3 875	4 287	4 906	5 255	5 992	7 659
Cereals and bakery products	569	334	355	474	467	476	547	640	673	769	958
Meats, poultry, fish, and eggs	961	586	581	788	784	849	906	1 035	1 172	1 244	1 659
Dairy products	449	247	297	351	359	374	429	511	520	634	769
Fruits and vegetables	858	484	537	694	671	733	851	937	985	1 181	1 503
Other food at home	1 627	1 022	975	1 348	1 303	1 444	1 554	1 782	1 905	2 164	2 770
Food away from home	3 459	1 502	1 299	2 097	2 343	2 822	2 931	3 770	4 771	5 192	7 849
Alcoholic Beverages	583	208	125	296	320	443	531	524	823	840	1 716
Housing	20 091	9 875	11 233	13 807	14 779	17 122	18 600	20 963	23 473	28 381	42 640
Shelter	11 747	5 962	6 748	8 206	8 217	9 725	10 816	12 280	13 860	16 075	25 567
Owned dwellings	6 678	1 748	2 446	3 256	3 450	4 350	5 152	6 762	8 485	11 556	19 543
Rented dwellings	4 249	4 028	4 112	4 691	4 319	4 858	5 071	4 846	4 418	3 150	3 009
Other lodging	821	186	190	259	448	517	594	672	956	1 369	3 014
Utilities, fuels, and public services	4 049	2 130	2 699	3 200	3 609	3 874	4 036	4 452	4 814	5 414	6 259
Household operations	1 522	501	673	804	1 003	1 025	1 125	1 434	1 622	2 377	4 652
Housekeeping supplies	747	489	417	528	631	746	604	802	878	1 026	1 351
Household furnishings and equipment	2 025	793	695	1 068	1 320	1 753	2 019	1 994	2 299	3 489	4 812
Apparel and Services	1 866	762	736	1 305	1 254	1 308	1 729	1 793	2 411	2 735	4 624
Transportation	9 761	3 483	3 953	6 169	7 352	7 891	9 385	10 324	12 254	16 427	20 352
Vehicle purchases (net outlay)	3 975	1 195	1 310	2 329	3 001	2 944	3 757	3 981	5 058	7 647	8 513
Gasoline and motor oil	2 109	967	1 005	1 396	1 746	1 968	2 177	2 439	2 781	3 240	3 369
Other vehicle expenses	2 859	1 032	1 417	1 997	2 176	2 515	2 814	3 195	3 384	4 338	5 719
Public and other transportation	818	288	220	447	430	464	637	710	1 031	1 203	2 751
Health Care	4 968	1 919	3 030	3 678	4 316	4 491	4 783	5 465	6 267	6 944	8 789
Health insurance	3 405	1 331	2 159	2 555	2 998	3 043	3 292	3 835	4 369	4 706	5 758
Medical services	909	317	380	567	689	783	818	927	1 165	1 467	1 973
Drugs	483	227	383	407	513	505	505	509	520	552	714
Medical supplies	172	45	109	150	117	160	167	194	213	219	343
Entertainment	3 226	1 369	1 368	1 535	2 830	2 679	2 405	3 503	3 485	5 309	7 758
Personal Care Products and Services	768	334	358	459	564	634	673	893	886	1 189	1 690
Reading	108	65	71	106	84	93	85	117	115	144	198
Education	1 407	1 215	317	363	459	632	828	972	1 416	2 524	5 332
Tobacco Products and Smoking Supplies	347	286	327	327	381	411	388	390	409	324	227
Miscellaneous	993	442	405	710	833	938	951	1 042	1 086	1 414	2 105
Cash Contributions	1 888	490	775	1 112	1 107	1 253	1 402	1 762	1 952	3 011	6 004
Personal Insurance and Pensions	7 296	687	746	1 543	2 566	4 650	5 245	7 604	9 634	14 630	25 612
Life and other personal insurance	465	129	214	258	337	328	327	435	560	718	1 339
Pensions and Social Security	6 831	558	531	1 285	2 228	4 322	4 918	7 169	9 074	13 911	24 273

Table 11-3. Consumer Expenditures, Averages by Income Before Taxes, 2018

(Number, dollar, percent.)

Item	All consumer units	Less than $15,000	$15,000 to $29,999	$30,000 to $39,999	$40,000 to $49,999	$50,000 to $69,999	$70,000 to $99,999	$100,000 to $149,999	$150,000 to $199,999	$200,000 and over
NUMBER OF CONSUMER UNITS (THOUSANDS)	131 439	17 156	20 575	13 022	10 683	17 003	19 074	17 243	8 118	8 566
CONSUMER UNIT CHARACTERISTICS										
Income Before Taxes	78 635	7 604	22 316	34 729	44 763	59 313	83 370	120 778	171 314	320 317
Income After Taxes	67 241	7 875	22 804	34 527	43 037	54 767	74 403	103 583	140 987	238 560
Age of Reference Person	51.1	50.6	58.3	54.0	51.2	49.2	48.0	47.9	48.8	49.7
Average Number in Consumer Unit										
All persons	2.5	1.6	1.9	2.3	2.4	2.5	2.8	3.1	3.1	3.2
Children under 18 years	0.6	0.3	0.4	0.5	0.5	0.6	0.7	0.8	0.8	0.8
Persons 65 years and over	0.4	0.3	0.6	0.6	0.5	0.4	0.3	0.2	0.2	0.2
Earners	1.3	0.5	0.6	0.9	1.2	1.4	1.7	2.0	2.1	2.1
Vehicles	1.9	0.9	1.3	1.7	1.8	1.9	2.2	2.5	2.7	2.9
Percent Distribution										
Male	47	38	40	45	45	50	52	52	56	58
Female	53	62	60	55	55	50	48	48	44	42
Percent Homeowner	63	35	54	58	59	62	70	80	87	91
With mortgage	37	11	16	22	31	35	50	60	68	71
Without mortgage	26	23	38	36	27	27	20	20	19	20
AVERAGE ANNUAL EXPENDITURES	61 224	25 346	32 386	42 611	46 850	53 104	65 814	85 730	108 909	158 738
Food	7 923	4 130	4 628	6 077	6 286	7 168	8 753	10 854	13 195	16 392
Food at home	4 464	2 690	3 011	3 744	3 633	4 228	4 900	5 759	6 764	8 002
Cereals and bakery products	569	340	396	486	442	541	629	735	869	988
Meats, poultry, fish, and eggs	961	588	642	786	844	892	1 042	1 253	1 453	1 717
Dairy products	449	258	299	386	341	422	505	579	695	816
Fruits and vegetables	858	485	589	700	690	817	933	1 111	1 344	1 567
Other food at home	1 627	1 019	1 085	1 386	1 315	1 554	1 791	2 082	2 403	2 913
Food away from home	3 459	1 440	1 617	2 334	2 653	2 941	3 854	5 095	6 431	8 391
Alcoholic Beverages	583	201	190	326	383	512	569	854	1 108	2 052
Housing	20 091	10 083	12 664	14 744	16 552	18 274	21 281	25 957	32 737	47 553
Shelter	11 747	6 089	7 584	8 229	9 485	10 538	12 460	14 959	18 687	29 025
Owned dwellings	6 678	1 891	2 908	3 480	4 137	4 952	7 050	10 097	13 678	22 430
Rented dwellings	4 249	4 010	4 446	4 312	4 846	5 015	4 693	3 783	3 003	3 018
Other lodging	821	187	230	437	502	571	717	1 079	2 006	3 577
Utilities, fuels, and public services	4 049	2 205	3 005	3 599	3 808	4 002	4 539	5 107	5 684	6 553
Household operations	1 522	513	774	940	1 015	1 116	1 415	2 044	3 065	5 398
Housekeeping supplies	747	486	457	629	699	648	799	964	1 181	1 406
Household furnishings and equipment	2 025	790	844	1 348	1 544	1 970	2 069	2 883	4 120	5 172
Apparel and Services	1 866	753	933	1 265	1 307	1 514	2 009	2 579	3 570	5 169
Transportation	9 761	3 411	5 177	7 301	7 250	9 158	11 303	14 167	16 523	22 698
Vehicle purchases (net outlay)	3 975	1 110	1 881	3 104	2 489	3 613	4 799	6 158	6 227	10 271
Gasoline and motor oil	2 109	952	1 217	1 720	1 922	2 151	2 520	3 036	3 293	3 402
Other vehicle expenses	2 859	1 090	1 717	2 035	2 402	2 805	3 202	3 899	5 136	5 909
Public and other transportation	818	258	363	442	437	590	782	1 074	1 866	3 116
Health Care	4 968	2 134	3 438	4 293	4 334	4 739	5 519	6 836	7 664	9 031
Health insurance	3 405	1 485	2 419	3 029	2 930	3 236	3 864	4 676	5 086	5 942
Medical services	909	327	496	635	785	828	950	1 382	1 721	1 982
Drugs	483	263	390	515	475	497	509	562	610	729
Medical supplies	172	59	134	114	144	178	196	217	247	378
Entertainment	3 226	1 348	1 431	2 807	2 577	2 392	3 407	4 677	5 913	8 409
Personal Care Products and Services	768	340	393	571	603	668	837	1 077	1 353	1 867
Reading	108	60	86	109	70	93	115	130	148	231
Education	1 407	1 011	343	478	631	731	979	2 087	3 315	6 251
Tobacco Products and Smoking Supplies	347	306	328	359	408	391	401	350	289	216
Miscellaneous	993	398	584	771	1 069	930	983	1 188	1 867	2 338
Cash Contributions	1 888	511	994	1 116	1 231	1 369	1 751	2 433	3 382	7 607
Personal Insurance and Pensions	7 296	659	1 197	2 395	4 150	5 163	7 907	12 542	17 845	28 923
Life and other personal insurance	465	150	243	321	338	317	457	658	868	1 545
Pensions and Social Security	6 831	509	955	2 074	3 812	4 846	7 449	11 884	16 978	27 378

Table 11-4. Consumer Expenditures, Generation of Reference Person, 2018

(Number, dollar, percent.)

Item	All consumer units	Birth year of 1927 and earlier[1]	Birth year from 1928 to 1945[1]	Birth year from 1946 to 1964	Birth year from 1965 to 1980	Birth year of 1981 or later
NUMBER OF CONSUMER UNITS (THOUSANDS)	131 439	34 845	35 498	43 763	16 206	1 128
CONSUMER UNIT CHARACTERISTICS						
Income Before Taxes	78 635	67 076	106 506	80 086	41 710	32 832
Income After Taxes	67 241	58 628	88 794	67 950	39 185	30 565
Age of Reference Person	51.1	29.0	45.2	62.1	79.0	92.3
Average Number in Consumer Unit						
All persons	2.5	2.6	3.1	2.1	1.7	1.3
Children under 18 years	0.6	0.9	1.1	0.2	(1)	(2)
Persons 65 years and over	0.4	(1)	(1)	0.6	1.4	1.3
Earners	1.3	1.5	1.7	1.2	0.3	0.1
Vehicles	1.9	1.6	2.1	2.1	1.6	1.0
Percent Distribution						
Male	47	49	47	48	43	46
Female	53	51	53	52	57	54
Percent Homeowner	63	37	64	77	81	64
With mortgage	37	29	52	39	19	8
Without mortgage	26	8	13	38	62	56
AVERAGE ANNUAL EXPENDITURES	61 224	52 874	74 683	63 325	45 551	34 824
Food	7 923	7 061	9 826	7 889	5 887	3 146
Food at home	4 464	3 724	5 377	4 597	3 784	2 045
Cereals and bakery products	569	465	694	573	522	312
Meats, poultry, fish, and eggs	961	792	1 174	1 002	760	450
Dairy products	449	378	544	452	400	191
Fruits and vegetables	858	717	1 008	890	759	444
Other food at home	1 627	1 372	1 958	1 681	1 344	648
Food away from home	3 459	3 338	4 449	3 292	2 102	1 101
Alcoholic Beverages	583	560	693	617	317	68
Housing	20 091	18 329	24 050	20 003	15 511	18 350
Shelter	11 747	11 415	14 193	11 159	8 644	12 439
Owned dwellings	6 678	4 096	8 623	7 722	5 369	3 494
Rented dwellings	4 249	6 895	4 589	2 372	2 577	8 621
Other lodging	821	425	981	1 064	698	324
Utilities, fuels, and public services	4 049	3 183	4 757	4 359	3 621	2 574
Household operations	1 522	1 522	1 892	1 286	1 287	2 425
Housekeeping supplies	747	512	905	819	722	464
Household furnishings and equipment	2 025	1 697	2 302	2 380	1 237	447
Apparel and Services	1 866	1 979	2 343	1 741	990	293
Transportation	9 761	9 435	11 775	10 044	5 836	1 677
Vehicle purchases (net outlay)	3 975	4 289	4 560	4 128	1 870	148
Gasoline and motor oil	2 109	2 053	2 639	2 114	1 172	411
Other vehicle expenses	2 859	2 428	3 537	2 928	2 252	680
Public and other transportation	818	665	1 039	874	542	438
Health Care	4 968	2 831	4 786	6 025	7 046	5 907
Health insurance	3 405	1 955	3 252	4 122	4 843	4 513
Medical services	909	568	961	1 069	1 122	487
Drugs	483	217	418	621	813	680
Medical supplies	172	91	155	213	268	227
Entertainment	3 226	2 391	3 921	3 801	2 065	987
Personal Care Products and Services	768	668	935	771	623	478
Reading	108	64	104	129	152	154
Education	1 407	1 308	2 156	1 322	304	67
Tobacco Products and Smoking Supplies	347	331	410	394	136	15
Miscellaneous	993	671	1 129	1 128	1 029	811
Cash Contributions	1 888	890	1 985	2 252	2 804	2 370
Personal Insurance and Pensions	7 296	6 355	10 570	7 210	2 850	503
Life and other personal insurance	465	203	527	617	505	138
Pensions and Social Security	6 831	6 153	10 043	6 593	2 345	365

[1]Value is too small to display.
[2]No data reported.

Table 11-5. Consumer Expenditures, Averages by Quintiles of Income Before Taxes, 2018

(Number, dollar, percent.)

Item	All consumer units	Lowest 20 percent	Second 20 percent	Third 20 percent	Fourth 20 percent	Highest 20 percent
NUMBER OF CONSUMER UNITS (THOUSANDS)	131 439	26 333	26 315	26 196	26 221	26 374
CONSUMER UNIT CHARACTERISTICS						
Income Before Taxes	78 635	11 285	31 237	54 900	90 478	204 975
Income After Taxes	67 241	11 695	31 199	51 211	79 944	161 954
Age of Reference Person	51.1	53.7	55.1	49.9	47.9	48.9
Average Number in Consumer Unit						
All persons	2.5	1.7	2.1	2.5	2.9	3.2
Children under 18 years	0.6	0.3	0.5	0.6	0.7	0.8
Persons 65 years and over	0.4	0.4	0.6	0.4	0.3	0.2
Earners	1.3	0.5	0.8	1.3	1.8	2.1
Vehicles	1.9	1.0	1.6	1.9	2.3	2.7
Percent Distribution						
Male	47	37	44	48	51	56
Female	53	63	56	52	49	44
Percent Homeowner	63	41	56	61	72	87
With mortgage	37	12	20	34	52	67
Without mortgage	26	29	36	27	20	20
AVERAGE ANNUAL EXPENDITURES	61 224	26 399	39 968	51 729	69 131	118 781
Food	7 923	4 109	5 840	6 958	9 353	13 348
Food at home	4 464	2 709	3 620	4 081	5 081	6 827
Cereals and bakery products	569	344	470	511	657	864
Meats, poultry, fish, and eggs	961	584	786	878	1 104	1 452
Dairy products	449	272	355	401	515	701
Fruits and vegetables	858	510	683	792	961	1 343
Other food at home	1 627	999	1 326	1 499	1 844	2 467
Food away from home	3 459	1 400	2 220	2 877	4 272	6 522
Alcoholic Beverages	583	166	308	487	674	1 279
Housing	20 091	10 553	14 293	17 860	22 217	35 501
Shelter	11 747	6 355	8 212	10 270	13 069	20 814
Owned dwellings	6 678	2 097	3 353	4 750	7 623	15 544
Rented dwellings	4 249	4 070	4 505	4 964	4 632	3 080
Other lodging	821	188	354	555	814	2 190
Utilities, fuels, and public services	4 049	2 415	3 404	3 955	4 633	5 836
Household operations	1 522	587	904	1 075	1 528	3 513
Housekeeping supplies	747	453	579	675	840	1 188
Household furnishings and equipment	2 025	744	1 194	1 886	2 147	4 150
Apparel and Services	1 866	749	1 280	1 519	2 103	3 680
Transportation	9 761	3 718	6 761	8 636	11 288	18 387
Vehicle purchases (net outlay)	3 975	1 253	2 665	3 350	4 519	8 079
Gasoline and motor oil	2 109	986	1 571	2 072	2 610	3 304
Other vehicle expenses	2 859	1 225	2 086	2 665	3 289	5 028
Public and other transportation	818	254	439	550	870	1 976
Health Care	4 968	2 475	3 997	4 637	5 866	7 865
Health insurance	3 405	1 745	2 776	3 167	4 102	5 232
Medical services	909	348	628	801	1 046	1 720
Drugs	483	305	460	505	515	633
Medical supplies	172	77	133	164	204	281
Entertainment	3 226	1 369	2 183	2 542	3 494	6 532
Personal Care Products and Services	768	346	512	653	890	1 439
Reading	108	68	95	89	116	171
Education	1 407	766	411	730	1 194	3 926
Tobacco Products and Smoking Supplies	347	306	354	399	399	275
Miscellaneous	993	424	772	944	1 064	1 759
Cash Contributions	1 888	633	1 109	1 327	1 857	4 505
Personal Insurance and Pensions	7 296	716	2 054	4 947	8 618	20 112
Life and other personal insurance	465	172	298	327	498	1 028
Pensions and Social Security	6 831	545	1 757	4 620	8 120	19 084

Table 11-6. Consumer Expenditures, Averages by Occupation of Reference Person, 2018

(Number, dollar, percent.)

Item	All consumer units	Self-employed workers	Wage and salary earners						Retired	All others, including those not reporting
			Total wage and salary earners	Managers and professional workers	Technical sales and clerical workers	Service workers	Construction workers and mechanics	Operators, fabricators, and laborers		
NUMBER OF CONSUMER UNITS (THOUSANDS)	131 439	7 856	80 288	33 102	19 838	16 263	3 383	7 702	26 786	16 509
CONSUMER UNIT CHARACTERISTICS										
Income Before Taxes	78 635	146 075	91 571	121 879	75 281	66 478	71 352	65 134	42 643	42 029
Income After Taxes	67 241	113 666	77 697	100 124	65 333	59 000	62 934	59 119	40 026	38 450
Age of Reference Person	51.1	51.1	44.2	44.5	43.1	44.9	43.6	44.7	73.8	47.9
Average Number in Consumer Unit										
All persons	2.5	2.7	2.6	2.6	2.5	2.6	2.7	2.9	1.8	3.0
Children under 18 years	0.6	0.7	0.7	0.7	0.7	0.7	0.8	0.9	0.1	1.0
Persons 65 years and over	0.4	0.3	0.1	0.1	0.1	0.2	0.1	0.1	1.3	0.0
Earners	1.3	1.7	1.7	1.8	1.7	1.7	1.7	1.8	0.3	1.0
Vehicles	1.9	2.2	2.0	2.1	2.0	1.7	2.0	2.1	1.8	2.0
Percent Distribution										
Male	47	62	50	48	41	48	89	75	44	30
Female	53	38	50	52	59	52	11	25	56	70
Percent Homeowner	63	73	60	68	56	51	52	56	82	47
With mortgage	37	48	44	53	40	35	35	36	23	24
Without mortgage	26	25	16	15	16	17	17	20	59	23
AVERAGE ANNUAL EXPENDITURES	61 224	88 884	65 834	83 129	56 671	51 606	54 386	50 732	49 441	44 745
Food	7 923	9 877	8 460	10 176	7 618	7 320	7 631	6 270	6 489	6 723
Food at home	4 464	5 235	4 562	5 230	4 259	4 083	4 390	3 654	3 997	4 368
Cereals and bakery products	569	704	576	664	533	514	548	458	522	550
Meats, poultry, fish, and eggs	961	1 078	978	1 046	941	946	1 066	796	835	1 023
Dairy products	449	534	457	538	426	396	386	368	409	436
Fruits and vegetables	858	1 044	876	1 055	772	784	770	653	785	796
Other food at home	1 627	1 875	1 676	1 928	1 587	1 442	1 620	1 379	1 446	1 563
Food away from home	3 459	4 642	3 898	4 945	3 359	3 236	3 241	2 616	2 492	2 355
Alcoholic Beverages	583	908	650	898	565	426	442	432	428	353
Housing	20 091	27 786	21 339	26 422	18 643	17 560	17 262	16 262	16 681	15 869
Shelter	11 747	16 345	12 712	15 958	11 034	10 449	9 873	9 102	9 097	9 171
Owned dwellings	6 678	10 487	7 106	9 861	5 573	5 030	4 737	4 645	5 775	4 245
Rented dwellings	4 249	4 246	4 809	4 873	4 846	4 952	4 802	4 142	2 446	4 450
Other lodging	821	1 612	796	1 224	616	468	333	316	876	476
Utilities, fuels, and public services	4 049	5 011	4 144	4 492	3 915	3 837	3 815	4 032	3 824	3 490
Household operations	1 522	2 204	1 656	2 340	1 349	1 068	943	1 065	1 321	872
Housekeeping supplies	747	1 301	727	867	682	610	580	584	748	572
Household furnishings and equipment	2 025	2 924	2 100	2 766	1 662	1 594	2 051	1 478	1 691	1 764
Apparel and Services	1 866	2 615	2 106	2 569	1 804	1 998	1 527	1 438	1 145	1 524
Transportation	9 761	12 142	10 902	13 074	9 419	8 455	11 089	10 504	7 264	7 114
Vehicle purchases (net outlay)	3 975	3 631	4 648	5 530	3 887	3 302	5 234	5 399	2 755	2 844
Gasoline and motor oil	2 109	2 680	2 376	2 573	2 221	2 082	2 619	2 444	1 431	1 636
Other vehicle expenses	2 859	4 093	3 058	3 784	2 703	2 443	2 842	2 272	2 375	2 075
Public and other transportation	818	1 738	820	1 187	609	629	394	389	702	558
Health Care	4 968	6 462	4 516	5 586	4 075	3 509	3 507	3 627	6 801	3 481
Health insurance	3 405	4 285	3 111	3 793	2 886	2 498	2 283	2 420	4 805	2 139
Medical services	909	1 321	868	1 143	718	576	682	770	985	785
Drugs	483	670	382	457	332	320	434	305	743	460
Medical supplies	172	185	154	193	138	115	108	131	267	96
Entertainment	3 226	4 444	3 394	4 598	2 889	2 284	2 064	2 524	2 805	2 510
Personal Care Products and Services	768	991	833	1 044	784	666	570	534	657	530
Reading	108	157	92	121	84	67	56	54	172	59
Education	1 407	2 833	1 653	2 519	1 109	1 073	973	851	473	1 048
Tobacco Products and Smoking Supplies	347	295	363	269	382	390	625	546	212	508
Miscellaneous	993	1 430	970	1 248	786	826	733	666	1 099	727
Cash Contributions	1 888	2 952	1 677	2 406	1 266	994	1 268	1 229	2 572	1 295
Personal Insurance and Pensions	7 296	15 992	8 879	12 199	7 247	6 039	6 639	5 795	2 644	3 003
Life and other personal insurance	465	870	445	623	366	312	179	283	511	293
Pensions and Social Security	6 831	15 122	8 434	11 576	6 881	5 727	6 460	5 512	2 133	2 711

Table 11-7. Consumer Expenditures, Averages by Number of Earners, 2018

(Number, dollar, percent.)

Item	All consumer units	Single consumer		Consumer units of two or more persons			
		No earner	One earner	No earner	One earner	Two earners	Three or more earners
NUMBER OF CONSUMER UNITS (THOUSANDS)	131 439	16 156	22 573	13 625	25 674	41 662	11 748
CONSUMER UNIT CHARACTERISTICS							
Income Before Taxes	78 635	20 385	50 437	36 263	69 671	119 476	136 818
Income After Taxes	67 241	19 353	41 931	35 038	62 241	98 946	117 563
Age of Reference Person	51.1	68.1	43.9	67.4	50.3	44.4	48.6
Average Number in Consumer Unit							
All persons	2.5	1.0	1.0	2.3	3.0	3.0	4.4
Children under 18 years	0.6	X	X	0.3	1.0	0.9	1.0
Persons 65 years and over	0.4	0.7	0.1	1.4	0.4	0.1	0.2
Earners	1.3	X	1.0	X	1.0	2.0	3.3
Vehicles	1.9	0.9	1.1	2.0	1.9	2.3	3.0
Percent Distribution							
Male	47	36	52	50	44	51	44
Female	53	64	48	50	56	49	56
Percent Homeowner	63	56	41	80	63	70	76
With mortgage	37	14	25	20	36	53	59
Without mortgage	26	42	16	60	27	17	17
AVERAGE ANNUAL EXPENDITURES	61 224	28 370	41 581	52 537	61 427	79 340	89 285
Food	7 923	3 676	4 968	7 513	8 058	10 118	11 730
Food at home	4 464	2 439	2 408	4 621	4 877	5 459	6 453
Cereals and bakery products	569	317	280	595	649	681	850
Meats, poultry, fish, and eggs	961	458	492	1 030	1 035	1 199	1 442
Dairy products	449	268	244	465	467	561	629
Fruits and vegetables	858	462	454	876	950	1 050	1 245
Other food at home	1 627	934	939	1 656	1 776	1 968	2 287
Food away from home	3 459	1 236	2 559	2 893	3 181	4 659	5 277
Alcoholic Beverages	583	219	518	448	478	854	629
Housing	20 091	11 799	15 224	17 335	20 357	24 963	26 108
Shelter	11 747	7 251	10 197	9 137	11 407	14 478	14 997
Owned dwellings	6 678	3 213	3 818	5 717	6 239	9 166	10 186
Rented dwellings	4 249	3 729	5 917	2 493	4 307	4 241	3 693
Other lodging	821	309	462	927	860	1 071	1 118
Utilities, fuels, and public services	4 049	2 475	2 474	4 027	4 384	4 774	5 957
Household operations	1 522	886	737	1 250	1 422	2 368	1 441
Housekeeping supplies	747	444	565	859	762	826	1 077
Household furnishings and equipment	2 025	743	1 251	2 062	2 382	2 516	2 636
Apparel and Services	1 866	687	1 175	1 280	1 929	2 465	3 227
Transportation	9 761	3 306	6 024	7 992	9 903	13 001	16 034
Vehicle purchases (net outlay)	3 975	1 132	2 054	3 119	3 941	5 673	6 620
Gasoline and motor oil	2 109	673	1 378	1 648	2 120	2 774	3 639
Other vehicle expenses	2 859	1 191	2 013	2 427	2 996	3 499	4 678
Public and other transportation	818	310	579	799	846	1 056	1 098
Health Care	4 968	3 633	2 507	7 324	5 290	5 491	6 246
Health insurance	3 405	2 503	1 597	5 108	3 587	3 834	4 223
Medical services	909	542	563	1 079	1 019	984	1 372
Drugs	483	461	254	838	510	490	457
Medical supplies	172	127	92	299	174	183	194
Entertainment	3 226	1 444	2 089	3 013	3 523	4 217	3 901
Personal Care Products and Services	768	395	556	682	758	959	1 133
Reading	108	122	76	160	106	107	103
Education	1 407	320	1 068	637	1 205	1 914	3 089
Tobacco Products and Smoking Supplies	347	221	274	304	377	373	552
Miscellaneous	993	714	745	1 099	1 013	1 107	1 299
Cash Contributions	1 888	1 335	1 258	2 688	2 190	1 903	2 215
Personal Insurance and Pensions	7 296	499	5 101	2 063	6 241	11 868	13 017
Life and other personal insurance	465	226	222	516	476	599	699
Pensions and Social Security	6 831	273	4 878	1 547	5 764	11 269	12 318

X = Not applicable.

Table 11-8. Consumer Expenditures, Averages by Size of Consumer Unit, 2018

(Number, dollar, percent.)

Item	All consumer units	One person	Two or more persons				
			Total	Two persons	Three persons	Four persons	Five or more persons
NUMBER OF CONSUMER UNITS (THOUSANDS)	131 439	38 730	92 709	44 633	18 886	16 490	12 701
CONSUMER UNIT CHARACTERISTICS							
Income Before Taxes	78 635	37 901	95 652	83 500	97 858	114 797	110 218
Income After Taxes	67 241	32 512	81 748	70 781	83 757	97 620	96 696
Age of Reference Person	51.1	54.0	49.9	55.7	46.9	43.5	42.6
Average Number in Consumer Unit							
All persons	2.5	1.0	3.1	2.0	3.0	4.0	5.7
Children under 18 years	0.6	X	0.8	0.1	0.7	1.6	2.8
Persons 65 years and over	0.4	0.4	0.4	0.7	0.3	0.1	0.2
Earners	1.3	0.6	1.6	1.2	1.8	2.0	2.3
Vehicles	1.9	1.0	2.3	2.2	2.3	2.4	2.5
Percent Distribution							
Male	47	46	48	52	43	47	44
Female	53	54	52	48	57	53	56
Percent Homeowner	63	47	70	73	68	70	65
With mortgage	37	21	44	37	48	56	49
Without mortgage	26	27	26	36	20	14	16
AVERAGE ANNUAL EXPENDITURES	61 224	36 087	71 623	65 535	72 696	80 795	79 693
Food	7 923	4 436	9 323	8 226	8 964	10 899	11 731
Food at home	4 464	2 421	5 282	4 583	5 057	6 128	7 048
Cereals and bakery products	569	295	679	554	639	816	1 013
Meats, poultry, fish, and eggs	961	478	1 154	983	1 114	1 363	1 559
Dairy products	449	254	527	461	518	601	684
Fruits and vegetables	858	457	1 018	906	968	1 176	1 287
Other food at home	1 627	937	1 904	1 678	1 818	2 172	2 505
Food away from home	3 459	2 015	4 041	3 643	3 906	4 771	4 683
Alcoholic Beverages	583	395	658	804	511	577	463
Housing	20 091	13 797	22 708	20 640	23 217	25 550	25 606
Shelter	11 747	8 968	12 908	11 891	13 156	14 578	13 949
Owned dwellings	6 678	3 566	7 978	7 181	8 042	9 627	8 543
Rented dwellings	4 249	5 004	3 933	3 616	4 216	3 940	4 619
Other lodging	821	398	997	1 094	898	1 011	787
Utilities, fuels, and public services	4 049	2 475	4 706	4 229	4 808	5 146	5 663
Household operations	1 522	799	1 824	1 326	2 169	2 747	1 861
Housekeeping supplies	747	515	840	772	835	818	1 146
Household furnishings and equipment	2 025	1 040	2 429	2 422	2 248	2 262	2 986
Apparel and Services	1 866	974	2 226	1 817	2 210	2 885	2 810
Transportation	9 761	4 892	11 789	10 175	13 121	13 507	13 271
Vehicle purchases (net outlay)	3 975	1 669	4 938	4 076	6 223	5 639	5 145
Gasoline and motor oil	2 109	1 084	2 537	2 118	2 582	2 979	3 369
Other vehicle expenses	2 859	1 672	3 349	3 028	3 452	3 811	3 738
Public and other transportation	818	467	965	954	863	1 078	1 019
Health Care	4 968	2 977	5 799	6 162	5 515	5 538	5 286
Health insurance	3 405	1 975	4 002	4 238	3 883	3 784	3 632
Medical services	909	555	1 056	1 056	979	1 124	1 086
Drugs	483	340	542	634	500	448	406
Medical supplies	172	107	199	234	153	182	162
Entertainment	3 226	1 822	3 805	3 897	3 519	3 793	3 969
Personal Care Products and Services	768	490	882	835	850	1 014	923
Reading	108	94	114	127	92	114	98
Education	1 407	756	1 679	1 134	2 015	2 278	2 319
Tobacco Products and Smoking Supplies	347	252	386	341	421	389	493
Miscellaneous	993	732	1 101	1 125	868	1 276	1 133
Cash Contributions	1 888	1 290	2 137	2 539	1 717	1 651	1 981
Personal Insurance and Pensions	7 296	3 181	9 014	7 713	9 676	11 322	9 609
Life and other personal insurance	465	224	566	552	513	675	548
Pensions and Social Security	6 831	2 957	8 449	7 160	9 163	10 647	9 061

X = Not applicable.

Table 11-9. Consumer Expenditures, Averages by Composition of Consumer Unit, 2018

(Number, dollar, percent.)

Item	All consumer unit	Married couple consumer units							Other married couple consumer units	One parent, at least one child under 18 years	Single person and other consumer units
		Total	Married couple only	Married couple with children							
				Total	Oldest child under 6 years	Oldest child 6 to 17 years	Oldest child 18 years or over				
NUMBER OF CONSUMER UNITS (THOUSANDS)	131 439	65 254	30 106	29 906	5 248	14 530	10 128		5 242	6 780	59 405
CONSUMER UNIT CHARACTERISTICS											
Income Before Taxes	78 635	109 223	93 651	124 937	114 877	123 289	132 513		109 009	43 445	49 052
Income After Taxes	67 241	92 122	78 763	104 650	95 991	103 881	110 241		97 375	41 447	42 853
Age of Reference Person	51.1	51.7	59.3	44.3	33.4	41.5	54.0		50.7	40.4	52.0
Average Number in Consumer Unit											
All persons	2.5	3.1	2.0	4.0	3.5	4.2	3.9		4.9	2.9	1.7
Children under 18 years	0.6	0.8	(1)	1.6	1.5	2.2	0.6		1.4	1.7	0.2
Persons 65 years and over	0.4	0.5	0.8	0.1	(1)	(1)	0.3		0.6	(1)	0.3
Earners	1.3	1.6	1.1	2.0	1.7	1.8	2.4		2.4	1.1	1.0
Vehicles	1.9	2.5	2.4	2.5	2.0	2.3	3.0		2.8	1.2	1.3
Percent Distribution											
Male	47	55	59	51	61	49	48		52	19	42
Female	53	45	41	49	39	51	52		48	81	58
Percent Homeowner	63	79	84	76	64	74	85		74	37	49
With mortgage	37	50	41	60	56	61	59		52	29	24
Without mortgage	26	29	43	16	8	12	25		22	9	25
AVERAGE ANNUAL EXPENDITURES	61 224	79 869	72 945	86 966	80 447	88 716	87 780		79 261	47 945	42 298
Food	7 923	10 345	9 064	11 498	9 502	12 013	11 752		11 191	6 733	5 418
Food at home	4 464	5 816	5 000	6 518	5 473	6 622	6 911		6 543	3 901	3 054
Cereals and bakery products	569	753	610	876	669	932	894		890	526	373
Meats, poultry, fish, and eggs	961	1 261	1 066	1 397	1 138	1 391	1 545		1 625	843	647
Dairy products	449	593	517	669	587	679	698		595	360	303
Fruits and vegetables	858	1 136	1 004	1 259	1 084	1 266	1 341		1 200	719	570
Other food at home	1 627	2 072	1 803	2 318	1 996	2 353	2 433		2 233	1 453	1 161
Food away from home	3 459	4 529	4 065	4 979	4 028	5 392	4 841		4 648	2 833	2 364
Alcoholic Beverages	583	758	927	624	714	646	539		535	312	425
Housing	20 091	24 633	22 060	27 225	28 792	27 665	25 755		24 646	17 149	15 445
Shelter	11 747	13 855	12 463	15 353	15 572	15 998	14 316		13 298	10 141	9 616
Owned dwellings	6 678	9 559	8 543	10 691	9 898	10 892	10 814		8 927	3 600	3 865
Rented dwellings	4 249	3 064	2 498	3 524	5 008	3 961	2 127		3 695	6 152	5 332
Other lodging	821	1 232	1 421	1 138	666	1 145	1 374		675	390	419
Utilities, fuels, and public services	4 049	4 981	4 526	5 321	4 064	5 285	6 023		5 654	3 785	3 055
Household operations	1 522	2 105	1 491	2 792	5 995	2 497	1 556		1 715	1 304	907
Housekeeping supplies	747	963	898	1 008	730	1 048	1 091		1 082	517	541
Household furnishings and equipment	2 025	2 730	2 683	2 751	2 431	2 838	2 770		2 896	1 401	1 326
Apparel and Services	1 866	2 396	1 950	2 816	2 779	2 877	2 752		2 582	1 892	1 284
Transportation	9 761	13 150	11 345	14 833	14 048	14 704	15 441		13 938	7 731	6 272
Vehicle purchases (net outlay)	3 975	5 593	4 676	6 498	7 282	6 237	6 467		5 689	2 729	2 340
Gasoline and motor oil	2 109	2 735	2 236	3 133	2 543	3 127	3 448		3 329	1 749	1 462
Other vehicle expenses	2 859	3 708	3 303	4 050	3 388	4 001	4 482		4 105	2 563	1 962
Public and other transportation	818	1 115	1 130	1 151	834	1 339	1 044		815	690	508
Health Care	4 968	6 775	7 434	6 109	5 479	5 732	6 976		6 785	2 729	3 241
Health insurance	3 405	4 652	5 074	4 196	3 864	3 926	4 754		4 823	1 939	2 202
Medical services	909	1 259	1 292	1 246	1 159	1 179	1 387		1 143	476	573
Drugs	483	636	784	489	321	459	617		619	228	347
Medical supplies	172	229	284	179	134	167	218		200	86	119
Entertainment	3 226	4 365	4 584	4 297	3 411	4 781	4 045		3 500	2 428	2 066
Personal Care Products and Services	768	960	895	1 032	880	1 056	1 079		924	718	564
Reading	108	133	151	126	77	117	169		68	92	82
Education	1 407	1 964	1 251	2 693	651	2 894	3 458		1 903	1 225	816
Tobacco Products and Smoking Supplies	347	319	274	319	193	325	377		580	286	384
Miscellaneous	993	1 200	1 219	1 195	827	1 223	1 358		1 114	781	790
Cash Contributions	1 888	2 590	3 248	2 064	1 336	2 258	2 163		1 814	963	1 222
Personal Insurance and Pensions	7 296	10 281	8 544	12 135	11 759	12 425	11 915		9 681	4 904	4 289
Life and other personal insurance	465	695	693	709	577	656	853		623	234	239
Pensions and Social Security	6 831	9 586	7 851	11 427	11 182	11 769	11 062		9 057	4 670	4 050

[1]Value is too small to display.
. . . = Not available.

Table 11-10. Consumer Expenditures, Averages by Selected Age of Reference Person, 2018

(Number, dollar, percent.)

Item	All consumer units	Under 30 years	30 years and older	Under 50	50 years and older	Under 55 years	55 years and older	Under 65 years	65 years and older
NUMBER OF CONSUMER UNITS (THOUSANDS)	131 439	17 383	114 056	62 291	69 148	73 936	57 503	98 417	33 023
CONSUMER UNIT CHARACTERISTICS									
Income Before Taxes	78 635	51 965	82 700	83 298	74 434	87 485	67 256	87 698	51 624
Income After Taxes	67 241	46 053	70 470	71 369	63 522	74 262	58 212	74 036	46 990
Age of Reference Person	51.1	24.6	55.1	35.3	65.3	38.0	68.0	43.3	74.4
Average Number in Consumer Unit									
All persons	2.5	2.2	2.5	2.9	2.1	2.9	1.9	2.7	1.8
Children under 18 years	0.6	0.5	0.6	1.0	0.2	0.9	0.1	0.8	0.1
Persons 65 years and over	0.4	(1)	0.5	(1)	0.7	(1)	0.9	0.1	1.4
Earners	1.3	1.4	1.3	1.6	1.0	1.6	0.9	1.6	0.5
Vehicles	1.9	1.4	2.0	1.8	2.0	1.9	2.0	1.9	1.8
Percent Distribution									
Male	47	47	47	48	46	48	47	48	46
Female	53	53	53	52	54	52	53	52	54
Percent Homeowner	63	25	69	49	77	52	79	58	80
With mortgage	37	19	40	39	36	41	33	42	24
Without mortgage	26	6	29	10	41	11	46	16	56
AVERAGE ANNUAL EXPENDITURES	61 224	43 313	63 990	61 989	60 536	64 177	57 421	64 682	50 860
Food	7 923	5 692	8 282	8 321	7 565	8 464	7 223	8 353	6 607
Food at home	4 464	2 934	4 711	4 474	4 455	4 564	4 334	4 612	4 009
Cereals and bakery products	569	367	602	569	570	581	554	582	532
Meats, poultry, fish, and eggs	961	620	1 016	973	950	987	927	1 003	830
Dairy products	449	283	476	450	449	461	434	459	419
Fruits and vegetables	858	561	906	848	867	867	846	880	790
Other food at home	1 627	1 103	1 712	1 635	1 620	1 669	1 573	1 689	1 438
Food away from home	3 459	2 758	3 571	3 847	3 110	3 900	2 888	3 741	2 598
Alcoholic Beverages	583	410	611	623	546	627	526	627	446
Housing	20 091	15 359	20 819	20 847	19 409	21 225	18 632	21 147	16 940
Shelter	11 747	10 209	11 982	12 626	10 956	12 777	10 424	12 550	9 357
Owned dwellings	6 678	2 319	7 342	6 021	7 270	6 450	6 971	6 935	5 910
Rented dwellings	4 249	7 529	3 749	5 988	2 682	5 604	2 506	4 807	2 585
Other lodging	821	361	891	617	1 005	723	947	808	861
Utilities, fuels, and public services	4 049	2 577	4 273	3 842	4 234	4 009	4 100	4 130	3 806
Household operations	1 522	865	1 623	1 742	1 324	1 678	1 321	1 576	1 361
Housekeeping supplies	747	391	805	671	816	721	781	743	759
Household furnishings and equipment	2 025	1 317	2 137	1 966	2 078	2 040	2 005	2 148	1 657
Apparel and Services	1 866	1 675	1 897	2 132	1 627	2 165	1 480	2 083	1 207
Transportation	9 761	7 927	10 043	10 419	9 169	10 648	8 621	10 596	7 270
Vehicle purchases (net outlay)	3 975	3 527	4 043	4 418	3 576	4 437	3 381	4 414	2 667
Gasoline and motor oil	2 109	1 737	2 165	2 311	1 926	2 362	1 783	2 332	1 442
Other vehicle expenses	2 859	2 093	2 978	2 881	2 840	2 998	2 681	2 996	2 450
Public and other transportation	818	570	856	809	827	851	777	854	711
Health Care	4 968	1 994	5 423	3 631	6 173	3 894	6 350	4 354	6 802
Health insurance	3 405	1 357	3 717	2 490	4 229	2 645	4 381	2 945	4 776
Medical services	909	411	984	734	1 066	791	1 060	879	998
Drugs	483	154	535	291	656	331	680	389	768
Medical supplies	172	72	187	116	222	127	230	142	260
Entertainment	3 226	1 980	3 418	3 084	3 353	3 168	3 300	3 313	2 958
Personal Care Products and Services	768	561	800	782	756	800	727	796	682
Reading	108	49	117	81	132	86	137	89	165
Education	1 407	1 629	1 373	1 378	1 433	1 760	953	1 753	375
Tobacco Products and Smoking Supplies	347	275	357	358	336	378	306	397	196
Miscellaneous	993	459	1 075	849	1 122	914	1 094	980	1 032
Cash Contributions	1 888	590	2 086	1 307	2 411	1 467	2 428	1 641	2 625
Personal Insurance and Pensions	7 296	4 713	7 689	8 174	6 504	8 580	5 644	8 550	3 556
Life and other personal insurance	465	94	521	323	593	382	572	449	512
Pensions and Social Security	6 831	4 619	7 168	7 851	5 912	8 199	5 072	8 101	3 044

[1]Value is too small to display.

Table 11-11. Consumer Expenditures, Averages by Race of Reference Person, 2018

(Number, dollar, percent.)

Item	All consumer units	White, Asian, and other races			Black
		Total	White and other races	Asian	
NUMBER OF CONSUMER UNITS (THOUSANDS)	131 439	114 227	108 069	6 159	17 212
Income After Taxes	67 241	69 827	68 399	94 889	50 076
Age of Reference Person	51.1	51.5	51.9	44.0	48.7
Average Number in Consumer Unit					
All persons	2.5	2.5	2.5	2.7	2.4
Children under 18 years	0.6	0.6	0.6	0.6	0.6
Persons 65 years and over	0.4	0.4	0.4	0.2	0.3
Earners	1.3	1.3	1.3	1.5	1.3
Vehicles	1.9	2.0	2.0	1.6	1.4
Percent Distribution					
Male	47	48	48	58	40
Female	53	52	52	42	60
Percent Homeowner	63	67	67	57	42
With mortgage	37	38	38	39	28
Without mortgage	26	28	29	18	14
AVERAGE ANNUAL EXPENDITURES	61 224	63 721	63 188	72 971	44 752
Food	7 923	8 336	8 220	10 257	5 228
Food at home	4 464	4 692	4 635	5 626	2 982
Cereals and bakery products	569	599	593	707	374
Meats, poultry, fish, and eggs	961	990	967	1 362	772
Dairy products	449	482	487	407	233
Fruits and vegetables	858	905	872	1 444	549
Other food at home	1 627	1 715	1 716	1 705	1 054
Food away from home	3 459	3 645	3 585	4 631	2 246
Alcoholic Beverages	583	635	647	435	243
Housing	20 091	20 647	20 403	24 963	16 413
Shelter	11 747	12 040	11 759	16 978	9 803
Owned dwellings	6 678	7 126	6 978	9 723	3 703
Rented dwellings	4 249	4 026	3 895	6 322	5 730
Other lodging	821	889	886	934	369
Utilities, fuels, and public services	4 049	4 077	4 090	3 857	3 860
Household operations	1 522	1 595	1 581	1 831	1 040
Housekeeping supplies	747	792	803	621	455
Household furnishings and equipment	2 025	2 142	2 170	1 677	1 255
Apparel and Services	1 866	1 921	1 849	3 123	1 511
Transportation	9 761	10 107	10 116	9 964	7 473
Vehicle purchases (net outlay)	3 975	4 120	4 154	3 519	3 011
Gasoline and motor oil	2 109	2 161	2 164	2 107	1 765
Other vehicle expenses	2 859	2 966	2 982	2 704	2 158
Public and other transportation	818	861	816	1 632	539
Health Care	4 968	5 247	5 298	4 346	3 123
Health insurance	3 405	3 549	3 564	3 270	2 449
Medical services	909	990	1 010	638	368
Drugs	483	520	533	301	242
Medical supplies	172	188	191	136	64
Entertainment	3 226	3 474	3 531	2 519	1 585
Personal Care Products and Services	768	779	778	783	699
Reading	108	116	119	75	52
Education	1 407	1 460	1 361	3 209	1 054
Tobacco Products and Smoking Supplies	347	359	373	112	265
Miscellaneous	993	1 005	987	1 309	915
Cash Contributions	1 888	1 983	2 009	1 516	1 258
Personal Insurance and Pensions	7 296	7 652	7 497	10 360	4 932
Life and other personal insurance	465	472	468	534	420
Pensions and Social Security	6 831	7 180	7 029	9 826	4 512

Table 11-12. Consumer Expenditures, Averages by Hispanic Origin of Reference Person, 2018

(Number, dollar, percent.)

Item	All consumer units	Hispanic[1]	Not Hispanic		
			Total	White, Asian, and other races	Black
NUMBER OF CONSUMER UNITS (THOUSANDS)	131 439	17 572	113 868	96 916	16 952
CONSUMER UNIT CHARACTERISTICS					
Income Before Taxes	78 635	65 298	80 693	85 082	55 600
Income After Taxes	67 241	58 828	68 539	71 792	49 941
Age of Reference Person	51.1	44.5	52.1	52.7	48.8
Average Number in Consumer Unit					
All persons	2.5	3.2	2.3	2.3	2.4
Children under 18 years	0.6	1.0	0.5	0.5	0.6
Persons 65 years and over	0.4	0.2	0.4	0.4	0.3
Earners	1.3	1.6	1.3	1.2	1.3
Vehicles	1.9	1.7	1.9	2.0	1.4
Percent Distribution					
Male	47	44	48	49	40
Female	53	56	52	51	60
Percent Homeowner	63	47	66	70	42
With mortgage	37	31	38	40	28
Without mortgage	26	16	28	30	14
AVERAGE ANNUAL EXPENDITURES	61 224	53 762	62 380	65 464	44 741
Food	7 923	7 906	7 925	8 398	5 217
Food at home	4 464	4 304	4 490	4 750	3 005
Cereals and bakery products	569	526	576	611	377
Meats, poultry, fish, and eggs	961	1 003	954	984	782
Dairy products	449	411	455	495	231
Fruits and vegetables	858	885	853	906	554
Other food at home	1 627	1 479	1 651	1 754	1 062
Food away from home	3 459	3 601	3 435	3 648	2 212
Alcoholic Beverages	583	374	617	682	244
Housing	20 091	19 409	20 197	20 864	16 380
Shelter	11 747	11 771	11 744	12 090	9 766
Owned dwellings	6 678	4 998	6 937	7 508	3 674
Rented dwellings	4 249	6 348	3 925	3 610	5 722
Other lodging	821	424	882	972	370
Utilities, fuels, and public services	4 049	3 882	4 074	4 111	3 864
Household operations	1 522	1 130	1 583	1 678	1 039
Housekeeping supplies	747	704	754	807	451
Household furnishings and equipment	2 025	1 922	2 042	2 178	1 261
Apparel and Services	1 866	2 043	1 838	1 895	1 509
Transportation	9 761	9 188	9 850	10 260	7 509
Vehicle purchases (net outlay)	3 975	3 599	4 033	4 203	3 057
Gasoline and motor oil	2 109	2 360	2 070	2 122	1 771
Other vehicle expenses	2 859	2 596	2 900	3 031	2 151
Public and other transportation	818	632	847	903	529
Health Care	4 968	3 173	5 246	5 618	3 122
Health insurance	3 405	2 223	3 587	3 786	2 452
Medical services	909	575	960	1 065	361
Drugs	483	261	518	566	245
Medical supplies	172	113	181	201	65
Entertainment	3 226	2 282	3 373	3 687	1 574
Personal Care Products and Services	768	656	786	799	709
Reading	108	56	116	128	52
Education	1 407	946	1 478	1 550	1 065
Tobacco Products and Smoking Supplies	347	155	376	395	269
Miscellaneous	993	671	1 043	1 066	909
Cash Contributions	1 888	855	2 047	2 183	1 269
Personal Insurance and Pensions	7 296	6 050	7 488	7 938	4 913
Life and other personal insurance	465	270	495	508	420
Pensions and Social Security	6 831	5 780	6 993	7 430	4 493

[1]May be of any race.

Table 11-13. Consumer Expenditures, Averages by Education of Reference Person, 2018

(Number, dollar, percent.)

Item	All consumer units	Less than a college graduate					College graduate or more		
		Total	Less than a high school graduate	High school graduate	High school graduate with some college	Associate's degree	Total	Bachelor's degree	Master's, professional, or doctoral degree
NUMBER OF CONSUMER UNITS (THOUSANDS)	131 439	74 123	8 214	24 789	26 769	14 351	57 316	33 374	23 942
CONSUMER UNIT CHARACTERISTICS									
Income Before Taxes	78 635	51 387	29 131	41 259	57 933	69 407	113 874	96 641	137 896
Income After Taxes	67 241	46 526	28 392	38 532	51 308	61 793	94 029	81 504	111 488
Age of Reference Person	51.1	51.7	56.3	53.7	49.1	50.3	50.4	49.5	51.6
Average Number in Consumer Unit									
All persons	2.5	2.4	2.2	2.2	2.4	2.6	2.6	2.5	2.6
Children under 18 years	0.6	0.6	0.7	0.5	0.6	0.7	0.6	0.5	0.6
Persons 65 years and over	0.4	0.4	0.4	0.5	0.4	0.4	0.4	0.4	0.4
Earners	1.3	1.1	0.8	1.0	1.3	1.4	1.5	1.5	1.5
Vehicles	1.9	1.7	1.2	1.5	1.8	2.3	2.1	2.1	2.2
Percent Distribution									
Male	47	44	43	45	42	45	52	50	53
Female	53	56	57	55	58	55	48	50	47
Percent Homeowner	63	56	42	54	56	68	73	70	77
With mortgage	37	29	14	23	31	41	48	46	51
Without mortgage	26	28	28	31	25	27	25	24	25
AVERAGE ANNUAL EXPENDITURES	61 224	45 064	30 285	38 173	48 164	59 252	81 923	72 264	95 446
Food	7 923	6 314	4 998	5 472	6 630	7 736	9 912	9 145	11 010
Food at home	4 464	3 790	3 282	3 448	3 872	4 427	5 292	4 924	5 822
Cereals and bakery products	569	496	432	462	501	568	660	609	732
Meats, poultry, fish, and eggs	961	849	818	789	852	955	1 097	1 061	1 150
Dairy products	449	367	317	325	383	430	550	500	621
Fruits and vegetables	858	676	628	615	666	811	1 081	970	1 240
Other food at home	1 627	1 402	1 086	1 257	1 471	1 664	1 904	1 783	2 079
Food away from home	3 459	2 524	1 716	2 024	2 758	3 308	4 620	4 221	5 188
Alcoholic Beverages	583	331	141	253	387	452	894	838	973
Housing	20 091	15 320	11 693	13 808	16 062	18 591	26 234	23 132	30 570
Shelter	11 747	8 696	6 854	7 833	9 090	10 507	15 693	13 853	18 258
Owned dwellings	6 678	4 128	1 976	3 304	4 486	6 114	9 975	8 401	12 169
Rented dwellings	4 249	4 201	4 773	4 268	4 187	3 783	4 311	4 369	4 230
Other lodging	821	368	105	262	416	610	1 407	1 084	1 858
Utilities, fuels, and public services	4 049	3 648	2 788	3 370	3 818	4 306	4 566	4 356	4 860
Household operations	1 522	877	561	705	953	1 214	2 356	1 796	3 137
Housekeeping supplies	747	638	506	542	729	691	882	792	1 011
Household furnishings and equipment	2 025	1 461	984	1 358	1 472	1 872	2 737	2 335	3 305
Apparel and Services	1 866	1 333	1 150	1 101	1 426	1 630	2 527	2 299	2 851
Transportation	9 761	7 842	4 580	6 716	8 279	10 811	12 232	11 300	13 534
Vehicle purchases (net outlay)	3 975	3 269	1 573	2 902	3 383	4 660	4 888	4 517	5 404
Gasoline and motor oil	2 109	1 899	1 243	1 659	1 981	2 538	2 379	2 341	2 433
Other vehicle expenses	2 859	2 306	1 330	1 901	2 522	3 123	3 565	3 396	3 802
Public and other transportation	818	368	435	254	394	490	1 400	1 045	1 895
Health Care	4 968	3 869	2 601	3 547	3 935	5 024	6 387	5 919	7 041
Health insurance	3 405	2 688	1 840	2 551	2 679	3 428	4 332	4 028	4 755
Medical services	909	643	372	510	685	952	1 252	1 155	1 386
Drugs	483	413	310	389	429	480	572	533	628
Medical supplies	172	125	79	98	142	164	232	203	272
Entertainment	3 226	2 395	1 138	1 776	2 492	3 951	4 286	3 912	4 808
Personal Care Products and Services	768	554	390	435	600	751	1 040	957	1 156
Reading	108	69	26	59	82	84	158	121	209
Education	1 407	557	117	217	861	831	2 505	1 857	3 408
Tobacco Products and Smoking Supplies	347	462	333	473	478	490	197	234	145
Miscellaneous	993	740	375	503	833	1 175	1 319	1 189	1 500
Cash Contributions	1 888	1 095	598	823	1 357	1 363	2 912	2 079	4 074
Personal Insurance and Pensions	7 296	4 183	2 143	2 991	4 742	6 363	11 321	9 281	14 165
Life and other personal insurance	465	305	154	267	318	432	672	524	878
Pensions and Social Security	6 831	3 878	1 989	2 724	4 425	5 931	10 649	8 757	13 287

Table 11-14. Consumer Expenditures, Averages by Housing Tenure and Type of Area, 2018

(Number, dollar, percent.)

Item	All consumer units	Housing tenure: Homeowner: Total	Housing tenure: Homeowner: Homeowner with mortgage	Housing tenure: Homeowner: Homeowner without mortgage	Housing tenure: Renter	Type of area: Urban: Total	Type of area: Urban: Central city	Type of area: Urban: Other urban	Type of area: Rural
NUMBER OF CONSUMER UNITS (THOUSANDS)	131 439	83 433	48 849	34 584	48 007	120 518	47 626	72 892	10 921
Income After Taxes	67 241	80 831	96 835	58 226	43 621	68 830	62 191	73 168	49 701
Age of Reference Person	51.1	55.7	50.1	63.7	43.1	50.7	47.9	52.5	55.9
Average Number in Consumer Unit									
All persons	2.5	2.6	2.9	2.2	2.2	2.5	2.3	2.5	2.5
Children under 18 years	0.6	0.6	0.8	0.3	0.6	0.6	0.5	0.6	0.6
Persons 65 years and over	0.4	0.5	0.3	0.8	0.2	0.4	0.3	0.4	0.6
Earners	1.3	1.4	1.7	0.9	1.2	1.3	1.3	1.4	1.1
Vehicles	1.9	2.3	2.4	2.1	1.2	1.9	1.5	2.1	2.4
Percent Distribution									
Male	47	48	50	46	45	47	46	48	46
Female	53	52	50	54	55	53	54	52	54
Percent Homeowner	63	100	100	100	X	62	49	70	82
With mortgage	37	59	100	X	X	38	30	42	32
Without mortgage	26	41	X	100	X	24	19	27	51
Food	7 923	8 956	9 976	7 173	6 137	8 064	7 378	8 501	6 451
Food at home	4 464	5 061	5 522	4 242	3 432	4 502	3 932	4 865	4 066
Cereals and bakery products	569	649	703	552	432	573	493	624	533
Meats, poultry, fish, and eggs	961	1 085	1 197	884	746	969	832	1 057	871
Dairy products	449	512	552	442	340	451	395	486	432
Fruits and vegetables	858	974	1 056	827	656	877	793	930	658
Other food at home	1 627	1 841	2 013	1 536	1 257	1 632	1 418	1 769	1 572
Food away from home	3 459	3 894	4 454	2 931	2 706	3 561	3 446	3 636	2 385
Alcoholic Beverages	583	687	778	528	403	612	611	612	280
Housing	20 091	21 954	26 144	15 981	16 855	20 780	19 582	21 555	12 512
Shelter	11 747	11 758	15 016	7 156	11 729	12 317	12 194	12 397	5 459
Owned dwellings	6 678	10 466	13 664	5 949	94	6 923	5 578	7 802	3 971
Rented dwellings	4 249	168	156	186	11 340	4 552	5 919	3 658	904
Other lodging	821	1 124	1 196	1 021	295	842	697	938	584
Utilities, fuels, and public services	4 049	4 833	5 162	4 369	2 685	4 052	3 615	4 337	4 014
Household operations	1 522	1 926	2 217	1 514	820	1 574	1 403	1 685	957
Housekeeping supplies	747	910	955	830	466	757	623	843	643
Household furnishings and equipment	2 025	2 527	2 794	2 113	1 155	2 080	1 747	2 292	1 439
Apparel and Services	1 866	2 035	2 404	1 401	1 575	1 915	1 895	1 928	1 348
Transportation	9 761	11 538	13 448	8 804	6 675	9 751	8 827	10 352	9 871
Vehicle purchases (net outlay)	3 975	4 806	5 891	3 272	2 531	3 934	3 729	4 069	4 421
Gasoline and motor oil	2 109	2 440	2 755	1 995	1 533	2 092	1 741	2 322	2 287
Other vehicle expenses	2 859	3 319	3 748	2 679	2 061	2 873	2 459	3 140	2 709
Public and other transportation	818	973	1 053	858	550	851	898	821	455
Health Care	4 968	6 305	6 221	6 431	2 645	4 944	4 242	5 403	5 234
Health insurance	3 405	4 307	4 269	4 361	1 837	3 398	2 895	3 727	3 476
Medical services	909	1 175	1 200	1 138	446	910	778	996	897
Drugs	483	604	552	684	274	467	420	498	664
Medical supplies	172	220	200	249	88	169	150	182	198
Entertainment	3 226	4 023	4 439	3 381	1 842	3 203	2 759	3 491	3 473
Personal Care Products and Services	768	874	956	744	585	787	749	811	563
Reading	108	131	120	152	69	110	112	109	85
Education	1 407	1 597	1 995	1 031	1 078	1 476	1 385	1 536	646
Tobacco Products and Smoking Supplies	347	333	347	314	370	320	293	338	636
Miscellaneous	993	1 214	1 308	1 085	608	988	867	1 068	1 047
Cash Contributions	1 888	2 491	2 188	2 919	840	1 859	1 774	1 914	2 205
Personal Insurance and Pensions	7 296	9 090	11 395	5 835	4 176	7 530	7 051	7 842	4 712
Life and other personal insurance	465	625	690	534	186	467	385	520	445
Pensions and Social Security	6 831	8 465	10 705	5 302	3 990	7 063	6 666	7 322	4 267

X = Not applicable.

Table 11-15. Consumer Expenditures, Averages by Selected Cities, 2017–2018

(Number, dollar, percent.)

Item	Washington, D.C.	Miami	Dallas-Fort Worth	New York	Philadelphia	Boston	Chicago	Detroit	Minneapolis-St. Paul	Los Angeles	Seattle	Anchorage
NUMBER OF CONSUMER UNITS (THOUSANDS)	2 536	2 294	2 829	7 329	2 185	1 961	3 477	1 957	1 657	6 605	1 872	210
CONSUMER UNIT CHARACTERISTICS												
Income Before Taxes	115 585	79 436	78 854	100 911	93 210	99 908	82 422	80 089	93 986	82 119	117 499	93 396
Age of Reference Person	48.8	53.5	46.9	51.7	54.1	51.2	50.1	52.5	47.5	49.2	45.5	51.8
Average Number in Consumer Unit												
All persons	2.6	2.5	2.5	2.5	2.4	2.3	2.5	2.4	2.3	3.0	2.0	2.4
Children under 18 years	0.7	0.5	0.7	0.5	0.5	0.5	0.6	0.6	0.5	1.0	1.0	0.5
Persons 65 years and over	0.3	0.4	0.2	0.4	0.5	0.4	0.3	0.4	0.3	0.0	0.0	0.3
Earners	1.5	1.4	1.4	1.3	1.4	1.3	1.4	1.3	1.5	2.0	2.0	1.5
Vehicles	1.8	1.5	1.6	1.2	1.7	1.7	1.7	1.9	2.3	2.0	2.0	2.4
Percent Homeowner	63.0	59.0	54.0	49.0	69.0	57.0	63.0	70.0	61.0	52.0	55.0	63.0
AVERAGE ANNUAL EXPENDITURES	91 118	57 555	66 282	70 875	70 813	79 747	63 726	64 998	72 382	68 129	84 864	71 855
Food	11 211	6 763	7 330	8 706	8 919	9 667	8 481	7 998	8 403	8 974	11 412	9 031
Food at home	5 582	4 001	3 861	4 821	5 085	5 870	4 761	4 429	4 809	4 543	6 195	5 779
Cereals and bakery products	664	427	452	638	708	827	575	585	588	563	763	790
Meats, poultry, fish, and eggs	1 276	1 086	917	1 166	1 055	1 110	1 070	934	990	1 030	1 217	1 202
Dairy products	562	420	330	492	512	571	467	407	479	431	645	550
Fruits and vegetables	1 104	912	758	1 025	1 070	1 268	983	876	921	955	1 358	1 011
Other food at home	1 977	1 157	1 403	1 500	1 740	2 094	1 666	1 626	1 833	1 563	2 212	2 226
Food away from home	5 629	2 761	3 469	3 885	3 835	3 797	3 720	3 569	3 594	4 431	5 217	3 252
Alcoholic Beverages	1 111	530	766	603	598	913	657	735	809	657	1 124	878
Housing	30 872	21 450	24 339	27 626	23 225	29 871	22 501	19 587	24 335	24 326	29 269	22 619
Shelter	20 502	13 960	15 292	19 298	13 592	18 805	14 426	10 670	14 685	16 613	18 966	13 688
Owned dwellings	12 712	7 007	7 699	10 083	8 550	10 644	8 920	6 881	9 118	7 767	10 040	8 133
Rented dwellings	6 153	6 250	6 802	8 121	3 663	7 007	4 608	2 960	4 334	8 063	7 764	4 682
Other lodging	1 637	703	791	1 094	1 379	1 154	898	829	1 233	783	1 162	873
Utilities, fuels, and public services	4 164	3 857	4 395	4 109	4 403	4 354	3 892	4 052	3 559	3 787	4 004	4 744
Household operations	3 289	1 245	1 478	1 798	1 987	2 006	1 405	1 636	1 936	1 554	2 399	1 254
Housekeeping supplies	901	724	806	680	965	987	714	810	703	757	923	845
Household furnishings and equipment	2 017	1 664	2 368	1 742	2 278	3 719	2 063	2 419	3 451	1 616	2 977	2 088
Apparel and Services	2 754	1 690	2 352	2 574	2 435	2 629	2 017	2 370	2 607	2 089	3 155	2 277
Transportation	13 095	8 820	11 140	8 494	11 065	9 571	8 443	12 541	9 318	9 273	11 999	11 290
Vehicle purchases (net outlay)	5 703	2 843	4 655	2 015	4 034	3 538	3 438	4 432	3 132	2 966	4 412	5 025
Gasoline and motor oil	2 040	2 284	2 211	1 514	1 972	1 820	1 819	2 039	2 104	2 706	2 175	2 366
Other vehicle expenses	3 253	3 061	3 588	3 149	3 939	2 886	2 232	5 219	2 891	2 683	3 978	2 509
Public and other transportation	2 099	631	688	1 815	1 120	1 327	954	850	1 190	918	1 434	1 390
Health Care	6 301	4 554	4 954	4 787	5 669	5 703	5 476	4 930	5 517	3 890	5 355	5 233
Entertainment	4 191	2 064	3 075	3 154	3 221	3 942	2 863	4 228	4 347	2 853	4 334	4 376
Personal Care Products and Services	1 271	978	857	858	838	817	1 056	752	895	811	911	784
Reading	151	65	85	110	173	189	156	86	239	94	157	108
Education	2 566	909	1 954	3 007	2 649	4 144	1 968	1 171	1 864	2 334	2 047	1 116
Tobacco Products and Smoking Supplies	147	211	174	257	349	285	186	513	449	211	298	535
Miscellaneous	1 846	1 289	859	1 112	1 675	1 228	1 003	1 333	980	1 247	1 454	1 069
Cash Contributions	2 672	773	1 561	1 508	2 013	1 848	1 597	1 565	4 263	1 654	2 630	1 802
Personal Insurance and Pensions	12 930	7 458	6 836	8 079	7 984	8 940	7 322	7 190	8 355	9 716	10 719	10 736
Life and other personal insurance	660	334	300	577	627	363	409	439	513	393	411	529
Pensions and Social Security	12 270	7 124	6 535	7 502	7 357	8 578	6 913	6 751	7 843	9 323	10 308	10 207

Table 11-16. Consumer Expenditures, Averages by Region of Residence, 2018

(Number, dollar, percent.)

Item	All consumer units	Region[1]			
		Northeast	South	Midwest	West
NUMBER OF CONSUMER UNITS (THOUSANDS)	131 439	23 357	28 305	50 576	29 201
CONSUMER UNIT CHARACTERISTICS					
Income Before Taxes	78 635	92 753	73 695	71 732	84 088
Income After Taxes	67 241	76 722	63 614	62 261	71 798
Age of Reference Person	51.1	52.6	51.3	51.1	49.8
Average Number in Consumer Unit					
All persons	2.5	2.4	2.4	2.4	2.6
Children under 18 years	0.6	0.5	0.6	0.6	0.7
Persons 65 years and over	0.4	0.4	0.4	0.4	0.4
Earners	1.3	1.3	1.3	1.2	1.4
Vehicles	1.9	1.6	2.1	1.9	2.0
Percent Distribution					
Male	47	47	47	46	49
Female	53	53	53	54	51
Percent Homeowner	63	61	67	66	58
With mortgage	37	34	40	37	37
Without mortgage	26	27	27	29	21
AVERAGE ANNUAL EXPENDITURES	61 224	66 076	58 241	56 667	68 113
Food	7 923	8 401	7 511	7 351	8 913
Food at home	4 464	4 845	4 255	4 127	4 938
Cereals and bakery products	569	662	534	523	609
Meats, poultry, fish, and eggs	961	1 063	892	926	1 004
Dairy products	449	509	450	385	512
Fruits and vegetables	858	987	772	769	988
Other food at home	1 627	1 624	1 607	1 524	1 825
Food away from home	3 459	3 557	3 255	3 224	3 975
Alcoholic Beverages	583	647	606	500	653
Housing	20 091	23 646	17 850	18 116	22 840
Shelter	11 747	14 531	9 935	10 058	14 204
Owned dwellings	6 678	8 510	6 206	5 822	7 152
Rented dwellings	4 249	5 020	2 965	3 513	6 151
Other lodging	821	1 001	764	723	901
Utilities, fuels, and public services	4 049	4 258	3 936	4 069	3 955
Household operations	1 522	1 732	1 349	1 403	1 728
Housekeeping supplies	747	762	699	750	777
Household furnishings and equipment	2 025	2 364	1 931	1 836	2 175
Apparel and Services	1 866	2 137	1 872	1 664	1 998
Transportation	9 761	9 324	9 279	9 789	10 530
Vehicle purchases (net outlay)	3 975	3 199	3 673	4 376	4 193
Gasoline and motor oil	2 109	1 855	2 051	2 115	2 357
Other vehicle expenses	2 859	3 144	2 819	2 670	2 998
Public and other transportation	818	1 125	737	629	981
Health Care	4 968	4 992	5 247	4 846	4 892
Health insurance	3 405	3 574	3 506	3 409	3 164
Medical services	909	831	990	816	1 053
Drugs	483	406	541	481	494
Medical supplies	172	182	211	140	180
Entertainment	3 226	3 117	3 630	2 778	3 696
Personal Care Products and Services	768	776	739	734	848
Reading	108	139	126	81	114
Education	1 407	2 103	1 189	1 176	1 462
Tobacco Products and Smoking Supplies	347	345	416	355	267
Miscellaneous	993	1 086	926	926	1 099
Cash Contributions	1 888	1 587	1 830	1 693	2 520
Personal Insurance and Pensions	7 296	7 775	7 019	6 660	8 281
Life and other personal insurance	465	526	495	458	399
Pensions and Social Security	6 831	7 248	6 524	6 202	7 882

[1]The states that comprise the Census regions are: Northeast—Connecticut, Maine, Massachusetts, New Hampshire, New Jersey, New York, Pennsylvania, Rhode Island, and Vermont; South—Alabama, Arkansas, Delaware, District of Columbia, Florida, Georgia, Kentucky, Louisiana, Maryland, Mississippi, North Carolina, Oklahoma, South Carolina, Tennessee, Texas, Virginia, and West Virginia; Midwest—Illinois, Indiana, Iowa, Kansas, Michigan, Minnesota, Missouri, Nebraska, North Dakota, Ohio, South Dakota, and Wisconsin; and West—Alaska, Arizona, California, Colorado, Hawaii, Idaho, Montana, Nevada, New Mexico, Oregon, Utah, Washington, and Wyoming.

Table 11-17. Consumer Expenditures, Averages for Single Men by Income Before Taxes, 2017–2018

Item	All single men	Complete reporting of income						
		Less than $15,000	$15,000 to $29,999	$30,000 to $39,999	$40,000 to $49,999	$50,000 to $69,999	$70,000 to $99,999	$100,000 and over
NUMBER OF CONSUMER UNITS (THOUSANDS)	17,263	4,584	4,326	1,843	1,486	2,155	1,578	1,291
CONSUMER UNIT CHARACTERISTICS								
Income Before Taxes	42,207	7,323	21,860	34,112	44,159	58,582	82,197	167,370
Income After Taxes	35,680	7,373	20,985	30,915	38,972	49,992	67,236	126,000
Age of Reference Person	50.2	48.8	57.5	46.5	49.2	45.4	46.7	49.5
Average Number in Consumer Unit								
All persons	1.0	1.0	1.0	1.0	1.0	1.0	1.0	1.0
Persons 65 years and over	0.3	0.3	0.4	0.2	0.2	0.1	0.2	0.1
Earners	0.6	0.4	0.5	0.8	0.8	0.9	0.9	1.0
Vehicles	1.2	0.7	1.3	1.3	1.5	1.5	1.5	1.5
Percent Homeowner	42	26	45	36	53	50	54	60
With mortgage	20	8	12	14	28	32	38	45
Without mortgage	22	19	33	21	25	18	16	16
AVERAGE ANNUAL EXPENDITURES	37,406	19,341	28,123	34,009	38,176	46,561	58,225	92,391
Food	4,725	3,125	3,654	4,403	5,241	5,519	6,483	9,029
Food at home	2,227	1,704	1,958	2,253	2,329	2,388	2,795	3,447
Cereals and bakery products	268	214	263	295	241	277	328	349
Meats, poultry, fish, and eggs	493	354	401	487	639	496	573	907
Dairy products	215	173	200	209	168	229	297	315
Fruits and vegetables	379	233	355	402	396	431	511	579
Other food at home	873	730	739	861	885	954	1,085	1,296
Food away from home	2,498	1,421	1,696	2,150	2,912	3,131	3,688	5,582
Alcoholic Beverages	549	215	233	603	524	714	868	1,780
Housing	13,718	8,057	11,057	12,462	13,838	16,500	20,766	30,627
Shelter	9,210	5,354	7,351	8,280	9,222	10,965	13,736	21,993
Owned dwellings	3,334	1,130	2,060	2,246	4,126	4,617	6,117	10,530
Rented dwellings	5,452	4,108	5,107	5,850	4,744	5,887	6,930	9,100
Other lodging	424	116	184	184	353	460	688	2,363
Utilities, fuels, and public services	2,316	1,512	2,250	2,298	2,669	2,744	2,914	3,570
Household operations	671	298	559	689	757	747	1,192	1,473
Housekeeping supplies	426	453	247	322	315	665	480	661
Household furnishings and equipment	1,095	440	649	873	875	1,380	2,444	2,931
Apparel and Services	914	576	505	540	890	1,125	1,477	2,680
Transportation	5,964	2,576	4,351	6,685	6,315	8,243	9,139	13,701
Vehicle purchases (net outlay)	2,157	727	1,701	3,129	1,947	3,500	4,033	3,075
Gasoline and motor oil	1,254	741	1,028	1,356	1,529	1,868	1,769	1,718
Other vehicle expenses	2,113	910	1,414	1,914	2,497	2,306	2,568	7,140
Public and other transportation	441	198	208	287	342	568	769	1,769
Health Care	2,601	1,399	2,775	2,205	2,611	2,942	3,440	5,168
Health insurance	1,780	1,028	1,856	1,590	1,912	2,001	2,253	3,370
Medical services	468	162	545	323	381	493	714	1,262
Drugs	282	181	307	236	214	371	335	412
Medical supplies	72	29	67	56	103	77	138	125
Entertainment	1,736	843	1,266	1,569	1,884	2,270	2,459	4,561
Personal Care Products and Services	270	156	204	235	301	313	475	528
Reading	68	31	57	48	54	122	119	109
Education	617	932	311	535	360	418	785	1,054
Tobacco Products and Smoking Supplies	336	296	393	379	348	314	247	351
Miscellaneous	794	389	675	496	687	951	1,642	1,809
Cash Contributions	1,350	378	897	1,048	1,478	1,386	2,099	5,631
Personal Insurance and Pensions	3,765	367	1,746	2,801	3,645	5,742	8,226	15,362
Life and other personal insurance	184	103	158	121	125	198	244	622
Pensions and Social Security	3,581	264	1,588	2,681	3,520	5,545	7,982	14,740

Table 11-18. Consumer Expenditures, Averages for Single Women by Income Before Taxes, 2017–2018

Item	All single women	Less than $15,000	$15,000 to $29,999	$30,000 to $39,999	$40,000 to $49,999	$50,000 to $69,999	$70,000 or more
NUMBER OF CONSUMER UNITS (THOUSANDS)	20 785	6 723	6 577	2 043	1 337	1 928	2 177
CONSUMER UNIT CHARACTERISTICS							
Income Before Taxes	32 516	8 183	21 183	34 417	44 689	58 694	109 463
Income After Taxes	28 608	8 270	20 443	31 614	40 124	50 340	86 955
Age of Reference Person	57.6	54.3	66.2	55.1	52.9	50.5	52.9
Average Number in Consumer Unit							
All persons	1.0	1.0	1.0	1.0	1.0	1.0	1.0
Persons 65 years and over	0.4	0.4	0.6	0.4	0.3	0.3	0.2
Earners	0.5	0.3	0.3	0.7	0.8	0.8	0.9
Vehicles	0.9	0.6	1.0	1.0	1.1	1.1	1.2
Percent Homeowner	52	34	62	54	56	54	70
With mortgage	20	8	16	20	35	34	45
Without mortgage	32	25	46	34	21	20	24
AVERAGE ANNUAL EXPENDITURES	34 817	20 918	29 612	36 380	42 587	49 528	71 916
Food	4 206	3 276	3 568	4 745	4 801	5 258	6 413
Food at home	2 482	2 133	2 305	2 988	2 419	2 642	3 262
Cereals and bakery products	310	261	313	374	306	303	374
Meats, poultry, fish, and eggs	459	421	437	560	411	473	545
Dairy products	268	235	252	319	264	293	322
Fruits and vegetables	512	437	465	621	502	525	713
Other food at home	933	780	837	1 114	935	1 048	1 308
Food away from home	1 724	1 142	1 263	1 757	2 382	2 616	3 151
Alcoholic Beverages	273	143	179	308	322	471	622
Housing	13 592	8 536	12 278	14 202	16 946	19 121	25 281
Shelter	8 533	5 317	7 376	8 863	10 887	12 654	16 555
Owned dwellings	3 745	1 653	3 299	3 662	5 041	5 014	9 713
Rented dwellings	4 367	3 484	3 800	4 867	5 352	6 890	5 494
Other lodging	422	180	278	334	495	750	1 349
Utilities, fuels, and public services	2 493	1 758	2 624	2 811	2 877	2 904	3 468
Household operations	851	406	874	857	985	1 167	1 777
Housekeeping supplies	537	388	508	649	507	680	774
Household furnishings and equipment	1 178	668	895	1 021	1 689	1 716	2 707
Apparel and Services	1 046	583	816	1 064	1 282	1 374	2 318
Transportation	4 255	2 266	3 612	4 715	5 673	6 583	8 649
Vehicle purchases (net outlay)	1 347	642	1 121	1 348	1 243	2 648	3 114
Gasoline and motor oil	866	556	758	1 165	1 169	1 243	1 350
Other vehicle expenses	1 583	864	1 392	1 770	2 574	2 023	2 893
Public and other transportation	459	205	341	432	686	669	1 292
Health Care	3 220	1 935	3 588	3 611	3 744	3 788	4 811
Health insurance	2 147	1 388	2 519	2 311	2 240	2 336	2 991
Medical services	559	240	484	641	940	903	1 151
Drugs	387	250	435	517	428	409	442
Medical supplies	127	56	150	142	136	141	228
Entertainment	1 747	1 155	1 369	1 631	1 744	2 301	4 232
Personal Care Products and Services	670	391	574	577	822	995	1 410
Reading	102	71	109	93	106	114	171
Education	859	1 197	348	464	815	1 298	1 358
Tobacco Products and Smoking Supplies	172	193	169	179	154	179	117
Miscellaneous	719	313	615	1 048	577	865	1 943
Cash Contributions	1 341	464	1 363	1 224	1 365	1 541	3 905
Personal Insurance and Pensions	2 614	396	1 023	2 518	4 238	5 641	10 685
Life and other personal insurance	221	123	197	215	250	211	594
Pensions and Social Security	2 393	273	827	2 303	3 988	5 430	10 092

Table 11-19. Consumer Expenditures, Averages for Age Groups by Income Before Taxes: Reference Person Under 25 Years of Age, 2017–2018

(Number, dollar, percent.)

Item	Complete reporting of income						
	Total under 25 years	Less than $5,000	$5,000 to $9,999	$10,000 to $14,999	$15,000 to $19,999	$20,000 to $29,999	$30,000 to $39,999
NUMBER OF CONSUMER UNITS (THOUSANDS)	7 589	3 057	1 434	746	661	806	886
CONSUMER UNIT CHARACTERISTICS							
Income Before Taxes	32 009	6 062	22 209	34 369	44 719	58 770	101 623
Income After Taxes	29 876	6 214	22 657	33 077	42 696	53 913	89 114
Age of Reference Person	21.3	20.4	21.5	22.1	22.3	22.2	22.3
Average Number in Consumer Unit							
All persons	1.9	1.2	1.9	2.1	2.5	2.5	2.9
Children under 18 years	0.3	0.1	0.4	0.4	0.5	0.4	0.5
Earners	1.3	0.8	1.2	1.3	1.7	1.9	2.3
Vehicles	1.1	0.5	1.0	1.3	1.8	1.8	2.1
Percent Distribution							
Male	43	40	39	52	39	53	51
Female	57	60	61	48	61	47	49
Percent Homeowner	13	3	11	9	21	23	38
With mortgage	8	1	3	6	12	14	29
Without mortgage	5	2	7	3	9	9	9
AVERAGE ANNUAL EXPENDITURES	32 718	17 248	26 577	34 943	43 719	50 031	65 489
Food	4 752	3 137	4 139	4 568	5 188	6 016	7 752
Food at home	2 405	1 272	2 098	2 457	3 112	2 994	4 152
Cereals and bakery products	316	166	291	352	401	378	526
Meats, poultry, fish, and eggs	513	255	443	466	722	652	918
Dairy products	245	124	211	257	393	327	372
Fruits and vegetables	458	196	419	455	575	563	879
Other food at home	872	530	734	928	1 021	1 075	1 457
Food away from home	2 348	1 864	2 041	2 111	2 077	3 022	3 600
Alcoholic Beverages	293	157	199	233	203	598	593
Housing	11 329	5 568	10 960	13 290	14 488	17 140	21 984
Shelter	7 627	4 051	7 598	8 554	9 454	11 411	14 428
Owned dwellings	983	180	527	512	1 200	1 667	4 105
Rented dwellings	6 349	3 658	6 786	7 881	8 056	9 183	9 792
Other lodging	294	212	285	[1]162	[1]198	561	532
Utilities, fuels, and public services	1 874	744	1 744	2 428	2 836	3 101	3 685
Household operations	509	177	499	565	838	814	1 095
Housekeeping supplies	320	145	241	293	363	428	684
Household furnishings and equipment	1 000	452	877	1 449	997	1 388	2 092
Apparel and Services	1 221	767	782	1 232	1 362	1 297	2 666
Transportation	6 094	2 367	4 640	6 555	10 506	11 747	11 980
Vehicle purchases (net outlay)	2 726	826	1 846	[1]3043	4 759	6 206	5 756
Gasoline and motor oil	1 416	717	1 246	1 620	1 945	2 395	2 649
Other vehicle expenses	1 518	583	1 014	1 625	3 454	2 470	2 739
Public and other transportation	433	240	534	268	348	677	835
Health Care	1 266	306	695	1 111	2 084	2 188	4 100
Health insurance	744	195	389	765	952	1 391	2 457
Medical services	350	44	182	202	961	469	1 244
Drugs	116	45	92	62	115	239	264
Medical supplies	56	22	32	[1]82	[1]56	89	135
Entertainment	1 446	796	1 024	1 661	1 939	2 310	2 747
Personal Care Products and Services	474	326	446	465	481	569	820
Reading	38	23	34	[1]44	[1]19	[1]53	84
Education	2 302	3 187	1 514	2 068	1 755	1 712	1 681
Tobacco Products and Smoking Supplies	225	98	177	293	336	417	401
Miscellaneous	332	75	198	383	1 241	533	419
Cash Contributions	326	113	236	365	524	519	855
Personal Insurance and Pensions	2 619	329	1 534	2 673	3 593	4 932	9 407
Life and other personal insurance	42	[1]3	[1]38	[1]31	[1]39	[1]68	171
Pensions and Social Security	2 577	326	1 496	2 642	3 554	4 864	9 236

[1]Data are likely to have large sampling errors.

Table 11-20. Consumer Expenditures, Averages for Age Groups by Income Before Taxes: Reference Person 25 to 34 Years of Age, 2017–2018

(Number, dollar, percent.)

Item	Total 25-34 years	Complete reporting of income: Less than $15,000	$15,000 to $29,999	$30,000 to $39,999	$40,000 to $49,999	$50,000 to $69,999	$70,000 to $99,999	$100,000 or more
NUMBER OF CONSUMER UNITS (THOUSANDS)	21 290	1 956	2 571	2 196	2 006	3 636	4 061	4 864
CONSUMER UNIT CHARACTERISTICS								
Income Before Taxes	71 573	7 348	23 028	34 536	44 779	59 224	82 890	150 612
Income After Taxes	62 832	8 307	25 478	34 985	43 112	54 028	73 167	123 159
Age of Reference Person	29.8	29.4	29.4	29.4	29.6	29.4	29.9	30.5
Average Number in Consumer Unit								
All persons	2.7	2.4	2.6	2.7	2.8	2.7	2.9	2.9
Children under 18 years	1.0	1.0	1.2	1.1	1.1	0.9	0.9	0.8
Earners	1.5	0.8	1.1	1.3	1.4	1.6	1.8	2.0
Vehicles	1.7	0.9	1.2	1.4	1.6	1.7	2.1	2.1
Percent Distribution								
Male	49	37	37	44	46	50	58	55
Female	51	63	63	56	54	50	42	45
Percent Homeowner	41	16	17	22	37	39	53	65
With mortgage	33	7	8	14	29	31	45	58
Without mortgage	8	9	9	8	7	7	8	7
AVERAGE ANNUAL EXPENDITURES	55 824	27 382	32 367	38 643	42 731	50 694	61 984	91 730
Food	7 367	5 065	4 942	5 682	6 026	6 742	7 909	11 006
Food at home	3 934	3 131	3 049	3 495	3 131	3 587	4 105	5 400
Cereals and bakery products	494	435	432	437	393	442	548	622
Meats, poultry, fish, and eggs	813	717	651	781	698	731	771	1 090
Dairy products	392	261	298	326	293	339	439	570
Fruits and vegetables	791	591	593	660	622	683	854	1 143
Other food at home	1 445	1 127	1 076	1 291	1 125	1 392	1 492	1 974
Food away from home	3 433	1 935	1 893	2 187	2 895	3 155	3 804	5 606
Alcoholic Beverages	603	132	167	299	427	573	639	1 233
Housing	19 765	11 340	12 814	14 341	16 584	17 690	21 465	30 768
Shelter	12 446	7 170	8 355	9 137	10 575	11 176	13 460	19 100
Owned dwellings	4 734	894	906	1 509	3 246	3 479	5 567	10 613
Rented dwellings	7 282	6 082	7 338	7 496	7 090	7 348	7 263	7 684
Other lodging	431	193	111	132	240	348	630	804
Utilities, fuels, and public services	3 306	2 264	2 485	2 858	3 192	3 247	3 642	4 171
Household operations	1 649	592	801	887	1 061	1 224	1 856	3 252
Housekeeping supplies	533	452	311	427	413	442	581	820
Household furnishings and equipment	1 832	862	862	1 032	1 344	1 602	1 926	3 425
Apparel and Services	2 083	1 331	1 313	1 534	1 447	1 671	2 060	3 651
Transportation	9 711	4 378	6 582	7 807	7 057	9 842	10 890	14 403
Vehicle purchases (net outlay)	4 400	1 655	3 049	3 805	2 628	4 773	4 659	6 722
Gasoline and motor oil	2 081	1 217	1 460	1 782	1 948	1 998	2 403	2 740
Other vehicle expenses	2 542	1 234	1 780	1 758	2 068	2 543	3 049	3 618
Public and other transportation	689	272	293	461	413	528	779	1 324
Health Care	3 063	854	1 067	1 812	2 494	2 882	3 938	5 213
Health insurance	2 167	553	739	1 327	1 822	2 028	2 871	3 607
Medical services	588	129	186	282	398	544	720	1 125
Drugs	218	143	101	138	191	219	256	328
Medical supplies	90	29	40	64	83	91	91	154
Entertainment	2 596	1 024	1 449	1 584	1 833	2 158	2 990	4 613
Personal Care Products and Services	659	341	456	440	479	553	776	1 067
Reading	64	[1]17	48	61	48	57	74	95
Education	1 165	1 555	556	705	537	970	1 058	2 033
Tobacco Products and Smoking Supplies	330	351	388	307	371	303	373	267
Miscellaneous	678	220	396	528	419	816	706	1 051
Cash Contributions	888	338	385	587	781	851	983	1 505
Personal Insurance and Pensions	6 851	435	1 803	2 956	4 228	5 585	8 123	14 825
Life and other personal insurance	194	38	63	83	152	138	225	408
Pensions and Social Security	6 658	397	1 740	2 873	4 075	5 447	7 897	14 417

[1]Data are likely to have large sampling errors.

Table 11-21. Consumer Expenditures, Averages for Age Groups by Income Before Taxes: Reference Person 35 to 44 Years of Age, 2017–2018

(Number, dollar, percent.)

Item	Complete reporting of income							
	Total 25-34 years	Less than $15,000	$15,000 to $29,999	$30,000 to $39,999	$40,000 to $49,999	$50,000 to $69,999	$70,000 to $99,999	$100,000 or more
NUMBER OF CONSUMER UNITS (THOUSANDS)	21 551	1 466	2 290	1 844	1 537	3 158	4 006	7 249
CONSUMER UNIT CHARACTERISTICS								
Income Before Taxes	91 784	7 377	22 713	34 615	44 822	59 404	84 052	173 551
Income After Taxes	79 068	8 126	25 703	36 005	43 834	55 270	75 676	140 939
Age of Reference Person	39.4	39.0	39.1	39.1	39.4	39.3	39.5	39.6
Average Number in Consumer Unit								
All persons	3.4	2.5	3.0	3.1	3.1	3.1	3.6	3.7
Children under 18 years	1.4	1.1	1.3	1.3	1.3	1.2	1.5	1.6
Earners	1.7	0.7	1.1	1.4	1.5	1.6	1.9	2.0
Vehicles	1.9	0.9	1.2	1.5	1.6	1.8	2.2	2.4
Percent Distribution								
Male	47	40	38	39	43	48	46	54
Female	53	60	62	61	57	52	54	46
Percent Homeowner	56	24	28	36	42	51	59	80
With mortgage	46	12	15	20	29	42	52	72
Without mortgage	10	11	13	16	12	9	8	8
AVERAGE ANNUAL EXPENDITURES	70 065	28 716	33 897	40 166	44 209	53 675	69 969	109 386
Food	9 603	5 405	5 596	6 711	7 442	7 816	9 411	13 428
Food at home	5 279	3 682	3 651	4 260	4 331	4 403	5 187	6 851
Cereals and bakery products	688	438	472	538	528	573	709	897
Meats, poultry, fish, and eggs	1 155	910	844	1 028	1 043	944	1 074	1 462
Dairy products	551	389	354	403	412	446	570	732
Fruits and vegetables	990	634	732	779	784	815	951	1 306
Other food at home	1 895	1 311	1 249	1 512	1 564	1 624	1 883	2 454
Food away from home	4 324	1 723	1 945	2 452	3 110	3 413	4 224	6 577
Alcoholic Beverages	676	275	225	225	310	400	709	1 151
Housing	23 747	12 090	13 614	15 273	16 308	19 078	22 886	35 457
Shelter	14 170	7 330	8 322	9 131	9 409	12 008	13 566	20 966
Owned dwellings	7 907	1 472	1 717	2 095	2 965	5 243	6 989	15 357
Rented dwellings	5 624	5 660	6 515	6 849	6 213	6 472	6 022	4 308
Other lodging	639	[1]198	89	187	231	293	555	1 301
Utilities, fuels, and public services	4 359	2 667	3 293	3 760	3 898	3 998	4 576	5 325
Household operations	2 164	624	620	803	796	1 090	1 525	4 417
Housekeeping supplies	830	473	508	518	785	638	796	1 153
Household furnishings and equipment	2 224	995	872	1 062	1 419	1 344	2 422	3 595
Apparel and Services	2 400	1 123	1 628	1 441	1 357	1 716	2 432	3 561
Transportation	11 455	4 611	6 309	7 241	6 074	8 652	12 963	17 052
Vehicle purchases (net outlay)	4 970	1 888	2 817	2 914	1 503	3 009	5 866	7 890
Gasoline and motor oil	2 516	1 261	1 713	1 899	2 208	2 360	2 786	3 165
Other vehicle expenses	3 129	1 164	1 520	2 075	2 067	2 850	3 601	4 379
Public and other transportation	841	297	260	354	296	433	710	1 619
Health Care	4 281	1 238	1 394	2 177	2 956	3 540	4 757	6 672
Health insurance	2 894	841	832	1 399	1 949	2 484	3 195	4 554
Medical services	890	165	302	479	568	663	1 009	1 429
Drugs	363	191	208	231	356	294	398	482
Medical supplies	134	41	52	67	83	99	155	207
Entertainment	3 782	1 528	1 339	1 489	2 272	2 472	3 460	6 556
Personal Care Products and Services	917	423	454	523	645	753	895	1 382
Reading	111	[1]75	27	71	71	98	110	170
Education	1 068	488	300	327	637	563	851	2 044
Tobacco Products and Smoking Supplies	388	439	370	557	392	521	378	288
Miscellaneous	1 074	325	528	376	772	1 233	898	1 664
Cash Contributions	1 631	272	528	836	994	1 187	1 632	2 786
Personal Insurance and Pensions	8 932	426	1 583	2 918	3 979	5 646	8 590	17 175
Life and other personal insurance	405	73	109	151	180	190	386	782
Pensions and Social Security	8 527	353	1 474	2 767	3 799	5 455	8 204	16 393

[1]Data are likely to have large sampling errors.

Table 11-22. Consumer Expenditures, Averages for Age Groups by Income Before Taxes: Reference Person 45 to 54 Years of Age, 2017–2018

(Number, dollar, percent.)

Item	Total 45-54 years	Complete reporting of income: Less than $15,000	$15,000 to $29,999	$30,000 to $39,999	$40,000 to $49,999	$50,000 to $69,999	$70,000 to $99,999	$100,000 or more
NUMBER OF CONSUMER UNITS (THOUSANDS)	23 315	2 087	2 231	1 677	1 607	2 779	4 085	8 849
CONSUMER UNIT CHARACTERISTICS								
Income Before Taxes	104 737	6 749	22 297	34 764	44 561	59 933	83 723	196 589
Income After Taxes	87 010	7 233	23 283	34 630	42 398	54 962	74 532	155 742
Age of Reference Person	49.6	50.0	50.0	49.7	49.4	49.5	49.7	49.5
Average Number in Consumer Unit								
All persons	2.8	1.9	2.1	2.5	2.5	2.8	2.9	3.3
Children under 18 years	0.7	0.4	0.5	0.6	0.6	0.7	0.7	0.9
Persons 65 years and over	0.1	([1])	0.1	0.1	[2]0.1	([1])	0.1	0.1
Earners	1.7	0.5	1.0	1.3	1.5	1.7	2.0	2.3
Vehicles	2.2	0.9	1.3	1.6	1.8	2.0	2.3	3.0
Percent Distribution								
Male	47	34	45	40	43	45	48	54
Female	53	66	55	60	57	55	52	46
Percent Homeowner	69	33	42	48	53	61	75	90
With mortgage	52	17	17	27	37	42	60	75
Without mortgage	17	17	25	21	16	19	15	15
AVERAGE ANNUAL EXPENDITURES	74 573	25 743	30 542	38 710	43 635	53 221	67 448	119 540
Food	9 400	4 219	5 114	5 703	6 268	7 455	8 618	13 906
Food at home	5 124	2 882	3 210	3 702	3 700	4 379	4 795	7 030
Cereals and bakery products	648	368	396	446	440	552	581	913
Meats, poultry, fish, and eggs	1 117	617	769	835	941	958	1 060	1 479
Dairy products	520	305	304	347	326	446	479	734
Fruits and vegetables	967	470	562	702	679	860	890	1 353
Other food at home	1 872	1 121	1 179	1 372	1 315	1 562	1 786	2 552
Food away from home	4 276	1 337	1 904	2 000	2 568	3 076	3 823	6 876
Alcoholic Beverages	645	241	210	266	269	418	467	1 142
Housing	23 358	11 442	12 061	14 567	15 859	17 828	21 898	34 459
Shelter	13 961	6 722	7 327	8 690	9 506	10 442	12 975	20 709
Owned dwellings	9 112	2 004	2 052	3 497	4 001	4 959	8 379	16 202
Rented dwellings	3 708	4 605	5 177	4 958	5 282	5 005	3 820	2 144
Other lodging	1 142	113	98	234	223	477	777	2 363
Utilities, fuels, and public services	4 711	2 606	3 022	3 614	3 762	4 290	4 876	6 070
Household operations	1 466	528	521	671	755	871	1 085	2 569
Housekeeping supplies	855	690	447	542	554	648	824	1 194
Household furnishings and equipment	2 364	896	744	1 050	1 282	1 579	2 137	3 917
Apparel and Services	2 316	888	1 192	1 467	1 439	1 503	2 047	3 626
Transportation	11 639	3 797	4 216	6 469	6 232	9 184	11 536	18 137
Vehicle purchases (net outlay)	4 646	[2]916	1 161	2 322	1 598	3 582	4 961	7 586
Gasoline and motor oil	2 560	1 086	1 405	1 948	1 915	2 258	2 637	3 492
Other vehicle expenses	3 471	1 531	1 349	1 855	2 430	2 741	3 250	5 286
Public and other transportation	962	264	301	344	289	603	688	1 773
Health Care	5 011	1 493	2 181	2 913	3 343	3 791	5 325	7 491
Health insurance	3 415	987	1 389	1 979	2 296	2 628	3 693	5 093
Medical services	957	242	398	412	669	653	974	1 510
Drugs	468	230	311	438	316	394	464	619
Medical supplies	171	34	84	84	63	117	194	268
Entertainment	4 008	1 141	1 279	1 468	2 595	2 676	3 314	6 843
Personal Care Products and Services	939	338	326	478	654	657	895	1 479
Reading	106	30	30	37	60	65	144	160
Education	3 013	183	595	477	754	1 253	1 814	6 287
Tobacco Products and Smoking Supplies	424	490	577	562	582	460	444	294
Miscellaneous	1 192	565	536	598	599	1 020	1 100	1 821
Cash Contributions	2 219	464	681	731	1 008	1 189	1 522	4 169
Personal Insurance and Pensions	10 304	451	1 546	2 975	3 973	5 721	8 324	19 728
Life and other personal insurance	553	113	179	197	216	299	455	1 005
Pensions and Social Security	9 751	338	1 366	2 778	3 757	5 422	7 869	18 723

[1]Value too small to display.
[2]Data are likely to have large sampling errors.

Table 11-23. Consumer Expenditures, Averages for Age Groups by Income Before Taxes: Reference Person 55 to 64 Years of Age, 2017–2018

(Number, dollar, percent.)

Item	Complete reporting of income							
	Total	Less than $15,000	$15,000 to $29,999	$30,000 to $39,999	$40,000 to $49,999	$50,000 to $69,999	$70,000 to $99,999	$100,000 or more
NUMBER OF CONSUMER UNITS (THOUSANDS)	24 597	3 464	3 417	2 000	1 819	2 930	3 429	7 537
CONSUMER UNIT CHARACTERISTICS								
Income Before Taxes	86 681	7 401	22 519	34 625	44 885	59 309	84 403	187 783
Income After Taxes	72 431	7 593	22 407	33 566	42 012	53 375	74 517	149 020
Age of Reference Person	59.4	59.5	59.9	59.8	59.6	59.4	59.5	59.0
Average Number in Consumer Unit								
All persons	2.2	1.5	1.8	2.1	2.1	2.2	2.5	2.7
Children under 18 years	0.2	0.1	0.1	0.2	0.2	0.2	0.2	0.2
Persons 65 years and over	0.1	0.1	0.1	0.2	0.1	0.1	0.1	0.1
Earners	1.4	0.4	0.7	1.1	1.3	1.5	1.8	2.1
Vehicles	2.2	1.1	1.6	1.9	1.9	2.3	2.5	3.0
Percent Distribution								
Male	49	43	40	43	45	46	51	59
Female	51	57	60	57	55	54	49	41
Percent Homeowner	77	48	59	72	72	83	87	94
With mortgage	44	17	23	29	41	47	55	62
Without mortgage	33	31	36	43	31	36	32	32
AVERAGE ANNUAL EXPENDITURES	65 528	26 618	33 083	40 137	46 018	54 774	66 165	113 405
Food	7 959	4 053	4 701	5 929	6 313	7 413	8 421	12 150
Food at home	4 710	2 863	3 249	3 870	3 893	4 544	5 061	6 522
Cereals and bakery products	591	352	422	507	483	582	616	816
Meats, poultry, fish, and eggs	1 062	699	726	922	1 030	1 010	1 104	1 426
Dairy products	458	276	318	342	360	454	499	641
Fruits and vegetables	882	486	571	729	647	831	977	1 272
Other food at home	1 716	1 050	1 211	1 369	1 374	1 667	1 865	2 366
Food away from home	3 248	1 190	1 452	2 059	2 420	2 869	3 360	5 628
Alcoholic Beverages	625	171	217	318	384	422	616	1 253
Housing	20 504	10 404	12 700	13 994	15 796	18 527	20 789	32 152
Shelter	11 731	6 027	7 112	7 321	8 818	9 618	11 546	19 226
Owned dwellings	8 377	2 918	3 381	4 219	5 064	6 945	8 853	15 394
Rented dwellings	2 290	2 989	3 500	2 652	3 374	1 971	1 944	1 346
Other lodging	1 064	120	231	450	380	701	750	2 487
Utilities, fuels, and public services	4 363	2 590	3 241	3 879	3 767	4 274	4 694	5 842
Household operations	1 217	502	623	717	760	1 005	1 135	2 178
Housekeeping supplies	837	441	542	660	596	749	840	1 296
Household furnishings and equipment	2 357	844	1 183	1 417	1 855	2 882	2 573	3 610
Apparel and Services	1 779	873	822	1 418	1 489	1 254	1 638	3 098
Transportation	10 314	3 473	5 237	6 741	7 790	8 772	9 892	18 101
Vehicle purchases (net outlay)	4 294	1 112	2 108	2 699	3 118	3 441	3 229	8 269
Gasoline and motor oil	2 166	990	1 277	1 746	1 983	2 176	2 653	3 038
Other vehicle expenses	3 026	1 189	1 579	2 055	2 285	2 628	3 344	4 964
Public and other transportation	828	181	273	241	404	526	667	1 830
Health Care	5 714	2 525	3 278	4 217	4 221	5 433	6 402	8 835
Health insurance	3 786	1 663	2 130	2 869	2 828	3 562	4 335	5 825
Medical services	1 170	480	612	681	778	1 113	1 244	1 952
Drugs	573	320	422	545	463	597	602	767
Medical supplies	185	62	114	122	151	161	221	291
Entertainment	3 598	1 879	1 690	2 001	2 007	2 811	4 235	6 026
Personal Care Products and Services	768	310	345	523	637	671	800	1 293
Reading	110	38	67	57	76	87	107	196
Education	1 688	345	350	269	382	494	1 028	4 369
Tobacco Products and Smoking Supplies	436	392	548	588	464	450	484	331
Miscellaneous	1 195	615	808	671	1 535	948	824	1 967
Cash Contributions	2 261	565	782	812	1 299	1 447	1 983	4 769
Personal Insurance and Pensions	8 579	976	1 539	2 600	3 624	6 043	8 946	18 866
Life and other personal insurance	635	216	306	447	394	476	643	1 144
Pensions and Social Security	7 944	760	1 234	2 153	3 230	5 568	8 303	17 721

Table 11-24. Consumer Expenditures, Averages for Age Groups by Income Before Taxes: Reference Person 65 Years of Age and Over, 2017–2018

(Number, dollar, percent.)

Item	Complete reporting of income							
	Total	Less than $15,000	$15,000 to $29,999	$30,000 to $39,999	$40,000 to $49,999	$50,000 to $69,999	$70,000 to $99,999	$100,000 or more
NUMBER OF CONSUMER UNITS (THOUSANDS)	32 378	4 991	9 537	4 566	3 040	3 727	3 076	3 441
CONSUMER UNIT CHARACTERISTICS								
Income Before Taxes	50 385	9 647	21 976	34 897	44 780	59 140	83 526	174 628
Income After Taxes	45 550	9 712	21 898	34 656	43 848	56 787	76 709	139 030
Age of Reference Person	74.3	75.9	76.2	74.4	73.2	73.1	71.9	70.9
Average Number in Consumer Unit								
All persons	1.8	1.3	1.4	1.9	1.9	2.1	2.2	2.4
Children under 18 years	0.1	([1])	([1])	0.1	([1])	0.1	0.1	0.1
Persons 65 years and over	1.4	1.1	1.2	1.6	1.6	1.6	1.5	1.6
Earners	0.5	0.1	0.2	0.3	0.5	0.8	1.1	1.4
Vehicles	1.8	0.9	1.4	1.9	2.0	2.2	2.3	2.7
Percent Distribution								
Male	46	36	38	47	48	54	56	61
Female	54	64	62	53	52	46	44	39
Percent Homeowner	80	58	76	87	88	87	90	91
With mortgage	24	11	16	22	29	28	38	42
Without mortgage	56	47	60	64	59	59	52	49
AVERAGE ANNUAL EXPENDITURES	50 165	25 964	34 100	47 841	52 564	56 402	65 446	107 395
Food	6 468	3 633	4 461	6 315	6 672	7 506	8 948	11 562
Food at home	3 913	2 434	3 006	3 986	3 896	4 438	5 138	6 171
Cereals and bakery products	519	317	395	555	538	615	677	760
Meats, poultry, fish, and eggs	815	457	639	807	789	963	1 044	1 336
Dairy products	414	253	322	433	391	464	566	637
Fruits and vegetables	773	515	605	731	730	862	1 051	1 231
Other food at home	1 392	893	1 046	1 460	1 449	1 534	1 800	2 207
Food away from home	2 555	1 199	1 455	2 329	2 775	3 069	3 811	5 391
Alcoholic Beverages	452	169	195	393	484	592	651	1 148
Housing	16 787	10 418	12 961	15 136	17 306	18 788	20 765	32 174
Shelter	9 296	6 136	7 506	7 912	9 272	9 802	11 533	18 148
Owned dwellings	5 915	2 678	4 061	5 386	6 762	6 584	8 418	12 740
Rented dwellings	2 557	3 213	3 095	1 822	1 626	2 291	1 906	2 785
Other lodging	823	245	350	704	884	927	1 209	2 622
Utilities, fuels, and public services	3 690	2 436	3 020	3 747	4 050	4 161	4 640	5 617
Household operations	1 299	563	924	1 205	1 401	1 473	1 520	3 044
Housekeeping supplies	810	478	603	879	811	1 055	961	1 213
Household furnishings and equipment	1 693	805	908	1 393	1 771	2 297	2 111	4 152
Apparel and Services	1 200	500	748	966	1 057	1 271	1 753	2 997
Transportation	7 390	3 085	4 538	7 632	7 992	9 504	9 598	16 074
Vehicle purchases (net outlay)	2 759	1 033	1 533	3 308	2 657	3 976	3 640	5 919
Gasoline and motor oil	1 367	671	964	1 442	1 541	1 727	1 924	2 358
Other vehicle expenses	2 610	1 086	1 713	2 380	3 176	3 104	3 076	5 816
Public and other transportation	654	295	328	502	618	697	958	1 981
Health Care	6 684	3 999	5 161	7 235	7 586	8 049	8 307	10 281
Health insurance	4 716	2 916	3 765	5 255	5 253	5 635	5 770	6 833
Medical services	955	501	617	896	1 158	1 103	1 283	2 000
Drugs	776	422	588	905	883	1 026	943	1 059
Medical supplies	237	160	191	179	291	286	311	391
Entertainment	2 800	1 322	1 600	3 725	2 901	2 835	3 400	6 176
Personal Care Products and Services	676	338	492	640	751	720	881	1 383
Reading	156	95	109	157	117	196	196	312
Education	381	239	245	130	276	208	310	1 631
Tobacco Products and Smoking Supplies	207	179	164	193	261	222	284	256
Miscellaneous	1 037	404	604	1 306	1 245	978	1 359	2 358
Cash Contributions	2 529	906	1 645	1 979	2 455	2 419	3 470	7 412
Personal Insurance and Pensions	3 395	676	1 178	2 035	3 460	3 115	5 524	13 631
Life and other personal insurance	489	267	309	461	602	525	708	1 011
Pensions and Social Security	2 906	409	869	1 574	2 858	2 590	4 816	12 620

[1]Value too small to display.

CHAPTER 12: AMERICAN TIME USE SURVEY

HIGHLIGHTS

This chapter presents data from the American Time Use Survey (ATUS). The survey was introduced in the sixth edition of the *Handbook of U.S. Labor Statistics*. Its purpose is to collect data on the activities people do during the day and the amount of time they spend on each one.

Figure 12-1. Average Hours Spent per Day in Primary Activities for Persons Reporting the Activity on the Diary Day, 2018

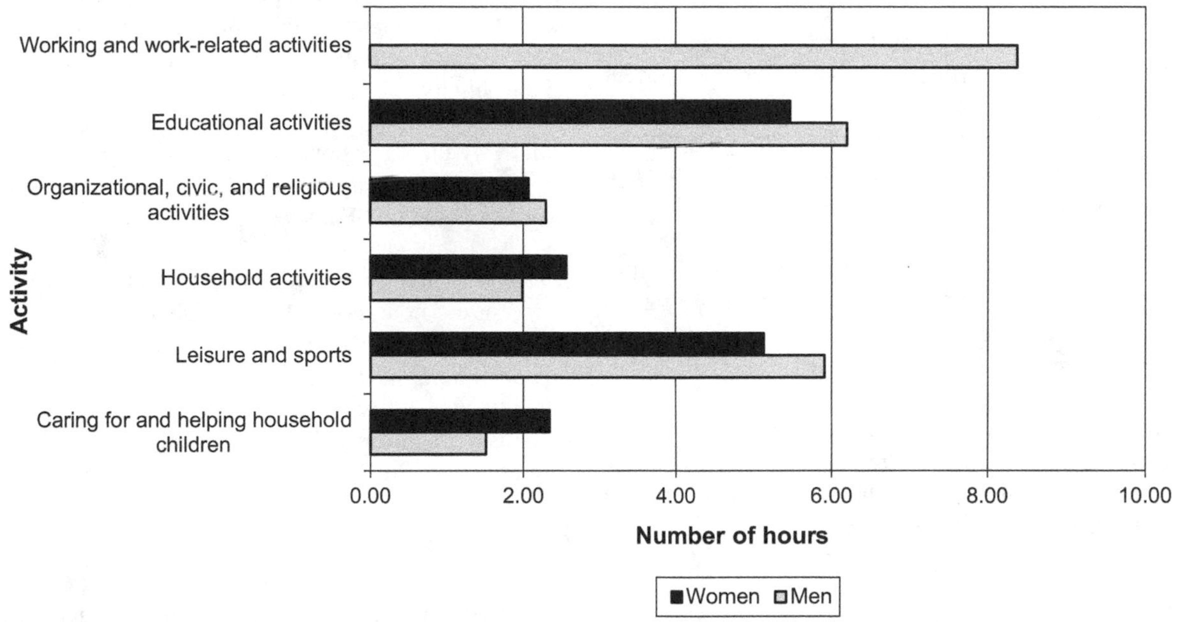

In 2018, on days that they worked, employed men worked 34 minutes more than employed women. Men also spent more time on leisure and sports; educational activities; and organizational, civic and religious activities. In contrast, women spent more time caring for and helping household members, purchasing goods and services, and household activities. (See Table 12-1.)

OTHER HIGHLIGHTS

- On an average day, 20 percent of men did housework—such as cleaning or laundry—compared with 49 percent of women. Forty-six percent of men did food preparation or cleanup, compared with 69 percent of women. Men were slightly more likely to engage in lawn and garden care than were women—11 percent, compared with 7 percent. (Table 12-1.)

- Hours spent in primary activities varied greatly by age. Persons aged 35 to 44 spent 4.08 hours in leisure activities compared with 7.75 hours for those 75 years and over. Specifically, individuals age 75 and over averaged 48 minutes of reading per day whereas individuals age 15 to 54 years read on average less than 10 minutes per day. (Table 12-2.)

- On the days they worked, nearly 82 percent of employed persons did some or all of their work at their workplace and 24 percent did some or all of their work at home. Employed persons spent more time working at the workplace than at home—7.9 hours compared with 2.9 hours. (Table 12-5.)

- On an average day in 2018, 24 percent of full-time employed workers spent some time working while at home. The share of full-time employed workers working at home rose from 19 percent per day in 2003 to 24 percent in 2009, and has remained relatively flat since then. (Table 12-5.)

NOTES AND DEFINITIONS

Survey Methodology

While the Bureau of Labor Statistics (BLS) has long produced statistics about the labor market, including information about employment, hours, and earnings, the American Time Use Survey (ATUS) marks the first time that a federal statistical agency has produced estimates on how Americans spend another critical resource—their time. Data collection for the ATUS began in January 2003. Sample cases for the survey are selected monthly, and interviews are conducted continuously throughout the year. In 2018, approximately 9,600 individuals were interviewed.

ATUS sample households are chosen from the households that have completed their eighth (final) interview for the Current Population Survey (CPS), the nation's monthly household labor force survey. (See Chapter 1 of this *Handbook* for a description of the CPS.) ATUS sample households are selected to ensure that estimates will be representative of the nation.

An individual age 15 years or older is randomly chosen from each sample household. This "designated person" takes part in a one-time telephone interview about his or her activities on the previous day (the "diary day").

All ATUS interviews are conducted using Computer Assisted Telephone Interviewing. Procedures are in place to collect information from the small number of households that did not provide a telephone number during the CPS interview.

ATUS designated persons are preassigned a day of the week about which to report. Preassignment is designed to reduce variability in response rates across the week and to allow oversampling of weekend days so that accurate weekend day measures can be developed. Interviews occur on the day following the assigned day. For example, a person assigned to report about a Monday would be contacted on the following Tuesday. Ten percent of designated persons are assigned to report about each of the five weekdays. Twenty five percent are assigned to report about each weekend day. Households are called for up to 8 consecutive weeks (for example, 8 Tuesdays) in order to secure an interview.

Concepts and Definitions

Average day reflects an average distribution across all persons in the reference population and all days of the week. Average day measures for the entire population provide a mechanism for seeing the overall distribution of time allocation for society as a whole. The ATUS collects data about daily activities from all segments of the population age 15 and over, including persons who are employed and not employed. Many activities are not typically done on a daily basis, and some activities are only done by a subset of the population.

Average hours per day refers to time spent in a 24-hour day (between 4 a.m. on the diary day and 4 a.m. on the interview day) doing a specified activity.

Average hours per day, persons reporting the activity on the diary day is computed using responses only from those engaged in the particular activity on the diary day.

Average hours per day, population is computed using all responses from the sample population, including those from respondents who did not do the particular activity on their diary day. These estimates reflect the total number of respondents engaged in an activity and the total amount of time they spent on the activity.

Diary day the day about which the designated person reports. For example, the diary day of a designated person interviewed on Tuesday would be Monday.

Household children refers to children under 18 years of age who reside in the household of the ATUS respondent. The children may be related to the respondent (such as their own children, grandchildren, nieces, nephews, brothers, or sisters) or not related (such as foster children or children of roommates). For secondary childcare calculations, respondents are asked about care of household children under 13 years of age.

Earnings

Usual weekly earnings represent the earnings of full-time wage and salary workers before taxes and other deductions and include any overtime pay, commissions, or tips usually received (at the main job in the case of multiple jobholders). Usual weekly earnings are only updated in ATUS for about a third of employed respondents—if the respondent changed jobs or employment status or if the CPS weekly earnings value was imputed. This means that the earnings information could be out of date because the CPS interview was done 2 to 5 months prior to the ATUS interview. Respondents are asked to identify the easiest way for them to report earnings (hourly, weekly, biweekly, twice monthly, annually, or other) and how much they usually earn in the reported time period. Earnings reported on a basis other than weekly are converted to a weekly equivalent. The term "usual" is as perceived by the respondent. If the respondent asks for a definition of usual, interviewers are instructed to define the term as more than half the weeks worked during the past 4 or 5 months.

Weekly earnings ranges refers to The ranges used represent approximately 25 percent of full-time wage and salary workers. For example, 25 percent of full-time wage and salary workers with one job only had weekly earnings of $500 or less. These dollar values vary from year to year.

Employment Status

Employed persons are those who, at any time during the seven days prior to the interview: 1) did any work at all as paid employees, worked in their own business professions, or on their own farms, or usually worked 15 hours or more an unpaid workers in family-operated enterprises; and 2) all those who were not working but had jobs or businesses from which they were temporarily absent due to illness, bad weather, vacation, childcare problems, labor-management disputes, maternity or paternity leave, job training, or other family or personal reasons, whether or not they were paid for the time off or were seeking other jobs.

Employed full time workers are those who usually work 35 hours or more per week at all jobs combined.

Employed part time workers are those who usually work fewer than 35 hours per week at all jobs combined.

Not employed includes persons are not employed if they do not meet the conditions for employment. Not employed workers include those classified as unemployed as well as those classified as not in the labor force (using CPS definitions).

The numbers of employed and not employed persons in this report do not correspond to published totals from the CPS. While the information on employment from the ATUS is useful for assessing work in the context of other daily activities, the employment data are not intended for analysis of current employment trends. Compared to the CPS and other estimates of employment, the ATUS estimates are based on a much smaller sample and are only available with a substantial lag.

Major Activity Category Definitions

Caring for and helping household members refers to time spent doing activities to care for or help any child (under age 18) or adult in the household, regardless of relationship to the respondent or the physical or mental health status of the person being helped, is classified here. Caring for and helping activities for household children and adults are coded separately in subcategories.

Caring for and helping non-household members includes time spent caring for and helping any child or adult who is not part of the respondent's household, regardless of the relationship to the respondent or the physical or mental health status of the person being helped, is classified in this category.

Eating and drinking includes all time spent eating or drinking (except when identified by the respondent as part of a work or volunteer activity), whether alone, with others, at home, at a place of purchase, in transit, or somewhere else, is classified in this category.

*Educational activitie*s include taking classes (including Internet and other distance-learning courses), doing research and homework, and taking care of administrative tasks, such as registering for classes or obtaining a school ID. For high school students, before- and after-school extracurricular activities (except sports) also are classified as educational activities.

Household activities are those done by respondents to maintain their households. These include housework, cooking, yard care, pet care, vehicle maintenance and repair, and home maintenance, repair, decoration, and renovation. Food preparation is always classified as a household activity.

Leisure and sports includes sports, exercise, and recreation; socializing and communicating; and other leisure activities, such as watching television, reading or attending entertainment events.

Organizational, civic, and religious activities captures time spent volunteering for or through an organization, performing civic obligations, and participating in religious and spiritual activities.

Other activities, not elsewhere classified includes security procedures related to traveling, traveling not associated with a specific activity category, ambiguous activities that could not be coded, or missing activities that were considered too private to report.

Personal care activities consist of sleeping, bathing, dressing, health-related self-care, and personal or private activities. Receiving unpaid personal care from others (for example, "my sister put polish on my nails") is also captured in this category.

Primary activity is the main activity of a respondent at a specified time.

Purchasing goods and service includes the purchase of consumer goods as well as the purchase or use of professional and personal care services, household services, and government services. Most purchases and rentals of consumer goods, regardless of mode or place of purchase or rental are classified in this category.

Secondary activity is an activity done at the same time as a primary activity. With the exception of the care of children under age 13, information on secondary activities is not systematically collected in the ATUS.

Telephone calls, mail, and email captures telephone communication and handling household or personal mail and email. Telephone and Internet purchases are classified in purchasing goods and services.

Working and work-related activities refers to time spent working, doing activities as part of one's job, engaging in income-generating activities (not as part of one's job), and job search activities. "Working" includes hours spent doing the specific tasks required of one's main or other job, regardless of location or time of day. Travel time related to working and work-related activities includes time spent commuting to and from one's job, as well as time spent traveling for work-related activities, generating income, and job searching.

Sources of Additional Information

Additional information, including expanded definitions and estimation methodology, is available from BLS news release USDL 19-1003 "American Time Use Survey—2018 Results" which is available on the BLS Web site at <http://www.bls.gov/tus/>.

Table 12-1. Average Hours Per Day Spent in Primary Activities[1] for the Total Population and for Persons Reporting the Activity on the Diary Day, by Activity Category and Sex, 2017 and 2018 Annual Averages

(Hours, percent.)

Activity	Hours per day, total population			Percent of population reporting the activity on the diary day			Hours per day for persons reporting the activity on the diary day		
	Both sexes	Men	Women	Both sexes	Men	Women	Both sexes	Men	Women
2017									
All Activities[2]	24.00	24.00	24.00	X	X	X	X	X	X
Personal care activities	9.59	9.35	9.81	100.0	100.0	100.0	9.59	9.35	9.81
Sleeping	8.80	8.70	8.90	99.9	99.9	99.9	8.81	8.70	8.91
Eating and drinking	1.18	1.22	1.14	95.1	95.3	95.0	1.24	1.28	1.20
Household activities	1.81	1.41	2.19	76.2	68.0	84.0	2.38	2.07	2.61
Housework	0.55	0.23	0.85	34.4	18.6	49.3	1.60	1.26	1.73
Food preparation and cleanup	0.60	0.36	0.83	57.6	45.7	68.9	1.04	0.79	1.20
Lawn and garden care	0.18	0.25	0.11	9.7	11.4	8.0	1.84	2.18	1.39
Household management	0.13	0.12	0.14	18.7	15.7	21.6	0.69	0.77	0.64
Purchasing goods and services	0.72	0.60	0.83	43.8	39.0	48.4	1.64	1.54	1.72
Consumer goods purchases	0.35	0.27	0.42	40.2	35.5	44.6	0.86	0.76	0.94
Professional and personal care services	0.08	0.07	0.10	7.3	5.6	8.8	1.12	1.19	1.08
Caring for and helping household members	0.52	0.36	0.68	24.6	20.0	29.0	2.13	1.79	2.34
Caring for and helping household children	0.40	0.26	0.53	20.1	15.6	24.3	1.99	1.69	2.17
Caring for and helping non-household members	0.18	0.15	0.22	10.4	8.7	12.1	1.76	1.70	1.81
Caring for and helping non-household adults	0.07	0.06	0.08	7.2	6.3	8.1	0.98	0.99	0.97
Working and work-related activities	3.59	4.32	2.89	43.6	50.0	37.7	8.21	8.66	7.67
Working	3.23	3.89	2.62	42.0	48.3	36.1	7.69	8.04	7.25
Educational activities	0.48	0.52	0.45	8.6	9.3	8.0	5.63	5.57	5.70
Attending class	0.26	0.29	0.23	5.2	5.5	4.9	4.94	5.29	4.58
Homework and research	0.18	0.18	0.17	6.0	6.4	5.6	2.97	2.89	3.06
Organizational, civic, and religious activities	0.33	0.26	0.39	14.0	10.2	17.5	2.35	2.53	2.25
Religious and spiritual activities	0.13	0.11	0.16	9.3	6.8	11.7	1.44	1.64	1.34
Volunteering (organizational and civic activities)	0.15	0.12	0.19	6.1	4.5	7.6	2.53	2.64	2.47
Leisure and sports	5.24	5.53	4.98	95.6	95.6	95.6	5.48	5.78	5.21
Socializing and communicating	0.65	0.60	0.70	35.7	33.3	37.9	1.84	1.81	1.85
Watching television	2.77	2.95	2.59	77.7	78.7	76.7	3.56	3.75	3.38
Participating in sports, exercise, and recreation	0.29	0.35	0.23	19.0	20.2	17.8	1.51	1.73	1.27
Telephone calls, mail, and e-mail	0.15	0.11	0.19	19.7	15.1	24.0	0.75	0.70	0.78
Other activities n.e.c.	0.20	0.18	0.22	17.1	15.8	18.4	1.20	1.16	1.22
2018									
All Activities[2]	24.00	24.00	24.00	X	X	X	X	X	X
Personal care activities	9.58	9.35	9.78	100.0	100.0	100.0	9.58	9.36	9.78
Sleeping	8.82	8.75	8.87	99.9	99.9	99.9	8.82	8.76	8.88
Eating and drinking	1.19	1.23	1.15	95.6	95.6	95.6	1.24	1.28	1.21
Household activities	1.78	1.36	2.17	76.7	68.5	84.4	2.32	1.99	2.57
Housework	0.55	0.24	0.83	34.8	20.2	48.5	1.57	1.20	1.71
Food preparation and cleanup	0.59	0.37	0.80	57.6	45.9	68.6	1.02	0.80	1.17
Lawn and garden care	0.18	0.25	0.11	8.8	11.0	6.8	2.02	2.28	1.61
Household management	0.14	0.12	0.16	19.1	15.6	22.4	0.73	0.75	0.71
Purchasing goods and services	0.72	0.61	0.82	43.6	40.2	46.9	1.65	1.52	1.76
Consumer goods purchases	0.33	0.25	0.41	39.7	36.6	42.7	0.84	0.69	0.96
Professional and personal care services	0.09	0.08	0.10	7.4	5.8	9.0	1.24	1.40	1.15
Caring for and helping household members	0.51	0.32	0.70	24.1	19.2	28.7	2.14	1.67	2.43
Caring for and helping household children	0.39	0.22	0.54	19.1	14.9	23.0	2.02	1.51	2.34
Caring for and helping non-household members	0.21	0.19	0.24	11.4	9.7	12.9	1.89	1.97	1.83
Caring for and helping non-household adults	0.07	0.08	0.07	7.2	6.4	8.0	1.00	1.24	0.82
Working and work-related activities	3.57	4.16	3.02	44.1	49.7	38.9	8.09	8.37	7.75
Working	3.23	3.75	2.75	42.5	47.6	37.6	7.61	7.87	7.30
Educational activities	0.46	0.49	0.43	7.9	7.9	7.8	5.83	6.20	5.47
Attending class	0.25	0.28	0.22	4.9	5.2	4.6	5.08	5.28	4.86
Homework and research	0.17	0.18	0.17	5.9	5.8	6.1	2.95	3.06	2.84
Organizational, civic, and religious activities	0.30	0.26	0.35	14.1	11.4	16.7	2.16	2.30	2.07
Religious and spiritual activities	0.14	0.11	0.17	9.8	7.5	11.9	1.44	1.47	1.42
Volunteering (organizational and civic activities)	0.13	0.12	0.14	5.7	5.1	6.3	2.25	2.29	2.21
Leisure and sports	5.27	5.69	4.87	95.6	96.2	94.9	5.51	5.91	5.13
Socializing and communicating	0.64	0.59	0.69	35.0	32.3	37.6	1.83	1.83	1.82
Watching television	2.84	3.09	2.61	78.4	79.1	77.7	3.63	3.91	3.36
Participating in sports, exercise, and recreation	0.29	0.36	0.23	19.1	21.1	17.2	1.51	1.68	1.31
Telephone calls, mail, and e-mail	0.15	0.09	0.20	19.2	14.8	23.4	0.76	0.62	0.84
Other activities n.e.c.	0.26	0.24	0.28	21.0	19.6	22.3	1.24	1.24	1.24

Note: Data refer to respondents age 15 years and over, unless otherwise specified.

n.e.c. = Not elsewhere classified.

[1]A primary activity is designated by a respondent as his or her main activity. Other activities done simultaneously are not included.
[2]All major activity categories include related travel time.
X = Not applicable.

Table 12-2. Average Hours Per Day Spent in Primary Activities[1] for the Total Population, by Age, Sex, Race, Hispanic Origin, and Educational Attainment, 2018 Annual Averages

(Hours.)

Characteristic	Hours per day spent in primary activities[2]											
	Personal care activities	Eating and drinking	Household activities	Purchasing goods and services	Caring for and helping household members	Caring for and helping non-household members	Working and work-related activities	Edu-cational activities	Organiza-tional, civic, and religious activities	Leisure activities	Telephone calls, mail, and e-mail	Other activities n.e.c.
Both Sexes, 15 Years and Over	9.58	1.19	1.78	0.72	0.51	0.21	3.57	0.46	0.30	5.27	0.15	0.26
15 to 19 years	10.34	1.17	0.84	0.53	0.17	0.12	1.22	3.06	0.29	5.79	0.19	0.29
20 to 24 years	9.96	1.12	1.12	0.49	0.38	0.16	3.52	1.70	0.13	5.02	0.16	0.24
25 to 34 years	9.54	1.14	1.53	0.66	0.99	0.15	5.01	0.28	0.14	4.22	0.09	0.24
35 to 44 years	9.26	1.13	1.80	0.62	1.18	0.11	5.08	0.09	0.27	4.08	0.09	0.29
45 to 54 years	9.30	1.17	1.83	0.89	0.41	0.23	4.93	0.04	0.34	4.54	0.12	0.20
55 to 64 years	9.40	1.18	2.10	0.79	0.16	0.31	3.79	0.05	0.35	5.49	0.13	0.25
65 to 74 years	9.65	1.28	2.45	0.84	0.16	0.42	1.05	0.03	0.42	7.17	0.22	0.30
75 years and over	9.90	1.41	2.14	0.83	0.12	0.19	0.49	*	0.58	7.75	0.27	0.31
Men, 15 Years and Over	9.35	1.23	1.36	0.61	0.32	0.19	4.16	0.49	0.26	5.69	0.09	0.24
15 to 19 years	9.94	1.16	0.73	0.39	0.11	0.09	1.24	3.61	0.24	6.09	0.13	0.26
20 to 24 years	9.96	1.09	0.69	0.38	0.10	0.14	3.75	1.58	*	5.90	0.09	0.22
25 to 34 years	9.27	1.18	1.07	0.58	0.47	0.19	5.88	0.24	0.12	4.72	0.07	0.22
35 to 44 years	9.08	1.15	1.28	0.50	0.72	0.12	6.05	0.03	0.28	4.46	0.05	0.30
45 to 54 years	9.07	1.25	1.34	0.71	0.39	0.16	5.67	0.03	0.24	4.88	0.07	0.20
55 to 64 years	9.25	1.22	1.78	0.70	0.12	0.24	4.18	*	0.29	5.88	0.08	0.23
65 to 74 years	9.41	1.34	2.03	0.76	0.18	0.39	1.29	*	0.34	7.81	0.15	0.26
75 years and over	9.56	1.52	1.89	0.83	0.08	0.17	0.71	*	0.64	8.12	0.18	0.29
Women, 15 Years and Over	9.78	1.15	2.17	0.82	0.70	0.24	3.02	0.43	0.35	4.87	0.20	0.28
15 to 19 years	10.74	1.18	0.94	0.67	0.23	0.15	1.20	2.49	0.33	5.49	0.26	0.33
20 to 24 years	9.95	1.14	1.56	0.61	0.66	0.18	3.29	1.82	0.16	4.13	*	0.27
25 to 34 years	9.82	1.10	1.99	0.74	1.52	0.11	4.16	0.31	0.15	3.72	0.12	0.26
35 to 44 years	9.43	1.12	2.30	0.74	1.61	0.10	4.15	0.14	0.27	3.71	0.14	0.29
45 to 54 years	9.52	1.10	2.31	1.06	0.43	0.30	4.22	0.04	0.44	4.21	0.17	0.20
55 to 64 years	9.53	1.15	2.40	0.87	0.19	0.37	3.43	0.08	0.40	5.13	0.18	0.26
65 to 74 years	9.86	1.22	2.82	0.92	0.15	0.44	0.85	0.03	0.49	6.60	0.29	0.33
75 years and over	10.15	1.33	2.32	0.83	0.16	0.20	*	*	0.54	7.48	34.00	0.33
White, 15 Years and Over	9.50	1.22	1.87	0.73	0.51	0.23	3.56	0.42	0.28	5.28	0.13	0.26
Men	9.26	1.26	1.47	0.61	0.33	0.21	4.24	0.45	0.24	5.62	0.08	0.24
Women	9.72	1.19	2.25	0.85	0.69	0.25	2.92	0.39	0.32	4.96	0.18	0.28
Black, 15 Years and Over	9.77	0.93	1.32	0.65	0.48	0.18	3.36	0.62	0.50	5.73	0.19	0.26
Men	9.67	0.94	0.87	0.56	0.25	0.15	3.39	0.76	0.48	6.55	0.12	0.26
Women	9.86	0.92	1.70	0.72	0.67	0.20	3.34	0.50	0.52	5.05	0.26	0.26
Asian, 15 Years and Over	10.03	1.36	1.58	0.71	0.65	0.13	4.32	0.55	0.18	4.00	0.22	0.28
Men	9.95	1.48	0.96	0.70	0.40	0.11	4.65	*	0.12	4.59	0.13	0.24
Women	10.11	1.22	2.27	0.72	0.93	0.15	3.95	*	0.24	3.33	*	0.34
Hispanic,[3] 15 Years and Over	9.86	1.20	1.90	0.68	0.64	0.12	3.67	0.49	0.26	4.82	0.13	0.23
Men	9.63	1.24	1.27	0.53	0.34	0.14	4.58	0.52	0.22	5.20	0.11	0.22
Women	10.09	1.15	2.52	0.83	0.93	0.11	2.76	0.47	0.29	4.45	0.14	0.25
Marital Status and Sex												
Married, spouse present	9.30	1.26	2.12	0.78	0.74	0.24	3.89	0.05	0.34	4.88	0.12	0.26
Men	9.06	1.31	1.64	0.68	0.51	0.21	4.66	0.04	0.31	5.25	0.08	0.25
Women	9.54	1.22	2.60	0.88	0.97	0.28	3.13	0.07	0.36	4.52	0.15	0.27
Other marital statuses	9.86	1.11	1.42	0.66	0.28	0.19	3.25	0.87	0.27	5.66	0.18	0.26
Men	9.67	1.13	1.07	0.54	0.12	0.17	3.63	0.98	0.21	6.15	0.11	0.23
Women	10.02	1.09	1.74	0.77	0.42	0.20	2.90	0.78	0.33	5.22	0.24	0.28
Educational Attainment, 25 Years and Over												
Less than a high school diploma	10.25	1.00	2.19	0.70	0.61	0.17	2.12	*	0.37	6.34	0.09	0.15
High school graduate, no college[4]	9.60	1.13	1.96	0.75	0.45	0.28	3.37	0.05	0.29	5.77	0.10	0.26
Some college or associate degree	9.41	1.14	1.97	0.74	0.53	0.27	3.88	0.12	0.31	5.20	0.17	0.25
Bachelor's degree and higher[5]	9.21	1.33	1.82	0.80	0.65	0.18	4.48	0.13	0.35	4.59	0.17	0.29
Some college or associate degree	9.20	1.33	1.92	0.75	0.62	0.19	4.43	0.09	0.34	4.67	0.16	0.30
Bachelor's degree and higher	9.23	1.33	1.67	0.87	0.69	0.16	4.56	0.19	0.36	4.47	0.18	0.27

Note: 0.00 = Estimates are approximately zero.

[1]A primary activity is designated by a respondent as his or her main activity. Other activities done simultaneously are not included.
[2]All major activity categories include related travel time.
[3]May be of any race.
[4]Includes persons with a high school diploma or equivalent.
[5]Includes persons with bachelor's, master's, professional, and doctoral degrees.
* = Figure does not meet standards of reliability or quality.

Table 12-3. Average Hours Worked Per Day by Employed Persons on Weekdays and Weekends, by Selected Characteristics, 2018 Annual Averages

(Number, percent.)

Characteristic	Total employed (thousands)	Employed persons who worked on an average day			Employed persons who worked on an average weekday			Employed persons who worked on an average Saturday, Sunday, or holiday[1]		
		Number (thousands)	Percent of employed	Hours per day[2]	Number[3] (thousands)	Percent of employed	Hours per day[2]	Number[4] (thousands)	Percent of employed	Hours per day[2]
Both Sexes[5]	165 269	110 785	67.0	7.62	135 994	82.3	7.99	50 885	30.8	5.27
Full-time worker	130 608	92 999	71.2	8.10	115 901	88.7	8.50	39 874	30.5	5.39
Part-time worker	34 662	17 785	51.3	5.10	20 373	58.8	5.17	11 041	31.9	4.81
Men[5]	85 959	60 191	70.0	7.88	73 581	85.6	8.27	28 567	33.2	5.49
Full-time worker	72 929	52 922	72.6	8.23	65 210	89.4	8.65	24 121	33.1	5.58
Part-time worker	13 030	7 269	55.8	5.32	8 412	64.6	5.39	4 450	34.2	5.00
Women[5]	79 311	50 594	63.8	7.31	62 424	78.7	7.66	22 299	28.1	4.99
Full-time worker	57 679	40 077	69.5	7.93	50 688	87.9	8.31	15 783	27.4	5.10
Part-time worker	21 632	10 517	48.6	4.96	11 980	55.4	5.01	6 570	30.4	4.67
Multiple Job Holding Status										
Single job holder	151 967	100 420	66.1	7.59	124 082	81.7	7.94	42 704	28.1	5.14
Multiple job holder	13 302	10 364	77.9	7.90	12 014	90.3	8.59	7 410	55.7	5.90
Educational Attainment, 25 Years and Over										
Less than a high school diploma	8 126	4 824	59.4	7.50	6 227	76.6	7.70	2 431	29.9	6.62
High school graduate, no college[6]	37 439	24 300	64.9	8.07	29 693	79.3	8.29	10 757	28.7	6.52
Some college or associate degree	33 763	23 386	69.3	7.90	28 783	85.3	8.19	9 457	28.0	5.60
Bachelor's degree or higher[7]	63 427	46 035	72.6	7.36	56 640	89.3	7.90	21 259	33.5	4.03

Note: Data refer to persons age 15 years and over, unless otherwise specified.

[1]Holidays are New Year's Day, Easter, Memorial Day, the Fourth of July, Labor Day, Thanksgiving Day, and Christmas Day.
[2]Includes work at main and other job(s) and excludes travel related to work.
[3]Number was derived by multiplying the "total employed" by the percentage of employed persons who worked on an average weekday.
[4]Number was derived by multiplying the "total employed" by the percentage of employed persons who worked on an average Saturday, Sunday, or holiday.
[5]Includes workers whose hours vary.
[6]Includes persons with a high school diploma or equivalent.
[7]Includes persons with bachelor's, master's, professional, and doctoral degrees.

Table 12-4. Average Hours Worked Per Day at Main Job Only by Employed Persons on Weekdays and Weekend Days, by Selected Characteristics, 2018 Annual Averages

(Number, percent.)

Characteristic	Total employed (thousands)	Worked on an average day			Worked on an average weekday			Worked on an average Saturday, Sunday, or holiday[1]		
		Number (thousands)	Percent	Hours per day[2]	Number[3] (thousands)	Percent	Hours per day[2]	Number[4] (thousands)	Percent	Hours per day[2]
Class of Worker										
Wage and salary workers	153 209	101 145	66.0	7.68	126 051	82.3	8.03	42 871	28.0	5.28
Self-employed workers[5]	11 985	7 902	65.9	5.98	8 932	74.5	6.30	4 925	41.1	4.36
Occupation										
Management, business, and financial operations	29 928	22 046	73.7	7.61	27 771	92.8	8.11	8 313	27.8	3.63
Professional and related	45 908	31 173	67.9	7.35	38 069	82.9	7.87	13 416	29.2	3.49
Services	26 566	16 227	61.1	7.12	18 454	69.5	7.24	10 506	39.5	6.61
Sales and related	12 982	8 273	63.7	7.24	9 817	75.6	7.54	5 245	40.4	6.15
Office and administrative support	18 931	11 725	61.9	7.63	15 495	81.9	7.78	3 851	20.3	6.32
Farming, fishing, and forestry	1 315	*	*	8.38	*	*	8.77	*	*	*
Construction and extraction	7 149	4 860	68.0	8.32	6 013	84.1	8.60	*	*	5.63
Installation, maintenance, and repair	4 970	3 629	73.0	8.40	*	*	8.59	*	*	5.51
Production	9 054	5 187	57.3	8.17	7 220	79.7	8.25	1 510	16.7	7.49
Transportation and material moving	8 466	5 023	59.3	8.23	6 502	76.8	8.34	1 906	22.5	7.50
Earnings of Full-Time Wage and Salary Earners[6]										
$0 to $630	27 323	17 733	64.9	7.94	22 296	81.6	8.15	7 613	27.9	6.62
$631 to $960	26 284	18 772	71.4	8.09	23 805	90.6	8.28	6 258	23.8	6.30
$961 to $1,530	28 388	19 147	67.4	8.32	24 779	87.3	8.64	5 864	20.7	5.22
$1,531 and higher	27 362	20 723	75.7	8.16	25 702	93.9	8.80	8 515	31.1	3.39

Note: Data refer to persons age 15 years and over, unless otherwise specified.

[1]Holidays are New Year's Day, Easter, Memorial Day, the Fourth of July, Labor Day, Thanksgiving Day, and Christmas Day.
[2]Includes work at main job only and excludes travel related to work.
[3]Number was derived by multiplying the "total employed" by the percentage of employed persons who worked on an average weekday.
[4]Number was derived by multiplying the "total employed" by the percentage of employed persons who worked on an average Saturday, Sunday, or holiday.
[5]Includes self-employed workers whose businesses are unincorporated. Self-employed workers whose businesses are incorporated are classified as wage and salary workers.
[6]These values are based on usual weekly earnings. Each earnings range represents approximately 25 percent of full-time wage and salary workers who held only one job.
* = Figure does not meet standards for reliability or quality.

Table 12-5. Average Hours Worked Per Day at All Jobs by Employed Persons at Workplaces or at Home, by Selected Characteristics, 2018 Annual Averages

(Number, percent.)

Characteristic	Total employed (thousands)	Employed persons who reported working on an average day[1]								
		Number (thousands)	Percent	Average hours of work	Location of work[2]					
					Persons who reported working at their workplaces on an average day			Persons who reported working at home on an average day[3]		
					Number (thousands)	Percent	Average hours of work at workplace	Number (thousands)	Percent	Average hours of work at home
Full- and Part-Time Status and Sex										
Both sexes[4]	165 269	110 785	67.0	7.62	90 515	81.7	7.94	26 240	23.7	2.94
Full-time worker	130 608	92 999	71.2	8.10	78 334	84.2	8.28	21 091	22.7	3.11
Part-time worker	34 662	17 785	51.3	5.10	12 181	68.5	5.75	5 149	28.9	2.25
Men[4]	85 959	60 191	70.0	7.88	50 443	83.8	8.04	14 017	23.3	3.11
Full-time worker	72 929	52 922	72.6	8.23	45 178	85.4	8.30	12 435	23.5	3.17
Part-time worker	13 030	7 269	55.8	5.32	5 265	72.4	5.78	1 581	21.8	2.64
Women[4]	79 311	50 594	63.8	7.31	40 072	79.2	7.82	12 223	24.2	2.74
Full-time worker	57 679	40 077	69.5	7.93	33 156	82.7	8.26	8 656	21.6	3.02
Part-time worker	21 632	10 517	48.6	4.96	6 916	65.8	5.73	3 567	33.9	2.08
Multiple Job Holding Status										
Single job holder	151 967	100 420	66.1	7.59	82 453	82.1	7.90	23 025	22.9	2.90
Multiple job holder	13 302	10 364	77.9	7.90	8 062	77.8	8.32	3 215	31.0	3.24
Educational Attainment, 25 Years and Over										
Less than a high school diploma	8 126	4 824	59.4	7.50	4 362	90.4	7.64	620	12.9	*
High school graduate, no college[5]	37 439	24 300	64.9	8.07	21 910	90.2	8.15	2 883	11.9	2.65
Some college or associate degree	33 763	23 386	69.3	7.90	19 875	85.0	8.05	4 876	20.8	3.09
Bachelor's degree or higher[6]	63 427	46 035	72.6	7.36	33 585	73.0	7.96	16 950	36.8	2.97
Bachelor's degree only	38 170	27 307	71.5	7.47	20 641	75.6	7.91	9 132	33.4	3.11
Advanced degree	25 257	18 728	74.2	7.20	12 944	69.1	8.03	7 818	41.7	2.80

Note: Data refer to persons age 15 years and over, unless otherwise specified.

[1]Includes work at main and other job(s) and excludes travel related to work.
[2]Respondents may have worked at more than one location.
[3]"Working at home" includes any time the respondent reported doing activities that were identified as "part of one's job"; this category is not restricted to persons whose usual workplace is their home.
[4]Includes workers whose hours vary.
[5]Includes persons with a high school diploma or equivalent.
[6]Includes persons with bachelor's, master's, professional, and doctoral degrees.
* = Figure does not meet standards for reliability or quality.

Table 12-6. Average Hours Worked Per Day at Main Job Only by Employed Persons at Workplaces or at Home, by Selected Characteristics, 2018 Annual Averages

(Number, percent.)

Characteristic	Total employed (thousands)	Employed persons who reported working on an average day[1]								
		Number (thousands)	Percent	Hours of work	Location of work[2]					
					Persons who reported working at their workplaces on an average day			Persons who reported working at home on an average day[3]		
					Number (thousands)	Percent	Hours of work at workplace	Number (thousands)	Percent	Hours of work at home
Class of Worker										
Wage and salary worker	153 209	101 145	66.0	7.68	85 409	84.4	7.95	20 847	20.6	2.73
Self-employed worker[3]	11 985	7 902	65.9	5.98	4 044	51.2	6.54	4 009	50.7	3.92
Occupation[4]										
Management, business, and financial operations	29 928	22 046	73.7	7.61	16 754	76.0	7.97	7 414	33.6	3.29
Professional and related	45 908	31 173	67.9	7.35	23 391	75.0	8.04	10 099	32.4	2.83
Services	26 566	16 227	61.1	7.12	14 170	87.3	7.33	1 625	10.0	2.60
Sales and related	12 982	8 273	63.7	7.24	6 220	75.2	7.52	2 268	27.4	3.35
Office and administrative support	18 931	11 725	61.9	7.63	10 635	90.7	7.81	1 763	15.0	2.75
Farming, fishing, and forestry	1 315	*	*	8.38	*	*	8.10	*	*	*
Construction and extraction	7 149	4 860	68.0	8.32	4 350	89.5	8.54	405	8.3	*
Installation, maintenance, and repair	4 970	3 629	73.0	8.40	3 385	93.3	7.98	*	*	*
Production	9 054	5 187	57.3	8.17	4 994	96.3	8.18	399	7.7	*
Transportation and material moving	8 466	5 023	59.3	8.23	4 661	92.8	8.12	352	7.0	1.73
Earnings of Full-Time Wage and Salary Earners[5]										
$0 to $630	27 323	17 733	64.9	7.94	16 543	93.3	7.85	1 394	7.9	2.62
$631 to $960	26 284	18 772	71.4	8.09	16 798	89.5	8.31	2 021	10.8	2.44
$961 to $1,530	28 388	19 147	67.4	8.32	16 460	86.0	8.53	4 402	23.0	2.60
$1,531 and higher	27 362	20 723	75.7	8.16	16 496	79.6	8.56	7 241	34.9	2.86

Note: Data refer to persons age 15 years and over, unless otherwise specified.

[1]Individuals may have worked at more than one location.
[2]Working at home includes any time persons did work at home and is not restricted to persons whose usual workplace is their home.
[3]Includes self-employed workers whose businesses are unincorporated. Self-employed workers whose businesses are incorporated are classified as wage and salary workers.
[4]These values were generated using the 2010 Census occupational classification system which was introduced with the 2011 estimates. Estimates are not strictly comparable to those from earlier years.
[5]These values are based on usual weekly earnings. Each earnings range covers approximately 25 percent of full-time wage and salary workers.
* = Figure does not meet standards for reliability or quality.

Table 12-7. Average Hours Per Day Spent by Persons Age 18 Years and Over Caring for Household Children Under 18 Years, by Sex of Respondent, Age of Youngest Household Child, and Day, 2014–2018 Combined Annual Averages

(Number.)

Activity	Hours per day caring for household children								
	Total			Weekdays			Weekends and holidays		
	Both sexes	Men	Women	Both sexes	Men	Women	Both sexes	Men	Women
Persons in Households with Children Under 18 Years									
Caring for household children as a primary activity	1.39	0.91	1.78	1.45	0.88	1.92	1.24	0.96	1.46
Physical care	0.44	0.23	0.61	0.46	0.23	0.64	0.40	0.23	0.53
Education-related activities	0.10	0.06	0.14	0.13	0.07	0.18	0.04	0.03	0.05
Reading to/with children	0.04	0.03	0.05	0.04	0.03	0.05	0.03	0.03	0.04
Talking to/with children	0.05	0.03	0.07	0.06	0.04	0.08	0.03	0.02	0.04
Playing/doing hobbies with children	0.29	0.26	0.32	0.25	0.22	0.29	0.37	0.35	0.38
Looking after children	0.09	0.06	0.12	0.08	0.05	0.11	0.11	0.09	0.14
Attending children's events	0.06	0.05	0.07	0.05	0.04	0.06	0.09	0.09	0.10
Travel related to care of household children	0.19	0.12	0.24	0.23	0.14	0.30	0.09	0.08	0.10
Other childcare activities	0.12	0.07	0.17	0.15	0.08	0.21	0.06	0.05	0.07
Persons in Households with Youngest Child 6 to 17 Years									
Caring for household children as a primary activity	0.83	0.55	1.06	0.90	0.56	1.19	0.64	0.53	0.74
Physical care	0.15	0.08	0.21	0.17	0.09	0.24	0.11	0.07	0.14
Education-related activities	0.12	0.07	0.16	0.15	0.08	0.20	0.05	0.04	0.06
Reading to/with children	0.02	0.01	0.02	0.02	0.01	0.02	0.01	0.01	0.02
Talking to/with children	0.06	0.04	0.08	0.07	0.05	0.09	0.04	0.02	0.06
Playing/doing hobbies with children	0.07	0.07	0.06	0.05	0.06	0.05	0.10	0.12	0.08
Looking after children	0.05	0.04	0.06	0.05	0.03	0.06	0.06	0.04	0.07
Attending children's events	0.08	0.07	0.10	0.06	0.05	0.08	0.13	0.11	0.14
Travel related to care of household children	0.17	0.11	0.22	0.20	0.13	0.26	0.09	0.07	0.11
Other childcare activities	0.10	0.06	0.14	0.12	0.06	0.17	0.06	0.05	0.06
Persons in Households with Youngest Child Under 6 Years									
Caring for household children as a primary activity	2.12	1.38	2.71	2.18	1.32	2.87	1.98	1.54	2.34
Physical care	0.81	0.43	1.12	0.83	0.42	1.16	0.76	0.46	1.00
Education-related activities	0.08	0.04	0.12	0.11	0.05	0.15	0.03	0.02	0.04
Reading to/with children	0.07	0.05	0.08	0.07	0.05	0.09	0.06	0.05	0.07
Talking to/with children	0.04	0.02	0.05	0.04	0.03	0.06	0.03	0.02	0.03
Playing/doing hobbies with children	0.58	0.50	0.64	0.52	0.44	0.59	0.71	0.65	0.76
Looking after children	0.14	0.09	0.19	0.12	0.07	0.17	0.19	0.15	0.22
Attending children's events	0.04	0.03	0.04	0.04	0.03	0.05	0.04	0.05	0.04
Travel related to care of household children	0.21	0.13	0.27	0.26	0.15	0.35	0.10	0.09	0.10
Other childcare activities	0.15	0.08	0.20	0.18	0.10	0.25	0.07	0.05	0.08

Note: Universe includes respondents age 18 years and over living in households with children under 18 years of age, whether or not they provided childcare.

CHAPTER 13: INCOME IN THE UNITED STATES (CENSUS BUREAU)

This chapter presents data on income and earnings in the United States collected by the Census Bureau. Income, as distinguished from earnings, includes income from pensions, investments, and other sources and is measured as real income in 2018 dollars.

Figure 13-1. Percent Distribution of Household Income, 1967–2018
(2018 CPI-U-RS-Adjusted dollars)

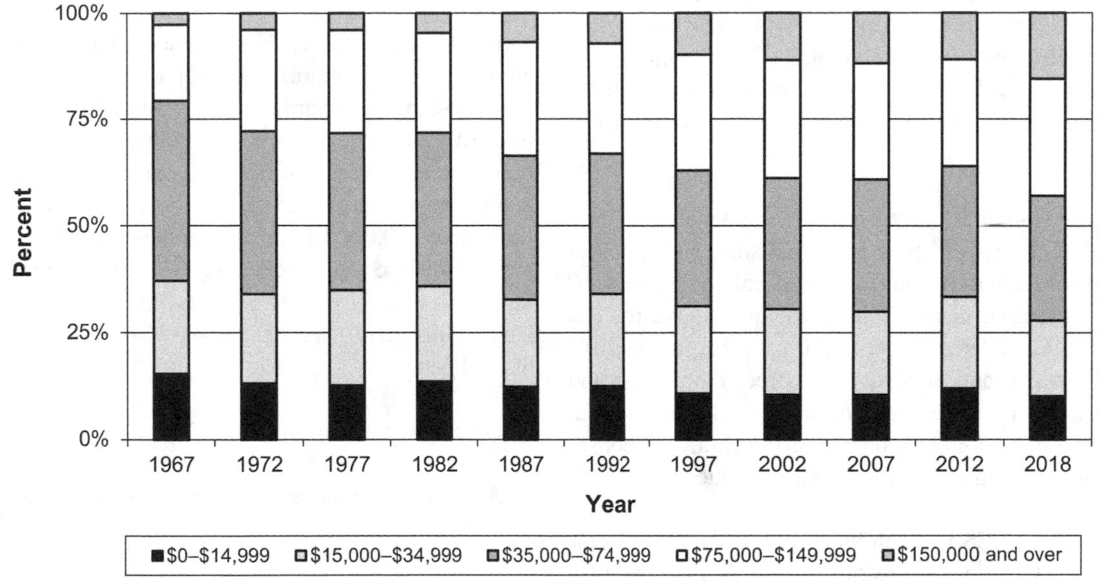

In 2018, 15.5 percent of households had an income above $150,000 and 8.5 had an income over $200,000—a slight decline from 8.6 percent in 2017. This is the first year since 2011 that the percent of households making over $200,000 has decreased. Meanwhile, the number of households making $25,000 or less decreased from 19.7 percent to 19.1 percent. (See Table 13-2.)

OTHER HIGHLIGHTS:

- Median income varied by race and ethnic origin. In 2018, Asians had the highest median income at $87,194 followed non-Hispanic Whites ($70,642), Hispanics ($51,450), and Blacks ($41,361). (See Table 13-1.)

- Real median income increased in all four regions listed on Table 13-1. The Northeast experienced the highest increase at 4.3 percent, followed by the Midwest at 2.3 percent, the West at 1.4 percent, and the South at 0.3 percent. (See Table 13-1.)

- Median household income increased in 2018 to $63,179. It has increased each year since 2013 after decreasing every year from 2008 to 2012. It varied significantly by state. Median household income was the highest in Massachusetts ($86,345) followed by Maryland ($86,223) and District of Columbia ($85,750). (See Table 13-5.)

- Mississippi continued to have the lowest family income at $57,380 in 2018 followed by West Virginia at $57,718. The District of Columbia had the highest median family income at $117,713 followed by Massachusetts ($101,548) and Maryland ($101,437). (See Table 13-7.)

NOTES AND DEFINITIONS

Collection and Coverage

The data in tables 13-1 through 13-5 are from the Annual Social and Economic Supplement (ASEC) to the Current Population Survey (CPS). The CPS ASEC provides timely estimates of household income and individual earnings, as well as the distribution of that income. The population represented is the civilian noninstitutionalized population living in the United States. Members of the Armed Forces living off post or with their families on post are included if at least one civilian adult lives in the household, hence, the CPS ASEC universe is slightly larger than the CPS universe which does not include persons who are on active duty in the armed forces.

The data in Tables 13-6 and 13-7 come from the American Community Survey (ACS). The ACS is an annual survey that covers the same type of information that had been collected every 10 years from the decennial census long form questionnaire. The ACS eliminated the need for a separate long form in the 2010 Census. The CPS ASEC and ACS surveys differ in the length and detail of its questionnaire, the number of households interviewed, the methodology used to collect and process the data, and, consequently, in the income and poverty estimates produced.

The sample size of the ACS is much larger (approximately 3 million compared with the sample size of the CPS ASEC 100,000). Although it is smaller, the CPS ASEC is a high quality source of information due to its detailed questionnaire and experienced interviewing staff. Another notable difference between the two surveys is that the ACS is a mandatory whereas the CPS ASEC is voluntary.

Concepts and Definitions

The *Gini index of income inequality* (also known as the Gini ratio, Gini coefficient, or index of income concentration) is a statistical measure that summarizes the dispersion of income across an entire income distribution. Values range from 0 to 1. A Gini value of 1 indicates "perfect" inequality; that is, one household has all the income and the rest have none. A value of zero indicates "perfect" equality, a situation in which all households have equal income.

Equivalence-adjusted income inequality is another way to measure income inequality. Equivalence adjusted income takes into consideration the number of people living in the household and how these people share resources and take advantage of economies of scale. For example, the household-income-based distribution treats income of $30,000 for a single-person household and a family household similarly, while the equivalence-adjusted income of $30,000 for a single-person household would be more than twice the equivalence-adjusted income of $30,000 for a family household with two adults and two children. The equivalence adjustment used here is based on a three-parameter scale that reflects:

1. On average, children consume less than adults.

2. As family size increases, expenses do not increase at the same rate.

3. The increase in expenses is larger for a first child of a single-parent family than the first child of a two-adult family.

Additional Information

Additional information is available in the Census publication "Income and Poverty in the United States: 2018 *Current Population Reports*, p60-266 (U.S. Census Bureau, September 2019)

Table 13-1. Income and Earnings Summary Measures, by Selected Characteristics, 2017 and 2018

(Numbers in thousands, dollars, percent; income in 2018 dollars.)

Characteristic	2017			2018			Percent change in real median income (2018 less 2017)	
	Number	Median income (dollars)		Number	Median income (dollars)			
		Estimate	Margin of error [1] (+/-)		Estimate	Margin of error [1] (+/-)	Estimate	Margin of error [1] (+/-)
ALL HOUSEHLDS	127 669	62 626	542	128 579	63 179	691	0.9	1.06
Type of Households								
Family households	83 523	79 693	884	83 482	80 663	664	1.2	1.14
Married-couple	61 869	93 556	863	61 959	93 654	1 125	0.1	1.16
Female householder, no husband present	15 303	42 669	862	15 043	45 128	1 116	5.8	3.00
Male householder, no wife present	6 351	59 636	2 072	6 480	61 518	1 246	3.2	3.90
Nonfamily households	44 146	37 229	512	45 096	38 122	825	2.4	2.38
Female householder	23 316	31 915	593	23 515	32 007	667	0.3	2.53
Male householder	20 830	43 843	1 680	21 582	45 754	868	4.4	3.98
Race[2] and Hispanic Origin of Householder								
White	100 113	66 413	862	100 528	66 943	646	0.8	1.25
White, not Hispanic	84 706	69 851	1 136	84 727	70 642	652	1.1	1.57
Black	17 019	40 324	1 430	17 167	41 361	906	2.6	3.67
Asian	6 750	83 376	1 822	6 981	87 194	2 805	4.6	3.66
Hispanic (any race)	17 336	51 389	776	17 758	51 450	735	0.1	1.83
Age of Householder								
Under 65 years	94 703	70 944	1 018	94 423	71 659	573	1.0	1.40
15 to 24 years	6 223	39 901	1 663	6 199	43 531	2 689	9.1	8.00
25 to 34 years	20 258	62 732	852	20 611	65 890	1 075	5.0	1.95
35 to 44 years	21 609	80 768	1 893	21 370	80 743	1 071	0.0	2.47
45 to 54 years	22 566	82 111	1 365	22 071	84 464	1 845	2.9	2.43
55 to 64 years	24 047	70 576	1 603	24 172	68 951	1 444	-2.3	2.95
65 years and older	32 966	42 303	808	34 156	43 696	816	3.3	2.48
Nativity of Householder								
Native born	107 720	63 377	580	108 560	64 243	712	1.4	1.21
Foreign born	19 949	57 795	1 233	20 019	58 776	1 588	1.7	3.03
Naturalized citizen	10 886	66 101	2 515	11 043	65 520	2 251	-0.9	4.76
Not a citizen	9 063	50 363	1 707	8 976	51 944	1 052	3.1	3.59
Region								
Northeast	22 513	67 192	1 707	22 054	70 113	1 886	4.3	3.21
Midwest	27 659	62 613	1 145	27 686	64 069	1 445	2.3	2.59
South	48 630	57 134	1 006	49 743	57 299	821	0.3	1.87
West	28 866	68 593	1 278	29 096	69 520	1 595	1.4	2.29
Residence								
Inside metropolitan statistical areas	109 804	65 142	869	110 789	66 164	609	1.6	1.31
Inside principal cites	42 573	56 299	1 306	42 983	59 358	1 223	5.4	2.87
Outside principal cites	67 230	71 627	1 076	67 806	70 928	757	-1.0	1.41
Outside metropolitan statistical areas	17 865	49 116	1 545	17 790	49 867	1 629	1.5	3.91

[1]A margin of error is a measure of an estimate's variability. The larger the margin of error in relation to the size of the estimate, the less reliable the estimate.
[2]Federal surveys now give respondents the option of reporting more than one race. Therefore, there are two basic ways of defining a race group. A group such as Asian may be defined as those who reported Asian and no other race (the race-alone or single-race concept) or as those who reported Asian regardless of whether they also reported another race (the race-alone-or-in-combination concept). This table shows data using the race-alone concept. The use of the single-race population does not imply that it is the preferred method of presenting or analyzing data; the Census Bureau uses a variety of approaches. Information on people who reported more than one race, such as White and American Indian and Alaska Native or Asian and Black or African American, is available from Census 2010 through American FactFinder. About 2.9 percent of respondents reported more than one race in Census 2010.
X = Not applicable.
N = Represents or rounds to zero.

Table 13-2. Households, by Total Money Income, Race, and Hispanic Origin of Householder, 1967–2018

(Numbers in thousands, percent, dollars; income in 2018 CPI-U-RS adjusted dollars.)

Race and Hispanic origin of householder and year	Number	Percent distribution										Median income (dollars)		Mean income (dollars)	
		Total	Under $15,000	$15,000 to $24,999	$25,000 to $34,999	$35,000 to $49,999	$50,000 to $74,999	$75,000 to $99,999	$100,000 to $149,999	$150,000 to $199,000	$200,000 and over	Value	Standard error	Value	Standard error
All Races															
1967[1]	60 813	100.0	15.0	10.3	11.1	17.6	24.2	12.0	7.0	1.6	1.1	47 085	171	52 662	171
1968	62 214	100.0	13.7	10.2	10.6	16.7	24.6	13.5	7.8	1.7	1.0	49 114	178	55 565	178
1969	63 401	100.0	13.4	10.1	9.6	16.4	24.3	13.9	8.9	2.1	1.3	50 940	188	57 954	182
1970	64 778	100.0	13.5	10.2	10.3	15.7	23.9	13.7	9.3	2.1	1.4	50 545	185	57 877	185
1971[2]	66 676	100.0	13.6	10.4	10.6	15.7	23.5	13.6	9.2	2.1	1.3	50 053	194	57 566	183
1972[3]	68 251	100.0	12.6	10.5	10.3	14.8	22.4	14.5	10.5	2.6	1.7	52 197	199	60 751	188
1973	69 859	100.0	11.9	10.9	9.6	14.4	22.5	14.7	11.4	2.9	1.8	53 251	203	61 584	187
1974[4,5]	71 163	100.0	12.2	10.8	10.3	15.3	22.5	14.3	10.6	2.5	1.5	51 565	198	60 301	189
1975[5]	72 867	100.0	12.7	11.4	10.9	15.0	22.2	13.9	10.2	2.2	1.4	50 214	204	58 636	183
1976[6]	74 142	100.0	12.3	11.5	10.4	14.9	21.9	14.2	10.7	2.4	1.6	51 048	189	60 045	185
1977	76 030	100.0	12.2	11.5	10.5	14.8	21.1	14.6	10.9	2.7	1.7	51 371	193	60 939	185
1978	77 330	100.0	11.9	10.8	10.0	14.7	21.2	14.6	11.9	3.0	1.9	53 359	216	62 802	241
1979[7]	80 776	100.0	12.1	10.5	10.3	14.6	20.9	14.8	11.8	3.1	2.0	53 257	252	63 264	239
1980	82 368	100.0	12.5	10.8	10.8	14.6	21.1	13.9	11.5	3.0	1.7	51 528	265	61 283	224
1981	83 527	100.0	12.7	11.1	11.4	14.3	20.7	13.8	11.4	2.9	1.7	50 709	266	60 580	221
1982	83 918	100.0	12.9	10.9	10.9	14.7	20.8	13.3	11.3	3.1	2.0	50 571	228	60 946	226
1983	85 407	100.0	13.0	11.0	10.8	14.9	20.3	13.2	11.4	3.2	2.1	50 216	228	61 075	228
1984[8]	86 789	100.0	12.4	11.0	10.7	14.4	20.1	13.4	12.1	3.6	2.3	51 742	235	63 397	233
1985[9]	88 458	100.0	12.4	10.8	10.2	14.5	19.9	13.3	12.7	3.7	2.5	52 709	286	64 868	257
1986	89 479	100.0	12.2	10.2	10.0	13.8	19.6	13.9	13.1	4.2	2.9	54 608	283	67 465	274
1987[10]	91 124	100.0	12.0	10.0	10.0	13.7	19.4	13.8	13.6	4.3	3.1	55 260	261	68 723	282
1988	92 830	100.0	11.8	10.1	9.9	13.2	19.5	13.7	13.8	4.6	3.4	55 716	272	69 615	311
1989	93 347	100.0	11.0	10.2	9.7	13.7	19.2	13.9	13.8	4.9	3.6	56 678	312	71 607	312
1990	94 312	100.0	11.5	10.1	9.7	14.0	19.9	13.5	13.4	4.5	3.4	55 952	286	69 892	295
1991	95 669	100.0	11.9	10.4	9.9	14.2	19.2	13.4	13.3	4.5	3.1	54 318	261	68 374	281
1992[11]	96 426	100.0	12.2	10.8	9.9	14.0	18.9	13.3	13.1	4.5	3.2	53 897	255	68 330	287
1993[12]	97 107	100.0	12.1	10.9	10.1	14.0	18.5	12.9	13.2	4.7	3.7	53 610	251	71 091	384
1994[13]	98 990	100.0	11.6	10.9	10.3	13.5	18.7	12.6	13.6	4.8	4.1	54 233	247	72 503	390
1995[14]	99 627	100.0	10.9	10.9	10.1	13.6	18.7	13.1	13.8	4.9	4.1	55 931	323	73 760	404
1996	101 018	100.0	10.9	10.7	9.6	13.9	17.9	13.6	13.9	5.3	4.3	56 744	286	75 340	422
1997	102 528	100.0	10.5	10.4	9.7	13.0	18.1	13.3	14.5	5.6	4.9	57 911	268	77 766	435
1998	103 874	100.0	10.0	10.1	9.1	13.3	17.7	13.5	15.1	6.0	5.3	60 040	355	80 067	432
1999[15]	106 434	100.0	9.2	9.8	9.4	13.1	17.5	13.5	15.1	6.4	6.0	61 526	287	82 754	429
2000[16]	108 209	100.0	9.6	9.5	8.8	13.3	18.0	13.1	15.3	6.5	5.9	61 399	193	83 545	329
2001	109 297	100.0	9.9	9.7	9.2	13.5	17.5	12.9	15.2	6.1	5.9	60 038	183	82 758	330
2002	111 278	100.0	10.1	9.9	9.8	13.0	17.5	12.8	15.3	6.1	5.6	59 360	195	80 975	304
2003	112 000	100.0	10.5	10.1	9.5	12.8	17.2	12.8	15.1	6.1	5.9	59 286	257	80 840	296
2004[17]	113 343	100.0	10.5	9.9	10.2	12.7	17.5	12.8	14.6	6.1	5.7	59 080	261	80 578	304
2005	114 384	100.0	10.3	10.0	9.8	12.6	17.8	12.9	14.5	6.2	5.9	59 712	200	81 647	308
2006	116 011	100.0	10.2	9.7	9.3	13.5	17.5	12.5	14.6	6.5	6.2	60 178	258	83 111	321
2007	116 783	100.0	10.2	10.1	9.1	13.1	17.3	12.6	15.1	6.5	6.1	60 985	170	82 081	287
2008	117 181	100.0	10.6	10.2	9.4	13.6	17.2	12.6	14.6	6.1	5.7	58 811	160	79 997	283
2009[18]	117 538	100.0	10.6	10.3	9.6	13.7	17.3	12.5	14.1	6.1	5.8	58 400	250	79 751	285
2010[19]	119 927	100.0	11.4	11.0	10.1	12.7	16.9	12.4	13.8	6.1	5.6	56 873	375	77 783	416
2011	121 084	100.0	11.9	10.4	10.3	13.1	17.3	11.8	13.6	6.0	5.5	56 006	281	77 962	412
2012	122 459	100.0	11.6	10.8	10.1	13.1	17.0	12.3	13.4	6.1	5.6	55 900	229	78 095	461
2013[20]	123 931	100.0	11.6	10.8	9.4	12.4	16.8	12.3	13.6	6.5	6.5	57 856	706	81 189	717
2014	124 587	100.0	11.8	10.4	9.7	12.8	16.9	11.7	14.0	6.3	6.5	56 969	416	80 413	474
2015	125 819	100.0	10.8	10.0	9.8	12.2	16.5	12.2	14.8	6.8	7.0	59 901	340	84 011	427
2016	126 224	100.0	10.6	9.1	9.4	12.5	16.8	12.4	14.6	7.0	7.7	61 779	456	87 001	491
2017	127 669	100.0	10.3	9.4	9.1	12.2	16.6	12.2	14.6	7.0	8.6	62 626	330	89 779	584
2018	128 579	100.0	10.2	8.9	8.8	12.0	17.2	12.5	14.9	7.0	8.5	63 179	420	90 021	546

[1]Implementation of a new Curent Population Survey (CPS) Annual Social and Economic Supplements (ASEC) processing system.
[2]Introduction of 1970 census sample design and population controls.
[3]Full implementation of 1970 census–based sample design.
[4]Implementation of a new CPS ASEC processing system. Questionnaire expanded to ask 11 income questions.
[5]Some of these estimates were derived using Pareto interpolation and may differ from published data that were derived using linear interpolation.
[6]First-year medians were derived using both Pareto and linear interpolation. Before this year, all medians were derived using linear interpolation.
[7]Implementation of 1980 census population controls. Questionnaire expanded to show 27 possible values from a list of 51 possible sources of income.
[8]Implementation of Hispanic population weighting controls and introduction of 1980 census–based sample design.
[9]Recording of amounts for earnings from longest job increased to $299,999. Full implementation of 1980 census–based sample design.
[10]Implementation of a new CPS ASEC processing system.
[11]Implementation of 1990 census population controls.
[12]Data collection method changed from paper and pencil to computer-assisted interviewing. In addition, the 1994 ASEC was revised to allow for the coding of different income amounts on selected questionnaire items. Limits either increased or decreased in the following categories: earnings limits increased to $999,999, Social Security limits increased to $49,999, Supplemental Security Income and public assistance limits increased to $24,999, veterans' benefits limits increased to $99,999, and child support and alimony limits decreased to $49,999.
[13]Introduction of 1990 census sample design.
[14]Full implementation of 1990 census–based sample design and metropolitan definitions, 7,000 household sample reduction, and revised editing of responses on race.
[15]Implementation of the 2000 census–based population controls.
[16]Implementation of a 28,000 household sample expansion.
[17]Data revised to reflect a correction to the weights in the 2005 ASEC.
[18]Median income is calculated using $2,500 intervals. Beginning with 2009 income data, the Census Bureau expanded the upper income intervals used to calculate medians to $250,000 or more.
[19]Implementation of 2010 census-based population controls.
[20]Data are based on the CPS ASEC sample of 68,000 addresses. The 2014 CPS ASEC included redesigned questions for income and health insurance coverage.

Table 13-2. Households, by Total Money Income, Race, and Hispanic Origin of Householder, 1967–2018 *—Continued*

(Numbers in thousands, percent, dollars; income in 2018 CPI-U-RS adjusted dollars.)

Race and Hispanic origin of householder and year	Number	Percent distribution										Median income (dollars)		Mean income (dollars)	
		Total	Under $15,000	$15,000 to $24,999	$25,000 to $34,999	$35,000 to $49,999	$50,000 to $74,999	$75,000 to $99,999	$100,000 to $149,999	$150,000 to $199,000	$200,000 and over	Value	Standard error	Value	Standard error
White[21]															
1967[1]	54 188	100.0	14.1	9.7	10.9	18.1	25.3	12.2	6.9	1.6	1.2	47 934	174	53 288	180
1968	55 394	100.0	12.9	9.9	10.0	18.0	25.6	13.3	7.6	1.6	1.1	49 921	186	56 193	186
1969	56 248	100.0	12.6	9.6	9.2	16.8	25.4	14.1	9.1	1.9	1.3	51 897	190	58 673	196
1970	57 575	100.0	12.7	9.7	10.0	16.1	25.1	13.6	9.3	2.0	1.4	51 393	198	58 477	192
1971[2]	59 463	100.0	12.6	10.1	10.3	16.2	24.2	14.0	9.2	2.1	1.3	51 108	195	58 231	189
1972[3]	60 618	100.0	11.8	9.9	9.8	15.2	23.6	14.7	10.6	2.6	1.7	53 456	205	61 612	200
1973	61 965	100.0	11.2	10.5	9.4	14.9	23.1	15.0	11.3	2.7	1.9	54 481	208	62 443	198
1974[4,5]	62 984	100.0	11.3	10.4	10.0	16.0	23.0	14.7	10.6	2.5	1.5	52 644	198	61 046	198
1975[5]	64 392	100.0	11.8	11.3	10.5	15.7	22.8	14.1	10.2	2.2	1.4	51 263	187	59 355	195
1976[6]	65 353	100.0	11.3	10.9	10.4	15.2	22.9	14.6	10.6	2.5	1.5	52 202	216	60 871	196
1977	66 934	100.0	11.3	10.8	10.4	15.0	22.4	14.8	11.0	2.7	1.7	52 735	222	61 813	200
1978	68 028	100.0	10.8	10.6	10.3	14.4	21.9	15.0	12.0	3.0	1.9	54 150	239	63 580	256
1979[7]	70 766	100.0	10.9	10.0	10.4	14.6	21.7	15.3	11.8	3.2	2.0	54 510	259	64 194	256
1980	71 872	100.0	11.3	10.4	10.8	14.8	22.2	14.2	11.6	3.0	1.7	53 068	273	62 239	239
1981	72 845	100.0	11.3	10.8	11.2	14.9	21.3	14.4	11.5	2.9	1.7	52 302	241	61 617	234
1982	73 182	100.0	11.9	10.7	10.8	15.4	21.3	13.4	11.5	3.1	1.9	51 683	235	61 948	242
1983	74 376	100.0	11.5	10.7	10.6	15.7	20.8	13.8	11.5	3.2	2.1	51 408	232	62 095	242
1984[8]	75 328	100.0	11.1	10.7	10.5	14.8	20.8	13.9	12.3	3.5	2.4	53 287	268	64 441	250
1985[9]	76 576	100.0	11.1	10.4	10.4	14.4	20.7	13.9	12.9	3.7	2.6	54 265	290	65 923	277
1986	77 284	100.0	11.0	9.7	10.2	14.0	20.2	14.4	13.3	4.3	2.9	56 045	272	68 603	293
1987[10]	78 519	100.0	10.5	9.9	9.7	14.1	20.2	14.3	13.9	4.3	3.1	56 837	286	69 954	302
1988	79 734	100.0	10.4	9.5	9.9	13.8	20.2	14.3	14.0	4.5	3.4	57 498	340	70 857	334
1989	80 163	100.0	9.6	10.1	9.6	14.0	19.6	14.6	13.9	4.9	3.6	58 200	283	72 814	337
1990	80 968	100.0	9.9	10.0	9.7	14.4	20.4	13.9	13.7	4.5	3.5	56 970	261	70 981	317
1991	81 675	100.0	10.3	10.5	9.6	14.9	19.7	13.8	13.6	4.6	3.2	55 565	269	69 565	303
1992[11]	81 795	100.0	10.5	10.6	10.3	14.0	19.4	14.0	13.4	4.5	3.3	55 316	268	69 717	311
1993[12]	82 387	100.0	10.5	10.5	10.2	14.0	19.3	13.5	13.4	4.8	3.8	55 214	322	72 510	419
1994[13]	83 737	100.0	10.4	10.8	10.2	13.9	19.1	13.0	13.7	4.9	4.1	55 837	313	73 897	430
1995[14]	84 511	100.0	9.6	10.7	10.0	13.8	19.1	13.6	14.0	4.9	4.2	57 308	300	74 874	434
1996	85 059	100.0	9.6	10.6	9.7	14.0	18.4	13.9	14.2	5.3	4.4	57 999	300	76 467	453
1997	86 106	100.0	9.3	10.3	9.5	13.4	18.4	13.8	14.7	5.7	4.9	59 538	377	79 292	483
1998	87 212	100.0	8.7	9.8	9.2	13.5	18.0	14.2	15.2	6.0	5.4	61 667	309	81 707	481
1999[15]	88 893	100.0	8.3	9.5	9.4	13.0	18.4	13.5	15.8	6.1	6.0	62 467	316	83 721	474
2000[16]	90 030	100.0	8.7	9.3	9.0	13.4	18.0	13.5	15.7	6.4	6.0	62 688	277	84 582	363
2001	90 682	100.0	8.8	9.9	9.4	13.2	17.7	13.2	15.6	6.1	6.1	61 786	290	83 986	361
White Alone[22]															
2002	91 645	100.0	8.7	9.5	9.5	12.7	17.7	13.2	16.1	6.4	6.0	63 107	256	84 214	343
2003	91 962	100.0	9.0	9.7	9.4	12.9	17.3	13.1	15.8	6.5	6.3	62 451	245	84 289	338
2004[17]	92 880	100.0	9.0	9.6	10.0	12.5	17.7	13.2	15.4	6.4	6.2	62 177	244	83 833	345
2005	93 588	100.0	8.8	9.5	9.6	12.7	18.0	13.4	15.2	6.6	6.4	62 584	273	85 022	352
2006	94 705	100.0	8.8	9.3	9.1	13.3	17.8	13.0	15.4	6.8	6.6	63 264	184	86 279	360
2007	95 112	100.0	8.6	9.8	8.9	12.9	17.5	13.1	15.8	6.8	6.6	63 270	187	85 385	325
2008	95 297	100.0	9.1	9.9	9.2	13.3	17.4	13.1	15.4	6.5	6.1	61 160	178	83 232	320
2009[18]	95 489	100.0	9.0	9.9	9.3	13.6	17.6	13.0	14.9	6.5	6.1	60 845	181	82 764	319
2010[19]	96 306	100.0	9.6	10.6	9.9	12.7	17.2	12.8	14.6	6.5	6.1	59 682	292	81 268	467
2011	96 964	100.0	10.1	9.9	10.1	13.2	17.7	12.2	14.3	6.4	6.0	58 423	252	81 470	472
2012	97 705	100.0	9.8	10.4	10.0	13.1	17.3	12.9	14.1	6.4	6.0	58 846	421	81 538	508
2013[20]	98 807	100.0	10.1	10.4	9.3	12.2	17.1	13.0	14.2	6.9	6.9	61 268	558	84 028	818
2014[20]	98 679	100.0	10.2	10.0	9.4	12.7	17.2	12.2	14.7	6.6	7.0	60 376	377	83 760	555
2015[20]	99 313	100.0	9.1	9.6	9.7	12.2	16.6	12.7	15.8	7.1	7.3	63 710	404	87 152	498
2016[20]	99 400	100.0	9.0	8.7	9.2	12.5	16.9	12.8	15.5	7.4	8.1	64 729	349	90 351	559
2017[20]	100 113	100.0	8.8	8.9	8.8	12.0	16.7	12.8	15.4	7.5	9.1	66 413	524	93 750	658
2018[20]	100 528	100.0	8.7	8.4	8.5	11.9	17.5	13.0	15.7	7.3	9.0	66 943	393	93 948	628

[1]Implementation of a new Curent Population Survey (CPS) Annual Social and Economic Supplements (ASEC) processing system.
[2]Introduction of 1970 census sample design and population controls.
[3]Full implementation of 1970 census–based sample design.
[4]Implementation of a new CPS ASEC processing system. Questionnaire expanded to ask 11 income questions.
[5]Some of these estimates were derived using Pareto interpolation and may differ from published data that were derived using linear interpolation.
[6]First-year medians were derived using both Pareto and linear interpolation. Before this year, all medians were derived using linear interpolation.
[7]Implementation of 1980 census population controls. Questionnaire expanded to show 27 possible values from a list of 51 possible sources of income.
[8]Implementation of Hispanic population weighting controls and introduction of 1980 census–based sample design.
[9]Recording of amounts for earnings from longest job increased to $299,999. Full implementation of 1980 census–based sample design.
[10]Implementation of a new CPS ASEC processing system.
[11]Implementation of 1990 census population controls.
[12]Data collection method changed from paper and pencil to computer-assisted interviewing. In addition, the 1994 ASEC was revised to allow for the coding of different income amounts on selected questionnaire items. Limits either increased or decreased in the following categories: earnings limits increased to $999,999, Social Security limits increased to $49,999, Supplemental Security Income and public assistance limits increased to $24,999, veterans' benefits limits increased to $99,999, and child support and alimony limits decreased to $49,999.
[13]Introduction of 1990 census sample design.
[14]Full implementation of 1990 census–based sample design and metropolitan definitions, 7,000 household sample reduction, and revised editing of responses on race.
[15]Implementation of the 2000 census–based population controls.
[16]Implementation of a 28,000 household sample expansion.
[17]Data revised to reflect a correction to the weights in the 2005 ASEC.
[18]Median income is calculated using $2,500 intervals. Beginning with 2009 income data, the Census Bureau expanded the upper income intervals used to calculate medians to $250,000 or more.
[19]Implementation of 2010 census-based population controls.
[20]Data are based on the CPS ASEC sample of 68,000 addresses. The 2014 CPS ASEC included redesigned questions for income and health insurance coverage.
[21]For 2001 and earlier years, the CPS allowed respondents to report only one race group.
[22]Beginning with the 2003 CPS, respondents were allowed to choose one or more races. White alone refers to people who reported White and did not report any other race category. The use of this single-race population does not imply that it is the preferred method of presenting or analyzing the data; the Census Bureau uses a variety of approaches. Information on people who reported more than one race, such as White and American Indian and Alaska Native or Asian and Black or African American, is available from Census 2010 through American FactFinder. About 2.9 percent of respondents reported more than one race in Census 2010.

Table 13-2. Households, by Total Money Income, Race, and Hispanic Origin of Householder, 1967–2018 —*Continued*

(Numbers in thousands, percent, dollars; income in 2018 CPI-U-RS adjusted dollars.)

Race and Hispanic origin of householder and year	Number	Percent distribution										Median income (dollars)		Mean income (dollars)	
		Total	Under $15,000	$15,000 to $24,999	$25,000 to $34,999	$35,000 to $49,999	$50,000 to $74,999	$75,000 to $99,999	$100,000 to $149,999	$150,000 to $199,000	$200,000 and over	Value	Standard error	Value	Standard error
White, Not Hispanic[21]															
1972[3]	58 005	100.0	11.4	9.5	9.6	14.5	23.3	15.5	11.6	2.9	1.9	55 540	264	63 846	285
1973	59 236	100.0	10.7	10.0	9.0	13.9	23.1	15.6	12.4	3.2	2.1	56 301	263	64 680	274
1974[4,5]	60 164	100.0	10.8	9.9	9.7	15.1	23.3	15.2	11.5	2.8	1.7	54 388	267	63 239	276
1975[5]	61 533	100.0	11.1	10.6	10.4	14.7	22.9	14.9	11.2	2.5	1.6	52 908	281	61 547	298
1976[6]	62 365	100.0	10.7	10.5	9.9	14.8	22.6	15.2	11.8	2.7	1.8	54 565	318	63 156	282
1977	63 721	100.0	10.7	10.6	10.0	14.5	21.7	15.7	11.9	3.0	2.0	55 091	310	64 104	303
1978	64 836	100.0	10.3	10.0	9.7	14.5	21.7	15.5	12.8	3.3	2.2	56 515	298	65 898	283
1979[7]	67 203	100.0	10.4	9.6	9.8	14.4	21.4	15.7	12.8	3.5	2.3	56 625	314	66 519	291
1980	68 106	100.0	10.6	9.9	10.3	14.5	21.8	14.9	12.6	3.4	1.9	55 325	314	64 594	291
1981	68 996	100.0	10.8	10.3	10.9	14.3	21.5	14.7	12.4	3.3	2.0	54 351	276	63 913	266
1982	69 214	100.0	10.9	10.1	10.5	14.8	21.5	14.1	12.5	3.5	2.2	53 830	271	64 390	276
1983	69 648	100.0	10.7	10.1	10.5	15.0	21.2	14.1	12.5	3.6	2.4	54 015	272	65 280	279
1984[8]	70 586	100.0	10.2	10.1	10.2	14.5	20.8	14.4	13.2	4.0	2.6	55 719	309	67 160	300
1985[9]	71 540	100.0	10.3	9.9	9.9	14.3	20.6	14.2	13.8	4.2	2.9	56 838	290	68 845	312
1986	72 067	100.0	10.1	9.3	9.6	13.6	20.2	14.8	14.3	4.7	3.4	58 716	303	71 670	329
1987[10]	73 120	100.0	9.6	9.1	9.6	13.5	20.1	14.8	14.9	4.8	3.5	59 823	333	73 061	339
1988	74 067	100.0	9.4	9.1	9.5	13.1	20.3	14.6	15.1	5.1	3.8	60 523	356	74 066	348
1989	74 495	100.0	8.7	9.5	9.3	13.5	19.7	14.8	14.9	5.4	4.1	60 901	298	76 084	373
1990	75 035	100.0	9.1	9.3	9.4	13.9	20.3	14.4	14.7	5.0	3.9	59 693	278	74 323	336
1991	75 625	100.0	9.4	9.7	9.5	14.1	19.7	14.3	14.6	5.1	3.5	58 279	287	72 790	325
1992[11]	75 107	100.0	9.6	10.0	9.6	13.7	19.6	14.3	14.5	5.1	3.8	58 566	362	73 230	338
1993[12]	75 697	100.0	9.6	10.0	9.6	13.7	19.2	13.9	14.5	5.3	4.2	58 641	343	76 235	455
1994[13]	77 004	100.0	9.2	10.1	9.9	13.2	19.3	13.4	14.9	5.4	4.6	59 044	313	77 626	461
1995[14]	76 932	100.0	8.5	9.8	9.5	13.2	19.3	14.1	15.2	5.6	4.8	61 023	318	79 201	474
1996	77 240	100.0	8.6	9.8	9.1	13.6	18.2	14.5	15.3	5.9	5.0	62 012	425	80 700	. . .
1997	77 936	100.0	8.3	9.5	9.2	12.6	18.2	14.2	16.0	6.3	5.7	63 501	332	83 827	. . .
1998	78 577	100.0	7.8	9.1	8.6	12.8	17.9	14.4	16.5	6.7	6.1	65 528	377	86 379	528
1999[15]	79 819	100.0	7.4	9.0	9.0	12.5	17.5	14.2	16.5	7.0	6.8	66 759	422	88 574	525
2000[16]	80 527	100.0	8.0	8.8	8.3	12.8	17.8	13.7	16.6	7.3	6.8	66 712	268	89 280	401
2001	80 818	100.0	8.1	9.1	8.7	12.9	17.5	13.5	16.6	6.8	6.9	65 835	273	88 780	402
White Alone, Not Hispanic[22]															
2002	81 166	100.0	8.3	9.2	9.0	12.3	17.6	13.5	16.9	6.8	0.0	65 646	258	86 942	370
2003	81 148	100.0	8.5	9.3	8.9	12.3	17.3	13.4	16.6	6.9	6.8	65 388	316	87 437	371
2004[17]	81 628	100.0	8.5	9.3	9.5	12.1	17.4	13.6	16.2	6.9	6.7	65 178	299	86 964	378
2005	82 003	100.0	8.3	9.1	9.2	12.2	17.7	13.7	15.9	7.0	6.9	65 458	222	88 426	391
2006	82 675	100.0	8.2	8.9	8.8	12.8	17.6	13.2	16.1	7.3	7.2	65 449	235	89 572	396
2007	82 765	100.0	8.1	9.4	8.5	12.4	17.3	13.3	16.7	7.3	7.2	66 676	300	88 847	358
2008	82 884	100.0	8.4	9.4	8.9	12.7	17.3	13.5	16.1	6.9	6.7	64 923	263	86 636	354
2009[18]	83 158	100.0	8.4	9.4	8.9	13.2	17.6	13.3	15.6	6.9	6.7	63 895	327	85 927	351
2010[19]	83 314	100.0	8.9	10.3	9.3	12.3	17.1	13.1	15.5	6.9	6.7	62 857	515	84 640	531
2011	83 573	100.0	9.4	9.4	9.6	12.7	17.6	12.6	15.1	6.9	6.6	62 001	367	85 108	535
2012	83 792	100.0	9.0	9.9	9.5	12.7	17.2	13.3	14.9	7.0	6.6	62 465	393	85 293	564
2013[20]	84 432	100.0	9.5	9.7	8.6	11.6	17.2	13.5	15.0	7.4	7.6	65 138	575	87 703	916
2014	84 228	100.0	9.6	9.5	8.9	12.2	17.1	12.4	15.3	7.2	7.7	63 976	391	87 555	615
2015	84 445	100.0	8.5	9.2	9.1	11.7	16.4	12.9	16.7	7.7	7.9	66 721	574	90 712	563
2016	84 387	100.0	8.5	8.3	8.8	11.9	16.7	12.9	16.1	7.9	8.9	68 059	534	93 922	637
2017	84 706	100.0	8.3	8.5	8.3	11.6	16.3	13.0	16.0	8.0	10.0	69 851	690	98 093	723
2018	84 727	100.0	8.1	7.9	8.0	11.3	17.3	13.1	16.5	7.8	9.9	70 642	396	98 261	711

[3]Full implementation of 1970 census–based sample design.
[4]Implementation of a new CPS ASEC processing system. Questionnaire expanded to ask 11 income questions.
[5]Some of these estimates were derived using Pareto interpolation and may differ from published data that were derived using linear interpolation.
[6]First-year medians were derived using both Pareto and linear interpolation. Before this year, all medians were derived using linear interpolation.
[7]Implementation of 1980 census population controls. Questionnaire expanded to show 27 possible values from a list of 51 possible sources of income.
[8]Implementation of Hispanic population weighting controls and introduction of 1980 census–based sample design.
[9]Recording of amounts for earnings from longest job increased to $299,999. Full implementation of 1980 census–based sample design.
[10]Implementation of a new CPS ASEC processing system.
[11]Implementation of 1990 census population controls.
[12]Data collection method changed from paper and pencil to computer-assisted interviewing. In addition, the 1994 ASEC was revised to allow for the coding of different income amounts on selected questionnaire items. Limits either increased or decreased in the following categories: earnings limits increased to $999,999, Social Security limits increased to $49,999, Supplemental Security Income and public assistance limits increased to $24,999, veterans' benefits limits increased to $99,999, and child support and alimony limits decreased to $49,999.
[13]Introduction of 1990 census sample design.
[14]Full implementation of 1990 census–based sample design and metropolitan definitions, 7,000 household sample reduction, and revised editing of responses on race.
[15]Implementation of the 2000 census–based population controls.
[16]Implementation of a 28,000 household sample expansion.
[17]Data revised to reflect a correction to the weights in the 2005 ASEC.
[18]Median income is calculated using $2,500 intervals. Beginning with 2009 income data, the Census Bureau expanded the upper income intervals used to calculate medians to $250,000 or more.
[19]Implementation of 2010 census-based population controls.
[20]Data are based on the CPS ASEC sample of 68,000 addresses. The 2014 CPS ASEC included redesigned questions for income and health insurance coverage.
[21]For 2001 and earlier years, the CPS allowed respondents to report only one race group.
[22]Beginning with the 2003 CPS, respondents were allowed to choose one or more races. White alone refers to people who reported White and did not report any other race category. The use of this single-race population does not imply that it is the preferred method of presenting or analyzing the data; the Census Bureau uses a variety of approaches. Information on people who reported more than one race, such as White and American Indian and Alaska Native or Asian and Black or African American, is available from Census 2010 through American FactFinder. About 2.9 percent of respondents reported more than one race in Census 2010.
. . . = Not available.

Table 13-2. Households, by Total Money Income, Race, and Hispanic Origin of Householder, 1967–2018 —*Continued*

(Numbers in thousands, percent, dollars; income in 2018 CPI-U-RS adjusted dollars.)

Race and Hispanic origin of householder and year	Number	Percent distribution										Median income (dollars)		Mean income (dollars)	
		Total	Under $15,000	$15,000 to $24,999	$25,000 to $34,999	$35,000 to $49,999	$50,000 to $74,999	$75,000 to $99,999	$100,000 to $149,999	$150,000 to $199,000	$200,000 and over	Value	Standard error	Value	Standard error
Black[21]															
1967[1]	5 728	100.0	27.3	17.5	15.6	16.5	14.6	5.1	2.5	0.6	0.3	28 510	475	34 258	382
1968	5 870	100.0	24.8	17.2	15.8	15.9	16.3	6.3	3.1	0.4	0.1	30 155	438	36 726	387
1969	6 053	100.0	24.2	16.6	14.2	17.9	16.5	6.6	3.5	0.5	0.1	32 134	474	38 255	407
1970	6 180	100.0	24.4	16.1	14.5	16.5	16.4	7.5	3.8	0.6	0.2	32 044	440	39 127	422
1971[2]	6 578	100.0	25.1	16.5	14.2	16.9	16.1	6.9	3.7	0.5	0.2	30 926	460	38 322	394
1972[3]	6 809	100.0	23.7	16.6	14.0	15.9	15.8	8.8	4.2	0.6	0.4	31 963	479	40 377	431
1973	7 040	100.0	22.0	16.9	13.0	16.3	17.7	8.3	4.6	0.8	0.4	32 851	512	40 795	405
1974[4,5]	7 263	100.0	23.4	16.5	14.2	16.1	16.6	8.1	4.3	0.6	0.2	32 071	387	39 886	355
1975[5]	7 489	100.0	24.8	17.0	12.9	15.9	16.7	7.9	4.1	0.7	0.1	31 524	464	39 350	349
1976[6]	7 776	100.0	23.5	17.8	12.6	14.9	17.4	8.3	4.6	0.6	0.2	31 797	394	40 626	362
1977	7 977	100.0	23.3	17.9	13.3	15.3	16.0	8.1	5.0	0.7	0.3	31 878	428	40 845	363
1978	8 066	100.0	24.0	16.0	11.9	15.2	17.2	8.5	6.1	1.0	0.2	33 335	705	42 601	556
1979[7]	8 586	100.0	24.0	16.0	12.9	14.7	16.3	9.1	5.7	0.9	0.3	32 784	599	42 066	518
1980	8 847	100.0	25.5	16.2	13.2	14.6	16.0	8.1	5.3	0.8	0.3	31 318	591	40 646	500
1981	8 961	100.0	27.0	16.0	13.9	13.4	15.7	8.1	5.1	0.8	0.1	30 065	505	39 495	479
1982	8 916	100.0	26.6	15.8	13.6	13.5	16.6	8.6	4.1	0.9	0.3	30 005	481	39 480	494
1983	9 236	100.0	27.5	16.1	12.7	14.1	15.2	7.9	5.3	1.0	0.2	29 885	560	39 747	491
1984[8]	9 480	100.0	25.8	16.2	13.0	14.5	15.1	7.7	6.1	1.1	0.4	31 096	598	41 472	510
1985[9]	9 797	100.0	25.3	15.5	12.1	14.7	15.7	8.4	6.7	1.1	0.5	33 072	643	43 151	560
1986	9 922	100.0	26.1	14.4	11.6	14.1	15.9	9.2	6.2	1.9	0.6	33 076	649	44 376	603
1987[10]	10 192	100.0	26.3	14.1	11.7	15.0	14.9	8.9	6.6	1.5	1.0	33 231	636	44 870	617
1988	10 561	100.0	26.1	14.8	10.9	13.9	14.9	9.0	7.7	1.8	1.0	33 577	700	45 999	671
1989	10 486	100.0	24.9	13.5	11.4	14.2	16.3	8.9	8.1	2.0	0.7	35 456	722	47 049	639
1990	10 671	100.0	25.6	13.5	10.9	14.1	17.1	9.0	6.9	2.0	0.8	34 898	796	46 368	626
1991	11 083	100.0	26.4	13.3	11.5	14.0	16.3	9.2	6.7	1.9	0.7	33 909	712	45 153	590
1992[11]	11 269	100.0	26.5	14.6	11.0	14.6	15.3	8.7	6.5	2.0	0.8	32 995	674	44 774	607
1993[12]	11 281	100.0	25.6	14.4	11.8	14.5	14.6	8.8	7.1	2.1	1.1	33 519	662	46 725	776
1994[13]	11 655	100.0	23.8	13.8	12.2	13.9	15.0	9.6	8.1	2.4	1.4	35 344	657	49 182	706
1995[14]	11 577	100.0	22.0	14.7	11.7	14.8	16.2	9.3	8.3	2.0	1.1	36 755	627	49 898	854
1996	12 109	100.0	21.7	14.4	11.3	14.6	16.3	10.2	7.7	2.3	1.3	37 543	739	51 897	1 014
1997	12 474	100.0	20.5	13.6	11.8	14.7	16.8	10.2	8.4	2.6	1.3	39 202	674	51 586	740
1998	12 579	100.0	21.0	13.8	11.2	14.2	16.1	10.0	9.2	2.6	1.7	39 143	613	52 712	704
1999[15]	12 838	100.0	18.3	12.9	11.2	14.8	16.1	11.3	9.3	3.8	2.4	42 196	786	58 149	835
2000[16]	13 174	100.0	18.1	12.1	11.1	14.9	17.9	10.8	9.5	3.7	1.9	43 380	575	57 288	581
2001	13 315	100.0	19.1	12.5	11.0	15.6	16.9	10.4	9.9	3.0	1.7	41 899	493	55 801	589
Black Alone[23]															
2002	13 465	100.0	19.3	13.1	12.3	15.2	15.9	9.8	9.4	2.9	2.2	40 628	547	56 003	647
2003	13 629	100.0	20.0	13.2	11.6	13.9	16.8	10.1	9.5	2.9	2.0	40 573	528	54 924	589
2004[17]	13 809	100.0	20.6	12.2	12.8	14.8	16.1	10.1	8.7	2.9	2.0	40 105	417	54 148	586
2005	14 002	100.0	20.1	13.9	11.7	13.5	17.2	9.6	8.9	3.1	2.0	39 774	388	54 721	594
2006	14 354	100.0	20.1	13.3	10.9	15.6	16.2	9.5	9.1	3.1	2.2	39 913	301	56 340	697
2007	14 551	100.0	19.7	13.4	10.6	14.8	16.7	9.7	9.9	3.1	2.1	41 176	577	56 612	631
2008	14 595	100.0	19.7	13.1	11.5	15.9	16.8	9.4	8.8	3.0	1.9	40 006	516	54 404	582
2009[18]	14 730	100.0	20.0	13.9	11.9	15.2	15.8	10.0	8.6	2.9	1.8	38 228	462	54 022	616
2010[19]	15 265	100.0	22.3	13.8	12.3	13.9	15.2	9.9	7.9	2.9	1.8	37 077	576	51 889	723
2011	15 583	100.0	23.0	14.4	11.8	13.3	15.4	8.8	8.4	2.9	2.0	36 061	570	52 874	898
2012	15 872	100.0	22.1	14.4	11.7	14.0	15.7	9.0	8.2	2.9	1.9	36 510	866	52 306	825
2013[20]	16 009	100.0	21.1	14.3	11.6	14.5	16.0	7.9	8.8	3.5	2.2	38 140	925	54 476	1 279
2014[20]	16 437	100.0	21.3	13.8	12.3	14.4	15.6	8.4	8.7	3.2	2.5	37 583	489	54 392	734
2015[20]	16 539	100.0	20.7	13.5	12.0	13.1	16.0	9.4	9.2	3.3	2.7	39 108	544	57 608	913
2016[20]	16 733	100.0	19.8	12.4	11.8	13.9	16.5	9.6	9.4	3.7	3.0	41 323	754	60 111	975
2017[20]	17 019	100.0	19.4	13.0	12.0	13.7	15.9	9.4	9.8	3.4	3.4	40 324	869	59 444	841
2018[20]	17 167	100.0	19.2	12.6	11.6	13.7	16.4	9.6	9.5	4.0	3.2	41 361	551	58 665	818

[1]Implementation of a new Curent Population Survey (CPS) Annual Social and Economic Supplements (ASEC) processing system.
[2]Introduction of 1970 census sample design and population controls.
[3]Full implementation of 1970 census–based sample design.
[4]Implementation of a new CPS ASEC processing system. Questionnaire expanded to ask 11 income questions.
[5]Some of these estimates were derived using Pareto interpolation and may differ from published data that were derived using linear interpolation.
[6]First-year medians were derived using both Pareto and linear interpolation. Before this year, all medians were derived using linear interpolation.
[7]Implementation of 1980 census population controls. Questionnaire expanded to show 27 possible values from a list of 51 possible sources of income.
[8]Implementation of Hispanic population weighting controls and introduction of 1980 census–based sample design.
[9]Recording of amounts for earnings from longest job increased to $299,999. Full implementation of 1980 census–based sample design.
[10]Implementation of a new CPS ASEC processing system.
[11]Implementation of 1990 census population controls.
[12]Data collection method changed from paper and pencil to computer-assisted interviewing. In addition, the 1994 ASEC was revised to allow for the coding of different income amounts on selected questionnaire items. Limits either increased or decreased in the following categories: earnings limits increased to $999,999, Social Security limits increased to $49,999, Supplemental Security Income and public assistance limits increased to $24,999, veterans' benefits limits increased to $99,999, and child support and alimony limits decreased to $49,999.
[13]Introduction of 1990 census sample design.
[14]Full implementation of 1990 census–based sample design and metropolitan definitions, 7,000 household sample reduction, and revised editing of responses on race.
[15]Implementation of the 2000 census–based population controls.
[16]Implementation of a 28,000 household sample expansion.
[17]Data revised to reflect a correction to the weights in the 2005 ASEC.
[18]Median income is calculated using $2,500 intervals. Beginning with 2009 income data, the Census Bureau expanded the upper income intervals used to calculate medians to $250,000 or more.
[19]Implementation of 2010 census-based population controls.
[20]Data are based on the CPS ASEC sample of 68,000 addresses. The 2014 CPS ASEC included redesigned questions for income and health insurance coverage.
[21]For 2001 and earlier years, the CPS allowed respondents to report only one race group.
[23]Black alone refers to persons who reported Black and did not report any other race category.

Table 13-2. Households, by Total Money Income, Race, and Hispanic Origin of Householder, 1967–2018 —*Continued*

(Numbers in thousands, percent, dollars; income in 2018 CPI-U-RS adjusted dollars.)

Race and Hispanic origin of householder and year	Number	Percent distribution: Total	Under $15,000	$15,000 to $24,999	$25,000 to $34,999	$35,000 to $49,999	$50,000 to $74,999	$75,000 to $99,999	$100,000 to $149,999	$150,000 to $199,999	$200,000 and over	Median income (dollars): Value	Median income (dollars): Standard error	Mean income (dollars): Value	Mean income (dollars): Standard error
Black Alone or in Combination															
2002	13 778	100.0	19.2	13.0	12.2	15.1	16.0	9.8	9.5	2.9	2.3	40 839	537	56 455	658
2003	13 969	100.0	19.9	13.3	11.6	13.9	16.8	10.2	9.5	2.9	2.0	40 633	510	55 177	584
2004[17]	14 151	100.0	20.4	12.2	12.7	14.7	16.2	10.1	8.8	2.9	1.9	40 292	369	54 316	577
2005	14 399	100.0	20.0	13.9	11.7	13.5	17.2	9.6	9.0	3.2	2.0	39 898	380	55 073	599
2006	14 709	100.0	19.9	13.3	10.8	15.7	16.3	9.4	9.2	3.1	2.3	40 116	297	56 797	697
2007	14 976	100.0	19.7	13.4	10.5	14.9	16.6	9.6	10.0	3.2	2.1	41 388	565	56 855	622
2008	15 056	100.0	19.6	13.1	11.5	15.8	16.8	9.3	8.9	3.0	1.9	40 154	513	54 574	571
2009[18]	15 212	100.0	19.9	13.8	11.9	15.1	15.8	10.0	8.5	2.9	1.9	38 423	490	54 297	605
2010[19]	15 909	100.0	22.1	13.8	12.4	13.9	15.1	9.8	8.0	3.0	1.9	37 114	542	52 514	724
2011	16 165	100.0	22.9	14.3	11.7	13.3	15.4	8.8	8.5	2.9	2.1	36 215	619	53 155	865
2012	16 559	100.0	21.9	14.3	11.7	14.0	15.6	9.0	8.5	2.9	2.0	36 945	874	52 769	809
2013[20]	16 723	100.0	20.6	14.2	11.8	14.5	16.1	7.8	9.0	3.6	2.3	38 615	840	55 793	1 428
2014	17 198	100.0	21.1	13.7	12.1	14.5	15.6	8.4	8.8	3.2	2.5	37 854	501	54 807	736
2015	17 322	100.0	20.5	13.4	11.9	13.0	16.1	9.5	9.3	3.4	2.8	39 440	579	58 088	919
2016	17 505	100.0	19.4	12.4	11.7	14.0	16.6	9.7	9.4	3.8	3.0	41 924	610	60 819	979
2017	17 813	100.0	19.1	13.0	11.9	13.7	16.1	9.5	9.9	3.4	3.5	40 963	704	59 800	812
2018	18 095	100.0	18.8	12.6	11.6	13.7	16.4	9.6	9.7	4.1	3.3	41 692	557	59 363	811
Asian and Pacific Islander[21]															
1987[10]	. . .	100.0	10.2	8.8	8.9	10.0	16.9	14.2	18.4	7.8	4.7	68 332	2 540	. . .	. . .
1988	1 913	100.0	8.5	9.2	8.9	10.9	18.3	14.9	16.3	7.1	6.1	66 034	2 714	82 557	2 466
1989	1 988	100.0	8.1	7.4	7.4	11.6	18.9	15.4	17.1	7.6	6.5	70 787	1 914	87 999	2 561
1990	1 958	100.0	8.7	7.4	8.0	10.5	18.2	15.8	17.4	7.3	6.7	71 848	2 128	86 726	2 455
1991	2 094	100.0	10.4	7.5	8.0	13.3	17.3	13.6	16.4	7.9	5.7	65 718	2 120	83 440	2 459
1992[11]	2 262	100.0	10.0	8.6	8.4	10.6	18.8	13.7	17.4	7.1	5.5	66 502	1 919	82 422	2 266
1993[12]	2 233	100.0	12.2	8.3	8.6	11.0	14.9	13.9	18.7	6.4	6.0	65 804	3 236	86 219	3 471
1994[13]	2 040	100.0	9.8	8.8	7.1	11.3	17.3	13.4	17.6	7.6	7.1	68 047	2 579	88 352	3 148
1995[14]	2 777	100.0	10.1	8.7	7.6	11.2	18.2	13.7	17.0	6.6	6.9	66 662	1 673	90 649	3 657
1996	2 998	100.0	10.4	7.5	7.3	10.6	17.9	12.7	18.2	9.5	6.0	69 189	2 480	90 407	3 242
1997	3 125	100.0	9.4	8.2	6.7	10.0	18.3	14.0	17.4	8.6	7.4	70 813	1 969	92 160	2 856
1998	3 308	100.0	8.8	7.7	6.7	11.7	17.0	12.4	19.7	8.4	7.5	72 010	2 004	92 964	2 685
1999[15]	3 742	100.0	8.6	7.1	6.1	10.8	16.6	12.7	17.1	9.6	11.6	77 044	2 715	101 879	2 582
2000[16]	3 963	100.0	7.8	6.3	6.0	10.7	16.1	13.4	19.1	10.2	10.5	81 530	1 391	106 447	2 209
2001	4 071	100.0	8.8	6.6	6.9	10.9	16.3	13.8	17.5	9.6	9.7	76 256	1 820	104 015	2 455
Asian Alone[24]															
2002	3 917	100.0	8.6	6.6	7.9	11.2	16.6	12.4	18.8	8.8	9.2	73 660	1 289	98 045	1 912
2003	4 040	100.0	11.7	8.0	5.8	8.5	15.3	13.4	18.4	8.9	9.9	76 231	1 497	95 766	1 696
2004[17]	4 123	100.0	8.5	6.7	7.5	9.3	17.0	13.7	17.7	9.5	9.9	76 631	1 628	101 968	1 972
2005	4 273	100.0	9.3	7.1	6.8	8.4	15.8	13.4	18.9	9.1	11.2	78 747	918	103 240	1 821
2006	4 454	100.0	8.4	6.3	6.7	9.9	16.0	12.6	17.8	11.4	10.8	80 200	2 090	110 232	2 372
2007	4 494	100.0	8.6	6.8	6.5	9.8	16.0	12.6	19.0	10.4	10.3	80 252	1 681	103 216	1 821
2008	4 573	100.0	10.1	7.0	6.6	11.0	14.5	12.4	18.1	9.9	10.5	76 739	1 620	100 763	1 757
2009[18]	4 687	100.0	10.4	6.7	6.6	10.5	15.1	12.2	17.4	9.9	11.3	76 810	1 486	106 542	2 165
2010[19]	5 212	100.0	9.8	7.8	7.6	8.9	16.4	11.9	17.0	10.7	9.9	74 167	1 818	97 625	1 957
2011	5 374	100.0	9.3	8.2	7.7	10.0	16.3	13.2	17.9	8.4	9.0	72 874	1 753	95 828	2 320
2012	5 560	100.0	9.8	6.5	7.3	9.9	16.4	13.3	16.5	9.9	10.2	75 205	2 071	100 147	2 012
2013[20]	5 818	100.0	9.8	7.5	5.1	9.9	15.3	13.2	17.9	8.5	12.8	78 153	3 630	109 276	4 822
2014	6 040	100.0	9.8	6.5	7.6	9.3	14.9	11.8	18.0	10.9	11.0	78 883	2 237	103 584	2 039
2015	6 328	100.0	9.4	6.3	6.2	9.5	15.2	11.8	16.8	10.9	13.9	81 788	1 799	111 732	2 360
2016	6 392	100.0	8.7	6.1	6.3	7.8	14.9	13.7	16.7	12.1	13.7	85 210	1 219	113 004	1 904
2017	6 750	100.0	8.1	6.5	5.8	9.8	14.9	12.1	16.6	11.3	14.8	83 376	1 107	117 202	2 697
2018	6 981	100.0	8.4	6.1	6.0	8.5	14.2	12.0	18.1	10.2	16.4	87 194	1 705	119 816	2 261
Asian Alone or in Combination															
2002	4 079	100.0	8.7	6.6	7.9	11.0	17.0	12.3	18.8	8.7	8.9	73 183	1 107	97 245	1 849
2003	4 235	100.0	11.5	8.0	5.9	8.6	15.6	13.4	18.4	8.8	9.6	75 632	1 686	94 998	1 634
2004[17]	4 346	100.0	8.6	6.7	7.4	9.3	17.1	13.9	17.6	9.5	9.8	76 557	1 543	101 453	1 915
2005	4 500	100.0	9.2	7.0	6.8	8.6	15.9	13.2	19.0	9.0	11.1	78 688	940	103 112	1 799
2006	4 664	100.0	8.4	6.3	6.7	9.9	16.2	12.8	17.9	11.5	10.5	79 778	2 019	109 277	2 287
2007	4 715	100.0	8.7	6.7	6.5	10.0	16.0	12.9	18.6	10.6	10.2	79 977	1 683	102 661	1 756
2008	4 805	100.0	9.9	7.1	6.6	11.2	14.5	12.5	18.1	9.7	10.4	76 657	1 652	100 924	1 739
2009[18]	4 940	100.0	10.4	6.7	6.6	10.8	15.1	12.0	17.4	9.7	11.2	76 345	1 684	105 719	2 077
2010[19]	5 550	100.0	9.6	7.9	7.8	9.2	16.5	11.9	16.9	10.5	9.7	73 322	1 691	96 620	1 856
2011	5 705	100.0	9.4	8.4	7.5	10.2	16.2	13.2	17.7	8.3	9.3	72 724	1 750	95 986	2 297
2012	5 872	100.0	9.7	6.6	7.3	10.0	16.7	13.3	16.4	9.8	10.4	74 707	1 903	100 479	2 075
2013[20]	6 160	100.0	9.8	7.3	5.3	10.1	14.9	13.7	17.5	8.7	12.6	78 249	3 446	109 135	4 561

[10]Implementation of a new CPS ASEC processing system.
[11]Implementation of 1990 census population controls.
[12]Data collection method changed from paper and pencil to computer-assisted interviewing. In addition, the 1994 ASEC was revised to allow for the coding of different income amounts on selected questionnaire items. Limits either increased or decreased in the following categories: earnings limits increased to $999,999, Social Security limits increased to $49,999, Supplemental Security Income and public assistance limits increased to $24,999, veterans' benefits limits increased to $99,999, and child support and alimony limits decreased to $49,999.
[13]Introduction of 1990 census sample design.
[14]Full implementation of 1990 census–based sample design and metropolitan definitions, 7,000 household sample reduction, and revised editing of responses on race.
[15]Implementation of the 2000 census–based population controls.
[16]Implementation of a 28,000 household sample expansion.
[17]Data revised to reflect a correction to the weights in the 2005 ASEC.
[18]Median income is calculated using $2,500 intervals. Beginning with 2009 income data, the Census Bureau expanded the upper income intervals used to calculate medians to $250,000 or more.
[19]Implementation of 2010 census-based population controls.
[20]Data are based on the CPS ASEC sample of 68,000 addresses. The 2014 CPS ASEC included redesigned questions for income and health insurance coverage.
[21]For 2001 and earlier years, the CPS allowed respondents to report only one race group.
[24]Asian alone refers to persons who reported Asian and did not report any other race category.
. . . = Not available.

Table 13-2. Households, by Total Money Income, Race, and Hispanic Origin of Householder, 1967–2018 *—Continued*

(Numbers in thousands, percent, dollars; income in 2018 CPI-U-RS adjusted dollars.)

Race and Hispanic origin of householder and year	Number	Percent distribution										Median income (dollars)		Mean income (dollars)	
		Total	Under $15,000	$15,000 to $24,999	$25,000 to $34,999	$35,000 to $49,999	$50,000 to $74,999	$75,000 to $99,999	$100,000 to $149,999	$150,000 to $199,000	$200,000 and over	Value	Standard error	Value	Standard error
Asian Alone or in Combination*—Continued*															
2014[20]	6 333	100.0	9.5	6.5	7.5	9.3	15.0	12.2	18.0	10.8	11.0	79 448	2 103	104 200	2 046
2015[20]	6 640	100.0	9.5	6.4	6.2	9.5	15.3	11.7	16.7	11.0	13.7	81 359	1 483	111 430	2 331
2016[20]	6 750	100.0	8.7	6.2	6.4	7.9	15.2	13.6	16.7	11.9	13.4	84 573	1 183	111 844	1 854
2017[20]	7 124	100.0	8.2	6.5	6.1	9.8	14.9	12.0	16.6	10.9	14.9	82 982	1 128	116 686	2 611
2018[20]	7 416	100.0	8.3	6.3	6.0	8.7	14.3	12.2	18.1	10.0	16.2	86 815	1 478	118 912	2 145
Hispanic[25]															
1972[3]	2 655	100.0	12.4	16.0	14.3	20.4	21.6	9.3	4.6	0.9	0.6	41 324	807	47 498	807
1973	2 722	100.0	12.5	14.4	14.4	18.9	22.2	10.9	5.5	0.9	0.4	41 255	937	47 932	780
1974[4,5]	2 897	100.0	13.6	15.2	14.0	18.3	22.1	9.8	5.4	1.1	0.5	41 014	898	47 512	774
1975[5]	2 948	100.0	16.8	15.2	15.0	17.5	21.3	8.7	4.3	0.7	0.5	37 725	834	44 785	796
1976[6]	3 081	100.0	16.7	15.7	13.4	18.1	19.9	10.0	4.8	1.0	0.3	38 505	821	45 503	740
1977	3 304	100.0	14.1	15.0	14.1	19.1	20.0	10.3	5.8	1.3	0.3	40 299	708	47 559	734
1978	3 291	100.0	14.4	13.8	12.5	19.2	20.7	11.4	6.3	1.3	0.5	41 808	1 013	49 385	999
1979[7]	3 684	100.0	14.7	13.1	13.4	17.2	21.2	10.6	7.4	1.5	0.9	42 195	1 216	51 054	1 026
1980	3 906	100.0	16.3	14.4	14.1	16.8	19.0	11.0	6.4	1.3	0.7	39 718	1 077	48 513	966
1981	3 980	100.0	15.5	14.2	13.7	16.9	20.2	10.5	7.0	1.2	0.6	40 675	1 114	48 845	933
1982	4 085	100.0	17.5	15.5	13.2	16.8	18.9	9.5	6.7	1.1	0.8	38 053	1 005	46 963	953
1983	4 326	100.0	18.8	14.8	13.1	16.3	19.1	9.4	6.7	1.3	0.5	38 245	969	46 571	894
1984[8]	4 883	100.0	18.1	14.4	13.3	14.7	19.8	10.1	6.9	1.7	0.8	39 224	983	48 773	951
1985[9]	5 213	100.0	17.5	15.8	12.1	16.2	18.7	9.6	7.9	1.5	0.7	38 977	911	48 703	792
1986	5 418	100.0	16.6	14.7	13.0	15.4	18.8	10.6	8.3	1.9	0.8	40 252	1 048	50 827	836
1987[10]	5 642	100.0	17.6	13.9	12.3	16.1	18.0	10.6	7.9	2.1	1.4	41 000	891	52 557	973
1988	5 910	100.0	17.1	13.2	13.2	15.2	18.6	11.2	7.8	2.2	1.5	41 664	1 056	53 194	1 128
1989	5 933	100.0	15.9	12.5	12.2	16.4	18.3	11.8	8.8	2.5	1.5	42 982	833	54 886	943
1990	6 220	100.0	16.1	14.9	11.9	16.1	19.7	10.0	8.0	2.1	1.3	41 726	856	52 269	861
1991	6 379	100.0	16.4	14.0	12.8	16.1	18.8	10.4	8.0	2.2	1.4	40 912	851	52 057	833
1992[11]	7 153	100.0	17.2	14.4	12.8	16.9	17.8	9.9	7.8	2.2	1.0	39 754	822	50 706	797
1993[12]	7 362	100.0	16.6	15.1	13.5	16.4	18.0	9.0	8.1	1.8	1.4	39 273	789	51 980	1 093
1994[13]	7 735	100.0	18.0	14.4	12.9	15.6	17.7	9.1	8.4	2.3	1.6	39 369	731	53 086	1 325
1995[14]	7 939	100.0	17.9	15.6	13.7	15.8	16.5	9.7	7.3	2.1	1.4	37 522	817	51 212	1 149
1996	8 225	100.0	16.1	15.3	13.0	16.2	17.3	10.0	8.1	2.3	1.7	39 819	772	54 367	1 258
1997	8 590	100.0	16.0	14.1	12.8	15.5	18.9	9.9	8.3	2.5	2.0	41 672	743	56 155	1 133
1998	9 060	100.0	14.6	14.2	11.5	16.4	18.0	11.1	9.0	3.0	2.1	43 743	843	59 106	1 257
1999[15]	9 579	100.0	11.7	13.6	11.9	16.9	18.7	11.4	10.5	3.0	2.4	46 484	676	61 064	1 084
2000[16]	10 034	100.0	11.5	12.5	11.1	16.4	20.1	11.7	11.0	3.2	2.5	48 500	699	64 306	926
2001	10 499	100.0	11.8	12.6	11.7	16.6	18.9	11.6	10.9	3.5	2.5	47 721	606	63 102	798
2002	11 339	100.0	12.2	12.0	13.1	16.5	18.4	11.6	10.4	3.3	2.5	46 334	675	62 828	840
2003	11 693	100.0	12.6	12.8	12.8	16.9	17.9	10.9	10.3	3.1	2.6	45 160	628	60 860	673
2004[17]	12 178	100.0	12.9	12.3	13.8	15.4	19.6	10.6	9.7	3.2	2.5	45 670	640	61 136	748
2005	12 519	100.0	12.7	12.3	12.7	16.0	19.4	11.3	9.7	3.4	2.5	46 360	460	60 759	611
2006	12 973	100.0	12.9	12.6	11.2	16.6	19.0	11.2	10.2	3.8	2.5	47 169	630	63 142	724
2007	13 339	100.0	12.7	12.6	11.5	16.8	18.6	11.9	10.2	3.3	2.4	46 958	631	61 708	650
2008	13 425	100.0	14.1	12.9	11.2	17.6	17.7	10.3	10.2	3.6	2.3	44 326	568	60 295	624
2009[18]	13 298	100.0	13.7	13.3	11.9	16.3	17.7	11.0	10.0	3.4	2.7	44 628	589	61 276	672
2010[19]	14 435	100.0	14.8	13.1	13.3	14.8	17.7	11.0	9.3	3.7	2.2	43 433	672	59 318	762
2011	14 939	100.0	15.1	12.7	13.2	16.0	18.3	9.5	9.5	3.5	2.3	43 217	612	58 577	665
2012	15 589	100.0	15.2	13.1	13.3	15.6	17.6	10.4	9.1	3.3	2.4	42 738	585	58 535	765
2013[20]	16 088	100.0	13.8	14.4	13.4	15.1	16.5	9.9	9.8	4.0	3.2	42 850	1 283	62 210	1 838
2014[20]	16 239	100.0	13.9	13.1	11.9	15.4	18.0	11.0	10.7	3.4	2.5	45 114	548	61 085	696
2015[20]	16 667	100.0	13.0	12.0	12.6	14.8	17.7	11.6	10.4	4.3	3.7	47 852	652	67 423	887
2016[20]	16 915	100.0	12.1	10.9	11.6	15.5	18.0	12.2	11.8	4.3	3.7	49 887	707	69 916	845
2017[20]	17 336	100.0	12.1	11.0	11.2	14.6	19.1	11.7	12.0	4.3	4.2	51 389	472	69 312	941
2018[20]	17 758	100.0	11.4	11.0	10.8	15.0	18.8	12.7	11.4	4.5	4.3	51 450	447	70 945	984

[3]Full implementation of 1970 census–based sample design.
[4]Implementation of a new CPS ASEC processing system. Questionnaire expanded to ask 11 income questions.
[5]Some of these estimates were derived using Pareto interpolation and may differ from published data that were derived using linear interpolation.
[6]First-year medians were derived using both Pareto and linear interpolation. Before this year, all medians were derived using linear interpolation.
[7]Implementation of 1980 census population controls. Questionnaire expanded to show 27 possible values from a list of 51 possible sources of income.
[8]Implementation of Hispanic population weighting controls and introduction of 1980 census–based sample design.
[9]Recording of amounts for earnings from longest job increased to $299,999. Full implementation of 1980 census–based sample design.
[10]Implementation of a new CPS ASEC processing system.
[11]Implementation of 1990 census population controls.
[12]Data collection method changed from paper and pencil to computer-assisted interviewing. In addition, the 1994 ASEC was revised to allow for the coding of different income amounts on selected questionnaire items. Limits either increased or decreased in the following categories: earnings limits increased to $999,999, Social Security limits increased to $49,999, Supplemental Security Income and public assistance limits increased to $24,999, veterans' benefits limits increased to $99,999, and child support and alimony limits decreased to $49,999.
[13]Introduction of 1990 census sample design.
[14]Full implementation of 1990 census–based sample design and metropolitan definitions, 7,000 household sample reduction, and revised editing of responses on race.
[15]Implementation of the 2000 census–based population controls.
[16]Implementation of a 28,000 household sample expansion.
[17]Data revised to reflect a correction to the weights in the 2005 ASEC.
[18]Median income is calculated using $2,500 intervals. Beginning with 2009 income data, the Census Bureau expanded the upper income intervals used to calculate medians to $250,000 or more.
[19]Implementation of 2010 census-based population controls.
[20]Data are based on the CPS ASEC sample of 68,000 addresses. The 2014 CPS ASEC included redesigned questions for income and health insurance coverage.
[25]Because Hispanics may be of any race, data in this report for Hispanics overlap with data for racial groups. Hispanic origin was reported by 15.0 percent of White householders who reported only one race, 4.3 percent of Black householders who reported only one race, and 2.4 percent of Asian householders who reported only one race. Data users should exercise caution when interpreting aggregate results for the Hispanic population and for race groups, because these populations consist of many distinct groups that differ in socioeconomic characteristics, culture, and recentness of immigration. Data were first collected for Hispanics in 1972.

Table 13-3. Income Deficit or Surplus of Families and Unrelated Individuals by Poverty Status, 2018

(Numbers of families and unrelated individuals in thousands, deficits and surpluses in dollars.)

Characteristic	Total	Size of deficit or surplus								Average deficit or surplus (dollars)		Deficit or surplus per capita (dollars)	
		Under $1,000	$1,000 to $2,499	$2,500 to $4,999	$5,000 to $7,499	$7,500 to $9,999	$10,000 to $12,499	$12,500 to $14,499	$15,000 or more	Estimate	90 percent confidence interval[1] (+/-)	Estimate	90 percent confidence interval[1] (+/-)
Below Poverty Threshold, Deficit													
All families	7 504	536	649	935	1 031	861	669	621	2 203	10 452	207	3 077	68
Married-couple families	2 938	281	274	412	396	333	236	219	787	9 789	346	2 735	105
Families with a female householder, no husband present	3 742	207	295	429	486	421	367	332	1 205	11 138	294	3 337	94
Families with a male householder, no wife present	824	48	80	93	149	106	66	69	211	9 704	536	3 223	186
Unrelated individuals	12 287	852	1 691	2 442	1 229	936	1 405	3 733	–	7 502	123	7 502	123
Male	5 301	313	729	1 004	557	374	632	1 693	–	7 688	207	7 688	207
Female	6 986	539	962	1 438	673	562	773	2 039	–	7 362	155	7 362	155
Above Poverty Threshold, Surplus													
All families	76 004	521	694	1 367	1 409	1 614	1 490	1 664	67 244	94 527	1 195	30 375	416
Married-couple families	59 033	275	344	663	738	914	852	969	54 279	106 184	1 368	33 719	467
Families with a female householder, no husband present	11 309	176	269	528	528	517	446	486	8 360	49 829	1 685	16 493	590
Families with a male householder, no wife present	5 661	70	82	176	143	184	192	209	4 605	62 265	3 229	21 425	1 147
Unrelated individuals	48 481	949	1 798	2 792	2 831	2 060	2 577	2 100	33 373	42 177	999	42 177	999
Male	24 586	393	725	1 154	1 214	868	1 179	909	18 144	47 170	1 577	47 170	1 577
Female	23 895	556	1 073	1 638	1 617	1 192	1 399	1 191	15 229	37 040	1 213	37 040	1 213

[1]A 90 percent confidence interval is a measure of an estimate's variability. The larger the confidence interval in relation to the size of the estimate, the less reliable the estimate.
– = Quantity represents or rounds to zero.

Table 13-4. Income Distribution Measures Using Money Income and Equivalence-Adjusted Income, 2017 and 2018

(Percent distribution.)

Measure	2017				2018				Percent change (2017–2018)			
	Money income		Equivalence-adjusted income		Money income		Equivalence-adjusted income		Money income		Equivalence-adjusted income	
	Estimate	90 percent confidence interval[1] (+/-)	Estimate	90 percent confidence interval[1] (+/-)	Estimate	90 percent confidence interval[1] (+/-)	Estimate	90 percent confidence interval[1] (+/-)	Estimate	90 percent confidence interval[1] (+/-)	Estimate	90 percent confidence interval[1] (+/-)
Shares of Aggregate Income by Percentile												
Lowest quintile	3.0	0.05	3.4	0.06	3.1	0.05	3.5	0.06	0.6	2.12	3.9	2.24
Second quintile	8.1	0.09	8.9	0.09	8.3	0.08	9.1	0.08	2.3	1.40	2.3	1.25
Middle quintile	14.0	0.12	14.4	0.11	14.1	0.11	14.7	0.11	0.9	1.14	1.5	1.11
Fourth quintile	22.6	0.16	22.4	0.15	22.6	0.16	22.4	0.15	-0.1	0.96	–	0.89
Highest quintile	52.3	0.35	50.9	0.34	52.0	0.34	50.3	0.33	-0.6	0.92	-1.1	0.89
Top 5 percent	23.2	0.44	22.7	0.42	23.1	0.42	22.5	0.40	-0.2	2.61	-0.8	2.43
Summary Measures												
Gini index of income inequality	0.489	0.004	0.471	0.004	0.486	0.004	0.464	0.003	-0.70	1.01	-1.40	1.00
Mean logrithmic deviation of income	0.617	0.012	0.643	0.015	0.616	0.014	0.628	0.012	-0.100	2.680	-2.500	2.830

[1]A 90-percent confidence interval is a measure of an estimate's variability. The larger the confidence interval in relation to the size of the estimate, the less reliable the estimate.
– = Quantity represents or rounds to zero.

Table 13-5. Median Household Income by State, 2005 to 2018

(Income in 2018 CPI-U-RS adjusted dollars.)

State	2005	2006	2007	2008	2009	2010	2011	2012	2013	2014	2015	2016	2017	2018
UNITED STATES	59 712	60 178	60 985	58 811	58 400	56 873	56 006	55 900	56 079	56 969	59 901	61 779	62 868	63 179
Alabama	47 885	47 382	51 248	51 999	46 905	47 244	47 654	47 624	44 679	44 888	47 175	49 412	52 359	49 936
Alaska	72 041	70 437	76 477	74 812	72 275	66 767	64 260	69 739	66 010	71 804	79 611	79 237	73 992	68 734
Arizona	58 319	58 250	57 321	54 849	53 662	54 127	54 403	51 546	54 635	52 294	55 378	59 750	62 615	62 283
Arkansas	47 250	46 265	49 527	46 282	42 867	44 536	46 213	42 752	43 101	47 695	45 362	48 037	50 019	49 781
California	66 710	69 065	67 664	66 658	65 858	62 652	59 713	62 477	62 113	64 221	67 448	69 729	71 459	70 489
Colorado	65 026	69 537	74 228	71 251	65 618	69 520	65 601	62 735	68 422	64 702	70 585	73 841	75 980	73 034
Connecticut	73 258	77 910	77 870	75 623	76 085	76 174	73 194	70 396	73 184	74 492	77 255	79 446	74 554	72 812
Delaware	66 039	65 468	66 274	59 278	61 141	63 727	61 160	53 659	56 381	61 073	61 216	60 740	63 837	65 012
District of Columbia	57 994	60 523	61 653	64 993	62 346	65 705	61 821	71 490	65 511	72 492	74 268	74 276	85 415	85 750
Florida	55 412	57 026	55 596	52 444	53 535	50 860	50 468	50 480	51 703	48 988	51 750	53 551	54 990	54 644
Georgia	59 196	61 605	59 053	54 046	50 848	50 919	51 440	52 726	51 220	52 614	53 809	56 011	58 406	55 821
Hawaii	76 803	75 496	77 726	71 927	65 289	68 719	66 068	61 648	66 303	75 619	68 379	75 480	75 369	80 108
Idaho	56 941	57 696	59 712	55 441	54 881	54 304	53 102	52 508	55 893	56 737	54 716	59 189	61 676	58 728
Illinois	62 383	60 765	63 745	62 262	62 028	58 549	56 658	56 690	61 755	58 306	64 032	64 235	66 184	70 145
Indiana	54 699	56 690	57 610	54 389	51 980	53 253	49 730	50 575	54 582	51 027	55 097	58 697	60 308	59 892
Iowa	59 936	60 084	59 377	58 623	59 507	56 573	56 191	58 557	59 227	61 379	64 500	61 836	65 028	68 718
Kansas	54 171	56 871	58 878	55 975	52 463	53 155	51 634	54 788	55 589	56 743	58 152	59 446	59 283	63 938
Kentucky	47 303	49 296	47 897	48 108	50 054	47 442	44 595	45 018	45 518	45 427	44 926	47 474	52 600	54 555
Louisiana	47 995	45 555	50 156	46 255	53 303	45 359	45 493	42 826	42 780	45 024	48 673	44 154	44 973	49 973
Maine	56 615	56 983	58 146	55 216	55 730	55 321	55 602	53 863	54 116	54 902	53 796	53 216	52 923	58 663
Maryland	77 997	79 488	79 678	74 487	75 305	74 100	77 066	78 711	70 464	80 867	78 002	77 183	83 061	86 223
Massachusetts	72 203	69 078	70 977	70 523	69 658	70 329	70 842	69 748	67 982	67 049	71 926	75 620	75 012	86 345
Michigan	59 205	60 735	59 938	58 209	53 961	53 411	54 691	54 802	52 691	55 215	57 450	59 740	59 107	60 449
Minnesota	69 880	70 178	70 485	64 215	65 806	60 388	64 695	67 709	65 762	71 395	72 847	73 477	73 673	71 817
Mississippi	42 374	43 363	45 259	42 611	41 154	44 044	45 976	40 148	44 106	37 714	42 435	43 006	44 500	42 781
Missouri	55 407	55 656	55 852	53 825	57 217	52 881	51 217	54 527	54 321	60 126	62 742	57 569	58 272	61 726
Montana	48 095	51 319	52 999	50 156	47 442	47 645	45 066	49 403	47 650	54 256	54 474	59 724	60 527	57 679
Nebraska	61 770	60 108	59 700	59 308	58 186	60 599	62 229	57 191	58 060	60 380	64 097	62 129	61 072	67 575
Nevada	62 139	65 273	65 629	64 004	60 344	59 094	52 637	51 863	48 985	52 954	55 123	58 003	57 929	61 864
New Hampshire	73 450	77 368	82 041	77 369	75 240	76 907	73 714	74 310	77 007	77 928	80 208	79 799	76 624	81 346
New Jersey	81 678	84 970	73 460	76 352	75 998	72 677	69 751	73 075	66 707	69 270	72 452	71 645	74 776	74 176
New Mexico	50 201	49 974	53 850	49 223	51 084	52 093	46 974	47 580	45 485	49 568	47 822	50 699	49 022	48 283
New York	60 808	60 204	59 421	58 996	58 915	57 456	56 657	52 243	58 135	57 662	61 480	64 288	63 969	67 274
North Carolina	54 208	49 686	52 827	50 191	49 165	50 588	50 581	45 530	44 493	49 672	53 840	56 259	51 570	53 369
North Dakota	54 383	51 246	57 309	58 026	58 749	58 870	63 063	61 103	57 104	64 479	60 854	62 977	61 346	66 505
Ohio	56 975	57 305	59 609	54 873	53 826	52 961	49 957	48 622	50 096	52 708	56 494	56 490	61 225	61 633
Oklahoma	48 523	48 488	52 466	53 910	53 825	49 749	54 217	53 040	47 266	50 113	49 897	53 307	56 347	54 434
Oregon	56 919	58 792	60 989	60 476	57 603	58 404	57 653	56 730	60 795	62 509	64 478	61 879	66 185	69 165
Pennsylvania	59 678	60 523	58 805	60 096	56 517	55 763	55 845	56 871	58 252	58 579	64 006	63 809	64 713	64 524
Rhode Island	63 782	67 088	65 814	62 246	60 578	59 582	54 864	61 431	62 420	62 252	59 038	64 383	68 008	62 266
South Carolina	51 854	49 461	53 677	49 285	48 221	48 127	44 850	48 650	47 236	47 702	49 137	56 858	56 311	57 444
South Dakota	55 620	56 715	56 354	60 328	53 764	52 344	52 838	54 144	58 793	56 328	58 364	60 116	58 281	59 463
Tennessee	50 792	50 804	50 013	46 417	47 535	44 541	47 306	47 110	45 887	46 415	50 165	53 727	56 587	56 060
Texas	53 391	54 068	55 911	54 353	55 699	54 554	54 879	56 896	57 254	57 201	59 856	60 844	60 740	59 785
Utah	70 651	68 202	64 987	73 115	68 623	65 443	62 092	63 924	67 986	67 296	70 227	70 613	73 058	77 067
Vermont	65 355	64 897	57 534	59 283	61 381	64 551	58 029	60 901	59 213	64 455	63 058	63 660	65 360	70 066
Virginia	66 915	71 312	71 824	72 469	70 981	69 675	70 062	70 818	73 010	70 239	65 169	69 535	73 031	77 151
Washington	65 280	68 321	70 512	66 210	70 853	64 822	63 610	68 139	64 897	62 714	71 271	73 573	77 256	79 726
West Virginia	46 976	47 965	51 101	44 420	47 504	49 372	46 794	47 721	43 449	41 993	45 389	46 412	46 499	50 573
Wisconsin	57 552	64 536	62 253	59 860	60 112	58 114	58 248	58 159	59 663	61 665	58 745	62 593	64 998	62 629
Wyoming	57 639	58 730	59 178	62 359	61 559	60 249	60 991	63 016	60 140	59 128	64 575	60 513	59 247	62 539

Table 13-6. Median Family Income in the Past Twelve Months, by the Number of Earners and State, 2018

(Income in 2018 inflation-adjusted dollars.)

State	Total	No earners	1 earner	2 earners	3 or more earners
UNITED STATES	76 401	39 417	52 557	98 586	120 837
Alabama	63 837	33 041	47 680	88 852	108 681
Alaska	89 847	39 880	62 858	109 067	131 547
Arizona	69 981	44 911	51 388	91 051	111 142
Arkansas	58 080	32 255	42 461	82 037	103 607
California	86 165	40 007	59 286	111 225	122 217
Colorado	88 955	49 809	60 819	107 990	127 149
Connecticut	98 100	47 146	65 502	123 864	148 769
Delaware	79 386	52 911	54 589	100 535	123 424
District of Columbia	117 713	20 622	62 285	182 594	164 039
Florida	66 995	42 900	50 641	86 074	107 774
Georgia	71 457	34 855	49 236	94 024	114 021
Hawaii	95 448	49 623	64 803	108 055	145 813
Idaho	65 987	42 365	51 189	80 307	99 449
Illinois	81 313	40 924	53 900	105 138	124 416
Indiana	70 150	40 570	47 965	88 484	113 542
Iowa	76 068	43 481	50 661	92 467	114 221
Kansas	74 042	42 205	50 944	90 517	115 957
Kentucky	62 228	31 791	43 800	86 213	113 824
Louisiana	61 847	27 598	44 822	91 300	118 314
Maine	72 390	38 230	50 537	87 954	120 826
Maryland	101 437	50 557	69 529	123 547	147 862
Massachusetts	101 548	39 839	65 924	127 817	149 103
Michigan	72 036	41 841	52 168	93 216	121 529
Minnesota	89 039	49 661	57 017	106 583	129 974
Mississippi	57 380	28 506	41 659	81 155	96 786
Missouri	69 188	39 074	48 212	87 579	114 063
Montana	68 940	44 018	50 165	84 826	114 705
Nebraska	75 990	43 350	48 796	91 433	111 919
Nevada	71 864	43 342	51 516	88 100	110 663
New Hampshire	93 930	46 336	65 400	111 121	138 087
New Jersey	101 404	44 699	68 464	125 654	155 176
New Mexico	58 760	32 687	44 833	79 112	99 995
New York	83 311	34 577	56 120	110 519	134 528
North Carolina	67 816	37 588	47 904	88 796	106 452
North Dakota	86 205	45 002	52 357	103 188	133 207
Ohio	72 028	38 794	50 384	93 923	117 525
Oklahoma	64 082	34 535	48 322	85 446	102 776
Oregon	77 655	45 906	55 943	100 050	117 966
Pennsylvania	77 491	39 477	53 633	99 752	122 574
Rhode Island	84 212	34 795	60 608	106 058	135 866
South Carolina	65 742	37 893	46 642	87 148	104 517
South Dakota	72 183	39 131	47 053	86 378	105 692
Tennessee	65 656	34 336	47 361	86 157	110 022
Texas	71 868	33 927	49 996	95 629	110 304
Utah	81 599	49 263	63 653	87 550	118 834
Vermont	80 452	37 088	56 829	96 609	104 435
Virginia	88 929	45 685	60 925	112 258	133 124
Washington	87 652	50 978	66 309	109 145	129 911
West Virginia	57 718	31 958	48 183	85 714	108 964
Wisconsin	76 814	42 779	51 792	94 718	118 574
Wyoming	78 352	43 314	60 985	93 977	116 072

Table 13-7. Median Family Income in the Past Twelve Months, by Size of Family and State, 2018

(Income in 2018 inflation-adjusted dollars.)

State	Total	2-person families	3-person families	4-person families	5-person families	6-person families	7-or-more-person families
UNITED STATES	76 401	67 277	78 835	94 593	86 697	84 511	85 999
Alabama	63 837	55 905	67 334	81 514	77 402	71 422	70 697
Alaska	89 847	76 208	100 494	101 221	99 139	93 533	79 964
Arizona	69 981	64 543	70 428	85 403	76 844	67 103	78 510
Arkansas	58 080	52 986	57 221	72 767	66 589	72 767	68 023
California	86 165	77 860	86 665	99 512	89 234	86 319	96 960
Colorado	88 955	79 711	92 517	105 947	96 685	95 502	93 872
Connecticut	98 100	87 017	99 857	123 477	109 307	136 220	110 820
Delaware	79 386	71 351	83 079	100 799	85 856	84 205	83 197
District of Columbia	117 713	113 034	127 467	138 112	87 423	121 964	70 022
Florida	66 995	61 619	67 717	81 091	75 920	74 797	77 895
Georgia	71 457	63 850	72 426	85 763	77 981	73 924	79 744
Hawaii	95 448	76 240	98 829	112 345	106 277	136 014	149 216
Idaho	65 987	60 814	66 222	76 536	71 769	76 340	81 700
Illinois	81 313	71 301	82 268	101 240	95 092	92 096	95 592
Indiana	70 150	61 811	72 228	86 076	82 884	85 377	74 872
Iowa	76 068	67 897	77 525	93 880	87 399	88 067	75 136
Kansas	74 042	66 025	75 629	87 119	81 771	82 742	84 022
Kentucky	62 228	55 256	65 544	78 689	76 106	74 119	70 115
Louisiana	61 847	54 424	61 917	80 818	75 681	72 080	66 157
Maine	72 390	63 734	76 984	93 912	87 528	88 088	76 996
Maryland	101 437	88 815	104 390	125 989	110 974	116 987	124 588
Massachusetts	101 548	82 628	106 206	132 026	128 661	129 340	124 063
Michigan	72 036	63 281	76 825	91 986	83 992	79 735	76 250
Minnesota	89 039	76 319	95 919	112 291	107 098	99 394	82 005
Mississippi	57 380	50 980	57 431	68 491	69 992	71 720	55 388
Missouri	69 188	60 424	72 543	90 489	82 325	76 217	71 525
Montana	68 940	63 278	73 586	85 739	80 034	56 229	68 074
Nebraska	75 990	68 061	77 274	93 746	84 533	91 820	79 083
Nevada	71 864	64 586	73 524	80 077	80 171	80 907	86 362
New Hampshire	93 930	78 998	100 278	120 342	109 854	124 674	121 348
New Jersey	101 404	82 249	104 752	128 994	124 988	123 682	110 635
New Mexico	58 760	55 325	59 538	66 358	60 987	69 104	66 527
New York	83 311	71 349	86 670	105 636	98 500	95 221	94 401
North Carolina	67 816	60 946	67 931	85 948	76 360	73 202	67 975
North Dakota	86 205	79 459	86 261	97 559	109 901	99 514	55 816
Ohio	72 028	63 514	76 260	91 580	87 025	78 436	77 392
Oklahoma	64 082	58 436	65 400	75 326	69 252	76 595	76 696
Oregon	77 655	70 559	79 262	97 311	83 181	93 626	83 936
Pennsylvania	77 491	66 338	82 375	101 477	96 068	84 671	77 022
Rhode Island	84 212	74 508	83 585	102 967	91 456	96 074	116 619
South Carolina	65 742	60 434	65 410	79 780	74 346	73 910	64 620
South Dakota	72 183	67 817	69 074	82 331	93 298	68 429	71 524
Tennessee	65 656	59 829	68 493	78 283	73 255	72 517	69 143
Texas	71 868	65 708	72 632	84 724	76 685	72 297	72 598
Utah	81 599	67 778	81 167	91 810	95 456	100 506	104 552
Vermont	80 452	74 256	80 232	101 783	90 287	71 855	58 063
Virginia	88 929	77 999	90 358	110 000	101 737	103 875	101 463
Washington	87 652	78 823	90 921	105 568	96 143	94 256	102 297
West Virginia	57 718	51 102	63 137	74 916	65 930	71 095	56 860
Wisconsin	76 814	67 146	82 119	98 317	91 208	82 709	79 237
Wyoming	78 352	72 964	76 916	96 120	86 422	72 425	86 763

CHAPTER 14: OCCUPATIONAL SAFETY AND HEALTH

HIGHLIGHTS

This chapter includes data on work-related illnesses and injuries and fatal work injuries from the Injuries, Illnesses, and Fatalities (IIF) program. Data are classified by industry and selected worker characteristics.

Figure 14-1. Fatal Occupational Injuries by Type of Injury, 2018

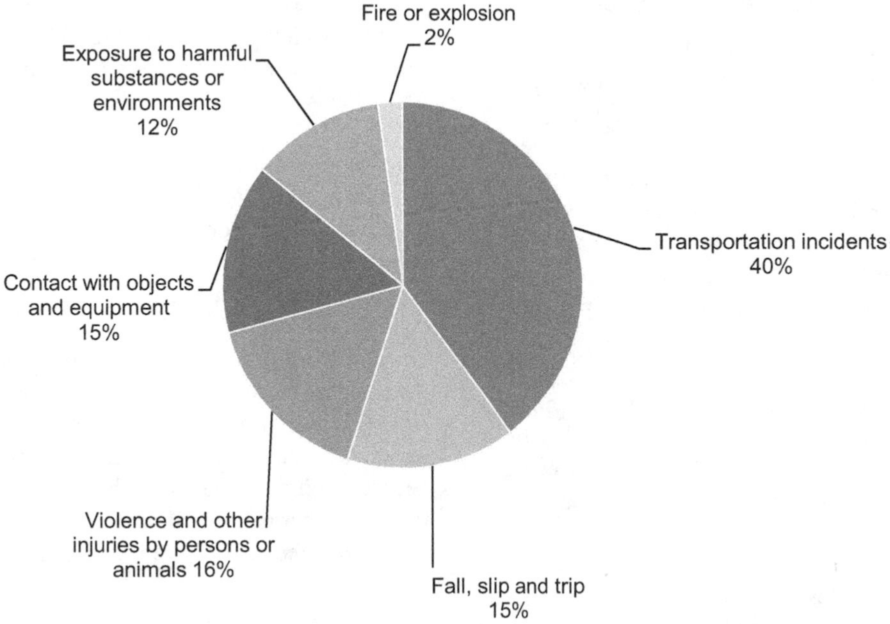

Transportation incidents remained the most frequent fatal event in 2018 accounting for 40 percent of all fatal occupational injuries. In 2018, the number of falls declined 10.8 percent to 791 accounting for 15.1 percent of all fatalities in the workplace. The number of suicides increased in 2018 while the number of homicides decreased for the second consecutive year. (See Table 14-9.)

OTHER HIGHLIGHTS

- Unintentional overdoses due to nonmedical use of drugs or alcohol while at work increased 12 percent from 272 to 305. This is the sixth consecutive annual increase. Since 2011, the percentage of unintentional drugs and alcohol overdoses increased 318 percent. (See Table 14-9.)

- In 2018, there were over 3.3 million nonfatal workplace injuries in the United States including private industry and state and local governments. This is the first year since 2012 that the total recordable cases did not decline. Agriculture, forestry, fishing, and hunting workers had the highest incidence rate in the private industry followed by those in accommodation and food services. (See Table 14-1.)

- Men accounted for over 92 percent of workplace fatalites in 2018. (See Table 14-8.)

- Poisonings accounted for 2,900 nonfatal occupational injuries and illnesses in 2018 while respiratory conditions accounted for nearly 20,000 and skin diseases and illnesses accounted for over 25,000 nonfatal occupational injuries and illnesses. (See Table 14-6.)

NOTES AND DEFINITIONS

Collection and Coverage

The Injuries, Illnesses, and Fatalities (IIF) program at the Bureau of Labor Statistics (BLS) provides annual reports on the number of workplace injuries, illnesses, and fatalities. BLS has reported annually on the number of work-related injuries, illnesses, and fatalities since 1972 after the Occupational Safety and Health Act of 1970 was passed.

Nonfatal Occupational Injuries and Illnesses

The Survey of Occupational Injuries and Illnesses is a federal-state program in which employer's reports are collected annually from over 200,000 private industry and public sector establishments and processed by state agencies cooperating with the BLS. Summary information on the number of injuries and illnesses is copied by these employers directly from their recordkeeping logs to the survey questionnaire. The questionnaire also asks for the number of employee hours worked (needed in the calculation of incidence rates) as well as its average employment (needed to verify the unit's employment-size class).

Occupational injury and illness data for coal, metal, and nonmetal mining and for railroad activities were provided by the Department of Labor's Mine Safety and Health Administration and the Department of Transportation's Federal Railroad Administration. The survey excludes all work-related fatalities as well as nonfatal work injuries and illnesses to the self employed; to workers on farms with 10 or fewer employees; to private household workers; and, nationally, to federal, state, and local government workers.

Injuries and illnesses logged by employers conform with definitions and recordkeeping guidelines set by the Occupational Safety and Health Administration, U.S. Department of Labor. Under those guidelines, nonfatal cases are recordable if they are occupational illnesses or if they are occupational injuries which involve lost worktime, medical treatment other than first aid, restriction of work or motion, loss of consciousness, or transfer to another job. Employers keep counts of injuries separate from illnesses and also identify for each whether a case involved any days away from work or days of restricted work activity, or both, beyond the day of injury or onset of illness.

Occupational injuries, such as sprains, cuts, and fractures, account for the vast majority of all cases that employers log and report to the BLS survey. Occupational illnesses are new cases recognized, diagnosed, and reported during the year. Overwhelmingly, those reported are easier to directly relate to workplace activity (e.g., contact dermatitis or carpal tunnel syndrome) than are long-term latent illnesses, such as cancers. The latter illnesses are believed to be under recorded and, thus, understated in the BLS survey.

Concepts and Definitions

Days away from work are cases that involve days away from work, days of restricted work activity, or both.

The data are presented in the form of *incidence rates*, defined as the number of injuries and illnesses or cases of days away from work per 100 full-time employees. The formula is (N/EH) x 200,000, where N = number of injuries and illnesses or days away from work, EH = total hours worked by all employees during the calendar year, and 200,000 represents the base for 100 full-time equivalent workers (working 40 hours per week, 50 weeks per year).

Median days away from work is a measure used to summarize the varying lengths of absences from work among the cases with days away from work. The median is the point at which half of the cases involved more days away from work and half involved less days away from work.

Occupational illness is an abnormal condition or disorder (other than one resulting from an occupational injury) caused by exposure to environmental factors associated with employment. It includes acute and chronic illnesses and diseases that may have been caused by inhalation, absorption, ingestion, or direct contact. Long-term latent illnesses can be difficult to relate to the workplace and are believed to be understated in this survey.

Occupational injury is any injury—such as a cut, fracture, sprain, or amputation—that results from a work accident or from exposure to an incident in the work environment.

Fatal Occupational Injuries

The Bureau of Labor Statistics (BLS) Census of Fatal Occupational Injuries (CFOI) produces comprehensive, accurate, and timely counts of fatal work injuries. CFOI is a federal-state cooperative program that has been implemented in all 50 states and the District of Columbia since 1992. To compile counts that are as complete as possible, the census uses multiple sources to identify, verify, and profile fatal worker injuries. Information about each workplace fatality—occupation and other worker characteristics, equipment involved, and circumstances of the event—is obtained by cross referencing the source records, such as death certificates, workers' compensation reports, and federal and state agency administrative reports. To ensure that fatalities are work-related, cases are substantiated with two or more independent source documents, or a source document and a follow-up questionnaire.

Data compiled by the CFOI program are issued annually for the preceding calendar year. These data are used by safety and health policy analysts and researchers to help prevent fatal work injuries by:

- Informing workers of life threatening hazards associated with various jobs;
- Promoting safer work practices through enhanced job safety training;
- Assessing and improving workplace safety standards; and
- Identifying new areas of safety research.

The National Safety Council has adopted the Census of Fatal Occupational Injuries figure, beginning with the 1992 data year, as the authoritative count for work related deaths in the United States.

Sources of Additional Information

For more extensive definitions and description of collection methods see the *BLS Handbook of Methods* and BLS news release USDL 19-1909, "Employer-Reported Workplace Injuries and Illnesses, 2018" and USDL 19-2194"National Census of Fatal Occupational Injuries in 2018" available on the BLS Web site at <https://www.bls.gov/iif/>.

Table 14-1. Incidence Rate[1] and Number of Nonfatal Occupational Injuries by Industry and Ownership, 2018

(Number, rate.)

Industry[2]	Incidence rate	Number of cases (thousands)	Percent relative standard cases	
			Incidence rate[2]	Number of cases (housands)
All Industries Including Private, State and Local Government[3]	2.9	3 368	0.5	0.5
Private industry[3]	2.7	2 708	0.5	0.5
Goods-producing[3]	3.1	652	0.9	0.8
Natural resources and mining[3,4]	3.5	61	3.3	2.8
Agriculture, forestry, fishing and hunting[3]	5.1	52	3.3	3.2
Mining, quarrying, and oil and gas extraction[4]	1.3	9	5.8	5.3
Construction	2.9	196	2.1	2.1
Manufacturing	3.1	395	0.9	0.8
Service-providing	2.6	2 056	0.6	0.6
Trade, transportation, and utilities[5]	3.4	781	0.9	0.9
Wholesale trade	2.8	157	2.6	2.5
Retail trade	3.4	401	1.3	1.2
Transportation and warehousing[5]	4.3	213	1.6	1.5
Information	1.2	32	8.9	7.9
Finance, insurance, and real estate	0.9	71	4.2	4.0
Finance and insurance	0.5	26	5.6	5.5
Real estate and rental and leasing	2.3	45	5.6	5.5
Professional and business services	1.2	196	2.8	2.5
Professional, scientific, and technical services	0.8	66	5.8	4.9
Management of companies and enterprises	0.7	17	5.9	5.9
Administrative and support and waste management and remediation services	2.1	113	3.3	3.1
Educational and health services	3.5	580	0.9	0.8
Educational services	1.8	35	3.4	3.4
Health care and social assistance	3.7	545	0.9	0.8
Leisure, entertainment, and hospitality	3.2	325	1.5	1.5
Arts, entertainment, and recreation	3.9	54	3.3	3.2
Accommodation and food services	3.1	271	1.6	1.6
Other services (except public administration)	2.2	71	5.5	5.3
State and local government[3]	4.5	660	1.4	1.4
State government[3]	3.3	129	1.3	1.2
Local government[3]	4.9	531	1.7	1.6

[1]The incidence rates represent the number of injuries and illnesses per 100 full-time workers and were calculated as: (N/EH) x 200,000 (where N = number of injuries and illnesses; EH = total hours worked by all employees during the calendar year; 200,000 = base for 100 equivalent full-time workers working 40 hours per week, 50 weeks per year).
[2]Totals include data for industries not shown separately.
[3]Excludes farms with fewer than 11 employees.
[4]Data for Mining include establishments not governed by the Mine Safety and Health Administration rules and reporting, such as those in Oil and Gas Extraction and related support activities.
[5]Data for employers in railroad transportation are provided to BLS by the Federal Railroad Administration, U.S. Department of Transportation.

Table 14-2. Highest Incidence Rates[1] of Total Nonfatal Occupational Injury and Illness Cases, 2018

(Rate per 100 full-time workers.)

Industry sector[2]	NAICS Code[3]	Incidence rate
All Industries Including State and Local Government[4]		3.1
Nursing and residential care facilities	623	11.9
Pet care (except veterinary) services	81 291	11.4
Veterinary services	54 194	10.4
Steel foundries (except investment)	331 513	10.2
Skiing facilities	71 392	10.0
Manufactured home (mobile home) manufacturing	321 991	9.7
Travel trailer and camper manufacturing	336 214	9.3
Motor home manufacturing	336 213	9.2
Other animal production	1 129	8.9
Beef cattle ranching and farming, including feedlots	11 211	8.5
Aluminum foundries (except die-casting)	331 524	8.5
Couriers and express delivery services	4 921	8.2
Consumer electronics and appliances rental	53 221	8.2
Hospitals	622	8.1
All other miscellaneous wood product manufacturing	321 999	7.8
Hog and pig farming	1 122	7.7
Interurban and rural bus transportation	4 852	7.7
Concrete block and brick manufacturing	327 331	7.5
Ambulance services	62 191	7.5
Psychiatric and substance abuse hospitals	6 222	7.4
Pet and pet supplies stores	45 391	7.3
Nursing and residential care facilities	623	7.3
Correctional institutions	92 214	7.3
Ice cream and frozen dessert manufacturing	31 152	7.2
Truss manufacturing	321 214	7.1
Truck trailer manufacturing	336 212	7.1

[1]The incidence rates represent the number of injuries and illnesses per 100 full-time workers and were calculated as: (N/EH) x 200,000 (where N = number of injuries and illnesses; EH = total hours worked by all employees during the calendar year; 200,000 = base for 100 equivalent full-time workers working 40 hours per week, 50 weeks per year).
[2]High rate industries were those having the highest incidence rate of total recordable cases of injuries and illnesses and at least 500 total recordable cases at the most detailed level of publication based on the North American Industry Classification System—United States, 2012.
[3]North American Industry Classification, United States 2012
[4]Excludes farms with fewer than 11 employees.

Table 14-3. Highest Incidence Rate[1] of Nonfatal Occupational Injuries and Illness Cases With Days Away From Work, Restricted Job Activity, or Job Transfer, 2018

(Number, rate per 100 full-time workers.)

Industry[2]	NAICS Code[3]	Incidence rate
All Industries Including State and Local Government[4]		1.7
Manufactured home manufacturing	321 991	7.2
Nursing and residential care facilities	623	7.2
Couriers and express delivery services	4 921	6.5
Motor home manufacturing	336 213	6.3
Steel foundries	331 513	5.9
Scheduled pasenger air transportation	481 111	5.6
Hog and pig farming	1 122	5.3
Soft drink manufacturing	312 111	5.3
Concrete block and brick manufacturing	327 331	5.3
Beef cattle ranching and farming, including feedlots	11 211	5.0
Prefabricated wood building manufacturing	321 992	5.0
Amusements and theme parks	71 311	5.0
Skiing facilities	71 392	5.0
Framing contractors	23 813	4.9
Steel wire drawing	331 222	4.9
Nursing and residential care facilities	623	4.9
Crop harvesting, primarily by amchine	115 113	4.8
Aluminum foundries	331 524	4.7
Other animal production	1 129	4.6
Truss manufacturing	321 214	4.6
Urban transit systems	4 851	4.6
Hospitals	622	4.6
Used households and office goods moving	48 421	4.5
Ambulance services	62 191	4.5
Psychiatric services	6 222	4.5

[1]The incidence rates represent the number of injuries and illnesses per 100 full-time workers and were calculated as: (N/EH) x 200,000 (where N = number of injuries and illnesses; EH = total hours worked by all employees during the calendar year; 200,000 = base for 100 equivalent full-time workers working 40 hours per week, 50 weeks per year).
[2]High rate industries were those having the highest incidence rate of injury and illness cases with days away from work, restricted work activity or job transfer and at least 500 total recordable cases at the most detailed level of publication, based on the *North American Industry Classification System*—United States, 2012.
[3]*North American Industry Classification System*—United States, 2012.
[4]Excludes farms with fewer than 11 employees.

Table 14-4. Highest Incidence Rate[1] of Nonfatal Occupational Injuries and Illnesses With Cases Away From Work, 2018[2]

(Incidence rate per 100 full-time workers.)

Industry[3]	NAICS code[4]	Incidence rate
All Industries Including State and Local Government[5]		1.0
Nursing and residential care facilities	623	5.7
Scheduled passenger air transportation	481 111	3.9
Correctional institutions	92 214	3.5
Couriers and express delivery services	4 921	3.4
Hospitals	622	3.4
Marinas	71 393	3.3
Beef cattle ranching and farming, including feedlots	11 211	3.1
Urban transit systems	4 851	3.1
Consumer electronics and appliances rental	53 221	3.1
Nursing and residential care facilities	623	3.1
Bituminous coal underground mining	212 112	3.0
Framing contractors	23 813	3.0
Crop harvesting, primarily by machine	115 113	2.9
Ambulance services	62 191	2.9
Dairy cattle and milk production	11 212	2.8
Logging	1 133	2.8
Psychiatric and substance abuse hospitals	6 222	2.8
All other miscellaneous wood product manufacturing	321 999	2.7
Interurban and rural bus transportation	4 852	2.7
Solid waste collection	562 111	2.7
Truss manufacturing	321 214	2.6
Overhead traveling crane, hoist, and monorail system manufacturing	333 923	2.6
Ice cream and frozen dessert manufacturing	31 152	2.5
Seafood product preparation and packaging	3 117	2.5
Other animal production	1 129	2.4

1 The incidence rates represent the number of injuries and illnesses per 100 full-time workers and were calculated as: (N/EH) x 200,000 (where N = number of injuries and illnesses; EH = total hours worked by all employees during the calendar year; 200,000 = base for 100 equivalent full-time workers working 40 hours per week, 50 weeks per year).
2 Days-away-from-work cases include those that result in days away from work with or without job transfer or restriction.
3 High rate industries were those having the highest incidence rate of injury and illness cases with days away from work and at least 500 total recordable cases at the most detailed level of publication based on the North American Industry Classification System —United States, 2012.
4 North American Industry Classification System —United States, 2012.
5 Data for mining operators in this industry are provided to BLS by the Mine Safety and Health Administration U.S. Department of Labor. Independent mining contractors are excluded. These data do not reflect the changes the Occupational Safety and Health Administration made to its recordkeeping requirements effective January 1, 2002; therefore, estimates for these industries are not comparable to estimates in other industries.

Table 14-5. Highest Incidence Rate[1] of Nonfatal Injury and Illness Cases With Job Transfer or Restriction, 2018

(Rate per 100 full-time workers.)

Industry[2]	NAICS code[3]	Incidence rate
All Industries Including State and Local Government		0.7
Manufactured home (mobile home) manufacturing	321 991	5.3
Motor home manufacturing	336 213	5.2
Steel foundries (except investment)	331 513	3.7
Amusement and theme parks	71 311	3.7
Soft drink manufacturing	312 111	3.6
Steel wire drawing	331 222	3.5
Prefabricated wood building manufacturing	321 992	3.3
Hog and pig farming	1 122	3.2
Couriers and express delivery services	4 921	3.2
Concrete block and brick manufacturing	327 331	3.1
Skiing facilities	71 392	2.8
Specialty canning	311 422	2.7
Aluminum foundries (except die-casting)	331 524	2.7
Light truck and utility vehicle manufacturing	336 112	2.7
Animal (except poultry) slaughtering	311 611	2.6
Secondary smelting, refining, and alloying of nonferrous metal (except copper and aluminum	331 492	2.6
Postharvest crop activities (except cotton ginning)	115 114	2.4
Home centers	44 411	2.4
Pet and pet supplies stores	45 391	2.4
Used household and office goods moving	48 421	2.4
Fruit and tree nut farming	1 113	2.3
Automobile manufacturing	336 111	2.3
Truck trailer manufacturing	336 212	2.3
Grocery and related product merchant wholesalers	4 244	2.3
Continuing care retirement communities and assisted living facilities for the elderly	6 233	2.3
Linen supply	812 331	2.3

[1]The incidence rates represent the number of injuries and illnesses per 100 full-time workers and were calculated as: (N/EH) x 200,000 (where N = number of injuries and illnesses; EH = total hours worked by all employees during the calendar year; 200,000 = base for 100 equivalent full-time workers working 40 hours per week, 50 weeks per year).
[2]High rate industries were those having the highest incidence rate of injury and illness cases with days away from work and at least 500 total recordable cases at the most detailed level of publication based on the North American Industry Classification System —United States, 2012.
[3]North American Industry Classification System —United States, 2012.

Table 14-6. Nonfatal Occupational Illnesses by Major Industry Sector and Category of Illness, 2018

(Number, rate.)

Characteristic	Total cases		Skin diseases or disorders		Respiratory conditions		Poisionings		Hearing loss		All other illnesses	
	Number of cases (000s)	Incidence rate[1]	Number of cases (000s)	Incidence rate[1]	Number of cases (000s)	Incidence rate[1]	Number of cases (000s)	Incidence rate[1]	Number of cases (000s)	Incidence rate[1]	Number of cases (000s)	Incidence rate[1]
All Industries Including Private, State and Local Government[2]	176.9	15.4	25.1	2.2	19.6	1.7	2.9	0.3	17.5	1.4	111.8	9.7
Private Industry[2]	126.8	12.6	19.2	1.9	12.1	1.2	1.7	0.2	15.3	1.4	78.5	7.8
Goods-Producing[2]	41.5	19.7	5.6	2.7	2.1	1.0	0.3	0.2	11.8	5.3	21.7	10.3
Natural resources and mining[2,3]	2.9	16.9	0.8	4.8	0.3	1.7	0.1	0.5	0.3	1.8	1.4	8.2
Construction	3.6	5.3	0.9	1.4	0.3	0.4	0.2	0.3	0.1	0.2	2.1	3.2
Manufacturing	35.0	27.7	3.9	3.1	1.6	1.2	0.1	0.1	11.4	8.4	18.1	14.3
Service-Providing	85.3	10.7	13.6	1.7	10.0	1.3	1.3	0.2	3.5	0.4	56.8	7.2
Trade, transportation, and utilities[4]	21.8	9.5	2.5	1.1	...	...	0.3	0.1	2.5	0.9	13.3	5.8
Information	1.6	6.3	0.4	1.5	0.2	0.7	0.1	0.2	0.1	0.4	0.9	3.5
Finance, insurance, and real estate	3.4	4.4	0.3	0.3	0.2	0.3	([5])	([5])	...	...	2.8	3.7
Professional and business services	11.0	6.9	2.1	1.3	1.6	1.0	0.4	0.2	0.6	0.2	6.3	3.9
Educational and health services	34.5	20.7	5.0	3.0	3.9	2.3	0.3	0.2	0.1	0.1	25.1	15.1
Leisure, entertainment, and hospitality	11.1	10.8	3.0	2.9	0.8	0.7	0.3	0.3	0.1	0.1	6.9	6.7
Other services (except public administration)	1.9	6.0	0.3	0.8	0.1	0.2	...	0.1	...	0.1	1.6	4.8
State and Local Government[2]	50.2	34.0	5.8	4.0	7.5	5.1	1.2	0.8	2.2	1.3	33.3	22.6
State government[2]	12.6	32.0	1.2	3.0	1.1	2.8	0.2	0.4	0.6	1.5	9.6	24.3
Local government[2]	37.6	34.8	4.7	4.3	6.4	6.0	1.1	1.0	1.6	1.2	23.8	22.0

[1]The incidence rates represent the number of injuries and illnesses per 100 full-time workers and were calculated as: (N/EH) x 200,000 (where N = number of injuries and illnesses; EH = total hours worked by all employees during the calendar year; 200,000 = base for 100 equivalent full-time workers working 40 hours per week, 50 weeks per year).
[2]Excludes farms with fewer than 11 employees.
[3]Data for Mining (Sector 21 in the North American Industry Classification System—United States, 2012) include establishments not governed by the Mine Safety and Health Administration rules and reporting, such as those in Oil and Gas Extraction and related support activities. Data for mining operators in coal, metal, and nonmetal mining are provided to BLS by the Mine Safety and Health Administration, U.S. Department of Labor.
[4] Data for employers in railroad transportation are provided to BLS by the Federal Railroad Administration, U.S. Department of Transportation.
[5] Data too small to be displayed.
... = Figure does not meet standards of reliability or quality.

Table 14-7. Number of Fatal Work Injuries by Employee Status, 2003–2018

(Number.)

Year	Total	Wage and salary workers	Self-employed workers
2003	5 575	4 405	1 170
2004	5 764	4 587	1 177
2005	5 734	4 592	1 142
2006	5 840	4 808	1 032
2007	5 657	4 613	1 044
2008	5 214	4 183	1 031
2009	4 551	3 488	1 063
2010	4 690	3 651	1 039
2011	4 693	3 642	1 051
2012	4 628	3 571	1 057
2013	4 585	3 535	1 050
2014	4 821	3 728	1 093
2015	4 836	3 751	1 085
2016	5 190	4 098	1 092
2017	5 147	4 069	1 078
2018	5 250	4 178	1 072

Table 14-8. Fatal Occupational Injuries Counts and Rates by Selected Demographic Characteristics 2017–2018

(Number, rate.)

Characteristic	Counts		Rates[1]	
	2017	2018	2017	2018
TOTAL[2]	5 147	5 250	3.5	3.5
Employee Status				
Wage and salary workers[3]	4 069	4 178	2.9	2.9
Self-employed[4]	1 078	1 072	13.1	12.7
Sex				
Men	4 761	4 837	5.7	5.7
Women	386	413	0.6	0.6
Age				
Under 16 years	15	13	. . .	. . .
16 to 17 years	7	9	0.8	1.0
18 to 19 years	62	56	2.6	2.3
20 to 24 years	293	282	2.2	2.1
25 to 34 years	872	946	2.5	2.7
35 to 44 years	907	966	2.9	2.9
45 to 54 years	1 059	1 114	3.3	3.4
55 to 64 years	1 155	1 104	4.6	4.3
65 years and over	775	759	10.3	9.6
Race and Hispanic Origin				
White	3 449	3 405	3.6	3.6
Black	530	615	3.2	3.6
Hispanic[5]	903	961	3.7	3.7
American Indian or Alaskan Native	38	42	. . .	. . .
Asian	144	153	1.6	1.7
Native Hawaiian or Pacific Islander	17	10	. . .	. . .
Multiple races	9	14	. . .	. . .
Other or not reported	57	50	. . .	. . .

[1]Fatal injury rates are per 100,000 full-time equivalent workers (FTEs).
[2]The Census of Fatal Occupational Injuries (CFOI) has published data on fatal occupational injuries for the United States since 1992. During this time, the classification systems and definitions of many data elements have changed.
[3]May include volunteers and other workers receiving compensation.
[4]Includes self-employed workers, owners of unincorporated businesses and farms, paid and unpaid family workers, and members of partnerships; may also include owners of incorporated businesses.
[5]May be of any race. The race categories shown exclude data for Hispanics and Latinos.
. . . = Not available.

Table 14-9. Fatal Occupational Injuries for Selected Events or Exposures, 2011–2018

(Number.)

Characteristic	2011	2012	2013	2014	2015	2016	2017	2018
TOTAL	4 693	4 628	4 585	4 821	4 836	5 190	5 147	5 250
Violence and Other Injuries by Persons or Animals	791	803	773	765	703	866	807	828
Intentional injury by person	718	725	686	689	646	792	733	757
Homicides	468	475	404	409	417	500	458	453
Shooting by other person—intentional	365	381	322	307	354	394	351	351
Stabbing, cutting, slashing, piercing	42	35	38	40	28	38	47	44
Suicides	250	249	282	280	229	291	275	304
Transportation Incidents	1 937	1 923	1 865	1 984	2 054	2 083	2 077	2 080
Aircraft incidents	145	127	136	135	139	130	126	133
Rail vehicle incidents	50	38	41	57	50	50	48	48
Pedestrian vehicular incident	316	293	294	318	289	342	313	325
Pedestrian struck by vehicle in work zone	63	65	48	53	44	58	56	58
Water vehicle incident	72	63	60	55	44	48	68	58
Roadway incident involving motorized land vehicle	1 103	1 153	1 099	1 157	1 264	1 252	1 299	1 276
Roadway collision with other vehicle	525	565	564	611	660	628	663	677
Roadway collision moving in same direction	150	124	144	146	166	168	189	183
Roadway collision moving in opposite directions, oncoming	172	204	192	230	224	199	214	243
Roadway collision moving perpendicularly	111	134	136	131	154	150	149	141
Roadway collision with object other than vehicle	313	338	332	317	360	342	377	373
Vehicle struck object or animal on side of roadway	292	318	311	292	335	321	348	345
Roadway noncollision incident	262	247	201	228	240	278	252	222
Jack-knifed or overturned, roadway	208	202	171	193	201	238	197	170
Nonroadway incident involving motorized land vehicle	222	233	227	248	253	245	209	225
Nonroadway noncollision incident	169	175	181	191	182	182	166	164
Jack-knifed or overturned, nonroadway	113	115	118	127	131	120	111	105
Fire or Explosion	144	122	149	137	121	88	123	115
Fall, Slip, Trip	681	704	724	818	800	849	887	791
Fall on same level	111	120	110	138	125	134	151	154
Fall to lower level	553	570	595	660	648	697	713	615
Fall from collapsing structure or equipment	38	35	45	44	55	65	48	50
Fall through surface or existing opening	60	72	68	82	87	87	85	83
Exposure to Harmful Substances or Environments	419	340	335	390	424	518	531	621
Exposure to electricity	174	156	141	154	134	154	136	160
Exposure to temperature extremes	63	41	38	26	40	48	38	60
Exposure to other harmful substances	144	110	124	182	215	268	317	355
Nonmedical use of drugs or alcohol unintentional overdose	73	65	82	114	165	217	272	305
Inhalation of harmful substance	57	40	39	59	45	39	43	42
Contact with Objects and Equipment	710	723	721	715	722	761	695	786
Struck by object or equipment	476	519	509	503	519	553	503	566
Struck by powered vehicle nontransport	196	201	197	202	216	232	197	215
Struck by falling object or equipment	219	241	245	243	247	255	237	278
Caught in or compressed by equipment or objects	145	124	131	132	99	117	108	137
Caught in running equipment or machinery	118	93	105	105	74	103	76	106
Struck, caught, or crushed in collapsing structure, equipment, or material	84	73	78	74	90	82	70	73

Table 14-10. Fatal Occupational Injuries Counts and Rates for Selected Occupations, 2017–2018

(Number, rate.)

Occupation	Counts		Rates[1]	
	2017	2018	2017	2018
TOTAL[2]	5 147	5 250	3.5	3.5
OCCUPATION (SOC)[3]				
Management	396	387	2.1	2.0
Business and Financial Operations	29	38	0.4	0.5
Computer and Mathematical	11	12	0.2	0.2
Architecture and Engineering	23	30	0.7	0.9
Life, Physical, and Social Science	13	18	0.9	1.1
Community and Social Services	37	23	1.4	0.8
Legal	11	15	0.6	0.8
Education, Training, and Library	30	27	0.4	0.3
Arts, Design, Entertainment, Sports, and Media	47	71	1.6	2.3
Health Care Practitioners and Technical	57	65	0.6	0.7
Health Care Support	28	32	0.9	1.0
Protective Service	266	270	7.7	7.4
Fire Fighting and Prevention Workers	35	33	. . .	. . .
Law enforcement workers	117	127	. . .	. . .
Food Preparation and Serving Related	89	100	1.4	1.5
Building and Grounds Cleaning and Maintenance	326	350	6.4	6.8
Building cleaning and pest control workers	68	66	. . .	. . .
Grounds maintenance workers	191	225	15.5	18.6
Personal Care and Service	69	63	1.2	1.2
Sales and Related	232	241	1.6	1.7
Supervisors, sales workers	98	102	. . .	. . .
Retail sales workers	89	99	. . .	. . .
Office and Administrative Support	101	69	0.6	0.4
Farming, Fishing, and Forestry	264	262	20.9	22.8
Agricultural workers	155	158	. . .	. . .
Fishing and hunting workers	41	31	. . .	. . .
Forest, conservation, and logging workers	57	57	. . .	. . .
Construction and Extraction	965	1 003	12.2	12.2
Supervisors, construction and extraction workers	121	144	17.4	21.0
Construction trades workers	747	731	. . .	. . .
Extraction workers	41	64	. . .	. . .
Installation, Maintenance, and Repair	414	420	8.1	8.2
Vehicle and mobile equipment mechanics, installers, and repairers	143	152	. . .	. . .
Production	221	225	2.6	2.6
Transportation and Material Moving	1 443	1 443	15.9	15.0
Air transportation workers	59	71	. . .	. . .
Motor vehicle operators	1 084	1 044	. . .	. . .
Material moving	235	255	. . .	. . .
Military	72	82	. . .	. . .

Note: Data for all years are final. Totals for major categories may include subcategories not shown separately.

[1]Fatal injury rates are per 100,000 full-time equivalent workers (FTEs).
[2]The Census of Fatal Occupational Injuries (CFOI) has published data on fatal occupational injuries for the United States since 1992. During this time, the classification systems and definitions of many data elements have changed.
[3]CFOI has used several versions of the Standard Occupation Classification (SOC) system since 2003 to define occupation.
. . . = Not available.

Table 14-11. Fatal Occupational Counts and Rates by Selected Industries, 2017–2018

(Number, rate.)

Occupation	Counts		Rate	
	2017	2018	2017	2018
TOTAL	5 147	5 250	3.5	3.5
NAICS INDUSTRY				
Private Industry	4 674	4 779	3.7	3.7
Goods-Producing	1 967	2 055	6.7	6.8
Agriculture, Forestry, Fishing and Hunting	581	574	23.0	23.4
Crop production	263	250	20.9	20.1
Animal production and aquaculture	152	161	16.4	18.6
Forestry and logging	76	84	...	...
Mining, Quarrying, and Oil and Gas Extraction	112	130	12.9	14.1
Mining (except oil and gas)	31	34	15.5	15.0
Support activities for mining	73	83	12.8	13.7
Construction	971	1 008	9.5	9.5
Construction of buildings	196	200	...	...
Heavy and civil engineering construction	152	180	...	...
Specialty trade contractors	610	609	...	...
Manufacturing	303	343	1.9	2.2
Food manufacturing	51	41	2.8	2.2
Fabricated metal product manufacturing	50	56	4.3	4.4
Service-Providing	2 707	2 724	2.8	2.8
Wholesale Trade	174	202	4.8	5.3
Retail Trade	287	274	2.0	1.9
Motor vehicle and parts dealers	54	68	2.5	3.2
Food and beverage stores	60	42	2.3	1.6
Transportation and Warehousing	882	874	15.1	14.0
Truck transportation	599	607	28.0	28.3
Utilities	28	29	2.6	2.6
Information	43	31	1.6	1.2
Finance and Insurance	32	30	0.5	0.4
Real Estate and Rental and Leasing	69	78	2.4	2.6
Professional, Scientific, and Technical Services	69	87	0.6	0.7
Administrative and Support and Waste Management and Remediation Services	460	497	...	...
Educational Services	43	30	1.0	0.7
Health Care and Social Assistance	146	138	0.8	0.8
Arts, Entertainment, and Recreation	91	78	3.2	3.0
Accommodation and Food Services	171	175	1.9	1.9
Other Services, Except Public Administration	205	195	2.9	2.6
Government	473	471	2.0	1.8
Federal Government	116	124	1.3	1.2
State Government	91	69	1.4	1.1
Local Government	265	276	2.6	2.7

... = Data not available.

Table 14-12. Fatal Occupational Injury Counts and Rates by State of Incident, 2017–2018

(Number, rate.)

State	Counts		Rates[1]	
	2017	2018	2017	2018
Total	5 147	5 250	3.5	3.5
Alabama	83	89	4.3	4.5
Alaska	33	32	10.2	9.9
Arizona	90	82	3.0	2.5
Arkansas	76	76	6.1	6.3
California	376	422	2.2	2.3
Colorado	77	72	2.8	2.6
Connecticut	35	48	1.9	2.8
Delaware	10	7	2.4	1.6
District of Columbia	13	10	3.4	2.8
Florida	299	332	3.3	3.5
Georgia	194	186	4.1	3.8
Hawaii	20	22	2.2	3.4
Idaho	37	45	4.8	5.8
Illinois	163	184	2.8	3.1
Indiana	138	173	4.5	5.6
Iowa	72	77	4.7	4.9
Kansas	72	61	5.2	4.5
Kentucky	70	83	3.8	4.2
Louisiana	117	98	6.3	5.1
Maine	18	17	2.7	2.5
Maryland	87	97	3.0	3.4
Massachusetts	108	97	3.2	2.7
Michigan	153	155	3.4	3.4
Minnesota	101	75	3.5	2.7
Mississippi	90	78	6.2	6.7
Missouri	125	145	4.4	5.1
Montana	32	28	6.9	5.5
Nebraska	35	44	3.6	4.7
Nevada	32	39	2.4	2.8
New Hampshire	11	20	1.6	2.9
New Jersey	69	83	1.6	2.0
New Mexico	44	43	4.7	4.7
New York (including NYC)	313	271	3.5	3.1
New York City	87	73	2.3	2.0
North Carolina	183	178	3.9	3.8
North Dakota	38	35	10.1	9.6
Ohio	174	158	3.3	3.0
Oklahoma	91	91	5.5	5.2
Oregon	60	62	3.2	3.1
Pennsylvania	172	177	3.0	3.0
Rhode Island	8	9	1.6	1.8
South Carolina	88	98	4.2	4.6
South Dakota	30	32	7.3	6.9
Tennessee	128	122	4.4	4.1
Texas	534	488	4.3	3.8
Utah	43	49	2.9	3.4
Vermont	22	11	7.0	3.5
Virginia	118	157	2.9	3.5
Washington	84	86	2.5	2.4
West Virginia	51	57	7.4	7.9
Wisconsin	106	114	3.5	3.8
Wyoming	20	31	7.7	11.5

[1]Fatal injury rates are per 100,000 full-time equivalent workers (FTEs).

CPSIA information can be obtained
at www.ICGtesting.com
Printed in the USA
BVHW011054060720
582404BV00027B/25

9 781641 434065